Turkey

THE ROUGH GUIDE

D0366971

There are more than one hundred Rough Guide titles
covering destinations from Amsterdam to Zimbabwe

Forthcoming titles include
Jamaica • New Zealand
South Africa • Southwest USA

Rough Guide Reference Series
Classical Music • The Internet • Jazz • Opera • Rock Music • World Music

Rough Guide Phrasebooks
Czech • French • German • Greek • Hindi & Urdu • Indonesian •Italian
Mandarin Chinese • Mexican Spanish • Polish • Portuguese
Russian • Spanish • Thai • Turkish • Vietnamese

Rough Guides on the Internet
http://www.roughguides.com/
http://www.hotwired.com/rough

ROUGH GUIDE CREDITS

Text editor: Paul Gray
Series editor: Mark Ellingham
Editorial: Martin Dunford, Jonathan Buckley, Jo Mead, Samantha Cook, Amanda Tomlin, Ann-Marie Shaw, Vivienne Heller, Sarah Dallas, Chris Schüler (UK), Andrew Rosenberg (US)
Production: Susanne Hillen, Andy Hilliard, Judy Pang, Link Hall, Nicola Williamson, Helen Ostick

Cartography: Melissa Flack and David Callier
Online Editor: Alan Spicer (UK)
Finance: John Fisher, Celia Crowley, Catherine Gillespie
Marketing & Publicity: Richard Trillo, Simon Carloss, Niki Smith (UK), Jean-Marie Kelly, Jeff Kaye (US)
Administration: Tania Hummel

ACKNOWLEDGEMENTS

Collectively, the authors and updaters would like to thank the following individuals who provided assistance during the research of this guide: Merih Kılıçaslan, Turkish Embassy Press Attaché, for arranging accreditation, and Nazif Ezken and Anna-Maria Allmark at the London Turkish Tourist Office for facilitating travel arrangements. At Rough Guides, all credit is due to Paul Gray for thorough editing, Andy Hilliard and Helen Ostick for typesetting, and Margo Daly and Pete Schmidt for keying. Thanks also to MicroMap, Romsey, Hants for Cartographic Production, and Susannah Walker and Elaine Pollard for proofreading.
Individually, the authors and updaters would like to thank:

Bradley – H. Engin, British Pro-consul in Ankara; Mahmut Arslan, head of the Adıyaman tourist office; Bilge Ilter of the Ankara Press Directorate; Asaf Yağlici in Adana; Ahmet Khan in Alanya; Ali Sabah in Antalya; and Kelli Hahn.

Marc – Philip Buckley, Ufuk Güven and the gang at *Bougainville Travel* in Kaş; Haluk Tosunlar and Kemal Tanrıseven in Kuşadası (again); Çiçek Park in Çeşme (for the third time); Victor Ananias, Kim Gould and the staff of the *Su Otel* in Bodrum; Muzaffer Otlu at Patara; Naci Dinçer in Fethiye; Nikiforos and Vasiliki on Heybeliada for the new music; Salih at Melodi Music for the discography check; and Sevan for pitching in at short notice.

Rosie – Howard Chung and Rachel Fisher, for watching out for baby Mia and her mum; Jamie, Ayşe and Gordon Dobie, for their hospitality and help with İstanbul restaurant and nightlife listings; Aytekin Saruhan in Yıldız Sarayı; Lillian and Galip Kırıkçı in Avanos, not least for Lillian's potent nappy-rash remedy; Mehmet Bozlak in Göreme; and Elkie Dixon and Temur Köran for their help and company on the Black Sea coast.

PUBLISHING INFORMATION

This third edition published March 1997 by Rough Guides Ltd, 1 Mercer St, London WC2H 9QJ. Previous editions 1991, 1994.
Distributed by the Penguin Group:
Penguin Books Ltd, 27 Wrights Lane, London W8 5TZ
Penguin Books USA Inc., 375 Hudson Street, New York 10014, USA
Penguin Books Australia Ltd, 487 Maroondah Highway, PO Box 257, Ringwood, Victoria 3134, Australia
Penguin Books Canada Ltd, 10 Alcorn Avenue, Toronto, Ontario, Canada M4V 1E4
Penguin Books (NZ) Ltd, 182–190 Wairau Road, Auckland 10, New Zealand
Typeset in Linotron Univers and Century Old Style to an original design by Andrew Oliver.
Printed in the UK by The Bath Press, Bath.
Illustrations in Part One & Part Three by Edward Briant.

Illustrations on p.1 and p.739 by Henry Iles.
No part of this book may be reproduced in any form without permission from the publisher except for the quotation of brief passages in reviews.
© Rosie Ayliffe, Marc Dubin and John Gawthrop 1997, 864pp, includes index
A catalogue record for this book is available from the British Library.
ISBN 1-85828-242-X

THE AUTHORS OF THE ROUGH GUIDE TO TURKEY

Rosie Ayliffe first went to Turkey in 1985 to work in Marmara University as an English teacher. On discovering the taste of fresh figs she decided to stay, working for three years in the west and south of the country as an English teacher and travel guide, while learning Turkish. She has returned several times – in fig season – to travel and write about Turkey, most recently with Mia, her eight-month-old daughter.

Since 1982, **Marc Dubin** has coached, trained, hiked, flown, driven or floated through most of Turkey's provinces. Having travelled extensively across the Mediterranean, he is also author of the Rough Guides to Rhodes and the Dodecanese, Cyprus and the Pyrenees, and co-author of the Rough Guide to Greece. He divides his time between London and Greece.

Born in the UK in 1965, **John Gawthrop** made his first visit to Turkey at the age of 22 and has been returning at every available opportunity since then. He has travelled throughout the country, from İstanbul to the mountains of the far southeast, but can't ever imagine tiring of the place.

THANKS TO THOSE WHO WROTE IN WITH COMMENTS ON THE LAST EDITION

Ayad Andrews; Babak Alizadeh; Hilary & Pippa André; Q. Atcha; A. Baldwin; the Bechis family; Frances Beg; Gill Blake; A.J. Boyle; Eleanor Brucken; Joyce Burgess; Robin Cave; Chris Carver; Mary Chan; Paula Chilvers; S. Chivers; Carol Clowes; Rowan Collier-Wright; John Cowler; Giles P. Croft; Maureen Donnelly; Christine Eida; Ken Elliott; Nick Fiddes; Gillian Ellison & Rob Lambert; Yasmine Estaphanos & Lars Laamann; Alex Everitt; Michael Forinton; Nicola George; Eilane Gietzen; Charlie Gillett; John C. Gilroy; Dr. Kurt Gingold; Kim Gould; Jill Goulder; Urur Gönülsen; Brooke E. Graham; Ellen Grande; W. Haelman; C.P. Hall; Clare Hambly & Caroline Skinner; James Hamilton; Pat Haynes; Maurice Heneghan; Peter & Joyce Hernon; Elizabeth Heslop; Stuart Howard & Carole Smith; Ian Hughes; Peter Hughes; D. Hussein; Jonathan Hollow; Lynne Jakubauskas & Robert Sherman; Paul Jay; Natasha Johns; Clive Jones & Sue Massie; Felix & Jane Jones; Mark T. Jones; the Jongerins; Kate Jordan; Norman Kan; Kaili Kidner; Regan Kilpin; P. Knight; Maggie & Simon Krabbendam; Mary Larkin & Felicity Fallon; Chris Leay; Carole Lee; Mack Lennon; Paul Lewis; Gordon W. McLachlan; Ian McLelland; Peter Macek; Monica Mackaness & John Garratt; George Main; Barth A.C. de Man; Roger Mantel; Ann May; Heather Meldrum; J. Milbourn; Ida Miller; Alan Newland; Patricia & Yehuda Nuriel; Helen O'Hanlon; Joel Palombo; Fiona Paterson & Brian Tait; Clair Parkinson & Matthew Wells; A.J. & B.J. Paterson; Richard Pell; Phil; Gianguido Piani; Joan R. Pryor; Tim Pope; Louise Rathbone; Kay Rawson; Elizabeth Raymont; Simon Richmond; Penny Roberts & Kieran Walker; Edward Rosenthal & Bryony Kay; Gillian Russell; Stefan Russell; James Ryan; Michael St John; Irene Sharp; V. Simm; Andrew J. Smith; Neil Spratt; Andy Stables; James Stafford; Janet Stevenson; R.M. Sweeney; Esther Thomson; Dave Tootell; Leon Vallet; Ahmet Velioqlu; Florence Vuillet; Joyce Whyte; Jenny Wells; Susan & Michael Weingarten; David Whitehead; Lucy Williams; Steve Witts; Vivienne Wood; Louise Woollett; R. Yeldham; Susi Zanatta; David Zilkha.

CONTENTS

Introduction xii

• CHAPTER 3: THE NORTH AEGEAN 228-265

• CHAPTER 4: THE CENTRAL AND SOUTHERN AEGEAN 266-380

• CHAPTER 5: THE TURQUOISE COAST 381-436

• CHAPTER 6: THE MEDITERRANEAN COAST AND THE HATAY 437–490

• CHAPTER 7: SOUTH CENTRAL ANATOLIA 491–559

• CHAPTER 8: NORTH CENTRAL ANATOLIA 560-618

• CHAPTER 9: THE BLACK SEA COAST 619-660

• CHAPTER 10: NORTHEASTERN ANATOLIA 661-698

This edition does not cover Lake Van & the southeast because of the political unrest in the region – see p.xvii.

MAP SYMBOLS

REGIONAL MAPS			Cliffs
			Pass
– – –	Chapter division boundary	◔	Cave
■ ▪ ■ ▪	International boundary		
═══	Road		TOWN MAPS
▬▬	Railway		
———	River	═══	Road
— —	Ferry route	⊓⊓⊓⊓	Steps
- - - -	Footpath	▪▪▪▪▪	Fortification
♜	Castle	▬–▪	Gate
⚲	Lighthouse	★	Bus/Dolmuş stop
⚑	Waterfall	♦	Museum
⥲	Marsh land	⊠	Post office
▦	Parkland	ⓘ	Tourist office
▲	Campsite	⊙	Hospital
▲	Mountain peak	◉	Accommodation
〰	Mountain range		

MAPS, PLANS, CHARTS

INTRODUCTION

Turkey is a country with a multiple identity, poised uneasily between East and West – though, despite the tourist brochure cliché, it is less a bridge between the two than a battleground, a buffer zone whose various parts have long been fought over from both directions. The country is now keen to be accepted on equal terms by the West, and is the only NATO ally in the Middle East region. But it is by no stretch of the imagination a Western nation, and the contradictions – and fascinations – persist. Mosques coexist with Orthodox churches; remnants of the Roman Empire crumble alongside ancient Hittite sites; and, despite the fact that Turkey is a secular state, strong Muslim fundamentalist currents now draw the country in a more southeasterly direction.

Politically, modern Turkey was a bold experiment, founded on the remaining, Anatolian kernel of the **Ottoman Empire**, once among the world's largest, and longest-lasting, imperial states. The country arose out of the defeat of World War I, almost entirely the creation of a single man of demonic energy and vision – **Kemal Atatürk**. The Turkish war of independence, fought against those victorious Allies intending to pursue imperialistic designs on Ottoman territory, was the prototype for all Third World "wars of liberation" in this century. It led to an explicitly **secular republic**, though one in which almost all of the inhabitants are at least nominally **Muslim** (predominantly Sunni).

Turks, except for a small minority in the southeast, are not Arabs, and loathe being mistaken for them; despite a heavy lacing of Persian and Arabic words, the **Turkish language** alone, unrelated to any neighbouring one, is sufficient to set its speakers apart. The **population** is, however, despite official efforts to bring about uniformity, ethnically remarkably **heterogeneous**. When the Ottoman Empire imploded early this century, large numbers of Muslim Slavs, Kurds, Greeks, Albanians and Circassians – to name only the largest non-Turkic groups – streamed into the modern territory, the safest refuge in an age of anti-Ottoman nationalism. This process has continued in recent years, so that the diversity of the people endures, constituting one of the surprises of travel in Turkey.

It's a vast country – France would fit within its boundaries with plenty of room to spare – incorporating characteristics of Middle Eastern and Aegean, even Balkan and trans-Caucasian countries. There are equally large **disparities** in levels of development. İstanbul boasts clubs as expensive and exclusive as any in New York or London, yet in the chronically backward eastern interior you'll encounter standards and modes of living scarcely changed from a century ago – an intolerable gap in a society aspiring to full EU membership and other accoutrements of **Westernization**. The government has attempted to address the anomalies over recent years, but it's debatable as to whether the modernization process begun during the late nineteenth century has struck deep roots in the culture, or is doomed to remain a veneer, typified by a fax- and credit-card-equipped, urban elite.

But one of the things that makes Turkey such a rewarding place to travel is the Turkish people, whose reputation for friendliness and **hospitality** is richly deserved; indeed you risk causing offence by refusing to partake of it, and any transaction can be the springboard for further acquaintance. Close to the bigger resorts or tourist attractions, much of this is undoubtedly mercenary, but in most of the country the warmth and generosity is genuine – all the more amazing when recent Turkish history has demonstrated that outsiders usually only bring trouble in their wake.

Turkey has been continuously inhabited and fought over for close on ten millennia, as the layer-cake arrangement of many **archeological sites** and the numerous fortified heights, encrusted with each era's contribution, testify. The juxtaposed ancient monuments mirror the bewildering **succession of states** – Hittite, Urartian, Phrygian, Hellenistic, Roman, Byzantine, Armeno-Georgian – that held sway here before the twelfth century. There is also, of course, an overwhelming number of graceful **Islamic monuments** dating from the eleventh century onwards, as well as magnificent city **bazaars**, alive and well despite the encroachments of more recent shopping practices. The country's modern architecture is less pleasing, the consequence both of government policy since 1950 and of returned overseas workers eager to invest their earnings in real estate; an ugliness also manifest at the **coastal resorts**, where the beaches are rarely as good as the tourist-board hype. Indeed it's **inland** Turkey – Asiatic expanses of mountain, steppe, lake, even cloud forest – that may leave a more vivid memory, especially when accented by some crumbling *kervansaray*, mosque or castle.

Where to go

Western Turkey is not only the more economically developed but also by far the more visited half of the country. **İstanbul**, straddling the straits linking the Black and Marmara seas, is touted as Turkish mystique par excellence, and understandably so: it would take months to even scratch the surface of the old imperial capital, still the cultural and commercial centre of the country. Flanking it on opposite sides of the **Sea of Marmara** are the two prior seats of the Ottoman Empire, Bursa and Edirne, each with their complement of attractions and regal atmosphere. The sea itself is flecked with tranquil, frequently overlooked islands, ideal havens when the cities get too much – and just beyond the Dardanelles and its World War I battlefields lie two larger Aegean islands, only opened to outsiders in the late 1980s.

As you move south, the classical character of the **Northeast Aegean** comes to the fore in the olive-swathed country around Bergama and Ayvalık, perhaps the two most compelling points in the region. Just outside **İzmir**, the old Ottoman princely training ground of Manisa and the originally Lydian city of Sardis, lost in vineyards, make a fine pair, while İzmir itself is the functional introduction to the **Central and Southern Aegean**, a magnet for travellers since the eighteenth century. The archeological complex at Ephesus overshadows in visitors' imaginations the equally deserving ancient Ionian sites of Priene and Didyma, and the ruins of Aphrodisias, Labranda and Alinda in old Caria. Be warned that the coast itself is heavily developed, though the star resorts – of which Çeşme is perhaps the quietest and Bodrum the most characterful – make comfortable bases from which to tour the interior. Don't overlook such evocative hill towns as Şirince, Birgi or Tire, which still exist in something of an Ottoman time warp.

Beyond the huge natural harbour of Marmaris, the Aegean becomes the Mediterranean; tourism levels drop slightly and the shore becomes more convoluted and piney. Yacht and schooner cruises are popular and easily arranged in Marmaris or the more pleasant town of Fethiye, principal centre of the **Turquoise Coast**. Two of the finest and largest beaches in the country sprawl at Dalyan and Patara, close to the eerie tombs of the Lycians, the fiercely independent locals of old. Kaş and Kalkan, further east, are other busy resorts, both good places to rest up, and well-situated bases for explorations into the mountainous hinterland. Beyond the relatively untouched beaches around ancient Olympos, Antalya is Turkey's fastest growing city, a sprawling place located at the beginning of the **Mediterranean Coast** proper. This is a lengthy shore, reaching as far as the Syrian border, with extensive sands and archeological sites – most notably at Perge, Side and Aspendos – though its western parts get swamped in high season. Once past castle-topped Alanya, however, the numbers diminish, and the stretch between Silifke and Adana offers innumerable minor points of interest, particularly the Roman city of Uzuncaburç and the romantic offshore

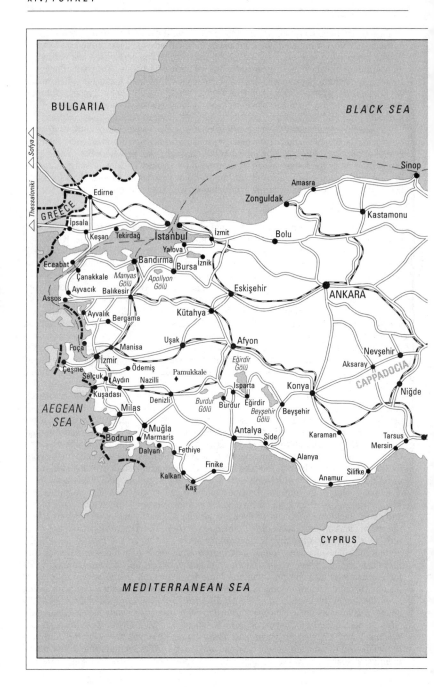

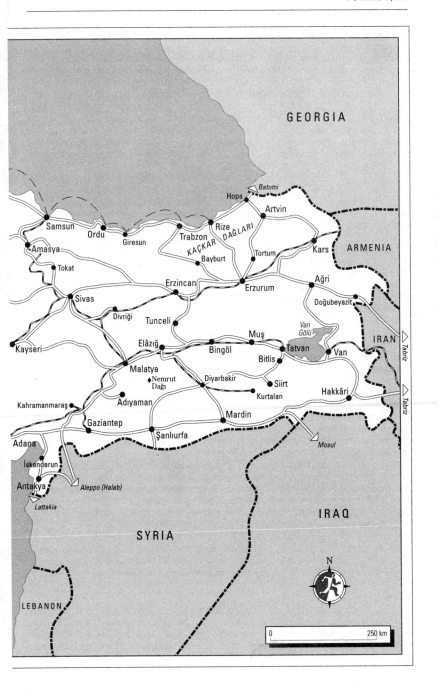

fortress at Kızkalesi. Further east, Arabic-flavoured Antakya is the heart of the **Hatay**, once part of Syria.

There are spectacular attractions inland, in **South Central Anatolia**, where you're confronted with the famous rock churches, subterranean cities and tufa-pinnacle landscapes of Cappadocia, in many ways the centrepiece of the region. The dry, bracing climate, excellent local wine, the artistic and architectural interest of the area, not to mention the chance to go horse-riding, could occupy you for as much as a week here, taking in the largest town in the area, Kayseri, with its bazaar and tombs, on the way north. You might pause, also, at Eğirdir or Beyşehir – historic towns fronting two of the numerous lakes that spangle the region – or in Konya, which, for both its Selçuk architecture and associations with the Mevlevi dervishes, makes for an appealing stopover on the way to or from the coast.

Ankara, hub of **North Central Anatolia**, is Turkey's capital, a planned city whose contrived Western feel gives some concrete indication of the priorities of the Turkish Republic; it also has the outstanding Museum of Anatolian Civilizations. Highlights of the region include the bizarre, isolated temple of Aezani, near Kutahya to the west; the Ottoman museum-town of Safranbolu; and the remarkable Hittite sites of Hatuşaş and Alacahöyük. If you're travelling north to the Black Sea, you should also look in on the Yeşilırmak valley towns of Sivas, Tokat and Amasya, each with their quota of early Turkish monuments. The **Black Sea** shore itself is surprisingly devoid of architectural interest other than a chain of Byzantine-Genoese castles, but the beauty of the landscape and beaches goes some way to compensate. The oldest and most interesting towns between utilitarian Samsun and Zonguldak are Sinop, the northernmost point of Anatolia, and Amasra, also easily reached from Safranbolu. East of Samsun, the coast gets wilder and wetter until you reach fabled Trabzon, once a seat of empire and today a base for visits to the marvellous monasteries of Aya Sofya and Sumela.

The Ankara–Sivas route also poises you for the trip along the Euphrates River and into the hitherto invisible "back half" of Turkey – the east. Your first stops in **Northeastern Anatolia** might be the outstanding early Turkish monumental ensembles at Divriği and Tercan. You'll inevitably end up in Erzurum, highest and bleakest major city of Turkey, from where you can head on to visit the temperate and church-studded valleys of southern medieval Georgia or go trekking in the Kaçkar mountains – Turkey's most popular hiking area – walling off the area from the Black Sea. Dreary Kars is worth enduring for the sake of nearby Ani, the ruined medieval Armenian capital, and various other Armenian monuments in the area – though many of these require some ingenuity and resourcefulness to seek out.

South of here, the **Euphrates and Tigris Basin** represents Turkey at its most Middle Eastern. Gaziantep, approached from points west, is the functional gateway to some centres of genuine interest. Urfa and nearby Harran are biblical in both appearance and history; Mardin, with its surrounding monasteries, is the homeland of Turkey's Syrian Orthodox minority. The colossal heads of Nemrut Dağı, however, reproduced endlessly on brochures and travel posters, are the real attraction here, and still mightily impressive, though now heavily commercialized. Diyarbakır, a swarming, vivid metropolis on the Tigris, is currently about the furthest east you should travel. East of Diyarbakır lies the largely Kurdish-populated – and violently troubled – basin of Lake Van, where travel is at the moment emphatically not recommended.

When to go

Turkey has a wide variety of climates, and there's a good chance that no matter when you want to go, somewhere in the country will be at least tolerable, if not ideal – although you should also pay attention to the basic seasonal patterns of tourist traffic.

Of the coastal areas, **İstanbul** and the area around the **Sea of Marmara** have a relatively damp, Balkan climate, with muggy summers and cool, rainy (though seldom snowy) winters. Bear in mind that competition for facilities between June and August can be a drawback. Things are similarly busy during summer on the popular **Aegean and Mediterranean coasts**; climatic conditions, too, can be difficult during July and August, especially between İzmir and Antakya, where the heat is tempered only slightly by offshore breezes. Perhaps the best time to visit these coastal regions is in spring or autumn, when the weather is gentler and the holiday crowds a little thinner. Indeed, even during winter, the Turquoise and Mediterranean coasts are – except for brief rainy periods in January and February – still fairly pleasant, and beyond Alanya up to the Hatay winters can be positively balmy, though you may still not be able to brave the water. The **Black Sea** is something of an anomaly, with temperate summers and exceptionally mild winters for so far north, and rain likely during the nine coolest months of the year, lingering as mist and humidity during summer – but it does have the advantage of being less crowded during the summer.

Anatolia is a natural fortress, its entire coast backed by mountains or hills, cutting off the interior from any moderating maritime influences. **Central Anatolia** is mostly semi-arid steppe, with a healthy, bracing climate – warm but not unpleasant in summer, cool and dry in the relatively short winters – though Ankara is exceptionally nasty during the central-heating season, when noxious soft coal is burnt (though this is being gradually phased out in favour of natural gas). Cappadocia in particular is a colourful, quiet treat throughout spring and autumn – indeed well into December, when its rock formations dusted with snow are especially beautiful. As you travel east, into **Northeast Anatolia** and around Lake Van, the altitude increases and conditions are deeply snowy between October and May, making high summer by far the best (in some cases the only) time to visit, when you'll also find it more comfortable and less populated than on the teeming coast. As you move into the lower **Euphrates and Tigris Basin**, a Middle Eastern influence exerts itself, with winters that are no worse than in central Anatolia but torrid summers – and without the compensation of a nearby beach.

THE LAKE VAN REGION

This edition of the *Rough Guide to Turkey* omits the chapter on **Lake Van and the southeast** which appeared in previous editions. In our opinion, travel in the region is now highly inadvisable owing to the ongoing Kurdish insurrection and to general lawlessness, including large-scale heroin smuggling between Lake Van and the Iranian frontier. Reprisals for PKK actions have often entailed the security forces placing local towns under formal curfew or even shooting up the main streets at random.

From 1992 to 1994, the Van region repeatedly made headlines overseas by virtue of the multiple kidnappings of foreign tourists by PKK operatives. Turkish authorities have responded by imposing a ban on domestic (and sometimes international) reporting of such incidents, depriving the PKK of the desired publicity – but also making it difficult for outsiders to evaluate the safety of venturing into the region. No kidnappings were reported in 1995 or 1996 (mainly because there were no tourists to kidnap), but there's always a chance you could end up the object of a sudden policy change.

Both the PKK and Turkish authorities are, in a sense, competing for your recognition and compliance. Kurdish sources announced that travellers to the region will not be molested if they're equipped with a Kurdish-language *laissez-passer* recognizing PKK sovereignty. The Turkish authorities, however, have made it clear that they are debriefing (ie interrogating) all released abductees for any evidence of voluntary collaboration with the PKK, including possession of such a document. For more on the Kurdish question, see p.780.

AVERAGE MIDDAY TEMPERATURES IN °C & °F

	Jan	Feb	Mar	Apr	May	Jun	Jul	Aug	Sep	Oct	Nov	Dec
İstanbul	6	6	7	12	17	21	24	24	20	16	12	8
	43	43	45	54	63	70	75	75	68	61	54	47
İzmir	9	10	12	16	21	25	28	28	24	19	15	11
	48	50	54	61	70	77	82	82	75	66	59	52
Antalya	11	12	13	17	21	23	29	29	25	21	16	12
	52	54	56	63	70	77	84	84	77	70	61	54
Ankara	1	1	5	12	17	20	24	24	19	13	8	3
	34	34	41	54	63	68	75	75	66	56	47	37
Trabzon	8	8	9	12	16	20	23	24	20	17	14	10
	47	47	48	54	61	68	73	75	68	63	57	50
Diyarbakir	2	4	9	14	20	26	31	31	25	18	10	5
	35	39	48	57	68	79	88	88	77	65	50	41

PART ONE

THE

BASICS

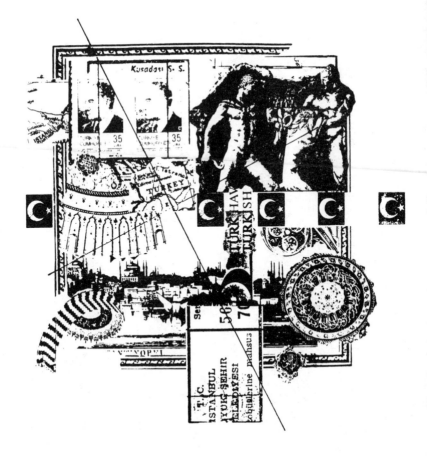

GETTING THERE FROM BRITAIN AND IRELAND

The easiest way to get to Turkey from Britain or Ireland is to travel by air. There are several gateway airports at each end, though London and İstanbul are still the busiest year-round; fares almost always undercut those of a train journey. Driving is perhaps the most expensive and time-consuming option, but once inside the country the effort can prove worthwhile. Using any overland means, you'll save bother and time – though not necessarily money – by taking ferries between Italy, Greece and Turkey, or between outlying Greek islands and the Turkish coast, thus avoiding long detours through theft- and corruption-ridden eastern Europe and the general turmoil in ex-Yugoslavia.

BY PLANE

British Airways, Turkish Airlines (THY), İstanbul Airlines, Cyprus Turkish Airlines and *Onur Air* all offer direct **scheduled services** to Turkey from the UK throughout the year. Of the two biggest carriers offering flights from **London Heathrow to İstanbul**, *Turkish Airlines* has two flights daily all year, continuing to Ankara or İzmir for a slight add-on fare; low-season APEX fares to İstanbul begin at £279 (including tax), climbing in high season (Christmas, Easter, and late March to October) to £319 (including tax). *British Airways* also has twice-daily services year-round for slightly more, ranging from £321 low season to £352 at peak times. These prices on both airlines entail a spec-

ified advance-purchase period, a stay of seven to ninety days involving at least one Saturday night, and heavy penalties for any date changes.

The **smaller airlines** tend to offer much better deals on scheduled flights, especially to southwestern Turkey. *İstanbul Airlines* – although notorious for cancelling, postponing and overbooking their flights – fly three times weekly **from London** (either Gatwick or Heathrow according to day) **to İstanbul** year-round, and return fares are a modest £187 tax inclusive in winter, climbing to about £210 in summer. They also fly once weekly in summer at comparable fares **from Manchester** to İstanbul, though often with a stop at London Stansted. If you're heading for southwestern Turkey, the most frequent and economical service is on *Cyprus Turkish Airlines*, which flies three times weekly in winter from **London Heathrow to İzmir or Antalya**, two times a week in summer. The return fare is £218 in winter, about £240 in summer; in summer they often ply the **Stansted–İzmir/Antalya** route at a similar frequency for roughly £230. *Onur Air* has two or three weekly scheduled flights from **London Gatwick to İstanbul**, at a very reasonable £149 or so in winter, about £169 in summer, tax inclusive. During the tourist season, they go once weekly from Gatwick **to Dalaman** on the Turquoise Coast for £160 (fare valid only for a stay of 2 weeks), İzmir for £165 (same time restriction), and Antalya for £160 (ditto); *Onur* also provides many charter flights from regional centres such as London Stansted, Bristol, Cardiff and Manchester.

AIRLINES WITH DIRECT SCHEDULED SERVICES TO TURKEY

British Airways, 156 Regent St, London W1R 5TA (☎0345/222111).

Cyprus Turkish Airlines, 11–12 Pall Mall, London SW1Y 5JG (☎0171/930 4851).

İstanbul Airlines, c/o *President Holidays*, 92 Park Lane, Croydon, Surrey CR0 1JF (☎0181/688 7555).

Onur Air, 23 Prince's Street, London W1R 7RG (☎0171/499 9939).

Turkish Airlines (Türk Hava Yolları), 11–12 Hanover St, London W1R 9HF (☎0171/499 9249).

FLIGHT AGENTS IN BRITAIN

Alpha Flights, 173 Uxbridge Rd, London W11 (☎0171/579 8444). Competitive airfares.

APA Travel, 138 Eversholt St, London NW1 (☎0171/387 5337). Competitive airfares.

Avro PLC, 1 Weir Rd, London SW19 8UX (☎0181/715 0000; or ☎0161/489 2989). Bottom-end, seat-only operator with seasonal charters to Dalaman from several UK airports.

Campus Travel, 541 Bristol Rd, Selly Oak, Birmingham B29 6AU (☎0121/414 1848); 61 Ditchling Rd, Brighton BN1 4SD (☎01273/570226); 39 Queens Rd, Clifton, Bristol BS8 1QE (☎0117/929 2494); 5 Emmanuel St, Cambridge CB1 1NE (☎01223/324283); 53 Forest Rd, Edinburgh EH1 2QP (☎0131/668 3303); 52 Grosvenor Gardens, London SW1W 0AG (☎0171/730 3402); 166 Deansgate, Manchester M3 3FE (☎0161/833 2046); 105–106 St Aldates, Oxford OX1 1DD (☎01865/242067). Student/youth travel specialists, with branches also in YHA shops and on university campuses all over Britain.

Council Travel, 28a Poland St, London W1V 3DB (☎0171/437 7767). Discounted student/youth flights only; "adults" need not apply.

The Flight Company, 2 Upper Teddington Road, Hampton Wick, Kingston upon Thames, Surrey KT1 4DP (☎0181/977 9455; or ☎0161/228 2330). Typically uncivilized flight times but good prices on charter tickets.

North South Travel, Moulsham Mill Centre, Parkway, Chelmsford, Essex CM2 7PX (☎01245/492882). Friendly, competitive travel agency, offering discounted fares worldwide – profits are used to support projects in the developing world, especially the promotion of sustainable tourism.

Nouvelles Frontières, 11 Blenheim St, London W1Y 9LE (☎0171/629 7772). UK branch of the biggest French discount agency.

Soliman Travel, 113 Earl's Court Rd, London SW5 (☎0171/244 6855). Very accommodating flight consolidators.

STA Travel, 25 Queens Rd, Bristol BS8 1QE (☎0117/929 4399); 38 Sidney St, Cambridge CB2 3HX (☎01223/366966); 88 Vicar Lane, Leeds LS1 7JH (☎0113/244 9212); 86 Old Brompton Rd, London SW7 3LH, 117 Euston Rd, London NW1 2SX, and 38 Store St, London WC1 (Worldwide ☎0171/361 6262; Europe ☎0171/ 361 6161); 75 Deansgate, Manchester M3 2BW (☎0161/834 0668); 36 George St, Oxford OX1 2OJ (☎01865/792800); and branches in Birmingham, Canterbury, Cardiff, Coventry, Durham, Glasgow, Loughborough, Nottingham, Sheffield and Warwick. Worldwide specialists in low-cost flights for students and under-26s.

Trailfinders, 22–24 The Priory, Queensway, Birmingham B4 6BS (☎0121/236 1234); 48 Corn St, Bristol BS1 1HQ (☎0117/929 9000); 254–284 Sauchiehall St, Glasgow G2 3EH (☎0141/353 2224); 42–50 Earls Court Rd, London W8 6FT (European flights ☎0171/937 5400), and 194 Kensington High St, London W8 7RG (☎0171/938 3939); 58 Deansgate, Manchester M3 2FF (☎0161/839 6969). One of the best-informed and most efficient agents, especially if you're not a student or are over 26.

Travel Bug, 125 Gloucester Rd, London SW7 (☎0171/835 1111); 597 Cheetham Hill Rd, Manchester M8 5EJ (☎0161/721 4000). Large range of discounted tickets; *Trailfinders'* closest competitor.

Union Travel, 93 Piccadilly, London W1 (☎0171/493 4343). Competitive airfares.

At the time of writing, scheduled services on *Istanbul Airlines* **from Ireland**, which formerly connected Belfast, Cork and Dublin with İzmir in the summer, have been discontinued.

Given the competitive fares from minor airlines, all of which are used as carriers by specialist Turkish travel agents, you'll probably save very little if anything by using a **charter**. Major seat-only brokers such as *Avro* offer fares to Dalaman from virtually every UK airport hovering in the £160–210 range, depending on season, for a two-

week ticket, while *The Flight Company* has similar prices to Dalaman from Gatwick as well as £150–190 services to İzmir and Antalya from Gatwick, plus slightly pricier Manchester departures to Dalaman and İzmir. Most charter durations are one or two weeks, but occasionally you can pay a supplement and get a four-week interval or even more by arrangement.

Sometimes **discounted scheduled flights** can be had from either Turkish specialists (see box on pp.8–9) or flight discount shops; specialist

TRAVEL AGENTS IN IRELAND

Aran Travel, 52 Dominick St, Galway (☎091/62595).

Discount Travel, 4 South Great Georges St, Dublin 2 (☎01/679 5888).

Flight Finders International, 13 Baggot St Lower, Dublin 2 (☎01/676 8326).

Inflight Travel, 92–94 York Rd, Belfast 15 (☎01232/740187 or 743341).

Joe Walsh Tours, 8–11 Baggot St, Dublin (☎01/676 3053). General budget fares agent.

JWT Holidays, 34 Grafton St, Dublin 2 (☎01/671 8751).

Lee Travel, 23 Princes St, Cork (☎021/277111).

Liffey Travel, Abbey Mall, 13 Lower Liffey St, Dublin 1 (☎01/873 4900). Package tour specialists.

McCarthy Travel, 56 Patrick St, Cork (☎021/270127).

Specialized Travel Services, 32 Bachelor's Walk, Dublin 1 (☎01/873 1066).

Student & Group Travel, 71 Dame St, Dublin 2 (☎01/677 7834). Student specialists.

Thomas Cook, 11 Donegall Place, Belfast (☎01232/240833); 118 Grafton St, Dublin (☎01/677 1721). Package holiday and flight agent, with occasional discount offers.

Travel Shop, 35 Belmont Rd, Belfast 4 (☎01232/471717).

USIT, Fountain Centre, Belfast BT1 6ET (☎01232/324073); 10–11 Market Parade, Patrick St, Cork (☎021/270900); 33 Ferryquay St, Derry (☎01504/371888); Aston Quay, Dublin 2 (☎01/679 8833); Victoria Place, Eyre Square, Galway (☎091/565177); Central Buildings, O'Connell St, Limerick (☎061/415064); 36–37 Georges St, Waterford (☎051/72601). Student and youth specialists for flights and trains.

youth and student agencies are especially good if you are a student or under 26, and often have a wide choice of scheduled deals. A scan of the travel section of weekend editions of the quality papers is usually the best way to find a bargain.

BY TRAIN

Travelling to Turkey by train makes very little sense unless you're European, under 26 and are equipped with an *InterRail* pass, making it possible to take in other countries en route. *British Rail International* no longer even quotes a through fare to İstanbul from London, requiring passengers to buy two separate fares, London–Munich and Munich–İstanbul, for a whopping total of £485, adult second-class return; *Eurotrain's BIJ* fare for this itinerary is a scant £4 cheaper. The usual **route**, taking the better part of four days, threads through Belgium, Germany (Munich), Austria (Vienna), Hungary (Budapest), Yugoslavia (Belgrade) and Bulgaria (Plovdiv). Alternatively, get yourself to Italy and then proceed by ferry to Greece or even all the way to Turkey (see p.7).

A far better deal, though still more than most air fares, is provided by the wide range of **InterRail youth passes**, which are available to European residents and valid for virtually the entire continental European rail network, plus Turkey and Morocco. To reach Turkey from the UK or Ireland, you'd need to cross at least two of the seven zones into which Europe is divided; a two-zone, one-month pass (£220) would allow you to cross France, Italy, Greece (including free passage on the *Adriatic/Hellenic Mediterranean's* Brindisi –Patras ferry) and Turkey, whilst an all-zone, one-month pass (£275) would permit transit along the all-overland route quoted above, which involves four zones. The **adult InterRail**, dubbed the 26+, is distinctly less worthwhile (1 month for £275) because it's not valid for Belgium, France, Spain, Portugal, Italy, Switzerland or Morocco; the absence of Belgium from the scheme means you'll pay £69 extra to cross from a British ferry port to the German frontier.

A **Eurail Pass**, which must be purchased before arrival in Europe, is unlikely to interest North Americans or Australasians bound for Turkey unless they plan to travel extensively in Europe beforehand; for a start, it's not valid in Turkey, but only in sixteen countries en route, the most obvious being Austria, Belgium, France, Germany, Greece, Hungary, Italy and Switzerland. (For travel within Turkey, you might consider buying a *Freedom* or *Eurodomino* pass, or a *TrenTur* card – see p.26.) Getting to the frontier as part of a wider trip through Europe, count on US$398/A$575 for a fifteen-day *Eurail Youthpass*

TRAIN INFORMATION AND TICKETS ABROAD

NORTH AMERICA

CIT Tours, 342 Madison Ave, Suite 207, New York, NY 10173 (☎1-800/223-7987).

DER Travel, 9501 W Divon Ave, Suite 400, Rosemont, IL 60018 (☎1-800/421-2929).

Rail Europe, 226 Westchester Ave, White Plains, NY 10604 (☎1-800/438-7245 in USA; ☎1-800/361-7245 in Canada).

ScanTours, 3439 Wade St, Los Angeles, CA 90066 (☎1-800/223-7226 or 310/636-4656).

AUSTRALIA AND NEW ZEALAND

CIT, 123 Clarence St, Sydney (☎02/9299 4754); offices in Melbourne, Brisbane, Adelaide and Perth. No NZ office; all enquires through the Australian offices.

Thomas Cook World Rail, Australia: ☎1800/422 747; New Zealand: ☎09/263 7260.

UK

British Rail International, opposite Platform 2, Victoria Station, London SW1V 1JY (☎0171/834 2345).

Eurotrain, 52 Grosvenor Gardens, London SW1W 0AG (☎0171/730 3402).

Wasteels, opposite platform 2, Victoria Station, London SW1V 1JY (☎0171/834 7066).

IRELAND

Continental Rail Desk, Iarnrod Eireann, 35 Lower Abbey St, Dublin 1 (☎01/703 1888).

Northern Ireland Railways, 28–30 Wellington Place, Belfast 1 (☎01232/230671).

(for those under 26); if you're 26 or over you'll have to buy a first-class pass, at US$498/A$720 for fifteen days; both of these passes are also available in one-month or two-month versions. You stand a better chance of getting your money's worth out of a **Eurail Flexipass**, which is good for a certain number of travel days in a two-month period. Five days cost US$255/A$370 for under-26s, US$348/A$505 for over-26s (first class); ten- and fifteen-day versions are also available. Another alternative is to attempt to buy an *InterRail* pass in Europe – most agents don't check residential qualifications, but once you're in Europe it'll be too late to buy a *Eurail* pass if you have problems.

TRAVELLING THROUGH BULGARIA: VISAS

In order to travel through Bulgaria, all EU citizens, Australians and New Zealanders need a visa, whilst Americans and Canadians do not at present. In theory visas are available at rail frontier crossings, but they're better value if obtained in advance from a Bulgarian embassy or consulate (see box). There are two kinds of visa: **transit visas**, which allow you to stay in Bulgaria for 30 hours and cost £25 or £40 if obtained in advance, depending on whether they're valid for single or double entry, and **tourist visas** permitting up to

twenty days' stay. The latter cost £54 on the spot or with less than 7 days' notice from an embassy or consulate, for fifteen days' stay, £34 for 20 days with 7 days' notice from an embassy or consulate. This visa type seems to be regarded more favourably by border guards; it also gives the option of stopping off for longer if you wish – especially worth it if you're using *InterRail*. Applying in person at a Bulgarian embassy or consulate should get you either kind of visa on the same day, subject to the noted surcharge; only

BULGARIAN EMBASSIES AND CONSULATES

Australia, 4 Carlotta Rd, Double Bay, Sydney, NSW 2028 (☎02/367581 or 9327 7592).

Canada, 325 Stewart St, Ottawa, ON K1M 6K5 (☎613/789-3215).

Turkey, Atatürk Bul 124, Kavaklıdere, Ankara (☎0312/436 1653); Talat Paşa Cad 31, Edirne (☎0284/225 1069); Zincirlikuyu Cad 44, Ulus, Levent, İstanbul (☎0212/269 0478).

UK, 186–188 Queen's Gate, London SW7 5HO (☎0171/584 9400; Mon–Fri 9.30am–12.30pm).

USA, 1621 22nd St NW, Washington, DC 20008 (☎202/387-7969); 121 E 62nd St, New York, NY 10021 (☎212/935 4646).

cash is accepted. Postal applications take a week; enclose your passport, a note specifying the type of visa required, a photo, a postal order as payment (no cheques), and an SAE.

DRIVING AND HITCHING

In theory you can do the car journey from Britain to Turkey in three to four days. However, this allows little time for stopping and sleeping, and it makes sense to spread the journey over a longer space of time and take in a few places en route. The most direct approach is through Germany, Austria, Hungary, Yugoslavia and Bulgaria, broadly sticking to the following route: London –Ostend–Frankfurt–Munich–Vienna– Budapest–Beograd–Sofia–Plovdiv–Edirne– İstanbul. For details on Balkan visas, see above; for the full story on customs formalities and insurance cover once in Turkey, see "Getting Around", p.32.

If you're hitching, follow roughly the same route as given above; rides are notoriously scarce through France, Switzerland and Italy. From Germany or Austria, though, there are plenty of TIR lorries and private cars en route to Turkey, making lifts relatively easy to find.

FERRIES FROM ITALY OR GREECE

If you're travelling overland to Turkey, particularly by car, concluding the journey with a boat ride from Italy or Greece is a tempting (and sensible) option.

Full-sized **long-haul ferries** ply a half-dozen routes between Italy and Turkey, most of them direct. *Turkish Maritime Lines*, the most consistent operator, runs a year-round ferry from **Venice to İzmir**, weekly (on Sat) from mid-March until mid-November, fortnightly otherwise. The 63-hour crossing is roughly comparable in price to the *Marlines* Ancona–Kuşadası route (see below) at about US$230 for a Pullman seat, US$360 for a third-class cabin, with small cars costing an additional US$230 (one-way, low-season fares, taxes inclusive). Better value in terms of sea miles covered is *TML's* identically priced weekly service (on Sat) from Venice to either **Antalya** or **Marmaris** (alternating each week), a three-day sail in operation between early June and early October.

Cheapest and briefest is *TML's* 32-hour **Brindisi–Çeşme** crossing, sailing twice weekly (Wed and Sat) between mid-June and mid-September; off-peak fares, taxes inclusive, run to US$160 for a seat, US$250 for a low-class cabin including meals, US$190 for a small car. There's competition on this route, with comparable fares, from private companies, including *Med Link Lines* (2 weekly late June to mid-Sept) and *European Seaways* (1–2 weekly year-round). **Çeşme**, the second westernmost point of Anatolia, is also served from **Bari** by *European Seaways* (2 weekly June–Sept; 38hr), with sample one-way passenger fares of US$250 for a middling cabin, plus US$190 a small car, and from **Ancona** by the somewhat less reliable *Topaş* (1 weekly May–Oct; 65hr), with specimen fares of US$330 for a mid-range cabin, meals included, plus US$240 for a saloon car.

From late June to mid-September, *Marlines* runs a weekly ferry from **Ancona to Kuşadası** on the Aegean coast, with stops at Patras and Crete in Greece. The total journey time is 75 hours, with one stop-over allowed. Tax-exclusive fares for the whole distance range from US$180 deck-class to US$280 for a mid-range cabin berth; a car costs US$270. Although there are no student or railpass concessions, return fares are ten percent cheaper than two one-ways.

Many travellers take the **short-hop ferries** over from the Greek islands of Lésvos, Híos, Sámos, Kós and Rhodes, to the respective Turkish ports of Ayvalık, Çeşme, Kuşadası, Bodrum and Marmaris. Except for the Lésvos and Kós services, these still run after a fashion in winter, but you may have to wait a week or two between boats. One-way prices of US$14–35 (plus US$16–30 more for Greek and Turkish port taxes) make these vastly overpriced for the distances involved; full details of every service are given at the end of the *North Aegean* and *Central and Southern Aegean* chapters.

One thing you should bear in mind if you're holidaying in Greece is that a quick **overnight** jaunt over to the Turkish side on one of these ferries will, if you're on a charter flight, **invalidate the return half of your ticket**, since the Greek government, having subsidized cheap landing fees for charter airlines, is loath for you to spend your money elsewhere. Day excursions (ie not staying in Turkey overnight) are exempt from this, but otherwise there is no way around it, since the Turkish authorities will clearly stamp your passport both when you enter the country and when you leave.

FERRY AGENCIES

European Seaways, c/o *Pan Sped*, Stazione Marittima, Corso de Tullio 26, 70 126 Bari (☎080/523 0420), and *Italian Ferries*, 96–98 Corso Garibaldi, 72 100 Brindisi (☎0831/590305).

Marlines, Via XXIX Settembre 8A, 60 122 Ancona (☎071/202566).

Med Link Lines, c/o *Discovery Shipping Agency*, Corso Garibaldi 49, 72 100 Brindisi (☎0831/527667).

TML, c/o *Sunquest Holidays*, 23 Prince's St, London W1R 7RG (☎0171/499 9991). In Italy, c/o *Bassani*, Via XXII Marzo 2414, Venice (☎041/522 9544).

Viamare Travel, Graphic House, 2 Sumatra Rd, London NW6 1PU (☎0171/431 4560). Agents for all major companies – including *Fragline, Poseidon, AK Ventouris* and *Arkadia* – plying the Italy–Greece crossing.

PACKAGES AND SPECIAL INTEREST TOURS

Like Greece and Spain, Turkey is now firmly on the circuit of inclusive tours, with nearly seventy companies in the UK offering some sort of hotel, villa, city-break or sailing holiday. Most of these target İstanbul and the coast between Çeşme and Alanya – Cappadocia is curiously missing from almost all brochures – but you needn't feel tied to a rigid programme, since most outfits also pitch advantageous fly-drive plans. As southern Turkey has such short, balmy winters, coastal yachting and accommodation packages are available from April to November; further north, a few companies handle winter skiing holidays and İstanbul city breaks. More esoteric special activity programmes include trekking, bird-spotting, scuba-diving and whitewater rafting. Prices for an ordinary, two-week, beach-front package, staying in a resort *pansiyon* or two-star hotel start at around £250 per person (double occupancy) for bed and breakfast, flight included; quality self-catering villas tend to cost over £500 for the same period (flight included), with a four-star hotel setting you back about £450. Fly-drive-only deals weigh in at around £300 per person for four adults travelling for two weeks in high season, around £400 if there are only two of you.

Following is a selection of package tour operators, in the UK and Turkey, selected for their unique offerings or high level of service, or both.

GENERAL TOUR OPERATORS

Anatolian Sky, IMEX House, 52 Blucher St, Birmingham B1 1QU (☎0121/633 4018). Fairly upmarket packages; particular strengths are Kalkan, Fethiye and Ölü Deniz, and classic hotels in İstanbul.

Bakhus Tourism, 1135 Great Cambridge Rd, Enfield, Middlesex EN1 4DB (☎0181/482 3224). One of the few operators to offer inland destinations, including Cappadocia; also arranges timely accommodation in Edirne (grease wrestling festival) and Konya (dervish performance).

Dolunay Holidays, Spreadeagle Court, Northgate St, Gloucester GL1 1SL (☎01452/501978). Features unique hotels at Assos, Bozcaada and Sultaniye (near Dalyan).

Metak Holidays, 70 Welbeck St, London W1M 7HA (☎0171/935 6961). Competent, long-running packager, with offerings in Kaş and Antalya as well as most other major coastal resorts.

President Holidays, 92 Park Lane, Croydon, Surrey CR0 1JF (☎0181/688 7555). Durable agency, strongest in İstanbul, but also offering glitzy hotels in Marmaris, Alanya and Kuşadası. UK reps for *İstanbul Airlines*.

Regent Holidays, Regent House, 31A High St, Shanklin, Isle of Wight PO37 6JW (☎01983/864212). Strong İstanbul programme, including Sile and Kilyos beaches; also tailor-made arrangements.

Simply Turkey, Chiswick Gate, 598–608 Chiswick High Rd, London W4 5RT (☎0181/747 1011). Probably the best outlet for quality self-catering villas in exclusive locations like Gümüşlük, Akyaka, Şirince and Ocakköy, as well as gourmet hotels in more frequented destinations; also guided walking and botanical tours, painting and cooking courses.

Sunquest, 23 Prince's St, London W1R 7RG (☎0171/499 9991). Long-established generalists, with a budget-to-mid-range presence in most coastal resorts between Ayvalık and Alanya, plus İstanbul; also the UK representatives for *Turkish Maritime Lines*, and affiliated with *Onur Air*.

Suntours, 10 Hills Place, London W1R 1AF (☎0171/434 3636). Virtually the only UK packages for Çeşme/Ilıca.

Tapestry Holidays, 24 Chiswick High Rd, London W4 1TE (☎0181/742 0055). Wide selection of small but high-quality *pansiyons* and hotels on the Turquoise Coast, with emphasis on Kalkan, Akyaka and Turunç Bay; also excellent villas at Gümüşlük, yachting and water sports, and İstanbul too.

Turkey & Beyond, 29 Marylebone Rd, London NW1 5JX (☎0171/486 3338). Well-balanced selection of accommodation on the southwest coast; particularly good Bodrum and Marmaris area programmes.

TREKKING/INLAND ADVENTURE HOLIDAYS

Adrift, Collingbourne House, 140–142 Wandsworth High St, London SW18 4JJ (☎0181/874 4969). Whitewater rafting on the Çoruh River from late May to late July; eight- or ten-day programme.

Alternatif Turizm, Bağdat Cad 36/8, Kızıltoprak, Turkey (☎0216/345 6650). Trekking and mountain-bike trips near İstanbul and throughout Turkey; also springtime whitewater rafting along the Turquoise Coast.

Explore Worldwide, 1 Frederick St, Aldershot, Hants GU11 1LQ (☎01252/319448). Camping treks in Lycia, the Toros ranges and the Kaçkar, plus an array of less strenuous overland minibus tours across the country, which can be combined with *gület* (caique) cruises.

Imaginative Traveller, 14 Barley Mow Passage, London W4 4PH (☎0181/742 8612). One- to three-week overland explorations of the best of Turkey, travelling by train or coach, camping out or staying at *pansiyons*. Some unusual stops and opportunities for light walking.

Sobek Travel, İstasyon Cad 42, 51100 Niğde, Turkey (☎0388/213 2117). Wide variety of outdoor programmes, including treks in virtually every mountain range, Cappadocian horse-riding, winter volcano skiing, and rafting on the Çoruh and Göksu.

Talking Turkey, 2 St Christophers Ave, Ashton-under-Lyne, Lancs OL6 9DT (☎0161/330 1404). Scuba, sea-kayaking, mountain-biking, trekking, and village/rural programs off the beaten track in Lycia. UK reps of *Bougainville Travel* in Kaş.

WATERSPORTS AND SAILING HOLIDAYS

Dive and Sail, Nastfield Cottage, The Green, Frampton-on-Severn, Glos GL2 7DY (☎01452/740919). One- or two-week, boat-based diving instruction programmes near Bodrum or Marmaris.

Nautilus Yachting, 42 Croydon Rd, Caterham, Surrey CR3 6QB (☎01883/340525). Broad selection of *gület*, yacht (with or without skipper) and catamaran holidays out of Göcek, Datça, Marmaris and Bitez.

Sunsail, The Porthouse, Port Solent, Portsmouth PO6 4TH (☎01705/219847 or 222222). Land-based yachting and windsurfing in the Bodrum, Datça, Fethiye and Marmaris areas; also flotilla holidays.

Sunworld Sailing, 120 St Georges Rd, Brighton, Sussex BN2 1EA (☎01273/626284). Windsurfing and small-boat programmes at Bitez and Farilya on the Bodrum peninsula.

Templecraft Yacht Charters, 33 Grand Parade, Brighton BN2 2QA (☎01273/695094). Offers *tirandels* (the local equivalent of the Greek *trehandíri* wooden fishing boat) for independent cruising.

SKIING HOLIDAYS

Seriously Turkey Holidays, Enterprise Centre, 4 Duke Close, Andover, Hants SP10 5AP (☎01264/333319). Skiing holidays in the Uludağ range, operating out of Bursa.

Sunquest (for address, see above). Skiing holidays based in Bursa.

SPECIAL INTEREST HOLIDAYS

British Museum Traveller, 46 Bloomsbury St, London WC1B 3QQ (☎0171/323 8895). Offers a pair of two-week tours led by experts: one focuses on Roman, Byzantine and Selçuk sites, the other takes in very early settlements.

Fotoğrafevi, Zambak Sok 15/4, Beyoğlu, İstanbul, Turkey (☎0212/251 0566 or 245 4008). Photographic minibus safaris to the most beautiful and exotic corners of Turkey (Lycia, the Kaçkar range, Cappadocia), led by English-speaking Faruk Akbaş.

Gullivers Natural History Holidays, Oak Farm, Stoke Hammond, Milton Keynes, Bucks MK17 9DB (☎01525/270100). Bird-watching and botanizing near Dalyan.

Holt's Battlefield Tours, Golden Key Building, 15 Market St, Sandwich, Kent CT13 9DA

(☎01304/612248). One-week tours centred on Gallipoli, designed to coincide with ANZAC Day commemorations.

Inter-Church Travel, Middleburg Square, Folkestone, Kent CT20 1AZ (☎01303/300444). Seven Churches of Revelations and other Saint Paul-oriented pilgrimages, based in and around west- and south-coast resorts.

Sunbird, PO Box 76, Sandy, Bedfordshire SG19 1DF (☎01767/682969). Offers a twelve-day birding tour of promising sites across Anatolia (May/June).

TEFS Limited Railway Tours, 77 Frederick St, Loughborough, Leics LE11 3TL (☎01509/262745). Yearly, two-week spring itineraries along 2500km of Anatolian train track, hauled by antique steam locomotives.

ALTERNATIVE ACTIVITIES

Gölköy Centre, Bodrum peninsula (☎0252/357 7202; in the UK, ☎0181/291 7981). Yoga "farm", which also functions as a guesthouse between the seven week-long courses offered from May to October.

Huzur Vadısı (☎01545/570742 in the UK). One- and two-week holistic programmes of light walks, tai chi, massage and so on at a secluded, three-acre *yurt* complex inland from Fethiye; open April–Oct.

Tohum Centre for Natural Living & Healing Arts, PK 2, Kaş (☎0242/839 5001). Yoga and travel programmes, wholefood meals and stone-house accommodation at this organic farmstead in the hills above Kaş.

GETTING THERE FROM THE US AND CANADA

From the US and Canada, flying to Turkey, directly or indirectly, is the only realistic option for vacations devoted solely to the country; of course, many travellers visit Turkey as part of an overland trip through Europe or Asia, in which case the remarks on crossing Europe in "Getting there from Britain and Ireland", above, will be of interest. No matter where you're flying from, it will almost certainly be cheaper to land in İstanbul: other cities such as Ankara and İzmir may be "common-rated" with İstanbul in airlines' published fares, but competition on routes into İstanbul results in heavier discounts off these published fares.

Low **season** on air fares to Turkey is early November to mid-December and late December to late March; high season is early June to mid-September, plus Christmas time; the rest of the calendar falls within the "shoulder" season. The **fares** below are those published by the airlines (consolidators may be able to knock off a couple of hundred dollars) and assume midweek travel; travelling on Friday, Saturday or Sunday will add about US$40 or Can$60. **Taxes** usually run an extra US$30–40 or Can$50–80, depending on the airports involved.

Round-the-world tickets rarely include Turkey because North American consolidators can't access discounted onward one-way tickets out of İstanbul. You'll find it much easier to get a ticket with a stop-over in Athens, starting at about US$2200, and treat Turkey as a side trip.

FROM THE US

Turkish Airlines is the only carrier to fly direct from the US to **İstanbul**, with a daily service from New York JFK, usually non-stop but sometimes with a stop in Brussels. Many other European carriers (see the box) fly via their respective capitals but, depending on your starting point, might offer better or cheaper connections than flying to New York to pick up *Turkish*. All the airlines listed in the box discount their tickets through consolidators – indeed, airlines like *Tarom* and *Malev* sell

AIRLINES IN THE US AND CANADA

Air France (in US, ☎1-800/237-2747; in Canada, ☎1-800/667-2747). Major US and Canadian cities to İstanbul via Paris.

Alitalia (☎1-800/223-5730; in New York, ☎1-800/442-5860; in Canada, ☎1-800/361-8336). Boston, Chicago, Los Angeles, Miami, New York JFK and Newark, and Toronto to İstanbul via Rome.

Austrian Airlines (☎1-800/843-0002). Atlanta, Chicago, New York and Washington to İstanbul, Ankara and İzmir, all via Vienna.

Delta Airlines (in US, ☎1-800/241-4141; in Canada, call directory inquiries, ☎1-800/555-1212, for local toll-free number). Atlanta, Cincinnati, Los Angeles, New York and Orlando to İstanbul via Frankfurt.

Finnair (☎1-800/950-5000). New York to İstanbul via Helsinki.

KLM (in US, ☎1-800/374-7747; in Canada, ☎1-800/361-5073). In partnership with *Northwest*,

flies from many US and Canadian cities to İstanbul via Amsterdam.

Lufthansa (in US, ☎1-800/645-3880; in Canada, ☎1-800/563-5954). Many US and Canadian cities to İstanbul, Ankara, İzmir and Anatalya, via Frankfurt.

Malev Hungarian Airlines (☎1-800/223-6884). Atlanta and New York to İstanbul via Budapest.

Sabena (☎1-800/955-2000). Atlanta, Boston, Chicago and New York to İstanbul via Brussels.

Swissair (in US, ☎1-800/221-4750; in Canada, ☎1-800/267-9477). Many US and Canadian cities to İstanbul via Zurich or Geneva.

Tarom Romanian Air (☎212/687-6013). Chicago and New York to İstanbul via Bucharest.

Turkish Airlines THY (☎1-800/874-8875). New York (JFK) non-stop or via Brussels to İstanbul, with onward connections to all major Turkish airports.

nearly all their tickets this way. The ones that sound cheapest usually are, but beware of long layovers in obscure airports.

Sample APEX fares to İstanbul include, from **New York**, US$690 in low season, US$910 in high season; from **Washington**, US$780 /US$1100; from **Miami**, US$860/US$1200; from **Chicago**, US$810/US$1140; from **Los Angeles**, US$980/US$1310; and from **San Francisco**, US$960/US$1290.

Turkish Airlines has the most comprehensive selection of connecting flights within Turkey, of

DISCOUNT TRAVEL AGENTS IN THE US AND CANADA

Airtech, 584 Broadway, Suite 1007, New York, NY 10012 (☎1-800/575-TECH or 212/219-7000). Standby seat broker; also deals in consolidator fares and courier flights.

Club America, 51 E 42nd St, Suite 1406, New York, NY 10017 (☎1-800/221-4969 or 212/972-2865). Consolidator.

Council Travel, 205 E 42nd St, New York, NY 10017 (☎1-800/226-8624 or 212/822-2700), and branches in many other US cities. Student/budget travel agency.

Educational Travel Center, 438 N Frances St, Madison, WI 53703 (☎1-800/747-5551 or 608/256-5551). Student/youth and consolidator fares.

International Student Exchange Flights, 5010 E Shea Blvd, Suite 104A, Scottsdale, AZ 85254 (☎602/951-1177). Student/youth fares, plus student IDs.

New Europe Holidays (☎1-800/642-3874). Consolidator.

Now Voyager, 74 Varick St, Suite 307, New York, NY 10013 (☎212/431-1616). Courier flight broker and consolidator.

Skylink, 265 Madison Ave, 5th Floor, New York, NY 10016 (☎1-800/AIR-ONLY or 212/573-8980), with branches in Chicago, Los Angeles, Montréal, Toronto and Washington DC. Consolidator.

STA Travel, 10 Downing St, New York, NY 10014 (☎1-800/777 0112 or 212/627-3111), and other branches in the Los Angeles, San Francisco and Boston areas. Worldwide discount travel firm specializing in student/youth fares; also student IDs, travel insurance, car rental, rail passes, etc.

Travel CUTS, 187 College St, Toronto, ON M5T 1P7 (☎416/979-2406), and other branches all over Canada. Organization specializing in student fares, IDs and other travel services.

Turkish Tursan Travel, 20 East 49th St, New York, NY 10017 (☎212/888-1180). Consolidator.

course, but *Lufthansa* and *Austrian Airlines* also offer direct connections from European hubs **to Ankara**, **İzmir** and **Antalya**. *Turkish* charges about US$50 extra for these cities, but specialist consolidators such as *Turkish Tursan Tours* can often book you straight through for no extra charge, or book you through with a stop in İstanbul for an extra US$25 or so.

FROM CANADA

There are no direct flights from Canada to Turkey, but several European airlines fly **to** İstanbul via their capital cities (see the box); alternatively, you could fly to New York JFK to link up with *Turkish Airlines'* non-stop flight to İstanbul (see above). Flights out of **Toronto** and **Montréal** via Europe are invariably cheapest: APEX fares tend to come in at around Can$1360 in low season, Can$1560 in high season. From **Vancouver**, figure on Can$1710/1960. If you're flying **to Ankara** or **İzmir**, you'll probably find it cheaper to book through an American consolidator on *Turkish*, via New York.

TOUR OPERATORS IN THE US AND CANADA

Although phone numbers are given here, you're better off making tour reservations through your local travel agent. An agent will make all the phone calls, sort out the snafus and arrange flights, insurance and the like – all at no extra cost to you. Sample prices (all excluding air fare) range from $1200 to $2400 for 15–17 days on a *gület* cruise; $700–2400 for 15–17 days of trekking, whitewater or other adventure travel; and $800–3000 for 14–17 days of escorted sightseeing.

Adventure Center (☎1-800/227-8747). Village-to-village hikes, camping treks, *gület* cruises, historical tours; usually booked through a UK adventure company.

Archeological Tours (☎212/986-3054). Tours of ancient sites guided by experts.

Inner Asia (☎1-800/777-8183). Deluxe trekking, *gület* cruises, Silk Road tours.

Mountain Travel-Sobek (in US, ☎1-800/227-2384; in Canada, ☎1-800/282-8747). Deluxe *gület* cruises.

Overseas Adventure Travel (☎1-800/221-0814). Deluxe *gület* cruises.

Safaricentre (☎1-800/223-6046). Walking, cycling, sailing, rafting, sightseeing.

Tohum Travel, PO Box 972, Bernardston, MA 01337 (☎413/774 4140). North American agents for the Tohum Centre near Kaş (see p.10).

Wilderness Travel (☎1-800/368-2794). Deluxe *gület* cruises.

GETTING THERE FROM AUSTRALIA & NEW ZEALAND

There are no direct flights of any kind from Australia or New Zealand to Turkey. However, several weekly scheduled flights will get you there after either a plane change or short layover in the airline's hub – typically Bahrain, Rome, Athens or Bangkok – before the final leg of the journey. A marginally less expensive, but far more time-consuming strategy would involve taking a flight to London and then proceeding from there with the benefit of the well-developed package industry (see "Getting There from Britain and Ireland", above). You're well

AIRLINES IN AUSTRALIA AND NEW ZEALAND

Alitalia, Orient Overseas Building, 32 Bridge St, Sydney (☎02/9247 1308); 6th Floor, Trustbank Building, 229 Queen St, Auckland (☎09/379 4457).

Gulf Air, 64 York St, Sydney (☎02/9321 9199). No NZ office.

Malaysia Airlines, 16 Spring St, Sydney (☎132627); Floor 12, Swanson Centre, 12–26 Swanson St, Auckland (☎09/373 2741).

Olympic Airways, Floor 3, 37–49 Pitt St, Sydney (☎02/9251 2044). No NZ office.

Qantas, 70 Hunter St, Sydney (☎02/9951 4294); Qantas House, 154 Queen St, Auckland (☎09/357 8900).

THY Turkish Airlines, Level 16, 388 George St, Sydney (☎02/9233 2105). No NZ office.

DISCOUNT AGENTS IN AUSTRALIA AND NEW ZEALAND

Anywhere Travel, 345 Anzac Parade, Kingsford, Sydney (☎02/9663 0411).

Brisbane Discount Travel, 260 Queen St, Brisbane (☎07/3229 9211).

Budget Travel, 16 Fort St, Auckland; other branches around the city (☎09/366 0061, toll-free 0800/ 808 040).

Destinations Unlimited, 3 Milford Rd, Milford, Auckland (☎09/373 4033).

Flight Centres *Australia*: Level 11, 33 Berry St, North Sydney (☎02/9241 2422); Bourke St, Melbourne (☎03/9650 2899); plus other branches nationwide. *New Zealand*: National Bank Towers, 205–225 Queen St, Auckland (☎09/209 6171); Shop 1M, National Mutual Arcade, 152 Hereford St, Christchurch (☎03/379 7145); 50–52 Willis St, Wellington (☎04/472 8101); other branches countrywide.

Northern Gateway, 22 Cavenagh St, Darwin (☎08/8941 1394).

Passport Travel, 320b Glenferrie Rd, Malvern (☎03/9824 7183).

STA Travel, *Australia*: 702–730 Harris St, Ultimo, Sydney (☎02/9212 1255, toll-free 1800/637 444); 256 Flinders St, Melbourne (☎03/9654 7266); other offices in state capitals and major universities. *New Zealand*: Travellers' Centre, 10 High St, Auckland (☎09/309 0458); 233 Cuba St, Wellington (☎04/385 0561); 90 Cashel St, Christchurch (☎03/379 9098); other offices in Dunedin, Palmerston North, Hamilton and major universities.

Thomas Cook, *Australia*: 321 Kent St, Sydney (☎02/9248 6100); 257 Collins St, Melbourne (☎03/9650 2442); branches in other state capitals. *New Zealand*: Shop 250a St Luke's Square, Auckland (☎09/849 2071).

Topdeck Travel, 65 Glenfell St, Adelaide (☎08/8232 7222).

Tymtro Travel, 428 George St, Sydney (☎02/9223 2211).

advised to contact the specialist agencies (p.13) for assistance on what could otherwise prove to be a pricy itinerary. Flights booked directly through the airlines tend to be more expensive than those bought from discount agents, who will have the latest information on limited specials offered sporadically across the year.

The cheapest through fares **from Australia** are with *Olympic Airlines*, twice weekly via Bangkok/Singapore and Athens from Sydney, Melbourne and Auckland; budget on A\$1620–2020, depending on season. Next up is *Gulf Air's* A\$1637–1923 from Sydney and Melbourne, with a free overnight in Bahrain included, while *Malaysia Airlines* offer several flights weekly from most major Australian cities with a Kuala Lumpur layover for A\$1880–1980. *Alitalia* flies to İstanbul via Rome for A\$1880–2330 several times weekly; in conjunc-

tion with *Qantas*, *Turkish Airways* serves İstanbul four times weekly via Singapore for A\$1950–2020. Fares out of any of the east-coast cities are common-rated; exact fare **seasons** vary by airline, but Christmas and May–August is considered high, mid-January to February and October–November low. **From New Zealand**, *Alitalia*, *Olympic* and *Malaysia Airlines* fly to İstanbul via their various hubs for NZ\$2200–2800, depending on season; linking flights to Australian centres are provided where needed by code-sharing *Air New Zealand*.

Round-the-world tickets that pause in Turkey use combinations of airlines, and could be worth considering for a long trip taking in many destinations; generally six free stop-overs are allowed, with fares starting at A\$2400/NZ\$3380. Backtracking and southern-hemisphere travel (other than the starting point) are generally not allowed.

SPECIALIST TOUR OPERATORS IN AUSTRALIA AND NEW ZEALAND

Adventure World (wholesaler), 73 Walker St, North Sydney (☎02/9956 7766, toll-free 1800/221931); Level 3, 33 Adelaide St, Brisbane (☎07/3229 0599); 8 Victoria Ave, Perth (☎08/9221 2300); 101 Great South Rd, Remuera, Auckland (☎09/524 5118). 15-day sailing expeditions from Marmaris to Fethiye.

Exodus (wholesaler), Suite 5, Level 5, 1 York St, Sydney (☎02/9251 5430, toll-free 1800/800 724). 8- to 15-day trips exploring southern Turkey by boat, foot or expedition vehicle, or relaxing in the secluded bay of Domuz Buku.

Kompas Holidays, Level 3, 257 Boundary Rd, Spring Hill (☎1800/269968); 71 Grey St, Brisbane (☎07/3846 4006). Accommodation, city-stays, car hire, yacht charter, historical and scenic tours.

PADI Dive Network, Level 4, 372 Eastern Valley Way, Chatswood, NSW (☎1800/678100). Individual dive-snorkling packages that allow you to visit out-of-the-way places along Turkey's coastline.

RED TAPE AND VISAS

To enter Turkey you'll need a full passport. Citizens of the UK and Ireland require visas, available only at the port of entry for £10; US citizens are charged $20. Note that while cashiers at much-frequented ports of entry, such as İstanbul's Atatürk Airport, nonchalantly convert between different currencies and give change for large notes, officials at less-used land border crossings can be highly inflexible: for example, UK nationals may be required to pay only in sterling, not Scottish pounds, dollars or marks, and change for £20 notes will not be given, even when proffered for two visas. Citizens of most other countries do not require visas to enter Turkey. Most visitors are allowed to remain in Turkey for three months (South Africans, however, are given only one month), during which time it is forbidden to take up employment.

If you want to stay longer you can apply for an *ikamet tezkeresi* or **residence permit**. In order to be granted one of these you'll have to show evidence of means of support – either savings, a steady income from abroad or legal work in Turkey (not easy to come by – see p.65). Many people nip into Greece or Bulgaria (even Northern Cyprus) every three months for at least 24 hours and re-enter for a new three-month stamp, rather than go through the trouble of applying for a residence permit.

BORDER INSPECTIONS

Entering Turkey usually entails a cursory customs inspection: commodity **import limits** worth knowing about include 200 cigarettes (plus 400 more from a Turkish duty-free shop), 200g of loose tobacco (plus 500g more from a Turkish duty-free shop), five litres in total of wine or spirits (foreign booze is now readily available in Turkey at approximately overseas prices) and 1500g of instant coffee, which is exorbitantly priced in Turkey. A record of laptop computers, video cameras, etc, may be made in your passport to ensure that you take them out with you when you leave. A **vehicle** will most definitely result in a passport entry, making it impossible for you to leave Turkey without it – unless you can prove that the vehicle has been wrecked or stolen (see p.32).

Checks on the way out may be more thorough, and you should arrive at the airport or ferry dock in good time in case the customs officers decide to be slow and inquisitive. Only an idiot would try and take drugs through Turkish customs, although it's more likely that the guards will be on the lookout for **antiquities**. Penalties for trying to smuggle these out include long jail sentences, plus a large fine. For a discussion on what constitutes an antiquity, see the advice in "Bazaars and Shopping", p.49.

HEALTH AND INSURANCE

No special inoculations are required for visiting Turkey, although if you don't want to take any chances, jabs against typhoid and tetanus are suggested, particularly if you're travelling to eastern Anatolia. Some visitors also take the precaution of getting injections against hepatitis A.

HEALTH PROBLEMS AND HAZARDS

You're unlikely to encounter many health problems in Turkey. Many people experience bouts of **mild diarrhoea**, and the chances of this happening increase the longer you stay in the country. As a precaution take Diocalm or similar anti-diarrhoea tablets with you (you'll be able to buy a locally produced variant if you forget). Lomotil or Imodium, trade names for the antiparastaltic diphenoxylate, is easily available in Turkey and will allow you to travel without constantly running to the bathroom, but does not kill the bug that ails you. Buscopan, also on sale locally, is particularly good for stomach cramps resulting from food poisoning and sunstroke. For electrolyte replacement resulting from dehydrating diarrhoea, Ge-Oral powder dissolved in pure water is a good local remedy. Tap **water** is heavily chlorinated and probably safe to drink, though not exactly delectable (except in restaurants which serve it chilled and minimally filtered). Rural springs are labelled *içilir*, *içilbelir* or *içme suyu* (all meaning "potable"), or *içilmez* (not drinkable).

In the east, particularly during the hot summer months, more serious **food poisoning** is a possibility. In restaurants, avoid dishes that look as if they have been standing around, and if you have a sensitive stomach make sure meat and fish are well grilled. Don't, whatever you do, eat mussels in summer. If you're struck down, the best thing is to let the bug run its course and drink lots of fluids like sweetened tea (without milk), *gazoz* (lemon-flavoured pop), Coke and bottled water; plain white rice and yoghurt also help. Stubborn cases will need a course of antibiotics – pharmacists (see below) are trained to recognize symptoms and can put you in touch with the nearest state clinic for free treatment.

Turkey has a few **animal hazards**. Adders and scorpions can lurk among the rocks and stones of archeological sites. **Mosquitoes** are a problem in some places, and since no good repellents are available locally, you should bring your own – roll-on varieties are best. At night they're most easily dispatched with locally sold incense coils (*spiral tütsü*), or an *ESEM Mat*, a small electrified tray that slowly vapourizes an odourless pyrethrin disc during the course of a night. Malaria is generally a seasonal (April–July) problem in the regions between Adana and Mardin (mainly the area covered in *The Euphrates and Tigris Basin* chapter), and incidence has skyrocketed recently around Şanlıurfa in areas newly irrigated by the GAP (see box on p.702), though for brief visits you shouldn't need prophylactic drugs. Incidentally, the word for mosquito netting – all too rarely supplied in accommodation – is *çibindirik*.

Rabies is perhaps the greatest potential danger, and the giant Sivas-Kangal sheepdogs, while rarely aggressive unless their flock is closely approached, are the most obvious possible source. Be wary of any animal that bites, scratches or licks you, particularly if it's behaving erratically. First aid involves flushing a wound with soap and water after encouraging limited bleeding; apply antiseptic and bandage if necessary, but do not suture. As soon as possible – within a maximum of 72 hours – embark on a six-injection course of human diploid cell vaccine (HDCV) – given in the arm and nowhere near as painful as the old abdominal shots – followed by one of human rabies immunoglobulin (HRIG). If you've been pre-immunized, you'll only need two doses of HDCV and no HRIG.

OVERSEAS HEALTH INFORMATION AND TRAVEL CLINICS

UK AND IRELAND

British Airways Travel Clinic, 156 Regent St, London W1 (Mon–Fri 9am–4.15pm, Sat 10am–4pm, no appointments; ☎0171/439 9584); also appointment-only branches at Cheapside, London EC2 (☎0171/606 2977), and at the *BA* terminal in London's Victoria Station (☎0171/233 6661). If you live outside London, call ☎0171/831 5333 to learn of the closest regional *BA Travel Clinic*.

The Hospital for Tropical Diseases, 4 St Pancras Way, London NW1 (☎0171/388 9600 or 387 4411), and at Queen's House, 180–182 Tottenham Court Road, London W1 (☎0171/530 3500); ☎01839/337722 for a recorded health message.

Travel Medicine Services, P.O. Box 254, 16 College St, Belfast 1 (☎01232/315220).

Tropical Medical Bureau, Grafton St Medical Centre, Dublin 2 (☎01/671 9200).

US AND CANADA

International SOS Assistance, PO Box 11568, Philadelphia, PA 19116 (in the US, ☎1-800/523-8930; in Canada, ☎1-800/363-0263).

Travelers Medical Center, 31 Washington Square, New York, NY 10011 (☎212/982-1600).

AUSTRALIA AND NEW ZEALAND

Auckland Hospital, Park Rd, Grafton (☎09/379 7440).

Travellers' Medical and Vaccination Centre, Level 7, 428 George St, Sydney (☎02/9221 7133); Level 3, 393 Little Bourke St, Melbourne (☎03/9602 5788); Level 6, 29 Gilbert Place, Adelaide (☎08/8212 7522); Level 6, 247 Adelaide St, Brisbane (☎07/3221 9066); 1 Mill St, Perth (☎08/9321 1977).

MEDICAL ATTENTION

For **minor complaints** head for the nearest **eczane** or pharmacy. Even the smallest town will have at least one, where you'll be able to obtain remedies for ailments like diarrhoea, sunburn and flu. In larger towns, *eczane* staff may know some English or German. Pharmacists in Turkey are able to dispense medicines that would ordinarily require a prescription abroad. Medication prices are kept low by a combination of government control and cheap local production, but you may find it difficult to find exact equivalents to your home prescription, so bring it, and a good supply of the actual medication you may need, along. Night-duty pharmacies are known as *nöbet(ci)*; a list of the current rota is posted in every chemist's front window.

For more **serious ailments** you'll find well-trained doctors in larger towns and cities. Most of these are specialists, advertising themselves by means of signs outside their premises. A *diş tabibi* or *hekimi* is a dentist; a *tıbbî doktor* will treat ailments of all kinds; while an *operatör* is a qualified surgeon.

If you're not sure what's wrong with you, it's best to go instead to one of the **free state clinics** (*sağlık ocağı*), which can give diagnoses and prescriptions, or a **hospital** (*hastane*), indicated by a blue street sign with a large white "H" on it. Hospitals are either public (*Devlet Hastane* or *SSK Hastanesi*) or private (*Özel Hastane*); the latter are vastly preferable in terms of cleanliness, shortness of queues and standard of care, and since all foreigners must pay for any attention anyway, you may as well get the best available. Fees are lower than in northern Europe and North America but still substantial enough that you'd want insurance cover (see below). As a compromise in quality and expense, the medical faculties of major universities – eg in İstanbul, İzmir, Edirne and Bursa – have affiliated teaching hospitals which are infinitely better than the state hospitals, but less expensive than the private ones. Admission desks of private hospitals can also recommend their affiliated doctors if you don't want or need to be an in-patient, and your consulate or the tourist information office may also be able to provide you with the address of an English-speaking doctor. If you're too ill to

TRAVEL INSURANCE COMPANIES

UK

Columbus Travel Insurance, 17 Devonshire Square, London EC2M 4SQ (☎0171/375 0011).

Endsleigh Insurance, 97–107 Southampton Row, London WC1B 4AG (☎0171/436 4451).

Frizzell Insurance, Frizzell House, County Gates, Bournemouth, Dorset BH1 2NF (☎01202/292 333).

US AND CANADA

Access America (☎1-800/284-8300).

Carefree Travel Insurance (☎1-800/323-3149).

Desjardins Travel Insurance – Canada only (☎1-800/463-7830).

International Student Insurance Service (ISIS) – sold by *STA Travel* (☎1-800/777-0112).

Travel Assistance International (☎1-800/821-2828).

Travel Guard (☎1-800/826-1300).

Travel Insurance Services (☎1-800/937-1387).

AUSTRALIA AND NEW ZEALAND

AFTA (Australian Federation of Travel Agents), 144 Pacific Highway, North Sydney (☎02/9264 3299).

Cover More, Level 9, 32 Walker St, North Sydney (☎02/9202 8000, toll free 1800/251 881).

Ready Plan, 141–147 Walker St, Dandenong, Victoria (☎1800/337 462); 10th Floor, 63 Albert St, Auckland (☎09/379 3208).

UTAG (United Travel Agents Group), 347 Kent St, Sydney (☎1800/809 462).

---

move, but must summon a doctor, hotel-room visits will cost about US$50, with perhaps another US$25 for medication delivered from a local pharmacy.

INSURANCE IN THE UK AND IRELAND

Especially since EC health care privileges don't exist in Turkey, Brits would do well to take out an insurance **policy** before travelling to cover against theft, loss and illness or injury. Most travel agents will offer you insurance when you book your flight or holiday, and some will insist you take it. If you feel the cover is inadequate, or you want to compare prices, other travel agents, insurance brokers or banks should be able to help, with prices starting from about £20 a month. If you have a good "all risks" home insurance policy it may well cover your possessions against loss or theft even when overseas, and many private medical schemes also cover you when abroad – make sure you know the procedure and the helpline number.

If you need to make a **claim**, you should keep receipts for medicines and medical treatment, and in the event you have anything stolen, you must obtain an official statement from the police (called an *ifade* or a *hırsızlık raporu*).

In **Ireland**, insurance is best obtained through a travel specialist such as *USIT* (see p.5

for addresses). Their policies cost £20 for 6–10 days, £30 for one month, with discounts offered to students of any age and anyone under 26.

INSURANCE IN NORTH AMERICA

Before buying an insurance policy, check that you're not already covered. **Canadian provincial health plans** typically provide some overseas medical coverage, although they are unlikely to pick up the full tab in the event of a mishap. Holders of official **student/teacher/youth cards** are entitled to accident coverage and hospital in-patient benefits – the annual membership ($18 for Americans, Can$15 for Canadians) is far less than the cost of comparable insurance. Benefits provided include up to $3000 in emergency medical coverage and $100 a day for 60 days in the hospital, plus a 24-hour hotline to call in the event of a medical, legal or financial emergency.

Students may also find that their student health coverage extends during the vacations and for one term beyond the date of last enrollment. **Credit and charge cards** (particularly *American Express*) often provide certain levels of medical or other insurance, and travel insurance may also be included if you use a major card to pay for your trip. **Homeowners' or renters'** insurance often covers theft or loss of documents, money and valuables while overseas.

After exhausting the possibilities above, you might want to contact a specialist **travel insurance** company; your travel agent can usually recommend one, or see the box. **Policies** vary: some are comprehensive while others cover only certain risks. In particular, ask whether the policy pays medical costs up front or reimburses you later, and whether it provides for medical evacuation to your home country. For policies that include lost or stolen luggage, check exactly what is and isn't covered, and make sure the per-article limit will cover your most valuable possession. Most policies apply only to items lost, stolen or damaged while in the custody of an identifiable, responsible third party – hotel porter, airline, luggage consignment, etc. Even in these cases you will have to contact the local police within a certain time limit to have a complete report (an *ifade* or a *hırsızlık raporu*) made out so that your insurer can process the claim.

The best **premiums** are usually to be had through student/youth travel agencies. If you're planning to do any "dangerous sports" (skiing, mountaineering, etc), be sure to ask whether these activities are covered: some companies levy a surcharge.

INSURANCE IN AUSTRALIA AND NZ

Travel insurance policies in Australia and New Zealand are put together by the airlines and travel agent groups in conjunction with insurance companies. They are all roughly similar in premium and coverage, though those offered by *Ready Plan* probably have the edge in terms of value for money. Adventure sports are covered apart from mountaineering with ropes, bungee jumping (some policies), and unassisted diving without an Open Water licence. A typical policy covering Turkey will cost A$190/NZ$220 for 1 month, A$270/NZ$320 for two months and A$330/NZ$400 for three months.

COSTS, MONEY AND BANKS

While no longer as rock-bottom cheap as it was a decade ago, much of Turkey is still less expensive than other Mediterranean travel destinations. Prices at the main resorts, however, have steadily crept up to scarcely less than those in Greece, Spain and Portugal. Domestic inflation runs at 75–100 percent annually, depending on which set of statistics you believe; outsiders are spared the full effect of this by a constant devaluation of the Turkish currency against hard currencies, amounting to about 70 percent a year. We've therefore quoted all prices in the *Guide* in US$, including the ranges for our accommodation categories (see p.37 for an explanation). With minor upward adjustments from year to year, these should give a fairly reliable idea of what you'll be paying on the spot.

COSTS

You can pretty well get by on as much or as little as you want in Turkey, given the wide disparity in prices between the coastal resorts and relatively unvisited spots in the interior. In terms of a **daily budget**, a frugal existence relying exclusively on bus travel, food from simple soup kitchens and the cheapest grades of accommodation won't set you back more than £15 (roughly US$23) a day per person. If you're entitled to one, a student identity card – FIYTO being more influential than ISIC – will shave a bit off the cost of museum or entertainment tickets and some forms of transport. For any degree of comfort, including rooms with en-suite bath and the occasional splurge on a moped or at the bazaar, allow an average daily expenditure of £24/$36. Incidentally, you won't save much by assembling picnic materials at a grocer's – even the poorest Turks eat out frequently, and you may as well too.

As for specifics, **accommodation** costs range from about £2/$3 per person in the most basic dosshouses to five-star resort hotels with every mod con at £70/$100 a head; mid-range hotels with decent amenities weigh in somewhere around £8/$12 per person in large provincial towns and coastal centres. **Food** also varies widely in price: it's difficult to spend more than £5/$8 apiece for a meal once off the tourist circuit, but easy to drop three times that amount in a resort town. **Transport** is more consistent – coach fares hover around £1.50/$2.25 per 100km travelled, slightly more for popular routes and top-flight companies. The better long-distance trains charge about the same, with small surcharges for sleeping facilities. Domestic air ticket prices have reached parity with those in northern Europe, but a Pullman seat or low-class cabin on the limited long-haul ferry network is still good value.

MONEY, BANKS AND DÖVIZ (EXCHANGE) HOUSES

The Turkish **currency** is the lira, abbreviated as TL. Coins exist in denominations of 500, 1000, 2500, 5000, 10,000 and 25,000TL, all but the last two cited having strictly nuisance value except in paying for public toilets. Notes come in denominations of 10,000, 20,000, 50,000, 100,000, 250,000, 500,000 and 1,000,000; the 100,000 and 1,000,000 notes in particular are confusingly similar in colour and size. As in other countries which have suffered from hyperinflation, it seems only a matter of time before Turkey knocks off some zeros from these denominations and issues new notes.

Most **banks** are open Monday to Friday, 8.30am to noon and 1.30 to 5pm, though the *Garanti Bankası* operates throughout the day and on Saturday mornings; foreign exchange transactions won't be undertaken after 4.45pm. Bank branches themselves vary in their efficiency, with the time spent filling in triplicate forms and obtaining counter-signatures ranging from ten minutes in tourist hotspots to nearly an hour in the east of the country. As a rule of thumb, the more

remote and less touristed a place is, the longer you'll wait – often with tea served in the meantime. In certain east Anatolian towns only one or two banks are authorized to accept foreign currency, and often rates may lag slightly behind that in the west, sometimes with larger commissions charged. If you have a choice, the *Türk Ziraat Bankası* and the *Türk Ticaret Bankası* are the most competent and efficient banks in the interior.

Rates for foreign currency are always better inside Turkey, so don't bother buying TL at home unless you know you'll be arriving in the dead of night at some obscure land frontier, in which case a token amount is advisable. Because of the TL's constant devaluation you should only change money every few days as you need it, unless you're going east.

Rates and **commissions** (*komisyon* in the Frenchified Turkish) vary widely, from the one percent or so levied by the PTT (see below) to the downright unreasonable three percent charged by most banks. Free transactions and the best rates are to be had at the new **döviz** or **exchange houses** springing up all over western Turkey. They're open very long hours, especially in resorts, and buy or sell foreign currency of any sort instantly, though almost none take travellers' cheques. Outside of normal banking hours, you can also use the **special exchange booths** run by banks in coastal resorts, airports and ferry docks – the main advantage of an enforced halt in such places – where service is quicker and commissions small or nonexistent. The local **post and telephone office (PTT)**, particularly in a sizeable town, is often able to change foreign currency or Eurocheques. In small towns where no bank is authorized to take foreign currency, the PTT will give a reasonable rate of exchange for travellers' cheques, but levies the usual commissions.

Incidentally, keep all **foreign exchange slips** with you until departure, if only to prove the value of purchases made in case of queries by customs. In any event, don't leave Turkey with unspent TL – it's not illegal to take out up to the equivalent of $5000, but the stuff is utterly worthless once out of the country.

Having money transferred from overseas is inadvisable. All of the above caveats about bank bureaucracy will apply five-fold, with waits measured in days, commissions and fees in the tens of dollars. If you have a credit card it's far cheaper and quicker to get a cash advance by service till/ATM or over the counter (see below).

CASH, TRAVELLERS' CHEQUES AND PLASTIC

It's wise to take a fair wad of overseas **cash** with you to Turkey: although theft and pickpocketing are on the increase in tourist areas, leaving a money belt in hotel lockers is enough of a safeguard under normal circumstances. You can often pay for souvenirs or accommodation with foreign currency directly (prices for both are frequently quoted in hard currency) and it allows you to take advantage of the *döviz* brokers' convenient service and excellent rates.

Travellers' cheques, available from UK high street banks for a one-percent commission, entail considerably more difficulty – virtually no *döviz* takes them, and any bank you try must have a specimen for the brand you carry, or they'll refuse to serve you. This is less of a problem with *Thomas Cook* and *American Express* cheques; off-brand cheques will be harder to change. *American Express* cheques are sold through most American and Canadian banks; to buy cheques by phone, call *American Express* (☎1-800/673 3782) or *MasterCard International/Thomas Cook* (☎1-800/223 7373). For both cash and travellers' cheques transactions, US$, DM or sterling are the **preferred currencies**, in varying order depending on where you are in the country – though pounds are often disparaged except in resorts much frequented by those from the UK.

Eurocheques are widely accepted, but many banks flout rules on commissions. This should never exceed the equivalent of Swiss Franc 2.5, as printed in your bank's Eurocheque documentation, although some Turkish outfits – especially in the east – have been known to demand as much as seven percent of the transaction value or a flat £2 fee, plus postage and mysterious "taxes". Much of the time you'll pay the commission on the spot, as a separate sub-transaction; cheques can be written for a maximum of £100.

A major **credit card** is invaluable for domestic ferry and plane tickets, and also for waiver of a huge cash deposit when renting a car. You can also normally get **cash advances** at any bank displaying the appropriate sign. More simply, you can use *Visa* and *Mastercard* cards in the widespread cashpoint networks of several banks, including the *Yapı Kredi Bankası, İş Bankası, Ak Bank* and *Ziraat Bankası*, to get a cash advance in TL; the automatic teller machines of *Garanti Bankası, Yapi Kredi* and *Pamukbank* will also accept UK and North American **debit cards** that are part of the Cirrus and Plus systems. Screen prompts for such transactions will be given in English on request. An increasing number of shopkeepers are also able to process debit cards with a *Visa* logo on swipe readers. The daily withdrawal limit for any card is about £200/$300 equivalent, making this really the simplest way to get money while on the road. However, don't rely entirely on plastic, as Turkish service till/ATM networks are prone to crashing.

COMMUNICATIONS: POST AND PHONES

The Turkish postal and telephone service has historically been run by the state-owned PTT (*Posta Telefon ve Telegraf*), easily identified by a black-on-yellow logo. In 1996, however, some of its telecommunications functions began to be privatized as TT (*Türk Telekom*), distinguished by black-on-blue livery. In the larger towns and tourist resorts, the phone division of the main PTT building is open until midnight, with mail accepted from 8am until 7 or 8pm; separate TT buildings, where present, tend to keep roughly the same hours. Elsewhere expect the PTT to adhere to standard civil service hours, with complete closure Saturday afternoon and Sundays.

THE POST

Overseas letter rates are rapidly approaching uniformity with those in EC countries; stamps are only available from the PTT. The outgoing service is efficient, but make sure that the clerk has charged you for air mail (*Uçakla* – under $0.60 for up to 20g) and not the cheaper and painfully slow surface rate. *Acele* (express) service is available for a hefty surcharge ($17 for up to 500g to Europe, $20 to North America, with extra charges for each additional 50g). To Britain, for example, express delivery is promised within three days, as against seven to ten days for air mail.

Postboxes are clearly labelled with categories of destination: *yurtdışı* for overseas, *yurtiçi* for inland, *şehiriçi* for local. Street-corner postboxes are rare, and shouldn't be mistaken for lookalike rubbish bins. To receive mail **poste restante**, articles should be addressed to you, c/o "Postrestant, Merkez Postanesi, [city name], Turkey". However, if you carry *American Express* travellers' cheques, you may be better off having mail sent and held at the İstanbul or Ankara branches of *Türk Ekspres*, the local **American Express agent**.

The best advice on **sending packages** is not to – at least not anything over two or three kilos. If you must, do it in a medium-sized town with an airport and enlist the help of a sympathetic supervisor who understands the rules. Boxes must be left open for inspection, though at main branches folded packing kits are usually sold. Always come prepared with tape, twine, indelible marker, glue, scissors, supporting invoices and certificates – and plenty of patience. Basic surface rates to Europe are $4 for up to 500g, with substantial supplements for air service which vary by destination country.

PHONES

The PTT (or TT, where available) is the best place to make **phone calls**. Inside or just adjacent there is usually a range of alternatives: a *jeton* (token) phone, a card phone and or a *köntürlü* (metered, clerk-attended) phone, sometimes in a closed booth. Public phones elsewhere are relatively rare, though you will find them in public parks and at filling stations.

Jetons theoretically come in small (*küçük*), medium (*orta*) and large (*büyük*) sizes, for local, domestic long-distance and international use respectively. However, *jetons* work out more expensive than phonecards or metered booths for anything but local calls, and the medium-sized ones are often in short supply if not entirely absent. Partly used tokens are not returned, so don't use bigger sizes for local calls; despite notices to the contrary, you can usually exchange unused ones for postage stamps. While you're in Turkey it's a good idea to carry a few on you – they're not always on sale when you need them. Drop at least one token in the slot before dialling; when the red light comes on and a warning tone sounds, you have about ten seconds to feed in more. Don't attempt to call from a *jeton*-operated phone box where the square, red "out of service" light is illuminated. The standard Turkish phone replies are the Frenchified *Allo* or the more local *Buyurun* (literally, "Avail yourself/at your service").

For interurban or overseas calls, **phonecards** (available in 30, 60, 100, 120 and 180 units) are the best value, though you have little warning before being cut off; a 100-unit card, for example, costing $3.50, will allow about thirteen minutes of chat between İstanbul and Ankara. They're used in exactly the same manner as British or North American ones, though wait for the number of units remaining to appear on the screen before dialling. Remember, too, that cardphones are only common in the west and in big resorts: don't buy the more expensive cards and expect to be able to use them in eastern Anatolia. **Metered booths** inside PTTs or TTs work out more expensive than cards, but are certainly far cheaper than hotels or tokens, and also tend to be quieter (plus you won't be cut off).

In 1993, Turkey inaugurated an entirely new system of eleven-digit phone numbers nationwide, consisting of four-digit area codes (all starting with "0") with a seven-digit subscriber number. However, old numbers (which will not work) still appear on obsolete literature and business cards. To convert any lingering old numbers, refer to the nearest PTT, the only source of phone books and conversion tables.

Overseas rates are not cheap: well over $1.70 per minute at a cardphone to Britain, over $3 for the same time to North America, even higher to Australasia. But there is a 25-percent discount on normal rates from 10pm to 8am and on Sunday. Try not to make anything other than local calls from a hotel room – there's usually a minimum 100-percent surcharge on the already hefty rates.

USEFUL TELEPHONE NUMBERS

To reach **a number in Turkey from overseas**, dial your country's international access code, then 90 for Turkey, the area code minus the initial zero, and the seven-digit subscriber number.

WITHIN TURKEY

Directory assistance ☎118
International operator ☎115
Postal code assistance ☎119
Inter-city operator ☎131
Paging operator ☎133

INTERNATIONAL DIALLING CODES

Australia ☎0061
Ireland ☎00353
Netherlands ☎0031
New Zealand ☎0064
UK ☎0044
USA and Canada ☎001
* UK Direct Operator ☎00 800 441177
* ATT Direct Operator ☎00 800 12277

* These last two are for reversing the charges to your home number or billing a credit card; no money is required in theory, but in practice you'll need one small jeton or card unit.

Most hotels in our categories ③ and above (see "Accommodation", p.35) have **faxes**, and it is usually simpler to send and receive one there than to use the PTT's advertised fax service. At about a minute per transmitted page, this is a far cheaper way of staying in touch transcontinentally than chatting – as well as making reservations. We've listed hotel fax numbers where known.

INFORMATION AND MAPS

Before you set off on your trip it's worth a visit to a Turkish tourist office (officially known as the Information Office of the Embassy), where you'll be able to pick up a few very basic maps and glossy brochures. Don't overload your luggage with these, however, as much the same choice (or the same scarcity) of bumph is available within Turkey itself. What you should take with you are decent regional maps, since those on sale locally are generally inadequate.

INFORMATION IN TURKEY

Most Turkish towns of any size will have a *Turizm Danışma Bürosu* or **tourist information office** of some sort, in smaller places lodged inside the public library or *Belediye* (city hall). However, outside of the larger cities and obvious tourist destinations there's often very little actual information to be had, and the staff may well try to dismiss you with a selection of useless and very general brochures. And in more frequented spots – with some sterling exceptions – staff made world-weary by the steady stream of visitors can be perfunctory at best in the discharge of their duties. The best plan is to approach with specific questions, such as exact bus schedules, festival ticket availability or revised museum opening hours, although in out-of-the-way places there is no guarantee that there will be anyone who can speak English. Lists of accommodation for all budgets are sometimes a useful feature of the more heavily patronized offices; the staff, however, will generally not make bookings.

We've given precise **opening hours** of tourist information offices in most cases; generally they adhere to a standard schedule of 8.30am to 12.30pm and 1.30pm to 5.30pm, Monday to Friday. At big-name resorts and large cities summer hours extend well into the evening and through much of the weekend. In winter, by contrast, many tourist offices in out-of-the-way spots will be shut most of the time.

MAPS

Stock up on **touring maps** *before* you leave, as Turkish ones are neither detailed nor accurate. The best generally available series is that originally produced by the German *Reise und Verkehrsverlag*, but distributed in the UK and North America by *GeoCenter International*. They cover the entire country in a variety of formats (divided up as *EuroMap, EuroAtlas, EuroTour, EuroCity*), including "Western Turkey" and "Eastern Turkey", each with a scale of 1:800,000 (each £4.99 in the UK), and the entire country on the same scale, double-sided (£6.99). Drivers are best off with the ring-bound *EuroAtlas* version which divides the country into manageable pages (£6.99 full size, £3.99 pocket size). The only comparable alternative is the easy-to-read *Kümmerly & Frey* double-sided map of the whole country at 1:1,100,000 (£7.50). There are also regional

GeoCenter folding offerings: "South Coast", "West Coast", "Southeast Turkey" and "Black Sea and West", all at a scale of 1:600,000 (£2.99). Many of these are regularly on sale at Turkish resorts, either as the original edition or produced by a Turkish licensee, but don't count on this.

CITY MAPS

Complementing our own city maps, the tourist offices in İstanbul, Ankara, Antalya and İzmir stock reasonable complimentary **city street plans**, although the İstanbul one is restricted to the centre and lacks detail. The quality of local sketch plans available at provincial tourist offices varies widely, though as a rule of thumb, the more tourists a place gets the better the maps tend to be.

There are very few maps of Turkish cities on sale, and when available they are in any case rarely good value. Notable exceptions are *GeoCenter's* 1:7500 *EuroCity* plan of central İstanbul, plus their exhaustive, ring-bound A–Z atlas, including pages at scales of 1:15,000 and 1:7500. The latter is available only in good İstanbul bookshops (about $15), alongside the slightly less accurate, locally published *Asya* A–Z atlas (about $12). One or the other would seem a worthwhile investment if you plan to spend a lot of time in the city. Otherwise, *Hallwag* do a good street plan of central İstanbul (£4.50), and the *Falk Plan* of İstanbul (£5.95) is also acceptable, with additional coverage of outlying districts.

TREKKING MAPS

It is virtually impossible to obtain large-scale **topographical maps** of specific areas for trekking, though restrictions in Turkey were lifted in 1993 enabling visitors in theory to obtain 1:50,000 topographic sheets from the *Harita Genel Müdürlügü* (General Mapping Ministry) in the Dikimevi district of Ankara. However, you will need to speak reasonable Turkish to get in the door – it's best to have a local get them on your behalf. It is possible to obtain overseas a 1:200,000 series prepared with German assistance in 1944, but again with some difficulty: the Turks have security or copyright protocols with other NATO countries, and permission must be obtained from military authorities. In Britain you should consult the Map Room at the Royal Geographical Society (1 Kensington Gore, London SW7), who will then refer you to the Mapping and Charting Establishment in Surrey for a permit.

MAP OUTLETS AROUND THE WORLD

UK

Thomas Nelson and Sons Ltd, 51 York Place, **Edinburgh**, EH1 3JD (☎0131/557 3011).
John Smith and Sons, 57–61 St Vincent St, **Glasgow** (☎0141/221 7472).
London:
National Map Centre, 22–24 Caxton St, SW1 (☎0171/222 4945).

Stanfords, 12–14 Long Acre, WC2 (☎0171/836 1321); 52 Grosvenor Gardens, SW1W 0AG; 156 Regent St, W1R 5TA. Maps by mail or phone order available.
The Travel Bookshop, 13–15 Blenheim Crescent, W11 2EE (☎0171/229 5260).

IRELAND

Waterstone's, Queens Bldg, 8 Royal Ave, **Belfast**, BT1 1DA (☎01232/247355).
Dublin:
Easons Bookshop, 40 O'Connell St (☎01/873 3811).

Fred Hanna's Bookshop, 27–29 Nassau St (☎01/677 1255).
Hodges Figgis Bookshop, 56–58 Dawson St (☎01/677 4754).

US

California:
Book Passage, 51 Tamal Vista Dr, Corte Madera, CA 94925 (☎415/927-0960).
The Complete Traveler Bookstore, 3207 Filmore St, San Francisco, CA 92123 (☎415/923-1511).
Map Link, 30 S. La Patera Lane, Unit 5, Santa Barbara, CA 93117 (☎805/692-6777).
Phileas Fogg's Books & Maps, #87 Stanford Shopping Center, Palo Alto, CA 94304 (☎1-800/233-FOGG in California; ☎1-800/533-FOGG elsewhere in US).
Rand McNally, 595 Market St, San Francisco, CA 94105 (☎415/777-3131).
Sierra Club Bookstore, 730 Polk St, San Francisco, CA 94109 (☎415/923-5500).
Traveler's Bookcase, 8375 West Third Street, Los Angeles, CA 90048 (☎213/655-0575).

Forsyth Travel Library, 9154 W 57th St, Shawnee Mission, **Kansas** 66201 (☎1-800/367-7984).
Travel Books & Language Center, 4931 Cordell Ave, Bethesda, **Maryland** 20814 (☎1-800/220-2665).

New York:
British Travel Bookshop, 551 Fifth Ave, NY 10176 (☎1-800/448-3039 or 212/490-6688).
The Complete Traveler Bookstore, 199 Madison Ave, NY 10016 (☎212/685-9007).
Rand McNally, 150 East 52nd St, NY 10022 (☎212/758-7488).
Traveler's Bookstore, 22 West 52nd St, NY 10019 (☎212/664-0995).

Elliot Bay Book Company, 101 South Main St, **Seattle**, WA 98104 (☎206/624-6600).
Rand McNally, 1201 Connecticut Ave NW, **Washington DC** 20036 (☎202/223-6751).

NB For other locations of *Rand McNally* across the US, or for direct-mail maps, phone ☎1-800/333-0136 (ext 2111).

CANADA

Ulysses Travel Bookshop, 4176 St-Denis, **Montréal** (☎514/289-0993).
Open Air Books and Maps, 25 Toronto St, **Toronto**, M5R 2C1 (☎416/363-0719).

World Wide Books and Maps, 1247 Granville St, **Vancouver**, V6Z 1E4 (☎604/687-3320).

AUSTRALIA AND NEW ZEALAND

The Map Shop, 16a Peel St, **Adelaide** 5000 (☎08/231 2033).
Specialty Maps, 58 Albert St, **Auckland** (☎09/307 2217).
Hema, 239 George St, **Brisbane** 4000 (☎07/9221 4330).

Bowyangs, 372 Little Bourke St, **Melbourne** 3000 (☎03/9670 4383).
Perth Map Centre, 891 Hay St, **Perth** 6000 (☎09/9322 5733).
Travel Bookshop, 20 Bridge St, **Sydney** 2000 (☎02/9241 3554).

These are not granted automatically – you will need to present yourself as a serious researcher or someone organizing an expedition. Usable enough maps for the most popular trekking areas can be found in *Trekking in Turkey* (Lonely Planet, o/p). Barring that, the Turkish Tourist Office's A4-sized brochure entitled "Mountaineering" includes six sketch maps at varying scales of popular alpine areas, but these were issued in the early 1980s by the Turkish Mountaineering Federation and are now woefully out of date. The *Mountains of Turkey* (Cicerone/Hunter) reproduces these sketches without correction or elaboration.

GETTING AROUND

Public transport is fairly comprehensive in Turkey, and only on major routes and during public holidays do you need to book tickets in advance. Where a destination is not part of the rather skeletal train network, private bus companies more than compensate, with a system that is reasonably priced and efficient. Although terminals can be nightmarish at times, ample attention is paid to your comfort and safety while you're in transit. Short stretches are best covered by *dolmuş* – either shared taxis in towns and cities or minibuses linking rural villages. Moving around under your own steam is also an option, though car rental rates are among the highest in the Mediterranean, and road conditions can be challenging. The domestic ferry network is confined to the north Aegean and Black Sea coasts, while the internal plane network is constantly expanding as demand rises and an increasing number of private companies compete with the state carrier *THY*.

TRAINS

Turkey's **train network**, run by the *TCDD* or *Turkish State Railways*, is far from exhaustive, and it's best used to span the distances between the three main cities and the provincial centres. When the Germans laid the track in the late nineteenth century they were paid by the kilometre, and told not to leave lines exposed to bombardment from the sea, with the result that trains often follow tortuous routes and may take up to twice as long as buses. They do, however, have the considerable advantage of additional comfort at comparable or lower prices.

The better services, west of Ankara, denoted "*mavı tren*" or "*ekspresi*", almost match long-distance buses in speed and frequency; in the east, however, punctuality and service standards begin to flag. Avoid any departure labelled *posta* (mail train) or *yolcu* (local) – they're excruciatingly slow.

Takeaway **timetables** are theoretically issued once yearly as a pink booklet entitled *Yolçu Rehberi/Passenger Guide*, but these disappear quickly, and were last updated in 1992; neither is the internationally published Thomas Cook handbook reliable, so in fact the only way to get accurate information is to go to the station in person, scan the placards, and then confirm departures with staff.

On major train routes it's a good idea to make a **reservation**. In theory you can do this for any journey in the country in İstanbul, İzmir and Ankara, where the system is computerized, though in practice it can be difficult to book, for example, an Ankara–İstanbul journey from İzmir. Non-sleeper **prices** on the better trains are about the same per kilometre as the buses; buying a return ticket brings the fare down by twenty percent. *InterRail* **passes** are valid all over Turkey, but *Eurotrain/BIJ* tickets only take you as far as İstanbul. *Freedom* and *Eurodomino* passes for travel within Turkey, and the similar *TrenTur* card purchased in Turkey, represent poor value.

Within Turkey, foreign **students** with appropriate identification are entitled to a thirty-percent discount on train tickets. Credit cards are not yet accepted as payment for train fares.

On long-haul journeys you may still have a choice between a first- and second-class seat, though with time this distinction is being phased out in favour of a single standard of service; very few shorter runs are still equipped with dilapidated third-class carriages. **First class** features Pullman-style seats, and air conditioning/heating according to season; as an indication it costs about $14 for Ankara–İstanbul. **Second-class** wagons have either Pullman seating or (in the east) continental-style, six-person compartments with narrow corridors on one side, and cost about half as much as first class: $7 for Bandırma–İzmir is representative. **Third class**, where it still exists, consists of uncomfortable wooden seats but it is ludicrously cheap. In second- or third-class carriages, **single women** travelling alone will be looked after by the conductor, which generally means delivery into a family or mixed-gender compartment. **Non-smoking** cars are always available on first- and second-class trains; ask for an *içmeyen vagon* when booking.

There's almost always a **dining car** on trains west of Ankara – the limited menus aren't so bad or expensive as to require bringing your own food, though no one will object if you nurse a Coke. In the east you'd be well advised to check on the availability of food and drink, and possibly bring your own.

There are three different kinds of **sleeping facilities** on Turkish trains. *Küşetli* is a couchette in a six-seat, second-class compartment, where you share with strangers and pay a supplement of about $8; the bunks pull down from the wall at night, and no bedding other than a pillow is supplied. *Örtülü küşetli* is a recently introduced category with usually only four bunks per compartment, with bedding provided. *Yataklı* compartments are first-class, three- or four-bed suites that cost up to three times as much as basic *küşetli*, with full linen laid on; reckon on paying around $30, İzmir–Ankara, for a bed in such a compartment.

LONG-DISTANCE BUSES

An immensely popular form of transport, the Turkish **long-distance bus** is a crucial part of the country's modern culture. There is no single, national bus company in Turkey; most routes are covered by several firms, with ticket booths both at the **otogars** (bus terminals) from which they operate, and also in the city centre. To further complicate matters, there's no such thing as a comprehensive timetable, although individual companies often provide their own, making for a bewildering choice. Prices vary between the best and scruffiest companies, though convenience of departures and on-board service are equally important criteria. If in doubt, inspect the vehicle out in the loading bay (*peron* in Turkish), and ask at the ticket office how long the trip will take. It's worth bearing in mind that long-haul journeys (over 10hr) generally take place at night, and that because of rest stops (see below) buses never cover more than 60km an hour, no matter what you're told. As a broad example of **fares**, İzmir–Antalya costs around $10, Konya–Göreme $4.

Otogars, especially in touristed areas, are full of **touts** (see also p.62) waiting to escort you to their company's window once you state your destination – though it may not have the soonest departure, nor the best service and seats. Common, fallacious ploys to get you to sign on with a particular company include promise of non-smoking vehicles (never happens except with the very top-end companies), "free breakfasts" on early morning departures (which means tepid tea in a PVC cup, and a soggy, cello-wrapped bread roll) or "free" transfer to the lodging of your choice at your destination (which may end up being accommodation owned by the driver's relatives where you're taken for an extra fee).

When buying tickets, ask to see the **seating plan**: if you crave fresh, non-smoky air, request front-row seats behind the driver, whose window may be the only ventilation on the coach. **Non-smoking** zones don't exist on the cheaper Turkish buses – and most Turks hate open windows or vents. Seats over the wheels (usually numbers 5–8 and 33–36 on the standard Mercedes O302 model) have cramped leg room and take the worst of the road bumps. Unacquainted women and men are not allowed to sit next to each other, and you may be asked to switch your assigned seat to accommodate this convention.

Be warned that most buses play music – either *arabesk* or a Western equivalent – until the lights go out. Partial compensation for this is the attention of the **muavin** or driver's assistant, who can supply drinking water on demand, and will appear several times in a journey with aromatic cologne for freshening up. Every ninety minutes there will be a fifteen-minute *mola* (**rest stop**) for tea and toilet visits, and there are less frequent half-hour pauses for meals at purpose-built roadside cafeterias.

To avoid the worst drawbacks of Turkish bus travel, particularly on the main inter-city lines, you might consider going with one of the three **premium coach companies**, *Ulusoy*, *Bosfor* and *Varan*. Their seats are more comfortable than most, with non-smoking areas on the most popular routes, and they don't segregate single passengers by sex. *Kamil Koç* and *Pamukkale*, while not quite as enlightened, are two of the best standard outfits in that order of preference.

When you buy your ticket at a *yazıhane* (sales office) in a town centre, you should ask about **free service buses** to the *otogar*, especially if it's located a few miles out. Most companies provide small minibuses even for a single passenger; the question to ask is "*servis araba var mı?*". These buses will theoretically also take passengers from *otogar*s into town centres, but this is a more erratic system, the service often being provided with considerable grumbling and subject to hidden extras.

DOLMUŞES

The Turkish institution of the **dolmuş** or shared transport could profitably be imitated in the West: it's practical, economical and ecologically sound. The idea is that a vehicle – a car or minibus – runs along set routes, picking passengers up and dropping them off along the way. As on full-sized buses, you will be expected to switch seats on both urban and interurban dolmuşes so that women do not sit next to strange males. To stop a dolmuş, give a hand signal as for a normal taxi, and if there's any room at all (the word *dolmuş* means "stuffed"), they'll stop and let you on. To get out, say *inecek var* (literally, "there's a getting out") or *müsait bir yerde* ("at a convenient place").

On busy **urban routes** it's better to take the dolmuş from the start of its run, at a stand marked by a blue sign with a black-on-white-field "D", sometimes with the destination indicated – though generally you'll have to ask to find out the eventual destination, or look at the dolmuşes themselves, which generally have their journey's end written on a windscreen placard. On less popular routes the driver will often depart before the vehicle is full, in which case you're likely to be taken aboard wherever you hail it.

Inter-town and -village dolmuşes are always 12- to 15-seater minibuses. For the remotest villages there will only be two services a day: to the nearest large town in the morning and back to the village in mid-afternoon. Generally, though, dolmuşes run constantly between 7 or 8am and 7pm in summer, stopping earlier to match the hour of sunset in winter or extending until 10 or 11pm near popular resorts. In the chapter-end travel details we've given broad frequencies within this period unless otherwise stated.

There's no strict **vehicle specialization**: minibuses serve as dolmuşes in most cities, particularly İzmir, but in İstanbul classic Chevrolets, Packards, Studebakers, Chryslers and other American collectors' items, sold off by US military and embassy personnel four decades ago, long had the monopoly on most routes. However, of late the municipal authorities have declared war on them as pollution-prone, and they're sadly being phased out in favour of small diesel Ford transit vans with windows. Yellow taxis, confusingly still bearing signs saying "TAKSI", operate as dolmuşes in many towns – if you're not sure, ask; in İstanbul the remaining older dolmuş saloons often have a checked stripe on their flank.

Fares are low, hardly more than urban bus prices and about the same as coaches between towns, but it's always difficult to know how much to pay if you're only going part-way. Everybody else on board will know, however; just state your destination and hand over a pile of coins or notes, and you'll invariably get the right change. If you sit near the front, you'll have to relay other people's fares and repeat their destinations to the driver – no mean feat if you don't speak the language.

CITY BUSES AND TAXIS

In larger towns the main means of transport are the red-and-white **city buses**, which take **pre-purchased tickets** available from kiosks near the main terminals, newsagents, or from kerbside touts (at slightly inflated prices). The only **exceptions** are private buses in İstanbul, which look the same as those run by the *belediye*, and whose drivers issue tickets in exchange for cash.

Yellow city **taxis** are everywhere, and ranks crop up at appropriate places, though in rush hour finding a free cab can be difficult. Hailing one in the street is the best way to find a cab, but in suburban areas there are useful street corner telephones from which you can call cabs if you can make yourself understood. Urban vehicles all have working, digital-display meters, and fares are among the lowest in the Mediterranean – the flag falls at about $0.75, with double tariff applicable between midnight and 6am. In cities, it's illegal to ask for a flat fare, though attempted rip-offs of foreigners aren't unheard of. Out in the country, you'll have to bargain. Taxi drivers will promptly remind you to fasten your seat belt (*kemer* is the word), though strangely the drivers themselves aren't required to use them – perhaps, as some cynics say, there are too many taxis and lawmakers consider their drivers expendable.

HITCHING

Hitching is an option where public transport is scarce or nonexistent, and lifts tend to be frequent and friendly – you may be expected to share tea with the driver on reaching your destination. Rural Turks hitch too – if you see a group at the roadside waving you down in your own car, it's a good bet that no bus or dolmuş is forthcoming, and you'd be performing a useful service by giving them a lift.

On routes that are well served by buses and dolmuşes, the general consensus among Turks is that there's little point in hitching since public transport is so cheap, and they will be less inclined to view hitchhikers favourably.

You do sometimes see **Turkish women** – older, conservatively dressed villagers – hitching near the Aegean coast. However, you also see prostitutes soliciting truck drivers along the main highways, and on balance it's not a good idea for foreign women to hitch alone, especially in the east of the country. With male company, it need be fraught with no more peril, and possibly less, than elsewhere around the Mediterranean.

DRIVING

Given the excellent bus services, you don't need to **drive** in Turkey to get between the major centres, but it's often the only way to reach remote spots, and will enable you to see more of the country during a brief visit. However, you really need to be an experienced, level-headed driver in order to tackle highway conditions.

REGULATIONS

You drive **on the right**, and yield to those approaching from the right, even on the numerous roundabouts. **Speed limits**, seldom observed, are 50km/hr within towns, 40km/hr if towing a trailer or caravan; on the open road, limits are 90km/hr for saloon cars, 80km/hr for vans, 70km/hr if you're towing something. Turkey has the second highest **accident rate** in the Mediterranean (after Portugal), and it's easy to see why: Turkish drivers are in the main an impatient bunch who lean on the horn and tailgate liberally if they feel the traffic isn't moving fast enough.

Traffic control points at the approaches to major cities are frequent, and although the police manning them are mostly interested in overweight trucks, they may halt foreigners. They can be rude and unnerving, and if things get sticky you should pretend total ignorance of Turkish, whatever your linguistic abilities; however, you might well be waved through simply upon showing your foreign ID. If it's your own vehicle, it may be inspected for real or imagined equipment defects (especially lights), though you'll probably be sent to the nearest *sanayi* (repair shop zone) rather than cited. If you've rented a car (see p.31), make sure the rental company provides both the insurance certificate and the vehicle registration, or a certified copy thereof.

Despite the deficiences of many Turkish drivers, don't expect to get away with blatant **driving offences** without being noticed, as radar gun and helicopter surveillance has become intensive. Major violations such as jumping red lights, speeding or turning illegally carry heavy spot fines (though still risible sums by European standards); less serious stuff like passing on hills or failing to wear your seat belt nets a token $10 fine, though there is talk of tripling all of these amounts. You should always receive a receipt for any fine paid, otherwise it goes straight into the cop's pocket.

Do heed the internationally signposted **no-parking zones**, especially in resorts. Local police are very industrious with tow trucks, though you usually get advance warning in the form of slowly cruising patrol cars yelling out the plate numbers of offenders over their loudspeakers. Fines of about $20 are not outrageous by European standards, but you will waste considerable time hunting down the pound where your vehicle has been taken, not to mention overcoming the language barrier with staff. Generally it's wisest to patronize the covered (*katlı*) or open *otoparks*. Parking on the street, you may often be approached by roving attendants demanding parking fees (about $0.70 for all day); don't pay up unless an official ticket is produced – this is a popular beggars' scam.

ROAD CONDITIONS

Ordinary **main roads** are usually adequately paved, but often dangerously narrow. This is not so much of a problem in the relatively uncrowded east, but it makes driving quite hair-raising in the west. Archeological sites and other points of interest are marked by large **black-on-yellow signs**; however, side roads to minor sites or villages are often poorly signposted and inaccurately shown on maps. **Information** from the nearest filling station is usually reliable – roads optimistically shown on maps may be unfinished or submerged under a new reservoir.

Toll highways, marked with white-on-green signs, are springing up, and especially for novice foreign drivers are well worth the modest tolls ($1.50–4) to use. Main ones finished or under construction at the moment include İstanbul–Ankara, bypassing the hilly, curvy nightmare between Gerede and Adapazarı; İstanbul–Edirne; Adana–Gaziantep; İzmir–Çeşme; and İzmir–Denizli, cutting through the mountains to skirt the horrific E-24 between Selçuk and Denizli.

Typical **hazards** include the local flair for overtaking right, left and centre, preferably on a curve; failure to signal turns; and huge trucks (the ever-present TIRs) ambling along at walking pace or whizzing past at kamikaze speeds. Additionally, small towns form dangerous bottlenecks of trotting horsecarts, blithely reversing tractors and pedestrians or livestock strolling heedlessly out in front of you, as well as buses and dolmuşes halting without warning to take on passengers invisible to you.

The commonest **minor mishaps** involve smashed windscreens, for which passing lorries churning up barrages of gravel are the main cul-

prit, and shredded tyres. If you rip a tyre (not difficult to do on the many rocky tracks), go to a *lastıkçı* (tyre workshop) of a well-stocked *sanayi*. In many cases the damage may be skilfully repaired; otherwise a new tyre for a rented Fiat Serçe 124 or Şahin 131 runs to about $60, a slightly used but acceptably treaded specimen around half that amount. When installing your spare, it's as well to know that the socket for the jack (*griko*) on the commonly rented Şahin 131 is found halfway along the chassis, and the wheel is held on by four nuts, not five, covering the plastic hubcap which is quite difficult to re-install.

Night driving is best not attempted by beginners – be prepared for vehicles (especially tractors) with no taillights, one headlight or just parking lights, flocks of sheep (distinguished by massed green eye shine) and an extra quota of lumbering TIRs. If you're forced to drive after dark in isolated areas, it's not a bad idea to open windows enough to smell goat flocks and tractor exhaust in front of you! Oncoming cars will typically flash their lights at you whether or not your high beams are on – contrary to British or North American convention, this actually means "Don't even think of overtaking, *I'm* coming through". **Safety equipment**, such as flares or warning triangles, is nonexistent, and usually the first hint you'll have of a breakdown or wreck ahead, night or day, are either piles or lines of stones on the asphalt.

FUEL, FILLING STATIONS AND REPAIRS

Filling stations are amazingly frequent throughout most of the country, and open long hours, so it's pretty difficult to run out of fuel. Diesel is *mazot*, while petrol is *benzin*, available in *normal* or (more usually) *süper* grades, costing $0.51, $0.61 and $0.71 per litre respectively; car rental firms like you to fill up with *süper*. Lead-free or *kursunsuz*, suitable for catalytic convertors (about $0.80 per litre), is fairly common in the west of Turkey, but is still almost impossible to come by in the remote east.

In western Turkey, roadside **rest-stop culture** conforming to Italian or French notions has arrived in a big way. You can eat, pray, patch a tyre, phone home, shop at mini-marts and sometimes even sleep at what amount to small hamlets in the middle of nowhere, essentially the descendants of the medieval *kervansarays*. In the impoverished east, however, where it can often be difficult to tell a shabby but functioning station

---

ROAD SIGNS

Dur	Stop
Tek yön	One way
Araç çıkabilir	Vehicles exiting
Yol yapımı	Roadworks
Şehir merkezi	City centre
Park yapılmaz/edilmez	No parking
Giremez	No entry
Askeri bölge	Military zone
Tırmanma şeridi	Overtaking lane

from a closed-down one, you'll find much more primitive amenities.

Credit cards (*Visa, Mastercard/Worldwide*) are widely honoured for fuel purchases in much of Turkey, but you'll find this facility far less often east of a line connecting Gaziantep, Elazığ and Trabzon. Plastic purchases used to carry a three percent surcharge to cover inflation during the two-to-three-week interval before the presentation of hand-filled-in charge slips, but lately – in the west of the country, at least – signs prominently advertise "*Kredi Kart Komisyon Sıfır*" (No commission on credit cards), since the amount is charged virtually immediately to your account via the same sort of on-line apparatus prevalent in Europe and North America. In the more primitive east, if the phone connection to the bank (to get transaction approval) doesn't work, you're out of luck.

Car **repair workshops** and spare-part dealers are located in industrial zones called *sanayis* at town outskirts. Fiat, Renault, Ford, Skoda, Mercedes and Fargo are the most common brands

catered to, usually instantly, though Turkish mechanics will attempt to fix anything. If you have a foreign make, it's wisest to seek out a factory-authorized workshop in a large town. **Parts** cost the same or slightly more than abroad, and if not in stock can be ordered on a day's notice, while **labour** charges are very cheap by foreign standards – a third to a half of the cost in northern Europe or North America.

CAR RENTAL

Car rental in Turkey is usually exorbitant, with rates equalling or exceeding any in Europe. This is partly a consequence of the high accident rate but also because of the surprisingly high cost of Turkish-produced cars.

The minimum over-the-counter rates of the largest **international chains** are close to $75 a day in summer, all inclusive; **Turkish chains** may charge fifteen to twenty percent less, and occasionally you'll find a **one-off outlet** that's willing to let a Group A car go for less than $40 per day outside of peak season. Weekly rates are hardly

---

INTERNATIONAL CAR RENTAL AGENCIES

UK

Avis ☎0181/848 8733.
Budget ☎0800/181181.
Eurodollar ☎01895/233300.
Europcar/InterRent ☎0345/222 525.

European ☎0171/240 4711.
Hertz ☎0345/555888.
Holiday Autos ☎0990/300400.

IRELAND

Avis ☎01232/240404.
Budget ☎01232/230700.
Europcar ☎01232/450904 or 423444.

Hertz ☎01/660 2255.
Holiday Autos ☎01/454 9090.

US AND CANADA

Auto Europe ☎1-800/223-5555.
Avis ☎1-800/331-1084.
Budget ☎1-800/527-0700.
Dollar ☎1-800/421-6868.

Hertz in US, ☎1-800/654-3001; in Canada ☎1-800/263-0600.
National ☎1-800/CAR-RENT.

AUSTRALIA

Avis ☎1800/225 533.
Budget ☎13 2848.

Hertz ☎13 3039.

NEW ZEALAND

Avis ☎09/579 5231.
Budget ☎09/375 2220.

Fly and Drive Holidays ☎09/529 3790.
Hertz ☎09/309 0989.

better, ranging from $300 with small local outfits to about $500 with a multinational in summer. Especially if you rent from *Hertz, Avis, Budget, Eurodollar, European* or *Europcar/InterRent*, you'll have to exploit every **discount scheme** available to bring the price down: Frequent Flyer cards, *THY* boarding passes presented at airport agency desks, and discount vouchers obtained at home before departure are all effective bargaining chips.

If you're willing to sacrifice some flexibility and can commit to a rental period of one to four weeks, you should **pre-book**, either as part of a fly-drive scheme (see p.8), or with a major rental agency. Reserving from North America, count on a minimum of US$275 per week, all inclusive; rates vary somewhat by season, but much more by company – promotional deals come and go without warning, so call as many agencies as possible, and ask for a complete itemization of charges. The most advantageous UK rates – about £200–220 weekly, all-inclusive, according to season – are available through *Holiday Autos* or *European Car Rental* (see the box for phone numbers). Otherwise you're best off dealing in person with small Turkish companies, especially off-season.

There is some **regional variation** in rates: south-coast locations (Antalya, Fethiye) are noticeably cheaper than west-coast resorts (Kuşadası, İzmir). Prices and contract conditions on a given day within the same town may appear to be uniform, but there's often considerable scope for comparison – and bargaining. Rental companies will usually allow you to rent "one-way" (ie, begin in one town and drop off in another), provided they have an office in your destination. **Unlimited kilometrage** is invariably a better deal than any time-plus-distance rate. Basic **insurance** is usually included, but **CDW** (Collision Damage Waiver) is not, and given typical driving conditions taking this out is virtually mandatory. Along with the fifteen-percent **KDV** (Value Added Tax), all these extras can push up the final total considerably.

To rent a car you need to be at least 21 years of age (27 for Groups E and above), with a driver's licence held for at least one year. An **International Driving Permit**, from the *RAC* or *AA* in Britain/Australasia or the *AAA* in the US, is not essential – your own home licence will do at a pinch – but very helpful. You'll also need to flash a credit card or leave a substantial cash deposit to cover the estimated rental total.

The bottom-of-the-line, Group A **models**, now offered only by small local outlets, are either the barely adequate Serçe, the Turkish equivalent of a Fiat 124, or the sturdier but now discontinued Toros Renault 12. If you've pre-booked from overseas with a chain, you'll be furnished with the slightly more powerful, Category B Şahin (Fiat 131). If at all possible, for scarcely more money lay hands on a Fiat Doğan (131 SLX), Fiat Uno or a Renault 9 Spring, to get better design, space and overtaking power.

When checking a car out, agency staff will often make a thorough diagramatic notation of any **blemishes** on the vehicle. If you have an **accident** of any kind which leaves an ineradicable mark, go immediately to the nearest police station and get them to type out a *kaza raporu* or accident report – otherwise you'll invalidate the insurance. For minor scratches or dents – especially if you're at fault – it's far less of a palaver to go to the nearest *sanayi* and have them repaired for a few dollars. It's worth emphasizing that rental insurance *never* covers smashed windscreens or ripped tyres; it's up to you to fix these as cheaply as possible.

BRINGING YOUR OWN CAR

If you arrive in **your own car** as a tourist, it will be registered in your passport for a maximum stay of six months, and must leave the country when you do. If you leave Turkey briefly and then return in the vehicle, you'll get a shorter allowance the second time around – only six months of tourist use in any twelve-month period is permitted.

If your car is **written off** while in Turkey, the remains must be transported to a customs compound, and the full-page stamp in your passport cancelled. Similarly, if it's **stolen**, you'll have to get a report from the *Vilayet* (Provincial Authority) to get rid of the passport endorsement.

At the frontier you'll be asked for the following **documentation**: an International Driving Permit or home licence, registration papers or log book (originals or certified copy), and a Green Card or other proof of internationally valid insurance. You'll also need a *Carnet de Passage* (transit book) if you intend continuing through to the Middle East; in any case you'll be issued with a Turkish temporary registration (*araba tezkeresi*), separate from the passport stamp, valid for six months and to be mandatorily surrendered at your point of exit.

The British Green Card **insurance** system only covers you in Turkey upon payment of a supplemental charge – for example, £75 extra to upgrade a typical *AA* policy. You must keep the receipt of this payment for display to Turkish officials; it will be requested at the frontier, and your Green Card will not be considered valid without it.

British motoring associations provide comprehensive cover, including breakdown and recovery service, legal aid and car replacement. In Turkey they work in conjunction with the Turkish motoring organization, the **TTOK** (Turkish Touring and Automobile Association), which can advise on Turkish insurance and related matters, especially if you are planning on staying several months. They have branches in a number of cities (see the box) and at almost every land frontier post. You will have to pay for their breakdown service unless you've equipped yourself with vouchers or an insurance policy prior to arrival. North Americans will have to pay in any case since the *AAA* has no reciprocal agreement with the *TTOK*.

In Britain, the "Five Star" insurance policy from the *AA* (☎0990/500600 or 01256/474727) provides comprehensive cover abroad, including vouchers for the *TTOK*'s breakdown service. Prices are £85 for a month with a £5 surcharge for non-members, and an additional £35 for cars older than fifteen years. The *RAC* (☎0800/678000) have a similar "Eurocover" service costing members £88.20 for 30 days' cover, and a supplement of £34 for most cars older than ten years.

The 24-hour *TTOK* emergency **breakdown** number nationwide is ☎0212/280 4449; there is unfortunately no toll-free service or numbers for each province. If an English speaker is unavailable, you'll have to find someone to translate for you, or contact the main İstanbul headquarters during office hours. If you have a minor problem which doesn't require the breakdown service, contact the nearest *TTOK* branch, who will advise you to go to the closest authorized garage for your make of car, pay up front for repairs and then present them with a receipt when you arrive at their office.

BICYCLES AND MOTORBIKES

Touring Turkey by **bicycle** isn't as daft as it sounds, so long as you avoid the hottest months and the busiest roads. Flying in with a bike in your luggage is no more complicated than it is to any other destination, and often it's not even charged as excess baggage.

You do, however, have to be prepared for the **lack of maintenance** facilities, and your own **novelty value**. The only pushbikes Turks are used to seeing are old clunkers used strictly for sedate pedalling around town. A homegrown mountain-bike industry is emerging in İstanbul and Ankara, but you should bring **spares** of everything small or light (especially inner tubes), and not count on the admittedly ingenious local mechanics to improvise parts. Because you'll probably opt for back roads where few foreigners pass by, you'll draw crowds at any rest stop. Accept the inevitable and reckon that bike and bags are usually more, rather than less, secure guarded in this manner while you go have a tea.

The main **dangers** to you and your bike will be potholed pavements and the elements; most back-road drivers are surprisingly courteous, perhaps because they're so stunned at the sight of you, though be prepared for some gratuitous horn-honking. You can skirt many potential trouble spots or skip boring stretches by judicious use of the ferry and train network, on which you can transport your machine for free. It would, however, be unpleasant, not to mention suicidal, to pedal through İstanbul, and you're not allowed to cycle across the Bosphorus bridges anyway. **Rental facilities** are as yet few and far between in Turkey; the few outlets we know about are mentioned in the text.

Much the same advice applies to riding around Turkey on a **motorbike**, though these are not transported free on the ferries, but charged at their own special rates. In larger resorts and big cities there will be least one **motorbike rental agency**, or a car rental company which also rents out motorbikes and mopeds (*mobilet*) – indeed far more than one in such tourist hotspots as Bodrum, Marmaris and Side. You'll need an appropriate driving licence to rent a moped or motorbike, and most companies insist that it has been held for at least a year. Before renting any kind of bike, particularly a moped, make sure it's physically capable of coping with the terrain you want to use it for.

FERRIES

Turkey's domestic **ferries** are run by the *Türkiye Denizcilik İşletmesi* (literally "Turkey Maritime Services"), more commonly known as *Turkish Maritime Lines* (*TML*). There are three kinds of ferry: city shuttle services across the various waterways of İstanbul and İzmir, short-hop links to islands and across the Sea of Marmara, and longer-haul services connecting major domestic centres. Ferries to Italy and Greece are covered on p.7.

CITY AND SHORT-HOP FERRIES

The **city shuttle lines**, mainly serving foot passengers (a notable exception is the Harem–Sirkeci shuttle in İstanbul), are frequent, cheap and efficient, and run to very tight schedules, so they don't hang around waiting for passengers. Seasonally changing timetables (*saat tarifeleri*) are available cheaply from the ticket window (*gişe*) at the various docks. The municipality of İstanbul also operates the *Deniz Otobüsleri* or "**sea buses**", a fleet of catamarans supplementing the steam ferries across the Bosphorus but which also call at more remote points such as Yalova and the islands of the Sea of Marmara. In general they're twice as fast – and twice as costly – as conventional boats.

In addition to these are **short-hop ferries**, some of which serve foot passengers only, while others have provision for vehicles. Useful examples of the former include the services from İstanbul's Kartal, Kabataş or Sirkeci docks to Yalova, and from Saray Burnu to the islands of the Sea of Marmara. Vessels accepting foot passengers and cars include lines from İstanbul's Saray Burnu across the Sea of Marmara to Bandırma or Mudanya, and the Darica–Topcular crossing of

the Gulf of İzmit. Any of the trans-Marmara links save time compared to the dreary road journey, but are relatively expensive with a vehicle: İstanbul–Bandırma, for example, costs $30 for two people with a car, $16 without.

LONG-HAUL FERRIES

Long-haul domestic ferries, run by *TML*, are restricted to the coastal stretches where the road network remains substandard, specifically between İstanbul and Rize – with several intermediate stops, including Trabzon – and direct from İstanbul to İzmir. These services are very popular, and **reservations** must be made well in advance through one of the authorized agencies in the appropriate ports. Precise addresses and phone numbers are given in the town accounts, though the İstanbul *TML* headquarters at Karaköy, right behind the jetty on Rihtim Caddesi, is the best equipped.

Schedule pamphlets in Turkish and German are issued more or less yearly, though prices and timetables are subject to change. There are five classes of **cabin** on long-haul ferries, containing a variable number of berths. All are comfortable enough, if ruthlessly air conditioned, with en-suite showers and toilets. It's also possible to reserve a *pulman koltuk* or reclining chair, but if you leave booking to the last minute you won't even get one of these. No one will mind if you sleep up on **on deck** – bring a sleeping bag and mat, or just crash out on the loungers provided – but you do need a confirmed seat reservation to be allowed on the boat in the first place. **Fares** are reasonable – about $44 in a fifth-class, three-bunk cabin İstanbul–İzmir, $70 for the same facilities İstanbul–Trabzon, for example – and **students** with proper ID enjoy discounts ranging from ten to thirty percent, depending on the route; there are also concessions for groups and children up to age 12. **Cars** cost (eg $41 İstanbul–İzmir) almost as much again as a passenger berth, but most drivers consider the expense to be well worth it in terms of wear and tear (as well as fuel) saved.

Once aboard, the **atmosphere** is extremely convivial: the long-haul services are essentially budget cruises. However, the mediocre **food and drink**, whether at the bar, the self-service cafeteria or in the dining room, is marked up seventy percent above normal, and often only available in exchange for pre-paid, non-refundable **chits**, which you get from the purser's office on board.

TML and private competitors also have services from Taşucu, Mersin and Alanya to Girne and Famagusta in Northern Cyprus, which are described in the relevant town accounts.

PLANES

The state of domestic **air transport** in Turkey is in constant flux. *THY*, the state airline, has recently been subjected to competition from smaller private companies, and the list of destinations served tends to change rapidly both seasonally and from year to year as the market fluctuates. The general trend, though, is one of better services to established airports, and steadily climbing fares – as an example, you'll pay $90 İstanbul–Antalya, at full fare on *THY*, rather less with their private-sector competitors. *THY* inflight standards and punctuality have improved markedly in recent years, though Turkish wags are still apt to tell you that the initials stand for "They Hate You"!

Regardless of what you may be told, appearing at the airport 45 minutes to an hour before your scheduled flight departure is adequate leeway for completing the strict security procedures. Rarely posted in English is the requirement for you, on the way to the parked plane, to **identify your luggage** from amongst a pile of bags on the runway; this is a measure to prevent terrorists from checking a bomb and then not boarding, so if you don't point out your bag it won't be loaded on, and may be destroyed!

THY still flies between İstanbul, Ankara and İzmir, and from İstanbul to most other major Turkish centres except Bursa and Edirne; precise details and frequencies are found in the "Travel Details" concluding each chapter. Most flights to the east involve a connection in Ankara, with frequently long stop-overs there. Of the other airlines, *Sönmez* is thus far just a Bursa–İstanbul shuttle; *Maşair* operates only between İstanbul and Bodrum in summer season, as does *Top Air*, which also goes to Selçuk; *Han Air* links Bursa and Antalya; while *Onur Air* flies between İstanbul and Diyarbakır, Ankara and Antalya. The largest private company, *İstanbul Hava Yollari* (İstanbul Airlines), links İstanbul with Adana, Antalya, Dalaman, Erzurum, İzmir, Trabzon and Van, as well as selected overseas airports. We've listed local addresses and phone numbers of airlines or their agents throughout the *Guide*.

Fares vary by fifteen percent at most when more than one carrier serves a particular destination; *THY* is usually the most expensive, though it offers a variable student **discount**. Most airlines offer family and child discounts of ten to ninety percent – worth bearing in mind when comparing prices.

ACCOMMODATION

Finding a bed for the night is generally no problem in Turkey, except in high season at the busier coastal resorts and larger towns. Lists of category-rated hotels, motels and the better *pansiyons* are published by local tourist offices, and we've listed the best options throughout the *Guide*, although in practice where you end up can often be luck of the draw – and which tout, if any, you decide to follow.

If you are following a tout rather than our recommendations, note that certain outfits, particularly in İstanbul, Kuşadası, Antalya, Kaş and Cappadocia, have received serious complaints, ranging from dangerous plumbing to extortion and false imprisonment. If, on the other hand, you like where you have stayed, you may very well find that your accommodation proprietor keeps business cards on hand for similar establishments in other towns; often they have visited each other, or have some idea of what's on offer. This informal network can work very well indeed, with proprietors making a simple phone call to arrange both a stay and a retrieval from the *otogar* for you at your destination.

Prices, while cheap by most Western European standards, are no longer rock-bottom. To some extent facilities have improved correspondingly, though not surprisingly you often get less for your money in the big tourist meccas, and little choice between fleapits or four-star luxury in relatively untouristed towns of the interior. Singles generally go for just over half the price of a double, since proprietors are well used to lone (male) business travellers. Rooms with en-suite bath are generally about 25 percent more than unplumbed ones; triples are also usually available, costing about 30 percent more than a double. Rates quoted should be discreetly compared to those posted over the reception desk, which show the maximum permissible prices.

One thing to consider when choosing a room is **noise avoidance** – pick a room away from main thoroughfares or mosque minarets (not easy). You'll never cause offence by asking to see another room, and you should never agree on a price for a room without seeing it first. Though break-ins aren't the norm in Turkey, **security** should be at least a token consideration; paradoxically, many rooms in fancier hotels cannot be locked with a latch or button from the inside, only by key from outside – a particular hazard for women travelling alone.

Water should be tested to verify claims of *devamlı/24 saat sıcak su* (constant/24 hour hot water) – always to be treated sceptically. If provided by a solar heater, after 5pm or so it will be absent with astonishing regularity even in multi-starred hotels; in the absence of an electric back-up system, there is little you can do short of moving. Before giving up completely, however, try the right-hand tap; the nominal "hot" and "cold" convention is sometimes reversed in Turkey. Bathtubs and sinks almost never have plugs, so a universal plug is worth bringing from home.

Double beds for **couples** are relatively rare, but slowly catching on; the magic words are *Fransiz yatak* ("French" bed), not *çift yatak* ("double" bed), which actually refers to the number of beds in the room. Incidentally, in many conservative (read Refah-dominated) rural areas, hotel management may refuse to let a heterosexual couple share a room, let alone a bed, unless there is documentary evidence that they are married (just a ring may not work, especially if passport

names remain different). The police may make trouble for them if proprietors are lenient on this point, as a law exists to this effect, so there's little you can do in this situation short of finding other lodgings which will accept you as you are.

Button and light coding in **lifts/elevators** is a potential source of mystification. "Ç" stands for *çagır* or "call"; a lit-up "K" means "*katta*", that is, the car is already on your floor; illuminated "M" is *meşgül* or "in use"; "Z" stands for *zemin kat*, the ground floor.

HOTELS AND MOTELS

Turkish **hotels** are graded on a scale of one to five stars by the Ministry of Tourism; there is also a lower tier of unstarred establishments rated by municipalities. At the four- and five-star level you're talking international-standard mod cons and prices, at $56–200 per double. Two- or three-star outfits are less expensive and may have slightly more character; of late there has been a veritable craze to restore historic buildings as unique lodgings, with decidedly mixed results. While on the face of it pressing a disused *kervansaray* into a service as a hotel may seem commendable, in practice the presence of a noisy nightclub, complete with tacky singers, in the central courtyard completely negates their function as accommodation; additionally such venues usually serve as money-laundering operations for local mafiosi.

Less expensive still are the wide variety of no- or one-star but acceptable establishments, which range in price from $12 to $35 a double. Their exact price depends on the location and the presence or absence of bath, and to some extent on the season; out of season you can bargain prices down considerably. **Breakfast**, on the occasions when it's available, is often included in the rates, but it's almost invariably unexciting.

Motels, also graded from one to five stars, tend to be more expensive than hotels of the same class, and conform more to American notions of the term; they're essentially aimed at the drive-in trade, and often have imposing beachfront or panoramic settings to compensate for a nondescript layout. However, unless you're touring by car, their locations – generally way outside city centres – are too inconvenient to be of much use. Be warned also that the term "motel" is sometimes used to add a touch of class to an otherwise mediocre establishment.

The **unrated** hotels licensed by municipalities can be virtually as good as the lower end of the one-star class, sometimes with wall-to-wall carpeting, en-suite baths and phones. On average, though, expect spartan rooms with possibly a washbasin and certainly a shower (never a tub),

---

ACCOMMODATION PRICE CODES

In this book, nearly all hotels, motels and *pansiyons* have been categorized according to the price codes outlined below. The short description appended to each code should give a rough idea of what you'll get for your money, though predictably in a few of the busier resorts you'll sometimes pay ④ for ③ facilities, and ⑤ for ④ standards.

Category ranges are given in **US$**, since the high domestic Turkish inflation rate makes TL prices meaningless. They represent the minimum you can expect to pay for a **double room in high season**. For the very limited number of hostels and for the most direly basic hotels in the interior, where guests are charged per person, US$ rates, rather than a numerical code, are given in the *Guide*.

Prices for rooms at any establishment must by law be displayed at the reception desk; for band ③ and up breakfast will be automatically included, while below that taking it is negotiable. At slack times bargaining is virtually expected, and usually productive; for example lone travellers may be able to upgrade to a double room for the single price.

It is strongly recommended that you book establishments in bands ⑥–⑧ as part of a package, since by doing so you will guarantee yourself better service and may actually see the effective price code drop a category.

① Under $12. The most basic, 1970s-vintage *pansiyons* – some with sink or shower cubicles added at a later date – plus budget hotels in untouristed areas without en-suite facilities.

② $12–17. Nicer, recently purpose-built *pansiyons*, often with balconies, bedside furniture and sometimes other individual touches, as well as en-suite baths, toilets, linen and towels. Slightly more salubrious hotels in the interior, though these may not have full attached bathrooms.

③ $18–25. Establishments in touristed areas which straddle the border between a *pansiyon* and a hotel, often with roof terraces for breakfast, and perhaps a bar and small swimming pool; occasionally handled by package tour operators. Relatively hygienic hotels in the interior, with fully equipped bathrooms and room phones. Hot water more reliable than in lower categories, but still not guaranteed.

④ $26–35. Good-value one-star hotels and *pansiyons* in resorts, sometimes in restored old buildings; invariably handled by package tour operators. Often with extra touches like attached restaurant and rural-antique decor.

⑤ $36–45. Comfortable if sometimes small two-star hotels and *pansiyons*; this category includes many (often overpriced) places in İstanbul's Sultanahmet district, top-end establishments in the Anatolian interior, and restored *kervansarays*, which may appear to be underpriced but often suffer from creeping damp or on-site nightclub

noise. Attached bar/restaurant is more or less mandatory, as are room phones and winter heating. Ottoman antiques in common areas, kilims in rooms etc, more or less de rigueur.

⑥ $46–55. Three-star hotels and the smaller holiday villages, plus *özel* (special) architectural revival projects. Air conditioning and full-sized bathtubs usually present, as well as extra facilities such as a pool, private beachfront, watersports gear and tennis courts.

⑦ $56–75. More exclusive, four-star hotels and bungalow complexes. All of the preceding amenities will be provided, probably duplicated (ie two pools, two restaurants, two snack-bars) and more grandly laid out – rooms may resemble small suites. Additional touches like businessmen's telecom services, hairdresser, organized excursions etc. Standard of breakfast starts to be higher than usual; there should be no excuse for lack of hot water. On-site casinos make their appearance.

⑧ Over $75 (up to $200 if you wish). Restored classics, such as the *Pera Palas* or *Çirağan* Palace in İstanbul, plus five-star de luxe behemoths often affiliated with an international chain. At coastal resorts, luxury digs are often rather remote, necessitating use of the hotel's shuttle or a local taxi to get into the nearest town (the idea being to encourage you to spend more money onsite). Breakfasts, ideally, will be generous and varied. All other creature comforts and diversions to hand, including the all-but-obligatory casino for the benefit of the Israeli and Russian mafiosi.

with a squat toilet down the hall. Count on $5–7 per person for such comforts, with showers often carrying an additional $1–2 charge. Some places, especially in the east or interior, are jail-like dosshouses where the bedding, winter or summer, tends to be yellowed sheets topped by a thick quilt wrapped in a seldom-laundered slipcover anchored with safety pins. These establishments are listed only in the absence of anything better.

At the **roughest** end of the spectrum – again, not recommended in this guide except under duress – you may pay by the bed ($3–4 apiece) rather than the room, so potentially sharing quarters with strangers unless you buy up all the beds; there will often be no shower in the building, certainly not a hot one. Such places tend to be patronized by villagers in town on business and thus attract an exclusively male clientele; often they have a less than salubrious location as well.

PANSIYONS AND APARTMENTS

Often the most pleasant places to stay are **pansiyons** (pensions), small guesthouses which increasingly have en-suite facilities and proliferate anywhere large numbers of holiday-makers do. If there are vacancies in season, touts in the coastal resorts and other tourist targets descend on every incoming bus, dolmuş or boat; at other places or times, look for little signs with the legend *Boş oda var* ("Empty rooms free").

The typical Turkish *pansiyon* breakfast (about $2–4 a head when not included in the room price) is often served in the common gardens or terraces that are this kind of accommodation's strong point. Rooms tend to be sparse but clean, furnished in one-star hotel mode and always with two sheets (*çarşafs*) on the bed. Hot water is generally solar-heated at seaside locations (subject to the unreliability noted above), out of wood- or coal-fired boilers elsewhere. Laundry facilities – even if just a drying line and a plastic bucket – are almost always present, and laundry will often be done for you cheaply, a big advantage over most low-grade hotels. In addition, the proprietors are apt to be younger and friendlier than hotel staff – though this may be manifested in an unduly attentive attitude to lone female guests. Prices are often rigidly controlled by the local tourist authorities, according to what category the establishment is rated at. Hot showers

are rarely charged for separately; if they are, count on an extra dollar or so a shot, as in modest hotels.

Self-catering apartments are just beginning to become widespread in coastal resorts, and are mostly pitched at vacationing Turks, or foreigners arriving on pre-arranged packages at the larger resorts. If you come across any – either on the spot or through the local tourist office – they're certainly worth considering for an extended stay. The major negotiable outlay will be for the large gas bottle feeding the stove.

CAMPING, CHALETS AND HOSTELS

Wherever *pansiyons* are found, there will probably also be **campsites** – often run by the same people, who in the absence of a proper site may simply allow you to crash out in the *pansiyon's* garden. Charges per head run from a couple of dollars for such an arrangement to $5 in a well-appointed, if sterile, site at a major resort in season, plus fees of around $1–4 per tent. You may also be charged for your vehicle – anything from $2 to $7 depending on the site and season. Campsites often rent out tents to those showing up without canvas, or provide A-frame **chalet** accommodation, which can be anything from a stuffy garden shed with a bed inside to a fairly luxurious affair with bathroom. The value for money of chalets varies tremendously, as does their architecture: prices will be anything between $10 and $20.

Possibly more appealing than any of the preceding are the well-amenitied, shady **forest campsites** managed by the Ministry of Forestry; look for brown wooden signs with yellow lettering. There are 25 of them, scattered at strategic locations (mostly coastal) across the west of the country, and they make an ideal choice if you have your own transport, especially a combi-van or car and caravan. Most are open April to October inclusive, with maximum charges of $4 per tent, $5 per van, and $1 per person; inland sites are much cheaper, and half rates apply to holders of IYHF or FIYTO cards.

Various makeshift **roadside "kampings"**, essentially nothing more than some clumps of trees with parking space for Turkish weekenders, are unlikely to appeal to most foreigners. Camping rough is not illegal, but hardly anybody does it except when trekking in the mountains, and, since you can expect a visit from curious police or even nosier villagers, it's not really a choice for those who like privacy.

With the abundance of budget *pansiyons* and downmarket working-men's hotels, there are relatively few **hostels** outside İstanbul. Sometimes a *pansiyon* in a major resort will have roof space or a "group room" set aside. Most other hostels – called *yurts* – are rather poky dormitories aimed at local students on summer holiday and are unlikely to cater for you, making the purchase of an IYHF card before you leave a waste of money.

HAMAMS

One of the highlights of a stay in Turkey, especially during the cooler months, is a visit to a hamam or Turkish bath. A nearby hamam will also make a shower-less but otherwise acceptable budget hotel more palatable. Many tourists never partake because they (usually wrongly) anticipate sexual hassles or intense culture shock; in fact, after a day at the ruins or in the bazaar, a corner of a bath-house is likely to be an oasis of tranquillity in comparison.

Virtually all Turkish towns of any size have at least one hamam per neighbourhood; about the only exceptions to this pattern are some of the coastal resorts that were formerly populated by Greeks, who didn't build such structures. Baths, and routes to them, are usually signposted, but if in doubt look for the distinctive external profile of the roof domes, visible from the street. Baths are either permanently designated for men or women, or sexually segregated on a schedule – look for the words *erkekler* (men) and *kadınlar* (women), followed by a time range written on a placard by the door. Women, alas, tend to be allotted far more restricted hours, usually mid-week during the day.

On entering, you will usually leave your **valuables** in a rather small locking drawer, the key of which (often on a wrist/ankle-thong) you keep with you for the duration of your wash. Bring soap, shampoo and a shaving mirror, which are either not supplied or are expensive to buy on the spot. The basic **admission** charge varies depending on the level of luxury, but except in posh or tourist-oriented baths it should never be more than $4 a head, and is normally clearly indicated by the front desk. Men will be supplied with a *peştamal*, a thin, wraparound sarong; women usually have to specifically request one but, in fancier spas, more often wear bathing costumes. Both sexes get *takunya*, awkward wooden clogs, and later a *havlu* or proper drying towel. Changing cubicles (*camekân* in Turkish), equipped with a reclining couch, are sometimes shared and rarely lock except in the better hamams – thus the safe-drawer.

The *hararet* or **main bath chamber** varies from plain to ornate, though any hamam worth its salt will be dressed in marble at least up to chest height. Two or more *halvets*, semi-private corner rooms with two or three *kurnas* (basins) each, lead off from the main chamber. The internal temperature varies from tryingly hot to barely luke-warm, depending on how well-run the baths are. Unless with a friend, it's one customer to a set of taps-and-basin; refrain from making a big soapy mess in the basin, which is meant for mixing pure water to ideal temperature. Use the scoop-dishes provided to sluice yourself, being careful not to splash your neighbours; on Fridays especially they may have just completed their *abdest* (ritual ablution), and would have to start all over again if touched by an "infidel's" water. It's also considered good etiquette to clean your marble slab with a few scoopfuls of water before leaving.

It's not done for men to drop their *peştamal*: **modesty** is the order of the day, and washing your lower half through or under the cloth is an important acquired technique. Women are less scrupulous about covering up, though they too keep their knickers on.

More than one foreign female visitor has been brought up short by the sight of a matronly figure advancing on them, beckoning with a straight razor: religious Turkish women **shave** *all over*, though usually not at the baths. Alternatively, the locals stalk about swathed to waist height in green depilatory paste, like New Guinea mud-women. Men, incidentally, are expected to shave their faces in the *tıraşlık*, a section of the *soğuk-*

luk cooling-down room located between the foyer and the main chamber.

At the heart of the hamam is the *göbek taşı* or **"navel stone"**, a raised platform positioned directly over the wood- or coal-fired furnaces that heat the premises. In a good bath the *göbek taşı* will be piping hot, and covered with prostrate figures using their scoop-dishes or special pillows as head-rests. It's also the venue for vigorous (to say the least) **massages** from the *tellâk* or masseur/masseuse, whose technique is inspired more by medieval rack-and-wheel practices than by New Age touchie-feelie methods – be warned. A *kese* (**abrasive mitt**) session from the same person beside your basin, in which untold layers of dead skin and grime are whisked away, will probably be more to most people's tastes. Agree terms

in advance with the *tellâk*, which should be about equal to the basic bath charge. If you prefer, you can buy a *kese* at any chemist's and rub yourself down. Traditionally, only male *tellâk*s massaged men, and female masseurs women, but of late there has been increased incidence of men massaging women in the more touristy baths; if this is not to your liking, decline offers or even request a same-sex masseur from the management.

Upon return to your cubicle you'll be offered tea, soft drinks or mineral water, any of which is a good idea since the baths dehydrate you. These, like a massage, are **extras**; if in doubt, consult the price placard over the reception desk. Except in the heavily touristed establishments, tips above and beyond the listed fees are not required or expected.

EATING AND DRINKING

At its finest, **Turkish food is some of the best in the world.** There are enough climate zones in the country to grow most ingredients locally, and the quality (especially ripeness) of the raw materials has not yet been compromised by EC-type marketing standards. Prices, except for the fancier cuts of meat and for seafood – and of course at the major resorts, where standards have sadly declined as tourism has taken hold – aren't going to break your budget either; when in doubt, try to eat where the local tradesmen do. Unadventurous

travellers are prone to get stuck in a kebab rut, and come away moaning about the monotony of the cuisine; in fact, all but the strictest vegetarians should find enough variety to satisfy them.

BREAKFAST AND STREET SNACKS

The so-called "Turkish" **breakfast** (*kahvaltı*) served at modest hotels and *pansiyon*s is almost invariably a pile of day-old bread slices with a pat of margarine, a slice of processed cheese, a dab of pre-packed jam and a couple of olives. Only tea is likely to be available in quantity; seconds are likely to be charged for, as are English-style extras like *sahanda yumurtalar* (fried eggs). In the better hotels you can often, but not always, anticipate decent butter in bulk, iced; jar-jam that actually contains fruit chunks; a variety of breads and pastries; fresh fruit slices; a choice of olive types; and for protein, an array of cold and hot meats, plus eggs in various styles.

You can eat better on a budget by simply using street stands or snack joints, many of which serve some of Turkey's best food. Many workers start the morning with a *börek*, a rich, flaky, layered pastry containing bits of mince or cheese; these can be found either at a tiny *büfe* (stall-café) or from a street cart. Others content themselves with a simple *simit* (bread rings speckled with sesame seeds) or a bowl of *çorba* (soup) with lemon.

Later in the day, vendors hawk *lahmacun*, small, round Arab-style pizzas with a thin meat-based topping. Visitors from Britain may find, to their surprise, that kebabs are not generally considered takeaway food; try instead a sandwich (*sandviç*) with various fillings (often *kokoreç* – offal – or fish). In coastal cities *midye tava* (deep-fried mussels) are often available, as are *midye dolması* (mussels stuffed with rice, pine nuts and allspice) – though these are best avoided in summer months, especially when offered at unrefridgerated street stalls.

Not to be confused with *lahmacun* is *pide*, Turkish pizza – flat bread with various toppings, served to a sit-down clientele in a *pideci* or *pide salonu*. The big advantage of this dish is that it's always made to order: typical styles are *kaşarlı* or *peynirli* (with cheese), *yumurtalı* (with egg), *kıymalı* (with mince), and *sucuklu* (with sausage). This would be another ideal breakfast food, except that many *pideci*s don't light their ovens until 11am or so, thus making it an obvious lunchtime treat.

Other snacky specialities worth seeking out are *mantı* – the traditional central-Asian, meat-filled ravioli served drenched in yoghurt and spice-reddened oil – and *gözleme*, a crêpe-like delicacy often served in the same places. In any sizeable town you'll also find at least one *kuru yemiş* stall, also known as a *leblebeci*, where nuts and dried fruit are sold by weight – typically 100g a shot. Aside from the usual offerings, keep an eye out for *cezeriye*, a bar made of carrot juice, honey and nuts; the winter/spring snack of *peştil* or dried fruit, most commonly apricot and peach, pressed into sheets; and *tatlı sucuk*, a fruit, nut and molasses roll not to be confused with meat *sucuk* (sausage).

RESTAURANTS

Several kinds of eateries in Turkey fill the need for more substantial sit-down food. A **lokanta** is a restaurant emphasizing *hazır yemek*, precooked dishes kept warm in a steamtray; here also can be found *sulu yemek*, "watery food" – which is just that, hearty chunks swimming in broth or sauce. A *"restoran"*, a self-bestowed title for anything from a motorway bus pitstop to a white-tablecloth affair, will also provide *ızgara yemek* or meat dishes grilled to order. A **çorbacı** is a

soup kitchen; **kebapcıs** and **köftecis** specialize in the preparation of kebab and *köfte* respectively, with a limited number of side dishes – usually just an array of salad, yoghurt and desserts. **İskembe salonus** are a Turkish institution, aimed at revellers as they emerge from clubs or *meyhanes* in the early hours, and open until 5 or 6am. Their main dish is tripe soup laced liberally with garlic, vinegar and red pepper, an effective hangover preventive. They also sell *piliç* (small chickens), which can usually be seen spit-roasting in the window.

Most budget-priced restaurants are *içkisiz*, "alcohol-free"; any place marked *içkili* (licensed) is likely to be more expensive. A useful exception is a **meyhane** (tavern), in its truest incarnation a smoky dive where eating is considered secondary to tippling; in the fancier ones, though, the food – mostly unusual delicacies – can be very conspicuous, very good and not always drastically marked up in price. No self-respecting Turkish woman, however, would be caught dead in most of them, and unfortunately very few *meyhanes* are the sort of spot where an unaccompanied foreign woman can go without comment, and some will seem dodgy to Western men too – deviations from this pattern are noted in the *Guide*. That said, any foreign men or couples bold enough to visit the more decorous *meyhanes* will be treated with the utmost courtesy. In restaurants, unaccompanied women may be ushered into the *aile salonu* (family parlour), usually upstairs or discreetly behind a curtain.

Prices vary widely according to the type of establishment: from $2–3 a head at a simple boozeless soup kitchen up to $12–14 at the flashier (and often more exploitative) resort restaurants. **Portions** tend to be tiny, so if you're a big eater you'll need to order two main courses. Many places don't have **menus**: you'll need to ascertain the prices of the most critical main courses beforehand, and review bills carefully when finished. Tallying up items you never ate, or presenting diners with dishes they didn't order, are fairly common gambits by waiters; so is having your plate whisked away before you're done with it. This last habit is not so much a ploy to hurry you along, but derives from the Turkish custom of never leaving a guest with an "empty" plate before them. *Kalsın* (May it remain) is the term to stop this practice in mid-air.

WHAT TO EAT

In a *çorbacı*, soup (*çorba*) and salad (*salata*) predominate. The most frequently encountered **soups** are *mercimek* (lentil), *ezo gelin* (rice and vegetable broth – thick enough to be an appetizing breakfast), *paça* (trotters) or *işkembe* (tripe). *Çoban* (shepherd's) *salatası* is the generic term for the widespread cucumber, tomato, onion, pepper and parsley **salad**; *yeşil* (green) salad, usually just some *marul* (lettuce), is only seasonally available. A range of soups and salads can also, of course, be found in *lokanta*s and high-class restaurants; here the so-called *mevsim salatası* or seasonal salad – perhaps tomato slices, watercress, red cabbage and lettuce hearts, sprinkled with cheese and drenched in dressing – approximates to a Western salad and makes a welcome change from "shepherd's" salad.

In any *içkili restoran* or *meyhane*, you'll find more of the **mezes** (appetizers) for which Turkey is justly famous – usually a bewildering array of rich purees, vinaigrettes, and fried-then-chilled dishes kept (sometimes for too long) in refrigerated display cases. These are the best dishes for **vegetarians** to concentrate on, since many are free of meat and the variety of vegetables and pulses used, combined with vitamin-retentive cooking methods, will sustain your dietary needs.

Along with dessert (see below), *mezes* are really the core of Turkish cuisine, and are far too numerous to list exhaustively. The best and most common include *patlıcan salatası* (aubergine mash), *piyaz* (white haricot vinaigrette), *semizotu* (purslane weed), *mücver* (courgette croquettes), *sigara böreği* (tightly rolled cheese pastries), *beyin salatası* (whole brain), *turşu* (pickled vegetables), *imam bayıldı* (cold baked aubergine with onion and tomato) and *dolma* (any stuffed vegetable).

Bread is good if an hour or two old but otherwise is spongy and stale, best for scooping up *meze* and the like. The flat unadorned *pide* served during Ramadan (not to be confused with the almost identical *pide* served with toppings) and at *kebapcı*s, and the very rare loaves of *kepekli* (bran; only from a *fırın* or bakery) afford the only relief. In villages, *yufka* – like ultra-thin Indian chapati; also the basis of *börek* pastry – makes a welcome respite, as does *bazlama* (similar to an Indian paratha).

Main courses are nutritious if often plainly presented. In *hazır yemek* restaurants, *kuru fasulye* (bean soup), *taze fasulye* (French beans), *sebze turlu* (vegetable stew) and *nohut* (chickpeas) are the principal **vegetable** standbys. Vegetarians should, however, be aware that even though no meat may be visible in these dishes, they're often made with lamb- or chicken-based broth; even *bulgur* and rice may be cooked in meat stock. To find out, ask *İçinde et suyu var mı?* (Does it contain meat stock?).

Other dishes more obviously **containing meat** include *mussaka* (not as good as the Greek rendition), *karnıyarık* (a much better Turkish version), *güveç* (clay-pot fricassee), *tas kebap* (a meat and vegetable combo) and *saç kavurma*, an inland Anatolian speciality made from meat, vegetables, spices and oil, fried up in a *saç* (the Turkish wok).

Full-on meat dishes from the *ızgara* (grill) include several variations on the stereotypical kebab. *Adana kebap* is spicy, with a sprinkling of purple sumac herb betraying Arab influence; *İskender kebap*, best sampled in Bursa, is heavy on the flatbread and yoghurt. *Köfte* (meatballs) and *şiş* (stew meat chunks), usually mutton or beef and *çöp* (bits of lamb or offal), are other options. When ordering, if you've any appetite, specify *bir buçuk* (a portion and a half – adequate) or *çift* (double portion – generous). Grilled dishes normally come with a slice or two of *pide* and raw-vegetable garnish – never inside pitta bread as in Britain. Potentially more exciting are titbits like *pirzola* (lamb chop), *böbrek* (kidney), *yürek* (heart), *ciğer* (liver), and *koç yumurtası* (ram's egg) or *billur* (crystal) – the last two euphemisms for testicle. A *karışık ızgara* (mixed grill) is always good value. Chicken is *piliç* or *tavuk* and widely available in various forms, though not as cheap as you'd think.

Fish and seafood is good, if usually pricy, and sold by weight more often than by item. Buy with an eye to what's in season (as opposed to frozen and imported), and don't turn your nose up at humbler items, which in all likelihood will be fresher because they turn over faster. Budget mainstays include *sardalya* (sardines – grilled fresh, and streets ahead of the canned kind), *palamut* (autumn tuna – ditto), *kefal* (grey mullet, a south Aegean speciality) and *sarıgöz* (black bream).

DESSERTS AND SWEETS

After the occasionally functional presentation of main dishes, Turkish chefs pander shamelessly and elegantly to the sweet tooth. Sticky-cake addicts and pudding freaks will find every imaginable concoction at the closest *pastane* (sweet-shop).

The syrup-soaked **baklava**-type items are pretty self-explanatory on a glance into the glass display cabinet – all permutations of a sugar, flour, nut and butter mix. More mysterious, less sweet and healthier are the **milk-based** products, which are popular all over the country. *Süpangile* ("süp" for short, a corruption of *soupe d'Anglais*) is an incredibly dense, rich chocolate pudding; more modest are *keşkül*, a vanilla and nut crumble custard, and *sütlaç* (rice pudding) – one dessert that's consistently available in ordinary restaurants. Top honours for elaborateness go to *tavukgöğsü*, a cinnamon-topped morsel made from hyper-boiled and strained chicken breast, semolina starch and milk. *Kazandibi* (literally "bottom of the pot") is *tavukgöğsü* residue with a dark crust on the bottom – not to be confused with *fırın sütlaç*, which looks the same but is actually *sütlaç* pudding with a scorched top baked in a clay dish.

Grain-based sweets are some of the best that the country has to offer. Especially if you coincide with the appropriate holiday, you'll get to sample *aşure*, a sort of rosewater jelly laced with pulses, wheat berries, raisins and nuts.* The best-known Turkish sweet, *lokum* or "Turkish Delight", is pretty much ubiquitous, available from *pastanes* and the more touristy shops. It's basically solidified sugar and pectin, flavoured (most commonly) with rosewater, sometimes pistachios, and sprinkled with powdered sugar. There are also nearly a dozen recognized sorts of *helva*, including the *tahini*-paste chew synonymous with the concoction in the West, although in Turkey the term usually means any variation on the basic theme of baked flour or starch, butter, sugar and flavoured water.

Ice cream is an excellent summer treat, provided it's genuine *Maraşlı döşme dondurma* (whipped in the Kahraman Maraş tradition – a bit like Italian *gelato*), not factory-produced rubbish.

Consistent warm weather prompts the stationing at public parks, sea promenades and so on of outlandishly costumed young men with swords selling the stuff. Being served is half the fun: you may be threatened or cajoled at (blunted) sword point into buying, after which the cone is presented to you on the point of the sword after a twirl or three, and a bell rung loudly to celebrate the transaction.

If none of the above appeals, your last resorts include *kabak tatlısı*, candied squash usually served in autumn with walnut chunks and *kaymak* (clotted cream), or summer **fruit** (*meyve*), which generally means *kavun* (Persian melon, honeydew) or *karpuz* (watermelon).

DRINKING

Beverages are consumed in Turkey with or without food, on the hoof or sedately, in the open-air setting of a tea garden or café or the boozy environs of what are essentially all-male clubs.

TEA, COFFEE AND SOFT DRINKS

Tea, grown along the Black Sea, is the national drink and an essential social lubricant – you'll inevitably be offered some within twenty minutes of your arrival in Turkey. Tea is properly prepared in a double-boiler apparatus, with a larger water chamber underneath the smaller receptacle containing dry leaves, to which a small quantity of hot water is added. After a suitable wait the tea is decanted into tiny tulip-shaped glasses, then diluted with more water to taste: *açık* is weak, *demli* or *koyu* steeped. Sugar comes as cubes on the side; milk is never added. If you're frustrated by the usual tiny glass at breakfast, ask for a *düble çay* (a "double tea", served in a juice glass).

Coffee is not as commonly drunk in Turkey, despite the fact that the Ottomans first intro-

---

*****Aşure* is the Turkish variant of a food with deep religious symbolism, found in Muslim, Christian and Jewish communities throughout Anatolia and the Balkans. The word is derived from the Arabic word for "ten", referring to *aşure günü*, or the tenth of the month of Muharrem, when Hasan and Hussein, sons of the fourth caliph Ali and grandsons of Mohammed, were slain, becoming martyrs for the Shiites and their allied sects in Turkey, the Alevîs and the Bektaşis. The latter have incorporated *aşure* fully into their ritual: after fasting for the first ten days of Muharrem, Bektaşi elders invite initiates to a private ceremony where the fast is broken over a communal meal of *aşure*. It is supposed to be made from forty different ingredients, courtesy of a legend which claims that after the Ark's forty-day sail on the Flood, and the first sighting of dry land, Noah commanded that a stew be made of the remaining supplies on board – which turned out to number forty sorts of food. An alternative name for the dish is thus "Noah's pudding", but today you'll be fortunate to find half that number of ingredients, even in a devotional recipe. You can also buy bags of prepackaged *aşure* mix in Turkish markets, and many kebab joints or *pastanes* serve it much of the year.

A FOOD AND DRINK GLOSSARY

Basics

Su	Water	*Makarna*	Pasta (noodles)	*Yağ*	Oil
Buz	Ice	*Yoğurt*	Yoghurt	*Tuz*	Salt
(Kepekli) ekmek	(Whole bran) bread	*Süt*	Milk	*Şeker*	Sugar
		Yumurta	Eggs	*Kara biber*	Black pepper
Pilav, pirinç	Rice	*Tereyağı*	Butter	*Bal*	Honey
Bulgur	Cracked wheat	*Sirke*	Vinegar		

Useful words

Başka bir ...	Another ...	*Çatal*	Fork	*Peçete*	Napkin
Bardak	Glass	*Kaşık*	Spoon	*Hesap*	Bill, check
Tabak	Plate	*Bıçak*	Knife	*Servis ücreti*	Service charge

Cooking terms

Ezme	Puree, mash	*Sıcak/soğuk*	Hot/cold
Haşlama	Meat stew without oil, sometimes with vegetables	*İyi pişmiş*	Well-cooked
		Pişmemiş	Raw
Kızartma	Fried then chilled	*Yoğurtlu*	In yoghurt sauce
Zeytinyağlı	Vegetables cooked in their own juices, spices and olive oil (*zeytin yağı*), then allowed to steep and chill	*Soslu, salçalı*	In red sauce
		Acı	Hot, spicy
		Yumurtalı	With egg (eg, *pide*)
		Sucuklu	With sausage
Çevirme	Spit-roasted	*Kıymalı*	With mince
Izgarada(n), ızgarası	Grilled	*Peynirli, kaşarlı*	With cheese
Tava, sahanda	Deep-fried, fried	*Etli*	Containing meat
Fırında(n)	Baked	*Etli mi?*	Does it contain meat?
Pilaki	Vinaigrette, marinated	*Etsiz yemek var mı?*	Do you have any meatless food?
Buğlama	Steamed		

Soup (*Çorba*)

Mercimek	Lentil	*İşkembe*	Tripe
Tarhana	Yoghurt, sour grain and spice	*Yayla*	Similar to *tarhana*
Ezo gelin	Rice and vegetable broth	*Düğün*	"Wedding": egg and lemon
Paça	Trotters	*Yoğurt*	Yoghurt, rice and celery greens
Tavuk	Chicken		

Appetizers (*Meze* or *Zeytinyağlı*)

Çoban salatası	Chopped tomato, cucumber, parsley, pepper and onion salad	*Beyin salatası*	Lamb brains salad
		Pancar	Beets, marinated
		Bürülce	Black-eyed peas
Yeşil salata	Green salad	*Deniz bürülce*	Wild asparagus (approximately)
Zeytin	Olives		
Turşu	Pickled vegetables	*Deniz otu*	Rock samphire
Amerikan salatası	Mayonnaise and vegetable salad	*Patlıcan ezmesi*	Aubergine pâté
		Piyaz	White haricots, onions and parsley vinaigrette
Tere	Rocket greens		
İçli köfte	Bulgur, nuts, vegetables and meat in a spicy crust	*Barbunya*	Red kidney beans, marinated
Tarama	Red fish-roe	*Sigara böreği*	Cheese-filled pastry "cigarettes"
Haydarı	Dense garlic dip		

Yaprak dolması or		*Semizotu*	Purslane vinaigrette
yılancı dolması	Stuffed vine leaves	*Mücver*	Courgette frittata
Cacık	Yoghurt, grated cucumber	*İmam bayıldı*	Cold baked aubergine,
	and herb dip		onion and tomato

Meat and poultry (*Beyaz et*)

Sığır	Beef	*Orman kebap*	Roast lamb (expensive)
Dana eti	Veal	*Döner kebap*	Fatty lamb from a
Koyun	Mutton		rotisseried cone of
Kuzu	Lamb		meat slabs
Keçi	Goat	*İskender* or	Döner drenched in yogurt
Pastırma	Cured meat	*Bursa kebap*	and sauce
Tavuk	Boiling chicken	*Karışık ızgara*	Mixed grill
Piliç	Roasting chicken	*Kaburga*	Spare ribs
Pirzola	Chop, cutlet	*Yürek*	Heart
Bonfile	Small steak	*Ciğer*	Liver
Köfte	Meatballs	*Böbrek*	Kidney
Adana kebap	Spicy Arab-style kebab	*Dil*	Tongue
Şiş kebap	Shish kebab	*Billur, koç*	
Çöp kebap	Literally, "rubbish kebab"	*yumurtası*	Testicle
	– tiny chunks of offal or lamb		

Fish (*Balık*) and seafood

Barbunya, tekir	Red mullet, large and small	*Palamut, torik*	Two types of bonito
Kefal	Grey mullet (Aegean)	*Sarıgöz*	Black bream
Küpes	Bogue	*Kalkan*	Turbot
Levrek	Bass	*Karagöz*	Two-banded bream
Alabalık	Trout	*Çipura*	Gilt-head bream
Mezgit	Whitebait	*Kılıç*	Swordfish
İstavrit	Horse mackerel	*Orfoz*	Giant grouper
Hamsi	Anchovy (Black Sea)	*Kalamar*	Squid
Uskumru	Atlantic mackerel	*Ahtapod*	Octopus
Kolyoz	Club mackerel	*Midye*	Mussel
Lüfer	Bluefish (autumn, İstanbul)	*Yengeç*	Crab
Sardalya	Sardine	*Karides*	Prawns
Mercan	Common bream	*İstakoz*	Saltwater crayfish
Sinagrit	Dentex		

Vegetables (*Sebze*)

Domates	Tomato	*Nohut*	Chickpeas
Salatalık	Cucumber	*Kuru fasulye*	White haricots
Soğan	Onion	*Taze fasulye*	French beans
Sarmısak	Garlic	*Bakla*	Broad beans
Maydanoz	Parsley	*Patlıcan*	Aubergine, eggplant
Marul	Lettuce	*Karnabahar*	Cauliflower
Lahana	Cabbage (usually stuffed)	*Havuç*	Carrot
Turp	Radish	*Bamya*	Okra, lady's finger
Hardal	Mustard greens	*Bezelye*	Peas
Mantar	Mushrooms	*İspanak*	Spinach
Kabak	Courgette, zucchini	*Patates*	Potato
Acı biber	Hot chillis	*Tere*	Rocket greens
Sivri biber	Skinny peppers, hot or mild		

A FOOD AND DRINK GLOSSARY (cont.)

Snacks

Menemen	Stir-fried omelette with tomatoes and peppers	*Lahmacun*	Round Arabic "pizza"
		Cezeriye	Carrot, honey and nut bar
Börek	Rich layered cheese pastry	*Pestil*	Sheet-pressed dried fruit
Su börek	"Water börek" – runny cheese between layers of phyllo	*Badem*	Almonds
		Fıstık	Pistachios
Çiğ börek	"Inflated" hollow turnovers	*Yer fıstığı*	Peanuts
Kokoreç	Mixed innard roulade	*Leblebi*	Roasted chickpeas
Midye dolması	Mussels stuffed with rice, allspice, pine nuts	*Fındık*	Hazelnuts
		Kuru üzüm	Raisins
Pide	Elongated Turkish "pizza"	*Çerez*	Bar nibbles

Typical dishes

Sebze turlu	Vegetable stew	*Karnıyarık*	Aubergine and meat dish, firmer than *mussaka*
Tas kebap	Meat and vegetable stew		
Güveç	Meat and vegetable clay-pot casserole	*Gözleme yufka*	Crêpe-like village bread with various toppings
Saç kavurma	"Wok"-fried medley	*Otlu peynir*	Herb-flavoured cheese, found especially in eastern Anatolia
Mantı	Asian "ravioli" with yoghurt		

Cheese *(Peynir)*

Beyaz	White; like Greek feta	*Kaşar*	Kasseri, variably aged
Çerkez	Like edam	*Tulum*	Dry, crumbly, parmesan-like cheese made in a goatskin
Dil	Like mozzarella or string cheese		

Fruit *(Meyve)*

Elma	Apple	*Muz*	Banana	*Böğürtlen*	Blackberries
Armut	Pear	*Kiraz*	Cherries	*Ahudüt*	Raspberries
Üzüm	Grapes	*Nar*	Pomegranate	*Karpuz*	Watermelon
Portakal	Orange	*Erik*	Plum	*Kavun*	Persian melon
Limon	Lemon	*Papaz/hoca eriği*	Green plum	*İncir*	Figs
Mandalin	Tangerine	*Kayısı*	Apricot	*Ayva*	Quince
Şeftali	Peach	*Çilek*	Strawberries	*Hurma*	Persimmon

duced the drink to Europe from Yemen. Instant – usually Nescafé – is relatively costly but increasingly popular; much better is the traditional, fine-ground Turkish type, brewed up *sade* (without sugar), *orta şekerli* (medium sweet) or *çok şekerli* (cloying). For an extended session of drinking either tea or coffee, you retire to a *çay bahçesi* (tea garden), which often will also serve ice cream and soft drinks.

Herbal teas are also popular in Turkey, particularly *ıhlamur* (linden flower), *kuşburnu* (rose hip), *papatya* (camomile), and *ada çay* ("island" tea), an infusion of a type of sage common in all coastal areas. The much-touted *elma çay* (apple tea) in fact contains strictly chemicals and not a trace of apple essence.

Certain **traditional beverages** tend to accompany particular kinds of food or appear at set seasons. *Sıcak süt* (hot milk) is the perennial complement to *börek*, though in winter it's fortified with *salep*, the ground-up tuber of *Orchis mascula*, a phenomenally expensive wild orchid gathered in coastal areas. *Salep* is a good safeguard against colds (and also reputedly aphrodisiac), though because of its cost most prepackaged varieties are heavily adulterated with powdered milk, starch and sugar. *Ayran*, watered-down yoghurt, is always on offer at *pideci*s and *kebapci*s, and is good cold but not so appetizing if – as it sometimes is – lukewarm and lumpy. In autumn and winter, you'll find stalls selling *boza*, a delicious, mildly fermented millet drink. Similarly tangy is *şıra*, a faintly alco-

Sweets *(Tatlı)*

Pasta	Any pastry or cake	İrmik helvası	Semolina and nut *helva*
Acı badem	Giant almond biscuits	Tahin helvası	Sesame paste *helva*
Kurabiye	Almond-nut biscuit dusted with powdered sugar	Keşkül	Vanilla-almond custard
		Krem karamel	Crême caramel
Baklava	Layered honey and nut pie	Sütlaç	Rice pudding
Kadayıf	"Shredded wheat" in syrup	Muhallebi	Rice flour and rosewater pudding
Lokum	Turkish delight		
Mustafakemalpaşa	Syrup-soaked dumpling	Süpangile	Ultra-rich chocolate pudding
Kadın göbeği	Doughnut in syrup	Fırın sütlaç	Baked rice pudding
Komposto	Stewed fruit	Kazandibi	Browned residue of *tavukgöğsü*
Aşure	Pulse, wheat, fruit and nut "soup"	Zerde	Saffron-laced jelly
Tavukgöğsü	Chicken fibre, milk and semolina taffy	Dondurma	Ice cream
		Kaymak	Clotted cream

Drinks

Çay	Tea	Şıra	Grape must, lightly fermented
Ada çay	Sage tea	Meyva suyu	Fruit juice
Papatya çay	Camomile tea	Memba suyu	Spring water (non-fizzy)
Kahve	Coffee	Maden suyu	Mineral water (fizzy)
Salep	Orchid root powder-based drink	Bira	Beer
		Rakı	Aniseed-flavoured spirit distilled from grape pressings
Ayran	Drinking yoghurt		
Boza	Fermented millet drink	Şarap	Wine

Common toasts

The closest equivalents to "Cheers" are:	The following are more formal:
Şeref'e, şerefiniz'e To honour, to our honour	Sağlığınız'a To your health
or	Mutluluğ'a To happiness
Neşe'ye To joy	Cam cam'a değil, can can'a Not glass to glass, but soul to soul

holic grape juice acceptable to religious Muslims and available in late summer and autumn.

Fruit juice or *meyva suyu* can be excellent if it comes as pulp in a bottle, available in such flavours as *kayısı* (apricot), *şeftali* (peach) and *vişne* (sour cherry). The new wave of thin, preservative-spiked cardboard-packaged juices is distinctly less thrilling. The good stuff is so thick you might want to cut it with spring **water** (*memba suyu*), or fizzy mineral water (*maden suyu*). A PVC bottle of water costs about $0.50 in a restaurant; in many establishments chilled, potable tap water in a glass bottle or a jug is routinely provided at each table, for which there should be no extra charge. You can request lemon wedges to squeeze into this for improved taste. *Meşrubat* is

the generic term for all types of carbonated **soft drinks** such as *Coca Cola*, *Fanta* and the like – available pretty much everywhere now.

BEER AND WINE

Despite inroads made by Islamic fundamentalists, **alcoholic drinks** (*içkiler*) are available virtually without restriction in resorts, though you will have some thirsty moments in interior towns like Konya or Diyarbakır.

Beer (*bira*) is sold principally in returnable bottles but also in cans (expensive) and on draught (cheaper; *fıcı bira* in Turkish). There are two main brands, *Efes Pilsen* (which tends to be overyeasty) and the cleaner *Tuborg*, along with a recent, less common contender, *Marmara*. The birahane (beer hall), an imitation-German notion, has cropped up in many towns but often has a distinctly aggressive atmosphere compared even to a *meyhane* – best avoided. **Wine** (*şarap*), from vineyards scattered across western Anatolia between Cappadocia, the Euphrates Valley, Thrace and the Aegean, is often better than average; brands to watch for include *Kavaklıdere, Doluca, Turasan, Narbağ, Peribacası, Kavalleros,* and the small independent vintner *Feyzi Kutman.* Red is *kırmızı*, white *beyaz*, rose *roze*. In shops, count on paying $3–6 for a bottle of wine.

SPIRITS AND HARD LIQUOR

The Turkish national **aperitif** is *rakı*, not unlike Greek ouzo but rougher and stronger. The best batches of the ubiquitous Yeni Rakı are those distilled at Tekirdağ, using recycled sherry casks – when shopping, you can tell them apart by a unique date stamp in the lower left corner of the label. It's usually drunk over ice and topped up with bottled water. The *meyhane* routine of an evening is for a group of men to order a big bottle of *rakı*, a bucket of ice, a few bottles of water, and then slowly drink themselves under the table between bites of *meze*, or nibbles of *çerez* – the generic term for pumpkin seeds, chickpeas, almonds, etc, served on tiny plates.

Stronger stuff – domestically produced *cin* (gin), *votka* (vodka) and *kanyak* (cognac) – was long the province of the "Tekel" or government monopoly, but recently import duties on foreign-bottled items have plummeted. However, there is still a sharp price (as well as quality) difference between imported spirits and those of the Tekel (designated as *yerli* or "local" on bar placards). Domestically produced **liqueurs** are often given on the house at the end of a meal. For the most part they are quite cloying, but bearable exceptions include Mocca and Acıbadem (almond liqueur).

MOSQUES, MUSEUMS AND SITES

There's no admission fee for entry to mosques but you may be asked by the caretaker or *imam* to make a small donation. If so, put it into the collection box rather than someone's hand. Larger mosques frequented by tourists are open all the time; others only for *namaz*, or Muslim prayer, five times a day. Prayer times, which last around twenty minutes, vary according to the time of year, but generally occur at dawn, mid-morning, midday, sundown and mid-evening; often a chalkboard will be posted outside the door with exact hours for that day. Outside of prayer times it's sometimes possible to find the *imam* and ask him to open up; just ask passers-by where his house is.

Whether or not you're required to, it's a **courtesy** for women to cover their heads before entering a mosque, and for both men and women to cover their legs (shorts are considered particularly offensive) and upper arms – in some mosques pieces of material are distributed at the door. Shoes should always be removed: unless there's an attendant outside, pick your shoes up, carry them inside and place them on the racks near the door. It's better to wait until prayer is finished and then go in, rather than enter while it's in progress, although at any time you will find a few individuals at prayer. As long as you keep a distance and speak quietly you won't disturb anyone unduly.

MUSEUMS AND SITES

Museums are generally open from 8.30 or 9am until 5.30 or 6pm, and closed on Monday, though in the case of some smaller museums you may have to find the *bekçi* (caretaker) yourself and ask him to open up. All sites and museums are closed on the mornings of public holidays. İstanbul's palaces are generally closed on Mondays and Thursdays.

Major **archeological sites** have variable opening hours, but are generally open daily from just after sunrise until just before sunset. Some smaller archeological sites are only guarded during the day, and left unfenced, permitting (in theory) a free wander around in the evening. Others are staffed until dark by a solitary warden, who may have enough English to give you a guided tour, for which he will probably expect a tip. However, in recent years surveillance at sites both fenced and unenclosed has been improved in the wake of antiquities theft, and furtive visits after posted closing hours can result in your being picked up by the *jandarma*, summoned by a well-concealed guard lingering after dark.

Never pay **entrance fees** unless the wardens can produce a ticket, whatever other documentation they may have. Keep tickets with you for the duration of your visit and even afterwards, as sites often straddle the route to a good beach – in theory the ticket is valid for the entire day, sparing you repayment if you recross the area. Admission varies from the current equivalent of $1 at minor sites, to $5 for five-star attractions like Ephesus. Especially since the Refah party has taken control of various municipalities, there are often wide disparities between what locals and foreigners are charged

(the latter much more, of course). On the other hand, FIYTO **student cards** should ensure free admission to museums and sites; ISIC cards will usually – though not always – net you a fifty percent reduction. In theory, those over 65 are also supposed to gain free entrance to museums and sites; bring your passport as proof of age.

Some of İstanbul's most fascinating smaller Byzantine monuments, such as the Fethiye Camii, are only accessible **by permission** from the Directorate of Aya Sofya, located in the grounds of Aya Sofya. Certain monuments along the Armenian border also technically require permission to visit, which can be granted only by the military authorities in Ankara.

BAZAARS AND SHOPPING

Consuming interests are high on the agenda of most visitors to Turkey. Even those who come determined not to buy will be shortly persuaded otherwise by the myriad street merchants, store owners and affiliated touts who cannot resist the hard sell – as traditional to Turkish culture as tea and hospitality – and by the occasionally high quality of goods available.

THE BAZAARS

There are several kinds of bazaar in Turkey, with a common denominator of interest, if you're not too intimidated by the barrage of pestering touts or proprietors trying to guess your nationality and inveigle you into their premises.

First there are the **covered bazaars**, found in large towns like İstanbul, Bursa and Kayseri. These are basically medieval Ottoman shopping malls, comprising several *bedestens* or domed buildings from which particular types of goods are sold, linked by various covered arcades, which in turn were also originally assigned to a particular trade.

Surrounding these covered bazaars are large areas of **small shops**, essentially open-air extensions of the covered areas and governed by the same rules: each shop is a separate unit with an owner and apprentice, and successful businesses are not allowed to expand or merge. Prices on the street are often a bit lower than in the *bedestens* owing to lower rents.

In addition there are weekly or twice-weekly **street markets** in most towns or in different areas of cities, arranged on the same lines as those in northern Europe, and selling roughly similar everyday household products. More exotic are the semi-permanent **flea markets** (*bit pazarı*, literally "louse markets"), ranging in quality from street stalls where old clothes are sold and resold among the homeless, to lanes of shops where you can buy second-hand clothes, furniture or occasionally an antique of real aesthetic or monetary value.

BEST BUYS

The best selection of good-quality wares is to be found in the major tourist centres: İstanbul, Ürgüp, Bursa and the coastal resorts. Don't think that you'll find bargains in the production centres for a particular craft in the interior: wholesalers and collectors have been there long before you.

Apart from the variety and visual impact of goods on sale in Turkish bazaars, and the tantalizing prospect of picking up something worthwhile, the main reason to frequent them is for the challenge of **bargaining**. As a guideline, begin at a figure rather lower than whatever you are prepared to pay, usually around half of your shopkeeper's starting price. Once a price has been agreed on, you are ethically committed to buy, so don't commence haggling unless you are reasonably sure you want the item. There are other psychological tactics to engage in, such as enquiring about several articles in a shop before you even look at the thing you really want, or proposing to go elsewhere for some comparison shopping, but you'll only perfect your act with practice. "Assistance" from touts will automatically bump up the price thirty to fifty percent, as they will be getting a commission. Also, be prepared to pay between three and seven percent extra if paying by credit card; your bargaining position is strongest with crisp, bunched foreign notes.

CARPETS AND KILIMS

Turkish **carpets and kilims** are world famous, and can still be bought relatively cheaply in Turkey. The selection is best in İstanbul, whose shopkeepers scour the countryside, with the result that there are relatively few rugs on sale near their source. A kilim, or pile-less rug, is flat woven; a *cicim* is a kilim with additional designs stitched onto it; while *sumak* technique, confined in Turkey to saddlebags, involves wrapping extra threads around the warp.

Special attention must be paid when shopping for any kind of floor covering; it's easy to pay over the odds for inferior quality. One useful **test**, to ensure that the colours aren't going to run the first time you try to clean off a coffee stain, is to wet a white rag and rub the carpet, then check to see if any colour has come off. If it has, it doesn't bode well for the future, and the dyes certainly aren't natural. Since older, handmade, natural-dyed rugs are getting rarer all the time, genuine collector's items are often salvaged from deteriorated larger works, and more or less skilfully repaired; saddle or cradle bags may be opened to become small rugs. A handwoven rug will usually show its pattern clearly on the reverse, unlike a machine-made one. Hand-spun yarn can be identified by the fringe, which is unevenly twisted, tight and ravelled to the ends.

You can buy a small, new, artificially dyed kilim for around $15–20, and **prices** go up according to quality, age and design. A small woollen rug made with natural dyes would be $80–200 bought new, a larger one around $250–350. Silk carpets start in the hundreds of dollars for a tiny one, and go up to hundreds of thousands.

Natural dyes, especially in earth tones, are now being used in manufacturing again, and they tend not to fade as quickly as chemical ones. This renaissance has been pioneered by DOBAG, a cooperative project headquartered in Ayvacık (see box on p.239), dedicated to both ethical treatment of the weavers and traditional methods, pigments and designs. All of their carpets bear a distinctive leather certification tag, though except at the project's storefront in Ayvacık, they are not available in Turkey; however those of copy-cat projects are, so a better distinguishing factor is DOBAG's exclusive use of a natural purple pigment, whose recipe, partly based on madder root, is secret.

Chemical dyes are usually brighter (initially) unless the rugs are left out for sun-bleaching or are bleached in lye or chlorine. The latter two processes are undesirable because of the weakening effect on the fabric; bleach-faded rugs will smell of chlorine when you rub a wet finger on the pile.

The test for pure **wool** is to take a strand and set light to it. If the charred remains are crumbly, it's wool; if they're sticky, it's synthetic fibre. To test for **silk**, burn some of the fringe: silk will not flame, but makes an ash and smells organic when it burns; synthetic silk glows and smells of chemicals. The price of a silk carpet depends on the number of knots per square centimetre – this is usually 64 or 81, but very fine ones are made with 144 or 196 per square centimetre. There should be no flaws visible on the back of a silk rug.

It's worth finding out as much as you can about the origins of the carpet, the symbolic meanings of its motifs, and the techniques used in its production. This will increase the nostalgic value of the product, and during such discussions you should be able to decide if your dealer is trustworthy, and whether his final price will be fair or not. If you're very serious about carpet-buying, a visit to an ethnological museum or two – and a perusal of some of the recommended titles on the subject listed under "Books" in *Contexts* – might be a worthwhile use of time.

JEWELLERY

Jewellery should also be bought with care, since imitations abound. Fake amber can be identified with a naked flame, since it melts, but a test isn't advisable without the permission of the proprietor. Gold, silver and semiprecious stones, of which amber and turquoise are the most common, are sold by weight, with almost total disregard for the disparate level of craftsmanship involved. One particularly intricate method is *telkâri* or wire filigree, most of which comes from eastern Turkey, particularly Diyarbakır and Trabzon. Bear in mind that the price per gramme of silver or gold can be bargained down, making a substantial difference to the eventual total. Also remember that sterling silver items should bear a hallmark – anything else could well be a nickel or pewter alloy.

COPPERWARE

Copperwork is not as common as in the days when it was an essential part of a newlywed couple's household furnishings, and very little of it is still hammered out from scratch, or of really heavy gauge. Still, the articles are very handsome, and occasionally functional; if you want to buy at the source, keep an eye out in the bazaars of eastern Anatolia. Since copper is mildly toxic, vessels intended for use in the kitchen must be tinned inside – one layer for use as a tea kettle, three for use with food. If the layer is absent or deteriorated, have it (re)done at the nearest *kalaycı* or tinsmith. If you live in a hard-water area, or the vessel is from such a place in Turkey, a layer of mineral deposits will quickly build up, serving the same protective function.

Antique copperware is a cult in itself, though not quite as exalted as that of the carpet. Pieces from the Republican (post-World War I) era are sold roughly by weight at about $6 per kilo; Ottoman trays and vessels are priced ad hoc, depending on the age, weight and provenance. Cheap, newer thin-gauge ware with designs often pressed in by machine, comes from Kayseri, Gaziantep or Kahramanmaraş, and won't be older than 1960 or cost more than $25. At the opposite end of the price/quality scale is embossed work from Bosnia, such as turn-of-the-century *sefer tası* (lunchbox sets, tiffins) for about $40–60; older Greek- or Armenian-produced trays or vessels, identifiable by distinctive lettering, for $120–240; and incredibly heavy, early nineteenth-century Persian or Anatolian trays or vessels with a sultan's monogram, for which asking prices of $1000 and up are not unheard of. Best deals are in Ankara's Bakırcılar Çarşısı; antique shops in Kalkan and Bergama are well presented but vastly overpriced, while İstanbul's old copper market, near the Nuruosmariye Camii, is now completely gentrified.

CLOTHING

Turkey's **clothing** industry has raised its profile somewhat since Rifat Özbek and half-Turkish Nicole Farhi appeared on the scene with their lines of orientally influenced designer clothing, and Turkish designs are beginning to match the quality of local fabrics – including Bursa silk and Angora wool. Nowadays you will pay near-Western prices for decent items; otherwise most outlets (and street vendors) concentrate on **imitation** Lacoste, Levi Strauss and Benetton garments of decidedly varying quality, some made in Turkey under licence but much of it merchandise bootlegged in the best pirating tradition of Asia. Occasionally this is done with panache and humour (such as a sign in Bodrum reading "Genuine Fake Rolexes"), but most of the time the marketing and results are furtive and shabby: real Italian- or English-language labels slapped onto

---

MUSEUM PIECE OR COLLECTOR'S ITEM?

Some of the more popular **archeological sites**, particularly Ephesus, Pamukkale and Ani, are often the haunt of characters peddling "*antiks*" of doubtful authenticity. These freelance salesmen are remarkably tenacious but in the majority of cases you would simply be throwing money away; in the unlikely event you were sold something genuine, you would be liable for prosecution. Under Turkish law it is an offence to buy, sell, attempt to export or even possess museum-calibre antiquities. Exact age limits are not specified in lawbooks, suggesting that decisions by customs officials are arbitrary and subjective, though a principal measure of antiquity is rarity.

In the case of **carpets** handled by established dealers, you run a very slight risk of investing a lot of money in a supposed "collector's item" which turns out to be collectable only by the Turkish Republic. If you're apprehensive about a proposed purchase, you should ask the dealer to prepare both a **fatura** (invoice) recording the exact purchase price – also necessary to satisfy customs – and a declaration stating that the item is not an antiquity. If you're still not reassured, you may want to consult staff at the nearest museum.

Should you be caught **smuggling** anything restricted out, the Turkish authorities will be unimpressed by any excuses or connections, and will very likely make an example of you – as they did an American woman in 1986, who unsuccessfully claimed ignorance of a purchase's vintage, and served six months of a much longer prison sentence before escaping with the assistance of her legal counsel.

local products which shrink two sizes or fade at the first washing. Prices too good to be true are the dead giveaway.

LEATHER GOODS

There are always a number of well-stocked **leather** outlets in any important tourist centre, though the industry was originally based in western Anatolia where alum deposits and acorn-derived tannin aided the tanning process. Today İzmir and İstanbul still have the largest workshops, though the retail business also booms on the Mediterranean coast, particularly in Antalya and Alanya, where specialist (ie, S&M) tastes may be catered for. Jackets are the most obvious purchase, the prices of which vary from a paltry $60 to over $300, with a minimum of about $120 for anything half-decent. If you're not interested in big outlays, wallets – especially Maraş brand – are excellent and durable.

NARGILES

The *nargile* or **hookah** is doubtless one of those Ottoman hangovers, like fezzes and dervishes, that Atatürk might have wished to consign to the dustheap of history. However, it's still around, indulged in for hours along the central and north Aegean coasts by cafés-full of contentedly puffing gentlemen.

A functional *nargile* is not a plastic toy nor *objet d'art* as sold in so many trinket shops, but should have a lamb's-leather, wire-reinforced tube, all-brass or lathed hardwood plumbing and a clear glass or crystal chamber. If you find an older, crystal item, it will be an antique, and worth upwards of $70. Expect to pay $30 for an 18-inch model with a blown glass bowl; cast ones with visible mould marks aren't so valuable. A wood superstructure looks better but brass ones last longer.

If you intend to use the *nargile* when you get home, remember to buy *tömbeki*, or compressed Persian tobacco, as you won't find it easily outside of Turkey. You'll also have to convince customs authorities that your *nargile* isn't narcotics paraphernalia, and you'll need a source of live coals to drop into the *sönbeki* or brazier end – matches don't work well. Also, the *sönbeki* tends to be fitted with meltable plastic mesh inside, so for practical use you'll need to install a small copper mesh, easily available for a few pennies in north European and American head shops or hippy boutiques.

MUSIC AND MUSICAL INSTRUMENTS

Traditional Turkish **musical instruments** are sold cheaply all over Turkey. The most easily portable are the *ney*, the Mevlevi flute made from a length of calamus reed, the *davul* or drum, and the *saz*, the long-necked Turkish lute. In İstanbul the main sales points are along Atatürk Bulvarı below the Valens Aqueduct, and on Galipdede Caddesi, across from the Mevlevi *semahane*, near the top station of the Tünel in Beyoğlu. You are less likely to get a "toy" version if you buy instruments at specialist shops like these, or from the craftsmen themselves. A *kaval* (end-blown flute) is compact and inexpensive at about $8, and a *saz* is good value for around $35 and up.

Cassettes and **CDs** of foreign music, made under licence in Turkey and sold for about $5 and $10 respectively, are found in İstanbul and most coastal resorts; the selection is somewhat limited, but here's your chance to cheaply replace your worn-out Edith Piaf or Fleetwood Mac. If you'd rather concentrate on Turkish music, see the relevant section in *Contexts* for a discography.

TOYS, GAMES AND OTHER GOODS

A **tavla** or backgammon set makes another good souvenir of Turkish popular culture, since it's played in coffeehouses and gaming halls all over the country. The cheapest wooden sets cost around $4; a medium-size apparatus of inlaid, painted cedar wood (*şedir*) runs to about $20, and you can easily pay anything up to $100 for inlaid mother-of-pearl and ivory. Most of the boards come from Damascus, as any reputable dealer will admit; if you're not confident that the inlay material is genuine and not just stencilled on, it's better to settle for the painted wood kind, which is more difficult to fake. Dice and pieces should be included, and many boards have a chess/checkers grid on the exterior; an olive-wood chessmen set will set you back another $6.

Mavi boncuk (blue bead) key rings, lintel ornaments and animal collars are sold all over the place to ward off *nazar* (the evil eye). Other possible memorabilia easily found in the shops of any covered bazaar are probably best obtained from the towns in which they originate. These include **meerschaum pipes** carved from *lületaşı* stone quarried near Eskişehir; **Karagöz puppets**, representing the popular folk characters Karagöz and Hacıvat, preferably made from camel skin in Bursa; **towelling and silk goods**, again in Bursa – although the all-cotton bedding and towels at dedicated retail outlets nationwide are excellent value; **onyx**, available all over Cappadocia but especially Hacıbektaş; and **Kütahya ceramics**, which may not be the finest ever produced in Turkey, but since the kilns of İznik closed down are the best available. Enamelled tiles suitable for fireplace surrounds won't cost more than $2 apiece at either of the two Kütahya factories making them – in tourist resorts, boutiques will demand up to $7 for the same, so it's worth loading up a car with some if you're passing through Kütahya. Tiles, as opposed to kitsch objects, may not be obvious in the town itself – you have to ask to be taken to the factories outside of town.

SPICES AND FOODSTUFFS

Acknowledging the real risk of having such goods confiscated on return to the European Union or North America, locally produced spices and foodstuffs can be provisionally recommended as a compact, lightweight souvenir purchase. Low-grade saffron (*zafran*), the stamen of a particular kind of crocus, is still gathered in northern Anatolia. Sumac (*sumak*) is a ground-up purple leaf for sprinkling on barbecued meats, much encountered in districts with an Arab heritage. Vanilla (*vanilya*) pods are cheaper in Turkey than elsewhere, and pure *salep* powder (ground-up orchid root; see p.46), while not cheap by any standard, can be found nowhere else. *Pekmez* (grape molasses) is phenomenally nutritious and, though a potential mess in your baggage, makes a splendid ice-cream topping or baking ingredient; rural people typically mix it with *tahini* (sesame paste) to make an appetizing, high-calorie snack. Many visitors acquire a taste for Black Sea tea; the best blends change from year to year, with little quality control within a single brand, but go for the best available, and it still won't break the bank.

FESTIVALS AND NATIONAL PUBLIC HOLIDAYS

There are two kinds of celebration in Turkey: religious festivals, observed all over the Islamic world on dates determined by the Muslim Hijra calendar, and Turkish national holidays, which commemorate significant dates in the history of Ottoman and Republican Turkey. In addition there are a number of annual cultural or harvest extravaganzas held in various cities and resorts across the country.

As the **Islamic calendar** is lunar, the dates of the four important **religious festivals** drift backwards eleven days each year relative to the Gregorian calendar. See the box below for the specific dates of forthcoming religious festivals.

The month of **Ramadan** itself (*Ramazan* in Turkish) is perhaps the most important, the Muslim month of daylight abstention from food, water, tobacco and sexual relations, occurring during late winter in the 1990s. Ramadan is not a public holiday: life carries on as normal despite the fact that half the population is fasting from sunrise to sunset. Some restaurants close for the duration, others discreetly hide their salons behind curtains, but at most establishments you will be served with surprisingly good grace. By Koranic injunction pregnant and nursing mothers, the infirm and travellers are excused from obligatory fasting; immediately after dark there's an orgy of eating by the famished in places public and private, and you may well find restaurants sold out of everything within an hour of sunset.

Kadir Gecesi (The Eve of Power) takes place between the 27th and 28th days of the month of Ramadan, the time when Mohammed is supposed to have received the Koran from Allah, an event hailed with night-long prayer in mosques. The three-day **Şeker Bayramı** (Sugar Holiday) is held at the end of Ramadan, celebrated by family get-togethers and the giving of presents and sweets to children, and restrained general partying in the streets and restaurants. The four-day **Kurban Bayramı** (Festival of the Sacrifice), in which the sacrificial offering of a sheep represents Abraham's son Ismael – a Koranic version of the Old Testament story – is marked by the slaughter of over 2.5 million sheep. Only the wealthiest families can afford to buy a whole animal, so part of the meat is distributed to the poor of the neighbourhood. Sheep are brought from all over Anatolia to the big cities (as depicted in the Yılmaz Güney film *The Herd*), and sold on street corners in the weeks leading up to the festival. They are killed by the traditional Islamic method of a slit gullet, in any open space available (apartment block gardens are a favourite).

During *Şeker* and *Kurban Bayram*s, which are also public holidays, **travel** becomes almost impossible: from the afternoon leading up to the first evening of the holiday (a Muslim festival is reckoned from sunset) public transport is completely booked up, and unless you plan in advance you won't get a seat on any long-distance coach, train, plane or ferry. Many shops and all banks, museums and government offices close during the holiday periods (although corner grocery stores and most shops in resorts stay open). It's worth noting that when these festivals occur close to a national holiday, the whole country effectively grinds to a halt for up to a week, with resorts packed for the duration.

CULTURAL FESTIVALS

Cultural festivals are most interesting in the cities and resorts with the resources to accommodate and attract international name acts. Just about every sizeable town will have some sort of yearly bash, though many are of limited interest to outsiders; we've tried to select the best below, most of which are described in fuller detail in the *Guide*.

The most important event is the **İstanbul Festival of Arts and Culture**, which runs from the middle of June to the middle of July. This features Turkish and Western music in venues all over the city, including Topkapı Palace, where Mozart's opera *Abduction from the Seraglio* is

NATIONAL PUBLIC HOLIDAYS

National public holidays are generally marked by processions of schoolchildren or the military, or else by some demonstration of national strength and dignity, like a sports display. Banks and offices will normally be closed on these days; where they are not, we say so below.

January 1 *Yılbaşı* – New Year's Day.

April 23 *Ulusal Egemenlik ve Çocuk Bayramı* – Independence Day and Children's Day, celebrating the first meeting of the new Republican Parliament in Ankara.

May 19 *Gençlik ve Spor Günü* – Youth and Sports Day, also Atatürk's birthday.

May 29 Festival to commemorate İstanbul's capture by Mehmet the Conqueror in 1453 (İstanbul only).

July 1 *Denizcilik Günü* – Navy Day (banks and government offices open).

August 26 *Silahlı Kuvvetler Günü* – Armed Forces Day (banks and offices open).

August 30 *Zafer Bayramı* – Celebration of the Turkish victory over the Greek forces at Dumlupınar in 1922.

September 9 *Kurtuluş Günü* (Liberation Day) – parades and speeches marking the end of the Independence War (İzmir only).

October 29 *Cumhuriyet Bayramı* – commemorates the proclamation of the Republic by Atatürk in 1923.

November 10 The anniversary of Atatürk's death in 1938. Observed at 9.05am (the time of his death), when the whole country halts whatever it's doing and maintains a respectful silence for a minute. It's worth being on a Bosphorus ferry this morning, when all the engines are turned off, and the boats drift and blow their foghorns mournfully.

usually performed. The **International İzmir Festival**, which takes place at about the same time, runs a close second, with many performances at Ephesus and Çeşme. Another festival of interest to visitors is the **İstanbul International Film Festival**, held in early April, which provides a rare opportunity to see Turkish films with English subtitles.

Less spectacular but still meriting a look if you happen to be in the area are the Manisa Power Gum Festival in late April; the Ephesus Festival, in the second or third week of May; the Bergama Festival in late June; the international Pamukkale Song Festival in late June; the Bursa Festival in early July; Çanakkale's "Troy" Festival in mid-August; the Bodrum Culture Week in early September; and the Antalya Altın Portakal Film Festival in late September.

A number of more unusual events are also worth catching if you can, not least of them the **camel wrestling** at Selçuk in mid-January, though bouts (between two male camels in rut) occur throughout Aydın province during December and January. You might also try and see the **grease wrestling** in Kırkpınar near Edirne in early summer (usually mid-June), and the **bull-fighting** – again between beasts – which forms the climax of the Kafkasör Yayla Festival at Artvin in late June. Camel and grease wrestling are national sports with an exotic appeal for foreign visitors; if you can't attend any of the live performances, they beat Wimbledon for TV viewing.

One of the few public performances of a religious nature – and the emphasis is on the word "performance" – is the **Mevlâna Festival** at Konya on December 10–17, one of the few occasions when the so-called "Whirling Dervishes" appear in public. Preferable, however, are the more genuine Mevlevi turning ceremonies that take place at the same time in İstanbul – a marked contrast to the basketball-court setting at Konya. The only two other public devotional observances are the **Hacı Bektaş Veli** commemoration at the namesake village near Cappadocian Avanos, during the latter half of August, when Bektaşis, and their affiliates the Alevîs, meet for a weekend of ritual singing and dancing; this is preceded by a similar festival in mid-June, honouring the second most important Alevî saint, Pir Abdal Musa, in Tekke village near Elmalı in Antalya province.

Folk dance festivals are always worth a detour, providing an opportunity to see some of the country's best dance groups performing a sample of the widely disparate Turkish dances in traditional costumes. There are folk festivals in Silifke in May, Foça in June, and in Samsun in July. Less organized, more spontaneous and therefore more difficult to track down are the music-and-dance gatherings of the gypsies in Thrace during early summer.

Agricultural festivals play an important part in Turkish rural life. The Diyarbakır Watermelon Festival in mid- or late September is basically a competition for the most outsized of the region's fruit. Ürgüp's Grape Harvest Festival in mid-September culminates a season of celebrations in the Cappadocia region, including not only the above-noted Hacı Bektaş ceremonies but also a Handicrafts and Pottery Festival at Avanos during August. The trodden grape is honoured by drinking some of Turkey's finest white wines from the local thimble-sized, earthenware vessels. Other agricultural products are ingested at Bolu's Mengen Chefs' Contest in August – the region is purportedly home to the country's best cooks.

THE MEDIA

Newspapers and magazines weren't even allowed in the country until the middle of the nineteenth century; since then, however, lost time has been made up for with a vengeance, though it's estimated that fewer than three million Turks read the papers, with subscription figures boosted by "free" gifts, lotteries and soft porn. Dozens of mastheads, representing the full gamut of public tastes from respectable to gutter, compete for readers' attention. The airwaves were until recently controlled exclusively by the government, but with satellite dishes widely available and overseas transmitters now a reality, a growing number of private and cable stations are flourishing throughout Turkey.

NEWSPAPERS AND MAGAZINES

Doyen of the **high-end newspapers** has historically been *Cumhuriyet* (Republic), a serious, mildly left-of-centre institution which fell on hard times early in the 1990s following a takeover and subsequent mass staff turnover. It's slowly rebuilding its reputation for analytical stories and features, but the Turkish used is university level and thus hardly material for beginners. Foreigners will mainly be interested in the daily entertainment listings on pages four to six – just about the only way to find out about live events in İstanbul, Ankara and İzmir, aside from keeping an eye out for posters.

In terms of circulation, *Cumhuriyet* has long been outstripped by liberal latecomer *Yeni Yüzyıl*, plus the more centrist *Hürriyet* and *Milliyet*, while the former holdings of the notorious Turkish-Cypriot businessman Asil Nadir – *Güneş* and *Günaydın* – are struggling along in the wake of their forced sale. Though no rival to Nadir, another small family-run press cartel, based in İzmir, produces the middle-of-the-road *Sabah*, which has expanded nationwide, and *Yeni Asır*, the self-styled "Voice of the Aegean". Pro-Islamic national dailies *Türkiye* and the more radical *Zaman* are now also in the thick of the circulation war, thanks to their often bold and unconventional editorials.

At the **lower end** of the spectrum, cornering the girlie, crime and sport markets, are such four-colour fish-wrappers as *Tan* and *Bügün*, equivalent to Britain's *Sunday Sport*.

The principal **weeklies** are *Nokta*, a news-and-feature magazine, and *Panorama*, a picture-spread affair a bit like the North American *Life* of the 1970s. *İkibin'e Doğru* (Towards 2000), an influential leftist weekly with regular provocative scoops, the pro-Kurdish *Özgür Gündem*, closed down in 1994 and succeeded by the equally short-lived *Özgür Ülke* and then *Yeni Politika* (banned 1995), are just four of a dozen activist publications which in recent years have been subjected to closure, confiscation and worse (see below) by the authorities.

Spot-on, topical coverage is exceptional; the main explanation for the timidity and regular self-censorship of the press in Turkey is the simple fact that hard-hitting features can be hazardous to journalists' health. Publishing an article deemed to "damage the respectability and dignity of Turkey abroad", "weaken national feeling", or "incite strife by exploiting class, race, religious, sectarian or regional differences", as defined by the **Devlet Güvenlik Mahkemesi** (the State Security Tribunal, in session in each province), can net both reporter and editor a maximum seven-year term in the slammer, per article. Despite an alleged commitment to the full return of civil liberties in Turkey, such indictments by the *DGM*, based on the infamous Article 8 of the so-called Anti-Terror Law, are still returned with depressing regularity. Most "infractions" have to do with alleged insults or impertinence to government officials, accounts of official misdeeds and financial scandals, the history or current status of Kurds or Armenians, and anything resembling advocacy of communism (banned in Turkey).

In recent years the staff of publications like *Özgür Gündem* and its successors have been physically attacked, often fatally, by shadowy groups alleged to have links with security forces; most egregious was the assassination of *Cumhuriyet* columnist and national pundit Uğur Mumcu in early 1993.

Mostly immune from such processes are the weekly **satirical comics**, whose format, often quasi-pornographic, delivers an at times political message, even for non-readers of the extremely street-slangy text – Turkey's caricature artists are among the cruellest and most graphic in the world. *Gırgır*, the oldest, was long the third biggest-selling adult comic in the world after

America's *Mad* and the Soviet Union's *Krokodil*. With such a winning formula, the proprietors long let well enough alone, but in late 1989 a dispute between management and cartoonists over the copyright ownership of artwork resulted in a massive staff walkout. *Gırgır*'s loss was the gain of a host of competitors and spinoffs such as *Limon*, *Hıbır*, and particularly *Pişmiş Kelle* (Baked Head), a cooperative venture begun by the ex-*Gırgır* personnel, which set new standards for scurrilousness and pungency, leaving the parent magazine tame by comparison.

The only local **English-language** newspaper, sold wherever foreigners congregate, is the generally off-the-wall *Turkish Daily News* ($0.60), published in Ankara by affiliates of President Demirel and pretty turgid – though it does have useful cinema listings in its "Arts Guide" section. Glossy magazines include *Atlas*, published by *Hürriyet*, a monthly with in-depth articles on Turkish and foreign culture and travel, with good photography and English text summaries; it's cheaper and more down-to-earth than the quarterly *Cornucopia*, which seems to live in its own bubble-world of decadent food and interiors, plus sound-bite features.

British and American newspapers tend to be two days old when you can actually get them. For up-to-date news in English you may be better off with the *International Herald Tribune*, or the American weeklies *Time* and *Newsweek*.

TV, RADIO AND CINEMAS

TV and radio are run partly by the state, and partly by a long-established (but only recently legalized) private sector. The advent of satellite dishes late in the 1980s essentially broke the public-broadcasting monopoly, as it became possible to beam Turkish-language (and, sporadically, Kurdish-language) programmes in from European transmitters, reflected from stationary satellites. The proliferating private channels – which, even before 1994 legalization, operated their sound stages and recording studios in Turkey itself – were not slow to take advantage of this, and have now completely overtaken the public stations in terms of viewer numbers.

Up to six **television** channels of the **state-owned TRT** (Turkish Radio and Television) are available, depending on where you are and what time it is. Public programming veers between foreign historical drama series dubbed in Turkish,

American films (also dubbed) and talking-heads panel-discussions, punctuated by classical Turkish musical interludes, variety shows, soaps and chirpy, American-style advertisements. TRT-1 and TRT-2 broadcast from 7am to midnight or 1am; the latter channel is also known as GAP (*Güney Anadolu Programı* or "South Anatolian Programme"), reserved for reruns and easy-watching pap aimed at those whose first language is Kurdish or Arabic. TRT-3 operates from 3 to 11pm, TRT-4 is nominally educational, and TRT-5 beams from 6pm to 1.30am. TRT-International, also called AVRASYA, targets the Turkophone central Asian republics.

Backed as they are by right-wing or obscurantist interests, the content of the numerous **private TV stations** – when not an adaptation of the public format – varies from the mindless to the tasteless by way of the politically sensationalist. *Kanal D*, which started early in 1995, has quickly carved out the largest market share; *Show TV*, owned by the *Hürriyet* newspaper and a bank, claims number-two rank in the viewing statistics despite broadcasting only from 7pm to 2am, helped by a generous film schedule. Rivals *Star*, also movie-laden and funded by the *İmar* bank, and *TeleOn* operate around the clock; *HBB*, actually the initials of a company run by the controlling Has family, and *ATV*, owned by the *Sabah* newspaper cartel, are on until after midnight. *TGRT*, affiliated with the *Türkiye* Islamic newspaper, airs only in the evening, winding up with droning Koranic readings, but caused quite a stir in 1995 with a documentary asserting secret Ottoman support for the Republican revolution in return for a safe-conduct for the last sultan. Finally, there's *Kanal Altı*, run by late President Turgut Özal's son Ahmet; indeed the private broadcasting bill was stalled in parliament for years while Ahmet's many enemies searched for a way to prosecute him for breaking the state monopoly. The fancier **hotels** may provide CNN, SuperChannel, BBC Prime, or the French Canal Cinque on room TVs.

Radio is a bit more accessible, with up to four **public stations** broadcasting between 7am and 1am, though certain channels start earlier or end later. Because of the overwhelming number of transmitters and frequencies, precise details are fairly pointless, but by playing dial roulette on your personal stereo or car radio, you can often snare some decent jazz, rock, blues or classical programmes. **Radyo Üç** (The Third Programme), most commonly found at 88.4, 94 and 99MHz, broadcasts the highest proportion of Western music. It also airs news bulletins in English at 9am, noon, 2pm, 5pm, 7pm and 10pm, though these tend to be heavily edited snippets focusing mostly on the movements and utterances of government ministers. The **BBC World Service** can often be received on medium wave as well as short wave, particularly on the south coast closest to the transmitter on Cyprus.

As with television, **private radio stations** have multiplied, though they received a brief setback early in 1993 when most studios were raided by the authorities on the grounds that Islamic fundamentalists were abusing official indulgence. The crackdown was soon reversed, however, and the existence of the many resurgent stations and their televised counterparts was recognized in April 1994 by a law that established a licensing and certification board on the order of the US's Federal Communications Commission, and ostensibly forbade political parties, local authorities, banks and marketing companies from starting new channels.

There are fewer than sixty **cinemas** remaining in all of Turkey, concentrated in İstanbul (with about half the total), Ankara, İzmir, Adana and Antalya; fare has improved considerably in recent years, with Western first-run releases replacing the old diet of shoot-em-ups and kung-fu flicks. Most foreign films are now shown in the original language with subtitles; if in doubt, examine the posters outside for clues (*Asıl ses* means "original voice") and then ask the ticket seller. *Seans* (screening) times, up to six daily, are fixed from about midday to late evening. This means that films are sometimes cut to fit the time slot as well as the censors' considerations, and intervals are similarly arbitrary. For a detailed overview of the homegrown Turkish film industry, *see* p.793.

SEXUAL HARASSMENT . . . AND WOMEN IN TURKEY

Mutual mistrust and misapprehension are the hallmarks of relationships between Western women and Turkish men. Each approaches the other with woeful stereotypes fuelled partly by myth, partly by reality: Turkish men are seen as lecherous wide boys out for a good time with any passing piece of skirt, while foreign women are considered an easy lay, and rich to boot.

Turkish society is deliberately gender-segregated, and if you want to avoid men completely, even if you're travelling alone, it's not too difficult. Simply seek the company of Turkish women at every opportunity, and you will generally be protected by them. Turkish women suffer from **harassment** themselves, and their methods of dealing with it can be successfully imitated. Avoid eye contact with men, and try to look as confident and purposeful as possible. When all else fails, the best way of neutralizing harassment is to make a public scene. You won't elicit any sympathy by swearing in Turkish, but the words *Ayıp* (Shame!) or *Beni rahatsız ediyorsun* (You're disturbing me), spoken very loudly, generally have the desired effect — passers-by or fellow passengers will deal with the situation for you. *Defol* (Get lost!) and *Bırak beni* (Leave me alone) are stronger retorts.

WOMEN'S STATUS

Turkish women, particularly Western-style feminists, have been organizing to fight back since the 1980s, picking up a thread that has always run through Turkish society. Among the pre-Islamic Turkic tribes, men were only allowed one wife (as they are in today's Republican Turkey) and the king and queen ruled as equals, so that a decree was only valid if issued in both their names. Historically, Turkish women have had support from some impressive quarters: the two best-known Sufi mystics, Hacı Bektaş Veli and Celâleddin Rumi (aka Mevlâna), both strongly endorsed the need to educate women and treat them as equals, and Atatürk, the founder of the Turkish Republic, made numerous speeches on the subject of women's rights, lending support to efforts which culminated in full women's suffrage in 1934. Between 1993 and 1996 Turkey had a woman prime minister, Tansu Çiller – something that would be anathema in other Middle Eastern countries. Nowadays abortion is available on demand with or without the father's consent, and contraceptives are readily available over the counter.

But **feminism** still has a long way to go, both in the cities and the rural areas. Pornography is conspicuously exhibited daily on news-stands across the country, perhaps two racks down from the handful of women's magazines pitched at an urbanized, educated audience. The veil is becoming more prevalent rather than less, girls' education is still marginalized in village schools, and women are rarely seen outdoors after dark, alone or accompanied. Women have long worked as public employees and in private white-collar jobs, but are almost totally absent from the bazaars, restaurants and bars, even in tourist resorts, due partly to the fact that they need special permits to work anywhere alcohol is served. A woman's right to work without her husband's consent was only guaranteed by a 1992 court decision, in which a bar waitress married to a spendthrift gambler successfully sued for the right to support herself.

PROSTITUTION

Nowhere is Turkish women's subordinate status more apparent, however, than in Turkey's numerous **brothels**. Strange as it may seem in a nominally Muslim culture, prostitution is legal and highly organized by every large municipality – the idea being that some women protect the virtue of others by acting as foils for male lust. Prostitution tends to be a feature of certain obvious hotels in a town's bazaar area, or more commonly is concentrated in purpose-built compounds, complete with gate and police guard, known as the *genelev* (general or public house). Activity is more widespread in the south and east of the country where single men may receive offers of red-light tours from taxi drivers ("Just to look, sir . . . ") – a rather sordid sort of voyeurism. İstanbul's notorious İkibuçuk *genelev*, just below the Galata Tower, was for years the largest, managed by the Armenian Mathilde Hanım, the nation's biggest taxpayer; in a typical eyewash manoeuvre for public consumption, it was shut down to great fanfare by Beyoğlu's Refah-run municipality in 1995, whereupon the complex simply moved to a remoter location in another borough.

The **prostitutes** themselves are licensed, and supposedly examined regularly for STDs, but are effectively the chattel of the mobsters who run most of the business across Turkey. If they attempt to flee the brothels to which they are tied by a system of debt bondage, the police are likely to work them over before returning them to their workplace. Many of the women (estimated at 100,000 nationwide) have literally been sold by their families or ex-spouse for real or imagined transgressions of the rural moral code; others, if suspected of "immoral acts", are committed – like lunatics to an asylum – to the *genelevs* by shadowy tribunals, which operate in each province "for the maintenance of public morality". A high proportion are dosed with amphetamines or other drugs much of the time, many attempt suicide, and few have a life expectancy of over 35 years. The UK-based Anti-Slavery Society has completed a thorough investigation into the racket (*Forced Prostitution in Turkey: Women in the Genelevs*), but little remedial action seems possible other than helping individual women escape these compounds. Perhaps the greatest obstacle to full civil rights for prostitutes is official policy; the Constitutional (Supreme) Court, for example, ruled in 1989 that the rape of a prostitute should carry a prison term only one-third as long as that for other rapes.

CAMPAIGNS AND ORGANIZATIONS

In the face of such entrenched reactionary attitudes, feminists face an uphill struggle. **Campaigns** like the *mor iğne campanyası*, the "purple needle campaign" of 1989, in which activists gave out purple-ribboned hat-pins to women on İstanbul buses and ferries – urging them to use them in response to groping – and the *mor çatı* or "purple attic", a refuge for battered women, are clearly only a beginning. The problem of raising male and female awareness without provoking a spectacular Islamic backlash is still to be resolved; what's already happening is a distinct trend of previously "liberated" profes-

sional women attending Refah-organized seminars on how to be content housewives.

Mor Catı, the organization running the women's refuge in İstanbul, is located at Cumhuriyet Cad, Fransız Hastanesi Sokak, Özbakır İşhanı 3/2, Harbiye (☎0212/248 6045). There's also a **women's study and information centre** at Fener Mahalle, Abdülezel Paşa Cad, İstanbul (Mon–Sat 9am–5.30pm; ☎0212/534 9550).

GAY LIFE

It would be an understatement to say that Turkish society is deeply ambivalent about male homosexuality; it has been so since Ottoman times, when the imperial culture was randily bisexual, and transvestite dancers and entertainers were the norm. Atatürk tried to stamp out such decadent holdovers, but in recent years transvestite – or transsexual – *arabesk* singers like the late Zeki Müren and Bülent Ersoy have become national heroes. That has not, however, stopped macho males from verbally or physically abusing such personalities in public – and getting away with it.

Homosexual acts between adults over 18 are legal, but "spreading homosexual information" in print – ie, advocating the lifestyle – isn't. A

"Gay Pride" festival was to have been held in İstanbul during 1993, but at the last minute was banned by the local governorate for being "contrary to society's values"; under the new Refah administration, repeat attempts are unlikely. The few gay bars in İstanbul have been raided in the past by the police, who forced customers to submit to STD testing; they still routinely beat drag queens on the streets. Except for the adulated entertainers cited above, public attitudes are generally intolerant – or closeted – except in resorts like Side or Alanya, and surprisingly enough in the otherwise religious stronghold of Bursa, considered the gay capital of Turkey. *İbne* (catamite, passive male partner) is a deadly Turkish insult, while there is no specific word for the other role.

POLICE AND AVOIDING TROUBLE

Despite popular stereotypes, you're unlikely to encounter any trouble in the western part of Turkey. Violent street crime is uncommon, theft is rare (though pickpocketing and purse-snatching are on the rise), and the authorities generally treat tourists with courtesy. Keep your wits about you and an eye on your belongings just as you would anywhere else, and make sure your passport is with you at all times, and you shouldn't have any problems. Indeed, most people are still scrupulously honest: it is far more likely that someone draws your attention to money fallen from your pocket onto the pavement, rather than pocket it themselves, or for a merchant to point out that you've given them a million-lira note rather than the lookalike hundred-thousand note.

THE POLICE, ARMY AND GENDARMERIE

Civilian police come in a variety of subdivisions, treated with a healthy respect – mixed with fear – by the locals, though theoretically (if not in practice), police are no longer allowed to beat suspects or address motorists disrespectfully and familiarly as *sen* (as opposed to the formal *siz*). Some of the attitude problems stem from the fact that most police are recruited from the slums, poorly trained and contemptibly paid. If you are arrested for any reason, you have the right to make a phone call to a friend, hotelier or consul; if you are refused this, asking for or getting the officer's name often brings about a swift attitude adjustment.

The blue-uniformed *Polis* are the everyday security force in cities and towns with populations over 2000; the most you'll probably have to do with them is a request for help in finding a street. The *Trafik Polis*, recognized by their white caps and two-toned Renault 12s, are a branch of this service, and their main responsibility seems to be controlling intersections and doing spot checks on vehicles at approaches to towns. İstanbul now has a rapid-response squad of red-and-black-uniformed motorbike police known as the *yunus* (dolphin) *polis*; they are generally courteous and helpful to tourists. The *Trafik Polis* in İstanbul also have a black-and-yellow-liveried motorbike branch, not particularly known for their courtesy towards anyone.

The small corps of *Turizm Polis* should have some knowledge of English, German or Arabic, and patrol tourist areas dressed in blue uniforms basically identical to the main *Polis*. In the towns you're also likely to see the *Belediye Zabitası*, the navy-clad market police, who patrol the markets and bazaars to ensure that tradesmen aren't ripping off customers. If you have reason for complaint, your best recourse is to approach one of the *Zabita* force, though restaurant prices and portion sizes are no longer controlled by law.

Although the country nominally returned to civilian rule in 1983, Turkey's huge armed forces still play a fairly high-profile role in maintaining law and order. In most rural areas where villages do not exceed 2000 in population, law enforcement is in the hands of the *Jandarma* or **gendarmerie**, a division of the regular army charged with law enforcement duties. Gendarmes, despite their military affiliation, are kitted out not in fatigues but well-tailored gear, modelled on the French pattern, to make them appear less threatening; most of them are conscripts and will be courteous and helpful if approached. However, their officer corps have been reported to be less than helpful in complicated or touchy cases such as rape complaints.

Another branch of the army much in evidence is the **military police** or *Askeri İnzibat*. You'll recognize them by their white helmets bearing the letters *As İz*, white holsters and lanyards. Officially they are supposed to keep order among the large numbers of conscripts you'll see on the streets of many Turkish towns.

PROBLEMS AND RESTRICTED AREAS

In addition to the expected caveats on drugs and antiquities, there are a number of other **situations to avoid**. Don't insult Atatürk or Turkey in any way, even in jest, nor should you deface or tear up currency or the flag; drunkenness will likely be considered an aggravating, not a mitigating factor. Try not to be drawn into serious disputes, since while things rarely turn violent in Turkey, when they do they can turn *very* violent – if anybody seems to be insulting or provoking you, walk away. Don't take photographs near the numerous, well-marked military zones. Don't "raid" archeological sites after posted closing hours (see "Mosques, Museums and Sites", above). And last but not least, don't engage in any missionary or proselytization activities among the locals, or attempt to import evangelical literature. Touring the Christian sites with the Bible or a scholarly work is certainly okay, but any tract intended for distribution isn't. Many foreigners have been arrested and/or deported for offending Muslim sensibilities on this point.

Despite the courtesy and honesty of most Turks, certain crimes aimed specifically at tourists should be guarded against: there have been an increasing number of instances of Italian-style **gas-and-rob** operations in train compartments, and of **knockout drugs** being introduced into food and drink. Be suspicious, especially if travelling alone, of young men working in pairs or trios who befriend you too assiduously – by proposing to share a hotel with you, for example – and ply you with comestibles procured out of sight; you're quite likely to wake up hours later with a splitting headache, minus your bags and valuables.

In the twelve southeastern provinces still under **martial law**, the army or gendarmerie patrol the streets in the towns and cities, and man numerous checkpoints on rural roads. In the mountains around the towns of Hakkâri and Siirt, all around Mardin, Doğubeyazit, Bitlis, Diyarbakır, Muş and Bingöl, and between Kemah and Tunceli, there's a full-scale insurrection under way, for which reason this guide does not presently advocate travel to most of these areas, and omits coverage of them. You're unlikely to have any direct experience of the insurrection – unless you're kidnapped by the insurgents – but you will notice a certain level of tension in nearby urban areas.

In remote areas of the east you're likely to attract the attention of the military or the police,

who'll want to know what you're doing and where you're going. This may involve, at most, a rather tedious day or evening of polite interrogation. The only areas where you absolutely need a **permit** are within 5km (sometimes 10km) of the frontiers with Georgia, Armenia and Iran, and we've detailed the specific instances in the *Guide*. Areas under threat from insurgent activities fall into a sort of grey zone: while it is not, strictly speaking, illegal for outsiders to visit them – tourism authorities are often loath to admit that there's a problem – local authorities may prevent you from going if they can, and will take no responsibility for your safety should you manage to get past the roadblocks. Currently this isn't recommended: were you to encounter any guerrillas, you can count on being kidnapped immediately, and possibly getting caught in any crossfire involved in your rescue.

TOUTS

The Turkish argot for **touts** – *avcılar*, "hunters" – gives a good idea of how these individuals, who haunt bus stations (see p.27 for more on *otogar* touts), restaurants, ferry quays and bazaars in particular, view foreigners. Whether and how you decide to use their services is a personal matter; just occasionally, they may lead you to acceptable or better accommodation, but more often they will be collecting commissions on accordingly marked-up lodging, food and goods, all of which may be dodgy. Sometimes, especially at certain western resorts, they can be stubbornly persistent or even abusive if spurned; at such times, it's best to use some of the techniques mentioned under "Sexual Harassment . . . and Women in Turkey" above, without, however, being too provocative. From time to time measures have been mooted by the more successful hoteliers and restaurateurs to control a practice which gives certain tourist meccas a bad name, but intense competition within the tourist industry – and Turkey's stubbornly high unemployment – together guarantee that the art and its practitioners will be around for the foreseeable future.

AVOIDING MISUNDERSTANDING: ETIQUETTE AND BODY LANGUAGE

Hospitality, *misarfirperverlik* in Turkish, remains one of the pillars of rural Turkish culture away from touristed areas, and dealing gracefully with invitations is crucial to avoid risk of causing offence. Such offers usually have no ulterior motives, with nothing expected in return except your company and possible entertainment value. If you really can't spare the time, you can mime "thanks" by placing one hand on your chest and pointing with the other to your watch and then in the direction you're headed. Even a **tea-break** will take a while, because you should stop for at least two, or none at all; drinking only one glass may be interpreted as a slight on their tea. The first offer of **food** or a full meal should be declined on your part – if it's sincere it will be repeated at least twice, and convention demands that you accept the third offer. Attempting to reciprocate in kind is extremely bad form; far more appreciated than grubby food from your pack will be a postcard from your hometown after your return, or a print of a snapshot you take of your new friends.

If you're invited **into a home**, remove your shoes at the door, and if a meal is served at a low table with seating on the floor, hide your stockinged feet under the table or a dropcloth provided for the purpose. You should in fact never point your feet, shod or otherwise, at anyone, as they're considered unclean in every sense. When scooping food with bread sections from a communal bowl, use your right hand – the left is reserved for intimate toilet operations. Do not pick your teeth or blow your nose at table or on the street.

Couples should refrain from making excessive gestures of **affection** in public; canoodling on a park bench, for instance, could result in an open, half-full soft drink can (or worse) being lobbed in your direction by the irate. Nudism at the beach is not on, though in the more decadent resorts like Side, Gümbet, İçmeler or Alanya you can get away with some discreet **topless** sunning. **Beachwear** (as in bikini tops and bottoms, briefs, etc) should be confined to the beach and, except in the most tolerant resorts, wearing halter tops or ultra-tight shorts on the street is just asking for abuse.

If you venture much off the tourist track, you will have to accept that being **stared at** is part of the experience, and not considered rude, as is possibly being mobbed by small children who may or may not wish to guide you to the local ruins, beg for pens and candy, or even pelt your car with stones. **People of colour** may find themselves ogled everywhere in unnerving fashion, along with unsolicited comments – ranging from *Arap!* (A Black!) to the notionally more appreciative *çok güzel* (very pretty!). Little can be done about this short of staying inside; read the box about "The Sudanese of Turkey" on p.277 to get an idea of what place Africans occupy in the Turkish consciousness.

Turks employ a variety of **body language** not immediately obvious to most outsiders. Clicking the tongue against the roof of the mouth and simultaneously raising the eyebrows and chin means "no" or "there isn't any"; the economical of movement will rely on the eyebrows alone. By contrast, wagging the head rapidly from side to side means "Explain, I don't understand", while a single, obliquely inclined nod means "yes". Rubbing bunched fingers and thumb together means "loadsamoney", usually when referring to nefarious dealings or local corruption. Clicking fingers sharply indicates "good, top quality (merchandise, football player, etc)". The length of things is measured on the outstretched arm, from the fingers up to the point where a flat hand is laid; chopping sharply at the elbow indicates hugeness.

SPORT AND OUTDOOR ACTIVITIES

The Turks have been sports fanatics since the inception of the Republic, but success in the international arena has thus far been confined to Naim Süleymanoğlu's spectacular Olympic weightlifting coup in 1988, when everyone in the country was treated to infinite television replays of his winning clean-and-jerk. He repeated this feat in the 1992 and 1996 Olympiads for a hat trick.

FOOTBALL

Football (soccer) claims pride of place in the hearts of Turks, with the history of organized clubs in İstanbul going back to the first decade of this century. Venues are mammoth, and matches, usually on Saturday or Sunday afternoons between September and May, are well attended. If anything Turks are more footie-obsessed with every passing year, and in season there are televised matches from somewhere nearly every night of the week.

The most conspicuous **first-division teams** are the three İstanbul rivals Beşiktaş, Galatasaray and Fenerbahçe, and the surprisingly good provincial sides Trabzonspor, Samsunspor and Kocaelispor. Oddly enough, İzmir's Karşıyaka and Altay are continually threatened with relegation to second-division status. Foreign players are limited to two per team.

Unfortunately, Turkish football has been quick to adopt some of the more unsavoury aspects of the Western European game. Charges of bribery and corruption are regular, and crowds, while generally less liquored up and not yet up to levels of hooliganism seen elsewhere, can get rowdy – as Manchester United supporters found out during the 1993 European Cup. In a 1995 rematch with Galatasaray, Man United fans were involved in violent incidents which culminated in their hotel being vandalized and the tenants being briefly arrested. It's becoming commonplace for a losing team to be attacked by their own supporters after a game, while victories are celebrated deliriously, with flag-waving maniacs leaning on the horns of cruising cars embroiled in massive traffic jams.

SKIING

Turkey is normally thought of as a summertime holiday destination, but if you're around during the cooler seasons there are a number of serviceable **ski resorts**, though none is as yet up to European standards. The oldest, most famous and perhaps most overrated resort is Uludağ, above Bursa, with easy and intermediate runs, but tourism authorities are pinning current hopes on the Saklıkent complex in the Beydarları near Antalya – potentially ideal for an early spring sea-cum-ski holiday, though snow cover is apt to be thin. Roughly midway between İstanbul and Ankara, near Bolu, Kartalkaya is probably better than either of these two, with a mixture of beginners' and intermediate runs, but only one T-bar lift. The best snow conditions and toughest, half-hour runs are at Palandöken near Erzurum, where the Turkish Olympic team trains, and Sarıkamış, near Kars, which boasts the highest and snowiest runs in the country. Other facilities are planned throughout Turkey but up to now this has resulted in just a rather token resort at Tekir Yaylası on Erciyes Dağı near Kayseri. For details of **ski package operators**, see p.9.

MOUNTAINEERING AND HIKING

Although the Turks themselves are only just beginning to **trek and hike** for pleasure, there is plenty of scope for these activities. You'll find details on specific hiking routes through the Kaçkar Dağları, and a selection of walks on Bursa's Uludağ, in the *Guide*, but if you're daunted at the prospect of going alone, contact one of the adventure travel companies listed in the "Getting There" sections above.

At present, the **Kaçkar Dağları** running parallel to the Black Sea is the most rewarding area for treks, and a number of companies organize expeditions there. The **Cilo and Sat massifs** along the Iraqi border are reportedly even more spectacular but have regrettably been off-limits to outsiders for most of the past 25 years, owing to the ongoing Kurdish troubles. Next up in interest are the **Toros (Taurus) ranges**, which form a long chain extending from central Turkey to above the main Turquoise Coast resort areas; again various tour companies can take you to the best places.

Aside from this, **mountaineering** in Turkey consists mostly of climbing the volcanoes of the central plateau – not nearly as satisfying; Ağrı Dağ (Ararat) – currently out of bounds – is likely at the best of times to be a crashing non-event for most, and Erciyes or Hasan Dağı near Cappadocia little better.

If you go alone, you'll need to be fully kitted out, since alpine huts are nonexistent. **Water** can be a problem in the limestone strata of the Toros; **detailed maps** are very difficult to obtain (see p.24); and **trails** (when present) are faint. But the unspoilt quality of the countryside and the friendliness of other mountaineers goes a long way in compensation.

OTHER ACTIVITIES

Opportunities for engaging in various **watersports** abound at the Turkish coastal resorts. You can count on renting windsurfing, kayaking and snorkelling gear just about anywhere, and at the more developed sites waterskiing, sailing and yachting will be on offer – the yachts chartered either bare-boat or (more likely) as part of a guided, skippered three-to-fifteen day **coastal cruise**. For the possibilities of pre-booking such a cruise, see the "Getting There" sections above; for advice on arranging something on the spur of the moment, see the box on p.355.

Because of the presumed number of antiquities still submerged off Turkey, **scuba-diving** is strictly regulated and is principally available out of Bodrum, Marmaris, Fethiye and Kaş, where there's something appreciable to see; of late, wreck diving around the Gallipoli peninsula has also become popular.

Only two rivers – the Çoruh, in the Kaçkar, and the Göksu, in the Toros mountains – are suitable for **whitewater rafting**, and both of these are chronically under threat from hydroelectric projects. Both rivers receive increasing attention from adventure travel operators; again, see the "Getting There" sections for specifics.

FINDING WORK

Turkey has a surplus of qualified graduates, a 25-percent unemployment rate, low wages and no special privileges for EC citizens – hardly a bright picture for potential job-seekers. Still, many foreigners do work in Turkey for varying periods, even on a tourist visa, though this is strictly speaking illegal. If you intend to work from the start, it's far preferable to contact the Turkish embassy or consulate in your home country, or failing that in a country bordering Turkey, to obtain a **çalışma tezkeresi** or **work permit; you'll need a written offer of employment from inside the country, two passport photos, and the requisite embassy forms filled out and fees paid.**

TEACHING

Year-round employment and reasonable working conditions are best achieved by **teaching English** as a foreign language in one of the major cities. Even so, contracts should be examined carefully. In government-run institutions, including universities, high schools and *Anadolu Liseleri* (the equivalent of British grammar schools), you will need some kind of degree, and your first pay packet can be delayed until the vetting procedure (checking your credentials and political background), which can take up to three months, is completed. Other schools generally – but not always – require proof of teaching qualifications and experience, though smaller schools often just want native English speakers, so it's worth enquiring for work even if you're not qualified.

Teaching posts in the bigger outfits are advertised in the *Guardian's* education section and in the *Times Educational Supplement* in Britain, and in the *International Herald Tribune*, but private schools are probably best approached on the spot, since the work will be temporary anyway. Check whether the job will enable you to apply for a work permit, because if it doesn't you will have to leave the country every three months. The better organizations will in any case normally sort out the legalities for you.

OTHER OPTIONS

There is always plenty of work available in **tourist resorts**, at least during the summer months. Very little of it is legal, but since the authorities generally turn a blind eye this simply means you will find yourself crossing a border into some neighbouring country every three months to renew your tourist visa.

Foreigners are not allowed to work as certified archeological tour guides – one rule that is enforced – though tour companies may employ you to do PR work in the office, or as couriers to meet groups from the airport and take them to their hotel. Carpet and leather shops will often employ English-speakers on a commission basis,

in which case you will work long hours trying to pull in your quota of likely tourists, but the pay can be rewarding. Bars, restaurants and hotels also like English-speaking staff, particularly women; you won't be well paid but board and accommodation should be provided. Yacht and *gület* crews are also often prepared to take on foreign staff to cook and clean, or host guests.

Au pair work is equally easy to find, especially on short contracts. Contact *Anglo Pair*, 40 Wavertree Rd, Streatham Hill, London SW2 3SP (☎0181/674 3605), or their branch office in Turkey: *Derin Ltd Şirketi*, Mazhar Paşa Sok, Bulvar Palas Apt 2/9, Beşiktaş, İstanbul (☎0212/258 5342).

Voluntary work in Turkey is organized by *Gençtur*, Yerebatan Cad 15/3, 34410 Sultanahmet, İstanbul (☎0212/520 5274, fax 519 0864). Their camps generally involve manual labour in Turkish villages or in holiday resorts. Basic accommodation is provided either in guest houses or in the village school, and food is prepared by the villagers. *Gençtur* is affiliated with the *International Voluntary Service*, 162 Upper New Walk, Leicester LE1 7QA (☎01533/549430).

DIRECTORY

ADDRESSES In Turkish addresses street names precede the number; if the address is on a minor alley, this will usually be included after the main thoroughfare it leads off. If you see a right-hand slash between two numbers, the first is the building number, the second the flat or office number. A letter following a right-hand slash is more

ambiguous: it can mean either the shop or unit number, or be part of the general building number. Standard abbreviations, also used in this book, include "Cad" for *Cadde(si)* (avenue or main street), "Bul" for *Bulvarı* (boulevard), "Meyd" for *Meydan(ı)* (square), "Sok" for *Sokak/Sokağı* (alley) and "PK" for *Posta Kutu* (Post Box). Other useful terms are *kat* (floor), *zemin* (ground floor), *han(ı)* (office block), *mahalle* (district or neighbourhood) and *çıkmaz(ı)* (blind alley). *Karşısı* means "opposite to", as in *PTT karşısı*. A five-digit postcode system has been introduced, but is sporadically used; it is much more important to include the district when addressing mail. For example: Halil Güner, Kıbrıs Şehitler Cad, Poyraz Sok, Ulus Apartmanı 36/2, Kat 1, Delikliçınar, 34800 Direkköy, which means that Halil Güner lives on Poyraz Sokak no. 36, just off Kıbrıs Şehitler Caddesi, on the first floor, Flat 2, of the Ulus apartments, in the Delikliçınar area of a larger postal district known as Direkköy.

BARGAINING You can haggle for souvenir purchases, minor repair services, rural taxis, car rental, hotels out of season, and meals – especially seafood ones – at eateries where a menu is absent. You shouldn't have to bargain for dolmuş or bus tickets, though some of the stewards selling fares on long-distance coaches are less than honest; if in doubt, check to see what others are paying for the same distance.

BRING a water container for summertime ruin-tramping; a torch (flashlight) for dark corners of same, and for night-time in rural areas; roll-on mosquito repellent; a travel alarm clock for early transport; suntan cream of at least factor 15; camera film (see below); and contact lens accessories – only a very basic range of solutions is available. Bath plugs are still hard to find in most places, and good toiletries are pricy in Turkey. A powerful Walkman is invaluable for combatting the unbearable Turkish pop music played on most long bus journeys; ear plugs work nearly as well, and are a godsend in noisy low-rent hotels. A multipurpose penknife and a small sewing kit can also be very useful.

CAMPING GAS One factory near İzmir has begun making it, but it's mostly imported from Greece and impossible to find away from the west coast – bring lots unless you're flying in.

CHILDREN They're adored in Turkey; childless couples will be asked when they plan to have some, and bringing children along guarantees red-carpet treatment almost everywhere. Three- or four-bedded hotel rooms are easy to find, and airlines, ships and trains offer substantial discounts. Baby formulas are cheap and readily available; disposable nappies aren't.

CIGARETTES AND TOBACCO SMOKE Turkish ones can be rough, but if you're keen to try them, *İkibin* are the mildest followed by *Maltepe* – though even these are not recommended in large quantities. Better are the cigarettes made in Turkey under licence from foreign brands, notably *Marlboro*, which are milder than their European equivalent. If you're not a smoker, tobacco smoke can be a major nuisance. There are, however, designated no-smoking cars on most trains, and smoking is forbidden on all domestic flights; in buses the smoke is not quite so bad as it used to be, a result of a nationwide anti-smoking campaign launched in 1991.

CONTRACEPTIVES Birth control pills (*doğum kontrol hapı*) are sold over the counter at pharmacies, though you should have your own brand with

you to check against the Turkish formula. Condoms used to be rare but are now sold in most pharmacies and off street carts, though you'll want to bring a supply along. Should you need them on the spot, the "proper" word is *preservatif*, the slang term *kılıf* ("hood") – the best brand is called Okey. AIDS and other sexually transmitted diseases are now prevalent in Turkey.

DEPARTMENT STORES The two chains are *Gima* and *Yeni Karamürsel*, with outlets in İstanbul, İzmir and Ankara, plus several other large towns.

DEPARTURE TAX None currently charged.

DISABLED TRAVELLERS Turkey makes poor provision for disabled travellers. Sidewalk corners and archeological sites do not have ramps, hotels below three stars in rating lack lifts, and there is no adapted public transport. For advice and current information on any improvements within the country, contact: *RADAR*, 12 City Forum, 250 City Rd, London EC1V 8AS (☎0171/250 3222; Minicom ☎0171/250 4119); *Irish Wheelchair Association*, Blackheath Drive, Clontarf, Dublin 3 (☎01/833 8241); *Directions Unlimited*, 720 N Bedford Rd, Bedford Hills, NY 10507 (☎1-800/533-5343), or *Mobility International USA*, PO Box 10767, Eugene, OR 97440 (Voice and TDD: ☎503/343-1284); the *Jewish Rehabilitation Hospital*, 3205 Place Alton Goldbloom, Montréal, PQ H7V 1R2 (☎514/688-9550); *ACROD* (Australian Council for Rehabilitation of the Disabled), PO Box 60, Curtin ACT 2605 (☎06/682 4333), or 55 Charles St, Ryde, NSW (☎02/9809 4488); or the *Disabled Persons Assembly*, PO Box 10, 138 The Terrace, Wellington (☎04/472 2626).

ELECTRIC POWER 220 volts, 50 cycles, out of double round-pin sockets. British appliances need a 3-to-2 plug adaptor; North American ones both a square-to-round-pin adaptor and a transformer (except for dual voltage shavers, which need only the former).

EMERGENCIES Police ☎155; rural gendarmerie ☎156; road rage incidents (yes, there's a special number) ☎154; fire brigade ☎110; rural forest fires ☎177; ambulance ☎112. These calls cost one small *jeton*, or one card unit.

FILM This is expensive in tourist resorts and provincial towns; most Fuji products are reasonable if bought in the bazaars of İstanbul, İzmir and Ankara, though it's best to bring enough with you. You won't find anything faster than ASA 100 outside of the three largest cities. The *Refo* chain used to offer decent E-6 processing but quality has taken a tumble of late – wait until you get home, or find a custom lab like *Kayacık* (Spor Cad 126, Maçka, İstanbul).

LAUNDRY Laundrettes are slowly appearing in tourist resorts, but there are dry cleaning (*kuru temizleme*) establishments in most large towns, and *pansiyon*s and large hotels will do loads of washing for a small consideration.

LEFT LUGGAGE An *emanet* (left-luggage) service is available at virtually all *otogar*s and train stations: there are no lockers, you pay the attendant upon return of article(s) in exchange for your claim ticket. Prices vary according to the amount of insurance applicable – for nice foreign backpacks or holdalls, staff will charge you the most expensive rate, about \$3 per item.

OPENING HOURS White-collar workers keep conventional Monday-to-Friday 9am–6pm schedules, with a full lunch hour; civil servants (including tourist offices and museum staff) in theory work 8.30am–5.30pm, but in practice hours can be much more erratic, including two-hour lunches – don't expect to get important official business attended to the same day after 2.30pm. Ordinary shops are open continuously from 8.30 or 9am until 7 or 8pm, depending on the owner. Craftsmen and bazaar stallholders keep marathon hours, often working from 9am to 8 or 9pm, Monday to Saturday, with only the hastiest of breaks for meals, tea or prayers. Even on Sunday the tradesmen's area may not be completely shut down – though don't count on this.

TAMPONS Tampax are available from pharmacies for the same price as in the UK; avoid Orkid, the disastrous domestic brand of "sanitary towels".

TIME Two hours ahead of GMT in winter; as in Europe, daylight saving is observed between the last weekend in March and the last one in October (GMT + 3hr).

TIPPING A service charge of ten to fifteen percent is levied at the fancier restaurants, but as this goes directly to the management, the waiters and busboys should be left five percent again if they deserve it. Round odd taxi fares upwards (you may not have a choice, as the driver may genuinely not have small change); hotel and train-sleeper porters should be tipped appropriately, with the latter presenting you with a chit stating the required amount.

TOILETS Except in the fancier resort hotels and restaurants, most public toilets are of the squat-hole variety, found either in public parks or (more infallibly) next to any mosque. They usually cost about \$0.20, so keep small coins handy. Also keep a supply of toilet paper with you (available in Turkey) – Turks wash themselves off either with the bidet or toilet-rim spout, or the special vessel filled from the handy floor-level tap. You may well become a convert to this method, reserving the paper – which shouldn't be thrown down the hole – for drying yourself off.

VALUE ADDED TAX The Turkish variety *(Katma Değer Vergisi* or *KDV)*, ranging from 8 to 23 percent depending on the commodity, is included in the price of virtually all goods and services (except car hire, where the 15 percent figure is usually quoted separately). Look for the notice *Fiatlarımız KDV Dahildir* (VAT included in our prices) if you think someone's trying to do you for it twice. There is a VAT refund scheme for large souvenir purchases made by those living outside the European Customs Union, but it's such a rigmarole to get that it's probably not worth pursuing; if you insist, ask the shop to provide a *KDV İade Özel Fatura* (Special VAT Refund Invoice), assuming that it participates in the programme.

CHAPTER 1 ISTANBUL

CHAPTER 2 AROUND THE SEA OF MARMARA

CHAPTER 3 THE NORTH AEGEAN

CHAPTER 4 THE CENTRAL AND SOUTHERN AEGEAN

CHAPTER 5 THE TURQUOISE COAST

CHAPTER 6 THE MEDITERRANEAN COAST

CHAPTER 7 SOUTH CENTRAL ANATOLIA

CHAPTER 8 NORTH CENTRAL ANATOLIA

CHAPTER 9 THE BLACK SEA COAST

CHAPTER 10 NORTHEASTERN ANATOLIA

CHAPTER 11 THE EUPHRATES AND TIGRIS BASIN

This book does not cover Lake Van and the southeast because of political unrest in the region

CHAPTER ONE

İSTANBUL

A rriving in **İSTANBUL** comes as a shock. You may still be in Europe, but a walk down any backstreet will be enough to convince you that you have entered a completely alien environment. Traders with handcarts, *hamal*s (stevedores) carrying burdens of merchandise twice their own size and weight, limbless beggars and shoeshine boys all frequent the streets around the city centre, loudly proclaiming their business until late at night. Men monopolize public bars and teahouses while women scurry about their business, heads often covered and gazing ever downcast. In summer, dust tracks take the place of pavements, giving way in winter to a ubiquitous slurry of mud. Where there are pavements, they are punctuated at intervals with unmarked pits large enough to swallow you without trace. And this is before you even begin to cross any bridges into Asia.

Yet İstanbul is the only city in the world to have played capital to consecutive **Christian and Islamic empires**. Their legacies are much in evidence, nowhere more prominently than in the cultural centre of the city, where the great edifices of **Aya Sofya** and **Sultan Ahmet Camii** glower at each other across a small park. The juxtaposition of the two cultures would be fascinating enough in itself, but it's made more so by the fact that the transition between them was a process of assimilation and adoption. The city walls of Theodosius have been preserved because they were refortified by Mehmet the Conqueror, and most of the city's **churches** were reconsecrated as mosques: not least Aya Sofya itself, which was a constant source of inspiration to Islamic architects.

Monumental architecture aside, the very confusion of sights and sounds – initially so alienating – soon becomes one of İstanbul's greatest fascinations. Even if the city did not have such a varied and vivid history, it would still take any number of return visits to begin to discover the source and meaning of the cacophony. Exploration reveals ancient **bazaars** which still function as they have done for centuries, including the largest covered bazaar in the world, the **Kapalı Çarşı**. The modern city, located around **Taksim Square**, offers further diversions: the sense of space created by the square's vast emptiness affords to some a feeling of relief after days spent in crowded, dirty backstreets, and at night Taksim takes on a new lease of life, as the streets, which in daylight are frequented by suited business types, are taken over by club-, theatre- and opera-goers, transvestites, prostitutes and their potential clients. The area has much to offer by way of **nightlife**: the Atatürk Cultural Centre on Taksim Square; most of the city's theatres and cinemas, as well as several bars and clubs – mainly seedy – in the area between Taksim and Galata; and some of the city's best restaurants. The **Bosphorus** – the straits dividing Europe and Asia – should be visited as often as possible during the course of a trip, since how much you enjoy İstanbul may well depend on how often you can escape to its shores. The **coastal villages** offer incredible views as well as some of the city's most interesting historical sites, parks and even open forestland, and the best fish restaurants in this part of the world. The **Princes' Islands**, traditional refuge from political turmoil on the mainland, are worth visiting for their unspoilt natural beauty and for the possibility of finding a secluded beach an hour's ferry ride away from Eminönü.

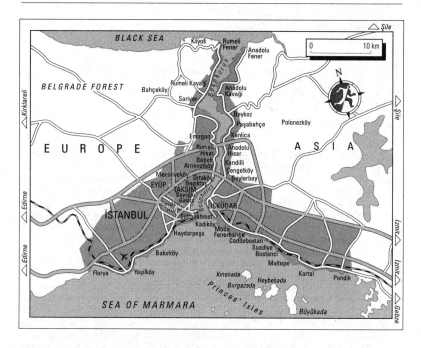

Perhaps one of the most pleasant aspects of a visit to İstanbul lies in the fact that an appreciation of its merits plays a part in the consciousness of locals of every race and creed, particularly evident in a diffident pride in the city's past. Ankara may have replaced İstanbul as the capital of Turkey, but the old imperial capital will never be replaced in the affections of the populace. Yaşar Kemal, in *The Sea-Crossed Fisherman*, summed up these feelings well:

> In the distance, sunk in shadow, its leaden domes, its minarets and buildings only vaguely discernible in the bluish haze, İstanbul was still asleep, its face hidden from the world. In a little while the city would awaken, with its buses, cars, horsecarts, its ships, steam launches, fishing boats, its hamals sweating under their loads of heaped crates, its streets and avenues overflowing, its apartment buildings, mosques, bridges, all surging, interlocking in a furious turmoil and, pressing through the tangle of traffic, wondering how this city could still move, was not entirely paralyzed, people would be making superhuman efforts to reach their destination. Fishvendors in their boats by the waterfront would be setting up their gear, lighting their coals or butane cookers, heating the oil into which they would drop the flour-coated fish, and soon the odour of fried fish would spread through the early-morning air right up to Karaköy Square, to the Flower Market and to the fruit-trading wharf. Hungry workers, tramps who had nowhere to sleep but had somehow got hold of a little money, carousers with a hangover, drowsy young streetwalkers, homeless children who subsisted by picking pockets, sneak-thieving or selling black-market cigarettes would line up in front of the bobbing boats to buy a slice of bluefish, a quarter of tuna, three or four pickerel or scad, sandwiched in a half-loaf of bread, and devour it hungrily, the fat dripping down their chins. And the dull heavy roar of the awakening city would reach us from across the sea, and gradually the domes and minarets, and also the ugly apartment buildings so out of keeping with the city, would emerge from the haze, and like a strange giant creature İstanbul would spread itself out in the light of day, down to its age-old battlements along the seashore.

Some history

Considering that this city was to have such an auspicious history, its origins were surprisingly humble. While there is archeological evidence of a **Mycenaean settlement** dating to the thirteenth century BC on the old acropolis, little is known about it, and popular tradition has it that the city was founded by **Byzas the Megarian** in the seventh century BC – hence the original name of Byzantium – and inhabited by what one ancient historian described as "a feeble colony of Greeks" until the third century AD. The site was chosen in accordance with a Delphic oracle instructing the settlers to found a city "opposite the city of the blind", and they concluded that this must refer to Chalcedon, modern-day Kadıköy, since earlier settlers had built their city in blithe ignorance of the obvious strategic merits of the peninsula, Saray Burnu, in front of their eyes.

Over the next thousand years, Byzantium became an important centre of trade and commerce, but always as a vassal of one overlord or other, and it was not until the early fourth century AD that a decision was taken that would elevate the city to the pinnacles of wealth, power and prestige. For more than 350 years, Byzantium had been part of the Roman province of Asia. On the retirement of Diocletian in 305, Licinius and **Constantine** fought for control of the empire. Constantine finally defeated his rival on the hills above Chrysopolis (Üsküdar) and chose Byzantium as the site for the new **capital of the Roman Empire**.

It was a fine choice. Rome itself was virtually uncontrollable: hidebound by tradition and effectively ruled by the mob. The seven hills on which Constantine was to build the new capital (a deliberate echo of Rome – indeed the city was originally to be called New Rome) commanded control of the **Bosphorus** and had easy access to the natural harbour of the **Golden Horn**. The site was protected by water on two sides, and its landward side was easily defensible. It was also well placed for access to the troublesome frontiers of both Europe and the Persian Empire.

In 395 the division of the Roman Empire between the two sons of Theodosius I left Constantinople as capital of the eastern part of the empire, and it rapidly began to take on its own distinctive character, dissociating itself from Rome and adopting the Greek language and **Christianity** (despite Constantine's earlier espousal of the religion, Christians were still in the minority during his reign). Long and successful government was interrupted briefly by the Nika riots in 532, during the reign of Justinian, after which the city was rebuilt on a grander scale than before. The church of Aya Sofya in particular was rebuilt to proportions hitherto unimagined.

Half a century later, however, the dissolution of the Byzantine Empire had begun, as waves of Persians, Avars and Slavs attacked from the north and east. The emperor Heraclius managed to stem the tide with a brilliant military campaign, but over the following centuries decline was constant, if slow. The empire was overrun by Arabs in the seventh and eighth centuries, and by Bulgars in the ninth and tenth centuries, and it was only the Theodosian land walls that saved the city of Constantinople itself from attack and invasion. At the beginning of the thirteenth century, however, not even the city's great fortifications could keep out the **Crusaders**. They breached the sea walls in 1204 and proceeded to sack and destroy the city. By the time the Byzantines, led by Michael Palaeologus, had succeeded in regaining control, not only had many of the major buildings fallen into disrepair and disuse, but the empire itself had greatly diminished in size.

Parallel to this decline ran the increasing strength of the **Ottoman Empire**, whose capital moved between Bursa and Edirne from 1362 onwards, and whose territory effectively surrounded the city long before it was taken. Most importantly, in 1452, Mehmet II demanded and received a section of land on the Bosphorus, the lifeline of the fading city, on which to build the fortress of Rumeli Hisarı. This meant he could besiege vital supply lines and starve the city into submission.

The **siege** of the city lasted for seven weeks, and ended when the Ottoman forces breached the land walls at their weakest point, between Topkapı and Edirnekapı. After

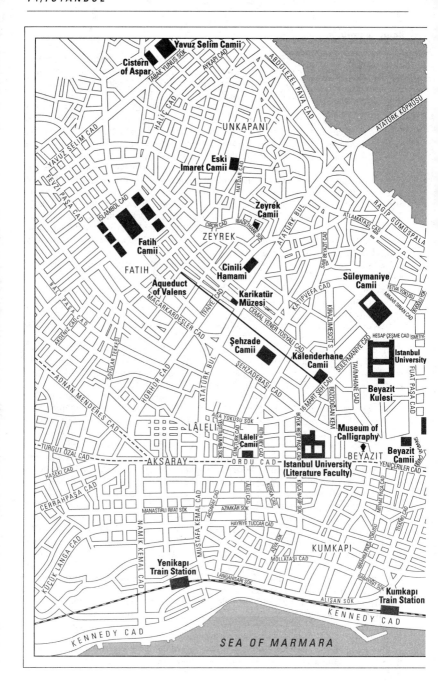

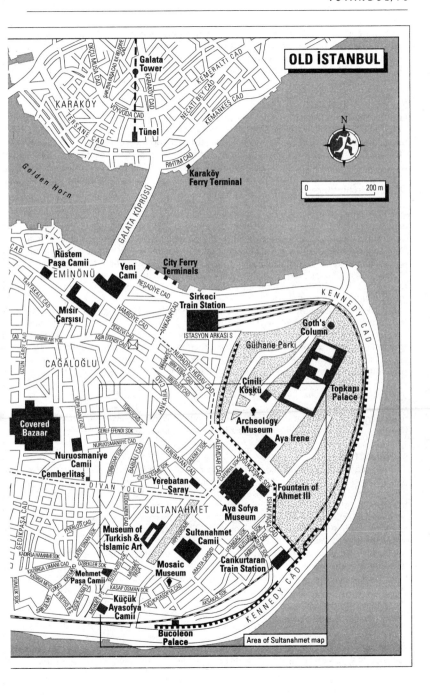

OLD İSTANBUL

the capture and subsequent pillage, **Mehmet the Conqueror** (Fatih Sultan Mehmet) began to rebuild the city, beginning with a new palace to replace the Great Palace of Byzantium. Later the Mosque of the Conqueror (Fatih Camii) and many smaller complexes were established. This did not mean that other religions were not tolerated – indeed Mehmet actively encouraged Greeks and Armenians to take up residence in the city, a policy followed by his successor Beyazit II, who settled Jewish refugees from Spain in an attempt to increase the flagging population figures and inject life into the economy and expertise into the workforce.

In the century following the Conquest the victory was reinforced by the great military achievements of **Selim the Grim**, and by the reign of **Süleyman the Magnificent** (1520–1566), "the Lawgiver". This greatest of all Turkish leaders was confounded in his plans for domination in the Western hemisphere only at the gates of Vienna, and the wealth gained in military conquests was used to fund the most magnificent of all Ottoman architecture, the work of Mimar Sinan.

It was another century after the death of Süleyman before the empire began to show signs of **decay**. Territorial losses abroad combined with corruption at home, which insinuated its way into the very heart of the empire, Topkapı Palace itself. The institution called the Cage, introduced by Ahmet III (see p.101), had proved a less than humanitarian solution to the customary fratricide committed by newly crowned sultans, since many of its occupants were completely insane by the time their turn came to take office. Many of the sultans preferred to spend their time in the harem rather than on the battlefield, and the women of the harem became involved in grand-scale intrigue and power struggles.

By the end of the eighteenth century these problems could no longer be ignored. As the Ottoman Empire lost more and more territory to the West, succeeding sultans became more interested in Western institutional models. This movement of **reform**, which began with Selim III's new model army, culminated in the first Ottoman constitution and a short-lived parliament in 1876. Parliament was dissolved after a year by Abdülhamid II, but eventually the forces of reform led to his deposition in 1909. After the War of Independence, Atatürk created a new capital in Ankara, a small provincial town in central Anatolia. İstanbul retained its importance as a centre of trade and commerce, however, and although the modern office buildings, hotels and high-rise flats may not have the glamorous appeal of the finer imperial architecture, they are evidence that the city still plays an important part in the life of its country.

Modern İstanbul

The **population** of Greater İstanbul is now around ten million (fourteen percent of the population of the entire country) and, with an influx of more than 300,000 new residents a year, there is no evidence of a slowdown in its growth – even though forty percent of the city's population live in shanty towns. The effects of this overcrowding are obvious even on a whistle-stop visit. İstanbul has the least **green space** per head of population among a random sample of twenty European cities (two square metres per head as opposed to Stockholm's eighty square metres), and it's becoming increasingly difficult to escape the city's perimeters, as they move further into Thrace and Anatolia. Indeed, **traffic congestion** and an overcrowded public transport system on all major routes make it hard to move at all, even within the city boundaries. The Refah Partisi (Islamic Welfare Party), who at present control the municipality of Greater İstanbul, have initiated clean-up programmes in some outlying neighbourhoods where their support is strongest, but still have no effective programme to deal with the expansion of shantytown dwellings other than to authorize more construction. In the summer of 1996 a cosmetic job was performed on İstanbul city centre in preparation for the United Nations habitat conference – ironically, given that the conference was concerned with improving living conditions for all in urban areas, this entailed further wholesale **slum clearances**.

ARRIVAL, CITY TRANSPORT AND ACCOMMODATION

İstanbul's transport infrastructure is improving slowly, with a new Bosphorus bridge, a ring road, better boats and faster trams, but traffic jams are still a part of everyday life, and you may prefer to stay around Sultanahmet, the main sightseeing centre of the city, to avoid the worst of the problems. The main points of arrival in İstanbul are Atatürk airport (*Atatürk Hava Limanı*), Esenler bus station and Sirkeci train station, none of which are in areas particularly renowned for their selection of accommodation. Getting into town from the airport has always been an especial nightmare because of lack of public transport, but this situation will improve considerably when the new metro reaches the airport. The metro, which will in time include Taksim Square and outlying neighbourhoods to the north, is the next stage of a grand plan to link all major suburbs of İstanbul by tram and train routes.

Arrival, orientation and information

İstanbul is divided in two by the **Bosphorus**, a narrow strait that runs roughly southwest between the Black Sea and the Sea of Marmara, separating Europe from Asia. At right angles to the strait is an inlet which feeds it, the **Golden Horn**, commencing in two small streams about 7km from the mouth of the Bosphorus. The majority of İstanbul's residential suburbs are located along the shores of the Sea of Marmara and on the hills above the Bosphorus, with the quarters along the Golden Horn dominated by light industry.

İstanbul effectively has two city centres, separated by the Golden Horn but both situated on the European side of the Bosphorus. The **Sultanahmet** district is the historical core of the city, while **Taksim** is the heart of culture and commerce. The two can easily be made out from the water, distinguished respectively by the landmarks of the Topkapı Palace and the Sheraton Hotel. As a visitor you're likely to spend much of your time in and around the Sultanahmet area, the centre of both the Byzantine and Ottoman empires. The most visited sites, **Topkapı Palace**, **Aya Sofya**, **Sultan Ahmet Camii** (the Blue Mosque) and the **Hippodrome** (now a strip of municipal park), are all within a stone's throw of each other, and of the major museums and the **Kapalı Çarşı**, the covered bazaar.

The relative concentration of these major sites also means that it is an easy matter to leave fellow tourists in the hands of the numerous self-appointed guides who frequent Sultanahmet, and head off alone in search of lesser-known but equally convincing evidence of the glory of İstanbul's imperial past. The Byzantine city of **Constantinople** occupied the area bordered by the Marmara Sea and the Golden Horn, delimited landwards by Theodosius' city walls, the greater part of which are still standing. The majority of the sites in this area are within easy walking distance of Sultanahmet; others – such as Theodosius' city walls, which are about 6km from Topkapı Palace – are accessible by bus, train or dolmuş.

Across the Golden Horn is the area centring on Taksim, often referred to as the **modern city**, although it includes the former Genoese colony of Galata, which is as old as the acropolis itself. The two sides of the inlet are connected at its mouth by the **Galata Bridge**, spanning the water between Eminönü and Karaköy. There are buses and dolmuşes from Eminönü to Taksim; an excellent way to get up the steep hill to Galata and İstiklâl Caddesi from Karaköy is to take the **Tünel**, the ancient French-built underground funicular railway, which takes eighty seconds to reach its destination.

The Bosphorus is spanned by two **bridges**, the original Boğaziçi Köprüsü and the Fatih Sultan Mehmet Köprüsü, opened in 1988. The villages along the shores of the Bosphorus can be visited by ferry, in small rented motorboats or by bus.

The most helpful **tourist information office** in the city is on Divanyolu Caddesi near the Hippodrome (☎0212/518 1802; daily 9am–5pm). Others can be found in the international arrivals area of Atatürk airport (☎0212/633 6363; daily 24hr), in Sirkeci train station (☎0212/511 5888; daily 9am–5pm), and at Karaköy International Maritime Passenger Terminal (☎0212/249 5776; Mon–Sat 9am–5pm); the office in the *Hilton Hotel* arcade on Cumhuriyet Caddesi (☎0212/233 0592; Mon–Sat 9am–5pm) has a few maps and pamphlets to hand out. The Directorate of Tourism, at Meşrutiyet Cad 57, Galatasaray (☎0212/243 3472 or 243 3731, fax 243 6564; Mon–Fri 9am–5pm), won't answer run-of-the-mill queries, but can help in the preparation of long trips and can recommend guiding companies.

Arriving by air

İstanbul has two **airport terminals**, international (*dışhatları*) and domestic (*içhatları*), a kilometre apart and around 25km west of the city centre near the Sea of Marmara. **Buses** ferry passengers between the two free of charge at half-hourly intervals (at least between 7am and 9pm – outside these hours services are erratic). Unfortunately these double as the *Havaş* bus service into İstanbul, so if you choose to make use of this service from the international terminal your first experience of public transport in Turkey may include a frustating delay as you wait for a late arrival at the domestic airport. The bus stops are situated outside the main door of the domestic airport and immediately across the car park from arrivals at the international airport. The service into İstanbul costs $2 and goes via Aksaray (see "Accommodation") to the *THY* office on the north side of Taksim Square.

The *hızlı tramvay* (high-speed tram), also known as the **metro**, has reached Yeni Bosna at the time of writing, and will soon reach the airport itself, with a station on the airport–Yeşilköy road, 500m from international arrivals. It will be the fastest, most comfortable and economical way of getting to and from the airport, but at present you need to take a taxi to the Yeni Bosna metro station, 2km away, from where 4–10 trains an hour go east to Esenler and Aksaray between 6am and 11.15pm.

If you decide that the bus or tram journey is rather too grim a proposal, you will have to resign yourself to the mercies of a **taxi** driver. You should insist before setting out that the driver uses his taxi meter (*taksi metre*, pronounced exactly the same in Turkish) and ensure on departure that he switches it on. The trip should cost $10–15, depending on where you want to go. You can save money by going to Yeşilköy train station, and taking a local train to Sirkeci (the last stop on the line). You buy a *banliyö* (suburban) ticket of fixed price (around $0.30) from the *gişe* (ticket office) on the platform and then take any train going east. From Sirkeci you can either take a tram (see below) or another taxi up to the hotels in Sultanahmet.

Arriving by train

İstanbul has two mainline **train stations**, one in Europe, at Sirkeci, the other, Haydarpaşa, across the Bosphorus in Asia. Trains from Western Europe arrive at **Sirkeci station**. From here it's easy to find a taxi to the hotels in Sultanahmet or Lâleli, and there's a tramway from outside the station going uphill directly to Sultanahmet and on to Lâleli and Topkapı *otogar*.

Trains from Moscow, Baghdad and all of Asian Turkey, with the exception of İzmir, arrive at **Haydarpaşa station**. If you want to cross the Bosphorus to Sultanahmet, the easiest way is to board a ferry immediately in front of the station; this will take you to Karaköy from where buses cross the Galata Bridge to Sultanahmet. Alternatively it's a two-kilometre walk to the hotels further along the waterfront in Kadıköy, or you can take a #12 or #14 bus to Üsküdar, also on the Bosphorus. There's a taxi rank outside the main entrance, on the road between the station and the quay.

Arriving by bus

There are two major **otogars** (bus stations) in İstanbul, a new one in **Esenler** 10km northwest of the centre on the E800 (İstanbul–Edirne toll road), and one at **Harem** on the Asian side of the city, on the coast road between Üsküdar and Kadıköy.

The new bus station is well organized, and companies have numbered ticket stands in the building around the periphery of the bus stops. To get into town from Esenler, take the *hızlı tramvay* (marked "metro"), from the station in the centre of the *otogar* (platform marked "Aksaray"); trams leave every fifteen minutes between around 6am and 11.15pm. If you arrive any later than this, take a taxi into town – the only hotel in the region of the *otogar*, the *Elit* (☎0212/658 3780; ⑧), is way overpriced for fairly basic, functional rooms.

If you're arriving in İstanbul by bus from Asia, it's worth disembarking at Harem, thus saving yourself a tedious journey to Esenler. From Harem half-hourly ferries cross the Bosphorus to Sirkeci, near Eminönü (7am–9pm, until 10pm April–Oct). There are also dolmuşes every few minutes to Kadıköy and to Üsküdar, leaving from the south side of the complex, beyond the ticket offices surrounding the main courtyard. From either of these suburbs, it's an easy matter to take a ferry across to Eminönü, or from Üsküdar to Beşiktaş for Taksim. Taxis are also easily found in this area, but a taxi across the bridge is expensive, as you pay the bridge toll on top.

Arriving by boat

Car ferries from Bandırma on the İzmir–İstanbul route, from the Black Sea and from Harem across the Bosphorus arrive at **Sirkeci** off Kennedy Caddesi. From here, it's a short walk to the tram terminal on Reşadiye Caddesi; trams go up to Sultanahmet via Topkapı Palace, and on to Aksaray.

Boats from the Marmara islands (Avşa and Marmara) dock on the other side of the Golden Horn at **Karaköy**, next to the passenger terminal on Rıhtım Caddesi. To get to Sultanahmet from here, walk across the Galata Bridge to Eminönü and catch the tram.

City transport

For any one journey within İstanbul there's invariably a whole gamut of possible permutations of route and means of transport. The latter may vary from an antiquated Oldsmobile or even a horse and carriage to the more efficient services such as the **metro**, also known as the *hızlı tramvay* service, and the **catamarans**, *deniz otobüsler* (meaning "seabuses"). The traffic infrastructure has improved with the building of the Fatih Sultan Mehmet bridge and its arterial roads, but traffic is still slowed by frequent snarl-ups around the inadequate lanes of Sultanahmet and parts of Taksim.

Buses

Buses (*otobus* in Turkish) are orange for the most part, but recent deregulation of advertising has given rise to some interesting variations. Most are run by the municipality, and you'll need to buy tickets in advance of boarding. They're sold at *otogar* ticket offices and newspaper, cigarette or fast-food booths, as well as some small grocery shops and newsagents; or by ticket touts at slightly inflated prices around some bus terminals. It's as well to lay in a good stock of tickets whenever you get the chance, since you can walk for miles trying to find one in more remote areas of the city. Tickets are sold in blocks of ten: either full price (*tam*) at around $0.25 each, or half-price tickets for students and teachers with passes issued by Turkish educational institutions. Tickets should be deposited into the metal dispensary next to the driver on boarding (don't be alarmed if this is on fire, tickets are disposed of in this way). Occasionally you may board a privately run bus where a conductor seated at the side will require a cash payment.

Trains

The **municipal train network**, consisting of one line on either side of the Bosphorus, is hardly comprehensive, but trains are frequent and cheap, though crowded at rush hours. One line runs from Haydarpaşa out to Göztepe, Bostancı, and along the Gulf of İzmit to Gebze, and the other from Sirkeci out to Halkalı, along the shores of the Marmara, stopping at Kumkapı, well known for its fish restaurants, at Yedikule museum, at Yeşilköy, not far from the airport, and at Florya, handy for the government-run campsite. For enquiries, call Sirkeci on ☎0212/527 0051, Haydarpaşa on ☎0212/336 0475. Tickets ($0.50 flat fare) are bought on the platform and should be retained until leaving the station as there is a fine for travelling without one. There is also an underground funicular line between Karaköy and Beyoğlu, known as the *tünel*. *Jeton*s are bought at the kiosks on entry.

Trams

There are three **tramlines** in the city. From Aksaray, the *hızlı tramvay*, also called the *metro*, is planned to go to Atatürk airport in Yeşilköy, but presently only reaches as far as Yeni Bosna, via the new bus station in Esenler. The other main line runs from Topkapı gate to Aksaray, Lâleli, Beyazit, Çemberlitaz, Sultanahmet and downhill to Eminönü. Approaching trams signal their arrival with a bell and passengers must wait on the concrete platforms at regular intervals along the tracks. Tickets are bought at booths on the platforms and are deposited in boxes on entry. The third tramline is more of a novelty ride, comprising original turn-of-the-century trams and mustachioed ticket collectors in appropriately antiquated uniform; but it does provide a useful service between the *tünel* station at the Beyoğlu end of İstiklâl Cad and Taksim. Tickets can be purchased from kiosks at either end and you can get off en route at specific tram stops.

Trams are frequent and run until at least 11pm year-round. However, they're overcrowded at all times, and pickpocketing is not unknown. If you have any trouble with this or sexual harassment on any form of public transport, make other passengers aware of the fact (try *beni rahatsiz etme*, meaning "leave me alone") and invariably you will be assisted.

Dolmuşes

One of the most economical yet elegant forms of public transport, the **dolmuş** is a most endearing Turkish institution. The basic principle is one of a shared taxi with a predetermined route and a range of set fares for all or part of that route. The original cars employed for the purpose were exported to Turkey as part of the Marshall Plan in the decade or so after World War II. Enthusiasts will enjoy a working museum of 1950s Fords, Cadillacs, Dodges, Plymouths and Chevrolets, while others can take a back seat and relish the ride. Less romantic but equally practical **minibuses** are now superseding the old-style dolmuşes on many routes; to further confuse the issue, some routes are run by yellow taxi cabs operating as dolmuşes.

All dolmuşes of whatever shape should have their point of departure and destination displayed somewhere about the windscreen and you can board and alight where you will en route. Flag them down as you would a taxi, and ask to get out at a convenient place with the polite *müsait bir yerde* or simply *inecek* (pronounced "inejek") *var*.

Taxis

Taxis are everywhere, but insist they use the meter and be careful that they don't try to charge you ten times what's written on it; if you get into bother start discussing the *polis*, especially if any suggestion of a flat fare is mooted. If you cross either Bosphorus bridge in either direction, you'll be charged the toll (currently over $1). Fares go up after midnight, when a sign on the meter saying *gece* should light up; otherwise the sign should read *gündüz* (daytime).

Ferryboats, motorboats and catamarans

Many useful routes are covered by the various **passenger boats** that work the waterways of the city, including crossings of the Bosphorus and Golden Horn, and regular services to the Princes' Islands in the Sea of Marmara. The boats get extremely crowded during rush hours (8–9am and 5.30–8pm) but otherwise are relaxing: however frantic the hurry you may be in, you might as well resign yourself to your fate on this leg of your journey as the boats will always take more or less the same time over a crossing. On the ferryboats, many of which were constructed in Tyneside shipyards after the war, you can drink tea or *sahlep* (a sweet drink made from a kind of root and sprinkled with cinnamon) or take a tour of the ship to admire wooden and brass fittings and possibly a steam engine. You'll need a small **token**, a *jeton* ($0.30), which you can buy at the kiosks by the entrance to the *iskele* (jetty), or from ubiquitous touts at slightly inflated prices. Smaller boats do journeys up and down the Horn, between Bostancı and the islands, and between Üsküdar and Beşiktaş; on these, cash fares are generally collected by one of the passengers.

The catamarans or *deniz otobüsler* are by far the fastest waterborne form of transport. Their most useful route for visitors to İstanbul is between Karaköy and Kadıköy, but they also have services in the Sea of Marmara between Kabataş and Yalova, Kartal and Yalova, and an infrequent service between Kabataş and Büyükada. For short hops across the Bosphorus, the fare is around $0.50 (buy a *jeton* and deposit it at the turnstile on entry); the longer trip to the islands is expensive at $3, but takes a mere 25 minutes.

Accommodation

Finding **somewhere to stay** in İstanbul is rarely a problem, as supply generally exceeds demand and new hotels appear all over the place every year. But this doesn't mean that you will necessarily be able to get into the place of your choice: it's best to **phone ahead** to avoid a lot of trudging from one full *pansiyon* to the next, and in mid-season anything up to a week's **advance booking** wouldn't go amiss, especially if you're hoping to stay somewhere pleasant that's also good value and central.

It's essential, and expected, that you should have a look at a room before you book in, even though **prices** are generally a reliable indication of the kind of accommodation on offer (if rates are quoted in Turkish lira, for example, you probably won't have a bathroom in the room, and the emphasis will be on function rather than appearance). **Hotels** (as opposed to *pansiyons* or youth hostels) generally quote prices in a strong currency – at present this is US dollars – so you need an idea of exchange rates before you start searching. Prices should by law be displayed in the foyer, but don't feel you can't **bargain**, especially in cheaper places, out of season, or if you intend to stay for a few nights.

There is a current trend for converting **old buildings** into hotels, or – in order to get planning permission despite tricky laws protecting old buildings – dismantling a building, using some of the original materials in a completely new construction, and calling it "renovated". Some, though, have been converted with a degree of sensitivity and respect for their original appearance, and many of these have been included in the listings.

ACCOMMODATION PRICE CODES

In this guide, motels and nearly all hotels and *pansiyon*s have been categorized according to the price codes outlined below, which are based on US$ because of the high domestic Turkish inflation rate. These categories represent the minimum you can expect to pay for a **double room in high season**. Rates for hostels and for the most basic hotels and *pansiyon*s, where guests are charged **per person**, are given in US$, instead of being indicated by price code. For further information, including a rough outline of what you might expect in each category, see p.37.

① under $12	② $12–17	③ $18–25
④ $26–35	⑤ $36–45	⑥ $46–55
⑦ $56–75	⑧ over $75	

Sultanahmet

Some of the city's nicest small hotels and *pansiyon*s – and many of its worst hostels – are situated in **Sultanahmet**, right at the heart of touristic İstanbul. You will have to weigh up whether you want to be offered the same guidebook as you step out of the front door each morning, but for short visits the hotels surrounding the **Hippodrome** couldn't be much better placed – without actually being part of the imperial harem – to give an on-location sense of history. A high concentration of cheap accommodation is to be found in and around **Yerebatan Caddesi**, while the hotels off **Divan Yolu Caddesi** have the advantage of being handy for the Topkapı–Eminönü tram. Rooms can also be found in the less prominent but equally atmospheric backstreets in **Cankurtaran**, between the Hippodrome and the sea.

Around the Hippodrome (Atmeydanjı)

Hotel Alzer, Atmeydanı 72 (☎0212/516 6262). Extremely comfortable rooms with TVs and mini-bars; terrace and breakfast bar. ⑦.

Hotel Antique, Küçük Ayasofya Cad, Oğul Sok 17 (☎0212/516 4936, fax 517 6370). Pleasant, comfortable hotel with small rooms which are excellent value for the level of service. Quiet neighbourhood, roof terrace. ④.

Hotel Ayasofya, Demirci Rasit Sok 28, off Mehmetpaşa Sok (☎0212/516 9446, fax 518 0700). An indoor winter garden, kilims and old-world charm feature at this nineteenth-century wooden *koşk*, or mansion. Not to be confused with *Ayasofya Pansiyonlar* near Topkapı. ⑦.

Hippodrome Pansiyon, Üçler Sok 9 (☎0212/516 0902). Cheap and convenient, with clean doubles and triples and friendly staff. One bathroom for every two rooms. ③.

Küçük Ayasofya Hotel, Şehit Mehmetpaşa Sok 25 (☎0212/516 1988, fax 516 8356). Lovely converted mansion, with kilimed and shuttered rooms. ⑦.

Optimist Guesthouse, Atmeydanı 68 (☎0212/516 2398). Good value for small rooms in this central location. ④.

Rose Pansiyon, Aksakal Sok 20, Küçükayasofya (☎0212/518 9705). Pleasant little *pansiyon*, well located in the atmospheric old city. ②.

Hotel Sokullu Paşa, Mehmetpaşa Sok 5/7, just below the Hippodrome (☎0212/518 1790). An original nineteenth-century *koşk* (mansion) with stained glass, Ottoman antiques, a Turkish bath, bar and garden. ⑧.

Hotel Spectra, Şehit Mehmet Paşa Yokusu 2 (☎0212/516 3546, fax 638 3379). Newly converted Ottoman house, comfortable and well furnished with good views from the terrace. ⑧.

Turkoman Hotel, Asmalı Çeşme Sok, Adliye Yanı 2 (☎0212/516 2956, fax 516 2957). Upmarket converted house in nineteenth-century Turkish style. Each room is named after the carpet on the floor, and carpets are on sale in the breakfast room downstairs. Fine views from the roof terrace. ⑦.

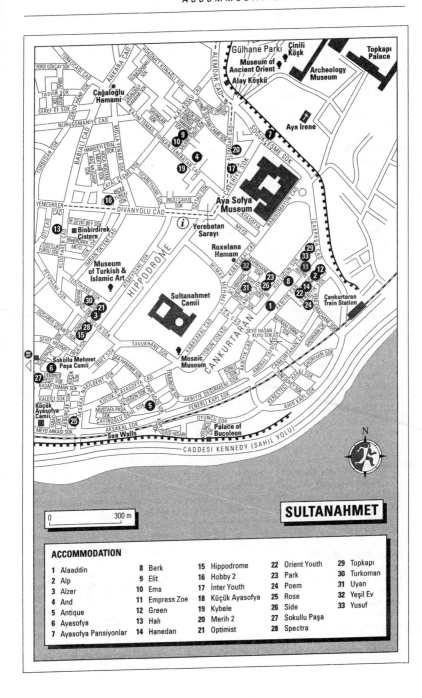

SULTANAHMET

0 _____ 300 m

ACCOMMODATION

1 Alaaddin	8 Berk	15 Hippodrome	22 Orient Youth	29 Topkapı
2 Alp	9 Elit	16 Hobby 2	23 Park	30 Turkoman
3 Alzer	10 Ema	17 İnter Youth	24 Poem	31 Uyan
4 And	11 Empress Zoe	18 Küçük Ayasofya	25 Rose	32 Yeşil Ev
5 Antique	12 Green	19 Kybele	26 Side	33 Yusuf
6 Ayasofya	13 Halı	20 Merih 2	27 Sokullu Paşa	
7 Ayasofya Pansiyonlar	14 Hanedan	21 Optimist	28 Spectra	

Around Topkapı and Cankurtaran

Alaadin Guest House, Akbıyık Cad 32 (☎0212/516 2330, fax 638 6059). Small doubles in a prime location, with the edge over others of the same ilk in this area in terms of value. ⑤.

Alp Guesthouse, Akbıyık Cad, Adliye Sok 4 (☎0212/517 9570). Clean place with en-suite bathrooms. Terrace and breakfast room with garden. ④.

Ayasofya Pansiyonlar, Soğukçeşme Sok (☎0212/513 3660, fax 513 3669). A row of houses reconstructed in nineteenth-century style, tucked away behind Aya Sofya and convenient for major sites. ⑧.

Berk Guesthouse, Kutluğun Sok 27 (☎0212/517 6561). Family-run, with half-a-dozen standard rooms, all with baths, plus a couple of luxury rooms, with minibar, air conditioning and TV. Great view of the former prison – now converted into a five-star luxury hotel – from the terrace. ⑥–⑧.

Empress Zoe, Akbıyık Cad, Adliye Sok 10 (☎0212/518 2504, fax 518 5699). American owned, with a Greek flavour. Previously a hamam, with remaining fixtures quaintly incorporated into the decor; the sun terrace has panoramic views of the Blue Mosque and Aya Sofya. ⑦.

Green Hotel, Akbıyık Cad 5 (☎0212/638 6600, fax 638 3104). Comfortable, with a reasonable restaurant attached. ⑦.

Hanedan Hostel, Akbıyık Cad, Adliye Sok 3 (☎0212/516 4869). Another good clean cheap option in this area, including en-suite doubles. ④, dorm $3–4.

Inter Youth Hostel, Caferiye Sok 6 (☎0212/513 6150, fax 512 7628). Affiliated to IYHF, with reasonable prices for one of İstanbul's prime locations. Rooms are basic but clean, with good facilities, including hot showers (shared bathrooms), safe, laundry, roof bar and a little library. Airport service for under $4. ①, dorm $3–5.50.

Hotel and Hostel Merih 2, Alemdar Cad 20 & 24 (☎0212/526 9708 or 527 5070). Double rooms are small and poky, with cramped bathrooms, but the place is clean and friendly, with a cafeteria and garden. Hot showers throughout. ④, dorm $4.50.

Orient Youth Hostel, Akbıyık Cad 13 (☎0212/516 0171 or 516 0194). Clean and recently refurbished, but still quite basic. Five bedrooms per bathroom. ①, dorm $4.

Hotel Park, Utangaç Sok 26 (☎0212/517 6596, fax 518 9602). Comfortable hotel with good service, guaranteed hot water, and great views from the terrace. ⑥.

Hotel Poem, Terbıyık Sok 12 (☎0212/518 7071). Well-furnished rooms with good views, each with a poem by a different Turkish poet on the wall. Friendly female proprietor. ④.

Side Pansiyon, Utangaç Sok 20 (☎/fax 0212/517 6590). Friendly staff, clean rooms, and great views of the Princes' Islands from the terrace. Some en suites, otherwise five bedrooms to each bathroom and toilet. (They've recently built a hotel in what used to be their tea garden, where rooms will cost around $50.) ③–④.

Topkapı Hostel, Işakpaşa Cad, Kutluğun Sok 1 (☎0212/527 2433). Simply furnished, with five rooms to each bathroom, but in an excellent situation. Doubles ③, dorm $8, roofspace $6.

Uyan Hotel, Utangaç Sok 25 (☎0212/516 4892, fax 517 1582). Attractively renovated 1920s home: large, comfortable rooms, some with air conditioning, and excellent views from the terrace. ⑦.

Yeşil Ev, Kabasakal Cad 5 (☎0212 517 6785, fax 517 6780). An important landmark, as it's right on the park between Aya Sofya and the Blue Mosque. With rising prices in this area, a room in the "Green House", as its name translates, is almost beginning to look like good value. Built in the style of the house which originally occupied this site, Yeşil Ev is furnished in period (mid-nineteenth century), and has an attractive garden restaurant with a central marble fountain. ⑧.

Yusuf Guesthouse, Işakpaşa Cad, Kutluğun Sok 3 (☎0212/516 5878). Simple, clean, family-run guesthouse, with hot water in the shared bathrooms. ①, dorm $4.

Yerebatan Caddesi

And Otel, Yerebatan Cad, Camii Çıkmazı Sok 40 (☎0212/512 0207). Comfortable option at the heart of things, with wonderful views of the Golden Horn and Bosphorus from the restaurant. ⑧.

Elit Hotel, Yerebatan Cad, Salkım Söğüt Sok 14 (☎0212/512 7566 or 526 2549, fax 512 4878). Clean, fairly quiet rooms with private facilities, above a carpet shop. ④.

Ema Hotel, Yerebatan Cad, Salkım Söğüt Sok 8 (☎0212/511 7166). Clean and quiet double rooms with showers. ②.

Kybele Hotel, Yerebatan Cad 35 (☎0212/511 7166). Beautifully furnished, spacious rooms, a garden and an excellent restaurant. Ask for a room at the back or high up on the third or fourth floor to avoid traffic noise. ⑦.

Off Divan Yolu Caddesi

Hotel Halı, Klodfarer Cad 20, Çemberlitaş (☎0212/901 516). Spacious, clean and tastefully decorated, run by a carpet export company. ⑦.

Hotel Hobby 2, Bicki Yurdu Sok 12 (☎0212/614 1003). Plain, reasonably priced rooms in the centre. ⑤.

Otel Nuruosmaniye, Nuruosmaniye Cad 7 (☎0212/527 1695). Good value for such a prime location: friendly and helpful, with shared hot showers. ①.

Lâleli (Aksaray)

If you can't find anywhere in Sultanahmet but want to stay relatively close to the centre, İstanbul's other main concentration of hotels is situated about 1500m up Ordu Caddesi, past the University, in the area called **Aksaray**, where you arrive if coming from Esenler *otogar* by metro. Aksaray encompasses the smaller district of **Lâleli**, immediately to the east of Aksaray Meydanı (where busy Turgut Özal Cad, Adnan Menderes Cad and Atatürk Bul meet), north and south of Ordu Caddesi. The area has become the unofficial marketplace for Eastern Europeans selling anything for which there's a market, including sex – single women walking alone here may be mistaken for "Natashas", as Eastern European prostitutes are called. On the plus side, trams into Sultanahmet along Ordu Caddesi are frequent, the traffic on what was once a very busy road has been restricted to one-way, and you may get better value for your money than in Sultanahmet.

The main concentration of accommodation is in the north of Lâleli, between Atatürk Bulvarı and Büyük Reşit Paşa Caddesi up as far as Şehzade Camii, with a few other options south of Ordu Caddesi. Expect to pay around $30–60 a double room in Lâleli, since cheaper options have nearly all been renovated from *pansiyon* to hotel. Since there's so little to choose between the hotels and they're so numerous, it's easy to walk about and find one that suits.

Hotel Altınışik, Yeşiltulumba Sok 37, Lâleli (☎0212/522 5892). Rooms with TVs, on the next street up from Gençtürk Cad; not as good value as the *Seren* in the same street, but still a reasonable option. ⑤.

Hotel Burak, Fethi Bey Cad, Ağa Yokuşu 1, Lâleli (☎0212/511 8679 or 522 7904). Quite ordinary but well situated and cheap. ④.

Hotel Grand Lord, Azimkâr Sok 22–24, Lâleli (☎0212/518 6311). Modern 3-star hotel with excellent service. ⑦.

Grand Yildiz Hotel, Gençtürk Cad 25, Lâleli (☎0212/513 5188, fax 513 6811). Rooms with TV and minibar, popular with Russian traders. ⑤.

Hotel Kul, Büyük Reşit Paşa Cad, Zeynep Kamil Sok 27, Lâleli (☎0212/526 0127 or 528 2892). Basic rooms with showers. ③.

Seranda Hotel, Namik Kemal Cad, Manastırlı Rıfat Sok 23, Aksaray (☎0212/529 5030, fax 529 5033). Modern hotel with a classic feel to its white-tablecloth restaurant and marble lobby. Large rooms with air conditioning and minibars. ⑧.

Hotel Seren, Yeşiltulumba Sok 26, parallel to Gençtürk Cad, Lâleli (☎0212/513 7982, fax 519 2319). Good-value three-star comfort, including minibar and air conditioning; popular with Russian business people. ⑥.

Taksim and around

Taksim may be the city's business centre, but it's also a remarkably convenient base from which to sightsee. It affords easy access to the Bosphorus and comes into its own at night, when it becomes the centre of entertainment, and of cultural and culinary activity. At the other end of İstiklâl Caddesi, seedy, cosmopolitan Beyoğlu has several well-established hotels in the district known as **Tepebaşı**, which lies just northwest of

İstiklâl, centred on Meşrutiyet Caddesi. To get to Meşrutiyet Caddesi by public transport from Taksim, take a tram along İstiklâl. On either side of Sıraselviler Caddesi, **Cihangir** is an atmospheric backwater with splendid views of the Bosphorus, handy for the antiques district of Çukurcuma.

For the locations of hotels in this area, see the "Around Taksim" **map** on p.138–39.

Off Taksim Square

Otel Avrupa, Topçu Cad 32 (☎0212/250 9420). Newly converted apartment building, on a quiet street in an area where most other hotels are in the luxury class. Small rooms with small beds and en-suite bathrooms, but a pleasant breakfast room down by the lobby on the first floor. ④.

Gezi Hotel, Mete Cad 42, Taksim (☎0212/251 7430, fax 251 7473). The service in this centrally located hotel is excellent, and rooms are well furnished, with nice bathrooms, minibars and hair-driers. ⑦.

Hotel Yeni My Fair, Abdülhakhamit Cad 54 (☎0212/256 2539, fax 237 8415). Plain, uninspiring rooms, not as good as the *Avrupa*, but still good value for the area. ⑤.

Tepebaşı

Otel Ali Baba, Meşrutiyet Cad 119 (☎0212/251 5648). Simple doubles (shared bathrooms) that are a bit dusty and run-down. ①.

Büyük Londra Oteli, Meşrutiyet Cad 117 (☎0212/249 1025, fax 249 0438). Mid-nineteenth-century, Italian-built and palatial, with a good restaurant and cocktail bar. Rooms are a little the worse for wear, but some have fridges – ask for a view across the Golden Horn. Baby-sitting service and airport transfers. ⑥.

Hotel Dünya, Meşrutiyet Cad 79 (☎0212/251 5648). Run-down and peeling but clean and cheap, with a lift, and views of the Princes' Islands from the sixth floor. Doubles with bathroom ③, without ②.

Monopol Hotel, Meşrutiyet Cad 223 (☎0212/251 7326, fax 251 7333). Friendly staff, and all in all excellent value for comfortable, well-furnished rooms with shiny new en-suite bathrooms and (Turkish) cable TV. ⑤.

Pera Palas, Meşrutiyet Cad 98–100 (☎0212/251 4560, fax 251 4089). Built in the nineteenth century to accommodate passengers of the Orient Express, this contender for classiest hotel in İstanbul deserves a visit if only for a cup of coffee in the chandeliered American Bar and a visit to the "powder room". It's worth checking out package deals from Britain if you want to stay here. ⑧.

Cihangir

Cihangir Hotel, Sıraselviler Cad, Arslan Yatağı Sok (☎0212/251 5317, fax 251 5321). Situated in a quiet backstreet in one of the town's more atmospheric quarters: excellent service, large rooms with TVs and minibars, some with tremendous Bosphorus views. ⑧.

Family House, Kutlu Sok 53 (☎0212/249 7351, fax 249 9670). Worthwhile if there are enough of you and you intend to do some self-catering, since these flats accommodate up to four people and have fully equipped kitchens; transport to and from the airport and a baby-sitter service are laid on. Interiors are rather gloomy and cheaply furnished, but the building is in a pleasant backstreet. In season it's essential to book in advance. ⑧.

Hotel Oriental, Cihangir Cad 60 (☎0212/252 6870). Some rooms with sea view and balcony; garden café. Twenty percent reduction in winter. ⑦.

Vardar Palace Hotel, Sıraselviler Cad 54 (☎0212/252 2888, fax 252 1527). Renovated turn-of-the-century Beyoğlu apartment building; no views at the back, and rooms at the front are noisy, but a reasonable option for the Taksim area, with period furniture and a friendly atmosphere. ⑧.

The Bosphorus

The suburbs and villages along the shores of the Bosphorus can be relaxing places to spend time and get to know Turkey while still not too far from the city centre. There are several cheap hotels on the **Asian side** in **Kadıköy** and **Üsküdar**. The former is almost devoid of tourist sites (and tourists), lively, scruffy and genuine, but its growing poverty manifests itself to the visitor in the form of young boys with solvent habits. Üsküdar is a wealthier suburb, retaining some of its Ottoman character and buildings, and a friendly small-town atmosphere. Between the two is **Harem** with its *otogar*, car ferry and one hotel.

There are no budget options on the **European shore** of the Bosphorus – you pay a massive premium for a waterfront location here, in some of the best hotels in İstanbul.

Asian shore

Hotel Acar, Uzun Hafiz Sok 23, Kadıköy (☎0216/337 8037). Not immune to traffic noise, and the place is down-at-heel once you get beyond the flowery facade, but it's away from the worst of the street action. ③.

Hotel Eysan, Rıhtım Cad 26, Kadıköy (☎0216/346 2440). Old-fashioned comfort with great views from the rooftop bar. ⑦.

Harem Otel, Ambar Sok 2, Harem (☎0216/333 2025). Large modern hotel in busy but convenient location above the *otogar*. Outdoor swimming pool and poolside bar. Ask for a room with a Bosphorus view. ⑦.

Konut Oteli, Selmanipak Cad 25, Üsküdar, over *Kanaat Lokantası* (☎0216/333 2284). A bit grim but reasonably clean: eight rooms to one bathroom, no hot water. ①.

Hotel Okur, Rıhtım Cad, Reşitefendi Sok 3, Kadıköy (☎0216/336 0629). The best of several in this street, but the street is a bit hectic with minibuses and street kids until around midnight. ③.

Yeni Saray Oteli, Selmanipak Cad, Çeşme Sok 33, Üsküdar (☎0216/333 0777 or 334 3485). Pleasant family hotel with restaurant, bar, café and a terrace overlooking the Bosphorus. ④.

European shore

Bebek Hotel, Cevdetpaşa Cad 113–115, Bebek (☎0212/263 3000, fax 263 2636). Pleasant location in this wealthy suburb for one of the best small hotels in İstanbul, but a long way from the sights. All rooms have balconies and satellite TV, and those by the water offer tremendous views of the Bosphorus. ⑦.

Çırağan Palace Hotel, Çırağan Cad 84, Beşiktaş (☎0212/258 3377, fax 259 6686). Elaborately restored Ottoman palace right on the Bosphorus, with spacious rooms (most of them in a modern building on the side of the palace), gourmet cuisine and a large outdoor pool. ⑧.

The Princes' Islands

The paradisiacal nature and proximity to İstanbul of these romantic retreats make it well nigh impossible to find accommodation on the **Princes' Islands** in the summer months, and the closure of most hotels out of season means that the same is generally true in winter. It's certainly worth some time and patience to search something out, however, since there is no nicer place to stay in the vicinity of İstanbul.

Kayambayan Endoğan, Cennet Yolu, Burgazada (☎0216/281 1504). Tiny establishment next to the sea, 2km from the ferry landing (take the coast road to the right as you disembark). Four simple rooms above a restaurant – which is also good value – and friendly management. Advance booking required. ③.

Merit Halki Palas, Refah Şehitler Cad 88, Heybeliada (☎0216/351 9550, fax 351 8483). Nineteenth-century villa originally used by families visiting students at the Greek Orthodox school of the Patriarchate, now restored in dubious taste by the Merit Hotel group, incorporating gymnasium, jacuzzi, outdoor pool and horse-riding. ⑧.

Panorama Hotel, Ayyıldız Cad, Heybeliada (☎0216/351 8543). Comfortable and old-fashioned if rather run-down, with friendly staff. Rooms have own bathrooms. Situated on the sea front with an outdoor café. ④.

Prenset Pansiyon, Ayyıldız Cad 74, Heybeliada (☎0216/351 9388, fax 351 8583). On Heybeli's main street (which runs parallel to Rihtim Cad on the front), this converted apartment building with wood-trimmed exterior is the best value on the islands. Friendly management, comfortable rooms with immaculate modern bathrooms and central heating in winter. They've also got a sauna and a tiny swimming pool on their roof terrace. ④.

Saydam Planet, İskele Meydanı, Büyükada (☎0216/382 2670, fax 382 3848). Beautiful old renovated mansion with comfortably furnished rooms and great bathrooms, but overpriced. ⑧.

Splendid Palas, 23 Nisan Cad 71, Büyükada (☎0216/382 6950, fax 382 6775). Serious *fin de siecle* grandeur, with cupolas, balconies, a good restaurant, excellent service, and a garden with a swimming pool. ⑧.

Villa Rifat, Yilmaz Turk Cad, Büyükada (☎0216/382 3081 or 382 6068). Quite a walk from the town centre and beaches on the shore road running round the east side of the island, but pleasant and comfortable. ④.

Yörük Ali Turistik Tesisleri, Yörük Ali beach, Büyükada (☎0216/321 9320). Less than 2km southwest of the ferry landing. Simple bungalows with kitchens and TV, in a secluded location by the sea, with a private beach and a reasonable restaurant. Book well in advance in season. ⑤.

Campsites

The city's **campsites** are all located along the Marmara coast out near the airport. Coming into town by car, follow signs to the airport, then drive around it to Yeşilköy on the coast; from here, Ataköy is the next suburb to the east and Florya a few hundred metres to the west. Both are easily accessible from Sirkeci by commuter train, and a cheap cab ride ($2–3) from the airport.

Ataköy Tatil Köyü, Rauf Orbay Cad, Ataköy (☎0212/559 6000–1). Attractive setting on the sea, 16km from the city centre. Bar, pools, disco and tennis courts, but a bit close to the main road for comfort so make it clear you want a seaside position if you book. Train to Ataköy station from Sirkeci, or bus #82 from Unkapanı via Kumkapı.

Florya Tourist Camping, Yezilköy Halkalı Cad, Florya (☎0212/573 7991). Pleasant and leafy, well served by public transport, and run by the municipality, so it's cheap; close to the airport but therefore noisy. About 25km from the city by #73 bus from Taksim, Topkapı–Florya dolmuş, or train from Sirkeci (Florya train station is 500m away).

Long-term residence

Flat-hunting in İstanbul can be a time-consuming business. Most landlords want prohibitively vast sums of money up front, generally a month's deposit and six months' rent, and banks are reluctant to lend money without material security, even to known customers.

The best way to go about **finding a place** is to choose an area you find particularly attractive and then look around for "*kiralık daire*" (flat to let) signs in windows. This way you will avoid paying agents' fees, generally another month's rent. Otherwise house agents (*emlak*) do have control of much of the best property in İstanbul and will generally be able to offer you something as soon as you can come up with the money.

The other problem with rented accommodation is that it's almost bound to be unfurnished: Turkish people don't generally move from the parental home until they marry, and they don't usually marry until they can afford to furnish a house. Still, buying furniture in the flea markets (*bit pazarları*) of İstanbul can be good fun, especially if you enjoy bargaining.

THE IMPERIAL CENTRE

The area bordered by the Theodosian city walls, by the city's natural harbour of the Golden Horn and by the Marmara Sea to the south is termed the **old city**, or "Stamboul" in some books. This quarter has been a **seat of government** since Byzas the Megarian founded his colony here, and there is enough evidence of this illustrious past – from the palaces and places of worship of successive empires to their city walls and cisterns – to imbue the entire area with a sense of history.

The old city is still very much alive today, with its own particular dilemmas and idio-syncrasies. Although the political factions of **İstanbul University** have been dispersed to some degree by the removal of a number of its faculties to Avcilar beyond Atatürk airport, the nation's press is still located in **Cağaloğlu**, and journalists are occasionally the target of assassination. The Refah Partisi are finding money to beautify the main Islamic touristic sites, in particular the Süleymaniye region, but the slum dwellings in the suburbs along the Theodosian city walls are rumoured to be centres of hard drug manufacture. These suburbs are still some of the roughest places in the city, with a long history of working-class defiance (Edirnekapı was a no-go area in the seventies). The worst of these areas along the walls is **Topkapı**, which now lacks even an *otogar* to give it character and is distinctly dangerous after dark. **Fatih** and surrounding districts are strongholds of Islamic fundamentalism, though they coexist peaceably enough with the nearby Christian and Jewish districts of Fener and Balat.

Sultanahmet

A large percentage of short-stay visitors spend all of their time in the **Sultanahmet** dis-trict, for here are the **main sightseeing attractions**: the Topkapı Palace, heart of the Ottoman dynasty, Sultan Ahmet Camii itself, known as the Blue Mosque, and the great-est legacy of the Byzantine Empire, the church of Aya Sofya. Here also are the ancient Hippodrome, the Museum of Islamic Culture, housed in the former Palace of İbrahim Paşa, the Yerebatan underground cistern, and the Kapalı Çarşı, the largest covered bazaar in the world. The monumental architecture, attractive parks and gardens, and the benefits of a traffic-free main road courtesy of the tramline combine to make this area pleasant for both sightseeing and staying over.

And yet initial impressions of Sultanahmet – for many their first experience of Turkey – may be negative, especially for young women, whether alone or in groups. The very worst of the country's most persistent **hustlers** gather here to plague new arrivals, who haven't yet learnt to deal summarily with such irritants. You may find that good-humoured tolerance combined with a no-nonsense air are the best antidotes to hassle, but on the other hand, maybe his uncle really does have just the *yahyalı* you're looking for tucked away in some hidden recess of his carpet shop.

Aya Sofya

For almost a thousand years **Aya Sofya**, or Haghia Sophia (daily except Mon 9am–4.30pm, until 5pm in July and August; galleries 9.30–11.30am & 1–4pm; $4), was the largest enclosed space in the world, designed to impress the strength and wealth of the Byzantine emperors upon their own subjects and visiting foreign dignitaries alike. Located between Topkapı Saray and Sultan Ahmet Camii on the ancient acropolis, the first hill of İstanbul, it must have dominated the city skyline for a millennium, until the domes and minarets of Sinan's mosques began to challenge it in the sixteenth century. A huge restoration programme is currently in progress, its time span as yet unknown. Scaffolding will undoubtedly be a major feature of the decor for the next few years.

Some history
Aya Sofya, "the Church of the Divine Wisdom", was commissioned in the sixth centu-ry by the Emperor Justinian after its predecessor had been razed to the ground in the Nika revolts of 532. The architects, **Anthemius of Tralles** and **Isidore of Miletus**, were to create a building combining elements in a manner and on a scale completely unknown to the Byzantine world, and no imitation or rival would subsequently be attempted until the sixteenth century. It remained an important symbol of Byzantine

power long after the empire itself had been destroyed, and it proved fatal to at least one Ottoman architect – **Atık Sinan**, who was executed by Mehmet the Conqueror when the dimensions of the dome of Fatih Camii failed to match those of Aya Sofya – and became the inspiration, not to say obsession, of the greatest of all Ottoman architects, **Mimar Sinan**, who devoted his lifetime to the attempt to surpass its technical achievements.

For a hundred-foot-wide **dome** to hover over a seemingly empty space, rather than being supported by solid walls, was unprecedented, and the novelty and sheer dimensions of the projected structure meant that the architects proceeded with no sure way of knowing that their plans would succeed. The building was initially constructed in five years, but various crises arose during the process, which suggested that the design was unsound. Twenty years and several earthquakes later the central dome collapsed. By this time both the original architects had died, so the task of rebuilding the dome went to **Isidorus the Younger**, the nephew of one of the original architects. He increased the height of the external buttresses and of the dome itself, and it is possible that he effected the removal of large windows from the north and south tympanum arches, thus initiating the gradual blockage of various of the windows that has resulted in the dim half-light in which visitors now grope.

First impressions on entering are of an overwhelming gloom and general neglect. It's sad to see the dome in such a bad state of repair, but judging from a letter written by Mary Montague Wortley, the process of decay had begun well before she arrived there in 1717:

> . . . *the whole roof [is] mosaic work, part of which decays very fast and drops down. They presented me a handful of it.*

Considering the vicissitudes undergone by the building over the centuries, and bearing in mind its size and the cost of its upkeep – a crippling burden to the Byzantines themselves once decline had set in and the population of Byzantium had decreased in the Middle Ages – it's surprising to find it still standing at all.

The worst **desecration** of the church occurred in 1204, when it was ransacked by Catholic soldiers during the **Fourth Crusade**. The altar was broken up and shared among the captors, the hangings were torn, and mules were brought in to help carry off silver and gilt carvings. A prostitute was seated on the throne of the patriarch, and she "sung and danced in the church, to ridicule the hymns and processions of the orientals". One Crusader said that Constantinople contained more holy relics than the rest of Christendom combined and that "the plunder of this city exceeded all that has been witnessed since the creation of the world".

Two and a half centuries later, in 1452, the Byzantine church became Catholic in the hope that Western powers would come to the aid of Constantinople against the Turks, but they were too late. On May 29, 1453 those who had said they would rather see the turban of a Turk than the hat of a cardinal in the streets of Constantinople got their way when the city was captured. **Mehmet the Conqueror** rode to the church of Aya Sofya and stopped the looting that was taking place there. He had the building cleared of relics, its "idolatrous images" covered over, and he said his first prayer there on the following Friday. Later a wooden minaret was built at the southwest corner of the building, not to be replaced until the late sixteenth century, when Mimar Sinan was called upon to restore the building.

Extensive restorations were carried out on the mosaics in the mid-nineteenth century by the Swiss **Fossati brothers**, but these were later covered over again, and the angels the Fossatis had painted in the west pendentives of the nave, to match the two mosaic angels in the east pendentives, were even given medallions to hide their faces.

The building continued to function as a **mosque** until 1932, when further renovations were carried out, and in 1934 it was opened as a **museum**. To the credit of progressive members of the Turkish government, they have not yielded to popular pressure – which has included a petition of several thousand signatures – to convert Aya Sofya back into a mosque.

The museum

The **exterior** of Aya Sofya gives no hint of the delights within. Always rather hidden by the heavy buttresses that were added after the first dome collapsed, it is now crowded in by buildings on two sides, which makes it almost impossible to get a good look at the exterior. This may be just as well, since it has been covered in cement which is given a new coat of increasingly lurid paint every few years: currently it's an interesting deep pink.

The main body of the building approximates to a **domed basilica**, with a basic octagonal shape split in two and a domed rectangle inserted. Thus Aya Sofya is both centralized and domed – forms which were gaining in popularity for prestigious monuments of the sixth century – but it retains a longitudinal axis and side aisles. At the diagonals of the octagon are semicircular niches (exedrae). The galleries, which follow the line of these exedrae around the building, are supported by rows of columns and by four piers, which are also the main support of the dome.

Most interesting of the internal decorations are the marbles and the mosaics. The **marbles** include purple-coloured Egyptian porphyry, which was not quarried at the time, so must have been pilfered from elsewhere. In revetments, small pieces are given undulating edges to conceal the joints, and the disparate sizes of the porphyry columns in the exedrae are compensated for in their pedestals. The columns supporting the galleries and the tympanum walls are verd antique marble while those in the upper gallery of the exedrae are Thessalian marble. These ranges of columns, above and below the gallery, are not aligned one above the other, an irregularity thought outrageously daring by contemporaries, who considered it structurally unsound as well as a dangerous departure from classical norms. Of those in the exedrae the poet Paul the Silentiary wrote: "One wonders at the power of him, who bravely set six columns over two, and has not trembled to fix their bases over empty air". Upstairs in the western gallery a large circle of green Thessalian marble marks the position of the **throne of the empress**.

Byzantine **mosaics** were designed to be seen in lamp- or candlelight. These conditions showed off the workmanship to its best advantage: flickering light reflected in pieces of glass or gold, which had been carefully embedded at minutely disparate angles, gave an appearance of movement and life to the mosaics. Nowadays visitors must rely on natural light, frequently wanting in İstanbul, and consequently the effect can be disappointing. What remains of the **abstract mosaics** and the large areas of plain gold which covered the underside of the dome and other large expanses of wall and ceiling dates from the sixth century. Some of the prettiest of this abstract work can be seen under the arches of the south gallery and in the narthex (the entrance porch), from which some impression can be gained of what the original four acres of such mosaics must have looked like.

The **figurative mosaics**, all of which date from after the Iconoclastic era (726–843), are located in the narthex, the nave, the upper gallery and the vestibule. Some of the most impressive are in the south gallery where, beyond a pair of false marble doors on the west face of the pier, there's a comparatively well-lit mosaic of a **Deisis**, depicting Christ, the Virgin and St John the Baptist. Although this mosaic is partly damaged, the three faces are all well preserved and there is no problem in making out their expressions. The face of John the Baptist is especially expressive, betraying great pain and suffering, while the Virgin has downcast eyes and an expression of modesty and humility.

On the east wall of the gallery, contiguous with the apse, is a **mosaic of Christ flanked by an emperor and empress**. The inscriptions over their heads read "Zoë, the most pious Augusta" and "Constantine in Christ, the Lord Autocrat, faithful Emperor of the Romans, Monomachus". It is believed that the two figures are those of Constantine IX Monomachus and the Empress Zoë, who ruled Byzantium in her own right with her sister Theodora before she married Constantine, her third husband. The explanation of why the head of Constantine and the inscription over his head have been changed may be that they were formerly those of one or other of his predecessors. The other mosaic in the south gallery, dating from 1118, depicts the **Virgin and Child between the Emperor John II Comnenus and the Empress Irene**, and their son Prince Alexius, added later. This is a livelier, less conventional work than that of Zoë and Constantine, with faces full of expression: the Virgin appears compassionate while Prince Alexius, who died soon after this portrait was executed, is depicted as a wan and sickly youth, his lined face presaging his premature death.

Other mosaics include a Virgin and Child in the apse and, one of the most beautiful of all the Aya Sofya mosaics, a **Virgin and Child flanked by two emperors**. The latter is located in the Vestibule of Warriors, now serving as an exit, and to see it you have to turn around and look upwards after you have passed through the magnificent Portal of the Emperor. Dated to the last quarter of the tenth century, it shows Emperor Justinian, to the right of the Virgin, offering a model of Aya Sofya, while the Emperor Constantine offers a model of the city of Constantinople. This is the only mosaic which has been properly spotlit, and the effect must be near to that originally intended by the artists.

What is left of the structures from Aya Sofya's time as a **mosque** are a *mihrab*, a *mimber*, a sultan's loge and the enormous wooden plaques which bear sacred Islamic names of God, the Prophet Mohammed and the first four caliphs. These and the inscription on the dome by the calligrapher Azzet Efendi all date from the time of the restoration by the Fossati brothers.

Topkapı Palace

The **Topkapı Palace** (daily 9.30am–5pm; winter closed Tues; $4) was both the symbolic and the political centre of the Ottoman Empire for nearly four centuries, from the construction by Mehmet the Conqueror of its oldest buildings – of which the present-day arms museum is the most complete example – until the removal of the imperial retinue to Dolmabahçe, by Sultan Abdül Mecid I in 1853. It is a beautiful setting in which to wander and contemplate the majesty of the Ottoman sultanate, as well as the cruelty exemplified by institutions like the harem and "the Cage".

In accordance with Islamic tradition, the palace consists of a collection of buildings arranged around a series of courtyards, similar to the Alhambra in Granada or a Moghul palace in India. The effect is extremely satisfying aesthetically, though it creates an initial impression of disorder. In fact the arrangement is meticulously logical, and the various adjustments made to the structure and function of the buildings over the centuries are indicative of shifting emphases in power in the Ottoman Empire (for example, a passageway was opened between the Harem and the Divan during the "Rule of the Harem", and in the eighteenth century, when the power of the sultan had declined, the offices of state were transferred away from the "Eye of the Sultan", the window in the Divan through which a sultan could monitor proceedings, and indeed from the palace altogether, to the gateway that led to the palaces of the Grand Vezir known as the Sublime Port).

Originally known as *Sarayı Cedid* or "new palace", Topkapı was built between 1459 and 1465 as the seat of government of the newly installed Ottoman regime. It was not at first a residence: Mehmet the Conqueror had already built what would become known as the old palace on the present site of İstanbul University, and even after he himself moved, his harem stayed on at the old site. The first courtyard was the service area of the palace, and open to all, while most of the second court and its attendant buildings were devoted to the Divan, the Council of State, and to those who had business with it. The pavilions of judges were located at the Orta Kapı (the entrance to the palace proper, between the first and second courtyards), in accordance with the tradition that justice should be dispensed at the gate of the palace.

The third courtyard was mainly given over to the palace school, an important imperial institution devoted to the training of civil servants, and it is only in the fourth courtyard that the serious business of state gives way to the more pleasurable aspects of life. Around the attractive gardens here are a number of pavilions erected by successive emperors in celebration of their victories and of the glorious views and the sunsets to be enjoyed in privileged retreat from their three- to four-thousand-member retinue.

The first courtyard and Aya Irene

Entering the first courtyard from the street through Mehmet the Conqueror's **Bab-ı Hümayün**, the great defensive imperial gate opposite the fountain of Ahmet III, all is taxi ranks and coaches and their disembarking tour parties: it's hard to believe that this is the outer courtyard of a former imperial palace. Such a mêlée, however, is entirely in keeping with the origins of the first courtyard, which, as the palace's service area, was always open to the general public. The **palace bakeries** are behind a wall to the right of the courtyard, and the buildings of the **imperial mint and outer treasury** are behind the wall north of Aya Irene (none of these is presently open). In front of Aya Irene were located the quarters of the straw-weavers and carriers of silver pitchers, around a central courtyard in which the palace firewood was stored, while the former church itself was variously employed as an armoury and storage space for archeological treasures.

Today, **Aya Irene**, "the Church of the Divine Peace", is closed to visitors, and it's next to impossible to obtain the necessary entrance papers. If you are prepared to enter into lengthy negotiations, you should approach the Directorate of Aya Sofya, located at the entrance of Aya Sofya, and proceed from there. Otherwise the only way to get in is for one of the occasional concerts of the İstanbul festival held here. The original church was one of the oldest in the city, but it was rebuilt along with Aya Sofya after being burnt down in the Nika riots of 532. Around the semicircular apse is the only **synthronon** (seating space for clergy in the apse of a church) in İstanbul to have survived the Byzantine era. It has six tiers of seats with an ambulatory running behind the fourth tier.

The second courtyard and the Divan

To reach the second courtyard you pass through the Bab-üs Selam, the Gate of Salutations, otherwise known as the **Orta Kapı** or middle gate. To the right of the gate, still in the first courtyard, is the ticket office and a useful list of the apartments and exhibitions open for viewing on the day in question (you'll need to pay separately for the guided tour of the Harem when you get there). Entering through Orta Kapı, with the gateway to the third courtyard straight ahead of you, the **Privy Stables of Mehmet II** (closed to the public) are on your immediate left, while beyond them are the buildings of the Divan and the Inner Treasury, and the entrance to the Harem. Opposite the Divan, on the right side of the courtyard, is the kitchen area.

The gardens between the paths radiating from the Orta Kapı are planted with ancient cypresses and plane trees, rose bushes and lawns. Originally they would also have been resplendent with peacocks, gazelles and most importantly with fountains. Running water, considered to have almost mystical properties by Muslims, was supplied in great quantity to the palace from the Byzantine cistern of Yerebatan Saray (see p.111). This **second courtyard** would have been the scene of pageantry during state ceremonies,

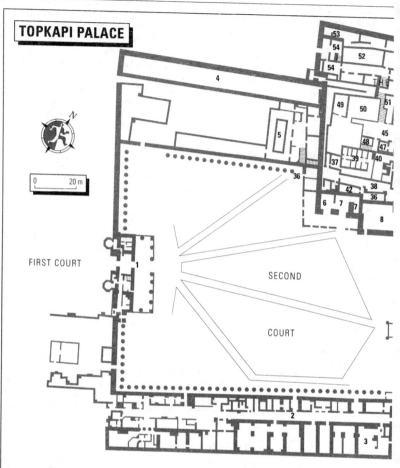

TOPKAPI PALACE

FIRST COURT

SECOND

COURT

1 Ortakapi or Middle Gate
2 Kitchens and cooks' quarters
   (Porcelain & glass collection)
3 Reconstructed kitchen
4 Stables and Harness rooms
5 Barrack of the Halberdiers
6 Hall of the Divan
7 Offices of the Divan
8 Inner Treasury (Arms & armour collection)
9 Gate of Felicity
10 Quarters of the White Eunuchs (Costume collection)
11 Throne room
12 Ahmet III library
13 Mosque of the school, now the library

14 Harem mosque
15 Court of the Room of the Robe
16 Room of the Robe of the Prophet
17 Rooms of the Relics of the Prophet
18 Hall of the Treasury
   (Sultans' portraits & miniture collection)
19 Hall of the Pantry (Museum Directorate)
20 Pavilion of Mehmet II, now the Treasury
21 Disrobing chamber of Selim II hamam
22 Site of Selim II hamam
23 Site of Selim II hamam boilers
24 Hall of the Expeditionary Force
25 Circumcision Köşkü
26 Terrace and bower

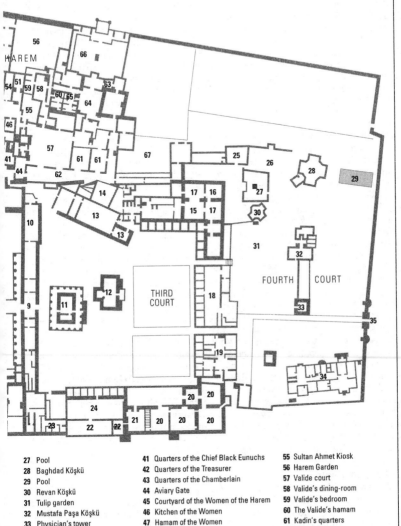

27 Pool
28 Baghdad Köşkü
29 Pool
30 Revan Köşkü
31 Tulip garden
32 Mustafa Paşa Köşkü
33 Physician's tower
34 Mecidiye Köşkü-restaurant
35 Third Gate
36 Entry to the Harem
37 Mosque of the Black Eunuchs
38 Court of the Black Eunuchs
39 Barrack of the Black Eunuchs
40 Princes' school

41 Quarters of the Chief Black Eunuchs
42 Quarters of the Treasurer
43 Quarters of the Chamberlain
44 Aviary Gate
45 Courtyard of the Women of the Harem
46 Kitchen of the Women
47 Hamam of the Women
48 Stairs to bedrooms
49 Laundry
50 Women's dormitory
51 Apartments of senior women
52 Court of women's hospital
53 Hospital hamam
54 Hospital kitchen quarters

55 Sultan Ahmet Kiosk
56 Harem Garden
57 Valide court
58 Valide's dining-room
59 Valide's bedroom
60 The Valide's hamam
61 Kadin's quarters
62 Golden Road
63 Ahmet III dining-room
64 The Throne Room Within
65 The Sultan's hamam
66 Osman III Terrace
67 Terrace of Selâmlik Garden

when the sultan would occupy his throne beneath the Bab-üs Saadet, the Gate of Felicity. At all times, even on one of the three days of the week when the courtyard was filled with petitioners to the Divan, silence reigned here, as people obeyed the rules of conduct imposed in the presence – actual or potential – of the sultan.

The buildings of the **Divan**, to the left of the courtyard, just beyond the entrance to the Harem, are historically fascinating. The metal grille in the Council Chamber (the first room on the left), is called "the Eye of the Sultan", through which he could observe the proceedings of the Divan, the eminent institution that took its name from the couch running around the three walls of this room. The building dates essentially from the reign of Mehmet the Conqueror, though it has been subsequently much altered. The Council Chamber was restored to its sixteenth-century appearance in 1945, with some of the original İznik tiles and arabesque painting. The other two rooms of the Divan have retained the Rococo decorations of Ahmet III.

The **Divan tower** is visible from many vantage points all over the city. It was rebuilt in 1825 by Mahmut II, to replace a squat-looking version with a pyramidal cap. The classical lines of the octagonal structure, with its tall windows between engaged Corinthian columns and its lead-covered conical spire, look rather out of place here, but it's certainly an impressive landmark, and a nice foil for the domes of the Divan. The tower is opened for strictly chaperoned guided tours twice a day: admission to the balconies is not allowed, but the panoramic Bosphorus views through the windows are exceptional. Ask at the entrance in the first courtyard for times of tours.

Next to the Divan is another building from Mehmet the Conqueror's original palace, the **Inner Treasury**, a six-domed hall preceded by a double-domed vestibule, and supported internally by three piers. The **exhibition of arms and armour** here juxtaposes much exquisite craftsmanship with barbaric-looking exhibits such as a seventeenth-century executioner's sword, and some seven-foot-long double-handed swords which wearied Europeans were relieved of during one Turkish campaign or another. It is also interesting to compare the swords of various Ottoman sultans, that of the Conqueror appearing altogether more effective than the more finely wrought example attributed to that patron of the arts, Süleyman the Magnificent.

Across the courtyard are the **palace kitchens**, with their magnificent rows of chimneys, best seen in profile from a distance (for example from Kennedy Bulvarı, which runs around the Marmara shore). Much of this complex was destroyed by fire in 1574, and the chimneys were reconstructed by Mimar Sinan, as were eight of the ten domes behind them (the two southernmost domes date to the reign of Mehmet the Conqueror). The ten kitchens, which had a staff of 1500, all served different purposes. The two at the far end, where sweets and *helva* were made, have been restored complete with a fascinating array of utensils. The other rooms of the kitchen complex house a collection of some of the finest porcelain in the world, an ever-changing display continually replenished from the vast Topkapı collection.

The third courtyard

Passing through the **Bab-üs Saadet**, the Gate of Felicity, the throne room is immediately in front of you. This building, mainly dating from the reign of Selim I, was where the sultan awaited the outcome of sessions of the Divan in order to give his assent or otherwise to their proposals. The grey marble building at the centre of the third courtyard, the **library of Ahmet III**, is not generally open to the public. It is restrained and sombre compared to his highly decorative fountain outside the gates of the palace.

On the southwest side, to either side of the Bab-üs Saadet, are the rooms of the **Palace School**, where boys aged ten or more recruited from Christian families (a process known as the *Devşirme*) were converted to Islam and educated to become members of the janissary corps or even future administrators of the empire. The room to the left of the entrance houses a collection of embroidery and a very small selection from the imperial costume collection. The latter includes a charming little outfit of Selim I's – red with yellow circles – begging the question of where he could have acquired his epithet "the Grim". Beyond the school to the right are the **Seferli Odası**, used as lodgings or a gym for pages, and the hamam of Selim the Sot, who fell there in a drunken stupor and died later of his injuries.

The Treasury

The **Pavilion of the Conqueror** takes up most of the southeast side of the third court-yard, to the right of the entrance. The building is on two floors, and a colonnaded ter-race leads from the courtyard into the lower rooms, which would originally have been employed as service rooms. The interior plasterwork of these apartments, including shell-shaped niches, stalactite capitals and ogee (slightly pointed) arches over the win-dows, is typical of the fifteenth century. The first two rooms – the right-hand one of which was used as the *camekân* or changing room of the hamam of Selim II – are beau-tifully proportioned and domed. The last two rooms are at right angles, with an attrac-tive loggia at the angle where they meet.

The **Topkapı treasury** is housed in these four rooms of the Conqueror's Pavilion. The first room contains a number of highly wrought and extremely beautiful objects, including a delicate silver model of a palace complete with tiny crabs and birds in the trees, a present to Abdül Hamid II from Japan, and a seventeenth-century music box decorated with palm trees and an elephant. The next two rooms – memorials to the excesses and bad taste of the megalomaniacal – are always thronged, and there are cer-tainly plenty of thrills to be had if you like your gemstones big and your precious met-als abundant. In any case, you may as well give up struggling with your sense of pro-portion and resign yourself to the larger-than-life dimensions of imperial wealth and ostentation.

The big crowd-puller in room two is the **Topkapı Dagger**, which starred alongside Peter Ustinov in the Sunday matinee classic *Topkapı*. A present from Murat I to Nadir Shah, which was waylaid and brought back when news of the Shah's death reached Topkapı, the dagger is decorated with three enormous emeralds, one of which conceals a watch (suggesting rather different attitudes to time and mortality than those you'll find in modern-day crime fiction, where watches are more likely to conceal weapons than vice versa).

In the third room the **Spoonmaker's Diamond**, the fifth largest diamond in the world, is invariably surrounded by a gawping throng, who perhaps give some impres-sion of the effect it must have had during its first public appearance, on Mehmet IV's turban at his coronation in 1648. The golden ceremonial throne which was presented by the governor of Egypt to Murat III on his accession in 1574 is accompanied by an unfortunate photograph of Selim III, made to look dreadfully puny and insignificant by its odd dimensions. The rest of this room is a succession of exhibits increasingly grotesque and jewel-studded, and you might well be tempted to make good your escape.

The fourth room boasts another jewel-encrusted throne (believed to have been pre-sented to Mahmut I by Nadir Shah, who never received his return gift of the Topkapı Dagger), and the hand and occipital bone of John the Baptist, but otherwise it's a rela-tive haven of restraint and good taste. Ivory and sandalwood objects predominate, refreshingly simple materials whose comparative worth is determined by craftsman-ship rather than quantity, so you don't feel obliged to make interminable calculations of the current market value of every object on display.

Across the courtyard from the treasury, the **Pavilion of the Holy Mantle** houses the holy relics brought home by Selim the Grim after his conquest of Egypt in 1517. The relics were originally viewed only by the sultan, his family and his immediate entourage on days of special religious significance, but were opened to the public in

1962. They include a footprint, hair and a tooth of the Prophet Mohammed, as well as his mantle and standard, swords of the first four caliphs, and a letter from the Prophet to the leader of the Coptic tribe. The most precious of the relics are kept behind glass, attractively arranged and lit.

Next to this, the former Hall of the Treasury now houses a selection from Topkapı's **Collection of Paintings and Miniatures**. The miniatures date from the reign of Süleyman the Magnificent to that of Ahmet III, the Tulip Age, but above all they come from the reign of Murat III. He commissioned three works, the *Hürname* (the "Book of Accomplishments"), the *Shahanshahname* (the "Book of the King of Kings") and the *Surname* (the "Book of Festivals"), the first two of which glorified the exploits of the sultans, while the last was a depiction of the circumcision ceremony of the sultan's son (nowadays Turks make home videos on the same theme). One of the illustrations from the *Surname*, "A Parade of Mule Drivers", shows the Serpentine Column from the Hippodrome (see p.104) complete with its three heads, and the sultan seated in a pavilion next to the Palace of İbrahim Paşa. A very small selection of the works of Siyah Kalem ("the Black Pen") are also on display, and feature unique and beautiful depictions of wrinkled old men and highly animated devils, as well as meticulously observed animal life. No longer believed to be by the hand of a single artist, they are thought to relate to a fourteenth- or fifteenth-century nomadic society, from either Turkestan or Transoxania, which held shamanistic beliefs. Upstairs in the gallery are rarely displayed portraits of the sultans.

The fourth courtyard

The **fourth courtyard** is entered through a passageway running between the Hall of the Treasury and the display of clocks and watches in the Silahdar Treasury (closed at the time of writing). It consists of several gardens, each graced with pavilions where sultans would take their pleasure. There are spectacular views of the setting sun and the sea, and sprawling gardens complete with fountains and darkened retreats. The most attractive of the pavilions, from which you get a totally new perspective of the city from Galata to Fatih, are located around a wide marble terrace beyond the tulip gardens of Ahmet III.

The **Baghdad Köşkü**, the cruciform building to the north of the terrace, is the only one presently open to the public. It was built by Murat IV to celebrate the conquest of Baghdad in 1638. The exterior and cool, dark interior are tiled in blue, turquoise and white, and the shutters and cupboard doors are inlaid with tortoiseshell and mother-of-pearl. Only the recent repainting of the dome – red on leather – is out of keeping with the general effect.

If you think the pavilion is redolent of unseemly excess, take a look at the attractive pool and marble fountain on the terrace, scene of debauched revels among İbrahim I and the women of his harem. Deli İbrahim, also known as **İbrahim the Mad**, emerged dangerously insane from 22 years in the Cage, his reign culminating in a fit of sexual jealousy when he ordered death by drowning in the Bosphorus for the 280 concubines of his harem – only one of them lived to tell the tale, when she escaped from the sack in which she was bound and was picked up by a passing French ship and taken to Paris. In one of his calmer moments İbrahim built the **İftariye Köşkü**, the little balcony with a bronze canopy set into the white marble balustrade of the terrace, naming it after the evening meal at which the day's fast is broken during Ramadan.

The **Sünnet Odası** (Circumcision Room), in the Portico of Columns above the terrace, also dates from the reign of İbrahim the Mad. During renovation you'll have to peer through the windows to get any idea of the interior, but outside it's covered in İznik tiles of the sixteenth and early seventeenth centuries. There doesn't seem to be much of a design about these – any number of different patterns are represented – but they include some of the most beautiful panels from the very best İznik period. At the other end of the Portico of Columns is the Revan Köşkü, built to commemorate the capture of Erivan in the Caucasus by Mehmet IV.

The **Mecidiye Köşkü** – the last building to be erected at Topkapı – commands the best view of any of the Topkapı pavilions; on a clear day from its garden terrace you can identify most of the buildings on the Asian shore of the Bosphorus, and appropriately it's been opened as a restaurant and terrace **café**. It's pricy, so best not to time things so that you arrive here famished, but it's a lovely place to while away a few hours over a long drink.

The Harem

The **tour of the Harem** (daily 10am–4pm, hourly from the Harem entrance in the second courtyard; $2.50) is the most popular aspect of a visit to Topkapı, so arrive early as tickets can sell out in mid-season, and the queues are massive later in the day. The best of the rooms include Ahmet III's dining room with its fruity frescoes, and the newly renovated women's dormitories – all now open to the public. The tour is conducted at breakneck speed, but can be interesting with a little background knowledge and a few pertinent questions.

The word *harem* means "forbidden" in Arabic; in Turkish it refers to a suite of apartments in a palace or private residence where the head of the household lived with his wives, odalisques (female slaves) and children. The harem in Topkapı lies between the sultan's private apartments – the Circumcision Room, Revan Pavilion and Apartment of the Holy Mantle of the Prophet – and the apartments of the Chief Black Eunuch. It consists of over four hundred rooms.

The **harem women** were so shrouded in mystery that they became a source of great fascination to the world in general. The most renowned among them was probably Haseki Hürrem, or Roxelana as she was known in the West, wife of Süleyman the Magnificent. Prior to their marriage, it was unusual for a sultan to marry at all, let alone to choose a wife from among his concubines. The marriage, and the subsequent installation of the harem women in the palace, established the women of the harem, and especially the **Valide Sultan** (the mother of the reigning sultan), in a position of unprecedented power. This was the beginning of a new age of harem intrigue, in which women began to take more control over affairs of state.

Roxelana began this new order in characteristic vein: she persuaded Süleyman to murder both his grand vizier, İbrahim Paşa, and his son, the heir apparent, Mustafa – the latter in order to make way for her own son, Selim the Sot. The favourite of Selim the Sot, **Nur Banu**, made a significant change to the layout of the harem when she became Valide Sultan in her turn. She moved her suite of apartments from one end of the Golden Road to the other, so that it was located next to that of her son, Murat III. She was now lodged near to the entrance of the Divan, and could easily listen in on affairs of state. Nur Banu encouraged her son in debauchery (he fathered a total of 103 children, 54 of whom survived him) and persuaded him to murder his most able minister, the grand vizier Sokollu Mehmet Paşa.

The number of **odalisques** employed in the harem increased steadily with the decline of the Ottoman Empire. During the reign of Mahmut I (1730–1754) there were 688 odalisques in Topkapı, excluding those who served the sultan personally. Most of these were servants to the Valide Sultan, the first wives and favourites. By the reign of Abdülaziz (1861–1876) this number had increased to 809. Many of the Ottoman odalisques were imported from Georgia and Caucasia for their looks, or they were prisoners of war, captured in Hungary, Poland or Venice. Upon entering the harem, they would become the charges of the *haznedar usta*, who would teach them how to behave towards the sultan and the other palace inhabitants. The conditions in which the majority of these women lived were dangerously unhygienic, and many of them died from vermin- and waterborne diseases, or from the cold of an İstanbul winter. The women who were chosen to enter the bedchamber of the sultan, however, were promoted to the rank of imperial odalisque, given slaves to serve them and pleasant accommodation, and if they bore a child, they would be promoted to the rank of favourite or wife, with their own apartments. If the sultan subsequently lost affection for one of these women, he could give her in marriage to one of his courtiers. The following account of life in the Topkapı harem, given by Hafsa Sultan, a wife of Mustafa II (1695–1703), dispels a couple of popular myths about life there:

The claims that the sultan throws a handkerchief at the girl he prefers are quite untrue. The sultan asks the Chief Black Eunuch to call whichever of the girls he desires, and his other women take her to the baths, perfume her body and dress her gracefully in clothes appropriate to the circumstances. The sultan sends the girl a gift, and afterwards goes to the room where she is. There is no truth either in the claim that the girl crawls to the sultan's bed.

THE BUILDINGS

The harem centred around the suites of the sultan and the Valide Sultan. Around these, in descending order of rank, were the apartments of the wives, favourites, sultan's daughters, princes, housekeepers, maids and odalisques. The harem was connected to the outside world by means of the **Carriage Gate**, probably so-called because the odalisques would have entered their carriages here when they went on outings. To the left of the Carriage Gate as you enter the Harem are the barracks of the Halberdiers of the Long Tresses, who carried logs and other loads into the Harem. The Halberdiers, who also served as imperial guardsmen, were only employed at certain hours, and even then they were blinkered. The Carriage Gate and the Aviary Gate were both guarded by black eunuchs, who were responsible for running the harem, but only allowed to enter in daylight hours. At night the female housekeepers took charge, and reported any unusual occurrences to the Chief Black Eunuch.

The **Court of the Black Eunuch**, the first area to be visited on a tour, dates mainly from a rebuilding programme begun after the great fire of July 24, 1665. The fire, started by a malicious servant, damaged most of the Harem as well as the Divan. The tiles in the eunuchs' quarters date from the seventeenth century, suggesting that the originals were destroyed in the fire.

The *Altın Yol* or **Golden Road** ran the entire length of the Harem, from the quarters of the Black Eunuch to the Fourth Courtyard. It was down this road in 1808 that the last of the great Valide Sultans, Aimée Dubbucq de Rivery, fled with her son Mahmut to escape the deaf mutes, hired assassins of the janissaries. The life of the prince was saved by a Georgian odalisque called Cevri Khalfa, who flung a brazier of red-hot coals into the faces of the pursuers. The prince escaped to become Mahmut II, later given the title of "reformer". Strategically located at the beginning of the Golden Road were the **apartments of the Valide Sultan**, also rebuilt after 1665. They include a particularly lovely domed dining room. A passageway leads from her apartments to those of the women she controlled, the senior women of the court. These were well-designed, compact apartments, with an upper gallery in which bedding was stored, windows and a hearth.

Beyond the Valide Sultan's apartments, to the north, are some of the most attractive rooms of the palace. These were the apartments and reception rooms of the *selâmlik*, the sultans' own rooms. The largest and grandest of them is the **Hünkar Sofrası**, the Imperial Hall, where the sultan entertained visitors. Another important room in this section is a masterwork of the architect Sinan: the **bedchamber of Murat III**. This is covered in sixteenth-century İznik tiles, including an inscription of verses from the Koran, and is kitted out with a marble fountain and, opposite, a bronze fireplace surrounded by a panel of tiling representing plum blossom.

THE CAGE

The Cage was adopted by Ahmet I as an alternative to fratricide, which had become institutionalized in the Ottoman Empire since the days of Beyazit II. To avoid wars of succession, Beyazit ruled that a sultan should execute his brothers upon his accession to the throne. The Cage was introduced as a way around this practice, but in the event proved a less than satisfactory solution. After the death of their father, the younger princes would be incarcerated along with deaf mutes and a harem of concubines, while their eldest brother acceded to the throne. They remained in the suite of rooms of the Harem known in Turkish as *Kafes* (the Cage) until such time as they were called upon to take power themselves. The concubines never left the Cage unless they became pregnant, and great care was taken to prevent this, either by the removal of their ovaries or by the use of pessaries, since if it did occur they were immediately drowned.

The decline of the Ottoman Empire has in part been attributed to the institution of the Cage. The sultans who spent any length of time there emerged crazed, avaricious and debauched. Osman II, for example, enjoyed archery, but only when using live targets, including prisoners of war and his own pages. He was assassinated by the janissaries, to be replaced by Mustafa I, who had all but died of starvation in the Cage, and was even more mad than his predecessor. He too was assassinated. The worst affected of all, however, was İbrahim, better known as Deli İbrahim (İbrahim the Mad). He spent 22 years in the Cage, and when they came to take him out he was so sure he was about to be assassinated that he had to be removed forcibly. His reign was characterized by sexual excess and political misrule (his mother Közem once complained that there was not enough wood for the Harem fires, and he responded by having his grand vizier executed). Eventually, in response to a rumour of harem intrigue, İbrahim had all of his 280 concubines (excluding his favourite, Şeker Para) drowned in the Bosphorus.

The northernmost rooms of the Harem are supported by immense piers and vaults, providing capacious basements used as dormitories and storerooms. Below the bedchamber is a large indoor **swimming pool**, with taps for hot and cold water, and is where Murat is supposed to have thrown gold to women that pleased him. Next to the bedchamber is the light and airy **library of Ahmet I**, with windows overlooking both the Bosphorus and the Golden Horn; beyond this is the **dining room of Ahmet III**, whose walls are covered in wood panelling painted with bowls of fruit and flowers, typical of the extravagant tulip-loving sultan. To the southwest of the bedchamber are two rooms originally thought to be the notorious **Cage**, though this is no longer believed to be the case: the Cage was actually situated in various rooms on the floor above.

Other rooms which you may visit on a tour of the Harem are the newly restored **dormitories** of the favourite women, located up stone stairs on a beautiful terrace overlooking the fourth courtyard, and the **boating pool** of Murat III.

It's usual for tours to depart from the Harem by way of the **Aviary Gate**, or Kuzhane Kapısı. One of the most infamous of all the Valide Sultans, Mahpeyker Sultan, also known as *Köşem*, "the leader", was assassinated here. She was the effective ruler of the Ottoman Empire during the reigns of her two sons, Murat IV and İbrahim the Mad, and since she was not banished to the old palace after the death of İbrahim (as was customary), she also ruled during the reign of her grandson Mehmet IV. She was eventually murdered on the orders of a jealous rival, the new Valide Turhan Hatice, by the Chief Black Eunuch. At the age of eighty the toothless old woman was stripped naked and strangled, after allegedly putting up a ferocious struggle.

Gulhane Parkı, the archeological museums and the Çinili Köşk

Gulhane Parkı was once the gardens of Topkapı Palace. It is now a public park and the location of free open-air concerts. Performers include *arabesk* musicians and belly dancers, neither of which can be broadcast by the Turkish media because they're considered to be low-class and Arabic-influenced. The park is also home to a rather sordid little **zoo**, with exhibits like caged dogs.

THE ARCHEOLOGY MUSEUM

The Archeology Museum complex can be entered either through Gulhane Parkı or from the first courtyard of the Topkapı Palace. Here you will find the **Archeology Museum** itself (daily except Mon 9.30am–4.30pm; $2.50, includes the Museum of the Ancient Orient or Çinili Köşk), built in the nineteenth century to house antiquities previously stored in the Çinili Köşk and acquisitions of the director of ancient antiquities, Hamdi Bey. It was his excavations at Sidon in 1887 that brought to light the group of sarcophagi, including the Alexander Sarcophagus, the Sarcophagus of the Mourning Women and the Lycian Sarcophagus, which are the chief exhibits of the museum. The monuments found at Sidon are of Phoenician origin but of quite disparate styles, evidence of the variety of influences absorbed into Phoenician culture from neighbouring civilizations.

Downstairs, the **Alexander Sarcophagus** is immediately to the left of the entrance lobby, in Room 8. It's covered with scenes of Alexander the Great hunting and in battle, but since Alexander himself is known to have been buried in Alexandria this is no longer believed to be his sarcophagus. Despite its Hellenistic influences, different sources variously ascribe it to a ruler of the Seleucid dynasty or to the Phoenician Prince Abdolonyme, but there seems to be agreement in dating the sarcophagus to the end of the fourth century BC. The metal weapons originally held by warriors and huntsmen on the sarcophagi were stolen prior to the excavations of Hamdi Bey, presumably when the burial chambers were looted.

The Ionic architecture of another of the Sidon sarcophagi, the **Sarcophagus of the Mourning Women**, is repeated in the exterior of the museum itself. This one shows eighteen members of the harem of King Straton (who died in 360 BC) in various poses of distress and mourning. To drive the point home, a funeral cortege is shown proceeding around the lid of the sarcophagus. As with the Alexander Sarcophagus, traces of the original paintwork can still be seen on the surface of the marble.

The **Lycian Sarcophagus** (Room 9) depicts centaurs, sphinxes and griffons, as well as scenes from Greek mythology. It is in the Lycian style, but the carvings show a Peloponnesian influence in the stocky bodies and broad faces of the human figures. In the same room are the anthropoid sarcophagi from Sidon, which illustrate the fifth-century BC fashion for Egyptian models in Greek sculpture. The **Tabnit Sarcophagus**, the oldest Sidon discovery, is in fact Egyptian in origin. A hieroglyphic inscription on the chest of this alabaster mummy case states that it belonged to an Egyptian commander named Penephtah, and a later inscription suggests that Tabnit, himself the father of a pharaoh, was its second occupant.

The **Sidamara Sarcophagus** (Room 3) dates from the third century AD and is the most important remaining example of its type. This room is full of similar sarcophagi, discovered elsewhere in Anatolia; on many of them a hand-held drill has been used for much of the carving, especially of the foliage, which is roughly executed in comparison with the Sidon sarcophagi.

The **upper rooms** of the museum have been renovated, a project which earned the museum the 1993 Council of Europe award for its contribution to European culture. This may be an anomaly since the exhibits are exclusively non-European artefacts, but recognition is well deserved for beautiful, well-lit displays, thorough explanatory aids, audiovisual back-up and a comfortable environment that encourages visitors to linger, a far cry from Turkey's provincial museums where nervous curators follow you about switching lights on and off. Exhibits worth mentioning range from jewellery discovered at Troy – some beautiful gold work including a head ornament with leaves as fine as paper – and Phrygian finds from near Arslantaş, the lion rock-cut tomb near Afyon Karahisar. Photos associate finds with their place of discovery, giving them space which is usually robbed by museum showcases.

If you really want to get a thorough perspective on the exhibits then the explanatory video (10am, 11.30am, 1.30pm & 3.30pm) is obligatory viewing. It explains the continuing traditions of building, storage and nutrition from 10,000 BC to the present day in Anatolian Turkey.

THE MUSEUM OF THE ANCIENT ORIENT

The **Museum of the Ancient Orient** (Wed, Fri & Sun 9.30am–5pm) contains a small but dazzling collection of Anatolian, Egyptian and Mesopotamian artefacts. The late-Hittite basalt lions flanking the entrance look newly hewn, but they actually date from the ninth century BC, giving a taste of the incredible state of preservation of some of the exhibits inside.

These include the oldest peace treaty known to mankind, the **Treaty of Kadesh** (1280–1269 BC), which was signed when a battle fought on the River Orontes (today's Ası Nehri in Anatolia), between Pharaoh Ramses II and the Hittite king Muvatellish, ended in a stalemate. The treaty includes an agreement of bilateral ceasefire and pledges of a mutual exchange of political refugees, and was originally engraved onto silver tablets. None of these survive, though the treaty was also inscribed in hieroglyphics on the mortuary temple of Ramses II in Thebes, and the copy on display in the museum was uncovered during excavations at the site of the Hittite capital of Hattuşaş (see p.600). A recent copy of the treaty decorates the entrance to the UN building in New York.

The blue and yellow **animal relief** in the corridor (Room 2) beyond the first room dates from the reign of Nebuchadnezzar (604–562 BC), the last hero-king of Babylonia, when it would have lined the processional way in Babylon, leading from the Ishtar gate to a sanctuary where New Year festivities were held. Other of the exhibits in the museum were taken from the palace-museum of Nebuchadnezzar, located at the Ishtar gate. Another massive relief, in Room 8, depicts the **Hittite king Urpalla** presenting gifts of grapes and grain to a vegetation god three times his own size, wearing a rather attractive pair of curly-toed boots. This is a plaster copy of a relief found at İvriz Kaya near Konya, dating from the eighth century BC.

Other exhibits include a **Sumerian** love poem and a tablet of Sumerian proverbs dating from the eighteenth century BC, and a figure of a duck (Room 2), with an inscription which identifies it as a standard weight belonging to a priest called Musallim Marduk. It weighs about 30 kilograms and has been dated to around 2000 BC, making it the oldest known standard measure.

ÇİNİLİ KÖŞK

The graceful **Cinili Köşk** (Tiled Pavilion) is the oldest secular building in İstanbul, its design and decoration influenced by Selçuk art. Built in 1472 as a kind of grandstand from which the sultan could watch sporting activities like wrestling or polo, it now houses a museum of ceramics (Tues, Thurs & Sat 9.30am–5pm). Tiles of equal quality to those in Topkapı Palace and İstanbul's older mosques can be seen here, and while there is no substitute for seeing tile panels *in situ*, here they can be inspected at close quarters and in good lighting conditions, along with well-written explanations of the different periods in the history of Turkish ceramics. Look particularly for polychrome tiles of the mid-sixteenth to mid-seventeenth centuries, the longest and most successful period of tile production. Interesting exhibits include a mosque lamp from the

Sokollu Mehmet Paşa Camii, a ceramic coffee cooler in which beans were placed after roasting and before grinding, and Murat III's attractive little fountain in the wall of the last room of all, after the İznik collection.

The Hippodrome

The arena of the **Hippodrome**, formerly the cultural focus of the Byzantine Empire, is now the site of a long and narrow municipal park, the **At Meydanı** or Square of Horses. This rather unprepossessing strip of land with a road running around its perimeter is overshadowed by the Palace of İbrahim Paşa on one side and Sultan Ahmet Camii on the other, but its historical significance predates that of most other major monuments in İstanbul.

Nowadays taxis rather than chariots perform laps of honour around the stadium, which was constructed by the Byzantine emperor Septimius Severus in 200 AD, and later enlarged by Constantine the Great for the performance of court ceremonies and games. The original orientation and dimensions of the 480-metre-long arena have been more or less preserved by the present-day park, although its amphitheatre was destroyed in the construction of the Sultan Ahmet mosque, and its semicircular south end is now the site of the Marmara University rectorate. Part of an arcade of columns was still in place at the south end until 1550, when it was pulled down to be used as building material. But, as can be seen from miniatures in the *Surname* of Murat III (see p.98), the Hippodrome continued to be a focus of state ceremony for the Ottoman sultans.

The large open space would now be little more than a pleasant respite from the surrounding hubbub if interest in its origins were not aroused by the monuments strewn in seemingly haphazard fashion throughout its length. Down at the south end of the park are three survivors of the array of obelisks, columns and statues that originally adorned the spina, the raised central axis of the arena, around which chariots raced.

The northernmost of these, the **Egyptian Obelisk**, was originally 60m tall, but only the upper third survived shipment from Egypt in the fourth century. The obelisk itself was commissioned to commemorate the campaigns of Thutmos III in Egypt during the sixteenth century BC, but the scenes on its base commemorate its erection in Constantinople under the direction of Theodosius I. Among the figures depicted are dancing maidens with musicians, Theodosius and his family watching a chariot race (south side), and a group of captives kneeling to pay homage to Theodosius (west side).

The **Serpentine Column** comes from the Temple of Apollo at Delphi, where it was dedicated to the god by the 31 Greek cities which defeated the Persians at Plataea in 479 BC. It was brought to Constantinople by Constantine the Great. The three intertwining bronze serpents originally had heads, which splayed out in three directions from the column itself. The jaw of one of the serpents was lopped off by Mehmet the Conqueror on his arrival in Constantinople, as an act of defiance against such symbols of idolatry, and the remaining heads were probably removed in an act of vandalism at the beginning of the eighteenth century. As a result of this dismemberment and of the discoloration of the bronze, the statue is now sadly lacking in grace or beauty. One of the heads is on display in the "İstanbul through the ages" exhibit at the archeological museum.

The third ancient monument on the spina is a huge lump of masonry, a 32-metre-high column of little or no decorative or practical worth. The emperor Constantine Porphyrogenitus was presumably of this opinion in the tenth century, since he restored the pillar and sheathed it in gold-plated bronze. This ornamentation was taken and melted down by the Crusaders during the Sack of Constantinople in 1204. The origins of the column, known as the **Column of Constantine**, are uncertain, but an inscription records that it was already decayed when Constantine restored it.

CROWD TROUBLE IN CONSTANTINOPLE

The **Hippodrome factions** originated in ancient Roman trade guilds, which in Byzantine times developed further associations: "the Blues" were generally upper-class, politically conservative and orthodox regarding religion, while "the Greens" were from the lower classes, more radical in their political and religious views.

The factions were a focus for serious rivalry in Constantinople, centred on the circus events in the Hippodrome. In 532 the rivalry was forgotten when members of the Blue faction combined forces with the Greens against the emperor Justinian in protest at heavy taxation, and in the resulting riots – which derived their name from the battle cry *Nika* (Victory) – much of the city, including the church of Aya Sofya, was destroyed. It was the former courtesan, Empress Theodora, who eventually shamed Justinian to action, and as a result 30,000 Greens and a few hundred Blues were trapped and massacred by the forces of General Belisarius in the Hippodrome. Chariot racing was banned for some time after this, and it was a number of years before the Green faction recovered to the extent where they could compete in either the sporting or the political arena.

A work of rather more aesthetic merit at the north end of the park is the **fountain of Kaiser Wilhelm II**, funds for which were donated by the Kaiser to Abdül Hamid II in 1895 – evidence of the close relationship between these two rulers. As Crown Prince, Wilhelm had been charmed by the sultan and described his meeting with him as "one of the most interesting encounters I have ever had with foreign princes".

Sultan Ahmet Camii: the Blue Mosque

It is impossible to remain for long in the Hippodrome without becoming aware of the **Sultan Ahmet Camii**, the Blue Mosque, on its southeast side. In the unlikely event that the mosque's imposing size fails to impress itself upon you, your attention will doubtless be drawn to it by some persistent youth who wishes to guide you around it. Despite its fame, however, Sultan Ahmet is not really the place to start developing a taste for oriental interiors: here it's size and visibility that counts rather than any architectural or aesthetic merits.

Before construction was begun, in 1609, objections were raised to the plan of a **six-minareted mosque** – partly because it was said to be unholy to rival the six minarets of the mosque at Mecca, but also because it would be a great drain on state revenues at a time when the empire was contracting in size. The true cause of the objections, however, probably had more to do with the need to destroy several palaces belonging to imperial ministers to make way for construction.

From the **outside**, the building is undeniably impressive, particularly on the all-important approach from the Topkapı Palace. An imposing mass of grey stone, it's visible for miles around on its hilltop vantage point and instantly recognizable thanks to the its six minarets. Above the level of the courtyard the mosque is a mass of shallow domes and domed turrets, hardly broken by a single straight line. Its courtyard is best approached from the attractive and graceful west portal, which bears a calligraphic inscription by the father of the travel writer Evliya Celebi. The courtyard is surrounded by a portico of thirty small domes, recently repainted, and has the same dimensions as the mosque itself.

The mosque is best entered through the courtyard, despite signs in English and German asking visitors to use the side entrance facing Aya Sofya. Lone tourists, as opposed to groups, will not create ill-will by entering here as long as they are suitably covered (limbs for men and women, heads for women) and do not intrude on worshippers. At the side entrance, you will invariably encounter large crowds, and shoe keepers will demand money as you leave – don't feel obliged to contribute since their behaviour makes a mockery of the Islamic faith.

The main disadvantage of entering through the courtyard is that the glaring sun reflected from pale marble dazzles the eyes, and the first impression on entry can be one of total darkness. When this subsides, piled semidomes and vast spaciousness combine with the overall blue of the gallery tiles to create a pleasant effect – it is only when the architecture is considered in perspective that its imperfections become evident.

Four **"elephant foot" pillars** (so called because of their size and clumsiness) of five metres in diameter impose their disproportionate dimensions, appearing squashed against the outer walls and obscuring parts of the building from every angle. The pillars also dwarf the modest dome they support, rendering their immense proportions ridiculous. The mosque has a four-leaf-clover shape, with semidomes flanked by smaller semidomes to north, south, east and west, and is made more interesting by a balcony running around three sides. The corners are a pleasing arrangement of semidomes and stalactite pendentives, with arches connecting the pillars to the wall.

The name "Blue Mosque" is derived from the predominantly blue colour of the decoration. The walls and arches are covered in **arabesque stencilling**, unattractive and of poor quality. The **windows** are brightly coloured but badly designed – the original stained glass was best-quality Venetian but even that caused an effect of gloominess – and many of the carpets on the floor are worn. The main attraction are the **tiles**: over twenty thousand of them, constituting such a tall order that the İznik kilns were practically exhausted. Still in evidence are the clear bright colours of the best period of late sixteenth-century İznik ware, including flower and tree panels as well as more abstract designs. They are difficult to see in the gloominess of the interior, and the best panels, in the galleries, are all but obscured by the columns of the arcades while renovation continues.

A more serious obstacle is the **fence** that prevents non-Muslim visitors from entering two-thirds of the mosque interior. This renders any examination of the attractive *mihrab* and *mimber* and the sultan's loge impossible, so after a cursory inspection of what is visible from behind the fence it might be as well to curtail your visit in favour of some other more welcoming environment.

At the northeast corner of the Sultan Ahmet complex is the richly decorated and elegant **royal pavilion**, approached by ramp and giving access to the sultan's loge inside the mosque – the ramp meant that the sultan could ride his horse right up to the door of his chambers. The royal pavilion now houses a **museum of carpets** (*Halı Müzesi*; Tues–Sat 9am–noon & 1–4pm; $1), while the old stables of the mosque, reached by taking the road downhill past the ramp and turning right, house a **kilim and flatweave museum** (*Kilim ve Düz Dokuma Müzesi*; same opening hours, included in price). Both museums trace the history of their respective art forms through the ages, and include some ancient, priceless pieces.

The Tomb of Sultan Ahmet

Outside the precinct wall to the northwest of the mosque is the *türbe* or **tomb of Sultan Ahmet** (daily except Mon 9.30am–4.30pm). Buried here along with the sultan are his wife and three of his sons, two of whom (Osman II and Murat IV) ruled in their turn. This successive rule of brothers was only possible because Sultan Ahmet had introduced the institution of the Cage, thus relieving himself and his sons of the burden of fratricide upon accession to the throne. Unfortunately both Ahmet's own brother Mustafa and his son Osman were completely mad and unfit to rule by the time they left the Cage to take up the reins of office, and Murat IV only escaped this fate by succeeding to the throne at the age of ten, before the conditions in the Cage had affected him. The tomb, like the mosque, is decorated with seventeenth-century İznik tiles and contains various **holy relics**, including a turban from Yahya Efendi's tomb.

İbrahim Paşa Sarayı: The Museum of Turkish and Islamic Art

The **İbrahim Paşa Sarayı** (Palace of İbrahim Paşa), on the other side of the Hippodrome, is now the Türk ve İslam Eserleri Müzesi, the **Museum of Turkish and Islamic Art** (Tues–Sun 10am–5pm; $2.50), an attractive, well-planned museum, containing what is probably the best-exhibited collection of Islamic artefacts in the world. It is certainly more impressive than the Museum of Islamic Art in Paris, partly because the sixteenth-century setting of cool, darkened rooms around a central garden courtyard obviate the necessity for expensive technology to keep the sun off the exhibits, but also because it gives a better idea of the wealth and complexity of Islamic art and culture. The museum also boasts an excellent courtyard café, serving good-value homemade cake.

The İbrahim Paşa Sarayı is one of the few private Ottoman residences to have survived – at least in part – the fires which periodically destroy large areas of the city. Much of the building has, however, disappeared, and what remains was rebuilt in stone – to the original plan – in 1843. Completed in 1524 for İbrahim Paşa, Süleyman the Magnificent's newly appointed grand vizier, the palace is a fitting memorial to one of the most able statesmen of his time, whose abilities were matched only by his accumulation of wealth and power. His status can be judged from the proportions of the palace's rooms, and by its prominent position next to the Hippodrome: later sultans were to use its balconies to watch the festivities below. İbrahim controlled the affairs of war and state of the Ottoman Empire for thirteen years, and fell from grace partly as a result of the schemings of Süleyman's wife Roxelana. Even so, it doesn't seem unreasonable that Süleyman should distrust a servant who could say to a foreign ambassador: "If I command that something should be done, and he [the sultan] has commanded to the contrary, my wishes and not his are obeyed". The body of İbrahim Paşa was found in a room of Topkapı Palace with strangulation marks around its neck. Süleyman the Magnificent ordered it to be buried in an unmarked grave, and his possessions, not least the palace, reverted to the crown.

The main concentration of **exhibits** in the museum deals with Selçuk, Mamluk and Ottoman Turkish art, but there are also several important Timurid and Persian works on display.

The Selçuk Empire, centred in Konya, preceded that of the Ottomans in Anatolia and it is interesting to trace influences between the two cultures. Ceramic techniques, for example, were obviously well developed by the Selçuks, judging from the wall tiles on display in the museum, and the wood carvings from Konya also suggest a high level of craftsmanship and artistry, which may have influenced later Ottoman work.

Other impressive exhibits include sixteenth-century Persian miniatures, which like many Ottoman works defy the Islamic stricture against depicting human or animal forms. Pictures in lacquer and leather-bound Persian manuscripts feature a tiger ripping into an antelope, and a dancing girl dated 1570. The tiny Sancak Korans were meant for hanging on the standard of the Ottoman imperial army in a jihad (holy war), so that the word of God would precede the troops into battle.

The **Great Hall** of the palace, İbrahim Paşa's audience hall, is devoted to a collection of Turkish **carpets** that is among the finest in the world. It includes tattered remains dating from the thirteenth century. On the ground floor, in rooms off the central courtyard, is an exhibition of the **folk art** of the Yörük tribes of Anatolia. This includes examples of a *kara cadır* (literally "black tent", a domicile woven from goat hair that can still be seen in central and eastern Anatolia) and a *topakev* (a tent constructed around a folding frame, which was used by nomads in Anatolia and Mongolia for over a thousand years). There is also an invaluable if rather faded exhibition concerning the dyes used in Turkish kilims and carpets, and the plants and insects from which they are derived. The use of natural dyes was almost forgotten in Anatolia after the introduction of chemical dyes in 1880, and the exhibition pays homage to the work of Marmara University's government-sponsored project, piloted in the province of Çanakkale, to encourage the reintroduction of natural dyes into the carpet- and kilim-making processes.

The Hamam of Roxelana

The double-domed building between the Sultan Ahmet Camii and Aya Sofya is the **Hamam of Roxelana** (daily except Tues 9.30am–5pm), built by Mimar Sinan in 1556 to replace the Byzantine baths of Zeuxippus on the same site. The 75-metre-long hamam served the worshippers at the mosque of Aya Sofya. The hamam has been restored with stained-glass windows and varnished wooden doors, and original marble fountains in the changing rooms, but the effect is rather diminished since after renovation the building was converted into a salesroom for handwoven carpets. One consequence of this unfortunate decision is that the hamam now has electric lighting, which destroys the characteristic effect – especially attractive when viewed through a veil of steam – produced by the skylights in the dome of a hamam.

Sokollu Mehmet Paşa Camii

A pleasant walk from the southwest corner of the Hippodrome leads down the steep Mehmet Paşa Yokuşu to **Sokollu Mehmet Paşa Camii** (open at prayer times only, but the *imam* may be around to unlock it during the day). This, one of Mimar Sinan's later buildings (1571), appears to have been omitted almost entirely from tourist itineraries. **Sokollu Mehmet Paşa**, who commissioned the mosque, was the last grand vizier of Süleyman the Magnificent, and it was his military expertise that later saved the Ottoman Empire from the worst effects of the dissolute rule of Selim the Sot. He was eventually assassinated as a result of the intrigues of Nur Banu, the mother of Murat III, who was jealous of his power.

The large mosque **courtyard** is surrounded on three sides by the rooms of the *medrese*, now occupied by a boys' Koran school (the boys, ten- to twelve-year-olds, inhabit the dervish lodge at the back of the mosque and can be seen seated in the porch studying the Koran during term time). At the centre of the courtyard is a handsome fountain with a pretty upcurved parapet to its dome.

The **interior** of the mosque is distinguished by the height of its dome and by the impressive display of İznik tiles on its east wall. These are from the best period of Turkish ceramics: the white is pure, the green vivid and the red intense. Calligraphic inscriptions are set against a jungle of enormous carnations and tulips, and the designs and colours are echoed all around the mosque and in the conical cap of the *mimber*, the tiling of which is unique in İstanbul. While the stained-glass windows are copies, some of the original, extremely delicate **paintwork** can be seen in the northwest corner below the gallery, and over the entrance. Embedded in the wall over the entrance and above the *mihrab* are pieces of the Kaaba from Mecca.

Around three sides of the mosque, a **gallery** is supported on lozenge-capitalled marble columns. With permission from the *imam*, who will hover during your visit, you can have a look up here and see the mosque interior from a different angle.

Küçük Ayasofya Camii

Küçük Ayasofya Camii (the "small mosque of Aya Sofya"; open prayer times only) was, like its larger namesake, built as a church in the sixth century. It was originally named after two Roman soldiers, **Sergius** and **Bacchus**, who were martyred for their faith and later became the patron saints of Christians in the Roman army, but it was renamed, aptly, because of its resemblance to Aya Sofya. It is believed to have predated the larger church, but this is not certain; all that is known is that it was built between 527 and 536 to service the palace of Hormisdas. This means that the church was part of the vast rebuilding programme carried out by Justinian to accommodate a growing population and to encourage the spread of Christianity, and also to consolidate his power after near-humiliation in the Nika riots. The church was converted into a mosque comparatively early in the sixteenth century during the reign of Beyazit II.

Despite imperfections in its execution, this is an attractive building, and it makes an interesting comparison with Aya Sofya since it is virtually a scale model of the larger building. The lesser dimensions mean that the various component parts are easier to comprehend as a whole.

Like most Byzantine churches of this era, its **exterior** is unprepossessing brick, and only inside can the satisfying proportions be properly appreciated. It is basically – like Aya Sofya – an octagon with semicircular niches at its diagonals, inscribed in a rectangle, but both these shapes are extremely irregular. This has been variously ascribed to a pragmatic solution to an awkward space at planning stage, or to shoddy workmanship, and while the latter seems to be the more likely explanation, the irregularities certainly don't detract from the general effect. The original marble facing and gold leaf have vanished, but a frieze honouring Justinian, Theodora and St Sergius runs around the architrave under the gallery – it's worthwhile, for the sake of the view, to ask permission for a visit to the **gallery**, but put on a pair of wooden clogs before you go up as it's filthy upstairs.

The sea wall and the Byzantine imperial palace

At the Küçük Ayasofya Camii you're almost down at the Marmara, close to the best-preserved section of the **sea walls**, built in 439 by Cyrus, Prefect of the East. They originally stretched from Saray Burnu to the city walls of Constantine the Great, and were later extended by Theodosius to meet his land walls, with thirteen gates piercing the eight-kilometre course. Theophilus, the last Iconoclast, rebuilt the walls in the ninth century to hold off a possible Arab invasion.

Nowadays the best way to see the walls is by train, since the tracks run along their length and on out of the city; indeed parts were destroyed when the rail lines were built. The best-preserved remains are a stretch of a couple of kilometres between Ahır Kapı, near the Cankurtaran train station, and Kumkapı, with a walkway along Kennedy Caddesi.

About halfway between the Küçük Ayasofya Camii and the Cankurtaran train station, the facade of the **Palace of Bucoleon** is one of the most melancholy and moving survivors of Byzantine Constantinople. This is a last remnant of the Great Palace of the Byzantine emperors, which once covered an enormous area from the Hippodrome down to the sea walls (see "The Mosaic Museum", below). The palace was begun by Constantine and added to by later emperors, until the Comneni dynasty abandoned it. It was later rehabilitated, and a description by one of the Crusaders illuminates why they took up residence after the Sack of Constantinople in 1204:

Within the palace there were fully 500 halls all connected with one another and all made with gold mosaic. And in it were fully 30 chapels, great and small, and there was one of them that was called the Holy Chapel, which was so rich and noble that there was not a hinge or a band nor any other small part that was not all of silver, and there was no column that was not of jasper or porphyry or some other precious stone.

By the time the Latins left in 1261, the palace was virtually destroyed, and funds were never found to repair it. Mehmet the Conqueror was so saddened by what he found there that he is said to have recited lines from the Persian poet Saadi:

> *The spider holds the curtain in the Palace of the Caesars*
> *The owl hoots its night call in the towers of Aphrasiab.*

It's easy to miss what's left of the Bucoleon Palace, especially if you pass at speed along Kennedy Caddesi. It is draped in beautiful red vine, and set back from the road with a little park in front. Three enormous marble-framed windows set high in the wall offer glimpses of the remains of a vaulted room behind. Below the windows, marble corbels give evidence of a balcony that would have projected over a marble quay (the waters of the Marmara once reached almost as far as the palace walls). For the rest, you'll need a lively imagination.

Walking from Küçük Ayasofya Camii along Kennedy Caddesi in the other direction, after about ten minutes you come to the little suburb of **Kumkapı**, the fish centre of İstanbul. A large number of increasingly expensive but excellent fish restaurants here cater to both locals and visitors, and there's also a fabulous **fish market**, which should be visited between 5 and 6am in the morning. At that time you'll witness the daily catch from the Marmara Sea – a vast array of marine life from squid and tuna to thousand upon thousand of *hamsi* – performing its death throes under the disrespectful boots of fishermen, stallholders, hoteliers and restaurateurs. The atmosphere of the place is frantic, but if you find a safe place from which to observe you'll be practically ignored in favour of the business of the day.

The Mosaic Museum

The only other remains of the Great Palace are the mosaics displayed in the **Mozaik Müzesi** (daily except Tues 9.30am–5pm; $1), inland from here on Torun Sokak. The museum is at the time of writing closed for refurbishment but should reopen some time in 1997. It can be reached by running the gauntlet of salespeople in the Arasta Çarşısı (formerly Kabasakal Caddesi), a renovated street selling tourist gifts, whose seven-teeth-century shops were originally built to pay for the upkeep of the nearby Sultan Ahmet Camii. The street was built on part of the site of the Great Palace, and until recently some of the mosaics, now removed to the museum, could be seen in the shops themselves.

A basic Nissen hut-type structure shelters the mosaics, many of which are still *in situ*, so that some idea of their original scale and purpose can be imagined. The building has been constructed so that some of the mosaics are viewed from a catwalk above but can also be examined more closely by descending to their level. These remains were part of a mosaic peristyle, an open courtyard surrounded by a portico. To the south of the portico and down to the Bucoleon on the Marmara were the private apartments of the emperor, while the public sections of the palace were located to the north. Among the mosaics, which probably date from Justinian's rebuilding programme of the sixth century, are various portrayals of animals in their natural habitats, as well as in domestic scenes. These include a vivid portrayal of an elephant locking a lion in a deadly embrace with its trunk, and two children being led on the back of a camel.

From Sultanahmet to Beyazit

Beyazit, which centres around the buildings of İstanbul University and is also home to the covered bazaar, is relatively little explored by tourists, but it's a quarter that deserves some time. The university and its surrounding mosques – Nuruosmaniye, Beyazit Camii and Süleymaniye – are all interesting, and then there's the bazaar itself, as well as the most famous of İstanbul's second-hand book markets.

The Yerebatan Saray

Before leaving Sultanahmet, it's worth taking a detour along Yerebatan Caddesi to the Basilica Cistern or **Yerebatan Saray** ("Sunken Palace"; daily 9am–5pm; $2.50), one of several underground cisterns that riddle the foundations of the city. This is the only one which has been extensively excavated and renovated, and although it's always thronged with people it's worth devoting time to a prolonged exploration of the furthest recesses. Probably built by the emperor Constantine in the fourth century, and enlarged by Justinian in the sixth century, the cistern was supplied by aqueducts with water from the Belgrade Forest, and it in turn supplied the Great Palace and later Topkapı Palace.

The cistern fell into disuse in the century after the Ottoman conquest, and its existence was only brought to public attention in 1545 by the French **Petrus Gyllius**. He had been led to it by local residents, whose houses were built over the cistern and who had easy access to it. They had sunk wells into it and even kept boats on the water from which they could fish its depths – allegedly Gyllius' interest was aroused when he found fresh fish being sold in the streets nearby.

Restorations were undertaken in 1987: 50,000 tons of mud and water were removed; the walls were covered to make them impermeable; and eight of the columns were sheathed in concrete to fortify the structure. The construction of concrete pathways to replace the old boats may seem a desecration, but they do facilitate a leisurely examination of interesting bits of masonry, as does the careful spotlighting. In addition, the piped music and the café at the exit add an element of mystery to the place: their purpose is wholly obscure.

The largest covered cistern in the city at 140 by 70 metres, Yerebatan holds 80,000 cubic metres of water. The small herringbone **domes** are supported by 336 columns, many of which have Corinthian capitals, and the whole fragile-seeming structure supports the buildings and a busy main road overhead. There is evidence that building material for the cistern was pillaged from elsewhere. The two **Medusa heads** at the southwest corner, brought to light when the cistern was drained, are thought to have been used simply as construction material – this would explain the fact that they would have been totally submerged and invisible. In addition, the marble **columns** may be recycled: some are square-shaped, others in two parts, and one has a tree-trunk effect patterned on its surface, resembling the various remains of columns found beyond the University on Ordu Caddesi.

Divan Yolu

The main approach to Beyazit is along **Divan Yolu**, a major thoroughfare which, if you're staying at one of the hotels in Lâleli or Aksaray, you may well be following in the other direction on your way to the better-known sights around Sultanahmet. It gained its name because it was the principal approach to the Divan, down which hordes of people would pour three times a week to make their petitions to the court. It's still hideously overcrowded, its narrow pavements barely passable at any hour of the day or night, its shops run-down, the restaurants shabby, and the major attractions, crowded in by buildings, are easy to miss as you fight for passage on the street below. Nevertheless there's plenty to see as you push your way through.

The **Binbirdirek Cistern**, or Cistern of a Thousand and One Columns, is on the Binbirdirek Meydanı at the end of Işık Sokak (to the left off Divan Yolu as you walk away from Aya Sofya), underneath a small building presently serving as the regional *muhtarlık*, the municipal directorate. If you ask here, the *muhtar* should produce the keys and take you down a flight of stone stairs to view the cistern, dimly lit by holes in the wasteland behind the *muhtarlık*. The second largest cistern in the city at 64 by 56 metres, Binbirdirek contains 224 columns, twelve of which were walled in not long after the cistern was completed. Originally the hall would have been over twelve metres high, and the columns actually consist of two separate units placed one on top of the other, but it's filled with soil almost to the top of the lower columns. The cistern is thought to have been built originally under the palace of Philoxenus, one of the Roman senators who accompanied Emperor Constantine to the city, and was restored and enlarged under Emperor Justinian. It dried up completely around the fifteenth century, and was later used as a spinning mill until the beginning of this century.

Continuing along Divan Yolu you'll come to a burnt column of masonry known as Çemberlitaş (the hooped stone). This is the **Column of Constantine**, erected by Constantine the Great in 330 AD to commemorate the city's dedication as capital of the Roman Empire. For the next sixteen centuries the city was known as Constantinople, and the Christian religion Constantine introduced was to be associated with it for almost as long. The column itself was originally sheathed in porphyry – the most prestigious of coloured marbles, found only in Egypt – and surmounted by a statue of the emperor. The iron hoops from which it derives its Turkish name were bound around the joints in the porphyry after an earthquake in 416 damaged the column and suggested its imminent collapse.

Across Vezirhanı Caddesi from the column is the **Çemberlitaş Hamamı** (daily 6am–midnight; $3 without massage), founded in the sixteenth century by Nur Banu, one of the most powerful of the Valide Sultans. Its central location means that the masseurs are well used to foreigners, and this might not be a bad place to be initiated into the rites of the Turkish bath.

If you turn up Vezirhanı Caddesi you'll come to the **Nuruosmaniye Camii** at the back of the covered bazaar; coming from the other direction, the mosque's courtyard provides a refreshing open space after the dark convolutions of the bazaar. Nuruosmaniye, begun by Mahmut I in 1748 and finished seven years later by Osman III, was the first and most impressive of the city's Baroque mosques, setting the fashion in Baroque and Rococo architecture for the following century. The designer is unknown – it has been attributed to both Turkish and foreign architects – but since it was such a radical departure from anything that had gone before it seems likely that foreign influence was at work.

The covered bazaar

With over four thousand shops, five banks, a mosque, store houses and moneychangers, İstanbul's **Kapalı Çarşı** (Mon–Sat 9am–7pm) is said to be the largest **covered bazaar** in the world. In addition to the retail outlets, the *han*s or market halls in and around the bazaar are the location of many workshops, where craftsmen make some of the goods sold in the bazaar.

The whole place is laid out street by street, and originally a particular type of shop was found in a certain area, with street names reflecting the nature of the businesses. While these areas have become blurred with an influx of new establishments, they still hold true to a certain extent. There are several good **carpet** shops around the fountain at the intersection of Keseciler and Takkeciler caddesis, and cheaper, rather scruffier places on Halıcılar Çarşısı Caddesi (Carpet Sellers' Market Street). Carpets can also be bought at **auction** on Wednesdays at 1pm in the Sandal Bedesteni, but you'll need a good grasp of your numbers in Turkish and some idea of what you want. You'll notice that the dealers inspect anything interesting with some care before bargaining, and many avoid the place altogether since you can't really see what you're buying, but it's fun to watch. There are also auctions of furniture and ornaments on Tuesday, and jewellery on Thursday, both at 1pm in the Sandal Bedesten. The best old **silver** is sold in and around the old bazaar or **İç Bedesten**, more or less at the centre, and traditionally reserved for

the most precious wares because it can be locked at night. **Ceramics** can be found along Yağlıkçılar Caddesi and off it in Çukur Han; leather and kilim **bags** are sold on Keseciler Caddesi and around Kürkçüler Çarşısı; and glittery, mainly poor-quality **gold** is sold around Kuyumcular Caddesi (the Street of the Jewellers) and Kalpakçılar Başı Caddesi. For details of specific shops, see under "Shops and markets", p.169.

Craftsmen at work in the *han*s of the bazaar include custom jewellery makers in Zincirli Han, silversmiths in Kalcılar Han, just outside the bazaar off Mahmut Paşa Yokuşu, and a carpet repair service in Mercan Ali Paşa Han, also outside the bazaar near Mercan Ağa Mescidi.

When you need a break, the nicest **café** in the bazaar is the *Şark Kahvesi* on Yağlıkçılar Sokak, almost opposite Zenneciler Sokak; play backgammon and drink strong tea while devising your plan of attack or gloating over hard-won booty.

In Ottoman times the bazaar was a vital part of the town, and consisted of both a covered and an open area centred on a *bedesten*, a domed building where foreign trade took place and valuable goods were stored. In İstanbul the commercial centre was based around two *bedesten*s, both inside the covered bazaar. The **İç Bedesten** probably dates from the time of the conquest, while the **Sandal Bedesten** was added during the reign of Süleyman to cope with the quantity of trade in fine fabrics which the capital attracted in the sixteenth century. In effect the bazaar extends much further than the limits of the covered area, sprawling into the streets that lead down to the Golden Horn, and this whole area was controlled by the strict laws laid down by the trade guilds, thus reducing competition between traders. Each shop could support just one owner and his apprentice, and successful merchants were not allowed to expand their businesses. Similar unwritten laws control market forces among traders in the covered bazaar even today.

Whether or not you actually enjoy the experience of the bazaar is very much a matter of temperament and mood: you'll either find the hassle from traders intolerable, or you'll be flattered to be paid more attention in one afternoon than you've received in your entire life. The only way to avoid this would be to go out of season, dress à la Turk, and move so fast they can't see you – in normal circumstances you might as well resign yourself to the bantering hard sell. If you have time to spend in idle chat you may discover some of the more interesting characters who work in these parts, and at least everyone is friendly and cheerful, in summer anyway. In winter the bazaar goes into hibernation; profit and loss are assessed, the ranks close and the season's sport is football, played in the alleyways between the shops, rather than tourist-baiting.

Beyazit Meydanı

If you carry straight on up the main road, you'll arrive at Beyazit Meydanı, the main square of Beyazit and the principal approach to İstanbul University. Here, approached through a small *bit pazarı* or flea market, is the famous **Sahaflar Çarşısı**, the second-hand booksellers' market, a little enclave of wonderful shops run by some of the quarter's best-known and worst-tempered characters. The Ottoman book market dates back to the eighteenth century, but long before that it was the site of a Byzantine book and paper market. After the conquest it lost its original identity to the spoonmakers, but gradually other tradesmen were replaced by booksellers when printing and publishing were legalized in the Ottoman Empire in the second half of the eighteenth century. On the west side of the square the tradition is reflected in a small **Museum of Calligraphy** (Tues–Sat 9am–4pm; $1.25), with some interesting examples of this highly developed Ottoman art form. It occupies an attractive old building, formerly a theological college.

To the east of the square, **Beyazit Camii**, completed in 1506, is the oldest surviving imperial mosque in the city. It has a beautiful, sombre courtyard full of richly coloured marble, including twenty columns of verd antique, red granite and porphyry. Inside, the building is a perfect square of exactly the same proportions as the courtyard (although the aisles make it feel elongated), and its plan is basically a simplified version of Aya Sofya, with the same balancing semidomes to east and west, but without the lateral galleries. The sixteenth-century fittings, including the carvings of the balustrade, *mihrab* and *mimber*, are all highly crafted and beautiful. If you walk straight past the mosque from Beyazit Square and on through the Sahaflar Çarşısı, you'll arrive at another of the entrances to the covered bazaar.

The university

Located on the site of the Old Palace of Mehmet the Conqueror, **İstanbul University** commands an impressive position at the crown of one of the city's seven hills. The fire tower located in the grounds, Beyazit Kulesi, is a landmark all over the city, and the main building and some of its subsidiaries have a certain style and grandeur, especially when approached through the main gateway (the best time to do this is at 9am in term-time, when the national anthem, the *İstiklâl Marşı*, is played, and everyone in the vicinity freezes for the duration).

There's a possibility that as a foreigner you won't be permitted to enter the grounds, since the gates are manned periodically by police who check identity cards. İstanbul University has been a centre of political activity of both the left and Muslim fundamentalists, with occasional demonstrations, lock-ins and even violence on the campus. Since the main campus was relocated to Avcilar on the Edirne highway, however, student unrest has died down to a large extent, though feelings still run high about the new relaxed attitude to religious garb on campus (formerly this was banned). Whoever is demonstrating, one of the main causes of ill feeling is the existence of the controversial body that controls all higher education in Turkey, *YÖK*, the Higher Education Council. It is *YÖK* that determines the national syllabus (which still includes compulsory classes on the life of Atatürk and the history of the republic) and the protocol which, in theory, forbids headscarves and beards on campus and bans all but one, officially controlled, society per university.

The **Old Palace** of Mehmet the Conqueror was the official imperial residence from its inception, after the Conquest of İstanbul in 1453, until it burnt to the ground in 1541, when the residential quarters and harem were relocated next to the Divan in Topkapı Palace. The Old Palace was then rebuilt to serve as a residence for concubines who had been retired after the accession of a new sultan. However, most of the buildings which now serve as draughty lecture halls were constructed by the French architect Bourgeois in 1866, and housed the Ministry of War until this moved to Ankara along with the other departments of state. At that time the university, which until then had been scattered around the city in various *medrese*s of the imperial mosques, was relocated here.

Apart from the monumental gateway where you enter the campus, the most impressive building on the site is a small *köşk*, to the right of the entrance, now used as the staff dining room. This is part of the original Bourgeois complex and has retained its Baroque interior decoration.

The Süleymaniye complex

Heading downhill through the university grounds, you will emerge in front of a collection of buildings considered to be the finest of all the Ottoman mosque complexes. Built by the renowned architect Sinan in honour of his most illustrious patron, Süleyman the Magnificent, they are arguably his greatest achievement.

When the imperial entourage moved to Topkapı, the grounds of the Old Palace were given over to the new complex, in what must have been a most attractive location overlooking the Golden Horn and its waterside parks and gardens. **Süleymaniye Camii** and its satellites, completed in just seven years from 1550, are built along traditional Islamic lines – the mosque is centralized beneath a dome at the very centre of the entire complex – but the whole achieves a perfection of form and a monumentality of appearance, dominating the skyline from Galata and the Horn, that set it apart from other Ottoman architecture.

Approaching from the university side, the first street encountered before entering the mosque precincts is Sıddık Sami Onal Caddesi, formerly **Tıryakı Çarşısı**, "market of the addicts". The name derives from the fact that the coffee houses in this street, whose rents augmented the upkeep of the foundation, used also to serve hashish, to be smoked on the premises or taken away. The present line of student cafés here may be seedy but are evidently nothing like as interesting as the establishments they replaced.

Behind the shop fronts in this street is the famous **Süleymaniye library**, housed in the Evvel and Sani *medrese*s. These buildings, mirror images of each other, are situated around shady garden courtyards. The library was established by Süleyman in an effort to bring together collections of books scattered throughout the city: works were gathered from eleven palaces and date from the reigns of six different sultans. The library is open to the public and all of the works are on microfilm, to protect the originals. There is also a book restoration department, where the original bindings are closely imitated.

MİMAR SİNAN (1489–1588): MASTER BUILDER

Many of the finest works of Ottoman civil and religious architecture throughout Turkey can be traced to one man, a genius who had the good luck to come of age in a rich, expanding empire willing to put its considerable resources at his disposal. **Mimar Sinan** served as court architect to three sultans – Süleyman the Magnificent, Selim II and Murat III – but principally to the first, who owed much of his reputation for "magnificence" to this gifted technician.

Little is known of Sinan's early life except that he was born in a small village near Kayseri, the son of Greek or Armenian Christian parents; even his birthdate is open to question, since it is established that he was conscripted into the janissaries in 1513, which would have made him a good ten years older than the typical recruit. In any case, prolonged military service in all of the major Ottoman campaigns of the early sixteenth century compelled Sinan to travel the length and breadth of southeastern Europe and the Middle East, giving him the opportunity to become familiar with the best Islamic – and Christian – monumental architecture there. Sinan was immediately able to apply what he had learned in the role of military engineer, building bridges, siegeworks, harbours and even ships which earned him the admiration of his superiors. These included Sultan Süleyman, who in recognition of his abilities appointed him Court Architect in April 1536.

During Sinan's first twelve years in the job, he did little out of the ordinary, undertaking only relatively minor public works such as aqueducts, bridges, hamams, *kervansaray*s and *imaret*s (soup kitchens) throughout Anatolia and the Balkans. In 1548 he completed his first major religious commission, İstanbul's Şehzade Camii, and shortly thereafter embarked on a rapid succession of ambitious projects in and around the capital, including the waterworks leading from the Belgrade Forest and the Süleymaniye Camii. After presumably exhausting the potential of the great city Sinan again turned his matured attention to the provinces, gracing Edirne with the Selimiye Camii in 1569–75, and a decade later fulfilling a longstanding wish as a devout Muslim by overseeing the restoration of the Harem-i-Zerif mosque in Mecca.

Unusually for his time, Sinan could make an objective assessment of his talents: he regarded most of his pre-1550 works as apprentice pieces, and posterity has generally agreed with the self-evaluations in his memoirs, the *Tezkeret-ül-Bünyan*. Despite temptations to luxury he lived and died equally modestly, being buried in a simple tomb he made for himself in his garden on the grounds of the Süleymaniye Camii – a tomb which was perhaps the last of more than 500 constructions by Sinan, large and small, throughout the empire.

Other buildings of interest in the vicinity include the **Türbe of Mimar Sinan**, on the corner of Şifahane Sokak and Mimar Sinan Caddesi. The tomb is in a triangular garden, which was the location of the architect's house during construction work. At the corner of the triangle is an octagonal eaved fountain. Perhaps there is no nicer way of being remembered than by providing the gift of water to passing strangers, but in Sinan's case it nearly caused his downfall: the fountain, as well as Sinan's house and garden, were liberally supplied with water, but when the mosques further down the pipeline began to run short, Sinan was charged with diverting the water supply for his household needs. The garden beyond the fountain now houses the tomb of Sinan, with its magnificent carved turban, a measure of the architect's high rank. The eulogy written on the south wall of the garden picks out the bridge at Büyükçekmece as Sinan's greatest achievement.

Otherwise, the buildings of the Süleymaniye complex served the usual functions: on Şifahane Sokak are a soup kitchen (*imaret*), which used to be the museum of Turkish antiquities and is usually open to wander around, and a *kervansaray*; a *mektep* or primary school stands on the corner of Sıddık Sami Onal Caddesi and Süleymaniye Caddesi; and there are Koran schools and a language school, which taught the proper pronunciation of Arabic for reading the Koran. The **hamam** on the corner of Mimar

Sinan Caddesi and Dökmeciler Hamamı Sokak is a beautiful building in a terrible state of repair; there's also a wrestling ground, located to the south of the cemetery.

The **mosque** and **cemetery**, enclosed by a wall with grilled openings, are located in the midst of these buildings, part of a harmoniously integrated ensemble, but at the same time independent enough to take dominion over the whole, and to be visible from all sides.

The mosque is preceded by a rectangular courtyard whose portico stands on columns of porphyry, Marmara marble and pink Egyptian granite (which are said to have come from the royal box of the Hippodrome), and by four tapering minarets. In the centre of the courtyard stands a small rectangular fountain, which serves to emphasize how big the open area is. On the exterior of the mosque itself, semidomes supporting the huge central dome to east and west alternate with arches, in front of which is a set of three domes. The east and west flanks of the mosque are distinguished by two-storey loggias, accessible from within the mosque, which support an eave protecting those performing their ablutions at the taps below.

The doorway into the mosque is high and narrow, its wooden doors inlaid with ebony, mother-of-pearl and ivory. Inside, a sense of light and spaciousness is paramount, the majestic effect only slightly tempered by the tackiness of more Fossati interior decor. The proportions are perfectly balanced: a dome 53m high (twice its diameter), surmounting a perfect square of 26.5m. The effect of space is helped by the fact that there are no side aisles, an airiness enhanced by 200 windows, including 32 in the central dome, and 23 in each tympanum, whose double panes ensure a softly filtered light.

The dome collapsed during the earthquake of 1766, and in the nineteenth century further damage was done by the Fossati brothers, whose attempt at Ottoman Baroque redecoration jars with the simplicity of other aspects of the building. The original crystal lamps have also been replaced by glassware supported on a rather cumbersome iron frame, which is a bit distracting. The original stained glass of İbrahim the Mad remains, however, above a simply graceful marble *mimber*, along with a few İznik tiles, a first cautious use of tiling by Sinan before he was swept away by enthusiasm in the Rüstem Paşa Camii down the hill.

In the **cemetery** (Wed–Sun 9.30am–4.30pm) are located the tombs of Süleyman the Magnificent and of Haseki Hürrem, or Roxelana, his powerful wife. Süleyman's tomb is particularly impressive: as you enter, passing through doors inlaid with ebony and ivory, silver and jade, and a peristyle supported by four verd antique columns, you are confronted by the huge turban of Süleyman the Magnificent. Above, the spectacular inner dome has been faithfully restored in red, black and gold inlaid with glittering ceramic stars. Both here and in the neighbouring tomb of Roxelana, you'll see the very beautiful original tiles and some fine stained glass in the centre that has survived.

Eminönü and the Golden Horn

Descending from Beyazit down the hill to Eminönü is not an experience for the fainthearted. The streets are steep, narrow and badly paved, and invariably thronged with *hamal*s (stevedores) bent double under burdens of merchandise twice their size. Even the smallest of these roads is open to traffic, and the resulting confusion can be awesome to behold.

Immediately below the covered bazaar is the region known as **Tahtakale**, formerly the unofficial moneychangers' market, now the place to buy a second-hand camera (or buy back one you thought you'd lost), from stallholders who set up shop here on Saturdays. The whole area around the bazaar and down to Sirkeci, generally known as **Eminönü**, is effectively an extension of the covered bazaar, with streets specializing in ironware, wooden implements, cheap rugs, dentists' chairs, or small nameless pieces of cheap metal. East of Tahtakale is the area known as **Cağaloğlu**, best known as the location of the nation's press, whose offices are mainly along Babıali and Turkocağı *caddesi*s. In recent years increasing violence – including a murder in 1990 over a bad restaurant review – has established the press as one of the country's high-risk industries, providing ample copy for the most sensationalist among them. Turkish *Playboy* also has its offices in Cağaloğlu, soft pornography being a major growth industry.

For visitors, though, Cağaloğlu's major attraction is its **hamam** on Kazım Ismail Gürkan Caddesi, an extension of Yerebatan Caddesi (women's entrance on Cağaloğlu Hamam Sok; daily 7am–10pm for men, 8am–9pm for women), the most popular baths this side of town, famous for their beautiful *hararet*s or steam rooms, open cruciform chambers with windowed domes supported on a circle of columns. The baths were built in 1741 by Mahmut I to pay for the upkeep of his library in Aya Sofya, and the arches, basins and taps of the hot room, as well as the entries to the private cubicles, are all magnificently Baroque. Weight-watching visitors should take note of the masseurs in the baths, to appreciate what pride of bearing can do for a little fat.

Sirkeci, the area immediately below the main train station, is a major ferry port, with boats for the Princes' Islands, the Bosphorus and the Golden Horn all leaving from landings around here. Seen from the Galata Tower across the Horn, the buildings above the water form a foreground to the skyline of Beyazit and Sultanahmet, with Yeni Cami directly below Nuruosmaniye, the Spice Bazaar below Beyazit Camii, and Rüstem Paşa Camii below the Beyazit fire tower.

Yeni Cami and the Spice Bazaar

The **Yeni Cami** is a large, grey and rather ugly building, whose steps form a popular stamping ground for hawkers, pickpockets and pigeons. It was the last of İstanbul's imperial mosques to be built in the classical era, however, and its history gives an interesting perspective on harem power struggles. It was built for the Valide Sultan Safiye ("the light one", a beautiful Venetian woman who some said was a Venetian spy), mother of Mehmet III and one of the most powerful of the Valide Sultans, who ruled not only the harem but effectively the whole empire through the weakness of her son. This was the only imperial mosque complex to be built during the reign of Mehmet III, and the site chosen by Safiye was regarded as wholly inappropriate. It occupied a slum neighbourhood inhabited by a sect of Jews called the Karaites, who were relocated down the Horn in Hasköy, and a synagogue and church had to be demolished to make room for it. The site was also dangerously close to the water's edge, and the building programme was constantly plagued by seepage from the Horn. The foundations that eventually withstood this seepage are a series of stone "bridges" reinforced with iron.

An even greater plague to the building programme, however, was court politics. The original architect was executed for heresy, and the work was interrupted again by the death of Mehmet III and the banishment of his mother to the Old Palace. Construction had reached as far as the lower casements when it was halted, and the Karaites returned to camp out in the rubble; sixty years passed before the Valide Sultan Turhan Hatice, mother of Sultan Mehmet IV, completed the building. Today the mosque, which is more or less a copy of the Şehzade Camii, is characterized above all by its gloominess, partly due to the heavy eaves that cover the washing area, but also a result of the thick layer of soot from the nearby ferry port that covers its walls and windows. The interior is dominated by arabesque stencilling and poor-quality tiles.

Mısır Çarşısı

The nearby **Mısır Çarşısı** or Egyptian Bazaar, also known as the **Spice Bazaar** because the main bulk of produce on sale here has always been spices, was part of the same complex and is far more atmospheric. Still a good place to buy anything from saffron to spice mixtures sold as aphrodisiacs, the bazaar is also nowadays good for towels, bed linen, *lokum* (Turkish delight) and basketware; the large courtyard outside is lined with aviaries crowded with parrots and lovebirds, as well as house plants and garden supplies. Completed a few years before Yeni Cami, the L-shaped bazaar was endowed with customs duties from Cairo (which explains its Turkish name); it has 88 vaulted rooms and chambers above the entryways at the ends of the halls. One of these, over the main entrance opposite the ferry ports, now houses the famous Greek *Pandeli Restaurant*, moved here after anti-Greek riots in 1955.

Rüstem Paşa Camii and around

One of the most attractive of İstanbul's smaller mosques, the **Rüstem Paşa Camii** lies just a short walk west of the Spice Bazaar. Built for Süleyman the Magnificent's grand vizier Rüstem Paşa (who was responsible along with Roxelana for the murder of the heir apparent Mustafa), the mosque is dated to the year he died, 1561, and was probably built in his memory by his widow Mihrimah, Roxelana's daughter.

Despite its setting in the midst of the city's bustling bazaar area, surrounded still by darkened backstreets of workshops and store rooms, Rüstem Paşa is no workaday piece of architecture. Designed by Sinan on an awkward site that seems to offer no room for such a building, it could almost escape your attention as you wander about in the streets below. At ground level an arcade of shops occupies the vaults, and climbing up to the mosque itself is like ascending to some higher realm. There are steps up to the terrace from the Golden Horn side of the mosque and from Kutucular Sokak behind it. Through an attractive entrance portal on the Golden Horn approach, you encounter a wide courtyard and a tiled double portico along the west wall. It's almost like entering a theatre, with the tiles of the portico as backdrop and the mosque interior, whose dimensions are not immediately apparent, backstage.

The **tiles**, inside and out, are among the most profuse in any mosque in Turkey, and mainly of the very best quality from the finest period of İznik tile production, when the techniques for producing tomato-red – slightly raised above the other colours – had been perfected. Designs, covering the walls, piers and pillars, and decorating the *mihrab* and *mimber*, include famous panels of tulips and carnations, and geometric patterns in such profusion that it pays to concentrate on them panel by panel to appreciate the subtlety of individual designs.

Inside are galleries supported by pillars and marble columns, and about as many windows as the structure of the mosque will allow, a common phenomenon in sixteenth-century mosques, which has been contrasted with a simultaneous Dark Age in learning, when sciences and logic were suppressed in favour of religious orthodoxy. Here it ensures that there is plenty of light to appreciate the surface irregularities of the tiles. Even the pendentives are tiled, with circular medallions containing inscriptions and surrounded by designs of flowers; only the ugly nineteenth-century painting, thoroughly incongruous and jarring, detracts from the overall effect.

Ancient warehouses

The area on the Beyazit side of Rüstem Paşa is a warren of antiquated streets, containing a few buildings that were there when the mosque was built. These alleys and their peculiar little specialist shops are interesting in themselves, but detailed exploration uncovers one of the best of all the city's Byzantine buildings, fascinating for its simple ordinariness. This is the remains of a commercial warehouse known as the **Balkapan Hanı** (the Han of the Honey Store). Situated on Balkapan Sokak off Hasırcılar Caddesi, it is one of several ancient *hans* in the neighbourhood (others include Kızılhan and Hurmalı Han), about which practically nothing is known apart from their Byzantine origins. Aside from the original courtyard, which is surrounded by later Ottoman structures, the remains of the Balkapan Hanı are all underground. The space is still being used to store imported goods – Japanese watch parts rather than Egyptian honey these days – but it's possible to look around with the help of one of the workmen who can be found in the courtyard. Steps lead down to the vaults from the middle of this courtyard, and below is a gloomy, cavernous space whose brick herringbone vaulting is supported by rows of columns. The vaults are reminiscent of a Byzantine cistern, and the fact that they are still used for their original purpose – and that they are practically unknown to tourists – makes them all the more exciting to visit.

The Golden Horn

The derivation of the name **Golden Horn**, *Chrysokeras* in Greek, is obscure (*Halic*, the Turkish name, simply means "estuary"), but one suggestion is that it was coined during the Turkish siege of the city, when all the gold and precious objects that the Byzantine citizens could collect were thrown into the inlet. Whatever the story, the name has become singularly inappropriate in recent years, since this stretch of water has become a dump for the worst of the city's filth and pollution. A clean-up programme was initiated by İstanbul's former right-wing mayor Dalan, but the best time to make a trip up the Golden Horn is still winter, before the stench gets too high. Yaşar Kemal's description of the Horn from *The Sea-Crossed Fisherman* still rings true for those who have experienced the reek of this once-beautiful stretch of water:

> *The Golden Horn, that deep well surrounded by huge ugly buildings and sooty factories, spewing rust from their chimneys and roofs and walls, staining the water with sulphur-yellow rust, a filthy sewer filled with empty cans and rubbish and horse carcasses, dead dogs and gulls and wild boars and thousands of cats, stinking . . . A viscid, turbid mass, opaque, teeming with maggots . . .*

Despite its unwholesome condition, the Golden Horn is still one of the finest natural harbours in the world, and its fortunes have been closely linked with those of the city it serves. On two separate occasions, capture of the Horn proved to be the turning point of crucial military campaigns. The first occasion, in 1203–4, was when the Crusaders captured the Horn and proceeded to besiege the city for ten months, until they breached the walls separating the inlet from the city. The second occasion was a spectacular *tour de force* by Mehmet the Conqueror, who was prevented from entering the Horn by a chain fastened across it, and so carried his ships overland at night and launched them into the inlet from its northern shore. Mehmet then proceeded to construct a pontoon across the top of the Horn over which he transported his army and cannons in preparation for the siege of the land walls, which were finally breached in 1453.

For the Ottoman Empire the Horn was a vital harbour, supplying the Genoan, Venetian and Jewish trading colonies which had become established on its northern shore. Nowadays the shipyards at Hasköy turn out copies of Scandinavian naval vessels and cruisers in a convincing attempt to establish Turkey as a seafaring nation.

Both banks of the Horn have long been settled by İstanbul's minority communities, and the suburbs of **Balat** and **Fener** were once respectively Jewish and Greek ghettos. Nowadays these areas retain much of their individual character through the buildings, institutions and community life of their respective faiths. Fener is still the location of the recently refurbished Greek Patriarchate, as well as a number of churches and the gigantic red-brick Greek Lycée, high on a hill overlooking the water. If you are thinking of taking to the water, however, the most interesting trip would be to the Muslim district of Eyüp (see p.134), a centre of pilgrimage for the Islamic world.

The old **Galata Bridge**, a pontoon bridge spanning the Horn between Eminönü and Karaköy, was gutted by fire in 1993, as its replacement, a characterless six-lane monstrosity, neared completion. The owners of the excellent – and sleazy – restaurants which used to occupy the premises on the lower tier of the bridge are rumoured to have set it alight and gutted the interiors of their establishments for insurance purposes. Two years in restoration, it's now is back in service as a footbridge. Small **ferry boats** ply up and down the Horn, starting from near the new Galata Bridge and ending up in Eyüp, beyond Theodosius' city walls. The boat service isn't as effective as the one serving the Bosphorus, being infrequent and none too strictly timetabled, but it's an enjoyable ride of 10 minutes to Fener, 35 minutes to Eyüp. Times are posted up on blackboards outside the boat stations.

Hasköy

Across on the Karaköy side of the Golden Horn, Hasköy was the location of an Ottoman naval shipyard and of a royal park, which was cultivated as a fruit orchard throughout the centuries of Ottoman rule. Among the ugly industrial developments that have sprung up along this shore, there still stands a timber royal pavilion, the **Aynalıkavak Kasrı** (daily except Mon & Thurs 9.30am–4pm; $1), the last surviving vestige of a large complex of buildings. The pavilion is situated off the Kasımpaşa–Hasköy road, to the south of the Hasköy ferry station. To get there, take a ferry boat, or bus #47 from Eminönü, or a #54HM from Taksim.

Inscriptions dated 1791 can be found in the palace, but it is thought to date from an earlier era, because of vestiges of an older style of architecture. This is confirmed by a poem inscribed on the walls of the composition room, which praises Ahmet III for renovating the palace.

Aynalıkavak retains some beautiful Ottoman features, particularly in the composition room, a private room of Ahmet III where he is thought to have composed music. Here there are a central brazier and low divans which were typical of early Ottoman interiors. The whole of the southwest facade, nearest the sea, has two sets of windows, another early Ottoman feature seen in some of the pavilions of Topkapı, with the second, "head windows" decorated with stained glass. On exhibition in the pavilion is a collection of Turkish musical instruments which are no longer in use, or have been modified. In summer, concerts of traditional music are held in the grounds.

The **Rahmi Koç Industrial Museum** at Hasköy Cad 27 (Tues–Sun 10am–5pm; $1.50) is one of İstanbul's better museums, both in terms of its exhibits, and the building in which they are housed. Constructed in the eighteenth century as a factory where anchors and their chains were made, it's recently been converted, but with many of its original attributes, like the arching brickwork of its ceiling and spacious halls, still in evidence. The restoration was carried out by Rahmi M. Koç, one of Turkey's most famous industrialists, to house his private collection of models, machines, vehicles and toys, originating from all over Turkey and Europe but mainly from Britain. The best time to visit is Saturday afternoon, when there are special exhibitions around slot machines, the old Kadıköy–Moda tram, and the history of flight.

Upstairs, the starboard main engine of the Kalender steam ferry, made in Newcastle-upon-Tyne in 1911 and decommissioned in the 1980s, is the main exhibit – press a button and and you can see its pistons move. Downstairs are a number of old bikes, from penny-farthings to an early Royal Enfield motorbike complete with basket chair for side carriage. The model railway is disappointing in terms of moving parts; far better is the ship's bridge, reconstructed from a number of Turkish and British vessels of the 1920s to 1940s. All the instruments are explained in English, with sound effects and working parts, including an echo sounder, an early dimmer switch and a very loud alarm bell.

For those disinclined to contemplate the marvels of the industrial age, the *Café du Levant* (closed in August) in the museum grounds is a good French **bistro**, with authentic decor and French chefs.

Lâleli and Aksaray

Heading west from Beyazit up Ordu Caddesi, you arrive at an appalling tangle of road intersections, the main focus of **Aksaray** and of **Lâleli** to the east. Both districts are run-down and short of any sense of community, partly because of the dispiriting effect of the roar of traffic on the main street but also because, in Lâleli especially, many of the inhabitants have not really settled or become accepted in Turkey, being Iranian refugees and Arab students, and more recently Eastern Europeans selling everything and anything the Turks might have a mind to buy. Turks often express antagonism or at least emphasize their cultural differences to other Islamic ethnic groups, and in Lâleli this manifests itself in a feeling of ill will that is certainly more pronounced than anything you are likely to feel in an area of İstanbul with a predominantly Greek or Jewish community.

Both quarters, though, have interesting mosques and converted churches, and it's certainly worth wandering away from the main road to explore some of them, especially if you're staying around here.

Lâleli Camii

The **Lâleli complex**, right on Ordu Caddesi, is in the Ottoman Baroque tradition of Nuruosmaniye and the Ayazma Camii in Üsküdar, but the mosque itself owes more to traditional Ottoman architecture. It was founded by Mustafa III, whose octagonal *türbe* (tomb) is located at the southeast gate; Selim III, who was assassinated by his janissaries, is also buried there.

The main Baroque elements in the mosque complex are the use of ramps, including one which the reigning sultan would have used to ride up to his loge; the grand staircases; and the detail, for example in the window grilles of the *türbe* and in the carved eaves of the *sebil* (drinking fountain). Inside, a mass of pillars dominates, especially to the west, where the columns beneath the main dome seem to crowd those supporting the galleries into the walls. The paintwork is coarse and dull, and enlivened only a little by a flood of light from the huge windows punctuating the dome.

Back outside, the foundations of the mosque have been exploited to make space for a covered **market** or *arasta*. This is supported on eight piers and its central hall is lit by high windows, adding an extra tier to the west facade of the mosque. The market is very much in use today, selling the cheapest of clothes and acting as an inducement for the local populace to worship at the mosque.

The Aqueduct of Valens and Kalenderhane Camii

An alternative route from Beyazit into Lâleli takes you up towards the Şehzade Camii, following the line of the magnificent **Aqueduct of Valens**. Presently undergoing renovation, the aqueduct was built as part of the late fourth-century waterworks rebuilding programme carried out by the emperor Valens, part of a distribution network that included the reservoirs in the Belgrade Forest and various cisterns located around the city centre. It was in use right up to the end of the nineteenth century, having been kept in good repair by successive rulers, who maintained a constant supply of water to the city in the face of both drought and siege (which is more than can be said for the present administration). More than six hundred of its original thousand metres are still standing in the valley between the two hills of Fatih and Beyazit, at a height above Atatürk Bulvari of 18.5 metres.

The ninth-century Byzantine Church of Kyriotissa, near where the aqueduct now ends (Kalenderhane Camii Sok, 16 Mart Şehitler Cad; open for *namaz* only), was renamed **Kalenderhane Camii** after the Kalender dervishes who converted it into a *tekke* (Dervish monastery) after the conquest. It has the cruciform ground plan typical of Byzantine churches of its time, but few of its original features now remain inside: where mosaics once covered the walls and ceiling only bare brick is now visible (though this has been scrupulously restored, and some of the original coloured marble revetments and sculptural decoration have survived); the apse has been closed off (the *imam* doesn't know why, or where the key to the door is); and a truly vile carpet laid on the floor. Worst of all, the famous fourteenth-century frescoes of the life of St Francis of Assisi were removed after restoration in the 1970s, and are no longer on public display.

Zeyrek

Across Atatürk Bulvarı, the aqueduct continues into **Zeyrek**, an attractively tatty area notable for its steep, cobbled streets and ramshackle wooden houses interspersed with small mosques. There are also wonderful views of the Süleymaniye mosque complex. Crossing Atatürk Bulvarı can be something of an ordeal, as local drivers seem to regard it as a Grand Prix test track. Once across, take İtfaiye Caddesi then turn onto Zeyrek Caddesi and right onto Yeni Akıl Sokak, and carry straight on up İbadethane Arkası Sokak to reach **Zeyrek Camii**, the former Church of the Pantocrator.

This twelfth-century church was converted into a mosque at the time of the conquest and is officially open only at prayer times, though you may be able to persuade the *imam* to open the door for you (his house is up the stone steps behind the wooden door, next to the mosque). The building originally consisted of two churches and a connecting chapel, built between 1118 and 1136 by John II Comnenus and Empress Irene. The chapel was built as a mausoleum for the Comneni dynasty, and continued to be used as such by the Paleologus dynasty. Although the tombs have been removed, there is still evidence of the graves beneath the pavement. Empress Irene also founded a monastery nearby, which was to become one of the most renowned religious institutions in the empire, and later the official residence of the Byzantine court, after the Great Palace had been reduced to a ruin. No trace remains of the monastery nor of its hospice, asylum or hospital.

The **mosque**, which occupies the south church, is also in an advanced state of dilapidation, and it's difficult to believe that it was once an imperial mausoleum. Among the surviving features are the revetments of the south apse and the original marble door frames. The floor, naturally, is covered in carpets, but the *imam* may pull one of these back to give a glimpse of the coloured marble underneath: an interlacing geometric pattern with figures of animals in its borders.

Another attractive Byzantine church can be found within walking distance, albeit by a rather convoluted route. To get there, return to İbadethane Sokak, and follow this to Çirçir Caddesi. Take a right off here onto Nevşehirli İbrahim Paşa Caddesi, then a left into Hanedan Sokak, and you'll see the church, now known as the **Eski İmaret Camii**, ahead of you. To get in you'll need to arrive at prayer time or hope to find the *imam* at home (his house is connected to the mosque down a flight of stone steps). Founded at the end of the twelfth century by Empress Anna Delessena, the mother of Alexius I Comnenus, this four-column structure is similar to the south church of the Pantocrator, evidence of a return to traditional Byzantine forms, perhaps in reaction to the encroaching political threat from east and west.

Eski İmaret has one of the most interesting exteriors of all the Byzantine churches in İstanbul. As ever it's hemmed in by surrounding buildings, but in this case the wooden houses provide an attractive frame as you approach down Küçük Mektep Sokak. The roof and twelve-sided dome retain their original curved tiles, while the eaves are decorated with a zigzag of bricks. Other designs in the brickwork include swastikas and Greek keys. Inside, some of the original fittings remain, notably the red marble door frames and a floral decoration around the cornice supporting the dome. The two side apses also retain their original windows and marble cornice.

Back towards the aqueduct, the **Çinili Hamamı** or "tiled baths" on İtfaiye Caddesi make a refreshing antidote to sightseeing. This double hamam, built for the great sixteenth-century pirate-admiral Barbarossa, has been beautifully restored to working order and has a particularly friendly atmosphere. Notice the huge dome and the marble floors and fountain of the *camekân* (changing room), the enormous octagonal marble massage table in the main room of the *hararet* (steam room), and the toilets, which are continually flushed by water draining from the *hararet*. There are still a few of the original tiles on the walls in the men's section, but none are evident through the continual clouds of steam in the women's baths. The blissful bath experience can be nicely rounded off in the *Gül Lokantası*, behind the basketball court on the other side of İtfaiye Caddesi. This little basement kebab joint has a discreet but friendly atmosphere peculiar to establishments in areas slightly off the tourist agenda, and as such is a rarity in İstanbul.

The **Karikatür ve Mizah Müzesi** or Museum of Caricatures (daily 9am–6pm) is back on Atatürk Bulvarı between Cemal Yener Tosyalı Caddesi and the aqueduct, housed in the rooms of Gazanfer Medrese around a pretty garden courtyard with a marble fountain. Cartoons are an important popular art form in Turkey: most papers employ a number of cartoonists, and the weekly *Gırgır* was the third best selling comic in the world before many of its employees left to set up the rival *Avni*. The exhibition changes every week, and the museum organizes silk screen and other workshops, including some for children.

Fatih

Initial impressions of the area called **Fatih** ("the Conqueror") may be favourable: it is quieter than the centre of town, and can at first seem to have a more relaxed atmosphere. In fact, this is one of the few areas in İstanbul, and even in Turkey generally, where Islamic orthodoxy is coupled with an air of intolerance towards visitors of different religious and cultural persuasions. If you spend any time here, you'll notice that people dress differently – there are more covered women about the streets, many of them in full *chador*, little girls wear headscarves, while old men sport long white beards and knitted caps – and even the language spoken on the streets is different, full of guttural-sounding Arabic borrowings long ago discarded elsewhere in Turkey. People are more likely to take exception to naked limbs, or (perhaps understandably) to having their picture taken without due warning. Not to say you shouldn't visit: only a very small minority of people are likely to show hostility towards foreigners even in Fatih, and it's certainly worth braving such a minor cold front to see the Fatih, Yavuz Selim and Fethiye mosques.

To get to Fatih, simply follow the line of the Valens Aqueduct from the north side of Atatürk Bulvarı and keep going in the same direction when you run out of aqueduct; or from Sultanahmet take any bus going to Edirnekapı and get off at the Fatih mosque complex. On the southwest side of the aqueduct, nearest to the main road, there is a pleasant tea garden situated in a park alongside the **Fatih monument**. This bronze statue commemorates the events of 1453, when İstanbul fell to Mehmet II, the Conqueror (Fatih Sultan Mehmet as he is known in Turkish). The Conqueror and his horse are suspended from a concrete pillar between two groups of figures, one of learned men in turbans, including Mehmet's *hoca* (teacher), and the other of his standard bearer and two janissaries. The inscription notes that the monument was erected not in memory of the conquest but of the Conqueror, universally remembered for effecting the transition between two eras, and that even the figure of Ulubatlı Hasan, the standard bearer, has not been given a weapon for this reason.

Fatih Camii

The **Mosque of the Conqueror**, on İslambol Caddesi, was begun ten years after the conquest of İstanbul, in 1463, and completed in 1470. In 1766, however, it was almost completely destroyed in an earthquake: only the courtyard, the entrance portal of the mosque, the south wall of the graveyard and the bases of the minarets survived; the rest was rebuilt.

The **outer precinct** of the mosque – which is always open – is large enough to accommodate the tents of a caravan. It is enclosed by a wall and, to north and south, by the *medrese* (theological academy) buildings, which accommodated the first Ottoman university. The inner courtyard of the mosque is one of the most beautiful in the city. Verd antique and porphyry columns support a domed portico with polychrome edges, and the eighteenth-century fountain with its wide canopy is surrounded by four enormous poplar trees. Over the windows outside the courtyard in the west wall the first verse of the Koran is inscribed in white marble on verd antique, while at either end of the mosque portico there are inscriptions in the early İznik *cuerda seca* technique, whereby coloured glazes were prevented from running into each other by a dividing line of potassium permanganate, which outlined the design. The inscription over the mosque portal records the date and dedication of the mosque, and the name of the architect, Atik Sinan, who was supposedly executed the year after its completion on the orders of Mehmet, because the dome wasn't as large as that of Aya Sofya.

The **interior**, painted in drab colours without a tile in sight, is most remarkable for being so well frequented that it is rarely empty, even outside prayer times. It appears to be a social meeting place as well as a centre of serious Koranic study for both women and men. As in all mosques, the men occupy the main body of the building while the women's section is confined to the anterior regions, where you'll find an unusual old bronze water pump with silver cups.

The **tombs** of Mehmet II and of one of his wives, Gülbahar (Wed–Sun 9.30am–4.30pm), are situated to the east of the mosque. The originals were destroyed in the earthquake, and while that of Gülbahar is probably a facsimile of the original, the *türbe* of the Conqueror is sumptuous Baroque. **Çorba Kapısı**, the Soup Gate, to the southeast of the mosque, is original, inlaid in porphyry and verd antique. The gate leads to the nearby *tabhane*, the hospice for travelling dervishes, which has recently been restored and is now used as a Koran school.

Other mosques in Fatih

Yavuz Selim Camii (also known as the Selimiye), on Yavuz Selim Caddesi, is a twenty-minute walk from Fatih Camii. Alternatively you could take a ferryboat up the Golden Horn from Eminönü to Aykapı İskelesi and walk up to the mosque, again about twenty minutes. Built on a terrace on the crest of one of İstanbul's seven hills (the fifth, counting from Topkapı's), the mosque holds a commanding position over the surrounding suburbs, and viewed on the approach down Yavuz Selim Caddesi it presents one of the most impressive facades to be seen in the city. This is mainly because of its position next to the **Cistern of Aspar**, one of three open cisterns built during the fifth and sixth centuries in Constantinople; more recently this space housed market gardens and a village, but these were cleared away as part of Mayor Dalan's slum clearance programme, and although a brand new covered market was promised in its place, the cistern is still a wasteland, across which you get a clear view of the mosque.

The mosque of Yavuz Selim (**Selim the Grim**) was probably begun in the reign of Selim and completed by Süleyman, but its dates are not certain. Close up, the exterior is rather bleak, a fitting memorial to a man with such a reputation for cruelty. Here there's no pretty cascade of domes and turrets, just a large dome sitting squat on a square room with a walled courtyard in front of it. Once inside the courtyard walls, however, this simple, restrained building emerges as one of the most attractive of all the imperial mosques. The central fountain is surrounded by tall cypress trees, and the floor of the portico is paved with an attractive floral design, while its columns are a variety of marbles and granites.

The **domed rooms** to the north and south of the mosque – which served as hostels for travelling dervishes – are characteristic of early Ottoman architecture, seen particularly in the Yeşil Camii at Bursa. In the mosque itself, long pendentives alternate with tall arches supporting the great shallow dome, which is hardly painted at all but inset with stained-glass windows. The lack of decoration, combined with an expanse of green carpet and grey marble, is very attractive. Under the sultan's loge (supported on columns in a variety of rare marbles) is paintwork in designs reminiscent of the delicacy of Turkish carpets or ceramics, a great relief after an excess of arabesque stencilling; in places there are bunches of flowers tied with painted bows, which cannot predate the eighteenth century, but the rest of the paintwork may be original.

The **tomb of Selim the Grim** (Wed–Sun 9.30am–4.30pm), beside the mosque, has lost its original interior decoration, but retains two beautiful tiled panels on either side of the door. Other tombs in the complex include that of four of Süleyman the Magnificent's children, probably the work of Sinan.

A fifteen-minute walk from Yavuz Selim Camii – follow Daruşşafaka Caddesi northwest until it becomes Manyasizade Caddesi – is **Fethiye Camii**, the former **Church of Theotokos Pammakaristos** (Sat & Sun 9.30am–5pm; $0.50). This twelfth-century church was one of the few that remained in the hands of the Byzantines after the conquest, and was home to the Patriarchate from 1456 to 1568. Mehmet II would come here to discuss matters of theology with the patriarch Gennadius, leading to the supposition in the West that he intended to convert to Christianity. The church and chapel were converted into a mosque in 1591 and called Fethiye ("Victory") Camii to commemorate the end of the Persian wars. At the time of writing it's not worth making this trip unless you've received permission to visit in advance from the Directorate of Aya Sofya, located in the grounds of Aya Sofya museum – you won't be admitted to see the mosaics without some kind of official sanction, preferably a written document.

The **mosaics** – which are really what you come here to see – are all located in the memorial chapel erected in memory of General Michael Doukas Glabas Tarchaniotes, who died in 1310, by his widow Maria. This small chapel, crammed with mosaics, is situated to the south of the mosque, closed off by partitions, and can only be opened by its curator. Among the highlights are, in the dome, Christ Pantocrator surrounded by twelve prophets; a Deisis with Christ in the apse; the Virgin on the left wall; John the Baptist on the right; and four archangels in the vault above. There is also a mosaic of the baptism of Christ on the vault of the south aisle. The inscription on the south wall, in gold letters on a blue ground, is a poem by Manuel Philes commemorating the love of Maria for her husband:

Therefore I will construct for thee this tomb as a pearl-oyster shell,
Or shell of the purple dye, rose of another clime,
Even though being plucked thou art pressed by the stones
So as to cause me shedding of tears . . .

Ask to climb the stairs to the little balcony to the west of the chapel, as there is a better view of some of the mosaics from this angle.

The city walls and Eyüp

Theodosius II's **city walls** are among the most fascinating Byzantine remains to be found in Turkey. Remnants in varying states of preservation can be found along the whole of their six-and-a-half-kilometre length. The walls are currently being renovated, a process scorned by local and international historians and archeologists, who consider the work unnecessary and historically invalid. Worse still, it is feared that important historical evidence may have been lost in the course of the renovations.

If time is limited, the best places to visit are the Yedikule fortifications and surrounding district; or Edirnekapı, which could include a tour of Kariye Camii, a mainly fourteenth-century former Byzantine church with some of the best-preserved mosaics and frescoes in the world, and a Mimar Sinan mosque, Mihrimah Camii. Although there's a fair amount to be seen in the Topkapı area, it's a rough and dangerous place further marred by one of the city's major bus garages.

A walk along the walls takes at least a day, longer if some of the major sites scattered along the way are to be explored at the same time. Some of the areas you will have to negotiate in an attempt to follow the lines of the walls are unsafe, particularly the stretch between Belgrat Kapısı and Silivri Kapısı, which is a deserted wasteland.

The land walls were named after Theodosius II, even though he was only twelve years old when their construction was started in 413. The walls – which stretch from the Marmara to Tekfur Saray, approximately 2km further out than the previous walls of Constantine – were planned by Anthemius, Prefect of the East, to accommodate the city's expanded population. They were almost completely destroyed by an earthquake in 447 and had to be rebuilt in haste, since Attila's forces were on the point of attack. An ancient edict was brought into effect whereby all citizens, regardless of rank, were required to help in the rebuilding, and the Hippodrome factions of Blues and Greens (see box on p.105) provided 16,000 labourers and finished the project in just two months. The completed construction consisted of the original wall, 5m thick and 12m high, plus an outer wall of 2m by 8.5m, and a 20-metre-wide moat. This was sufficient to repel Atilla's Huns: they numbered several thousand but did not have the skill or patience for siege warfare.

Buses from Eminönü and Sultanahmet include the #80 to Yedikule, #84 to Topkapı and #86 to Edirnekapı, but the best way of reaching the walls is to take a local *banliyö* train to Yedikule on the Marmara shore. Bring a torch if you want to explore the fortifications thoroughly.

Yedikule and the Golden Gate

Yedikule is a quaintly attractive quarter, full of churches since it is a centre of Rum Orthodoxy: the dwindling congregations of such churches, scattered throughout İstanbul, are the last remaining descendants of the Byzantine Greeks. When you leave the train station, on Yedikule İstasyon Caddesi, head away from the sea along Halit Efendi Sokak and you reach İmrahor İlyas Bey Caddesi, Yedikule's main street. Here you'll find a concentration of quaint, Greek-influenced houses and some attractive churches.

İmrahor Camii

The only ancient building of any note in the vicinity of Yedikule is the **İmrahor Camii**, the former Church of St John of Studius, at İmam Aşır Sokak, off İmrahor İlyas Bey Caddesi. Even this is almost completely ruined. To get there, walk straight up Halit Efendi Sokak from the train station and you'll see the remains on your right. Whatever anyone may suggest to the contrary, there is no entrance fee to see them.

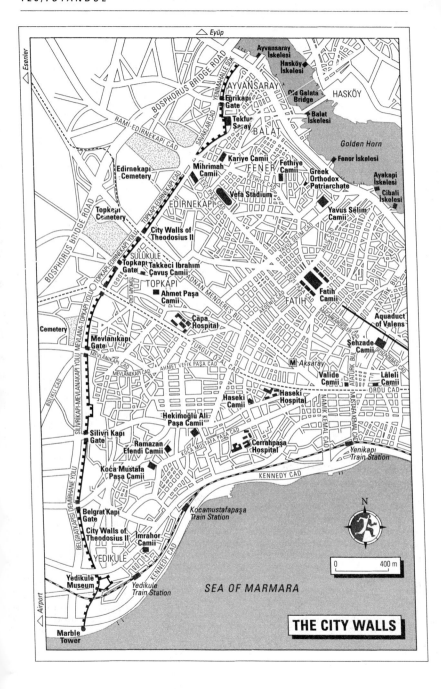

THE CITY WALLS

The church, built in 463, was connected to a monastery of the *akoimetai* or "unsleeping", who prayed in relay around the clock. The monks lived according to the strict rules of St Basil: even melancholy was considered a sin and the monks were required to keep before them the spectre of death by repeating the words "We shall die!" over and over. They still found time, however, to transcribe books for mass circulation, and monks even came to the monastery from Russia to learn the trade and prepare books for distribution at home. The monastery gained particular renown under the auspices of **Abbot Theodore**, an outspoken defender of images and critic of the Byzantine court, who established it as the centre of a renaissance in Byzantine scholarship. Although he died in exile on the Princes' Islands, the reputation of the institution survived him, and the monastery was home to the University of Constantinople during the first half of the fifteenth century. Its greatest claim to historical fame, though, came in 1042, when the tyrant **Michael V** took refuge here from a popular revolution. He made his way to the church by ship, but was discovered, dragged from the altar and blinded.

As you approach the **church entrance** you'll see four large columns with acanthus capitals, supporting a horizontal carved entablature. This is the entrance to the narthex and the east wall of the atrium, which was square and probably colonnaded. The interior of the church was a simple, almost square basilica: the aisles were partitioned off by rows of columns, six of which have survived, and again these are capped with acanthus capitals and support a horizontal entablature. The interlace floor is twelfth-century, but what remains of the original fittings suggests that the church was sumptuously decorated, in contrast to its simple structure.

The Yedikule fortifications

The most impressive sections of wall here have been designated the **Yedikule museum** (Tues–Sun 9.30am–4.30pm; $1), situated to the southwest of İmrahor Camii on Yedikule Meydanı Sokak, Yedikule Caddesi. Follow Kuyulu Bakkal Sokak (or, from the station, Yedikule İstasyon Cad) straight to the entrance.

The **Golden Gate**, flanked by two marble towers, was constructed on this site by Theodosius I in 390, before even the walls themselves. This monumental entranceway stood alone, a triumphal arch in the path of important visitors of state and of conquering emperors (generals were never permitted to pass through the gate even after successful campaigns). Nowadays the shape of the three arches is still visible on both sides of the wall, but it takes a degree of imagination to invest the structure with the glamour and dignity it must once have possessed. Michael Palaeologus was the last emperor to ride through the gate in triumph, when the city was recaptured from occupying Crusaders. After the empire went into decline, the gold-plated doors were removed and the entryway bricked up.

The other five towers of the Yedikule ("seven-tower") fortifications were added by Mehmet the Conqueror, and with their 12-metre-high curtain walls they form the enclave which can be seen today. Despite appearances this was never used as a castle, but two of the towers served as prisons and others were used as treasuries and offices for the collection of revenue of the *Vakıf* or pious foundation.

For those possessing a morbid disposition, the two **prison towers** are those immediately to the left of the entrance: the "tower with inscriptions" and the tower on the north side of the Golden Gate. The inscriptions around the outside of the first of these were carved into the walls by prisoners, many of whom were foreign ambassadors on some hapless errand. The prison in the second tower doubled as an execution chamber: the wooden gallows and "well of blood", into which heads would roll, are still to be seen, and the odd instrument of torture can be found lying about outside in the courtyard. The most famous victim of the execution chamber was Osman II, deposed and murdered in 1622 by his janissaries, thus providing Ottoman history with its first case of regicide.

Your visit to Yedikule is worth spending some time over, climbing around the battlements with the lizards. **Views** include the Marble Tower, where the sea and land walls meet beyond the railway line on the Marmara coast, and a good stretch of the walls to the south.

Towards Topkapı

When leaving Yedikule to walk along the walls you'll come across the first of the public gateways, the **Yedikule Kapısı**. This is still in use: self-appointed and official traffic wardens compete to direct traffic through the narrow entry, while a Byzantine eagle cut in the blackened marble overhead remains serenely oblivious to the commotion below.

Most of the outer wall and its 96 towers are still standing, and their **construction** can be examined in detail if you are dressed to clamber in the dirt and brick dust. The stone used is limestone, and the bricks, about a foot square and two inches thick, were sometimes stamped with the name of the manufacturer or donor and bear the name of the emperor in whose reign they were made. Mortar mixed with brick dust was used liberally to bind the masonry. The towers had two levels, separated by the small brick domes used in Byzantine architecture to strengthen roof structures so that they would support weight overhead.

You can walk between the first gate and the second, **Belgrat Kapısı**, along a path which leads along the top of the inner wall and then down to the terrace between the two walls. Belgrat Kapısı was a military gate, distinguished from a public gateway in that there was no bridge crossing the moat beyond the outer walls. It was named for the captives who were settled in this area by Süleyman the Magnificent after his capture of Belgrade in 1521. The walls here have been substantially renovated – they're floodlit at night – and a cannonball from the cannon of Mehmet the Conqueror has been stuck into the wall with the claim that it became embedded there during the siege of Constantinople in 1453.

Silivri Kapısı

The area immediately to the north of Belgrat Kapısı is a deserted wasteland, unsafe for lone tourists, so it's advisable to take a dolmuş on to **Silivri Kapısı**, a gate that's been extensively renovated, though the walls on either side remain untouched so far.

A diversion from Silivri Kapısı, which needs about an hour to complete, takes you through the Muslim and Christian graveyards to the west of the walls. Cross the main Belgratkapısı–Demirhane Yolu Caddesi to the road leading off nearly opposite the gate, Seyit Nizam Caddesi, and take a right fork into Silivrikapı–Balıklı Caddesi. On the left of this street is the **shrine of Zöodohou Piyi**, the "Life-Giving Spring", called Balıklı Kilise or the "Church of the Fish" in Turkish. Buried in the graveyard here are several patriarchs of the Greek Orthodox Church, including the last patriarch, whose body was brought from the United States in 1972. The gravestones bear interesting masonic symbols, and marks of vandalism perpetrated during the anti-Greek riots of 1955.

The Christian shrine was built by Leo I and dedicated to the Virgin, although it is thought that it could be on the site of a pre-Christian sanctuary of Artemis. Successive emperors visited the shrine once a year, on Assumption Day, and it was rebuilt several times during the Byzantine period, although the present building dates from 1833. A flight of steps leads down to the chapel of the sacred spring, where you can peer into the hallowed depths for fish.

Mevlanikapı

Back at the walls, the walk to Mevlevihane Kapısı is best done along the backstreets on the opposite side of the main road, partly because the walls themselves are in too bad a state of repair to be worth exploring, but also because these are interesting suburbs, where wooden houses are interspersed with foundries and other fascinating workplaces.

There is more restoration work at the **Mevlanıkapı**, and also some interesting inscriptions on the outer wall. The Theodosian walls reached completion at this gate, since the Greens, building from the Marmara, met the Blues, who were working southwards from the direction of the Golden Horn. A Latin inscription to the left of the gate celebrates this fact: "By the command of Theodosius, Constantine erected these strong fortifications in less than two months. Scarcely could Pallas [Athena] herself have built so strong a citadel in so short a time."

Topkapı and around

The Topkapı gate is barely 1km further on, but again it's difficult to walk along the walls themselves, because of the gypsy encampments on this stretch. It's probably better to stick to the backstreets. Just south of Topkapı the walls have been destroyed to make way for the enormous thoroughfare of Turgut Özal Caddesi, and you will somehow have to cross this to reach Topkapı itself. On the other side, walk up the steep, stony path from Turgut Özal Caddesi to Paşa Odaları Caddesi, inside the walls, until you reach the area called Kaleiçi and the **Topkapı** gate. The "Gate of the Cannonball" is named after the most powerful cannon of Mehmet the Conqueror (see below), some of whose enormous stone cannonballs have been placed around the inside of the gate. To get here by public transport, take a tram from Sirkeci, Sultanahmet or Aksaray.

On the other side of the walls is the **Topkapı Bit Pazarı** (literally "louse market"), where poverty reveals its worst side in the painful sale and resale of dirty, disintegrated pieces of clothing.

At Kaleiçi you can get a decent midday meal at any of the *lokanta*s and *pide* or kebab salons on Topkapı Caddesi . At the bottom of this street, on the left, is the **Ahmet Paşa Camii**, a Sinan mosque dating from 1554. In the porch there are original tiles made in the *cuerda seca* technique, and despite some heavy-handed renovation it's worth having a look inside at the original arabesque painting under the galleries.

Another attractive mosque in this region is on Topkapı–Davutpaşa Caddesi (south off Davutpaşa Cad). The wooden **Takkeci İbrahim Çavuş Camii** (open for *namaz* only) is delightful and retains much that is original, including its wooden dome and some fine tile panels from the best İznik period (a few botched copies only serve to highlight the beauty of the real thing). The underside of the galleries and the stalactite pendentives also retain their original paintwork. The mosque was founded in 1592 by the eponymous *takkeci*, a maker of the distinctive felt hats (*takke*) worn by dervishes. The income of an artisan could not have been equal to the cost of building a mosque, however modest, and around this fact no doubt has grown the myth of its origins.

It is said that the hatmaker was told in a dream to go to Baghdad, where he would find a great treasure buried under a vine tree in the garden of an inn. He duly set off on his donkey and, arriving at the place of his dream, he began to dig under said vine. The innkeeper came out and enquired his business, admonished him and advised him to return to the place from which he had started his journey. On arriving back in Topkapı, the *takkeci* found two bags of gold on the present site of the mosque. Burying one in the ground, he used the other to finance the building of his mosque, the idea being that if this mosque were destroyed then another could be built in its place with the buried gold. The *imam* who tells this story to visitors points out a panel of faience tiles depicting plump red grapes hanging on vines, jokingly suggesting that these are corroborative evidence of his story. And in such a poor parish who can blame him for clinging to the fond hope that sufficient funds are buried beneath the wooden mosque to finance its rebuilding should the need arise.

Towards Edirnekapı

Between Topkapı and Edirnekapı there is a pronounced valley, formerly the route of the Lycus river, now taken by Vatan Caddesi. At this point the walls are at their least defensible, since the higher ground outside gives the advantage to attackers. The famed **Orban cannon** of Mehmet the Conqueror was trained on this part of the walls during the siege of 1453 – hence their ruinous state – and it was here that Constantine XI rode into the midst of the Turkish army after he realized that all hope of holding out was gone.

Beyond Vatan Caddesi, just inside the walls, lies **Sulukule**, where late at night travellers are persuaded to part with vast sums of money by gypsy dance troupes who live in the ramshackle houses in this area. The idea is that the brothers play *kemençe* (a bowed string instrument) while you stuff money into their sisters' bodices to get them to dance for you as you eat mother's home cooking. Turks who used to frequent the place will no longer go near it; but if you don't mind being ripped off to the tune of forty or fifty dollars in an evening, this is an enjoyable place to lose it. It's advisable to go with someone who knows the area, though, or at least a Turkish speaker, since it's potentially a little dangerous for lone foreigners.

Edirnekapı itself is a small-time suburb with a large *otogar* for local buses and no decent restaurants. The gate of Edirnekapı takes its name from the route to modern Edirne, which passed through even in Byzantine times. Also left over from the Byzantine era is the smallest of the ancient city's open cisterns, located about 50m from the *otogar* on the left of Fevzi Paşa Caddesi (Edirnekapı's main street), below the level of the road. It's now the site of the Vefa sports stadium, but the original dimensions of the cistern can still be seen. Buses straight to Edirnekapı from town include the #28 from Eminönü.

The **Mihrimah Camii** is a little to the left of the *otogar* as you face the walls. Mihrimah, the favourite daughter of Süleyman the Magnificent, had a passion for architecture as great as that of her husband Rüstem Paşa, and the couple commissioned many of Sinan's early works, both in İstanbul and elsewhere. The Mihrimah Camii, situated on the highest of İstanbul's seven hills, dates from somewhere around the middle of the sixteenth century. Raised on a platform, the area beneath is occupied by shops, and can be seen from all over the city and especially as you approach from Edirne.

The mosque and its dependencies have suffered in two earthquakes, the second of which brought the minaret tumbling down onto the mosque itself, and during renovation the interior was filled with twentieth-century arabesque stencilling. Other aspects of the interior compensate, however, especially the light flooding in through the vast number of windows – fifteen in the tympana of each arch – and the graceful white marble *mimber*. Note the skilful fake marbling of the arches under the eastern gallery. The mosque's nearby **hamam** has also been poorly restored but at least is still functioning.

Kariye Camii

To get to **Kariye Camii** (daily except Tues 9.30am–4.30pm; $2) from Edirnekapı, take Vaiz Sokak off Fevzi Paşa Caddesi, and a second right onto Kariye Bostanı Sokak. This street has a number of picturesquely renovated wooden houses, painted in pastel colours as they would have been originally. At the bottom of the street the *Asitane,* the garden restaurant of the renovated *Kariye Hotel*, is expensive, but you may feel like splashing out for good service and food in such a peaceful location.

Kariye Camii, formerly the Church of St Saviour in Chora, contains a series of superbly preserved frescoes and mosaics, among the most evocative of all the city's

Byzantine treasures. The church was probably built in the early twelfth century on the site of a building predating the walls: hence "in Chora", meaning "in the country". The nave and central apse are all that remain of that church. Between 1316 and 1321 the statesman and scholar Theodore Metochites rebuilt the central dome and added the narthexes and mortuary chapel.

The narthexes

The **mosaics and frescoes** date from the same period as the renovations carried out by Metochites, and depict the life of Christ in picture-book sequence. The first series to be followed is a set of dedicatory and devotional panels located in the two **narthexes**. On entering the church, the most prominent of the mosaics is that of Christ Pantocrator, bearing the inscription "Jesus Christ, the Land of the Living". Opposite this, above the entrance, is a depiction of the Virgin and angels, with the inscription "Mother of God, the Dwelling Place of the Uncontainable". The third in the series is located in the inner narthex and depicts Metochites offering a model of the building to a seated Christ. The hat he is wearing is called a *skiadon*, or "sunshade". Saints Peter and Paul are portrayed on either side of the door leading to the nave, and to the right of the door are Christ with his Mother and two benefactors, Isaac (who built the original church) and a female figure, described in the inscription as "Lady of the Mongols, Melane the Nun".

In the two domes of the inner narthex are medallions of Christ Pantocrator and the Virgin and Child; and in the fluting of the domes, a series of notable figures – starting with Adam – from the **Genealogy of Christ**. The **Cycle of the Blessed Virgin** is located in the first three bays of the inner narthex. These mosaics are based on the apocryphal gospel of St James, which gives an account of the birth and life of the Virgin and was very popular in the Middle Ages. Episodes depicted here include the first seven steps of the Virgin (taken when she was six months old); the Virgin caressed by her parents, with two beautiful peacocks in the background; the Virgin presented as an attendant at the temple (where she remained from the age of three to twelve); the Virgin receiving a skein of purple wool, as proof of her royal blood; Joseph taking the Virgin to his house, in which is also depicted one of Joseph's sons by his first wife; and Joseph returning from a six-month business trip to find his wife pregnant.

The next cycle, to be found in the lunettes of the outer narthex, is that of the **Infancy of Christ**. The mosaics can be followed clockwise, starting with Joseph dreaming, the Virgin and two companions, and the journey to Bethlehem. Apart from well-known scenes like the Journey of the Magi and the Nativity, there are depictions in the seventh bay (furthest right from the main entrance) of the Flight into Egypt, which includes the apocryphal Fall of Idols (white and ghostly looking figures) from the walls of an Egyptian town as the holy family passes by. In the sixth bay is the Slaughter of the Innocents, complete with babies impaled on spikes. The inscription accompanying the picture of Herod says "Then Herod, when he saw that he was mocked of the Wise Men, was exceeding wroth and sent forth and slew all the children that were in Bethlehem, and in all the coasts thereof, from two years and under".

The **Cycle of Christ's Ministry** fills the vaults of the outer narthex, and parts of the south bay of the inner narthex. It includes wonderful scenes of the Temptation of Christ, with dramatic dialogue (Matthew 4: 3–10) that could almost be in speech bubbles, beginning:

Devil: If thou be the Son of God, command that these stones be made bread.
Christ: It is written, Man shall not live by bread alone, but by every word that proceedeth out of the mouth of God.

Other scenes in this cycle deal with the miracles.

The nave and funerary chapel

In the **nave**, the main frescoes echo the mosaics, featuring the death of the Virgin, over the door, and to the right of this, another depiction of Christ with the inscription "Jesus Christ, the Land of the Living". To the left, the inscription accompanying the picture of the Virgin again reads "Mother of God, the Dwelling Place of the Uncontainable". The best known of all the works in the church, however, are the frescoes in the **funerary chapel** (known as the paracclesion) to the south of the nave. These comprise depictions of the Resurrection, the Last Judgement, Heaven and Hell, and the Mother of God. Below the cornice are portraits of the saints and martyrs.

The most spectacular of the frescoes is the **Resurrection**, also known as the Harrowing of Hell. This is a dramatic representation of Christ in action, trampling the gates of Hell underfoot and forcibly dragging Adam and Eve from their tombs. A black Satan lies among the broken fetters at his feet, bound at the ankles, wrists and neck, but still writhing around in a vital manner. To the left of the painting, animated onlookers include John the Baptist, David and Solomon, while to the right Abel is standing in his mother's tomb, behind him another group of the righteous.

Other frescoes in the chapel, in the vault of the east bay, depict the **Second Coming**. In the east half of the domical vault Christ sits in judgement, saying to the souls of the saved, on his right, "Come ye blessed of my Father, inherit the kingdom prepared for you from the foundation of the world". To the condemned souls on the left he says: "Depart from me, ye cursed, into everlasting fire, prepared for the devil and his angels". Below, a river of fire broadens into a lake in which are the souls of the damned. Their torments are illustrated in the lunette of the south wall, and comprise the Gnashing of Teeth, the Outer Darkness, the Worm that Sleepeth Not and the Unquenchable Fire.

The tomb in the north wall of the paracclesion has lost its inscription, but is almost certainly that of Metochites, the donor of the church.

Tekfur Saray

The remains of a late thirteenth-century Byzantine palace, **Tekfur Saray**, which was originally known as the Palace of the Porphyrogenitus (meaning "born into the purple", the royal colour in Byzantium), are located alongside the walls between Edirnekapı and Eğri Kapı. A sign above the entrance proclaims the entrance fee as 200TL, but the occupants of the cottage inside the palace walls may try to charge you more. In actual fact, entrance is free. What you'll see are the bare walls of a simple rectangular structure – originally it was three-storeyed – decorated with brick and marble geometric designs, notably on the courtyard's north facade.

From Tekfur Saray towards the Horn, the Theodosian walls were replaced in the twelfth century by a single, thicker wall without a moat, and with strong, high towers placed close together. This section is presently being restored with gaudy white breeze blocks and red brick.

Eyüp

Beyond the walls, though more obviously reached up the Golden Horn by boat from Eminönü, there's one final place worth seeing. **Eyüp** is the last ferry stop before the Horn peters out into two small streams (there are also bus and minibus services from the centre), or it's an attractive twenty-minute walk from Eğrikapı, just below Tekfur Saray. The only problem is crossing the Bosphorus Bridge arterial road; once you've done this go north along Aşhane Sokak (where there's an attractive little mosque, the Aşçıbaşı Camii) and continue in the same direction, parallel to the Horn, until you come out at Eyüp.

Eyüp is one of the holiest places in Islam, and Muslims come here from all over the Islamic world on pilgrimage. It's now one of the districts of İstanbul controlled by the Islamic Welfare Party, who are carrying out an extensive restoration programme in the suburb, spending large amounts of money to create a showcase for the party. As a consequence, Eyüp has a refreshingly well-heeled atmosphere – as long as you're not over-concerned about who might be backing the Refah Partisi and making these good works feasible.

The beautiful complex of **Eyüp Camii** is famous above all as the site of the tomb of Eyüp Ensari, the Prophet Mohammed's standard bearer. One of the small group of companions of the Prophet, Eyüp Ensari was killed during the first Arab siege of Constantinople (674–678); a condition of the peace treaty signed following the siege was that his tomb be preserved. Later, the complex hosted the investiture ceremonies of the Ottoman sultans, described by Pierre Loti (see below):

> In the holy mosque of Eyoub, amid scenes of great pomp, Abdül Hamid girded the scimitar of Osman. After this ceremony, he marched at the head of a long and brilliant procession all through Stamboul, on his way to the Palace of the old Seraglio, pausing at every mosque and funerary kiosque in his path to pay the customary acts of worship and prayer . . .
>
> On the heights of Eyoub were massed a swaying multitude of Turkish ladies, their heads veiled with the white folds of the yashmak, while their graceful forms, in vivid silken draperies that swept the ground, could hardly be distinguished from the painted and chiselled tombstones beneath the cypresses.

The mosque and tomb are about a ten-minute walk from the ferry dock, on Camii Kebir Caddesi. They face each other across the courtyard that was the scene of the girding of the sultans, the exact site marked by a raised platform surrounded by railings, from which two plane trees grow. The original mosque, built by Mehmet the Conqueror in honour of Eyüp Ensari, was destroyed in the eighteenth century, probably by the same earthquake that put paid to Fatih Camii. The present Baroque replacement, filled with light, gold, pale stone and white marble, was completed in 1800. The **türbe of Eyüp Ensari** is far more compelling, however (footwear should be removed and women should cover their heads before entering). Its facade and vestibule are covered in tile panels from many different periods, and although the overall effect is a bit overwhelming, the panels constitute a beautiful and varied display of the art form: you could spend weeks visiting individual buildings to see as many different designs and styles.

There are a number of other important tombs in the Eyüp district, as it was a popular place of burial for Ottoman dignitaries. Two of these, the **tombs of Sokollu Mehmet Paşa and Siyavus Paşa** (Tues–Sun 9.30am–4.30pm), stand opposite each other on either side of Cami Kebir Caddesi, five minutes' walk from Eyüp Camii towards the Golden Horn. Sokollu Mehmet Paşa commissioned Mimar Sinan to build his tomb in around 1574, five years before his assassination. It is an elegantly proportioned octagonal building notable for its stained glass, some of which is original; connected to the tomb by an elegant three-arched colonnade is a former Koran school. Decorated with beautiful İznik tiles, Siyavus Paşa's tomb was probably actually built by Sinan for the children of Siyavus Paşa, who had died young.

Eyüp is still a popular burial place, and the hills above the mosque are covered in plain modern stones interspersed with beautiful Ottoman tombs. To the north of the mosque, off Silahtarağa Caddesi, Karyağdı Sokak leads up into the Eyüp cemetery. Following the signs up this lane through the graveyard – most beautiful at sunset – you'll reach, about twenty minutes' walk from Eyüp Camii, the **Pierre Loti Café**, where waiters in Ottoman costume serve up Turkish coffee. The café was made famous by the autobiographical novel of Pierre Loti (pen name of Julien Marie Viaud), a young French naval officer and writer of romantic novels and travel books, who fell in love with the green eyes of a Circassian harem girl called Aziyade in nineteenth-century İstanbul. Perhaps his most fitting memorial is this romantic little café overlooking the Golden Horn.

ACROSS THE HORN TO TAKSİM

Life across the Horn revolves around the massive open plaza of **Taksim**, the modern
business centre of İstanbul. Such a large, airy space – wholly untypical of traditional
Islamic city planning – is a glorious relief after you've been grubbing around in the
backstreets of the old quarters, but as an imitation of a Western-style plaza it's not a
great success, lacking the essential monumental architecture to balance its broad
expanse. *Taksim* in Turkish means "distribution", and in late Ottoman times the reservoir at the top of İstiklâl Caddesi was the main water distribution centre for the whole
city.

You're most likely to arrive on this side of the Horn across the Galata Bridge to
Karaköy and into the old Levantine areas of **Galata** and **Pera**, formerly inhabited by
İstanbul's various ethnic minorities. The first of these were the Genoese, who built one
of the city's most famous landmarks here, the Galata Tower. Not far from the northern
end of the bridge is the entrance to the **Tünel**, İstanbul's underground system, which
runs less than a kilometre up to the start of İstiklâl Caddesi. Built in 1875 by French
engineers, this is one of the oldest underground systems in Europe. From the top you
can follow İstiklâl Caddesi all the way through to Taksim.

The wayward carousing that takes place in the drinking establishments, strip joints,
and most recently the transvestite bars of the European quarters of İstanbul has afforded it notoriety since the sixteenth century. Taksim is still central to İstanbul's nightlife,
whether this be classical opera and ballet, cinemas, or gay bars. At night, the suited
business types give way to transvestite prostitutes who cruise the square and the city's
gay bars, located on Saraselviler Caddesi off Taksim Square. Daytime pleasures on this
side of the Horn include a number of interesting monuments and museums, the İstiklâl
tramway, and the opportunity to explore – away from the tourist trail – the steep, mysterious backstreets of İstiklâl, with their hidden bars, junk shops and hamams.

Any number of **buses** cross the Horn via the Galata and Atatürk bridges. Take ones
marked "Beyoğlu" or "Taksim" from Aksaray, or buses from Eminönü marked
"Karaköy" or "Taksim". It's also pleasant to walk up to Beyoğlu, taking the steep
Yüksek Kaldırım Caddesi past the Galata Tower and on up to Galipdede Sokak, well
known for its book and musical instrument stores.

Galata and Beyoğlu

The settlement at **Galata** is as old as the city itself. In the fifth century the area already
had city walls, which were restored by Justinian, and towards the end of the century
Tiberius is said to have built a fortress on this side of the Horn, to facilitate the closure
of the water to enemy shipping.

The **Genoese** occupation of Galata began when they gave active support to Michael
Palaeologus in his attempt to drive out the Crusaders. In return he signed a treaty in
March 1261, granting them preferential treatment throughout his dominions, present
and future, and signing Galata over to them as a semi-independent colony. From that
date until the Turkish conquest of Constantinople, the Genoese busied themselves with
fortifying their stronghold and expanding its territory. The Byzantines no doubt lived
to regret the privileges granted to the colony when the Genoese repaid them with neutrality during the final siege of Constantinople by Mehmet the Conqueror. The new sultan, however, showed his gratitude by allowing the Genoese to retain their commercial
and religious establishments, although arms were to be handed over and walls torn
down.

During the early centuries of Ottoman rule, Galata became established as the city's **European quarter**. The Jews invited from Spain by Beyazit II settled here, as well as Moorish, Greek and Armenian refugees. In time, foreign powers set up their embassies in the area, and it was also a popular haunt of visiting merchants, seamen and dignitaries. Lady Mary Montague Wortley wrote in a letter in 1718 that very few Europeans were prepared to brave the journey across the Horn to "Constantinople", or old Stamboul:

> *Christian men are loath to hazard the adventures they sometimes meet amongst the Levents or seamen . . . and the women must cover their faces to go there, which they have a perfect aversion to do. 'Tis true they wear veils in Pera, but they are only such as serve to show their beauty to more advantage, and which would not be permitted in Constantinople. Those reasons deter almost every creature from seeing it, and the French Ambassadress will return to France (I believe) without ever having been there.*

The word **Pera** is Greek for "beyond" or "across", and it was originally used interchangeably with Galata to refer to the area across the Horn. Later it came to denote the district above Galata, present-day **Beyoğlu**, to which the European quarter, in particular the diplomatic corps, gradually spread as Galata became too crowded. The *Pera Palas Hotel* was built here in the late nineteenth century to accommodate a new influx of travellers from Europe, encouraged by the completion of the Orient Express Railway in 1889. Around the same time Pera became a favoured haunt – and subject matter – of a school of artists heavily influenced by European "salon" painting of the nineteenth century. The best-known member of the Pera school was Osman Hamdi Bey (1842–1909), the first Ottoman Muslim painter to have his work displayed abroad.

The **nightlife** of the quarter was notoriously riotous even in the seventeenth century, when Evliya Çelebi could write:

> *Whoever says Galata says taverns, because they are as numerous there as at Leghorn or Malta. The word Gumrah (seducing from the road) is most particularly to be applied to the taverns of Galata, because there are all kinds of playing and dancing boys, mimics and fools flock together and delight themselves day and night.*

By the nineteenth and early twentieth centuries, the area had become fashionable for its operettas, music halls, taverns, cinemas and restaurants; and it was only after the exodus of the Greek population from İstanbul in the 1920s that Galata and Pera began to lose much of the cosmopolitan flavour on which they had thrived. Other minorities followed, partly as a result of the wealth tax imposed on ethnic communities between 1942 and 1944, and until recently it looked as if the area would be entirely destroyed by office building and lack of planning.

In recent years, however, there have been moves to restore the appearance of Beyoğlu, starting with its most famous food emporium, the Çiçek Pasajı. Attempts have also been made at an historical revamp of Beyoğlu's main boulevard, **İstiklâl Caddesi**, once known as the Grand Rue de Pera. The street is now a pedestrian precinct, with a tramline complete with 1920s trams running along its 1.2-kilometre length.

Attempts have also been made to clean up the sleazier side of Beyoğlu's image. The side streets off İstiklâl Caddesi are still lined with "adult" cinemas and nightclubs that are as big a rip-off as their counterparts anywhere else in Europe, but the city's official **brothels** (known collectively as İki Buçuk or "two-and-a-half", from the days when this was the going price charged, in lira) have been closed down by the Islamic Welfare Party, who now run the Greater Istanbul municipality. Prostitution now takes place on the streets or in taxis, with no police to protect the women. Meanwhile, Beyoğlu is still good for bars, *meyhane*s, restaurants and art cinemas, the area of Çukurcuma off İstiklâl Caddesi has the best antique shops in town, and the best of Turkey's clothing

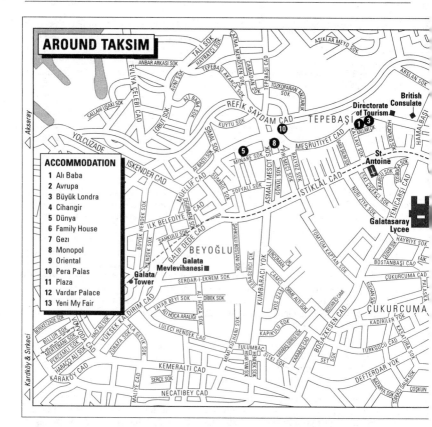

outlets are reappearing among İstiklâl's rejuvenated shopfronts. While there's little hope of recapturing the district's cosmopolitan past, when it was almost entirely populated by the city's European minorities, given the chance the new Beyoğlu may flourish in its own right.

From Galata Tower to Taksim

Galata Kulesi (daily 10am–6pm; $1) is the area's most obvious landmark, and one of the first places to head for on a sightseeing tour, since the tower's viewing galleries, reached by means of a modern lift, offer the best possible panoramas of the city, and are an invaluable means of orientation; it also has some of the cleanest toilets in the city. Built in 1348, the tower was originally known as the Tower of Christ. The inscription on its side records how, on Tuesday May 29, 1453, the Genoese surrendered the keys of the colony of Galata to Mehmet the Conqueror.

As you walk from here up Galipdede Sokak towards Taksim, an unassuming doorway on the right leads to the courtyard of the **Galata Mevlevihane** (Tues–Sun 9.30am–4.30pm), a former monastery and ceremonial hall of the "Whirling Dervishes" (see p.000). The building now serves as a museum to the Mevlevi sect, which was

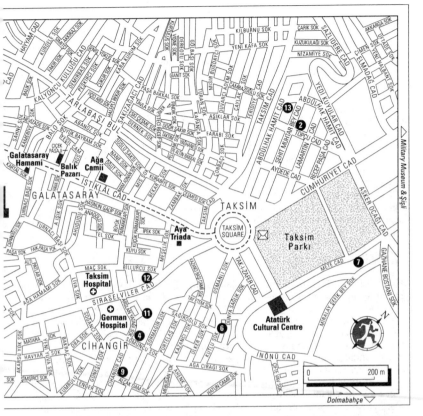

banned by Atatürk along with other Sufi organizations because of its political affilia-
tions. Exhibitions include musical instruments and dervish costumes, and the building
itself has been beautifully restored to late eighteenth-century splendour, complete with
the fake marbling that was so popular at the time. Dervish ceremonies take place sporadically at the Mevlevihane, and almost certainly on December 17, the annual Mevlana
holiday: information on this should be available at the museum.

Continuing to the bottom of İstiklâl Caddesi, you pass the top station of the Tünel.
Although the shops, seedy nightclubs and cinemas are the real attraction, **İstiklâl
Caddesi** is also the location of an impressive number of churches. One of the best-
known of these is the **Church of St Antoine**, in a courtyard just after Postacılar Sokak
at no. 325. A Roman Catholic church run by Franciscan monks, it was demolished to
make way for a tramway at the beginning of the century but rebuilt in 1913, a nice
example of red-brick neo-Gothic architecture. Also situated at the Tünel end of İstiklâl
Caddesi, in the grounds of the Dutch consulate, is the **Union Church of İstanbul**, a
seventeenth- or early eighteenth-century building whose basement once served as a
prison. At the Taksim end, next to the *Hacı Baba Restaurant* at Mezelik Sok 11/1, **Aya
Triada** is a large Greek Orthodox church founded in the late nineteenth century (open
daily at 4pm for mass).

Taksim

The size of **Taksim Square** is undeniably impressive, which is just as well since there's little else to be said in its favour. Poor planning and confused traffic rob it of any real atmosphere: a busy *otogar* on the north side does nothing to enhance the ambience, nor do the large, impersonal hotels – including the luxury *Marmara* – and other examples of misguided modern architecture. One exception to this otherwise grey and uninviting prospect is İstanbul's main centre for the performing arts, the **Atatürk Cultural Centre** (Atatürk Kültür Merkezi), to the east of the square. Its attractive foyer provides an ideal viewing gallery from which to observe the action below, whether this be daytime traffic jams or street life at night. Another plus is that the streets leading off the square, including Inönü Caddesi and Tarlabaşı Bulvarı, are the best place in town to find the few remaining genuine 1950s American **dolmuşes**.

The immediate environs of the square are disappointing if you're looking for decent **food**. There's a *McDonalds* at the beginning of Cumhuriyet Caddesi, whose novelty is beginning to wear off even for the Turks, and a good restaurant, the *Park Café* (see p.161), on Dünya Sağlık Sokak behind the *Marmara Hotel*.

The Military Museum

The **Military Museum** (Wed–Sun 9am–5pm; $1), about 1500m north of Taksim Square along Cumhuriyet Caddesi, is well worth visiting, not least for the janissary marching band which plays outside the museum every afternoon that it's open, between 3 and 4pm. The museum also plays host to a comprehensive collection of military memorabilia, proudly displayed and labelled in English. To get there, turn right after İstanbul Radyoevi and follow the road around to the left behind the military barracks; continue along Gümüz Sokak, past the *Lutfi Kırdar Spor Salonu*, and the museum entrance is on the right.

The **Mehter Band** originated in 1289 when the Selçuk Sultan Alâeddin Keykubad II sent a selection of musical instruments to Osman Gazi, founder of the Ottoman Empire. The band became an institution, symbolizing the power and independence of the Ottoman Empire; its members were janissaries, and they would accompany the sultan into battle. During public performances, members of the band sang songs about their hero-ancestors and Ottoman battle victories. They had considerable influence in Europe, helping create new musical styles such as Spanish *a la turca*, and inspiring numerous composers (examples include Mozart's *Marcia Turca* and Beethoven's *Ruinen von Athens, Opus 113*). The kettledrum, *kös* in Turkish, was also introduced into the West as a result of interest in the Mehter Band. The band was abolished by Mahmut II along with the janissary corps in 1826, and only re-established in 1914, when new instruments were added. The pieces played nowadays include some dating from the seventeenth and eighteenth centuries, and others written by Giuseppi Donizetti for Mahmut II's new army.

Housed in the military academy where Atatürk received some of his education, the museum is one of the most impressive in the country, evidence of the Turks' intense pride in their military history. Inside the most striking exhibits are the cotton and silk tents used by campaigning sultans. You'll also find a rich collection of Ottoman armour and weaponry, including beautifully ornamented *jambiyah* daggers, and a piece of the chain used by the Byzantines to close off the entrance of the Golden Horn in 1453.

ALONG THE BOSPHORUS

One of the world's most eulogized stretches of water, the **Bosphorus** is a source of pride for İstanbul's residents – even those who have to commute across it daily on perilously overcrowded ferryboats – and of admiration for its visitors. The thirty-kilometre strait divides Europe and Asia and connects the Marmara and Black seas, its width varying from 660 to 4500 metres, and its depth from fifty to several hundred metres. The main current flows from the Black Sea to the Marmara, with a strong undercurrent flowing in the opposite direction. The importance of the Bosphorus can be measured by the extent and variety of traffic it supports, but its recreational assets are equally evident, whether you're boating or enjoying one of the many bars and restaurants overlooking the water. The Bosphorus has numerous mythical and historical associations, too; indeed its name is derived from the Greek myth of Io, lover of Zeus, whom the god transformed into a cow to conceal her from his jealous wife Hera. She plunged into the straits to escape a gadfly, and hence Bosphorus, or "Ford of the Cow". The straits were also visited by Jason in his quest for the Golden Fleece.

For residents, the straits are a daily fact of life, one of İstanbul's most important transport arteries; as a visitor, too, you can use the Bosphorus to get around, but the ferry journeys often turn out to be a pleasure in themselves, one of the city's highlights. Along the way *yalıs*, or waterside residences, many in a state of precarious disrepair, overhang the banks. The regular ferryboats that weave their way up and down from shore to shore share the waterways with oil tankers, ocean liners and cargo ships of every nationality. But despite the resulting pollution the Bosphorus is full of **fish**: from porpoise and swordfish to red mullet and *hamsi* (a small fish belonging to the anchovy family), all caught by professionals and amateurs throughout the year.

There are various ways of touring the Bosphorus and its shoreside villages by **public transport**, and probably the best idea is to use a combination of ferries, buses and dolmuşes, so that you can see exactly what you want to in your own time. If you prefer to have your itinerary planned out in advance, however, there are special **sightseeing boats** throughout the year (2 daily in winter; 3 on weekdays and 5 on Sundays in summer), leaving from the first ferry landing in Eminönü. They're relatively expensive, and only take an hour and forty minutes to get to their final destination in Anadolu Kavağı, but you can always get off and wait for the next one at a landing stage on the way. To ensure a good seat in summer, arrive at least half an hour before departure – it's not worth making the trip if you have to sit in the bowels of the boat with screaming children, missing all the views.

To explore more economically and with greater independence you'll need a **ferry** timetable (*vapur tarifesi*, normally available from ferryboat *gişe*) and a handful of ferryboat tokens (*jetonlar*, also available from any *gişe*) and bus tickets. The normal ferries are reasonably frequent, and if you get stranded up the Bosphorus after they stop running (the last one from Anadolu Kavağı is at 5pm in summer, in winter at 3pm), you can always resort to a bus or dolmuş, both of which run along the Asian and European shores from village to village. There are jetties at every small village on either side of the strait.

The European shore

The **European shore** of the Bosphorus borders the modern city for some distance, and almost as far as the Bosphorus Bridge it's really the backyard of Taksim and commercial İstanbul. A backdrop of shipping companies and merchant banks, not to mention the central sorting office of the PTT, make **Karaköy** rather less than a tourist's

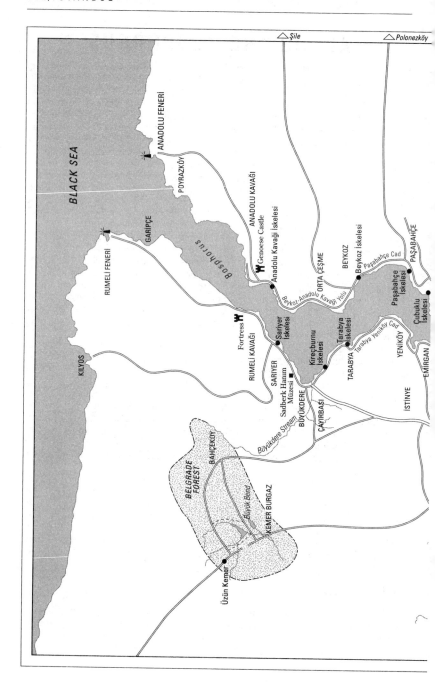

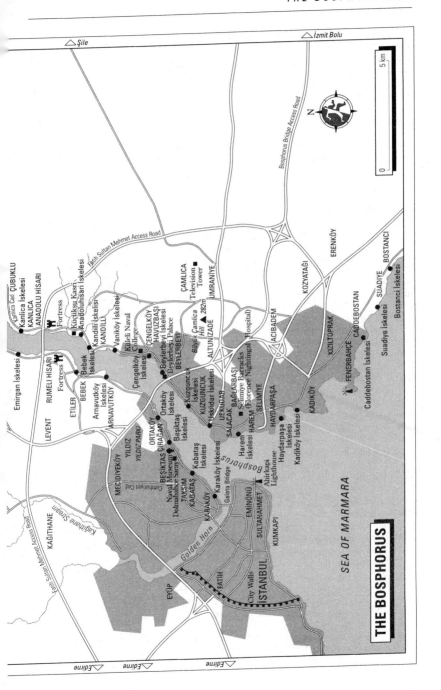

THE BOSPHORUS

mecca, while **Beşiktaş** is dominated by major roads and a bus terminal. Further up towards the Black Sea the scenery mellows, but, as a result of their relative proximity to the centre of town, the most charming of the villages on this side – traditionally **Bebek** and **Trabya**, but now **Ortaköy** too – are popular haunts for the rich and careless, who are responsible for the growing commercialization of what were once attractive waterside retreats.

Beşiktaş

Most visitors to **BEŞİKTAŞ** are here to see the Dolmabahçe Palace, successor to Topkapı as the residence of the Ottoman sultans. It's worth spending time in the neighbourhood, however, since it's also the location of the naval museum, as well as a couple of decent art galleries, and the Yıldız Parkı and palace.

Dolmabahçe Palace

Dolmabahçe Palace (Oct–Feb daily 9am–3pm; March–Sept daily 9am–4pm; guided tours only: Selâmlik $5, Harem $5, combined ticket $8) is the largest and most sumptuous of all the palaces on the Bosphorus built in the nineteenth century by various members of the Balian family. To the modern eye it's not so much magnificent as grotesque, a grossly excessive display of ornament and ostentatious wealth, suggesting that good taste suffered along with the fortunes of the Ottoman Empire. Classical Turkish architectural forms were being replaced by those of eighteenth- and nineteenth-century Europe, and while elsewhere these were successfully adapted into an oriental idiom, in Dolmabahçe there's a feeling that the wholesale adoption of Western architectural forms constitutes a last-ditch effort to muster some respect for a crumbling and defeated empire.

The palace is situated on the site of the harbour from which Mehmet the Conqueror launched his attack on Constantinople, later to be used as a conveniently public location for the **naval ceremonies** of the Ottoman fleet. The harbour was completely filled with stones on the order of Ahmet I at the beginning of the seventeenth century (*dolmabahçe* means "filled garden"). It later became a **shoreside grove** set aside for imperial use, with a number of small palaces and pavilions, which were demolished to make way for Sultan Abdül Mecid's new enterprise: a palace to replace Topkapı as the imperial residence of the Ottoman sultans. This was built by Armenian architect Karabet Balian and his son Nikoğos between 1843 and 1856.

It is often pointed out on a guided tour of the palace that everything you see coloured yellow is **gold**. The decor is excessively ornamental to the extent that it is an assault on the senses, but it's worth trying to ignore the worst of the excesses and concentrating on more wholesome aspects of the tour, like inlaid parquet floors, translucent pink alabaster imperial baths, or the famous double staircase with crystal balusters.

The palace retains an oriental feel in the organization of its rooms: it is divided into **selâmlık** and **harem** by the 36-metre-high **throne room** (double the height of the rest of the rooms). The ceremonies conducted here were accompanied by an orchestra playing European marches and watched by women of the harem through the *kafes*, grilles behind which women were kept hidden even in these days of Westernization and reform. Other onlookers included members of the foreign press, installed on their own balcony, who certainly had plenty to keep them scribbling within these decadent walls. The four-tonne chandelier in the throne room, one of the largest ever made, was a present from Queen Victoria.

In the east wing of the palace, the former apartments of the heir to the throne – entered from the side of the building nearest to Beşiktaş – now house the **Museum of Fine Arts** (*Resim ve Heykel Müzesi*; Wed–Sun 12.30–4.30pm; free). The best of the collection dates from the late nineteenth and early twentieth centuries, and gives an intriguing insight into the lifestyle and attitudes of the late Ottoman Turks. Look out especially for the works of Osman Hamdi (1842–1910), including *Mimosalı Kadın* (Woman with Mimosas), and the wonderful painting of a mosque doorway by Osman Hamdi's pupil Şevret Dağ.

The Maritime Museum

Back towards the ferry landing in Beşiktaş, the Deniz Müzesi or **Maritime Museum** (Wed–Sun 9am–12.30pm & 1.30–5pm; $1) is one of the really fun museums in İstanbul. The collection is divided between two buildings, the one facing the water housing seagoing craft while the other, on Cezayir Caddesi, is devoted to the maritime history of the Ottoman Empire and the Turkish Republic.

Most of the labels are in Turkish, but the best of the exhibits, such as the enormous wooden figureheads depicting tigers and swans, and the display of items from Atatürk's yacht, the *Savarona*, can't fail to capture the imagination and need little explanation. Next door the exhibition continues with a collection of **caiques** belonging to the sultans, some with models of the oarsmen in fez and *şalvar*. The largest of these, dating from 1648, needed an incredible 144 oarsmen to power it. The lovely mother-of-pearl inlay of the sultan's kiosk can be viewed from above via a purpose-built walkway.

Çırağan Sarayı

In the main square in front of Beşiktaş's ferry station, a **statue of Hayrettin Paşa**, or Barbarossa as he was known in the West, stands on a base inscribed with the poem "From whence this sound of cannons on the horizons of the sea?" by Yahya Kemal. He was a North African corsair taken into the employ of Süleyman the Magnificent and eventually appointed First Admiral of the Fleet. Opposite the statue is his tomb, an early work of Mimar Sinan.

A ten-minute walk from this main square in the direction of Ortaköy brings you to the **Çırağan Sarayı**, on Çırağan Caddesi. This sumptuous Balian construction was completed in 1874 during the reign of Abdül Aziz, and was the palace where he was murdered or committed suicide – the cause of death was never established. Murat V was later imprisoned here after being deposed by his brother, and following a period of abandonment, the palace housed the Turkish parliament for a short time from 1908. In 1910, Çırağan was reduced to a blackened shell by fire and was only restored in 1991 to its present magnificence as İstanbul's foremost luxury hotel.

Like Dolmabahçe, Çırağan was designed along the lines of a European palace, but Arabic touches were added on the orders of Abdül Aziz. Externally this is evident in the honeycomb stalactites decorating the windows. Unfortunately the modern block of the hotel slightly mars the view of the palace from the Bosphorus, and the restoration work has been further criticized for making no attempt to restore the interior to its original plan or decor, but the garden restaurant is a truly magnificent setting for a buffet breakfast or salad lunch. A bridge crosses Çırağan Caddesi from the palace to Yıldız Parkı, which allowed the harem women private access to the park, on the odd occasion they were given permission to enter of course.

Yıldız Parkı

Close by on Çırağan Caddesi is the public entrance to **Yıldız Parkı** (winter daily 9am–5.30pm; summer daily 9am–6pm; free), a vast wooded area dotted with *koşks*, lakes and gardens, which was the centre of the Ottoman Empire for thirty years during the reign of Abdül Hamid II. The buildings in and around the park constitute **Yıldız Palace**, a collection of structures in the old Ottoman style, and a total contrast to Dolmabahçe. The park and pavilions were restored by the Touring Club of Turkey in

1979, but not landscaped to such an extent as to detract from the natural beauty of their superb hillside location. Since then Yıldız Parkı has been one of the most popular places in İstanbul for city-dwellers thirsting for fresh air and open spaces: on public holidays the park is always crowded.

Most of the **pavilions** date from the reign of Abdül Aziz, but it was Abdül Hamid – a reforming sultan whose downfall was brought about by his intense paranoia – who transformed Yıldız into a small city and power base. Among its many buildings were the Mabeyn, the great palace used for official business; the Şale Köşkü, where receptions were held; and the Küçük Mabeyn, where the sultan lived; also in the park were a factory for Yıldız porcelain and a theatre.

The most important surviving building in the park is the **Şale Köşkü** (daily except Mon and Thurs 9.30am–5pm; Oct–Feb closes 4pm; guided tours obligatory, $1.50). It's a long hot walk uphill from Çırağan Caddesi, so you may consider getting a taxi up. The first of the Şale Köşkü's three separate sections was modelled on a Swiss chalet, while the second and third sections were built to receive Kaiser Wilhelm II on his first and second state visits, in 1889 and 1898. The most impressive room, the Ceremonial Hall, takes up the greater part of the third section of the palace, with a Hereke carpet so big (approximately 400 square metres) that part of a wall was knocked down to install it. In the attractive dining room, at the top of the central stairway in the central section, the dining chairs were carved by the reclusive Abdül Hamid himself.

The Malta Köskü, also in the park, is at present closed for restoration; to reach the other palace buildings it's best to return to the main square in Beşiktaş and take any bus or minibus up Barbaros Bulvarı (it's not far to walk, but it's another steep hill). Follow the signs to Yıldız Üniversitesi and Şehir Müzesi off to the right. The main buildings of the palace are not open to the public, but a subsidiary building houses the **Belediye Şehir Müzesi** (Tues, Wed & Fri–Sun 9am–4.30pm; $1). This State Museum includes a miscellaneous collection of knick-knacks, ornaments and paintings from the eighteenth and nineteenth centuries, many of them peculiar to the Ottoman way of life, such as an instrument for making *tesbih* (Islamic worry beads) and a janissary's chin support. In the same complex is the **Yıldız Sarayı Theatre**, complete with stage set and Abdül Hamid's chair left in splendid isolation in its own balcony, while on display backstage are fascinating theatre costumes and portraits of some of the stars who appeared here, including Sarah Bernhardt.

Ortaköy

The first suspension bridge across the Bosphorus, built in 1974, crosses the straits at Ortaköy, a former Bosphorus backwater whose character has been submerged by gentrification into a zone of nightclubs, expensive restaurants and theme bars. For **Ortaköy** take a #23B, #B2, #40A or #40 bus from Taksim, or a #25 from Eminönü, or take a bus or ferry to Beşiktaş and walk (about 15min). This last way is the best bet on public holidays and weekends as the traffic is dreadful on this road. The village now has a **Sunday market** largely frequented by the *entel* set, "intellectuals" with a penchant for large crowds and small talk: the stalls aren't very exciting but you can get hold of some nice ceramics. Ortaköy is also a popular **evening haunt** of the same crowd, and consequently restaurant decor and prices have gone way upmarket; anything on the waterfront will certainly be overpriced.

The small **Sinan hamam** in the centre of town is, by contrast, much better value than many of the larger baths, at under $3 per person, $4 with a massage. The waterfront is a favourite with anglers, and it's also the location of an attractive little Baroque mosque and some of the liveliest teahouses on the Bosphorus.

Arnavutköy and Bebek

One of the most beautiful of all the Bosphorus villages, especially when seen from the water, **Arnavutköy** is famous for its line of *yalıs*, wooden waterfront mansions with their boat moorings carved out beneath them. Some of the *yalıs* here have been restored, but there's a dilapidated feel about the whole village suggesting that it's nothing like as wealthy as neighbouring Bebek. The inner village, its streets lined with wooden houses, is worth exploring, and it's also worth trying out the tavernas run by the surviving Greek community, which feature live entertainment. There's an evening boat to Arnavutköy and Bebek from Eminönü; to get back, take the #25E **bus**, which stops running at around 11.30pm.

Bebek is the beginning of real wealth on the Bosphorus, and the suburbs from here to Sariyer encompass some of the most beautiful, priceless Bosphorus *yalıs*. The most famous building in Bebek is the waterfront Hıdıv Sarayı (the Khedive's Palace), an Art Nouveau-style mansion located to the left of the ferry landing as you leave the boat – notice especially the wrought-iron vine on the railings on the waterfront (these can be seen from a little jetty beside the consulate building). City dwellers drive to Bebek to eat ice cream, especially at night, and the *Café Pate* on the village square is the gathering place for rich-kid bikers. Above Bebek, up the extremely steep Küçük Bebek Caddesi, there's a little park known as the *balkon* (balcony) where the views of the Bosphorus are particularly extensive. Tea is served – and you'll need it if you've walked up here.

One of the most impressive sights on this side of the Bosphorus is the **fortress of Rumeli Hisarı** (Tues–Sun 9am–5pm; $2.50), just beyond Bebek. Larger and grander than its counterpart across the straits, this early Ottoman fortress was constructed in just four months in 1452, before the Ottoman conquest of the city. It houses a small open-air theatre, a summer evening venue for concerts and plays.

Sariyer and Rumeli Kavağı

It's an easy enough matter to get right up the Bosphorus as far as the delightful fish restaurants in **Sariyer** and **Rumeli Kavağı** but you may have trouble getting back again. If you're intending to make an evening of it, the last bus from Rumeli Kavağı to Eminönü, the #25A, leaves at 10pm from the bus stop near the jetty. The last dolmuş to Sariyer leaves at 11pm, and there are later buses from there.

Just before Sariyer, an essential place to visit is the **Sadberk Hanım Museum**, located 300m south of the Sariyer jetty at Piyası Cad 25–29, Büyükdere (daily except Wed 10am–6pm; $1.20). Bus #25 to Sariyer from Eminönü and Beşiktaş passes by. This excellent collection of miscellaneous archeological and ethnographical objects is located in two wooden houses, the largest of which formerly belonged to an Armenian civil servant who became a politician and died in the great Beyoğlu fire of 1922. The collection was put together in memory of Sadberk Hanım, wife of the millionaire business entrepreneur Vehbi Koç, herself a keen collector of Turkish needlecraft. The artefacts in the museum are well lit and beautifully displayed with excellent commentary explaining their significance. The oldest exhibits in the archeological section include sixth-millennium mother goddesses and Hittite cuneiform tablets from the second millennium BC. In the ethnography section there are maternity and circumcision beds, needlework, clothing and jewellery, and a thorough examination of İznik and Kütahya pottery.

Belgrade Forest

The land west of Sariyer is occupied by the **Belgrade Forest**, originally a hunting preserve of the Ottomans. The only sizeable piece of woodland in the vicinity of İstanbul,

Belgrade Forest has always been popular among Turks, and with expats seeking a pastoral, not to say elite and Christian, retreat from the rigours of the city. The forest and Belgrade village, of which only a few remnants remain, were inhabited from Byzantine times by the caretakers of the reservoirs that supplied the city with water. The name came about after the capture of Belgrade in 1521, when a community of Serbian well-diggers, prisoners-of-war of Süleyman the Magnificent, were settled here to take over the care and upkeep of the water supply system. In the seventeenth century its attractions were discovered by the foreign community of İstanbul, who came to the village to seek refuge from a particularly nasty pestilence that was wiping out half the city, and for the next century or so many wealthy Christians had second homes here. In the 1890s the village was evacuated by Abdül Hamid II, who in his paranoia believed that the inhabitants were polluting the city's water supply. To get to the edge of the forest take a **dolmuş** from Çayırbaşı, between Sariyer and Büyükdere on the Bosphorus, to Bahçeköy.

A sophisticated system of dams, reservoirs, water towers and aqueducts is still in evidence around the forest. The water towers, or *su terazı*, were an ingenious device for transporting water over long distances and storing it en route: water descends into underground conduits where pressure builds up and forces the water up into the tower. When the tank is full the water is sent underground with enough force to travel up into the next tower, and so the process continues. By this means, and by aqueducts, water was brought from the forest to the city.

The most impressive of the aqueducts in the forest is the *Uzun* or **Long Aqueduct,** beyond Kemer Burgaz on the way to Kısırmandıra. Its tiers of tall, pointed arches across the Kağithane Suyu, one of the streams that forms the Golden Horn, were built by Sinan for Süleyman the Magnificent in 1563. Easier to get to from Bahçeköy is the **Büyük Bend** reservoir. Follow the blue sign marked "Bentler" out of the village to Neşet Suyu, half an hour's walk from the town, where there's a small tea garden and a first-aid stand. From here it's another beautiful half-hour (2km) to the reservoir. Gymnastic equipment, including parallel bars and a wooden horse, can be glimpsed through the trees on the road between the Neşet picnic area and Büyük Bend, having been provided for the benefit of the amateur athletes who make for the forest in droves to partake in jogging and working out away from the fumes of the city. The reservoir, which was originally built in Byzantine times, is one of the oldest parts of the water system.

The Asian shore

On the Asian side of the Bosphorus are vast suburbs and small villages which all have one thing in common: they are virtually unknown to tourists. The best base from which to explore this area is probably **Üsküdar**, one of the most beautiful of all the Bosphorus suburbs, with some impressive imperial and domestic architecture and a uniquely tranquil atmosphere. There are one or two decent hotels here and buses leave regularly to all the other villages up and down the Bosphorus from the main bus station in front of the İskele Camii.

Kadıköy and Moda

Kadıköy, which sprawls dirtily between the Bosphorus and the Marmara, may at first seem to have only views of the European shore to recommend it, but despite an unpromising appearance it's a lively and busy place, with good shops, restaurants and cinemas. After dark the ferry landing area comes alive – a good place to buy a bottle of cheap alcohol after closing time, which may explain the number of drunken brawls in the area – and there are scores of street vendors along the windswept shorefront esplanade, from whom you can buy a disposable watch or pair of socks for next to nothing. Kadıköy has now taken over from Beyazit as the city's main centre for leftist political demonstrations – Gen Azim Gündüz Caddesi is the favourite location, and can be hazardous at such times if the army are called in.

The main road south from Kadıköy to Kartal is **Bağdat Caddesi**, part of the old silk route from China. Nowadays the street is better known as a place to pose and to shop for the clothes to pose in (labels should be external, prominent and preferably foreign). As all good Bağdat people know, the best way to see the *caddesi* is from daddy's BMW, but failing the daddy you can take a seabus to Bostancı – from Bakırköy, Yenikapı, Karaköy or Kabataş – and then a dolmuş from behind the *Dolphin Hotel* back to Kadıköy (Bağdat Caddesi is one-way, so you can't tour it from Kadıköy). Dolmuşes can be hailed anywhere along the street, which is just as well since the shops are generally massive and quite far apart, and you may need transport between them. Best areas for shops are Şaşkın Bakkal and Suadiye (see "Shops and Markets"), and there are good restaurants the whole way along.

In Kadıköy itself, the best place for clothes is Gen Azim Gündüz Caddesi (formerly Bahariye Cad), which is a right turn off Söğütlüçeşme Caddesi, the wide, steep street leading from the ferry jetty uphill, but there's more fun to be had sorting through the great mounds of junk, old carpets and kilims that can be found for sale in the **bit pazarı** on Özellik Sokak. **Moda**, the district to the south of Kadıköy jetty, is reached by taking Mühürdar Caddesi along the shore away from Haydarpaşa, and turning left up any of its side streets. It's a pleasant area for aimless wandering, particularly popular with courting couples. On Moda Caddesi there's the *Benadam* art gallery, the *Café Bonjour*, and at no. 266 a very well-known ice-cream parlour, *Ali Usta*, that attracts vast queues on summer evenings. On Kadife Sokak, off Moda Caddesi, *Kadife Chalet* is an old wooden mansion serving salads and vegetable dishes with ingredients from their own garden. Around the corner on Feritek Sokak, the *Café Kırıntı* serves *durum*, a delicious meat sandwich affair, and at the end of the street is a nice little tea garden overlooking the sea.

Haydarpaşa

The **Selimiye Barracks**, which house the former **hospital of Florence Nightingale** (Sat 9am–4pm, otherwise by appointment only; phone even if you're planning to go on a Saturday as they're notoriously unreliable, ☎0216/343 7310; free), are on the road between Kadıköy and Üsküdar in **Haydarpaşa**. To get there, take a dolmuş between Kadıköy and Üsküdar and ask for Selimiye Kışlası, or walk for fifteen minutes from Kadıköy up Haydarpaşa Rıhtım Caddesi, which becomes Tıbbiye Caddesi. You can also take a ferry directly from Sirkeci station to Harem and head for the large white towered building to the left as you disembark. After passing the military hospital and the imposing turreted building that now houses Marmara University's faculties of law and medicine, turn left onto Çeşme-i Kebir Sokak and continue straight towards the sea until you reach the entrance of the massive Selimiye barracks to your left. Despite appearances parts of the barracks are open to the public, though you will be required to take a **guided tour**, probably given by a conscript thanking his lucky stars that military service has turned up such an easy option. Take means of identification (passport or driving licence) or you may not be allowed in.

The barracks were originally built by Selim III in 1799 for his Western-style *Nizam-i Jedid* or **New Order**, which was established to undermine the power of the janissaries. The building was positioned some distance from the city so that the new corps would not cause too much trouble among the janissaries, but in this it failed and Selim was forced to dissolve the corps. The barracks were burned down in 1808, the same year that Selim was deposed and assassinated, but were rebuilt in stone in 1828, two years after Mahmut II had finally massacred and destroyed the janissaries. Additional wings were added by Abdül Mecit in 1842; as it stands today the building has over 1100 exterior windows.

The northwest wing was used as a hospital by the British during the **Crimean War** (1854–56), and Florence Nightingale lived and worked in the northern tower. Access is through the barracks library via a central spiral staircase. This section has been organized as a museum to Nightingale by the Turkish Nurses' Association, who have preserved the original furnishings and some of her personal belongings. During her stay here she reduced the death toll among patients from twenty to two percent, and established universally accepted principles of modern nursing. On display are some of the pamphlets written by Nightingale, such as *Notes on Nursing for the Labouring Class* and *The Sanitary State of the Army in India, 1863*, as is a copy of the lady's lamp, rather more oriental in design than that pictured in British history books.

On the opposite side of Çeşme-i Kebir Sokak, on Selimiye Camii Sokak, is the **Selimiye Camii**, constructed, along with the nearby hamam, for the use of soldiers of the New Order. With its imposing entrance portal and window-filled tympana arches, it does more than justice to the quiet and attractive suburb in which it is situated, elevated above the surrounding streets in a garden of plane trees.

Also in Haydarpaşa, not far from the hospital, is the **British War Cemetery**, a beautifully kept, peaceful spot, sheltering the dead of the Crimean and two world wars. To find it, return to Tıbbiye Caddesi and walk in the direction of Kadıköy, past Marmara University law and medicine faculties; take a left turn up Burhan Felek Caddesi between the university building and the military hospital, and continue past the hospital entrance down the leafy lane which leads to the cemetery.

The largest Muslim graveyard in İstanbul, the **Karaca Ahmet Mezarlığı** is a ten-minute walk away on Tıbbiye Caddesi, in the direction of Üsküdar. A beautiful, sprawling place shadowed by ancient cypresses, it's ideal to wander around and study Ottoman gravestones. Women's graves are marked by carved flowers, each bloom signifying a child, while men's are surmounted by headgear that indicates the lifetime office of the deceased. The **Karaca Ahmet Türbesi**, on Tunus Bağı Caddesi in the north of the cemetery (easily reached by taking a right off Tıbbiye Caddesi through the graveyard), commemorates a sainted warrior who fought beside Orhan Gazi. It is still used as an almshouse and a kind of youth club by the Bektaşi dervishes, where boys and girls learn poems and the ritual *sema* of these Sufi mystics, whose activities were first restricted during the reign of Mahmut II because of their connections with the janissaries.

Üsküdar

Although there's plenty of evidence of religious conservatism in **Üsküdar** (formerly Scutari), particularly in the dress of its inhabitants, the town has a relaxed atmosphere, and a feeling of old-fashioned hospitality and a prosperity more akin to Black Sea villages than to İstanbul's suburbs. The atmosphere may have been affected by dervish attitudes of religious tolerance and open-mindedness, since this has long been a centre of Islamic mystical sects, but whatever the reason it's certainly a more comfortable and friendly place than other similarly conservative centres like Fatih. To get to Üsküdar take a ferry from Eminönü or Beşiktaş, a #500B bus from either Edirnekapı or Mecidiyeköy, or from Kadıköy a #12 or #14 bus or a dolmuş. Üsküdar's main square and quayside is an enormous bus park. Buses up the Bosphorus, as far as Anadolu Hisarı, leave from in front of the İskele Camii on Paşa Liman Caddesi. It's also possible to get dolmuşes from here to Çengelköy and Beykoz.

Although there are some fine imperial mosques in and around the suburb, modern Üsküdar is primarily renowned as a shopping centre for Bosphorus villagers. In the main square, lorries park in a great circle to sell market produce in bulk, while the small streets offer fresh produce, particularly fish and vegetables, as well as all kinds of kitchen hardware. Second-hand furniture and ornaments are sold at the Üsküdar flea market in Büyük Hamam Sokak, and there are some reasonable jewellery and clothes shops. Along the quayside at **Salacak** are some good restaurants (see p.166), pavement cafés and bars, and fantastic views of Topkapı Palace and İstanbul generally.

The **İskele** or **Mihrimah Camii** is located opposite the ferry landing on the İskele Meydanı, sitting on a high platform with an immense covered porch in front of it. This porch is a favourite viewing platform where old men in knitted hats shelter from all weathers and complain about the changing times while they peruse the square below. Inside it's all rather gloomy and cluttered, and the lateral domes are dwarfed by the large central dome. Designed by Sinan and built in 1547–8, this is the only Ottoman mosque with three semidomes (rather than two or four), a result of the requirements of a difficult site against the hillside behind.

Directly across the main square from the İskele Camii is the **Yeni Valide Camii**, and it's worth being in the vicinity of these two mosques for the call to prayer: the two muezzins call and answer each other in a poignant refrain across the bus park below. The Yeni Valide Camii, built between 1708 and 1710 by Ahmet III in honour of his mother, is most easily identified by the Valide Sultan's green, birdcage-like tomb, the meshed roof of which was in fact designed to keep birds out while allowing rain in to water the garden tomb below (now rather untidily overgrown). There is an attractive *şadırvan* (ablutions fountain) in the courtyard: the grilles of its cistern are highly wrought with their pattern echoed in the stone carvings above.

One of the most attractive mosques in Üsküdar is the **Çinili Cami** (tiled mosque), which dates from 1640. To get there on foot, take Hakimiyet-i Milliye Caddesi out of the centre and do a left into Çavuşdere Caddesi. After passing Çavuşdere fruit and veg market, continue to climb the same street, and you'll see the mosque on your right. The tiles are mainly blues and turquoise, but there's a rare shade of green to be found in the *mihrab*. Below the mosque, in the same street, is the beautifully restored **Çinili Hamamı**. The restorations in the men's side have the edge over those in the women's, but both parts have their original central marble stone for massage, and acres of marble revetments. It's an extremely clean hamam, and the pride of its workers.

The **Atık Valide Külliyesi** is just a short walk from Çinili Cami: go back down Çavuşdere Caddesi and turn left into Çinili Hamam Sokak, and you'll find the mosque and its dependencies on the right. Dating from 1583, the complex is a work of the master architect Mimar Sinan, built for Nur Banu, wife of Selim II and mother of Murat III. The dependencies, including an *imaret*, a Koran school, a *kervansaray* and a hamam, line the surrounding streets, although none of them are open to the public. The mosque courtyard, meant to be the most beautiful in İstanbul, is presently closed for restoration, and the mosque, in which renovation work is also in progress, is now entered through a side door. Worth inspecting are the underside of the wooden galleries on three sides of the interior, which are beautifully painted, and the İznik tiles covering the *mihrab*.

From Üsküdar's main square minibuses to Ümraniye run past the foot of **Büyük Çamlıca**, the highest hill on the Asian side. If you get off at Kısıklı Camii you can walk up Kısıklı–Büyük Çamlıca Caddesi, turning right just before the *Büyük Çamlıca Et Lokantası* to reach the park: a walk of fifteen minutes or so. The effort is rewarded by refreshingly cooler temperatures and spectacular views, not only of İstanbul but also of the Uludağ mountain range to the south, near Bursa. Büyük Çamlıca used to be covered with shantytown *gecekondu* dwellings, but these were demolished in a slum clearance programme to make way for the park. The **café** on the hill (daily 9am–midnight) has been tastefully refurbished by the Greater İstanbul Municipality.

On to Beylerbeyi

The next village along the Bosphorus, just before you reach the first bridge, is **Kuzguncuk**. There's a good fish restaurant on the shore here, with a fine view of Ortaköy Camii on the other side, and a **Jewish cemetery** a half-hour's walk from the village up İcadiye Sokak. From a distance the cemetery looks like a hill littered with pieces of white paper: this is because the white marble gravestones, some of which are coffin-shaped, lie flat on the ground instead of standing upright. The Jewish community in İstanbul originates from 1492, when Beyazit II gave refuge to Jews escaping the Spanish Inquisition. As the Spanish economy suffered from the exodus, so the Ottomans benefited from the commercial activities and know-how of the Jewish community, which still plays an important part in the Turkish economy.

The main attraction of **Beylerbeyi**, the next village along, is the **Beylerbeyi Palace** (daily except Mon & Thurs 9.30am–4pm; guided tours only; $1.50). This nineteenth-century summer residence and guesthouse of the Ottoman sultans is another palace that was built by members of the Balian family, in this case Sarkis and Agop, and was much admired by contemporary visitors from Europe – after her stay in 1869, the Empress Eugénie had its windows copied in the Tuileries Palace in Paris. The palace is still popular with Western visitors who are repelled by the extravagances of Dolmabahçe. The interior decoration was planned and designed by Sultan Abdül Aziz himself, while some of the furniture, including the matching dining chairs in the harem and the *selâmlık*, was carved by Sultan Abdül Hamid II during his six years of imprisonment here up to his death in 1918. Downstairs, the reception room was lit by three Bohemian crystal chandeliers, with a marble pool and fountain, supported on the tails of dolphins, cooling the air of the building. The central staircase, with its fanciful twisting shape, is perhaps the highlight, but all kinds of details, from the neo-Islamic patterns on the ceilings down to the beautiful Egyptian *hasır*, the reed matting on the floor, are worth spending time to investigate.

Çengelköy to Anadolu Hisarı

Çengelköy is a pretty, atmospheric village, but its fish restaurants are overpriced and its main attraction, the *kuleli*, is closed to the public, so there's not much point stopping here unless you want a good look at the Baroque fountain in the square. The *kuleli*, the long yellow building on the seashore beyond the village, was originally built, along with the Selimiye Barracks, as a military training school and barracks by Selim III, and like that building it served as a hospital under the direction of Florence Nightingale in the Crimean War. Since the end of World War I the building has been an officers' training school, offering the best education to be had in Turkey in exchange for the adult working life of its students.

Küçüksu Kasrı, a palace built by Nikoğos Balian, son of the architect of Dolmabahçe, is a ten-minute bus ride from Çengelköy (daily except Mon & Thurs 9.30am–4pm; $0.50). After passing a boatyard to your left you'll cross a bridge over the Küçüksu Deresi; get off at the next stop, walk back to the sign saying "Küçük Saray Aile Bahcesi", and you'll find the palace at the end of a drive. Its exterior is ornate, with Rococo carving probably best seen from the Bosphorus, which was the intended approach. From the water you also get the best view of the staircase doubling back on itself to create the illusion of being free of any means of support. The whole of the palace interior is decorated with lace and carpets from Hereke and lit by Bohemian crystal chandeliers. The floors are mahogany, inlaid with rose-, almond-wood and ebony, and upstairs is an ebony table on which Sultan Abdül Aziz was wont to arm-wrestle with visitors of state.

The **Küçüksu Deresi** and the **Göksu** further up the Bosphorus are the streams formerly known to Europeans as the "Sweet Waters of Asia". Their banks were graced by picnicking parties of Ottoman nobility, and the image they presented was much admired by European visitors. The Ottoman castle of **Anadolu Hisarı**, a short walk through the village on the other side from Küçüksu Kasrı, is open at all times to wander around and clamber over, but its main interest is historical. Close as they were to Constantinople, this and the fortification across the Bosphorus were built while the city was still in Byzantine hands, this one in around 1390 by Beyazit I and the other sixty years later by Mehmet the Conqueror. The Anatolian fortress is by no means as impressive as its counterpart across the water, but nevertheless it's a measure of the extent of the decline of the Byzantine Empire that the Turks could build such fortifications on the shores of a stretch of water that was so important strategically and economically.

On the coastal path towards Anadolu Hisarı there's a **tea garden** serving *midye tava* (fried mussels), with a good view of Rumeli Hisarı across the Bosphorus. Just before the Göksu Deresi, behind the *spor klübü*, is the *Hisar Köftecisi*, a tiny **café** where you can eat a rough meal of steak or *köfte* and salad for next to nothing. The unsightly pieces of reinforced concrete littering the field next to the restaurant are the supports on which the second Bosphorus bridge was made. There are **boats for rent** at Anadolu Hisarı: smaller ones for trips up the Göksu Deresi or larger ones (about $18) in which you can tour the Bosphorus at leisure.

On to Anadolu Kavağı

Kanlıca, the next ferry stop up, beyond the new Fatih Sultan Mehmet bridge, is famed for its yoghurt, which can be eaten at any of the little quayside restaurants. Not far beyond is the glass factory of **Paşabahçe**, which after its inception in 1933 produced delicate glassware that's still to be found in second-hand shops around Turkey. Standards inevitably slipped, but Paşabahçe glass is now making something of a comeback with some imaginative designs. The factory shop is not the best place to buy the glass, however, as the better-quality pieces are sold in İstanbul's wealthier suburbs (see "Shops and markets") – though it might be fun to get a group of people together for a tour of the factory (☎0216/322 0018; tours Mon–Fri 2.30 & 4.30pm, minimum of 10 people).

Anadolu Kavağı is the last stop on the official sightseeing boats from Sirkeci, with a stop of a couple of hours, giving you time to have a good look around. The village has a distinct if dilapidated charm – balconied houses with boat mooring stations overlooking the Bosphorus, and a main street lined with restaurants and food stands – but the real reason to make the trek is to visit the **Byzantine fortification** on the hill above the town, from which the village takes its name. This used to be part of a military base and has only recently been opened to the public: there are still a number of apartment blocks housing military families on the steep road up to the fortress, and various signs forbidding entry. These appear to be universally ignored, but proceed with caution anyway in case the situation has changed.

To get to the fortification, take Mirşah Hamam Sokak from the dock and walk uphill for half an hour. The fortress sprawls across a hilltop overgrown with blackcurrant, gorse, heather and grasses, affording excellent views of the Bosphorus and of migratory birds in spring. The best approach to the castle itself is to walk to the top of Anadolu Kavağı Fener Yolu, with the defences on your left, to the uppermost entrance. The fortress is sometimes known as the Genoese castle, since it was controlled by them from the mid-fourteenth century, but approaching from above you'll see various Greek inscriptions, and even the imperial motto of the Palaeologus dynasty (a cross with the letter "b" in each corner, which stands for "King of Kings, who Kings it over Kings"), as clear evidence that it was in fact Byzantine in origin.

FURTHER OUT: ESCAPES FROM THE CITY

The longer you stay in İstanbul the greater your desire to escape will probably become, as the pollution and overcrowding take their toll on your nerves and general health. Fortunately, it's not hard to escape for a day or more to one of the beaches beyond the immediate reach of the city's pollution. Şile, Ağva and Kilyos, with some of the best beaches on the Black Sea, are all surprisingly unspoilt, while the Princes' Islands manage to maintain some of their independent character and wild beauty despite the hordes of partying teenagers who descend through the summer months.

Princes' Islands

The **Princes' Islands**, in the Sea of Marmara between 15 and 30km southeast of the city, have always been a favourite retreat from the mainland. Nowadays four of the nine islands are easily accessible by ferry from İstanbul, and in the summer months public holidays see a steady stream of visitors threatening to destroy the peace and tranquillity of these sleepy havens. Many Turkish families take full advantage of the proximity of the islands and move out here for the duration of İstanbul's sticky summer.

The islands have been inhabited since Classical times, but their first claim to fame derived from the copper mines of Chalkitis (Heybeliada), which have long since been exhausted but are still visible near Çam Limanı. In the Byzantine era numerous convents and monasteries were built on the islands, and these became favoured – because of their proximity to the capital and ease of surveillance – as luxurious prisons for banished emperors, empresses and princes (often after they had been blinded).

After the conquest, the islands were largely neglected by the Ottoman Turks, and became another of the city's refuges for Greek and Armenian communities. Armenian Protestants acquired **Heybeliada** from the Turkish government in 1821. In 1846 a ferry service was established from the mainland to the islands; they became popular with Pera's expatriate community, and in 1857 the British Ambassador Sir Henry Bulwer bought Yassıada and built a castle there. But it was only in the early years of the republic that the islands entered popular Turkish culture as İstanbul's favourite summer resort. Mosques began to appear in the villages, hotels and bougainvillea-draped villas followed, and many beautiful wooden *konak*s were built, which contributed to the turn-of-the-century Ottoman gentility of the larger islands. A Turkish naval college was established on Heybeliada, and the islands received the rubber stamp of republican respectability when Atatürk's private yacht was moored here as a training ship.

Not all of the islands have romantic connotations, however. **Sivriada**, which is uninhabited and cannot be visited, gained public notoriety in 1911 when all the stray dogs in İstanbul were rounded up, shipped out there, and left to starve; and **Yassıada** is best known as a prison island, used for the detention of high-risk political prisoners. It was here that Adnan Menderes and two of his former ministers were hanged on the night of September 16, 1961 after a military coup (Menderes has recently been publicly rehabilitated and his remains reburied in a mausoleum on the mainland).

Recently, **development** has become a serious worry. Apart from unsightly building projects – legislation restricting the height of new buildings has been flouted, and many exceed the 7.5-metre, two-storey limit – other direct results of the new development on the islands include deforestation and pollution caused by earth being dumped into the sea. Little is being done by the authorities to prevent any of this: in 1992 a preservation order lasted for about six weeks before the islands were once again opened up to development, and Büyükada and Heybeliada were declared centres of tourism, which meant that substantial incentives were offered to would-be developers.

All this means that the islands are changing rapidly, but at least they are still traffic-free. Plans to introduce a bus service were eventually dropped by the municipality under pressure from *Ada Dostları* (Friends of the Islands), and this pressure group continues to do what it can to preserve what's left of the islands' heritage. Despite the changes, the essence of a trip to the islands is still escape, from the noise, stress and pollution of the city.

For details of **accommodation** on the Princes' Isles, see p.87.

Getting there

The Princes' Islands are easy to get to. The furthest is less than two hours by boat from Sirkeci pier no. 5 (3 hourly departures in the morning; 1hr 30min–2hr journey; $2.50 per *jeton*), and there is even a catamaran (*Deniz Otobüs*) service three times a day at the weekends and on public holidays from Kabataş (near Beşiktaş on the Bosphorus), and from Bostancı on the Asian shore, to Büyükada, which takes about 25 minutes.

Island hopping among the four larger islands – **Büyükada, Heybeliada, Burgazada** and **Kınalıada** – is a simple matter as long as you check ferry times at the dock and don't simply rely on a timetable: the service is notoriously changeable, but you can estimate a ten-minute journey between islands. In season there are around twenty boats a day from Büyükada to Heybeliada alone. The other islands are equally well served by the steady old boats, some of which are steam-powered, beautifully trimmed in varnished wood, and furnished with armchairs and tables like something out of an Agatha Christie novel.

Büyükada

BÜYÜKADA (the "Great Island", the original *Prinkipo*, or "Prince's Island", in Greek) is the largest of the islands and has always been the most popular and populated of them. Its elaborate wooden mansions date from the nineteenth century when the Greek and Armenian bankers of Galata and the Ottoman dignitaries built them as hol-iday villas. Like all the islands, Büyükada has long been inhabited by minorities, and İslam is not taken as seriously as it is on the mainland. Nowadays young city-dwellers come here to enjoy the relaxed atmosphere, away from the ever growing pressure of İslamic fundamentalism in the city. In summer the late boats bring scores of adoles-cents dressed to party, who then congregate in the main square, eat ice cream and return to İstanbul on the last ferry.

Büyükada has traditionally been a place of retreat or exile. Long-term visitors to the Monastery of St George included the granddaughter of Empress Irene, and the royal princess Zoë, in 1012. Leon Trotsky lived here in exile from 1929 to 1933, when he began to write his *History of the Russian Revolution*. He spent most of his time here at **İzzet Paşa Köşkü**, an attractive wooden mansion at 55 Çankaya Cad, built by a Greek banker and later owned by Abdül Hamid's Chief of Police. On the same road further back towards the ferry landing is another fine wooden mansion, the **Con Paşa Köşkü**, with a two-storey colonnaded portico, elaborately carved in honey-coloured wood. These large mansions of Büyükada tend to have beautiful gardens full of magnolia, mimosa and jasmine, and in the surrounding pine forests myrtle, lilac and rock roses grow wild, so the scents of the island on a summer's evening are one of its most memorable aspects.

The island consists of two hills, both surmounted by monasteries, with a valley between them. The south of the island is wilder and unpopulated, and is most easily vis-ited by **phaeton** (horse and carriage). These expensive tours (the short tour is $7, long tour $10, leaving from the main square off Isa Çelebi Sok) are evidence of considerable tourist development, which includes paying beaches and good hotels. There are **bike** rental shops (Çınar Cad 10B and 51A; around $2 an hour), and good **restaurants**, including the *Kaptan Restaurant* for fish, at Liman Çıkmazı Sok 11 beside the ferry landing; the *Yörük Ali Restaurant* at the beach of the same name, reached by following Çankaya Caddesi 2km southwest from the ferry landing; and *Hamdi Baba*, at Gülistan Cad 18 (immediately to the left of the ferry on landing), where the best dish is *kiremette balık*, fish baked in a clay dish. **Donkeys** to ride up the hills start from a little park up Kadıyoran Caddesi from the centre of town (about $2 a ride).

The southern hill, **Yüce Tepe**, is the location of the **Monastery of St George**, probably on the site of a building dating from the twelfth century. Lady Hornby described riding up to the monastery in the nineteenth century: "Perched on the very highest peak of mountain above, it looks no bigger than a doll's house, left there by some spiteful fairy, to be shaken by winter tempests and scorched by the summer glare." Close up, it consists of a series of chapels on three levels, presently undergoing renovation work, with the oldest, containing a sacred spring, on the lowest level. In Byzantine times the monastery was used as an insane asylum, and iron rings set into the floor of the chapels were used for restraining the inmates. The monastery on the northern hill, **Ísa Tepe**, is a nineteenth-century building. Three families still inhabit the precincts, and there are services in the chapel on Sundays.

Heybeliada

HEYBELİADA, or the "Island of the Saddlebag", is popular for its natural beauty and for the beaches to which İstanbul residents flock in their hundreds at weekends. It's also the location of a highly fashionable watersports club – situated near Değirmen Burnu to the northwest of the island – where the annual membership fee runs to thousands of dollars. Heybeli has retained much of its village identity, however, and there is a strong community spirit among its permanent residents. The unique character of the island is enhanced by a plague of cats, who stalk the streets and feed off the rats and mice living in the old wooden buildings of the village.

Heybeli is not completely devoid of motorized transport, but what there is is either *Belediye*- or naval-owned, so there's no chance of hitching any lifts. Once again, you're at the mercy of semi-wild animals and their taciturn owners in your travels: prices for **phaetons** from Ayyıldız Caddesi (which runs parallel to the front) to various destinations around the island are posted on a board in the street, and tours of the island are also available (short tours for $4, longer ones $8). The **restaurants** cater to locals all year round, and consequently they are generally good, simple and cheap. Most are on Ayyıldız Caddesi: at no. 75, for example, there's a cheap *pide salon* where you can eat Turkish pizza for next to nothing. The *Güleryüz* restaurant on the same street is slightly classier, and *Başak Et ve Balık Lokantası* at no. 38 serves fried fish and meats, seafood, and some cheaper home-style cooking. There's also an extremely good cake shop, *Mehtap Pastanesi*, down towards the ferry landing.

On a tour of the island you'll see one of its most prominent landmarks, the nineteenth-century **Greek Orthodox School of Theology**, the Aya Triada Manastiri, which is the site of an important collection of Byzantine manuscripts. The school, majestically situated on the peak of the island's northernmost hill, is only accessible with permission from the Greek Orthodox Patriarchate in Fener. Other buildings you'll be shown include the Heybeliada Sanatorium, a private home for TB sufferers located off Çam Limanı Yolu on the south side of the island. The Naval High School (*Deniz Harp Okulu*), on the east side of the island along the coast road from the main jetty, was originally the Naval War Academy, situated on the island since 1852. When the academy was transferred to Tuzla in 1985, it became a high school, where young boys are given an education, and pay for it with a lifetime's service.

Walking and **cycling** are good ways to enjoy Heybeli, its pine forests and hills making for scenic rambles; bikes can be rented from near the quayside at Imralı Sok 3. The best way to find an isolated **beach** is to head up Refah Şehitler Caddesi out of the village until you arrive at Alp Görüngen Yolu, which encircles the western half of the island. The northern shore especially, before you reach Alman Köy, is a good bet for a quiet swim if you climb down off the road to one of the tiny pebble beaches below. You can also reach Yeni İskele from Refah Şehitler Caddesi, and from here it costs around $4 to take a small boat across to **Kaşıkadı** ("Spoon Island", so called because of its shape), although the new holiday complex on this island has scarred its former wildness.

Burgazada and Kınalıada

The other two islands served by public ferry are Burgazada and Kınalıada, both small and relatively unspoilt, although development is proceeding apace. They are still popular with escapees from the strict Islamic codes more evident in mainland İstanbul, and on both holiday homes already outnumber those of permanent residents. In winter the villages around their jetties are practically ghost towns, with little to see or do.

BURGAZADA has a fascinating small **museum** (Tues–Fri & Sun 10am–noon & 2–5pm, Sat 10am–noon; free) at Burgaz Çayırı Sok 15, on the other side of a square from the Church of St John the Baptist (the dome of which is the town's most prominent landmark). The museum is dedicated to the novelist **Sait Faik** (often described as the Turkish Mark Twain) who lived here, and the house has been so carefully preserved – as if the writer were still there – that you get an unsettling sense that you're trespassing. This becomes stronger when you go up to the bedroom and find a pair of pyjamas neatly folded on the bed, and a towel on the rack beside it. You get an immediate impression of the man, whose exceptional character is evidenced by the simple bohemian style of furnishings in his island home (the floor, for example, is covered in reed matting, generally associated with impoverishment).

KINALIADA, "Henna Island", takes its name from the red colouring of its eastern cliffs; in Greek it was known as *Proti*, since it's the nearest of the islands to the mainland. Like Heybeliada, Kınalıada's history is notable for exiles, including Romanus IV Diogenes, deposed after his disastrous defeat at the Battle of Manzikert by the Selçuk Turks. Now its population is seventy percent Armenian.

The island is rather bare and barren, and hotels are scarce. There are a few reasonable **restaurants**, though: the *Mimosa*, to the left of the ferry landing, is probably the best, but only open in the summer season; *the Kayambayan Endoğan*, on Cennet Yolu 2km north of the ferry landing, is a pleasant seaside establishment, only open in summer, where you can eat *izgara* and salads.

Black Sea resorts

The **Black Sea** and a few of its resorts are easily accessible from İstanbul, and if you're staying in the city for any length of time and want a short break, these seaside villages make ideal day trips or weekend breaks. The resorts nearest to İstanbul are actually some of the most attractive on the entire Black Sea coast, with very good sand beaches – though bathing can be dangerous, especially at Ağva.

Kilyos, on the European side of the Bosphorus, is accessible by minibus-dolmuş from Sariyer, from where there's a direct road of about 12km. Şile is a two-hour drive from Üsküdar, with buses from the westernmost bus depot on the hour every hour from 9am; it's another hour to Ağva. Tickets are sold from the bus station in Üsküdar on Doğancilar Caddesi, and cost $1.50 to Şile, $2 to Ağva. If you're driving, the easiest route to take out of İstanbul is along the coast road via Beykoz (a quicker route is via Kısıklı near Büyük Çamlıca, but it's not as well marked).

As the closest real resort to the metropolis, ŞİLE suffers from overfamiliarity: as far as locals are concerned, it's all right for a lark at the weekend, but if you get the chance to go further afield, then take it. Consequently the place is sad and abandoned – and peaceful like no other Turkish beach resort – on public holidays of any length, but jam-packed at weekends. Without the crowds it's undeniably attractive, perched on a clifftop overlooking a large bay and tiny island, with white sandy beaches stretching off to the west. To add to the holiday feel, there's a pretty French-built black-and-white-striped lighthouse which can be visited, but only in the evenings after sunset, when the keeper arrives. The fourteenth-century Genoese castle on a nearby island cannot be visited, but it makes a romantic backdrop for the town's harbour.

Şile's main historical claim to fame is that it was visited by Xenophon and his Ten Thousand, the army which was left leaderless when its officers were all murdered by the Persians. They stayed in Şile, then known as Kalpe, and Xenophon wrote in his memoirs about how well the site suited the establishment of a city. Apart from the few who are doing very well out of tourism, the town is essentially quite poor. Their main product, sold all over Turkey, is *Şile bezi*, a kind of cheesecloth which local women embroider by hand.

Practicalities

Hotels are plentiful, but prices go up at weekends, and anything cheap fills fast. If you get stuck for somewhere to stay, walk up the main street, Üsküdar Caddesi, and ask if anyone knows anyone with a room: locals often have *pansiyon* rooms in their houses, which they're happy to rent out.

Well signposted from the *otogar*, there's a group of hotels near the beach, including the *Otel Değirmen* (☎0216/711 5048; ⑤) whose rooms are disappointingly old and shab-by for the price (its swimming pool costs an outrageous $12 for non-residents). Above the *Değirmen* at Aynalı Mevki 14, the *Motel Garden* (☎0216/711 4343; ③) is not partic-ularly well run or comfortable but it's cheap for Şile, and steps from the end of this street give direct access to the beach. The *Ruya* on the harbour below the *Değirmen* at Plaj Yolu 7 (☎0216/711 5070; ③), 500m from the beach, has very basic rooms with (cold) water and breakfast.

Following Üsküdar Caddesi out of town in the opposite direction to the beach, the *Taunay*, at Vali Muhittin Cad 21 (☎0216/711 2144; ③), has rooms with en-suite bath-rooms, as well as flats with two double bedrooms for $36.

Uzunkum Beach to the east of town is the best beach in Şile, being sandy and absolutely spotless, partly because the proprietors of the massive *Resort Hotel* next to the beach rake it every day. To get here, take a dolmuş labelled "Resort" from the bus station. On the other side of the road from the *Resort*, the *Uzunkum Motel and Restaurant* (☎0216/711 2880; ④) is comfortable, clean, friendly and generally has empty rooms. The local **campsites** are the *Doğuş* further round the coast at the equal-ly beautiful Ağlayan Beach (for which you pay entry), or *Şile Kamping* back on Halk Plajı near the *otogar*.

The *Fener* **restaurant** on Fener Caddesi near the lighthouse has excellent views, pleasant white-tablecloth surroundings and good but somewhat pricy food. Or try the low-key *Turhan Kardeş Lokanta*, off Üsküdar Caddesi at Çıkrıkçı Pasajı 130, with sea views and cheap steamtray food, but a loud TV.

Ağva

About 30km further along the coast from Şile, **AĞVA** is a lovely, quiet and sleepy little haven, even more worthy of the journey from İstanbul. To get there, catch one of the

Şile buses from Üsküdar that continue to Ağva. Be warned that the last buses back to İstanbul leave at 6pm in summer, in winter at 5pm at the weekend, 3pm on a weekday.

There are a few small **hotels** in the village, some with fish restaurants attached. On the banks of the Yeşilçay River, the *Motel Tahir* (☎0216/721 8012; ②) has simple clean doubles without en-suite facilities, and serves *kiremit kebap* in the evenings by the river. If you require a higher degree of comfort, the *Kurfal Otel* at Plaj Cad 15 (☎0216/721 8493; ④) has nicely furnished rooms with en-suite bathrooms and balconies looking onto the beach.

The beauty of this tiny village lies in its location between two rivers, the Yeşilçay and the Göksü, both of which are fished to provide the livelihood of the local community. It's an easy matter to take a boat around the cove from the Yeşilçay River to the **Karabatak beach** at Kilimli (about $18 return, $30 to be dropped and picked up later), where it's possible to camp in absolute seclusion (it's also accessible from the Kilimli road out of Ağva); there's a good chance of spotting a school of dolphins in these waters. **Ağva beach** is fine golden sand, but the currents are notoriously strong and it's not recommended that you swim unless there are plenty of people around to help out should you get into any trouble.

Polonezköy

The small Polish village of **POLONEZKÖY** could be visited on your way to the coast if you were driving, though it's not easy to reach by public transport. Some of the village's charm has been destroyed by over-commercialization, but its most interesting aspect remains its unusual history. Polonezköy ("village of the Poles") was established in 1848 by **Prince Czartorisky**, the leader of the Polish nationals, who was granted exile in the Ottoman Empire to escape Russian oppression in the Balkans. His main aim, along with other Eastern European exiles such as the poet Adam Mickiewicz and Hungarian nationalist leader Kossuth, was to establish a union of the Balkan races, including Romanians, Circassians and Turks, to counteract Panslavic expansion. He continued this work during his years of exile, while establishing the community which still survives on the plot of land sold to him by a local monastery. The village has long attracted international interest, and among its most famous visitors have been Liszt, Flaubert, Pope John Paul, and most recently Lech Walesa, who visited the village in 1994. A few of the present inhabitants of the village are the sixth generation of Poles in İstanbul. Since the establishment of the Turkish republic they have not been allowed to educate their children in Polish and now only a few of the permanent community of the village speak Polish.

The village became known to tourism in the 1970s, when it was popular among İstanbulites on the track of illicit pig meat, hard to find in the city. A change has taken place in recent years, however, and the new generation of visitors to the village are more interested in illicit sex than *charcuterie*. Consequently the latter is practically unobtainable, while a number of insalubrious landlords and ladies offer rooms for rent at hourly rates.

Since the building of the new Bosphorus Bridge, Polonezköy has become the fashionable place for İstanbul residents to own a "dublex villa", a two-storey second home away from İstanbul's deathly pollution. Of the original Central-European-style wooden houses with their balconies and flower gardens, few remain, and most of these are brothels or seedy hotels at best; in their place are purpose-built travesties of the originals. On the plus side, the designation of the village as İstanbul's first national park has slowed the development that threatened to ruin the surrounding countryside as well as the village. A forest keeper has been employed, and locals have waived their legal rights to cut trees for firewood. An influential organization, the Association for the Conservation of the Natural Environment, has become involved with the project, and illegally constructed buildings in the village have been demolished. There's a 4.5-kilometre jogging and walking track to the north of the village (beginning near the *Adampol Hotel*), which wends through the forest of pine, chestnut, oaks and hornbeams, crossing streams over little wooden bridges.

Most of the **restaurants** in the town now sell chicken in place of pork, but if you've been in Turkey for a long time and you're desperate for pig meat, it's served at the *Leonardo Restaurant* on the road into the village. The service in their walled garden courtyard is excellent, and so is the food, but beware that a salad with sausage and chips for two – albeit very special sausages – comes to $26. The **hotels** are mostly the aforementioned sleaze pits or very expensive. The *Adampol* (☎0216/432 3154, fax 432 3218; ④) at Polonezköy 23 comprises a large, luxurious hotel complex with a swimming pool, but prices rise and rooms are booked well in advance at the weekend and on public holidays.

The main problem of a visit to the village is that **getting there** is so difficult: there is no longer any public transport from İstanbul. Possible options are to take a taxi from Beykoz on the Bosphorus, or to take the #15K bus from Üsküdar to Cavuşbaşı and hitch the final 13km. To get there by car, take the first turning off the Mehmet the Conqueror bridge on the Asian side, and follow the signs from Ruzgarlıbahçe to Polonezköy. Alternatively, ask for the Polonezköy road from Paşabahçe on the Bosphorus.

Kilyos

On the European shores of the Black Sea, **KİLYOS** is an attractive place with an impressive stretch of beach. This expanse of sand, with resort paraphernalia like umbrellas and deck chairs in season, is kept spotlessly clean. The most imposing monument, the medieval Genoese castle on a cliff above the town, is closed to the public because of the Turkish army unit installed there. To get to Kilyos, take a **dolmuş** from the Bosphorus suburb of Sariyer, from where it's a twelve-kilometre drive.

There are a couple of restaurants down near the shore, and plenty of **hotel** options, although accommodation tends to be pricy. The plush, modern *Kilyos Kale Hotel*, on a cliff overlooking the sea in Kıyıköyü, has *pansiyon* rooms below its expensive hotel rooms. Another cheaper option is the clean and basic *Kilyos Yuva Hotel*, near the minibus stop some distance from the beach.

FOOD, ENTERTAINMENT AND SHOPPING

İstanbul may not be the political capital of Turkey, but in terms of gastronomy and culture it certainly leads the nation. Despite twenty percent unemployment and an average wage of around $40 a month, it's not at all difficult to part with large amounts of cash when you go out to eat or drink. For food and nightlife, the liveliest areas of the city are across the Horn, in Taksim and Galata, though there are restaurants everywhere.

Restaurants

Eating out is an everyday activity for most Turks, and the best **restaurants** in Turkey, some would even say in the world, are located in İstanbul, including several that lavish time and skill on old Ottoman cuisine. If you're just after a snack, however, you can find it almost anywhere: **street-food** options in the city vary from the excellent fish sandwiches served off boats by fishermen in Kadıköy, Karaköy and Eminönü, to disgusting piles of sheeps' innards (*kokoreç*) which are sold from booths in less salubrious areas. There's no real way of knowing what standards of hygiene will be, but then there isn't in a restaurant either, however much you pay.

Taksim and Galata

Most of İstanbul's best restaurants and bars are located around Taksim and Galata, catering for theatre- and cinema-goers, or for people who want to spend all night over a meal and a bottle of *rakı*. For the latter, the **Balıkpazarı**, the fish market in Nevizade Caddesi behind the Çiçik Pasajı (Flower Passage), is the place for pavement cafés and excellent fish and *mezes*. The musicians have followed the alleycats, and one will serenade you while the other pesters you through the course of a meal. A less fraught culinary experience might be had at any of a number of *lokanta*s, restaurants and cafés scattered around this area.

Budget options

Ayazpaşa Russian Restaurant, İnönü Cad 77/1, Taksim, entrance on Miralay Zefik Bey Sok (☎0212/143 4892). Basement restaurant with friendly atmosphere and good service, offering a selection of Russian favourites like borscht and *palaçinka*, though the interpretation of some is unmistakably Turkish. The eventual outcome is OK though, and it's cheaper than *Rejans*.

Burç Pastanesi, İstiklâl Cad 463–465, Beyoğlu. Good breakfasts and midday snacks.

Cumhuriyet Meyhanesi, Balıkpazarı Sahne Sok 47, Beyoğlu. Good value for fish, and an excellent selection of *mezes*. Sit outside in the pedestrian walkway in the fish market for lively musical entertainment and the devoted attention of the neighbourhood cats.

Damgâh Restaurant, Nevizade Sok 15, Balıkpazarı, Beyoğlu. One of the best in the fish market for food and service, with a lively atmosphere.

Hacı Abdullah, Sakızağacı Cad 19, Beyoğlu. Opposite the Ağa Camii, the only mosque on İstiklâl Cad. Excellent little place, unusually decorated with huge jars of pickles. Well-known among locals as a cheap, reliable alternative to the flashier places on İstiklâl. Only catch is they don't serve alcohol.

Hasır I (also known as *Asır*), Kalyoncu Kulluğu Cad 94/1, Tarlabaşı, Beyoğlu. Very popular Turkish *meyhane*, about ten minutes' walk from the PTT on İstiklâl Cad. Excellent food and lots of veggie options. Order a minimal selection from the menu as the best food will periodically be brought around on a large tray. Closed Aug.

Ocakbaşı, Sıraselviler Cad 52. Specializes in kebab cooked on a grill in the middle of the restaurant. Friendly service and good value at under $10 a head with beer.

Park Café, Sağlık Sok 27, Ayazpaşa, near the *Marmara Hotel*. Good, reasonably priced food and friendly staff; popular with locals, though a bit smoky.

Tadim Köfte Salonu, Sıraselviler Cad, Taksim, near the Armenian High School. Inventive lunchtime menu and good, cheap grills, hot plates and desserts.

Yakup 2, Asmalı Mescit Sok 35–37, İstiklâl Cad, Tünel. A noisy, down-to-earth *meyhane* popular with local artists and journalists. Open till 2am.

Vegetarian

Nature and Peace, Büyükparmakkapı Cad 21, İstiklâl Cad (third left from Taksim Square as you go towards the *tünel*). Service can be slow but that's because your food's being freshly prepared, and it's worth waiting for. Specialities are green lentil *köfte* and a vegetable platter. They also serve meat dishes.

Safran, Ezine Apartment 1/1, Balo Sok, İstiklâl Cad, very near the Balıkpazarı. Excellent health-food restaurant, further distinguished by having a female chef-owner, whose home-made breads are renowned. Alcohol served.

Zencefil Cafe, Kurabiye Sok 3, Beyoğlu, around the corner from *Pia*, behind the *Fitaş* cinema passage. All ingredients home-grown: a small, ever-changing menu includes home-made breads, herbal teas and local wines.

Upmarket Turkish

Çatı Restaurant and Bar, İstiklâl Cad, Orhan A. Apaydın Sok 20/7, Barohan, floor 7, Tünel, Beyoğlu (☎0212/251 0000 or 251 5107). Well-established among İstanbul's intelligentsia but little known to tourists, this attractive restaurant deserves its glowing reputation. There's live jazz entertainment with the odd class act. Food is reasonably priced, and there are unusual items, like a dessert made from tomatoes. Closed Sun.

Galata Tower Restaurant, in the tower. Expensive, and with no real atmosphere. It's better to go up in the daytime for the views and eat elsewhere.

Garibaldi Bar-Rötisserie, İstiklâl Cad, Perukar Çikmazı 1, Beyoğlu (200m from the PTT opposite the Galatasaray Lycee; ☎0212/149 6895 or 151 9591). Excellent cheap salad buffet and some good Turkish standards, as well as a dodgy selection of "international" dishes. Jazz and Turkish folk music as background accompaniment.

Hacı Baba Restaurant, İstiklâl Cad 49. The food is good, though overpriced, and there's an attractive, peaceful balcony at the back overlooking the churchyard of Aya Triada.

Revan Restaurant, *Sheraton Hotel*, Taksim (☎0212/131 2121). A fixed menu of ten courses for around $30 without drinks, and the ingredients are the best from all over Turkey.

International

Four Seasons, corner of İstiklâl and Şahkula Bostanı Sok, near the *tünel* (☎0212/245 8941). Popular among expats for its classy, English-style old-world charm and sweet trolley. Not cheap, but you get what you pay for. Closed Sun.

Guang Zhou Ocean Restaurant, İnönü Cad 53, Taksim. Chinese restaurant with good-value lunch and evening set menu, and good service. Popular with local Orientals. **Lebanese Restaurant**, Lamartin Cad 41, off Cumhuriyet Cad. Popular for its fresh, authentic food.

Mezzaluna, Abdi İpekçi Cad 38, off Vali Konağı Cad, Nişantaşı. Excellent Italian restaurant which only uses authentic ingredients and recipes. Expensive, but you may be ready to fork out for a change from Turkish.

Pia, Bekar Sok 4, off İstiklâl Cad, Beyoğlu. Friendly chic café with a small but tasty international menu, a bar, and good coffee.

Rejans, Emir Nevruz Sok 17, Galatasaray, Beyoğlu; opposite the church of St Antoine off İstiklâl Cad (☎0212/444 1610). Frequented by diplomats from the nearby consulates and generally by people who know where to eat, this famous establishment was founded by White Russians in the 1930s and thrives on a well-earned reputation. Considering the quality of food and service it's not expensive. *Zindan* in the basement is a newly opened upmarket *meyhane* quickly acquiring recognition for its informal but classy atmosphere. Both closed Sun.

Taksim Sanat Evi, Sıraselviler Cad 69/1, Taksim (☎0212/244 2526 or 152 0273). Large, well-decorated place with splendid Bosphorus view. Popular with media people. Excellent menu includes Chinese, Turkish and Albanian food for around $25 a head. Open daily noon–3.30pm & 10pm–2am.

The China, Lamartin Cad 17, Taksim. The first Chinese restaurant in Turkey, with excellent food – their speciality is chicken with vegetables and almonds – and a friendly atmosphere. Closed Sun.

Urban, Kartal Sok 6/A, near the PTT and the Galatasaray Lycee. One of the many establishments to have sprung up in Beyoğlu since the opening of the new tramline, which is injecting life and colour into a neighbourhood that ten years ago looked as if it had kissed goodbye to its bohemian past. This café serves Italian pasta and Greek bread in the daytime, and becomes a jazz bar in the evenings.

Cafés and sweets

Café Gramofon, Tünel Meydanı 3, near the Beyoğlu entrance to the *tünel*. Run by the same family who manage the excellent *Kathisma* in Sultanahmet, this is a turn-of-the-century-style French-influenced café, where you can eat *tartines*, salads or hot sandwiches, listen to jazz in the evenings, and soak up the unique Beyoğlu atmosphere.

Café Kaktüs, İstiklâl Cad, Imam Adnan Sok 4 (fifth on the right from Taksim Square), Beyoğlu. Further evidence of the gentrification of this area. Very French; serves light food and drinks (and real coffee) from 8am to 2am.

Café Wien, Atiye Sok 5, off Abdi Ipekçi Cad, Teşvikiye. Elegant nineteenth-century townhouse with shady garden – a fitting location for weekend breakfasts or a schnitzel for lunch. The coffee and desserts are wicked on the calorie count.

Patisserie de Pera, *Pera Palas Hotel*, Tepebaşı. It would be worth splashing out for a chance to savour the Art Nouveau elegance, even if the delicious cakes and coffee, and the excellent service, weren't enough in themselves.

Saray, İstiklâl Cad 102–104, Beyoğlu, just above Çiçek Pasajı. Emphasis on milk-based desserts; classic and cheap.

Saray, Teşvikiye Cad 105, just east of the police station; a 10- to 15-minute walk from the Military Museum or Dolmabahçe. No relation to the above but just as good, serving simple egg and noodle snacks until 1am.

The imperial centre

The restaurant situation in old İstanbul has improved significantly in recent years, and now you can find good food at reasonable prices both day and evening, although it still doesn't compete with Taksim or the Bosphorus for variety or quality. The area on the other side of Kennedy Caddesi in Kumkapı, long known for its fish restaurants and convivial atmosphere, has recently been cleaned up and the waterside establishments here are a pleasant option on a summer evening. We've also listed several restaurants below in Eminönü and Sirkeci, which despite unpromising locations maintain excellent reputations.

The Hippodrome (At Meydanı)

Cafer Ağa Medresesi, Caferiye Sok, Soğukkuyu Çıkmazı. A cafe in the courtyard of a former *medrese*, which now sells Turkish handicrafts in its beautifully renovated rooms. This is a good place for a budget breakfast or to quench the thirst after a trip round Aya Sofya.

Doy Doy, Zıfa Hamamı Sok 13, off Küçükayasofya Cad at the Hippodrome end. Small and insignificant in appearance but with a well-deserved reputation for simple, cheap and well-prepared kebabs and *pide*.

Hippodrome Restaurant Cafeteria, At Meydanı 74. The "Hippodrome kebab", a fresh, mainly vegetable pie, comes highly recommended. Two set menus for around $4.50 each.

Hotel Alzer, At Meydanı. Good central restaurant next to the *Hippodrome* restaurant, with reasonable prices, excellent *et sote* (sautéed meat).

Türkistan Aşevi, Tavukhane Sok 36. A rather shiny rebuild of a nineteenth-century family house (only the ceiling upstairs is original). The family now run the restaurant and have introduced some quaint customs, usually reserved for the home, such as removing your shoes as you enter and eating at low tables. Mum prepares traditional Turkish and Turkestan dishes; the *düğün çorbası* (wedding soup) is especially good.

Cankurtaran

Kathisma Restaurant, Yeni Akbıyık Cad 26. Fish and meat dishes, with a wine menu and excellent sweets to follow, in a pleasant environment. On Wed lunchtimes catch the street market outside the front door.

Rami Restaurant, Utangaç Sok 6, opposite the Arasta Bazaar, near the Mosaic Museum (☎0212/517 6593). Candlelight, antiques and muted music combine to intimate effect in this restored Ottoman townhouse with great views from the roof terrace. A good option to soothe your nerves after a day in Sultanahmet. Fish of the day $8.50; their speciality is *karidesli dolması* or shrimp pie.

Around Divanyolu and the covered bazaar

Altın Sofrası, Süleymaniye Cad 33 (☎0212/522 5518). A good bet for lunch after a visit to Süleymaniye; certainly much better than any of the touristy restaurants that face the mosque.

Cennet, Divanyolu Cad 90, Çemberlitaş. Two traditional Turkish dishes, *gözleme* and *mantı*, served at low tables. This is mock-up ethnic, with Turkish women seated in the centre rolling out pastry for the *gözleme*, and a band of extremely noisy live musicians doing the rounds – it's the sort of place you might visit once for the experience, then look elsewhere for better cooking without the gimmicks.

Darüzziyafe, Şifahane Cad, Süleymaniye. Ottoman cuisine, live sixteenth-century-style music and non-alcoholic Ottoman drinks in Sinan-built annexe to his masterpiece mosque. Unforgettable and moderately priced.

Havuzlu Lokantası, Gani Çelebi Sok 3, Kapalı Çarşı (☎0212/527 3346). This is probably the best eating establishment in the covered bazaar, reasonably easy to locate since it's next to the PTT. The lofty, unadorned hall gives a good impression of the architecture of the bazaar. After an explosion in 1954 gas was banned in the bazaar, and the food is cooked on cast-iron coal-fired stoves to good effect.

Karadeniz Pide Salonu, Divanyolu Cad, Bıckı Yurdu Sok 1/1. Cheap and popular with the locals; serves a good *kiremit kebap*.

Pudding Shop, Divanyolu Cad 18. World-famous restaurant serving fast food à la Turk at reasonable prices. Featured in the drug deal scenes in *Midnight Express*.

Rumeli Cafe, Divanyolu Cad, Ticarethane Sok 8. Friendly, cosmopolitan atmosphere in nicely restored bare brick and wood surroundings. Reasonable prices for simple filling fare: breakfasts, omelettes, salads, and steak and mash in addition to a Turkish menu. Live music Fri nights.

Subaşı Restaurant, Nuruosmaniye Cad 48, Çarsıkapı, next to the Covered Bazaar. A spit-and-sawdust place (with real sawdust), located behind Nuruosmaniye Camii near the covered bazaar, serving excellent lunchtime food, far better than anything else in the same price range and area. Go early (noon–1pm) as it gets packed and food may run out.

Vitamin Restaurant, Divanyolu Cad 16, next door to *Pudding Shop*. Popular meeting place and information exchange mart serving Turkish fast food.

Eminönü and Sirkeci

Borsa Lokanta, Yalıköşkuşkü Işhanı 60–62, Yalı Köşkü Cad, Eminönü (☎0212/522 4173). Excellent restaurant: you won't find better Turkish meat dishes anywhere in the country.

Konyali, Ankara Cad 233, Sirkeci (☎0212/513 9610). Excellent pastry shop frequented by the quarter's business people, who eat their breakfast standing at the marble-topped counters. Open Mon–Fri 7am–6pm, Sat 7am–5.30pm. Tucked away round the back in Mimar Kemalettin Cad is one of the city's best self-service restaurants, part of the same establishment, which serves excellent meat stews and pastries.

Pandeli, Mısır Carşısı 51 (☎0212/522 5534). Unusually for a commercial establishment, this restaurant is deliberately located out of the way: as a result of anti-Greek riots in the 1950s it was moved here on the advice of then prime minister Adnan Menderes. To get in, go through the main entrance of the Mısır Carşısı and then turn back towards the doorway; on your right is a staircase leading up to the restaurant. The restaurant is run by a Greek and a Turk, and the food is some of the best to be found anywhere in İstanbul. Open daily 11.30am–3.30pm.

Kumkapı

Doğan Restaurant, Kennedy Cad, Balıkçılar Carşısı. Fish are caught and sold here, so feature highly on the menu. You can even watch the boats go out in the evening from the waterside terrace. Fixed menu for $13.

Merkez, Çaparı Sok. Serves excellent fish stews and the region's speciality sweet of honey, clotted cream and nuts, called *kaymak*.

Olimpiyat 2, Kumkapı Meydanı. Favourite among locals for its excellent service, guaranteed high quality and large range of fish, which includes swordfish kebab when available.

Yengeç, Telli Odalar Sok 6. This enormous three-storey affair specializes in seafood: jumbo prawns, octopus, swordfish kebab and crab all regularly make an appearance.

Aksaray and Lâleli

Aksu Oçakbaşı, Aksaray Cad, Azımkar Sok 5, Lâleli. Well-prepared, interesting food that's not too pricy. Friendly service.

Konyalı Kebabcı, İnkilap Cad 8–10, Aksaray. Simple, basic and cheap.

Hotel Merit Antique Asian Restaurant, Ordu Cad 226, Lâleli (☎0212/513 9300 ext 5092). Well-cooked Chinese food: *dim sum* lunch served from noon to 3pm at around $10, but an evening meal will set you back $20–30. Their Turkish restaurant, the **Lale** (ext 5054), is similarly priced and a good bet for superlative Turkish food which hasn't been standing in trays since mid-morning. The food and service at the **Metsou-Yan**, the only kosher restaurant in town, are also excellent. The hotel comprising several buildings on the opposite sides of a street brought together under one roof, and renovated beyond recognition, is worth a look in itself.

Taşhan Restaurant, Fethi Bey Cad 55, Lâleli. *Mezes*, kebabs and grills in an atmospheric market building. The food's good, if a bit overpriced, and the location is atmospheric and a pleasant respite from the more tawdry aspects of Lâleli.

The Bosphorus

The straits dividing Europe and Asia certainly provide the most romantic setting in which to eat fish, drink *rakı* and muse over how your budget will be affected by the evening's final outcome. The best value and the best fish are to be found way up near the Black Sea, in **Rumeli Kavağı** and **Sariyer** on the European side, but if you don't have your own transport it can be difficult to get back into town afterwards. Otherwise you can try your luck in **Ortaköy**, which has become pricy as a result of its recent rise in popularity, **Arnavutköy**, or possibly one or two of the villages across the straits. Don't expect the fish to be cheap, though, especially if there's a good view as well. There's less chance of meeting other tourists if you take the trouble to work out ferry times and cross the straits to the Asian side.

European shore

Ahtapot, Köyiçi Meydanı 50, Beşiktaş. Small, friendly fish restaurant located near the fresh produce market in lively Beşiktaş. Serves all the standards but charges less than establishments right on the Bosphorus.

Bosfor Restaurant, Çayirbaşı Cad 312–314, Büyükdere. No Bosphorus view to speak of – it's on the wrong side of the main road – hence reasonably priced, with good service.

Café Caliente, İskele Cad 3, Ortaköy. Mexican food may make a welcome break on a prolonged stay. Around $20 a head with mesquitas. Three sittings: noon–2pm, dinner 8–10pm and late 10pm–1am.

Café Creme, Camii Meydanı, Değirmen Sok 12, Ortaköy. Young atmosphere and good food, including crêpes, salads and herbal teas. Live music at the weekends.

Cuisine Restaurant, Nispetiye Cad 38/3, Alkent, Etiler. Imaginative European and Turkish dishes on the terrace. They also serve Sunday brunch and an open buffet on Wednesdays.

Dergah Pastanesi, Yıldız Yolu 20, Beşiktaş. Very good strawberry cakes and pastries.

Hanedan, Beşiktaş İskelesi. Large, fairly formal establishment, popular with locals and tourists alike for its reliable menu, served with abundant fresh *pide*. It's on the front next to the ferry jetty in Beşiktaş, so window tables afford good views of shoreside activities along the Bosphorus. Downstairs is a meat restaurant, upstairs fish.

İskele Balik Lokantası, İskele Meydanı 4/1, Rumeli Kavağı. Rather large and impersonal, but the food's good.

Japan Club (Hana Shiki), Mürbasan Sok, Koza İş Merkezi, A Blok, off Barbaros Bulvarı, Beşiktaş. The best sushi bar and restaurant in town, popular with Japanese businessmen. Open Mon–Fri noon–2pm & 6.30–11pm; dinner only on Sat, closed Sun.

Mor Fil Izgara Salonu, Osmanzade Sok 27, Ortaköy (☎0212/136 0169). Lunchtime and supper bistro, a bit tacky outside, but the food's good and cheap.

Süper Yedigün, Rumeli Kavağı İskele Cad 27, Sariyer. Reasonably priced fish restaurant (around $10 a head), with an open terrace on the roof.

Tahta Kaşık, Muallim Naci Cad 90, Ortaköy. Good for lunchtime snacks, with meat dishes and sweets as well as tripe soup; views too.

Tuğra, Çıragan Palace Hotel, Çıragan Cad 84, Beşiktaş (☎0212/258 3377). Ottoman restaurant in one of the most spectacular settings in the city. Excellent service and some unexpected items on the menu. However oriental the decor and cuisine, expect to pay Western prices. Closed Mon.

Uçurtma, Osmanzade Sok 11, Ortaköy. Good for breakfasts and home-made jams, snacks and pastries until 10pm.

Yaselam Arabian Restaurant, Cevdet Paşa Cad 294, Bebek. Excellent Arabic food amid chintzy over-the-top decor. Overlooks the harbour and has a pleasant garden out the back. Open daily noon–midnight.

Asian shore

2ler Et Lokantası, Bağdat Cad 289, Caddebostan (☎0216/355 2253). Meat restaurant with a good reputation, though sometimes the service isn't all it could be.

Angel Balık Restaurant, Semişipaşa Sahil Yolu 46, Üsküdar. Modern, classy affair with English-speaking waiters and views of the river. Choose your fish from an array in the fridge. Full dinner around $25.

Borsa Lokanta, Fener Kalamız Cad 87, Fenerbahçe (☎0216/348 7700). Recently taken over by the *Borsa* chain (see "Eminönü" above), this restaurant lives up to the reputation: food and service are marvellous, and unusually it all takes place in an enormous greenhouse affair. If you sit too near the windows you may feel a bit exposed.

Divan Pastanesi, Bağdat Cad 319, Erenköy (☎0216/358 5451). Very classy joint selling the best pastries and cakes in the street. You can sit outside and watch the Bağdat people as you indulge yourself. Good line, too, in attractively boxed sweets and *lokum* (Turkish delight).

Eski Osmanlı Mutfağı, Bağdat Cad, Cinardıbı 342/1, Şaşkinbakkal. Good traditional Ottoman cooking.

Hasir, Beykoz Korusu, Beykoz. Good food and a bar in plush modern surroundings with a Bosphorus view. Around $10 a head without drinks.

Huzur Restaurant/Arabin Yeri, Salacak, Üsküdar (☎0216/333 3157). Run by a group of Arabic-speaking Turks from the Hatay, serving grilled fish. The restaurant has a degree of old-world, rather faded charm, and an undeniably wonderful view of the Bosphorus, but unfortunately it's let down by service that is often plain shabby.

İsmet Baba, İcadiye Cad 96–8, Kuzguncuk (☎0216/333 1232). Twenty varieties of *meze*, fish of the day and *raki* in one of those genuine old establishments it's hard to find on the Bosphorus, all for $15–20 per person.

Kanaat Lokantasi, Selmanipak Cad 25, Üsküdar (next to *Migros*). Recently renovated with copies of İznik tile panels from the Selimiye Camii in Edirne and a copper chimney piece. Meals, though not as good as they used to be, are still reasonably cheap at about $3 a head. Despite the waiters – grumpy and taciturn at best – this is probably the best *lokanta* in the area.

Katibim, Şemsipaşa Sahil Yolu 53, Üsküdar. One of the few affordable restaurants on the seafront here, probably because it's meat not fish. White tablecloth service, and good views of the front.

Sarı Çiçekler, Tabyasi Cad, Anadolu Kavaği, south of the ferry landing. Good-value fish at the end of the Bosphorus cruise, in a village devoted to food.

Uludağ Kebabcısı, İskele Cad 8, off Bağdat Cad, Caddebostan. Only one item on the menu here and an atmosphere like a school dining room, but the *İskender kebap* is the best to be had outside Bursa.

Nightlife: clubs, bars and discos

Traditional İstanbul **nightlife** centres around restaurants and *gazinos* (clubs where *meze* are served, accompanied by singers and oriental dancers), but new bars and Western-style clubs are gaining in popularity among the younger middle class and *entel* (pseudo-intellectual) set. These are generally uncomfortable imitations of Western models with little real atmosphere, but a few of them have the charm of a good location, or attract an interesting clientele which provides a distraction from bad decor or obsequious service. The locations tend to centre around Taksim and its nearby suburbs, and along the Bosphorus, mainly on the European side.

Bars

For a Muslim city, İstanbul is far from dry, and in most areas away from Islamic fundamentalists (forget Fatih and Eyüp, for example), you'll find bars ranging from the dangerously seedy to the chic and overpriced.

Sultanahmet

Adı Bar, Ancili Çavuz Sok 8/1. Nice decor, friendly atmosphere and good music which is turned off when the nearby mosques call *namaz*. Daily 3pm–2am.

Orient Youth Hostel Bar, Yeni Akbıyık Cad 13, opposite Aya Sofya. The bar has a good view of the Bosphorus and Marmara Sea, and is frequented by travellers from surrounding hostels in the evening.

Sultan Pub, Divanyolu Cad 2. Pleasant café-bar with tables outside in summer.

Around Taksim

Alkazar Cinema Bar, İstiklâl Cad 179. Tranquil, intellectual café-bar, in a restored old building, popular with cinema buffs.

Cazibe Café Bar, Turnacı Başı Sok 5, İstiklâl Cad, Galatasaray. Live reggae and rock after 10.30pm; occasional evenings of gypsy music.

Hayal Kahvesi, Büyükparmakkapı Sok 19, Beyoğlu. Attractive bare brick and wood decor and good live jazz and blues. Food and drink served day and night.

İstanbul Sanat Merkezi, Sakızağacı Cad, Eski Çeşme Sok 12, Taksim. Huge, very expensive ex-monastery with great decor and views, roof terrace and good jazz. Pool bar downstairs.

Limon, İmam Adnan Sok, İstiklâl Cad (fourth right coming from Taksim Square). Run by satirical cartoonists from the magazine of the same name, a favourite meeting place before a visit to the cinemas in this area.

Tribunal, Muammer Karaca Çıkmazı, off İstiklâl Cad, just before Sainte Antoine Kilisesi. Basement bar in a medieval French courthouse. Live Greek *rembetika* and gypsy music.

Zihni, Bronz Sok 1/B, Maçka (☎0212/146 9043). Opened by a local sculptor who is often seen mixing drinks. The walls are covered with Ottoman calligraphy and most of the furniture is antique. After work it's crowded with local bankers meeting their wives, in the daytime it's a good place for lunch. The menu features salads and brunch-type dishes as well as more substantial meat and seafood. Daily noon–10pm.

On the Bosphorus

Bebek Hotel Bar, Cevdet Paşa Cad 113, Bebek (☎0226/163 3000). Popular with expats and older examples of the local beautiful people. Nondescript inside, so only worth it in the summer when you can sit by the water: be prepared to wait for an outside table, especially at weekends. Daily 1pm–2am.

Bilsak, Soğancı Sok 7, Cihangir (fourth left off Sıraselviler Cad as you head away from Taksim Square). Aspiring cultural centre with a restaurant, small informal bar and occasional music, as well as acting and ceramics classes.

Eylül, Birinci Cad 23, Arnavutköy. In an old, wooden waterside residence, this three-storey café-bar serves coffee on the first floor and good French and Turkish wine at the top, with a jazz bar in the middle.

Hayal, Kanlıca–Çubuklu Cad, Çubuklu. Located on an old wharf, this Asian branch of Büyükparmakkapı's well-known rock bar occupies a converted nineteenth-century warehouse – tables on the promenade risk being splashed by the Bosphorus. Live music is mostly Hispanic. Get there from İstinye İskele, whence the *Hayal*'s motor launch will ferry you across the Bosphorus (and back).

Kalem Bar, Cevdetpaşa Cad 306/1, Bebek (☎0212/165 0448). Popular with students from the nearby Bosphorus University and with the rich kids from the neighbourhood. The tiny balcony gets almost unbearably packed in summer; there's a jazz pianist most nights. Open daily noon–1am.

Kedi Bar, Arnavutköy Deresi Sok, Arnavutköy. Although *Kedi* only opened a couple of years ago, it feels ancient, mainly because it's the hangout of much of İstanbul's sizeable 1968-obsessed population. The music, mostly cover versions of old Bob Dylan tunes, adds to the atmosphere. Despite this, *Kedi* is very popular with the aspiring *entel* set. Open till 1am.

Kortan Café, Hakkak Yumni Sok 15, Emirgan (after the Bosphorus Bridge between Rumeli Hisarı and Emirgan ferry landing, turn left after the petrol station). Great café with a stunning view and very low prices. Virtually devoid of foreigners, *Kortan* is frequented by local teenagers whose parents came here when they were young. Open daily 11am–midnight.

North Shields, Çalıkuşu Sok Levent, off Barbaros Bul, about 4km out of Beşiktaş. Typical British pub with a real beer garden, serving all kinds of malt whisky and British and other European beers. Go and make your excuses to all the other sad expats.

Rock House Café, *Princess Hotel*, Dereboyu Cad, Ortaköy. İstanbul's version of the *Hard Rock Café* chain. Bar and restaurant (ribs, chilli, steaks, burgers) with live bands after 10pm. A barn of a place, but very busy at weekends.

Uno, Bağdat Cad 406, Suadiye. Chrome-and-glass aquarium bar with occasional singers. Not worth making a detour for, but if you're over this side of the Bosphorus it has quite a relaxed atmosphere.

Ziya Bar, Muallim Naci Cad, just past Ortaköy. One of the older, more established bars, with an oyster bar on its first floor. In the winter, it caters largely to the middle-management business crowd; summers are much more alive as *Ziya*'s has a big garden and outdoor bar. Open daily noon–1am.

Dancing

İstanbul's dance clubs may surprise Western visitors. The best ones are imaginative in decor with sounds that are bang up to date. Expect to spend no less than you would in London, New York or Sydney on a night out. Most places have entry charges (anything from $2 to $8) and are open from around 9pm until 2 or 4am.

Around Taksim

Andon, Sıraselviler Cad 89. Different bars on three floors plus a snug in the basement. Booze, nosh, babes, hunks.

Harry's Bar, *Hyatt Regency Hotel*, Taşkışla Cad, Taksim. Avant-garde, designer decor in a five-star hotel, with live blues and rock from a resident American band. Sixteen-monitor video wall where you can watch important sports events, laser discs or your karaoke performance.

Gitanes, Tel Sok, off Büyükparmakkapı Sok, which is three streets down on the left from Taksim Square. Crowded, lively rendezvous for a grungy, student crowd.

Kemanci Bar, Sıraselviler Cad 69, under *Reks Duğun Salonu* and cinema (☎0212/245 3048). Hard rock basement bar-disco with live music at least five times a week, including the weekends.

Roxy, Aslanyatağı Sok 113, Sıraselviler Cad. DJs and live bands play rock, R&B, jazz and dance music in this posy, pricy, pokey bar-disco; fairly exclusive, yuppy groove.

On the Bosphorus

2019, Atatürk 100 Yil Oto Sanayi, Maslak, between Taksim and Arnavutköy. Set in the middle of a car workshop area, you have to practically clamber over body parts to make an entrance. Still, it's the place to be seen, so it must be worth it. Hard rock music, waiters in miner's helmets.

Çubuklu 29, Paşabahçe Yolu 24, Çubuklu. Large outdoor club right on the water, tables shaded by canvas umbrellas and lit by flaming torches. Music is mamba and soul; the crowd is all ages and very energetic.

Memo's, Salhane Sok 10/2, Ortaköy (☎0212/261 8304). With its beautiful Bosphorus views from the terrace, this is a class joint and you won't get in unless they like the look of you. Disco starts at 11pm. Free entry, but high drink prices.

Paşa Beach, Muallim Nacı Cad, Kuruçeşme (☎0212/259 7061). Drinking outside until dawn for the bright young things who manage to get through the door. Dance floors on different levels, video screens and bars all directly overlooking the Bosphorus.

Şamdansa, Turkbostan Sok 22, Yeniköy (☎0212/262 1313). Landscaped gardens and sculpture provide a backdrop for the best sounds in the city.

Gay İstanbul

Despite the widespread enthusiasm for transvestite and transsexual singers and entertainers in Turkey, homosexuality is still taboo and it is possible to be arrested for cruising. The following are all located around Taksim, the main centre of the Turkish gay scene.

1001, Sıraselviler Cad. Transvestite bar and disco serving food.

Ceylan, Abdülhak Hamit Cad, Belediye Dükkanları 14. Gay bar frequented by all ages.

Taxim Night Park, Nizamiye Sok 13/45, off Taksim Cad, Taksim. Transvestite floor shows. Attracts both straight and gay clientele.

Valentino, Taksim Square. Male gay bar open 10pm–7am.

Vat 69, 7 İmam Adnan Sok, İstiklâl Cad. Western-style disco open 11pm–4am. Gay at the weekends, otherwise it's fairly straight.

Cabaret

Cabaret is one of the best – and probably the most expensive – way to develop a feel for the Orient over your gin and tonic. Belly dancers expect to be given generous amounts of money (stuffed in their bras) by foreign tourists; you may like to budget accordingly.

Gar Music Hall, Mustafa Kemal Paşa Cad 3, Yenikapı (☎0212/588 4045). Folk dancing, belly dancing and a good three-course meal for around $50.

Kervansaray, Cumhuriyet Cad 30, Harbiye, not far from the *Hilton* (☎0212/247 1630). A huge pillared and chandeliered hall where you won't feel comfortable unless you dress up a bit. Expensive at around $60 a head, $30 without food, but the club has an excellent reputation for its floor show, which includes oriental and folk dancers. Daily 7.30pm–midnight.

Orient House, Tiyatro Cad 27, Beyazit (☎0212/517 6163). Traditional Turkish and folk music and belly dancing in good-value venue. A four-course meal with wine and show is $40 a head; wine but no meal costs $20. Ask about a taxi service to and from your hotel.

Shops and markets

At times İstanbul seems like one enormous bazaar, and as long as you know where to look you can purchase anything. Knowing where to look is always the tricky bit, of course: the best, and cheapest shopping is as elusive in İstanbul as in any major European city. Given that there's a fairly comprehensive public transport system, however, nothing is inaccessible once you start finding your way about. Shopping is most satisfying in the bazaars of the old city, but for practical stuff or designer clothes you'll find the going easier along İstiklâl Caddesi or over the Bosphorus on Bağdat Caddesi.

Shopping centres are taking off in a big way in Turkey, not surprising since they are the modern-day equivalent of the covered bazaar; they're open until at least 8pm, and on Sundays. **Galeria** is five minutes' walk south along the main Bakırköy highway (Rauf Orbay Cad) from the seabus landing. It's designed to incorporate Western features such as an ice-skating rink surrounded by fast-food cafés, but the shops are grouped by genre in typical Turkish bazaar fashion. The best of Turkish names, as well as some European chains like *Printemps*, have outlets here, and contrary to expectations they don't seem to be charging over the odds even though the rents for premises are phenomenal. **Akmerkez** on Nisbetiye Cad in Etiler (daily 10am–10pm, bus #59R from Taksim) is the largest of the new Western-style shopping centres. It has most of the top Turkish brands, many European outlets, *Bazaar 54* for carpets, restaurants, and a cinema. Prices are clearly marked (no room for bargaining, but Turks still do), and it's an altogether too comfortable place to lose a few pounds. On the Asian side of the Bosphorus, **Capitol** shopping centre which dominates the Altunizade area (take an Altunizade dolmuş from Üsküdar to get there) is nearly as big and even more user-friendly than Akmerkez.

Clothes

Turkish **fashion** designs are beginning to compete on the European catwalks, thanks to Rıfat Özbek, the darling of the European fashion world. Other names to watch out for in Turkey are Neslihan Yargıcı, Gönül Paksoy, Zeynep Tunuslu and Arif Ilhan, all of whom are working with the best Turkish **fabrics**, including leather so fine that it is now processed for the Italian market and sold at inflated prices under Italian labels; Bursa silk; and the universally famous Angora wool. Paksoy also uses hand-processed vegetable dyes. While Turkish designers often imitate European styles, they do occasionally flirt with eastern motifs and designs to more interesting effect; a vernacular style is evident in the work on sale through the *Academia* label, which *Beymen* (see below) has developed as a platfom for new designers.

Leather is big business in Turkey, not surprising in a country where so much meat is consumed: something has to be done with all those hides after *kurban bayram* (the annual ritual slaughter). Turks wear a lot of leather and, increasingly, designs are matching the quality of the raw material. Prices are also very attractive to foreign buyers; and if you go home without buying a leather item then count yourself in the minority. The classiest outlets are listed below; cheaper shops are located in and around the covered bazaar, particularly in Vezirhan Sokak. Bursa **towelling**, among the best in the world, is available from *Özdilek* in Galeria.

Clothing outlets in İstanbul are mainly located in Nişantaşı, Osmanbey and Şişli, beyond Taksim in the modern city (any bus from Taksim Square and Cumhuriyet Cad to Mecidyeköy passes through these areas); on Bağdat Caddesi on the Asian side of the Bosphorus near Kadıköy; at the Galeria shopping complex in Bakırköy; and at the Akmerkez centre in Etiler. İstiklâl Caddesi in Beyoğlu is also gaining prestige as a result of its new facelift.

Designer clothes

Beymen, Halazkargazı Cad 230, Şişli; İstiklâl Cad 2/1, Beyoğlu; Rumeli Cad 81, Nişantaşı; and Akmerkez.

Dreams Designer, Mim Kemal Öke Cad 11/2, Nişantaşı; and Bağdat Cad 412, Suadiye. Top women's designers.

Gönül Paksoy, Atiye Sok 6A, Teşvikiye.

IGS, Galeria; Akmerkez; and Halazkargazı Cad 198, Şişli.

Karaca, Matbaacı Osmanbey Sok, Bekiroğlu İş Merkezi 38, Osmanbey. Woollen separates.

Kenzo, Abdi İpekçi Cad 38, Nişantaşı.

Neslihan Yargıcı, Kuyulu Bostan Sok 6, Nişantaşı.

Park Bravo, Halazkargazı Cad 214/D and Bağdat Cad 399.

Pierre Cardin, Akmerkez; Baytar Ahmet Sokak 42; and Capitol.

Silk and Cashmere, Akmerkez and Galeria.

Vakko, İstiklâl Cad 123–5, Beyoğlu; and Akmerkez. Oldest of İstanbul's fashion houses.

Yargıcı, Valikonağı Cad 30, Nişantaşı; Galeria; and Bağdat Cad 313/1.

Shoes

Desa, Halazkargazı Cad 216, Osmanbey; İstiklâl Cad 140, Beyoğlu; Akmerkez; Galeria; and Capitol. Best leather, functional designs.

Elle, Rumeli Cad 12, Nişantaşı. Younger designs.

Hotiç, Teşvikiye Cad 135/1 and Akmerkez.

Seyitağaoğulları, Tavukhane Sok 30, Sultanahmet. Unusual shoes and bags made from kilims.

Casual clothes

BM Club, Galeria; İstiklâl Cad, Vakıf Göçek Hanı, Beyoğlu.

Mudo, Rumeli Cad 44, Osmanbey; and Bağdat Cad 395/1A.

OXXO, İstiklâl Cad 146; Galeria; and Akmerkez. Inexpensive young fashions.

Tiffany and Tomato, Rumeli Cad 67, Osmanbey; and Bağdat Cad 396/2, Suadiye.

Vakkorama, Osmanlı Sok 13, Taksim; and Bağdat Cad 407.

Leather

Angel Leder, Vezirhan Cad 67.

BB, Kuyulu Sok 9–12, covered bazaar; and Yağlıkçılar Cad 143, covered bazaar. European designers, competitive prices.

Derishow, Bağdat Cad 381, Suadiye; Akkavak Sok 18A, Nişantaşı; Akmerkez; and Galeria.

Desa, İstiklâl Cad 140, Beyoğlu; Akmerkez; Capitol; and Galeria. Top-quality Turkish designs, and representatives of Samsonite.

De-Sa, Ortakazlar Cad 8–10, covered bazaar. Good selection of leather and kilim bags.

Sultan Deri, İskele Cad 14, Beylerbeyi.

Food

The best places for food shopping are the **Halk Pazarları**, located in residential areas all over the city. These are permanent markets with small cubicle-like shops including grocers, butchers and delicatessens, usually open from Saturday to Monday, and specializing in fresh, cheap produce. If you're looking for specialist produce and Western commodities that you can't find elsewhere, the best place is the Balık Pazarı, the **fish market** off İstiklâl Caddesi behind the Çiçek Pazarı. Here you can buy otherwise unobtainable pork and bacon at a shop called *Şutte*, Duduodalar Sok 21. **Spices** that can be difficult to obtain elsewhere, such as curry spices, are available at Duduodalar Sok 26 and 32, and you can find Western-style sauces and other specialist **imports** at *Saraylar*, Balık Pazarı 17. Another outlet for exotic herbs and spices is *Zencefil*, Kurabiye Sok 3, Beyoğlu, where they also sell health food alongside their veggie café. *Kurukahveci Mehmet*, Tahmiş Cad 66, Eminönü, next to the spice bazaar, is the most famous outlet for **Turkish coffee** in Turkey.

Books

There are only a few stockists of English-language **books** around the city, and foreign publications are hideously expensive. It's often rewarding to spend time and energy raking the second-hand book markets and shops, however. The best-known of all the *sahaflar çarşısı* (old book markets) is the one at **Beyazit** (next to Beyazit Camii off Beyazit Meydanı), where antique and new history and art books, English novels and language textbooks, as well as old prints, can all be bought.

ABC Kitabevi, İstiklâl Cad 461. Reasonably up-to-date foreign newspapers and magazines.

Beyoğlu Sahaflar Çarşısı. Another good book market, in the Çiçek Pasajı, where there are several shops, some of which specialize in English-language texts.

Divan Book Exchange, Divanyolu, Hoca Rüstem Sok 5, Sultanahmet. Buy, sell, or swap your books. Many English-language texts.

Dünya Aktüel, Cevdet Paşa Cad 232, Bebek, opposite *Bebek Hotel*. Upmarket outlet specializing in coffee-table hardbacks.

Eren, Sofyalı Sok 34, Tünel. Art and history books, old maps and miniatures.

Gallery Alpha, Hacıoğlu Sok 1/A, Beyoğlu. Old prints, maps and documents, as well as antique books.

Haşet Kitabevi, İstiklâl Cad 469, Beyoğlu (☎0212/144 9470). Good selection of guide and art books in English.

Librairie de Pera, Galıpdede Cad 22, Tünel. Excellent selection of antiquarian books, including English-language ones.

Pandora, İstiklal Cad, Büyükparmakkapı Sok 3, Beyoğlu. Excellent selection of foreign-language books on three storeys.

Redhouse, Rızapaşa Yokuşu 48, Tahtakale (☎0212/522 8100). Highly respected publishing house. You may have to knock in order to obtain entrance, or ring in advance, since the shopfront is closed.

Remzi Kitabevi, basement floor, 121 Akmerkez Shopping Mall, Etiler. A good selection of books and magazines in English, for adults and children.

Robinson Crusoe Kitabevi, İstiklâl Cad 389, Beyoğlu. Reasonably priced, extensive collection of English-language books, and a number of good guides and maps. They will order books from abroad.

Zambakoğlu, Altıpatlar Sok 63, off Sıraselviler Cad, Çukurcuma. Good antique bookshop where you can also find antique magazines and sheet music.

Carpets and kilims

There are **carpet shops** all over the city, particularly in and around the covered bazaar (Takkeciler Cad has a good concentration), but also in the flea markets of Kadıköy and Üsküdar, and in second-hand shops around Altıpatlar Sokak off İstiklâl Caddesi. Buying a carpet involves a psychological game called bargaining. The rules of the game are learnt by playing it with the right people, otherwise you will be ripped off. See *Basics*, p.50.

Music and musical instruments

Turkish music aside, you'll find a good general selection of world music, including classical, pop and jazz, in the music shops listed below. Traditional **musical instruments** are sold in the covered bazaar, but prices are much better at *İstanbul Müzik Merkezi*, Galipdede Cad 23, Tünel, for quality instruments.

Akusta CD and Hi-fi Showroom, Abdi İpekçi Cad 40, Nişantaşi. Classical, jazz, rock and world music.

Deniz Kitabevi, İstiklâl Cad 390, Narmanlı Han 3/B, Beyoğlu. Jazz, rock and classical cassettes and records.

Lale Plak, Kaset, CD, Galıpdede Cad 1, Beyoğlu. A good selection of European classical and pop music.

Unkapani, Atatürk Bulvarı. The nerve centre of the Turkish music business is just over the Atatürk Bridge on the Golden Horn. It's a normal-looking urban shopping precinct but every outlet sells cassettes, CDs and discs. Downstairs you can have bootlegs made – only they're legal.

Vakkorama Music Store, Rumeli Cad 80, Nişantaşi. R&B, soul, jazz, funk.

Markets, crafts and antiques

Bit pazarları or **flea markets** (literally "louse markets") make for excellent shopping: whether you're settling in the city and need furniture, or simply looking for souvenirs, it's well worth having a root around these areas, which are really streets full of junkshops. Remember that while antiquities may be bought and sold, it's illegal to export them (punishable with 5–10 years' imprisonment).

The **Çukurcuma** *bit pazarı* is located in the streets below the Galatasaray Hamam off İstiklâl Caddesi, particularly Çukurcuma Sokak. It encompasses some very classy antique shops, some of which are listed below. **Üsküdar** *bit pazarı* is on Büyük Hamam Sokak, off Hakimiyet-i Milliye Caddesi; and **Kadıköy** *bit pazarı*, selling mainly furniture, is off Soğutluçeşme Cad, on Özellik Sokak.

The **arts and crafts market** in Ortaköy may be pretentious and trendy, but it's an enjoyably relaxing place to spend a Sunday afternoon if you don't mind crowds. Among the best stalls are those selling obscure music cassettes and dissident literature. The market is held every Sunday on the waterfront square (take the road which leads off the main street to the Bosphorus, from behind the petrol station).

Open-air **street markets** are also an important aspect of the city's commercial life. The biggest is probably the *Salı Pazarı*, the **Tuesday Market**, which confusingly takes place every Tuesday and Friday at Altıyol in Kadıköy, but every residential district has its own little string of stalls on a particular day of the week. They are very much what you'd expect of a European street market, selling cheap fresh produce, spices, kitchen utensils and clothing.

Below is listed an assortment of **market stalls**, and odd shops selling **crafts** and **antiques**.

Sultanahmet

İstanbul Handicrafts Centre, beside the *Yeşil Ev Hotel*, Kabasakal Cad 5. Restored *medrese* where artists and craftsmen are keeping alive traditional skills such as *ebru* marbling, calligraphy, lace-making and embroidery. Products and antiques are on sale.

Caferağa Medresesi, between the *Interyouth Youth Hostel* and the *Konuk Evi Hotel* on Caferiye Sok. Similar venture to the above. The central courtyard is a pleasant tree-shaded café, while the shops in the surrounding rooms sell leather goods, jewellery, calligraphy, carpets and miniatures.

The covered bazaar

Emin Çömez, Yağlıkçılar Cad 101–103. Excellent hat stall, well stocked with Russian and Turkish wool, leather, and fur in winter. This street is also good for handprinted cloth and other Anatolian textiles.

İç Bedesten. The "Old Bazaar" is where the most precious objects have traditionally been kept, since it's possible to lock the doors at night. The place to go for antiques of every kind, from Ottoman hamam slippers to pistols. There are also a number of shops here selling silver jewellery.

May, Kolancilar Kapısı Sok 7. Kilim bags, belts, purses etc, and ceramics.

Sarnıçlı Han, Çadırcılar Cad 5. A wholesale and handicraft bazaar: lots of copperware.

Sivaslı İstanbul Yazmacısı, Yağlıkçılar Cad 57. Hand-woven and hand-embroidered old and new textiles.

Sofa, Nuruosmaniye Cad 42, Cağaloğlu. Old prints, maps, calligraphy and ceramics.

Çukurcuma and Beyouğlu

Aslı Gunsıray, Çukur Camii Sok 72/A. Antique furniture and prints.

Gallery Alpha, Hacioğlu Sok 1/A, Firuşağa, Beyoğlu. Prints, maps, postcards and ephemera relating to Turkey and İstanbul.

Leyla Seyhanlı, Altıpatlar Sok 30, Çukurcuma. Antique lace shop.

Ortaköy

Artisan, İskele Sok. Specializes in Kütahya pottery.

Ayşe Gallery, İskele Sok, next door to the above. Designer jewellery, some inspired by Ottoman motifs, some high-tech.

Hazal, Mecidiye Köprüsü Sok 27–29. Some colourful, quality carpets and kilims, beautifully displayed.

Medisa, Cami Sok 6. Glassware painted with *ebru* marbling techniques, and a range of modern ceramics.

Listings

Airlines İstanbul offices of **international airlines** include: *Aeroflot,* Mete Cad 30, Taksim (☎0212/243 4725); *Alitalia*, Cumhuriyet Cad 14, Elmadağ (☎0212/231 3391); *American Airlines,* Cumhuriyet Cad 263/1, Harbiye (☎0212/230 2211); *Austrian Airlines* in the *Sheraton Hotel,* Cumhuriyet Cad, Elmadağ (☎0212/232 2200); *British Airways*, Cumhuriyet Cad 10 (☎0212/234 1300); *Casio Airlines* (for flights to Slovenia), Ordu Cad 291, Lâleli (☎0212/638 0506); *Gulf Air,* Cumhuriyet Cad 213, Harbiye (☎0212/231 3450); *Iberia*, Topcu Cad, Taksim (☎0212/237 3104); *İstanbul Airlines,* Cumhuriyet Cad 289 (☎0212/231 7526, fax 246 4967); *KLM*, Abdi Ipekçi Cad, Ünsal Apt 6–8, Nişantaşi (☎0212/230 0311); *Malaysian Airlines*, Cumhuriyet Cad 14, Elmadağ, (☎0212/241 0909); *Northern Cyprus-Turkish Airlines*, Abdi Ipekçi Cad 8, Nişantaşi (☎0212/267 0973); *Olympic Airlines*, Cumhuriyet Cad 171/A (☎0212/246 5081); *Onur Air*, Halazkargazı Cad

79/1, Harbiye (☎0212/256 4622); *Sabena*, Topcu Cad, Taksim (☎0212/254 7254); *Swissair*, Cumhuriyet Cad 6, Taksim (☎0212/231 2845); *THY Turkish Airlines*, Cumhuriyet Cad 199–201, Harbiye (☎0212/248 2631), off Taksim Square at the beginning of Cumhuriyet Cad (☎0212/251 1106), and Atatürk Bul 162, Gülpalas Apt, office no. 3, fourth floor, Aksaray (☎0212/514 0022). For **domestic flights**: *İstanbul Airlines*, Cumhuriyet Cad 289 (☎0212/231 7526, fax 246 4967), for Ankara, Antalya, Erzurum, İzmir and Trabzon; *Sönmez Holding Hava Yolları* (Bursa daily), Atatürk Airport (☎0212/573 9323 or 573 7240), or through *Moris Şey Acentesi*, Tünel Pasajı 11, Beyoğlu (☎0212/249 8510); *Onur Air*, Halazkargazı Cad 79/1, Harbiye, (☎0212/256 4622); *THY* fly all over Turkey (though not to Bursa; see addresses above).

Airport Domestic and international flights from Atatürk Airport, Yeşilköy: for international flights, *Dış Hatları*, call ☎0212/663 6400; domestic flights, *İç Hatları*, ☎0212/574 2443 or 573 2920. Half-hourly buses to the airport leave from 5.30am to 11pm from the *THY* office on Cumhuriyet Cad (☎0212/244 0296); it costs $2 and takes about one hour. A number of the travel agents on Divanyolu Cad, and certain hotels in Sultanahmet and Taksim, can arrange a transfer service to the airport, for around $4. Trams go from Aksaray to Yeni Bosna, which is a ten-minute taxi ride from the airport.

Art galleries Good ones include *Aksanat Cultural Centre*, İstiklâl Cad 16–18, Beyoğlu, for exhibitions and auctions; *Maya*, İstiklâl Cad 140/20, Halep İşhanı Beyoğlu; *Opera*, *Marmara Hotel*, Taksim Square (☎0212/251 4696); *Toprakbank Galeri*, Halazkargazı Cad 204, Osmanbey (☎0212/233 2663).

Banks and exchange Exchange offices (**döviz**) can now be found all over the city; they change cash, usually at good rates, are open long hours at weekends, and are generally faster and more efficient than banks. *Fast Forex*, Meşrutiyet Cad 22, Beyoğlu, opposite the British Consulate, stock 18 different currencies, and don't charge commission. A few, like *Paradöviz*, at İstiklâl Cad 117 in Beyoğlu, Taksim Cad 28/8 in Taksim, and Carşıkapı, Nuruosmaniye Cad 36 in Kapalı Çarşi, take travellers' cheques. Opening hours for most **banks** are Mon–Fri 9am–12.30pm & 1.30–5pm. The *Garanti Bankası* stays open through lunchtime and opens on Saturdays, and *İşbank* at the airport is open 24hr. The change window in Sirkeci station is open at weekends from 9am–5pm, and takes travellers' cheques. There are two banks at Esenler *otogar*, *İşbankası* (Mon–Fri 9.30am–12.30pm & 1.30–5.30pm) and *Vakıfbank* (Mon–Fri 8.30am–11pm). Neither take travellers' cheques, but there is a money dispenser at the *İşbankası*. Don't pay commission for cash unless you're really needy: you can always change hard currencies in the covered bazaar, at a better rate than you get in the banks (make sure they give you the rate in a current newspaper). The **PTT** has an exchange booth outside Sultanahmet Camii in the summer (daily 9am–5pm) and there's a 24-hour **credit card** booth next to it. Most of the major banks are now members of the International Credit Card Centre and will take Visa, Mastercard and American Express. Credit card hotlines in İstanbul are: Visa International ☎0212/282 5263; American Express ☎0212/224 4363; Mastercard ☎0212/281 8548. Most banks in İstanbul now have money dispensers which take major credit cards.

Bus companies For further information on national bus services from İstanbul, see "Travel details" at the end of the chapter. For western and southern destinations, try *Varan*, Esenler *otogar* bays 1–2 (☎0212/658 0277), with a non-stop executive luxury service to Ankara; *Ulusoy*, bay 127 (☎0212/658 3000), who have a non-smoking service to major cities; *Pamukkale*, bays 41–42 (☎0212/658 2222); or *Kamil Koç*, bays 144–146 (☎0212/658 2010). For the Black Sea coast, *Dağıştanlı*, bay 73 (☎0212/658 0922); *Metro*, bays 51–52 (☎0212/658 3235); *Birçik*, bay 154 (☎0212/658 1714); *Barış* (☎0212/658 4002); or *Ulusoy* again. For Cappadocia, try *Nevtur/Göreme*, bay 24 (☎0212/658 0771), and for the east, *Mersin* (☎0212/658 3527) and *Kamil Koç*.

Caravan rental *Anadolu Caravan*, Çiragan Müvezzi Cad 9/1, Beşiktaş (☎0212/258 0041), and *Hewa Caravan*, Atatürk Sahil Yolu, Mocamp Tatil Köyü, Ataköy (☎0212/661 4143).

Car rental Local companies which offer good deals are: *Airtour*, Cumhuriyet Cad, Dr Celal Öker Sok 1/1, Harbiye (☎0212/232 8486 or 232 8488); *Comet*, Şehit Muhtar Cad 19/B, Taksim (☎0212/237 4087); *Fiesta*, Topar Cad 5/1, Taksim (☎0212/254 6009); *Globcar*, Şehit Muhtar Cad 17, floor 1, Taksim (☎0212/237 4479); *Manager Rent a car*, Abide Hürriyet Cad 251, Şişli (☎0212/234 2223); and *Sun Rent a Car*, Cumhuriyet Cad 26, Elmadağ (☎0212/246 0815). International companies – with the advantage of countrywide outlets – include *Avis* at Atatürk Airport (☎0212/573 1452) and the *Hilton Hotel*, Cumhuriyet Cad, Harbiye (☎0212/248 7752); *Budget*, Cumhuriyet Cad 19, Taksim (☎0212/253 9200), and the airport (☎0212/663 0858); *Eurodollar*, Aydede Cad 1, Taksim (☎0212/254 7719); *Europcar*, Cumhuriyet Cad 47/2, Taksim (☎0212/254 7788); *Hertz*, Atatürk Airport (☎0212/663 6400), and Cumhuriyet Cad 295, Harbiye (☎0212/526 1465).

Car repairs İstanbul's highly skilled mechanics are used to keeping old cars roadworthy, and charge very little for the service. Mechanics and part shops are located at *Oto Sanayı* in outlying areas of the city. Nearest to Sultanahmet is the *sanayı* at Topkapı, on the other side of the walls off Davutpaşa Cad around Latif Ağa and Gürün Sok. The largest *Oto Sanayı* is 10km north of Taksim Square off Büyükdere Cad in 4th (Dördüncü) Levent. Most spare parts can be found at Tarlabaşı Cad in Taksim.

Consulates *Britain*, Meşrutiyet Cad 34, Tepebaşı, Beyoğlu (☎0212/252 6436); *France*, İstiklâl Cad 8, Beyoğlu (☎0212/228 2878); *Germany*, İnönü Cad 16–18, Beyoğlu (☎0212/251 5404); *Greece*, Turnacıbaşı Sok 32, Galatasaray (☎0212/245 0596); *Iran*, Ankara Cad, Cağaloğlu (☎0212/513 8230); *Ireland*, Cumhuriyet Cad 26/A, Harbiye (☎0212/246 6025); *Netherlands*, İstiklâl Cad 393, Galatasaray, Beyoğlu (☎0212/251 5030); *Norway*, Bilezik Sok 2, Fındıklı (☎0212/249 9753); *Russian Federation*, İstiklâl Cad 443, Tünel, Beyoğlu (☎0212/244 2610); *Syria*, İkıncı Bayırı Sok 8, Mecidiyeköy (☎0212/275 4396); *United States*, Meşrutiyet Cad 104–108, Beyoğlu (☎0212/251 3602).

Crime Turkey as a whole is relatively crime-free, but in İstanbul pickpocketing is on the increase. More worryingly, there is an increase in the use of sleep-inducing drugs on victims who are subsequently divested of all their valuables. The police are generally sympathetic to foreigners. Reports of theft or loss should be made to the tourism police, while any commercial misdealings should be reported to the *Zabita* (see "Police", below).

Dentists Reliable options are *Cosmodent Dental Clinic*, Beytem Plaza, 4th floor, Şişli (☎0212/296 1862); *Reha Sezgin*, Halazkargazi Cad 48, Şeker Apt, 5th floor no. 9, Harbiye (☎0212/240 3332); *Unident* at Korukent Sitesi, R Blok D/1, Levent (☎0212/288 1717); and the dental clinic at the German Hospital, Sıraselviler Cad 119 (☎0212/293 2150).

Festivals The International Film Festival (end March to mid-April) takes place at cinemas all over town: information and bookings from the *Atatürk Kültür Merkezi* (Atatürk Culture Centre) in Taksim (a programme is published in *Cumhuriyet* fairly early in March). This is the only chance you'll get to see the best of the previous year's Turkish films with English subtitles. The Theatre Festival takes place in May: programmes are available from the *Atatürk Kültür Merkezi*, where most of the events take place. The Jazz Festival takes place over two weeks in July, and includes big international names, as well as the best of the Turkish performers. Tickets are available from the *Atatürk Kültür Merkezi*. The İstanbul Book Fair is held in the İstanbul Sergi Sarayı on Meşrutiyet Cad, near the *Pera Palas Hotel*, in late October. The İstanbul Festival of Arts and Culture runs from mid-June to mid-July. Its venues include the *Atatürk Kültür Merkezi* on Taksim Square, the *Açik Hava Tiyatrosu* (Open Air Theatre) on Taşkışla Cad, Harbiye, the Aya Irene church, Sultanahmet, and Topkapı Palace, and the programme includes international classical, jazz and rock music as well as opera, ballet and traditional dancing. Tickets are available from early June, from the *Atatürk Kültür Merkezi*. The İstanbul Arts Fair takes place in mid-September in the Tuyap Exhibition Centre, Sergi Saray, Meşrutiyet Cad in Tepebaşi. The Akbank International Jazz Festival takes place in early October and includes world-class musicians at venues all over town; details from *Pozitif Productions* (☎0212/252 5167).

Football Football is Turkey's national sport, and top teams, most of which are İstanbul-based, receive fanatical support across the country. Major games are played at the İnönü Stadium, on Kadırgalar Cad between Taksim and Beşiktaş, and the Bahçe Stadium on Bağdat Cad, in Kızıltoprak.

Hamams Most central, and the most frequented by tourists, are *Çemberlitaş Hamam*, on Divanyolu; *Cağaloğlu Hamam*, Hilali Ahmed Cad 34, Cağaloğlu; and *Galatasaray Hamam*, Turnacıbaşı Sok (for men), Çapanoğlu Sok (for women), Beyoğlu. Other good ones are the *Çinili Hamam* off Itfaiye Cad in Zeyrek, the *Çinili Hamam* opposite the Çinili Cami in Üsküdar, the *Ortaköy Hamam*, the *Beylerbeyi Hamam*, and the *Turistik Ağa Hamam* on Turnacıbaşı Sok, Beyoğlu, which is cheaper and friendlier than *Galatasaray Hamam* on the same street.

Hospitals Foreign hospitals include the American *Admiral Bristol Hospital*, Güzelbahçe Sok 20, Nişantaşı (☎0212/231 4050); the French *Pasteur Hospital*, Taşkışla Cad 3, Harbiye (☎0212/248 4756); *German Hospital*, Sıraselviler Cad 119, Taksim (☎0212/293 2150); *International Hospital*, İstanbul Cad 82, Yeşilköy (☎0212/663 3000); the *Italian Hospital*, Defterdar Yokuşu 37, Cihangir (☎0212/249 9751), and the *Jewish Hospital*, Hisarönü Cad 46–48, Balat (☎0212/524 1151). Otherwise the teaching hospitals are a safer bet than state hospitals. The *Cerrahpaşa Faculty of Medicine* is at Cerrahpaşa Cad 97, Cerrahpaşa (☎0212/588 4800); the *Çapa Medical Faculty Hospital* is at Millet Cad, Çapa (☎0212/534 0000); and the *Marmara University Hospital* is at Fahrettin Kerim Gökay Cad, Okul Sok, Altunizade (☎0212/340 0100). The *Taksim First Aid Hospital* is at 112 Sıraselviler Cad (☎0212/252 4300).

Laundry You might find a laundry service in your hotel or *pansiyon*, otherwise try the *Active Laundry*, Divanyolu Cad, Dr Eminpaşa Sok 14 (daily 8am–8pm); *Hobby*, at Caferiye Sok 6/1, Sultanahmet (daily 9am–8pm); or *Star Hostel Laundry*, Yeni Akbıyık Cad 18, Çankurtaran (☎0212/638 2302). Dry cleaners (*kuru temizlemecisi*) are also good value in Turkey; there's a good one, *Morve-Site*, at the far end of the Hippodrome, at Üçler Sok 4/A.

Left luggage Left luggage offices (*Emanet* in Turkish) can be found in both Sirkeci and Haydarpaşa train stations.

Libraries The *American Culture Centre* has a library in the American Consulate (Meşrutiyet Cad 104–108, Tepebaşı, Beyoğlu; ☎0212/251 2675; Mon–Fri 12.30–4.30pm). The *British Council* library is in the *ÖRS Turistik İş Merkezi*, İstiklâl Cad 251–253, third floor (☎0212/249 0574; only open to members, $5 to join; Tues–Fri 10am–5.30pm, Sat 9.30am–2.30pm). The *Süleymaniye Library*, Ayşekadın Hamam Sok 35, Beyazit (☎0212/520 6460), has a rich reference collection on Ottoman history and Culture. The *Turkish Touring Club* has a library of books concerning the history of İstanbul, on Soğukçeşme Sok, Sultanahmet (☎0212/512 5730; Mon, Wed & Fri 10am–noon & 1.30–4.30pm). The *Women's Library*, across from the Fener jetty on the Golden Horn (☎0212/534 9550; Mon–Sat 9am–5.30pm), is a new venture with a growing collection of books by and about women, plus art on display.

Listings Good publications include *İstanbul: The Guide*, available in hotel lobbies or bookshops for $3, with comprehensive restaurant, club and café listings; and *Cornucopia*, with discursive articles and great photos, available in bookshops that stock foreign press.

Opticians Turkish opticians are cheaper than their British or US equivalents, and reasonably fast, even though the stock is mostly imported. There are a number of outlets in Sirkeci, particularly on Hamidiye Cad.

Police For work and resident permits, contact the *Yabanci Sübe* of the *Emniyet Müdürlüğü*, next to the *Vilayet* on Hükümet Konağı Sok, Cağaloğlu. The tourist police are at Alemdar Cad 6, Sultanahmet (☎0212/528 5369; 24 hr), and have an English translator on the premises Mon–Fri 9am–5pm; there are also *Zabita* (market police) offices all over town, including a handy one in the centre, at the far end of the Hippodrome.

Post offices The main post office is on Yeni Posthane Cad in Sirkeci, open daily 9am–5.30pm (8am–8pm for stamps). Large branch offices, for example those at Cumhuriyet Cad, immediately to the north of Taksim Square, at Kadıköy İskele Meydanı, at Beşiktaş Shopping Arcade and on Hakimiyeti Milliye Cad, Üsküdar, are open for air mail and parcels daily from 8.30am–12.30pm and 1.30–5pm; for normal post 8.30am–8pm; and for telegraph and phone *jeton*s 8.30am–midnight. Small branch offices are open Mon–Fri 8am–6pm.

Poste restante Address mail to Büyük PTT, Yeni Posthane Cad, Sirkeci.

Swimming pools Public pool at the *Burhan Felek Spor Sitesi*, Nuh Kuyusu Cad, Bağlarbaşı (on the minibus route between Kadıköy and Üsküdar); indoor pools in the *Merit Antique*, Ordu Cad 226 (☎0212/513 9300), and the *Büyük Sürmeli Hotel*, Saatçı Bayırı Sok, Gayrettepe (☎0212/272 1160); outdoor pools in the *Hilton*, Cumhuriyet Cad 152, Harbiye (☎0212/231 4646), the *Sheraton Hotel*, Mete Cad, Taksim (☎0212/231 2121), and the *Harem Hotel*, above the bus station in Selimiye, Üsküdar (☎0216/333 2025); pools connected to gymnasiums include the *Planet Health Club*, Eski Çaykur Binası, Kuruçeşme (☎0212/263 1067), and the *Moda Kondisyon 2000*, on the ground floor of the *Moda Deniz Külübü*, Moda, Kadıköy (☎0216/346 2126).

Travel agents For plane and bus tickets try *Marco Polo*, Divanyolu Cad 54/11, Sultanahmet (☎0212/519 2804); *Imperial*, Divanyolu Cad 30, Sultanahmet (☎0212/513 9430); *Kirkit Voyage*, Ticarethane Sok 8, Divanyolu, above *Rumeli Café* (☎0212/512 0547); or any of the outlets on Alemdar Cad, which can book for destinations anywhere in Turkey, and also book hotels and car rental. Most of these companies can arrange service buses out to Atatürk Airport ($4) and Esenler otogar (free).

Turkish language classes The *Turkish-American Universities Association* (*TAUA*), Osmanbey (☎0212/247 2188), run a 5-week summer course (3 hours' teaching a weekday), and courses throughout the year on a 3-term basis; *Persona*, Nispetiye Cad, Başa Sok 13/7, Birinci Levent (☎0212/ 270 7120), run private and group classes; *English Fast* in Mecidiyeköy (☎0212/275 4398), Kadıköy (☎0216/338 9100) and Bakırköy (☎0212/542 5627) offer an intensive, 5-days-a-week course; *Bosphorus University* (☎0212/257 5039) run an intensive 8-week summer course, and a regular 2-term Turkish course; and the *Tömer* school in Gümüşsuyu (☎0212/293 0307) has an intensive 3-week summer course, as well as courses through the year.

Turkish Touring and Automobile Club (TTOK, or *Turing* as they're known), Şişli Meyd 364, Şişli (☎0212/231 4631); or next to the *Oto Sanayi* off Büyükdere Cad in 4th (Dördüncü) Levent, İstanbul (☎0212/282 8140). They provide an invaluable rescue service and insurance for motorists through affiliation with major insurers.

Women's Movement An active women's group meets at Türkbeyi Sok 33/1 in the "Pink Apartment" in Pangaltı (☎0212/248 8683). They are running a campaign against male violence and have established a women's refuge, the *Mor Çatı*, for victims.

travel details

Buses

The main bus terminals are located at Esenler (☎0212/658 0036) and Harem (☎0216/333 3763). All national bus services stop at both, regardless of where they are going in Turkey (see "Listings" above for company locations and phone numbers). All international buses use Esenler *otogar* only.

MEDITERRANEAN AND AEGEAN COASTS

(Served by *Varan, Ulusoy, Pamukkale, Kamil Koç*) Alanya (hourly; 14hr); Antalya (several in the evening from 6pm; 12hr); Ayvalık (hourly; 9hr); Bodrum (4 daily, evening; 13hr); Datça (1 daily; 17hr); Fethiye (hourly; 15hr); İzmir (hourly; 9hr 30min); Kuşadası (3 daily; 10hr); Marmaris (4 daily; 14hr); Side (1 daily; 13hr).

BLACK SEA COAST

(Served by *Ulusoy, Dağıştanlı, Metro, Birçik, Barış*) Artvin (1 daily; 22hr); Hopa (3 daily; 21hr); Karabük (4 daily; 6hr); Ordu (3 daily; 14hr); Rize (4 daily; 19hr); Samsun (4 daily; 11hr); Trabzon (7 daily; 18hr); Zonguldak (6 daily; 6hr).

WESTERN TURKEY

(*Kamil Koç, Pamukkale, Varan, Uludağ Hakiki Koç*) Ankara (hourly; 6hr); Balıkesir (3 daily; 8hr); Bandırma (hourly; 6hr); Bursa (hourly; 5hr); Çanakkale (hourly; 5hr 30min); Denizli (hourly; 10hr); Edirne (hourly; 2hr 30min); Kütahya (4 daily; 5hr 30min); Uşak (4 daily; 8hr 30min).

CAPPADOCIA

(*Nevtur/Göreme Seyahat* has the most direct service, and is the most comfortable, reliable and fast of the companies serving Cappadocia, and the only one which drops in Göreme village.) Avanos (5 daily; 12hr 30min); Göreme (5 daily; 12hr 30min); Kayseri (4 daily; 13hr); Nevşehir (5 daily; 12hr); Ürgüp (2 daily; 12hr 30min).

EASTERN TURKEY

(*Mersin, Kamil Koç*) Adana (2 daily; 19hr); Antakya (2 daily; 18hr); Antep (1 daily; 20hr); Diyarbakır (3 daily; 19hr); Doğubeyazit (1 daily; 24hr); Erzurum (3 daily; 18hr); İskenderun (2 daily; 18hr); Konya (7 daily; 11hr); Mardin (1 daily; 22hr); Tokat (3 daily; 16hr); Urfa (1 daily; 21hr).

OUT OF TURKEY

To Bulgaria (with *Avar, Trakya* and *Alpar*): Sofia (3 weekly; 12hr)
To Georgia (with *Ortadoğu* and *Buse*): Batum (1 daily; 22hr); Tiflis (1 daily; 22hr).
To Greece (with *Bosfor Turizm* and *Varan*): Athens (6 weekly; 23hr 30min); Thessaloniki (6 weekly; 12hr 30min).
To Russia (with *Ortadoğu*): Moscow (2 weekly; 36hr)

Trains

For inter-city journeys, it's advisable to purchase tickets in advance from stations or travel agents who liaise with the TCDD.

Haydarpaşa Station to: Adana (3 weekly; 29hr); Adapazarı (11 daily; 2hr 45min); Afyon (3 daily; 13hr 30min); Ankara (6 daily; 7hr 30min–9hr); Arifiye (3 daily; 3hr); Denizli (1 daily; 14hr 25min); Erzurum (1 daily; 35hr); Eskişehir (3 daily; 6hr 20min); Gaziantep (3 weekly; 38hr 40min); Gebze (2/3 hourly; 30min); Halep (2 weekly; 40hr); İzmir (2 daily; 11hr); Kahraman (3 weekly; 36hr); Kars (1 daily; 42hr); Kayseri (2 daily; 21hr); Konya (2 daily; 13hr 35min); Tatvan (3 weekly; 45hr).

Sirkeci Station to: Athens (1 daily; 32/46hr); Belgrade (1 daily; 23hr); Edirne (3 daily; 5hr 10min–7hr); Halkalı (4 daily; 45min); London (1 daily; 65hr); Milan (1 daily; 46hr); Moscow (1 daily;

39hr); Munich (1 daily; 39hr); Paris (1 daily; 52hr); Prague (1 daily; 30hr); Rome (1 daily; 51hr); Sofia (1 daily; 12hr); Thessaloniki (1 daily; 16hr); Üzünköprü (2 daily; 6hr 5min); Venice (1 daily; 41hr); Vienna (1 daily; 37hr).

Boats

All the following services are run by Turkish Maritime Lines (*TML*), Rihtim Cad, Karaköy (☎0212/249 9222).

PASSENGER SERVICES

Sirkeci to: Bandirma (4 weekly; 4hr 30min; 3 of these boats connect with a train to İzmir).

Karaköy to: Avşa (1 daily June–Sept, 3 weekly Oct–May; 6hr); Marmara Island (1 daily June–Sept, 3 weekly Oct–May; 5hr).

CAR FERRIES

Karaköy to: Giresun (1 weekly; 31hr); İzmir (1 weekly; 18 hour); Ordu (1 weekly; 39hr); Samsun (1 weekly; 62hr); Sinop (1 weekly; 68hr); Trabzon (1 weekly; 41hr).

For Bursa by car, drive to Eskihisar, beyond Pendik, and take the ferry to Topçular (every 30min; 20min).

Internal flights

All the following are with *THY* unless otherwise stated; see "Listings" above for company addresses.

Atatürk Airport to: Adana (at least 6 daily; 1hr 35min); Ankara, with *THY*, *İstanbul Airlines* or *Onur Air* (15 or more daily; 55min); Antalya, with *THY or İstanbul Airlines* (at least 3 daily; 1hr 15min); Batman (1 daily; 4hr); Bodrum (2–4 daily; 1hr 20min); Bursa, with *Sönmez Holding* (1 daily; 45min); Dalaman (3 daily; 1hr 15min); Denizli (2 weekly; 1hr); Diyarbakir, with *THY* or *Onur Air* (1/2 daily; 4hr); Elaziğ (3 weekly; 3hr); Erzurum, with *THY* or *İstanbul Airlines* (2 weekly; 1hr 50min); Gaziantep (6 weekly; 3hr); İzmir, with *THY or İstanbul Airlines* (10 or more daily; 55min); Kars (at least 1 daily; 3hr 30min); Kayseri (2 daily; 1hr 15min); Samsun (4 weekly; 1hr); Şanlıurfa (5 weekly; 3hr 30min); Sivas (2 weekly; 2hr 30min); Trabzon with *THY* or *İstanbul Airlines* (1/2 daily; 1hr 30min); Van (5 weekly; 3hr).

CHAPTER TWO

AROUND THE SEA OF MARMARA

Despite their proximity to İstanbul, the shores and hinterland of the Sea of Marmara are the part of Turkey most neglected by foreign travellers. This is not altogether surprising – here the country is at its most Balkan and, at first glance, least exotic – but there are good reasons to come: above all the exquisite early Ottoman centres of **Edirne** and **Bursa**. If your appetite is whetted for more of the same, **Lüleburgaz** and **İznik** make good postscripts to the former imperial capitals.

For many citizens of Commonwealth nations, a pilgrimage to the extensive and moving World War I battlefields and cemeteries on the **Gallipoli peninsula** may involve personal as well as national history. The northern Marmara port of **Gelibolu** makes a good base for excursions to the memorial sites, and local attempts are being made to develop tourism in **Eceabat**, though Çanakkale, described in the next chapter, is the more commonly used jump-off point.

With more time at your disposal, you might consider sampling some of the **coastal resorts**, notably **Şarköy** on the north shore or **Erdek** on the south, or the three inhabited and easily accessible **islands** in the sea. The resorts attract local tourism due to their proximity to İstanbul, Edirne and Bursa, but their short summer season and unglamorous image mean that much of the Marmara coastline and its islands are relatively unspoilt, and you may enjoy the status of being the only foreigner in town. For evocative – but hardly pristine – inland scenery, visit **Uluabat Gölü** or **Uludağ**, both easily reached from Bursa.

Before 1923 much of the Marmara region's population was Greek Orthodox; following the establishment of the republic and the exchange of populations, massive immigration – both internal and from abroad – filled the vacuum. The result is an ethnic stew that includes people of Çerkez (Circassian), Artvinli and Greek Muslim descent, but consists predominantly of **Pomak**, **Bosnian** and **Macedonian Muslims**, and especially **Bulgarian Turks**. All of them had in fact been trickling in since well before the

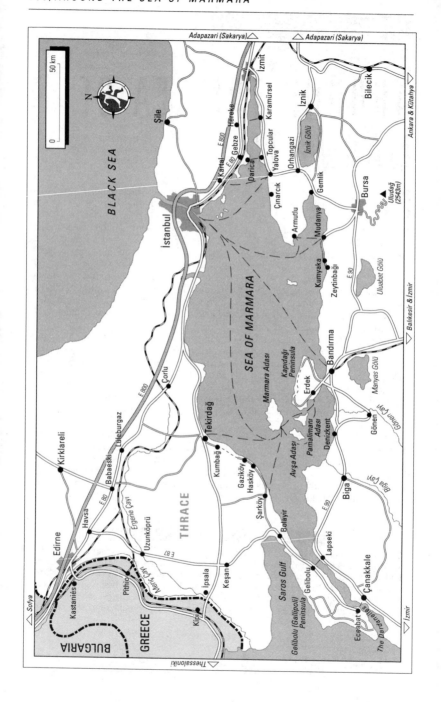

turn of the century, as Austro-Hungarian or Christian nationalist victories in the Balkans made their previous homes inhospitable to Turks or Slavic Muslims. This trend received a huge reinforcement following the disturbances in Bulgaria during 1989, when hundreds of thousands of ethnic Turks fled to Turkey, though many of the new arrivals subsequently returned to post-Communist Bulgaria.

THRACE (TRAKYA)

Thrace, the historic term for the territory bounded by the rivers Danube and Nestos and the Aegean, Marmara and Black seas, is today divided roughly equally among Greece, Bulgaria and Turkey. In ancient times it was home to warlike, stock-breeding tribes credited by various historians with bizarre religions and habits, and with being a continual headache for rulers bent on subduing them.

Contemporary life is decidedly less colourful, and the three-percent proportion of Turkey lying in continental Europe is best regarded as the anteroom to the country. The terrain is mostly nondescript, with monotonously rolling hills flecked with copses of stubby oaks; it's a major agricultural area too, with the grain and tobacco fields green- or dun-coloured according to season. Until the late 1960s nearly all of it was a military security zone and strictly off-limits to foreigners; most of the area is open to travel now, but all towns remain heavily garrisoned, and no major tourist excitements were unveiled by the new ease of access.

The E80 highway from İstanbul to Edirne follows almost exactly the route of the Roman and Byzantine **Via Egnatia**, which later became the medieval route to the Ottoman holdings in Europe: keep an eye out for various fine **old bridges**, which like the road itself may be Ottoman reworkings of Roman or Byzantine originals. The best of these is the quadruple **Büyükçekmece** span, crossing the neck of an estuary a few kilometres west of İstanbul and built by the great architect Sinan in 1563. Many towns along the road not surprisingly began life as Roman staging posts, a role continued under the Ottomans, who endowed all of them with a civic monument or two. Yet few places have anything else to detain you; except for those detailed below, they can be glimpsed well enough from the window of a passing vehicle.

Edirne and around

More than just the quintessential border town, **EDİRNE** makes an impressive and easily digestible introduction to Turkey. It's a lively and attractive city of around a hundred thousand people, occupying a rise overlooking the meeting of the Tunca, Arda and Meriç rivers, a short distance from the Greek and Bulgarian frontiers. The life of the place is derived from day-tripping foreign shoppers, TIR trucks and their drivers, a growing number of discerning tourists, and from students (the University of Thrace is here). Downtown, teeming bazaars and elegant domestic architecture almost distract you from the clutch of striking early Ottoman monuments that lifts Edirne out of the ranks of the ordinary. The best of these Ottoman offerings, crowning the town hillock and sufficient reason in itself for a detour here, is the architect Sinan's culminating achievement, the **Selimiye Camii**.

There has always been a settlement of some kind at this strategic point, and its military importance has fated it to be captured – and sometimes sacked for good measure – repeatedly over the centuries. Thracian Uscudama was refurbished as Hellenistic Oresteia, but the city really entered history as **Hadrianopolis**, designated the main centre of Roman Thrace by the emperor Hadrian. Under the Byzantines it retained its significance, not least as a forward base en route to the Balkans – or, more ominously from the Byzantine point of view, first stop on the way to attempts on the imperial capital itself. Unsuccessful besiegers of Constantinople habitually vented their frustration on Hadrianopolis as they retreated, and a handful of emperors met their end here in pitched battles with Thracian "barbarians" of one sort or another.

The **Ottomans**, more disciplined and enduring than the usual marauders, had by the mid-fourteenth century enmeshed the Byzantines in a web of mutual defence treaties and links by marriage, and gained their first permanent foothold on the coast of Thrace. In 1361 Hadrianopolis surrendered to the besieging Murat I, and the provisional Ottoman capital was effectively transferred here from Bursa. A century later, Mehmet the Conqueror trained his troops and tested his artillery here in preparation for the march on Constantinople; indeed the Ottoman court was not completely moved to the Bosphorus until 1458, and because of its excellent opportunities for hunting and falconry, Edirne, as the Turks renamed it, remained a favourite haunt of numerous sultans for three more centuries.

Decline set in in the eighteenth century, prompted largely by an earthquake in 1751. During each of the Russo-Turkish wars of 1829 and 1878–79, the city was occupied and pillaged by Tsarist troops; far worse were the Bulgarians, who in 1913 presided over a four-month spree of atrocities. The Greeks, as one of the victorious World War I Allies, annexed Edirne along with the rest of Turkish Thrace from 1920 to 1922, and Turkish sovereignty over the city was only confirmed by the 1923 Treaty of Lausanne. Though most physical marks of this turbulence have long since been repaired, the litany of invasions makes it easier to understand the persisting atmosphere of tension with the Greeks and Bulgarians. Never an easily defendable strongpoint, Edirne is once again an appetizer, in all senses, for İstanbul.

Arrival and information

From elsewhere in Turkey, you'll most likely arrive at Edirne's **otogar**, just over 2km southeast of the centre; a service minibus or dolmuş will whisk you to points opposite the town hall. The **train station**, a more likely entry point from abroad, is another kilometre out in the same direction; from here, the only transport is a red city bus, but these are infrequent, and a taxi ($2) is the easiest option. If you're coming directly from the Greek or Bulgarian highway border posts, see "Border crossings" below.

There are two **tourist information offices** in Edirne, both on Talat Paşa Caddesi: the main one about 500m west toward the Gazi Mihal bridge at no. 76/A (☎0284/225 1518; Mon–Fri 8.30am–5pm), stocking heaps of glossies on all of Turkey as well as Edirne, and the equally important annexe (summer daily 8.30am–5.30pm or sometimes 7pm; winter daily 8am–5pm; ☎0284/213 9208) up near Hürriyet Meydanı, Edirne's "Ground Zero" by the traffic signals. There's also a booth at the Bulgarian (Kapıkule) frontier gate.

If you need to **change money** you'll find several banks along Talat Paşa Caddesi; the only one open on Saturdays is the *Garanti Bankası*. None of the banks will change Turkish lira for drachma, so you'll need to do this at a *Döviz* office; the *Araz* on Hürriyet Meydanı gives reasonable rates. The 24-hour **PTT** is on Saraçlar Caddesi. The **Bulgarian consulate** (Mon–Fri 9am–noon; ☎0284/225 1069) is out on Mithat Paşa Cad, about halfway to the *otogar*; the **Greek** one at Cumhuriyet Cad 1, in Kale İçi district (same hours; ☎0284/225 1074). There's a **hospital** behind the Bulgarian consulate.

Border crossings

At the time of writing, the **Turkish-Greek frontier posts** are open only from 9am to 1pm weekdays, and 9am to noon at weekends. The Turkish post of Pazarkule, separated from the Greek one at Kastaniés by a kilometre-wide no-man's-land, is 7km west of Edirne and 2km beyond the last Turkish village of Karaağaç.

Red **city buses** ($0.15) run from behind the *Belediye* building in Edirne **to Karaağaç** every twenty minutes; **dolmuşes** ($0.25) depart with similar frequency from Saraçlar Cad, opposite the PTT. Buses to Kastaniés in Greece (from where there are connections to Alexandhróupoli) leave from Karaağaç; look for signs for *Yunanistan* ("Greece" in Turkish), in travel agent windows. At present you can walk the final stretch from Karaağaç to the border, but this may change, so enquire about the current situation at the tourist information office before setting out. Another alternative is to take a **taxi** ($4.50) all the way from Edirne **to Pazarkule**. Once at Pazarkule, you'll have to take a Greek taxi to the Kastaniés post; this applies coming from Greece too – budget on $5 per car for the one-kilometre gap. On the Greek side three trains daily, and about as many buses, make the three-hour run down from Kastaniés to Alexandhroúpoli, the first major Greek city, between 8am and 1pm, with a couple more later in the day. If all this seems too much bother, compare the more southerly rail and road crossings into Greece described on p.190.

The **Bulgarian-Turkish border** is slightly less problematic. The vast complex at Kapıkule, 18km northwest of Edirne, straddles the busy E5/100 expressway and is open around the clock. Unless the Bulgarian government has a change of heart on such matters, most nationals will still need a **visa** of some kind: $46 for a transit visa obtained from the Edirne consulate; $60 for one issued at the border (not available at weekends). "Express" visas can also be obtained at the consulate, issued within an hour of application at a cost of $60.

Getting to Kapıkule is no problem: **dolmuşes** ply the route half-hourly from 6.30am to 9pm, leaving from the minibus *garajı* off Talat Paşa Asfaltı behind the Eski Cami, for a fare of $0.40. Opposite the Bulgarian consulate *Hakiki Koç* run six **coaches** daily to Kapıkule, for under $1. A taxi will set you back well over $10.

If your interest lies further afield in the Balkans, consider the Balkan Express **trains**, which have couchettes and depart daily from Kapıkule at 2.50am for Bucharest and 4.20pm for Sofia, Belgrade and Budapest (check times beforehand with the tourism information in Edirne).

Accommodation

With the few genuinely budget hotels either substandard or booked solid by TIR drivers, accommodation is always tight in Edirne; during the Kırkpınar greasy wrestling festival – generally the first week of July – you'll need to book a hotel at least a month in advance. The central **Rüstem Paşa Kervansarayı** on İki Kapalıhan Caddesi, half of which is now used as an upmarket hotel (☎0284/215 2195, fax 212 0462; ③) while the other half is a student hostel, is the best the town has to offer by a long way. The hotel is located in a *kervansaray* built by Mimar Sinan, and its restoration earned the Ağa Khan Prize for Architecture in 1980. The cool, well-furnished rooms are set around a pleasant garden courtyard, which is also location of a bar and billiard hall (noise is minimal from either at nights as the substantial walls of the *kervansaray* are quite soundproof). In term-time, the courtyard is a good place to meet local students from Edirne University.

A recommended option if the *Rüstem Paşa* is full is the *Otel Şaban Acikgöz*, nearby at Çilingirler Cad 9 (☎0284/213 1404; ②), for comfort (TVs and a bar) and good service. Maarif Caddesi is lined with a few serious dives, which are best avoided, but does play host to the newly opened *Efe Hotel*, at no. 13 (☎0284/213 6166; ③), a clean, modern, family-run business; the *Efe* is better looked after than the nearby *Park*, Maarif Cad 7 (☎0284/223 5276; ③), which is nevertheless comfortable and calm. The three-star *Sultan Hotel*, Talat Paşa Asfaltı 170 (☎0284/225 1372; ⑤), which have an imposing exterior and comfortable if dreary rooms on gloomy corridors, is only worth considering if you can't get a room in one of the above. Similarly overpriced, the *Hotel Kervan*, Talat Paşa Asfaltı 134 (☎0284/213 8491; ⑤), is central and newly renovated, but noisy.

Fifi Mocamp (☎0284/235 7908), 8km along the E5/100 towards İstanbul, is the best **campsite** in the region; *Turing*, along the Kapıkule road, isn't particularly clean.

The City

You can tour the main sights of Edirne on foot, but as the Ottoman monuments are widely scattered you'll need a full day to do it. If the weather's fine this is a pleasure, especially since you'll walk along the willow-shaded banks of the Tunca River for some distance. It's difficult if not impossible to move among the outlying sites by public transport – which is organized radially – and hiring a taxi will be your only other option.

The Eski Cami and the Bedesten

The logical starting point is the **Eski Cami**, the oldest mosque in town, right across from the *Belediye*. This boxy structure, topped by nine vaults arranged three-square, is reckoned a more elaborate version of Bursa's Ulu Cami. Emir Süleyman, son of the luckless Beyazit I, began it in 1403, but it was his younger brother Mehmet I – the only one of three brothers left alive after a bloody succession struggle – who dedicated it eleven years later. The mosque is famous for its giant works of calligraphy; unfortunately the fussy late Ottoman stencil work in the domes and arches doesn't compliment their bold strokes, and neither does the scaffolding which still fills the interior as renovation work slowly proceeds.

Just across the way Mehmet constructed the **Bedesten**, Edirne's first covered market, a portion of whose revenue went to the upkeep of the nearby mosque. The barn-like structure with its fourteen vaulted chambers – again indebted to a Bursa prototype – has recently been restored.

Semiz Ali Paşa Çarşısı and Kale İçi

The other main covered bazaar in Edirne is the nearby **Semiz Ali Paşa Çarşısı**, whose north entrance lies about 250m west, on the corner of Talat Paşa and Saraçlar *caddesi*s. The bazaar was begun by Sinan in 1568 at the behest of Semiz Ali, one of the most able and congenial of the Ottoman grand viziers. Many of its shops, however, were burnt out by in a massive fire in 1992; the renovations – particularly impressive that of the beautiful multi-domed ceiling – are at the time of writing nearing completion and the bazaar should soon be open again. Just opposite the north entrance looms the **Kule Kapısı** (Tower Gate), sole remnant of the town's Roman/Byzantine fortifications; the Ottomans, in a burst of confidence after expanding the limits of empire far beyond Edirne, demolished the rest. Today the gate is occupied by the fire brigade. West of the Semiz Ali market sprawls the **Kale İçi** district, a rectangular grid of streets dating from Byzantine times and lined with much-interrupted terraces of medieval houses. A stroll through here will uncover some surviving stumps of Byzantine wall.

The Üç Şerefeli Cami and the Sokullu Paşa Hamamı

Slightly north of Semiz Ali and Hürriyet Meydanı stands the **Üç Şerefeli Cami**, which replaced the Eski Cami as Edirne's Friday mosque in 1447. It is also undergoing restoration at present, and its interior will be filled with scaffolding for the next couple of years at least. Ten years in the making, its conceptual daring represented the pinnacle of Ottoman religious architecture until overshadowed by the Selimiye Camii a short time later. The name, meaning "three-balconied", derives from the presence of three galleries for the muezzin on the tallest of the four whimsically idiosyncratic **minarets**; the second highest has two balconies, the others one, and their bases are all different. Each of the multiple balconies is reached by a separate stairway within the minaret.

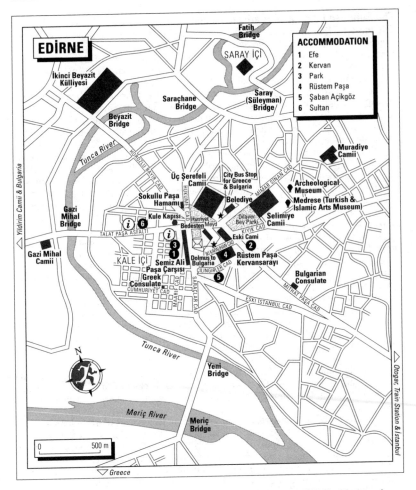

The **courtyard**, too, was an innovation, centred on a *şadırvan* (ritual ablutions fountain) and ringed by porphyry and marble columns pilfered from Roman buildings.

The experimental nature of the mosque is further confirmed by its **interior**, much wider than it is deep and covered by a dome 24m in diameter, the largest that the Turks had built at the time. To impart a sense of space the architect relied on just two free-standing columns, with the other four recessed into front and back walls to form a hexagon. Sadly the design doesn't quite work: two smaller domes to each side, hovering over areas reserved for the dervishes favoured by the ruling sultan Murat II, each had to be flanked by a pair of rather lame space-filling subsidiary domes.

Right across from the Üç Şerefeli Cami is the **Sokullu Paşa Hamamı** (daily 6am–10pm; separate wings for men and women; $2), but it's not as friendly, hot or well maintained as it might be, especially when you consider its pedigree: it was built by Mimar Sinan.

The Selimiye Camii and nearby museums

The masterly **Selimiye Camii**, widely considered to be the finest mosque in Turkey, was designed by the 80-year-old Sinan in 1569 at the command of Selim II (for more on Sinan, see p.116). The work of a confident craftsman at the height of his powers, it's visible from some distance away on the Thracian plain, and is virtually the municipal symbol, reproduced on the sides of Edirne's buses, among other places.

You can approach the Selimiye across the central park, Dilaver Bey, then through the **Kavaflar Arasta** (the Cobbler's Arcade), which was built by Sinan's pupil Davut Ağa and is still used as a covered market, full of household goods and cheap clothing aimed at local custom. The **courtyard**, approached from the Kavaflar Arasta up a flight of stone steps, is even grander than the Üç Şerefeli's, surrounded by a colonnaded portico with arches in alternating red and white stone, the usual appropriated ancient columns (in proconessian marble and verd antique), and domes of varying size above the arcades. Its delicately fashioned *şadırvan* is likewise the finest in the city. The four identical slender **minarets** each have three balconies – Sinan's nod to his predecessors – and at 71m are the second tallest in the world after those in Mecca. The detailed carved portal once graced the Ulu Cami in Birgi (see p.290) and was transported here in pieces, then reassembled.

But it is the celestial **interior**, specifically the dome, that attracts and impresses visitors. Planned expressly to surpass that of Aya Sofya in İstanbul, it manages this – at 31.5m in diameter – by a bare few centimetres, and Sinan thus achieved a lifetime's ambition. Supported by eight mammoth but surprisingly unobtrusive twelve-sided pillars, the cupola floats 44m above the floor, covered in calligraphy proclaiming the glory of Allah. No trace remains of the original painting of the dome, but the current work is not as intrusive as such late Ottoman restorations often are. Immediately below the dome the muezzin's platform, supported on twelve columns, is an ideal place from which to contemplate the proportions of the mosque. The delicate painting on the platform's underside is not original either, but it's a faithful restoration, and gives some idea of how the mosque dome must once have looked. The water of the small marble drinking fountain beneath symbolizes life, under the dome of eternity. The most ornate stonecarving is reserved for the *mihrab* and *mimber*, backed by fine İznik faïence illuminated by sunlight streaming in through the many windows allowed by the pillar support scheme.

Other than the Kavaflar Arasta, there were few dependencies of the Selimiye Camii. An associated *medrese*, at the southeastern corner of the exterior, is now the **Museum of Turkish and Islamic Arts** (summer daily 8.30am–5.30pm; winter daily 8am–5pm; $1), consisting of fifteen rooms around a pleasant garden courtyard, and housing assorted wooden, ceramic and martial knick-knacks from the province. One of the rooms is dedicated to *yağlı güreş* (see box), including a portrait gallery of its stars, a pair of greasy wrestler's leather trousers, and blow-ups of miniatures depicting this 600-year-old sport through the ages. The main **Archeological/Ethnographic Museum** (summer Tues–Sun 8.30am–5.30pm; winter Tues–Sun 8am–5pm; $1), the modern building just east of the mosque precincts, contains a predictable assortment of Greco-Roman fragments; the ethnographic section focuses on carpet-weaving and other local crafts, including colourful village bridal wear, which preceded the bland white confectionery that's been inherited from the West.

Peripheral sites and bridges

Many of Edirne's monuments are north and west of town, deliberately rusticated by the early sultans to provide a nucleus for future suburbs. Because of the many depopulations suffered by the city during the last three centuries, urban growth has never caught up with some of them and many have a forlorn, lonely atmosphere.

KIRKPINAR YAĞLI GUREŞ AND THE GYPSY SPRING FESTIVAL

Yağlı güreş (grease-wrestling) is popular throughout Turkey, but reaches the pinnacle of its acclaim at the doyen of tournaments, the annual Kırkpınar Festival, staged early each summer on the Saray İçi islet outside Edirne; the preferred date is the first week of July, but the five-day event is moved back into June if Ramadan or either of the two major bayrams (religious holidays) following it interfere.

The matches have been held annually, except in times of war or Edirne's occupation, for more than six centuries, and their origins are shrouded in legend. The most commonly repeated story asserts that Süleyman, son of Orhan Gazi, was returning from a battle in 1360 with forty of his men and decided to camp at a village near Edirne. To pass the time the soldiers paired off to wrestle; the last two were unable to best each other after several days of tussling, and in a final elimination match expired simultaneously after midnight. Their companions buried them on the spot and, returning to visit the graves the next season, were astonished to find instead a lush meadow with forty springs (kırk pınar in Turkish) bubbling away. Forty is one of the sacred numbers of Islam, and the Ottomans needed little encouragement to inaugurate a commemoration.

Despite the less than atmospheric environment of the stadium that now hosts the wrestling on Saray İçi, tradition still hedges the event. The contestants – up to a thousand per year – dress only in leather knickers called kisbet, and are slicked down head to toe in diluted olive oil. Wrestlers are classed by height, not by weight, from toddlers up to the pehlivan (full-size) category. Warm-up exercises, the peşrev, are highly stereotyped and accompanied by the davul (deep-toned drum) and zurna (single-reed Islamic oboe). The competitors and the actual matches are solemnly introduced by the cazgır or master of ceremonies, usually himself a former champion.

The bouts, several of which are often going on simultaneously, can last anything from a few minutes to a couple of hours, until one competitor collapses or has his back pinned to the grass. Referees keep a lookout for the limited number of illegal moves or holds, and victors advance more or less immediately to the next round until, after the second or third day, only the başpehlivan (champion) remains. Despite the small prize purse, donated by the Kırkpınar Ağaları – the local worthies who put on the whole show – a champion is usually well set-up in terms of appearance and endorsement fees, and should derive ample benefit from the furious on- and off-site betting. In the main, gladiators tend to be simple villagers from all over Turkey who have won regional titles, starry-eyed with the prospect of fame and escape from a rural rut.

A couple of days of folkloric exhibitions laid on by the Edirne municipality precede the gladiatorial events; if you're interested in tickets to the latter, best ring the tourist office (☎0284/225 1518) well in advance for information.

In addition to providing the music of the peşrev, gypsies descend in force during the Kırkpınar, setting up a combination funfair, circus and carnival at the outskirts of town. The gypsies also have their own spring festival, which takes place at Kırkpınar, in the fields around the stadium, during the first week of May. The Gypsy King lights a bonfire on the evening of the 6th of May, and a flaming torch is paraded around to light a number of other bonfires in the area; a dish of meat and rice is given to the gathered picnickers. The next morning, young gypsy girls are paraded through the streets on horseback around the Muradiye Camii (where a number of settled gypsies live) to the accompaniment of davul and zurna, wearing their own or their mothers' wedding dresses.

Isolated to the northeast of the centre, but simple enough to reach, the **Muradiye Camii** is an easy ten-minute, down-then-up walk along Mimar Sinan Caddesi from the Selimiye mosque. According to legend, Celâleddin Rumi, founder of the Mevlevi dervish order, appeared in a dream to the pious Murat II in 1435, urging him to build a sanctuary for the Mevlevis in Edirne. The result is this pleasing, T-shaped zaviye (dervish convent) crouched on a hill looking north over vegetable patches and the

Tunca; a final bucolic touch is lent by the grassy entry court. Inside – it's best to come at prayer time to guarantee admission – the mosque is distinguished by the best İznik tiles outside of Bursa: the *mihrab* and walls up to eye level are solid with them. Higher surfaces once bore calligraphic frescoes, but these have probably been missing since the catastrophic earthquake of 1751. The dervishes initially congregated in the *eyvan*s (transepts), that form the ends of the T's cross-stroke; Murat later housed them in a separate *tekke* (gathering place) in the garden.

The other outlying attractions are all on the far bank of the Tunca, crossed here by the greatest concentration of **historic bridges** in Thrace, better suited to pedestrians and horsecarts than the single file of motor vehicles which barely fits on most of them. The pair furthest upstream, the fifteenth-century **Saray (Süleyman)** and **Fatih** bridges, join the respective left and right banks of the Tunca with **Saray İçi**, an island in the river that used to support the **Edirne Sarayı**, a royal palace begun by Murat II. Unhappily it was blown to bits by the Turks themselves in 1877, to prevent the munitions stored inside from falling into Russian hands, and today nothing is left of this pleasure pavilion except the rubble of some baths, and a tower, next to which is an incongruously modern concrete stadium, venue for the Kırkpınar wrestling matches.

The next bridge below the island is the **Saraçhane**; you can descend directly on foot from Muradiye Camii to this or the preceding two, but with a vehicle you'll have to retrace your steps to the town centre. The riverbanks are officially a military zone, but you can certainly take snaps of the old bridges as long as you're not brazen and don't point your camera at soldiers or modern installations.

If time is short, cross on the double-stage **Beyazit Bridge** – accessible along Horozlu Bayır Caddesi – directly to the **İkinci Beyazit Külliyesi**, built between 1484 and 1488 by Hayrettin, court architect to Beyazit II, and the largest Ottoman spiritual and physical welfare complex ever constructed. Within a single irregular boundary wall, and beneath a hundred-dome silhouette familiar from many an M. C. Escher engraving, are assembled not only a mosque but a food storehouse, bakery, *imaret*, dervish hostel, medical school and insane asylum. Unfortunately most of the buildings are completely closed to the public these days, the keys being in the possession of the university. The imam or his son may appear in order to give you a short tour of the complex, which will mean peering frustratedly though windows and gates.

On the east side, the **storehouse and bakery** are appropriately enough given over to ceramic kilns; the low platform in the **imaret**, around which the itinerant dervishes dined, is now completely closed up and inaccessible. Except for its handsome courtyard and the sultan's loge inside, the **mosque** itself is disappointing, a single-dome affair disfigured by some unfortunate Ottoman Baroque mural work. The dervish hospices to either side are not generally open to the public.

West of the mosque lie the most interesting parts of the *külliye*. The **medical school** in the furthest northwest corner was conveniently linked to the *timarhane* or madhouse, built around an open garden, which in turn leads to the magnificent **darüşşifa** or therapy centre. This hexagonal, domed structure consists of a circular central space with six *eyvan*s opening onto it; the inmates were brought here regularly, where a fountain – slightly elevated to drain to the rim of the chamber – and musicians would play together to soothe the more intractable cases. Strange five-sided rooms with fireplaces open off three of the *eyvan*s.

More walking parallel to the dykes and water meadows of the Tunca's right bank will bring you to the misnamed **Yıldırım Camii**, credited not to Yıldırım Beyazit I but to Murat I, who built it over a Byzantine church shortly after his capture of Edirne in 1361 – consequently it lacks a proper *mihrab*. The mosque is reached via its own recently repaired bridge, just past the *Mihal Et Lokantası*; currently it's undergoing what appears to be a ham-handed restoration.

Return to town over the **Gazi Mihal Bridge**, an Ottoman refurbishment of a thirteenth-century Byzantine span and hence the oldest around Edirne. The river can also be crossed here by means of a modern structure, which affords good views and photo opportunities of the older bridge. Gazi Mihal was a Christian nobleman who became an enthusiastic convert to Islam – hence the epithet *Gazi*, "Warrior for the Faith". His namesake mosque, at the western end of the bridge, is presently undergoing restoration.

Eating and drinking

Restaurants are adequate but not especially cheap in Edirne, an exception being the tiny *ciğerci* booths serving up the city speciality, deep-fried liver, on and around Saraçlar Caddesi; the *Saray Ciğer ve Çorba salonu* in Tahmiş Carşışı near the PTT is especially recommended for a cheap lunch. Some of the other obvious eateries on Saraçlar Caddesi aren't bad: the *Aile Restaurant* on the first floor of the Belediye İşhanı next to the post office has a good selection of kebabs and steamtray stews combined with excellent service. For **dessert**, every imaginable kind of pudding, pastry and ice cream is on offer at various stalls lining Saraçlar Caddesi.

On the Meriç River a kilometre south of town on the road to Karaağaç, the *Lalezar* has beautiful views of the Meriç and its elegant, honey-coloured bridge. They serve kebabs and *meze*s at reasonable prices in their waterfront garden, one table of which is located in the branches of a tree; to get there take the Karaağaç dolmuş from in front of the PTT. On the way, between the Yeni and Meriç bridges, the *Doruk* is a friendly, lively *meyhane*, with reasonably priced *meze*s and alcohol.

East of Edirne: Lüleburgaz

If you've become a Sinan-ophile, you can visit yet another of his substantial creations which dominates the town of **LÜLEBURGAZ**, 76km east of Edirne on the main route to İstanbul. The **Sokollu Mehmet Paşa Külliyesi**, originally commissioned by that governor of Rumeli in 1549, was built in fits and starts, not being completed until 1569 during Sokollu's term as grand vizier. Today what's left is an imposing mosque and *medrese* abutted by a covered bazaar and guarded by two isolated towers.

The **mosque** proper is peculiar, possessing only one minaret; where the others might be, three stubby turret-like towers jut instead, all joined by a mansard crenellation. The **medrese**, still used as a children's Koran school, is arrayed around the mosque courtyard, entered by two tiny arcades on the east and west sides; in the middle of the vast space stands the late Ottoman caprice of a **şadırvan**. The mosque's portico, built to square with the *medrese*, is far more impressive than the interior, and most visitors will soon drift out of the north gate to the **market promenade**, whose shops are still intact and in use. Just outside the gate, a huge dome with a stork's nest on top shades the centre of the bazaar.

Beyond, there was once a massive *kervansaray*, equal in size to the mosque and *medrese* complex; this was the last part to be finished, and all of it has vanished save for a lone tower, balanced by another, the **Dar-ül-Kura**, at the south edge of the entire precinct, beyond the mosque's *mihrab*. The former **hamam**, across the street from the complex and also constructed as an afterthought, is now chock-a-block with tiny **restaurants** in its outer bays, though the main dome has collapsed.

There are a few simple but acceptable **hotels** 200m south of Sokollu Mehmet, plus the more luxurious *Hongurlar Oteli* at İstanbul Cad 73. There's little point stopping over, though, as the town is otherwise utterly undistinguished and, given the frequent buses, moving on toward either İstanbul or Edirne is easy at any time.

South of Edirne: Greek border crossings

There's little reason to stop at any point along the E87/550 highway as it heads down from Havsa, the junction 27km southeast of Edirne. This road does, however, connect Uzunköprü and Keşan, one of which you're likely to pass through if in transit to or from Greece.

UZUNKÖPRÜ (Long Bridge) gets its name from the 173-arched Ottoman aqueduct at the north end of town. You wouldn't make a special trip to see it, though, and while Uzunköprü is an official rail entry and exit port for Turkey, the station is 4km north of town and you'd have to be pretty perverse to catch either the late-night international "express" from Greece to İstanbul or the pre-dawn train to Greece here – certainly when connections out of Edirne are so much better. If you insist, you may end up waiting for the Greece-bound train at the one-star *Ergene Oteli*, on the main square.

The main Greek–Turkish road crossing, far busier and somewhat less paranoiac than the Edirne–Kastaniés one, is at Kípi in Greece, leading over the border to **İPSALA**, astride the E25/110 highway. The two posts here are open 24 hours, but the banking facilities on both sides and the tourist information booth in İpsala (☎0284/616 1577) only operate sporadically, so it's not a bad idea to show up with a certain amount of currency for the country you'll be entering (though if you have dollars or another hard currency, the Turkish immigration officials will be happy to exchange it for Turkish lira). As at the Edirne frontier, there's a 500-metre-wide military zone that you're not allowed to cross on foot; during daylight hours at least, it's fairly easy to arrange a ride over.

From the village of Kípi there are six buses daily further into Greece; at the Turkish immigration post you'll meet just taxis. It's cheaper to take a bus from **KEŞAN** (30km east), a cipher of a town but with frequent bus connections from İstanbul, Edirne and Çanakkale, and into Greece via İpsala. There are also a couple of cheap **hotels** in Keşan, the *İşçimen* (②), and the *Erikli Oberj* (①). As long-haul bus connections out of Edirne to anywhere but İstanbul are very poor, if you're making for Çanakkale, İzmir or Bursa, you'll almost always have a change of vehicle – with an hour or two stopover – in Keşan.

The Thracian coast: Tekirdağ to the Gelibolu Peninsula

Heading west from İstanbul, you don't really outrun the straggling suburbs until the junction where the Edirne-bound E5/100 splits off from the E25/110, headed for the İpsala frontier station. Fifty-five kilometres beyond the junction, **TEKİRDAĞ**, in a hilly setting at the head of a gently curving bay, is a fairly pleasant seaside port, with a few remaining wooden apartments, landscaped gardens on its shoreline esplanade, and a good beach, Alkaya Plajı, 3km back on the İstanbul road. Down on the shore boulevard there's a **tourist information office** (daily 8am–noon & 1–6pm; ☎0186/261 2083) just next to the *TML* dock. From the dock in summer boats ply to and from the islands of the Sea of Marmara and on to Erdek (see p.221; at least three competing car ferries go to Marmara and Avşa every day in the evenings). Out of season service drops to three a week to Marmara and Avşa, weather permitting. The **otogar** is 200m from the ferry landing off Atatürk Bulvarı on the road to İstanbul.

If you should miss the boat, the *Yat Hotel* opposite the ferry jetty (☎0282/261 1054; ②–③) on İskele Caddesi is well established as the most comfortable **hotel** in town, and has rooms either just with toilets, or with full bathrooms. East of town on the İstanbul road, there are a number of *pansiyon*s near Alkaya Plajı including the *No Problem*

(☎0282/262 4207; ③); take a yellow minibus 3km out of town, from the tea garden on Atatürk Bulvarı near the tourist information office. Tekirdağ's speciality is *köfte*, which can be eaten cheaply with a salad and beer at any of the very competitive **restaurants** opposite the ferry jetty, including the *Meşhur Tekirdağ Köftecisi*, where a meal for two will cost under $10.

Time to kill between connections could be spent in the sixteenth-century **Rüstem Paşa Camii** designed by Mimar Sinan, situated opposite the *Belediye* building on Hükümet Caddesi, or in the **Rakoczi Museum** (Tues–Sun 8.30am–4.30pm). Prince Ferenc II Rakoczi was leader of an unsuccessful revolt against the Austrian Hapsburgs, and this house, where he lived in exile as a Carmelite friar, was converted to a museum in his memory in 1932 by the Hungarian government. Among the exhibits are Hungarian weapons, paintings relating to Rakoczi's life, and his flag.

West from Tekirdağ

More interesting than Tekirdağ are a row of tiny resorts and fishing villages out to the west. There are regular dolmuşes from Tekirdağ *otogar* to the most developed, **KUMBAĞ**, 8km along the coast, with a marvellous beach, around 3km of clean sand with crystal-clear water. Most of the prime beachfront sites have been bagged by private developers and sold off as timeshares, but there's a small campsite, the *Deniz*, on the waterfront, and the very comfortable and modern *Bilge Hotel* (☎0282/283 4104; ②), with its own restaurant, beach and pedal boats for hire.

A couple of villages further along from Kumbağ, the Şarköy coast road becomes a dirt track, passable only in a four-wheel-drive – though a few Şarköy-bound minibuses do take this route. On the other side of this poor stretch of road, most easily accessible by dolmuş from Şarköy, 20km to the west, the pretty fishing village of **HASKÖY** has a pebbly beach and clean water, set against rolling, vine-covered hills. There's very little tourism development, apart from a couple of waterfront **guest houses**, the *Başkır*, a quaint house-*pansiyon* with comfortable rooms overlooking the harbour (③), and the slightly upmarket *Durak* (③). Both have their own fish restaurants, and the *Durak* also boasts a swimming pool.

Şarköy

One of the few human-scale resorts remaining near İstanbul, **ŞARKÖY** is also one of the longest established, having catered to İstanbul-dwellers and Thracians since the 1960s. There's an actual town behind the plane-tree esplanade fringing a kilometre of decent sand, with a few signs in English aimed at foreigners, although it's mostly Turks who pour through here in summer; regular boats link the town with Marmara Island (see p.223).

The **otogar** is about a fifteen-minute walk from the beach, at the extreme north-western edge of town on the road to the E87/550 highway. If you decide to **stay**, the *Sedef Motel* (☎0282/518 1094; ③) is probably the best choice, with its garden courtyard, small pool, and simple but comfortable rooms, although at the height of summer, from July 15 until October 1, rooms are available only on a half-board basis ($42 for two people sharing a room); it's located near the pier right on the beach, on Atatürk Caddesi. Next door the *Otel İmen* (☎0282/518 1188) has a few nicely furnished rooms overlooking the beach, but the rooms at the back aren't so pleasant, and can be noisy as they're near a *gazino*; they offer only half-board rates, at $13 a head. To the east of town at Sarıcapaşa Cad 10, Cumhuriyet Mah, the *Elif Motel Pansiyon* (☎0282/518 2752; ①) is small and packed in season, so bookings are advisable; rooms are clean, with tiny bathrooms.

When thoughts turn to **food**, you could try the *Sevecen Restaurant*, in one of the few old buildings standing on the shore plaza, or, a notch up but still good value, the *Deniz* on İskele Meydanı. A more atmospheric fish restaurant for sampling the local catch and a limited selection of *meze*s is the *Limaniçi* on the harbour which juts out to sea to the west of town. At night the location is peaceful, away from the shoreside fairground and the general hubbub of the promenade, and you can eat your fish overlooking the boat that brought it in.

The Gelibolu peninsula: Gallipoli

Burdened with a grim military history but endowed with some fine scenery and beaches, the slender **Gelibolu Peninsula** forms the northwest side of the **Dardanelles**. Whether you approach from Şarköy or (more likely) Keşan, the road there is pretty, swooping down in long arcs past the Saros gulf, scene of recent friction between Greece and Turkey because of the latter's intention to prospect for undersea petroleum.

If you're travelling under your own steam you could stop off at one of a handful of motels overlooking the gravelly Saros beaches, absolutely the northernmost in the Turkish Aegean. At **BOLAYIR**, where the peninsula is a mere 4km across, you might also pause for a glance at the obvious **castle** and two **tombs**: one of Prince Süleyman, he of the Kırkpınar rites (see p.187), killed on this spot in a riding accident in 1359; the other of **Namik Kemal**, poet and reform advocate of the late nineteenth century, who spent much of his life in exile.

Gelibolu

Principal town of the peninsula, which served as Anglo-French headquarters during the Crimean War, **GELİBOLU** is a moderately inviting if slightly windy place perched just where the Dardanelles (*Çanakkale Boğazı* in Turkish) begin to narrow in earnest. At the heart of town is a colourful, square fishing harbour, ringed by cafés and restaurants, its two pools separated by a stump of a **medieval tower**. This is the sole survivor of Byzantine Callipolis' fortifications, greatly enlarged by the Ottomans when they took the place from Catalan mercenaries in 1354. The only other significant monuments are a historic mosque in the marketplace and, well inland to the northeast, a few handsomely sturdy but otherwise unremarkable Ottoman **türbes**.

Practicalities

The **ferry jetty** is right at the inner harbour entrance; ferries cross to Lapseki on the hour between 6am and 1am, and cost $4. There is no reasonable accommodation in Lapseki, so if it's a toss-up between the two, opt for Gelibolu. The **bus terminal** is over on the opposite side of the anchorage, next to the old tower.

The *Yelkenci* (☎0286/566 1022; ②), at Liman Meydanı on the harbour, offers pleasant **rooms** without showers but with balconies overlooking the harbour. A short walk up the main street, Liman Caddesi, at Yukarı Çarşı 64, the *Hotel Turkmen* (☎0286/566 2164; ②) is surprisingly upmarket for such a small town, with very well-furnished rooms. Between the lighthouse and an army camp extends a serviceable beach, with a **campsite**; there's also the *Obidi* campsite at the opposite edge of town.

The Yılmaz clan, who run the unprepossessing, old-fashioned *Hotel Yılmaz* (☎0286/566 1256; ③) and the equally unappealing but cheaper *Anzac Pansiyon* opposite (☎0286/566 3596; ①), both on Liman Caddesi, offer morning and afternoon **tours** of the World War I sites for $14 in a guided group; or you can take their cassette ($12) for your walkman, which gives a commentary as you go around the battlefields and ceme-

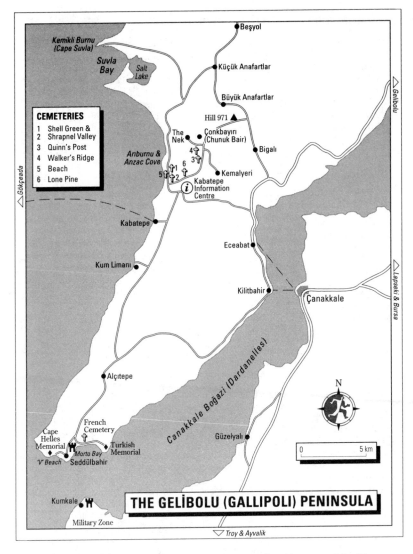

THE GELİBOLU (GALLIPOLI) PENINSULA

CEMETERIES
1. Shell Green & 2. Shrapnel Valley
3. Quinn's Post
4. Walker's Ridge
5. Beach
6. Lone Pine

teries. They also run their own bus company serving major cities around the Marmara. When **eating out**, don't miss the local catch of **sardalya** (sardines), best grilled fresh before they find their way to Gelibolu's canneries. The *Yelkenci Pansiyon* has a good cheap fish restaurant, with a large rooftop balcony looking out to sea. The *İmren Restaurant* by the ferry landing is also cheap, licensed and excellent. For something slightly more upmarket, and a good view across the straits, head for the *Gelibolu Restaurant* on the seaward side of the harbour, which serves enormous fish dishes for less than $10 a head.

The battlefields, cemeteries and beaches

The **World War I battlefields and Allied cemeteries** scattered along the Gelibolu peninsula are by turns moving and numbing in the sheer multiplicity of graves, memorials and obelisks, the past violence made all the more poignant by the present beauty of the landscape. The whole area is now either fertile, rolling farm country, or cloaked in thick scrub and pine forest alive with birds, making it difficult to imagine the bare desolation of 1915. Recently the last 20km or so of the landmass has been designated a **national historical park**, and since 1985 some effort has been made by the Turkish authorities to signpost road junctions and sites. This was complemented in 1990 by the Australian and New Zealand governments, who took the occasion of the 75th anniversary observations to add various facilities and markers of their own to join those previously placed by the Commonwealth War Graves Commission.

The open-air sites have no admission fees or restricted hours, and there's now a reasonable choice of **transport** options for touring the cape. **Tours** from Gelibolu, Çanakkale (see p.230) or Eceabat, cost $10–14 a head, lasting 3–4hr and taking in the Kabatepe Information Centre and the main sites to the north. All the companies listed are supposed to be working with Ministry of Tourism licensed guides, who should have excellent English and a thorough knowledge of the sites – if you find your guide is going too fast, ask questions to slow him or her down. You can also visit all the sites in the northern and southern parts of the peninsula less comfortably but with more freedom, by a combination of short **dolmuş** rides and **walking**. Dolmuşes run from Gelibolu to Kilitbahir via Eceabat, and from Eceabat to Alçitepe via the Kabatepe Information Centre. You can then walk around the main sites to the north of the information centre inside a couple of hours. At Kilitbahir, dolmuşes meet the Çannakkale car ferries in summer and take passengers to Alçitepe and Seddülbahir, from where you can tour the surrounding cemeteries and memorials on foot. They also ferry passengers to the Turkish memorial (*Çanakkale Abidesi* in Turkish). It's also possible to **rent bicycles and cars** in Eceabat, which gives you all the freedom you could possibly require.

Some history

Soon after the start of World War I it became obvious to the Allies that Russia could not be supplied by sea, nor a Balkan front opened against the Central Powers, unless Ottoman Turkey was eliminated. **Winston Churchill**, in his earliest important post as First Lord of the Admiralty, reasoned that the quickest way to accomplish this would be to force the Dardanelles with a fleet and bombard İstanbul into submission. A combined Anglo-French armada made several half-hearted attempts on the straits during November 1914, which were repulsed, but they returned in earnest on March 18, 1915. This time they managed to penetrate less than 10km up the waterway before striking numerous Turkish mines, losing half a dozen vessels and hundreds of men. The Allies retreated, and command squabbles erupted as a result of Lord Kitchener's insistence that the Commonwealth armies should hereafter be paramount. Regrouped at Mudros harbour on the Greek island of Limnos, the joint expeditionary forces took several months to prepare an amphibious assault on the Turkish positions along the peninsula. During this time another naval sprint down the Dardanelles may have succeeded, but instead the delay gave the Turks the chance to strengthen their own defences.

The plan eventually formulated by the Commonwealth and French commanders called for an Anglo-French landing at Cape Helles, Seddülbahir and Morto Bay at the mouth of the straits, and a simultaneous ANZAC (Australia–New Zealand Army Corps) assault at Kabatepe beach 13km north. The two forces were to drive towards each other, link up and neutralize the Turkish shore batteries controlling the Dardanelles.

This rather hare-brained scheme ran into trouble from the start. At dawn on April 25, 1915, the Anglo-French brigades at the southernmost cape were pinned down by accurate Turkish fire; a toehold was eventually established, but it was never expanded during the rest of the campaign, and the French contingent was virtually annihilated. The fate of the **ANZAC** landing was even more horrific: owing to a drifting signal buoy, the Aussies and Kiwis disembarked not on the wide, flat sands of Kabatepe, but at a cramped and Turkish-dominated cove next to Arıburnu, 2km north. Despite appalling casualties the ANZACs advanced inland in staggered parties over the next day, goaded by their commanders, to threaten the Turkish strongpoint of Çonkbayırı overhead. As at the other landing, however, little permanent progress was made despite a supplementary British landing at Cape Suvla to the north; except during ferocious battles for the summit in early August, both sides settled into long-term trench warfare, every bit as gruesome as its north European counterpart despite the Mediterranean latitude. Finally, around Christmas 1915, the Allies gave up, with the last troops leaving Seddülbahir on January 8, 1916. Churchill's career, among others, went into temporary eclipse.

The reasons for the **Allied defeat** are many. In addition to the chanciness of the basic strategy, the callousness and incompetence of the Allied commanders – who often countermanded each other's orders or failed to press advantages with reinforcements – cannot be underestimated. With hindsight you cannot help but wonder why the Allies didn't concentrate more on Cape Suvla and the flat, wide valley behind, skirting the fortified Ottoman heights to reach the Dardanelles' northwest shore. On the **Turkish side**, much of the credit for the successful resistance must go to one Mustafa Kemal, then a relatively obscure lieutenant-colonel, later better known as **Atatürk**. As ranking officer at Çonkbayırı for the duration of the campaign, his role in the Turkish victory is legendary. He seemed to enjoy a charmed life, narrowly escaping death on several occasions and, aside from his tactical skills, is credited with various other extraordinary accomplishments, but primarily that of rekindling morale, by threats, persuasion or example, among often outgunned and outnumbered Ottoman infantrymen.

Half a million men were deployed by defenders and attackers alike, albeit in stages; of these well over fifty percent were killed, wounded or missing, with Turkish deaths estimated at 86,000, and Allied forces at 160,000. The carnage among the ANZACs in particular was grossly disproportionate to the island nations' populations; indeed the Allied top brass cavalierly regarded the "colonials" as expendable cannon fodder, an attitude that has not been forgotten in certain circles. This baptism by blood had several long-term effects: a sense of Australia and New Zealand having come of age as sovereign countries; the designation of April 25 as a solemn holiday in Australia and New Zealand; and a healthy antipodean scepticism, pending an evaluation of actual national interest in the face of blandishments to join international adventures.

Central and northern sites

Three kilometres north of Eceabat (see below), a signposted side road heads west toward "Kemalyeri" and "Kabatepe". The first stop of most tours is the **Kabatepe Orientation Centre and Museum** 6km along (daily 8.30am–5pm; $0.50), which has an interesting, well-labelled selection of war memorabilia, including touching letters home, photos of the trenches, weapons and uniforms. However, the centre's full title is a bit of a misnomer since orientation is available only through the expensive glossy literature sold at the reception desk – a relief map or scale model of the area showing the main battle sites and lines of attack and defence would be welcome for those not visiting on a guided tour. A worthwhile and not too pricy publication is *Gallipoli Plaques* ($3, available at the centre), designed to flesh out the information given on ten explanatory plaques that are scattered around various battlefield sites to the north of the information centre. In the foyer there's a display of photographs and a map of the forest fire which swept the peninsula in July 1994, killing one local man and destroying 4000 hectares of pine forest.

The first points encountered along the coast road are the **Beach**, **Shrapnel Valley** and **Shell Green** cemeteries, followed by **Anzac Cove** and **Arıburnu**, site of the first, bungled ANZAC landing and ringed by more graves. At Anzac Cove a memorial bears Atatürk's famous quotation which, translated into English, begins "Those heroes that shed their blood and lost their lives . . . you are now lying in the soil of a friendly country". Looking inland, you'll see the murderous badlands that gave the defenders such an advantage. Beyond Arıburnu, the terrain flattens out and the four other cemeteries (Canterbury, No. 2 Outpost, New Zealand No. 2 Outpost and Embarcation Pier) are much more dispersed.

At a fork north of Arıburnu, a left turn leads toward the beaches and salt lake at **Cape Suvla**, today renamed Kemikli Burnu; most tourists bear right for Büyük Anafartalar village and Çonkbayırı (Chunuk Bair). The road curls up the long, flat valley partly occupied by the British during that fateful spring; if you're at the wheel you need to take another right at an inconspicuous sign facing away from you: "Çonkbayırı 6, Kabatepe 13".

The main features of **Çonkbayırı hill** are the massive New Zealand memorial obelisk and the five-monolith Turkish memorial describing Atatürk's words and deeds – chief among the latter being his organization of successful resistance to the Allied attacks of August 6–10. The spot where the Turkish leader's pocket watch stopped a fragment of shrapnel is highlighted, as is the grave of a Turkish soldier discovered in 1990 when the trenches were reconstructed.

Working your way back down toward the visitors' centre, you pass the strongholds-turned-cemeteries of **The Nek**, **Walker's Ridge** and **Quinn's Post**, where the trenches of the opposing forces lay within a few metres of each other; the modern road corresponds to the no-man's-land. From here the single, perilous supply line ran down-valley to the present location of Beach Cemetery. The line of furthest ANZAC advance continues down a little further to **Lone Pine (Kanlı Sırt)**, lowest strategic position on the ridge and the largest graveyard-cum-memorial to those buried unmarked or at sea. Action here was considered a sideshow to the main August offensive at Çonkbayırı; a total of 28,000 men died in four days at both points. Just before the Lone Pine memorial to the right of the road, opposite Johnston's Jolly Cemetery, is an unrestored and heavily eroded section of **trench**, peaceful now beneath the pine trees.

To the southern cape

The harbour of **KABATEPE** village, boarding point for the ferry to Gökçeada (Imvros; twice weekly in winter, daily in summer), is 2km south of the orientation centre. There's a good beach here – intended site of the ANZAC landing – but if you're after a swim wait until you reach **KUM LİMANI**, 5km south of the museum, where an even better strand fringes a warm, clean, calm sea, unusual this far north. Except for the *Kum Motel* (☎0286/814 1466; ③), there's been little development of this beautiful setting, but you probably won't be alone: a number of tour companies bring their clients here for a dip after battlefield sightseeing. If you're relying on public transport, this is one place you can get to fairly easily, since Eceabat–Alçıtepe dolmuşes pass the junction just over a kilometre inland.

The **Cape Helles** British naval obelisk adorns the Turkish equivalent of Land's End, 16km beyond Kum Limanı and just past the village of **SEDDÜLBAHİR**. It's worth stopping off in Seddülbahir to visit the quirky private **battle museum** (free, donations appreciated) run by Mutlu Salim, who has amassed an extensive collection of shell splinters, bullets, uniform fragments and other grizzly military remains from local fields and beaches; it's on the right-hand side of the road leading into the village from the north. From Cape Helles itself, the views south to Bozcaada (Tenedos), west to Gökçeada (Imvros) and east to Asia are magnificent, and abundant **Ottoman fortifications** hint at the age-old importance of the place. (The Kumkale castle on the other side of the straits is still out of bounds to visitors.) Tucked between the medieval bulwarks is an excellent beach, the **"V Beach"** of the Allied expedition, behind which is a

campsite – and the biggest of five British cemeteries in the area. The beach partly explains the five local **pansiyons** such as *Fulda* and *Helles Panorama*, but so far little impact has been made on a basically sleepy hamlet.

A turning just before Seddülbahir leads to the **French cemetery** above Morto Bay, one of the most striking of all the memorials, with its serried rows of named black crosses; and the nearby **Turkish memorial**, resembling a stark, tetrahedral footstool.

Kilitbahir and Eceabat

You'll need to retrace your steps to the Seddülbahir–Alçıtepe road to make an approximately complete circuit of the peninsula. The tiny village of **KİLİTBAHİR**, 5km south of Eceabat, is dwarfed by its massive and perfectly preserved **castle**. Unpublicized, privately run **car ferries** chug across to Çanakkale at half-hourly intervals at this narrowest point (1300m) of the Dardanelles. In summer, regular **dolmuşes** meet the Çanakkale car ferry at Kilitbahir and take passengers to Alçıtepe, Seddülbahir and the Turkish memorial.

ECEABAT is a transit point, less attractive than Gelibolu and smaller than Çanakkale but handy for the battlefield sites, and you may consider making it your base. There's a **PTT booth** by the jetty, changing money and offering a metered phone until 9pm, and an excellent hotel, the *Eceabat* (☎0286/814 2460; ②), on İskele Meydanı overlooking the harbour: clean, good value and comfortable, it has a pleasant breakfast room with picture windows looking out to sea. A downmarket alternative, the *RSL Pansiyon* (☎0286/814 1065, fax 814 2323; ①), has basic rooms with en-suite facilities, a bar and serves up veggie food. The owners, who all speak English, also offer **tours**, which begin with a yacht cruise to ANZAC Cove (snorkelling opportunities and a fish barbecue), followed by a conventional tour of the northern memorials and battlefield sites ($20 per person), as well as **diving** to the wrecks ($75 for two dives). *Anatur*, whose main operation base is Çanakkale (see p.231), have an office in Eceabat, opposite the ferry jetty (☎0286/217 5482). They offer **bicycle** ($4 per day) and **car rental** ($50), and tours of the area for $10 a head, but you'll need to go over to Çanakkale to see the Mel Gibson video and the "Fatal Shore" documentary.

Local **dolmuşes** depart from in front of the *Atlanta* restaurant for Gelibolu, Kabatepe (which can also drop you at the Kabatepe Orientation Centre and Museum) and Alçıtepe, and south to Kilitbahir, where you can find regular dolmuşes to the southern battlefield sites.

THE SOUTHERN MARMARA SHORE

The **southern shoreline** of the sea of Marmara is not as rewarding as the northern one, consisting mainly of a heavily urbanized, polluted dormitory community for İstanbul. Inland, **İznik**, despite a fascinating history as an important centre of Christianity and, briefly, capital of the Nicaean Empire, does not merit a prolonged stay, and if you're pushed for time you will probably head straight for **Bursa**, one of Turkey's most attractive and fascinating cities.

Approaching Bursa: coastal ports and resorts

The southern Marmara shore from İzmit to Bandırma offers little of compelling interest; for the most part this is rocky coast, with inland contours softened somewhat by ubiquitous olive groves. If you're travelling between İstanbul and Bursa, though, you're likely to catch a glimpse of at least one of the **ferry ports** that like to call themselves resorts – which they are for numbers of locals.

If you're relying on public transport, probably the best option for getting to the southern Marmara shore from İstanbul is to cross the sea to **YALOVA**. There's no reason to linger, since touts for buses to İznik, Bursa and the nearby spa meet incoming ferries and hydrofoils. If you're heading back towards İstanbul and you miss the last hydrofoil to Kabataş near Beşiktaş (Mon–Fri 3 or 4 daily, last one at 5.10pm; ☎0216/814 1020 to check times), or the passenger ferry to Kartal (four a day, last one at 7.30pm), you'd be better off taking a dolmuş, bus (Taşköprü-Termal) or cab from the ferry terminal to Termal (see below) than staying in any of the awful hotels in Yalova.

Note that there is no **car ferry** service to or from Yalova; if you're driving yourself or you're on a bus, you must cross the Gulf of İzmit via **Topcular**, 15km east. Here there are regular ferries to and from the Eskihisar/Darica docks below **Gebze**, on the main dual carriageway (and suburban rail system) to İstanbul – both ferries and trains run every twenty minutes around the clock. Foot passengers get a final chance to cross the gulf between **Karamürsel** and **Hereke**. These services are a far better option than undergoing the dull and congested drive along the gulf shore through **İzmit**, the Marmara region's industrial tip.

The famous hot springs at **TERMAL**, with their Ottoman Belle Epoque surroundings, are 12km southwest of Yalova, just inland from Çinarcik. The spa resort is completely dominated by two luxury **hotels**, both owned by the *Turban* hotel group, the *Turban* (☎0226/835 7400, fax 835 7413; ⑤–⑦, depending on the location of the room) and the *Çamlık* (same numbers and prices). Located right in the pine-clad valley, these pseudo-rustic lodges afford easy access to the baths and swimming pool of the spa complex. A cheaper alternative can be found in an idyllic location on one of the surrounding hills: the *Dinana* (☎0226/675 7293; ④) in the village of Üvezpinar is family-run and clean, with pleasant rooms all with balconies overlooking the beautiful forested mountains; the hotel also has a restaurant serving simple meals. Üvezpinar is a two-kilometre hike up the road leading from the *jandarmarie* station to the left of the entrance to Termal, or up steps leading from within the resort itself.

Though visited by Byzantine and Roman emperors, Termal's springs only became fashionable again at the turn of the century, and most of the present buildings date from that era. Atatürk had a house built here, now open as a **museum** (Tues–Sun 8.30am–noon & 1–5pm; $1), which preserves a certain rustic charm, its original handcrafted furniture still in place. The **baths**, all open from 8am to 11pm, are popular for their beneficial effect on rheumatism and skin diseases. The two main hamams are the *Valide*, which has massive communal pools ($1.50), and the *Sultan Bath*, with separate compartments ($4 for two people, couples accepted). The separate outdoor swimming pool of *Kurşunlu Hamam* ($2) is small and mainly dominated by an aggressive male clientele.

The closest beach for a safe swim on this stretch of coast would be **ARMUTLU**, 50km southwest of Yalova on a dirt road, where a few hotels line a pebble beach. Gemlik, just off the Bursa–Yalova expressway, might have been attractive once, but its polluted gulf now mocks the superfluous breeze-block hotels on the waterfront.

MUDANYA is the closest harbour to Bursa, and another useful transit point from İstanbul, with two daily passenger ferries. Despite its moment in history as the place where the provisional armistice between Turkey and the Allies was signed on October 11, 1922, Mudanya's modern ranks of concrete high-rises are no more appealing than those of Yalova. Fortunately, Mudanya is well connected by **public transport**: the daily catamaran from Yenikapı in İstanbul leaves at 8am and arrives in Mudanya at 9.30am (except on Sundays when it leaves at 6.30pm arriving at 8pm), and the lone normal ferry service leaves İstanbul at 9am, arriving at noon. Bursa, İznik, and Çannakale buses and dolmuşes are frequent, all connecting with the ferry and the catamaran from İstanbul. There's an excellent **hotel** here should you get stuck: the *Montania*, in a renovated 150-year-old station building on the seaside esplanade of Eski İstasyon Caddesi

(☎0224/544 6000; ⑦, negotiable), has an outdoor pool and well-equipped modern rooms, some with sea views.

KUMYAKA, 7km west of Mudanya, and **ZEYTINBAĞI**, 3km further, both have **Byzantine churches** that are worth a look. The latter village was the Greek Trilya, and the Fatih Camii here is thought to have started life as a thirteenth-century church; a more ruinous church just out of town dates from the eighth century. Once you've seen these, you can get a good fish meal by the little anchorage. Both villages are served by bus from Mudanya and Bursa.

İznik

It's hard to believe that **İZNİK**, today a somnolent farming community at the east end of the lake of the same name, was once the seat of empires and scene of desperate battles for their control. But looking around the fertile, olive-mantled valley, you can understand the attraction for imperial powers needing a fortified base near – but not too near – the sea lanes of the Marmara. On closer examination, İznik proves to be a poky, even dilapidated one-horse town, slumbering away among its orchards after the exertions of history, waking only recently – and fitfully – to the demands of tourism. Compared to the sophistication of Bursans, the townspeople can seem unhelpful, while its most famous attribute, the famous sixteenth-century ceramics, the best ever produced in Turkey, are all but absent from the museums and mosques of modern İznik – even the tiles sheathing the minaret of Yeşil Cami, the town's most famous landmark, are poor substitutes made in Kütahya. Most people visit İznik as a long day out of İstanbul or Bursa, staying a night at most – more than enough time for the handful of mostly overrated monuments.

Some history

Founded by Alexander's general Antigonus in 316 BC, the city was seized and enlarged fifteen years later by his rival Lysimachus, who named it **Nicaea** after his late wife. He also gave Nicaea its first set of walls and the **grid plan** typical of Hellenistic towns; both are still evident. When the Bithynian kingdom succeeded Lysimachus, Nicaea alternated with nearby Nicomedia as its capital until bequeathed to Rome in 74 BC. Under the Roman emperors the city prospered as capital of the province, and it continued to flourish during the Byzantine era.

Nicaea played a pivotal role in early Christianity, by virtue of hosting two important **ecumenical councils**. The first, convened by Constantine the Great in 325, resulted in the condemnation of the Arian heresy – which maintained that Christ's nature was inferior to God the Father's – and the promulgation of the Nicene Creed, affirming Christ's divine nature, which is still central to Christian belief. The seventh council (the second to be held here) was presided over by Empress Irene in 787; this time the Iconoclast controversy was settled by the pronouncement, widely misunderstood in the West, that icons had their proper place in the church so long as they were revered and not worshipped.

Nicaea's much-repaired walls seldom repelled invaders, and in 1081 the Selçuks took the city, only to be evicted by a combined force of Byzantines and Crusaders sixteen years later. The fall of Constantinople to the Fourth Crusade in 1204 propelled Nicaea into the spotlight once more, for the Byzantine heir Theodore Lascaris retreated here and made this the base of the improbably successful **Nicaean Empire**. The Lascarid dynasty added a second circuit of walls before returning to Constantinople in 1261, but these again failed to deter the besieging Ottomans, who, led by Orhan Gazi, the victor of Bursa, broke through in March 1331.

Renamed İznik, the city embarked on a golden age of sorts, interrupted briefly by the obligatory pillaging of Tamerlane in 1402. Virtually all of the surviving monuments predate the Mongol sacking, but the most enduring contribution to art and architecture – the celebrated **İznik tiles and pottery** – first appeared during the reign of Çelebi Mehmet I, who brought skilled potters from Persia to begin the local industry. This received another boost in 1514 when Selim the Grim took Tabriz and sent more crafts-men west as war booty; by the end of the sixteenth century ceramic production was at its height, with more than 300 functioning kilns. The tiles produced here adorned pub-lic buildings in every corner of the Ottoman Empire. It was to be a brief flowering, since within another hundred years war and politics had scattered most of the artisans. By the mid-eighteenth century the local industry had packed up completely, with products from nearby Kütahya serving as inferior substitutes. İznik began a long, steady decline, hastened by near-total devastation during the 1920–22 war.

The Town

With its regular street plan, İznik is easy to navigate; the main north–south boulevard **Atatürk Caddesi** and its east–west counterpart **Kılıçaslan Caddesi** link four of the seven ancient gates, dividing the town into unequal quadrants. You'll probably arrive at the tiny **otogar** in the southeast quarter, three or four blocks south of the **tourist infor-mation office**, opposite the *Belediye* on the first floor at Kılıçaslan Cad 130 (☎0224/757 1454; June–Aug daily 8.30am–noon & 1–5.30pm; closed Sat & Sun in winter), which hands out rather blurry city plans.

The southeast quadrant

In the immediate vicinity of the *otogar* are a few minor sites worth a passing glance. The fourteenth-century **Yakub Çelebi Zaviyesi**, one block southeast, was founded by the luckless prince slain by his brother Beyazit I at Kosovo in 1389 (see p.214); it has been compromised by too many bad restorations. A block to the east, nothing but founda-tions remain of the **Kimisis Kilisesi** (Church of the Assumption), the presumed bur-ial place of Theodore Lascaris, which was destroyed in 1922. Nearby is a dank, sunken **ayazma** or sacred spring.

It makes more sense if time is limited to head directly to İznik's central roundabout, southeast of which is the **Aya Sofya Museum** (daily 9am–noon & 1–5pm; $1), housed in all that remains of the Byzantine Church of Holy Wisdom, founded by Justinian. The current structure was built after an earthquake in 1065, and as the cathedral of the pro-visional Byzantine capital hosted the coronations of the four Nicaean emperors. The Ottomans converted it to a mosque directly on taking the city, and Mimar Sinan restored it, but the premises were already half-ruined when reduced to their present, sorry condition in 1922. Inside there's not much to see except some damaged floor mosaics and a faint but exquisite **fresco of Christ, John and Mary**, at ground level behind a glass panel to the left as you enter.

Returning to Kılıçaslan Caddesi, take a right before the tourist information office, and opposite the İkinci Murat Hamamı you'll see the **excavations of the İznik kilns**, still in progress. The site can be viewed from the road, but visitors are not allowed to enter; finds from the excavations are on display in the archeological museum (see below). Local attempts to revive the art of **ceramics** in the town are in their infancy, and the finished products as yet mainly consist of poor copies of sixteenth-century orig-inals, on sale in the *Babacan Pansiyon* and in Yusuf Bardakçı's boutique, Kılıçaslan Cad 205. The tile research centre, on the lake to the south of Kılıçaslan Caddesi, was found-ed in 1995 to investigate the technology behind ceramic manufacture, and to advance the art form in İznik. If you'd like to see how work is progressing, the tourist informa-tion office should be able to give advice on which workshops are open to visitors.

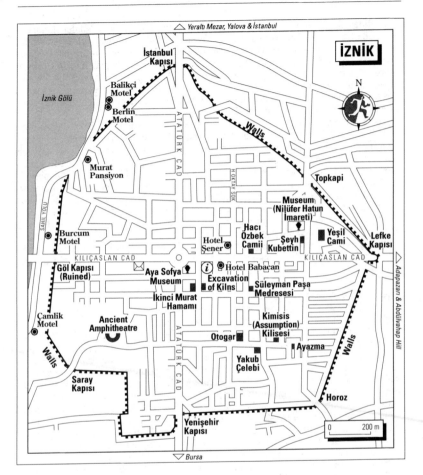

The northeast quadrant

Most of İznik's Ottoman attractions are in the northeast quarter of town. Just north of Kılıçaslan Caddesi squats the **Hacı Özbek Camii**, the earliest known Ottoman mosque, built in 1333 but much adulterated; the portico was senselessly pulled down in 1939. Three blocks due south stands the **Süleyman Paşa Medresesi**, likewise the oldest such Ottoman structure in Turkey and still used as a Koran school.

Resuming an amble along Kılıçaslan, you'll soon reach a vast landscaped park to the north, dotted with İznik's most famous monuments. The **Yeşil Cami**, erected toward the end of the fourteenth century by Murat I's grand vizier, is a small gem of a building, its highlight the fantastic marble relief on the portico. Tufted with a stubby minaret that looks back to Selçuk models, the mosque takes its name from the green İznik tiles that once adorned this minaret; they've long since been replaced by mediocre, tri-coloured Kütahya work.

Across the park sprawls the **Nilüfer Hatun İmareti**, commissioned by Murat I in 1388 in honour of his mother, by all accounts a remarkable woman. Daughter of a

Byzantine noble (some say Emperor John VI Cantacuzenos himself), Nilüfer Hatun was married off to Orhan Gazi to consolidate a Byzantine–Ottoman alliance. Her native ability was soon recognized by Orhan, who appointed her regent during his frequent absences. The T-form building, whose ample domes perennially play host to storks, is more accurately called a *zaviye* than a mere soup kitchen, and is one of the few that never doubled as a mosque. It was originally the meeting place not of dervishes but of the Ahi brotherhood, a guild drawn from the ranks of skilled craftsmen that also acted as a community welfare and benevolent society.

Today the *imaret* (hostel) contains the **archeological museum** (daily 8.30am–noon & 1–5pm; $1), which is sadly lacking in the expected **İznik ware**. The pieces of four-teenth-century İznik tiles excavated from the town's kilns have been painstakingly restored but are all incomplete, and there are few of the beautiful sixteenth-century mosque ornaments and massive plates produced in İznik, which are commonplace in the museums of İstanbul. More interesting is an exhibition of **Selçuk tile fragments** found in the area around the Roman theatre and in local kilns – this area was not known to be a centre of Selçuk occupation and it's uncertain whether these tiles were locally produced or imported. The museum also has such Roman bits as a bronze **dancing Pan**, some Byzantine gold jewellery and, standing out among the nondescript marble clutter, a **sarcophagus** in near-mint condition. For a more perilous adventure, and a fine view of Nilüfer Hatun's cupolas, climb the minaret of the adjacent **Şeyh Kubettin Camii**.

The walls and Roman theatre

Only enthusiasts will want to walk the entire perimeter of the double **walls**, now missing most of their hundred original watchtowers, but three of the seven portals are worth some time. Heavy traffic has been rerouted through modern breaches in the for-tifications to prevent vibration damage to the original openings, now restricted to trac-tors and pedestrians. Closest to the Yeşil Cami is the eastern **Lefke Kapısı**, a three-ply affair including a triumphal arch dedicated to Hadrian between the two courses of walls. Just outside is a stretch of the ancient **aqueduct** that until recently supplied the town. It's possible to get up on the ramparts here for a stroll, as it is at the northerly **İstanbul Kapısı**, best preserved of the gates. A Hadrianic arch is sandwiched here as well, opposite two relief **masks** in the inner portal, but the whole effect is rather dull because of the flat ground. By contrast the southern **Yenişehir Kapısı**, though the most recent gate, is in woeful condition – not least because the Selçuks, the Byzantines and finally the Ottomans successfully stormed the city at this point.

The only traces of Roman Nicaea are both in the southwestern quarter: the all-but-collapsed **theatre** just inside the Saray Kapısı, and a course of **ancient wall** that delim-its the so-called "Senatus court", extending from the surviving tower next to the gate.

Beyond the walls

If time permits, you might walk or drive to the obvious **hill** 2.5km outside the Lefke Kapısı for a comprehensive view over İznik, its walls and lake. The tomb on top belongs to a certain Abdülvahap, a semi-legendary character in the Arab raids of the eighth cen-tury.

Seven kilometres north of İznik in the village of Elbeyli is the **Bespekli Hipojesi Yeraltı Mezar**, a subterranean tomb for which the archeology museum staff in İznik control the keys. Thought to be the fourth-century burial chamber of a Roman couple (there are two graves here), the single chamber is covered in excellent **frescoes**, including a pair of peacocks. The museum custodian takes individuals and groups after the museum closes at 5pm.

Practicalities

Maple-canopied Kılıçaslan Caddesi has a few good **restaurants**, including two facing each other near the *Belediye* building: the *Konya Pide Salonu* for *lahmacun* and fresh *pide*, and the *Inegöl Köftecisi*, which sells the tremendous local meatballs and steamtray food. Most outsiders, however, will want to eat by the lakeshore, where all the restaurants are licensed; try grilled or fried *yayın*, the excellent local catfish. On the inland side of Sahil Yolu to the north as you approach from Kılıçaslan Caddesi, the *Burcum* is an unpretentious, reasonably priced fish restaurant, with tables in the garden. The *Kırıkçatal*, on the same street to the north of the *Burcum*, is also a good choice, but it's only open from June to October. Going south along the lakeside from Kılıçaslan Caddesi, however, will bring you to the best-value waterside restaurant, the *Çamlık Motel*, dishing up fish and kebabs. For snacks or dessert there are plenty of tea gardens, cafés and ice cream parlours overlooking the lake.

Rooms, singles in particular, are at a premium, and reservations are recommended between mid-June and mid-September – especially at the weekends, when inhabitants of neighbouring towns come to bathe in İznik lake. The most appealing **midtown** option is the *Hotel Şener* (☎0224/757 1480, fax 757 2280; ④), at H. Oktay Sokak 7 behind the *Belediye* building. It has a walled garden with a fountain where breakfast is served, and it's lighter with better rooms and service than the *Hotel Babacan*. The latter, at Kılıçaslan Cad 104 (☎0224/757 1623; ②), is unfriendly and not particularly comfortable, but cheap for a room with en-suite bathroom. The *Çamlık Motel*, like its attached restaurant, offers the best value on the **lakeshore** (☎0224/757 1613; ③); rooms are small but comfortable, with balconies overlooking the lake. The *Burcum Motel* (☎0224/757 1011; ③) has similar amenities, including a front garden, but the location isn't as pleasant. Both are open in winter. Alternatives at the extreme north end of the waterfront include the *Balıkçı Motel* (☎0224/757 1152; ③; closed in winter), and the *Berlin* next door (☎0224 757 1152; ③; closed in winter) with similar good facilities and secluded location. Your only hope of anything cheaper on the lake would be the tiny *Murat Café Pansiyon* (☎0224/757 3300; ①), with waterless rooms. There's a **campsite** on the lake just north of the city walls.

The **lake** itself is quite swimmable in summer, but the town beaches are scrappy and uninviting; you really need a car to reach more attractive spots. Both roads out of town along the lakeshore stay close to the water, and both offer swimming possibilities at various tiny beaches along their lengths. Both men (evenings) and women (daytime) can get steam-cleaned at the **İkinci Murat Hamamı**, just southeast of İznik's central roundabout and Aya Sofya.

Bursa

Draped ribbon-like along the leafy lower slopes of Uludağ, which towers more than 2000m above it, and overlooking the fertile plain of the Nilüfer Çayı, **BURSA** does more justice to its setting than any other Turkish city besides İstanbul. Gathered here are some of the finest early Ottoman monuments in the Balkans, focuses of a few neighbourhoods that, despite being marooned in masses of concrete, remain among the most appealing in Turkey.

Industrialization over the last three decades, and the quadrupling in population to over a million, mean that the city as a whole is no longer exactly elegant. Silk and textile manufacture, plus patronage of the area's thermal baths by the elite, were for centuries the most important enterprises; they're now outstripped by automobile manufacture (both Renault and Murat have plants here), canneries and bottlers processing the rich harvest of the plain, and the presence of Uludağ University. Vast numbers of settlers from Artvin province have been attracted by job opportunities at the various factories, while the students provide a necessary leavening in what might otherwise be a uniformly stodgy, conservative community. Some of this atmosphere derives from Bursa's role as first capital of the Ottoman Empire and burial place of the first six sultans, their piety as well as authority emanating from the mosques, social welfare foundations and tombs built at their command.

Bursa is sometimes touted as a day out from İstanbul, but this is really doing both the city and yourself a disservice: it deserves at least one and preferably a two-night stay. The spirit of the place really can't be gauged amid the whisked-in coach parties gawping at the overexposed Yeşil Cami and Yeşil Türbe. And despite dire warnings in other guidebooks, Bursa is a good city for walking, whether through the hive of the bazaars, the linear parks of the Hisar district, or the anachronistic peace of the Muradiye quarter.

Some history

Though the area had been settled at least a millennium before, the first actual city was founded here early in the second century BC by Prusias I, a king of ancient Bithynia, who in typical Hellenistic fashion named the town **Proussa** after himself. Legend claims that Hannibal helped him pick the location of the acropolis, today's Hisar.

Overshadowed by nearby Nicomedia (modern İzmit) and Nicaea (İznik), the city stagnated until the Romans, attracted by its natural hot springs, began spending lavish amounts on public baths and made it capital of their province of Mysia. Justinian introduced silkworm culture, and Byzantine Proussa flourished until Arab raids of the seventh and eighth centuries, and the subsequent tug-of-war for sovereignty between the Selçuks and the Greeks, precipitated decline. During and after the Latin interlude in Constantinople (1204–1261), the Byzantines reconsolidated their hold on Proussa, but not for long.

The start of the fourteenth century saw a small band of nomadic Turks, led by one **Osman Gazi**, camped outside the walls of Proussa. After more than a decade of siege, the city capitulated in 1326 to Orhan, Osman's son, and the **Ottomans** ceased to be a wandering tribe of marauders. Orhan marked the acquisition of a capital and the organization of an infant state by styling himself sultan, giving the city its present name and striking coinage. Bursa began to enjoy a second golden age: the silk industry was expanded and the city, now outgrowing the confines of the citadel, beautified and graced with monuments.

In the years following Orhan's death in 1362 the imperial capital was gradually moved to Edirne, a more appropriate base for the reduction of Constantinople, but Bursa's place in history, and in the hearts of the Ottomans, was ensured; succeeding sultans continued to add buildings, and to be laid to rest here, for another hundred years. Disastrous fires and earthquakes in the mid-nineteenth century, and the 1920–22 war of independence, only slightly diminished the city's splendour.

Arrival, orientation and information

Bursa's position at the foot of the mountain has dictated an elongated layout, with most of the major boulevards running from east to west, changing their names several times as they go. The northernmost artery, the **E23/200 dual carriageway** linking Çanakkale and Ankara, passes beside the **otogar**, where you'll arrive unless you've flown in and taken the airport coach to the centre. The area around the *otogar*, with its perpetual chaos of roundabouts and no concessions whatsoever to pedestrians, is the worst introduction to the city imaginable; don't lose heart. **Fevzi Çakmak Caddesi** is the quickest walking route up to the centre if you're lightly laden.

Most people, however, instantly find a dolmuş just outside the terminal on Kıbrıs Şehitler Caddesi; the cars are prominently marked "**Heykel**", the commonest alias of **Cumhuriyet Alanı**, nominal focal point of the city. Your vehicle will inch along **İnönü Caddesi**, one of the few north–south arteries besides Fevzi Çakmak to tackle the slope, sparing you a one-kilometre-plus walk.

Though Bursa is narrow, with many points of interest bunched together, it's sufficiently long that you'll want to consider public transport to reach the outlying attractions. Of the **city buses**, only the #2/A – connecting Emir Sultan in the east of town with Çekirge to the west – and the #3/A, linking Heykel with the Uludağ *teleferik*, are of much use, and you need to buy tickets for them at designated booths. Especially if you're newly arrived, it's simpler, and well worth the extra $0.50 or so, to avail yourself of Bursa's many **dolmuşes**. If your luggage won't fit in the boot, you'll have to buy a seat for it – at $0.50 each, still a lot cheaper than a private taxi. Useful routes, many starting at Heykel, are indicated where appropriate in "The City", below.

Bursa's main lengthwise thoroughfare begins life just east of Heykel as **Namazgah Caddesi**, becomes **Atatürk Caddesi** west of İnönü Caddesi as it passes through the city's central bazaar and hotel district, and changes its name again to **Cemal Nadir Caddesi** right below Hisar, the nucleus of the Byzantine settlement. After being fed more traffic by Cumhuriyet Caddesi, which divides the bazaar, and by the roundabout at the top of Fevzi Çakmak Caddesi, the boulevard metamorphoses into **Altıparmak Caddesi**, and then into **Çekirge Caddesi** as it heads west past the Kültür Parkı. There are, though, numerous delightful secondary streets, noted in the city account, all better suited for walking between Bursa's historical sites.

Bursa's main **tourist information office** (☎0224/220 1848; summer Mon–Fri 8.30am–noon & 1–5.30pm; winter Mon–Fri 8am–noon & 1–5pm) is opposite Orhan Gazi Camii, in a row of shops under the north side of Atatürk Caddesi. The Directorate of Tourism is located at Fevzi Çakmak Cad 75 (☎0224/223 8308; Mon–Fri 9am–5pm); they can give out maps and brochures, but for more detailed information will direct you to the central office.

Accommodation

There are generally enough reasonably priced **hotel** beds to go around in Bursa, even during the July festival season, thanks to the mentality that sees the city primarily as a day trip from İstanbul. Rich foreigners, particularly Arabs, gravitate toward the luxury spa hotels at Çekirge, but there is also a cluster of modest, acceptable establishments out here, around the Birinci Murat Camii. If you're interested in monumental Bursa, then midtown accommodation, preferably above (south of) Atatürk Caddesi, makes more sense. Hotels around the *otogar* are mostly pretty grim, and only a few are listed here for the benefit of late arrivals. Incidentally, Bursa's **youth hostel** is now permanently closed, whatever you may read in *IYHF* handbooks.

Near Atatürk Caddesi and Tophane

Hotel Bilgiç, Ressam Şefik Bursalı Cad 30 (☎0224/220 3190). Clean, quiet rooms with little character, but friendly owners; on a quiet street, with good views from the upper floors. ③.

Hotel Çeşmeli, Gümüşçeken Cad 6 (☎0224/224 1511). Immaculate hotel with fridges and TVs in the rooms, run by women; buffet breakfasts offered. ③.

Hotel Dikmen, Maksem Cad 78 (☎0224/224 1840, fax 224 1844). Slightly impersonal two-star, with a garden courtyard where breakfast is served. Some rooms have TVs, minibars and balconies, all have pleasant bathrooms; bargaining possible for the less luxurious rooms. ⑤.

Hotel İpekçi, Çancılar Cad 38 (☎0224/221 1935). In the fascinating bazaar area west of İnönü Cad, with bright, airy and surprisingly quiet rooms. ①.

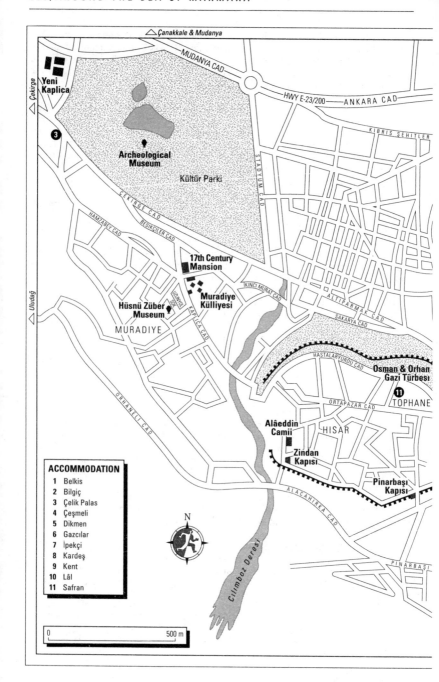

△ Çanakkale & Mudanya

MUDANYA CAD

HWY E-23/200 — ANKARA CAD

KIBRIS ŞEHITLER

△ Çekirge

Yeni Kaplıca

❸

Archeological Museum

Kültür Parki

STADIUM CAD

ÇEKIRGE CAD

HAMZABEY CAD

BEŞIKÇILER CAD

UZUNYOL

KAPLICA CAD

17th Century Mansion

İKINCI MURAT CAD

ALTIPARMAK CAD

SAKARYA CAD

Muradiye Külliyesi

Hüsnü Züber Museum

MURADIYE

△ Uludağ

ORHANELI CAD

HASTALARYURDU CAD

Osman & Orhan Gazi Türbesi

❶❶

TOPHANE

ORTAPAZAR CAD

Alâeddin Camii

HISAR

Zindan Kapısı

Pınarbaşı Kapısı

ALACAHIRKA CAD

PINARBAŞI

N

Cılımboz Deresi

ACCOMMODATION

1 Belkis
2 Bilgiç
3 Çelik Palas
4 Çeşmeli
5 Dikmen
6 Gazcılar
7 İpekçi
8 Kardeş
9 Kent
10 Lâl
11 Safran

0   500 m

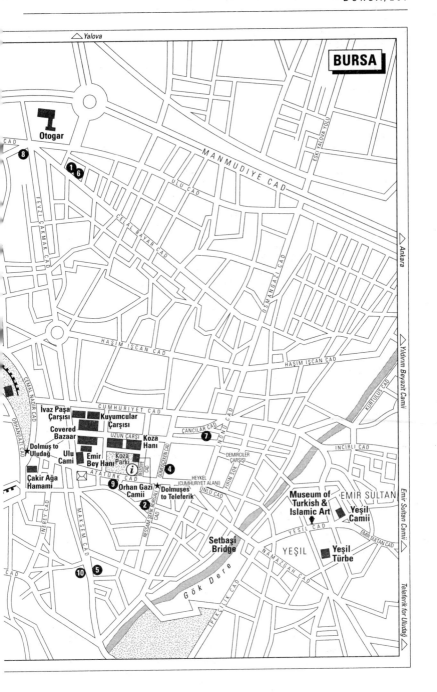

Kent Hotel, Atatürk Cad 119 (☎0224/223 5422, fax 224 4015). Being the most prominent hotel in the town centre, the front rooms suffer badly from traffic noise, but it's three-star comfortable, with satellite TV, fridges and minibars. ⑥.

Lâl Hotel, Maksem Cad 79 (☎0224/221 1710). Old tumbledown building with clean, waterless rooms, acceptable if you choose one at the far end of the corridor away from the smelly toilets. ①.

Safran Hotel, Ortapazar Cad, Arka Sok 4, Tophane (☎0224/224 7216, fax 224 7219). Beautifully restored wooden house, in an atmospheric part of the old town. Rooms are modern, with TVs and minibars. ④.

Çekirge

Atlas Termal, Hamamlar Cad 35 (☎0224/234 4100). A brand new hotel with comfortable rooms, excellent bathrooms, a garden courtyard and terrace, and good service. The decor is mock Art Nouveau including stained glass windows and a glass lift, and downstairs there are two shiny new marble hamams. Excellent value, but it's bound to go up in price. ④.

Boyugüzel Termal Hotel, opposite the military hospital on Birinci Murat Cad (☎0224/233 3850, fax 233 9999). Rooms – with or without bathrooms – are much plainer than in the smarter hotels in this area, but adequately comfortable, and the hotel has its own hamam downstairs. ②–③.

Hotel Çelik Palas, Çekirge Cad (☎0224/233 3800). A refined, elegant hotel, which still retains some of its turn-of-the century chandeliers and other trimmings, but rooms are ultra-modern with air con, cable TV and hot spring water in the bathtubs. The Turkish bath is the hotel's major selling point, with top-to-toe marble and a magnificent domed ceiling. ⑧.

Hotel Dilmen, Birinci Murat Cad 20 (☎0224/233 9500, fax 233 2568). Four-star with sauna, Turkish bath, rooftop terrace and all the en-suite comforts you might expect at this price. ⑨.

Hotel Eren, Birinci Murat Camii Aralığı 2 (☎0224/220 7105). Boring decor but rooms with bathrooms, and a hamam downstairs. ③.

Hakki Paşa, Birinci Murat Cad 14, in front of the old mosque (☎0224/234 2406). Very rundown and rooms have no showers (you're expected to use the hamam downstairs), but the hotel is in a great location, with views across the city. ②.

Konak Palas Oteli, Birinci Murat Camii Arkası 11 (☎0224/236 5113). Simple rooms but clean and quiet, with a good clean hamam downstairs. ②.

Yıldız Hotel, Birinci Murat Cad (☎0224/233 9610, fax 233 9615). Above the four-star *Dilmen*, but on the other side of the road, so no views. The level of comfort, with fridges and a marble hamam in the basement, is comparable to the more expensive luxury establishments, and it's friendlier. ⑦.

Near the otogar

Hotel Belkis, Celal Bayar Cad 168 (☎0224/254 8322). Plain but relatively quiet. ②.

Gazcılar Oteli, Celal Bayar Cad 156 (☎0224/251 8118). Comfortable hotel, where the management are open to bargaining; higher prices for en-suite bathrooms. ②–③.

Hotel Kardeş, southwest of the *otogar*, on the corner of Fevzi Çakmak and Kıbrıs Şehitler *caddesi*s. The decor's unexciting, but if you need to stay near the *otogar*, this is the most comfortable in the area, with very clean rooms.

Camping

The best **campsite** in the region is *Caravan Camping*, 5km out of town on the Yalova road – get off the Yalova dolmuş at the BP garage, and walk back in the Bursa direction, crossing to the road that runs parallel to the main road.

The City

There's little point in touring Bursa's monuments in strictly chronological order, though not surprisingly many of the oldest ones are clustered just outside Hisar, in today's city centre. The points grouped under each heading can be visited in a leisurely morning or afternoon, adding up to two full days if you want to see everything comfortably. If you can't spare this much time, you could just manage to see the most spectacular monuments around the Koza Parkı and at Yeşil in a few rushed hours.

Central sites

Just across from the main tourist information office stands the **Orhan Gazi Camii**, whose 1336 foundation makes it the second oldest mosque in Bursa. Originally built as a *zaviye* for itinerant dervishes, this is the earliest example of the T-form mosque with *eyvan*s flanking the main prayer hall. Unfortunately it's been clumsily restored at least four times in as many centuries, and is now mostly of use as a landmark. **Karagöz puppets**, the painted camel-leather props used in the Turkish national shadow play, are supposed to represent workers who were involved in building the Orhan Gazi Camii. According to legend, the antics of Karagöz and his sidekick Hacıvat so entertained their fellow workmen that Orhan had them beheaded to end the distraction. Later, missing the comedians and repenting of his deed, he arranged to immortalize the pair in the art form which now bears the name of Karagöz.

Just west of Orhan Gazi, the compact **Koza Parkı**, with its fountains, benches, strolling crowds and street-level cafés, is the real heart of Bursa – never mind what they say about Heykel. Though animated through the day and early evening, the plaza empties soon after, with the illuminated fountains dark and still, and the walkways deserted by 11pm. On the far side of the Koza Parkı looms the tawny limestone **Ulu Cami**, built between 1396 and 1399 by Yıldırım Beyazit I, from the proceeds of booty won from the Crusaders at Macedonian Nicopolis. Before the battle Yıldırım (Thunderbolt) had vowed to construct twenty mosques if victorious. The present building of twenty domes supported by twelve freestanding pillars was his rather loose interpretation of this promise, but it was still the largest and most ambitious Ottoman mosque of its time. The interior is dominated by a huge *şadırvan* pool in the centre, whose skylight was once open to the elements, and an intricate walnut *mimber* pieced together, it's claimed, without nails or glue. Less convincing is the tradition stating that the main north portal was remodelled by Tamerlane when he occupied Bursa in 1402–3.

From the north porch you can descend stairs to the two-storeyed **Emir (Bey) Hanı**, originally a dependency of the Orhan Gazi Camii and now home to various offices and shops. A fountain plays under the trees in the courtyard, but with no teahouse or public seating it's not a place to linger. Beyond the Emir Hanı begins Bursa's **covered market**: assorted galleries and lesser *han*s jumbled together in a cartographer's nightmare – but a delight for shoppers hunting for ready-to-wear clothing, silk goods ranging from scarves to jump suits, towels, bolts of cloth, and furniture, all Bursa province specialities. The whole area was devastated by fire in 1955, though, and despite careful restoration both form and function are a bit bogus. There's more genuine continuity in the nearby **Bedesten**, another Yıldırım Beyazit foundation, today as ever given over to the sale and warehousing of jewellery and precious metals.

The centrepiece of the bazaar has to be the **Koza Hanı** or "Silk-Cocoon Hall", flanking the park close to the Orhan Gazi Camii. Built in 1451 on two levels like the Emir Hanı, it's far grander, and still entirely occupied by silk and brocade merchants. In the middle of the cobbled courtyard, under the plane trees, a minuscule **mescit** (small mosque) perches directly over its *şadırvan*, while a U-shaped subsidiary court bulges asymmetrically to the east; there are teahouses and public benches to pause at.

Highlight of the year is the **cocoon auction** of late June and early July, when silk-breeders from around the province gather to hawk their valuable produce. Then the *han* becomes a lake of white torpedoes the size of a songbird's egg; the moth, when it hatches, is a beautiful, otherworldly creature with giant onyx eyes and feathery antennae. You can watch the mêlée from the upper arcades, or, so long as you're careful, the merchants don't mind you walking the floor. After being sent into a tailspin by French and Italian competition 200 years ago, the Bursa silk trade has recently experienced a tentative revival, though the quality of contemporary fabric cannot compare to museum pieces from the early Ottoman heyday, and most of the better designs are made up in imported material, which is still better quality than the Turkish material. If you're buying silk here, make sure the label says *ipek* (silk) and not *ithal ipek* (silky).

Bursa's most central **food market** is in the Nilüfer Koylu Pasajı on Belediye Caddesi. This is the place to stock up for picnics, with an excellent selection of the fruits (strawberries and cherries in spring, peaches and pears in summer), nuts and dairy products for which the region is noted. In the same area, near the *Sezende Restaurant*, handmade lace and other handicrafts are on sale in Hanımelsanatlar Sokak (meaning "the street of women's handicrafts").

Another area of the bazaar that has kept its traditions intact despite quake and blaze is the **Demirciler Çarşısı**, the ironmonger's market. This is just the other side of İnönü Caddesi, best crossed by the pedestrian underpass at Okcular Caddesi. Stall upon stall of blacksmiths and braziers attract photographers, but be advised that some expect a consideration for posing. From here you can easily continue past a small mosque and some cabinet-makers' workshops to **Fırın Sokak**, which is lined with some of the finest old dwellings in town. At the end of this short street a bridge spans the **Gök Dere**, one of two streams that tumble through Bursa, forming an approximate eastern boundary for the centre.

East of the Gök Dere: Yeşil and beyond

However you cross the stream, it's only a few minutes' walk up to **Yeşil**, as the neighbourhood around the namesake mosque and tombs is known. Designed by the architect Hacı Ivaz atop a slight but panoramic rise, the **Yeşil Cami** was begun soon after the civil war caused by the death of Beyazit I ended in 1413, with Çelebi Mehmet I the victor. Despite being unfinished – work ceased in 1424, three years after Mehmet himself died – and catastrophic damage from two nineteenth-century earth tremors, it's easily the most spectacular of Bursa's imperial mosques. The incomplete entrance, faced in a light marble, is all the more easy to examine for the lack of a portico; above the stalactite vaulting and relief calligraphy you can see the supports for arches never built.

Next you'll pass through a foyer supported by pilfered Byzantine columns to reach the **interior**, a variation on the T-plan usually reserved for dervish *zaviye*s. The prayer hall here is flanked by not two but six *eyvan*s, and it's thought that the front pair were used for audiences and councils of state rather than religious purposes. A fine *şadırvan* occupies the centre of the "T", but your eye is monopolized by the hundreds of **polychrome tiles** that line not just the *mihrab* but every available vertical surface up to 5m in height, particularly two recesses flanking the entryway. Green and blue pigments matching the carpets predominate, and praying amid this dimly lit majesty must be something like worshipping inside a leaf. Tucked above the foyer, and usually closed to visitors, is the **imperial loge**, the most extravagantly decorated chamber of all. Several artisans from Tabriz participated in the tiling of Yeşil Cami but the loge is attributed to a certain Al-Majnun, which translates most accurately as "intoxicated on hashish".

On the same knoll as the mosque, and immediately across the pedestrian precinct separating them, the **Yeşil Türbe** (daily 8.30am–noon & 1–5.30pm; free) contains the sarcophagus of not only Çelebi Mehmet I but also assorted offspring. The same Hacı Ivaz is responsible for the octagonal structure, though the outside is no longer green but blue with inferior replacement tiles applied after 1855; inside, however, the walls and Mehmet's tomb glisten with the glorious original Tabriz material.

Regrettably, the immediate environs of the two monuments swarm with tour groups and are twee in the extreme: the café nearby overcharges mercilessly for the view, and a clutch of converted, vehemently repainted old houses are glutted with souvenir dross. There's not a genuine antique-seller to be found, with the possible exception of one eccentric old man next to the *medrese* (theology academy), the largest surviving dependency of the mosque. A hundred metres from the summit, this now houses Bursa's **Museum of Turkish and Islamic Art** (daily except Mon 8.30am–noon & 1–5.15pm; $1). It's not a bad ethnographic collection, though some find the courtyard with its fountain, trees and picnic tables equally interesting. If the museum is short-staffed, certain rooms may be closed, but in theory you can view İznik ware, Çanakkale ceramics, kitchen utensils, inlaid wooden articles, weapons, glass items and the inevitable mock-up of an Ottoman *sünnet odası* or circumcision chamber. The exhibition of hamam para-phernalia has a local relevance because of the history of bathing in the area, which is probably why Bursa towelling has developed world prominence. In the nineteenth cen-tury however, in place of towels, beautifully embroidered linen cloths were used as wraps. Other signs of wealth would have been silver bathbowls, bone or tortoiseshell combs, and clogs inlaid with mother-of-pearl, all of which are on display here.

A 300-metre walk east of Yeşil leads to the **Emir Sultan Camii**, lost in extensive graveyards where every religious Bursan hopes to be buried. The mosque was origi-nally endowed by a Bokharan dervish and trusted adviser to three sultans, beginning with Beyazit I, but it has just been restored again after enduring an Ottoman Baroque overhaul early last century, so you can only guess what's left of the original essence. The pious, however, seem to harbour no doubts, coming in strength to worship at the tombs of the saint and his family.

If you're short of time Emir Sultan Camii is the obvious site to omit: climb down steps through the graveyard instead and cross the urban lowlands to the **Yıldırım Beyazit Camii**, perched on a small hillock at the northeast edge of the city. If you're coming directly from downtown, this is a substantial hike, so you might want to take a dolmuş marked "Heykel–Beyazit Yıldırım", or the more common "Heykel–Fakülte", which passes 200m below the mosque.

Completed by Beyazit I between 1390 and 1395, the Beyazit Camii is essentially the prototype for the Yeşil Cami, with little difference in the exterior marble used or in the modified-T floor plan. Here there's a handsome, five-arched portico defined by square columns. The **interior** is unremarkable except for a gravity-defying arch bisecting the prayer hall, its lower supports apparently tapering away to end in stalactite moulding. The only other note of whimsy in this spare building are the elaborate niches out on the porch.

The associated **medrese**, exceptionally long and narrow because of its sloping site, huddles just downhill; today it's used as a medical clinic. The **türbe** of the luckless Beyazit, kept in an iron cage by the rampaging Tamerlane until his death in 1403, is usu-ally locked; perhaps the mosque custodians fear a revival of the Ottoman inclination to abuse the tomb of the most ignominiously defeated sultan.

The Hisar

The **Hisar**, Bursa's original nucleus, nowadays retains just a few clusters of dilapidated Ottoman housing within its warren of narrow lanes, and some courses of medieval wall along its perimeter. Atop the ramparts, the city planners have scattered ribbons of park interspersed with tea gardens – excellent vantage points over the lower town.

From where Atatürk Caddesi becomes Cemal Nadir Caddesi in a whirl of traffic, you can climb up to the Hisar plateau via pedestrian ramps negotiating the **ancient walls**, or, less enticingly, walk along Orhangazi Caddesi, home to a rather contrived artists' colony. Where Orhangazi stops climbing, the **türbes of Osman and Orhan Gazi** stand side by side at the edge of the fortified acropolis that they conquered, on the site of a Byzantine church which has long since disappeared except for some **mosaic traces** near Orhan's sarcophagus. Unfortunately the superstructures are post-earth-quake restorations in gaudy late-Ottoman style.

Far better is the view from the cliff-top **park** sprawling around the tombs and clock-tower, with reasonable cafés at the head of the walkways down to Cemal Nadir and Altıparmak *caddesi*s. Most of the city's posher shops and cinemas line Altıparmak, but for now it's preferable to back away from the brink and explore Hisar itself, where the wreckers took a heavy toll of the vernacular houses before preservation orders went into effect.

You must choose whether to follow signs west to Muradiye along the most direct route, or to veer inland on a random walk around the neighbourhood. At the southernmost extreme of the citadel you'd exit at the **Pınarbaşı Kapısı**, lowest point in the circuit of walls and the spot where Orhan's forces finally entered the city in 1326. From there you can stroll parallel to the walls, re-entering at the **Zindan Kapısı**, inside of which is the **Alâeddin Camii**, erected within a decade of the conquest and so the earliest mosque in Bursa. It's a simple box surmounted by a single dome, the norm for Ottoman mosques before the advent of the T-plan *zaviye*.

A more straightforward route follows Hasta Yurdu Caddesi, the continuation of Yiğitler, until another generous swathe of **park** studded with teahouses opens out opposite the public hospital. The furthest teahouses have fine views of the Muradiye district, and from the final café and course of wall, obvious stairs descend to the **Cılımboz Deresi**, the second major stream to furrow the city.

Muradiye

Across the stream lies medieval **Muradiye**, where Bursa's best-preserved dwellings line streets at their liveliest during the Tuesday **street market**. If you're coming directly from the centre, take one of the frequent dolmuşes marked "Muradiye".

The **Muradiye Külliyesi** is easy enough to find, following the district's high street past two simple lunchtime restaurants. If you were disappointed by the circus at Yeşil, this is the place to more accurately capture the early Ottoman spirit; while trinket sellers and an antique shop do show the flag, there's no pressure to buy and no coachloads to shatter the calm. The complex, begun in 1424 by Murat II, was the last imperial foundation in Bursa, though the tombs for which Muradiye is famous were added piecemeal over the next century or so. The sultan's **mosque** is similar to the Orhan Gazi Camii in ground plan and so does not represent any advance of imagination, but the profuse **tiles** low on the walls, spare calligraphy up high and double dome above are satisfying. The nearby **medrese** is now a clinic, like the one at Yıldırım Beyazit.

The ten **royal tombs** (summer daily 8.30am–noon & 1–5.30pm; winter daily 8am–5pm) are set in lovingly tended gardens, and open on a rota basis; to get into the locked ones you must find the gardener-*bekçi* with the keys – no tip is expected for the service. The first tomb encountered is that of **Şehzade Ahmet** and his brother Şehinşah, both murdered in 1513 by their cousin Selim I to preclude any succession disputes. The luxury of the İznik tiles within contrasts sharply with the adjacent austerity of **Murat II's tomb**, where Roman columns inside and a wooden awning out front are the only superfluities. Murat, as much contemplative mystic as warrior-sultan, was the only Ottoman ruler ever to abdicate voluntarily, though pressures of state forced him to leave the company of his dervishes and return to the throne after just two years. He was the last sultan to be interred at Bursa, and one of the few lying here who died in his bed; in accordance with his wishes, both the coffin and the dome were originally open to the sky "so that the rain of heaven might wash my face like any pauper's".

Next along is the *türbe* of **Şehzade Mustafa**, Süleyman the Magnificent's unjustly murdered heir; perhaps a sign of his father's remorse, the tomb is done up in extravagantly floral İznik tiles, with a top border of calligraphy. Nearby stands the tomb of **Cem Sultan**, his brother Mustafa and two of Beyazit II's sons, decorated with plain green tiles below as in Ahmet's, but a riot of abstract, botanical and calligraphic paint strokes up to the dome. Cem, the cultured and favourite son of Mehmet the Conqueror, was one of the Ottoman Empire's most interesting might-have-beens. Following the death of his father in 1481, he lost a brief dynastic struggle with the successful claimant, brother Beyazit II, and fled abroad. For fourteen years he wandered, seeking sponsorship of his cause from Christian benefactors who in all cases became his jailers: first the Knights of St John at Rhodes and Bodrum, later the papacy. At one point it seemed that he would command a Crusader army organized to re-take İstanbul, but all such plans came to grief for the simple reason that Beyazit anticipated his opponents' moves and each time bribed them handsomely to desist, making Cem a lucrative prisoner indeed. His usefulness as a pawn exhausted, Cem was probably poisoned in Italy by the pope in 1495, leaving nothing but reams of poems aching with nostalgia and homesickness.

The last ornate tomb, that of **Şehzade Mahmut** and his sons, victims respectively of father Beyazit II and uncle Selim I, also sports tiles and badly deteriorated paintings. This, however, and all the much plainer tombs by the southwestern fence are scheduled for restoration and closed to the public.

With such a preponderance of princes suffering unnatural deaths, it's clear that the Ottoman spirit included a broad, dark patch of sanguinary ruthlessness. Successful claimants of the throne who showed reluctance to murder their male relatives would be warned by Koranic scholars that rebellion was worse than fratricide; their rivals could be honoured more safely in death, with magnificent tombs, than in life.

Directly across the street from the *külliye* is a restored **seventeenth-century mansion,** though at the time of writing it's closed for restoration. The best room is the upstairs corner one, with carved and painted wood ceilings and cupboards, though the liberal use of foam-rubber cushions instead of authentic furniture is disconcerting.

More compelling is the **Hüsnü Züber House**, a minute's walk from the Muradiye Külliyesi at Uzunyol Sok 3, Kaplıca Cad (Tues–Sun 10am–5pm; $1). This former Ottoman guest house, built in 1836, sports a typical overhanging upper storey, wooden roof and beams, and a garden courtyard. It now houses a collection of wood carving: musical instruments, spoons and farming utensils, many of which were carved by Hüsnü Züber himself, the present owner who inhabits the house still. The main exhibit, however, is the house itself, one of the few of its era to have been well restored and opened to the public. The large room upstairs with its carved ceilings was originally open on one side like a massive balcony and must have been a wonderful place to sit and contemplate the fine view. There's also a room devoted to the history of the restoration of the house, which was completed in 1992.

The Kültür Parkı

From Muradiye it's just a short walk down to Çekirge Caddesi and the southeast gate of the **Kültür Parkı** (token admission charge when entry booths are staffed). Inside there's a popular tea garden, a small boating lake, a disgraceful mini-zoo that ought to be either upgraded or disbanded, and a number of restaurants and nightclubs. As you stroll, however, it soon becomes obvious, as in similar parks in İzmir and Ankara, that there's no potential for solitude – though courting couples try their best – and no wild spots among the regimented plantations and too-broad driveways: something that speaks volumes about Turkish attitudes towards public life, conformity and authority.

At the west end of the park, just below Çekirge Caddesi, is the **open-air theatre** with its hoardings (see "Entertainment and nightlife", p.216), and next to it the **archeological museum** (daily except Mon 8.30am–noon & 1–5.30pm; $1). Inside the museum, exhibits in the right-hand Stone Room vary from the macabre (a Byzantine ossuary with a skull peeking out) to the homely (a Roman cavalryman figurine), but the adjacent hall featuring **metal jewellery** from all over Anatolia – watch chains, breast plates, belts, buckles, bracelets, anklets, chokers – steals the show. The left wing houses a modest coin gallery and miscellaneous small ancient objects, the best of which are the **Roman glass** items and **Byzantine and Roman bronzes**. Oil lamps, pottery, a token amount of gold and far too many ceramic figurines complete these poorly labelled exhibits; the sparseness of the collections is a shame, since the halls are well lit and could accommodate better finds. A predictable garden of sarcophagi, stelae and other statuary fragments surrounds the building.

Çekirge

Most of the "Realm of the Cicada", as Çekirge translates, is too remote to reach on foot except by the keenest walkers; luckily dolmuşes (marked "Çekirge") as well as city buses shuttle often in either direction.

The **Yeni Kaplıca** ("New Baths"; daily 6am–10pm; $2, full works $5) are just beyond the Kültür Parkı, accessible by a steep driveway beginning opposite the luxury *Çelik Palas Oteli*. There's actually a clutch of three facilities here: the **Kaynarca baths**, for women only, which is really rather grim and unappealing; the **Karamustafa spa**, for men only; and the Yeni Kaplıca, dating in its present form from the mid-sixteenth century, which has a women's section, but nothing like as splendid as the men's. According to legend, Süleyman the Magnificent was cured of gout after a dip in the Byzantine baths here and had his vizier Rüstem Paşa overhaul the building.

The results are not obvious in the unpromising changing rooms and *soğukluk* (cool room) of the men's section, but the main chamber boasts, instead of the usual *göbek taşı*, a vast **pool** of drowning depth – a sign warns non-swimmers not to enter. Fragments of mosaic paving stud the floor, and the walls are lined with once-exquisite but now blurred **İznik tiles**.

The multiple cupolas of the **Eski Kaplıca** (Old Baths), huddled at the far end of Çekirge Caddesi next to the *Termal Kervansaray Oteli*, are indeed Bursa's most ancient, though recently well restored. Byzantine rulers Justinian and Theodora improved a Roman spa on the site, and Murat I in turn had a go at the structure in the late fourteenth century.

The baths, with both men's and women's sections open from 7am to 10.30pm daily, are more interesting architecturally than the Yeni Kaplıca – this is much the nicest public bath for women – and also much more expensive ($5 basic admission, $4.50 extra for a massage). As at the Yeni, huge but shallow keyhole-shaped **pools** dominate the *hararetler* or hot rooms of the men's and women's sections, whose domes are supported by eight Byzantine columns. Scalding (113°F) water pours into the notch of the keyhole, the temperature still so taxing in the main basin that you'll soon be gasping out in the cool room, seeking relief from the fountain in the middle. Some of the natural springs on the mountainside in fact run as high as 160°F – and as low as 45°F. Afterwards, the bar in the men's *camekân*, where you recuperate swaddled in towels on a chaise longue, serves alcoholic beverages should you wish to pass out completely. Alternatively, head for the swimming pool of the *Kervansaray Hotel* (daily 8am–11pm; $5), where you swim indoors and then under a partition to their heated outdoor section.

On a hillock just west of the thermal centre stands the **Hüdavendigâr (Birinci) Murat Camii**, which with its five-arched portico and alternating bands of brick and stone seems more like a church teleported from Ravenna or Macedonia. Indeed tradition asserts that the architect and builders were Christians, who dallied twenty years at the task because Murat I, whose pompous epithet literally means "Creator of the Universe", was continually off at war and unable to supervise the work. The interior plan, consisting of a first-floor *medrese* above a highly modified, T-type *zaviye* at ground level, is unique in Islam. Unfortunately the upper storey, wrapped around the courtyard that's the heart of the place, is rarely open for visits.

Murat himself lies in the much-modified **türbe** across the street, complete apart from his entrails, which were removed by the embalmers before the body began its long journey back from Serbia in 1389. In June of that year Murat was in the process of winning his greatest triumph over the Serbian king Lazarus and his allies at the **Battle of Kosovo**, in the former Yugoslavia, when he was stabbed to death in his tent by Miloš Obilič, a Serbian noble who had feigned desertion. Murat's son Beyazit, later better known as Yıldırım, immediately had his brother Yakub strangled and, once in single command, decimated the Christian armies. Beyazit's acts had two far-reaching consequences: the Balkans remained under Ottoman control until early this century, and a gruesome precedent of blood-letting was set for most subsequent Ottoman coronations.

Eating and drinking

Bursa's cuisine is solidly meat-oriented, dished out in an alcohol-free environment. The most famous local recipes are *İskender kebap*, named after its supposed inventor, İskender (Alexander) Usta, a Bursan chef, and essentially *döner kebap* soaked in a rich butter, tomato and yoghurt sauce; and *İnegöl köftesi*, rich little pellets of mince often made even more so by being laced with cheese (*kaşarlı köfte*). If you're hungry, ask for "*bir buçuk porsiyon*" as a single portion of these recipes is not a meal. You can get also fish and *soğuk meze* if you're in the mood to splurge, and the city is famous for its chestnut-based sweets. If you're sick of Turkish white bread there are a lot of *kepekli* (whole bran) loaves about – ask at promising-looking bakeries. If you want alcohol with your evening meal, head for Sakarya Caddesi, between Altıparmak and Hastalaryurdu *caddesi*s, near the clocktower, or the Kultur Parkı, where you can dine in a peaceful environment and maybe take in a club later. A pedestrianized street of restored houses, the accent here is on fish, and most places have outdoor seating during summer. In one or two establishments, food takes second place to raki and beer consumption.

Kebapcıs and köfte salons

Adanur Hacibey, Unlu Cad, Yılmaz Işhanı Girişi, Heykel. Large impersonal dining room but great service and excellent *İskender*, much cheaper than its namesake described below.

Çiçek İzgara, Belediye Cad 5, upper floor, behind the town hall. Flawless service despite its popularity, tablecloth elegance and extremely reasonable prices – in short, the best midtown value for lunch and dinner. Emphasis on *İnegöl* variations.

Hacibey İskender, Taşkapı Sok 4, off Atatürk Cad (opposite the *Belediye* building). The original, famous *İskender* salon, not to be confused with the one at Heykel. It's a tiny, two-storey establishment where decor is old wood and fake Ottoman tiles – very quaint, and the *İskender* is excellent, but you pay for the ambience.

Kebapcı İskender, Unlu Cad 7, Heykel. Claims to be the place where the namesake dish was invented – and that's all they serve, not even salads. Open lunchtime only, and always crowded to feed-trough density, even though it's moderately expensive.

Konyalı Lokantası, in the central courtyard of Koza Hanı. With its tree-canopied setting, the most atmospheric of a dozen *pide* ovens, tea booths, *büfe*s and tiny restaurants scattered throughout the bazaar. Excellent *saç kavurma* (lamb in onion and tomato sauce made and served in a Turkish wok), which locals mop up with bread. Lunch only.

Üç Köfte, İvaz Paşa Çarşısı 3, to the north of the covered bazaar. The name means "three meatballs", which is what you get, served up three times over for a portion so the food on your plate is always piping hot.

Traditional Turkish and international restaurants

Daruzzifaye, İkinci Murat Cad 36. This new establishment is located in the former *medrese* of the Muradiye Cami, now lovingly restored and elegantly furnished; fittingly, they concentrate on Ottoman traditional cuisine.

Konyalı Mutfağı, Altıparmak Cad. A shiny-clean three-storey restaurant serving an excellent selection of *meze*s and kebabs, including all sorts of stuffed veg and baked lamb, followed by baked rice pudding.

Mercan Restaurant, *Kervansaray Hotel*, Çekirge Meydanı. A rooftop restaurant with great views and an outdoor section. International treats include smoked salmon, Chateaubriand and extravagant sweets such as pineapple flambé. Expect a bill in the region of $25–30 for two, with wine.

Safran Restaurant, Ortapazar Cad, Arka Sok 4. Chic little restaurant in a renovated Ottoman mansion. The menu includes cold and hot *mezes*, meat and mushroom stews, good salads, and sweets such as the heavenly *kaymaklı ayva tatlısı* (quince with clotted cream).

Sezende Restaurant, Hamamlar Cad 37, off Belediye Cad. Restored Ottoman house in the bazaar area serving a wide selection of dishes from soup and *pide* to *izgara*.

Yusuf Restaurant, Kultur Parkı. One of many licensed establishments in the park, where two can eat *mezes* and kebabs, with a bottle of wine, for around $15. The *Yusuf* has a large peaceful garden, and a relaxed atmosphere.

Fish

Arap Sükrü, Kuruçeşme Mah, Sakarya Cad 6 and 29. Fish in all shapes and sizes with beer, wine or raki to wash it down. Reasonable prices with set meal deals available.

Canlı Balık, Yeni Balık Pazarı 14, about 200m below *Çiçek İzgara* in the fish market. Licensed and reasonable; can close for spring cleaning during the May spawning season.

Snacks, desserts and sweets

Bahar Muhallebecisi, Altıparmak Cad 64. One of the best places in town for *dondurma*.

Hünkar Kebab Salonu, Yeşil Cami Yanı 17–19. Great pastries in the basement next to Yeşil Cami, with views across the city from the valley-side windows.

La Perla, Maksem Cad 73. A restored old house with seating on three levels. Snacks, puddings and soft drinks served amid magenta decor.

Öz Akay, Pars Çıkmazı, off Atatürk Cad. Nothing but *mantı* and *çiğ börek* (once-cooked, rather than twice-cooked ingredients) served noontime and evening.

Drinking and hubble-bubbles

Barantico, Kuruçeşme Mah, Sakarya Cad 55. "Mixology and gastronomy" for Bursa's fashionable youth in this trendy bar. Cocktails are their speciality, and they serve snacks.

Teahouse, opposite the junction of İnebey and Atatürk *caddesi*s. This is a good place to try a *nargile* (hubble-bubble pipe) in an easy-going environment; see p.52 for an introduction to *nargiles*.

Tino Bar, at the Setbaşı bridge over the Gök Dere, where Atatürk Cad becomes Namazgah Cad. Reasonably priced to attract a student crowd. The outdoor terrace looks over the creek to the next bridge down; indoor seating too. Open noon–midnight.

Entertainment and nightlife

For a city of its size Bursa has relatively few nocturnal or weekend events; the student contingent is probably responsible for the concerts that do occur. Keep an eye peeled for hoardings at the tourist information office, art galleries and shop windows around the Koza Parkı. The most common **venues** are, in summer the **open-air theatre** in the Kültür Parkı, behind the archeological museum, and in winter the **Vefik Paşa Theatre** up at Heykel. Rather touristy musical performances and folkloric presentations form a big part of the annual **festival** in the last three weeks of July.

Bongo Bar, Clup Altınceylan, Kültür Parkı. Fashion-conscious Euro-style nightclub.

Club S, İpekiş entrance, Kültür Parkı. Bar and disco, with live music most Fri and Sat nights.

Listings

Airlines *Han Air*, Çekirge Cad, İş Merkezi İntam 101, first floor (☎0224/236 8934), twice weekly to Antalya; *Sönmez Airlines*, in the airport (☎0224/246 5445 or 247 7715), and from *Ottomantur*, Cemal Nadır Cad, Kızılay Pasajı, Çakırhamamı district (☎0224/221 1167), with daily flights to İstanbul. The following don't fly from Bursa, but have offices here: *THY*, Haşim İşhan Cad, Tuğtaş İşhanı 73 (☎0224/221 1167); and *Onur Air*, Çekirge Cad 2 (☎0224/224 6361).

Airport bus Departs 45min before flight time from in front of the *Ottomantur* offices (see above).

Books Good stock of English-language books including Penguins at the *Haşet Kitabevi,* Altıparmak Cad 48–50.

Car rental The big international chain outlets are *Avis,* Çekirge Cad 139 (☎0224/236 5133); *Budget,* Çekirge Cad 39/1 (☎0224/222 8322); *Europcar/InterRent,* Çekirge Cad 41 (☎0224/223 2037); and *Hertz,* Çekirge Cad 39 (☎0224/236 3719). Two local independent agencies that offer substantial off-peak discounts are *Can,* Zübeydehanım Cad, İnce Sok 4 (☎0224/235 0571); and *Vezir,* Çekirge Cad 53 (☎0224/233 8079).

Exchange There are plenty of banks, including *Garanti Bankası,* on Atatürk Cad, and exchange offices in the covered bazaar (Mon–Sat 8am–8pm).

Hamams See p.214, or try the central, historic *Çakır Ağa,* located just below Hisar on Cemal Nadir Cad (6am–midnight men and women; $1.75); or *İkinci Murat* next to the Muradiye tomb complex (10am–6pm; Fri & Sun men only, all other days women only; $2).

Hospitals *Devlet* (State) *Hastanesi,* on Hasta Yurdu Cad in Hisar district (☎0224/220 0020); *Üniversite Hastanesi,* P. Tezok Cad, Hastane Sok (☎0224/442 8400); and *Özel Bursa,* on Zübeyde Hanım Cad, Çekirge, with a dental clinic.

Left luggage At the *otogar,* open 24hr.

PTT Main branch at the corner of Atatürk and Maksem *caddesi*s, open daily 24hr for phone service, 8am–9pm for letters.

South of Bursa: Uludağ

Presiding genius of Bursa, the 2543-metre-high **Uludağ** (or "Great Mountain") is a dramatic, often cloud-cloaked massif, its northern palisades dropping dizzyingly into the city. In ancient times it was known as the Olympos of Mysia, one of nearly twenty peaks around the Aegean so named (Olympos was possibly a generic Phoenician or Doric word for "mountain"). Early in the Christian era the range became a refuge for monks and hermits, who were replaced after the Ottoman conquest by Muslim dervishes.

These days the scent of grilling meat has displaced the odour of sanctity, since Bursa natives cram the alpine campsites and picnic grounds to the gills on any holiday or weekend. Uludağ is considered a year-round recreation area, with a dense cluster of unplanned hotels, most with their own **ski lift**, at the 1800m level (a day pass for each lift costs around $7). Skiing is possible from December to March, and you can hire skis and ski clothes at booths in **Oteller**, as the accommodation and skiing area is known.

Much of the dense middle-altitude forest has been designated a national park, with a pitiful few kilometres of marked hiking trails in addition to the above amenities. As so often happens in Turkey, though, the best part of the mountain is outside the park, east of Oteller. A few hours' **walking** will bring you to some glacial **lakes** in a wild, rocky setting just below the highest summit, but don't let the relatively short distances lull you into overconfidence: because of its closeness to the Sea of Marmara, the high ridges trap moist marine air, and whiteouts or violent storms can blow up most months of the year. The best and safest seasons for a visit are May–June, when the wildflowers are blooming, or September–October, when the mist is less dense.

Getting there and accommodation

Getting there is definitely half the fun if you opt for the **teleferik**, which links the Teleferüç borough of Bursa with the Sarıalan picnic grounds at 1635m, where a cluster of *et mangal*s (barbecue grillhouses) and *kendin pişin, kendin ye* (rent-a-barbecue establishments) await your custom. To reach the lower cable car terminus, take a dolmuş labelled "Teleferik" from the corner of Ressam Şefik Bursalı and Atatürk *caddesi*s. The unnervingly wobbly gondolas make the trip up from Teleferüç to Sarıalan every half-hour or so between 8am and 9pm, but are cancelled in high winds; if all goes well the journey takes just under thirty minutes, with a pause part way up at Kadıyayla. Tickets cost $5 each way (half-price Wed); try to avoid mid-afternoon and weekends, when hour-long queues at either end are the norm. From Sarıalan another dolmuş makes the journey to Oteller.

Alternatively you can take a **dolmuş** all the way to Oteller, which winds the 32km of paved road up from Yiğitler Caddesi. The one-way fee is $6 per person, though it can occasionally be difficult to muster the necessary number of passengers (6).

You'd follow the same route in your own vehicle, the road veering off above Çekirge and climbing rapidly through successive vegetation zones and past beckoning *et mangal*s and *kendin pişin, kendin ye*. Staff at the Karabelen **national park** gate, 20km into the park, charge $2.50 per car when they're in the mood, and sometimes have information to hand out. The final stretch of road from just below the gate to the hotels is very rough cobble, designed to prevent drivers from skidding – or speeding, so allow nearly an hour for the trip. In bad weather conditions you will be advised to put chains on your wheels, and may not be allowed to make the journey without them.

There's little to choose between the mostly hideous **hotels** at the road's end, but since the national park **campsites** are far from the better hiking, not to mention squalid and full in summer, you might well consider a room. Out-of-ski-season rates can dip as low as $45 for a double with full board at the *Kar Otel* (☎0224/285 2121), the highest and quietest of them, but will climb to $85 full board in season; similar rates are available at the nearby *Beceren* (☎0224/285 2111, fax 285 2119) or the *Genç Yazıcı* (☎0224/285 2040, fax 285 2045). The latter is not to be confused with the *Grand Yazıcı* (☎0224/285 2050, fax 285 2048; ⑤) the most consistently open in summer, offering B&B.

Walking routes

The closest trailhead to the Karabelen gate is at **Kirazlıyayla**, about halfway along to Oteller; you'll have to look sharp for a little sign, "Patika no. 7, Kirazlıyayla–Sarıalan, 2700m" tacked onto the Uludağ University research facility placard, next to the *Genç Osman* grill. Upon reaching the end of the indicated driveway, you'll set out on what passes for a trail (*patika* in Turkish) in the ravine behind the research building. The path is really just the way originally cleared for the giant power pylons overhead and, now clogged with vegetation, doesn't offer quality hiking. About an hour of up-and-down progress through the trees – more with a full pack – will suffice to bring you to **Sarıalan**.

Once free of the teeming car parks, souvenir stalls and picnic meadows here, a ten-minute process, you should find another placard marked "3 [ie Trail 3], 2565m; 1, 4135m", a few hundred metres to the east. After another half-hour under power lines, take a right fork at the signed "3385m" option. Soon you forsake the high-tension wires for a real trail through stream-creased fir forest, but the idyll is short-lived as you collide with bulldozed driveways just below Oteller, a bit less than three hours from Kirazlıyayla.

You might be better off taking a car or dolmuş directly to the top of the hotel zone, from where a jeep track leads in under ninety minutes to the **tungsten mine** managed by a Turkish bank. An obvious path beginning behind the mine's guardhouse slips up onto the broad but barren watershed ridge, just below the secondary summit of **Zirve** (2496m); follow this trail for a total of ninety minutes to a fork. Right leads to the main peak of **2543**; the cairned left-hand choice is more rewarding, descending slightly to overlook the first of Uludağ's lakes, **Aynalıgöl**, reachable by its own side trail a half-hour beyond the junction.

There are some campsites here but none at **Karagöl**, the second and most famous lake, fifteen minutes southeast of the first one, sunk in a deep chasm and speckled with ice floes. **Kilimligöl**, the third substantial lake, is tucked away on a plateau southeast of Karagöl and offers good high-altitude camping. There are two smaller, nameless tarns, difficult to find in the crags above Aynalıgöl.

Returning to Oteller, as long as the weather is good you can stay with the ridge rather than revisiting the tungsten works, passing below the ruined hut on Zirve to meet a faint trail. This soon vanishes and thereafter it's cross-country downhill along the watershed as far as **Cennetkaya**, a knoll above the hotels, served by a marked trail. High above the trees, crowds and jeep tracks here, you just might strike lucky and glimpse patches of the distant Sea of Marmara to the north.

West of Bursa: the Mysian lakes

The tedious 120-kilometre drive from Bursa to Bandırma is enlivened only by two large but shallow lakes: one supporting a bird sanctuary, the other rarely visited. The latter, **Uluabat (Apollyon) Gölü**, just outside Bursa, is the more rewarding lake for the casual visitor and is somewhat more accessible by public transport, although surprisingly few people make it here. If you're driving yourself, you need to keep an eye out for an inconspicuous sign, "Gölyazı", 38km west of Bursa, which marks the 6-kilometre side road to that village.

GÖLYAZI proves to be an atmospheric community of half-timbered houses, with the odd daub of purple or green paint, built on an island now lashed by a causeway to the shore. Bits of Roman and Byzantine **Apollonia** – the lake's alias – have unconcernedly been pressed into domestic service, and extensive courses of wall ring the island's shoreline; on the mainland you can see a huge, ruined Greek **cathedral**, large enough for a few hundred parishioners.

Appearances would lead you to pronounce Gölyazı the quintessential **fishing village**: there's a lively open-air fish market each morning at the island end of the causeway, nets and rowboats are much in evidence, and the women – who don't appreciate gratuitous snaps being taken of them – patiently mend traps. All this conceals the sad fact that pesticide and fertilizer runoff from the surrounding fields is constantly diminishing the lake catch, and a handful of families now emigrate every year. The lake itself, speckled with islets, is murky and not suitable for swimming.

All in all, Gölyazı is best visited on a day trip from Bursa, if **dolmuş** schedules permit. Otherwise, there's only the *Apollonia Motel*, on the landward side of the causeway, to **stay** at – it's very rough and open only in July and August. More promising is the co-managed **restaurant** of the same name at the extreme north edge of town, where you can sample inexpensive *turna* (lake pike) fresh from a tank. The staff have the key to the motel, or there's a makeshift, mosquito-plagued **campsite** across the road from the outdoor tables. There aren't yet any organized outings around the village, though you can easily arrange for one of the fisher families to take you out in a small boat to some remote ruins on the nearby islets.

Manyas Gölü, to the west, attracts visitors mainly because of the **Kuşcenneti National Park**, a bird sanctuary established in 1938 astride a stream delta and swamps at the northeast corner of the lake. The "Bird Paradise", as the name translates, is a total of 18km south of Bandırma: 13km along the Balıkesir road and then 5km on the signposted side road. There's no public transport along this last stretch.

The park (daily 7am–5.30pm; $0.50) consists mostly of a small **visitor centre** full of dioramas, labelled in Turkish, but with a handy poster giving translations into English, and stocked with stuffed geese, orioles, spoonbills, herons, pelicans, ducks, egrets and owls.

Next you're directed to a wooden **observation tower**, with a pair of binoculars, unfortunately not powerful enough for the job in hand. The most spectacular sightings are of pelicans (white and Dalmatian), spoonbills, spotted eagles and night herons, with cormorants and gray herons commonplace. Hundreds of other species stop by during migration.

Despite the fact that no walkways or boats are provided to get you through or around the delta and out onto open water, the experience is still worthwhile. The best months are alleged to be November – after the first rains and coincident with various migratory species' southward movements – and April–May, when the swamps are at their fullest and the birds are flying north. There are no facilities in the park grounds; the closest are a **pansiyon** and restaurant by the roadside at Eski Sığırcı, 1500m before the gate.

Bandırma, the Kapıdağı peninsula and the Marmara islands

In the western half of the Sea of Marmara lie several inhabited islands and a large land mass that just misses being one. These are well known to Turks – especially İstanbul people – but rarely visited by foreigners. In all honesty they're never going to attract many overseas visitors, not when the south Turkish resorts offer more of intrinsic interest and a longer season, but they make an interesting overnight or two between İstanbul or Bursa and the north Aegean.

Except for parts of Erdek and Avşa island (Avşa Adası), these places exist in a 1970s time warp; the holiday centres have all lost whatever pretences to trendiness they once claimed, bypassed in the stampede to the south that increased affluence, better roads

and more frequent internal flights have made possible. The only foreigners about tend to be expatriates weekending from İstanbul or those brought here by Turkish friends, plus increasing numbers of expatriate Turks returning from Europe for nostalgic visits to childhood haunts. The major settlements are nondescript, with little conscious preservation ethic, but the swimming – and cycling – are fine and the scenery, with the horizon studded with islets, is as close to the Greek archipelagos as you'll see in Turkey.

The islands are accessible by ferry from İstanbul, from Tekirdağ and from Erdek, main town of the Kapıdağı peninsula and just a short bus ride from Bandırma. **BANDIRMA** itself, which was knocked flat during battles in 1922 and is now neighbour to a NATO airbase, is a definite finalist in the ugliest town in Turkey sweepstakes. Given its status as a major transit point you may well have to spend some time here, but all you really need to know is how to get from one transport terminal to another.

The main **otogar** is at the southern outskirts of town, 800m above the **ferry port** and adjoining **train station**; if you don't want to walk up the hill or take a taxi between the two, use the red-and-white city buses labelled "Garaj/600 Evler", which depart from a marquee 200m east of the harbour gate, or a service bus into the town centre. The smaller **garaj** or local bus station, halfway between the *otogar* and the bay on the main thoroughfare, Atatürk Caddesi, is not well marked: look for the *Petrol Ofisi* pump next to the entry driveway; buses to Erdek and Kuşcenetti leave from here. If by some misfortune you're stranded for the night here, the *Eken Hotel* (☎0266/718 0840; ⑤), at Uğur Mumcu Cad 9 off the main square in the centre of town, is very comfortable, while the *Otel Özdil* (☎0266/712 2200; ②), right in front of the shoreline city-bus ranks, is tolerable enough.

Erdek and around

A leafy, cobbled, pedestrianized shore esplanade sets the tone for **ERDEK**, the closest jump-off point for the islands, tucked at the base of the Kapıdağı peninsula. The closest of the islands guards the harbour entrance, and there's another islet further out to sea, with the hills of the "mainland" looming beyond. The rest of town, with its landscaping and patches of park, is pleasant enough, but if you're going to stay any length of time you'll probably prefer to be behind the strip of beach to the northwest.

Practicalities

The **otogar** is by the road in from Bandırma, at the northeast edge of town, but many coaches go all the way down to the water, so ask if you want to be set down there.

Almost everything else of interest stands either along the shore promenade or just behind it – the **tourist information office** (daily 8am–noon & 1–5pm) for example, is on Neyyire Sıtkı Caddesi, opposite the ferry landing, and they have a booth beside the landing stage in summer (daily 8am–7pm). The **PTT** is also on Neyyire Sıtkı near the ferry landing.

If you want to **stay in town** proper, first nose about behind Cumhuriyet Meydanı, the obvious swelling in the shore promenade. The *Ümit Hotel*, on Balıkhanı Sokak (☎0266/835 1092; ①), is the nicest of the cheaper deals in town, and nearer to the tourist information office, the *Emin*, İstiklal Cad 17 (☎0266/835 1213; ①) is also fine, if you don't need en-suite facilities. The *Deniz Palas* (☎0266/835 1008; ①) at Zafer Sok 3 is the most consistently open in winter and two rooms have en-suite bathrooms.

Standards **along the beach north of town**, where there must be at least forty establishments, are a bit higher. Towards the end of the promenade, the *Otel Gül Plaj* (☎0266/835 1053) is a swish option directly on the seafront, but they only offer half-board, at $33 for two people sharing a room. Further along the shorefront, the *Hotel Alevok* (☎0266/835 1116) has a similar ambience, again on the beachfront and the same price for half-board. Both are closed in winter. The best value for money on this stretch, however, is the two-star *Hotel Özgün* (0266/835 4722; ②), a friendly establishment, with small but well-furnished rooms. Top hotel is the luxury four-star *Agrigento* (☎0266/835 4973, fax 835 1399; ⑨), with mock-classical trimmings, large indoor and outdoor pools, comfortable air-conditioned rooms, and a massive fifty percent reduction out of season. The staff are all on work placements from the local catering school, so the service is good. Right at the end of the beach, there's a **campsite**, *Ay Camping.*

For **eating** in the town centre, head for the excellent *Uludağ Pide Salonu*, one block inland from Cumhuriyet Meydanı, or the *Rıhtım* fish restaurant on the seafront promenade.

Touring the peninsula

You'll have already seen some of the **Kapıdağı peninsula** if you approached Erdek from Bandırma, and it's difficult to imagine a less promising preview. Between Erdek and the two-kilometre-wide isthmus that joins the peninsula to the rest of Anatolia, the shore is almost wholly given over to private and military facilities, or to campsites firmly oriented toward automobile or caravan custom. The ruins of ancient Kyzikos are so negligible that the archeological service hasn't even bothered posting the usual sign; the only visible monuments are those of a huge tank farm, unhappily sited opposite some of the few public beaches west of the isthmus.

On the eastern shore, facing Bandırma, things are initially even worse: despite good beaches and a motel or two at Tatlisu and beyond, a huge fertilizer plant on the horizon discourages swimming. **KARŞIYAKA**, a few kilometres further on, has similar amenities and water that looks a bit more inviting. Really the best thing to do here would be to **cycle**: the landscape is green, the grades gentle, the road paved (if potholed) and little travelled. The sole disincentive to a complete loop of the Kapıdaği peninsula is the long, and at times precipitous, dirt stretch between Ballıpınar and İlhan.

Heading the other way (northwest) out of Erdek is in most respects a better bet; from the west coast the 800-metre-high peninsula shows its green profile, tufted with olives, poplars and willows, to full advantage. There are **dolmuş** services from the *otogar* to the villages of Ocaklar, Narlı and Turan. The one-street village of **OCAKLAR** is lost in vegetation 5km north of Erdek. An excellent, partly shaded **beach** extends 1500m to the north, only about half-developed with motels and restaurants, the best of which is the *Çakıl (Pir Ramis'in yeri)*, serving cheap seafood.

NARLI, 4km further on, has more of a village feel with its ruined Greek church in the centre, and an evocative setting on a slope overlooking Paşalimanı Island, but the tiny beach can't compare with Ocaklar's. There's a handful of *pansiyon*s on the outskirts and an equal number of eateries by the jetty where dolmuşes pull up and private boats set off for the island. Beyond Narlı there are a couple more *pansiyon*s and new villas, but nothing overwhelming yet; the short season and the heavy military presence (patrol boats are ubiquitous) have combined to put a damper on commercialization – as have the narrow and rocky beaches between Narlı and **İLHAN**, a rickety fishing port where it's possible to hire boats across to Paşalimanı Island.

The islands

Four of the islands off Erdek are inhabited and can be visited with varying degrees of ease. The largest, Marmara, was a colony of Miletus in ancient times, as were Erdek (Artaki) and Kyzikos on the peninsula. A Greek identity persisted until this century, and the old names are still used by the older generation: Elafonisos for Marmara, Ophioussa for Avşa, Haloni for Paşalimanı. As elsewhere in west Anatolia, the Greeks began leaving the archipelago at the turn of the century, with emigration acquiring a more compulsory character after some were caught cooperating with British submarine captains during World War I. Occasional elderly, forlorn Greeks still return each summer, searching for the houses they were born in, but the islanders claim they rarely find them – too much has changed.

For such a tightly bunched group, the islands are markedly different. Avşa is the most commercialized – some say ruined; its dependency Ekinlik and Paşalimanı are the least spoiled, with Marmara falling somewhere in between. Incidentally, while cars are not expressly forbidden on the islands, neither are they encouraged, making the archipelago relatively quiet by Turkish standards. Finally, if you show up much before June 1 or after September 30, the sea will be cool – and hardly anything open.

It should be stressed that **boat timetables** to the islands are notoriously changeable. Generally, boats from Erdek are not as frequent as from Tekirdağ. At the time of writing, there are two *TML* car ferries in winter **from Erdek** at 3.30pm, one **to Avşa**, the other **to Marmara**, while in summer one daily *TML* car ferry goes to Marmara and Avşa. Smaller boats leave in the morning in summer, but don't operate in winter. The cost on any of these craft is at present $3 per person, $7 per car, to either island. You may be able to hire a fishing boat in Erdek to take you to the island of your choice, at a going rate of $45 – though it should be possible to get this down if you can find someone who is visiting the islands anyway.

From Tekirdağ, at least three competing private companies run car ferries daily in season at 4, 5, and 7pm, to both Marmara and Avşa islands ($3 per person, $7 per car, to Marmara or Avşa one-way). Out of season this drops to three a week, to both Marmara and Avşa, weather permitting. There are also connections on to Erdek, but it would be a shame to make the journey without seeing any of the islands. Four times a week in summer there's also an evening *TML* car ferry from Tekirdağ to both Marmara and Avşa, costing about the same as the private ferries. In winter, this boat is less useful as it only goes to Avşa (still four times a week) and leaves Tekirdağ at 2am.

From İstanbul Karaköy docks, one daily passenger ferry visits Marmara and Avşa in summer ($10 one-way); in winter, this drops to two weekly (☎0212/244 4233 for details). There's also a thrice-weekly passenger ferry **from Şarköy** ($6 one-way) which goes first to Çınarlı on Marmara island, then visits Marmara village, and finally goes to Avşa. It returns to Şarköy on the evening of the same day, visiting the same ports in reverse order.

Paşalimanı is very difficult to access. At the time of writing, there's only an island tour boat, which takes no cars, from Avşa. Otherwise, access is by private craft from Erdek or Narlı, at $45 a head return (if you can find someone who is making the trip anyway, they may take you for less). **Ekinlik** is presently better served, with a *TML* car ferry from Erdek visiting daily in summer, once weekly in winter.

Marmara

Largest of the islands at roughly 17km by 8km, **Marmara** acquired its name during the Middle Ages thanks to the giant marble quarries (*ta marmara* in Greek) that are still worked on the north shore. Marmara is the ancient Proconnesus, from where the famous blue-streaked Proconnesian marble, used for many of the columns of Aya Sofya in İstanbul, originates. Sailing in from the south, you'll see the rocky ridge of 700-metre İlyas Dağı, with a ruined Byzantine tower, plunging down to the west tip of the island. Except for its valley-bottom oases, Marmara is bleak – downright windswept and cliff-girt in the north – so most of its villages huddle on the southern, lee shore.

The ferry will stop first at the pretty but facility-less port of Gündoğdu; don't get off here, but wait to reach the main town. This, simply called **MARMARA**, is backed up against a hill with steep, stepped streets penetrating inland, an enchanting setting from a distance, though seen up close its modern domestic architecture is nothing special. A remaining cluster of old houses at the west end of town, due to be demolished for a *gazino* complex, recently received a stay of execution, courtesy of a new preservation rule.

There's a **PTT** and a **bank** in Marmara. The best places to **stay** are at the far west end of the shore esplanade, facing the sunset. The *Marmara Otel* (☎0266/885 5476; ①) has its own restaurant; quieter and more secluded is the *Şato Motel* (☎0266/885 5003; ③) around the corner, with sea view terraces, en-suite baths, and a good breakfast, but it suffers from noise from the nearby *gazino*s. Handy for early ferries, the friendly *Murat* (☎0266/885 5222; ③) has small rooms with hot water near the passenger jetty. **Restaurants** are fairly unpretentious: the *Bursa* is good and cheap, the *Şato Motel* has a small restaurant serving one or two good dishes a night, and the *Birol*, the first establishment over the footbridge from the car ferry landing, has excellent fish, meat and *meze*s, slightly more expensive than elsewhere on the island but worth it for the waterside location and good service.

Heading off around the island, you'll find a few really good **beaches**. The beach to the northwest of Marmara town is sandy, but you'll have to accustom yourself to the extremely low salinity of the Sea of Marmara, and occasional swarms of disgusting but usually stingless white jellyfish, which plague all the islands from time to time, according to weather conditions. In cooler weather you might entertain thoughts of hiking up through the mostly barren interior, but there are only goat-trails along the ridges, and most of the time you'll be restricted to the skeletal network of dirt roads that almost completely rings the island.

The north side of the island is dominated by marble quarries, the sole attempt to attract tourists being a collection of marble fragments collected together in the Open Air Museum in **Saraylar**. Exhibits include a large, fairly complete but undistinguished Roman soldier, but other than this all is tombs and column bases.

The only other village equipped to handle visitors is **ÇINARLI**, 6km northwest of the main harbour by dirt road; there's no bus service, only taxis and the occasional boat (including some ferries from Tekirdağ and the ferry from Şarköy). Çınarlı is a pretty place, with cottage gardens bursting with flowers and a village green; its 700-metre swathe of sand and pebbles is backed by a scruffy esplanade so it's not particularly private. The *1071 Pide Salonu* on this stretch does a wickedly spicy *kuşbaşi pide* (meaning "bird's head", or tiny pieces of meat). You can try your luck **staying** at the *Gül Pansiyon*, the *Ketenci Pansiyon*, the *Viking Motel* or the *Alp*, behind the calmest and sandiest stretch.

On the road to Çınarlı, **Manastır** is a more private beach, where you can buy beer and light lunches from *Sevim Hanım's Restaurant* situated on a terrace next to the beach. There's no access to Manastır by road but there is a boat service from Marmara village in the early afternoon.

Avşa

Low-lying and partly covered in vineyards, **Avşa** is surrounded by beaches and crystal-clear water that are both its raison d'être and its curse. The somewhat down-at-heel resort of **TÜRKELI** on the west coast is virtually a suburb of İstanbul in season and, unlike on Marmara where most outsiders have a villa, development here has taken the form of more than a hundred *pansiyon*s and hotels. Prime beachfront locations were snapped up 25 years ago, and built on in the spartan style of the time; if you want something more plush you'll usually have to move inland, though that's still no guarantee of much comfort. The sole cultural point of interest is the abandoned **Aya Triada church**, awash somewhere in the concrete sprawl of Türkeli. The **PTT** is located to the north of town on Posthane Caddesi, on the road running uphill parallel to the beach.

The island is awash with **accommodation**, but some names to look out for include the *Ayberk* (☎0266/845 5151; $33 per person for half-board), 3km from Türkeli at the extreme north end of the beach; and the *Uzun* (☎0266/896 1081; ①), five minutes north along the front from the ferry landing, which has rooms with kitchens right on the beach. On the road to the PTT, the excellent, very clean *Berlin Pansiyon* (☎0266/896 4032; ①) is possibly the best value on the island unless you particularly want a beachfront location; they also have family suites of two or three rooms joined together. The *Geçim* (☎0266/896 1493) is a comfortable *pansiyon* off the beachfront esplanade, offering rooms with kitchens and bathrooms on the landing (①), or very modern well-furnished self-catering flats, big enough for four (④).

When **eating out**, be sure to sample the island's excellent **wine**, whether red, rosé or white. *Kavalleros* is the usual brand and stores do a brisk business in souvenir bottles. Atatürk Caddesi to the south of the ferry landing is a street of restaurants, bars and street vendors, particularly lively at evening promenade time. The *Yakamoz* is a good option for reasonably priced fish, while the *Cafe Bar 353* is an old wooden house with a balcony and live music in summer.

If the main town gets too much, remember that the island is only about 7km by 3km, so no point is more than ninety minutes away on foot. A tractor-pulled "train" heads off 8km northeast of Türkeli to **Mavıköy**, which has a good stretch of beach backed by waterfront villas. Alternatively, you could stalk off south past *Motel 78* towards **Manastır Burnu** (Monastery Cape) to find isolated sandy coves. **Çınaraltı** beach, 1km south of Manastır Burnu, is hard to access by road so it's almost deserted, though boat tours to Paşalimanı stop here. The *Tarihi Çınar* **restaurant** near the beach has a large selection of *izgara*, *et sote* (sauteed meat in sauce), cold *mezes* and *köfte*, served in a congenial beachside atmosphere.

Taxis and dolmuşes from Türkeli (next to Hal Çarşısı on Okullar Caddesi) run to **Yiğitler** on the east coast of Avşa, populated almost entirely by settlers from the former Yugoslavia. One kilometre southeast of the village, there's a large sandy beach called **Altınkum** and perched above it the *Şahintepesi* **restaurant** serves fish and meat in a very laid-back atmosphere; staff can give information about cheap **rooms** in Yiğitler.

Ekinlik

A *TML* ferry leaves Erdek daily in summer for **Ekinlik**, also known as Kaşık Adası or "spoon island" because of its shape. Although there are no beaches and consequently no tourism development here, the island has a pretty harbourside village with a ruined church to the left of the jetty and several Greek houses, as well as some more recent Turkish architecture of merit. The harbour is full of fishing boats (refreshingly, no pleasure craft) and is overlooked by a shaded tea garden.

Paşalimanı

Reached in summer by daily tour boat from Avşa, but otherwise difficult to access, and lacking enough beaches to make it the target of development, **Paşalimanı** is a sleepy, friendly place, greener than Marmara and Avşa and distinguished mainly by its giant plane trees. Balıklı village is the "capital", but there's no bank or PTT, so come prepared. Accommodation is likewise very basic – certainly nothing beyond a few *pansiyon*s.

West of Bandırma: the coast road to Çanakkale

Once past Bandırma, the old highway veers sharply south to pass through **GÖNEN**, a cobbled-street market town famous for its thermal baths and the giant *Miş* dairy on its outskirts. However, a new bypass road now runs parallel to the coast to **DENİZKENT**, bang on the Çanakkale–Balıkesir provincial border. It's a strange relic, the first planned holiday village in Turkey, laid out in the 1950s by Ankara civil servants and fulfilling a fantasy of American suburbia of that era. The beach is narrow but very long, with views out to the islands of the Marmara; if you want to **stay** there's a single motel and a separate restaurant.

Subsequently the road heads inland again, crossing the Biga Çayı, formerly the Granicus, at **Biga**, where Alexander the Great won his first victory over the Persians in 334 BC. The local hill villages are populated almost entirely by Pomaks from the Rhodope mountains of the Greek–Bulgarian frontier, who are renowned for the costumes of their women and their skill in weaving goathair mats – though without a prolonged acquaintance you're unlikely to see either.

Beyond Biga you eventually emerge on the southeast flank of the Dardanelles; the drive is pleasant enough, but there's really no place to stop except **LAPSEKİ**, 40km northeast of Çanakkale, and even here, **accommodation** possibilities are exceedingly dire. Neither of the two *pansiyon*s, the *Yılmaz* and the *Mutlu*, are worth recommending, but if you arrive in school holidays, you may be able to get a room at the somewhat institutional but clean *Öğretmenevi* (teacher's lodgings), opposite the ferry landing (☎0286/512 1504). Successor to the Lampsacus of yore, Lapseki still bears a medieval **fortress** designed to act in concert with the one across the water at Gelibolu. Otherwise there's little to it besides the ferry jetty where all long-distance buses halt, looking for disembarking passengers.

travel details

Trains

Bandırma to: İzmir (2 daily; 5hr 30min).

Edirne to: Belgrade (1 daily; 18hr); Bucharest (1 daily; 10hr); Budapest (1 daily; 25hr); İstanbul (2 daily; 5hr 30min); Sofya (1 daily; 10hr).

Buses and dolmuşes

Bandırma to: Balıkesir (hourly; 1hr 45min); Bursa (hourly; 2hr); Çanakkale (hourly; 3hr 30min); İzmir (7 daily; 6hr); Manyas (7 daily; 30min).

Bursa to: Ankara (every 30min; 7hr); Bandırma (hourly; 1hr 30min); Çanakkale (hourly; 6hr); İstanbul, with ferry transfer (hourly; 5hr); İzmir, via Balıkesir and often Ayvalık (every 30min; 7hr); Kütahya (3 daily; 3hr); Mudanya (every 30min; 40min); Yalova (every 30min; 1hr 20min).

Edirne to: Çanakkale (3 direct daily; 4hr 30min); İstanbul (every 30min; 3hr); Keşan (hourly; 2hr); Kapıkule (every 30min; 30min).

Erdek to: Bandırma (every 30min; 25min); Bursa (8 daily; 2hr).

Gelibolu to: Eceabat (hourly; 50min); Kilitbahir (hourly; 1hr).

İznik to: Adapazarı (hourly; 1hr 30min); Bursa (every 30min; 1hr 30min); İstanbul (1 daily; 3hr 30min); Yalova (several daily; 1hr).

Şarköy to: Edirne (1 daily, early morning; 3hr 30min); İstanbul (every 30min; 4hr); Tekirdağ (20 daily; 1hr 30min).

Short-hop ferries

Eceabat to: Çanakkale, car ferry (hourly 6am–midnight; 20min).

Gelibolu to: Lapseki, car ferry (15 daily 6.30am–midnight, hourly after 4pm; 20min).

Karamürsel to: Hereke, passenger ferry (6 daily 6am–7pm; 30min).

Kilitbahir to: Çanakkale, car ferry (according to traffic 6am–9pm; 10min).

Topcular to: Eskihisar/Darica, car ferry (every 30min 6am–midnight, hourly midnight–6am; 20min).

Ferries, catamarans and hydrofoils: island & long-haul

Avşa to: İstanbul (summer 1 daily; winter 2 weekly; 6hr); tour boat to Paşalimanı (1 daily; 30min).

Bandırma to: İstanbul (4 weekly; 4hr 30min).

Erdek *TML* liners to: Avşa (1 daily; 3hr); Ekinlik (summer 1 daily; winter 1 weekly; 2hr 30min); Marmara (1 daily; 2hr 15min).

Kabatepe to: Gökçeada (Imvros) island (June–Oct 1 daily; Nov–May 2 weekly; 1hr 30min).

Marmara to: Avşa (1 daily; 1hr); İstanbul Karaköy docks (summer 1 daily; winter 2 weekly; 5hr).

Mudanya to: İstanbul (2 daily; 1hr 30min–3hr).

Şarköy to: Avşa (3 weekly; 3hr); Marmara (3 weekly; 1hr 30min).

Tekirdağ to: Avşa (summer 3/4 daily; winter 1/2 daily; 3hr 30min); Erdek (2 daily in summer; 5hr 30min); Marmara (summer 3/4 daily; winter 3 weekly; 3hr).

Yalova to: İstanbul-Sirkeci via Princes' Isles, passengers only (3 daily; 2hr 15min); Kabataş (Mon–Fri 3/4 daily; 1hr); direct ferry to Kartal (winter 3 daily, summer 4 daily; 1hr 15min); catamarans to Kartal (every 30min; 35min).

Flights

Bursa to: Antalya with *Han Airlines* (2 weekly; 2hr); İstanbul with *Sönmez Airlines* (Mon–Fri at 9.30am & 6pm; 1hr).

CHAPTER THREE

THE NORTH AEGEAN

urkey's North Aegean coast sees far fewer visitors than the shoreline further south. Although the proportion of sandy beaches to rocky ones is in fact the equal here of better-known resorts, it's the shorter season, lower sea temperature and lack of an international airport that together protect the region from widespread development. Most summer visitors are Turks, and while tourism is inevitably important to the local economy, even in August the number of visitors doesn't match those at the country's internationally renowned destinations. Away from the resort towns, life goes on much as it always did, farming and fishing providing the livelihood of the bulk of the population.

This area, which roughly constitutes ancient **Aeolia**, has been settled since Paleolithic times; civilization bloomed early here under the Phrygians, who arrived in Anatolia during the thirteenth century BC. Later waves of Greek colonists established settlements on the coast, leaving the region rich in Classical and Hellenistic remains. Although the ruins of **Troy** in the north don't quite live up to their literary and legendary reputation, the ancient cities of **Assos** and **Pergamon** display some tangible reminders of the power and wealth of the greater Greek empire. The Lydian city of **Sardis**, the ancient capital of King Croesus (and Midas before him), located a little way east of the lively town of **Manisa**, is also one of Aegean Turkey's most impressive sites.

Coming from İstanbul or anywhere else in northwestern Turkey, **Çanakkale** is the obvious entry point – useful as a base for both the war sites at Gelibolu (Gallipoli; see p.192) and the ruins at Troy. Further south, the best stretches of beach lie near **Ayvalık** – the area's longest-established resort – and along the coastal strip running from **Assos** to **Ören**, on the northern shore of the **Gulf of Edremit**. **Bergama**, the modern town beside ancient Pergamon, presents an alternative introduction to the region, being just a short bus ride away from Soma on the İzmir–Bandırma railway. In general there's less to write home about further **inland**, where a mountainous landscape harbours a few predominantly industrial cities, with only the town of **Alaşehir** worth any kind of detour.

ACCOMMODATION PRICE CODES

In this guide, motels and nearly all hotels and *pansiyon*s have been categorized according to the price codes outlined below, which are based on US$ because of the high domestic Turkish inflation rate. These categories represent the minimum you can expect to pay for a **double room in high season**. Rates for hostels and for the most basic hotels and *pansiyon*s, where guests are charged **per person**, are given in US$, instead of being indicated by price code. For further information, including a rough outline of what you might expect in each category, see p.37.

① under $12	② $12–17	③ $18–25
④ $26–35	⑤ $36–45	⑥ $46–55
⑦ $56–75	⑧ over $75	

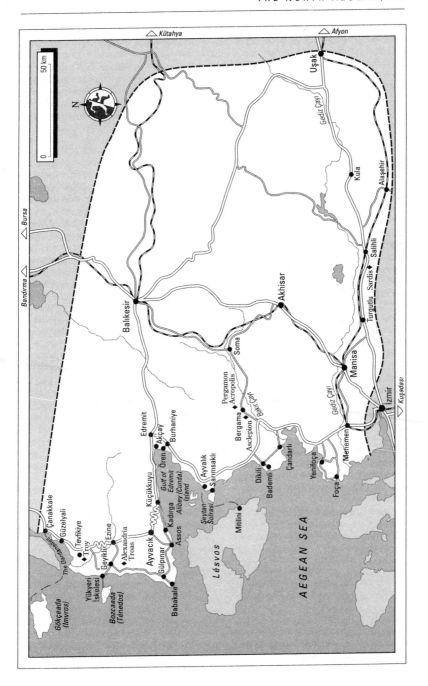

ÇANAKKALE TO EDREMİT

The road running from **Çanakkale** to **Edremit** is justifiably characterized as scenic on most maps, with much of the route wooded and gently hilly, giving way to a coastal strip with the mountains of the **Kaz Dağı** range rising behind. **Troy** is the obvious first stop, after which **Assos**, a few kilometres south of the main road past **Ayvacık**, is the place to head for. Beyond Ayvacık the road follows the coast, passing a number of small resorts before reaching Edremit.

Çanakkale

Though celebrated for its setting on the Dardanelles, **ÇANAKKALE** has little to detain you except for a good archeological museum. However, it is the most strategic base for visiting the Gelibolu (Gallipoli) sites on the European side of the Dardanelles straits, and for the sparse ruins of Troy. Also, if you're intent on going to the Turkish Aegean islands of Gökçeada or Bozcaada, then Çanakkale is the most convenient jump-off point.

It's the **Dardanelles** (*Çanakkale Boğazı* in Turkish) that have defined Çanakkale's history and its place in myth. The area's Classical name, "**Hellespont**", is owed to one Helle, who, while escaping from her wicked stepmother on the back of a winged ram, fell into the swift-moving channel and drowned. From Abydus on the Asian side, the youth Leander used to swim to Sestos on the European shore for trysts with his lover Hero, until one night he too perished in the currents; in despair Hero drowned herself as well. Byron narrowly escaped being added to the list of casualties on his swim in the opposite direction in 1810.

In 480 BC Xerxes' Persian hordes crossed the waters on their way to Greece; and in 411 and 405 BC the last two naval battles of the Peloponnesian War took place in the straits, the latter engagement ending in decisive defeat for the Athenian fleet. Twenty centuries later Mehmet the Conqueror constructed the elaborate fortress of Kilitbahir directly opposite the Çimenlik Kale in Çanakkale (which he also built), to tighten the stranglehold being applied to doomed Constantinople. In March 1915, an Allied fleet attempting to force the Dardanelles and attack İstanbul was repulsed, with severe losses, by Turkish shore batteries, prompting the even bloodier land campaign at Gelibolu. The straits are still heavily militarized and modern Çanakkale is very much a navy town.

Arrival and information

Coming by **ferry** from European Eceabat or Kilitbahir, you'll arrive close to the start of Demircioğlu Caddesi, which barrels inland, roughly splitting the town in two. Everything you might want to see or do in Çanakkale, except for the archeological museum, is within walking distance of the ferry docks. The **tourist information office** (summer Mon–Fri 8.30am–7.30pm, Sat & Sun 10am–6pm; winter Mon–Fri 8.30am–5.30pm; ☎0286/217 1187), next to the main dock, is worth a stop as they have detailed information on the town and surroundings and are happy to divulge it. Buses use the **otogar** out on Atatürk Caddesi, the local name for the coastal İzmir–Bursa highway, a little way north of the end of Demircioğlu Caddesi. It's a fifteen-minute walk from the centre, though many drivers seem to loop down to the waterfront to drop passengers by the tourist office.

If you're planning to visit the **Gelibolu battlefields** from here, the principal **tour operators** in Çanakkale are *Troy Anzac Tours*, just west of the Saat Kulesi at Yalı Cad

CENTRAL ÇANAKKALE

△ Ecabat

Dardanelles

△ Gökçeada

△ Kilitbahir

BALIKESIR CAD

KAYSERILI AHMET PAŞA CAD

▷ Lapseki & Bursa

ACCOMMODATION

1 Anafartlar
2 Anzac
3 Anzac House
4 Kervansaray
5 Temizel

**Emniyet
Müdürlüğü**

**Ferry Ticket
Office**

CUMHURIYET
MEYDANI

ALI CAD

INÖNÜ CAD

❶
ⓘ ❸
❷❺
FETVAHANE SOK   KEMAL YERI
❹   VENI SOK
YALI SOK
MATBAA SOK

DEMIRCIOGLU CAD

✉

**Passport
Police**

⚓ **Naval
Museum**
● **Nusrat**

ÇARŞI CAD

Hamam

ARALIK SOK

Çimenlik Kale

✛

Otogar

ATATÜRK CAD

N

0   200 m

Fairground

**Dolmuşes
for Troy** ★

Archeological Museum, Troy & Ayvalik ▽

2 (☎0286/217 5849), whose four-hour outings leave daily at 10am (plus 3pm in summer); and *Anzac House/Anatur*, at Cumhuriyet Meyd 61 (☎0286/217 1392, fax 217 2906). Both have fully qualified English-speaking guides, and charge $10 per person (for information on the other options for visiting the battlefields, see p.194). *Anatur* shows an Australian-made documentary plus *The Fatal Shore*, a Mel Gibson movie, as part of the tour, at 6pm in the evening at *Anzac House*. A new venture operating from *Troy Anzac* is the *Neptun Diving Centre*, which offers **dives** to the 1915 shipwrecks around the peninsula (from $35 per dive). **Rental cars** can be found at *Kandemir*,

Cumhuriyet Meyd 40 (☎0286/212 8136), and English-language newspapers from *Orka Kitabevi*, Yalı Cad 5, behind the *Entellektüel Restaurant*.

Accommodation

Except during mid-August when the Çanakkale/Troy Festival is being staged, you'll have little trouble finding a **room**. Just south of the tourist office, the Saat Kulesi (clock-tower) signals the entrance to a warren of alleys – Fetvahane Sokağı, Aralık Sokağı, Yeni Sokak – that are home to various inexpensive hotels and *pansiyons*; moving across Demircioğlu Caddesi or closer to the water, you'll also be moving upscale hotel-wise.

The most obvious budget option is a couple of minutes' walk from the ferry landing on the main thoroughfare: *Anzac House*, at Cumhuriyet Meyd 61 (☎0286/217 1392, fax 217 2906; ②), is Aussie-run (they even sell *TNT*) and backpacker-friendly. They're connected to *Anatur* and share premises, with a bar and restaurant, plus video room. Housed in a 200-year-old mansion, the *Kervansaray*, at Fetvahane Sok 13 near the Saat Kulesi (☎0286/217 8192; $3.50–5.50 per person), has recently been taken over and is now a quiet, family-run affair with rather dilapidated rooms, some en suite, and a pleasant garden courtyard. There's a washing machine on the premises and the kitchen is available for use by guests. Another good option, slightly upmarket of the preceding, is the *Hotel Temizel*, Cumhuriyet Meyd 15, a very professionally run and clean establishment (☎0286/212 8760, fax 217 5885; ④). In a similar vein, the two-star *Hotel Anzac* at Saat Kulesi Meyd 8 (☎0286/217 7772; ③) is a popular option. The *Hotel Anafartlar* on the water next to the ferry landing (☎0286/217 4454; ⑤) is overpriced unless you particularly want a room with a sea view.

There are several **campsites** at Güzelyali, 12km southwest of town, though this is a rather overdeveloped place with a narrow, windswept beach. All sites are accessible by minibus but none is as good as those on the Gelibolu peninsula, across the Dardanelles.

The Town

The name *Çanakkale* means "Pottery Castle", after the garish Çanakkale ware that finds its way into the ethnographic section of every Turkish museum. Fortunately none of this is conspicuous, the only nod to the plastic arts in a few appealing, turn-of-the-century buildings in the tiny **bazaar**, just south of the nucleus of cheap hotels. Continue past the bazaar area to **Çimenlik Park, Kale and Naval Museum** (park daily 9am–10pm; museum daily except Mon & Thurs 9am–noon & 1.30–5pm; $0.50). Beached on the park esplanade, from where you get the best views of Kilitbahir fort across the way, is a replica of the minelayer **Nusrat** (same hours and ticket as museum), which stymied the Allied fleet by re-mining at night zones that the French and British had swept clean by day. It's festooned inside with fairly forgettable newspaper clippings of the era. The **museum** itself is more worthwhile, featuring archival photos – Seddülbahir in ruins after Allied shelling, Atatürk's funeral – and military paraphernalia, including (on the upper floor) Atatürk's shattered pocket watch, which stopped a shell fragment at Gelibolu and saved his life.

An hour should be enough to take in the **Archeological Museum** (daily 8.30am–noon & 1–5.30pm; $1), nearly 2km from the centre of town. To avoid walking there, flag down any dolmuş along Atatürk Caddesi labelled "Kepez" or "Güzelyali". The collection is strong on brass implements, delicate glass and glazed pottery, unfired lamps and figurines, and wooden objects, most of them from the nearby Bozcaada and Dardanos tumuli, and is uncluttered by the usual doorstop statuary of Turkish archeological museums. There's also a coin case spanning all cultures from Lydian to Ottoman, but the most exquisite items are the gold and jewellery grave finds, and the bone and ivory work by the exit.

Eating and drinking

Most **places to eat** are within a block or two of the straits. Of the conspicuous quayside restaurants south of the main ferry jetty, the *Entellektüel* has the widest range of *meze* and fish – try the banded bream (*karagöz*). They give a handy chart of Turkish fish with their English names, and pictures, in case you're still in doubt. The *Şehir Lokantası*, at the southern end of the esplanade, has the quietest and most sheltered outdoor seating.

Inland near the bazaar, the food is more modest and cheaper. Best and friendliest of the bunch is the *Yılmaz Restaurant*, one street back from the water. Further down the same block, almost to the Çimenlik park, the *Engin Pastanesi* has the best puddings and ice cream in town, and around the corner on Çarşı Caddesi, the *Ozan Pide ve Lahmacun Salonu* is another worthy option. The *Trakya Lokantası* consists of two premises on either side of Demircioğlu Caddesi, and is probably the best of its kind in town.

For **drinking**, *Anzac House* bar is a popular meeting place for travellers; they also run a bar, the *TNT*, round the corner on Fetvahane Sokağı.

The Turkish Aegean islands

Strategically straddling the Dardanelles, **Gökçeada** and **Bozcaada** were the only Aegean islands to remain in Turkish hands after the 1923 Treaty of Lausanne, which concluded the Greek-Turkish war. Under the terms of the agreement the islands' predominantly Greek inhabitants were exempt from the population exchange of the same year, but after 1937 both Gökçeada and Bozcaada were re-militarized along with the Greek islands of Samothraki and Limnos, and in subsequent decades the Turkish authorities began to assert their sovereignty more forcefully. Access to foreigners was banned until 1987, with special permits from the police in Çanakkale still required up until 1991, and even now few overseas visitors make their way over from the mainland; what they find are inexpensive, basic facilities, good beaches and a rather uneasily shifted sense of identity.

Ferries to Gökçeada leave from Çanakkale and from Kabatepe on the Gelibolu peninsula daily in season; check current schedules carefully at Çanakkale tourist information office. The Çanakkale boat costs under $2 per passenger, $10 per car, while the Kabatepe boat costs $1 per passenger, $8.50 per car (all one-way prices). Ferries **to Bozcaada** leave from **Yükyeri İskelesi**, a tiny port with a hotel, the *Belediye* (②), and several kilometres of excellent beach, 60km southwest of Çanakkale and linked by dolmuş. In season there are three or four boats daily, costing $0.50 per passenger, $3.50 per car (one-way); out of season, service drops to two daily ferries.

Gökçeada (Imvros)

The larger of the two Turkish Aegean islands, **GÖKÇEADA** hovers just northwest of the Dardanelles, tantalizingly visible from any of the Gelibolu battlefields. It's a rollingly hilly island – still heavily militarized – and large enough to make your own vehicle necessary.

Assigned to Turkey for its strategic value after the 1923 peace conference, the island's majority population of seven thousand Orthodox Greeks was more or less left to itself for forty years, save for a token force of a hundred or so Turkish gendarmes and officials. When the Cyprus conflict came to a head in 1964, the Turkish government decided to "claim" the island more pointedly, instituting policies of forced land expropriation without compensation, heavy garrisoning, the closure of schools for

Greek children, settlement of Turkish civilians from the mainland, and the establishment of an open prison – it was from here that William Hayes, of *Midnight Express* notoriety, escaped. These measures were taken specifically to make continued residence for the ethnic Greeks impossible, and they've had the desired effect – today there are only about three hundred demoralized Greeks left, the bulk of the population having fled to Athens and further afield.

Ferries dock at the new, functional harbour of **KUZU LİMANI**, where a small motel fails to attract much foreign custom. A dolmuş meets the boat and takes you the 6km inland to **ÇINARLI**, formerly Panavia, the island's capital. Here you'll find a couple of hotels and restaurants – including the *Gökçeada Belediyesi Otel* at Belediye Meydanı (☎0286/887 3473; ②), with its own good *lokanta* – as well as two or three huge, shuttered Greek churches. But the streets are dusty or muddy according to season, and the grim official architecture on the main drag overwhelms the old houses on the slope. Most visitors continue a further 4km by minibus to **KALE** (formerly Kastro) on the north shore, where a ruined castle built during Süleyman the Magnificent's reign overlooks a good beach and the Greek island of Samothraki. Along the quay are a handful of *pansiyon*s and excellent, cheap fish tavernas with roof-terrace seating. The beach, though, is encroached upon by a huge officers' club, and the upper village around the castle is a virtual ghost town; the life of the place pretty much left it when the main anchorage was shifted to Kuzu Limanı.

From Kale you can easily walk the 1500m south to **BADEMLİ** (Glyki), passing on the way the hideous new prefab settlement of Yeni Bademli. Old Bademli is also virtually deserted, its 25 or so inhabitants split evenly along ethnic lines and coexisting uneasily. There's more of an illusion of normality at **ZEYTİNLİ** (Ayii Theodhori), 3km northwest of Çınarlı, where most of Gökçeada's remaining Greek Orthodox population lives, but you'll quickly notice that no one is younger than sixty. They're understandably bitter about the turn of events, and often reluctant to talk to – or be photographed by – outsiders for fear of subsequent Turkish interrogation.

There are another three villages close to the prison in the west of the island, but there's no public transport to them, only a rumoured service van making the journey to the jail every morning. **Kefalo Burnu**, the southeastern tip of the island, offers better beaches than those around Kale, but you'll need your own transport if you plan to visit it.

Bozcaada (Tenedos)

The island of **BOZCAADA** is a more cheerful place, if only because it's far less militarized and more architecturally of a piece. It's too close to the mainland to have avoided the attention of any power ruling Turkey, and the population, as evidenced by a handful of medieval mosques, has historically been about one-fourth Muslim. Covered mostly in vineyards that produce the justly famous Bozcaada wine, the island is small enough to walk around – and it has some excellent beaches, though the water is freezing cold until September.

Ferries dock at the northeast tip of the island, in the shadow of the **castle**, which has been successively enlarged by Byzantine, Genoese, Venetian and Turkish occupiers, and most recently restored by the archeological service in the 1960s. The result is one of the hugest citadels in the Aegean, easily equal to Bodrum's; thankfully it's not a military area, so you can explore every inch – the locals use the keep to graze sheep, and the lower courtyard as a football pitch.

Guarded by the castle, the only town, **BOZCAADA**, though built on a grid plan along a slight slope, is surprisingly elegant: there's a minimum of concrete and a maximum of old overhanging upper floors and cobbled streets. The feel is much like that of a Greek island of twenty or thirty years ago – or a Turkish southern Aegean resort of a mere decade ago. The architecture is protected by law so the exteriors of the old houses cannot be radically altered. The old Greek quarter extended east from the church to the sea, though nowadays fewer than a hundred elderly Orthodox remain, following the same sort of campaign as occurred on Gökçeada.

The interior of the island consists of gently undulating countryside, flatter than Gökçeada and treeless except for the clumps marking farms. The three best **beaches** are the consecutive strands of Ayazma, Sullubahçe and Habbelle, 5–6km away on the south coast; take the right at the first fork out of town and then two lefts, or catch one of the three daily dolmuşes to Ayazma. Just above Ayazma is an abandoned monastery, home to the *ayazma* (sacred spring) that gives it its name, while closer to the sand are a couple of restaurants. A dirt track leads thirty minutes east to **Ayiana beach**, a marvellous site if you're after complete solitude.

Taking the left at the first fork leads to some more **beaches** – narrower and more exposed – on the east shore, along the 4km of asphalt ending at Tuzburnu.

Practicalities

A haven this convenient not surprisingly fills up in summer, mostly with people from İstanbul and Athens visiting relatives, but **accommodation** is not a big problem even in high season, except at weekends and on public holidays. All the same, advance booking is advisable if you want to stay in anything better than average in summer. One drawback of the island is that its water, drawn from deep wells, is highly brackish – though it's rumoured that water will be piped from the mainland sometime in 1997. In the meantime, sniff the water from the taps in your *pansiyon* before you take a room.

Nicest of all the *pansiyon*s is the *Emiroğlu* on the far side of the castle from the dock (☎0286/697 8037; ③). It's half built of stone, with an overhanging wooden upper storey and a conservatory out the back where breakfast is served; all bathrooms are en suite. The *Ergin Pansiyon* in the same area, visible from the coast road as you walk away from the castle (☎0286/697 8429; ②), has good clean rooms with kitchens and bathrooms and a roof terrace. Another excellent establishment, at the far end of the esplanade, is the *Ege*, located in an immaculately restored nineteenth-century Greek school (Cumhuriyet Mah, Mektep Sok; ☎0286/697 8189; ③).

The *Güler Hotel* on the front, to the left of the ferry landing, is old and rather rundown but their annexe, the *Güler Ada* (☎0286/697 8844; ②), inland behind the **PTT** (which is on the main square), is clean, modern and pleasant, with breakfast served by the water at the hotel. Right in the town centre the *Bozca*, over a market of the same name, has immaculate rooms with bathrooms (☎0286/ 697 8336; ②).

The luxury options are the *Zafer*, which has a reputation for bad service, and the *Thenes* (☎0286/697 8888; ⑤), 5km round the coast south of town at Alaybey *mahalle*, which has its own concreted "beach" and rather basic rooms for the price. Beyond the *Thenes*, the *Güler Pansiyon* (☎0286/697 8454; ③) is beautifully situated with only vines between it and the sea, its own strip of beach and boats to rent. Rooms are very simple, but guests have use of a kitchen.

There's a **campsite** with showers and shade at Ayazma beach behind the *Boruzan Restaurant* (camping rough is not really appreciated by the authorities, though it is practised). The *Ada Café* (☎0286/697 8795) in town **rents bikes** for $6 a day, as well as arranging tours of the island and renting out camping equipment.

For **food**, the *Paşa Café Restaurant* on the front near the ferry landing has a varied menu, including *güveç*, *pide*, steak and chips, octopus and *mantı*, served in a congenial atmosphere. The nearby *Café at Lisa's* – which doubles as an information centre and meeting place – is a real break if you've had too many Turkish breakfasts, serving scrambled eggs, cornflakes, herbal teas and fruit. Local seafood is usually accompanied by the equally characteristic and ubiquitous island **wine**; good brands include *Doruk*, *Halikarnass*, *Talay*, *Dimitrakopoulou* and *Ataol*.

Troy

> *But Aunt Dot could only think how Priam and Hecuba would have been vexed to see the state it had all got into and no one seeming to care anymore. She thought the nations ought to go on working at it and dig it all up again, and perhaps do some reconstruction, for she belonged to the reconstruction school, and would have liked to see Troy's walls and towers rising once more against the sky like a Hollywood Troy, and the wooden horse standing beside them, opening mechanically every little while to show that it was full of armed Greeks.*

Rose Macaulay, *The Towers of Trebizond*

Although by no means the most spectacular archeological site in Turkey, **TROY**, thanks to Homer, is probably the most celebrated. Known as *Truva* in Turkish, the remains of the ancient city lie just west of the main road around 20km south of Çanakkale. It's a scanty affair on the whole, but if you lower your expectations and use your imagination, you may well be impressed. The ruins are now a lot less obscure than previously: recent excavation work led by Dr Manfred Korfman, which has used modern scientific methods to try to fill in the gaps left by earlier excavations, has served to clarify the site greatly, to the extent that laypeople can now at least grasp the basic layout, and gain a knowledge of the different settlement periods discovered. If you visit independently, it's well worth buying a copy of Korfman's *A Tour of Troia* from a small shop by the entrance to the site, consisting of two books and a map ($9), which will guide you around with pages of information corresponding to numbers on the signs at the site.

Until 1871 Troy was generally thought to have existed in legend only. The Troad plain, where the ruins lie, was known to be associated with the Troy that Homer wrote about in the *Iliad*, but all traces of the city had vanished completely. In 1868 **Heinrich Schliemann** (1822–1890), a German businessman who had made his fortune in America, obtained permission from the Ottoman government to start digging on a hill known to the Turks as Hisarlık, where earlier excavators had already found the remains of a classical temple and signs of further, older ruins.

Schliemann was born into a poor Mecklenburg family and became obsessed at an early age with the myths of ancient Greece. Unable to pursue the interest professionally (although he did teach himself ancient Greek, in addition to several modern languages), he amassed his considerable fortune during the Californian Gold Rush of 1849, forsaking commerce at the age of 46 to become the world's most celebrated and successful amateur archeologist.

Schliemann's sloppy trenching work actually resulted in a certain amount of damage to the site, and he was also responsible for removing the so-called **Treasure of Priam**, a large cache of beautiful jewellery that was taken back to Berlin and subsequently displayed there until 1941, when it was squirrelled away for safety under Zoo Station. The horde disappeared during the Red Army's sacking of the city in May 1945; long suspected of having been spirited back to the USSR, it resurfaced spectacularly in Moscow in August 1993. A two-way legal tussle between Germany and the Russian Federation to determine ownership is now in progress – as well as careful forensic examination of the precious items to answer allegations that Schliemann fraudulently assembled the treasure from scattered sites in Asia Minor.

Whatever Schliemann's shortcomings, his initial, unsystematic excavations did uncover nine layers of remains, representing distinct and consecutive city developments that span four millennia. The oldest, Troy I, dates back to about 3600 BC and was followed by four similar settlements. Either Troy VI or VII is thought to have been the city described by Homer: the former is known to have been destroyed by an earthquake in about 1275 BC, while the latter shows signs of having been wiped out by fire about a quarter of a century later, around the time historians generally estimate the

Trojan War to have taken place. Troy VIII, which thrived from 700 to 300 BC, was a Greek foundation, while much of the final layer of development, Troy IX (300 BC–300 AD), was built during the heyday of the Roman Empire.

Although there's no way of being absolutely sure that the Trojan War did take place, there's a fair amount of circumstantial evidence suggesting that the city was the scene of some kind of armed conflict, even if it wasn't the ten-year battle described in the *Iliad*. It's possible that Homer's epic is based on a number of wars fought between the Mycenaean Greeks and the inhabitants of Troy, who, it seems, were alternately trading partners and commercial rivals. Homer's version of events, however, dispensed with these pedestrian possibilities, turning the war into a full-scale heroic drama, complete with bit parts for the ancient Greek gods.

The site

The **site** (summer daily 8am–7.30pm; winter daily 8am–5pm; $1.50) is signalled by the ticket office – marked "Gişe" – just opposite the drop-off point. Note that the little hut near the ticket office, described as "Schliemann's house", is a fake – he actually stayed in the village of Tevfikiye. From here a long, straight road leads to a giant wooden horse that would have delighted Macaulay's fictional Aunt Dot, and the **excavation house**, with a scale model of the site and an excellent video explaining the history of Troy and the excavations.

Just beyond is the ruined city itself, a craggy outcrop overlooking the Troad plain, which extends about 8km to the sea. It's a bleak sight, leaving you in no doubt as to the thinness of Troy's remains, but as you stand on what's left of the ramparts and look out across the plain that stretches out at your feet, it's not too difficult to imagine a besieging army, legendary or otherwise, camped out below. Most impressive of the extant remains are the **east wall and gate** from Troy VI (1700–1275BC), of which 330m remain, curving around the eastern and southern flanks of the city. The inward-leaning walls, 6m high and over 4m thick, would have been surmounted by an additional brick section. A ramp paved with flat stones from Troy II (2500–2300 BC), which would have led to the citadel entrance, also stands out. It was near here that Schliemann found what he believed to be Priam's treasure, using the evidence that Troy II had been burnt down in a fire to come to the erroneous conclusion that this was Homer's city. Just inside the citadel entrance is the most impressive of the dwellings unearthed at Troy, the **Pillar House**, dating from Troy VI.

The most important monument of Roman Troy IX, or Ilium, is the **temple of Athena**, which was rebuilt on a promise of Alexander the Great by his general, Lysimachus, after Alexander himself had visited the temple and left his armour as a gift. Remains found by Schliemann proved the temple to be of the Doric order, and fragments of its coffered ceiling can still be seen on site; the most famous relief from the temple, however, depicting Apollo astride four pawing stallions, is now in Berlin. Troy was an important religious centre during Greek and Roman times, and the remains of two other **sanctuaries**, which were also renovated after the visit of Alexander the Great, can be seen at the westernmost point of the site. It's thought that the female deities Cybele and Demeter were worshipped here, because the layout, with altar and grandstand, is similar to the sanctuary in Pergamon.

Practicalities

Çanakkale is without a doubt the most sensible base for seeing Troy, with both *Anatur* and *Troy Anzac Tours* (see p.230) running worthwhile guided tours of the ancient site for $10 per person. Alternatively, fairly frequent dolmuşes leave from the station just before the bridge on Atatürk Caddesi, for the half-hour journey through a rolling landscape of olive groves and cotton fields. Failing either of these options, you can stay in the village of Tevfikiye, just before Troy, although the only budget accommodation is at the none-too-luxurious *pansiyons Yarol, Akçin* and *Deniz* (all ②). There's also the rather overpriced *Hısarlık Hotel*, just before the ticket office on the road to the site, opposite the *Helen Restaurant* (☎0286/283 1026, fax 283 1087; ④).

The dolmuş to the site drops you off just beyond the village, in front of a burgeoning cluster of tourist shops and **restaurants**, highlight of which is the reasonably decent *Helen Restaurant*. There's also a **bank**, a **PTT** and the car park.

Alexandria Troas

About 20km to the south of Troy is Ezine, a small wayside town from where infrequent dolmuşes run to Dalyan village, close by the ruins of **ALEXANDRİA TROAS**, a city founded in about 300 BC by Antigonus I, a general of Alexander the Great and ruler of one of the successor kingdoms established when Alexander's empire finally broke up. Antigonus forced the inhabitants of the surrounding area to move into his city, which he named Antigonia after himself. His stab at immortality was unsuccessful: Lysimachus, king of Macedonia, conquered Antigonia, after killing Antigonus and his son Demetrius in battle, and renamed the city Alexandria Troas in honour of Alexander the Great.

Apparently a large area of the thousand-acre city remained intact until as late as 1764, when the British traveller and antiquarian Richard Chandler visited and reported having seen substantial city walls and fortifications, enclosing what he assumed to be a ruined temple. These days, however, the **ruins** ($1 admission if the ticket booth is staffed) consist of nothing more than a few courses of wall and the vaults of baths, perched on a rise overlooking the island of Bozcaada. As Eric Newby wrote in *On the Shores of the Mediterranean*, "it was perfectly possible . . . to walk into it through one of the now enormous gaps in the walls and walk out through a similar gap on the far side, without, apart from tripping over some low-lying remains or else bumping into something shrouded in vegetation which loomed unidentifiable overhead, seeing much of Alexandria Troas at all".

Ayvacık and Assos

Thirty kilometres south of Ezine lies **AYVACIK**, a market town with about four or five dolmuşes a day to the Classical settlement of Assos. It's not likely that you'll find much to detain you in Ayvacık, although the village is the headquarters of the **DOBAG carpet project**, based in new premises opposite the *Elif* petrol station on the Çanakkale road into town (☎0286/712 1274, fax 712 1705; note that the carpets sold in the Friday market in Ayvacık, and elsewhere in the bazaars of Turkey, although they may be produced in the area, are not those of the DOBAG cooperative). The best time to be in town is Friday – **market day** – when the local people, mostly settled nomads, converge from the surrounding villages to trade their produce at stalls adjacent to the bus stop and ticket offices. It's a particularly noisy and colourful affair, worth spending some time at between dolmuş connections: women in traditional patterned *şalvar* (baggy pantaloons) and headscarves sell all kinds of fruit and vegetables, honey, cheese and pre-prepared *börek*. If you decide to spend more time in Ayvacık, there's a **hotel**, *B Hotel*, next to the PTT (☎0286/712 2888; ②).

ASSOS, 25km south of Ayvacık, combines the two mainstays of tourism in coastal Turkey: ruins and an attractive harbour. The site of an ancient Greek settlement, it is officially called **Behramkale** after the village that has grown up around it, but many of the locals, including dolmuş drivers, still know it as Assos. Until the mid-1980s the site was more or less undiscovered, but now it's a well-established stopover on most itineraries, attracting a good share of visitors in summer. Most people, however, arrive for day trips on buses, leaving the village relatively tourist-free by evening.

DOBAG CARPETS

The **DOBAG** carpet project was initiated by a German schoolteacher, **Harold Böhmer**, who became interested in Turkish carpets and natural dyes while working in Istanbul in the 1970s. He started by analysing traditional carpet dyes using a technique called thin-layer chromatography, then went on to the more difficult task of reconstructing the processes used to produce the colours. He eventually took his project to Marmara University in 1981, who decided to fund the Doğal Boya Araştırma ve Geliştirme Projesi (natural dye research and development project). The project was set up in the Ayvacık region, at the request of the local forestry commission to give the locals something to do other than cut down trees, and because of the long tradition of carpet weaving in the area. At that time the settled nomads were still producing carpets, but using imported chemical dyes, and the demand for them was decreasing.

Böhmer adapted commercial techniques for the preparation of dyes to suit the village lifestyle, and he and his wife started to teach the recipes to the villagers. Now these techniques, particularly the production of indigo dye, are practised all over Turkey. Other dyes are produced using madder, indigo, oak galls and other plants to produce blue, red, apricot, yellow, green and black. The production process of the purple dye, however, is a secret, a way of keeping the DOBAG carpets distinctive.

The villagers have set up a worker's **cooperative**, choosing their own colours and patterns, adapted from traditional designs learnt by heart. The project encourages personal inventiveness, in order to keep the tradition alive. Standards are high, and if corners have been cut in the production process, the carpet will not be accepted to be sold by DOBAG – only the best-quality, handspun long stapler winter wool and dyes that will retain their lustre are used. A square metre of a DOBAG carpet has a hundred thousand knots, and consequently costs around $340. The plants used in the dying process are now being farmed in the region, and a spin-off project has been set up in Yuntdağ near Manisa.

The half-hour ride, a journey of winding hill roads and impressive rocky scenery, takes you past a fourteenth-century, hump-backed **Ottoman bridge**, built with masonry from the ancient settlement. Shortly after this, a left fork leads up into the village and the dolmuş drop-off point, on a small square in front of a café. **Accommodation** in this part of the village is confined to two *pansiyons*, the *Sidar* on the left as you enter (☎0286/721 7047; ①), offering good clean doubles with en-suite bathrooms, and the *Halıcı Hanı*, just below the ancient site, a restored old house that's open in winter (☎0286/337 8321; ④) – it's a bit overpriced but you can bargain them down when things are slow.

Ancient Assos

According to some sources, Assos was the site of a thirteenth-century BC Hittite colony, although history only really began here during the eighth century, when Greek colonists from neighbouring Lesbos established a settlement, later building a huge temple to Athena in 540 BC. Hermias, a eunuch and disciple of Plato, ruled here, attempting to put Plato's theories of the ideal city-state into practice. From 347 to 344 BC Aristotle made his home in Assos as the guest of Hermias, before the arrival of the Persians forced him to flee. During medieval times, the Ottomans plundered the town for dressed stone, as did local villagers.

Take the road into the village via a cluster of kids and old people selling trinkets until you reach the **Murat Hüdavendigâr Camii**, an austere fourteenth-century mosque that probably began as a church, built with stone quarried from the earlier settlement. Beyond is the enclosed site of the sixth-century **Temple of Athena** (open daylight hours; $1), with Doric columns recently re-erected by an American university archeological team. One only hopes, for the sake of architectural harmony, that the concrete replacement column-segments lying about remain unused. As yet it's beautiful, although overshadowed somewhat by views to Lesbos and over the Gulf of Edremit.

The rest of ancient Assos is a jumble of ruins falling away from the temple, enclosed by the old and partly intact **city wall**, which is accented with towers and quite impressive; the most recognizable part is the old **necropolis** (same hours; $1), littered with sarcophagi, which can be viewed on the way down from the village to the harbour.

The harbour and around

Assos **harbour**, a good half-hour's walk from the upper village and site by way of a steep winding road, is entirely different in feel. Tourism is the main means of livelihood here: there are several comfortable hotels and *pansiyon*s, plus a few campsites, and at the height of summer it's totally overrun. Since between here and the Greek island of Lésvos there's nothing but 8km of open water, the harbour has its own platoon of gendarmerie.

The harbour resort, all of a dozen basalt buildings large and small, is very compact and you'll have no trouble locating the **accommodation**, although during the season free rooms are a precious commodity. Budget options by the harbour are the *Plaj Pansiyon*, with simple rooms (one has a tree growing through it) sharing cold-water bathrooms (☎0286/721 7193; ②). Next to it, the *Hotel Mehtap* also has basic rooms fronting the beach, but with en-suite hot-water bathrooms (☎0286/721 7221; ③). Going up a notch, the *Küçük Ev* is a nicely restored old village house set back from the harbour (☎0286/721 7011; ⑤); above it, the *Sen Pansiyon* also has pleasant rooms (☎0286/721 7209; ④); and the good-value *Behramkale*, further up from the harbour again (☎0286/721 7016; ④), is immaculate and well run. If you're prepared to pay a bit more, the larger hotels offer reasonable half-board options. The nicest are the *Hotel Assos*, with its own beach (☎0286/721 7017, fax 721 7249), and the *Assos Kervansaray* (☎0286/721 7093, fax 721 7200), which both charge $48 for half-board per double room.

Most of the hotels have good **restaurants**. The one at the *Assos* overlooks the sea and is probably the most pleasant, but the handful of inland *pansiyon*s do reasonable food a bit cheaper. Both the *Plaj* and the *Mehtap* have beachfront restaurants. For better-value food there are a number of outlets up in the village selling typical village food like *mantı* and *gözleme*, to be washed down with a glass of *ayran*.

Beaches to the east: Kadırga

If you do stay during summer, you'll find beach space at a premium, particularly at weekends. Less than an hour away on foot from Assos harbour is the beach resort of **KADIRGA**, reached by cutting across the base of the headland beyond the pebble beach: at the first livestock gate, twenty minutes along, bear left instead of descending to the pebble cove. Red paint-splodge waymarks facing you suggest that this is a common outing. Kadırga is also accessible by a paved four-kilometre road signposted from the upper village.

The beach itself is reasonable, over a kilometre of volcanic gravel and sand, and by Turkish standards still relatively undeveloped – but that means no showers and little shade. Its peaceful days are numbered, however, what with co-op villas sprouting on the nearby cape and two new luxury hotels behind. So far, though, there are only about a half-dozen cheaper **places to stay**; the least pretentious are *Hunters*, at the northwest end (☎0286/721 7058; ③), and *Yıldız Saray* (☎0286/721 7204; ③).

Well worth knowing about, and not properly shown on most maps, is the very pleasant twenty-kilometre **shore road** east from Kadırga to Küçükkuyu (see below), the next major coastal settlement. Though narrow, it is entirely paved, travelled by the occasional dolmuş (or mountain bike), and it allows you to bypass the tortuous mountain curves of the main inland route.

West of Assos: Gülpınar and Babakale

West of Assos, a good road leads 26km to Gülpınar, also served by direct dolmuş from Ezine. The villages en route, built uniformly of the local basalt, are some of the most attractive in western Turkey, and for the first few kilometres out of Assos the old cobbled path linking them still survives, just north of the modern asphalt.

GÜLPINAR is notable mainly as the site of a **temple to Apollo Smintheos**, well signposted at the western edge of the village. The shrine is dedicated to one of the more bizarre manifestations of the god, as Lord of Mice: when the original Cretan colonists found themselves harrassed by mice, they remembered a previous oracle advising them to settle wherever overrun by the "sons of earth". This they took to mean the rodents, founding the now mostly vanished ancient town of Chryse around the temple. Of the remaining Hellenistic temple, oddly aligned northeast, scarcely more remains, just the platform and some column stumps. Yet it's an atmospheric, lonely site, and worth the detour.

The feeling of desolation intensifies as you ride nine paved kilometres southwest from Gülpınar to **BABAKALE**, the westernmost point of Asia. This working fishing port is dominated by a fine eighteenth-century castle that can be visited; a plaque informs you, in fractured English, that a certain valiant admiral expelled the infidel pirates molesting the Allah-fearing Mohammedans at this approach to the Dardanelles. If you're seized by the urge to stay or eat, there's just the aptly named *Karayel* (north wind) **motel-restaurant**. The only local **beach** is about 3km before the port, overlooked by phalanxes of standard-issue villa projects.

Ayvacık to Ören – and inland

From Ayvacık, the main Çanakkale–İzmir road winds through pine-forested hills, offering occasional glimpses out across the Gulf of Edremit, before straightening out at **KÜÇÜKKUYU** – the first major settlement and the only real town before a succession of resorts leading up to Edremit. Küçükkuyu was originally a small fishing port, with a fleet still in evidence and plenty of reasonable seafood restaurants, and on Fridays farmers from the surrounding villages come here to sell their produce at the street market, while mostly Turkish tourists swim on the nearby beaches. The handful of **hotels** are affordable and never more than a few minutes from the sea; near the port, the *Marina Hotel* (☎0286/752 5686; ③) is worth trying, though most of the beach-front premises are west of town, along the start of the minor coast road to Kadırga (see above).

After Küçükkuyu a series of small resorts, one with the baldly descriptive name of Moteller ("motels"), is unlikely to appeal to foreigners. You're best off staying in your vehicle until Akçay, the next place of any size and only a modest improvement on what has preceded.

Akçay

From the main road, where long-distance buses will drop you (Edremit-bound dolmuşes continue to the centre), it's about a ten-minute walk into **AKÇAY**, a middle-class resort with plenty of hotels, restaurants and discos, filled with mainly Turkish tourists during the summer months but deadly quiet out of season.

The **tourist information office** is on Edremit Caddesi (daily 8.30am–noon & 1.30–5pm), clearly signposted on the left as you walk into town, although it's not particularly helpful. If you're **staying**, a good budget option in the town centre is the *Set Motel* at Cami Kordon Yolu (☎0266/384 2636; ②), run by a friendly family. *The Erzade Motel* on Leman Akpınar Caddesi (☎0266/384 1058; ②) is also good value, for clean rooms with showers, close to the beach. The one-star waterfront *Otel Özsoy*, Leman Akpınar Cad 3 (☎0266/384 1190; ③), is about the classiest central option, all rooms boasting sea views. Along Etiler Caddesi, which runs southeast out of town, parallel to the seafront, there are numerous other hotels of all shapes and sizes. One of the best is the *Otel Çimen*, Etiler Cad 34, 1500m from the centre of town past Sarıkız, but they only do half-board ($42 per double room). They have a restaurant, snack bar, roof bar and a private beach for their guests.

There are plenty of places to **eat and drink** in town, and cheap *pide* places abound. Taner Nuran Sokak in the centre is a good hunting ground for restaurants, including the *Yat* with steamtrays and *izgara*. For something more substantial, head for the *Sarıkız Plaj Restaurant*, which overlooks the sea from Etiler Caddesi in the area known as Sarıkız. There are another two reasonable restaurants on Turgut Reis Caddesi, heading west out of town: the *Pinar Motel-Restaurant* and the *Yeni Faruk Restaurant*, both towards the sea about 1km along.

Edremit and Ören

Easily reached by dolmuş from Akçay, **EDREMİT** is the Adramyttium of the *Iliad*, which was sacked by Achilles. After destroying the town, Achilles kidnapped Chryseis, the daughter of the priest at the temple of Apollo Smintheos (see "Gülpınar", above), only to have her claimed by Agamemnon, leader of the Greek force; this provoked the "wrath of Achilles" (more like a long-drawn-out sulk), one of the major sub-plots of the *Iliad*.

These days the legends far outshine the reality of the place, and you're most likely to stop in Edremit only for services such as post and banks, as these are not good in the coastal resorts. The *Otel Bılgıçler*, however, at Menderes Bul 63 opposite the Yunus Emre Park, is pretty good value should you get caught between connections (☎0266/372 2255; ③), with clean, pleasant **rooms** and good service, though it can be noisy. Menderes Bulvarı – the main thoroughfare – is also location of the main **PTT** (summer 9am–11pm, winter 9am–7pm), a very efficient branch of *İşbankası* (Mon–Fri 9am–12.30pm & 1.30–5pm), and a change office, *Huzur Döviz*, on Cumhuriyet Meydani at the end of the *bulvarı*. Edremit is a major **public transport** node, with buses to destinations all over Turkey; the **bus station** is 800m out of town on Yılmaz Akpınar Bulvarı.

From Burhaniye, 14km south of Edremit, there are dolmuşes to **ÖREN**, about 4km northwest, a small resort popular with Turkish holidaymakers, with a beautiful beach overlooked by Kaz Dağı, the ancient Mount Ida; during the summer you can also reach Ören by boat from Akçay. Much smaller and sleepier than Akçay, Ören has managed to retain a village feel, with development restricted to the outlying areas. In the centre there is little new building allowed, leaving space for flower-filled gardens between old-fashioned holiday villas. The town has a long history of wine and olive oil production, dating back to Greek occupation, with an olive festival held between August 16 and 18.

Accommodation possibilities are mainly located on Çarşı Caddesi, the street running from the *otogar* to the beach. The *Kösem* here (☎0266/422 1327; ③) is good value, with en-suite bathrooms and breakfast included. For a bit more comfort, try the *Motel Karakaş* right on the beach (☎0266/422 1393; ③). The nearby *Altay Restaurant* serves fish and *izgara*, but for better-value **food**, head for the market which runs parallel to Çarşı Caddesi, where fast-food stands dish up *pide* and *lahmacun*, baked potatoes and kebabs. Further up the market street, *Sevinç Patisserie* sells great sweets, cakes and breakfasts.

Balıkesir

Frequent bus services link Edremit with the provincial capital of **BALIKESİR**, about 70km inland and east, but there isn't really much to take you there. An important focus and market centre for the surrounding area, it suffers from the pollution churned into the atmosphere by huge nearby cement factories. If you do pass through, it will certainly be on your way to somewhere else: the town is an important train junction, with twice-daily trains to İzmir and Bandırma, and twice-nightly expresses to Kütahya and Ankara; plus frequent buses to İzmir, Çanakkale and Bursa. Those forced to stop over might like to know that there are a few medieval mosques in town, including the sturdy and well-preserved **Zağanos Paşa Camii**, built in 1461 by one of Mehmet the Conqueror's viziers.

The best-value **hotel** is the *Molam Oteli* on Yeşil Caddesi (☎0266/241 8075; ②); further up the price scale is the *Yilmaz Otel*, Milli Kuvvetler Cad 37 (☎0266/241 7493; ③).

AYVALIK TO MANISA

South of Edremit, the road follows the coastline more closely, and although the journey down to **Ayvalık** is an unspectacular one, Ayvalık itself makes an excellent place to stop for a few days. It has some good beaches nearby and offers easy access to **Bergama** a little way inland, with its unmissable Hellenistic ruins. Further down the coast there are more resorts, most notably **Çandarlı** and **Foça**, with a final duo of more monumental attractions inland: the hillside city of **Manisa** and the nearby site of **Sardis**, ancient capital of Croesus and Midas.

Ayvalık and around

From Burhaniye, it's forty minutes by bus to **AYVALIK**, which lies a couple of kilometres west of the main road. You can either take a direct bus all the way there, or catch any bus going south and walk or hitch the rest of the way from the turnoff.

Ayvalık is growing in popularity among Turkish and European visitors for the charm of its cobbled streets lined with picturesque old buildings. In stark contrast to the strings of motels further north, or resorts to the south which have been completely taken over by tourism, the town has retained a fishing fleet and other light industry (mainly olive oil and soap production), and tourism feels like just another string to its bow. The closest good beaches are in the recently developed resort of Sarımsaklı, with some remoter, less sandy ones on the island of Alibey. Ayvalık is also convenient for ruin-spotting at Bergama, 60km southeast, and stands opposite the Greek island of Lésvos, to which there's a regular ferry service in summer.

Arrival, information and accommodation

Ayvalık is a fairly small place and most of what you'll need is concentrated around İskele Meydanı, the small plaza with the Atatürk bust, 1500m south of the main **otogar**. If you're heavily laden, any red-and-white city bus labelled "Çamlık" will take you into town for about $0.25. Northbound buses coming from İzmir usually pass through this square and will drop you here if you ask. Just north of İskele Meydanı you'll find the **banks**, **PTT** and most midtown bus company offices. The **tourist office** is a booth on İskele Meydanı (May–Sept daily 9am–1pm & 2–7pm; ☎0266/312 3158). On the fishing-harbour quay, you'll find the regular (in season) **shuttle launch** to Alibey (Cunda) island, vastly preferable to the circuitous city bus trip there. If you're arriving from Lésvos by **international ferry**, these dock near the customs, some 250m north.

Accommodation
As far as **accommodation** goes, there's something for almost everyone in either central Ayvalık or nearby Çamlık.

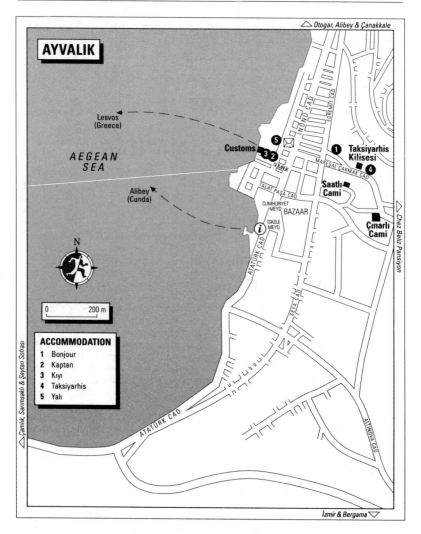

Among the most characterful central choices, immediately behind the church of the same name (see below), the *Taksiyarhis Pansiyon* (☎0266/312 1494; ①) takes up what was the priest's house and offers fine views, along with a multilingual Austrian/Turkish management. There are only sixteen beds, and a preference for family groups, so booking is mandatory in summer. The place doubles up as an information centre, bike rental outlet and book exchange. *Chez Beliz Pansiyon* is another highly recommended establishment (☎0266/312 4897; ③), based at the family home of ex-actress Beliz, the charming patron who cooks lavishly at dinner time and breakfast. The interior is comfortable (though no en-suites), and there's a relaxing, friendly atmosphere in the garden courtyard where dinner is served. The *pansiyon* is located at Fethiye Mahallesi, Mareşal Çakmak Cad 28; to get there, follow the signs from the seafront deep into the old town.

In a similar vein, the newly opened *Bonjour Pansiyon*, Mareşal Çakmak Cad, Bezinci Sok 6 (☎0266/313 8085; ③), occupies one of the grandest houses in town and has been beautifully renovated with a wing of rooms added and a charming courtyard in which breakfast is served. Ask for a room in the older Greek-built mansion house with its lavishly painted ceilings and wood fittings.

Down on the water there are two more excellent *pansiyon*s, the *Yalı*, behind the PTT (☎0266/312 2423; ③), with its large high-ceilinged rooms and lush garden, and the beautifully converted old soap mill, the *Hotel Kaptan*, Balıkhane Sok 7 (☎0266/312 8834; ③). The latter has bathrooms in all rooms, and balconies looking out to sea, as well as a seaside terrace where breakfast is served. The *Kıyı Motel* is handy for ferries to Lésvos, en suite throughout and good value (②); it's on Gümrük Meydanı, next to the ferry terminal.

If all of the foregoing are full, you'll have to extend your search to the south, to **ÇAMLIK**, a suburb of Ayvalık where the summer villas of turn-of-the-century İzmir Greeks still peek out from between the pines. Here a number of modest *pansiyon*s, such as the *Sözer* (☎0266/312 4474; ③), are clearly marked from the coast road. A bit beyond these you'll find the slightly upmarket *Çadır* (☎0266/312 1678; ③).

The Town

Ayvalık occupies the site of ancient Kydoniae, "Quinces" in Greek, and indeed the modern Turkish name means much the same. The present settlement was founded during the sixteenth century by Ottoman Greeks, and rapidly grew to become the most prosperous and imposing town on the Aegean coast after İzmir. However, its fortunes declined after a serious earthquake at the beginning of this century, plus another one in 1944, though the most devastating recent event for Ayvalık was the expulsion of its mainly Greek Orthodox inhabitants in the exchange of populations that followed the Greek-Turkish war of 1920–22. The largest Greek Orthodox churches have been converted to mosques, sporting concrete minarets added in the 1950s. Ironically, most of the people resettled here after 1923 were Greek-speaking Muslims from Crete and Mitilini, and many of Ayvalık's older inhabitants still speak Greek.

A few streets back from the waterfront, Ayvalık is anything but a modern tourist town, its essential nature little changed despite the inroads of commercialization at the fringes. Riotously painted horsecarts clatter through the cobbled bazaar, and this is one Turkish place where you're far more likely to be mown down by one of these than by a car. In the bazaar itself, crafts are still alive and well, as cobblers, copper- and tinsmiths and watch-repairers ply their trades from ramshackle wooden premises. Ayvalık is also famous for its fine yoghurt, cheese and *kepekli* (wholegrain) bread, a veritable godsend for vegetarians after weeks of the typical Turkish foam-rubber loaves and overprocessed foil-wrapped dairy products. Thursday is the special market day, when the backstreets overflow with produce and tattier dry goods.

Above all, however, Ayvalık presents the spectacle – almost unique in the Aegean – of a perfectly preserved Ottoman bourgeois town, a fact recently recognized by both UNESCO and the Turkish tourism authorities. There are few specific sites other than the **converted nineteenth-century churches** punctuating the warren of inland streets, and little point in asking directions: just use the minarets as landmarks, and give yourself over to the pleasure of wandering under numerous wrought-iron window grilles and past ornately carved doorways.

The most conspicuous church, Ayios Ioannis, is now the **Saatlı Cami**, renamed after its clock tower. Just north of here and up the hill lies the **Taksiyarhis Kilisesi**, which was never converted into a mosque but is now undergoing restoration in preparation for its imminent opening as a museum. Southeast of the Saatlı stands ex-Ayios Yioryios, now the **Çınarlı Camı**, misnamed insomuch as not one of the half-dozen trees gracing its courtyard is a plane (*çınar* in Turkish).

Eating, drinking and other practicalities

The choice of **restaurants** in Ayvalık doesn't quite match up to the variety of hotels and *pansiyon*s, and if you get to stay at *Chez Beliz* you may be tempted by her lavish cuisine and stay put. If you do venture out, head for *Bengi Lokantası* near the front on Talatpaşa Caddesi. The *Bengi* serves good-value steamtray fare and excellent sweets in clean premises. On the street leading from here to Cumhuriyet Meydanı, *Celal Ustanin Yeri* serves home-style Turkish food at tables outside, but is more pricy. Opposite the PTT on İnönü Caddesi, the *Kardeşler Pide ve Kebab Salonu* does nine different sorts of kebabs including *beyti* and *İskender*, while the *Odak Cafeteria* opposite the information booth on İskele Meydanı is popular for *İskender* and durum filled with *döner*. Going up in price and quality of service, the *Özcanli Balık* on the front has good *meze*s from under $2, with fish and seafood starting at $3 a piece. Between Edremit and İnönü *caddesi*s there are a number of **beer** outlets in a vine-covered street, with the *Hüsünün Yeri Meyhane* round the corner. The *Atarabası Bar* off Gümrük Sokak is the nearest approximation to a European bar, serving spaghetti and sangria in a friendly atmosphere where women are welcome.

Avis **car rental** is at Talatpaşa Cad 67/B (☎0266/312 2456). **Currency** can be changed at *Gunaydın Döviz* on İnönü Cad, travellers' cheques at the PTT. There's an astonishing range of English **newspapers** and periodicals on sale at the newspaper booth on Cumhuriyet Meydanı; if it's time to do your **laundry**, head for *Ak Pak*, Edremit Cad 38.

Boat tours and ferries to Lésvos

One of the most pleasant excursions from Ayvalık is a **boat trip** around its islands. This costs a mere $6, includes lunch, and lasts around six hours or more, taking in stops for swimming, and sightseeing at Alibey harbour (see opposite). Plenty of boats tout for custom between around 9.30 and 11am every morning, near the tourist information booth.

From Ayvalık there are supposedly regular **ferries to Lésvos** in summer, but it's worth stressing at the outset that the two communities exist in a state of semi-permanent feud, which inevitably affects sailings: schedules are the least reliable of any of the Greek island–Turkish mainland crossings, and for years a rule has been applied to the effect that you have to do the outward and return journeys with the same boat, whether it be Turkish or Greek. The two agencies who deal with the crossing are *Ayvalık Tour*, also known as *Jale*, at Gümrük Cad 41/A (☎0266/312 2740), and *Yeni İstanbul Tur* next to the *Aziz Arslan Otel* off Cumhuriyet Meydanı (☎0266/312 6123). The service runs from May to September, with three boats a week leaving Ayvalık at 9am and returning at 4pm. The round trip costs $65, one way $50, and a car is $60 extra; in Greece, you pay a $20 port tax.

Sarımsaklı

Some of the best beaches in the area are 6km south of Ayvalık at **SARIMSAKLI** (literally "Garlic Beach"), a growing resort accessible by dolmuş or one of the municipal buses from İskele Meydanı. The development is now frankly out of hand, with streets here perennially torn up by the constant construction. You could stay here too – there are plenty of big tourist hotels – but, in season at least, most of these cost an arm and a leg, and if you aren't on a package and haven't got vast amounts of cash to spare, or an overt taste for grossness, it's far better to remain in Ayvalık and take the bus or dolmuş to Sarımsaklı for the beach life. The sandy shore is admittedly attractive, getting less crowded and developed as you head away from town in either direction along its three-to-four-kilometre length.

If you're determined to **stay** in Sarımsaklı, there are a couple of budget *pansiyon*s off the main drag near the PTT, the *Ankara Anı Pansiyon* and the *El Pansiyon* next door (☎0266/324 1161), both ②. Good value at a higher price is offered by the comfortable *Varol* (☎0266/324 0999; ③), which has big rooms with balconies overlooking a garden, on the other side of the road from the beach.

For **food**, try the reasonably priced *köfte*, *börek*, soup and *mantı* at the *Hanımeli Sofrası*, on the seafront road leading to the *Varol*. There's a **car rental** agency, *Gold*, at Atatürk Meydanı, Rüya Apt 6 (☎0266/324 2331), which also rents **mopeds** for $24 a day.

Up to Şeytan Sofrası

Between Ayvalık and Sarımsaklı, the headland that juts out into the Aegean levels off at Şeytan Sofrası (The Devil's Dinner Table). This distinctive rocky outcrop sits virtually at the centre of a vast array of islands and almost-islands, of which Alibey (see below) and more distant Lésvos are just two. Such convoluted topography is typical of volcanic archipelagos like this one; in clear weather it's certainly worth the trip up for views extending a hundred kilometres around, and perhaps also to spot otherwise hidden beaches below, to be reached later with your own vehicle.

In summer a **bus** leaves for Şeytan Sofrası at 7pm from the minibus stand near Ayvalık's PTT (returning after sunset), but if you come to watch the sun go down, you'll probably be accompanied by massive crowds intent on the same haunting experience. At the northern edge there's a small cavity in a rock, supposedly Satan's footprint, into which people throw money for luck; more prominent, however, are the numerous votive rags tied onto bushes by the country folk to placate the presiding genius of the place, Satan or otherwise.

Alibey (Cunda) Island

Across the bay from Ayvalık, the island of **ALİBEY** – known also as **Cunda Adası** – constitutes either a good day-trip destination or an overnight halt, with its couple of patches of beach and some quayside fish restaurants. The best way to **get here** in summer is by boat from Ayvalık: in addition to tour boats (see opposite), a regular ferry service runs every half-hour from the landing near the tourist information office at İskele Meydanı (20min; $1). At other times you'll have to rely on the half-hourly bus service from İskele Meydanı or a taxi (expensive – establish the fare first) to cross the bridge linking island to mainland.

Alibey seems a quieter, less grand version of Ayvalık: behind the harbour sprawls a grid of sleepy backstreets lined by dilapidated but still imposing stone houses and the odd remnant of life before 1922, when Cunda was known as Moskhonissi to its largely Greek-speaking inhabitants. After the Greeks were deported, the island was resettled with Cretan Muslims from around Hania, and you'll find that most people over fifty speak Greek as a matter of course. Recently the place has slowly woken up to outsiders, many of whom are buying up and restoring the old houses for an Aegean retreat feasibly close to İstanbul.

Halfway up the slope from the waterfront stands the Orthodox **Cathedral of Taksiarhis**, now all but deserted and home only to a Greek-speaking caretaker, its interior retaining a few defaced and faded frescoes. The church was heavily damaged in the earthquake of 1944 and rumoured restoration has yet to materialize. Above the town on a hill, there's a small, roofless chapel, now used as a stable, from where you can gaze out across the bay to Ayvalık.

The northern half of Alibey, known as Patrica, has some relatively deserted sand-and-gravel beaches, though as ever horrible villa complexes are beginning to sprout. Pleasure launches on the quay offer trips to these coves, as well as to an enormous derelict Greek monastery accessible only by sea.

Accommodation possibilities on the island include the rather basic *Altay Pansiyon* (☎0266/327 1204; ①), situated a couple of blocks inland from the harbour, and the slightly upmarket *Altun Pansiyon*, with en-suite bathrooms, further back into the village (☎0266/327 1554; ②). Prices and comfort levels increase toward the waterside, where the best value is on offer at the *Artur* (☎0266/327 1014; ③), with en-suite bathrooms, TVs and fridges, right on the quay. The **restaurant** attached to the *Artur* is excellent, with a great selection of *mezes* and kalamari, at reasonable prices for this standard of preparation. Keep an eye out for the inexpensive local seafood speciality, *papalina*, a sort of small, tasty smelt. For breakfast look no further than the *Ada Mandıra* on the inland market square, which doles out yoghurt made of milk from the island's contented cows.

You may see some of these on the way to Alibey's main **campsite**, *ADA Camping* (3km southwest of town on a rough road), which provides good facilities and access to the best beach on the island. *Ortunç Camping*, 1km beyond, has a restaurant, some rooms and a scrappy beach.

Bergama

Though frequently touted as a day-trip destination from Ayvalık, **BERGAMA**, site of the ancient city of Pergamon, rates a full day or two in its own right. The stunning acropolis of the tyrant Eumenes II is the main attraction, but there is a host of lesser sights, and an old quarter of chaotic charm, to detain you a little longer. Bergama is unpromising at first: the long approach to the centre reveals a dusty modern-looking place, and the monuments to which it owes its reputation are nowhere to be seen. In fact, most of ancient Pergamon is some distance from the modern town and takes a little effort to reach.

Arrival and information

Bergama has **two otogars**: the second, unpublicized one, is just south of the Kızıl Avlu, with valuable supplemental services from and to points east and north. Most useful are the links with Bursa (until evening) and Soma, 45km away, on the **main rail line** between İzmir and Bandırma (it's a short taxi ride between Soma's train and bus stations). When leaving Bergama, you can easily connect with either the morning or evening trains to Bandırma and its ferry to İstanbul – by far the easiest and cheapest way of reaching the city from Bergama. So-called "direct" night buses to İstanbul from the main *otogar*, incidentally, tend to be uncomfortable, slow and expensive. If you're visiting on a day trip from Ayvalık, note that the last direct dolmuş back departs from the main *otogar* at 5pm; if you miss it, there'll be a few more minibuses to Ayvalık via Dikili with *Dikili Ko-op* until about 8pm.

Bergama's **tourist information office** is on Atatürk Meydanı next to the archeological museum (summer daily 8.30am–7pm; winter daily 8.30am–5.30pm; ☎0232/633 1862).

Accommodation and eating

The town's bigger and more expensive **hotels** announce themselves loudly enough on the approach to town, as do the two local **campsites**. The latter are signposted near an onyx shop just south of the town limits. Bergama's best budget accommodation, however, tends to be located in the old town, although there are also a few possibilities **near the main otogar**. Here, the *Pension Manolya*, Maltepe Mahallesi, Tanpınar Sok 5

(☎0232/633 4488; ②), is excellent value for very clean rooms with en-suite facilities. The friendly *Böblingen Pansiyon*, Asklepion Cad 2 (☎0232/633 2153; ①–③), has an annexe at the back with very comfortable rooms, but otherwise suffers from traffic noise. They offer rooms with or without bathrooms and serve a good breakfast on their terrace.

In the **old town**, the *Athena* at Barbaros Mah, Imam Çıkmazı 5 (☎0232/633 3420; ①–②), occupies a 150-year-old Greek house as well as a new annexe with en-suite facilities. On the other side of the old stone bridge, Tabak Köprü, the *Nike Pansiyon* is justifiably popular in season (☎0232/633 3901; ①); bathrooms are shared and they do an excellent breakfast in their fine garden courtyard. If you can't get into either of these, try the *Pergamon Pansiyon*, another atmospheric old house, with some en-suite but rather run-down rooms, at Bankalar Cad 5 (☎0232/633 2395; ①); the courtyard restaurant is a good option whether or not you're staying.

Of the **upmarket hotels** on the way into Bergama on the İzmir Asfaltı, the *Berksoy* (☎0232/633 2595; ⑥) is probably the most comfortable, with its extensive grounds and outdoor pool; the *Otel Asude*, at İzmir Asfaltı 63 (☎0232/633 0512; ⑥), is another reasonable option, as long as you ask for a room at the back.

In general, the **restaurant** situation in Bergama is pretty dismal: menus are dull and expensive, especially at the blatantly tourist-pitched establishments along the approach to the Kızıl Avlu, so many give up and settle for *pide*. Exceptions are *Sağlam 2*, on Istiklâl Meydanı, and *Sağlam 3*, at Hükümet Meyd 29, not far down from the tourist information office. The former specializes in *kiremit kebap*, baked in the oven, with cheese, and serves excellent *lavaş pide*, massive puffed flat bread with melted butter and cheese. *Sağlam 3* has a wide variety of *lokanta*-style *sulu yemek* and *izgara*, but they specialize in eastern food from the Urfa region, including *içli köfte*, a really spicy *güveç*, and *beyti sarma* (a roll of spicy *Adana kebap* covered in unleavened bread, then sliced and served with salad), the chef's speciality. They have a garden courtyard out back and rooms upstairs where you can dine seated on cushions around low tables. The *Sarmaşık Lokantası* is another reliable option on İstiklâl Meydanı. Beware of signs at the *Kardeşler* on the way out of town on the İzmir Asfaltı offering as much food as you can eat for $4 a head: the food comes cold and bland, and drinks are priced through the roof.

The Town

The foremost attraction in Bergama itself is probably the **Kızıl Avlu** or "Red Basilica" (daily 8.30am–5.30pm; $2), a huge redbrick edifice on the river below the acropolis, originally built as a second-century AD temple to the Egyptian god Serapis and converted into a basilica by the Byzantines. Early in Christianity it was one of the Seven Churches of Asia Minor addressed by St John in the Book of Revelation – he refers to it as home of the throne of the devil, perhaps referring to the still-extant Egyptian cult. It's now a crumbling ruin containing a mosque in one of its towers, with the ancient Selinus River (today called the Bergama Çayı) passing underneath the basilica via two intact tunnels; just downstream you'll see a handsome, equally well-preserved Ottoman bridge.

The area around and uphill from the basilica is given over to the **old quarter** of the town, a jumble of Ottoman buildings, antique and carpet shops, mosques and maze-like streets full of vitality and colour. The antique stalls are full of very beautiful and very overpriced copperware, costing even more than in İstanbul – too many coach tours have had their effect. Similarly, the formerly good reputation of Bergama carpets has been besmirched by too much synthetic dye and machine-weaving – beware.

Back on the main drag into town you'll find the **Archeological Museum** (daily 8.30am–5.30pm; $2), which not surprisingly has a large collection of locally unearthed booty, including a statue of Hadrian from the Asclepion, and various busts of figures like Zeus and Socrates. There's also a model of the Zeus altar, complete with the Berlin-resident reliefs.

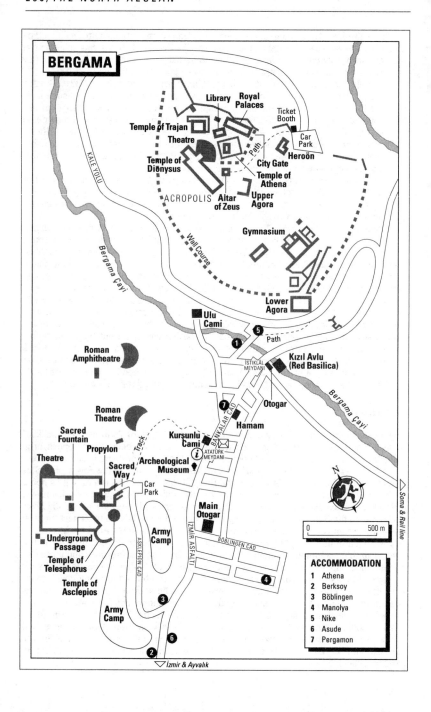

BERGAMA

Library
Royal Palaces
Ticket Booth
Temple of Trajan
Car Park
Theatre
KALE YOLU
Path
Temple of Dionysus
City Gate
Heroön
Temple of Athena
ACROPOLIS
Altar of Zeus
Upper Agora
Wall Course
Bergama Çayı
Gymnasium
Lower Agora
Ulu Cami
Path
Roman Amphitheatre
İSTIKLÂL MEYDANI
Kızıl Avlu (Red Basilica)
Bergama Çayı
Otogar
Roman Theatre
Hamam
Sacred Fountain
Kurşunlu Cami
Propylon
Track
ATATÜRK MEYDANI
Theatre
Archeological Museum
Sacred Way
Car Park
Underground Passage
Main Otogar
Temple of Telesphorus
Army Camp
İZMIR ASFALTI
BANKALAR CAD
BÖBLINGEN CAD
Temple of Asclepios
ASKLEPION CAD
Army Camp
Soma & Rail line

0   500 m

N

İzmir & Ayvalık

ACCOMMODATION
1 Athena
2 Berksoy
3 Böblingen
4 Manolya
5 Nike
6 Asude
7 Pergamon

The ancient sites

The first recorded mention of **Pergamon** dates from 399 BC, but the town only gained prominence when it became the base of Lysimachus, one of Alexander the Great's generals. He left some of his accumulated wealth in the hands of his officer Philetarus, who inherited the lot when Lysimachus was killed in battle fighting Syria for control of Asia Minor. By skilled political manoeuvring Philetarus was able to hang on to his new-found riches, passing them on to his adopted son Eumenes, who again defeated the Syrians at Sardis and extended further the domain of Philetarus.

Eumenes, generally recognized as the founder of the Pergamene dynasty, was succeeded in 241 BC by his nephew, Attalus I, whose immediate task was to defeat the Gauls; this he did with the help of the sacrifice of an animal whose liver turned out to bear the word "Victory". Attalus was a cunning ruler – it later emerged that he had secretly imprinted the word onto the liver with a specially made ring – and his authority was soon assured, the fame of his kingdom spreading across the Hellenistic world. Thus installed, he went on to build the Temple of Athena and the library in Pergamon.

Attalus's son and successor, Eumenes II, consolidated his father's gains, allied himself with the Romans and set about building Pergamon into a great city. He later helped the Romans to defeat the Syrians at the Battle of Magnesium, extending his sphere of influence. Under Eumenes II, the gymnasium and theatre were built, and the acropolis was secured with a wall. The last king of Pergamon, Attalus III, was less interested in ruling than in chemistry (he spent a lot of time conducting experiments with poisons on criminals), and died after a short reign, perversely leaving his realm to the Romans. Under them Pergamon thrived, growing into a city of 150,000 people that was a renowned artistic and commercial centre. With the arrival of the Goths in 262 AD, the city began a gradual decline, and passed through the hands of a succession of invaders before falling into ruin.

The German railway engineer Karl Humann rediscovered ancient Pergamon in 1871, when he found a strange mosaic in the possession of some local road workers that turned out to be part of the relief from the Altar of Zeus. Humann bought the mosaic from the farmers, gave notice to his Ottoman employers on the rail line, and five years later began excavating the acropolis. Work was completed in 1886, and unfortunately most of the finds were carted off to Germany, not least the reliefs from the Zeus altar, which you can only view in the Pergamon Museum in Berlin.

Getting around the sites

The **acropolis**, the ancient city of the kings of Pergamon, sits atop a rocky bluff towering over modern Bergama, while just out of town, to the west, is the **Asclepion**, the ancient medical centre. The old town with its Kızıl Avlu lies at the foot of the acropolis, about ten minutes' walk from the main *otogar*. As soon as you get off the bus at this *otogar* you'll probably be approached by a **taxi driver** offering to ferry you around the ruins for over $12. If there are a few of you or you're in a hurry, this can make sense, but otherwise it's a bit of a racket, limiting you to one hour at the acropolis (you'll almost certainly want to spend more time there), ten minutes at the red basilica and half an hour at the Asclepion.

If you're not pushed for time, it's easy enough to walk to both the basilica and Asclepion without too much trouble. The acropolis is readily accessible on foot by way of a **path** up from the old town – though this is one attraction you may want to reach by taxi, at least on the way up, since the path can be difficult to find in that direction. The trail actually begins on the far side of the second bridge upstream from the Kızıl Avlu, angling obliquely up to the road, then across into the lower agora (see below for specifics of all these sites). If you set off early before it gets hot, it's not a difficult trek for anyone of average fitness. In any case, try not to walk there following the main road, which is steep and not particularly direct, doubling back on itself for about 5km.

The acropolis

Taxis up to **the acropolis** (daily 8.30am–5.30pm, summer until 7pm; $2, plus $1 for own vehicle) drop you off in the site car park, where a ramp leads up to the former **city gate**, though this has almost completely disappeared. On your left is the **Heroön**, an ancient temple built to honour the kings of Pergamon and reportedly lined with white marble in Roman times.

From here a path leads southwest to the huge square **Altar of Zeus**, standing in the shade of two great pine trees. The altar was built during the reign of Eumenes II to commemorate his father's victory over the Gauls, and was decorated with reliefs depicting the battle between the Titans and the gods, symbolizing the triumph of order over chaos, and, presumably, that of Attalus over the Gauls. Even today its former splendour is apparent, though it has been much diminished by the removal of the reliefs to Berlin. The main approach stairway was on the west, though this is the most deteriorated side today.

THE TEMPLE OF ATHENA AND THE LIBRARY

Directly northeast of and exactly parallel to the Zeus altar, on the next terrace up, lie the remains of the **Temple of Athena**, dating back to the third century BC. Only some of the stepped foundations on which it was built have survived, although the entrance gate, with the inscription recording its dedication by "King Eumenes to Athena the Bearer of Victories", has been reconstructed in Berlin.

The scanty north stoa of the temple once housed Pergamon's famous **Library**, which at its peak rivalled that of Alexandria. Founded by Attalus II, it came to have a catalogue of 200,000 books. Eumenes II was particularly active in building it up, interestingly enough augmenting the collection by borrowing books from other libraries and not returning them. He is also said to have paid for books by Aristotle and Theophrastus with their weight in gold. Eventually the Egyptian kings, alarmed at the growth of the Pergamon library, which they saw as a threat to their own library in Alexandria, banned the export of papyrus, on which all books were written – and of which they were sole producers – thereby attempting to stem the library's expansion.

In response Eumenes offered a reward to anyone who could come up with a replacement, and the old custom of writing on specially treated animal skins – parchment – was revived, leading to the invention of the codex or paged book, since it wasn't possible to roll up parchment like papyrus. The words "parchment", and the more archaic "pergamene", are both actually derived from "Pergamon". The library was ransacked by Mark Antony, who gave the choicest items to Cleopatra as a gift, but enough remained for it to be consulted up until the fourth century AD.

Despite this illustrious history, not much more than the library foundations remain at the moment, but the German archeologists who have been digging here more or less continuously since 1878 are set to commence restoring it now that they've finished work on the Temple of Trajan.

THE TEMPLE OF TRAJAN AND AROUND

Still further north and higher up looms the Corinthian **Temple of Trajan**, where Trajan and Hadrian were both revered during Roman times – their busts were taken from the temple and are also now in Berlin. The Germans recently completed the re-erection of the temple columns, plus those from the stoa that surrounded the shrine on three sides. The north architrave is lined with Medusa heads, two of them modern recastings.

Behind the temple are mounds of rubble and collapsed walls – the remains of barracks and the highest reaches of the city's **perimeter wall**. Nearby yawns a cistern with a pillar, either a level indicator or core of a vanished stairway, in the centre – this was fed by an **aqueduct**, traces of which are still visible running parallel to a modern one on the hillside to the northwest. A reliable water supply was an obvious preoccupation for those dwelling atop this arid plug, though judging from the huge modern reservoir to the north and the town's perennial rivers, contemporary Bergama is well served in this regard.

Finally, as you begin your descent back down toward the main entrance, you'll pass – east of the library and Athena temple – the extensive but jumbled ruins of the **royal palaces**.

THE THEATRE

From the Temple of Athena a narrow staircase leads down to the **theatre**, the most spectacular part of the acropolis. Dating from Hellenistic times, it was cut into the hillside and was capable of seating 10,000 spectators. According to the architectural conventions of the day, the auditoria of Greek theatres were always greater than a semicircle, but at Pergamon, the steepness of the site made this impossible, and the architects compensated by building upwards, creating a narrow, sharply raked auditorium with eighty rows of seats. The stage was built from wood and removed after performances – the holes into which supporting posts were driven can still be seen on the terrace at the foot of the auditorium. One of the reasons for the use of a portable stage was to allow free access to the **Temple of Dionysos**, built just off-stage to the audience's right.

THE UPPER AND LOWER AGORAS

Just south of the Altar of Zeus lies a terrace, formerly the **Upper Agora** of Pergamon. There isn't much to see today, other than Karl Humann's grave, although this was once the commercial and social focal point of the city. A path leads down from here to the **Lower Agora**, where the common people lived and went about their business.

In among the remains of various houses, at the foot of the path to the agora, is the **Temple of Demeter**, where the local variant of the Eleusinian Mysteries, a cultic ceremony supposed to guarantee a better life after death, was enacted. On the northern side of the temple are the remains of a building, containing nine rows of seats with space for about a thousand people, which it's thought were for spectators at the ritual. Below the temple are a fountain for ritual ablutions and a pit designed to receive the blood of animals sacrificed in the temple. Nearby is a **gymnasium**, spread out over three terraces, where the children of the city were educated. The upper level, with its sports ground, was for young men, the middle was used by the adolescents, while the lower served as a kind of playground for younger children. In the area around are the remains of various houses and the **lower agora**.

Once you've reached the lower agora, it should be a simple matter to find the path from here back down to town – the cirular blue waymarks are much easier to see on the way down.

The Asclepion

Bergama's other significant archeological site is the **Asclepion** (daily 8.30am–5.30pm, summer closes 7pm; $2), a Greco-Roman medical centre that can be reached on foot from the old aqueduct in the modern town or, more straightforwardly, along the road starting opposite the PTT, by the Kurşunlu Cami – a drive or walk of 1500m. Note that the ruins lie within a large and clearly marked military zone, which is closed to traffic at dusk – avoid entering any surrounding army camps and don't take photographs away from the site itself.

The Asclepion was devoted to Asclepios, son of Apollo and the god of healing, who supposedly served as a doctor in the army of Agamemnon during the siege of Troy. According to myth, Asclepios learned how to bring the dead back to life using the blood of the Gorgon which Athena had given to him. Zeus, worried that Asclepios's activities were endangering the natural order of things, struck him down with a thunderbolt but elevated him to the stars in compensation.

In part, the healing methods practised at the Asclepion were ritualistic in nature, with patients required to sleep in the temple in order that Asclepios might appear to them in a dream to relay his diagnosis and suggest treatment. However, dieting, bathing and exercise also played an important role in the therapeutic regime. Galen (131–201 AD), the greatest physician of the ancient world, who laid down the basis of much of modern medical science and served as personal physician to the emperor Marcus Aurelius, was trained here.

Much of what can be seen today was built in the reign of the emperor Hadrian (117–138 AD), the early stages of the first- and second-century heyday of the Pergamene Asclepion, when its function was similar to that of a nineteenth-century spa. Some patients came here to be cured of ailments, but for others a visit to the Asclepion was simply a social event, part of the habitual existence of the wealthy and leisured.

THE SITE

From the site entrance, a long, colonnaded sacred way known as the **Via Tecta** leads to the **Propylon** or monumental entrance gate. The propylon was built during the third century AD, after an earthquake which had seriously damaged the complex in the previous century. Northeast of the propylon is a square building which housed a **library** and the statue of Hadrian now on display in the local museum (see p.249).

To the south of the propylon lies the circular **Temple of Asclepios**, dating from 150 AD and modelled on the Pantheon in Rome. The domed roof of this graceful structure was 24m in diameter and had a circular opening in the centre to allow light and air to penetrate. The floor and walls would have been decorated with mosaics, and recesses housed statues of the gods. To the west of the propylon and temple, the broad, open area was originally enclosed by colonnaded walkways, the bases of which can still be seen. At the western end of the northern colonnade is a **theatre** with a seating capacity of 3500, which served to keep patients entertained. At the centre of the open area, the **sacred fountain** still gushes with weakly radioactive drinking water. Nearby an 80m-long underground passage leads to the **Temple of Telesphoros** (a lesser deity associated with Asclepios) – a two-storey circular building, which, like the Temple of Asclepios, served as a place for patients to sleep while awaiting dream diagnoses. The lower storey survives in good repair.

The coast south of Ayvalık

The coast road south from Ayvalık takes you near a number of small resort towns, although the best stretch of sandy **beach** is en route, beginning just south of Altınova and continuing for about 15km to Dikili. It is, however, only really accessible if you have your own transport, and in any case has very few facilities.

Dikili and around

Easily reached by dolmuş from Ayvalık or Bergama, **DİKİLİ**, with a population of about 10,000, is smaller and less touristy than many of the resorts along this stretch of coast. Cruise liners occasionally dock in the harbour, allowing their passengers to make day excursions to Bergama and Ayvalık, or head for the beaches to the north; there's a decent beach, and in the town itself there's a promenade lined with cafés and restaurants. But it's small and the kind of place whose possibilities are soon exhausted; a day, or less, is really the most you could spend here before getting itchy for somewhere else.

From the *otogar*, the tree-lined high street leads south to the centre of town. Several decent **accommodation** possibilities lie further out from the *otogar* along the same road: the *Pension Dikili* (☎0232/671 2454; ②) and the *Halat Pansiyon* (☎0232/671 4825; ②), behind the similarly priced *Palmiye*, are all clean and reasonable. A good mid-range choice is the *Sinka ve Antur* (☎0232/671 4717; ③), directly behind the main square and its equestrian Atatürk statue – there's traffic noise but some sea views. Slotting into the next bracket up is the *Tanriverda Perla Hotel*, on the road to Çandarlı (☎0232/6714849; ④), well south of the centre and with unobstructed sea views.

There are numerous **cafés and restaurants** along the shore esplanade, but better value is the restaurant of the *Sinka ve Antur*, where you can eat excellent *mezes* or sardines cooked in three different ways.

A few kilometres south of Dikili, accessible by dolmuş from opposite the *Ziraat Bankası*, **BADEMLİ** is a tiny village with a **campsite**, the *Çamlımanı*, about 500m before you reach the village. The sea here, however, is rather distant, and stagnant when you do get to it. There's another attractive campsite in the village itself, as well as a handful of **teahouses and restaurants** – the local speciality is *koruk şurubu*, a drink made from young grapes.

Although the village is practically untouched by tourism, there's an excellent **pansiyon**, run by *Er Turistick Tesisleri* (☎0232/671 8084; ①–②), offering double rooms or well-furnished flats with kitchens. They have a private beach, called Temenos, a couple of kilometres out of town off the Pisa road.

Çandarlı

About half an hour to the south of Dikili by several daily buses, is the small fishing port and resort of **ÇANDARLI** , catering mainly for İzmir-resident weekenders. It occupies a headland that was formerly the site of ancient Pitane, the northernmost Aeolian city, though nothing remains of this. Despite its pedigree, the oldest building in Çandarlı is a perfectly restored fourteenth-century **Genoese fort**, not open to the public, incorporating recognizable chunks of the ancient city. This is one of several such forts dotting the northwestern Turkish coast and the Greek islands immediately opposite, a reminder of the days when the military and commercial might of Genoa dominated the North Aegean.

The beach is coarse sand, but – except in high summer – Çandarlı is not a bad place to get away from the crowds for a day or two of relaxation. It's remarkably clean and well kept, with excellent *pansiyon*s and a welcoming atmosphere absent in some larger resort towns.

The most comfortable **accommodation** is on the harbour, visible from the dolmuş drop-off point, the excellent-value *Hotel Diamond* (☎0232/673 2893; ③). Right next to the dolmuş stop, the *Kaya Pansiyon* is also good value and friendly (☎0232/673 3058; ③). It's a pleasant ten-minute walk to the beach from the dolmuş drop-off through Uğur Mumcu Parkı and the town's produce market. The *Gül Pansiyon* is a good option near the beach, with a kitchen per floor, shared bathrooms and a terrace with sea views (☎0232/673 3347; ②).

Most of Çandarlı's fancier **restaurants**, **cafés** and **bars** line the shore road: for reasonably priced seafood, look no further than the *Kalender Restaurant*. The ordinary life of the town, though, has gravitated decisively to the east side of the peninsula, near the bus stop. Here the lively market square is surrounded by simple soup-and-*pide* kitchens, beer halls, old Greek houses, the **PTT** and a **bank**. Six or seven buses a day run each way between Çandarlı and İzmir in summer, but beware of sharply reduced connections out of season.

Foça

The town of **FOÇA** lies 65km south of Çandarlı, west of the main road. To reach it, take any İzmir-bound bus and ask to be let off at the turning for Foça. From here a dolmuş or one of the almost-hourly direct buses from İzmir itself should take you the remaining 26km into town.

Foça is the modern successor (and linguistically a corruption) of ancient **Phocaea**, founded around 1000 BC by Ionian colonists; it was thus later reckoned a member of the Ionian confederation, despite lying squarely in Aeolian territory. The Phocaeans became renowned seafarers whose enormous, state-of-the-art boats plied the principal trade routes of the Mediterranean throughout the fifth century BC, establishing among other places the city of Massilia, now Marseilles. Powered by fifty oarsmen, the galleys were capable of carrying five hundred passengers or the equivalent in precious metals. On the basis of excavations carried out in 1913, it is claimed that the prodigious Phocaeans also introduced writing into southern France and were responsible for olive cultivation in the Mediterranean basin. In later times, the Byzantines gave Phocaea as a wedding present to the Genoese, who restored its castle and managed to retain the city during the fourteenth century by paying tribute to the Saruhan emirs and later the Ottomans.

The original name *Phocaea* is derived from the ancient Greek word for "seal", and the beast features in modern local statues, promotional signs, and so forth. The small local colony of endangered **monk seals** – whose barking may have given rise to the myth of the sirens luring sailors onto the rocks, which features in Homer's *Odyssey* – has now been afforded special protection by Turkey's council of ministers and is the target of a World Wildlife Fund conservation project (visitors are welcome at their public information office at Küçükdeniz just behind Sahil Yolu). Frankly you'd have to *be* a seal to really enjoy the ocean here, which owing to strong currents and sharp drop-off is notoriously chilly most of the year. The other fortuitous restraint on development has been the pervasive military presence: Foça is an important naval base, and the land to the north is out of bounds.

None of this has prevented Foça from becoming a favourite summer retreat for İzmir and Manisa people, who crowd out the long-term, multistorey flats that dominate the town's accommodation scene. They have recently been joined by a few German, Dutch and Norwegian package groups in conventional hotels, but the town has accommodated the tourist swell fairly graciously.

The Town

Today, sadly, little remains intact of ancient Phocaea: 9km before the town, just north of the main road, is the **Taş Kule**, an unusual-looking tomb believed to date from the fourth century BC, squatting beside an Ottoman bridge and a modern cemetery, while a small **ancient theatre** marks the east entry to Foça. Recently some mosaic pavements from a Roman villa, including an almost perfectly preserved portrayal of four Bacchus heads and birds, have been unearthed in what was to be a car park off 193 Sokak near the *Aydın Pansiyon*.

The oldest structure in Foça itself is the **Genoese fortress**, originally incorporating liberal quantities of ancient masonry; it has recently been rather crudely restored, and stage-set towers added, to serve as a touristic backdrop. More authentic are some wonderful old Greek fishermen's cottages and a few more opulent Ottoman mansions lining the cobbled backstreets inland. There are also two interesting mosques: a small, unheralded but beautiful, fifteenth-century **Fatih Camii**; and one, at the very summit of the castle enclosure, sporting a distinctly lighthouse-like minaret. In the same street as the Fatih Camii are two **hamams**, one of which is 150 years old and has been converted into a pottery workshop by local artists, while the other continues to operate daily from 8am to midnight, taking families on Wednesdays.

The castle headland lends Foça an interesting layout, splitting the bay into two smaller harbours: the northerly, more picturesque **Küçükdeniz**, where most of the action is; and the southern, rather bleak **Büyükdeniz**, which looks as if it could be anywhere in Turkey, and whose pair of hotel-restaurants is not really recommended – go only for a view of the huge fishing fleet and the *kale* on its promontory. Neither bay has a decent beach, with the shore apt to be weedy.

Practicalities

The local **tourist information office** (summer Mon–Fri 8.30am–6.30pm, Sat & Sun 10am–1pm & 5–8pm; winter Mon–Fri 8.30am–5.30pm; ☎0232/812 1222) is at the rear of the central square, opposite the bus stop, at the south end of town, though it's easy enough to find **accommodation** unassisted. If you want to stay affordably by the sea, head towards 139 Sokağı, just off the Küçükdeniz esplanade near its north end, where you'll find the *Huzur* (☎0232/872 7203; ③), the best **inexpensive** option in the area, with nicely furnished rooms and a waterside terrace. The adjacent *Fokai* is a possible option if this is full (☎0232/812 1765; ③). The nearby *Sempatik Güneş*, set one block back from the water (☎0232/812 2195; ③), is well kept and comfortable. Further away from the water, the *Zeki Pansiyon* at Fevzipaşa Mah 32 (☎0232/812 2126; ③) has plain, clean rooms, while the *Ensar Pansiyon*, 161 Sok 15 (☎0232/812 1777; ③), has sea views from the terrace and a kitchen for guests. The *Siren* next door is similarly basic and clean (☎0232/812 2660; ③).

Most comfortable of the Küçükdeniz **mid-range** premises is the *Karaçam* (☎0232/812 3216, fax 812 2042; ⑥), though you'll be lucky to squeeze in between the tour groups patronizing this restored Greek mansion. Another likely upmarket alternative is the *Minoza Hotel* on the headland above the fortress wall, between the two bays (☎0232/812 2897; ④). The owner, charming and knowledgeable about local politics and the area in general, serves evening meals and fresh coffee at breakfast.

There's a **campsite** at the Halk Plajı, 2km north of town, served by frequent dolmuşes from the *otogar* behind the main square.

For **food**, the *Sempatik Güneş* isn't cheap but it's different, serving the kind of international cuisine – Mexican steak, stroganoff with rice and spaghetti carbonara – that's very hard to find out of the big cities. The *Kordon* on Küçükdeniz esplanade isn't cheap either, but it's popular with the locals for its *çipura* (gilt-headed bream, a regional speciality) and lobster. At the extreme south end of the quay, inland among trees, the *Sedef* offers the best value in town, though choice is more limited than the boards outside would have you believe – try the *kiremit kebap* (lamb cooked on a tile).

An excellent local company, *The Nem* at Aşıklar Yolu, Küçükdeniz (next to the *Sempatik Güneş*), offers **tours** of the region by bus, horse or boat, trips to Pergamon and Efes, and **car rental** (☎0232/812 1368). *Kybele rent-a-car*, off Aşıklar Yolu at Mazhar Zola Bedesteni 110 (☎0232/812 6819), **rent bikes** for $6 a day, **motorbikes** for $18 a day.

Around the coast to Yenifoça

Around the coast towards Yenifoça, 23km by road from Foça, are some excellent beaches, often difficult to access but worth the effort for their seclusion. About 8km from Foça, you'll run into the *Turina* and the *Acar* **campsites**, each with its own good beach. Further on the *Azac*, 2km before Yenifoça, has a bar, campsite, restaurant and **pansiyon**, as well as a decent beach – a far better place to stay than Yenifoça itself. The military presence along this stretch is unobtrusive, but they do have their own beach next to the *Turina* campsite.

The scenic countryside is ideal for touring by rented motorbike, though any illusions of completely escaping development as the shore heads east are shattered by the huge Club Med complex just before **YENİFOÇA**. This too has its core of old Greek houses, but here the beach is grubby, rocky and suffers from full northern exposure. The only budget accommodation option is the unfriendly *Hotel Palmıye* (☎0232/814 6159; ③), with its own fish and meat restaurant near the PTT. All in all, the town is merely the turnaround point for heading back to Foça via an inland road, past crumbling hamlets abandoned since 1923.

Menemen: the road to İzmir

Between Foça and İzmir the coast is virtually inaccessible, since the Turkish military controls vast tracts of land and shore flanking the vital approaches to İzmir. Indeed one of the motives for building the city's modern Adnan Menderes airport was so that the airforce could have the airfield at Ciğli all to itself. Civilian habitation is accordingly very sparse, so the main road cuts inland toward the city.

The one place of consequence, 30km north of İzmir, **MENEMEN** sprawls near the Gediz River and its clay banks, which support a thriving **ceramics** industry, whose kitsch products line the bypass road. Otherwise it's a fairly forgettable town except for an old central quarter of fine Ottoman houses, mainly worth knowing about as the only place besides İzmir that has decent **dolmuş connections** with Manisa.

Manisa and around

The site of the ancient town of Magnesia ad Sipylus, **MANİSA** lies about 40km east of Menemen and is easily reached from either there or İzmir by way of pleasant mountain roads. Over ninety percent of the historic centre was destroyed by the Greek army during its 1922 retreat so that today the town has a modern feel; but despite this, Manisa remains an interesting place with a few fine Selçuk and Ottoman monuments, reminiscent of Bursa as it spills out from the foot of the Manisa Dağı mountain range. These by themselves may not seem enough to pull you so far off the main route to the attractions of the central Aegean, but the nearby ruins of Sardis – the ancient capital of Croesus – tip the balance in favour of a detour. An overnight stop suggests itself as a strategy: arriving in Manisa at noon, visiting Sardis in the afternoon, and spending the following morning looking around Manisa itself before moving on. In practice, however, sleeping and eating options in Manisa are both dreadful unless you've got money to burn. For visits to Sardis, you may prefer to carry on to Salihli, which boasts some good-value accommodation beyond the ancient site on the İzmir–Afyon road (see p.262).

According to Homer, Manisa was founded after the Trojan War by warriors from the area. Alexander the Great passed through during his campaign, and in 190 BC there was a huge battle here between the Romans and the Syrians, under King Antioch III. The day was decided in favour of the Romans by the cavalry of the king of Pergamon, who was given control over the city as a reward. The town finally came under direct Roman rule – and entered a period of great prosperity – after the death of Attalus III of Pergamon. For a short time during the thirteenth century Manisa was capital of the Byzantine Empire, after the sacking of İstanbul by the Fourth Crusade. In 1313 the city fell into the hands of the Selçuk chieftain Saruhan Bey; from this century date the earliest of Manisa's surviving monuments. Later, the Ottomans sent heirs to the throne here to serve an apprenticeship as local governors, in order to ready them for the rigours of İstanbul palace life.

The Town

Manisa still has a lot to recommend it; the relatively modern town centre with its extensive parklands strikes you as clean, orderly and evidently prosperous, altogether a better place to live than to stay as a tourist. The lower area, around the town's **otogar**, is an old quarter undergoing extensive redevelopment, where modern blocks, rickety old houses and building sites vie for space. Upon arrival, walk south away from the *otogar* toward the mountains for about ten minutes until you come to Doğu Caddesi – the town's main commercial street, where most of the banks and larger shops are located.

The Sultan Camii and around

The principal central attractions in Manisa are three **mosques**. At the south end of Ören Caddesi, the extension of İbrahim Gökçen Caddesi, the **Sultan Camii** was built in 1522 by the architect Acem Alisi for Ayşe Hafize, the mother of Süleyman the Magnificent, who lived here with her son while he was serving as governor. This rectangular mosque is much wider than it is deep, its single central dome flanked by two pairs of satellite domes. The decor is plain except for the blue-and-ochre painted outlines of windows and most curved surfaces. Late Ottoman Baroque paint decoration and a tiny wood-railed pulpit on the west enliven the porch – actually a *son cemaat yeri* (latecomers' praying place). The mosque was once the focus of a large *külliye* (mosque complex) that included a *medrese*, mental hospital and even an official clock-setting shop.

Every year on April 21, the *Mesir Şenlikleri* **Power-Gum Festival** – now in its 456th year – takes place around the Sultan Camii, to commemorate the occasion when a local doctor called Merkez Efendi concocted a special resin to cure Ayşe Hafize, of an unspecified ailment. The gum or *mesir macunu*, concocted from 41 herbs, is scattered from the minaret by the *muezzin* to the waiting crowd, who believe that consuming the paste will protect one from pain, especially that of snake and insect bites, until the next festival; it is also reputed to have an aphrodisiac effect.

Across the street stands the **Saruhan Bey Türbesi**, the tomb of Saruhan Bey, who took Manisa in 1313, ending Byzantine sovereignty. His army is said to have attacked Sandıkkale, the city's castle, driving a flock of goats with candles on their horns before them to give the impression that a huge army was attacking. The defenders panicked and the castle fell – an event commemorated here by a festival each November 13.

The Muradiye complex

Barely a hundred metres further east along the same side of Murat Caddesi you'll find the **Muradiye Camii**, built for Murat III in 1583–85 while he was governor here. The interior, with its stained-glass windows and relatively restrained decoration – despite the use of twelve kilos of gold – is impressive: the carved marble *mimber* or pulpit and the sultan's loggia are particularly fine, as are the İznik tiles around the *mihrab* and the windows. Unusually, a large women's gallery runs the full length of the cross-stroke of the reverse-T groundplan, a design more typical of dervish *zaviye*s (hostels), and indeed the mosque, like the Sultan Camii, was originally part of a *külliye*.

Next door to the Muradiye Camii, housed in the former *imaret* or soup kitchen for religious scholars, is the **Manisa Museum** (daily except Mon 8.30am–12.30pm & 1.30–5.30pm; $1), where you'll find rather poorly lit local archeological exhibits from the Bronze Age onwards. Among the most memorable items are weird zoomorphic and abstract Bronze Age pottery, two painted sarcophagi, Hellenistic figures of Hercules and Aphrodite, a huge *kratir* (drinking goblet), and the fountain from the Sardis synagogue. Most impressive, though, are two mosaics from Sardis: one from

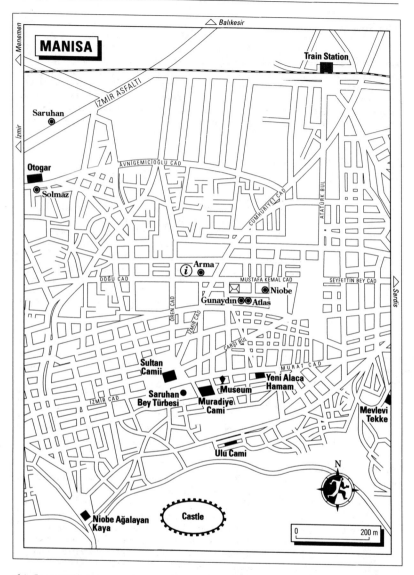

the floor of the synagogue apse, the other vivid bestiary scenes from a villa on the banks of the Pactolus. An adjacent *medrese* contains an ethnological section with Ottoman objects – weapons, caskets inlaid with mother-of-pearl, and so forth – though this wing was closed indefinitely in 1993.

Further along the same street, the still-used **Yeni Alaca Hamam** is one of the oldest bath houses in town. On Thursdays Murat Caddesi is the site of the town's large

market, where you'll find just about any kind of vegetable or fruit you could desire, as well as cheap household items and clothing.

The Ulu Cami and peripheral sites

Manisa's oldest surviving mosque, the **Ulu Cami**, sits on a natural terrace amid a panoramic park 250m directly above the museum. Built on the site of a Byzantine church in 1366 by Işak Çelebi, the grandson of Saruhan Bey, it is basically a square walled compound divided into two rectangles, with a *medrese* – still functioning as a children's Koran school – tacked onto the west side. Entering the open-roofed courtyard via the ornate portal, you confront the glory of the place, a forest of **dissimilar columns**, some double and some with distinctly pagan-looking capitals but many presumably recycled from the former church. There are more in the interior, supporting a very large central dome with the aid of Moorish arches between the pillars. Back outside, the minaret is striped with patterns of green- and grape-coloured İznik bricks.

Follow the maze of streets leading west from here to the foot of Mount Sipylus (Sipil Dağ) and you'll eventually come to **Niobe Ağlayan Kaya**, the so-called "Weeping Rock of Niobe", which appears to take the form of a woman's head, from which tears can supposedly be seen issuing every Friday. According to legend, Niobe was the daughter of Tantalus and had seven daughters and six sons. She taunted the nymph Leto – who had only borne the divine twins Apollo and Artemis – for her relative infertility until the latter became jealous and ordered her own offspring to kill Niobe's. Niobe wept for a long time over the bodies of her children until Zeus put an end to her suffering by turning her to rock.

That's about it for sightseeing in Manisa, apart from the remnants of the **Sandıkkale** fortress above the town, and the **Mevlevihane** – a former *tekke* or gathering place of the Konya-based dervish order – housed in a solid stone building on the southeastern edge of town.

Practicalities

Manisa's **tourist office** is on the third floor at Doğu Cad 8, Eylül Işhanı 14 (Mon–Fri 8am–noon & 1–5pm; ☎0236/231 2541); they should be able to give you a town plan, and may also have someone on hand who can speak English.

On the **accommodation** front, Manisa leaves so much to be desired that most travellers visit only on a day trip. The five cheaper hotels are all fairly unpleasant, and the solitary upmarket one is vastly overpriced. The *Arma* next to the tourism information on Doğu Caddesi (☎0236/231 1980; ④) provides good service but tatty rooms, and is run by the same people as the overpriced *Saruhan* on the main İzmir–Balıkesir through road (☎0236/233 2380; ⑦). The *Otel Niobe* (☎0236/231 3745; ③) opposite the *belediye* building on Sınema Park Caddesi has surly staff and, in summer, boiling hot rooms, and the *Atlas* and *Gunaydın* are similarly dire. The only other option is the *Solmaz* opposite the *otogar* at Avnigemicioğlu Cad 163 (☎0236/232 1857; ②), which is pretty basic but probably the best inexpensive fallback in town.

As with accommodation, so with **food and drink**: substandard. Your initial overriding impression will be of the improbable number of sleazy, luridly lit, all-male "beer halls" along Doğu and İzmir *caddesi*s; in the park just to the east of the Atatürk Bulvarı and Mustafa Kemal Caddesi intersection there's a pavilion with a couple of teahouses that act as a more decorous kind of social focus. Greasy-spoon-type **restaurants** are the norm, doling out a stomach-churning repertoire of soup, sheep's head, and *tereyağlı kebap* (greasy meat steeped in butter), so specific recommendations are pretty futile; the row of eateries right opposite the *otogar* offers the most variety. About the only bright spot might be the autumn recipe of stewed quince in *pekmez* (grape molasses), the latter courtesy of the province's vineyards.

Ancient Sardis (Sart)

About 50km east of town, the major archeological site of **SARDİS** (Sart in Turkish) represents the main attraction close to Manisa, and it is easily reached by taking the Salihli dolmuş from Manisa – or the Salihli bus from İzmir. The site can also be reached by means of two morning trains from İzmir and Manisa, which are a more relaxed way of doing the trip, and can be better for the return journey since they run a bit later (7.15pm) than the dolmuşes.

As **accommodation** in Manisa is so dire, you may prefer to carry on to Salihli, a market town 8km beyond Sardis on the İzmir–Afyon road. There's nothing of historical interest in the town, but its three hotels represent far better value than Manisa's. At the budget option, the *Hotel Yener*, Dede Çelık Sok 7 (☎0236/712 5003; ③), rooms at the front have showers but may suffer a little from traffic noise, especially on market day (Wed). The upmarket *Berrak*, behind the *Yener* at Belediye Cad 59 (☎0236/713 1452; ④), and *Akgül*, clearly visible from the marketplace next to the *otogar* (☎0236/713 3737; ④), are both new and extremely comfortable.

The road to Sardis

If you're travelling by dolmuş and have the time and inclination to stop on the way, there's a 3300-year-old relief, known as the **Taş Suret**, carved into the rock of **Mount Sipylus**, above the road about 7km east of Manisa. It's generally reckoned to be a Hittite version of Cybele, the mother goddess. Ask to be let out at the Akpınar pool and climb a few hundred metres up into the cliffs above the road. The image, none too distinct, is tucked into a five-metre-high niche and was probably placed here in the hope of making the valley of the Gediz River below more fertile.

Mount Sipylus, incidentally, is associated with the ancient king **Tantalus**, whose daughter Niobe was turned into the rock back in Manisa. According to legend, Tantalus also had two sons, Pelops and Broteas, the latter of whom supposedly carved this image of Cybele on the mountainside. Pelops ended up being served up in a dish Tantalus prepared for the gods, and narrowly escaped with only his shoulder being eaten. He was later restored to life with a new ivory shoulder and Tantalus was punished by being sent to Hades, where water and food were kept eternally just out of his reach – hence the verb "to tantalize".

Continuing the journey to Sardis takes you initially through an uneventful agricultural landscape, not enlivened by the huge brickworks at Turgutlu. The fertile Gediz plain from Manisa until well past Alaşehir is totally given over to the cultivation of various kinds of grapes, particularly sultanas, for which the region is the number-one world producer.

Things pick up beyond Turgutlu as the Boz Dağları mountain range rears up to the south. When you see the ruins of ancient Sardis, get off at **SARTMUSTAFA**, a small and traditional village centred around a cluster of teahouses, where local farmers like to put their feet up while their wives and daughters work the vineyards.

Some history

Sardis is another one of those places in Turkey that is so old that it's difficult to separate its true history from myth. The area was probably inhabited as far back as 1200 BC and was later settled by the Lydians, descended from native Anatolians and Greek invaders, who rate a bizarre sociological footnote for their promotion of prostitution as a viable way for a girl to earn her dowry.

Pursuing this vein of kinkiness, another story relates how an early (690 BC) Lydian king, Candaules, was so proud of his wife's beauty that he arranged for one of his bodyguards, Gyges, to glimpse her naked. The queen realized what had happened and told Gyges that he could either kill her husband and marry her, or face immediate execution. Not surprisingly Gyges opted for the former and founded a new dynasty that was to last over a century, ending with Croesus (see below).

Sardis grew to be incredibly wealthy thanks to the gold that was washed down from the nearby mountains and caught in sheepskins by the locals. According to legend, the source of these riches was the Phrygian king **Midas**, whose touch turned everything to gold. Unable to eat, his curse was lifted when the gods had him wash his hands in the River Pactolus, which flowed down to Sardis from the south. Wherever the gold came from, the Lydians were happy enough and celebrated their wealth by inventing coinage.

The first coins were issued under the city's most celebrated king, **Croesus**, under whose rule (563–546 BC) the kingdom's prosperity grew, attracting the attention of the Persians under Cyrus the Great. Worried about this threat, Croesus consulted the Delphic oracle as to whether or not he should attack first. The oracle replied that if he did he would destroy a great empire. Croesus went to war and was defeated, and after a two-week siege Sardis fell and Croesus was supposedly burned alive by the victors.

As a Persian city, Sardis was sacked during the Ionian revolt of 499 BC. It made a comeback under Alexander the Great and the Macedonians, but was destroyed by an earthquake in 17 AD. The Romans rebuilt it, having taken it at the same time as Manisa, and the town was the site of one of the Seven Churches of Asia addressed by Saint John in the Book of Revelation. This didn't save Byzantine Sardis from conquest by Saruhan and destruction at the hands of Tamerlane in 1401, after which the city never really recovered. It only came to light again early this century, when American archeologists began excavating mostly Roman and Byzantine remains.

The sites

There are two main clusters of ruins, both easily reached on foot from the main road. The first, primarily made up of the gymnasium and synagogue (daily 7.30am–8pm; $1), lies just north of the road on the eastern edge of the village and includes the **Marble Way**, a Byzantine shopping street complete with latrines, whose holes and drainage channels are still visible. The various shops are labelled and include a restaurant, an office and a hardware shop. Foundations and low walls with discernible doorways are all that remain, although in some places Greek inscriptions and engraved basins with carved crosses can still be seen.

A left turn leads into the restored **synagogue**, whose walls are covered with impressive mosaics – though these are copies, the originals being housed in the Manisa museum; the extensive floor mosaics are, however, original. The intact walls and pillars are covered with ornate patterned tiles, and explanatory text includes a plaque honouring the donors, mostly North American Jews, for the renovation work.

Almost right next door to the synagogue is the third-century AD **gymnasium and bath complex**, the most prominent building in the city, covering five and a half acres. Its **Marble Court**, the entry from the palaestra to the baths, has been spectacularly restored to its original state when first built in AD 211 – though some features of its renovation in the second half of the fifth century have been included. The walls behind the columns would have had marble revetments, and the podia would have supported statues, forming a multi-storeyed facade so visually splendid as to suggest that the baths must have been associated with observance of the imperial cult.

Behind the court are the remains of a swimming pool and rest area. Following the main road east from here toward Salihli, you'll come across more ruins – none as impressive as the Marble Court but including what's left of a Roman stadium, an agora, a basilica and a theatre.

From the village teahouses, a paved track – very poorly marked on the far side of the highway west of the synagogue – leads 1200m south from the main road to the other main site, the **Temple of Artemis**. You pay a separate fee of $1 to enter this partly enclosed site – in the past the ruins have been left exposed to vandalism, with only plaintive signs in English and Turkish attempting to dissuade graffiti artists. There are no facilities other than a nearby barbecue area by the Pactolus stream.

The temple, once among the four largest in Asia Minor, was built by Croesus, destroyed by Greek raiders during the Ionian revolt and later rebuilt by Alexander the Great. Today a baker's dozen of massive **Ionic columns**, dating from both Hellenistic and Roman times, remain standing, though only two are completely intact. Enough of the foundations are visible to make clear just how large the building, constructed to rival the temples of Ephesus, Samos and Didyma, used to be. In the southeastern corner of the site are the remains of a small brick Byzantine church. More than anything, however, it's the beauty of the setting, enclosed by wooded and vined hills, and accented by weird Cappadocia-like pinnacles, that leaves a lasting impression.

Alaşehir

Perched between high mountains and a vine-covered valley leading down to the Gediz flood plain, **ALAŞEHİR** is a pleasant although nondescript town easily reached from Sardis or Salihli. Founded originally by Attalus II of Pergamon, and later the Philadelphia of the early Church (one of St John's Seven Churches of Revelations), its residents always astonished historians by their loyalty to the site despite repeated destruction by earthquakes. This strategic location also wasn't spared the tug of war between Turks and Byzantines, though amazingly it held out as an enclave against the Ottomans until 1390.

Generally the only outsiders passing through today are North American Christians on whirlwind tours of St John's Seven Churches, though the sole evidence of the one here consists of four squat brick stumps that once supported the seventh-century dome of the **basilica of St John**, in the Beş Eylül district. Finding it is easy enough: stand facing the mid-range *Hotel Benan* on Cumhuriyet Meydanı (☎0236/652 3026) – incidentally the only comfortable place to stay – and take the street leading diagonally uphill to the left, then look right just after the Atatürk obelisk. On Tuesdays the church neighbourhood is host to a lively **street market**. If you're pressed for other things to do, there's a small **Roman odeion** up on Toptepe, the hill overlooking town. The **Byzantine walls**, which only a few decades ago girded much of Alaşehir, have been allowed to crumble; what little remains can be seen at the northeast edge of town, by the bus stand.

travel details

Trains

Balıkesir to: Bandırma (2 daily; 2hr); Kütahya (4 daily; 5hr).

Manisa to: Afyon (1 daily; 10hr); Ankara (2 daily; 12hr); Balıkesir (3 daily; 3hr); İzmir (9 daily; 1hr 30min); Salihli (2 daily; 1hr 30min); Sart (2 daily; 1hr 30min).

Buses and dolmuşes

Alaşehir to: Denizli (4 daily; 1hr 45min); İzmir (hourly; 2hr); Salihli (hourly; 2hr).

Ayvalık to: Balıkesir (hourly; 2hr); Bergama via Dikili (11 daily; 1hr); Bursa (10 daily; 4hr 30min); Çanakkale (hourly; 3hr 30min); İstanbul (10 daily; 8hr); İzmir (every 30min; 2hr 30min).

Bergama to: Afyon (1 daily; 7hr); Ankara (1 daily; 11hr); Ayvalık (6 daily; 1hr); İstanbul (2 daily; 10hr); İzmir (hourly; 1hr 45min); Soma (hourly; 1hr).

Çanakkale to: Ayvacık (several daily; 1hr 30min); Ayvalık (every 1hr 30min; 3hr 30min); Bursa (16 daily; 6hr); Ezine (several daily; 1hr 30min); İstanbul (hourly via Thrace; 6hr); İzmir (every 1hr 30min; 6hr); Lapseki (every 30min; 45min); Troy (every 20min; 30min); Yükyeri İskelesi (timed to meet the Bozcaada ferry; 1hr).

Manisa to: Alaşehir (2 daily; 2hr); İzmir (every 15min; 1hr); Salihli via Sart (every 20min; 1hr 30min).

Ferries

Ayvalık to: Lésvos, Greece (May–Sept 3 weekly; 2hr).

Çanakkale to: Eceabat (hourly on the hour 6am–midnight; 20min); Gökçeada (1 daily; 3hr); Kilitbahir (every 30min; 10min).

Kabatepe to: Gökçeada (daily in July & August, otherwise 2 weekly; 1hr 30min).

Ören to: Akçay (numerous small boats daily in season; 30min).

Yükyeri İskelesi to: Bozcaada (3–4 daily in summer, 2 daily in winter; 1hr 10min).

CHAPTER FOUR

THE CENTRAL AND SOUTHERN AEGEAN

T he Turkish **Central and Southern Aegean coast** and its hinterland have seen foreign tourism longer than any other part of the country, if you include the first European adventurers of the eighteenth and nineteenth centuries. The territory between modern İzmir and Marmaris corresponds to the bulk of ancient **Ionia**, and just about all of old **Caria**, and is home to a concentration of Classical Greek, Hellenistic and Roman antiquities unrivalled in Turkey. **Ephesus** (*Efes* in Turkish) is usually first on everyone's list of dutiful pilgrimages, but the understated charms of exquisitely positioned sites like **Priene**, **Labranda** and **Alında** have at least as much appeal, if not more.

The landscape, too, can be compelling, most memorably at eerie **Bafa Gölü**, towering **Samsun Dağı** and the oasis-speckled **Bodrum peninsula**. Towns, however, not least sprawling, polluted İzmir, are in general functional places, best hurried through en route to more appealing destinations. But there are some pleasant surprises inland, particularly **Muğla**, **Birgi** and **Şirince**: the first two unselfconscious Ottoman museum towns, the last a well-preserved former Greek village still just the right side of tweeness.

The biggest disappointment, however, may be the **coast** itself. Despite the tourist brochure hype, most beaches are average at best, and west-facing shores are mercilessly exposed to winds and waves in the afternoon. Worse still, of the various **resort towns** on the so-called "Turkish Riviera", only **Bodrum** and (to a far lesser extent) **Çeşme** retain much intrinsic whitewashed charm, and even there it's increasingly impinged upon by shoreline villa development. Turkey has embraced *costa*-style tourism with a vengeance, and even the shortest and most mediocre sandy stretch will be dwarfed by serried ranks of holiday flats. Most of the development is aimed at the rapidly growing domestic middle class, since in most locales Turkish law stipulates that the surplus can only be leased long-term, not sold outright, to foreigners. Runaway con-

---

ACCOMMODATION PRICE CODES

In this guide, motels and nearly all hotels and *pansiyon*s have been categorized according to the price codes outlined below, which are based on US$ because of the high domestic Turkish inflation rate. These categories represent the minimum you can expect to pay for a **double room in high season**. Rates for hostels and for the most basic hotels and *pansiyon*s, where guests are charged **per person**, are given in US$, instead of being indicated by price code. For further information, including a rough outline of what you might expect in each category, see p.37.

① under $12	② $12–17	③ $18–25
④ $26–35	⑤ $36–45	⑥ $46–55
⑦ $56–75	⑧ over $75	

struction is further fuelled by Turkey's pernicious inflation rate: with an essentially worthless currency, real estate was until the early 1990s a far better investment than any interest-bearing account. There is now excess capacity of shoddily built villas, and belatedly many local authorities – perhaps learning from similar Spanish disasters – have imposed height limits, so that most new projects are only two (at most three) storeys high.

It takes determination, a good map and, in some places, your own vehicle to get the best out of this coast – though if you choose not to use your own wheels, **public transport** is excellent. The area is well served by **international flights** to İzmir, with an additional airport near Güllük and Milas, designed to replace local reliance on Dalaman, approaching completion. Four of the six **international ferry/hydrofoil links** with neighbouring Greek islands are found here too, making a visit to or from Greece feasible; the Turkish authorities rarely cause problems for holders of charter tickets who wish to do this.

İZMİR AND AROUND

For most travellers, **İzmir** is an unavoidable obstacle on the way to more enticing destinations. But on closer examination the city is not without charm: its setting and ethnological museum are unique, and the bazaar here offers some of the better shopping opportunities in the region. Should you be catching a flight home or otherwise be short of time or resources, it's definitely worth having a look around. The city might also serve as a base for day trips or short overnight jaunts, either to nearby **Çeşme** and its peninsula – mostly stark but with some well-preserved villages and a beach or two – or to the valley of the **Küçük Menderes River**, where a pair of utterly untouristed old towns give a hint of what the whole of Turkey was like just a few decades ago.

İzmir

Turkey's third city and its second port after İstanbul, **İZMİR** – the ancient Smyrna – is home to over two million people. It is blessed with a mild climate (aside from summer) and an enviable position, straddling the head of a fifty-kilometre-long gulf fed by several streams and flanked by mountains on all sides. But despite a long and illustrious history, most of the city is relentlessly modern; even enthusiasts will concede that a couple of days here as a tourist are plenty.

The possibilities of the site suggested themselves as long ago as the third millennium BC, when aboriginal **Anatolians** settled at Tepekule, a hill in the modern northern suburb of Bayraklı. The place has a better claim than most contending candidates as the birthplace of **Homer**, said to have lived here during the ninth century BC. Around 600 BC, Lydian raids sent the Bayraklı site into a long decline; it was recovering tentatively when **Alexander the Great** appeared in 334 BC. Spurred by a timely dream corroborated by the oracle of Apollo at Claros, Alexander decreed the foundation of a new, better-fortified settlement on Mount Pagos, the flat-topped hill today adorned with the Kadifekale. His generals Antigonus and Lysimachus carried out Alexander's plan after his death, by which time the city bore the name – Smyrna – familiar to the West for centuries after. This and its variants appear to be a corruption of Samornia, an Amazon queen who once had her stronghold on Mount Pagos.

Under the **Romans**, who endowed it with numerous impressive buildings, the city prospered and spread north onto the plain, despite the destructive earthquakes to which the region is subject. It continued to do so with the advent of **Christianity**, spurred by the decline of Ephesus, its nearest rival. The martyrdom of local bishop

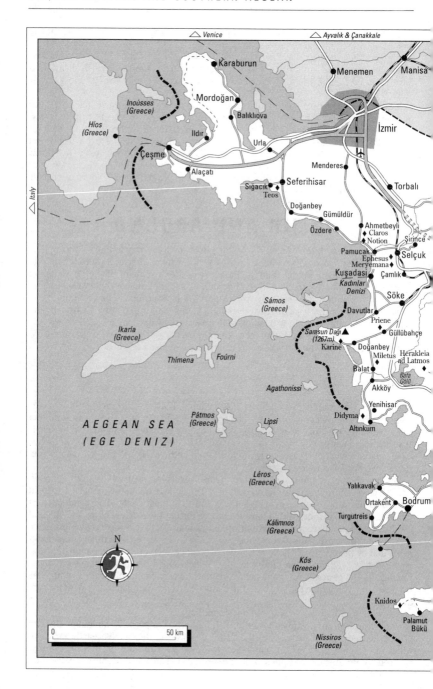

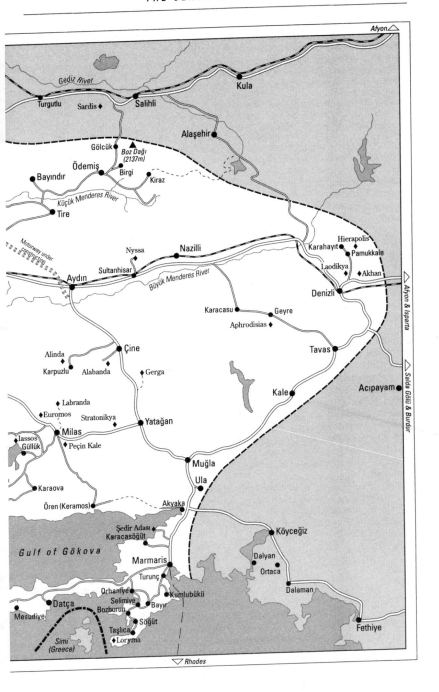

Saint Polycarp (156 AD) occurred soon after Saint John the Divine's nomination of Smyrna as one of the Seven Churches of Asia Minor.

The **Arab** raids of the seventh century AD triggered several centuries of turbulence. **Selçuk** Turks held the city for two decades prior to 1097, when the **Byzantines** recaptured it; the thirteenth-century Latin tenure in Constantinople provoked another era of disruption at Smyrna, with Crusaders, Genoese, Tamerlane's Mongols, and minor Turkish emirs jockeying for position. Order was re-established in 1415 by Mehmet I, who finally incorporated the town into the **Ottoman Empire**, his successors repulsing repeated Venetian efforts to retake it. Encouraged by the stability under imperial rule, and despite more disastrous earthquakes in 1688 and 1778, traders flocked to Smyrna (now also known as İzmir), whose population soared above the 100,000-level of late Roman times.

The city was predominantly Christian, mostly Greek Orthodox but with a generous sprinkling of Armenians, Levantine Latins and Sephardic Jews; Muslims rarely made up more than a quarter of the population. It was both the empire's window to the West, and as in ages past a major terminus of the "Silk Route" from the East: a cosmopolitan entrepôt in which many of the inhabitants were not even Ottoman subjects. The Ottoman ruling class habitually referred to it as *gavur İzmir* or "infidel İzmir" – a necessary evil, within the confines of which the "heathens" enjoyed one of the most cultured lifestyles on the Mediterranean. Following the defeat of the Ottoman Empire in World War I, Greece was given an indefinite mandate over İzmir and its hinterland. Foolishly, a huge Greek expeditionary force pressed inland, inciting the resistance of the Nationalists under Atatürk.

The climactic defeat in the two-year-long struggle against Greece and her nominal French and Italian allies was the entry into Smyrna of the Turkish army on September 9, 1922. The secular republic not having yet been proclaimed, the reconquest of the city took on the character of a successfully concluded *jihad* or holy Muslim war, with three days of murder and plunder. Aided by civilian mobs, and in a vengeful mood after wholesale atrocities perpetrated by the retreating Greek armies, the victors rounded off their sacking by setting fire to the Armenian and Greek quarters. Almost seventy percent of the city burned to the ground in two days, and thousands of non-Muslims died; a quarter of a million refugees huddled at the quayside while British, American, French and Italian vessels stood idly by and refused to grant them safe passage until the third day.

These incidents are in part attested to by the look and layout of the modern city, built from scratch on the ashes. The central boulevards are wide and often tree-lined, the high-rises – except for the forty-storey *Hilton*, the tallest building in town – almost tasteful, but the effect seems sterile, unreal, even melancholy, an almost deliberate exercise in amnesia.

Nowadays, İzmir is a booming commercial and industrial centre, home to major trade expositions, with chemical plants, paper mills and textile works on the outskirts supplanting the traditional export trade in figs, raisins, tobacco and cotton. The people are generally easy-going and have more time for you than in Ankara or İstanbul, a reflection of the prevailing villagey atmosphere, belying İzmir's size. Yet the city is also home to some of the more persistent street hustlers in Turkey, in part a product of life in the teeming *gecekondu* shanties that line the banks of the Yeşildere east of the city centre – the grim flip side of İzmir's burgeoning development. Even in the better-off working-class boroughs, cloth-weaving sweatshops clank on until late at night. Street hassles are further aggravated by the large numbers of foreign servicemen around, due to the city's role as headquarters of NATO Southeast.

Whether İzmir appeals to you or not is a matter of your ability to forget or ignore the negatives, at least for the duration of your visit. Certainly nothing can detract from the grandeur of the city's setting, and it's this that may well be your most enduring memory.

Arrival, city transport and information

Arrival in İzmir can be either painless or traumatic, depending on your means of transport. If you fly into Adnan Menderes Airport, 18km southeast of town, use either the frequent shuttle train from the **airport** to Alsancak train station, or the special *Havaş* airport bus, which will deposit you – somewhat more conveniently – by the *THY* terminal on the ground floor of the *Büyük Efes* hotel on Gaziosmanpaşa Bulvarı. The half-hour journey costs about $2 and is geared primarily to arrivals of *THY* flights. If you arrive late at the airport, you may have quite a time getting out of it: the shuttle trains stop before midnight, *Havaş* coaches cease just after the last *THY* flight, and promised tour-company transfer vehicles often fail to materialize. Taxis are pricy, but not unbearably so if shared between four passengers: $54 to the centre of Kuşadası, $44 to Selçuk, or $13 to downtown İzmir.

Ferries anchor at the Alsancak terminal, almost 2km north of the city centre; take a taxi into town (for around $2), or walk 250m south and pick up a #2 blue-and-white bus from next to the Alsancak suburban train station.

Long-distance **trains** pull in at Basmane station, almost in the middle of our city plan, with virtually all of İzmir's affordable accommodation within walking distance.

The main **otogar** is over 2km northeast of the centre and getting into town with luggage from here can be problematic. If you don't take a taxi, use a relatively infrequent red-and-white #53 bus which links the *otogar* with Konak Meydanı, the heart of the city's transport system, pausing at Montrö Meydanı en route.

If you are coming from points south by **bus**, you should ask the driver to set you down at the "Tepecik" stop, which will spare you an unnecessary trip out to the main terminal and back. From the roadside, walk down underneath the flyover, turn left, and continue 700m further along Gaziler Caddesi until you come to Basmane station. For details of bus departures heading south see "Listings", p.281. Arriving from (and departing to) anywhere on the Çeşme peninsula, buses halt at a special terminal in the coastal suburb of Üçkuyular, 6km west of downtown. From there, take any urban, red-and-white urban bus labelled "Konak"; to get out there from Konak Meydanı, merely take the same service in reverse. If you're coming from the north on a morning train, and only want to transfer to a bus for Ephesus, Kuşadası or other more compelling attractions, alight at Çınarlı station, the stop before Basmane, and walk 300m south to the *otogar*.

City transport

Replete with oddly angled intersections and roundabouts, the modern city is quite confusing to negotiate, with the added complication – if you're driving – of one-way traffic on Gazi Bulvarı (toward the sea) and Fevzipaşa Bulvarı (inland). Parking outside of designated car-park structures may appear to be free, but you'll be approached by roving wardens and dunned $0.60.

The good news is that İzmir's core is relatively compact, and most points of interest close together. Much the quickest and most enjoyable way of exploring is on foot; when you're better off taking a bus we've said so. The municipality's numbered **bus routes**, based at Konak Meydanı – also the departure point for **ferries** to Karşıyaka, the quarter across the bay – underwent a computer-assisted rethink in 1992 to vastly improving effect. Two separate organizations, *ESHOT* and *IZULAŞ*, administer the red-and-white city vehicles between them, and ticket prices vary from $0.25 to $0.50, according to how many zones you cross; you must buy tickets in advance from white kiosks near most stops, cancelling them on board.

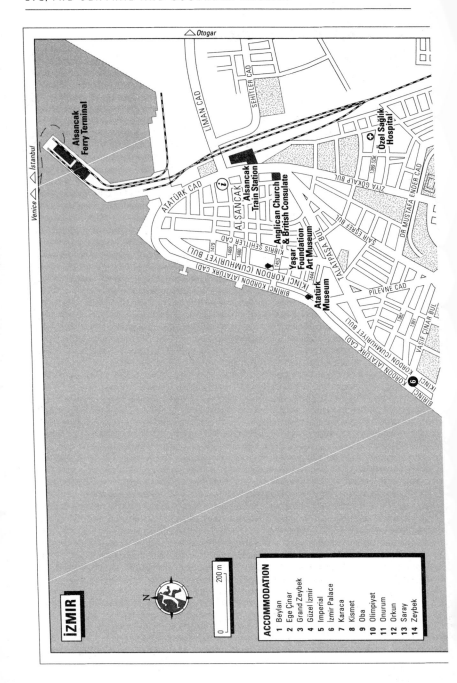

IZMIR

ACCOMMODATION

1 Beylan
2 Ege Çinar
3 Grand Zeybek
4 Güzel İzmir
5 Imperial
6 İzmir Palace
7 Karaca
8 Kismet
9 Oba
10 Olimpiyat
11 Onurum
12 Orkun
13 Saray
14 Zeybek

0   200 m

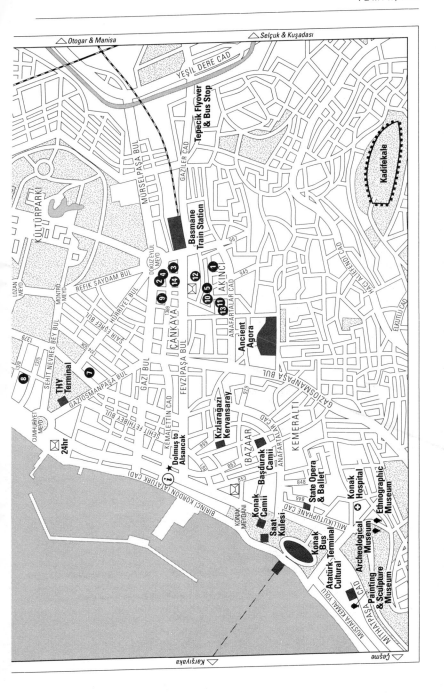

Otogar & Manisa

Selçuk & Kuşadası

YEŞİL DERE CAD

Tepecik Flyover & Bus Stop

GAZİLER CAD

MÜRSELPAŞA BUL

Basmane Train Station

Kadifekale

KÜLTÜRPARKI

DOKUZ EYLÜL MEYD

HACI ALİEFENDİ CAD

LOZAN MEYD

REFİK SAYDAM BUL

MONTRÖ MEYD

967

945

1

12

2 4 3

9 14

AKINCI

ELKUTLU CAD

1379

1378

1376

ŞAİR EŞREF BUL

HÜRRİYET BUL

İKİ SOK

ÇANKAYA

10 5

13 11

ANAFARTALAR CAD

8

SEHIT NEVRES BEY BUL

GAZİOSMANPAŞA BUL

7

GAZİ BUL

FEVZİPAŞA BUL

Ancient Agora

929

THY terminal

KEMALETTİN CAD

ŞEHİT FETHİBEY BUL

Kızlarağası Kervansaray

GAZİOSMANPAŞA BUL

CUMHURİYET MEYD

24hr

Dolmus to Alsancak

898

BAZAAR

Başdurak Camii

ANAFARTALAR CAD

863

KEMERALTI

ANAFARTALAR CAD

State Opera & Ballet

Konak Hospital

BİRİNCİ KORDON (ATATÜRK CAD)

853

848

848

Ethnographic Museum

KONAK MEYDANI

Konak Camii

MİLLİKÜTÜPHANE CAD

Saat Kulesi

Konak Bus

Atatürk Cultural

Archeological Museum

Painting & Sculpture Museum

MİTHATPAŞA CAD

MUSTAFA KEMAL YOLU

Karşıyaka

Çeşme

Information

İzmir has two **tourist information offices**: one in the airport arrivals hall (☎0232/274 2110), and the helpful, English-speaking central bureau, moved in 1996 to refurbished premises at 1344 Sok 2, Pasaport district, across from the Borsa (June–Oct daily 8.30am–7pm; Nov–May Mon–Sat 8.30am–5.30pm; ☎0232/484 2147). They don't book, but only suggest, **accommodation** (mid-range and up), and have been known to run out of their very useful free city plan. Programmes for İzmir's various festivals and entertainment venues are also kept on hand here, with the possibility of ticket sales.

Accommodation

Accommodation in İzmir tends to be either very basic or very luxurious, with a relative shortage of mid-range establishments, and everything is fairly expensive for what you get, with street noise a nearly universal problem. Don't plan on staying overnight during the big annual fair between late August and mid-September, when most hotels are uniformly packed; more minor expositions occur until November. At other times, however, you should find something quickly – the city is not exactly a tourist mecca.

The main area for budget hotels is **Akıncı** (also called Yenigün), which straddles Fevzipaşa Bulvarı immediately in front of Basmane train station. Hotels in the zone to the south, between Fevzipaşa and Anafartalar Caddesi, are often much plainer and cheaper than those to the north, between Fevzipaşa and Gazi *bulvarı*s. Above all, don't be fooled by the charming old wooden facades of certain rock-bottom hotels on, and just off, 1294 and 1296 *sokak*s; they usually mask dire interiors with chipboard partitions, roach-infested toilets and lobby-lurkers.

Apart from the recommended exceptions, you'll be more comfortable on the other side of Fevzipaşa, an area also called **Çankaya**. A pedestrianization programme centred on 1369 Sokak has made nearby hotels a good deal quieter and more appealing. But for out-and-out luxury, you'll have to head for the streets around seafront Cumhuriyet Meydanı.

South of Fevzipaşa Bulvarı (Akıncı)

Beylan, 1299 Sok 8 (☎0232/483 1426, fax 483 3844). Air-conditioned, two-star comfort, off-street parking. Nominally overpriced but amenable to bargaining a price category or two downwards. ⑦.

Imperial, 1296 Sok 54, İş Bankası Arkası (☎0232/425 6883). Better than most en-suite budget hotels in this area. ②.

Olimpiyat, 945 Sok 2 (☎0232/425 1269). Rooms have washbasins only; extra charge for hot showers. ①

Onurum, 1298 Sok 10 (☎0232/483 3565, fax 484 9858). New (1996), quietish one-star outfit, though en-suite rooms are small and it's a bit overpriced. ④.

Orkun, 1294 Sok 4 (☎0232/441 4503). No air conditioning, but within walking distance of Basmane station, in a quiet lane. Officially ⑥, but usually a snip at ③.

Saray, Anafartalar Cad 635 (☎0232/483 6946). Heated rooms with washbasins surround a pleasant, glassed-over court. This is where the tourist office sends impecunious backpackers. ①.

North of Fevzipaşa Bulvarı (Çankaya)

Ege Çınar, Dokuz Eylül Meydanı (☎0232/489 4298). Clean, well run and surprisingly quiet for the location. ⑤.

Grand Zeybek, 1368 Sok 6 (☎0232/441 9590). Recently opened three-star outfit that's the fanciest on this alley. ⑤.

Güzel İzmir, 1368 Sok 8 (☎0232/483 5069). One of the better-value mid-range hotels in this area, though the single rooms are tiny; en suite. ②.

Oba, 1369 Sok 59 (☎0232/483 5474). Refurbished in 1993, this offers a choice of rooms with and without baths; clean, with helpful management. ③.

Zeybek, 1368 Sok 5 (☎0232/489 6694). Same management as the *Grand Zeybek* across the street, only less grand; smallish rooms have fans and TV. Rates include breakfast. ④

Around Cumhuriyet Meydanı

İzmir Palace, Vasıf Çınar Bul 2 (☎0232/421 5583, fax 422 6870). Older, three-star standby with a good seafront location; amenable to bargaining. ⑦.

Karaca, 1379 Sok 55, aka pedestrianized Sevgi Yolu (☎0232/489 1940, fax 483 1498). Above the eponymous cinema and recently renovated, popular with NATO personnel. ⑦.

Kismet, 1377 Sok 9 (☎0232/463 3850, fax 421 4856). Calm location on leafy side street; redecorated in 1992, and run by the same family managing the Kuşadası namesake hotel. ⑥.

Camping

OBA Dinleme Tesisleri, Güzelbahçe (☎0232/234 2015). Open all year, with chalets for the tent-less and a swimming pool. It's 20km out, but has good bus connections west and east, with useful restaurants nearby.

The City

From Basmane station and Dokuz Eylül Meydanı respectively, **Fevzipaşa Bulvarı** and **Gazi Bulvarı** shoot straight west toward the bay, clearly visible from the front steps of the station. North of these two one-way streets lies the bulk of the largely radial modern city, wrapped around the vast expanse of the **Kültür Parkı**. From the middle of Gazi Bulvarı, **Gaziosmanpaşa Bulvarı** aims straight for Cumhuriyet Meydanı, a seashore half-roundabout with most of İzmir's upmarket tourist facilities clustered nearby.

The area south of Fevzipaşa Bulvarı is home to the majority of the buildings that survived the fire. The backbone of this district is **Anafartalar Caddesi**, beginning just south of Basmane station and snaking its way to Konak Meydanı. Once across Gaziosmanpaşa Bulvarı, the **bazaar** begins in earnest, sprawling mostly on the north side of Anafartalar; this street exits inconspicuously onto **Konak Meydanı**, lined by government buildings, banks and cultural facilities and bounded by sea and parkland to the west. In 1993, Konak was gentrified by virtue of landscaping and pedestrianization, and the installation of a "Galeria" mega-shopping centre like the one in İstanbul. Buses, in what has always been İzmir's main transport hub, are now confined in orderly ranks to a long serpentine around the park areas and municipal buildings, with private traffic diverted to the seaward edge. Birinci and İkinci Kordon end here too, though three continuation roads – **Mithatpaşa Caddesi**, **Mustafa Kemal** and **İnönü** – follow the gulf to the Üçkuyular bus terminal.

Around Konak Meydanı: the major museums

İzmir cannot really be said to have a single centre; among several possible contenders, **Konak** might win by default, simply because it's the spot where visitors will spend much of their time. The ornate **Saat Kulesi** (clock tower), dating only from 1901 but the city's official logo, stands on the opposite end of the Konak pedestrian bridge from the **Konak Camii**, distinguished by its facade of enamelled Kütahya tiles. Both seem lost in the modernity and bustle around, though they have been showcased somewhat by the surrounding improvements.

The area southwest of Konak forms the undisputed cultural focus of İzmir, home to the **Atatürk Kültür Merkezi** (Cultural Centre), the **Devlet Opera ve Balesi** (State Opera and Ballet – see "Entertainment, festivals and nightlife", p.280) and virtually all of the city's **museums**.

THE ARCHEOLOGICAL MUSEUM

The **Archeological Museum** (daily 8.30am–5.30pm; $2) features an excellent collection of finds from all over İzmir province and beyond, housed in a building that could – and may, eventually – hold more. Labelling is scant, but large explanatory wall hoardings make up for this, and the museum is well worth an hour or so of your time.

The ground floor is largely given over to statuary and friezes of all eras: standouts include a rather Hebraic-looking Roman priest, a headless but still impressive archaic *kore* (idealized maiden), and the showcased bronze statuette of a runner. The top floor, whose foyer features a large Roman mosaic from İzmir, contains smaller objects, with an emphasis on Bronze Age and Archaic pottery – more exciting than it sounds, particularly the so-called "orientalized" terracotta and bestiary amphoras from Pitane (Çandarlı). The section of small finds from Erythrae (Ildır) is especially good, as is a case of embossed seals, helpfully displayed with full-colour enlargements. The oddest item is a unique mushroom-form column capital from the seventh century. The single best piece, though, is a graceful, if peculiar Hellenistic statuette of Eros, clenching a veil in his teeth.

THE ETHNOGRAPHIC MUSEUM

The **Ethnographic Museum** (daily 8.30am–noon & 1–5.30pm; open at lunch during high season; $1), immediately across from the archeological museum, is housed in an Ottoman Belle Epoque structure which was a hospital before becoming a museum in 1984. A helpful brochure with a plan of the galleries is provided at the ticket booth, and overall it's a more enjoyable collection than the archeological one.

One of the first exhibits on the lower floor is of the two types of İzmir area house: the traditional wooden Turkish residence, and the more substantial "Levantine" (Christian and Jewish merchants') house, helpfully illustrated with photographs showing the districts or town where surviving mansions may still be found. There are also reconstructions of a kiln for blue beads to ward off the evil eye, and of the first Ottoman pharmacy in the area; dioramas of felt and pottery production; and a photo-and-mannequin presentation of camel-wrestling and the *zeybek*s – the traditional warrior caste of western Anatolia. The upper floor has a more domestic focus, with recreations of a nuptial chamber, a sitting room and circumcision recovery suite, along with vast quantities of household utensils and Ottoman weaponry. The galleries finish with flat weavings, saddlebags and fine carpets, accompanied by potted histories of the crafts.

THE PAINTING AND SCULPTURE MUSEUM

If time is short, the **Painting and Sculpture Museum** (ground floor daily 10am–6pm; upper levels Mon–Fri 10am–5pm; free) is the obvious one to miss. The lower level hosts changing exhibits; the two upstairs galleries contain almost two hundred works by artists active since the foundation of the Republic. Some are awful, some decent, though most are stylistically derivative renderings of pastoral or populist themes reminiscent of Socialist Realism. The modern stuff is probably the best of the lot.

Along the Kordon to Alsancak

Cumhuriyet Meydanı, another traditional orientation point, lies less than a kilometre northeast of Konak. The *meydan* itself is unremarkable except for the equestrian statue of the Gazi completing his long ride from inland Anatolia and poised in the act of chasing the infidels into the sea. Today the infidels are back, in limited measure, as evidenced by the member nations' flags undulating in amity outside the nearby **NATO Southeast Division Headquarters**.

For the most part luxury seaside apartment blocks line **Birinci Kordon** along its entire length, until it doubles back on itself before the ferry terminal. For several hundred metres either side of Cumhuriyet, the İzmir smart set convenes for drinks and snacks in the evening; by day, crowds queuing for visas gather outside the German consulate, housed in one of several substantial buildings which escaped the 1922 destruction. Next door stands the Greek consulate, ministering surreptitiously to the spiritual needs of the city's few thousand Greek Orthodox, descended from those who elected to stay – by laying claim to English or Italian passports – after 1923. Yet another mansion is the home of the all-but-obligatory **Atatürk Museum**, Atatürk Caddesi 248 (Tues–Fri 8.30am–5pm; $0.50), occupying the building where the premier stayed on his visits to İzmir, now containing a standard assortment of Atatürkian knick-knacks in amongst kitsch Belle Epoque sculpture.

The museum more or less marks the southern margin of **Alsancak**, where the 1922 blaze was less severe than elsewhere in the flatlands; just inland, particularly on 1453, 1469, 1482, 1481 and 1480 *sokak*s, plus the east side of İkinci Kordon, are entire intact terraces of sumptuous **eighteenth- and nineteenth-century mansions** that once belonged to European merchants, who knew the area as Punta (a term still used). These add direction to wanderings out here, and have predictably become targets for gentrification, with expensive eateries and bars opening among the ranks of daytime offices and private homes. One, at Cumhuriyet Bul 252, houses the **Yaşar Foundation Art Museum** (Mon–Fri June–Sept 10am–7pm), a privately run gallery emphasizing modern Turkish painting and hosting temporary exhibitions.

Returning from Alsancak to the city centre, you unavoidably pass by or through the **Kültür Parkı** (daily 8am–midnight), a 75-acre lozenge midway between Alsancak point and Kadifekale hill, built on the ruins of the pre-1922 Greek quarter. "Culture" in this case means a parachute tower, İzmir TV headquarters, permanent exhibition halls for the city's yearly trade fair, a mini-golf course and funfair, a zoo, an artificial lake, an open-air theatre, plus a dozen *gazino* nightspots and tea/beer gardens. Only the theatre, occasional venue for summer concerts, is likely to be of interest to foreigners, plus of course the greenery and the city's quietest phone booths.

THE SUDANESE OF TURKEY

Many travellers to western Turkey, and İzmir in particular, are startled by the sight of Africans who are obviously not visitors. They are in fact descendants of the large numbers of Sudanese blacks who were brought to the Ottoman Empire as household slaves, beginning in the sixteenth century.

The most prominent of them, ensconced in the Topkapı Sarayı, was the Kızlarağası or "Black Eunuch", responsible for the administration of the Sultan's harem and by his very nature not capable of giving rise to Turkey's contemporary African population. This is owed to the fact that, before World War I, virtually every urban household – especially in İstanbul – had a Sudanese manservant and a nanny for the children, often a married couple; any Turkish dictionary still gives "Negro wetnurse" as the primary meaning of *bacı*, today used as a form of address to any woman a few years older than the speaker. Although slavery was formally abolished by Sultan Abdul Mecid, many of these domestic slaves chose to remain in the families with whom they had grown up. The sons of the household, and those of the wetnurse herself, were termed *süt kardeşleri* (milk brothers), and between them existed bonds of affection and mutual obligation which usually endured throughout their lives.

After the collapse of the Ottoman Empire, however, the Sudanese were forced to move out on their own, gravitating mostly to southwestern Anatolia, where they occupy secluded villages scattered in the mountains between İzmir and Mersin. To this day, though devout Muslims and fluent Turkish-speakers, they do not intermarry with other Turks; this segregation has predictably engendered, as in the case of their neighbours the Alevis (see p.418), the vaguely similar sensational allegation that their women earn their dowry for marriage by prostitution, with no shame accruing to the practice.

From the bazaar to Kadifekale

İzmir's **bazaar**, though a distinct second to İstanbul's, warrants losing yourself in for a half-day or so, and is large enough to include several distinct city districts, notably Kemeraltı and Hisarönü. Anafartalar Caddesi, the main drag, is lined with clothing, jewellery and shoe shops; Fevzipaşa Bulvarı and the alleys just south are strong on **leather** garments, for which the city is famous. İzmir is not, however, known for its carpets, those displayed in the Kızlarağası Hanı (see below) notwithstanding. Any distance away from these principal streets, humbler, more practical merchandise – irrigation pumps, live chickens, canaries and rabbits, plastic pipes, tea sets, olives, pickles, bath tiles, rubber stamps – predominates.

In contrast to many other Turkish town bazaars, there is little of architectural interest here, though several late Ottoman mosques are worth a glance in passing. Most of İzmir's commercial wealth resided in harbour warehouses wiped out in 1922; with a pre-Republican population two-thirds non-Muslim, there were correspondingly few historic *medrese*s or mosques. One exception, the **Kızlarağası Hanı**, a handsome Ottoman *kervansaray* near the late sixteenth-century Hisar mosque, was restored from the ground up between 1989 and 1993. The vaulted shops inside are overwhelmingly of touristic orientation, though there are a few catering to local interests; the shady square in front of Hisar Camii is now chock-a-block with eateries and teahouses.

The only surviving pre-Ottoman monument in the flatlands is the nearby **agora** (daily 8.30am–5.30pm; $1), the most accessible of İzmir's ancient sites, and the most visited. From Anafartalar Caddesi turn south onto 943 Sokak, then west onto 816 Sokak; typical black-on-yellow signs confirm the way. The agora probably dates back to the early second century BC but what you see now are the remains of a later reconstruction, financed during the reign of the Roman Emperor Marcus Aurelius, after the catastrophic earthquake of 178 AD. Principal structures, unearthed between the world wars, include a **colonnade** of fourteen Corinthian columns on the west side, and an elevated north stoa resting on a vaulted basement. In the eastern part of the area sit hundreds of unsorted Ottoman gravestones and earlier fragments of sculpture, the best of which have been removed to the archeological museum — which frankly, if time is limited, is far more deserving of a visit.

Rising just southeast of the agora, the **Kadifekale** (Velvet Castle), as visible by night as by day owing to skilful floodlighting, is perhaps the one sight in the city you shouldn't miss. The less energetic can take a city bus from Konak and cover the final 300m on foot, but the best introduction to the citadel is to walk up from the agora, the route threading through a once-elegant district of narrow streets and dilapidated pre-1922 houses that offer just a hint of what life must be like in the sprawling shantytowns the other side of Yeşildere. Once you reach Hacı Ali Effendi Caddesi – probably via 977 or 985 *sokak*s – cross it and finish the climb up the obvious pedestrian stairs opposite, which thread through the city's gypsy quarter. The irregularly shaped fortress itself is permanently open, serving as a daytime playground for local kids but not lit inside after dark. Virtually nothing is visible of its Hellenistic foundations; the present structure dates from Byzantine and Ottoman times. Late afternoon is the best time to go, to wait for the kindling of thousands of city lights below to match the often lurid sunsets over the bay, but the views over the city are unrivalled at any hour. In the warmer months, a **tea/beer garden** operates until late at a prime location under the pines; otherwise there are several more along the stretch between the castle gate and the bus stop.

Karşıyaka and the bird sanctuary

Karşıyaka means "the opposite shore", and that's really all this suburb is. Before 1922 its population was about seventy-percent Greek Orthodox, and it's said that title to much of the land still legally resides with their descendants now in Greece. Ethnic demographics aside, Karşıyaka still provides an excuse for the nice short trip from

İzmir proper, the twenty-minute ferry cruise across from Konak ending next to a waterfront park studded with pubs and snack bars that directly overhang the bay. At evenings and weekends, Karşıyakans turn out here in force to eat the *lokma* (dough fritters) for which the district is famous, for example at *Kemal'in Yeri* on Yalı Caddesi across from the ferry dock. The sole monumental destination might be the **Tomb of Zübeyde Hanım**, Atatürk's mother, some way inland; otherwise the cool breeze on the ride over seems to be most of the point,

The only other destination of interest on the north shore of the bay is the *kuş cenneti* or **bird sanctuary** around the salt evaporation pans at Çamaltı. This is signposted near the Çiğli airfield turn-off, and while there's a commuter train to the Çiğli station, you'll need a taxi or your own vehicle to effectively tour the eight hectares of wetlands.

Eating and drinking

For a city of İzmir's size, **restaurants** are remarkably thin on the ground, and fast-food joints (eg *McDonald's* and *Burger King* in Karşıyaka) have made destructive inroads. The obvious clutch of eateries within sight of Basmane station, usually full of transient male travellers with nowhere else to go, make for a pretty depressing – and undistinguished – meal. As so often in Turkey, there's a far better selection of inexpensive outfits in the bazaar, but unfortunately most of them close by 7.30pm; also, despite their promising position in the city grid, both the Karşıyaka and Kadifekale districts offer little in the way of food, merely the previously noted tea and beer gardens. Meals close to the Birinci Kordon waterfront represent a definite notch up in price, though not always as much as you'd think, since at most of these places the emphasis is on drinking. Of late, some attractive establishments have opened among the restored inland mansions of Alsancak, but even without a sea view these are generally pretty expensive.

While **mussels** are fairly common along the Aegean, İzmir is particularly noted for them, and half a dozen stuffed with rice and pine-nuts make a wonderful cheap snack for well under a dollar – don't be conned into paying more. The street vendors are everywhere, but it's a good idea not to patronize them between late May and early September, when you stand a good chance of food poisoning.

Bazaar

Aksüt, 863 Sok, corner 873 Sok. Somewhat more expensive, but better, than the *Tarihi Kemeraltı* (see below). Shiny decor, excellent dairy products and breakfast pastries. Closes 7.30pm.

Bolulu Hasan Usta, 853 Sok 13/B, behind the Kemeraltı police station. Some of the best puddings and *dondurma* (Turkish ice cream) in town; shuts at 8pm.

Doğu Karadeniz Lokantası, Yeyisel Çıkmazı 39/E. A late-opening (11pm) *meyhane*, just off the beginning of Anafartalar Cad. All male as a rule, but decorous – outdoor seating, impromptu music with your grilled items and cold hors d'œuvres.

Halikarnass Balık Lokantası, overlooking the fountain at the junction of 870, 871 and 873 *sokak*s. A simple fish restaurant near the Bazdurak Camii fish market, where an adequate meal won't cost over $7. Unlicensed; closes 7.30pm.

Mennan, 899 Sok 30/A, along the pedestrian entry from Fevzipaşa Bulvarı to the Hisar Camii and Kızlarağası Meydanı. Puddings and ice cream to rival *Bolulu Hasan*, and slightly better seating facilities.

Ömür Balık, **Ödemiş Kebap**, **Kismet Kebap**: immediately north of the Kızlarağası Kervansaray, three contiguous, attractive venues, now restored and predictably pricy for the fare on offer.

Öz Ezo Gelin, corner 848 Sok and Anafartalar Cad. Soups, kebab and pudding in an elegant dining room with a family atmosphere. No alcohol; closes at 9pm.

Şükran Lokantası, Anafartalar Cad 61, adjacent to the *Doğu Karadeniz*. A cavernous, once-premier restaurant come down in the world; the food is average but prices are still stiff. The big draws are the setting – outdoor summer seating around a fountain-courtyard of an old "Levantine" building – and its licensed status, giving the opportunity to nurse your drink until midnight unmolested by traffic.

Tabaklar, 872 Sok 134. Around the corner from, and similar to, the *Halikarnass*.
Tarihi Kemeraltı Börekcisi, Anafartalar Cad 93. Good for a breakfast of *börek* and hot milk, or puddings later; closes at 7pm.

Birinci Kordon

Gemi Restoran, Birinci Kordon, moveable site. Seating in an anchored pleasure boat with cheap fish fries and alcohol, but check the freshness of the catch – and your waiter's arithmetic.
Liman Çay Salonu, Birinci Kordon 128. Extremely varied crowd of locals having unbelievably cheap tea, soft drinks and juices, also puffing hookahs; a good place to try your first one.
Palet, Birinci Kordon, beyond the Alsancak Kordon dock. If you want to eat in style and drop a wad of banknotes, this is the place, though food quality has slid a bit since the early 1990s.
Sera, Birinci Kordon 206; **Sirena**, Birinci Kordon 194. The first does English/continental breakfast; the second is a pub with food, okay for a mild splurge. These are just two of several such establishments cropping up at this point as you move north along the Kordon.

Inland Alsancak

Altınkapı, 1444 Sok 14/A, near Atatürk Museum. Good for *döner* and other reasonably priced meat grills; long established and popular with the trendy set, who weather permitting sit outside on the pedestrianized street.
Chinese Restaurant, 1385 Sokak, behind the *Hilton*. Not brilliant, but the least expensive and most central of the city's three oriental food outlets, with good-value lunch specials.
Kemal'in Yeri, 1453 Sok 20/A (☎0232/422 3190). One of several on this lane, and famous for its excellent (but expensive) seafood; reservations suggested.
Vejetaryen Restaurant, 1375 Sok 11. Run by the city's Vegetarian Foundation, just across from the American Hospital. Tiny – about six tables indoors, seven out – but cheerful; count on $5 for a meal.

Entertainment, festivals and nightlife

As with the eating and drinking situation, the city's evening **entertainment** options are surprisingly limited. The Atatürk Cultural Centre and the State Opera and Ballet go some way to satisfying **classical music** lovers, but only between late September and May. The **Atatürk Cultural Centre** is home to the local symphony orchestra, which plays regularly Friday evening and Saturday at noon, and hosts random concerts of "serious" soloists; strangely, **tickets** for these events are not always sold on the spot – read the hoardings outside the building for directions, or ask at the information desk. More varied is the programme offered by the **State Opera and Ballet**, housed in a wonderful Ottoman Art Deco specimen on Milli Kütüphane Caddesi, which encompasses everything from chamber music to pop and jazz. Tickets are sold on the premises.

With the onset of the hot weather, events move to the open-air theatre in the Kültür Parkı. Linchpin of the summer season, however, running from mid-June to early July, is the **International İzmir Festival**, inaugurated in 1987 and something of a misnomer since many events take place at either various restored venues at Ephesus or Çeşme castle. Tickets tend to run to $10–18 a head, but fifty percent student discounts are available and the acts featured are often world-class – past names have included Sarah Vaughan, the Moscow Ballet, Paco Peña, Ravi Shankar and Chris de Burgh. Get this year's **programme** from the İzmir Culture Foundation at Şair Eşref Bul, Park Apt 58/4, 35220 Alsancak (☎0232/463 0300, fax 463 0077), or the city tourist office; **tickets** have in the past been available from the Opera and Ballet box office, the museum in Selçuk, the İzmir *Hilton*, or the tourist office in Kuşadası.

Mid-April sporadically sees the **İzmir International Film Festival**, featuring many foreign releases, all shown in their original languages with subtitles. The favourite venue is usually the *Karaca Sineması*, 1379 Sok 55/A (aka Sevgi Yolu), a pedestrian lane near the *Hilton*. The town's other quality cinemas functioning year round are *Çınar*, in the SSK building on Konak Meydanı; and *İzmir*, Cumhuriyet Bulvarı, next to the *Dünya* bookshop.

Upper Alsancak has lately blossomed as the district for trendy **nightlife**, with assorted bars and clubs tucked inland along pedestrianized side streets invisible from Birinci Kordon. It should be stressed that ownership and themes of each establishment tend to roll over on roughly a two-year cycle, so specific recommendations are fairly pointless; however, a stroll along the various *sokak*s should turn up the latest possibilities. Longest-lived, if hardly state-of-the-art, places include *Mask*, 1435 Sok 18, a bistro-bar with dance floor; and for the better dressed, *Punta Bar*, in an old merchant's villa at 1469 Sok 26 (open Wed–Sat), with live music some nights, and *Sheriff*, 1453 Sok 18, a bar with Wild West decor and live gigs.

Listings

Airlines *British Airways*, Şair Eşref Bul 3, Suite 304 (☎0232/441 382); *Delta*, İkinci Kordon 143/H (☎0232/421 4262); *İstanbul Hava Yolları*, Gaziosmanpaşa Cad 2/E (☎0232/489 0541); *KLM*, Alsancak (☎0232/421 4757) or Adnan Menderes Airport (☎0232/251 3423); *KTHY* (*Cyprus Turkish Airways*), Şehit Nevres Bul 13/A (☎0232/422 7164); *THY*, on the ground floor of the *Büyük Efes Oteli*, Gaziosmanpaşa Bul 1/F–G, though they intend to move 100m south in 1997 (daily 8.30am–7.30pm, Sun closes 5.30pm; information ☎0232/484 1220, reservations ☎0232/425 8280).

Airport bus Operated by *Havaş*, this runs from in front of the *THY* office 90min before each domestic *THY* flight, 2hr before overseas ones (non-*THY* passengers welcome), taking 20–30min to reach Menderes Airport, 18km south of town; the fare is about $2, with 12–15 departures daily between 4.45am and 8.30 or 9.30pm. Other airline companies occasionally provide a service coach; ask when reconfirming your return ticket.

Books *Dünya*, Cumhuriyet Bul 143 F/G (mostly English magazines); *Elt Haşet*, Şehit Nevres Bey Bul 3/B; and *NET*, Cumhuriyet Bul 142/B, next to Dokuz Eylül Üniversitesi.

Buses Leaving İzmir to the south, it's easy to flag down buses from the pavement along the Tepecik expressway. You can buy tickets at the *otogar* or from sales offices on Dokuz Eylül Meydanı, the roundabout just north of Basmane.

Car rental İzmir is by no means the best spot for this; sparse tourist numbers mean there's little resort-style competition to drive prices down, and additionally agencies have been spoilt by NATO personnel with too much money and too little sense. If you insist, though, local chains include *Airtour*, Şair Eşref Bul, 1371 Sok 5 (☎0232/441 6252); *DeCar*, Hürriyet Bul 3/1, Yusuf Dede İş Hanı (☎0232/446 0707); *Intercity*, 1370 Sok 7/1, 2nd Floor, Suite 8 (☎0232/446 0165); *Lets*, Şehit Fethi Bey Cad 122/C (☎0232/484 8053); and *Sun*, Şehit Nevres Bey Bul 2/D (☎0232/489 9493). International chain branches include *Avis*, Şair Eşref Bul 18/D (☎0232/441 4417); *Budget*, Şair Eşref Bul 22/1 (☎0232/441 9224); *Eurodollar/Yes*, Şehit Nevres Bey Bul 11/A (☎0232/422 7107); *Europcar/InterRent*, Şehit Fethi Bey Cad 122/F (☎0232/441 5141); and *Hertz*, Cumhuriyet Bul 138 (☎0232/446 1441). Many of these have airport offices too.

Consulates *Belgium*, Birinci Kordon 228 (☎0232/421 8847); *Britain* (also *Canada/Australia/New Zealand*), Mahmut Esat Bozkurt Cad 49, an annexe of the Anglican church by Alsancak train station (☎0232/463 5151); *Denmark*, Akdeniz Cad 1, Alsancak (☎0232/489 5401); *Netherlands*, Cumhuriyet Meydanı 10/A (☎0232/463 4963); *Sweden*, 1378 Sok 4/1, Suite 201 (☎0232/422 1038). The *US* consulate has closed; in emergencies refer to the cultural centre (see below).

Cultural centres *Turkish-American Cultural Association*, Şehit Nevres Bey Bul 23/A (library open Mon–Fri 1.30–6.30pm); also the *Alliance Française*, Cumhuriyet Bul 13, and *Centro Italiano*, 1452 Sok 37, Alsancak – the last two possible venues for exhibitions and film showings.

Exchange You can change money round-the-clock at standard bank rates (and commissions) in the PTT on Cumhuriyet Meydanı; much better are the private exchange booths such as *Odak Döviz*, 1369 Sokak, and *Kaynak Döviz*, 895 Sok 5/E. These are both open Mon–Sat 8.30am–7pm and offer premium rates for cash only. As ever, it's best to avoid the larger hotels, which offer poor rates with high commissions.

Ferries Tickets and information on weekly international services to Venice (☎0232/421 0094) and the weekend domestic line to İstanbul (☎0232/421 1484) from the *Turkish Maritime Lines* facilities at the Alsancak dock; the gate of the complex is on Atatürk Caddesi, opposite 1475 Sokak.

Football The dismal record of local teams Altay and Karşıyaka fails to dampen enthusiasm; matches, at the Alsancak or Atatürk stadiums, frequently sell out. Ticket information from the tourist office.

Hamam The cleanest, securest and best-maintained baths are *Hoşgör*, on an alley inland from Mithatpaşa Cad 10, opposite Karataş Lisesi (daily 6.30am–11.30pm; $3; mixed-gender groups by arrangement, otherwise men only).

Hospitals Most central are *Alsancak Devlet Hastanesi*, on Ali Çetinkaya Bulvarı; the *Çocuk Hastanesi* (Children's Hospital) on 1374 Sok 3/A and the *Konak Hastanesi*, including a dental section, across from the ethnographic and archeological museums. Much better, if you can afford them or carry insurance, are the *American Hospital*, 1375 Sok – staffed with NATO doctors and intended primarily for NATO personnel – or the *Özel Sağlık Hastanesi* on 1399 Sok, considered the best in town.

Left luggage On the left side of Basmane station as you face it (daily 7.30am–7.30pm).

Parcels If you don't trust the PTT for shipping souvenirs or personal effects, or can't face the bureaucracy involved, try *United Parcel Service*, Akdeniz Cad 8/K, which provides cost-effective air delivery to North America and the UK.

PTT Besides the 24-hr one on Cumhuriyet Meydanı (quiet phones), there's a branch at 858 Sok, just off 857 Sok, Kemeraltı (also with quiet phones), and another on Fevzipaşa Bulvarı, 300m west of Basmane train station – though the last has uselessly noisy phones.

Shopping Traditional Turkish musical instruments are best bought from *Bağdat Saz Evi*, Kızlarağası Hanı 19/P/22, now that the row of shops along Gaziler Caddesi in Basmane has been demolished. The best hookahs on the Aegean can be found at *İlhan Etike*, also inside the Kızlarağası Hanı near *Bağdat Saz Evi*, or at *Mehmet & Osman Kaya*, 856 Sok 7/C, in Kemeraltı.

Swimming Due to pollution the bay is off-limits until well past İncialtı. There are pools at the *Büyük Efes Oteli*, though these are expensive, and (less expensive) the *Balçova Termal* resort – known also as the legendary Baths of Agamemnon – 10km west of town.

Çeşme and around

The claw-like mass of land extending west from İzmir terminates near **Çeşme**, most low-key of the central Aegean's main coastal resorts. You can make detours off the eighty-kilometre highway out there to visit the isolated **Karaburun peninsula** to the north, or medieval **Sığacık** and ancient **Teos** to the south, but the several attractions within shouting distance of Çeşme, most notably **Ildır/Erythrae**, the town of **Alaçatı**, and **Altınkum** beach, are easier ways to fill a day or two.

The immediate environs of Çeşme are bleak scrubland, the only note of colour introduced by the deeply aquamarine sea. It's a deceptive barrenness: before 1922 the area, almost entirely Greek-populated, was famous for its vineyards and market gardens, nurtured by artesian wells surging up from hundreds of metres below ground level. After 1922, the newly arrived Muslim settlers, mostly from the Aegean islands, Macedonia or Thrace, turned their goats loose on the farmland, and now little remains except for the odd vine or melon patch. Agricultural reclamation is further hampered by the fact that most deep ground water is now diverted to support the ever-increasing number of villas on the peninsula's north shore.

One historical constant here is the **climate**: noticeably drier, cooler and healthier than anywhere nearby on the Turkish coast, especially in comparison to occasionally hellish İzmir or muggy Kuşadası. These conditions, combined with the presence of several thermal springs, have made the peninsula a popular resort for over a century. This is the second westernmost point of continental Turkey, subject to currents from the Dardanelles and maritime breezes that make the sea chilly and the nights pullover weather at any time of the year. For warmer, sheltered swimming on sand beaches unshadowed by villas, make for the **coast south of Çeşme**, where development has been slowed, as most land belongs to the forestry department or various municipalities.

Çeşme

An often sleepy, two-street town of old Greek houses wrapped around a Genoese castle, **ÇEŞME** ("drinking fountain" in Turkish) doubtless takes its name from the many Ottoman fountains, some still functioning, scattered around its streets. Despite guarding the mouth of the İzmir Gulf, it has figured little in recent history other than as the sight of a sea battle on July 5, 1770, when the Russian fleet annihilated the Ottoman navy in the straits here.

The place makes an agreeable, brief stopover on the way to or from Híos in Greece, and it's hard to work up a great deal of indignation about the current scale of tourism here – which, despite the long-delayed completion of the six-lane dual carriageway linking İzmir and Çeşme, and wishful thinking on the part of municipal authorities, seems permanently stalled at its present level where not actually decreased. There simply isn't enough in and around the town to hold foreigners' interest for even one week of a two-centre package holiday, and Çeşme seems permanently destined for a turnstile role, processing long-haul ferry passengers en route to and from various ports in Italy, and those on the short hop to Híos in Greece.

Arrival and information

Coming **by ferry** from Híos, you arrive at the small jetty in front of the castle; larger ferries from Italy use the newer dock across the bay. Arriving by bus from İzmir, you'll be set down at the **otogar**, 1km south of the ferry port, although most drivers make a preliminary stop on the east edge of town at the top of İnkilap Caddesi. At the time of writing İzmir is the only long-distance destination served, but the *otogar* has obviously been built for growth, and as soon as the expressway is opened, facilitating a detour to Kuşadası, you can expect some minibus-type services to bypass İzmir. **Dolmuşes** to Dalyan, Ovacık and Ildır leave from the roundabout and victory statue at the top of İnkilap Caddesi; others, serving Ilıca, Altınkum and Alaçatı, depart from next to customs and the somewhat helpful **tourist information office** (May–Sept Mon–Fri 8.30am–7pm, Sat & Sun 9am–noon & 1–5pm; Oct–April daily 8.30am–noon & 1–5pm; ☎0232/712 6653), which dispenses the usual brochures and town plans, and lets you have a peek at comprehensive accommodation listings.

Accommodation

The decline in tourist numbers at Çeşme has inevitably taken its toll on the range of accommodation available, with marginal or overextended premises recently shutting their doors. Outside of high season, designated price categories are somewhat negotiable, since capacity exceeds demand for most of the year. The most desirable location to stay is the hillside above and to the right of the castle as you face it; if establishments there are full, other options cluster near the intersection of Çarşı Caddesi and Müftü Sokak, and even further south in the flatlands towards the *otogar*.

The obvious *Çeşme Kervansaray Hotel* (☎0232/712 7177, fax 712 6491) might do for a mild splurge, especially at ④ rates for the quieter rear units, but the rooms, though preserving their original vaulting and fireplaces, are a bit worn and plagued by damp in the colder months owing to sloppy restoration. The *Tarhan Pansiyon* (☎0232/712 6599; ②), behind the *kervansaray* and to the right, offers nine modern rooms with bath; the *Yalçin Otel*, Kale Sok 38 (☎0232/712 6981; ③), above the *Tarhan*, is larger, of recent vintage and also good value.

Down in the flatlands, the large *Alim Pansiyon*, Müftü Sok 3 (☎0232/712 7828; ②), is similarly recent, with baths in the rooms, and breakfast served in your choice of front or rear garden. In the same neighbourhood there's also the *Otel A*, Çarşı Cad 24 (☎0232/712 6881; ③). Even closer to the *otogar*, the well-signposted *Yaprak Pansiyon*

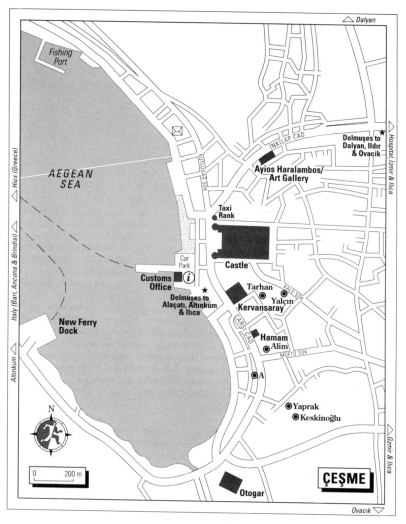

(☎0232/712 6036; ②) enjoys a peaceful setting amidst a wonderful garden; 200m beyond on the same street stands the rather less inspired *Keskinoğlu Pansiyon* (☎0232/712 8193; ②). Finally, the *Avrupalı Pansiyon*, Sağ Sok 12 (☎0232/712 7039; ②), run by two friendly retired schoolteachers, comes highly recommended for its clean rooms with baths and garden, as does the *Aras Pansiyon* (☎0232/712 7375; ②).

The Town

The town's two main streets are **İnkilap Caddesi**, the main bazaar thoroughfare, and **Çarşı Caddesi**, its continuation, which saunters south along the waterfront past the castle, *kervansaray* and most travel agencies before veering slightly inland. Unless you're a fan of nineteenth-century domestic architecture, though, Çeşme's sights are soon exhausted. You are free to clamber about every perilous inch of the waterfront **castle** (daily 8.30am–noon & 1–5.30pm; $1), much repaired by the Ottomans and today home to an open-air theatre (see "Eating, drinking and nightlife", below) and a small **museum** containing a paltry collection of finds from nearby Erythrae. The **kervansaray**, a few paces south, dates from the reign of Süleyman the Magnificent and has been predictably restored as a "luxury" hotel (see above). The huge old **Greek basilica** of Ayios Haralambos, in the centre of town, has been refurbished to serve as an art gallery and exhibition hall (irregular opening times).

Eating, drinking and nightlife

As with accommodation, so with food: a decline in choice and quality, with many recent closures and changes of ownership or format. Of the three quayside **eateries** down by the post office, the *Körfez* is about the best of a pricy lot. Otherwise it's back up along İnkilap, where the *Lezzet Aş Evi* at no. 14 revels in zero atmosphere but provides sustaining lunchtime steamtray fare. Just behind the old church you'll find the *Özen Pide Salonu*, preferable to the nearby *Fatih*. About halfway up İnkilap at no. 44 is the *Rumeli Pastanesi*, a local legend, with some of the best ice cream – including *sakız*- or mastic-resin-flavoured – on the Aegean; their home-made fruit preserves (*reçel*) are also on sale.

In terms of **after-dark** action, the favourite pastime seems to be promenading along roped-off İnkilap Caddesi, ice-cream cone in hand. Discos such as *Dokuz Buçuk* and *On* east of town on the Ilıca road are now considered passé, having yielded to a small number of bars near the castle which rarely maintain style or ownership for more than a season. The only cinema, the *Kale*, devotes itself to soft porn; more high-brow programmes characterize the **Çeşme Song Contest and Sea Festival** during early July, when the castle hosts performances ranging from the painfully amateurish to mediocre by way of the obscure.

Ferries

This is the main business of Çeşme and accordingly there are plenty of agencies. You can't miss the *Ertürk* agency (☎0232/712 6768, fax 712 6223), opposite the tourist office, which runs a namesake morning ferry **to Híos**. The Greek afternoon boat is represented by *Karavan*, next to *Ertürk* at Belediye Dükkanları 3 and also new premises closer to the *otogar* (☎0232/712 7230, fax 712 8987); this is also the most helpful full-service travel agency in town, with rare – and reliable – information on schedules elsewhere on the Turkish Aegean. *Karavan* also sells tickets for *European Seaways* liners to Bari or Brindisi, the only **Italy-bound service** to operate during the off-season. *Tamer Tours*, Beyazit Cad 15 (☎0232/712 7932), is the representative for the *Topaş* direct boats to Ancona and Bari, Italy, while *Maskot*, İnkilap Cad 93 (☎0232/712 7654, fax 712 8435), handles *Med Link* sailings to Brindisi. Do, however, take all this apparent abundance of choice with a grain of salt; in practice, long-haul companies suspend departures without notice, or drop services entirely when proven unprofitable, and it's unwise to advance-purchase a ticket to Italy unless the boat is in harbour, engines running.

Listings

Car rental *Sultan*, İnkilap Cad 68 (☎0232/712 7395), is about the cheapest; they also rent motorbikes, perfectly adequate for exploring the peninsula. Otherwise try *Blue Rent a Car*, Gümrük Sok 11/B (☎0232/712 9674).

Exchange The *Ziraat Bankası* has an automatic bill-changer, the *İş Bankası* the usual Visa-accepting ATM.

Hamam On Çarşı Cad, 200m down from the *kervansaray*.

Horse riding *Çaka Bey Riding Center*, 3km southeast of town (☎0232/712 8466, fax 712 9455), offers English instructors, tack and saddles; track and cross-country riding in the surrounding hills.

Hospitals *Devlet Hastanesi*, at the very top of İnkilap Cad, past the turning for Dalyan; however either the *Sağlak Hastanesi* in Ilıca (summer only), or the public health centre in Alaçatı (see below), are preferable.

PTT On the water 300m north of the ferry dock; open daily 8am–midnight. Look for a separate branch of *Türk Telekom* to open soon.

South of Çeşme: Alaçatı and some beaches

Nine kilometres southeast of Çeşme, **ALAÇATI** is a handsome, formerly Greek town, overlooking a plain at the head of a long, shallow inlet, and backed by three windmills. Architecturally it's still of a piece – much like Çeşme must have been twenty years ago – and a wander through its old lanes makes for an excellent morning or afternoon. The old church has not only been turned into a mosque by the Bosnian Muslims who came after 1923, but its former portico has become the heart of the meat and produce market – a strangely effective adaption. There are two or three **restaurants** between the windmills and the main square, plus one very plain *pansiyon*, the *Sarı* (☎0232/716 8315; ①). Alaçatı is strangely juxtaposed with a futuristic, American-run environmental technology park at its southern outskirts; the sea is 4km distant in the form of a 300-metre sandy beach, though lots of seaweed washes up. Facilities include one simple restaurant, the *Çınar*, and the *Çark Pansiyon* (☎0232/716 7309; ②).

By way of contrast, **OVACIK**, 5km due south of Çeşme on a road starting just east of the *otogar*, is dusty and half-inhabited, another ex-Greek village on a hill overlooking the straits to Híos. The paving ends here and you'll need your own means to continue 4km down a dirt road – with a right fork at an old fountain – to the small beach at **Çatal Azmak**. There's a single café there, and a better, more isolated beach five minutes' walk west, but neither can compare to the beaches at **Altınkum**, a series of sun-baked coves 9km southwest of Çeşme, beyond the rather forgettable seaside township of Çiftlik, and easily reached by dolmuş.

The **westernmost** of these is the smallest, taken up by the *Tursite* motel/camping/restaurant (⑥), whose fifty detached bungalows become sauna-like in summer and can only be occupied on a full-board basis. Between June and September the dolmuş continues a kilometre or so to the **central cove**, which is probably the best beach between Bozcaada and the Turquoise Coast, with multi-hued water lapping hundreds of metres of sand – and even dunes, which conceal a handful of scattered tent and caravan **campsites**. You can rent kayaks and windsurfers from impromptu beach stalls; though it's often windy here, the water is very clear and warm. Similarly ephemeral drink stalls sprout here in season next to the more permanent *Baba Camping* and *Antik Turgut* **restaurants**.

In high summer you have to walk pretty far east to lose the crowds – possibly over the headland to the **easternmost cove**, equal in all respects to the central one. However, even here a few villas have made their appearance; the only short-term accommodation hereabouts is at the small motel *Saraçoğlu* (③), which offers some A-frame chalets, tent space and a restaurant as well. The motel and by extension the eastern cove are accessible along a direct, unsignposted road from Çiftlik (bear left at the north edge of town).

Northeast of Çeşme: more resorts and a ruin

The approach to **DALYAN**, 4km north of Çeşme, is announced by a strange, four-storey tower looming over the village's remaining Greek-built houses. On the whole this is a peculiar, straggly, fishing settlement, built on the west shore of an almost completely landlocked harbour, which could become the area's main yacht anchorage should Çeşme harbour ever become overcrowded. There are, however, few short-term

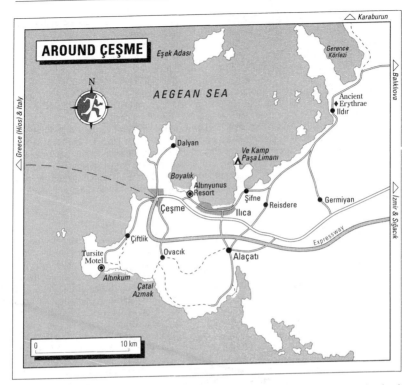

places to stay, and even less in the way of sandy beach, so for most people a clutch of **fish restaurants**, appealingly set by the narrow channel to the open sea, will be the extent of Dalyan's interest. Avoid the *Çınar* and the small neighbouring outfits; the best by a long way, right where the channel bends, is the *Liman*, with salubrious (but not cheap) *meze* and seafood. If you want to **stay**, you might try the *Güven Pansiyon* (☎0232/724 7031; ②), or the small *Alihan Hotel* (☎0232/712 6038; ④).

If you can fight your way past the tangles of villas – and the giant *Altın Yunus* holiday complex – lining **Boyalık** beach, 1500m east of Çeşme, you'll find the sand is actually okay, but painfully exposed – like most beaches on this side of the peninsula – to north winds, cold currents and washed-up rubbish. Far better to bypass it in favour of **ILICA**, 4km due east of Çeşme, where the degree of development – the name means "spa" – is justified by the excellent, kilometre-long beach. This can also get grubby in season but is less encroached upon east of the *Turban Ilıca* luxury hotel (closed for renovation until 1998), which grooms its own stretch of sand. The waterfront has been refurbished in recent years, and a yacht harbour set up, but despite these blandishments few foreigners are found outside the two aforementioned multi-starred facilities; the place has been and always will be primarily a weekend retreat for İzmir people.

If you're inclined to **stay** in Ilıca town, you'll find inexpensive non-package options are thin on the ground, and virtually no British package presence here. A characterful establishment near the yacht anchorage is the *Rasim Palas* (☎0232/723 1010; ③), a century-old Greek period piece with its own thermal baths where Atatürk once took a cure in the spa-tubs out back; his upstairs room is preserved as a shrine. Moving up in comfort, there's the *Lord Hotel* (☎0232/723 3823; ④), a small outfit with views of the bay from its hilltop position near the luxury *Altın Yunus* complex.

Eating possibilities are similarly limited, mostly to rather dubious takeaway sandwich stalls, though *İsmet Usta*, near the PTT, is excellent for hygienic soup and stays open late. Other exceptions, along Şifne Caddesi, include *Dost Pide*, with some meat dishes on offer, and – in the easterly Şantiye district, Turkey's earliest, German-designed holiday housing development – a branch of İzmir's famous *Altınkapı Döner* kitchen, with kebabs and real fruit (not fruit essence) ice cream. **Nightlife** is pretty tame, though *İlayda* is a sympathetic bar near the *Rasim Palas*.

Ve Kamp, the peninsula's most luxurious **campsite**, with its own beach and natural thermal pool, sprawls 3km past the east end of Ilıca beach at **PAŞA LİMANI**. At the base of the same promontory hides the tiny, shabby, German-founded and -patronized spa of **ŞİFNE**, where you can retire for a hot bath, should the urge seize you, at the municipally run *Termal Otel*, or for an outdoor mud bath at the head of the sumpy inlet here. But if you've come this far, you're probably on the way to Ildır and ancient Erythrae, 27km from Çeşme.

Ildır

ILDIR itself is a poky little village with minimal tourist facilities, its Greek houses underinhabited and un-"improved" owing to an archeological preservation order: Ildır is built just to one side of the acropolis of **old Erythrae**, an important site during Hellenistic and Roman times. The ancient city was renowned for two local cults: that of a sibyl or prophetess, second in importance only to the one at Cumae in Italy, and that of Hercules, venerated in a temple containing a miraculous statue of the god. All traces of either have long since vanished, along with quite a bit of the rest of Erythrae, villagers of all subsequent eras having helped themselves to the masonry.

A well-defined path leads from the edge of Ildır up the conical hill behind to the caretaker's white sentry box. If he's around he'll take you on a fifteeen-minute tour of the highlights, though the trodden paths lead obviously enough to most attractions. Only a few courses of **wall** and a recent, battered **Greek church** remain on the summit; the **theatre**, disfigured by concrete stairs, spills down the north slope. North of a wheat-field-cum-pear orchard, you'll be shown an old **tomb** and several **houses** standing to waist height, including a large **Roman villa** with a fieldstone floor and storage cistern. Panoramas west over the islet-flecked gulf, and north to the mountains looming over the Gerence Körfezi, seem the main recompense for the trip up.

Because of the village's listed status, amenities for outsiders are limited to the expensive *Mutlu* taverna just north, the *Ildır Pansiyon* (☎0232/725 1109; ②), and two fine fish restaurants, the waterside *Ildır* (tasty but pricy at $25 for two), and the *Deniz Kızı* just inland, both right on the road 500m south of the village.

The Karaburun Peninsula

Until recently isolated and little visited, the **Karaburun peninsula**, which spears northeast of Çeşme, is the newest suburb of İzmir. While there is a **bus service** as far as Karaburun town, near the tip of the peninsula, there are few other facilities – such as *pansiyons* – for casual visitors; the east shore is very much villa-land, and not terribly rewarding unless you have your own vehicle.

The turn-off from the old highway is 12km west of Urla; from the new expressway, about 9km west of the Urla exit. The first place you'd be tempted to stop is **BALIK-LIOVA**, a sheltered bay with some patches of beach and a restaurant or two. **MOR-DOĞAN**, about halfway up the east coast, is a proper town, but its sand beach is completely overshadowed by the renovated harbour and new development. The final stretch to Karaburun is dramatic, with villages and orchards clinging to the crags of

1212-metre Akdağ, although **KARABURUN** itself is a letdown, with an exposed, rocky shore and a port redeemed only by a few fish restaurants.

Beyond here, the road – paved until Küçükbahçe, dirt thereafter – loops completely around the peninsula to Ildır, winding through several crumbling, half-inhabited villages that were Greek before 1922. Several **pebble beaches** face Híos and Inoússes, but they're difficult to get at without a motorcycle. The most accessible and protected lie in the embrace of the Gerence Körfezi, but by this point you're within 6km of Ildır, or 10km from Balıklıova via another dirt road spanning the narrow neck of the peninsula.

Sığacık and Teos

Thirty kilometres south of Güzelbahçe on either the new or old İzmir–Çeşme highways, **SIĞACIK** huddles inside a low-slung Genoese castle, with many of its houses built right into the perimeter. Otherwise the village is of middling architectural interest, and although you might want to wander the maze of alleys inside, foreigners come to Sığacık primarily for the sake of its good yacht anchorage, with no decent beaches in sight. For a swim, you'll need to continue 1500m over the hill to the west to **Akkum**, a 150-metre-wide sandy cove ($0.50) that's gradually becoming oversubscribed.

The journey to Sığacık by **bus** is complicated by loop routes and the frequent need to change vehicles. From İzmir, some, but not all, routes to Ürkmez and Gümüldür (see p.300) go through **Seferihisar**, a large town 6km east of Sığacık – here you can catch a red-and-white *Belediye* bus to cover the remaining distance to Akkum. A few of the Kuşadası–Seferihisar **dolmuşes** continue to Sığacık, but again you'll usually have to change in Seferihisar.

If you want to **stay** in Sığacık, the pick of a limited bunch is the *Burg Pansiyon* (☎0232/745 7716; ②), a recent but traditional-style building right on the quay. Otherwise there's the *Liman* (☎0232/745 7019; ①) and the *Huzur* (☎0232/745 7923; ②), set well back from the water on the way out of town. At Akkum there's a **campsite**, the imaginatively named *Bungalow Kamping*, on the cape past the large *Neptun* windsurfing resort whose patrons crowd out the beach. **Eating** at Sığacık's low-key port, the *Liman* restaurant is a bit fancier – and cleaner – than the *Burç*.

Teos

The same road serving Akkum continues for just under 5km to ancient **TEOS** (site unenclosed), though approaching on foot you can considerably short-cut the final zigzags.

Teos was once one of the most important Ionian cities, renowned for its colossal temple to Dionysos, deity not only of wine but of the arts and the generative forces of nature. Accordingly, in early Roman times Teos was chosen to host the Guild of Dionysos, the union of all artists, actors and musicians who performed throughout Asia Minor. They soon proved so insufferable that the Teans exiled them to backwaters down the coast. An earlier, more genial embodiment of the Dionysian ethic was the city's famous son, the sixth-century poet **Anacreon**, who choked to death on a grape seed after a long life of wine, women and song.

Appropriately, the second-century BC **Temple of Dionysos** is the most interesting remain, excavated – with three columns partly re-erected – in a bucolic setting of olive trees and grazing cattle. You can also pick your way 400m northeast to a hillside supporting the **Hellenistic theatre**, though only the stage foundations are left of this, and it's debatable whether it's worth snaking around the wheat fields and buzzing cow-pat flies for the view south over assorted islets to Sámos. About 100m southeast of the theatre you might find the eleven remaining rows of the Roman-era **odeion**. When you've finished sightseeing, call at the small drinks stand that operates in high season, at the road's end in front of the temple.

Inland: the Küçük Menderes valley

With a spare day, most of the towns and villages of the **Küçük Menderes valley**, inland a little way to the southeast of İzmir, are easily seen by public transport, as connections with both İzmir and Selçuk are good. Visit **Birgi**, the most remote and unusual, first.

Birgi and Gölcük

A sleepy community of half-timbered houses lining both slopes of a narrow valley at the foot of Boz Dağ, **BİRGİ** is an excellent example of what small-town Turkey looked like before the wars and cement mania of this century. The main thing to see is the currently unsignposted **Aydınoğlu Mehmet Bey Camii**, also called the Ulu Cami, an engaging fourteenth-century construction on the site of an earlier church. It's across the ravine from the Çakırağa Konağı (see below), and a bit upstream. Quite a lot of ancient Pyrgion, including a sculpted lion, is incorporated into the exterior walls; inside, it's an understated masterpiece, with the tiled *mihrab* and a single arch betraying Selçuk influence. Most impressive, though, are the carved hardwood *mimber* and shutters, some of them replacements for those carted off to the Selimiye Camii in Edirne. The sloping wooden roof is supported by a forest of Roman columns, the whole effect more like Spanish Andalucia than Turkey. The minaret features zigzag belts of glazed green tiles, like the Yeşil Cami in İznik, while the dome of the adjacent **türbe** of the Aydınoğlu clan is fashioned in concentric rings of alternating brick and the same faïence. A couple of other mid- to late Ottoman mosques perch next to or above the stream, along with some ruined baths and a *medrese*, but while these add to the atmosphere of the place none can compare to the Ulu Cami.

Birgi's houses, ensembles of wood and either brick, stone, lath-and-plaster or half-timbered mud, run the gamut from the simple to the sumptuous. Many are dilapidated, but the recently restored eighteenth-century **Çakırağa Konağı**, one of the largest and most ornate in Turkey, operates as a museum (Tues–Sun 9am–noon & 1–6pm; $1). Built by one Şerif Aliağa in 1761, this mansion is one of the best surviving specimens of many which sprung up in the wake of the decentralizing reforms of the eighteenth century, which allowed local potentates (the *derebey*s) to rule and live in grand style. Most *konak*s were two-storeyed, but the slope here dictates a three-storey plan: the ground floor in stone, the upper floors in lath-and-plaster. Many have burned down or simply rotted away owing to the extensive use of wood in coffered and painted ceilings, lattices, and built-in cupboards (*mısandra*s). The extensive and vivid murals depict, as was the vogue of the time, stylized skylines of favourite coastal cities; the presence or absence of particular structures allows dating of the paintings to the nineteenth century.

Despite the increased tourist traffic which the mansion attracts, Birgi actually boasts fewer facilities for outsiders than in previous years. Down in the bazaar, there are currently no places to **eat**, other than a single, rather threatening *birahane*. If you're forced to stop over, you can beg a **room** at the inn in the *belediye* building (no phone; $6 per person) – not as grim as it looks with proper beds and hot water, but you'll need plenty of lead time during weekday working hours to track down the warden with the key.

Gölcük

GÖLCÜK, 20km above Birgi, is just about the last thing you'd expect to see in the Aegean region: a six-acre **lake** in a wooded cavity tucked nearly halfway up 2129-metre Boz Dağ. The coolness and the greenery make it a favourite local summer retreat. You can come just for the day to **eat catfish** (*yayın* in Turkish) at the *Rıhtım Restaurant*, with a gazebo on stilts over the water, or you might **stay** at the rather overpriced *Gölcük*

Motel (☎0232/544 3530; ④), though it's frequently full in high season. A few summer villas are sprouting here and there, but the lakeshore itself is surprisingly undisturbed, probably because it's reedy, with no real beach and murky water.

Arrival via Ödemiş

To reach both Birgi and Gölcük you have to travel via **ÖDEMİŞ**, 9km west of Birgi. There are six or seven **dolmuşes** daily to Gölcük, and a like number of daily buses to Birgi run by its _belediye_. Failing these, anything plying the mountain road to Salihli passes within 3km of the lake and 1km of the village, or you'll have to arrange a taxi ($2 per car to Birgi). Gölcük services leave from the corner of Hatay and Namik Kemal _caddesis_, some 200m distant from the adjacent **train station** and **otosar**. That's pretty much all you have to know about the place, an undistinguished market town famed mostly for the export of _salep_ root – derived from a variety of orchid and ground up to make a hot winter drink. Its only pretension to things cultural is the **Archeological/Ethnographic Museum** (daily except Mon 8.30am–noon & 1–5pm; $1), 1500m out on the route to Birgi. Predictable pottery vies with too many headless statues and, in the ethnographic section, a clothed store mannequin pathetically labelled "modern dress".

Tire

Thirty kilometres across the valley floor from Ödemiş, **TİRE**, clustered at the base of Güme Dağı, is an altogether different kettle of fish. Much fought over by Byzantines and Selçuks, it eventually became one of the Aydınoğlu clan's first important strongholds, and the conservatism and religious fervour of the inhabitants is still apparent (and disparaged by secular Turks). If you've had an overdose of the touristed coast, Tire makes the perfect antidote – though being stared at may be part of the experience.

The **old quarter** with its rickety houses is uphill from the main traffic roundabout in the northwest of town; you might have a look at the map placard outside of the kitschy **museum** (same hours and price as in Ödemiş), but the best strategy is just to wander. First, find the **Yeşil Imaret Zaviyesi**, also known as the Yahşi Bey Camii, built in 1442 by a general of Murat II as the core of a dervish community. Its minaret sports the same type of faïence as that of the Ulu Cami in Birgi; an unusual scallop-shell halfdome looms over the _mihrab_, as does stalactite vaulting over the front door. No other monument cries out for attention – your main impression will be of a staggering number (reputedly 37) of indifferently restored Ottoman mosques, and older _türbes_ or tombs, including two by the _otogar_.

Tire's atmosphere is, however, considerably enlivened by a large gypsy presence from the surrounding villages, most in evidence at the weekly Tuesday market, reputedly the best in the Aegean region. The gypsies are probably the source of the lace articles sold in the bazaar, and of the local horse-cart painting technique, imitated by some wealthy city-dwellers on their kitchen cabinets.

THE HEART OF ANCIENT IONIA

Although old **Ionia** – including half of the ancient league of thirteen cities known as the Panionium – extended north of the Çeşme peninsula, what the term usually evokes is the often startlingly beautiful territory around the deltas of the Küçük and Büyük Menderes rivers. Few other parts of Turkey can match this region for the sheer concentration of ancient cities, which in their time were at the forefront in the emergence of the sciences, philosophy and the arts.

The Ionian coast was first colonized by Greek-speakers in the twelfth century BC and the culture reached its zenith during the seventh and sixth centuries BC. Enormous advantages accrued to those who had chosen to settle here: an amenable climate, fertile, well-watered terrain, and a strategic location between the Aegean – with its many fine harbours – and inland Anatolia. The Persian invasions, Alexander the Great's contrary campaigns and the chaos following his death only temporarily hampered local development, and under the Romans and the Byzantines the region perked up again; urban life might have continued indefinitely in the old nuclei were it not for the inexorably receding coastline – thanks to the two silt-bearing rivers. By mid-Byzantine times virtually all of the Ionian cities had been abandoned, and with the declaration of Christianity as the state religion, religious centres and oracles met a similar fate.

Today's inhabitants have found the silver lining to the cloud of the advancing deltas, cashing in on the rich soil brought down from the hills. Vast tracts of cotton, tobacco, sesame and grain benefit from irrigation works, while groves of pine, olive and cypress, which need no such encouragement, adorn the hills and wilder reaches. And the sea, though more distant than in former times, still beckons when tramping the ruins palls; indeed, tourism is threatening to outstrip agriculture as a moneymaker.

This is nowhere more obvious than in **Kuşadası**, an unabashedly utilitarian base for excursions to the major antiquities. There are some beaches and minor sites, particularly to the north at **Pamucak** and **Claros**, to delay your progress inland, but the main show of the area is undoubtedly the ensemble of ruins further south, spanning numerous eras: most notably at **Ephesus**; at **Priene** – perhaps the most dramatic site of all the Ionian cities; at **Miletus**, further south – probably the least impressive; and at **Didyma**, with its gargantuan temple. Oddly, considering the proximity of the river mouths, the **beaches** near these ruins unfortunately tend to be functional at best and always exposed; the immensely popular exception is **Altınkum**, now a densely developed, tatty package venue.

Kuşadası

KUŞADASI is Turkey's most bloated resort, a brashly mercenary Las Vegas-on-Sea that extends along several kilometres of coast, and well inland. In just three decades its population has swelled from about 6000 to almost 40,000, though how many of these are year-round inhabitants is debatable.

The town – whose name means "Bird Island" – is many people's introduction to the country: efficient ferry services link it with the Greek island of Sámos, and the resort is an obligatory port of call for Aegean cruise ships, which disgorge vast crowds in summer, who delight the local souvenir merchants after a visit to the ruins of Ephesus just inland. Not to be outdone by Bodrum and Marmaris, and in a studied attempt to siphon off some business from the Greek islands opposite, the local authorities have also constructed a huge yacht marina at the north end of town. It's the largest and best-equipped marina northwest of Marmaris, but it can't help but seem a strange venture, since the coast nearby is largely exposed leeward shore and unsuitable for cruising.

Not surprisingly, all this rapid development has affected local attitudes, to say the least. New arrivals are usually besieged by aggressive touts offering accommodation, carpets, escort service for unaccompanied foreign women and so forth. Stay here for the sake of the excellent connections to nearby attractions, the adjacent beaches and some sophisticated nightlife, rather than the town's minimal charm. Of late, Kuşadası has opted for downmarket tourism in a big way, in a bid to bolster flagging visitor numbers. Flights from Britain and Ireland plus a week's hotel stay are offered for as little as £159, in the usually vain hope that takers will make up the difference by shopping in the local bazaars; instead their main concern seems to be finding the cheapest beer in the greatest quantities possible. If that leaves you cold, you might prefer Selçuk as a base (see p.301).

Kuşadası's origins are obscure; no proven trace has been found of any ancient settlement. The Venetians and Genoese rechristened the Byzantine anchorage of Ania as Scala Nuova when they established the harbour here to replace Ephesus's silted-up one, but only in the Ottoman era did the port acquire its current name, derived from the small fortified islet – Güvercin Adası or "Pigeon Island" – tethered to the mainland by a causeway. The little castle on the island (now home to various cafés and a disco) is actually the southernmost of several Aegean fortresses built by the Genoese during the fourteenth and fifteenth centuries. Sepia-toned postcards for sale, re-issued by the local Lion's Club, show the town as it was from the 1920s until the 1950s: handsome, tiered ensembles of tile-roofed nineteenth-century houses grouped in distinct neighbourhoods (of the Jews, the Greeks, the Muslim immigrants from Crete or the Peloponnese) – especially poignant souvenirs in light of what has transpired here since the 1970s.

Arrival and information

Arriving by **ferry** from Sámos, you'll exit customs directly onto Liman Caddesi, and walk right past the **tourist information office** at no. 13 (May, June, Sept & Oct daily 8am–6pm; July & Aug daily 7.30am–8pm; Nov–April Mon–Fri 8.30am–noon & 1.30–5.30pm; ☎0256/614 1103), which hands out an insufficiently detailed town plan (see "Listings" for a better one) and keeps exhaustive lists of accommodation.

The **long-distance** *otogar*, where you're dropped if coming from the south, is over a kilometre out, past the end of Kahramanlar Caddesi on the ring road (*çevre yolu*) to Söke. **Dolmuşes**, for example those to and from Selçuk, Söke and the national park (see below), share the same facilities, but often accept passengers at a stop slightly closer to the centre, on the corner of Adnan Menderes Bulvarı and the ring road; all long-distance services make a stop near here too. Coaches and most minibuses have been effectively banned from the former in-town stop at the corner of Atatürk and İnönü *bulvarı*s, with the exception of local dolmuşes linking the northern Tusan beach with the town centre and its southern annexe of Kadınlar Denizi.

If you're bound for İzmir on *Elbirlik*'s frequent shuttle service, you really have to trudge out to the *otogar* to be sure of getting a seat, since they often sell out. Little publicized is the fact that these coaches pass the airport gate, 700m from the terminal proper; *havalimanı kavşağı* means "airport junction" – allow ninety minutes for the trip. Taxis usually wait to transfer you the final distance, and you pay $2.50 maximum per car.

Accommodation

The tourist office lists over 300 **hotels and pansiyons** of all categories in Kuşadası, so you're spoilt for choice – except in high season. As ever, prices within a given class are rigidly controlled, so it's more what you get for your money that's the issue. Sometimes you can get far more than you bargained for: the notionally five-star *Hotel Imbat* at Kadınlar Denizi spent a month shut down during 1995 owing to comprehensive contamination by legionnaire's disease – a fitting conclusion to Kuşadası's recent ethic of pack-em-in-cheap-and-never-mind-the-infrastructure.

One area for reasonably priced, hygienic accommodation is just south of the core of the town, uphill from Barbaros Hayrettin Bulvarı, particularly the upper reaches of Yıldırım, Aslanlar and Kıbrıs *caddesi*s. For a relatively central location with a sea view, try Bezirgan Sokak, above Kıbrıs Caddesi, reached quickest via stairs from behind the new shopping centre with its clock tower. For more comfort, there are a number of sea-view establishments scattered along the entire length of the shore road. Kadınlar

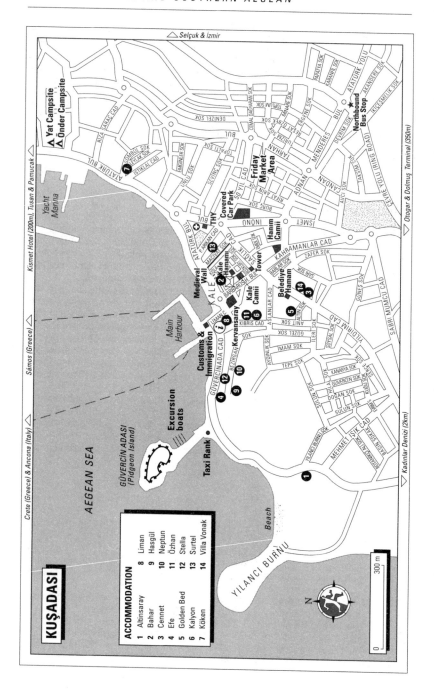

KUŞADASI

ACCOMMODATION

1	Altinsaray	8	Liman
2	Bahar	9	Hasgül
3	Cennet	10	Neptun
4	Efe	11	Özhan
5	Golden Bed	12	Stella
6	Kalyon	13	Surtel
7	Köken	14	Villa Vonak

AEGEAN SEA

GÜVERCİN ADASI
(Pidgeon Island)

Main Harbour

Excursion boats

Taxi Rank

Beach

YILANCI BURNU

Customs & Immigration

Medieval Wall

KALE

Kale Camii

Kervansaray

Belediye Hamam

Kale Tower

Hanim Camii

Friday Market Area

Covered Car Park

THY

Northbound Bus Stop

Yacht Marina

Selçuk & İzmir

Kismet Hotel (200ml, Tusan & Pamucak)

Sámos (Greece)

Crete (Greece) & Ancona (Italy)

Otogar & Dolmuş Terminal (350m)

Çevre Yolu (RING ROAD)

Kadinlar Denizi (2km)

Yat Campsite
Önder Campsite

300 m

Denizi may suggest itself as a cheap and cheerful base, but legionella aside it can also be squalid, and the poor beach can't compensate for its relative remoteness.

It's advisable to choose in the first instance from amongst the hotels and *pansiyon*s we recommend below, as we have received serious complaints about a number of establishments and proprietors, particularly those who tout at the *otogar* or the pier.

Bezirgan Sokak

Hasgül (☎0256/614 3641). At the quiet end of Bezirgan Sok, past the co-managed *Hotel Stella*. En suite, with some rooms overlooking the bay; terrific roof terrace, plus pool privileges at the *Stella* (see below). ③.

Hotel Neptun, alley off Bezirgan Sok (☎0256/614 1540). Very quiet position, some ocean glimpses from this older but en-suite hotel. ③.

Hotel Stella, Bezirgan Sok 44 (☎0256/614 1632, fax 614 5100). Kilim decor for the common areas, good-sized tile-floor rooms with view balconies, a swimming pool and friendly management make this the choice establishment on this street. ⑤.

Kıbrıs Caddesi and Kale

Bahar Pansiyon, Cephane Sok 12, Kale (☎0256/614 1191). Down in the flatlands in an area better known for nightlife than quiet sleep, but double glazing in the well-appointed rooms defeats the noise. ④.

Hotel Kalyon, Kıbrıs Cad 7 (☎0256/614 3346). Rooms are larger than at the *Özhan*, but no heating and no roof terrace. ③.

Özhan Pansiyon, Kıbrıs Cad 5 (☎0256/614 2932). Small but reasonably kept *pansiyon* that's good value; terrace bar and heated rooms, convenient for winter ferry-waits. ③.

Yıldırım and Aslanlar caddesis

Cennet Pansiyon, Yayla Sok 1, corner Yıldırım Cad (☎0256/614 4893). Spotless, recent building, with a small garden. Table d'hôte meals by advance arrangement. ②.

Golden Bed, Aslanlar Cad, Uğurlu Birinci Çıkmazı 4 (☎0256/614 8708). A newish, dead quiet outfit with good views from both balconied rooms and rooftop breakfast terrace; signposted from Yıldırım Cad. Hot water can be unreliable, but the place is run partly by women, which can be a blessing for many female travellers. ②.

Villa Konak Hotel, Yıldırım Cad 55 (☎0256/614 6318). A 1990s building in traditional style, popular with groups. ③.

Seafront

Altınsaray Otel, Yılancı Burnu, 250m south of the islet (☎0256/614 4514, fax 612 7122). Only some of the smallish rooms have balconies, but there's a pool, it's near the beach if chlorine doesn't suit, and the tile-and-wood architecture with greenery behind is pleasant enough. ⑤.

Efe Hotel, Güvercinada Cad 37 (☎0256/614 3660, fax 614 3662). A formerly exemplary two-star hotel come down in the world and now the reputed haunt of some very shady characters, but still worth a mention for its excellent location. On-site restaurant and tiny "splash" pool out front by the roadside. ⑤.

Kismet Hotel, Yacht Marina (☎0256/614 2005, fax 614 4914). Part owned by Hümeyra Özbaş, a princess descended from the last Ottoman sultan. That, and the pictures of distinguished guests displayed in the lobby, set the tone for this elegant spot set in well-kept gardens. Ordinary rooms resemble small suites, while so-called "de luxe" rooms are palatial. Private lido and tennis court; limited package presence (*Simply Turkey* and *Anatolian Sky*), and mind your manners. If you enquire which price category it falls into, you can't afford it, but since you did, prices range from $80 double up to $250, with advantageous half-board rates. ⑧.

Köken Otel, İstiklal Cad 5 (☎0256/614 1460, fax 614 5723). Set back just inland from noisy Atatürk Bulvarı, this small, friendly hotel with a limited package allotment represents good value; there are reputable *pansiyon*s to either side if it's full. ④.

Liman Otel, Kıbrıs Cad, Buyral Sok 4 (☎0256/614 7770, fax 614 6913). Fair-sized rooms in a small, modern building, central but relatively calm; ask for a sea-facing or side room. ④.

Surtel Hotel, Atatürk Bul 20, Hacivat Sok (☎0256/612 0606, fax 614 5126). Three-star comfort on a pedestrian alley bordering the *kale* wall; roof-pool and bar. ⑤.

Campsites

Önder, Atatürk Bul, behind yacht marina. Reasonably priced, open year-round and popular, with good facilities and its own restaurant (see "Eating and drinking", below).

Tur-Yat Mocamp, Tusan beach. A well-appointed spot for tenting down, though its bungalows are downright unreasonable; open May–Oct.

Yat, Atatürk Bul, behind yacht marina. Next to the *Önder* and similar.

The town and beaches

Liman Caddesi runs 200m from the ferry port up to the sixteenth-century **Öküz Mehmet Paşa Kervansaray**, restored as a noisy, tawdry luxury hotel, before turning hard left to become **Atatürk Bulvarı**, the main harbour esplanade. **Barbaros Hayrettin Bulvarı** is a pedestrian precinct beginning next to the *kervansaray* and homing in on a little stone tower, a remnant of the town's medieval landwalls, up the slope. To the left as you ascend lies the **Kale district**, huddled inside the rest of the walls, with a namesake mosque and some fine traditional houses that help lend the town what little appeal it has – most of these have been done up as upmarket restaurants and bars. **Sağlık Caddesi** is the perpendicular street behind the tower, and bearing left down here takes you along the rear of Kale, where bits of old wall, including the landscaped stretch parallel to Hacivat Sokak leading down to the water, are visible; right leads up towards some of Kuşadası's more desirable *pansiyons*, scattered among the largest neighbourhood of handsome old dwellings. Continuing straight on, the walkway (emblazoned with a sign "Old Bazaar") changes its name to **Kahramanlar Caddesi**, dividing (the left fork becomes **Adnan Menderes Bulvarı**) just past the **Hanım Camii**.

Kuşadası's most famous **beach**, the **Kadınlar Denizi** (Ladies' Beach), just under 3km southwest of town, is a popular strand for both sexes and far too crowded – and filthy – for its own good in season. Dolmuşes for this beach trundle south along the seafront past the fortified islet, alert for custom.

Güvercin Adası itself is mostly landscaped terraces within its fortifications, dotted with tea gardens and snack bars – good spots to wait for an afternoon ferry to Greece. Swimming off the islet is rocky; for the closest decent sand, head 500m further south to the small beach north of Yılancı Burnu, or patronize one of the day trips to points north offered by excursion boats moored along the causeway.

Tusan beach, 5km to the north of town, is probably more worthwhile, despite noise from the coast road; the namesake luxury hotel behind it will rent you all manner of watersports equipment. All Kuşadası–Selçuk minibuses pass by, as well as the more frequent ones labelled "Kadınlar Denizi" and "Şehir İçi", whose routes end near the *Tusan Hotel*.

Much the best beach in the area is **Pamucak**, at the mouth of the Küçük Menderes River 15km north, a little way off the route to Selçuk. The main disadvantage of this exposed, four-kilometre-long stretch of sand is that it can't be used if the wind is up. Popular principally with local families, it's scarcely developed except for the two enormous luxury complexes situated near the far south end: just south of the river mouth, there's *Dereli Camping/Motel* (☎0232/892 3636), with a well-landscaped, tree-shaded camping area; north of the stream, there's just the jail-like *Tamsa Otel*, and the stop for the dolmuşes which call regularly from both Kuşadası and Selçuk in season.

Eating and drinking

Value for money is not the order of the day as far as **food** goes in Kuşadası, and if you're planning to head straight for Selçuk off the Greece ferry, a sensible impulse might be to quell rumbling stomachs until arrival there. As with certain dubious hotels and legionella, so with numbers of dodgy restaurants and salmonella. But if you're lingering, careful hunting will turn up a bare handful of acceptable (and even better) restaurants scattered about, though the best local eateries lie well south of town.

In the **Kale** area, you'll do no better for traditional Turkish food than *Avlu*, Cephane Sok 15/A, with rear-courtyard seating, serving reasonably priced grilled and steamtray specialities lovingly prepared by the owners; it's unlicensed, but open until about 11pm, with plans afoot for 24-hour operation. More touristically pitched with a wider menu, but still acceptable, is the *Melamet Sofrası* near the Kale Camii, while *BeBop*, Cephane Sok 20, is a well-regarded Italian bistro which becomes a jazz bar after-hours.

Moving a little further **inland**, beyond Sağlık Caddesi, the squeaky clean *Albatros Restaurant* at Emek Sok 4, Belediye Dükkanları Zabıta Karşısı (the sign is obscured by a huge climbing vine), serves outstanding stews and such for just over $5; again unlicensed, and open at lunch only, when the place is frequented by local tradesmen. Of a line of eateries along Kahramanlar Caddesi beyond the tower, the only half-decent place is the long-established *Konya* at no. 65.

There's little else worth singling out in the town centre, and the handful of **waterfront** fish-and-*meze* restaurants lurking closest to the cruise-ship and ferry jetties are without exception rip-offs. If you want to eat by the water without blasting away the entire contents of your wallet, you might try the second, no-name place beyond the tatty *Ada Restaurant-Plaj-Café*, on Güvercin Adası, though the food there is nothing special. About 1km north along Atatürk Bulvarı, the restaurant attached to the *Önder* campsite is run by three brothers and perennially packed out; it boasts good food, though of late the portions seem to have shrunk and prices risen.

For high-quality eating, however, you really have to leave the city limits, heading south on the road bound for Davutlar. About 3km before that village in **Saraydamları** district, a pair of large, extremely popular restaurants flank the road, both requiring advance booking. A meal at either place shouldn't exceed $14 a head with wine – money well spent.

The entree menu at the older, more traditional *Tarihi Çınar* (☎0256/681 1177; open year-round), which takes its name from the enormous plane tree on site, is limited to spit-roasted lamb and chicken, but there's a full *meze* tray and sweets on offer. Just opposite on a hilltop, *Değirmen* (☎0256/681 2150; also year-round) is a meticulous recreation of an old mill built from traditional and salvaged materials, with a menu featuring seldom-seen household breads, noodles and stews, as well as grilled items; summer tables on the lawn overlook an artificial lake and farm on the premises where chicken and quail are raised for the table.

Nightlife

After-dark activity in Kuşadası is distributed over perhaps three dozen bars, clumped into several groups: a dwindling number of arty, genteel theme bars of the Kale district; their more energetic neighbours, featuring live music with either Turkish- or English-language lyrics; and self-explanatory Irish/British pubs with karaoke tackle and recorded House/Techno tracks, culminating in the considerably more downmarket and foreigner-dominated "Barlar Sokak". As ever, making specific recommendations in a fluid resort environment is probably futile, even invidious; if you pace the streets named below, guided by the cranked-up sound systems, you'll certainly find something to suit.

The most durable of the **Kale** watering holes, and congenial environments for meeting educated Turks on holiday, include *Jazz Bar*, Bahar Sok 18, and the perennially popular *She*, at the corner of Bahar and Sakarya *sokak*s. Dancers will want to gravitate towards the disco-ish *Cool Bar* or *2021*, while *Ankara* on Cephane Sokak is representative of the Turkish-language format, and *Rock and Blues* at Kızla Sok 14 of the Western style.

Just off the foot of Yıldırım Caddesi, Eskipazaryeri Sokak has been officially renamed **Barlar Sokak** (Pub Lane), as the entry arch proclaims. The decibels emanating from the dozen or so "Irish" and "London" pubs are deafening, with the Union Jack T-shirt brigade and rugby-song choirs out in force. Turkish men stroll by, motivated by a mixture of contempt and fascination, and the off-chance of finding an unescorted Shirley Valentine wannabe.

Listings

Antiques An unusually good shop in Kale district is *Hâki Baba*, Bozkurt Cad 19 (☎0256/614 3018 for viewing appointment), run by a Frenchified Turk who will dispense dervish philosophy with your purchase.

Books An exceptional and well-designed shop, totally at odds with the tacky ethos of the town, is *Kuydaş* at İnönü Bul 8/B. Besides books, there are newspapers, magazines, CDs and tapes, nautical charts and an upstairs art gallery. An annexe of used stock is planned.

Car rental After İzmir, Kuşadası is one of the most expensive places in Turkey to rent a vehicle, and it's advisable to pre-book from home. Many outlets cluster along İnönü Bul, just back from the sea; standard daily walk-in rates of $80 can be bargained down to $45–55 at slack times. Turkish chain and one-off outlets include *Airtour*, Atatürk Bul 64/10 (☎0256/614 2856); *DeCar*, Atatürk Bul 106/A (☎0256/612 6844); and *Start*, İnönü Bul 6/1 (☎0256/614 3126). Otherwise you're at the mercy of the major chains: *Avis*, Atatürk Bul 26/B (☎0256/614 4600); *Budget*, Sağlık Cad 58 (☎0256/614 4956); *Europcar/InterRent*, Atatürk Bul 68 (☎0256/614 3607); *Hertz*, İnönü Bul 38/3 (☎0256/612 1151).

Exchange Many of the bank booths at the junction of Liman Cad and Atatürk Bul stay open until dark in the summer, while further up Barbaros Hayrettin are a few premium-rate *döviz* brokers. Unwanted Greek drachmas can be exchanged fairly easily for Turkish lira, but at 25 percent below their actual value. All the most useful ATMs – *Garanti Bankası, Yapı Kredi, Pamukbank* – are present.

Ferries Agency for the Turkish morning boat *Sultan* is *Azim Tour*, Liman Cad, Yayla Pasajı (☎0256/614 1553); all other boats, including the *Diana, Kuşadası Prenses* (sic) and the Greek afternoon craft, are handled by *Diana*, on Kıbrıs Cad just above the shore road (☎0256/614 4900). Ticket prices are among the steepest of all the Greek–Turkish ferry lines, although they drop significantly in the off-season: peak time singles $20, day returns $25, open returns $35, plus $10 tax on the Turkish side, with an additional $10 levied if you stay overnight in Greece, plus 4000dr when leaving Greece. On recent trial, *Azim Tour* proved to be marginally cheaper for a return ticket than *Diana*. Cars incur charges of $50–75 depending on size. In the afternoon, Greek-based hydrofoils also ply to Sámos, for much the same price in half the journey time. The once-weekly *Mar Lines* ferry to Crete (Greece) and Ancona (Italy) is handled exclusively by *Kervan*, Kıbrıs Cad 2/1 (☎0256/614 1279).

Hamams *Kale Hamamı* behind the Kale Camii is very touristy; *Belediye Hamam* on Yıldırım Cad slightly less so; both open daily 9am–9pm, both are expensive.

Hospital The state hospital is at Atatürk Bul 32, near the park.

Map "City Plan, Kuşadası", published by Kuydaş, is the only reliable and detailed town plan, most reliably available from the eponymous bookstore.

Market day Friday, on Candan Tarhan Bul north of Adnan Menderes Bul, but inevitably skewed by tourist interests.

Parking Best to leave autos fairly far north along Atatürk Bul, or well out on Güvercin Adası Cad, or (for a fee) in the *kapanlı* (covered) car park on the site of the old *otogar*. Badly placed vehicles will be towed to a remote pound and drivers fined a minimum of $20.

PTT A few steps up Barbaros Hayrettin Bul; open 24hr in season, 8am–midnight otherwise.

Supermarkets *Migros* and *Tansaş*, flanking the *otogar* out on the inland bypass road.
THY *Osman Turizm*, İnönü Bul 18/A (☎0256/614 4205). Full-service agency with computerized booking capability.

North of Kuşadası: beaches and minor sites

Particularly if you have your own vehicle, it's worth pressing **north** from Kuşadası toward some relatively unspoiled beaches and two archeological sites. While neither site in itself would justify a detour, together with the chance for a swim they make a satisfying day trip.

At the roundabout where the roads from Kuşadası, Pamucak and Selçuk meet, continue straight toward Seferihisar; the highway ahead has been widened and surfaced and is no longer the narrow dirt road indicated on obsolete maps. After 25km there's a poorly marked junction, with a sign pointing inland to Ahmetbeyli and Menderes. This is a recognized stop for buses; in your own vehicle bear seaward for the moment and park behind the excellent 600-metre beach.

Notion

The artificially terraced promontory bounding the beach to the east, on the opposite side of a sluggish creek, is in fact the site of ancient **NOTION**. This obscure settlement was founded as the port annexe to the ancient city of Colophon, 15km inland, at least as early as the eighth century BC. In time the littoral community attained greater importance than the inland one, and came to be called Neocolophon. This process was accelerated when Lysimachus punished old Colophon for its support of Antigonus in the post-Alexandrian civil wars by semi-depopulating it in 302 BC. Both settlements dwindled as nearby Ephesus (see p.308) became prominent, and today Notion is ruinous in the extreme – the only recognizable monument, aside from the fragments of wall visible above the stream bed, being the foundations and column fragments of a Corinthian **Temple of Athina Polias** erected during the second century AD. For some it will be debatable whether the tricky scramble through the breaches in the walls is worth interrupting a tanning session, but the view over the sea from up top is superb.

Claros

The ancient oracle and temple of Apollo at **CLAROS**, 1500m inland from Notion in a lushly vegetated valley, is more rewarding. Though overshadowed in popular imagination by the nearby oracle of Apollo at Didyma (see p.318) and the more remote one at Delphi, Claros, particularly during the Roman period, equalled the other two in importance.

Though there was mention of a temple here as early as the seventh century BC, its role as a prophetic centre did not begin until three hundred years later, notably with its approval of the relocation of Smyrna. The sacred precinct was a dependency of ancient Colophon, and was similarly punished by Lysimachus, but under Hadrian its fortunes revived spectacularly; the premises were handsomely reconstructed, with clients from throughout the Roman Empire arriving to consult the oracle. Despite this, most of what is visible today – most poignantly seen at dusk – dates from early or even pre-Hellenistic times.

To get there, turn right at the yellow-and-black signpost, 1km along the asphalt road up to Ahmetbeyli village, then right again once over the bridge, following more crude signs. Beyond this point the track would be impassably muddy to two-wheel-drive cars after a rain, but it's only 400m further to the makeshift car park. Repeated scholarly expeditions have been undertaken since the turn of the century to keep the ruins clear of the silt deposited by the adjacent river, and to pump them free of the high water table – an ongoing problem, which has resulted in a permanent resident population of frogs and terrapins hereabouts. At present the site, like Notion, has unrestricted entrance, but French-supervised restoration works are continuing and the admission situation will certainly change when excavations are completed.

The site

The precinct was entered from the south via a **monumental gate**, of which a half-dozen sunken columns remain, flanked by a semicircular bench and a small stoa. Originally, a **sacred way** – now half-buried under dirt and shrubbery but still flanked by statue niches and adorned with inscriptions from grateful supplicants – led some 200m to the **Temple of Apollo**.

This, strewn with enormous toppled column drums, dates from the fourth or third century BC and – rare in Ionia – is of the Doric order. Pilgrims were admitted at night to the temple porch, and their names were relayed by a priest to the prophet residing in a sunken sanctuary underneath the great hall. After the seer had drunk from a sacred spring within, his mutterings were then phrased in more artful verse by an assistant. You can still see the vaulting of the subterranean chamber's roof, which supported the shrine's colossal 25-foot statue of Apollo, of which only fragments remain. The current excavators are slowly piecing together some of these.

Immediately east of the temple are the remains of the sacrificial altar, while next door, on the northern side, rest the foundations of a smaller Ionic **Temple of Artemis**, also with the ruins of an altar.

The back road to Teos and Çeşme

The coastal road **west from Claros** sweeps through magnificent scenery, with sandy coves at almost every turn, although the minimal traffic will increase in the future if the direct Urla–Kuşadası highway is improved again. İzmir looms barely 70km away, and most foreigners visit the area as a day trip. As a result, it can be difficult to find affordable short-term accommodation among the masses of villas and motels let by the week or month, which dwarf all but the largest beaches and cater principally to Turks or the occasional German. Of the settlements, only **ÖZDERE** has a trace of village character, but the beach here is not that great. The best strand is indisputably at **GÜMÜLDÜR**, 20km west of Notion and marked as Köprübaşı on some maps. A large grid of purpose-built civil servants' holiday quarters, motels, *pansiyon*s and grills close to the main road has not yet managed to engulf 4km of fine sand opposite a little islet. *Sunquest* is virtually the only UK package operator to work in the area, offering such multi-starred, beachfront hotels as the *Club Yalı* just west of Gümüldür and the *Grand Efe* and *Mavı Köy* near Özdere.

Beyond Gümüldür the road continues uneventfully to Seferihisar, turn-off point for Sığacık and Teos (see p.289) and the obligatory point to change dolmuşes if you are travelling from Kuşadası to Çeşme by public transport. There are a few inviting-looking beaches before Doğanbey, but many are posted as off-limits, ostentatiously tank-trapped and presumably mined against the absurdly remote possibility of an amphibious landing from the Greek island of Sámos opposite.

The only other possible diversion on the way – if you can find a safe way to it through the various marked military zones – is the islet studded with the fortifications of old **Myonessos**, tethered to the mainland by a half-submerged causeway. But you'll need your own vehicle to get there, since dolmuşes from Selçuk use the faster inland bypass to Seferihisar.

South of Kuşadası: Dilek Yarımadası Milli Parkı

The imposing outline of **Samsun Dağı** (the ancient Mount Mycale) dominates the skyline south of Kuşadası and may inspire notions of a visit. Tour operators and dolmuşes make light work of the 28-kilometre trip to the national park established around the mountain, so that the immediate environs of its north-shore beaches hardly count as wilderness any longer.

The **Dilek Yarımadası Milli Parkı** (daily spring & autumn 8am–5pm; summer closes 6.30pm; $0.50, cars $2.50) was set aside in 1966 for, among other reasons, the protection of its thick forest and diverse fauna, which is said to include rare lynx, jackal and wild cats. However, you are unlikely to see any of the species in question, since much of the 28,000-acre park is an off-limits military zone; try to walk out towards the tempting bits at the very tip of the peninsula and armed conscripts will bar the way.

Arguably the park performs its function as a wildlife preserve better than it does that of an all-purpose recreation area. The walk to the summit is also possible from the mountain's south flank (see p.315), and the undeniable beauty of the terrain, certainly the most unspoiled along the Turkish Aegean, is owed entirely to the military presence. The most visited portion of the unrestricted zone consists of a ten-kilometre-plus stretch of mostly paved road beyond the entrance and four good but often windswept **beaches** along it – İçmeler (hard sand shaded by plane trees), just beyond the gate; Aydınlık Koyu (pebbles); asphalt's end at Kavaklı Burun (pebbles); and the last and prettiest one, Karasu (700m of pea gravel). Each beach has its own small snack bar or drinks kiosk operating in high season.

Immediately past Karasu the onward dirt track is signposted as "Yasak Bölge", and armed patrols will turn you back should you venture further. A lone jeep track, gated against wheeled traffic and signposted as "Kanyon" complete with walking-man symbol, does saunter inland between Aydınlık and Kavaklı beaches, curling up to the summit ridge east of 1237-metre Dilek Tepesi, but better access to the ridge is possible by trail from Eskidoğanbey village to the south. Since the closure of most short-term accommodation in Eskidoğanbey, walkers tend to take an early dolmuş to one or other of the trailheads, hike over the mountain, and take an evening dolmuş back to Söke or Kuşadası from the walk's endpoint.

There are no facilities for staying overnight in the park; the closest *pansiyon*s and hotels, inexorably Turkish-pitched, are in and around **GÜZELÇAMLI**, a village 1km outside the reserve boundaries. The pebble beaches 300m below Güzelçamlı are not as good as those in the park, and hemmed in by massive overdevelopment.

Selçuk and around

Only two decades ago a laid-back farming town, **SELÇUK** has been catapulted into the limelight of first-division tourism by its proximity to the ruins of Ephesus – and a number of other attractions within the city limits or just outside. The flavour of tourism here, though, is markedly different from that at nearby Kuşadası, its less prestigious inland location and ecclesiastical connections making it a haven for a disparate mix of collegiate backpackers and Bible Belters from every corner of the globe. Some may find this characterization a bit harsh, but it's not meant as out-and-out disparagement – it means, among other things, that the numerous carpet-shop hustlers and accommodation touts here have a more realistic idea of their audience's financial limits.

Although evidence of settlement as early as 2000 BC has been found atop Ayasoluk Hill (Selçuk's logo), the town only really got going as a Byzantine enterprise during the fifth century AD, after the harbour of adjacent Ephesus had completely silted up. Like Birgi and Tire, the place was later a haunt of the Aydınoğlu clan, who yielded to the Ottomans in the early fifteenth century. Despite a venerable role in the events of the early church, including key events in the life of Paul, John and (supposedly) the Virgin, local Christianity thereafter was mostly restricted to the village of Kirkince (see p.307). In this century, the town's demographic profile has become an uneasy mix of Rumeliot (south Balkan) and Bosnian emigrants, who arrived in successive waves between 1890 and 1960; settled Yörük nomads wont to idle in the teahouses; Kurds and gypsies. Each group has its own designated quarter, socializing little with the others.

Arrival and information

At the base of the castle hill and across the busy E24/550 highway, a mock arch marks the start of a pedestrian precinct leading east to the **train station**. Along the way you'll pass the long-hours **PTT** and most of the town's restaurants. Following the main highway a bit further south brings you to the combined **bus and dolmuş terminal**; it's worth saying that the *Elbirlik* shuttle between Kuşadası and İzmir airport always makes a stop on the main highway. On the opposite side of this road, beyond the fountains of the central park, the cheerful **tourist information office** (May–Sept daily 8.30am–noon & 1–5.30pm; Oct–April Mon–Fri 9am–noon & 1–5.30pm; ☎0232/892 6945) has extensive lists of accommodation.

You will find them a more disinterested source of intelligence than the rug boys and *pansiyon* promoters, often one and the same person, who mob every bus arrival, sometimes boarding them at the town limits to deliver their sales pitch. Subsequent hustles are more refined, and include the time-honoured offer of a lift to Ephesus and loan of a site guidebook – bracketed by "coincidental" stopovers at a relative's carpet shop for tea and a "chat".

Accommodation

Staying overnight in Selçuk presents something of a puzzle. An entire category of lodging – ② in our scheme – is under-represented, so that little fills the gap between fairly basic, 1970s-vintage facilities with shared plumbing, and occasionally overpriced hotels. Since 1993 there's been a big shake-up in local tourism, with about half the town's more modest ① *pansiyon*s permanently closing their doors. Most recommendations from among the survivors cluster around the two pedestrian streets or just west of the through highway, near the museum, with additional desirable establishments scattered on and beyond Ayasoluk Hill. Another concentration of *pansiyon*s is found in the east of the town, mostly beyond the rail line.

Near the museum

Ak Hotel, Uğur Mumcu Sevgi Yolu 14, the pedestrianized way behind the central park (☎0232/892 2161, fax 892 3142). Enormous rooms distributed over two buildings; ask for one facing the garden. Rearmost rooms are quieter, but have no balcony. Some package-tour presence; attached restaurant. Nominally ④, but lately a snip at ③.

Australian Pansiyon, Miltner Sok 17 (☎0232/892 6050). Run by a family of returned Turkish-Australians, this *pansiyon* is proud of its courtyard-with-view, and there's a convenient tie-in with their carpet-and-book-exchange shop, run by the two sons. Shared bathrooms; ①.

Barım Pansiyon, Turgut Reis Sok 34 (☎0232/892 6923). Restored, rambling old house, with some en-suites. ①.

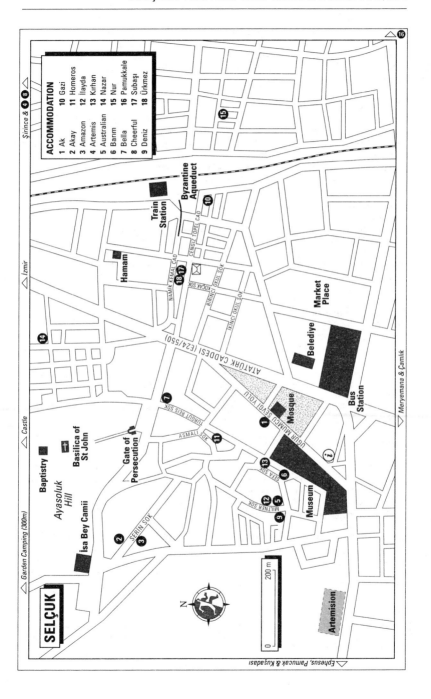

SELÇUK

ACCOMMODATION

1 Ak	10 Gazi
2 Akay	11 Homeros
3 Amazon	12 Ilayda
4 Artemis	13 Kırhan
5 Australian	14 Nazar
6 Barım	15 Nur
7 Bella	16 Pamukkale
8 Cheerful	17 Subaşı
9 Deniz	18 Ürkmez

Deniz Pansiyon, Sefa Sok 9 (☎0232/892 6741). Accepts the *Australian*'s overflow; similar bathless rooms. ①.

İlayda Pansiyon, Miltner Sok 15 (☎0232/892 3278). Another well-placed cheapie. ①.

Kırhan Pansiyon, Turgut Reis Sok 7 (☎0232/892 2257). Dormitory-type accommodation at rock-bottom prices. $5 a head.

West of Ayasoluk

Hotel Akay, Serin Sok 3 (☎0232/892 3172, fax 892 3009). Affordable comfort if somewhat dour management, with fine views of the mosque, castle and basilica from its roof restaurant. ③.

Amazon Pansiyon, Serin Sok 8 (☎0232/892 3215). Basic, non-en-suite rooms in an older building around a courtyard garden; kitchen facilities. ①.

Homeros Pansiyon, Asmalı Sok 17, near the top of the hill (☎0232/892 3995). Simple rooms but a fine roof terrace and English-speaking management. ①.

East of Ayasoluk

Hotel Bella, Saint Jean Sok 7 (☎0232/892 3944, fax 892 7045). Some tour-bus and carpet-shop bustle and hustle en route owing to its position near the basilica gate, but the hotel itself is well run, featuring smallish rooms with balconies and American-style showers en suite. Good value and bargainable. ③.

Nazar Hotel, Eski İzmir Cad 14 (☎0232/892 2222, fax 891 4016). Not the most inspiring location in the flatlands of the gypsy quarter, but gets rave reviews from many readers. New, en suite, clean, friendly and well run, with a good roof-restaurant. Underpriced at ②.

The pedestrian streets

Hotel Gazi, Cengiz Topel Cad 1, right by the train station (☎0232/892 6467). All rooms with en-suite baths, but slightly dubious air of late, and management can be unhelpful. ③.

Hotel Subaşı, Cengiz Topel Cad 12, across from the PTT (☎0232/892 6359). Another of the "storkview" hotels; clean if spartan. ③.

Otel Ürkmez, Namık Kemal Cad (☎0232/893 6312). The best by some way of several "stork view" hotels overlooking a Byzantine aqueduct with its nests. Some rooms have balconies, all have baths, but what makes the hotel is the sympathetic, non-pushy management style of the Özkan brothers, who speak excellent English. Roof terrace with laundry and kitchen facilities; good breakfasts by hotel standards. ③.

Eastern neighbourhoods

Artemis Pansiyon, Attila Sok 5, Zafer Mahalle, 250m walk from the centre east of the rail line (☎0232/892 2722). A 1970s breeze-block construction, but friendly, quiet and highly thought of by a loyal repeat clientele; excellent table d'hôte meals available for about $6 a head. The *Cheerful Pansiyon* (☎0232/892 2732) nearby is similar. Both ①.

Nur Pansiyon, Dere Sok 16, Zafer Mahalle, east of the train tracks (☎0232/892 6595). Run by a widow and particularly appropriate for single women travellers; serves optional breakfasts in the garden, and excellent evening meals. ①.

Pamukkale Pansiyon, Sedir Sok 1, Ondört Mayıs Mahalle (☎0232/892 2388). Smallish outfit with garden, some en-suite rooms; English-speaking proprietor, loyal international following. ①.

Vardar Pansiyon, Atatürk Mahalle, S. DD Cad 9 (☎0232/891 5451). 200m from the bus station. English-speaking female management, so a good spot for single women travellers; bad news is non-en-suite, some traffic noise. ①.

Campsites

Dereli, Pamucak beach, 9km west of town. See p.296.

Garden, in Selçuk itself, well signposted 300m beyond İsa Bey Camii. Shady, grassy, caravan-popular and well regarded.

The Town

Selçuk offers a variety of antiquities from diverse eras, which can easily be toured in a single day – but they're numerous and interesting enough that you can't just do them as a postscript after a day spent at Ephesus.

Ayasoluk Hill

Lodestone of settlement in every era, the **Hill of Ayasoluk** (daily 8am–6.30pm; $2, includes castle when open) is the first point you should head for. You enter the site through the **Gate of Persecution**, so called by the Byzantines because of a relief of Achilles in combat which once adorned it, mistakenly thought to depict a martyrdom of Christians in the amphitheatre of nearby Ephesus.

Traditionally Saint John the Evangelist – or "Theologian" as the Greeks knew him – came to Ephesus in the middle of the first century. He died here around 100 AD and was buried on Ayasoluk Hill, whose name is thought to be a corruption of "Ayios Theologos". The sixth-century Byzantine emperor Justinian decided to replace two earlier churches sheltering John's tomb with a basilica worthy of the saint's reputation, and until destruction by Tamerlane's Mongols in 1402 it was one of the largest and most ornate Byzantine churches in existence.

Today various colonnades and walls of the **Basilica of St John** have been re-erected, courtesy of a religious foundation based in Lima, Ohio, giving just a hint of the building's magnificence in its prime. The purported tomb of the evangelist is marked by a slab at the former site of the altar; beside the nave is the baptistry, where fundamentalist tourists may pose in the act of dunking for friends' cameras.

The **castle** (same times, shut for works until 1998) is 200m past the church, and virtually empty inside. Prior to its recent closure you were allowed to make a full circuit on the ramparts – if this isn't permitted in the future, the same views are available from the church.

The museum

Just behind the tourist office, the **Archeological Museum** (daily except Mon 8.30am–noon & 1–5.30pm, winter closes 5pm; $3) is permanently packed out with visitors but well worth setting aside the time to visit. Its galleries of finds (mostly from Ephesus) are, interestingly, arranged thematically rather than chronologically. The first, small-finds hall contains some of the most famous bronze and ceramic objects in the collection, including Eros riding a dolphin, effigies of the phallic gods Bes and Priapus – perennial postcard favourites – a humane bust of the comedian Menander, and various excellent miniatures from the Roman terrace houses at Ephesus, one of the rooms from which is mocked up at the far end.

Beyond here, past some relief and free-standing statuary from the fountains of Ephesus, a wall hoarding on oil lamp manufacture and an ivory furniture frieze, there are a couple of courtyards containing sarcophagi, column capitals and stelae, from which steps lead down to another courtyard with attractive fountains, an ethnography section on bazaar crafts and a restored sixteenth-century hamam.

Continuing through the main galleries, you'll enter a hall devoted to tomb finds and mortuary practices. Just beyond this is the famous **Artemis room**, with two renditions of the goddess studded with multiple testicles (not breasts, as is commonly believed) and tiny figurines of real and mythical beasts, honouring her role as mistress of animals. At Ephesus, Artemis adopted most of the attributes of the indigenous Anatolian mother-goddess Cybele, including a eunuch priesthood – the stone testicles possibly symbolize the ultimate votive offering.

The last gallery houses friezes and busts from imperial cult temples – the strangest fragments a giant forearm and head, the latter misshapen and infantile, part of a five-metre statue of the Emperor Domitian (81–96 AD).

West: the Artemision and İsa Bey Camii

Beyond the museum, 600m along the road toward Ephesus and to the right, are the scanty remains of the **Artemision** or Sanctuary of Artemis (daily 8.30am–5.30pm; free). The archaic temple here replaced three predecessors dedicated to Cybele, and was itself burned down in 356 BC by Herostratus, a lunatic who (correctly) reckoned his name would be immortalized by the act. The massive Hellenistic replacement was considered to be one of the Seven Wonders of the ancient world, though this is hard to believe today: the Goths sacked it in 263 AD, and the Byzantines subsequently carted off most of the remaining masonry to Ayasoluk and Constantinople, leaving just a lone column (re-erected in modern times) amid battered foundation blocks. It took the English archeologist J. T. Wood six years of trial soundings in the mud to locate the temple's foundations in 1869. Constant pumping is necessary to keep the area from flooding, and in winter the ducks come here for a swim anyway.

Within sight of the Artemision stands the **İsa Bey Camii**, the most distinguished of the various Selçuk monuments that give the town its name. It's a late fourteenth-century Aydınoğlu mosque, and represents a transition between Selçuk and Ottoman styles, with its innovative courtyard – where most of the congregation would worship – and stalactite vaulting over the entrance; the contemporary Ulu Cami in Manisa (see p.261), though much smaller, is conceptually quite similar in its use of a courtyard. Although recently restored, the İsa Bey's two minarets were snapped off long ago and the ablutions fountain in the court is missing. If you can get inside the main hall (often locked), you'll see a high, gabled roof supported by Roman columns, and some fine tile work in the south dome.

Eating, drinking and entertainment

Restaurants in Selçuk, virtually all in the town centre, tend to be on the samey side: not nearly so exploitative as some in Kuşadası, though not nearly as refined either. Marginally better value among establishments along pedestrianized Cengiz Topel Caddesi are the relatively elegant *Seçkin* and the cheap and abundant *Köfteci Turhan*, near the PTT, both of which have fish, mixed grill and *meze*; plus the *Artemis Pide Salonu* further east on 1010 Sokak, a deceptive hole-in-the wall with such oddities as sweet *tahin pide*. The *Seçil* is an okay fourth choice, with not as wide-ranging a menu. A sweet tooth can be satisfied at the *Dilek Pastanesi* on Cengiz Topel, while after-hours tippling takes place at several noisy **pubs** lining both parallel pedestrianized streets.

In terms of more formal **entertainment**, the second or third week of May sees the **Ephesus festival** occur nightly at the Ephesus amphitheatre, and mid-January brings **camel wrestling** between huge male camels, at the edge of town.

Meryemana

Eight kilometres southwest of Selçuk, beyond Ephesus (see below) and just below the summit of Bülbül Dağ, stands **MERYEMANA**, a monument to piety and faith. Though most orthodox theologians maintain that the Virgin Mary died and was buried in Jerusalem, another school of thought holds that the mother of Jesus accompanied Saint John the Evangelist when he left Palestine in the middle of the first century on his way to Ephesus.

After the medieval turmoil around Ephesus nobody from abroad was inclined to delve further into the matter until **Catherine Emmerich** (1774–1824), a German nun and seer who never left her country, recorded her visions of a small stone house, where, she claimed, the Virgin had lived her last years. In 1891 Lazarist priests from İzmir decided to follow her descriptions, and discovered a building that matched them – and which, in its role as the chapel of Panayia Kapılı, was already a focus of adoration by the Orthodox Greeks of nearby Kirkince, especially on August 15, the Feast of the Assumption. Things mushroomed predictably from there, spurred by a papal visit and imprimatur in 1967, and today the place is on the checklist of pilgrims from around the world.

The **site**, accessible only by private car, is enclosed in a Selçuk municipal park (dawn–dusk; $2, plus car-park fees) and subject to a generous dose of commercialism – though the dense forest and fountain are pleasant enough. The **house** itself, now a chapel aligned unusually southwest-to-northeast, probably dates from early Byzantine times, though its foundations may indeed be first-century. It overlooks a beautiful wooded valley and two terraces where a spring gushes forth; nearby, tree branches are festooned with the votive rag scraps left by Muslim pilgrims, for whom *Meryemana* (Mother Mary) is also a saint. Whatever you may believe about the historical likelihood of this being Mary's last home, the shrine is a tribute to the tenacity of mother-goddess veneration in Anatolia.

Şirince

Kirkince itself is today called **ŞİRİNCE**, a well-preserved, originally Greek-built hill village 8km east of and above Selçuk, surrounded by lush orchards and vineyards and now inhabited by Muslim settlers from near Thessaloníki. They make assorted wines that pack quite a punch – you can taste or even buy them at *Şarap Evi* on the single shopping street – and also export a certain quantity of peaches. Not too surprisingly the place has become a target of tour groups, but compared with Selçuk or Kuşadası it's low-key – though beware of invitations to private homes, which invariably serve as pretexts to foist lacework on you.

At the edge of Şirince as you approach stands a late nineteenth-century **church**, with a pebble-mosaic floor, plaster relief work on the ceiling and wooden vaulting – though much is crumbling away. Nearer the middle of the village there's a larger stone **basilica** dating from 1839, recently restored as an art gallery. But the main point of a visit is the idyllic scenery and the handsome domestic architecture, which since the late 1980s has attracted wealthy urban Turks in search of characterful vacation homes.

Six to seven daily **minibuses** serve Şirince, departing from next to Selçuk's train station between 8.30am and 5pm. If you want to **stay**, there are two *pansiyon*s: the simple but quiet *Ersa* near the north edge of the village (☎0232/898 3140; ②); and the *Şirince Evler*, two restored nineteenth-century houses flanking the main street leading to the bazaar. These self-catering units for up to five people must be booked in advance from either *Rea Turizm*, Plevne Bul Ünüvar Apt 6/14, İzmir (☎0232/489 8571, fax 421 0796; ⑤), or through *Simply Turkey* in the UK. At the east end of the single-lane bazaar now mostly lined by shabby trinket shops, a half-dozen indifferent **restaurants** and *gözleme* stalls cluster around the main square. One was formerly named after Dido Sotiriou, chronicler of the Greek Asia Minor experience and its post-1922 aftermath, in honour of a visit made by her in spring 1990; much of her classic novel *Farewell to Anatolia*, perennially popular in Turkey, was set in the village.

Çamlık Open-Air Rail Museum

Some 12km south of Selçuk on the main highway, the village of **ÇAMLIK** is the site of the **Open-Air Rail Museum** (unfenced; $0.60 when warden present), just southwest of the road after the village-limits sign. More than two dozen steam locomotives, most of them German-made and pre-World-War-I, are scattered about on disused sidings, with a half-dozen of the most impressive grouped around a turntable. There's no labelling or explanatory placards but then, if you're a train buff, you won't be needing any. Nothing to stop you from clambering up into the cabins either.

Ephesus (Efes)

With the exception of Pompeii and newly rediscovered Butrint in Albania, **EPHESUS** is the largest and best-preserved ancient city around the Mediterranean, and after the Sultanahmet district of İstanbul is the most visited tourist attraction in Turkey. Not surprisingly, the ruins are mobbed for much of the year, although with a little planning and initiative it's possible to tour the site in relative peace. Certainly it's a place you shouldn't miss, though you may come away disappointed at the commercialization and the extent of the off-limits areas. You'll need three or four partly shady hours to see Ephesus, and a water bottle – the acres of stone act as a grill in the heat of the day, and there are only two drinking taps within the site, close by the main entrance.

Some history

Situated by a fine harbour at the terminus of overland trade routes, and beneficiary of the lucrative **cult** of the Anatolian mother-goddess Cybele/Artemis, Ephesus led a charmed life from earliest times. Legends relate that Androclus, son of King Kodrus of Athens, had been advised by an oracle to settle at a place indicated by a fish and a wild boar. Androclus and his entourage arrived here to find natives roasting fish by the sea; embers from the fire set a bush ablaze, out of which charged a pig, and the city was on its way. The imported worship of Artemis melded easily with that of the indigenous Cybele, and the Ephesus of 1000 BC was built on the north slope of Mount Pion (Panayır Dağı), very close to the temple of the goddess.

The Ephesians needed their commercial wealth, since they rarely displayed much common sense, military strength or political acumen. When the Lydian king **Croesus** appeared in the sixth century, the locals could muster no other defence than to rope off the Artemis temple and retreat behind the barrier. Croesus, perhaps amused by this naivety, treated the city leniently and even contributed to the temple, but insisted on moving the population closer to the sea, north of Panayır Dağı. Still unfortified and ungarrisoned, Ephesus passed back and forth between Greek and Persian interests until the Hellenistic era.

Alexander the Great, on his visit in 334 BC, offered to fund the completion of the latest version of the Artemis shrine, but the city fathers tactfully demurred, saying that one deity should not support another, and dug deeper into their own pockets. Following Alexander's death his lieutenant **Lysimachus** moved the city to its present location – necessary because the sea had already receded considerably – and provided it with its first **walls**, traces of which are still visible on Panayır Dağı and Mount Koressos (Bülbül Dağı) to the south.

In subsequent centuries, Ephesus displayed flashes of its old fickleness, changing allegiance frequently and backing various revolts against Roman rule. Yet it never suffered for this lack of principle: during the Roman imperial period it was designated the **capital of Asia**, and ornamented with magnificent public buildings – the ones on view today – by a succession of emperors. As tolerant as it was shifty, Ephesus's quarter-million population was swelled substantially at times by the right of sanctuary pertaining to the sacred precinct of Artemis, which at one point encompassed much of the city limits, allowing shelter to large numbers of criminals. Of a somewhat less lurid cast was the more stable, mixed population of Jews, Romans and Egyptian and Anatolian cultists.

Despite or perhaps because of this, **Christianity** took root early and quickly at Ephesus. Saint John the Evangelist arrived in the mid-first century, and **Saint Paul** spent the years 51–53 AD in the city, proselytizing foremost among the Jewish community. As usual, Paul managed to foment controversy even in this cosmopolitan environment, apparently being imprisoned for some time – in a tower bearing his name near the west end of the walls – and later provoking the famous silversmiths' riot, described in Acts 19:23–20:1. Paul preached that the silver votive images of Artemis were not divine; the head of the silversmiths' guild, seeing his livelihood threatened, assembled his fellows in the amphitheatre where they howled "Great is Artemis of the Ephesians!" – as well as for the apostle's blood. The authorities managed to calm the crowd, but Paul was obliged to depart for Macedonia.

Under the Byzantines, Ephesus was the venue for two of the **councils of the church**, including one in 431 AD at which the Nestorian heresy (see p.707) was anathematized. However, the general tenor of the Byzantine era was one of decline, owing to the abandoning of Artemis-worship following the establishment of state Christianity, Arab raids, and (worst of all) the final silting up of the harbour. The population began to siphon off to the nearby hill crowned by the tomb and church of St John, future nucleus of the town of Selçuk, and by the time the Selçuks themselves appeared the process was virtually complete.

The site

Approaching the **site** (daily 8am–6.30pm; last ticket 6pm; winter closes 5.30pm; $5, $1.25 parking fee) from Kuşadası, get the dolmuş to drop you at the *Tusan Motel* junction, from where it's another easy kilometre to the lower, north gate. From Selçuk, don't bother with wheeled transport unless you have your own or succumb to the blandishments of horse-drawn cab drivers ($5 per cart) – it's a pleasant three-kilometre walk, the first two along a mulberry-shaded lane paralleling the busy highway. There is also a second entrance on the upper, southeastern side of Ephesus, on the way to Meryemana – perhaps a more sensible route in summer since it enables you to walk downhill through the site (tour buses tend to drop their clients there, retrieving them at the lower gate). Visiting Meryemana first by taxi from Selçuk will allow you to use the upper gate: $20 should include a half-hour wait at "Mary's house", then a drop-off at the top of the Ephesus site.

The Cave of the Seven Sleepers

Before reaching the lower gate, you can detour left off the approach road after 300m, and then proceed about 1km, to visit the **Cave of the Seven Sleepers**, the focus of a touching legend. Seven young Ephesian Christians, refusing to sacrifice to the second-century emperor Decius, took refuge in this cave, were walled in by the imperial guard and fell into a deep sleep. An earthquake shattered the wall and woke them; upon ambling down to town for food, they discovered that 200 years had passed and that Christianity was now the state religion. When the seven men died soon after – presumably from shock – they were re-interred in the grotto, and a commemorative church was built over their graves.

The place is in fact an extensive network of catacombs backed into the hillside on several levels which was used until late Byzantine times. Since 1993, however, the complex has been tightly fenced, and you can only view from the perimeter path which snakes above it. On the approach road you run a gauntlet of *gözleme* and *çay* stalls, rather more relaxed and pleasant than those crowding the entries to Ephesus proper.

The Church of St Mary

The first hint of the city, well before you reach the tacky parking lot with its souvenir stalls and tour buses, are the rather eroded (and pilfered) remains of the **gymnasium of Vedius** and the **stadium**, funded by Nero. Once past the entry gate, take a sharp right along a path signed "Meryem Kilisesi", which leads to the **Church of St Mary**,

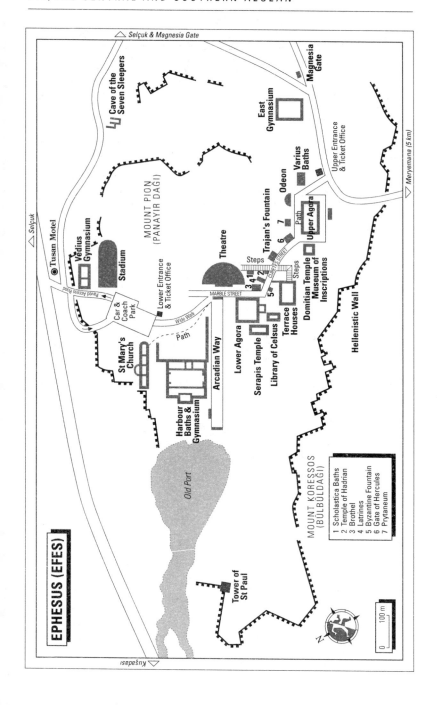

EPHESUS (EFES)

Selçuk & Magnesia Gate

Magnesia Gate

Cave of the
Seven Sleepers

East
Gymnasium

MOUNT PION
(PANAYIR DAĞI)

Upper Entrance
& Ticket Office

Varius
Baths

Meryemana (5 km)

Selçuk

Odeon

Tusan Motel

Vedius
Gymnasium

Trajan's Fountain

Stadium

Theatre

7

6

Upper Agora

Paved Access Road

Lower Entrance
& Ticket Office

Steps

Path

CURETES STREET

3 4 1 2

Domitian Temple
Museum of
Inscriptions

Car &
Coach
Park

Wide Walk

MARBLE STREET

5

Steps

Hellenistic Wall

St Mary's
Church

Path

Arcadian Way

Lower Agora

Serapis Temple

Terrace
Houses

Library of Celsus

Harbour
Baths &
Gymnasium

Old Port

MOUNT KORESSOS
(BÜLBÜLDAĞI)

1 Scholastica Baths
2 Temple of Hadrian
3 Brothel
4 Latrines
5 Byzantine Fountain
6 Gate of Hercules
7 Prytaneum

Tower of
St Paul

Kuşadası

0   100 m

N

an absurdly elongated hotch-potch constructed between the second and fourth centuries AD. The building, originally a Roman warehouse, was the venue of the ecumenical council in 431 AD; its baptistry is in good condition.

The Arcadian Way and the theatre

Beyond the church, the **harbour baths** and **gymnasium** are prominent, but overgrown and difficult to explore. They are usually approached along the splendid **Arcadian Way** (currently off-limits while adjacent digs are under way), so named after the fifth-century Byzantine emperor Arcadius who renovated it. Today tree- and bush-fringed, it's a forlorn echo of the era when it was lined with hundreds of shops and illuminated at night – although its neglect is refreshing when compared to the **ancient theatre**, recently and brutally restored to provide additional seating for the various summer festivals, with material that would be more appropriate buttressing a California freeway flyover. For all that, it has been shut recently, owing to slips occasioned by heavy winter rains. If you bother to climb past the 20,000 seats of half-modern masonry to the top, it's for the perspectives over the surrounding countryside.

Along the Marble Street

The so-called **Marble Street** begins near the base of the theatre and heads almost straight south; wheel-ruts in the road and the slightly elevated colonnade remnant to the right indicate that pedestrians and vehicles were kept neatly separated. Also to your right as you proceed is the main **agora**, currently closed for excavations, with an adjoining **temple of Serapis**, where the city's many Egyptian merchants would have worshipped. About halfway along the Marble Street, metal stanchions protect alleged "signposting" – a footprint and a female head etched into the rock – for a **brothel**, located in the very centre of the Roman city, at the junction with the city's other main street, the Street of the Curetes, named after a caste of priests at the Artemis shrine. Little remains above chest height at the house of pleasure, but there are some fine floor mosaics denoting the four seasons, and (appropriately enough) one of the priapic figurines in the Selçuk Museum was found here.

The Library of Celsus

Directly across the intersection of the two major streets looms the **Library of Celsus**, originally erected by the consul Gaius Julius Aquila between 110 and 135 AD as a memorial to his father Celsus Polemaeanus, still entombed under the west wall of the structure. The elegant, two-storey facade was fitted with niches for statues of the four personified intellectual virtues, today filled with plaster copies (the originals are in Vienna). Inside, twelve thousand scrolls were stored in galleries designed to prevent damp damage – a precaution that didn't prevent the Goths burning them all when they sacked the area in 262 AD. The library has been restored by the presiding Austrian archeological team and their commercial contractor, Kallinger, who get in your face as if the ruins were a mere building site, with self-promoting wall plaques and German-only labelling. Abutting the library, and designed to provide entry to the still off-limits *agora*, is the triple **gate of Mazaeus and Mithridates**, restored since 1980 with a bit more taste. (Mithridates was a wealthy freedman, not to be confused with the notorious Pontic nemesis of the Roman republic.)

Along Curetes Street

Just uphill from the Roman city's main intersection, a **Byzantine fountain** looks across the Street of the Curetes to the **public latrines**, a favourite of visitors owing to the graphic obviousness of their function. The toilets were conveniently connected with the brothel just downhill. Continuing along the same side of the street, you'll come to the

so-called **temple of Hadrian**, actually donated in 118 AD by a wealthy citizen in honour of Hadrian, Artemis and the city in general. Currently a drinks stand occupies its
left side. As in the case of the library facade, most of the relief works here are plaster
copies of the originals, which reside in the Selçuk Museum. The two small heads on the
arches spanning the four columns out front are of Tyche and possibly Medusa, respectively installed for luck and to ward off evil influences.

Behind and above the temple sprawl the **baths of Scholastica**, named after the fifth-
century Byzantine lady whose headless statue adorns the entrance and who restored
the complex, which was actually four hundred years older. There was direct access
from here to the latrines and thence the brothel, though it seems from graffiti that the
baths too were at one stage used as a bawdy house. Clay drainage pipes are still visibly
lodged in the floor, as they are at many points in Ephesus.

The terrace houses

On the far side of Curetes Street from the Hadrian shrine lies a huge patterned **mosaic**, which once fronted a series of shops. Nearby a stepped street leads up to the **terrace houses**, protected by an incongruous, constantly growing brick-and-cement
structure that many initially mistake for a motel. Until further notice the houses are
only open upon special application to the Selçuk Museum (see p.305), a measure calculated to minimize wear and tear to the mosaics and frescoes from shoes and human
breath-vapour.

If you do gain admission, the complex gives a good idea of everyday life during imperial and early Byzantine times, which appears to have been on a par with that at Pompeii
and Herculaneum. The first house is built around a fountained atrium paved in black-
and-white mosaics; a room leading off this to the east has walls covered in murals,
including one of Hercules battling the river-sprite Achelous. In the second dwelling
open to view, the central court features a fine mosaic of a triton cavorting with a nereid;
just south of this, in an overhead vault, Dionysos and Ariadne are depicted in an excellent, 3-D-ish glass mosaic, which, while damaged, is still recognizable.

The top of Curetes

Returning to Curetes, you pass the **fountain of Trajan**, whose ornamentation has been
removed to the museum, and then the street splits just above the **Hydreion** (another
fountain) and the **gate of Hercules**, where a remaining column relief depicts the hero
wrapped in the skin of the Nemean lion. Bearing right at the junction takes you to the
temple of Domitian, a paranoid megalomaniac even by imperial Roman criteria; only
the lower floor of the complex is left intact, housing a **museum of inscriptions** (daily
8am–5pm; free). Descriptions of residents and their doings, including chronicles of
gladiatorial combat, fights with lions and animal sacrifice, provide some insight into the
daily life of this Roman provincial capital.

The main thoroughfare skirts the large, overgrown **upper agora**, fringed by fountain skeletons on the side facing the Domitian foundations and by a **colonnade** to the
north, opposite the civic heart of the Roman community – the **prytaneum**. This
housed the inextinguishable sacred flame of Ephesus and two of the Artemis statues in
the Selçuk Museum, in spite of Hestia (Vesta) being the presiding goddess; it also
served as the reception area for official guests.

The adjacent **odeion**, once the local parliament, has been as insensitively restored as
the main theatre, though presumably the 27 rows of seats are the original number. The
baths of Varius mark the end of the paved Roman street system, and also the location
of the upper site entrance. Beyond the gate huddles the massive **east gymnasium**,
next to which the **Magnesia Gate** signals the true edge of the old city. The asphalt road
here leads 5km south to Meryemana (see p.356), but you'd have to hitch or hope for a
passing taxi – it's too steep and car-infested a walk to be enjoyable.

South of Selçuk: more Ionian cities

Twenty-four kilometres southeast of Kuşadası and 44km by road from Selçuk, **SÖKE** holds nothing of interest to a casual traveller other than its excellent bus and dolmuş services. If you pass up offers in Kuşadası or Selçuk of all-in tours to Priene, Miletus and Didyma – not at all a bad idea if you can negotiate a reasonable price – you'll probably spend some time here making connections. This is pretty hassle-free: Kuşadası-based dolmuşes deposit you right next to other vehicles leaving for the villages adjacent to the three noted sites, as well as for Milas.

Priene

Perched on a series of pine terraces graded into the south flank of Samsun Dağı, 35km south of Kuşadası, the compact but exquisite **PRIENE** (daily 8am–6.30pm, winter closes 5.30pm; $1.50) enjoys a situation that bears comparison with that of Delphi in Greece. The original settlement, legendarily founded by refugee Athenians and dating from perhaps the eleventh century BC, was elsewhere in the Meander basin; the townspeople, following the receding shoreline, refounded the city at its present site during the fourth century BC, just in time for Alexander to stop in and defray the cost of the principal temple of Athena. The Panionion sanctuary, cult centre of the league of Ionian cities, had always lain in Priene's territory, just the other side of Samsun Dağı; as a result its priest was usually chosen from Priene, whose secular officials also presided over the regular meetings of the confederacy. Under Roman – and later Byzantine – rule, however, the city enjoyed little patronage from the emperors, with the result that Priene represents the best-preserved Hellenistic townscape in Ionia, without any of the usual later additions. The town was laid out by Hippodamus, an architect from nearby Miletus, who favoured a grid pattern made up of various *insulae* (rectangular units) measuring roughly 42m by 35m. Within each rectangle stood four private dwellings; a public building had its own *insula*, sometimes two.

Arrival is by frequent dolmuş from Söke to the very spread-out village of **GÜLLÜBAHÇE**, scattered 200 to 700m east of the ruins. It is tempting to save Priene for late afternoon, when it is most beautiful, but **staying** overnight can be a problem. There is only one small and relatively expensive *pansiyon* and campsite in the village, *Pension Priene* (☎0256/547 1249; ②), which shares space with the local chapter of the Society for the Protection of Nature; it's prudent to book space first thing, or phone in advance. Of the handful of **restaurants**, best is *Pınar*, at the far west end of the village, right below the site car park; *Şelale*, in the village centre, has a wider menu.

The site: below the main street

Once through a gap in Priene's ancient walls at the east end of the central street, climb this wide thoroughfare, heading west, which before long is crossed by a myriad of smaller lanes, stepped in places. The first easily distinguished civic monument, just to the left of the main street, is the square **bouleuterion** or council house, the most intact in Turkey, consisting of seats on three sides enclosing the speakers' area, together with a sacrificial altar.

Just east of the bouleuterion are the scantier remains of the **prytaneion** or town administration offices, with traces of a dining area for the highest municipal officials. On the next terrace down lie the **temple of Zeus**, the **agora** and the **sacred stoa**, once graced by outer and inner series of Doric and Ionic columns, though nothing is left above knee level of any of these. The commanding views, however, suggest that this was the heart of public life in the city.

Clearly visible below, reached by way of a stairway from the agora, are the **gymnasium** and **stadium** – relatively neglected parts of the site due to the shadeless climb back up entailed by a visit. Some of the gymnasium walls are decorated with still-visi-

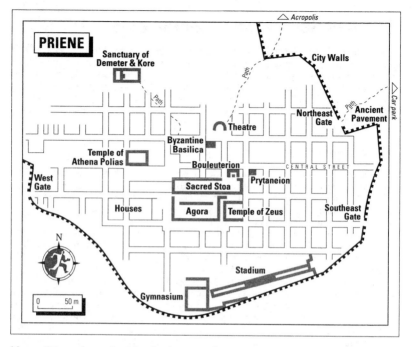

ble graffiti; nearby are **bathing basins**, complete with gutters and lion-head spouts, for use after athletics. On the west side of the stadium there are a few sets of **starting blocks** for foot races; spectators watched from the north side of the 190m-by-20m area, where some seats are still discernible.

Returning to the central street and continuing west down a gentle slope, you are soon in the midst of the densest surviving **residential district** in Priene. Though many of the houses, whose thick walls stand to five feet in some cases, are choked by pine and shrubbery, others permit entry. The usual ground plan was that of a narrow passage leading to a large central court, surrounded by various rooms; the discovery of occasional stairways demonstrated that some dwellings had two storeys. Priene's **west gate** marks the end of both the main street and the blocks of houses.

Above the main street

The city's most conspicuous monument, the **temple of Athena Polias**, stands two terraces above the main residential street. The temple took more than two centuries to complete, and in its time was considered the epitome of Ionic perfection; a manual written by its designer Pytheos was still considered standard reading in Roman times. Five of the original thirty Ionic columns were re-erected in the 1960s, and at certain seasons of the year they catch the sunset and glow in the dusk long after the rest of the archeological zone is plunged in darkness.

Directly north of the Athena temple, reached by a faint trail through the pines, is the **sanctuary of Demeter and Kore**, on the highest terrace of the urban grid. Other than the foundations – a good century or two older than those of any other shrine in Priene – little is visible today besides the few Doric column stumps and a pit for catching the blood of sacrificial animals.

The **theatre**, a little way southeast, is by contrast in an excellent state of preservation, its layout and seating unchanged from the Hellenistic original; a capacity of 5000 approximates Priene's population. Most prominent are five larger than average marble thrones for the municipal dignitaries. The stage buildings were extensively modified during the second century AD – virtually the only Roman tampering with Priene's public buildings; just behind them are the waist-high remains of a **Byzantine basilica**.

If you're keen on scrambling and the weather is not too hot, take the path beginning above the theatre, which leads in stages to the **acropolis**, on the bluff known as Teloneia in ancient times. A head for heights is useful as the path dwindles, after passing an aqueduct and some cisterns, to a series of paint-splodge-marked steps and goat traces zigzagging steeply up the cliff. Allow an extra hour and a half for the round trip.

The mandatory exit from the site is the former **main (northeast) gate**, still mostly intact.

Beyond Priene: Karine, Doğanbey and Samsun Dağı

If you have a car, don't be tempted by the notation on some maps of a long beach near the village of Karine, some 17km west of the site. In fact neither exists. Once past the village of Doğanbey (see below), the road deteriorates alarmingly before dead-ending at a small rocky cove with a derelict Ottoman customs station. This, you will be told by either the fishermen camped in the ruins or the gendarmes at the modern post ahead, is **KARİNE**, or rather ancient Carina, whose remains are somewhere in the overgrown bushes. No further progress is permitted, should it cross your mind to storm the peninsula-tip military zone from this side, though you are welcome to pitch a tent.

The main reason for making the bumpy journey out here is to **eat fish** at the *Karina Restaurant*, some 3km after Doğanbey, which serves some of the best and cheapest *kefal* (grey mullet) in Turkey, compliments of the fishermen's cooperative based at the giant lagoon to the south. The restaurant also runs a *pansiyon* nearby, but it's expensive (②) for what you get, and the "beach" – bits of sandbar and reef at the margin of the lagoon, Dil Gölü – is inaccessible.

DOĞANBEY itself makes a far more interesting destination if you've your own transport. It is actually two villages: a nondescript modern district down by the asphalt road (with occasional dolmuş service), and an upper, all-but-abandoned settlement of fine Greek-built houses, known as Domatça in Ottoman times and now signposted in yellow-and-black as **ESKİDOĞANBEY**. Most of the handsome ruins have been bought up for restoration at increasingly inflated prices by the urban intelligentsia; the feel here, with parched hills toward the sea and pine-forested mountain ridges above, is utterly different from lush (and permanently inhabited) Şirince.

Eskidoğanbey is in fact a good starting point for the **climb** of the twin 1237-metre summits of **Samsun Dağı**. A path, initially distinct, goes up first the west, then the east bank of the ravine furrowing the village, and recrosses the watercourse before snaking up to the only springs en route, in a beautiful grove of planes some two hours along. Chances of wildlife-spotting, particularly badgers, jackals and birds of prey, are probably better here than within the confines of the national park on the other side of the mountain. Within twenty minutes you attain the ridge at a pass with a T-intersection; the track straight down leads into national park territory, through the "Kanyon" indicated on p.301. Turn left and west instead, leaving the watershed road after a few hundred metres for the pathless scramble through bushes up to the easterly summit.

This is an all-day outing, best done in spring or autumn to avoid the heat; if you don't do it as a point-to-point trek to or from the north coast of the peninsula, you'll have to **stay** at the one remaining *pansiyon* in Eskidoğanbey, the *Natural* (①), basic but usually open. Its rival, *At the Riverside*, shut in 1995 despite the continued presence of signs indicating it.

Miletus (Milet)

The position of **MILETUS**, on an eminently defendable promontory jutting out into the ancient Gulf of Latmos, once outshone that of Priene. Its modern setting, marooned in the seasonal marshes of the Büyük Menderes, is by contrast one of the dreariest in Turkey, with little left to bear witness to the town's long and colourful past. Only the theatre, visible from some distance away, hints at former glories.

Up close, the site of Miletus is an often confusing juxtaposition of relics from dissimilar eras, widely scattered and disguised by weeds, mud or even water, depending on the season. Ironically, even the grid street plan championed by native son Hippodamus has largely failed to survive, swept away by the Romans and geological processes. If you're pressed for time, this might be the Ionian site to miss.

Access by public transport is fairly easy from Söke or Güllübahçe; all dolmuşes bound for Altınkum, Akköy or Balat – the last village 2km from the ruins – go past Priene and Milet. At Akköy, 6km away, there are simple **eateries** (but no accommodation); otherwise some expensive snack bars cater for a tour-bus clientele near the site entrance.

Some history

Miletus is at least as old as Ephesus, and far older than Priene; German archeologists working locally since the 1890s have uncovered remnants of a Creto-Mycenaean settlement from the sixteenth century BC. Ionian invaders made their first appearance during the eleventh century, and by the seventh century BC Miletus was in the first flush of a heyday which was to last more than 200 years, when the city was able to repulse the advances of the Lydians and found colonies all over Anatolia. It was also a highly evolved cultural centre, with a roll call of scholars and thinkers that included the mathematician Thales and the courtesan-orator Aspasia, friend of Socrates and Pericles.

While not strong enough to completely avoid Persian domination, Miletus did manage to secure favourable terms as an equal, and even took the opportunity to appropriate the nearby oracle of Didyma. But with Athenian instigation, the city was unwisely persuaded to take command of the abortive Ionian revolt against the Persians between 500 and 494 BC. After the rebels were finally defeated in the naval battle at nearby Lade Island, Darius punished the ringleader severely with wholesale massacre and pillage.

Within fifty years Miletus was rebuilt some distance to the northeast of its original site, but it was never again to be as great – or as independent. Alexander saw fit to "liberate" the city from a new, short-lived occupation by the Persians and their allies, including a huge fleet anchored hard by which sat motionless, perhaps in awe of the Macedonian's mystique. Later it was bequeathed to the Romans, under whose rule it enjoyed a brief renaissance – most of what you see today is a legacy of various emperors' largesse. The Byzantine town stubbornly clung to life, producing Isidorus, architect of İstanbul's Aya Sofya. In the ninth century Miletus was already dwindling, and by the time the Menteşe emirs, and then the Ottomans, took control, there was little left to prize.

The site

The most obvious attraction at the partly enclosed settlement of Miletus (summer daily 8am–7pm; $1) is behind the ticket stall: a **theatre**, whose Hellenistic base was modified and enlarged during the second century AD to a capacity of 15,000. One of

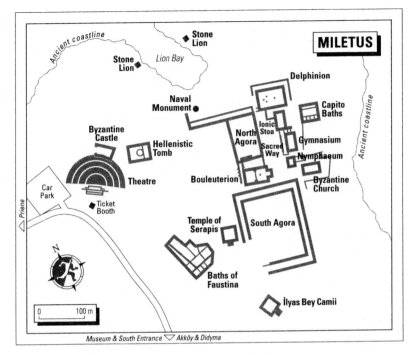

the first things you'll see on the orchestra floor is a stone block with two griffins carved in relief, one playing a lyre. The centre of the front row sports two pillars which once supported the emperor's canopy. Further up, the vaulted exit passage-ways are enormous and virtually intact; unfortunately the area above the *diazoma* (dividing terrace) is now off-limits.

An eighth-century **Byzantine castle** and some contemporaneous **ramparts** surmount the theatre, giving a marvellous 360-degree view over the flood plain, and the chance to get your bearings on the rest of the site. Visible on the plain a kilometre or so to the west is a scrubby hill, formerly the **Island of Lade**.

The harbour area

Descending from the walls, you pass a Hellenistic **tomb** featuring a circular burial chamber in the middle. Further east, a round base is all that remains of the **naval monument** commemorating an unknown victory of the first century BC, which once over-looked the most impressive of Miletus's four harbours, the "Lion Bay", so called for the two **stone lions** that guarded the entrance – now embedded up to their haunches in marsh silt.

The end of the tongue-shaped bay was lined by a colonnade that extended east to the sixth-century **Delphinion**, dedicated to Apollo Delphinius, patron of sailors, ships and ports. Not surprisingly in such a maritime community, it was the most important religious establishment in town; today you can still see the foundations of altars or semi-circular benches and the enclosing colonnade. Immediately south squat some incongruous **Selçuk baths**.

Along the Sacred Way

Both the Delphinion and baths stand at the north end of a handsomely paved sacred **processional way**, which in its time linked Miletus with Didyma; after a rainy winter, though, it's likely to remain submerged for some months. On the same side of the pavement as you walk south stands a first-century AD **Ionic stoa**, conspicuous owing to its rather clinical partial restoration, which partly shields the enormous **Capito baths** and a **gymnasium** of the same era. The most satisfying monument east of the Sacred Way is the **nymphaeum**, the largest public fountain of Miletus, once almost baroquely ornate but now standing to barely half its original height. Just south of here are the ruins of a sixth-century **Byzantine church**.

On the west side of the pavement, beginning at the harbour, are the jumbled and overgrown remains of the so-called **north agora**; marginally more interesting is the second-century BC **bouleuterion**, which faces the nymphaeum. The Sacred Way skirts the **south agora**, unexcavated except for a monumental gateway, which was carted off to Berlin in 1908. West of the agora are the recessed premises of a third-century AD **temple of Serapis**; you can make out a bas-relief representation of the deity Serapis Helios on a fallen pediment.

The Baths of Faustina

The Roman **baths of Faustina** (Marcus Aurelius' wife), west of here at the foot of the theatre hill, are distinctive for their position at an angle to what remains of the urban grid – and for their good state of repair. The most engaging sight inside is two spouts that once fed the cold pool – one in the form of a now decapitated statue of local river deity Meander, the other an intact lion-head.

The İlyas Bey Camii

About 200m south of the baths and marked by dense vegetation, the early fifteenth-century **İlyas Bey Camii**, built by that Menteşe emir to give thanks for his safe return from captivity by Tamerlane, is arguably more interesting than anything at the ancient site except the theatre. The mosque, dressed entirely in marble pillaged from the ancient city, lost its minaret in the 1958 earthquake that levelled nearby Balat, but otherwise fared well, retaining its fine carved-marble *mihrab*, stalactite vaulting and Arabic inscriptions. The entrance is particularly enchanting, with a carved marble screen flanking the door and triple bicoloured arches just outside. There was once a *medrese* and *imaret* adjacent, but only a peaceful, neglected courtyard with some adjoining cells and headstones has survived. It's a serene and contemplative corner, more frequented by storks than humans.

The museum

Exactly 1km separates the main ticket stall from the southerly toll gate and the site **museum** (daily 8am–5.30pm; $1), though unfortunately most of the important Miletian moveables have long since found their way to İstanbul or Berlin. The three-room collection spanning all periods makes do with the best of the leftovers, which include some fifth-century Byzantine mosaics depicting animals, a Roman comic theatre mask, and a headless, seated statuette of Cybele with a lion cub on her lap.

Didyma (Didim) and around

By the time you reach **DIDYMA**, site fatigue might be beginning to set in. However, the oracular sanctuary of Apollo here, though half-ruined and besieged throughout the middle of the day by swarms of tour groups, rarely fails to impress. The best time to visit – and the hour when, having worked their way through either Priene or Miletus or both, many people tend to show up – is late afternoon or early evening, when the masonry glows in the sunset.

Access is probably the simplest of all the remote Ionian sites: frequent dolmuşes and the odd full-size coach cover the route between Söke and Altınkum beach via Didim village, the modern name for Didyma. The village itself is something of a tourist trap, crammed with souvenir shops and tour coaches. All three of the **restaurants** across from the archeological zone are expensive and poor in quality; for a good feed at reasonable prices you'll have to walk a kilometre south to Yenihisar, a much larger, more untouched village. If **staying** the night appeals, the choice is between the *Pension Oracle* (①), bare-bones basic but with a fine terrace directly overlooking the ruins, and the more comfortable if viewless *Medusa Head* (②) just south, an old building restored with character.

Some history

An oracle and shrine of some sort apparently existed at Didyma long before the arrival of the Ionian settlers in the eleventh century BC – the name itself is an ancient Anatolian word – but the imported cult of Apollo quickly appropriated whatever previous oracle, centred around a sacred well and laurel tree, had worked here. Didyma remained a sacred precinct, under the jurisdiction of a clan of priests originally from Delphi, and was never a town as such, though it eventually became a dependency of nearby Miletus. Every four years the sanctuary was also the venue for the Didymeia, a festival of music and drama as well as athletics.

The Archaic shrine, begun during the eighth century BC, was finished within 200 years, and though similar in design to the current structure, it was half the size. After their defeat of the Ionian revolt in 494 BC, the Persians destroyed this first temple and plundered its treasures, including the cult statue of Apollo. The oracle puttered along in reduced circumstances until Alexander appeared on the scene, when the cult statue was retrieved from Persia and a new temple (the one existing today) commissioned, with the actual work undertaken by the Seleucid dynasty.

Despite continuing subsidy from the Romans, work continued at a snail's pace for more than five centuries and the building was never actually completed – not entirely surprising when you consider the formidable engineering problems presented, and the cost of the material; the columns alone, for example, are reckoned to have cost today's equivalent of £200 million. In the end Christianity put paid to the oracle, and when the edict of Theodosius in 385 AD proscribed all pagan practices, construction ceased for good, after which a medieval earthquake toppled most of the columns. Inhabitants of the Greek village of Yeronda (the Ottoman name for the hamlet overlooking the temple precinct) helped themselves liberally to the ancient masonry in their midst, and blocks can still be seen incorporated into some of the older village houses.

At its zenith Didyma was approached not only from Miletus but also from Panormos, a cove 6km west, via a sacred way whose final stretches were lined with statuary. Neither pavement nor statues are visible today, the latter having been abducted to the British Museum in 1858.

The site

Entry to the **site** (daily 8am–7pm summer, closes 5.30pm winter; $1) is now by way of a gate to the north of the enclosure. At the bottom of the steps look out for the **Medusa head**, which fell from a Roman-era architrave and is now the unofficial logo of the place, repeated ad infinitum on posters and cards all over Turkey.

Pilgrims would first visit a **well** below the resting place of the Medusa head and purify themselves, then approach a still-prominent **circular altar** to offer a sacrifice before proceeding to the **shrine** itself. Even in ruins this is still intimidatingly large, the surviving column stumps alone way taller than a man, and in its nearly complete state it must have inspired an attitude of reverence. The effect was accentuated by the shrine's positioning on a steep, stepped base and enclosure in a virtual forest of 108 Ionic **columns** – though only three of these stand to their original height. The remaining twelve stumps supported the roof of the entry porch, reached by a steep flight of steps, where supplicants would deliver their queries to the priest of Apollo, who would reappear after a suitable interval on a terrace some six feet higher to deliver the prophetess's oracular pronouncement. Questions ranged from the personal to matters of state; prophecies were recorded and stored for posterity on the premises. The cult statue of Apollo, his sacred laurel and the sacred well, were formerly enclosed in a miniature shrine of which only traces remain – though the **well** itself is still obvious, roped off to prevent accidents. As at Delphi in Greece, prophecies were formulated by a priestess, who either (accounts disagree) drank from, bathed in or inhaled potent vapours from the waters. Her subsequent ravings were rephrased more delicately to those waiting out front.

Petitioners did not normally enter the inner sanctum, except to watch the goings-on of the Didymeia from a monumental stairway providing access to the terrace from the interior; the steps still bear spectators' graffiti, though the terrace is currently off-limits – you enter the sanctuary proper by means of twin tunnels to either side. The innermost court was never roofed, though the height of the walls once exceeded 20m; today they're half that tall.

North of Didyma: some beaches

As you drive to Didyma from Akköy, the sea – with views across to the Greek island of Agathoníssi – is never far away, and the road soon actually runs alongside the water. Unfortunately the shore is scruffy and windswept, with a narrow strip of sand; at first there are merely a few primitive campsites and the odd *pansiyon* just south of a new fishing port. A state-run picnic ground and campsite at **Tavşanburnu**, sandier and protected by an islet, is more appealing, and there are shops for supplies nearby. But although the area is low-key compared to Altınkum, the campsite heralds the start of almost continuous development south to Didyma.

South of Didyma: Altınkum

Five kilometres south of Didyma, the information placard at the road's end in **ALTINKUM** says it all, listing well over a hundred hotels and *pansiyon*s arrayed behind a single kilometre of beach split by a headland. In midsummer it's standing room only on the sand, but at least it lives up to its name ("golden sand" in Turkish): a gently sloping beach with no surf, ideal for children and in total contrast to the exposed coast on the other side of Didyma. Of late the place has become the Turkish equivalent of Blackpool, with a large British package presence which has engendered a rash of "English" eateries with food, and prices, the way Turks imagine Brits like it ("Roast Beef and Yorkshire Pudding, £5.50") as well as totally inedible, widely advertised T-bone "steaks".

Altınkum is essentially the shore annexe of Yenihisar, 1km from Didyma, where you'll find most amenities (such as proper shops). However, to the right of the T-junction marked by the accommodation placard there's a **bank**, **PTT** and a sporadically staffed **tourist information** booth further along. However, the main interest of Altınkum to most overland travellers is its seasonal **ferry service** to Bodrum, most days in the morning, which allows one to shortcut the tortuous journey in by land.

Should you want to stay, the more inexpensive **pansiyons** can be found on the upper, parallel street behind the far western jetty, but these are block-booked by Turkish families all summer, and you'd probably have to strike lucky to find an unreserved room in season. Lodgings to the east of the accommodation placard are considerably more upmarket, though competition and lean tourist years have led to some three-star **hotels** which would ordinarily be priced at ④ or even ⑤ being let go for ③. Examples include the *Göçtur* (☎0256/813 2740) and the *Majestic* (☎0256/813 4615), also available in advance, along with several others here, through *Sunquest Holidays* in Britain.

ANCIENT CARIA: THE COASTAL REGIONS

In antiquity **Caria** was an isolated, mysterious region, inhabited by purportedly barbarous people indigenous to the area (a rarity in Anatolia), speaking a language distantly related to Greek. Following the advent of Alexander, and the Hecatomnid dynasty at Halicarnassus, Hellenization proceeded apace and the differences between the Carians and their neighbours diminished. After the Byzantine period, and the fifteenth-century absorption of the local Menteşe emirate by the Ottomans, the region again assumed backwater status; until the early Republican years internal exile to the coast here was an habitual and feared sentence for political offenders. In a strange echo of the ancient tendency, the dialect of **Muğla province** – whose territory corresponds almost exactly to that of coastal Caria – is still one of the most eccentric and difficult to understand in the entire country.

Bafa Gölü and ancient **Heracleia ad Latmos** on its northeast shore make a suitably dramatic introduction to coastal Caria. **Euromos** and **Labranda** are two of the more satisfying minor ancient sites in Turkey, particularly the latter; both are visitable from **Milas**, the nearest substantial town and by no means devoid of interest in its own right. Southeast of Milas, **Peçin Kale** constitutes a Turkish oddity – a ruined medieval city, in this case the Menteşe capital. **Ören**, still further southeast on the same road, is another rare beast: an attractive coastal resort that has not yet been steamrollered by industrial tourism. Southwest of Milas, however, neither **ancient Iassos** nor the small resort of **Güllük** live up to their hype in other sources. Most visitors bypass Güllük in favour of **Bodrum** and its peninsula, very much the big tourist event on this coast, with tentacles of development creeping over every available parcel of land around – though what attracted outsiders to the area in the first place still shines through on occasion.

Moving on, **Muğla** is a pleasant surprise: one of the best-preserved Ottoman townscapes in Turkey, coexisting with an unobtrusive, well-planned new city. Happy juxtaposition of old and new is about the last thing that comes to mind at nearby **Stratonikya**, a once-untouched ancient metropolis almost engulfed by a lignite quarry.

Further south, **Marmaris** is another big – and rather overblown – resort, from which the **Loryma (Hisarönü) peninsula** beyond, bereft of a sandy shoreline but blessed with magnificent scenery, offers the closest escape. As a compromise, **Datça** and its surroundings might fit the bill, some remote beaches nearby more rewarding than the much-touted but poorly presented ruins of ancient **Knidos**.

Bafa Gölü (Lake Bafa)

The hundred square kilometres of **Bafa Gölü**, one of the most entrancing spectacles in southwestern Turkey, were created when silt deposited by the Büyük Menderes River sealed off the Latmos gulf from the sea. The barren, weirdly sculpted pinnacles of ancient **Mount Latmos** (today's Beşparmak Dağ) still loom over the northeast shore, visible from a great distance west. Numerous islets dot Bafa, most of them sporting some sort of fortified Byzantine religious establishment, dating from the lake's days as an important monastic centre between the seventh and fourteenth centuries.

Bafa's separation from the ocean is not perfect: canals link the lake's west end with an oxbow of the Büyük Menderes close by. As a result the water is faintly brackish, and fish species tolerant of both salt and fresh water shuttle back and forth, spawning in the lake. The most important are *levrek* (bass), *kefal* (grey mullet), *yayın* (catfish) and *yılan balığı* (eel) – all good for eating and all exploited by a fishing cooperative based on the north shore, and by numerous migratory waterfowl for whom Bafa is an important stopover.

In the wake of wet winters between 1994 and 1996, the lake water level is now about normal; however, during dry years when the level falls up to a metre, the weeds that always hover in the shallows can burgeon, making access difficult – which is a shame since the water temperature is ideal for swimming.

Practicalities

Bus services past the lake are frequent, but Söke–Milas dolmuşes are more flexible than the big coaches in terms of stopping. The southern shore of Bafa, which the main highway follows, presents a strangely deserted prospect except for olive groves – and is the location of two combination **campsite-pansiyon-restaurants**. Heading east, the first is *Turgut*, rather sterile, regimented, and relatively expensive compared to *Ceri'nin Yeri*, a few kilometres further on. For the tentless, proprietor Ceri runs a rather basic, five-room *pansiyon* best considered as an emergency fallback (☎0252/512 4498; ②). The menu varies with the catch, and there are no shops anywhere along the lake (though Ceri sells perishables like eggs and yoghurt), so bring what you need.

Swimming is best from the far side of the monastery-capped islet joined to Ceri's restaurant in dry years by a muddy spit; once on the islet, some flattish rocks offer a weed-free corridor out onto the lake when the water level is normal. Failing that, dive off the end of the wooden jetty constructed to outrun the weeds.

Heracleia ad Latmos

Across the lake, most easily seen from *Ceri'nin Yeri*, is a patch of irregular shoreline with a modern village whose lights twinkle at the base of Mount Latmos by night. This is also the site of **HERACLEIA AD LATMOS**, one of Turkey's most evocatively situated antiquities.

A settlement of Carian origin had existed here long before the arrival of the Ionians, and Carian habits died hard, though Latmos – as it was then known – had far better geographical communication with Ionia than with the rest of Caria. Late in the Hellenistic period the city's location was moved a kilometre or so west, and the name changed to Heracleia, but despite adornment with numerous monuments and an enormous wall, it was never a place of great importance. Miletus, at the head of the then-gulf, monopolized most trade and already the inlet was beginning to close up.

Heracleia owes its fame, and an enduring hold on the romantic imagination, to a legend associated not with the town itself but with Mount Latmos behind. **Endymion** was a handsome shepherd who, while asleep in a cave on the mountain, was noticed by Selene, the moon goddess. She made love with him as he slept and in time, so the story goes, bore Endymion fifty daughters without their sire ever waking once. Endymion was reluctant for all this to stop and begged Zeus, who was also fond of him, to be allowed to dream forever; his wish was granted and, as a character in Mary Lee Settle's *Blood Ties* flippantly observed, thus became the only known demigod of the wet dream.

Later, Christian hermits who settled in the vicinity during mid-Byzantine times cleaned up Endymion's act, so to speak – in their version he was a mystic who after a lifetime of "communing" with the moon had learned the secret name of God. Once a year the anchorites, leaving their homes on the island cloisters or in various caves on Latmos, converged upon an ancient tomb believed to be Endymion's. The sarcophagus lid would be opened and the bones inside would emit a strange humming noise, the deceased saint's attempt to communicate the holy name.

The monastic communities, after producing a few minor saints, were dispersed for good early in the fourteenth century, and little is now left of any of the Byzantine monuments. But when a full moon rises over the serrated peaks across the water, it is easy to suspend disbelief in all the legends pertaining to the place. Indeed Endymion's fate has exercised a fascination on many subsequent eras: Shakespeare declared "Peace, ho! The moon sleeps with Endymion/And would not be waked!", and four centuries later Keats added: "What is there in thee, Moon! that shouldst move my heart so potently? . . . Now I begin to feel thy orby power/Is coming fresh upon me."

The site

Arriving by car, park your vehicle either next to the *Serçin* restaurant or in another area about 200m up the hill. The site is not enclosed, though you may have to pay a dollar or so admission if the warden is staffing the portakabin booth. The crudely signposted **bouleuterion** lies 100m to the east of the first parking area, though only the retaining wall and some rows of benches are left of the second-century BC structure. The **Roman baths** visible in the valley below, and a crumbled but appealing **Roman theatre** off in the olives beyond, can be reached via an unmarked trail starting between the first and second parking areas. The path up to the **hermits' caves** on Mount Latmos begins at the rear of the second parking area. Stout boots are advisable, as is a cool day in early spring or late autumn – for a place still so close to the sea, Heracleia can be surprisingly hot and airless. Similar cautions apply for those who want to trace the course of the **Hellenistic walls**, the city's most imposing and conspicuous relics, supposedly built by Lysimachus in the late third century BC.

The *Serçin* restaurant looks south over the **Hellenistic agora**, now mostly taken up by the village schoolyard; its south edge is buttressed by a row of **shops**, whose downhill side stands intact to two storeys, complete with windows. From the agora grounds you've a fine view west over the lake and assorted castle-crowned promontories. A boxlike Hellenistic **Temple of Athena**, perched on a hill west of the agora, is unmissable; less conspicuous is an inscription to Athena, left of the entrance.

From the agora a wide, walled-in path descends toward the shore and the final quota of recognizable monuments at Heracleia. Most obvious is the peninsula – or, in wet years, island – studded with **Byzantine walls** and a **church**. A stone causeway half-buried in the beach allowed entrance in what must have been drier medieval times. Follow the shore southwest to the *Zeybek* restaurant (one of three here), strategically astride another promontory, and then continue along its access drive to the junction with a slightly wider track. Across the way you should see the tentatively identified Hellenistic **Sanctuary of Endymion**, oriented unusually northeast to southwest. Five column stumps front the structure, which has a rounded rear wall – a ready-made apse for later Christians – with sections of rock incorporated into the masonry.

Striking out across the pasture opposite the Endymion shrine, and skimming the base of yet another Byzantine castle, you arrive at the ancient **necropolis**, which consists of a few dozen rectangular tombs hewn into boulders on the shore. Many are partly or completely awash, depending on the water level.

Practicalities

The most common **access** to Heracleia is by **boat** from *Ceri'nin Yeri*: reckon on paying about $2 a head, round trip, assuming a group of at least ten people, plus site admission. Tours generally depart between 9.30 and 10.30am, take twenty minutes to cross the lake, and allow just under two and a half hours at the ruins – enough for a look around and a quick meal. Alternatively, if you have your own vehicle, **drive** east to Çamiçi village (6km beyond *Ceri'nin Yeri*) and then turn left at the signpost ("Herakleia"). The ten-kilometre, all-weather dirt road leads through fields and finally a wilderness of Latmian boulders to the modern village of **KAPIKIRI**, built higgledy-piggledy among the ruins.

Scattered in and around Kapıkırı are a few simple restaurants such as those noted above, a campsite, and rumours of sporadically operating *pansiyon*s, though the opening periods of most establishments are erratic to say the least. The *Zeybek Restaurant/Camping* has a good view over the lake, serves moderately priced fish and seems the most consistently open; for a room, your best bet is the *Agora Pansiyon* in the village (☎0252/543 5445; ②).

Milas

A small, initially nondescript-seeming town of some 35,000 people, **MİLAS** is all too often given short shrift by tourists intent on reaching the fleshpots of Bodrum as quickly as possible. This is a shame, for although it's unlikely that most foreigners would want to stay the night here, there are more than enough sights of interest to fill a few hours between buses – Milas is a major regional transport hub, with dolmuş services in every direction. First impressions – sprawling towerblocks on the outskirts, traffic congestion in the bazaar – are not reassuring, but opinions may improve after a stroll around. The town's market is at its best on Tuesdays, when organized tours visit from Bodrum; local specialities are honey and earth-toned carpets.

Milas – or Mylasa, as it was formerly known – was an important Carian centre (its original location was at the nearby hill of Peçin Kale – see p.329), but it was the Halicarnassus-based Hecatomnid dynasty that really put it on the map, with the nearby quarries providing ample marble for numerous public monuments, and increased control over the sanctuary at Labranda bringing the city additional benefits. Mylasa's assignment by the Roman republic to the jurisdiction of Rhodes in 190 BC was too much for the locals to stomach and they rebelled within twenty years, declaring a brief independence of two more decades before eventual incorporation into the Roman Empire. Details of the Byzantine period are obscure, but the city experienced a resurgence during the fourteenth century when the Menteşe emirs, a Turcoman clan, made it the capital of their realms in southwestern Anatolia.

The Town

An elaborate early Roman tomb known as the **Gümüşkesen** (literally "cuts-silver") is the most intriguing relic of ancient Mylasa. The way there is poorly marked from the town centre, but the monument is easy enough to find by heading 500m west along Kadıağa Caddesi, which soon becomes the slightly sloping Gümüşkesen Caddesi. There are no formal visiting hours or admission fee to the landscaped site, which lies in a slight depression south of Hıdırlık hill.

The monument consists of a square burial chamber surmounted by a Corinthian colonnade with a pyramidal roof – a design presumed to be a miniature of the now-van-

CENTRAL MİLAS

ished mausoleum at Halicarnassus. A small ladder was once installed on the southwest side, allowing access to the platform, but this currently seems to have gone missing. The ceiling sports elaborate carvings and some flecks of paint; a hole in the floor allowed mourners to pour libations into the sepulchre below.

Milas's lively tradesmen's **bazaar** covers the western slopes of Hisarbaşı hill, which has been the focus of settlement in every era. Once past the warren of alleys perpendicular to the main longitudinal street, veer up to the summit and the late Ottoman Belen Camii. Immediately to its right stands the eighteenth-century **Çöllühanı**, one of the last functioning, unrestored *kervansaray*s in western Turkey. On many afternoons of the year the premises will be full of donkeys and carts, the former comical studies in patient waiting while their masters take tea or smoke hookahs in the shady galleries of the building. Leaving here, go through the archways of the more modern *han* opposite and continue downhill to the grounds of the fine, pink-marble late fourteenth-century **Firuz Bey Camii**, erected by the Menteşe emirs using bits of the ancient town.

Back past the Çöllühanı, heading southeast behind the PTT, there's a district of sumptuous **old houses**, the finest in Milas, built from the wealth engendered by tobacco or cotton during the nineteenth century, when the town (like Bodrum) was half-Greek Orthodox in population. Watch for yellow arrow-signs with the legend "Uzunyuva" (Tall Nest) and the single Corinthian column, adorned with a stork's nest (hence the name), of the first-century BC **Temple of Zeus**, adjacent to which a sign cryptically reads "*Kutsal Alan*" (Holy Clearing). Much of the foundation has been incorporated into later houses.

Downhill from here you'll pass a huge stretch of **ancient wall** – possibly a fort – and at the bottom of the slope an **Ottoman bridge** with an inscribed plaque. Across the bridge, a few minutes' walk past the Orhan (Ağa) Camii, oldest of the town's mosques (1330), stands the **Baltalı Kapı** (Gate-with-Axe) – all that remains of the ancient city walls. The axe in question, a double-headed attribute of Zeus, is faintly carved on the north-facing keystone.

The late fourteenth-century **Ulu Cami**, further south along the canal, is perhaps more engaging, an exotically asymmetrical building incorporating a vast quantity of plundered antiquities. Kufic inscriptions adorn the lintels, and a peculiar staircase leads up over the front door to a short and stubby minaret. In addition, the building has gables, buttressing and a dome over the *mihrab* end, and the whole effect is more that of a Byzantine church than a mosque.

Across the street, the **archeological museum** (daily 8.30am–noon & 1–5.30pm; $1), labelled almost exclusively in Turkish, has a sparse collection considering the size of the hall – merely pottery and figurines from the immediate environs of Milas, plus two cases of mediocre gold diadems and slightly better jewellery.

Practicalities

Milas's **otogar** is way out on the northern edge of town, near the junction for Labranda. You'll be left here unless you've come from Güllük or Ören, whose dolmuşes have separate terminals in the town centre. Getting into the centre from the *otogar*, take either a dolmuş marked "Şehir İçi" or the *servis araba* (complimentary shuttle) run by the big companies. The drop-off/pick-up point is the pavement south of the *Köşem* restaurant and city park; there's no fixed rank – just wait around. Quite nearby, on the south side of Muştak Bey Caddesi in the Sudi Özkan İş Merkezi, is Milas's recently opened **tourism information bureau**.

If you need or want to spend the night in Milas, the only savoury budget **accommodation** you'll find is on Kadıağa Caddesi, just west of a T-junction at the base of Hisarbaşı hill: the *Akdeniz* (☎0252/512 8661; ①), is the more basic, though en suite, while the nearby *Çınar* (☎0252/512 5525, fax 512 2102; ③) has more comfortable, balconied rooms. The town's most upmarket hotel is the *Sürücü* on Atatürk Bulvarı (☎0252/512 4001, fax 512 4000; ④), with an attached restaurant and café.

Eating out, simple lunches can be had at the *Pamukkale Pide Salonu*, near the produce market, or at several nearby holes-in-the-wall. Another good midday option is the *Özcan Kebap Salonu*, halfway up the main thoroughfare threading the bazaar on Hisarbaşı hill, on the east side of the street. The *Köşem* near the park and the *Sürücü Hotel*'s eatery are licensed and not too expensive, while the *Corner Bar Meyhane*, in the heart of the hillside bazaar on Türk Ocağı Caddesi, also offers food with booze. For dessert, there's nothing better than an ice cream in the park on a hot day; or try the *Nur Pastanesi*, over on the north side of town, below the Firuz Bey Camii and across from the *Bizim Birahanesi* – the last the only other moderate establishment serving both food and booze. For **drinking** only, there's a clutch of beer halls under some plane trees at the base of the Zeus temple hill.

Northeast of Milas: Euromos and Labranda

A short distance north of Milas are two impressive Carian ruins that together make a good day out from the town. **Euromos** is easily reached by public transport, although you really need your own vehicle to visit **Labranda**. If possible, try to see Labranda in the morning and Euromos in the afternoon.

Euromos

Between Bafa Gölü and Milas, 4km southeast of the town of Selimiye, a Corinthian **Temple of Zeus**, north of the road in an olive grove, is virtually all that remains intact of the ancient city of **EUROMOS** (site unenclosed; $1 if warden present). However, it's sufficiently unusual – only two other temples in Turkey are in a comparable state of repair – to justify a detour. You can get to the site from Milas by taking a dolmuş towards Selimiye, although if you're **returning** by public transport, be warned that long-distance buses will not stop to pick up passengers at the ruins. Even the Selimiye–Milas dolmuşes, often full by this point, may refuse you. Be prepared to walk back to Selimiye to find one at the start of its run.

There was a sanctuary to a native Carian deity on this spot as early as the sixth century BC, together with a city originally known as Kyromus. By the fourth century, under the Hellenizing influence of nearby Halicarnassus, the name had changed to Euromos and the cult of Zeus had merged with that of the earlier god. The city attained its greatest importance during the Hellenistic and Roman periods, when it nearly rivalled nearby Mylasa, but by Byzantine times it had sunk back into obscurity.

The **temple** is a legacy of the generous Roman emperor Hadrian, though the fact that several of the remaining columns are unfluted suggests that the shrine was never finished. Of the original 32 columns, arranged six by eleven, only sixteen remain, though all of these are linked to one or more neighbours by portions of the architrave. The city itself was built several hundred metres to the northwest of the temple, but the only easily found trace of it is a stretch of **wall** with a **tower**, up on the ridge overlooking the sacred precinct. The city's badly eroded **amphitheatre** lies about ten minutes' walk north, on the far side of the ridge, heading down and right from the tower.

Labranda (Labraynda)

The sanctuary of Zeus at **LABRANDA**, perched in splendid isolation on a south-facing hillside overlooking the plain of Milas, is arguably the most beautifully set archeological zone of ancient Caria, and one of its least visited – it takes a very sturdy tour bus to brave the horrendous road in. The site lies over 15km north of Milas, but dolmuşes only go as far as the hamlet of Kargıcak, roughly halfway, beyond which you must walk or beg lifts from passing trucks. The first 6km or so are paved and deceptively easy, but thereafter the road deteriorates markedly, the surface often thick dust or mud, depending on recent weather, and the gradient at times punishing. In summer you can normally get an ordinary car through with some alert driving in first gear, but after a heavy rain only four-wheel drive vehicles are up to it. Rumour has it that the way in will be paved in the near future, but this has been local gossip since 1987. A **taxi** from Milas, should you find a driver willing to risk his undercarriage, will set you back the better part of $20 return.

Excavations since 1948 have turned up no finds older than the seventh century BC, but it seems certain that some god was venerated here long before that. Oddly enough, the agreeable climate 600m up, coupled with a perennial spring, never prompted the founding of a city, but instead nurtured a grove of sacred plane trees that eventually

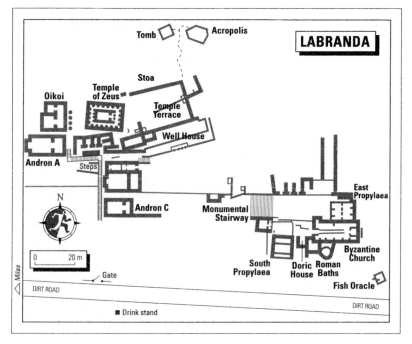

became the precinct of Zeus Stratius (the Warlike), alias Zeus Labrayndus (Axe-bearing), after his depiction on fourth-century coins struck at nearby Mylasa. The fourth-century BC Hecatomnid rulers of Halicarnassus and Mylasa did much to promote the cult, endowing various structures at the sanctuary which can still be seen. However, the priests of Zeus retained a large degree of autonomy, exerting their independence to advantage during the chaotic years after the death of Alexander. Roman and later Byzantine rule brought few material benefits to Labranda, and the place was finally abandoned during the late eleventh century.

The site

Just when you're beginning to wonder if you've made a wrong turn, a clump of poplars – replacing the long-vanished plane trees – heralds the location of the springs that still supply some of the water for modern Milas. A drinks stall and some beehives stand opposite the artificial terraces of the **sanctuary** (daily 8am–8pm; $1) and the rickety wooden gate giving onto them. The warden's family lives on the premises, and their children will usually escort you through the principal monuments in the following order, though they can only speak Turkish, and in any case the site is well marked, plus there's a helpful map-placard.

After skirting some unidentified ancient buildings, you climb up to the so-called **Andron A** – one of three such constructions at Labranda, used for sacred banquets held at the shrine. While roofless, it is otherwise complete, and includes a windowed niche in back. Immediately adjacent are the **oikoi** (priests' residences), fronted by four Doric column stubs. Like the Andron A, this was another foundation of the Hecatomnids, though authorities disagree on whether it was the actual quarters of the cult priests or merely the repository of temple records.

The **Temple of Zeus**, originally laid out in the fifth century and rededicated by Idrieus, sprawls east of here. None of it stands more than knee high, yet it is appealing, especially when viewed from the near edge of the temple terrace, lined with the rudiments of a stoa. From its far corner a path leads up the ruined **acropolis** and – more importantly – a massive fourth-century **tomb** thought to be that of Idrieus and his family. This is divided in two, with three sarcophagi in the rear chamber and a damaged pair up front.

Just below the south rim of the temple terrace is the recessed **well-house**, the original exit point of the spring; just across the flat area from here are **Andron B**, donated by Mausolus and relatively intact, and **Andron C**, a Roman contribution that has not weathered the ages as well.

From the level area in front of Andron C, it's a short distance to the prominent **monumental stairway** descending to the lowest terrace at the site. A right turn at the bottom of the steps leads to the **south propylaea**, one end of the sacred way to Mylasa, patches of which can still be followed; straight ahead takes you to the more prominent **east propylaea**, terminus of a processional way, long disappeared, from Alinda (see p.364). Wedged in between the two *propylaea* are the remains of a so-called **Doric house**, some adjoining **Roman baths** and a **Byzantine church**, beyond which are the probable foundations of Labranda's famous **fish oracle**. The resident fish, bedecked with jewellery according to several ancient sources, were thrown bits of food by their custodians. Depending on whether they accepted the morsels or not, the enquirer's fortunes were in the ascendant or decline.

South of Milas: Peçin Kale and minor resorts

The original site of Mylasa at **Peçin Kale** lies just off the road leading southeast to the Gulf of Gökova, though it is better known for its remains from the Menteşe emirate who appropriated the castle here and built a small settlement nearby. Further on, travellers usually skip ancient Keramos in favour of the adjacent beach resort of **Ören**. Southwest of Milas, **Güllük** is a wannabe resort making most of its living from fishing and ore shipment, while **Iassos** across the bay is a fairly scrappy ancient site close to some enticing fish restaurants.

Peçin Kale

Mylasa's shift to its current position during the fourth century BC means that its original site on the hill of **Peçin Kale** (*Beçin Kale* in local dialect and signposting) is more interesting for its **castle** (daily 8am–8pm; $1), originally Byzantine but adapted by the Menteşe emirs during their fourteenth-century tenure. The unmistakeable fortified bluff lies 5km east of Milas on the road to Ören (access via a marked, 800-metre dirt side road), but the citadel does not fulfil the promise of its imposing exterior; inside it is cluttered with the untidy ruins of Mutluca village, which relocated downhill 25 years ago, and the citadel's principal saving grace is the view of the plain 200m below.

The Menteşe complex itself lies about 400m from the castle, up a dirt track where a left fork leads to the unusual two-storeyed **Kızıl Han** and the fourteenth-century **Orhan Bey Camii**, featuring a far more ancient doorjamb. Bearing right takes you to the **medrese and türbe of Ahmet Gazi**, from the same era – tombs of a Menteşe governor and his wife that are venerated as those of minor Islamic saints, with coloured rags and candles. Most visitors, however, content themselves with a drink at the small, reasonably priced drinks stand, whose tables are set amidst the spring-fed olives, poplars and planes.

Ören

Frequented only in midsummer despite good transport links, **ÖREN** is an endangered Turkish species – a coastal resort that's not overdeveloped. It's virtually the only sizeable village on the north coast of the Gulf of Gökova, and owes its pre-tourism history to the narrow, fertile alluvial plain adjacent, and the lignite deposits in the mountains behind.

The route there is inauspicious, the landscape defaced by two giant power plants built with Polish aid – though Turkey's fledgling environmental movement has scored its first majory victory by successfully lobbying against the completion of the second plant. These installations are also one of the reasons tour operators have not seen fit to develop the area, although the industrial scenery of stacks and open-cast mining stops well short of Ören itself, and pollution has not yet perceptibly affected the crystalline waters offshore.

Inland Ören and ancient Keramos

The **upper village**, on the east bank of a canyon mouth exiting the hills, is an appealingly homogenous settlement, scattered among the ruins of **ancient Keramos**. No new works have been allowed for years but, following an earthquake in June 1989, permission was granted for "repairs". You can easily make out sections of wall, arches and a boat slip, dating from the time when the sea (now a kilometre distant) lapped the edge of town. There are no obvious visiting hours or admission charges – a do-it-yourself tour through the old, mostly Ottoman Greek houses should turn up various oddments.

The village has **shops** and a **post office** but no bank; most **dolmuşes** from Milas continue the final distance to the coast. For those driving themselves, a 45-kilometre **road** of sorts continues east from Ören past unspoiled, spectacular canyonland to the resort of Akyaka (see p.350), but only the first eight or so kilometres at each end have thus far been widened or improved in any way, leaving a horrendous middle section capable of shearing off exhausts: explore at your own risk!

The beach

The **beach** is a more than acceptable kilometre of coarse sand, gravel and pebbles, backed by handsome pine-tufted cliffs; in clear weather you can spy the Datça peninsula opposite. Once there was a working harbour at the east end of the town, but since the stuff is now burned locally rather than being shipped out, the lignite-loading conveyor there has been demolished, and the jetty has been allowed to crumble – what's left of it now serves a few fishing boats and the occasional wandering yacht. Overall Ören makes a great hideout from the commercialism that has engulfed the rest of the coast, and is an excellent spot to recuperate from the rigours of overland travel. People, mostly from Ankara, come to stay for weeks on end: a single day is really pointless, and since there are fewer than 250 beds to go around, the place fills up in high season, when reservations are strongly advised.

Practicalities

Should you plan on **staying**, mid-range comfort is best represented by the *Dolunay Motel* (☎0252/532 2194; ②) at the west end of the beach, with its own pier, pleasant garden and airy cottage units. Newer and somewhat posher is *Kardelen* (☎0252/532 2678; ③), though its inland location is a drawback. Other alternatives include the *Yalı Motel* (☎0252/532 2227; ②), on the beach next to the *Dolunay*; the *Kerme* (☎0252/532 2065; ②), with a rudimentary **campsite** and simple wooden cottages; or the rather plain *Yıltur Motel* (☎0252/532 2108; ①), in a rambling old compound at the far east end of the beach by the jetty. For **eating**, there are just a handful of unassuming restaurants – like the tasty *Çorumlunun Yeri*, or the *Keramos* – and a couple of stores. **Nightlife** consists of one pub-café and a couple of self-styled discos affiliated with *pansiyon*s.

Güllük

GÜLLÜK, 27km southeast of Milas, began life as a small fishing and bauxite-ore port, both of which are still the dominant enterprises. After enjoying a brief vogue among German trendies during the 1980s, it's now a rather déclassé resort, still patronized in the main by a few Germans. Despite delays in building the airport – it's scheduled for completion in 1997 – Güllük has already carpeted the surrounding hills with the standard-issue identikit villas, and has little to offer in the way of scenery, beaches or good hotels.

For the moment you can still watch wooden keels being laid at the giant **boatyards** beside the main port, where ore boats, fishing craft, yachts and the Turkish Navy all jostle for space. The minute town **beach** – really just a swimming platform – lies alongside the promontory closing off the bay to the south; beyond this is another bay, gated and off-limits to hoi polloi as it's the private preserve of *Türk Petrol* employees. Following the quay road north instead brings you to three other bays in succession, but none have anything much resembling a proper beach.

Practicalities

Access is easy, with frequent dolmuşes from Milas pulling in at a big inland plaza near the food market and **PTT** (there's no bank or tourist information). Peaceful **accommodation** tends to be scattered on either side of the commercial district: to the south there's the *Nazar Pansiyon* (☎0252/522 2132; ②), just inland from the boatyard, or the more comfortable, view-set *Özer Hotel* (☎0252/522 2221; ④) out on the lighthouse point, often full of German tour groups. Just inland from the first northerly bay sits the *Passala Pansiyon* (☎0252/522 2822; ③), perhaps the quietest of the three.

Eating and drinking options centre on the old customs building at mid-quay, where fish depots and chandleries alternate with such seafood restaurants as the *Çiçek* or *Eski Depo* (with prices just over half of those in Bodrum) and a pair of lively nocturnal bars which rule this area out for lodging.

Iassos

Covering a headland almost completely surrounded by the Gulf of Asim (*Asin* in local dialect), IASSOS would seem, from a glance at the map, to promise great things. Alas the ruins, after the first few paces, fizzle to virtually nothing, and swimming in the sumpy coves nearby is hardly an inviting prospect. Only the excellent local fish, the best reason to visit, represents an unbroken tradition from the past.

Fish stories abound at Iassos. In Hellenistic times the city's coinage even depicted a youth swimming with a dolphin that had befriended him. A more repeated tale concerns an itinerant musician that held his audience's attention until the ringing of the bell announcing the opening of the Iassian fish market. At that, the townspeople rose and trooped out, except for a partially deaf gentleman. The singer approached the man to compliment him on his manners; the deaf one, on understanding that the market had begun, hastily excused himself and fled after his peers.

The adjacent soil has always been poor, and from very early times Iassos must have attracted settlers, and made its living, by virtue of its good anchorage and fisheries. Traces of Minoan and Mycenaean habitation from as far back as 1900 BC have been found, though the city was damaged so badly during the Persian, Peloponnesian and Mithridatic wars that it never amounted to much until Roman imperial rule. Particularly during the second century AD, Iassos recovered substantially, and most of what can be seen today dates from those years. During the Byzantine era the city ranked as a bishopric, reflected by the presence of two basilicas. The hilltop castle was a medieval foundation of the Knights of St John, and after the Turkish conquest the place was known as Asimkalesi (Asim's Castle), Asim being a local *ağa* (feudal lord). The poor condition of most antiquities here can be attributed to the Ottoman policy of loading all easily prisable dressed stone onto waiting ships for transfer to building sites in İstanbul.

The site

On entering the modern village of Kıyıkışlacik next to the ruins, you first pass a Roman **mausoleum**, arguably far more interesting than anything within the city walls and recently converted to the site museum (erratic hours; $1). Inside, the star exhibit is a Corinthian temple-tomb resting on a stepped platform. Signposting and maintenance at the principal **site** of Iassos ($1 admission when staff present) have improved recently, though it's still debatable whether the entry fee is money well spent. Matters start promisingly enough as you cross the isthmus beyond the mausoleum to the **dipylon** (gate) in the **Hellenistic city wall**, repaired by the Byzantines. Once inside, the well-preserved Roman **bouleuterion**, with four rows of seats, lies immediately to your right but is currently off-limits. On your left, the **agora** has undergone a partial restoration of its Roman colonnade; at the south corner of the square is a rather obscure rectangular structure known as the **Caesarium**. Southeast of the castle there's a Roman **villa** with blurry murals and extensive floor mosaics, the latter hidden under a layer of protective sand. Close by, a wide stairway descends to the foundations of a small **Temple of Demeter and Kore**, while beyond is a partially submerged defensive **tower**.

From beside the tower a narrow but definite path threads past the large, dull **stoa of Artemis** on the right, before reaching the meagre hillside **theatre**, of which only the *cavea* walls and stumps of the stage building remain – the fine view over the northeast harbour partly compensates. Continue around, or (better) through, the obvious **castle**: there's little to see within the medieval walls, though again the panorama from atop the ramparts is excellent.

Practicalities

Like Heracleia ad Latmos, Iassos has both land and waterborne approaches. Coming **by land**, there's a turning 8km west of Milas – a pretty drive, narrow but paved all the way, first across a plain planted with cotton, then through pine- and olive-studded hills overlooking the airport-to-be. There are infrequent **dolmuş** services from Milas. Coming from Bodrum or Güllük, use instead the narrow but fair-standard dirt road beginning 3km north of Koru on the Bodrum–Milas road; just near a *Petrol Ofisi* station, the usual black-on-yellow sign announces "Iasos 17".

Without your own car, it's better to come **by sea**. Excursion boats from Güllük provide the link in season, and almost always include a swimming stop at a beach only reachable from the water. This is certainly a bonus, since there are no beaches worthy of the name accessible by foot or vehicle anywhere near Iassos.

In Kıyıkışlacık village, four or five **restaurants** predictably specialize in fish, in particular the cheap and excellent local *çipura* (gilthead bream); best of the bunch is the *Dilek*, behind the touristy *İasos Deniz*. If you want to **stay**, one of a half-dozen cheap *pansiyon*s can put you up for the night. Most eateries and lodgings overlook the rather murky harbour – due, perhaps, to become still murkier, as a formal yacht marina is planned.

Bodrum and its peninsula

In the eyes of its devotees, **BODRUM**, with its whitewashed square houses and sub-tropical gardens, is the longest-established, most attractive and most versatile Turkish resort – a quality outfit in comparison to its upstart Aegean rivals Marmaris and Kuşadası. However, its recent, almost frantic attempts to be all things to all tourists have made it hard to tell the difference, and the controlled development within the municipality – height limits and a preservation code are in force – has resulted in wholesale exploitation of the until recently little-disturbed peninsula. Until now, the lack of a convenient airport and the obligatory three-to-four-hour coach transfer in from İzmir or Dalaman has kept the place from going the way of Magalluf or Mykonos, but once the airport near Güllük has been completed, all bets are off.

The Bodrum area has long attracted large numbers of Britons, both the moneyed yacht set and the charter-flight trade. Most of the big UK package tour operators (including *Sunworld, Sovereign, Thomson* and *Airtours*) are active hereabouts, which can be either reassuring or offputting, depending on your viewpoint. If you want all water-borne distractions laid on by day, and some of the most sophisticated nightlife in Turkey by night, complete with imported DJs and lager louts, then Bodrum town and Gümbet in particular will be your dream come true; if you're after a coastal backwater with some vestiges of local character, then such peninsula outposts as Gümüşlük or Akyarlar will more closely answer to the description.

Some history

Bodrum was originally known as **Halikarnassos** (Halicarnassus), colonized by Dorians from the Peloponnese during the eleventh century BC. They mingled with the existing Carian population, settling on the small island of Zephysia, which in later ages became a peninsula and the location of the medieval castle. Along with Knidos, Kos and the three Rhodian cities of Lindos, Kamiros and Ialyssos, Halicarnassus was a member of the so-called Dorian Hexapolis, whose assembly met periodically at the sanctuary of Triopian Apollo at Knidos. At some point during the sixth century BC Halicarnassus was expelled from the confederation, on the pretext that one of the city's athletes had failed to show proper reverence to the god; in reality the increasing Ionian character of Halicarnassus offended the other five cities.

Later the city came under Persian influence, though managing to retain considerable autonomy. Halicarnassus' most famous son, **Herodotus** (484–420 BC), chronicled the city's fortunes in his acclaimed *Histories*. Eventually direct Persian rule was replaced by that of the **Hecatomnid satraps**, a capable if rather inbred dynasty, the most renowned of whose rulers was **Mausolus** (377–353 BC), a leader who greatly increased the power and wealth of what in effect was a semi-independent Carian principality. An admirer of Greek civilization, Mausolus spared no effort to Hellenize his cities, and was working on a suitably self-aggrandizing tomb at the time of his death – thereby giving us our word "mausoleum". **Artemisia II**, his sister and wife, completed the massive structure, which came to be regarded as one of the Seven Wonders of the ancient world. Like her ancestor Artemisia I, she distinguished herself in warfare, inflicting a humiliating defeat on the Rhodians, who were tricked into allowing her entire fleet into their port.

In 334 BC the rampaging Alexander's arrival coincided with a bitter succession feud between Artemisia's heirs. The Macedonian armies wreaked such havoc that the city never fully recovered, and its population was dispersed throughout Caria over the next two chaotic centuries. After a period of little importance under the Roman and Byzantine empires, and brief shuffling among Selçuk, Menteşe and Ottoman occupiers,

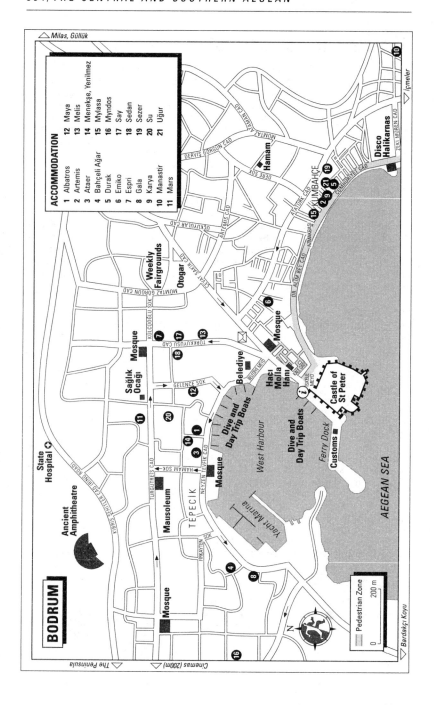

BODRUM

ACCOMMODATION

1	Albatros	12	Maya
2	Artemis	13	Melis
3	Ataer	14	Menekşe, Yenilmez
4	Bahçeli Ağar	15	Mylasa
5	Durak	16	Myndos
6	Emiko	17	Say
7	Espri	18	Sedan
8	Gala	19	Sezer
9	Karya	20	Su
10	Manastir	21	Uğur
11	Mars		

the **Knights of St John** slipped over from Rhodes in 1402 and erected the **castle** that is now Bodrum's most prominent landmark. Urgently needing to replace the fortress at Smyrna destroyed by the Mongols, the Knights engaged the best military engineers of the era to construct their new stronghold on the promontory. The name *bodrum*, meaning "cellar" or "dungeon" in Turkish, probably pays tribute to the stronghold's subterranean defences. After Süleyman the Magnificent compelled the order to depart in 1523, the castle's history was virtually synonymous with that of the town until early this century.

Arrival, orientation and information

Both international and domestic **ferries** dock at the jetty west of the castle, opposite the expanding yacht marina. In the more likely event that you arrive by **bus**, you'll be left at the **otogar**, some 500m up Cevat Şakir Caddesi, which links Belediye Meydanı with the main peninsular highway and divides the town roughly in two.

Cevat Şakir's approximate continuation, Kale Caddesi, defines one edge of the bazaar, huddling in the shadow of the medieval castle. Kale Caddesi ends at İskele Meydanı, officially known as Barış Meydanı and home to the **tourist information office** (summer Mon–Fri 8am–8pm, Sat 9am–7.30pm; ☎0252/316 1091) – as so often in Turkey, useless unless you have a specific query. Northwest of Cevat Şakir is the service-oriented side of town. Most travel and car rental agencies, plus the bus company offices, line Neyzen Tevfik Caddesi, which takes off from Belediye Meydanı. Its most important perpendiculars, especially when accommodation-hunting, are Menekşe Sokağı and Türkkuyusu Caddesi.

Driving is difficult in Bodrum, made all the more so by a strict, anticlockwise one-way system; you enter town via Cevat Şakir, proceed west along Neyzen Tevfik, curl north towards Turgutreis Caddesi via one of several minor streets, and then proceed east again. Türkkuyusu Caddesi and Hamam Sokağı are northbound (uphill) only. On the eastern side of town, Atatürk Caddesi is westbound only. **Parking** is even more frustrating; shelling out for car park fees or, even worse, getting a vehicle out of impoundment is disheartening, so we've noted accommodation with parking space.

Accommodation

Desirable **accommodation** tends to concentrate in three main areas: in Kumbahçe Mahalle, but away from Cumhuriyet Caddesi (where you'd get little sleep); in Tepecik district, along or just off Neyzen Tevfik Caddesi (passably quiet); and on the convenient and usually peaceful Türkkuyusu Caddesi, winding up from Belediye Meydanı. There are also several desirable locales along, or just off, Turgutreis Caddesi, as well as behind Bardakçı Koyu, the first sandy bay southwest of the town centre. Advance reservations are suggested in peak season, and out of season most hotels (except those with central heating) are closed. Air conditioning is a distinct bonus in mid-summer, when the less expensive *pansiyon*s tend to be airless shoeboxes.

Kumbahçe Mahalle

Artemis, Cumhuriyet Cad 117 (☎0252/316 1572, fax 316 2907). Some rooms at this *pansiyon* can be noisy, but all are very comfortable with good views across the bay. ⑤.

Durak, Rasathane Sok 8 (☎0252/316 1564). This quiet *pansiyon* has a front garden, kitchen and terrace; all rooms are en suite, some with balconies. ②.

Emiko, Atatürk Cad, Uslu Sok 11 (☎0252/316 5560). Run by a delightful Japanese woman, this *pansiyon* is quiet despite the central location, and a bargain for en-suite rooms. ②.

Karya, Cumhuriyet Cad 127 (☎0252/316 1535). Comfortable small hotel near the *Artemis*; similar facilities, plus central heating. Cheaper in winter. ⑤.

Manastır, Barış Mevkii, uphill from the *Disco Halikarnas* (☎0252/316 2775, fax 316 2772). Well run, with sympathetic architecture and great views over town; pool and air conditioning/heating. ⑥.

Mylasa, Cumhuriyet Cad 34 (☎0252/316 1846, fax 316 1254). Variable room size, but open in winter; least noisy of the several *pansiyon*s on this stretch. ④.

Sezer, Atatürk Cad 84 (☎0252/316 5262). A two-star hotel with a nice view from the terrace. Small pool and snack bar. ④.

Uğur, Rasathane Sok 13 (☎0252/316 2106). Similar to the *Durak* in all respects, but with limited parking space too. ②.

Türkkuyusu Caddesi

Espri, Türkkuyusu Cad 98, corner Külcüoğlu Sok (☎0252/316 1129). Basically a large *pansiyon* with hotel pretensions; en-suite rooms are nothing special – indeed on the dire side – but there's a fair-sized pool, and easy parking nearby. ③.

Melis, Türkkuyusu Cad 50 (☎0252/316 1487). Set back from the street, with a garden and popular bar; where Aussie backpackers tend to go straight off the boat from Kós. ③.

Say, Türkkuyusu Cad, Alibaba Çıkmazı 9 (☎0252/316 8874, fax 313 0247). Newish hotel with some rooms taken by package tours; small, tile-floored rooms, central pool. ④.

Sedan, Türkkuyusu Cad 121/A (☎0252/316 0355). A 1970s-vintage, "ethnic" *pansiyon* built around a shady courtyard with a disused irrigation pool; a choice of plumbed and unplumbed rooms, and limited parking. ②–③.

Tepecik

Albatros, Menekşe Sok 6 (☎0252/316 7117). The front garden and lobby are more impressive than the rather basic if en-suite rooms. ③.

Ataer, alley off Neyzen Tevfik Cad 94 (☎0252/316 5357). Quiet location just inland from the mosque. ②.

Bahçeli Ağar, 1402 Sok 4/A, an alley off Neyzen Tevfik Cad 190, behind the yacht marina (☎0252/316 1648). Rooms are very plain but clean; self-catering kitchen. ②.

Gala, Neyzen Tevfik Cad 224, Yat Limani (☎0252/316 2216, fax 316 1910). Good-value two star hotel, where yacht outfitters tend to place clients before or after cruises; rooms of variable size, with home-like rather than institutional furnishings, and a roof terrace. ⑤.

Maya, Gelence Sok 49 (☎0252/316 4741, fax 316 4745). Inland garden hotel, recently upgraded to three stars, with air conditioning, sauna and fitness centre. ⑥.

Menekşe, Menekşe Çıkmazı, the continuation of Menekşe Sokağı (☎0252/316 0537). Very peaceful garden setting for this good-value *pansiyon*; limited parking. ③.

Myndos, Myndos Cad 1 (☎0252/316 3080, fax 316 5252). Medium-sized, three-star hotel featuring in some package brochures; well managed, heated in winter. ⑥.

Yenilmez, Menekşe Çıkmazı (☎0252/316 2520). Central and quiet *pansiyon*; a good option if the next-door *Menekşe* is full. ③.

Turgutreis Caddesi

Mars, Turgutreis Cad, İmbat Çıkmazı 20 (☎0252/316 6559). Most sympathetic of three small hotels clustered here; mostly French clientele, but no organized groups. Small pool, simple rooms. ③.

Su, end of 1201 Sokak, off Turgutreis Cad (☎0252/316 6906, fax 316 7391). Delightful, dead-quiet small hotel, as no cars can get in here. Worth the extra for the bougainvillea-clad environment and tastefully done rooms; small pool with bar. ⑤.

Bardakçı Koyu

Azka Oteli (☎0252/316 8992, fax 316 8214). Four-star comfort right on the best part of the beach here; try and get a unit in the terraced north wing, facing the garden. That said, it's grossly overpriced. ⑧.

Salmakis Hotel (☎0252/316 6506, fax 316 6511). Units with mock-village decor, arrayed on several levels; has a share of the beach just down from the *Azka*. ⑥.

The Castle of St Peter

The centrepiece of Bodrum is the **Castle of St Peter** (Tues–Sun 8.30am–noon & 1–5pm; $2.50) – an attraction in itself and also home to separate **museums** of underwater archeology, though much of the grounds are relentlessly (and sometimes tastelessly) commercialized.

The castle was built by the Knights of St John over the small Selçuk fortress and older battlements they found on the site. An initial circuit of walls was completed in 1437, though as the new science of artillery ballistics advanced, the garrison saw fit to add more walls and moats, particularly on the landward side – with their powerful fleets, the Knights had less fear of attack by sea. Fourteen water cisterns were provided to guarantee self-sufficiency in the event of siege, increasingly probable after 1453, when the citadel became the sole Christian stronghold in Anatolia. Work proceeded slowly, and the finishing touches had just been applied in 1522 when Süleyman's capture of the Knights' headquarters on Rhodes made their position here untenable. Bodrum's castle was subsequently neglected until the nineteenth century, when the chapel was converted to a mosque, the keep to a prison and a hamam installed. During a siege in 1915, shells from a French battleship levelled the minaret and damaged various towers. The Italians repaired most of the harm done during their brief postwar occupation, though the place was not properly refurbished until the 1960s, when it was converted into a museum.

Entry and the lower courtyard

Initial entrance is no longer via the **north gate**, facing Barış Meydanı, but through the **west gate**, looking on to the water. Once inside the west moat, you'll notice bits of ancient masonry from the **mausoleum** incorporated into the walls, as well as some of the 249 Christian coats of arms. Stairs lead up to the seaward fortifications and then into the **lower courtyard**, where strolling peacocks animate a small drink stall, the first of a number scattered strategically across the huge grounds. On the left, a linear display on amphora production culminates in the "**medieval shop**", actually a clever pretext to sell unusual aromatic oils, herbal samples and souvenir foodstuffs.

To the right, the **chapel** (currently locked) formerly housed the local Bronze Age and Mycenean collection featuring artefacts recovered from three Aegean wrecks, including a provisional case of finds from the Uluburun site near Kaş; this is set, by 1998, to be housed in new premises on the east side of the castle precinct. A building at the base of the Italian tower holds a small **glass collection**, mostly Roman and early Islamic work, displayed in odd reverse illumination.

Glass Wreck Hall

Just downhill from this collection is a more substantial one, in the so-called **Glass Wreck Hall** (Tues–Fri 10–11am & 2–4pm; $1.50 separate admission), which houses a Byzantine shipwreck and cargo found 33m down at Serçe Limanı in 1973. Dating from 1025, this was a peacetime trading vessel plying between Fatimid and Byzantine territories. The craft – tubby and flat-bottomed to permit entry to the Mediterranean's many shallow straits – is displayed in a climate-controlled environment, though only twenty percent of the original timbers are preserved. The rest is a mock-up, loaded with a fraction of the cargo: two tonnes of raw coloured glass, finished glassware, and tamped-down broken shards intended for an early recycling programme. The archeologists' main task, which took eleven years to complete, was to separate 15,000 fragments into the three categories. When she sank, the ship was apparently headed for skilled glass workshops along the Black Sea, and returning empty pots to their owners – a frugal bunch, it would seem, as the amphoras were being used long after their spouts and handles had been badly damaged. Also displayed are the personal effects of the passengers and crew, including gaming pieces, tools and grooming items. All told, it's a well-labelled and -lit exhibit, worth the extra expense if you can coincide with the restricted opening hours.

Carian Princess Hall

On the next level up, the linked Italian and French towers are now home to a gift shop; just beyond, the recently inaugurated **Carian Princess Hall** (same hours as castle; $1.50 extra admission) contains artefacts from an ancient tomb found miraculously unlooted during hotel-building works in 1989. The sarcophagus with its skeleton, evidently that of a Carian noblewoman, is on view, along with a scant number of gold tomb finds, which were almost certainly imported, as the metal was (and is) not found locally. Items include the lady's favourite drinking cup, buried with her, and an elaborate diadem with floral motifs, which lends credence to the supposition of royalty.

The English tower

The **English tower**, at the southeast corner of the castle precinct, as presently laid out is a bald attempt to pander to Bodrum's major foreign constituency. Assorted standards of the Order of St John and of their Muslim adversaries compete for wall space with an incongruous array of medieval armour and weapons, and apparently contemporary hunting trophies; the medieval mood muzak of previous years has been replaced, in season at least, by a live clarinettist (tips accepted). Many visitors attempt to decipher extensive swathes of Latin graffiti incised into the window jambs by bored knights.

The upper courtyard and the dungeon

Finish your tour by crossing the **upper courtyard**, landscaped, like much of the castle grounds, with native flora, to the **German tower**, with an exhibit of Ottoman royal *tuğra*s that are for sale, and the **Snake tower** – named for the serpent relief plaque over the entrance, with an amphora display inside. East of these, it's possible to make a long, dead-end detour, past a horrible diorama on galley slavery, to the lowest exihibit in the Gatineau Tower. This, the Knights' former **dungeon**, has been done up in a feeble presumed imitation of the London Dungeon, complete with dangling chains, an infernal blacksmith fashioning fetters and bathed in lurid red light, plus pre-recorded moans and sighs. In case you missed the point, an original Latin inscription over the door reads "Here God does not exist".

The Town

Immediately to the north of the castle lies the **bazaar**, most of which is pedestrianized along its two main thoroughfares of Kale Caddesi and Dr Alim Bey Caddesi; traffic enters the dense warren of streets to the southeast via Atatürk Caddesi, 200m inland. East of the spot called Azmakbaşı (Creek-Mouth), Alim Bey becomes Cumhuriyet Caddesi, home to most of Bodrum's nightlife, and the two, completely pedestrianized, are jointly referred to locally as Uzunyol (Long Street). Halfway along Kale Caddesi is Bodrum's only other substantial medieval monument apart from the castle, the eighteenth-century **han of Hacı Molla**, now host to a luxury restaurant and various souvenir shops – a pattern that is repeated throughout the lanes of the surrounding bazaar, most workaday tradespeople having been exiled further inland.

From landscaped Belediye Meydanı, stroll up Türkkuyusu Caddesi and bear left onto Turgutreis Caddesi – centre of a small district of old stone houses with courtyards that give some hint of what pre-tourism Bodrum was like. Roughly 400m west along

Turgutreis Caddesi lies all that's left of the **Mausoleum** (Tues–Sun 8.30am–noon & 1–5.30pm; $1.50). Designed by Pytheos, architect of the Athena temple at Priene, the complete structure measured 39m by 33m at its base and stood nearly 60m high. A nine-by-eleven colonnade surmounted the burial vault and supported a stepped pyramidal roof bearing a chariot with effigies of Mausolus and his sister-wife Artemisia, now in the British Museum. Most available vertical surfaces were adorned with friezes and statues executed by some of the best sculptors of the age.

The tomb stood essentially intact for over sixteen centuries before being severely damaged by an earthquake; the Knights of St John finished its destruction between 1402 and 1522 by removing all the cut stone as building material and burning much of the marble facing for lime. Happily for posterity, they used most of the friezes for decorating their castle. When Stratford Canning, British Ambassador to the Sublime Porte, noticed them there in 1846, he obtained permission to ship them to the British Museum. Eleven years later Charles Newton discovered the site of the mausoleum and unearthed the statues of Mausolus and Artemisia, plus portions of the chariot team, which went to join the other relics in London.

Not surprisingly the mausoleum in its present condition ranks as a disappointment, despite diligent and imaginative work by Danish archeologists. Little is left besides the precinct wall, assorted column fragments, and some subterranean vaults, probably belonging to an earlier burial chamber. In a shed east of the foundation cavity are exhibited plans and models, as well as a copy or two of the original friezes in England. By way of contrast the **ancient theatre**, just above the main highway bounding Bodrum to the north, has been almost overzealously restored and is now used during the September

BODRUM IN LITERATURE AND MUSIC – AND IN DRAG

In recent years personalities have outshone monuments, as Bodrum has become something of a mecca for Turkish bohemian types. The earliest arrival was the writer-to-be **Cevat Şakir Kabaağaçlı**, who was first exiled here in 1908 for his political views, and returned compulsorily in 1923, under commuted death sentence for allegedly murdering his father, a wealthy pasha. He persistently declined all comment on the latter charge, but for the balance of his long life devoted himself to the welfare of the area, in particular to the preservation of its monuments (he once wrote to the British Museum demanding the return of the Halicarnassian artefacts pillaged by Charles Newton). He also recorded the lore and legends of the local seafarers, penning several collections of short stories based on these conversations under the *nom de plume* "Fisherman of Halicarnassus". To him is also owed the concept of the *Mavi Yolculuk* or "Blue Voyage", the title of a work of his describing his week-long Aegean forays, during the 1950s and 1960s, on a primitive sponge-fishing boat with a minimum of amenities. Kabaağaçlı is buried on a hill overlooking the bay of Gümbet, having died some years before his bohemian sea voyages with like-minded disciples had become the money-spinning *gület* cruises of today.

Ahmet and Nesuhi Ertegün, two more prominent Bodrum habitués, were the sons of the Turkish ambassador to the US during the 1930s and 1940s, and caught the jazz bug while living in America. Both later became big-time recording executives, notably establishing Atlantic's jazz label, which in the early 1960s launched the careers of (among others) Charles Mingus, John Coltrane and the Modern Jazz Quartet. The Ertegüns were influential in the process of introducing jazz to Turkey, and their careers go a long way toward explaining the music's popularity among the Turkish middle and upper classes. Nesuhi died in 1989 but his brother still occasionally visits the family villa in Bodrum.

Another long-term local villa-owner was **Zeki Müren**, foremost among a bevy of widely acclaimed transvestite (or transsexual) pop singers in Turkey. He lived in Bodrum – and circulated out of drag – from the 1970s until his death in 1996, and has a street named after him, appropriately enough leading to the biggest disco in Turkey.

BOAT TRIPS AROUND BODRUM

It's almost impossible to miss the touts for **boat day trips** in Bodrum, and if you're not planning to tour the area by land they are worth taking advantage of, since swimming anywhere near the pair of polluted town bays is inadvisable. Most of the craft are concentrated on the west harbour, and a typical day out starts between 9.30 and 10.30am and finishes between 4 and 5pm, costing roughly $10 per person in a minimum group of seven (lunch not included). Itineraries vary little, with most boats visiting a fixed list of attractions in the following order.

First stop is usually **Kara Ada**, a sizable island southeast of town, where you bathe in some hot springs issuing from a cave at the island's margin. Next halt is the "**Akvaryum**", a snorkellers' venue in the Ada Boğazı (Island Strait) near Gümbet, with claimed optimal underwater visibility of 30m; the fish, however, seem usually to be frightened off by the crowds of humans and motor noise. The final moorings, also accessible by land and detailed below, tend to be two of the following attractions: **Kargı** beach, where you can ride camels, **Bağla** cove, and **Karaincir** bay. Some craft head east from Kara Ada to visit **Orak Adası** and **Yalıçiftlik** beach instead.

festival. Begun by Mausolus, it was modified in the Roman era and originally seated 13,000, though it has a present capacity of about half that. The so-called **Myndos gate**, west of the junction of Turgutreis Caddesi and Cafer Paşa Caddesi, is the sole surviving section of Mausolus's ambitious city wall, though stubby bits of the fortifications crop up here and there on the west side of town.

Eating and drinking

You don't come to Bodrum to ease your budget, and **eating out** proves no exception. Almost everywhere you'll be paying over the odds, especially if you're close to the water or in a chi-chi restaurant.

Absolute rock-bottom is the classic, original branch of *Sakallı Köftecisi*, Çarşı İçi İkinci Sok 11, opposite the *Garanti Bankası* in the bazaar, and a firm tradesmen's favourite: lots of *hazır yemek* and kebabs, but predictably no booze. A more touristic annexe of the same management, also known as *Ali Doksan*, opposite the PTT and the *İş Bankası* on Cevat Şakir, has more pleasant seating, but the food tends to be a bit oilier. Near the fruit market on Cevat Şakir, the *Can Ciğer*, in Niyazi Saat arcade, is open long hours, serving sheep's head as well as more normal fare.

At Atatürk Cad 21, the licensed *Kebapçı Ata*, run by folk from Adana and with a mainly Turkish clientele, specializes in unusual grilled items (heart, liver, ribs), tasty *meze*, and wonderful flat bread with sesame; the entrance is a bit inconspicuous, so be alert. The *Ecem* nearby at no. 9 is also popular, though by no means as elegant.

Anywhere else, especially overlooking either bay, you can expect a considerable jump up in price, if not always quality. *Sohbet*, at Cumhuriyet Cad 99, is about the most Turkish of the score of places along Uzunyol, serving only moderately pricy *hazır yemek* in a stone-walled salon. Opposite the yacht harbour, *Gemibaşı*, on the corner of Firkayten Sokak and Neyzen Tevfik, and *Amphora* at Neyzen Tevfik 164 are old reliable fixtures, good for an unadorned, no-nonsense meat meal. The *Sünger* pizza restaurant at no. 218 is even cheaper and more cheerful, and additionally can be a good venue to find temporary work on yachts.

If you have the inclination and the funds, there are Chinese, Thai, Italian, Indian and even Mexican restaurants in Bodrum, most but not all of them along Atatürk or Neyzen Tevfik *caddesi*s. Of the Chinese eateries, the *Dragon*, at the corner of Gelence Sokağı and Neyzen Tevfik, is reckoned the best, while Thai-managed *Ladda's*, just up from the waterfront at Cizdaroğlu Sok 10, gets the trophy for Thai (☎0252/313 1504 for reservations); both cost about $20 a head for the works.

Well inland, the *Sapa Restaurant* at Külcüoğlu Sok 6 is a longstanding local favourite, serving "international cuisine" suppers in the garden of an old house – again, count on $20 for the works. Certainly the most unusual restaurant in Bodrum, indeed on the whole Turkish coast, is nearby at Türkkuyusu Cad 72: *Buğday Vegetarian Restaurant*, offering a few dairy dishes to liven up the original vegan menu. It's liveliest at lunchtime, with wonderful soups, but also a good bet in the morning, especially if you're bored of the standard *pansiyon* breakfast.

For dessert, the *Ladin* is a good, all-round *dondurma*, pudding and pastry shop on Alim Bey Caddesi.

Nightlife

There must be forty places to **drink and dance** in Bodrum, most of them lining Uzunyol in Kumbahçe district, packed and sweaty of a summer night. East of Azmakbaşı, the *Red Lion* and the adjacent *Kadir Sea Lion* are loud and among the more durable, as is the adjacent *Rick's Bar, Uno*, beyond the two "Lions", has live music, while *Sensi Bar*, between *Uno* and the "Lions", has beachfront seating and less emphasis on dancing. The ultimate, both in style and physical location, is *Disco Halikarnas*, at the east end of Cumhuriyet Caddesi, where a $12 cover charge (includes one drink) and proper dress sees you in with the beautiful people, up to two thousand of them on the mammoth dance floor. The external laser show, frequently aimed at the castle, is free.

To the west, along Alim Bey Caddesi, *Kef* is where young Turks dance on the tables, while nearby *Sokak* is a former warehouse transformed into a state-of-the-art disco. Also near the start of Alim Bey, the popular "live blues" bar, *Veli*, is the longest lived of Bodrum's watering holes, attracting an older, Turkish crowd. Nearby, across from the *Ora* disco, stands *Hadi Gari*, a music bar in an old fig warehouse that reopened to general acclaim in late 1996. Most outrageous in this area is the only rival to the *Halikarnas*, the *M&M* disco with live DJs and organized theme nights; reservations (☎0252/316 2725) may be necessary in peak season.

There's not much after-hours elsewhere, but you could try *Mola*, another jazz-and-blues bar at Neyzen Tevfik Cad 86, or *Chez Ahmet*, a French-speaking bar out on the ferry dock, past the castle entrance.

Bodrum has two full-fledged **cinemas**: the *Karia Princess*, in the basement of the eponymous hotel, and the outdoor *Sinema Bodrum*, 100m to the east, with screenings at least an hour after dark (usually 10pm). Films are subtitled, with the original soundtrack; playbills are posted at strategic locations.

Listings

Airlines *THY*, Neyzen Tevfik Cad, opposite the yacht harbour (☎0252/373 5780); *Top Air*, Neyzen Tevfik Cad 92 (☎0252/313 0626).

Books Just one proper store, as opposed to purveyors of tourist literature: *Bodrum Kitaplığı*, Cumhuriyet Cad, Adliye Sok 4.

Car rental International chain outlets include *Avis*, Neyzen Tevfik Cad 92/A (☎0252/316 2333); *Budget*, Neyzen Tevfik Cad 86/A (☎0252/316 7382); *Europcar/InterRent*, Neyzen Tevfik Cad 48 (☎0252/316 5632); *Hertz*, Neyzen Tevfik Cad 232 (☎0252/313 4905). Small chains or local operators include *Airtour*, Atatürk Cad 198 (☎0252/316 5927); *DeCar*, Neyzen Tevfik Cad 236/B (☎0252/313 2151); *Sun*, Neyzen Tevfik Cad 82/A (☎0252/316 4385); and *Unicar*, Neyzen Tevfik Cad 80 (☎0252/316 6252).

Consulate Honorary British consulate on ☎0252/316 4932.

Diving *Bodrum Reef* (☎0252/313 1341), or visit their boat *Mersed*, berthed near the Tepecik mosque; also *İlmer*, Menekşe Çıkmazı 2/A (☎0252/316 5890), whose slightly smaller boat berths opposite the entrance to the castle. A typical day excursion including all gear, two dives and a picnic costs about $55 – remember to bring your certification card, otherwise training courses run to about $300. If you want your own kit, or need spares, try *Bodrum Dive Store*, Kıbrıs Şehitler Cad, Alaman Centre E/3 (☎0252/316 0493).

Exchange *Döviz* houses are ubiquitous, or use the ATMs of *Pamukbank, Garanti Bankası, Yapı Kredi* or *Akbank*.

Ferry agents The big two are nearly adjacent, just outside customs on the jetty: *Bodrum Express* for hydrofoils (☎0252/316 1087) and the *Bodrum Ferryboat Association* (☎0252/316 0882). Domestic services to Marmaris, Datça and Altınkum are offered, as well as the international short hop to Kós (Greece). Fares for the latter are the least pricy of all the crossings to Greece: singles $14 ferry/$20 hydrofoil, day returns $21/$28, open returns $46/$54, including the 5000dr tax for leaving Greece.

Hamam Dere Umurca Sok (daily 8am–5pm, Wed & Sat afternoons for women only).

Hospitals The *Devlet Hastanesi* (state hospital) is 300m east of the ancient theatre on the ring road; *Sağlık Ocağı* (private clinic) is 300m east near the corner of Davut Sok. *Halikarnassos Klinik*, Kıbrıs Şehitler Cad 97 (☎0252/316 3635), and *Medicare*, Hamam Sok 4 (☎0252/316 7051), both promise 24-hour, 7-day attention.

Jeep safaris *Highland Jeep Adventures*, Seldır Şeyh Cad 2 (☎0252/316 8924), Dutch-run and committed to small (8-person) groups, bashes about in unlikely corners of the peninsula; coffees, swim and lunch stop included in $60 day-trip price.

Laundrettes *Neyzen*, Neyzen Tevfik Cad 236/A, and *Minik*, no. 236/C, compete for the yachtie trade near the marina gate; service wash $4.50. The *Can*, Türkkuyusu Cad 99, is slightly cheaper.

Map *Simpson's Map of Bodrum and Environs* is accurate and detailed enough for most requirements; failing that, use the one in the giveaway promo-paper *Aegean Sun*.

Market Thurs (produce) & Fri (cloth goods too), in the fairgrounds behind the bus station. Don't count on stupendous bargains.

Shopping *Yaban Sandalet*, Alim Bey Cad 39, *Taban* at no. 71, and *Sur Sandalet* on the same street are the places for handmade shoes and sandals, as well as leather trinkets. *Bodrum Havlu*, Atatürk Cad 66, is the outlet for domestically made towels and bedding – good value in the high-quality lines.

Supermarkets *Migros*, near the turning for Gümbet; *Tansaş*, by the *otogar*.

Yachting *S&J Travel & Yachting*, Neyzen Tevfik Cad 218/A (☎0252/316 0561, fax 316 8446), specializes in custom-itinerary *gület* hire; minimum six days, with a crew of 2–4 (including a cook). Most cruises hug the scenic Gökova Gulf coast en route to Marmaris. *Aegean Yacht Services*, Paşa Tarlası Cad 21 (☎0252/316 1517, fax 316 5749), and *Fora Tourism & Yachting*, Neyzen Tevfik Cad 210 (☎0252/316 3046), with weekly scheduled departures, are the main alternatives.

Around the peninsula

There is more of interest and beauty in the rest of the **Bodrum peninsula** than the often dreary immediate environs of the town promise, and no matter how long or short your stay, some time spent there is worthwhile. The north side of the peninsula tends to be greener, with patches of pine forest; the south, studded with tall crags, is more arid, with a sandier coast.

The population here was largely Greek Orthodox before 1923, and villages often still have a vaguely Hellenic feel, with ruined churches, windmills and the old **stone houses** that even the most brazen new developments attempt to imitate. The landscape in general, with bare rock (and sometimes castles) at the higher elevations and vast oases along the stream beds and shore, is not unlike that of the islands of Pátmos, Léros or Kálimnos across the water. An otherworldly atmosphere is imparted by the many large and small **islands**, floating out to sea, and an exotic touch lent by the ubiquitous, white-domed *gümbet*s (cisterns), and camel caravans – not all for tourist photo ops but working draft animals, especially during the off-season.

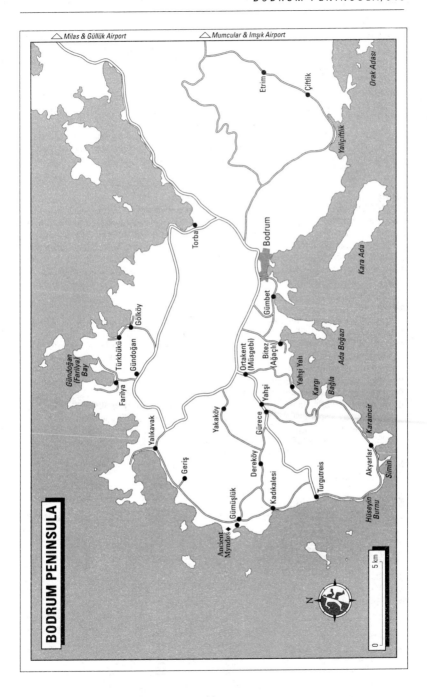

BODRUM PENINSULA

△ Milas & Güllük Airport   △ Mumcular & Imşık Airport

Etrim
Çiftlik
Orak Adası
Yalıçiftlik
Torba
Bodrum
Kara Ada
Gölköy
Gümbet
Ortakent
(Müsgebi)
Bitez
Ağaçlı
Ada Boğazı
Türkbükü
Gündoğan
Yahşi Yalı
Kargı
Gündoğan
(Farilya)
Bay
Farilya
Yahşi
Bağla
Yalıkavak
Yakaköy
Gürece
Karaincir
Geriş
Dereköy
Turgutreis
Akyarlar
Simin
Gümüşlük
Kadkalesi
Hüseyin
Burnu
Ancient
Myndos

N

5 km
0

There is also a relatively high concentration of serviceable **beaches,** and virtually every resort of any importance is served by **dolmuş** from Bodrum's *otogar*. The account of the coastline that follows covers the south, west and north shores in a clockwise direction from Bodrum.

Gümbet

Roughly 2km west of Bodrum on the peninsula's **south shore, GÜMBET** is the closest proper resort to the town – indeed, almost a suburb – and its 600-metre, tamarisk-lined gritty beach is usually wall-to-wall loungers, with parasailing, ringo-ing and water-skiing offshore. Development is exclusively package hotels and *pansiyons* – a hundred of them on the gradual slope behind, with more a-building – for the rowdy 18-to-30 set who have effectively claimed this bay.

Bitez

BİTEZ (Ağaçlı), the next cove west, reached by a different side road, is a little more staid and upmarket, and (along with Farilya, see below) seems to have adopted Gümbet's former role as a windsurfing and sailing centre, with *Sunworld* sailing packages prominently. There are quite a number of reasonable watering holes for the yachties, but the beach is negligible, even after artificial supplementing. Of the thirty-plus **hotels** here, the well-designed, three-star *Okaliptüs* (☎0252/343 1445, fax 343 1427; ⑦), nestled in a grove of said eucalyptus trees, is probably the pick of the bunch.

Ortakent

The south peninsular trunk road continues to **ORTAKENT** (still known by its old name Müsgebi), an inland village crowned by the early seventeenth-century Mustafa Paşa tower and blessed with abundant water and orchards. From both Ortakent and Yahşi, the next settlement, paved drives wind down several kilometres through oases to the longest, though not necessarily best, **beach** on the peninsula. Its two-kilometre extent has been closed to wheeled traffic, and the clutter of shops, mediocre restaurants and perhaps two-score of motels and small hotels just inland can make access problematic if you're not actually staying here. The resort is pitched almost totally to Turkish families, with lately a scattering of Czech and Russian tour groups. If you do choose to stay, you may as well plump for the top end of things here: the three-star *Club Petunya* (☎0252/348 3272, fax 348 3179; ⑦), right on the beach, with lodging in six separate garden buildings. It's available through several British package specialists, including *Sunquest* and *Turkey & Beyond*. Dolmuşes to the beach bear the legend "Ortakent Yahşi Sahil" or "Yahşi Yali".

Kargı, Bağla & Karaincir

Beyond Yahşi, a turning flanked with hotel signs at Gürece leads high above **KARGI** – a beach more commonly reached by boat from Bodrum (though there is good land-dolmuş service), and usually referred to in day-trip-speak as "Camel Beach" for obvious reasons. Curiously, there's little development as yet: just the three-star *Javelin Hotel* (☎0252/348 3189; ⑥) and a pair of waterfront restaurants, with the ubiquitous villas unobtrusively uphill and inland. The beach, and bay, are sandy and gently sloping.

BAĞLA, the next cove on, initially seems off-putting, with a water tank resembling an airport control tower planted amidst the villas that cover the the cape. But if you've arrived with your own transport, persevere by going straight past the old Greek chapel to the beachfront parking space, rather than following signs to a pair of mediocre restaurants' fee car park. A French-run scheme exploiting the oasis here as a paid-admission attraction seems thankfully to have expired, but then so apparently has the gushing spring which once fed a pond here. Nonetheless, the beach sand here is the softest – and the water the cleanest – in the vicinity of Bodrum town; accordingly, excursion boats arrive in force by noon.

KARAİNCİR, the next bay with public access, is nearly as good – 600m of sand guarded by a pair of headlands. Canoes and windsurfing boards are rented, and while mid-beach is completely crowded out by sunbeds and umbrellas, the south end of the strand inexplicably remains in its wild, natural state. Among places to **eat**, the adjacent *Dorya* and *Bal Mahmut'in Yeri* divide most of the custom between them, with a handful of snacky cafés or bars further south hemming in the beach a bit claustrophobically. Of a similar number of simple **motels** up by the main road, the *Bizimtepe* (☎0252/393 6322; ④) is recommended.

Akyarlar and beyond

Just around the bend, **AKYARLAR** (the former Greek port of Kefalouka) is more of an actual village, with a stone jetty, a mosque and a taxi rank. More to the point, this is your passport to good local **eating**, with cuisine and clientele far more Turkish, and prices far lower, than anywhere east of here. Current favourites include *Kücük Ev* and the restaurants attached to the *Akyarlar* and *Kılavuz* motels; you can **stay** most comfortably and quietly at the *Kılavuz* (☎0252/393 6006; ③) or the *Babadan* (☎0252/393 6002; ③). Akyarlar's beach is small and hardpacked, mostly given over to windsurfing, but with both Karaincir and the sandy cove below the *Simin Hotel* in the opposite direction within walking distance, this is no great loss.

Beyond Akyarlar the coast is completely packed out with villas and a very few *pansiyon*s, all staring across at nearby Kós (just two nautical miles distant here) and assorted Turkish islets. The good **beach** on the peninsula's southwesternmost cape is partly occupied by the *Armonia* time-share village, but the far end, under the **Hüseyin Burnu** lighthouse, offers free access and is popular with Turkish free-campers and caravanners, as well as a few German windsurfers, who repair to the *Fener* restaurant for sustenance; the cuisine here has been affected for the worse, but it's still the only place for a bite between here and Turgutreis.

Turgutreis

Once the road rounds the point to skirt the peninsula's **west shore**, the wind becomes stronger and the sand disappears, with nothing aside from villas until **TURGUTREİS**. As a strictly package resort, this runs a close second on the peninsula to Gümbet, with nearly a hundred hotels and a bona fide bus station inland, but the town is a sterile grid of streets, and the small exposed beach is closely pressed by the luckiest half-dozen **accommodation** outfits. Among these, the two-star *Sar Beach Hotel* (☎0252/382 3319; ⑤) is available through *Sunquest*.

Kadıkalesi

A side road starting by the Turgutreis *otogar* leads north to better things, through a fertile landscape of the tangerine groves for which the region is famous. After 4km you reach **KADIKALESİ**, with its long, partly protected sand beach and unbeatable views over to assorted islets. The old Greek church on the hill is about the most intact around Bodrum, but of the namesake "judge's castle" there seems to be no trace. As with Turgutreis, however, there is little **accommodation** available if you haven't arranged it in advance: the British tour operator *Mark Warner* owns the *Palm Beach* complex, French groups have taken over the *Yaprak Hotel*, and otherwise there's only another *Armonia* time-share scheme. Amazingly, only one **restaurant** – the *Körfez*, which does fish – survives, next to the parking lot and taxi rank behind the beach.

Gümüşlük

If you've had a bellyful of villa phalanxes, then sleepy **GÜMÜŞLÜK**, 2km past Kadıkalesi or 6km along a direct road from a turning at Gürece, is perhaps the perfect place. It partly occupies the site of **ancient Myndos**, so most new development has been prohibited by the archeological service. The majority of the sparse ruins litter the flat isthmus that links a giant, towering cape to the rest of the peninsula; you can scrabble around the unrestricted site, assisted by a placard map. Yachties are drawn here by the excellent deep anchorage between the headland and Tavşan Adası (Rabbit Island), with more traces of ancient Myndos; the namesake beasts are shy, and only emerge at night. The kilometre-long, sand-and-gravel **beach** extending south of the island is less protected but still attractive, with watersports gear for rent.

Among the bare handful of low-key **pansiyons** which have been allowed, the *Sisyphos* (☎0252/394 3016; ③), at the south end of the beach with a decent terrace restaurant, or the *Hera* at mid-beach (☎0252/394 3065; ③), cater well to independent travellers; other scruffier ones, such as the *Belde* or *Özak*, are worth avoiding – bedbugs and such await you. UK package companies *Tapestry* and *Simply Turkey* between them control the best of the often very characterful **self-catering villas** at the north end of things, overlooking the most sheltered part of the bay. Their presence has resulted in a surprising concentration of well-stocked shops in the shoreline hamlet here. The actual village of Gümüşlük lies 2km inland, from where you can climb to an abandoned ridgetop monastery.

A round dozen waterfront fish **restaurants** cater primarily to yacht passengers and seasonally resident Turks; most are outrageously priced, with expensive *meze*, obligatory service charges and (sometimes) stale fish. *Ali Reza* is the oldest, but rests on its laurels; the *Myndos*, aka *Cumhur'in Yeri*, at the opposite end of the waterfront, is better value, and open all year. The *Batı*, near *Ali Reza*, does meat as well as fish and has its own *pide* oven. *Gümüş Café*, much promoted locally, is overrated, with slow service and bland overpriced food – an unfortunate consequence of an undemanding clientele.

Yalıkavak

The **north flank** of the peninsula, served by a loop road out of Ortakent (or the narrower coastal route from Gümüşlük), in general has poor swimming and a relative lack of facilities. The trip over to **YALIKAVAK**, with glimpses of ocean from a windmill-studded ridge, is possibly more worthwhile than the destination itself. Formerly the area's main sponge-fishing port, it has now been ruthlessly gentrified in expectation of tourism, with its shorefront windmill marooned in a pedestrian zone which extends through most of the commercial district; vehicles can get little further than the small *otogar*. Few tourists, however, choose to brave the windswept, scrappy coast here, with just a handful of **hotels** exiled to either side of the town; these include the three-star *Gloria* (☎0252/385 4005, fax 385 4391; ⑥; available through *Sunquest*), 2km southwest, with a pool and sports facilities, and the relatively luxurious *Club Mirage* holiday village (☎0252/385 4437; ⑦), a similar distance north of town. Clifftop *Çimentepe*, on the coast road 2km southwest at Geriş Yalısa, is the best local **eatery**, with meat and fish dishes; it's inconspicuous, with no sign, so you recognize it by the *Hotel Gloria*'s swimming jetties below and the restaurant's own stone seating terrace.

Gündoğan (Farilya)

GÜNDOĞAN, three bays east, represents something of an improvement. Although the villas, as ever, are perched to right and left on the promontories framing the bay, the long, mostly narrow, but serviceable beach, divided by a small harbour, is little impinged upon. The tour company *Sunworld Sailing* maintains a big presence here with its windsurfers and small craft; the constant breeze does not, however, prevent swims. Mostly indifferent restaurants and bars extend right of the anchorage, while **accommodation** options clusters to the left; of these, the small *Villa Lale* motel (☎0252/387 7110; ④; available through *Tapestry*) sits right on the beach, while the *Hotel Gündoğan* (☎0252/387 7039, fax 387 7001; ④ without air conditioning, ⑤ with) has well-tended gardens but is apt to be monopolized by German groups. The main alternative is the simple *Farilya Motel* across the bay (☎0252/387 7015, fax 387 7105; ④), currently unaffiliated with any tour company. The old Greek name of Farilya has in fact been dusted off and enthusiastically pressed into service, part of a tentative reclamation of local Ottoman heritage. For more of that, you can walk a kilometre inland to Gündoğan village proper, where there's a ruined monastery to climb to, similar to the one at Gümüşlük.

Gölköy and Türkbuku

The turning for **GÖLKÖY**, 1km further east, is easy to miss, and indeed development is low-rise, with the improbably slender beach doubling as the shore path. Swimming platforms have been erected for diving into the cold, clear water by the half-dozen hopeful **motels**, which include the *Kaktüs Çiçeği* (☎0252/377 5253, fax 377 5248; ④). As at Farilya, restaurants are apt to be stuck in a snack-and-kebab rut; the only foreigners you're likely to see are those attending the local **yoga farm** run by Michael Cullingworth and Pervin Hakimoğlu (☎/fax 0252/357 7202, or in London ☎/fax 0181/291 7981). They run the place as a guesthouse (③) between the seven week-long courses offered between May and October.

TÜRKBÜKÜ, just around the corner and on the same dolmuş route, has lost what little beach it had following enlargement of the quay – everyone swims from platforms. The clientele is overwhelmingly forty-something İstanbul trendies, who often come ashore from the motor and sail yachts at anchor, with the indented local coast and island providing shelter for even more craft than at Gümüşlük. But accommodation is minimal, architecture relentlessly concrete, and restaurants indifferent, so if you're not a member of this constituency, give the place a miss.

Torba

Last stop on the loop road if you're travelling clockwise, **TORBA** has had its kernel of an old port utterly overwhelmed by several soulless purpose-built holiday complexes; a piney backdrop is the place's most conspicuous asset, as the bay is essentially beachless. As at so many spots on the peninsula, there's little for the independent traveller or day-tripper (other than ferry service to Didyma). However, *Club Galata* (☎0252/367 1572, fax 367 1574; ⑤; available through *Tapestry* or *Turkey & Beyond*), a small, gourmet hotel backing what little pebbly shore there is, may have room for non-package tourists.

East of Bodrum: carpet villages

The Bodrum peninsula extends east of the modern highway in from Milas, the twisty but paved old road winding through pine hills to Mumcular, past several of the so-called "carpet villages" where the tawny-hued Milas carpets are woven. **ETRİM**, on the dirt road down to Çiftlik, is the most famous target of special-interest tours from town, while unprepossessing **MUMCULAR** has the most retail carpet shops, but all told the area's not worth the detour unless you're intent on buying a carpet – and have your own vehicle. Dolmuşes come here rarely, and tend to stick to the Milas–Mumcular stretch of road.

Muğla and around

MUĞLA, capital of the province containing several of the biggest resorts on the Aegean, is something of a showcase town and an exception to the Turkish rule of dire urban architecture. A well-planned modern quarter incorporates spacious tree-lined boulevards and accommodates some hillside **Ottoman neighbourhoods** that are among the finest in Turkey. A leisurely stroll through lanes of well-maintained eighteenth-century white houses, with their tiled roofs, beaked chimneys and ornate doors, is well worth half a day. The **bazaar**, a grid of neat alleys nestling at the base of the old residential slope to the north, is divided roughly by trade (blacksmiths predominating) and contrasts sharply with Milas's untidy jumble; the **Yağcılar Hanı** is an even more serene shopping experience, being a restored *kervansaray* located on Kursunlu Caddesi. The **Konakaltı Hanı** on Saathkulealtı Caddesi is another restored *kervansaray*, now operating as an art gallery. More personal is a visit to **Hafıze Kaşıkara's house**, a 250-year-old *konak* with beautifully carved ceilings and a display of handmade carpets that the owner herself weaves on a loom.

Muğla is also much the best base for visiting **Stratonikya**, on the road to Milas, and Gerga (see p.365). It's also the closest town of note to the up-and-coming resort of **Akyaka**, the first coastal settlement you encounter at the bottom of the winding grade descending south from Muğla's plateau.

Practicalities

Muğla's **tourist information office** (summer Mon–Fri 8am–7pm; winter Mon–Fri 8am–noon & 1–5pm; ☎0252/214 3127), on the central roundabout sporting an Atatürk statue, is more enthusiastic than most and may have stocks of worthwhile handouts exhausted at other branches. They also provide a good map of the town.

Accommodation is somewhat limited, but since Muğla is not exactly deluged with tourists, this shouldn't be a problem. The quietest and least expensive mid-range option is the fairly new *Otel Saray* (☎0252/214 1594, fax 214 3722; ③), facing the produce market but dead calm at night, with comfortable rooms with baths and balconies. The gracefully ageing *Yalçın* (☎0252/214 1599, fax 214 1050; ③), across from the *otogar*, has larger, marginally more expensive rooms with enormous, refurbished bathrooms, but traffic noise is a nuisance. There's also the *Petek Hotel* on Marmaris Bulvarı (☎0252/214 3135, fax 214 2423; ④), but it's even noisier, with no balconies, and if you're going to splash out you may as well do so at the brand-new, strangely named *Grand Brothers*, with a swimming pool, on the road west out of town (☎0252/212 2700, fax 212 2610; ⑥).

Eating out, either the *Bolu Mengen Lokantası*, on Kursunlu Caddesi just below the Yağcılar Hanı, or the *Altın Sofrası Kebap Salonu*, on the ground floor of the (not recommended) *Zeybek Hotel*, Turgutreis Cad 5, are fine for lunch or a simple, booze-less supper. In the Mustafa Muğlali Işhanı near the *otogar* there's the licensed *Bulvar Ocakbaşi*, which has a good line in spit-roasted chickens but very limited *meze* or steam-tray food; a cheaper, more versatile option is the nearby *Sabah Lokantasi* opposite the *Saray Otel*, again licensed with both *meyhane* fare and *hazır yemek*, and well frequented for the sake of its pleasant outdoor seating opposite a fountain. For **dessert**, look no further than *Nazar Ün Mamulleri*, on the *otogar* side of Mustafa Muğlali Işhanı, which in addition to the bread and sticky cakes promised by the name does wonderful *dondurma*, with queues on summer nights for such flavours as kiwi, honey almond and chicken.

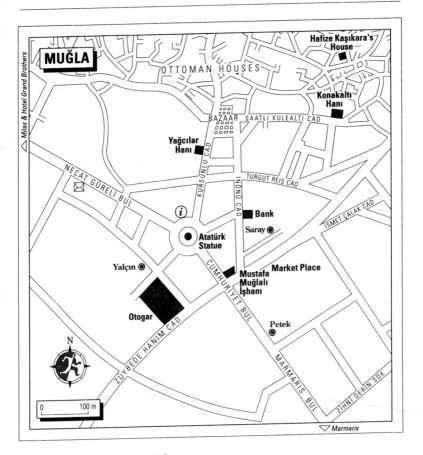

Stratonikya (Stratoniceia)

The ancient city of **STRATONİKYA**, 36km west of Muğla, would be more acclaimed if it weren't for a giant lignite quarry immediately west, whose noise and dust considerably reduce the peace and atmosphere; that the site continues to exist at all is a tribute to the Ministry of Culture's obstinace in the face of the coal company's demands to swallow it up. The archeological zone occupies the site of tumbledown Eskihisar village, nearly all of whose population has moved 3km west to a new settlement. Still, if you have your own vehicle or time to spare, the ruins are worth a visit. Signs direct you through the crumbling houses, themselves worthy museum pieces of 1930s architecture, past the abandoned teahouse and vandalized mosque to a parking area beside the makeshift sculpture depot noted below; $1 admission is payable when the portakabin is staffed.

Stratonikya was a third-century Seleucid foundation, but its heyday occurred during the Roman Imperial period, so everything you can see now dates from that time. A few paces north of the empty teahouse is the Roman **gymnasium**, an elaborate structure with a colonnaded semicircular chamber sandwiched between three quadrangles of massive masonry. At the edge of the village, overlooking the opencast mine, is the **north city gate**, flanked by a lone, unfluted Corinthian column, just outside of which is a fragment of a **sacred way** that once led to a shrine of Hecate at nearby Lagina. By the pavement stands a **subterranean tomb** in good condition, the sole survivor of a necropolis which, like the sacred way, has been sacrificed to mining interests. Bits of the substantial **city wall** are incorporated into houses on the west side of Eskihisar, with more chunks visible marching up the hillside to the south.

On the opposite side of the village is the most imposing remnant of Stratonikya, a vast rectangular precinct identified either as a **bouleuterion** or a **shrine of Serapis**. The first thing you'll see is an isolated, rectangular **monumental gateway** erected a few metres west, but currently entry is via twin staircases bored through the south and north side walls; the north wall's interior is covered with inscriptions. Its possible role as a council house is supported by the five rows of seats, overlooking the countryside to the east. Southeast of here, the garden of an ochre-stained building serves as an impromptu **museum-cum-warehouse**, where finds from the excavation have been temporarily stored.

Akyaka

Situtated at the very head of the Gökova Gulf, with steep Sakara Tepe looming overhead, scenic **AKYAKA** has always been popular with Turkish holidaymakers but is now attracting foreign tourists; in the UK, *Sunquest*, *Tapestry* and *Simply Turkey* all represent properties here. The resort itself is arrayed along a somewhat dull, if unobjectionable grid of streets on a slight slope amidst dense pine forest; private villas are interspersed between *pansiyon*s and small hotels, most built attractively in a sort of mock-Ottoman-*köşk* architecture mandated by a local preservation code. Although Akyaka's town beach consists of short, hard-packed sand, merely suitable for getting into the clear waters of the gulf, there's a much better gravel beach 2.5km west of town, beyond the old *iskele*, and another more utilitarian strand to the east, beyond the river mouth here.

On the river bank stands Akyaka's most unusual **accommodation**, a restored water-mill house represented exclusively by *Simply Turkey*. Totally opposite in style is the top-end, three-star *Yücelen* (☎0252/248 5108, fax 243 5434; ⑥; available through *Sunquest*), just inland at the village centre, with vast common areas and a large pool. The cosier *Engin* (☎0252/243 5727, fax 243 5609; ④), with a small pool, is isolated out by reed beds, east towards the river, while the two-star *Erdem* (☎0252/243 5849; ⑤), 1km out of mid-village, offers both a pool and easy beach access. If you're caravanning overland, there's a forestry **campsite** with good amenities on the west side of the "urban grid". In the village centre, there are few **restaurants** independent of the hotels: try the *Deniz*, at the old *iskele*, or one of several fish restaurants marooned on an island in the local river, with reedbeds and ducks for decor. **Dolmuşes** ply regularly to and from Marmaris and Muğla, though if you'd rather drive yourself there are several car-rental agencies in the resort.

Marmaris

MARMARIS runs a close second to Kuşadası as the largest and most developed Aegean resort. Boosters call it *Yeşil Marmaris* – "Green Marmaris" – which it certainly is, but they omit mention of the dampness, the ferocious mosquitoes and the amorphous concrete sprawl that extends for nearly 10km around the bay. All this dwarfs the old village core of shops and *lokanta*s lining narrow, bazaar-like streets, which form an intricate warren contrasting strongly with the slick European-looking marina and waterfront. According to legend, the place was named when Süleyman the Magnificent, not finding the castle here to his liking, was heard to mutter *"Mimarı as"* (Hang the architect), later corrupted to "Marmaris" – a command that ought perhaps still to apply to the designers of the seemingly endless tower blocks.

Marmaris's **Netsel yacht marina**, Turkey's largest, has more than anything else shaped the town's character – this is the main base for most yacht charter organizations operating on the Turquoise Coast. Proximity to Dalaman airport also means that both foreign and domestic tourists pour in non-stop during the warmer months, imparting to the town a certain pressure-cooker quality which may not be to everyone's liking. However, the construction craze which gripped Marmaris from the late Eighties until the early Nineties is over for the time being, and the town now seems intent on consolidating an image as a "quality" resort.

Marmaris's **history** has been determined above all by the stunning local topography: a deep, fjord-like inlet surrounded by pine-cloaked hills. This did not seem to spur ancient Physcus, the original Dorian colony, to any growth or importance, but Süleyman comfortably assembled a force of 200,000 here in 1522, when launching the successful siege of the Knights of St John's base in Rhodes. Shortly after this campaign Süleyman endowed the old town nucleus with the tiny castle and a *han*. In 1798 Nelson's entire fleet sheltered here before setting out to defeat Napoleon's armada at the Battle of Aboukir.

Arrival and information

The **otogar** is two blocks behind the yacht marina on the east side of town, just a few minutes' walk from the town centre. The *Havaş* **airport bus** from Dalaman leaves you in front of the *THY* office on Atatürk Caddesi, the long shore road usually known as Kordon Caddesi. The main bus companies – *Varan, Ulusoy, Pamukkale, Kamil Koç, Hakiki Koç* – all have offices at the Kordon Caddesi end of Ulusal Egemenlik Bulvarı, and all run service buses to connect with their company's major routes. It's always worth asking if they have a service to connect with your bus – they almost definitely provide something on request.

If you show up with your own **car**, be aware that no parking is allowed anywhere along the Kordon. Arriving by **ferry or hydrofoil** from the Greek island of Rhodes, the dock conveniently abuts İskele Meydanı, on one side of which stands the **tourist information office** (summer daily 8am–8pm; winter Mon–Fri 8am–noon & 1–5pm; ☎0252/412 1035), dispensing town plans, bus schedules and accommodation lists.

Accommodation

Accommodation in Marmaris is generally mega-hotel-oriented and thus expensive; there is no concentration of *pansiyon*s or small hotels as in Turkey's other coastal resorts. Since the completion of the yacht harbour, most *pansiyon*s have vanished from Barbaros Caddesi, as the waterfront east of the castle is known. A handful of very basic establishments survive in the bazaar district, and somewhat better value for money can be had out at the west end of the Kordon, close to its split into Kemal Seyfettin Elgin Caddesi and Uzunyalı beach. One consolation for budget travellers: Marmaris has two excellent, IYHF-affiliated **youth hostels**.

Town centre

There's little worth singling out here, as space considerations, noise levels and property values mean few hotels with either character or amenities.

Hotel Begonya, Hacı Mustafa Sok 101 (☎0252/412 4095). Delightful renovated barn with designer architecture and enclosed garden, but loud music from nearby bars can be a nuisance. ⑤.

Interyouth Hostel 1, 42 Sok 45, near the PTT (☎0252/412 3687). Double rooms as well as dorm accommodation; the usual hostel services, but hopelessly overcrowded in season. Dorms $6 per head, doubles ②.

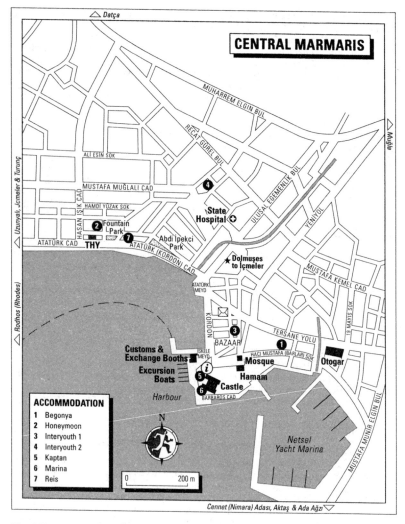

CENTRAL MARMARIS

△ Datça

MUHARREM ELGIN BUL

RECAİ GÜREL BUL

ALİ ESİN SOK

ULUSAL EGEMENLİK BUL

YENİYOL

△ Muğla

Uzunyalı, İcmeler & Turunç ▷

HASAN IŞIK CAD

MUSTAFA MUĞLALI CAD

HAMDİ YÜZAK SOK

4

State Hospital ✚

2 Fountain
Park
ATATÜRK CAD **THY** **7** ATATÜRK (KORDON) CAD

Abdi İpekci
Park

★ **Dolmuşes to İçmeler**

MUSTAFA KEMEL CAD

19 MAYIS SOK

ATATÜRK
MEYD.

◁ Rodhos (Rhodes)

KORDON

TERSANE YOLU

3

BAZAAR

1

Customs &
Exchange Booths

Excursion
Boats

İSKELE
MEYD.

i

5

6

Castle

BARBAROS CAD

Mosque

Hamam

HACI MUSTAFA (BARLAR) SOK

Otogar

MUSTAFA MÜNİR ELGİN BUL

Harbour

N

*Netsel
Yacht Marina*

ACCOMMODATION
1 Begonya
2 Honeymoon
3 Interyouth 1
4 Interyouth 2
5 Kaptan
6 Marina
7 Reis

0   200 m

Cennet (Nimara) Adası, Aktaş & Ada Ağzı ▽

Hotel Kaptan, Barbaros Cad 11 (☎0252/412 1251). The most central location in town, with plain but acceptable rooms. ④.

Hotel Marina, Barbaros Cad 37 (☎0252/412 6598). Somewhat better than the *Kaptan* for the same money, with neater rooms and less street noise. ④.

Uzunyalı beach and west

Some three hundred hotels line the five-kilometre beach strip west of town. Luxury, all-inclusive complexes, such as (in order of encountering them) the *Grand Azur*, *MGM*, *Altınyunus*, *Grand Yazıcı* and *Iberotel*, cluster towards the far end, as well as still further west in İçmeler, 9km west of town. Closer to the town centre, properties tend to be older – ie 1970s-built – and show it, but are no cheaper for that. For the best value try seafront establishments in the neighbourhood of the *Turban Hotel*, at the edge of the built-up area, or go a few blocks inland. Kenan Evren Bulvarı, incidentally, is the continuation of Kemal Seyfettin Elgin Caddesi, running parallel to the beach but slightly inland.

Pansiyon Cihan, at the start of the İçmeler road near the *Turban* (☎0252/412 5549). One of several, similarly modest and friendly establishments here. ③.

Pansiyon Honeymoon, passage off Uzunyalı 22 near the *Çubuk Otel* (☎0252/412 3001). Well maintained, and offering fair value. ③.

Interyouth Hostel 2, 300m beyond the state hospital on the Datça road (☎0252/412 6432). A newish, three-storey outfit with all mod cons; less convenient than *Interyouth Hostel 1*, but quieter. Dorms $6 per head, doubles ②.

Hotel Karadeniz, Atatürk Cad (Kordon) 68 (☎0252/412 3642). Comfortable and well run in a convenient location. ⑤.

Hotel Lidya, Kenan Evren Bulvarı, 4km from centre (☎0252/412 2940). The oldest luxury hotel in Marmaris still has the most character and smoothest service. Good beach facilities, casino on site. ⑥.

Reis Hotel, on the seafront at Uzunyalı 6 (☎0252/412 4417). Quieter than others in this area. ⑤.

Pansiyon Sembol 3, Turban Yolu 20, off the west end of Kenan Evren Bulvarı (☎0252/412 1356). Good value for a quiet seafront location. ④.

East of town

A handful of pleasant small hotels can be found at Aktaş, 4km east of the marina near a forest-fringed beach; further out are more secluded hotels frequented by the yacht set between trips.

Scotland Hotel, Aktaş (☎0252/412 7046). Newish hotel with pleasant garden, friendly management, live guitar music and singing promised nightly. ④.

Stardust Marine Yat Hotel, Ada Ağızı, 6km east of town (☎0252/412 3535). Delightful, French-managed spot on an isolated bay, with an excellent restaurant. ④.

Camping

Camping is probably not such a good idea in the immediate surroundings of Marmaris. With the skyrocketing value of real estate, most campsite owners plan to build villas or *pansiyon*s on their patch, so facilities tend to be rudimentary, poorly maintained and noisy. Your best bet near the centre is to stroll along Uzunyalı beach and see who's operating this year between the building sites. Better still, head out of town altogether: 20km or so away on the Datça road, there are several well-equipped sites; 8km south at Açmeler, *Karya Mocamp* and *Mustafa Camping* are permanent fixtures; and some 1500m east of Marmaris, past the Günnücek forestry reserve set aside to protect the resin-producing tree *Liquidambar orientalis*, is *Dimet Camping* (☎0252/412 1963).

The Town

Ulusal Egemenlik Bulvarı cuts Marmaris roughly in half, and the maze of narrow streets to the east of it is home to most of the monuments and facilities – including the castle, bazaar, banks, PTT – of interest to the average tourist. Numerous travel agencies and bus company ticket offices cluster a hundred or so metres to either side of Atatürk Meydanı, the seashore plaza at the base of Ulusal Egemenlik.

Little is left of the sleepy fishing village that Marmaris was a mere two decades ago. The bazaar, including its diminutive *kervansaray*, now rivals those at İstanbul or Kuşadası in its array of glitzy kitsch on offer, and only the **Kaleiçi** district, the brief warren of streets at the base of the tiny castle, offers a pleasant wander. The **fortress** itself (daily 8am–noon & 1–5pm; $1) is not yet up and running as a fully stocked museum; it mostly serves as a venue for events during the May festival (see "Listings" below).

In any case, you don't come to Marmaris for cultural edification, and you swim off the badly polluted **Kordon beach** at your peril – though this doesn't seem to to deter the hundreds of bathers who use it daily. Far safer to take a dolmuş out to **İçmeler**, 9km west of Marmaris (regular services from Ulusal Egemenlik Bulvarı), a recently developed resort of some fifty package hotels, plus a handful of inexpensive *pansiyon*s in the old village core, which survives precariously at the far edge of the resort. Here the sand is coarse but cleaner than at Kordon, as is the sea.

All in all a better way of spending time here is to take a **boat excursion**, whether a short outing or a two-week cruise (see box opposite). **Day trips** usually visit highlights of the inner bay, not venturing much beyond the straits separating Cennet and Keçi islands. Most skippers will take you to a beach on the north side of Cennet Adası, and caves on the south shore, then complete the day with a visit to Kumlubükü or Turunç coves (see "Around Marmaris" below for full descriptions). Since all of these spots are more or less difficult to reach by land, it's worth the effort – and the price of $8–20 per person may include a full lunch.

One offer that you definitely can refuse is an excursion to Kaunos from Marmaris: because of the distance involved, you'll spend six-plus hours sailing and at best two hours sightseeing. Kaunos (see p.398) is more usually reached from Dalyan or as part of a lengthy cruise.

Eating and drinking

Getting a decent **meal** at a reasonable price is something of a challenge in Marmaris: don't expect much solace even **in the bazaar**, where restaurants have been uniformly gentrified. Offering relatively good value among the latter are *Halil İbrahim Sofrası* (near the PTT) and *Yeni Liman Restaurant* (Kemeraltı Sok), where a Turkish home-style meal can be had for $10.

East of the castle, the waterfront spots along Barbaros Caddesi will run to $20 apiece for a meal with wine, provided you stay away from the seafood. *Mr Zek's*, run by a former chef of the *İstanbul Hilton*, and *Mona Titti*, noted for its eccentric menu (eg, chicken wings, crêpes), stand out in terms of quality here. The longest-running star of the local culinary scene is *Türkay Restaurant* at Hacı Mustafa Sokağı ("Bar Street") 107, which combines Turkish themes with a French touch to excellent effect – at about $40 a head. The *Antik* overlooking the Netsel Marina offers cosy atmosphere and impeccable service for about $30 per person.

Simple pizzerias and other spots serving light meals abound **along the Kordon** and further west, where homesick Britons seek relief at various English-named outfits serving indifferently cooked "English" food. An exception to this pattern is *Turhan* at Uzunyalı 26, offering pizza and Turkish dishes for about $8 a meal.

In **İçmeler**, *Küçük Ev* serves probably the widest selection of *hazır yemek* in the area, for $10–20 per head, including beer.

Nightlife

Most of Marmaris's tippling takes place along Hacı Mustafa Sokağı, which in recent years has become a full-fledged "Bar Street" along the lines of its namesake in Kuşadası. More than two dozen clubs here feature increasingly sophisticated designer profiles and various sorts of (usually live) music, often in spacious inner courtyards; names and favourites change yearly, if not more often. The yachties expand their liver capacities during happy hour at several pubs within the marina, such as *Scorpio* or *Pineapple* (the latter with snacks too). At the casinos of luxury hotels such as the *Altınyunus* and *Lidya*, buying a certain amount of chips entitles visitors to a sumptuous complimentary buffet dinner, which can be enjoyed even if one ends up cashing in most (or all) of said chips.

Listings

Airlines *İstanbul Hava Yolları*, Kenan Evren Bul 88/B (☎0252/412 6627); *THY*, Atatürk Cad 50/B (☎0252/412 3751); *Top Air*, Kenan Evren Bul 72/10 (☎0252/412 0015).

Airport Both *THY* (*Havaş*) and *İstanbul Hava Yolları* have service buses to Dalaman airport, 90km east, departing from their respective town offices 2hr 45min before flight departures. In addition, the *Marmaris Belediyesi* runs 2 daily buses to the airport.

Books *Şehrazat*, across from Hacı Mustafa Sok 49, behind the castle, has some used English books to trade. *NET*, in the bazaar, stocks nautical charts of the area for use on your coastal cruise. *Hittite*, the book and music store, is on Hacı Mustafa Sok; *Marmaris International Bookstore* at Talat Paşa Sok.

THE *MAVİ YOLCULUK:* COASTAL BOAT CHARTERS

As noted in the Bodrum account (p.339), Cevat Şakir Kabaağaçlı immortalized the *Mavi Yolculuk* (Blue Cruise) with his eponymous work, and now such a cruise is an all-but-obligatory feature of a visit to coastal Caria, for visiting Turks as well as foreigners. Life on deck is so rife with comic and romantic possibilities that there was even a Turkish TV soap during the late 1980s, entitled *Mavi Tur*.

Literary and media antecedents notwithstanding, chartering either a motor schooner (*gület*) or a smaller yacht out of Marmaris will allow you to explore the convoluted coast between Bodrum and Kaş. Especially out of high season, the daily cost isn't necessarily prohibitive – no more than renting a medium-sized car, for example – and in the case of a *gület*, a knowledgeable crew will be included. Virtually all of the shore described in this chapter and the next is fair game, plus many other hidden anchorages accessible only by sea.

You can pre-book a yacht charter from the UK through specialist operators (see *Basics* for details), or you can make arrangements on the spot; though prices are always quoted in US dollars or sterling, it's possible to pay in Turkish lira. Substantial deposits are required – usually fifty percent of the total price – so deciding to take a "Blue Cruise" is not something to be indulged in lightly.

If you're uncertain about your level of commitment, or have shown up alone or in a very small group, the best option is what's called a **cabin charter**. Several companies set aside one schooner whose berths are let out individually; the craft departs on a particular day of the week with a fixed, "sample" itinerary of seven days. Prices in April, May and October are $320 per person, including all food and watersports equipment – excellent value. From June to September the cost jumps to around $415.

If you can assemble a large group, and have more time at your disposal, consider a **standard charter** of a twenty-metre motor schooner. A group of twelve, for example, will during May or October pay $34 each daily, not including food or sporting equipment, while a group of eight will be more comfortable and less crowded but will pay $38 a day. From June to September, count on $42–50 each per day for the same-sized groups.

Companies often offer to supply food for about $15 minimum per day each passenger, though there's a sizable mark-up hidden in this, and you'd spend about the same eating two meals a day on shore. Probably the best strategy is to dine in restaurants at your evening mooring and to keep the galley stocked for breakfast and snacks; if you tip the crew appropriately they're usually happy to shop for you.

For the greatest degree of independence, so-called **bareboat yacht charter** is the answer. This assumes that at least one of your party is a certified skipper; otherwise count on at least $130 a day extra to engage one. Prices are usually quoted by the week, and in April or October work out around $250 per person. During June or September allow $320 each per week.

One of the oldest and more reliable charter **agencies** in Marmaris is *Yeşil Marmaris*, Barbaros Caddesi 11, PO Box 8, 48700 Marmaris (☎0252/412 2290). For bareboat yachts, one of the larger local operators is *Offshore Sailing* at the Albatros Marina, 3km east of Netsel Marina (☎0252/412 3430, fax 412 0755).

Car rental The majors include *Avis*, Kordon Cad 30 (☎0252/412 2771); *Budget*, Ulusal Egemenlik Cad 12 (☎0252/412 4144); *Europcar/InterRent*, Kordon Cad 12 (☎0252/412 2001); and *Hertz*, İskele Meydanı (☎0252/412 2552). Small chains and local independents include *Airtour*, Kenan Evren Bul, İlter Sok 18/A (☎0252/412 3915); *DeCar*, Ulusal Egemenlik Cad, Rodoslu Kemal İş Hanı 13 (☎0252/413 4669); *Intercity*, İskele Meyd 41 (☎0252/413 0106); *LeMar*, Kemal Seyfettin Elgin Bul 4 (☎0252/412 3222).

Consulate Honorary British consulate on Hacı Mustafa Sok near the marina (☎0252/416 2310, mobile ☎0532/262 7661, 24hr).

Exchange Assorted *döviz* booths along the Kordon and near the ferry jetty stay open until 8–9.30pm daily, including Sundays and holidays. In addition, Marmaris is well sown with the usual repertoire of foreign credit/debit-card-accepting ATMs.

Ferries and hydrofoils Authorized agents include *Yeşil Marmaris*, Barbaros Cad 11 (☎0252/412 2290), and *Engin Turizm*, Kordon Cad 10 (☎0252/412 1082). Hydrofoils, running twice daily in season to Rhodes at 9.30am and 4.30pm, have largely supplanted the slower ferries; fares, excluding Turkish and Greek port taxes totalling $25, are $24 single, $32 day return and $40 open return. *Yeşil Marmaris* still runs its own car ferry to Rhodes twice weekly (currently Tues and Sat at 9.30am) for much the same prices. There's also a twice-weekly domestic hydrofoil to Bodrum.

Festival Yachting regatta and arts presentations take place in the second week of May, when the accommodation situation will be tight. Another yacht race occurs during the first week of November.

Hamam The old one in the rear of the bazaar on Eski Cami Arkası 3 (daily 8am–midnight for both sexes) is not especially cheap: the works (massage, tea, etc) cost $7. The plush, newer *Ottoman Hamam* off the Datça road costs slightly less.

Hospitals The state hospital is at the junction of Ulusal Egemenlik and the Datça road; *Ahu Hetman* private hospital is in Armutalan suburb.

Around Marmaris: the Rhodian Peraea

In ancient times the peninsula extending from the head of the Gulf of Gökova to a promontory between the Greek islands of Symi and Rhodes was known as the **Rhodian Peraea** – the mainland territory of the three united city-states of Rhodes, which controlled the area for eight centuries. Despite this, and the fact that the natives were granted full Rhodian citizenship, there is little evidence of the long tenure; the peninsula was – and is – a backwater, today known as the Hisarönü, Loryma or Daraçya peninsula, depending on which map you look at or yacht skipper you ask. In fact, yachts have up to now been the principal means of getting around this irregular landmass, and although a proper road was completed in 1989, the difficulty of access has so far kept development to a minimum and the locals amazingly friendly. If you're not privileged enough to have a yacht handy, the most rewarding way of seeing the area is on foot.

North: the Gökova Gulf shore

The shores of the Gökova Gulf – see also Ören (p.330) and Akyaka (p.350) – were long the last remaining pristine seascape of southwest Turkey. So it was all the sadder when, in late July 1996, a massive **forest fire** roared along the southerly shore between the Muğla–Marmaris road and the Marmaris–Datça highway, reducing thousands of forested acres to ashes. Among the spots listed below, Karacasöğüt and Taşbükü were the hardest hit; it took weeks to reopen main roads and motels, though tourism should probably be almost back to normal by mid-1997.

In Marmaris you'll probably notice signs pitching an excursion to "Cleopatra's Isle". This is actually **SEDİR ADASI** (Cedar Island), an islet near the head of the Gulf of Gökova, which still sports extensive fortifications and a theatre from its time as Cedreae, a city of the Peraea. More evocative, however, is its alleged role as a trysting place of Cleopatra and Mark Antony, and the legend concerning the island's **beach** – the main goal of the day trips. The sand was supposedly brought from Africa at Mark Antony's behest, and indeed analysis has shown that the grains are not from local strata.

The usual way of getting to the island (where you may well be charged an additional $4 admission by the resident warden) is by tour boat, departing between 10 and 11am from **ÇAMLI İSKELESİ**, 6km down a side road beginning 12km north of Marmaris; there's no public transport to the departure point, so you must use the tour operator's shuttle bus. The boats return at 4 or 5pm.

Alternative access is by much briefer boat excursion from the hamlet of **TAŞBÜKÜ**, 4km further along the same road and just opposite the islet. Again there's no dolmuş in, but there are two **motel-campsites** with attached **restaurants**, of which the friendly *Çamlı* (☎0252/495 8085, fax 495 8080; ②) is the preferable; if you phone in good time the management might arrange to shuttle you in. This formerly well-vegetated area is idyllic if small-scale, and the sand-and-gravel beach is not nearly so stony as the name Taşbükü (Stone Cove) implies. Just inland from the two beach motels stand the self-catering *Mandalin Villas*, represented exclusively by *Simply Turkey* in the UK, but their appeal will likely be diminished if they've lost their green environment to the recent blaze.

Besides the obvious jaunt over to Sedir Adası, there are also boat outings available to **İNGİLİZLİMANI** – a beautiful fjord reachable only by sea, which got its name ("English Harbour") from a World War II incident when a British ship sought shelter from pursuing Germans in these neutral waters.

Boats based at Çamlı İskelesi also call at **KARACASÖĞÜT**, accessible by land via another side road 11km north of Marmaris. It's 13km (the occasional village-bound dolmuş will take you the first 11km) to this almost landlocked bay, girded by willows and what's remained of the local greenery post-conflagration, with the wall of mountains north of the open gulf as a backdrop. It's a big yacht and *gület* haven, and you can watch the action from several **restaurants** overlooking the bay. The main **beach**, alas, is muddy and has two creeks draining onto it, so you can really only swim off the purpose-built platform jutting out into the water, well away from the boats and the shore.

South to Bozburun

Overland access to the bulk of the **Loryma (Hisarönü) peninsula** is by way of a recently paved road, which branches south from the main Datça-bound highway, 21km west of Marmaris, and describes a loop back to Marmaris via Selimiye, Bayır, Turunç and İçmeler.

Orhaniye and Selimiye

The first place (9km along) anyone, including dolmuşes, stops is **ORHANİYE** – but mostly for the yacht anchorage. The two small hotels and mere half-dozen *pansiyon*s here are a reflection of the mostly muddy, sumpy shallows, though further out in the bay lurks a celebrated curiosity: a long, narrow, submerged sandspit known as **Kızkumu** (Maiden's Sand) extending halfway across the bay, which allows day-trippers apparently to emulate Jesus walking on the Sea of Galilee. Legend asserts that a local beauty, menaced by raiding pirates, filled her skirts with sand and attempted to escape across the water by creating her own causeway, but upon exhausting her supply at mid-bay, drowned herself rather than surrender her virtue to the marauders.

SELİMİYE, 9km further south, is the next coastal village where visitors tend to stop, again mostly by yacht. A hilltop Ottoman fort overlooks the port here, at the head of an all-but-landlocked arm of the giant Delikyol bay. Numerous quayside restaurants are aimed mostly at the passing boat trade, as are the half-dozen *pansiyon*s which have sprouted since the road was paved. You may decide to **stay** at the *Güvercin* (☎0252/446 4274; ③) by the small beach at the far western end of the straggly village – when the yachts are gone life passes very slowly. *Boşver* (literally "Never mind, not bothered"), the name of a fishing boat moored here, about sums up the mood of the place.

Bozburun and beyond

BOZBURUN, just over the hill from Selimiye, is more of a proper town, but still has a firm nautical orientation: yacht repairs and supplies are conspicuously on offer, and boatyards occupy a large area. The settlement itself is undistinguished, slumbering in dusty heat six months of the year, but its setting, on a convoluted gulf with a fat islet astride its mouth, and the Greek island of Sími beyond, is startling.

The place is unlikely to go the way of Datça (see below), even with the recently asphalted road, since there is precious little level land for villas, even less fresh water, and absolutely no sand beaches. Nonetheless Bozburun has long been a very "in" resort for certain Turks: former SDP party leader Erdal İnönü holidayed here, and various eccentrics – ex-journalists turned bartenders, recording executives turned restaurant proprietors, diehard Turkish hippies – collect in this most isolated corner of coastal Turkey.

Pansiyon proprietors will collar you as you alight the thrice-daily dolmuş from Marmaris, but if you're staying a while, it's best to fend them off and call for a boat to *Sabrina's House* (☎0252/456 2045; $350 per person per week B&B), a German-run, television- and traffic-free idyll set on the far edge of the harbour. This tasteful haven amidst burgeoning gardens has dissimilar, suite-like units and (of necessity) an excellent restaurant; without a boat shuttle, it's a thirty-minute walk there, partly along the road signposted to "Hotel Mete". Less expensive alternatives closer to town include (on the left as you face the sea) *Pembe Yunus* (☎0252/456 2154; ③), run by strong-willed Fatma Hanım, late of İstanbul. Cement swimming platforms dot the shore here so you won't miss a beach.

Most of the five or six quayside **restaurants** offer variable food and laconic service to the *Mavi Tur* crowd; best of the lot is probably the *Akvaryum*, owned by the wife of a former government minister. The trendy set, whether Turkish landlubbers or yachties, gathers at the *Mariners Bar*, run by yet another refugee from the İstanbul rat-race.

Unless you've eloped with someone, boredom could become a problem in Bozburun; the boat day trips advertised rarely leave the confines of the bay. In cooler weather you could walk east one valley to **SÖĞÜT**, essentially a farming oasis with a minimal shore settlement boasting two restaurants and a like number of *pansiyon*s. The dolmuş serving Söğüt terminates at **TAŞLICA**, a hilltop village girded by almonds and olives sprouting from what's otherwise a stone desert. From the square where the dolmuş leaves you, a three- to four-hour trail leads south to ancient **Loryma**, where a Rhodian-built fort overlooks the magnificent harbour of Bozukkale – which in turn holds several restaurants. If you don't want to walk back the same way, you just might be able to hitch a boat ride out from here.

The east coast of the Hisarönü peninsula

From Selimiye, the main loop road climbs inland to **BAYİR**, a mountain village spread across an amphitheatre of rocky terraces, whose distinctive feature is an ancient, much-venerated plane tree on its main square; there are teahouses adjacent to contemplate it. A side road leads down from here to **Çiftlik bay**, a once-isolated beach now dominated by a huge holiday village and signs of more development to come.

Turunç

The main route curls north back towards Marmaris, with another spur road leading down to **TURUNÇ**, which since the late 1980s has metamorphosed from a few farms and two ramshackle restaurants into an exclusively package venue rivalling İçmeler. The core of the resort is a 500-metre beach of coarse sand, backed by impressive, pine-tufted cliffs which formerly blocked easy overland access to Turunç. These are now dotted with hotels and villas, some of whose residents commute to sea level using cogwheel chair-lifts. UK-based *Tapestry Holidays* has a virtual hammerlock on **accommodation** here, offering something for all tastes from the exclusive *Physkos* and *Serena Suites* self-catering apartments down to the bare-bones *pansiyon*s *Sema* and *Alpin*. One outfit which, despite listing in other tour-op catalogues, does seem to expect walk-in trade is the *Otel Mavi Deniz* (☎0252/476 7190, fax 476 7007; ⑤), whose tower-block and bungalow units front the beach, with all watersports on offer; another likely to have vacancies on spec is the small, inland *Bilge Pansiyon* (☎0252/476 7162; ④), with two self-catering units in a forested setting.

A spur road (and sometimes a dolmuş) heads south, past ancient **Amos** (only Hellenistic walls and theatre remain) to **KUMLUBÜKÜ**, another large bay with decent amenities. Along with the above-noted Çiftlik bay, 4km southwest of here by rough tracks or paths, it's the only really big patch of sand on the whole peninsula.

The Datça peninsula

Once past ongoing roadworks and the turning for Bozburun, the main highway west of Marmaris ventures out onto the elongated, narrow **Datça (Reşadiye) peninsula**. You've glimpses through pine gullies of the sea on both sides, though the road is narrow, twisty, and inadvisable at night. There's nothing until Datça town except a pair of tiny villages, two huge, German-monopolized mega-hotels and two private **campsites** which escaped fire damage: the *Cennetköy*, just south of the road with a decent beach, and the *Özil*, 18km before Datça behind a larger, sandy beach.

Datça

Too built-up and commercialized to be the backpackers' haven it once was, **DATÇA** is still many times calmer than either Bodrum or Marmaris. It's essentially the shore annexe of inland Reşadiye village, but under the ministrations of visiting yachtspeople and tour operators has outgrown its parent. Carpet shops are big news here – a round dozen appeal to the yacht-bound (Datça is now an official port of entry) and to the paltry number of package clients, steadily dwindling owing to low local accommodation standards and the difficulty of access. Prices are still fifteen percent less than in Bodrum or Marmaris, and most villa development lies out of town to the east.

Practicalities

Datça's most striking feature is its layout: a single, kilometre-long high street meandering between two sheltered bays separated by a hillock and then a narrow isthmus, finally terminating on a cape. Along the way in you pass – more or less in this order – the **PTT**, some **banks** (*Ziraat* and *İş* have ATMs), the tiny **tourist office**, a traffic circle dominated by a large tree, with **taxi rank** and **bazaar** grounds (Fri & Sat) adjacent, and **travel agencies**.

Only two **bus** companies (*Kamil Koç* and *Pamukkale*) currently serve Datça, so there's no *otogar*, you're best off using a short-hop minibus to either Marmaris or Muğla, whence there will be more frequent onward departures. Domestic **ferries** to and from Bodrum run from Körmen Limanı, 9km north and connected by a short bus ride. It's worth taking the boat at least in one direction to avoid duplicating the wild bus journey in from the east. Any international ferries advertised to Kós or Rhodes actually go via Bodrum; owing to local squabbles, there are no longer services of any sort to Sími.

Accommodation is barely sufficient to meet demand – you may have to try several places. The most obvious desirable location is the hillock separating the two bays, where there are several *pansiyon*s to choose from: the *Huzur* (☎0252/712 3052; ③), which is the most modern, the *Kader* (☎0252/712 3553; ③), and the *Karaoğlu* (☎0252/712 3079; ③), with the best sea view and a pleasant attached restaurant. The *Kaya* and the *Yılmaz*, nearby facing the main drag, are newer, dearer and noiser. Another possible hunting ground is the east bay, where the *Yalı* (☎0252/712 3059; ③) and *Oya* are older establishments pitched mainly at Turkish families.

Out on the point, formerly an island called Esenada, the aging *Dorya Motel* (☎0252/712 3593, fax 712 3303; ④) is home to such package trade as Datça gets. Rooms are hardly state-of-the-art, but the place does offer well-kept gardens and common areas, a pool and a private lido. The only other establishment with comparable comfort and facilities is the aptly named *Hotel Panorama* (☎ and fax 0252/712 3764; ③), set 600m inland from the tree roundabout in a quiet hillside setting; with a large pool and bar, it's a snip at the price, and with tourist numbers down the management seems eager to please.

When foraging for **food**, the half-dozen restaurants overlooking the west cove are fairly indistinguishable in price and quality, and all tout aggressively. Some imaginative dishes rarely seen elsewhere may be on display, especially at the *Akdeniz* and *Liman*, but there are no bargains. If money's an issue, try the nicely decorated *Defne Pide Salonu* on the main drag or such inland sidewalk eateries as *Korsan*, *Valentino* and *Kemal*, on the west side of the main thoroughfare. A worthwhile find on the east beach is the versatile, friendly and not vastly overpriced *Dutdibi*, offering meat dishes, *pide* and occasionally fish. Various cafés overlooking this beach offer full **breakfast** for as little as $2.50. The most frantic activity you'll find in Datça is after dark at the handful of **music pubs** and **bars** along the west harbour and beyond on the west beach.

Beaches and boat excursions

Life in and around Datça mostly boils down to a matter of picking your swimming and sunbathing spot. The **east beach** of hardpacked sand, known as Kumluk locally, is oversubscribed but has some shade; the less crowded **west beach**, mixed pebble and sand and called Taşlık, is acceptable and gets better the further you get from the anchored yachts.

In contrast to the scenery on the drive in, the immediate surroundings of Datça are quite barren, softened only by a mineral spring-fed **lake** halfway along the west bay. Warm seeps from the lake bed, up to 2m down, make swimming here nicer than in the ocean; a line of appealing bar-cafés overlook the stone dam that augments the water level.

With limited swimming options in town, the **local boat trips** advertised on the west harbour make a good day out. Groups generally depart between 9 and 9.30am, returning between 5 and 6pm. Standard stops include Palamut Bükü, Domuz Çukuru, Mesudiye Bükü and ancient Knidos – most of these detailed below. The going price per person, excluding lunch (usually at Palamut Bükü) and allowing three swim stops, is $15, which compares well to the practicalities of taking a taxi to Knidos (see below). The boat *Kara Ada* is recommended for its attentive, English-speaking crew.

The way to Knidos

Beyond Datça the peninsula broadens considerably, and the scenery, almond or olive groves around somnolent, back-of-beyond villages at the base of pine-speckled mountains, is quite unlike that which came before. Of the 32km of road beyond Reşadiye village, the 24km to Yazıköy are paved (with more being currently oiled), but the last 4km are appalling, although an ordinary car with good clearance should make it in dry weather.

Some 9km out of Reşadiye, signs point down the five-kilometre side road to the shore hamlet at **MESUDİYE BÜKÜ**. There is an occasional **dolmuş** to Mesudiye from

Datça, but this ordinarily stops in the upper village, so you may have to cajole the driver into taking you the extra 3km to the shore. Here, the *Hoppala* and *Özdemir pansiyon*-campsites (no phones) separate the mixed sand-and-gravel beach from a spectacular backdrop of oasis greenery and mountains. Prices are slightly cheaper than in Datça but not much happens after dark.

Hayıt Bükü, one cove east with the necessary road-fork left well marked, hasn't such a good beach, but the bay itself is well protected by a scenic, clawlike headland on the west. Accordingly the place sees lots of boat traffic, as evidenced by a large dock, a few motels and **restaurants**. Best of the latter is probably *Olgun's Place*, with a friendly, laid-back staff and a surprising amount of *hazır yemek* rather than the cold *meze*s typical of yachtie havens.

Some 9km of coast road, rough but just passable in an ordinary car in low gears, links Mesudiye with **PALAMUT BÜKÜ**. Most vehicles (but no dolmuşes) take the main road to the point in Yaka Köyü, about 20km out of Reşadiye, where a side road drops 4.5km south to Palamut. The stark setting is balanced by a kilometre-long beach of tiny pebbles lapped by brisk, clear water, with an islet offshore. Of a handful of **pansiyons**, mostly occupied for weeks on end by Turkish families, the *Olgun* (☎0252/725 5165; ③), where the road hits the beach, and the *Bük* (☎0252/725 5136; ②), at the far east end of the bay, are the most appealing; the only drawback is that most **restaurants** are well to the west, by the harbour.

Knidos (Cnidus)

Hard as it is to believe from its current state, **KNIDOS**, out on windlashed Tekir Burnu (the Cape Krio of antiquity), was one of the most fabled and prosperous cities of antiquity. With its strategic location astride the main shipping lanes of the Mediterranean, it was also a cosmopolitan city, and illustrious personalities hailing from here were legion. In its heyday it was also home to an eminent medical school, rival to the Hippocratic clinic across the straits on Kós. However, the city was most notorious for a splendid statue of Aphrodite and the cult (and sacred brothels) that surrounded it.

The catch is that very little remains of this former greatness, and it's probably not worth punishing any vehicle the full distance in from Datça, though in compensation you do glimpse extensive patches of massively masoned city wall along the last 3km. At least until excavations are completed, a short halt on a boat tour is all that the site will merit for most visitors. Arriving **by boat** (a far better option than a taxi from Datça, which will cost $30, with only an hour at the ruins), you dock in the south bay, backed by a single restaurant and a police post. Leave **vehicles** at the small car park; a nearby sign requests that, although the site is unenclosed, you should observe the official visiting hours of 8am to 7pm and pay admission – $2 – if the keeper is manning his booth.

The site

With the ruins still under excavation, the site-plan placard near the entrance is of little use, though labelling and signposting have improved in recent years. Your overwhelming impression will be of an enormous, weedy mess, booby-trapped with deep, unguarded trenches – you may derive more satisfaction from the windswept, dramatic setting.

Most of Knidos's public buildings were on the mainland side, and of these the **Hellenistic theatre**, overlooking the south anchorage, is the best preserved. A military watchtower on the ex-island confirms that most of it is off-limits; visit instead the two **Byzantine basilicas**, one huge with extensive mosaics, overlooking the north harbour. Hellenistic Knidos was laid out in a grid pattern, though the hilly site necessitated extensive terracing, retaining walls and stairways. Clambering along these, you can take a self-guided tour by following arrow-signs to the agora (by the north port), the bouleuterion, a Corinthian temple, a purported sundial and an unidentified mosaic

THE APHRODISIAC CULT AT KNIDOS

Like several cities in Asia Minor, Knidos was a Peloponnesian Dorian foundation, circa 1000 BC, its original site near present-day Datça. The famous shrine of Apollo, religious focus of the Dorian Hexapolis, is thought to have been above today's Palamut Bükü. During the middle of the fourth century BC Knidos was moved to its present location – a shrewd step, taking advantage of the enforced stays of ships sheltering here from high local winds. The new town was built on both the tip of the mainland and what was then an island to the south; in ancient times the two were joined by a causeway sluiced by a bridged channel but the channel has long since silted up.

Undoubtedly Knidos's most famous "citizen" was an inanimate object, the **cult statue of Aphrodite** by Praxiteles, the first large-scale, freestanding nude of a woman, modelled by the famous Athenian courtesan, Phryne. This adorned the new city from its earliest days and became, even more than the menacing winds, Knidos's chief source of revenue. Set up in a sanctuary so that it could be admired from every angle, the marble Aphrodite attracted thousands of ancient tourists, not all of them mere art-lovers. According to legend the statue bore a dark stain in its crotch, not a flaw in the marble but the result of a youth conceiving such a passion for it that he hid in the temple until after closing time and made love to the effigy.

After paying their respects to the image, more conventional pilgrims were wont to observe the rites of love with one of the sacred prostitutes who worked in the temple precincts. Subsequently customers bought tacky pornographic souvenirs, whose nature will be familiar to anyone who has browsed a postcard rack or gift shop anywhere in the modern Aegean. All this licence was – perhaps predictably – too much for the Byzantine Christians, who destroyed Praxiteles' Aphrodite along with the temple, though aptly named Iris Love, chief of the American archeological team, claims to have discovered the goddess's head in a vault at the British Museum. Copies and incomplete versions of the statue still exist in New York, Paris, Rome and Munich.

floor. Of the Aphrodite shrine, on the very highest terrace, there remains only the circular foundation of either an altar or perhaps the *tholos* (round portico) where the image of the goddess was displayed.

INLAND CARIA

Away from the coastal regions, the major settlements in ancient Caria tended to be concentrated along the upper reaches of the Meander river, now the Büyük Menderes, and its tributaries, particularly the Marsyas – today's Çine Çayı.

Aydın, a pleasant if nondescript town easily reached from Kuşadası, is the base of choice for visiting ancient **Nyssa**, and also **Alinda**, **Alabanda** and **Gerga**, the archeological sites of the Çine valley. Of these, only Alinda is anything like required viewing, and it is also the easiest to reach by public transport; the other two are pretty remote and for most visitors don't repay the effort involved in driving or walking out to them. Further east, **Aphrodisias**, on a high plateau south of the Büyük Menderes, is similarly isolated but buses are more obliging since it's poised to become Ephesus' archeological rival in the southwest Aegean.

Still further inland, the functional city of **Denizli** has transport connections in every direction, most obviously with **Hierapolis/Pamukkale**, an ancient site-cum-geological-prodigy that's the star of every other Turkish tourist poster ever produced. Whether it figures as the high or low point of your stay depends on your temperament, but if escape becomes imperative, minor attractions such as **Laodiceia** and **Akhan** are conveniently close.

Aydın and around

AYDIN is a modern provincial capital, with clean, tree-lined main boulevards and a smattering of older buildings in the centre. If you don't have a car, its excellent dolmuş services make it the obvious jump-off point for the area's ancient ruins – Nyssa to the east, and the sites of the Çine valley, scattered either side of the scenic road south to Muğla.

Aydın started life as **Tralles**, the distinguished ancient town founded, according to legend, by colonists from the Greek Argive and Thrace; the site of the original settlement (now classified as a military zone and consequently requiring special permission to visit) was a plateau northwest of today's city. Despite its good natural defences Tralles submitted, or fell, to whatever conqueror was currently traipsing through Asia Minor, but enjoyed a period of prosperity during the Roman Imperial period, even eclipsing neighbouring Nyssa.

Contemporary Aydın's attractions fall squarely into the time-filling category. The oldest Turkish monument is the seventeenth-century **Süleyman Bey Camii**, across from the pleasant, mosaic-paved central park. The **museum** (Tues–Sun 8.30am–noon & 1.30–5pm; $1.50), west of the gardens, holds a wide collection of finds from around the province, spanning all eras and cultures, and includes a recently added ethnographic division. Don't bother pestering the authorities for permission to visit ancient Tralles – you'll see only the barest vestiges of a Roman gymnasium.

Practicalities

The **otogar** is 700m south of the centre on the main highway, just west of a large roundabout and the **tourist information office** (☎0256/225 4145), which offers excellent city maps; the *otogar* is connected with the centre of town by complimetary shuttle bus. Adnan Menderes Bulvarı shoots straight up to the heart of town, where the **train station** and **PTT** face each other just west of the central square. Hükümet Bulvarı, Menderes's narrower continuation, climbs past the bulk of the hotels and restaurants before intersecting Gazi Bulvarı, Aydın's main east–west thoroughfare and home to the important **dolmuş station**.

As for **accommodation**, the *Kabaçam*, Hükümet Bulvarı, 11 Sokak 2/B (☎0256/212 2794; ③), is the best value, with comfortable doubles with baths. Runner-up is the nearby *Baltaçı*, Gazi Bulvarı, 3 Sokağı (☎0256/212 1321; ③), with slightly more worn facilities for the same price. Directly opposite the *Kabaçam* stands the *Vardar*, but it's quite a step down in quality. There's one further two-star establishment, the *Orhan* up on Gazi Bulvarı (☎0256/225 1713; ④), but it's hard to imagine both the *Kabaçam* and the *Baltaçı* full up. Various inexpensive **restaurants** are tucked into the lanes of the small bazaar west of Hükümet: the *Şanlıurfa Kebab Salonu* is representative.

Nyssa

Awash in a sea of olive groves in the hills above the Büyük Menderes valley, ancient **NYSSA** is rarely visited – and except for its theatre, bouleuterion and unusual layout, there is little to interest non-specialist visitors. What's left above ground is mostly numerous arches of inferior masonry.

Originally founded by Peloponnesians, the city flourished from the first century BC until the third century AD, and remained an important Byzantine community subsequently. During the Roman era it was famous as an academic centre, attracting pupils from throughout Asia Minor. Strabo, while not a native, studied here and left detailed accounts of the city, which can still be partly verified even in Nyssa's present ruinous condition.

The archeological zone lies 2km above Sultanhisar, the modern successor to Nyssa, astride major bus and rail routes. There are simple eateries in Sultanhisar but nowhere to stay; nor is there any public transport up to the ruins.

The site

The paved access road from the ticket office ($1 admission) balloons out into a small car park flanked by picnic tables, just north of which lies an excellently preserved **Roman theatre** – a structure, with a capacity of well over 5000, that is slowly being taken over by wild olives sprouting quaintly amidst the seats. The paved road continues another 300m uphill to the start of the 200-metre walk to the **bouleuterion**, where twelve semicircular rows of seats face out onto an area graced with a **ceremonial basin** and **mosaics**.

Strabo described the city as built on both sides of a steep ravine, and some of the monuments that he listed are still clinging to the banks of the canyon. A path just to the east of the theatre descends to the mouth of an enormous, 115-metre-long **tunnel** burrowing under the car park, which in Roman times was the main city square. Beyond the southern exit are the remains of two **bridges** linking the halves of Nyssa, and the virtually unrecognizable rubble of a stadium and a gymnasium, well recessed into the flanks of the gully and currently both off-limits. The tunnel, in addition to functioning as a simple storm drain, could be used to fill the stadium with water for mock naval battles.

To the west of the access road, reached by another path beginning 100m north of the guard post, stand the remains of some **baths** (adjoining the theatre) and a **library**, alleged in many sources to be the most important in Asia Minor after the one in Ephesus. You wouldn't know it from today's muddled, two-storey building lost in more olives.

The Çine valley: Alinda, Alabanda, Gerga

The **Çine Çayı**, formerly the river Marsyas, is one of the largest tributaries of the Büyük Menderes. Its old name commemorates a legend concerning the satyr Marsyas, a devotee of the mother goddess Cybele. Upon finding a deer-bone flute discarded by Athena, he became entranced by its sound as he played in Cybele's processions, and was so bold as to challenge Apollo to a musical contest. The god accepted on condition that the winner could impose the punishment of his choice on the loser. Marsyas lost; Apollo tied him to a pine tree near the source of the stream that would bear his name, and flayed him alive.

These days most travellers hurry along the modern highway that runs parallel to the river, unmindful of the legend and the three ancient sites that lie just off the main route.

Alinda

The first and best of the ancient ruins in the valley, **ALİNDA**, studding a huge bluff that dominates the area, is closely linked with a colourful episode in the life of Alexander the Great. Ada, the sister of King Mausolus of Halicarnassus, after losing the battle for succession to the Hecatomnid throne during the middle of the fourth century, was exiled to Alinda, then a mere fortress, where she awaited an opportunity to reverse her fortunes. A few years later, upon the arrival of Alexander, Ada offered to surrender Alinda and all her personal resources in exchange for his aid in regaining her royal position. Her proposal was accepted, and Alexander holed up in Alinda for some time, preparing their combined – and eventually successful – siege of Halicarnassus. During this period they became close friends, and it seems that Ada even adopted Alexander as her son. After their victory Ada was left to rule over most of Caria, but she was the last of the remarkable Hecatomnid line; little of consequence occurred locally after her death.

Though the site of Alinda lies 28km off the main highway, a total of 58km from Aydın, public transport connections are decent. There are direct dolmuşes from Aydın to **KARPUZLU**, the fair-sized town at the base of the ruins; if you can't get one you'll have to use an Aydın–Çine dolmuş (departing across the road from the Aydın tourist office) and change vehicles in Çine town. The last direct service back from Karpuzlu to Aydın leaves at 4pm, to Çine at 6.30pm. Don't plan to stay over in shabby **ÇİNE**, whose lone hotel *Babadan* is an airless fleapit. In Karpuzlu there are several adequate restaurants but again only one bare-bones hotel.

The site

From the little square where the minibuses stop, follow the signs 400m up a dirt track to the unfenced site ($1 during daylight hours) and car park; close by, the oldest houses of Karpuzlu merge into ancient masonry just below the monstrous **market building**. One hundred metres long, this was originally three storeys high, with hefty interior columns; now only two floors stand, but these are in perfect condition, and, like so much Carian stonework, bear a strange resemblance to Inca construction half a world away. Cross the open agora behind to some courses of wall, where an obvious serpentine path leads up to the well-preserved **theatre**, retaining two galleries and most of its seats. These face south, giving superlative views over Karpuzlu and its valley. From here, continue further north up the hill, where an impressive, two-storey **Hellenistic watchtower** surveys a patchwork of fields and trees, with rings of mountains up to 50km distant. The flat space around the tower is peppered with cistern mouths and partly collapsed tunnels that supposedly once led to the lower levels of the city. Walk west along the neck of the ridge, past the foundations of **acropolis houses**, until you reach a gap in the **city walls**; just beyond are a couple of specimens from Alinda's extensive **necropolis**.

Alabanda and Gerga

Both of these Carian sites are considerably more difficult to get to and will really only reward archeology fanatics, although the walk to Gerga, providing you can reach the starting point, is enjoyable in itself.

Alabanda

Although originally a Carian settlement, **ALABANDA** figures in history only briefly as a Roman city, notorious for its scorpions. Today there is not much on view at all, and the site, 8km west of Çine, is perfunctorily signposted and not served by any public transport. Only the old **bouleuterion**, north of the road, is obvious, its walls standing up to six metres high. The **theatre**, up in the village across the road, has almost disappeared – houses have been built up against it, and vegetables are being raised in the old stage area.

Gerga

Near the headwaters of the Çine River, the valley narrows to a defile known as the Gökbel pass. The deserted landscape, with the water far below tumbling over huge boulders, is evocative of Marsyas and his fate – and hides **GERGA**, the most mysterious site in Caria.

Twelve kilometres south of Eskiçine, the graceful **İncekemer** Ottoman bridge spans the gorge. This is a recognized bus stop (though the driver will think you daft to alight here), and if you have a car you'll find parking space at the roadside. From here it's about a ninety-minute walk to Gerga. Cross the bridge, then another flimsy cement one across a tributary, and stay with the main trail, which soon becomes a dirt track. After

25 minutes you'll reach the village of İncekemer Mahalle, split in two by yet another watercourse. Change to the west bank of this, maintaining always a northerly course, and continue up the small valley between the big ridge and a smaller rock plug to the east. Near the top, make a hairpin left over a slight saddle to reach some drystone walls and thornbush barriers for livestock. Just past this is a small farm at the base of a terraced hillside, on which stand the remains of Gerga.

Virtually nothing is known for certain about Gerga, other than that it is of very early Carian vintage, with crude, monolithic masonry supposed to date from the Roman era. At first sight it would appear to have not been a town, but a sacred precinct like Labranda. The most conspicuous item is a **temple or tomb** in the form of a house, visible from afar and in perfect condition, despite use as a cow shed. Its stone roof is intact and on the lintel "GERGAS" is inscribed in Greek lettering – which some archeologists theorize is not the place name but that of an obscure Carian deity. You actually enter the site between two upright, flattened **monoliths**, irregularly shaped like African termite nests; adjacent is a large lustral **basin** carved from living rock. A giant headless **statue** lies on the ground beyond the tomb-temple, and at the far edge of the main terrace are two purported **fountains**: one backed into the hillside, the other freestanding and bearing another "GERGAS" legend. While none of the individual structures is that impressive, the total effect, and the outlandish location, are unsettling.

Aphrodisias

Situated on a high plateau over 600m above sea level, ringed by mountains and watered by a tributary of the Büyük Menderes, **APHRODISIAS** is among the most isolated and beautifully set of Turkey's major archeological sites. Acres of marble peek out from among the poplars and other vegetation that cloaks the remains of one of imperial Rome's most cultured Asian cities. Late afternoon visits have the bonus of often dramatic cloud formations spawned by the elevation, and the attendant dappled lighting, but both can turn murky – as can the transportation situation out.

Since 1961, excavations have been carried out with the conscious intent of rendering Aphrodisias on a par with Ephesus. The eventual results will certainly be spectacular, but in the meantime the digs can be a nuisance for tourists: much of the site is off-limits to both photography and entry, and the opportunity to watch any ongoing work from a distance is small consolation.

Some history

Aphrodisias was one of the earliest occupied sites in Anatolia. Neolithic and Bronze Age mounds have been found here, including the artificial hill supporting the theatre. There has also been a fertility cult of some sort here for just as long, fostered by the agricultural associations of the river valley. The Assyrian goddess of love and war, Nin, became syncretized with the Semitic Ishtar, whose attributes were eventually assumed by the Hellenic Aphrodite.

Despite a strategic position near the meeting point of ancient Caria, Lydia and Phrygia, and proximity to major trade routes, Aphrodisias for many centuries remained only a shrine, and never really grew into a town until the second century BC. The citizens of Aphrodisias were amply rewarded for their support of the Romans during the Mithridatic revolt; many special privileges – including the right of sanctuary within the Aphrodite temple precincts – were granted, and the rapidly burgeoning city was heavily patronized by various emperors, becoming a major cultural centre. It was renowned in particular for its school of sculpture, which took advantage of nearby quarries of high-grade marble, and Aphrodisian works adorned every corner of the empire, including Rome itself.

Perhaps because of this fixation with graven images, not to mention the lucrative cult of Aphrodite (similar to that at Knidos), paganism lingered here for almost two centuries after Theodosius proscribed the old religions. Even following conversion of the Aphrodite shrine to a more decorous basilica, and a change of name to Stavropolis, the Christianity professed here tended toward heretical persuasions.

The reputation of its love-cult had served to protect Aphrodisias since its inception, but by the fourth century AD a wall had become necessary. This failed singularly, however, to stave off the effect of two earthquakes and sundry raids, and decline was the dominant theme of Byzantine times. The town was abandoned completely during the thirteenth century, its former glories recalled only by the Ottoman village of Geyre – a corruption of "Caria" – among the ruins. Romantic travellers dutifully stopped, sketched and copied inscriptions, but none suspected the wealth of relics hidden from view. First French, then Italian researchers poked rather desultorily below the surface early this century, but it is only since 1961 that work by a New York University team under Dr Kenan Erim has permitted a fuller understanding of the site. Dr Erim's death in 1990 (he is buried on the site) marked the end of an era; no new monuments are currently being uncovered, with ongoing work concentrating on consolidation, cleaning and documentation of inscriptions.

The site

A loop path around the site (summer daily 8am–7pm; winter daily 8am–5.30pm; $2.50) passes all of the major monuments, though at the time of going to press, only the stadium, the theatre, the odeion and the Temple of Aphrodite have completely unrestricted access.

The route begins conspicuously across the old village square from the museum; first stop is the the magnificent, virtually intact **theatre**, founded in the first century BC but extensively modified by the Romans for their blood sports three centuries later. At the rear of the stage building are chiselled imperial decrees affecting the status of the town. Still further behind the stage is a large square, the **tetrastoön**, originally surrounded by colonnades on all sides, and one of several meeting places in the Roman and Byzantine city. South of the tetrastoön lies a large baths complex.

The path skirts the north flank of the theatre, right under the the hill's summit; down and to the north you may often see workmen pottering about in the **Sebasteion** – two parallel porticoes erected in the first century AD to honour the deified Roman emperors – and the **double agora**, two squares ringed by Ionic and Corinthian stoas. Numerous columns still vie with the poplars, and the whole area is bounded to the southwest by the **Portico of Tiberius**, which separates the agora from the fine **Baths of Hadrian** (currently out of bounds), well preserved right down to the floor tiles and the odd mosaic.

North of the baths, several blue-marble columns sprout from a multi-roomed structure commonly known as the **bishop's palace**, from its presumed use during Byzantine times. However its ground plan, particularly the large audience chamber, is typical of a governor's residence in Roman provinces and that is certainly how the building began life. East of here huddles the appealing Roman **odeion**, with nine rows of seats. Since the many earthquakes have disrupted the local water table, the orchestra is prone to springtime flooding and today frogs often croak where concerts were once given and the city council deliberated.

A few paces to the north, fourteen columns of the **Temple of Aphrodite** are all that's left of the city's principal sanctuary; the Byzantines mangled not only the idol within but also the ground plan when they converted it to a basilica during the fifth century, so considerable detective work was required to re-establish the first-century BC foundations. Even these were laid atop at least two older structures, with evidence of mother-

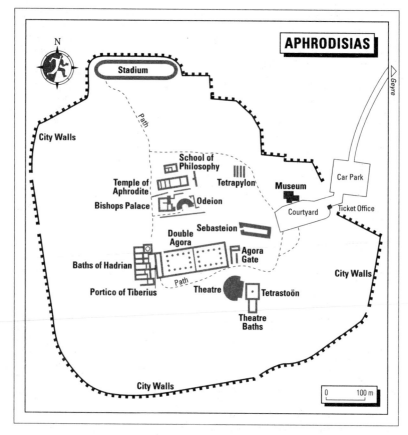

goddess worship extending back to the seventh century. The Hellenistic/Roman sanctuary had forty Ionic columns arranged eight by thirteen, with the cult image erected in the main hall. The Byzantines removed the columns at each end of the temple, fashioning an apse to the east, an atrium and baptistry on the west, and it's this architectural pastiche you see today. Immediately north is the so-called **school of philosophy**, tentatively identified, like the bishop's palace, on the basis of resemblance to other such structures elsewhere.

The northernmost feature of the site, 200m off the main path, is the 30,000-seat **stadium**, one of the largest and best preserved in Anatolia. Under the empire, and with official encouragement, many cities of Asia Minor held periodic festivals in imitation of the major Greek competitions. Those at Aphrodisias were a version of Delphi's Pythian Games, with sporting, musical and dramatic events. Returning to the main loop trail, the last thing you'll notice before exiting onto the museum square is the recently re-erected **tetrapylon**, a monumental gateway with two double rows of four columns, half of them fluted, supporting pediments with intricate reliefs. This second-century AD edifice is thought to mark the intersection of a major north–south street with a sacred way heading toward the Aphrodite shrine.

The museum

An earthquake in 1956 damaged the old village of Geyre, giving the authorities a time-ly pretext to relocate the villagers 1500m to the north and begin excavations. The old village square is now flanked by the archeologists' quarters and the attractive **muse-um** (same hours as site; separate $2.50 admission), whose collection consists almost entirely of sculpture recovered from the ruins. Given that Aphrodisias met most of the demand for effigies under the empire, even what remains after the loss of originals and the spiriting away of works to city museums is considerable. The so-called "Aphrodite Hall" contains statuary related to the cult, a rendition of the goddess, much defaced by Christian zealots, occupying the position of honour. In the "Penthesileia Hall", a joyous satyr carries the child Dionysos in his arms; the "Melpomene Hall" contains a wrench-ing version of the muse of tragedy, together with two suitably loutish-looking boxers and the completely intact, quasi-satirical portrait of Flavius Palmatus, Byzantine gover-nor of Asia. With a small head and thick body, he was an ugly, malproportioned man, but, judging from the facial expression, one you crossed at your peril. Recent notable additions to the collection include the remounted, so-called "Zoïlos" friezes, and por-trait busts of various philosophers. The first (or last) notable item you'll pass is a ver-sion of Nike carrying a trophy, opposite the souvenir stall.

Practicalities

Aphrodisias is situated 13km east of Karacasu, the nearest sizable town, which lies 25km from the E24/320 highway threading through the Menderes valley between Aydın and Denizli, and 40km from **NAZİLLİ**, whose *otogar* sits just north of the highway on the west edge of town. If coming in by **train**, exit Nazilli station and turn right onto the main town thoroughfare, or follow the tracks southwest – they pass very near the bus stand.

Dolmuşes leave for Karacasu, on demand, from the rear of the Nazilli *otogar*; dur-ing the warmer months the route may even extend to Geyre, the village next to the ruins. The *Dadaş* company runs **large coaches** from Nazilli station, mostly in the early afternoon, two of which continue to Geyre and Tavas.

If you're staying in Pamukkale, it's tempting to try and devise a loop back to Denizli through Tavas, but you must get to Tavas in time for the last dolmuş back to Denizli, and thence to Pamukkale, which is difficult. Indeed you're probably best off only trying to com-plete such an ambitious circuit under your own steam, or with a tour bus out of Pamukkale.

Whatever happens, try to avoid getting stranded at Aphrodisias – a distinct possibil-ity after 6pm, even in summer. A round trip by **taxi** from Karacasu will cost you $7, double that if you have to take it all the way back to the Nazilli–Denizli highway. If you are going to get stuck, you're best off doing so at **GEYRE**, which can offer the simple *Chez Mestan pansiyon*-campsite (①), 600m from the site on the main highway, and the more comfortable *Aphrodisias Hotel-Restaurant-Camping* (☎0256/448 8132, fax 448 8422; ④), 1km west of *Chez Mestan*. In **KARACASU** there is only the grimmest of dor-mitories built directly over the small bus terminal building.

Denizli

Devastated by earthquakes in 1710 and 1899, **DENİZLİ** is a gritty agricultural town and transport hub of just over 200,000 inhabitants, so your first and last thought will proba-bly be to move on – most likely to Pamukkale, 20km north, to which there are minibus-es until 11pm in season. The **train station**, containing an essentially useless **tourist information office**, lies right across the busy highway from the **otogar**. Çardak **air-port** lies 65km away near **Acıgöl**, a $25 taxi ride, so try not to miss the *Havaş* shuttle bus which departs from in front of the *THY* office at İstiklâl Cad 27/B (☎0258/264 8661).

Travellers' stays in Denizli are usually measured in minutes, not hours, and with the recent slump in Pamukkale tourism it's highly unlikely that you'd ever be forced to find a **place to stay** here. Moreover, most of the conspicuous hotels are luxury outfits for businessmen, and most of the cheaper places plagued by noise from the bus station or main streets. Two reasonable and relatively quiet alternatives are the comfortable *Arar Otel*, İstiklâl Cad, Delikli Çınar Meyd 9 (☎0258/263 7195; ④), and the nearby *Kuyumcu Oteli* (☎0258/263 3749; ④). These are a one-kilometre walk south of the train station, reached by taking İstasyon Caddesi opposite the station, and then its continuation Enverpaşa Caddesi. If you're heavily laden, you can pick up a dolmuş at any of the stops marked with "D" along İstasyon Caddesi.

You can **eat** well between buses at one of several places just southeast of the bus stand serving ready-prepared dishes. There are also numerous kebab and *pide* outfits, plus sweet shops, around Delikli Çınar, but these make little sense unless you're staying in Denizli.

Pamukkale/Hierapolis and around

As you approach the site of **PAMUKKALE/HIERAPOLIS** from Denizli, a long white smudge along the hills to the north suggests a landslide or opencast mine. Getting closer, this resolves into the edge of a plateau, more than 100m higher than the level of the river valley and absolutely smothered in white **travertine terraces**. Some are shaped like water lilies, others like shell-bathtubs with stalagmitic feet, with the simplest ones resembling bleached rice terraces out of an oriental engraving. The Turks have dubbed this geological fairyland *Pamukkale*, or "Cotton Castle".

The responsibility for this freak of nature rests with a spring, saturated with dissolved calcium bicarbonate, bubbling up from the feet of Çal Dağı beyond. As the water surges over the edge of the plateau and cools, carbon dioxide is given off and calcium carbonate precipitated as hard chalk (travertine). What you see now has been accumulating for millennia, but slowly but surely the solidified waterfall advances southwest. Seen at sunset, subtle hues of ochre, purple and pink are reflected in the water, replacing the dazzling white of midday.

The spring emerges in what once was the exact middle of the ancient city of **Hierapolis** but is now the garden of a motel. The ruins of Hierapolis would merit a stop even if they weren't coupled with this natural phenomenon, but as things are you can often hardly see them for the tour buses, souvenir hawkers and shabby motels. Pamukkale and Hierapolis are Turkey's closest equivalent to Disneyland, a tourist extravaganza in which the terraces fill in for the Matterhorn and the castle, and one "rides" the ruins (or the camels handily stationed in between). Of late the circus atmosphere has been augmented by the inauguration of a new, Russian-patronized casino nearby. Depending on your mood, taste or timing, it can either be a prime example of everything loathsome in modern tourism, or (in winter at least) a relatively deserted stage set and a chance for a warm outdoor bath.

Present restrictions on access to the travertine terraces mean that visitors are obliged to remove footwear before treading on anything vaguely resembling a calcium deposit, and in the near future visitors may be confined entirely to the major pathways around the site, as even the skin oil from bare feet has been demonstrated to damage the formations. UNESCO and the Turkish government also periodically talk of closing down some of the major hotels, or at least limiting their use of the precious spring water which is presently being diverted away from the travertine terraces to swimming pools and saunas. In tandem with their seriously depleted water supply, the terraces lately are grubbily discoloured and (sad to say) often strewn with litter and cigarette butts.

Some history

The therapeutic properties and bizarre appearance of the hot springs were known about for thousands of years before an actual town was founded here by one of the Pergamene kings during the second century BC. After incorporation into the Roman Empire in 129 BC, development proceeded apace, spurred by minor industries in wool and metals, plus a health spa practically the equal of the present one. Hierapolis seems to have enjoyed considerable imperial favour, especially after catastrophic earthquakes in 17 and 60 AD. No fewer than three emperors paid personal visits, stimulating local emperor-worship alongside the veneration of Apollo and his mother Leto, who was venerated in the guise of Cybele.

The presence of a flourishing Jewish community aided the rapid and early establishment of Christianity here. Hierapolis is mentioned in Paul's Epistle to the (neighbouring) Colossians, and Philip the Apostle is traditionally thought to have been martyred here along with his seven sons. However, as at Aphrodisias, paganism lingered well into the sixth century, until a zealous bishop supervised the destruction of the remaining focuses of ancient worship and the establishment of nearly one hundred churches, several of which are still visible.

Hierapolis slid into obscurity in late Byzantine times, nudged along by Arab and Turcoman raids. After the Selçuks arrived in the 1100s, the city was abandoned, not to figure much in the Western imagination until Italian excavations began in 1957; even as recently as 1939, George Bean reported much the same landscape as the romantic travellers of the eighteenth century had witnessed. A mere four decades have sufficed to re-create, if not the monumental taste, then certainly the commercialism of the Roman period.

Practicalities

PAMUKKALE KÖYÜ, a once-sleepy village at the base of the cliff, is where most foreign travellers stay. The majority arrive from Denizli, where **dolmuşes** labelled "Pamukkale/Karahayıt" set off from a rank on the west edge of the *otogar*, last departure in either direction is around 11pm in summer, much earlier in the cooler months. Red-and-white Denizli **city buses** also go to Pamukkale Köyü, but these are less frequent, begin their run from downtown Denizli and are altogether more inconvenient (if cheaper). If you fail to coincide, a **taxi** will set you back $12 per car-load; consider ringing one of the recommended *pansiyon*s, who may be able to fetch you for free or a reasonable charge.

There are also **long-distance bus connections** between Pamukkale Köyü and most of the larger resorts – Kaş, Marmaris, Kuşadası and Fethiye, among other places – up to several times daily, although the buses are really minibuses and not air-conditioned. Several companies, including *Pamukkale*, have ticket offices in the village, but be sure when purchasing tickets that the fare and itinerary includes a shuttle to the Denizli *otogar* (you'll rarely get through service except perhaps in peak season).

The village has in recent years acquired a rash of discos, carpet shops, hustlers (read on) and wretched restaurants in its centre. Despite all this, it's still a rural settlement, partly dependent on cotton; beyond the main drag, especially in the lower neighbourhood away from the travertine, little outward change is evident. For any nocturnal peace, it's indeed better to stay on the outskirts, whose limit seems to have stabilized about 500m west of the road leading up to the south gate of the ruins.

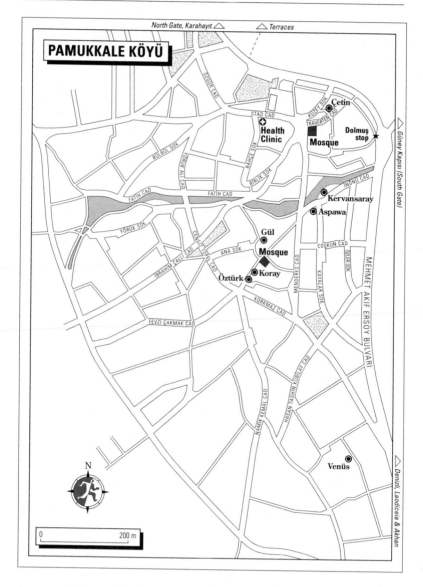

North Gate, Karahayıt △   △ Terraces

PAMUKKALE KÖYÜ

Çetin
STAD CAD
KUZEY SOK
TRAVERTEN CAD
Health
Clinic
Dolmuş
stop
Mosque
MIGRIR CAD
BÜLBÜL SOK
YÖRÜK ALT CAD
BAHÇE SOK
BIRLIK SOK
FATIH CAD
FATIH CAD
İNÖNÜ CAD
Kervansaray
Aspawa
YÖRÜK SOK
Gül
COŞKUN CAD
Mosque
İBRAHIM KALLI CAD
CENGİZ TOPEL CAD
ANA SOK
MENDERES CAD
KAYALAR SOK
OZLER SOK
Öztürk
Koray
KORKMAZ CAD
FEVZİ ÇAKMAK CAD
MEHMET AKİF ERSOY BULVARI
NAMIK KEMAL CAD
HASAN TAHSİN KOBİLA CAD
N
Venüs
Güney Kapısı (South Gate) △
Denizli, Laodiceia & Akhan △

0 — 200 m

Accommodation and eating

Of late there has been a vigorous winnowing of excess capacity in Pamukkale Köyü, spurred by falling tourist numbers; only about forty *pansiyon*s, and some thirty motels and small hotels, have survived, with substandard (ie non-en-suite) outfits folding. The effect of this has been to make the notorious local accommodation **touts**, rivalling those at Selçuk and Kuşadası for aggressiveness and mendaciousness, all the more desperate and resourceful. If you announce your intention to patronize one of the establishments listed below, you'll almost certainly be told that it's "full", "dirty", "closed down" or "I'm their cousin", as these individuals are, not surprisingly, skimming off commissions from *pansiyon*s that are chronically empty – usually for good reason. To spare yourself such an ordeal, which may include having your car door, backpack, or even person being clung to while pitch is delivered, it's well worth arranging a room in advance with one of the following lodgings, who (well aware of the touts' ploys) may offer to fetch you from Denizli, or meet you in the village, if informed of your likely arrival time. Most lodgings in the village advertise the presence of a **swimming pool**, but by the time the mineral water has made the long trip down from the cliff it's distinctly cool and murky – a summertime pleasure only.

Top billing **down in the village** currently goes to the small, professionally run *Koray Otel* (☎0258/272 2222, fax 272 2095; ③), built around a non-mineral pool and garden, with a good restaurant offering buffet breakfast, and wintertime heating and hot water. Overflow tends to be referred next door to the quiet, off-street *Öztürk Pension* (☎0258/272 2116; ③), also enclosing a pool-garden and managed by a friendly if slightly loopy family. Another long-standing favourite about 200m up the street is the *Hotel Kervansaray* (☎0258/272 2209, fax 272 2143; ③), owned by the welcoming Kaya family; many of the rooms overlook creek greenery, plus there's a rooftop café-restaurant, though the latter is shut in winter, and (like most places in the village) the rooms are unheated. If they're full, you'll be pointed a few metres down the hill to the *Aspawa* (☎0258/272 2094; ②), with an off-street mineral pool and good breakfasts, or further on to the *Gül* (☎0258/272 2289; ②). At the remote, south end of matters, on a backstreet near the junction of Korkmaz Caddesi and Mehmet Akif Ersoy Bulvarı, is the new, dead-quiet *Venüs Motel* (☎0258/272 2152; ②), with basic en-suite rooms, run by a woman. A final budget alternative is the *Arkadaş Pension* at the village centre (☎0258/272 2183, fax 272 2589; ②), en suite with English-speaking management. Also centrally convenient, the *Çetin Motel* (☎0258/272 2210; ④) is set back from the main shopping street and relatively comfortable.

For something approximating luxury, however, you'd need to stay at one of the half-dozen motels **up on the rim** of the travertine terraces. Mostly built during the 1970s and now distinctly showing their age, these places charge more for their location than superlative amenities. Additionally, as part of the proposed travertine preservation programme, some or all of them are periodically threatened with closure by the authorities, so don't be too surprised in future years to see a heap of rubble marking their location. Establishments listed below are those most likely to escape demolition.

Doyen of them all for the sake of its famous Roman-era pool (see below) is the slightly set-back *Pamukkale Motel* (☎0258/272 2024; ⑦); the rooms themselves are box-like and functional. Situated 300m northwest on the terrace edge, the *Motel Koru* (☎0258/272 2429, fax 272 2023; ⑥) is rather better value with its three pools – one indoors – and popular restaurant. By contrast the *Hotel Mistur* (☎0258/272 2421, fax 272 2013; ⑤), well out of the hubbub on the road out to Karahayıt just before the necropolis, is undersubscribed for unclear reasons, but merits inclusion for its distinctive igloo-like rooms.

Eating out, the situation is almost uniformly dire. Service is slack and prices nearly double what they'd be elsewhere. You'll usually get better value if you arrange half-board with your *pansiyon* or motel – sometimes obligatory in the fancier places.

The site

The combined **site** (daily dawn–dusk, ie 7.30am–7.30pm in summer; $3) of ancient Hierapolis and the travertines has two entrances. One, the signposted *Güney Kapısı* or **South Gate**, is at the end of a road describing a lazy loop up from the village; here you'll find a rather grandiose "visitor centre" plus a ticket booth, and will additionally be charged ($0.50) for the privilege of parking vehicles. The complex seems, however, a rather futile gesture, as you've a long, shadeless walk to the ruins and terraces from here. Most vehicles – including tour buses and a shuttle minibus up from the village – still use the other, **North Gate** (another ticket booth) for access to the central car parks next to the museum. If you plan to visit Karahayıt, beyond Hierapolis, retain your ticket stub so that you don't have to pay again when re-entering the fee zone.

There's also a quite conspicuous **path** up to the plateau (a 15-minute hike), from just before the point where the Karahayıt-bound road curls north out of the village. Intended originally to allow the villagers to enjoy the springs, it's still a way to get into the site for free, though it can't be long before the *Refah*-inspired authorities plug this long-standing loophole by stationing a guard astride the trail to extract toll from foreigners.

The **travertine terraces** are, deservedly, the first item on most people's agenda. Most face west-southwest, so if you can restrain yourself a late afternoon or dusk visit is most dramatic. The authorities, not yet prepared logistically to prevent visitors from walking out on the solidified lime, are for the moment reduced to pleading that you not wear shoes in the pools – a reasonable enough request. The main problem, other than the crowds, is that relatively few pools remain, their tepid waters ranging in depth from ankle to waist height; it's fairly evident – in the form of dried-up, abandoned sluices snaking in various directions – that the extent of the terraces was once much greater.

If you want to take a proper bath in the springs, visit the *Pamukkale Motel* up on the plateau, which encloses the **sacred pool** of the ancients, with mineral water bubbling from its bottom at 95°F. Time was when you could discreetly saunter in for an early-morning bath with the staff none the wiser, but admission is now highly regimented: dawn–11pm for guests, dawn–dusk for the public with $5 admission payable and non-locking changing cabins by the ticket office. Merely show, do not give, ticket stubs to the guards stationed at the pool entrances or you'll have trouble getting back in if you go to the rest rooms or have a drink. Notwithstanding all the foregoing expense and hassle, the irregularly shaped pool must be one of the most delightful around the Mediterranean, with surrounding gardens and the submerged columns of a portico that once stood nearby. Come as early or late as possible; midday is the province of large tour groups.

On your way to the pool you'll have passed the **tourist information office** (☎0258/268 6539; daily in season 8am–noon & 1.30–7.30pm), principally useful for its combined map of the site and village, and the **museum** (daily except Mon 9am–noon & 1.30–5pm; $1), housed in the restored, second-century AD baths. Its rather disappointing collection consists primarily of statuary, sarcophagi, masonry fragments and smaller knick-knacks recovered during excavations at Hierapolis. Behind the museum is a large sixth-century **basilica**, probably the Byzantine-era cathedral, with two aisles sandwiching the nave.

Hierapolis: eastern monuments

Access to the easterly monuments of ancient **Hierapolis** is via a narrow road winding up between the main car park and the museum. The first break – it can hardly be called a gate – in the roadside fence gives access to a **nymphaeum** or fountainhouse, the **Temple of Apollo** and the adjacent **Plutonium**. The Apollo shrine in its present, scanty form dates from the third century AD, though built on a second-century BC foundation. The grotto of the Plutonium, a quasi-oracular site sacred to the god of the underworld, is today a small, partly paved cavity beyond which you can hear rushing water and an ominous hissing – the emission of a highly toxic gas, probably a mixture of sulphurous compounds and carbon dioxide, capable of killing man and beast alike. In ancient times the eunuch priests of Cybele were reputedly able to descend into the

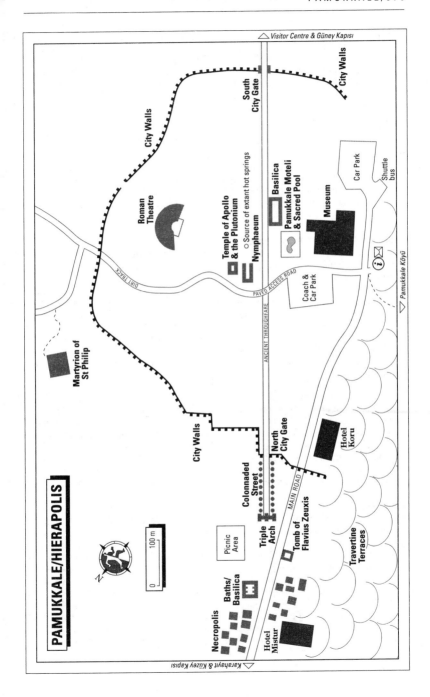

PAMUKKALE/HIERAPOLIS

△ *Visitor Centre & Güney Kapısı*

City Walls

City Walls

South City Gate

Source of extant hot springs

Roman Theatre

Temple of Apollo & the Plutonium

Nymphaeum

Basilica

Pamukkale Moteli & Sacred Pool

Museum

Car Park

Shuttle bus

▷ *Pamukkale Köyü*

DIRT TRACK

PAVED ACCESS ROAD

ANCIENT THROUGHFARE

Coach & Car Park

Martyrion of St Philip

City Walls

North City Gate

Hotel Koru

MAIN ROAD

Colonnaded Street

Picnic Area

Triple Arch

Tomb of Flavius Zeuxis

Travertine Terraces

N

0   100 m

Necropolis

Baths/ Basilica

Hotel Mistur

△ *Karahayıt & Kuzey Kapısı*

chasm with no ill effect; whether this was a result of their anatomical deficiency or some less obvious ruse is unknown. Today a formidable metal cage-grille keeps dare-devils out – before this was installed, two Germans died attempting to brave the cave.

The next feature – and the only monument that can really be sealed off after dark – is the restored **Roman theatre**, dating from the second century AD. Admittedly amphitheatres are a dime a dozen in Turkey but this one is in exceptionally good shape, including most of the stage buildings and their elaborate reliefs. During the **International Pamukkale Song Festival** (late June) performances are held here: the 46 rows of seats can still hold up to 7000 spectators comfortably, as against the former capacity of 10,000.

After seeing the theatre, return to the dirt track and follow it further east past a stretch of the **city walls**, turning left onto a smaller path and eventually halting before the **Martyrion of St Philip**, built in honour of the apostle martyred here in AD80. This fifth-century structure, comprising many rectangular cells converging on a central octagonal chamber, was almost certainly not Philip's tomb, nor even a church, but probably the venue for festivals and processions on the saint's day.

Hierapolis: northern monuments

Arguably the most interesting part of the city is the **colonnaded street**, which once extended for almost 1km from a gate 400m southeast of the sacred pool to another breach in the north wall. This thoroughfare, parallel to the plateau's edge, unevenly bisected the grid plan of the Hellenistic city, and terminated at each end in monumental portals a few paces outside the walls. Only the northerly one, a **triple arch** flanked by towers and dedicated to the emperor Domitian in 84 AD, still stands. The short stretch of intact paved way, flanked by various columns, was the commercial heart of the city. Immediately behind, a grove of conifers shelters a **picnic area**, a possible lunch stop and good landmark to navigate towards should you wish to descend directly from the Martyrion to the colonnaded street, rather than retrace your steps to the museum junction.

North of Domitian's triple arch, on the east side of the road, stands the squat bulk of some second-century AD baths, converted 200 years later into a **basilica**. Slightly closer to the archway, west of the asphalt, you'll notice the elaborate **tomb of Flavius Zeuxis**, a prominent Hierapolitan merchant – the first of more than a thousand tombs of all shapes and sizes constituting the **necropolis**, the largest in Asia Minor and extending for nearly 2km along the road. The more sumptuous ones bear epitaphs or inscriptions warning grave-robbers of punishments awaiting those caught, and there are even forecourts with benches for visits by the deceased's relatives. Nowadays camels and their drovers, instead of tomb-desecrators, lurk among the tumuli.

Karahayıt

Many dolmuşes cover the 7km or so from the lower village to **KARAHAYIT**, famous for its *Kırmızı Su* (Red Water). These hot (130˚F), iron-rich springs well up from within a single, blunt-topped rock formation and then flow, considerably cooled down, into a large rustic pool belonging to the small **campsite** next door. A fee is payable for pool use, though collection can be somewhat lax. Despite no less than ten luxury mega-complexes at the village outskirts – including the Russian-supported casino – Karahayıt seems a sort of downmarket Pamukkale Köyü, patronized almost exclusively by Turkish villagers after a soak; shops on the single high street offer tatty plastic goods rather than carpets or copper souvenirs. As at Pamukkale, overzealous tapping of the thermal springs by the various *pansiyons* has led to a similar reduction in flow and similar threats by the authorities to close down or at least regulate offending establishments.

Laodiceia and Akhan

Just off the road linking Pamukkale and Denizli are two minor archeological sites, ancient **Laodiceia** and Selçuk **Akhan** – worth a short detour if you've time or your own vehicle.

Laodiceia (Laodikya)

Thirteen kilometres south of Pamukkale, a standard issue black-on-yellow marker points 500m west to a larger placard detailing the delights of "Laodikya", the site of ancient **LAODICEIA**, which covers an elevated tableland squeezed between two river valleys, the bleak melancholy of the meagre remains accentuated by tractor furrows and power pylons. It's a setting redeemed principally by perennially snow-covered Honaz Dağı (2571m) to the southeast, matched in miniature by the white strip of Pamukkale to the north.

Founded by the post-Alexandrian Seleucid kings in the mid-third century BC at the junction of two major trade routes, Laodiceia came under Roman rule at the same time as the other cities of Caria. Under the empire, its prosperity – derived largely from soft black wool – was such that (unlike Hierapolis) it needed no imperial assistance to repair the earthquake damage of 60 AD. As with its northern neighbour, though, the presence of a large Jewish community aided in the rapid adoption of Christianity – albeit half-heartedly according to St John the Divine, whose pungent comment in Revelations 3:15–17 is notorious: "I know your works, you are neither hot nor cold. Would that you were cold or hot! So, because you are lukewarm, and neither cold nor hot, I will spew you out of my mouth" – a metaphor almost certainly derived from John's acquaintance with the springs at Pamukkale. Nonetheless, Laodiceia became an important bishopric during Byzantine times, and only began its final decline after a fifth-century earthquake. Shortly after the Selçuk conquest the city was abandoned in favour of nearby Denizli.

As befits a settlement of mostly Roman importance, the visible ruins date from that era. The track starting at the orientation placard dwindles away in the centre of the plateau, next to the rubble of a **nymphaeum**. Southeast of here, at the edge of the site, is the 350-metre-long **stadium**, the largest in Asia Minor but in parlous condition, constructed in the first century AD under the emperor Vespasian. Overlooking it are the fairly substantial remains of a Hadrianic **gymnasium** and **baths complex**. These, and the archeological zone in general, have suffered from systematic masonry pilferage in recent times; engravings from the 1820s show monuments standing to twice their present height. Return to the nymphaeum once more and cross the rudimentary track to find the foundations of an **Ionic temple**. Continue a short distance north and begin pacing the edge of the upland to find, in quick succession, the **small theatre** – facing northwest and with many seats intact – and the **large theatre**, facing northeast over the modern village of Eskihisar.

Akhan

If the weather's fine you might just want to walk the 3km between Laodiceia and the Selçuk *kervansaray* of **AKHAN**. Upon reaching Highway E24/320, the main Denizli–Afyon road, turn left and proceed 1500m to the lightly restored structure tucked just north of the asphalt, on the west bank of a creek. If you enter the modern village of Akhan, you've gone too far. The rectangular structure encloses a courtyard, with arches to either side and a covered hall at the rear. An inscription over the front gate, which looks southeast over the stream and a peach orchard, declares that the building was completed in 1252–53, under the reign of the sultan İzzedin Kaykavuş.

travel details

Trains

Denizli to: Afyon–Eskişehir–Haydarpaşa–İstanbul (1 daily; 14hr 30min); Afyon (1 daily; 5hr 30min).

İzmir (Alsancak) to: Menderes Airport (every hour, on the half-hour; 20min; return from the airport on the hour).

İzmir (Basmane) to: Denizli (2 daily, via Aydın & Nazilli; 6hr); Manisa–Balıkesir–Bandırma (1 daily; 6hr 30min; ferry connection at Bandırma for İstanbul's Sarayburnu dock, 4hr 30min more); Manisa–Balıkesir–Kütahya–Ankara (2 daily, both with couchettes or full sleepers; 14–15hr); Manisa–Balıkesir–Kütahya–Eskişehir (9hr 30min–12hr); Ödemiş (1 daily; 3hr 30min); Selçuk (2 daily; 1hr 45min); Söke, via Selçuk (1 daily; 2hr 15min).

Selçuk to: Aydın (3 daily; 1hr); Denizli (2 daily; 4hr 15min); İzmir (Basmane, 6 or 7 daily; 1hr 45min).

Buses and dolmuşes

Aydın to: Alinda via Karpuzlu (hourly; 1hr); Ankara (several daily; 10hr); Çine (hourly; 35min); Denizli (every 30min until 7pm; 2hr); Fethiye (8 daily; 4hr 30min); Konya (3 daily; 10hr); Marmaris (10 daily; 2hr 45min); Nazilli (every 30min; 50min); Söke (every 30min; 50min); Sultanhisar (every 30min; 30min).

Bodrum to: Ankara (several daily; 13hr); Bitez (every 30min; 15min); Fethiye (6 daily; 4hr 30min); Gölköy (hourly; 20min); Gümbet (every 15min; 10min); Gümüşluk (every 30min; 40min); Gündoğan via Torba (hourly; 25min); İstanbul (several daily; 15hr); Marmaris (8 daily; 3hr 15min); Muğla (10 daily; 2hr 30min); Ortakent (every 30min; 20min); Turgutreis (every 30min; 25min); Yahşi Sahil (every 30min; 20min); Yalıkavak (10 daily; 25min).

Datça to: Ankara (2 daily; 13hr); İstanbul (2 daily; 16hr); Marmaris (13 minibuses daily; 2hr 15min); Mesudiye (several minibuses daily; 30min); Muğla (11 minibuses daily; 3hr 15min).

Denizli to: Antalya via Burdur/Korkuteli (8 daily; 5hr 30min); Bodrum via Kale/Muğla (2–3 daily; 4hr 30min); Konya via Isparta and Eğridir (several daily; 7hr 15min); Marmaris via Kale/Muğla (2–3 daily; 3hr 30min). Minibuses from the same terminal to: Tavas (hourly till 6pm; 40min) and Yeşilova, for Salda Gölü (8 daily; 1hr 30min).

İzmir to: Afyon (8 daily; 5hr 30min); Ahmetbeyli (at least 8 daily; 1hr 20min); Ankara (8 daily; 9hr 30min); Antalya via Aydın and Burdur (8 daily; 8hr 30min); Aydın (every 30min; 2hr); Ayvalık (every 30min; 2hr 30min); Bergama (hourly; 2hr); Bodrum (hourly; 4hr); Bursa (hourly; 7hr); Çandarlı (6 daily in season; 1hr 40min); Çanakkale (6 daily; 5hr 30min); Çeşme (every 15–20min from Üçkuyular terminal; 1hr 30min); Datça (3 daily; 7hr); Denizli (hourly; 4hr); Edirne (6 daily; 10hr); Fethiye (12–18 daily; 6hr 45min); Foça (every 30min; 1hr 30min); Gümüldür (at least 8 daily; 1hr 40min); İstanbul (hourly; 11hr); Kuşadası (every 20min until 9pm; 2hr); Manisa (every 15min; 45min); Marmaris (hourly; 5hr); Milas (hourly; 3hr); Muğla (hourly; 4hr); Salihli (hourly; 1hr 30min); Sart (hourly; 1hr 30min); Seferihisar (at least hourly from Üçkuyular terminal; 1hr); Selçuk (every 20min; 1hr 40min).

Kuşadası to: Aydın (hourly; 1hr 15min); Bodrum (3 daily; 3hr); Dilek Yarımadası National Park (every 30min; 40min); İstanbul (6 daily; 13hr); Menderes Airport (every 20min until 9pm; 1hr 30min); Pamukkale (12 daily; 3hr 30min); Seferihisar (hourly; 1hr 30min); Söke (every 30min; 30min).

Marmaris to: Akyaka (every 30min; 30min); Ankara (14 daily; 13hr); Bodrum (4 daily; 3hr 15min); Bozburun (3 daily; 1hr 15min); Denizli (6 daily; 3hr); Fethiye (10 daily; 2hr 45min); İstanbul (4 daily; 16hr); Orhaniye (several daily; 35min); Ortaca (hourly; 1hr 15min); Selimiye (3 daily; 50min); Tavlica (1 daily; 1hr 40min); Turunç (hourly; 20min).

Milas to: Euromos (hourly; 15min); Güllük (every 30min; 35min); Muğla (hourly; 1hr 15min); Ören (at least 6 daily; 1hr); Selimiye (hourly; 20min).

Muğla to: Akyaka (every 30min; 30min); Fethiye (10 daily; 2hr 30min); Köyceğiz (hourly; 50min); Marmaris (every 30min; 1hr).

Nazilli to: Geyre (6–7 daily; 50min); Karacasu (6–7 daily; 40min).

Selçuk to: Kuşadası (every 20min until 10pm; 25min); Tire (every 20min; 40min).

Söke to: Altınkum (hourly; 50min); Bafa Gölü (every 30min; 30min); Balat (several daily; 40min);

Didyma (hourly; 50min); Dilek Yarımadasi National Park (every 30min; 40min); Güllübahçe (hourly; 20min); Güzelçamlı (every 30min; 40min); Milas (every 30min; 1hr 20min); Miletus (several daily; 40min); Priene (hourly; 20min).

Planes

Bodrum (İmsık) to: Antalya (3 weekly on *Top Air*, 40min); İstanbul (3–4 daily on *THY*, not winter; several weekly on *Top Air*, 1hr 10min); Selçuk (5 weekly on *Top Air*, 40min).

Denizli (Çardak Airport) to: İstanbul (3 weekly; 1hr 10min).

İzmir to: Ankara (2 or 3 daily on *THY*, 1hr 15min); Antalya (2 weekly on *İstanbul Hava Yolları*, 50min); Dalaman (1 weekly on *İstanbul Hava Yolları*, 1hr); İstanbul (7–8 daily on *THY*, 3–4 weekly on *İstanbul Hava Yolları*, 50min).

Domestic hydrofoils

All frequencies given apply to the reverse itinerary also, and are valid during the May–Oct season only. These services are currently operated by *Bodrum Express Lines*.

Altınkum to: Bodrum (1 or 2 weekly; 1hr). $10 one-way, $20 open return. This service usually uses Torba harbour, north of Bodrum; land transfer fees included.

Bodrum to: Marmaris (3 weekly; 2hr). $20 one-way, $35 open return.

Datça to: Bodrum (2 daily; 1hr). Hydrofoils actually arrive and depart Körmen Limanı, 9km north of Datça; shuttle bus included in prices, which vary from $10 one-way to $20 open return.

Domestic ferries

The first two, Bodrum-based services are operated by the *Bodrum Ferryboat Association*, the others by *TML*. All frequencies, except those for the Karşıyaka service, are valid during the May–Oct season only.

Altınkum to: Bodrum-Torba (1 daily; 2hr). $7.50 one-way, $12.50 open return.

Datça (Körmen) to: Bodrum (1 daily; 2hr). $6 one-way, $11 open return.

İzmir to: İstanbul (1 weekly, usually Sun; 19hr). $30 for a pullman seat, $50 for a middling cabin, $40 for a small car.

İzmir (Konak) to: Karşıyaka (every 30min; 15min).

Short-hop ferries and hydrofoils to the Greek islands

Most Greek islands opposite Turkey's Central and South Aegean coast are served by at least one Greek and Turkish boat each. Turkish vessels normally leave in the morning – usually between 8 and 9am – returning from Greece between 4.30 and 5.30pm, depending on the time of year; Greek craft arrive between 9 and 10am and return between 4 and 5pm. For a morning boat you must bring your passport to ticket agencies the evening before – or failing that, at the crack of dawn – so that your name is recorded on a passenger manifest; for an afternoon boat it should be enough to hand over your papers two hours before sailing time. Bear in mind that in high season the boats occasionally sell out a day in advance.

With the exception of Çeşme, fares are very nearly uniform in any given port, with significant reductions in slow seasons, but always overpriced for the distances involved. This is partly because any Turkish port controlled by *TML* – including Kuşadası and Marmaris – levies heavy docking fees on all craft, whether *TML*-owned or not; more obviously, such ports also demand departure and arrival taxes from passengers, while all Greek destination ports hit any passenger staying overnight with stiff departure taxes. The following prices do *not* include the cost of Turkish visas required by various nationalities. Taking a small car over on a ferry costs $40–80 one way depending on the port; combi vans and other favoured overlanding vehicles can cost almost double. Advance booking is essential since the boats often hold only two or three vehicles.

Çeşme–Híos (May–Oct 3–12 weekly, Nov–April 2 weekly; 1hr). $25–35 one-way (no Turkish tax), $51–68 open return (the latter includes Greek tax); small car $60–65.

Kuşadası–Sámos (early May to late Oct 9–11 weekly, dwindling to 1 weekly midwinter; 1hr 30min. Also 2–4 afternoon hydrofoils weekly; 45min). Hydrofoils and ferries much the same price at $30 one-way (includes Turkish tax), $66 open return (includes Turkish tax twice, plus Greek tax). Small car $50.

Bodrum–Kós (6–12 weekly, dwindling to 1 or 2 weekly in midwinter; 45min. Also daily hydrofoils in summer; 20min). Currently the cheapest crossing at $14 one-way, $46 open return (including Greek tax) for ferries, $20 one-way (no Turkish tax), $54 open return (including Greek tax) for the hydrofoils. Small car $50.

Marmaris–Rhodes (1–2 daily hydrofoils May–Oct, down to 1 or 2 weekly in mid-winter; 1hr 15min). $34 one-way (includes Turkish tax), open return $75 (two Turkish taxes and Greek tax included). Also 2 weekly car ferries (2hr 30min); slightly cheaper prices. Small car $80.

Long-haul international ferries

İzmir–Venice (Italy) (March–Sept 1 weekly, Oct–Feb every other week, on *TML*, usually Wed; 67hr). Sample one-way fares: $360 per passenger for a middling cabin, including taxes and meals, plus $230 for a small car.

Çeşme–Ancona (Italy) (mid-June to late Sept, weekly on *Topaş*, usually Wed; 65hr). Sample one-way fares: $330 per passenger for a middling cabin, plus $240 for a small car.

Çeşme–Bari (Italy) (June–Sept 2 weekly on *European Seaways*; 38hr). Sample one-way fares: $250 for a middling cabin, plus $190 a small car.

Çeşme–Brindisi (Italy) (mid-June to mid-Sept 2 weekly on *TML*; 31hr; late June to mid-Sept 2 weekly on *Med Link Lines*; 1–2 weekly year-round on *European Seaways*). Sample one-way fares (on *TML*): $250 per passenger for a middling cabin, including taxes and meals, plus $190 for a small car. Prices on the two private lines are comparable.

Kuşadası–Iraklion (Greece)–Patras (Greece)–Ancona (Italy) (late June to mid-Sept 1 weekly on *Marlines*, usually Tues evening or Wed morning; 75hr for the full run). Sample one-way fares: $280 per passenger for a middling cabin, plus $270 for a small car. Prices exclusive of taxes.

Marmaris–Venice (Italy) (early June to early Oct every other week, generally Wed, on *TML*; 70hr). Same fares for passengers and cars as the İzmir-based service.

CHAPTER FIVE

THE TURQUOISE COAST

urkey's southwesternmost shore is dominated by the Baba, Akdağ and Bey ranges of the Toros mountains, which drop precipitously to a road running along the coast, its curves sometimes skimming just above the water; this is the **Turquoise Coast**, noted for its fine beaches and beautiful scenery. Here, and some distance inland, lay the ancient kingdom of **Lycia**, peopled by an independent race who bequeathed a legacy of their distinctive rock tombs to Turkish tourism.

Until the late 1970s, there was no proper highway through these parts, and most of the seaside settlements were reachable only by boat. Many of the most attractive bays and islands are still inaccessible to land-based traffic, with yachting accordingly popular. But roads in the area have been vastly improved in recent years, penetrating to hitherto idyllic, isolated coves such as Kekova, Adrasan and Çıralı. There's a slender chance that the damage done to the area by large-scale development will be minimized by careful planning, however – the height of new buildings has been restricted, nearby archeological sites often prompt special protection measures, and touting in the streets and at *otogar*s is not yet at the level of, for example, Kuşadası or Pamukkale. And the greater accessibility is a blessing if you happen to be reliant on public transport rather than a yacht.

The usually excellent **Highway 400** runs from Marmaris to Antalya, linking most of the major sights along the way, and offering some impressively panoramic views. Arrival in the Turquoise Coast has also been eased overall by the construction of **Dalaman airport**, to which there are regular direct international flights, as well as domestic flights from İstanbul, Ankara, and even nearby Antalya. Another airport, somewhere between Fethiye and Demre, has long been proposed, though so far environmentalists and other anti-growth factions have succeeded in blocking the first proposed locations near Patara.

At the far west of the region, **Dalyan** is renowned for its sandy beach – a breeding ground of loggerhead turtles – as well as being an idyllically set, small resort with a bit more than lip-service paid to preserving the value of the area; it's also an excellent base for nearby **Köyceğiz Lake** and the ruins of **Kaunos**. East of here, **Fethiye**, along with the nearby lagoon of **Ölüdeniz**, is a full-blown town worth visiting in its own right, but also the Turquoise Coast's primary and most central resort, well placed for visiting some of the best of the area's numerous overgrown and crumbling Lycian ruins. Collectively these, located in spectacular settings, are perhaps the most compelling attraction of the region. **Pinara**, **Tlos** and **Xanthos** are close to Fethiye and situated in dramatic mountainous locations; further on, **Patara** abuts one of the coast's best beaches, making it perfectly possible to combine a sea-and-sun holiday with the odd cultural foray. Other convenient bases for such an outing will be the resorts of **Kalkan** and **Kaş** to the east, both smaller than Fethiye and pitched at slightly different audiences.

Proceeding east again, **Finike** is the next major town; though far less successful than Fethiye as a tourist centre, it still makes a good starting point for a precipitous inland route that takes in the sites of **Limyra** and **Arykanda** on the way up to the high plateau of **Elmalı**, whose rarefied air and marvellous setting repay the trip, especially if a return loop to the coast is made via Gömbe, jump-off point for the attractions of **Akdağ**.

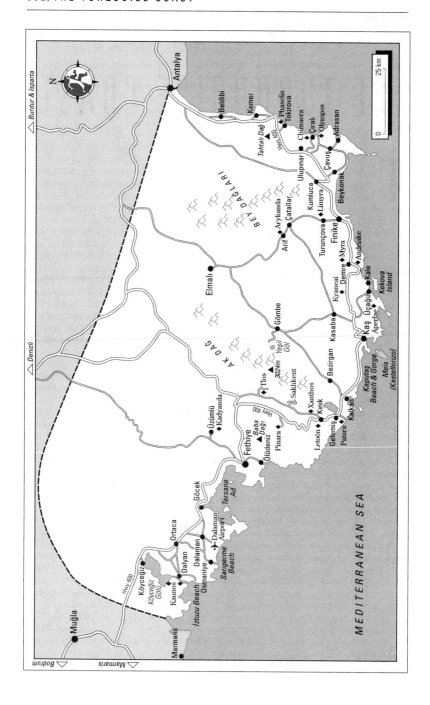

ACCOMMODATION PRICE CODES

In this guide, motels and nearly all hotels and *pansiyon*s have been categorized according to the price codes outlined below, which are based on US$ because of the high domestic Turkish inflation rate. These categories represent the minimum you can expect to pay for a **double room in high season**. Rates for hostels and for the most basic hotels and *pansiyon*s, where guests are charged **per person**, are given in US$, instead of being indicated by price code. For further information, including a rough outline of what you might expect in each category, see p.37.

① under $12	② $12–17	③ $18–25
④ $26–35	⑤ $36–45	⑥ $46–55
⑦ $56–75	⑧ over $75	

Beyond Finike, the scenery becomes increasingly spectacular as you enter a densely forested area on the slopes of **Tahtalı Dağ**, officially designated a national park, before passing the sites of ancient **Olympos** – set close to more good beaches at **Adrasan** and **Çıralı** – and **Phaselis**. Thereafter, however, a string of functional, even dreary purpose-built resorts lines the approach to Antalya, main centre for the Mediterranean Coast and detailed in Chapter 6.

Lycia in history

The mountainous, rugged territory of **Lycia** lies south of a line drawn roughly between Antalya and Köyceğiz; the peaks of the Bey Dağları and Akdağ, exceeding 3000m in altitude, form the core of the region and have always isolated it from the rest of Anatolia. Relatively secure in their mountain fastness, the Lycians – now thought to be an indigenous, pre-Hittite people rather than (as previous theories held) Cretan immigrants – held a distinctive place in ancient Anatolian history. Their notoriously fierce desire for independence prompted the citizens of Xanthos on two separate occasions to make a funeral pyre of their own city and burn themselves alive, rather than be conquered. They also had their own language and customs: Herodotus wrote, for example, that (unusually) "they reckon their lineage not by their father's but by their mother's side". The main ancient cities or conurbations of smaller towns organized themselves together against external authority in the **Lycian Federation**, a democratic grouping which consisted of 23 voting units, and was charged with electing national officials and municipal authorities – and, until control of Lycia was assumed by imperial Rome, making decisions of state. The Lycians are first mentioned in Homer's *Iliad*, in which they fought as allies of the Trojans. Later, in the sixth century BC, the region was subdued by the Persian general Harpagus, but was largely left to govern itself.

From 454 BC, after the Athenian general Kimon had cleared all Persian garrisons from the Mediterranean coast, the Lycians became members of the Delian League, a maritime alliance which required them to pay tribute to Athens. The League ceased to exist after the Peloponnesian War ended in 404 BC, and Lycia again fell under Persian domination, although this did not mean that they entirely accepted vassal status. Alexander the Great arrived in 333 BC, and after the conquest of Halicarnassus secured the surrender of Lycia without further trouble; following his death Lycia was ruled by Alexander's general, Ptolemy, also king of Egypt. During the Ptolemaic rule of the third century BC, the native Lycian language was replaced by Greek, and the cities adopted Greek constitutions. The Ptolemies were defeated by Antiochus III in 197 BC, who in turn was bested in 189 by the Romans, who handed the kingdom over to the Rhodians. As ever, the Lycians bitterly and forcefully resented Rhodian control, and succeeded in 167 BC in having this administrative relegation revoked.

Thereafter, the Lycians enjoyed over two centuries of semi-independence, during which time their Federation came back into prominence, resisting attack once again by the Pontic (Black Sea) King Mithridates in 88 BC and being subsequently rewarded by Rome for loyalty. During the Roman civil wars, Lycian reluctance to assist Brutus led to the destruction of Xanthos, and although Antony later reconfirmed the autonomy of Lycia, in 43 AD the region was joined to Pamphylia in a larger Roman province. Roman imperial rule was not unduly harsh; indeed the area reached its maximum ancient population of about 200,000, a figure not again equalled until this century, and the cities were graced by the Roman civic architecture which constitutes most of the ruins on view today.

During the fourth century the province was divided by Diocletian and a period of Byzantine-supervised decline set in, a process helped along by Arab raids in the seventh and eighth centuries. From this point on, the history of the region resembled that of the rest of western Anatolia, where after the establishment of Selçuk Turk sovereignty during the eleventh and twelfth centuries, and an interlude of minor emirates, a more comprehensive, durable Anatolian Muslim state was installed by the Ottomans. They continued a pattern of moving nomadic Turkic tribes into the Lycian uplands, leaving the coast to pirates and local chieftains, until in the eighteenth century the sultan ordered its settlement by more tractable, productive Greek Orthodox colonists from the offshore islands.

Fethiye

FETHİYE is advantageously situated for visits to some of the Turquoise Coast's more fascinating sites, and although adjacent beaches at **Çalış** and **Ölüdeniz** are now much too crowded for comfort in season, the town itself still has qualities that set it apart from many other Mediterranean holiday centres. While tourism is admittedly dominant, Fethiye remains a lively, Turkish-feeling market town, utterly unlike Marmaris, Bodrum or Kuşadası; plans may eventually materialize to have it designated the capital of a newly created province split off from Muğla province. Adding to the atmosphere are the numerous ore ships at anchor by the jetty, taking on cargoes of chromium, a major Fethiye-hinterland product, and the commercial tomato brokers' section of the extensive produce market.

Unlike tourism rival Kaş, which is confined by its sheer rock backdrop, Fethiye has been able to spread north to accommodate the increase in tourist traffic; it also boasts other nearby beaches – like **Sarıgirme** and **Kıdrak** – and there seems to be a good supply of more rugged coastline left when even these get out of hand. Moreover, the Gulf of Fethiye is speckled with twelve islands, and one of the greatest pleasures here is to embark on a boat tour from Fethiye harbour, in search of secluded coves in which to swim, fish and camp out.

The town occupies the site of the ancient Lycian city of **Telmessos**, and some impressive rock tombs are an easy stroll from the centre, itself enlivened by a recently excavated amphitheatre. A short drive or long walk out of Fethiye brings you to the "ghost village" of **Kaya**, a former Greek settlement abandoned after the 1923 population exchanges, whose ruined houses and churches conjure a sad, dramatic history.

Some history

Nothing much is known of the origins of Telmessos, except that it wasn't originally part of the Lycian Federation; indeed, in the fourth century BC the Telmessans actually fought against the Lycians. It may be that Pericles, a Lycian dynast, subdued the Telmessans and allowed them into the Federation around this time – Lycian inscriptions have been found in the city, and it is known that during the time of the Roman Empire the city was part of the Federation, if unique in having good relations with Rhodes.

Like most Lycian cities, Telmessos was captured by Alexander in 334–333 BC, but lost not long after. The city was recaptured by one of Alexander's companions by means of a famous strategem: Nearchus the Cretan asked permission to leave a number of captive women musicians and boys in the city, but the women concealed weapons in their musical instrument cases, and the prisoners' escort used them to seize the acropolis. In the eighth century, the city's name was changed to **Anastasiopolis** in honour of a Byzantine emperor. This name gave way to **Makri** in the following century (*Meğri* in Turkish), and became Fethiye during this century, in honour of a local pilot and war hero named **Fethi Bey**, after the expulsion of the predominantly Greek Orthodox population. Hardly anything now remains of the ancient or medieval city, partly because it suffered two immense **earthquakes** in 1857 and 1957, which toppled much of the town – whose rubble lies compacted under the present quay and shoreline boulevard.

Arrival, getting around and information

The **new otogar** is over 2km east of the town centre at the junction with the Ölüdeniz road; short-haul **dolmuşes** run from here as far as the popular accommodation district of Karagözler, sparing you the necessity of a three-kilometre-plus walk, or shelling out for a taxi. Other dolmuşes to Ölüdeniz, Çalış beach and Kaya arrive and leave from underneath wooden marquees at the **old otogar**, east of the central market area. The main **taxi ranks** are found near the PTT, and beside Şehit Fethi Bey Park, in front of the ancient amphitheatre. **Dolmuş boats** link Fethiye and Çalış regularly in mid-season (daily 9.30am–midnight; $0.85), departing from the seafront behind the Municipal Building.

Driving your own vehicle, you're forced to adhere to what is in effect a one-way system: westbound on **Atatürk Caddesi**, the main road leading toward the harbour, lined with most services and official buildings, and eastbound on inland **Çarşı Caddesi**, which threads through the heart of the commercial district. Parking can be nightmarish, so you'll probably want to patronize the handful of fee *otopark*s rather than risk being towed.

The **tourist information office** (May–Sept daily 8am–noon & 1–8pm; Oct–April daily 8am–5pm; ☎0252/614 1527), near the harbour at İskele Meydanı 1, has a reasonable amount of useful literature. The local **hoteliers association**, just next door, handles hotel bookings.

Accommodation

Fethiye has an abundance of lodging for all tastes and budgets, so unlike in other coastal resorts, you *will* eventually find something – even in high summer – though perhaps after a bit of trudging around.

Karagözler

Divided into Birinci (First) and İkinci (Second) Karagözler, this is the oldest enclave of hotels and *pansiyons* in Fethiye, desirable and quiet, with most premises enjoying a view of the bay. The only drawback is that it's a fair distance west of the transport terminals and restaurants, though if you have your own vehicle, parking is no problem.

Duygu Pension, Ordu Cad 64, İkinci Karagözler (☎0252/614 3563). Clean en-suite rooms, English-speaking owner. ②.

Ferah, Ordu Cad 21, İkinci Karagözler (☎0252/614 2816). Another long-running standby, near the preceding; garden bar, and sea view despite its location one block inland. ②.

Fethiye, Ordu Cad, İkinci Karagözler (☎0252/614 2483). Comfortable, small, quietish hotel with good bay views. ③.

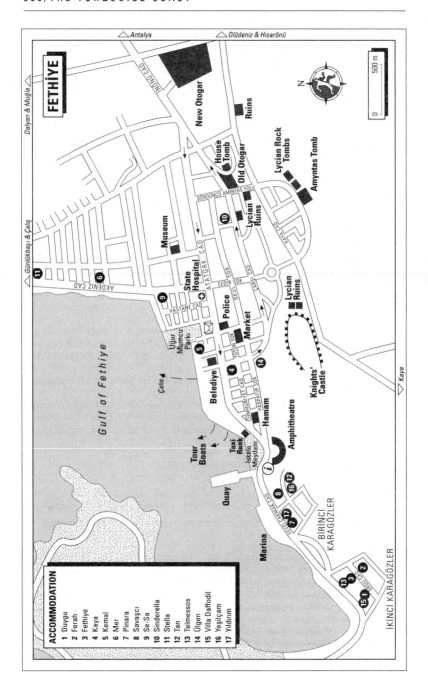

FETHİYE

△ Antalya
△ Olüdeniz & Hisarönü

◁ Dalyan & Muğla

◁ Günlükbaşı & Çalış

N

500 m

0

MÜNÜ CAD

New Otogar

Ruins

House Tomb

Old Otogar

Lycian Rock Tombs

Amyntas Tomb

DÖRDÜNCÜ AMINTAS YOLU

Museum

Lycian Ruins

10

KAYA CAD

State Hospital

ATATÜRK CAD

SEDİR SOK

Police

OKUL SOK

ÇARŞI CAD

Lycian Ruins

Market

HASTANE CAD

9

AKDENİZ CAD

11

6

Uğur Mumcu Parkı

5

Belediye

TÜTÜN SOK

4

14

Knights' Castle

Çalış

Gulf of Fethiye

CUMHURİYET CAD

ASPAIR SOK

Hamam

Amphitheatre

Tour Boats

Taxi Rank

İskele Meydanı

i

Quay

8

16

12

17

7

Marina

BİRİNCİ KARAGÖZLER

13

3

2

15

1

İKİNCİ KARAGÖZLER

▷ Kaya

ACCOMMODATION

1 Duygu
2 Ferah
3 Fethiye
4 Kaya
5 Kemal
6 Mer
7 Pinara
8 Savaşçı
9 Se-Sa
10 Sinderella
11 Stella
12 Tan
13 Telmessos
14 Ülgen
15 Villa Daffodil
16 Yeşilçam
17 Yıldırım

Pinara Pansiyon, Fevzi Çakmak Cad 39, Birinci Karagözler (☎0252/614 2151). Down on the shore road and thus a bit noisier, but highly rated for friendliness and reliable hot water. ②.

Savaşcı Pansiyon (aka *Feridun's Place*), Birinci Karagözler (☎0252/614 4108). Well-worn facilities but hospitable management, and a perennial favourite with backpackers for its roof breakfast-terrace. Perched well above the *Tan* and *Yeşilçam* (see below), so you need to be fit to stay here. ②.

Tan Pansiyon, Karagözler Cad 89, Birinci Karagözler (☎0252/614 1584). A steep hike above the marina quay, basic yet en suite, with flexible breakfast times. ②.

Telmessos Pansiyon, İkinci Karagözler, right opposite the *jandarma* post (☎0252/614 1042). 1970s-vintage building, but comfortable enough; run by an elderly couple whose daughter, a travel agent, is a mine of good advice. ②.

Villa Daffodil, Fevzi Çakmak Cad 115, İkinci Karagözler (☎0252/614 9595, fax 612 2223). Mock-Ottoman design, a pool and a sauna make this newish outfit a favourite; booking advised. ④.

Yeşilçam, Karagözler Cad 91, Birinci Karagözler (☎0252/612 3518). Next door to the *Tan*, slightly newer, and with sweeping views. ②.

Yıldırım, Fevzi Çakmak Cad, Birinci Karagözler (☎0252/614 3923). Next to, and newer than, the *Pinara*; large breakfast included in the price. ②.

The bazaar and waterfront

Fethiye's bazaar area, extending roughly two blocks to either side of Çarşı Caddesi, can be noisy, especially when competing sound systems from assorted bars and clubs raise a din, but it's obviously dead central; a few paces toward the water are some good, if more expensive, choices. Unless indicated, all of the following have en-suite plumbing.

Kaya, Cumhuriyet Cad 6 (☎0252/614 2469). One block inland and bang in the middle of the restaurant and souvenir-shop district, so some rooms can be noisy until past midnight, but comfortable for the price. ③.

Kemal, immediately behind the PTT (☎0252/614 5009). Fanless rooms can be stuffy in midsummer, but this is a relatively quiet, seaside location. ④.

Köln Pension, Beşkaza Sok, Akdeniz Cad (☎0252/614 3373). Balconied, en-suite rooms, with helpful, English-speaking management, near the *Stella*. ②..

Mer (formerly *Martı*), Dolgu Sahası district (☎0252/614 1177). 500m along the coast road to Çalış from the *Se-Sa*; more modest but perfectly comfortable. ③.

Se-Sa, Akdeniz Cad 17 (☎0252/614 4656). Well-run, modestly posh waterside hotel at the corner of the Çalış-bound road, convenient for the museum, *otogar* and bazaar. Of late the haunt of travelling salesmen, though it is used by the UK tour operator *Tapestry*. ⑤.

Sinderella Pension, off Çarşı Cad on Merdivenli Geçit 3; well signposted (☎0252/614 2288). Helpful, English-speaking proprietors and a location convenient for the old *otogar* are this inland pension's selling points. ②.

Stella Motel, Dolgu Sahası district (☎0252/614 1735). One of the last buildings in town, out past the *Mer* en route to Çalış; clean, small and simple. ③.

Ülgen Pansiyon, Üçüncü Merdevenli Yokuşu, off Paspatır Sok (☎0252/614 3491). A basic 1970s-style *pansiyon*, with shared bathrooms, whose main virtue is a relatively quiet but convenient location. ②.

Çalış and Günlükbaşı

If you're here specifically for a beach holiday, it might make sense to stay in one of these two districts, both 5km north of Fethiye; there's a direct road to **Çalış** from town, as well as boat dolmuşes, though ordinary dolmuşes arrive there in a roundabout way from the main highway via **Günlükbaşı**, which is considerably more inland and thus cheaper. Their final stop is way at the north end, near the *Seril* hotel; the Çalış esplanade itself is off-limits for cars. The gravelly sand of Çalış extends over 2km, with views over the bay islets to the sunset, but it's prone to pummelling from wind and waves, making the water very murky when not downright filthy. Çalış itself is essentially a tourist ghetto of leather shops, "minimarkets", resolutely mediocre restaurants and mushrooming hotels, overrun in season by Germans and Scandinavians, with lately a sprinkling of British. The navigable channels and marshes between Çalış and Günlükbaşı are picturesque but breed swarms of mosquitoes.

Bahar, Çalış shore road (☎0252/613 1073). Halfway along the developed shore frontage road – recently expanded, but still isolated from its neighbours and one of the few outfits here with a Turkish clientele. ④.

Cadianda, off the direct Fethiye–Çalış road, close to Günlükbaşı (☎0252/613 1773, fax 613 1774). This hotel stands out by itself in the reed beds, not near any beach – but is peaceful and well run. ④.

Fiesta, about 200m inland from the central junction at Çalış (☎0252/613 2871). Newish complex that compensates for its location by attentive service and a pool; available through *Tapestry Holidays*. ⑤.

König Pansiyon, on a road linking Günlükbaşı with the beach 700m away (☎0252/613 1299). As the name suggests, it's German-run, with a small swimming pool. ④.

Kumsal Pansiyon, right at the central junction in Çalış (☎0252/613 1265). Somewhat noisy because of the location; popular with independent travellers and one of the friendliest outfits in Çalış. Wood-floored rooms with sea-view balconies. ④.

Mutlu, at the desirable far southern end of the developed strip (☎ and fax 0252/613 1210). Prime setting and well laid-out grounds with a large pool make this popular with British and German package groups. ⑤.

Oykun Pansiyon, opposite the *Sesel Hotel*, 1500m inland along the main Günlükbaşı–Çalış road (☎0252/613 1605). Attractively arranged with a pleasant garden; breakfast included. The **Beşik** (☎0252/613 1418), next door, is similar. Both ③.

Poyraz, south end of the strip, near the *Mutlu* (☎0252/613 1220, fax 613 2471). Engaging wooden balconies and a pool area; a similar package clientele to its neighbour. ⑤.

Seril, at the north end of the strip near the dolmuş terminal (☎0252/613 1631). A good mid-range choice, though mostly given over to German tours; some rooms have a sea view. ⑤.

The Town

The remains of ancient Telmessos are immediately obvious as soon as you arrive in Fethiye. Covering the hillside above the bazaar area are a number of Lycian rock tombs, striking in their proximity to the city and in the grandeur of their setting. Most notable – and worth a closer inspection, despite swarms of children who will offer to guide you there unnecessarily and then demand money – is the **Amyntas Tomb**, so called because of the inscription *Amyntou tou Ermagiou* (Amyntas son of Hermagios) carved in Greek letters on the wall of the tomb. To get there, follow Kaya Caddesi from the *otogar* toward town and take a left turn after the fire station, onto Dördüncü Amintas Yolu, then along a path that leads directly to the tomb (daily 8.30am–sunset; $0.60). Its porch consists of two Ionic columns surmounted by a triangular pediment, carved in close imitation of a temple facade – even down to simulating the bronze nails with which the door frames were studded – giving an excellent impression of what the original wooden temple porches would have looked like. The tomb would have been entered through the bottom right-hand panel of the doorway, but this has now been broken by grave robbers. Traces of paint were still visible on the exterior until the nineteenth century.

Behind the tourist office and main quay sprawls the newly revealed, conspicuous **amphitheatre**, excavated only since 1994. Much of its masonry was carted away after the 1957 quake for construction material, so it's rather frayed at the edges; benefit concerts are often staged here in season to raise funds for a complete restoration of the stage building and seating, though authenticity is likely to be sacrificed in the rush to provide the town with a prestigious venue.

There's not all that much else to see in Fethiye, although you can visit the remains of the **medieval fortress**, on the hillside behind the harbour area. The path to the castle leads off Çarşı Caddesi through backstreets up to the acropolis, affording good views of the town on the way. The fortress is attributed to the Knights of St John, but a variety of architectural styles suggests additional work on the part of Lycians, Greeks, Romans, Byzantines and Turks.

In the centre of town, off Atatürk Caddesi, Fethiye's **museum** (Tues–Sun 8.30am–5pm; $1) has bad labelling and is very small, but some of the exhibits help to enhance the nearby archeological sights by contributing an element of human interest. The most compelling exhibit is the stele found at the Letoön (see p.404), dating from 358 BC, which was critically important in deciphering the Lycian language. The stone slab is covered in a trilingual text in Lycian, Greek and Aramaic concerning a sanctuary in Xanthos dedicated to the mythical god-king, Kaunos, the supposed founder of the city of that name. Other finds include a beautiful gold-leaf headdress dating from the third century BC, unearthed at the site of Pinara.

Eating, drinking and nightlife

Especially compared to unadulterated resorts like Dalyan and Göcek, the eating situation in Fethiye is quite satisfactory; the main thing to watch out for is the oft-used ploy of bringing you, or charging you for, items you haven't ordered – check bills carefully.

Long-running doyen of Fethiye eateries is the *Meğri*, with two branches: one at Çarşı Cad 13, best at lunchtime and specializing in home-style Turkish dishes you'll see nowhere else, and a more blatantly touristic but still tasty outlet at Likya Sok 8–9; beware of an unaffiliated namesake dive on Cumhuriyet Caddesi. Other good choices include: the fancy *Güneş* at Likya Sok 4–5; the simpler *Şedir* on Tütün Sok 3, with a good range of grills, *hazır yemek* and puddings; the *Kent*, a tiny cold *meze* and grilled meat spot under the (not recommended) eponymous hotel at the seaward end of Likya Sokak; and just around the corner on Cumhuriyet Caddesi, the tiny *Mutfak* ("Kitchen"), mobbed at lunch for the sake of its limited but inexpensive selection of goodies, including *mantı*.

Fethiye is well supplied with *pideci*s, each with their partisans. The *Özlem İzgara & Pide* on Çarşı Caddesi, opposite Tütün Sokağı, is the oldest, though lately *Pizza Villa* at Çarşı Cad 36 and *Nefis Pide*, one block west on Eski Cami Sokağı beside the mosque of the name, can match or exceed it in quality; they also offer a range of excellent cheap kebabs and meat dishes. For dessert or a drink, prime venues are the handful of cafés along the kilometre of waterfront leading up to Uğur Mumcu Parkı.

As for **nightlife**, there are plenty of outdoor drinking venues between Atatürk and Çarşı *caddesi*s, as well as further west along and above the harbour. Current favourites include the adjacent, always busy *Car Cemetery Bar* and *Bubon* on Hamam Sokağı. Up on the hillside above the amhpitheatre – itself an occasional venue for live spectacles – state-of-the art *Yasmin* often has live Turkish music. Dancing enthusiasts divide between *Yes! Bar* at Cumhuriyet Cad 9, and the perennial *Disco Marina* in Birinci Karagözler, on the shore road.

Listings

Airlines *İstanbul Airlines*, c/o *Lama Tours*, Hamam Sok 3/A (☎0252/614 4964); *THY*, c/o *Fetur*, ground floor of *Funya Otel*, beside the amphitheatre (☎0252/614 2034).

Boat rental The standard-issue, multi-island day tours cost about $10 a head and are well promoted at the quayside; however, they tend to be rushed (10am–6pm or so), taking in only a set repertoire of relatively spoilt islands with little time at each. It's far better to rent your own boat and crew to take in just one or two selected islands, or even arrange to stay overnight, sleeping on deck or camping on the shore. One recommended boat is the *Pınar 3*, which offers off-season, three-day cruises for an unbeatable $70, including full board.

Bookstore *Imagine*, Atatürk Cad 18/B, which also has a stock of very mainstream cassettes and CDs.

Car rental Local one-offs and small Turkish chains include *Hi-Car* at the yacht marina (☎0252/614 7434); *Focus*, Çarşı Cad, by the *Vakıfbank* (☎0252/6123519); *Light Tours*, Atatürk Cad 104 (☎0252/614 7161); *Intercity*, Atatürk Cad 106/B (252/612 2281); and *Active*, next to the amphitheatre (☎0252/612 3525). The big boys are *Avis*, ground floor of the *Dedeoğlu Hotel*, opposite the jetty (☎0252/612 1385); *Budget*, Karagözler Yokuşu (☎0252/614 6166); and *Europcar*, on the corner of Atatürk and Çarşı *caddesi*s (☎0252/614 4995).

Diving Underwater tours have recently taken off here, particularly between mid-April and mid-November. While the Gulf of Fethiye cannot match tropical oceans in the variety of species, there are plenty of turtles, rays, dolphins, fish and invertebrates in the warm, clear water, plus opportunities for ruin-, cave- and reef-diving. Most long-lived of the half-dozen local companies is the British-run *European Diving Center* (☎0252/614 9771), PO Box 26, 48301 Fethiye, with premises on Atatürk Caddesi by *Etibank*. However, *Mermaid Diving*, Eski Cami Sok 6/A (☎0252/612 3350), has smaller groups and more personable service. A day out with lunch and two dives typically costs $60, a five-day certification course about $400.

Exchange Beware souvenir shops and storefronts who claim to give cash advances on credit cards – shortchanging is common. Stick to the usual venues such as the PTT, banks and dedicated *Döviz* dealers. ATMs that accept foreign cards include *Yapı Kredi*, *Garanti* and *Akbank*, all within a few yards of each other at the west end of Atatürk Caddesi.

Hamam At Hamam Sok 2 (daily 7am–midnight); lukewarm, overpriced and touristy, this is not a good introduction to Turkish baths.

Hydrofoil From May to September, hydrofoils run twice daily on two or three selected days of the week directly to Rhodes in Greece (journey time 90min). Fares are $44 one-way, $63 open return. Though these may seem high, there is no departure tax here as in Marmaris, so in fact they work out cheaper. For current information, contact designated agent *Borina* (see below for address).

Motorbikes/mopeds These can be rented on the square (☎0252/614 5412) very close to the tourist information office, or at *Lib Tour* on the marina (☎0252/614 6952), among other spots.

PTT Atatürk Cad (Mon–Sat 8am–midnight, Sun 9am–7pm).

Shopping Fethiye is excellent for shopping, with a marvellous food market (the place to stock up for a trip to the islands) located between Çarşı Cad and Tütün Sok in the centre of town – also plenty of fake Calvin Klein jeans, fake Chanel, and a few pickpockets. Main market day is Tuesday, when villagers from surrounding districts flood into town with their produce; peak hours 10.30am–1pm. The place to hunt for carpets, leather and silver is Paspatır district, especially to either side of Hamam Sok.

Travel agents *Light Tours*, Atatürk Cad 104 (☎0252/614 4757) is about the most active locally, handling "Blue Cruises" and jeep safaris. Another helpful general agent, which arranges hotel bookings, dive tours and car rental, is *Borina*, currently at Cumhuriyet Cad, Ahmet Ağa İşhane 28/21, 4th floor, but set to move next to the amphitheatre in 1997 (☎0252/614 3429); Naci speaks excellent English.

Around Fethiye

Easily reached on a day trip from town are a variety of attractions: a huge abandoned village, an ancient Lycian city recently opened to tourism, and a handful of popular beaches. Most of them are well connected by public transport in season, and some can even be reached on foot from Fethiye.

Kaya Köyü and beyond

A paved seven-kilometre road – plus the remains of a much shorter trail – climbs up from behind the castle in Fethiye towards the ghost town of **KAYA KÖYÜ**. By dolmuş from the main terminal, however, it's a fifteen-kilometre journey, taking a roundabout route via the village of Ovacık (see p.392).

The deserted village, the largest late-medieval ghost town in Asia Minor, is located on the side of a hill 4km west of Hisarönü (see below), near the site of ancient **Karmylassos**. It was known as **Levissi** after the nineteenth century, when it was settled by Greek Orthodox from the Dodecanese islands just offshore; the present appela-

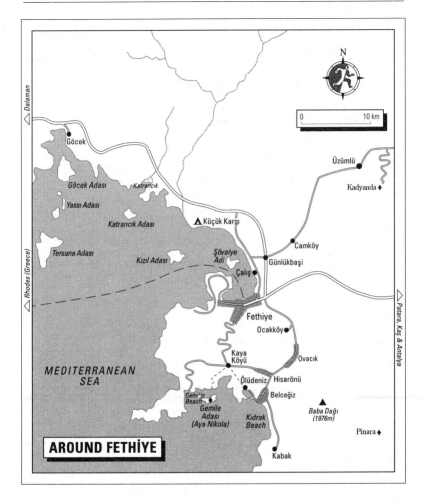

tion is taken from the rather inappropriately named Kaya Çukuru or "Stone Gulch", the small but fertile adjacent upland that partly supported the local population before 1923, and still produces substantial crops of tobacco and grain.

The place has been abandoned since then, when its Christian inhabitants were exiled, along with more than a million others, to a country that had never been their homeland. Kaya is one of the most dramatic and moving sites on the Turkish coast, and puts into painful relief the human suffering involved in the compulsory population exchange. The Macedonian Muslims who were sent here to occupy the abandoned buildings for the most part never did, believing that the Greeks had laid a curse on the village before leaving. In any event, most of their descendants currently live in the hamlets of Keciler and Kınık, at the far fringes of the Kaya Çukuru plateau, overlooked by the ruins.

All you can see now of Kaya is a hillside covered with more than 1500 ruined cottages and the attractive **Panayia Piryiotissa** basilica, the most important of three churches here, to the right of the main path, about 200m up the gentle slope from the road. The church, dated 1888 by a floor mosaic, retains some of its marble altar screen and murals, including faces of Christ and the apostles over the altar, but the general state of dereliction merely serves to highlight the plight of the village. A particularly grisly item in the southwest corner of the church precinct is the **charnel house** piled high with human leg bones (highlighted, in rather bad taste, by certain tour-agency posters); the departing Greeks took the exhumed skulls of their ancestors away with them.

Because of its desolation, proper title deeds for individual Kaya properties were never issued by the Republican Turkish government; consequently in 1988, mass acquisition of the village houses for package-holiday accommodation was proposed by a tour company. When the **Greek-Turkish Friendship Society** learned of this, there was a storm of protest and international lobbying, the government reasserted its claim to the village, and conventional development plans were withdrawn. So far, just a few houses near the edge of Kaya have been restored, and are available, if booked in advance, through the *Kaya Turizm Geliştirme Kooperatifi*, Cumhuriyet Cad 46, Fethiye (☎0252/614 6983, fax 614 6984). For spur-of-the-moment overnights, there are two conventional **pansiyons** in and around Kaya: the volubly friendly *Çavuşoğlu* (☎0252/616 6749; ③), at the edge of the village, with a big swimming pool and a good **restaurant**, and the more upmarket *Villa Rhapsody* (☎0252/616 6551; ④), 500m along the road to Gemiler, also with a pool. Kaya also has about a half dozen cafes and simple restaurants, some – like the *Agora* near the *Çavuşoğlu Pansiyon*, or the *Poseidon İkizler* by the signposted church car park – strategically straddling the paths into the ruined town, but none providing superlative fare.

Gemiler and Aya Nikola

Isolated **Gemiler** beach lies 7km beyond Kaya Köyü along a dirt-surface, minimally marked track, not served by any public transport – and not at present worth any special effort to reach, as the water is murky, the beach strewn with garbage, and all amenities were destroyed in 1991. The previously thriving campsite-restaurants here, whose management kept the place clean, were forced to close by the police, at the behest of local developers who still hope to erect a holiday village here. Now the place has the air of a refugee camp, with a few temporary shacks, offering little besides drinks, set up amid the ruins of the old facilities.

Just offshore looms a prime destination of local boat trips: **Gemile (Aya Nikola) Adası**, an island and yacht anchorage on which stand prominent remains of several eras, including a few rock tombs, a seventh-century Byzantine monastery, and a later, ruined hamlet complete with a nineteenth-century church. Without a boat, all you can do is walk from Kaya Köyü to the mainland directly opposite Gemile island, over the obvious saddle, in about two hours.

Ovacık and Hisarönü

The main road southeast out of Fethiye climbs to a pass, where a turnoff west leads to an abandoned ex-Greek village that met a different fate to Kaya Köyü's: it became *Ocakköy* (☎0252/616 6157, fax 616 6158; ⑤), an establishment of some thirty self-catering restored stone cottages dotting the hillside, plus more conventional rooms around two swimming pools; this is one of the few resorts in Turkey which actively caters for **disabled clients**, with wheelchair ramps and harness slings for lowering yourself into one of the pools.

Just beyond the pass, the straggly, linear village of **OVACIK** seems to consist entirely of about thirty *pansiyon*s and small hotels, which are being snapped up by foreign tour operators – surprisingly, in view of its inland, roadside location and the modest endowments of many of these establishments. The only one worth singling out in terms of facilities or location (though it's still by the busy road) is the *Orka Hotel and Villas* (☎0252/616 6794, fax 616 6706; ⑤; available through *Anatolian Sky*).

HİSARÖNÜ, the next "settlement", actually lies 1500m along the side road to Kaya and Gemiler; once a tiny hamlet, it now offers all the dubious delights of a landlocked concrete resort. Pick of the hotels here are the helpful *Motel Nevis* (☎0252/616 6766; ④), mercifully tucked away at the western edge of things, and the *St Nicholas* (☎0252/616 6353 or 616 6288, fax 616 6355 or 616 6289; ⑤; available through *Anatolian Sky*, *Sunquest* and *Tapestry*) with its own hamam and horse-riding facilities. Far and away the best place to **eat** in town is *Max Donald*, a welcome retreat, with hearty Turkish and Western dishes, a convivial bar and a thoroughly disarming host.

The cancerous growth of Hisarönü and Ovacık is something quietly deplored even by local tourism professionals, and seems all the more ill-advised in light of the local water scarcity; small-bore pipes bringing pumped water up from Kıdrak are inadequate, so water trucks are a daily sight.

Ölüdeniz

Beyond the Hisarönü junction, hotel signs proliferate, making an intimidating introduction by road to **Ölüdeniz**, the azure lagoon that features on every second Turkish travel poster. Frequent dolmuşes make the trip here from Fethiye until late at night, but by far the most attractive approach is on foot from Kaya Köyü. The mostly downhill walk takes you up through Kaya village, over the crest of a hill, down into beautiful woods, finally around the coast and down to the lagoon, with stunning views all the while.

The warm if occasionally turbid waters of Ölüdeniz ($0.60 per person, $2.50 per car, for admission to the fenced "national park") make for pleasant swimming even in April or May, or serve as a protected venue for a spin on a rented kayak. However, the environs of this once-pristine lagoon, whose name translates as "Dead Sea" in Turkish, rank as one of the country's most popular resorts, and in the past decade its beaches – both the spit enclosing the inlet (mostly Turks) and the more exposed strand of **Belceğiz** (mostly foreigners) – reach saturation level on summer weekends. At such times, perhaps it's worth avoiding Ölüdeniz altogether in favour of **Kıdrak** forest service beach (same admission), 3km east of Belceğiz beside the ultra-posh *Robinson Club Lykia* (☎0252/616 6410, fax 616 6488; ⑦), with basic camping facilities.

Just inland from Kıdrak lies a well-watered limestone canyon dubbed "Butterfly Valley" after the many species which can be seen at the right time of year – and when they haven't been frightened off by the numerous tours that target the place. Other, larger flying creatures regularly dot the skies above the area: in recent years **paragliding** has become a big thing locally, and for just under $100, several beachfront outfits will kit you up for a half-hour flight, taking off from the summit of 1976-metre Baba Dağı. A more predictable repertoire of **boat trips** – to sandy coves, seaside springs or waterfalls, and Byzantine ruins – is also on offer.

Practicalities

If you want to stay locally, most **accommodation** clusters behind the recently gentrified Belceğiz beach; the old car park has been transformed into a broad, landscaped promenade, and virtually all of the rough-and-ready bungalow-campsites which set up shop here for the hippie vanguard during the late 1970s have been swept aside by more permanent, lucrative development. You may as well be hung for a sheep as a lamb and plump for the comforts of the *Belcekiz Beach* (☎0252/616 6009, fax 616 6448; ⑥; available through *Anatolian Sky*, among others), a pastel-painted compound with attractive mock-rustic units (the fireplaces work in theory), on-site hamam and masseur, and a huge pool much frequented when the afternoon surf outside hurls egg-sized pebbles at bathers.

Tent/caravan **campsites** have been exiled to the north shore of the lagoon, where the *Ölüdeniz Kamp* (☎0252/616 1430), 1km past the official day-use entrance to the lagoon, is the grassiest of several sites here, with its own little beach and restaurant. Further on, the *Osman Çavuş* campsite also furnishes secure bungalows, without en-suite facilities (②). On a forested hillside overlooking Ölüdeniz and its own private beach facilities, *Hotel Meri* (☎0252/616 6060, fax 616 6456) is the only bona fide lodging around the lagoon itself, squeezed in with a bit of regulation-bending just at the time the national park here was designated. Cog-and-pinion elevators take you up through the gardens to large, recently overhauled rooms, some with private terraces; rates are steep (⑦ half-board only), discounted slightly by arranging things in advance through *Anatolian Sky*.

Besides the waterfront establishments, there must be three dozen other motels, hotels and makeshift camps crammed into the former orchardlands behind Belceğiz, and on the slopes flanking the road in. Undisputably the best of the latter bunch is the *Montana Pine Resort* (☎0252/616 7108, fax 616 6451; ⑦), a sympathetically designed complex, with large, well-appointed units, one of the best breakfasts on the Turquoise Coast, and no less than three pools.

Food in the Ölüdeniz area is generally bland and forgettable, **tippling** less so: on the Belceğiz pedestrian esplanade – tucked in between the excursion outlets – *Buzz Bar* and *Harry's* offer happy hours, televised soccer, and the like.

Kadyanda

Under an hour's drive north of Günlükbaşı on a well-marked secondary road, the ruined mountaintop city of **KADYANDA** was only in 1992 readied for tourism. The initial 16km to Üzümlü village (served by very sparse public transport) are quick and paved; enter the attractive village – which so far has made little of its proximity to the ruins – turn left at the usual black-on-yellow sign, then proceed 3km more on a good gravel road to just beyond the summit of a pass with a view of Akdağ. Now bear right, following a newish "Kadyanda" sign, to negotiate well over 5km of widened, improved dirt track to a small car park in the pines below the site.

Here there's a portable toilet, and a daytime guard, but as yet no admission fee or fencing; an arrow points you to the start of a self-guiding tour along a graded loop path. First you bear south past a few tombs of the **necropolis**, then close to presumed bits of the city wall on the left; next there's a climb to a false summit with a long, partly preserved **agora**, and the first views of Fethiye.

At the true top of things, matters fall into place with the highlight of the site: a long, narrow **stadium**, seven rows of its seats surviving. Steps in the seats lead up to a huge jumble of masonry, all that's left of a **temple** to an unknown deity; on the opposite side of the stadium stand the substantial **Roman baths**, looking much earlier with their polygonal masonry and entry archway. At the northeast edge of the stadium, a flat expanse is pierced by two deep cisterns that supplied the city with rainwater.

Finally the path angles south to the best-preserved stretch of **city wall**, punctuated by windows and affording incomparable views of the mountains on the horizon and the forested valleys in between. Crossing the top of a square bastion, you look down into the **theatre**, which retains its rear facing and stage wall, plus many seats. The descent to the roadhead completes a 45-minute walk through superb mountain scenery – good reason alone for a visit.

Göcek

Set at the far northwest corner of the Gulf of Fethiye, **GÖCEK** is an obligatory stop on yacht or *gület* tours. It has become trendy of late among both foreigners and Turks, with the late President Özal himself vacationing here on occasion during the late 1980s. While there's no beach to speak of, the passing boat trade has resulted in an astonishing concentration of facilities for such a small place: laundries, a chandlery, a half-dozen posh souvenir shops and even a *Yapı Kredi* ATM along the pedestrianized inland bazaar street. If as a landlubber (six **buses** daily to and from Fethiye) you are seized by the urge to **stay**, you have some ten *pansiyon*s to choose from, including the *Ünlü* (☎0252/645 1170; ③) overlooking the less busy, west end of the meticulously landscaped quayside, as well as two **campsites** just west of town, the *Göcek* and the *Sarıoğlu*. Be warned, however, that the smart set has had a deleterious effect on the half-dozen rather precious **restaurants** here, with obligatory service charges (often for haphazard or nonexistent service) and miniature portions even by Turkish resort standards.

Ten kilometres east of here along Highway 400 at Küçük Kargı, two forest-service **campsites**, *Katrancı* and *Günlüklü*, are served by the Kargı–Yanıklar–Fethiye dolmuş and have stony beaches backed by a beautiful forest.

Dalaman and Sarıgerme

The main town west of Fethiye is bleak, grid-planned **DALAMAN**, home to the southern Turkish coast's main airport and little else, apart from one of the country's two open prisons for the rehabilitation of long-term, low-risk convicts: they run a popular **restaurant** for the public (the *Cezaevi*, near the airport), serving excellent chicken.

You may, of course, arrive here, so it's worth knowing that the **airport** has a 24-hour tourist information desk and round-the-clock banking facilities, including a *Yapı Kredi* ATM, as well as a number of car rental booths. There are, however, no public transport links, so barring a transfer coach for your package holiday, you'll have to take a taxi 5km along Kenan Evren Bulvarı into town – count on paying about $9 for this. There are a few unexciting **hotels** to choose from if you are forced to stay in Dalaman itself; of these, the *Yıldız* off Atatürk Caddesi (③) and the *Dalaman Pansiyon*, 200m from the small *otogar* off Kenan Evren Bulvarı (☎0252/692 5543; ③), are recommended. For more comfort there's the two-star *Meltem*, Kenan Evren Bul 65 (☎0252/692 2901; ④), near the turning for Sarıgerme.

Sarıgerme

The main reason to pass through town is to reach **Sarıgerme beach**, 15km out of Dalaman and 22km from Ortaca, and even so there's a more direct but confusingly marked side road from Highway 400, just east of Ortaca, signposted as "*Sarıgerme Tatil Köyleri*". Sarıgerme is even longer than İztuzu beach near Dalyan and arguably more scenic, fringed at its western, developed end with pines and offering sweeping views east past the mouth of the Dalaman Çayı toward the mountains near Fethiye. Just offshore, **Baba Adası**, capped by a crumbling, tree-obscured stone pyramid thought to be an ancient lighthouse, protects the beach somewhat. Thus the water is likely to be cleaner than at İztuzu, though colder too owing to freshwater springs which dribble into the sea near the westernmost cove.

The pattern of development here – four enormous luxury complexes stuffed with German tour groups, but set well back from the sand – implies that this is another turtle-nesting beach. Cars are banned from the attractively landscaped park in the pines just behind, to which entering pedestrians are charged a fee ($0.40) during daylight hours. But sunbeds and umbrellas there are aplenty (most affiliated with the inland hotels), as well as windsurfing and diving on offer (pitched in German). Aside from a drinks stall and rudimentary snack cantina in the park, there's no food, so it's perhaps best to bring a picnic.

If you want to stay independently or eat more substantially, head for the village of **OSMANİYE**, 2km inland along the road and served by regular dolmuş from Ortaca (not Dalaman, as you'd think). A forest of signs in German suggest who's principally catered for, but you might try the *Sarıgerme Pension* (☎0252/286 8172, fax 286 8218; ③) or the *Şahin Otel*, perched in relative calm on the slope west of the high street (☎0252/286 8284, fax 286 8285; ④).

Dalyan and around

The landscape to the west of Fethiye more than holds its own in scenic appeal, although passing through by car or bus, you may not initially agree, as road-widening works will mean considerable mess, dust and delays until at least 1998. Westbound buses from Dalaman continue to Ortaca, from where plentiful dolmuşes make the twenty-minute journey to the little town of **Dalyan**, 13km off Highway 400 and a good base for the surrounding attractions: the ancient site of **Kaunos**, downriver from Dalyan, **İztuzu Beach**, and the beautiful freshwater lake of **Köyceğiz**.

Dalyan

DALYAN first achieved a measure of international fame in 1986, when its "turtle controversy" blew up into a major battle against developers, who wanted to build a luxury hotel on nearby **İztuzu Beach**, a breeding ground of the loggerhead turtle (*Carretta carretta*). Conservationists, among them Britain's David Bellamy, succeeded in halting the scheme, and now the beach is carefully protected between May and October, when the eggs are laid.

In the wake of this campaign, the town likes to present itself as politically and ecologically correct, but recently – with its mess of *pide*/pizza houses, carpet shops, T-shirt vendors and loud bars – it has proven little different from most other mainstream resorts. The **turtle motif** has been commercially harnessed ad nauseam: there's a turtle statue in the main square, restaurants and *pansiyons* are named after the beasts, they appear on postcards, T-shirts and taxi doors, and you can even buy ceramic statuettes of the infant turtles hatching.

Otherwise life in Dalyan revolves around the **Dalyan Çayı**, which flows past the village linking the Köyceğiz lake and the sea. Many choice *pansiyons* line the east bank of this river, and the boats that putt-putt up and down it, navigating swathes of reeds reflected bright green in the water, are the preferred means of transport to all of the major local sites. Craft heading downstream pass a series of spectacular fourth-century **rock tombs** set into the cliff on the west bank, many of them temple-style with two Ionic columns, similar to those at Fethiye.

Arriving **dolmuşes** drop you at the terminal just behind the centrally placed **PTT** (June–Sept daily 8am–midnight; Oct–May daily 8am–7pm). Near the PTT on Gülpınar Caddesi, there's a *Yapı Kredi* **ATM**, while the *Ziraat Bankası* by the boat co-op has both an ATM and an automatic foreign note-changer.

Accommodation

Many of the most desirable **pansiyons** are scattered around a swelling in the river locally referred to as the "*göl*" (lake), and accessible from **İskele (Maraş) Caddesi**, which links the middle of town with a dead end nearly 2km south, opposite the fish processing plant; another road heads southeast from the PTT toward İztuzu. Mosquitoes are a major plague everywhere, so bring anti-bug juice or a mosquito net, since your accommodation may not have window screens.

Closest river-view establishment to the centre is the *Çınar Sahil Pansiyon* (☎0252/284 2117; ③), actually in a small citrus grove, 20m from the rowboat ferry (see below) at the end of Yalı Sokak, though at last visit the *pansiyon* appeared to be barely functioning. A more reliable pair, just across the street, are the *Hotel Caria* (☎0252/284 2075, fax 284 3046; ④; available through *Sunquest*), some of whose en-suite rooms have river views, and the adjacent *Utku Otel* (☎0252/284 2134, fax 284 2135; ④). Both of these have rooftop breakfast terraces with views of the rock tombs, should you strike unlucky in choice of room.

The main concentration of perhaps a dozen waterside lodgings is further along İskele Caddesi, reached by taking the signposted road toward İztuzu and then bearing right at the second junction – though you'll have little hope of a vacancy in high season without calling well in advance. One of the first you'll come to, the *Aktaş Pansiyon* (☎0252/284 2042, fax 284 4380; ③), has upstairs rooms with baths and views of the half-dozen rock tombs on the river bank opposite – but they've no balconies and are apt to be hot and airless in season, and the owners offer no single rates. About 300m south on the same side of the road, the friendlier *Miletos Pansiyon* (☎0252/284 2532; ②) has just three rooms, two with shower, and a kitchen down the hall for the largely Turkish clientele.

A second cluster of choice accommodation lines the dirt side track off İskele Caddesi, Ada Sokağı, leading west through the area known as Maraş Mahallesi. Pick of these, set in a beautiful lakefront orchard, is the *Lindos Pansiyon*, managed by English-speaking Levent Sünger (☎0252/284 2005; ④). Just beyond, in rather bleaker grounds, is the *Midas Pansiyon* (☎0252/284 2195 or 284 3154; ③), with well-appointed doubles as well as a few camping pitches by the river; the owner's relatives at the *Likya* next door handle any overflow. At the start of this side road, the *Dalyan Camping* is the most central of the local **campsites**.

Just at the start of the road to İztuzu are two proper **hotels** whose greater comforts compensate for their inland location. The three-star *Binlik*, Sulungur Sok 16 (☎0252/284 2148, fax 284 2149; ⑤), features unusually large, well-appointed rooms and two pools (one with a bar operating until 1am). The nearby, mock-Ottoman-style *Arikan*, Karakol Sok (☎0252/284 2487, fax 284 2424; ⑤), has smaller rooms and a tiny pool for the same rates, though there is a hamam on the premises. Both are available on packages from *Sunquest*.

Eating and drinking

Restaurants in Dalyan are unfortunately pretty hard to distinguish between: don't expect much in the way of culinary expertise or portion size. About the best in the centre is the *Çiçek*, with a wide selection of *meze*s, good taped music and a pleasant garden setting – though none of this comes cheaply. The nearby *Adonis* is also reliable, though the streetside seating is hardly atmospheric. The oldest eatery in town is the riverside *Denizatı*, specializing in fish, which has recently exiled itself 4km northwest to new expanded digs, the better to cater for coached-in parties; a complimentary boat shuttle is laid on in the evenings, or you can go by car to the restaurant, 1500m west of the roundabout at the north edge of town. In Dalyan itself, at the north end of the waterfront, the *Sürmen* has inherited the *Denizatı*'s mantle for pricey seafood meals.

If main courses can be less than inspiring, sweet teeth are coddled at two establishments facing each other on Maraş Caddesi: *Riverside Pastry*, for puddings and tarts, and *Fruit Bar*, the place for fresh fruit juices and shakes, as well as souvenir homemade jams. **Nightlife** in the handful of bars along Maraş Caddesi, and at the town centre, is fairly self-evident; just choose according to the noise level and the crowd.

Boats and other local transport

Dolmuş boats to the river end of İztuzu beach will have all departed in season by 10.30am – don't dally – and they return every half-hour or so between 3 and 7pm; the return fare is about $2.50, for a forty-minute trip each way. Otherwise, there are **dolmuş vans** for slightly less every half-hour along the thirteen-kilometre road to the east end of the strand. The next most popular outing is the full-day **set tour** offered by the Dalyan motorboat cooperative based on the quayside. These excursions, taking in thermal springs on Köyceğiz lake, Kaunos ruins and the beach, are good value at about $3 a head (assuming 12 passengers), but a bit rushed; if you prefer to dictate the pace, you can **custom-rent** a whole boat, which costs around $50 for an entire day for groups of up to a dozen or so. Half- or two-third days can be arranged for about $25 – say for a visit just to the ruins and the mudbaths – slightly less for a shuttle to the beach if you've missed the morning dolmuş boats. Many of the *pansiyon*s along the river have their own small motorboats providing a once-daily service to the beach for a nominal fee, and will take you on evening rides upriver to sit and watch for the silent dark shapes of freshwater terrapins occasionally surfacing for air. You can sometimes get such boats on a **self-skippering** basis; more likely you'll only be entrusted with a canoe or rowboat.

Finally, if you just want a sunset stroll to the ruins, use the unpublicized **rowboat ferry** behind the *Caria Hotel* and the health centre, intended mostly for the inhabitants of Çandır, the closest village to ancient Kaunos (see below).

Renting a **mountain bike** in town is another possible strategy, at least in the cooler months; they're available for rent both at the better package hotels, and at certain street stalls. There's one nasty hill en route to İztuzu beach, with *ayran* and *gözleme* stalls to pause at for refreshment on the grade. This land route is recommended at least once, as you loop around the Sulungur lake and get glimpses of marsh and mountain not possible amid the claustrophobic reed beds of the Dalyan Çayı. If you cross the river – the rowboat ferry should take you after some grumbling – you can cycle to Kaunos and beyond along an extensive system of dirt tracks.

Kaunos

The excavation of ancient **KAUNOS** began in 1967 and still takes place each August, sometimes using labour from the minimum security prison at Dalaman. While the ruins are poorly labelled and by no means spectacular, the site is one of the most pleasant and underrated minor attractions on this coast, swarming with wildlife (not least mosquitoes – take precautions if you're prone to bites), including herons and storks in summer, flamingoes in winter, and small terrapins, tortoises, snakes and nodding lizards in all seasons.

Arriving by tour boat, you disembark either at a fish weir opened in recent decades to replace the one formerly located closer to the village, or at another jetty on the opposite side of the rock outcrop supporting Kaunos's acropolis. The fish caught (*dalyan* means weir) are mostly grey mullet and bass, and a fragmentary inscription found at Kaunos suggests that the river has been exploited for food since ancient times. From either landing point it is a ten-minute walk up to the **site** (daily dawn to dusk, but unenclosed; $1 when warden present).

If you don't want to arrive on a river tour, it's easy to walk to Kaunos, in slightly more time, from the north, using the **rowboat ferry** from Dalyan (behind the *Caria Hotel* and the health clinic), which lands just under the cliff-hewn temple tombs on the west bank. The boatmen – or sometimes boatwomen – will demand $0.75 each way (locals pay half that).

Although it is possible to drive to Kaunos from Köyceğiz via the Sultaniye baths and Çandır (see below), this is not recommended as the dirt road beyond the hot springs is very rough and meandering.

Some history

Although Kaunos was a Carian foundation of the ninth century BC, the city exhibited various Lycian cultural traits, not least the compulsion to adorn nearby cliffs with typically

Southwest USA
THE ROUGH GUIDE
Greg Ward

India
THE ROUGH GUIDE
David Abram, Devdan Sen, Harriet Sharkey and Gareth John Williams

China
THE ROUGH GUIDE

Vietnam
THE ROUGH GUIDE
Jan Dodd and Mark Lewis

Peru
THE ROUGH GUIDE
Dilwyn Jenkins

Paris
THE ROUGH GUIDE
Kate Baillie and Tim Salmon

Spain
THE ROUGH GUIDE
Mark Ellingham and John Fisher

Norway
THE ROUGH GUIDE
John Brown and Phil Lee

London
THE ROUGH GUIDE
Rob Humphreys

Mallorca
& Menorca
THE ROUGH GUIDE
Phil Lee

Indonesian
A ROUGH GUIDE PHRASEBOOK

French
A ROUGH GUIDE PHRASEBOOK

Mandarin Chinese
A ROUGH GUIDE PHRASEBOOK

Hindi & Urdu
A ROUGH GUIDE PHRASEBOOK

Thai
A ROUGH GUIDE PHRASEBOOK

The Internet
AND WORLD WIDE WEB
THE ROUGH GUIDE 2.0
Angus J. Kennedy from Internet

Jazz
THE ROUGH GUIDE

World Music
THE ROUGH GUIDE
Saha to Son via Johnny to Chyna: the complete handbook

Opera
THE ROUGH GUIDE
A SIMPLE GUIDE TO THE OPERA:
COMPOSERS, ARTISTS AND RECORDINGS
Matthew Boyden

Rock
THE ROUGH GUIDE
MORE THAN 5000 CD RECOMMENDATIONS
THE DEFINITIVE GUIDE TO 1000 ARTISTS
AND BANDS FROM THEN...TO NOW

100% Reliable

* illustrated are some of our latest publications   www.roughguides.com

Stay in touch with us!

ROUGH*NEWS* is Rough Guides' free newsletter.
In three issues a year we give you news, travel
issues, music reviews, readers' letters and the
latest dispatches from authors on the road.

I would like to receive ROUGH*NEWS*: please put me on your free mailing list.

NAME . . . .

ADDRESS . . . .

Please clip or photocopy and send to: Rough Guides, 1 Mercer Street, London WC2H 9QJ, England
or Rough Guides, 375 Hudson Street, New York, NY 10014, USA.

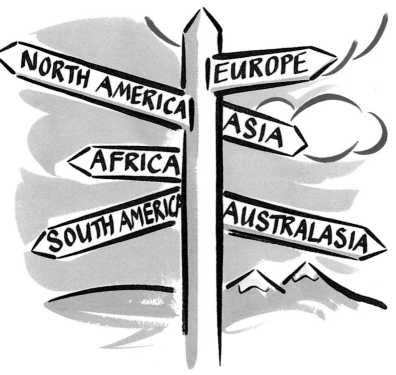

Travel the world
HIV *Safe*

Travel *Safe*

HIV, the virus that causes AIDS, is worldwide.

You're probably aware of the dangers of getting it from unprotected sex, but there are many other risks when travelling.

Wherever you're visiting it makes sense to take precautions. Try to avoid any medical or dental treatment, but if it's necessary, make sure the equipment is sterilised. Likewise, if you really need to have a blood transfusion, always ask for screened blood.

Make sure your travelling companions are aware of the risks and the necessary precautions. In fact, you should take your own sterile medical pack, available from larger high street pharmacies.

Remember, ear and body piercing, acupuncture and even tattoos could be risky, because they all involve puncturing the skin. And although you might not normally consider any of these things now, after a few drinks - you never know.

Of course, the things that are dangerous at home are just as dangerous when you travel. So don't inject drugs or share works.

Avoid casual sex and always use a good quality condom when having sex with a new partner (and each time you have sex with them).

And it's not just a gay disease' either. In fact, worldwide, it's most commonly transmitted through sex between men and women.

For information in the UK:

Ring for the TravelSafe leaflet on the Health Literature Line freephone 0800 555 777, or pick one up at a doctor's surgery or pharmacy.

Further advice on HIV and AIDS: National AIDS Helpline: 0800 567 123. (Cannot be reached from abroad).

The Terrence Higgins Trust Helpline (12 noon–10pm) provides advice and counselling on HIV/AIDS issues: 0171 242 1010.

MASTA Travellers Health Line: 0891 224 100.

Travel *Safe*

Travel the world HIV *Safe*

Lycian rocktombs. Kaunos was also closely allied to the principal Lycian city of Xanthos, and when the Persian Harpagus attempted to conquer the region in the sixth century BC, this pair were the only two to resist. Kaunos began to acquire a Greek character under the influence of the Hellenizing Carian ruler Mausolus – an apparently successful campaign, since no Carian words have been found on inscriptions here. Subsequently, the city passed from one ruler to another: to Ptolemy after Alexander's death; then to the Rhodians; and finally, after fierce resistance to Rhodes, to indirect Roman imperial administration.

Besides its fish, Kaunos was noted for its figs, and for the prevalence of malaria among its inhabitants; the fruit was erroneously deemed the cause of the disease by outsiders, rather than the anopheles mosquitoes that until 1948 infested the surrounding swamps. Another insidious problem was the silting up of its harbour, which continually threatened the city's substantial commercial interests. The Mediterranean originally came right up to the foot of the acropolis hill, surrounding Kaunos on all sides apart from an isthmus of land to the north. But the Dalyan Çayı has since deposited over 5km of silt, leaving an expanse of marshy delta in its wake.

The site

Much of Kaunos is yet to be unearthed, despite the long-running excavation, and only the "Roman bath" and "church", to either side of the upper ticket booth, are labelled. North of the city extend well-preserved stretches of **defensive wall**, some of which is thought to have been constructed by Mausolus early in the fourth century BC. Just below the **acropolis** outcrop, crowned by a medieval and Hellenistic fortified area, the second-century BC **theatre** is the most impressive building here. Resting against the hillside to the southeast, it's considerably greater than a semicircle in the Greek fashion and retains two of its original arched entrances. Between here and the Byzantine church, a **temple to Apollo** has recently been identified.

Northwest of the theatre and Apollo temple, closer to the upper ticket booth, the **Byzantine basilica** and the city's **Roman baths** are also in excellent condition. A paved stone street leads downhill from the baths to an ancient **Doric temple**, consisting most obviously of an attractive circular structure, possibly an altar, sacred pool or podium, flanked by bits of a re-erected colonnade. A path continues to the **agora**, on the lowest level, which boasts a restored **fountain-house** bearing an inscription to Vespasian, at the end of a long **stoa**. The ancient **harbour** is now the Sülüklü Gölü, or "Lake of the Leeches". According to ancient observers, the lake was once closed off by a chain in times of danger; nowadays it's merely dive-bombed by feeding waterbirds.

İztuzu beach

Whether you go to the roadhead end ($1 car fees; the barrier 2km before the end of the road shuts at dusk) or the river mouth end of **İztuzu Beach**, a big problem can be the lack of shade. Bring some sort of sun protection and consider renting an umbrella from one of the drink and snack kiosks (there are only two kiosks, one at each end of the beach, and their menus are expensive and limited, so you'll probably want to bring some food, too). Alternatively, you could swim or be ferried across the river mouth to a smaller, more peaceful beach shaded by some pines. Umbrellas, whose masts damage the turtle nests, are not permitted from a line of marker stakes down to the sea, and all access to the beach is banned between 8pm and 8am in summer – though these rules are apparently flouted regularly. During the day the entire length of the beach is open to the public; owing to wind exposure the water can be choppy and murky, but the gently shelving seabed makes this spot excellent for children. You should, however, remain wary of turtle nests, which are easily trampled on. Turtle tracks – scrapings in the sand where the creatures have hauled themselves up onto the beach to lay their eggs – are visible in June and July. The beach is often alive with other wildlife too, including lizards, snakes and tortoises, and its approach road is lined with profusely flowering oleander bushes, as well as deformed trees showing the effects of high winter winds.

Ilıca and Sultaniye Kaplıcaları

Ten minutes upriver from Dalyan in the direction of Köyceğiz are the **thermal baths** at **Ilıca**, a series of open-air mud pools ($0.75), worth investigating on a boat trip. These springs are claimed to increase male potency and cure rheumatism and gynecological problems, and reach temperatures of around 40°C. Whatever else they do, bathing in them certainly relieves stress, and the hog-wallow atmosphere somewhat dampens the chatting-up techniques of the local men. Beware, however, that the total area is small, and in season gets packed during the day with tour groups – you're better off going at an odd hour, or convincing your skipper to take you to a second, more secluded set of hot springs, further upstream toward the lake.

These, the **Köyceğiz Sultaniye Kaplıcaları**, are also accessible by a mostly paved, eighteen-kilometre road from Köyceğiz (see below); follow signposting for Ekincik on the west side of Köyceğiz town. The last kilometre or two along the sideroad from Karaağaç is dirt but perfectly passable for an ordinary car. The baths themselves ($0.75), housed in a conspicuous white domed structure right on the lakeshore, are claimed to be open around the clock despite the nominal posted hours of 6am to 10pm. The dome shelters a large round pool with a naturally rocky and uneven bottom from which the water wells up at 39–41°C; it's best appreciated at night or during the cooler months, otherwise you'll be needing to dive into the adjacent lake periodically. The modern chamber has walls marble-lined to waist height, but ancient masonry at the pool rim is evidence that the baths have been present in some form at least since Roman times.

Köyceğiz

With only its lakeside setting north of Dalyan to recommend it, **KÖYCEĞİZ** is a sleepy little town fast being written off the tourist agenda by its quickly developing rival. Nevertheless it boasts a healthy economy, based on local cotton, olive and citrus cultivation, and its position on the ten-metre-deep **Köyceğiz Gölü** – once a bay open to the Mediterranean that became dammed by silt deposits from mountain rivers – gives it a further source of income in the fish who swim up the Dalyan Çayı to spawn here.

There's no big advantage in staying here, but it's connected with Dalyan, Muğla and Marmaris by regular minibus, and you could use it as an alternative base for visiting the ruins at Kaunos. The **tourist information office** on the main square (Mon–Fri 8.30am–12.30pm & 1.30–5.30pm; ☎0252/262 4703) can advise on excursions and **accommodation**, though the two most obvious lakefront hotels are fairly grim. Better to choose among a handful of establishments west of the centre: the *Fulya Pansiyon* on Aliihsan Kalmaz Caddesi (☎0252/262 2301 or 262 4356; ③), clean and well placed within sight of the lake; the *Özbek Pansiyon* further east at no. 84 of the same lane (☎0252/262 1062, fax 262 2840; ③), with an attractive garden and limited off-street parking; or the newish, lakefront *Panorama Plaza Hotel* at Cengiz Topel Cad 69 (☎0252/262 3731, fax 262 3633; ⑤), with a pool and all mod cons – though the staff seems thoroughly unused to non-German clientele and quote prices in DM. Some 200m beyond the *Panorama Plaza*, a grassy **campsite**, the *International Anatolia*, shelters under a plantation of the local liquidambar (Oriental sweetgum) trees, with a tiny patch of sandy beach just across the shore road. For **eating out**, the *Çınaraltı* east of the main square has a pleasant environment, though the food – cold *meze* selection, fish and grills – could be better; however the main alternative, the *Çiçek* on the square, is more explicitly pitched at German tour groups and unlikely to be far superior.

The Xanthos valley

East of Fethiye lies the heartland of ancient Lycia, home to a number of archeological sites, including the two ancient citadel cities of **Tlos** and **Pinara**, on opposite sides of the **Xanthos river valley**. They were both important settlements, having three votes each in the deliberations of the Lycian Federation, but Tlos had the geographical advantage, lying above a rich open flood plain and sheltered to the east by the Massicytus range (today's Akdağ); Pinara's surrounding hilly terrain was difficult to cultivate. Both cities were unearthed by the English traveller Charles Fellows between 1838 and 1840, during the same period as his work – or pillaging, as some would have it – at **Xanthos**.

Indeed the seventy-kilometre stretch of road as far as Kalkan, for the most part following the valley of the ancient Xanthos River (now the Esen Çayı), is littered with beautifully set ruins, the lucky ones advantageously shielded to the east by the Massicytus (Akdağ) mountain range; it's an immensely fertile area too, home to fields of cotton and maize and a wide variety of fruit. Under the centre-right ANAP government of 1984–1991, an airport was proposed for the flat plain here, first near the ruins at the **Letoön** and then further up the valley, but thankfully it never materialized; this has had the effect of keeping growth at **Patara**, the main resort here, modest by Turkish coastal standards. Between Tlos and Patara, the magnificent river gorge of **Saklıkent** is easy to visit by dolmuş or with your own vehicle.

Tlos

One of the most ancient of the Lycian cities, **TLOS** is situated above the modern village of Kale Asar (also known as Yaka Köy). It is referred to in Hittite records of the fourteenth century as "Dalawa in the Lukka lands", and the discovery on the site of a bronze hatchet dating from the second millennium BC confirms the long heritage of the place. Little else is known about its history, however, although it was numbered among the six principal Lycian cities.

There's no reliable public **transport** the full distance to Tlos; under your own steam, veer left 22km out of Fethiye, toward Korkuteli, and once over the Koca Çayı bridge, bear immediately right onto the marked side road to both Tlos and Saklıkent. Nine kilometres along, turn left (east) onto a signposted dirt track; it's over 4km up here to the base of the acropolis hill – which stays in constant view – and a cluster of drink stands. In spring the route up, with snow-streaked Akdağ as a backdrop for the purple of flowering judas trees, is spectacularly beautiful.

The ruins themselves, while reasonably abundant, are confusing and barely excavated – densely overgrown or farmed, in fact – so that the precise identification of buildings is open to question. But the setting is impressive, a high rocky promontory which affords excellent views of the Xanthos valley. The acropolis hill of Tlos is dominated by a **Turkish fortress** from the Ottoman period, the residence of a nineteenth-century brigand and local chieftain, Kanlı Ali Ağa, who killed his own wayward daughter to defend the family reputation. Presently unoccupied except for use as a football pitch and pasture, and of minimal interest, it has obliterated all earlier remains on the hill. To the northeast, the acropolis ends in almost perpendicular cliffs; on the eastern slope are traces of the Lycian city wall and a long stretch of subsequent Roman masonry.

The site

Entry to the site (unenclosed but $1 admission when guard present) is via the still-intact northeastern city gate, next to the guard's Portakabin. Cobbled stairs ascend to the main **necropolis**, consisting of a few freestanding sarcophagi and a complex of rock-cut house tombs. If, however, you walk along a lower, level path from the gate, outside the city walls, you reach a second group of rock tombs; dip below and right of these along a zigzagging trail to reach the best of the graves, the **Tomb of Bellerophon**, at the northern base of the hill. Its facade was carved to resemble that of a temple, with roughly hewn columns supporting a pediment, and three carved doors. On the left wall of the porch is the carving that gives the tomb its name, representing the mythical hero Bellerophon riding the winged horse Pegasus, while facing them over the door is a lion – probably meant to stand guard over the tomb. Apparently one of the ruling families of ancient Tlos claimed descent from Bellerophon, so it can be assumed that this was the burial place of royalty. Be warned, however, that it's a fifteen-minute scramble down, requiring good shoes, with a ladder ascent at the end, and both figures, especially the lion's head, have been worn down by vandals or the elements.

Between the east slope of the acropolis hill and the curving onward track is a large open space seasonally planted with peas and hay, thought by some to be the site of the **agora**. Close to the base of the hill are traces of seats that were a part of a stadium, which unusually lay parallel to the marketplace. The opposite side of the agora is lined by a long, arcaded building presumed to be the **market hall**, with vines festooning its interior arches.

Well beyond this, reached by a broad path off the main eastbound track, lie the **baths**, where the sound of running water in nearby ditches lends credence to such an identification. This is a romantic vantage point, and perhaps the best bit of Tlos: two complete **rooms** and an apsidal projection known locally as **Yedi Kapı** (Seven Gates), after its seven intact windows, offer a good view of the Xanthos valley.

Just east of the approach path to Yedi Kapı are the remains of a Byzantine **basilica**, and to the southeast of this another open space that some believe to be the true site of the city's agora. Just north of a modern track stands a magnificent second-century BC **theatre**, with 34 rows of seats remaining. The stage building has a number of finely carved blocks, and its northern section still stands to nearly full height, vying with the backdrop of mountains.

From the theatre, the track continues 3km uphill to several fancy trout restaurants in the hamlet of **Yaka**; of these perhaps the most intriguing is the *Yaka Park*, formerly a watermill, where at the bar you keep your drink chilled in a sluice through which your potential dinner swims by.

Saklıkent

Once you've returned from Tlos to the paved road, the gauntlet of *saç böreği, gözleme* and *ayran* stands which you run as you move south (*Hüseyin Güseli'in Yeri* is as good as any) clues you in that you're headed the right way for the **Saklıkent** gorge. After 9km, you bear left for just over 3km along asphalt to the gorge mouth, 44km out of Fethiye. There's a dolmuş service in season – look for minibuses marked "Kayadibi/Saklıkent" in Fethiye.

The mouth of the gorge is deceptively modest; to reach it go under the road bridge onto a 150-metre catwalk spiked into the canyon walls, ending at the **Gökçesu/Ulupınar springs**, which bubble up under great pressure from the base of the towering cliffs, exiting the narrows to eventually mingle with the Esen Çayı. It's a magical place, seemingly channelling all the water this side of Akdağ, and only somewhat diminished by the tatty tea and trout stalls just downstream – and the regular descent of coached-in tour groups from Fethiye. The *Saklıkent Restaurant*, if no less touristy than the others, is at least charmingly suspended on wood platforms above the cascades.

Beyond this point, the evocatively water-sculpted chasm extends 18km upstream, though further progress for all except rock-climbers is blocked after about 2000m by a boulder slide. If you want to **explore** up to that point, it's initially a wading exercise – take submersible shoes, or rent a pair here for $0.50. In case you're wondering, in 1993 a technically equipped canyoning expedition descended the entire length of the gorge in eighteen hours (bivouacking halfway), with frequent abseilling down dry waterfalls and rock piles dropping up to thirty metres.

With your own vehicle, it's easy to continue from the gorge mouth down the unsign-posted road to Xanthos, the Letoön or Patara (all described later in the chapter); proceed over the auto-bridge past the half-dozen trout restaurants to follow the fairly good dirt road along the left bank of the river. After eleven rather lonely, unmarked kilometres, the asphalt resumes 3km before Palamut village; bear right at the fork immediately beyond the next village, and, just under 10km from Palamut, you'll pass right through ancient Xanthos, with the way on to the coast obvious.

Pinara

Some 45km out of Fethiye on the main Highway 400 toward Patara, you'll see the turning west (right) for ancient **PİNARA** (unenclosed but $1 admission when guard present). It's just over 3km from here to the edge of Minare village (drinks and snacks, but no public transport), from where at least 2km more of signposted but steep and rutted dirt track leads to the ruins. You can hike this final distance in about half an hour, or you can make it to the car park at the top if you're prepared for substantial wear and tear on two-wheel-drive vehicles. One of the guards, Fethi Parça, is quite knowledgeable and will point out (in Turkish) items you might otherwise miss.

Approaching the site, the **cliff** on which the original city was founded is unmissable, practically blocking out the horizon – indeed it's worth the trip up just to see this towering mass, whose east face is covered in rectangular openings, thought to be either tombs or food storage space. These can now only be reached by experienced rock climbers, and it's hard to fathom how they were ever cut in the first place.

Practically nothing is known about Pinara, inscriptions at the site being singularly uninformative. According to the fourth-century Xanthian historian Menecrates, it was founded to accommodate the overflow from Xanthos. Later on, however, Pinara – whose name means "something round" in the Lycian language, presumably because of the shape of the original, upper acropolis – grew to become one of the larger Lycian cities, minting its own coins and earning three votes in the Federation.

The site

The main part of the ruins of Pinara are situated on the lower acropolis hill, to the east of the cliff, where the city was relocated quite early in its history, when defence had become less of a priority. The **lower acropolis** is overgrown and most of its buildings are unidentifiable.

Pinara's **tombs** are probably its most interesting feature, especially a group on the west bank of the seasonal stream which tumbles through the site. On the east side of the lower acropolis hill, the so-called **Royal Tomb** is unique for its detailed carvings representing four walled cities with battlements, gates, houses and tombs, with one or two human figures on the walls of its porch; a frieze survives above, showing a large number of people and animals in a peaceful scene – perhaps a religious festival. Inside there is a single bench, unusually high off the ground, suggesting that it was the tomb of a single person, probably of royal blood.

On the same side of this lower hill but higher up, reached by a direct path north from the Royal Tomb, there's a house tomb with a roof in the form of a gothic arch, at whose point is a pair of stone **ox horns** thought to ward off evil spirits. This stands near the top of the lower acropolis, and at the south edge of the possible **agora**, now under the welcome shade of tall pines. A few short jambs are still upright amid the rubble; on the east side of the market precinct, the massive foundations of a **temple** to an unidentified god overlook the theatre (see below). Hairpinning back, smaller paths thread south between the pigeonholed cliff and the lower acropolis, first past a very ruinous **odeion** on the west slope of the lower acropolis, then through a jumble of walls, uprights and tombs clogging the narrow defile between the heights: there's nothing identifiable, but this was clearly the heart of the city.

At the far end, two sarcophagi flank a man-made terrace and a sharp drop to the stream valley. About the only building that can be identified with certainty by its apse is a **church**; above this juts a strange, intact **tower**, claimed by some to be a tomb but more likely a guardhouse controlling the way to the upper citadel, and offering a fine vantage point for making sense of the jumbled town. From the terrace, the path descends to the canyon floor, passing more rock tombs and a wonderful permanent spring en route to the car park.

Northeast of the town, easily accessible along the track, is the well-preserved **theatre**, backing into a hill and overlooking a tilled field as well as the "Swiss cheese" cliff; small but handsome, and never modified by the Romans, it gives an idea of Pinara's modest population.

The Letoön

Sixteen kilometres south of Pinara, the site of the **LETOÖN** (site unenclosed but $1 when warden present) lies 4.5km off Highway 400, the turning signposted 1.5km before Kınık. To go the whole way there by **public transport**, take a dolmuş from Fethiye to **Kumluova** and get off in the village centre near the signposted turnoff to the Letoön, a few hundred metres' walk away.

Some history

The Letoön, the shrine of the goddess **Leto**, was the official religious sanctuary of the Lycian Federation, where national festivals were celebrated, and the extensive ruins to be seen today bear witness to its importance. The sanctuary became a centre of Christian worship, and a church was consecrated here; it was not until the Arab raids in the seventh century that the site was eventually abandoned. The initial remains of the Letoön were discovered in 1840, although excavation work wasn't begun until 1962, since when it has been systematically uncovered and labelled, making the ruins easily appreciated even if you don't have a knowledge of classical architecture.

The nymph Leto was loved by Zeus, and jealously pursued by Hera, his wife. Wandering about in search of a place to give birth to her divine twins (Apollo and Artemis), she is said to have approached a fountain to relieve her thirst, only to be driven away by local herdsmen. Leto was then led to drink at the Xanthos River by wolves, and so changed the name of the country to Lycia, *lykos* being the Greek word for wolf. Later, after giving birth to her children, she returned to punish the herdsmen by transforming them into frogs.

It is thought that the name Leto could be derived from the Lycian word *lada*, meaning woman, and it is conceivable that the Anatolian mother goddess, Cybele, was worshipped on this site before her. Another similarity between the two goddesses is that they are both often mentioned in connection with incestuous mother-son unions – something believed to have been common in Lycian society. Most famous of all the prophecies supposed to have been given at the Letoön was that received by Alexander the Great, in which he was informed that the Persian Empire would be destroyed by the Greeks. Encouraged by this prophecy, says Plutarch, "he went on to clear the coastline of Persians as far as Cilicia and Phoenicia".

The site

Since excavations began, the remains of three temples, a nymphaeum and two porticoes have been uncovered, as well as a number of interesting **inscriptions**. One of these lays down the conditions of entry to the sanctuary, including a strict dress code, which stated that clothing must be simple, with rich jewellery and elaborate hairstyles forbidden. Another important inscription, found on the rock shelf to the east of the temples, is a trilingual text in Lycian, Greek and Aramaic, referring to the establishment in Xanthos of a cult of the Kaunian deity Basilens (meaning "king"), which proved invaluable in deciphering the Lycian language.

The low ruins of the three **temples** occupy the centre of the site, beyond the relatively uninteresting **agora**. The westernmost of them, straight ahead as you stand with your back to the entrance, bears a dedication to Leto. Once surrounded by a single colonnade with decorative half-columns around the interior walls, it dates back to the third century BC. The temple in the centre is a fourth-century BC structure, identified by a dedication to Artemis; its northern part incorporates a rocky outcrop. The easternmost temple was similar in design to the temple of Leto, surrounded by a Doric colonnade with half-columns around its interior. The mosaic on the floor of this temple – now buried under six inches of protective sand and covered by a low, corrugated-tin roof – depicts a lyre, bow and quiver, which suggests that it was dedicated to Artemis and Apollo, since the bow and quiver were symbols of Artemis, and the lyre that of Apollo. Not surprisingly, these children of Leto, legendarily born in the Xanthos valley, were the region's most revered deities. The style of architecture and mosaic date the temple to the second and first centuries BC.

Beyond the three temples, to the southwest, extends a **nymphaeum**, which consisted of a rectangular structure with two semicircular recesses on either side, with niches for statues. The remains of the building are bordered by a semicircular paved basin with a diameter of 27m, now permanently flooded by the high local water table and full of terrapins and noisy frogs, a fitting reminder of the vengeance of Leto on the herdsmen who wouldn't give her a drink. A **church** was built over the rectangular section of the nymphaeum in the fourth century, and destroyed by Arab invaders in the seventh, so that only its outline is now discernible.

Returning to the car park at the entrance, you'll come to a large, well-preserved Hellenistic **theatre** on the right, entered through a vaulted passage. Sixteen blank plaques, once adorned by comic and tragic masks, decorate the southwest entrance to this passage, and nearby is an interesting Roman **tomb** with a relief representation of its toga-clad occupant.

In theory it's possible to drive beyond the Letoön, following signs for 5km to **Kumluova Plajı**, but in practice it's a likely place to founder a car in the sand, and there are no facilities or shade at this entry point – skip it, and visit the enormous beach hereabouts from the access points detailed below.

Xanthos

The remains of the hilltop city of **XANTHOS**, with their breathtaking views of the Xanthos River – now the Esen Çayı – and its valley, are among the most fascinating in the whole of Lycia. The site was first made familiar to the British public in 1842, when traveller Charles Fellows visited it and carried off the greater part of its moveable art works, just four decades after the Elgin marbles had been similarly relocated. It took two months to strip the site of its monuments, which were loaded onto the *HMS Beacon* and shipped back to the British Museum in London.

Buses or (more likely) **dolmuşes** between Fethiye and Patara will drop you off in Kınık, less than 2km beyond the Letoön turn-off, from where it's a twenty-minute uphill walk. Alternatively you could rent a fourteen-seater minibus in Kalkan for about $40.

Some history

Part of the fascination of a visit to Xanthos lies in the city's history, which was dominated by the mercurial fortunes and unusual temperament of its inhabitants. In mythology the city was connected with the story of Bellerophon and Pegasus (see "Olympos and Çıralı", p.430). King Iobates – who originally set impossible tasks for Bellerophon and later offered him a share in his kingdom – ruled here, and the city was the home of the grandson of Bellerophon, Glaucus, who was described in the *Iliad* as hailing "from the whirling waters of the Xanthos".

Archeological finds from the site date back to the eighth century BC, but the earliest historical mention of the city dates from 540 BC and the conquest of Lycia by the Persian general Harpagus. From Caria he descended into the Xanthos valley and after some resistance succeeded in penning the citizens up in their own city. Their response was the city's first holocaust, in which they gathered their families and made a funeral pyre with their household belongings. The women and children died in the flames, and the men perished fighting, the only surviving citizens being eight families who were out of town at the time.

The subsequent fate of Xanthos resembled that of the rest of Lycia, with Alexander succeeding the Persians, and in time being succeeded by his general Antigonus and then by Antiochus III. After the defeat of Antiochus, Xanthos was given to Rhodes with the rest of Lycia.

The second Xanthian holocaust occurred in 42 BC during the Roman civil war, when Brutus besieged the city, causing the citizens again to make funeral pyres of their possessions and cast themselves into the flames. Xanthos prospered anew in Roman imperial times, and under Byzantine rule the city walls were renovated and a monastery built.

The site

The most important construction discovered at ancient Xanthos, the fourth-century Nereid Monument, a beautifully decorated Ionic temple on a high podium, is now in the British Museum, along with many other monuments and sculptures pillaged by Charles Fellows in 1842. However, there is still enough to see here to require a lengthy visit. The **site** is unfenced, but officially open 7.30am to 7pm in summer, 8am to 5pm in winter; the warden stationed at the car-park souvenir stall will collect $1 admission from you, as well as parking fees if you're arrived under your own power. Afternoons are scorchingly hot even by Lycian standards – go earlier or later in the day.

Very close to the entry booth, west of the road, stands a monumental pair: an **Arch of Vespasian**, and an adjoining **Hellenistic gateway** bearing an inscription recording that Antiochus the Great dedicated the city to Leto, Apollo and Artemis, the national deities of Lycia. Further up, east of the road, the former location of the Nereid Monument is marked by a plaque.

West of the car park, at the top of the access road, the Lycian acropolis and the overgrown Roman agora sandwich the Roman theatre, beside which are two conspicuous Lycian monuments. To the north looms the so-called **Harpy Tomb**, once topped with a marble chamber that was removed by Fellows; this has since been replaced by a cement cast of the original. The paired bird-women figures on the tomb's north and south sides have been identified as harpies, or, more likely, sirens, carrying the souls of the dead (represented as children) to the Isles of the Blessed. Other reliefs on all four sides portray unidentified seated figures receiving gifts. Beside the Harpy Tomb a **Lycian-type sarcophagus** stands on a pillar, an unusual structure thought to date from the third century BC. The remains of a body and some third-century pottery were found inside the tomb, along with a sixth-century relief – thought to have been brought from elsewhere – depicting funeral games.

Just northeast of the agora looms what's popularly known as the **Xanthian Obelisk**. It is in fact the remains of another pillar tomb, labelled as the "Inscribed Pillar" and cov-

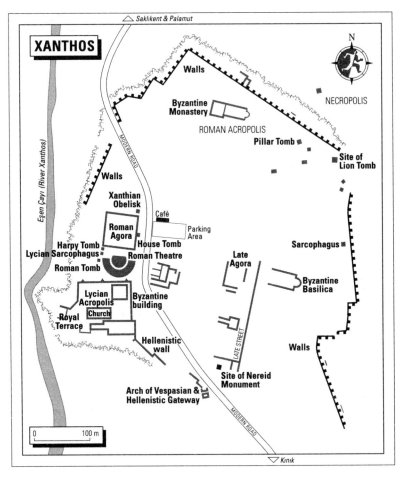

XANTHOS

△ *Saklıkent & Palamut*

N

Walls

Byzantine
Monastery

ROMAN ACROPOLIS

Pillar Tomb

NECROPOLIS

Site of
Lion Tomb

Eşen Çayı (River Xanthos)

MODERN ROAD

Walls

Xanthian
Obelisk

Café

Roman
Agora

Parking
Area

Harpy Tomb
Lycian Sarcophagus

House Tomb

Roman Theatre

Late
Agora

Sarcophagus

Roman Tomb

Lycian
Acropolis

Byzantine
building

Byzantine
Basilica

Church

Royal
Terrace

Hellenistic
wall

LATE STREET

Walls

Site of Nereid
Monument

Arch of Vespasian &
Hellenistic Gateway

MODERN ROAD

0   100 m

▽ *Kınık*

ered on all four sides by the longest known Lycian inscription, which runs to 250 lines and includes 12 lines of Greek verse. Since the Lycian language hasn't been completely deciphered, the understanding of the inscription is based on this verse, and on proper names appearing in the text, which tells the story of a youthful champion wrestler who went on to sack many cities, and generally to glorify his family name.

The nearby Roman **theatre** was built on the site of an earlier Greek structure and is pretty complete, missing only the upper seats, which were incorporated into the Byzantine city wall. Behind the theatre, overlooking the Xanthos valley, lies the **Lycian acropolis**, in the far southeastern corner of which are the remains of a square building believed to be the palace of the early Xanthian kings destroyed by General Harpagus. Under protective sand you can find patches of sophisticated mosaic, which would seem to indicate Roman or Byzantine use of the acropolis.

Moving east from the car park, paths lead through the residential sections of the Hellenistic, Roman and Byzantine city, where a **Byzantine basilica**, still being excavated and currently fenced off, is distinguished by its extensive abstract mosaics and a *synthronon* in the semicircular apse. On the hill north of here is the **Roman acropolis**, at the eastern side of which are a number of freestanding **sarcophagi**, and above, cut into the hillside, a group of picturesque **tombs** mainly of the Lycian house (as opposed to temple) type. A well-preserved early **Byzantine monastery**, containing an open courtyard with washbasins along one side, is located to the north of the acropolis hill.

Patara and Gelemiş

PATARA was the principal port of Lycia, famed for its oracle of Apollo, and as the birthplace in the fourth century AD of Saint Nicholas, Bishop of Myra, better known as Santa Claus. Today, however, the area is better known for its huge white sand beach, which has recently prompted considerable development in the form of *pansiyon*s, bars and restaurants in the village of **GELEMİŞ** almost 3km inland.

Gelemiş lies 3km off Highway 400 down a paved side road; the turn-off is signposted about midway between the villages of Ovaköy and Yeşilköy. **Dolmuşes**, stopping at a patch of ground near the PTT, arrive every half-hour from Kalkan; from Fethiye there are around fifteen a day; and many of these continue past the ruins of Patara to the beach at road's end.

Some history

There are many myths concerning the Greek origins of the city of Patara, but in fact the city was Lycian from the beginning, as evidenced by coins and inscriptions spelt PTTRA. The city was famous for its temple and oracle of Apollo, which was supposed to rival the one at Delphi in accuracy, probably because Apollo was said to spend the winter months near Patara. No verified traces of this temple have, however, been found so far.

Patara played an important part in Lycian and Hellenistic history, being used as a naval base during the wars between Alexander's successors. Later, in 42 BC, Brutus threatened the Patarans with a fate similar to the recent Xanthian holocaust if they didn't submit, giving them a day to decide. Plutarch claims that Brutus released the women hostages in the hope that they would change the minds of their menfolk. When this didn't work, Brutus freed all the remaining hostages, thereby proving his amiability and endearing himself to the Patarans, who subsequently surrendered. Whatever his tactics, his chief motive for taking the city was suggested by the fact that he took no prisoners, but merely ordered that all the city's gold and silver should be handed over.

The Patara site

At the southern edge of Gelemiş village, a gate bars traffic to the ruins and beach at night (open summer daily 7.30am–7pm; winter daily 8.30am–5pm; $1 admission from adjacent booth); although the ruins are unfenced, you are technically not allowed in on foot at other times. It should be stressed that most of the site has never been fully excavated, by and large presenting a spectacle of numerous unidentified and badly overgrown walls in polygonal masonry. Few clear paths link individual ruins, which means repeated, irritating backtracking to the main road, and there are no facilities or shade – bring water, stout shoes and a head covering during summer.

Two kilometres from the village, the entrance to the city is marked by a triple-arched, first-century AD **Roman gateway**, almost completely intact. To the west of the gate rises a little hill where a head of Apollo was discovered, prompting brief speculation that this was the site of the temple of Apollo. Just outside the gate, a **necropolis** is currently being excavated during August by a Turkish team from Akdeniz University in Antalya.

South of the hill sit a **baths complex**, not unlike the one at Tlos, with numerous arches and five square windows, and the foundations of a **basilica**, to which an exotic touch is lent by a shady palm grove sprouting up from the flooring. To the west of these, tacked onto the longest surviving extent of the **city walls**, and difficult to reach, is an attractive second-century **temple**. While too small and simple to be identified as the city's famous Apollo shrine, it has a richly decorated seven-metre-high door frame – its lintel long on the point of collapse – leading into a single chamber. Further south, reached by a different track from the main road, are more **baths**, built by the emperor Vespasian (69–79 AD), which are currently off-limits and impress mainly by their squat bulk.

The **theatre** sits southwest of these baths, under the brow of the acropolis hill and easiest reached by yet another track heading off the main road, a few paces before the beach car park. The cavea is now romantically half-full of drifted sand, but you can still count twenty rows of seats. The partly intact stage building has five doors, with five arched windows above them; on its exterior you can read a Greek inscription ascribing the erection of the stage to a woman, Vilia Procula, and her father, both of them citizens of Patara.

South of the theatre a reasonable path climbs uphill to the city's **acropolis**. At the top lurks an unusual circular pit, 10m in diameter, with a pillar rearing out of the bottom and badly damaged stairs down its side. Since it doesn't overlook the old harbour, the pit is more probably a **cistern**, and not a **lighthouse** as originally supposed; that is now thought to be the square, arched tower, its top collapsed, on the west side of the hill, which still has a fine view over the sea, beach and silted-up port. On the far side of this, reached by crossing the dunes, are the bulky remains of **Hadrian's granary**.

The beach

The harbour of Patara silted up gradually in the Middle Ages and consequently had to be abandoned; it is today a brackish swamp to the northwest of the theatre, separated from the beach by 300-metre-wide dunes stabilized by mimosa and fencing. The **beach** of fine white sand ranks as one of the longest continual strands in the Mediterranean: 9km from the access road to the mouth of the river (accessible from Gelemiş by a side road labelled "Çayığzı"; see below), then almost 6km further to the end. Most people prefer flagging down a beach dolmuş in summer, or taking advantage of transport laid on by hotels, to the hot, half-hour stroll out from the centre of Gelemiş; parking at road's end is limited, as the archeological authorities have refused permission to expand the space.

Flanking the entrance to the beach are two **restaurants**: one currently out of service, the other (*Patara*) taking advantage of its sudden monopoly and long-standing reputation for *mantı* of seasonably variable quality. There is also a single wood-built snack and drinks stall out on the sand itself. In season it gets crowded in the immediate vicinity of the beach entrance, but a walk along the dunes toward the river and the Letoön brings you to more than enough solitary spots. Once away from the roadhead, though, there are no amenities, and you're well advised to rent an umbrella and/or a sunbed ($1.25 apiece). Spring and autumn swimming is delightful, but in summer the exposed shoreline can get battered with a considerable surf by Mediterranean standards.

Less publicized but no less vigorous **anti-development battles** than at Dalyan have taken place here too. This beach is also a turtle-nesting area, off-limits after dark, and in winter the lagoon behind attracts considerable bird life from inner Anatolia. Conservationists have won the fight to exclude villas from the cape at the southeast end of the strand, while the protected archeological status of the area seems to have put a stop to most building inland at Gelemiş since the early 1990s. A proposed nearby airport has also been successfully resisted, with a change of venue to Çukurbağ, above Kaş, now contemplated.

If you wish to visit the beach after the Patara gate has closed – to watch the sunset, for example – you'll need to use the side road to **Çayağzı** ("river mouth"), well sign-posted from both Gelemiş (6.5km) and Highway 400 (7.5km). The beach here isn't as nice as at Patara, nor are there any umbrellas to rent, but you'll find some wooden tea-and-kebab stalls, and there are canoes available to paddle around the pool which forms at the river mouth.

Gelemiş practicalities

Gelemiş itself consists of little more than a busy T-junction, with a crescent-shaped neighbourhood, threaded by a single twisting high street extending west, ending in a small rise. Before 1950, the entire area was highly malarial; subsequently, a lake immediately northeast of the main highway (still erroneously shown on most maps) was drained by a canal running parallel to the Çayağzı road, and the Patara swamp shrunk by eucalyptus plantations in the village centre.

The most desirable **accommodation** is accordingly off the still-damp flatlands, either on the western rise, or on another ridge to the east of the T-junction. Even with this little boost in elevation, you'll need your lodging to furnish mosquito nets. There are a few establishments along the approach to the village from Highway 400, but the only one crying out for consideration – just as you enter Gelemiş, right of the road – is Mustafa Kirca's *Flower Pension* (☎0242/843 5164, fax 843 5078; ③).

Most versatile of the local hoteliers are the brothers Muzaffer and Arif Otlu, who cater to those on a budget with Arif's dead-central *Golden Pansiyon* (☎0242/843 5162, fax 843 5008; ③), or, for those seeking more comfort, Muzaffer's *Patara View Point Hotel* (☎0242/843 5184, fax 843 5022; ④; available through *Tapestry*), with an unbeatable setting on the **easterly ridge**, mosquito nets, tractor shuttle to the beach, a pool-bar and a Turkish-style breakfast terrace. The Otlus also run their own **travel agency** in the basement of the *Golden Pansiyon*, *Gelemiş Turizm*, which offers canoeing and trekking trips in addition to the standard excursions. The *Likya 2 Pansiyon* (☎0242/843 5211; ④), a bit to the south of the *Patara View Point*, is a more basic outfit but still good value, while the nearby *Mehmet* (☎0242/843 5032, fax 843 5078; ④) is a notch up with its pool and restaurant, and accordingly attracts some package tours. Still further south on this easterly ridge stands the small *Hotel Merhaba* (☎0242/843 5113, fax 843 5133; ④), with unique views of the ancient city and vegetarian food on offer. If all these are full, consider the well-appointed *Sisyphos* (☎0242/843 5044, fax 843 5156; ④), downhill close to the T-junction but calm enough.

On the **western hill**, good choices – though neither with much of a view – are the *Pansiyon Zeybek 1* (☎0242/843 5072; ③) and the nearby *Apollon* (☎0242/843 5048; ④), with a swimming pool. It is theoretically possible to walk from this neighbourhood past the west shore of the swamp and Hadrian's granary to the beach in about twenty minutes, but this puts you out on a part of the dunes completely devoid of facilities and is best considered an interesting way of returning to the village at the end of the day.

Choice in **eating out** is somewhat limited, and you're often best off arranging to be fed at your accommodation; the cuisine is often sustaining rather than *haute*, but then prices are hardly *haute* compared to Kalkan for example. The best **restaurants**, in no particular order, are those attached to the *Sisyphos*, the *Golden* (which sometimes has trout) and the *Flower pansiyons*; among unaffiliated eateries, the *Tlos Terrace* gets the best marks. If Turkish hotel **breakfasts** don't start the day well for you, you'll do no better than patronizing one of the two tasty *gözleme* stalls next to the *Golden Pansiyon*, run by the sisters of Arif and Muzaffer. Also on Gelemiş high street, the *Voodoo Bar*, the musical *Medusa*, the fruit-punchy *Vitamin Bar* and the *Sera Roof Bar* (above the PTT, with a pool table) together furnish adequate **nightlife**.

Kalkan

Thirteen kilometres beyond the turnoff for Patara, the former Greek village of Kalamaki, now **KALKAN**, appears to cling for dear life to the steep hill on which it is precariously situated. Occasionally the older, stone-built houses lose their fight with gravity, as in the case of the severe 1957 earthquake, traces of which are still discernible in unrepaired buildings of the original village core to the east. Tourism is a fairly new phenomenon in the town: until the early 1970s both Kalkan and its rival Kaş eked out a living from charcoal-burning and olives. The locals benefiting from the recent boom were those too poor to spend the summer tending grain and apples on the huge *ova*, or upland, around the mountain village of Bezirgan, and who therefore were on hand to staff the new establishments. The richer residents sold up their seaside property without realizing its value, and no doubt the speculators will eventually transform most of the olive groves they bought; the worst developments to date are the *Patara Club*, an unsightly complex of holiday villas situated to the east of the village, and the hulking *Hotel Pirat* complex, just west of the yacht harbour.

Nonetheless, Kalkan makes a good base from which to explore Patara and Xanthos, or even the Letoön. Compared with Kaş (see p.413), the place is more polished (if not to say twee), and the clientele more sedate and wealthier, even when not yacht-propelled – something reflected in the higher prices and a growing package-tour presence. Speaking of money, and despite all this glitz, there's thus far just a single **bank**, but it's worth shunning their poor service in favour of either their Visa-accepting ATM, the **PTT**, or the special **exchange booth** on the quayside.

Accommodation

Some excellent **pansiyons** are located in the converted old buildings lining the central grid of cemented lanes – a district known as **Yalıboyu** – that drops from the top of town down to the harbour. Down **near the water**, the *Pension Patara* (☎0242/844 3076; ③) is a well-restored Greek mansion with a terrace bar, and ten varying en-suite rooms; *Tapestry Holidays* have an allotment here, so if it's full, try its quiet neighbour, the *Çetinkaya* (☎0242/844 3307; ③), or, for the connoisseurs of 1970s funky, the friendly, basic *Çetin* (no phone; ①), one block inland but with some sea views. More in the centre of things, on the same level above the water, is the similarly restored *Balıkçı Han* (☎0242/844 3641, fax 844 3075; ④), which can be noisy owing to the ground-floor bar; their annexe, the *Balıkçı Han 2*, in the easterly neighbourhood, is far more tranquil for the same price. Proceeding further west from *Balıkçı Han* and slightly uphill, you'll find the excellent-value *Akın Pansiyon* (☎0242/844 3025, fax 844 2094; ②), with a mix of en-suite and unplumbed rooms.

Inland, the *Kalamaki Pansiyon* (☎0242/844 3312, fax 844 3654; ⑤), run by Durmuş and Christine Uşaklı and a few steps above the *Pension Patara*, was one of the first restoration jobs here, its name recalling the original Greek village. Like most of the conversions at or near the village centre, the rooms are on the small side, and available only by weekly or two-weekly periods; for bookings from the UK contact ☎0131/440 2444. Above the *Kalamaki*, Hasan Altan Sokağı becomes after dark the main pedestrianized drag linking the bus stop with the village centre. One block above this, on Süleyman Yılmaz Caddesi, you can try the simple, long-established *Çelik* (☎0242/844 3022; ③) for en-suite rooms; or, on the perpendicular lane heading up from the *Alternatif Restaurant*, the *Gül* (☎0242/844 3416; ③), a place of undistinguished modern architecture, which offers a particularly good breakfast and is run by friendly, if non-English-speaking, management. Even if money is no object, the arty, minimalist *Kalkan Han* (☎0242/844 3151, fax 844 2048; ⑥)), back on Süleyman Yılmaz Caddesi, seems overpriced considering the smallish rooms and the fact that only its rooftop bar has good views.

There's also a new "ghetto" of **modern, purpose-built hotels** extending a kilometre or so west from the edge of town, most block-booked in season by tour operators; larger room sizes, and often the presence of a swimming pool, offset the disadvantage of a potentially hefty walk into town. Some of the best among these, about 500m along, are the French-Turkish co-run *Diva* (☎0242/844 3175; ⑤; available through *Anatolian Sky* and *Tapestry*), with some rooms overlooking the sea and olives, and its neighbour the *Dionysia* (☎0242/844 3681; ⑤; available through *Anatolian Sky* and *Tapestry*); 500m further out again, the simple but highly recommended en-suite *Lizo Pansiyon* (☎0242/844 3381, winter 344 5527; ④; half-board rates available) is managed by two engaging sisters, Nükhet and Ruhsar, the elder of whom has written a Turkish cookery book and accordingly presides over the on-site roof restaurant. Finally, near the very top of town, prominently signposted from the approach road, the *Kelebek Otel* (☎0242/844 3770; fax 844 3771; ④), with pool and good views, compensates for its remoteness by underpricing itself at slow times.

Eating and drinking

Good **food**, in addition to that at *Lizo* (reckoned by some as the best in town), isn't a problem to find in Kalkan, albeit at a price. A common gimmick is the set-price (currently $3), fill-your-plate *meze* special, with the eatery making most of its money out of obligatory service charges, booze and entrees.

Time-tested, reliable options include the restaurant attached to the *Akın Pansiyon*; the waterfront *İlyada*, which serves up to 25 different cold *meze* a night; or perennial favourite *Korsan*, near the east end of the front, the second restaurant established here in 1979. One to avoid, by all accounts, is the tourist-trap *Köşk Restaurant*. A better choice inland is *Belgin's Kitchen*, popular for its mock-nomad, cavernous decor and live Turkish evenings; the limited menu's not bad either, featuring such delights as *mantı* and *çiğ börek*, and unusually for Kalkan it gets a partly Turkish clientele. Back down by the water, *The Steps Sandwich Shop* is reasonable for its location and features excellent homemade desserts, as well as a comfortable, after-dark roof bar serving light snacks.

Other **drinking** options narrow down to an inland trio: the long-lived, loud *Yalı* bar, up at the top of Yalıboyu; *Bar+Bar*, whose tables fill a perpendicular lane just below Hasan Altan Sokağı; and the more secluded *Aquarium Bar* well to the east, with a billiards room and occasional transvestite belly dancing.

Around Kalkan

Walking around the coast road west from town, you'll arrive at the **Taş Adamı** or "Stone Man", the local name for a disused quarry that originally provided the masonry for Kalkan's jetty. Beyond this is a pebbly **beach** traditionally reserved for women, although this doesn't mean you won't be followed on the way there.

It's only by exploring further afield into the Toros mountains or along the coast that the real advantages of Kalkan's situation are revealed. **Bezırgan**, 11km inland from Kalkan by a recently paved road, is the retreat of richer Kalkan residents in summer, and has a sprinkling of Lycian rock tombs; and near the adjacent hamlet of Islamlar, a flour mill is set in a cool green valley. You can visit on a day trip by donkey, arranged by Süleyman Bolukbaşı (☎0242/844 3324); the $25 price includes a meal in an attractive wooden village house.

The road from Kalkan to Kaş follows the harsh karstic coastline, the thin soil stained red from traces of metallic ores. Soon you cross the **Kaputaş Gorge**, a deep gash leading back into the cliff face. Steps from the road take you down to the popular **Kaputaş beach**, a 150-metre-long expanse of pebble that is normally fairly crowded, probably as a result of the poor quality of the beaches closer to Kalkan and Kaş. A plaque on the cliff face commemorates four workers who were killed here during the road-building in 1962–63.

Kaş

Tourism has transformed **KAŞ**, until 1923 the Greek-populated timber-shipping port of Andifli. It's still beautifully situated, nestled in a curving bay – the name Kaş means "eyebrow" or "something curved" – with a backdrop of vertical, 500-metre-high cliffs peppered with rock-tombs. But what was a sleepy fishing village until the early 1980s has become a holiday metropolis and *ilçe* (country seat), whose permanent population of five thousand is vastly outnumbered in summer by the vacationers – largely İstanbul and Ankara yuppies – on whom locals depend for a living. Attitudes towards outsiders have inevitably hardened, though they are still mild compared to those occasionally encountered in Kuşadası or Antalya.

Kaş is a major halting point on "Blue Cruise" itineraries, and **yacht and gület culture** is nearly as important here as at Kalkan – with day trips available on the latter craft for the less well-heeled. Plans are afoot to move all pleasure craft to a new marina being prepared at Bucak (formerly Vathy), the long fjord west of town, wedged between Highway 400 and the Çukurbağ peninsula which extends 5km southwest of Kaş. To avoid the necessity of a long detour around Çukurbağ if sailing in from the east, a canal will be blasted through the narrow isthumus joining the peninsula to the mainland, complete with drawbridge to allow tall ships to pass.

There's no beach to speak of in Kaş itself, or anywhere nearby for that matter, which together with a lack of a really convenient airport, and a spotty water supply (to be remedied by a pipeline from Saklıkent) has spared the town the worst excesses of modern tourism. Indeed, if you're not looking for leather and carpets, at first glance there seems little to keep you here; the town does get lively **at night**, however, mainly because shops stay open until 1am in season – the many bars much later. By day Kaş makes a handy base from which to reach Kekova and nearby Patara if you don't have your own transport, and local boosters hope that in the near future it can also serve as a springboard for various types of adventure and activity tourism. The modern town is built atop the site of ancient **Antiphellos**, whose remaining ruins still speckle the streets, as well as covering the base of the peninsula to the west.

Information and accommodation

The busy **tourist information office** is at waterfront Cumhuriyet Meydanı 5 (Mon–Fri 8.30am–noon & 1–8pm, Sat & Sun 10am–noon & 1–8pm; ☎0242/836 1238), and stocks town maps as well as hotel lists. Because of the town's nocturnal rhythms, it's worth walking a bit out of the centre – especially traffic-clogged Elmalı Caddesi, and the main bar district – in search of calm, views and privacy in your **accommodation**. Package tourism has been slow to take off here not only because of distance from any airport, but also the often indifferent standard of lodging – surprisingly few establishments can be recommended with unqualified enthusiasm. The main concentration of desirable hotels and *pansiyon*s within the town limits is now east of the centre, beyond the main cluster of government buildings and above Küçükçakıl Plajı; an older enclave of lodgings lies west of the main drag Elmalı Caddesi, along Hastane Caddesi and around the hilltop Yeni Cami, formerly a Greek church. The Çukurbağ peninsula has in recent years acquired a crop of multi-starred hotels, but few deserve their star rating, and there's no public tranport along the peninsula's eleven-kilometre loop road – local taxi

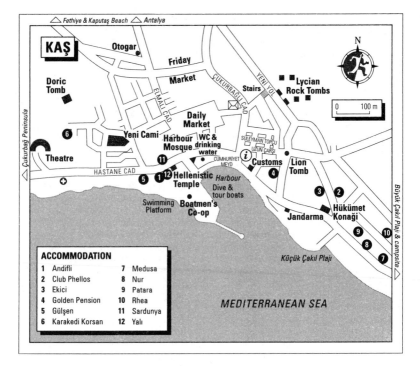

drivers, and the various remote resorts who prefer their clientele to spend all their money in-house, have together blocked the implementation of a shuttle bus service.

Hastane Caddesi and around Yeni Cami

Andifli Motel, Hastane Cad 13 (☎0242/836 1042). 1970s-style rooms with shared bathrooms charge 1990s rates strictly by virtue of the wonderful sea-view terrace and sea-facing rooms. ②.

Gülşen Pansiyon, Hastane Cad 23 (☎0242/836 1171). Modern, en-suite affair on several floors; lucky balcony rooms face the sea. ②.

Karakedi Korsan Motel, Yeni Cami Sok 7 (☎0242/836 1887, fax 836 3076). Despite the ominous name, which translates as "Pirate-Black Cat", this is the pick of a half-dozen outfits around the Yeni Cami, with a roof bar and view of the amphitheatre. ③.

Sardunya Otel, Hastane Cad (☎0242/836 3080, fax 836 3082). Viewless setting on landward side of the street, but new and comfortable for the price. ③.

Yalı Pansiyon, Hastane Cad 11 (☎0242/836 3226). Slightly more comfort than its neighbour the *Andifli*, identical views. ②.

Küçükçakıl

Club Phellos, Doğruyol Sok 4 (☎0242/836 1953, fax 836 1890). Large pool, fairly sympathetic architecture, air-con rooms and views make this a good three-star choice in the town centre; available through *Sunquest*. ⑤.

Ekici, Arısan Sok, opposite *Club Phellos* (☎0242/836 1417, fax 836 1418). Similar in most respects to its rival, though its medium-sized rooms are slightly older; available through *Sunquest*. ⑤.

Golden Pension, just south of Uzun Çarşı (☎0242/836 1736). Basic rooms with shared bathrooms in an ageing building; popular with backpackers, but close to several bars, so don't expect much sleep. ①.

Medusa, Küçükçakıl shore road (☎0242/836 1440). Good-value two-star hotel with a pool, private rock-beach and various comforts you'd associate with a category higher. ④.

Nur Hotel, Küçükçakıl shore road (☎0242/836 1828, fax 836 1388). Pool, bar, medium-sized rooms, beach access. ④.

Nur Pansiyon, Küçükçakıl shore road, a few doors west of the preceding (☎0242/836 1203). Co-managed with the namesake hotel, to which guests have pool access; simpler en-suite rooms, terrace restaurant. ③.

Patara Pansiyon (☎0242/836 1328). Co-run with the *Rhea/Linda* below, for which guests have pool privileges. ③.

Rhea/Linda Hotel, Doğruyol Sok, east end (☎0242/836 3084, fax 836 1788). Largish rooms, most with view, and tiny pool at this Siamese-twin hotel in a quiet spot; the Rhea wing has air conditioning. ③.

Çukurbağ peninsula

Aqua Park, end of the peninsula (☎0242/836 1901; fax 836 1992). Supposedly the best resort hotel in Kaş, with four stars, but only its dramatically set pool facing Greek Kastellórizo redeems it: cramped rooms and balconies, grouchy staff, limp breakfasts. German rather than British package availability. ⑥.

Hamarat, 3km out on the south shore loop (☎0242/836 1547). Cosy (eight-room) *pansiyon* with good views, kitchen facilities and a swimming platform just across the road. ②.

Campsites

Büyükçakıl, east of town at the far end of Hükümet Caddesi, 1km past the *jandarma* (☎0242/836 1968). Shade from olive trees; also rents out A-frames with cots.

Kaş Camping, 1km west of town along Hastane Caddesi, just past the amphitheatre (☎0242/836 1050). Long a favoured link in the Hippie Trail to Asia, this boasts a swimming platform, restaurant and a famous bar; also caravan space, and A-frames for the tentless.

The Town

The ruins of ancient **Antiphellos** are scattered around Kaş and across the approach to the Çukurbağ peninsula. This was the harbour of ancient Phellos, inland near the modern village of Çukurbağ and one of the few Lycian cities to bear a Greek name (*phellos* means "cork oak"). Excavations here have unearthed a settlement dating back to at least the fourth century BC, although Antiphellos only gained importance in Hellenistic times, when an increase in seagoing commerce meant it thrived while Phellos withered. By the Roman era, it was the most important city in the region, famed particularly for its exported sponges, which Pliny mentioned as being exceptionally soft.

The **remains** of the ancient city are few and scattered, but what there is to see is quite impressive. Out of town, 500m along Hastane Caddesi from the harbour mosque, sits a small, almost complete Hellenistic **amphitheatre** with 26 rows of seats. The theatre never had a permanent stage building, but in recent years a curved wall has been built in place of a stage to provide a backdrop for local wrestling matches. At other times it's a favourite venue to come and watch the sunset with a bottle of refreshment.

Above and behind the theatre, 100m away on the top of a hill, stands a unique **Doric tomb**, also almost completely intact. Its single chamber forms a slightly tapering cube cut from the rock on which it stands. The two-metre-high entrance was once closed by a sliding door, but can now be entered in order to examine the bench at the back (on which the body would have been laid out), decorated by a frieze of small female figures performing a dance.

The most interesting of the sarcophagi to have survived local pilfering for building materials is the **Lion Tomb** on Postane Sokak, right at the top of the Uzun Çarşı. This towering structure has two burial chambers, the lower one forming a base for the Lycian sarcophagus above it. On the side of the lower chamber is an undeciphered Lycian inscription, written in a poetic form similar to that of the obelisk at Xanthos. The

SCUBA DIVING AROUND KAŞ

The Mediterranean around Kaş has arguably the best visibility and greatest variety of sea life along the entire Turkish coast. A number of **dive operators** offer half-and full-day trips for qualified divers, as well as the usual certification courses. Beginners' dives visit a tunnel at 15 metres and a shoreline cave fed by an icy freshwater spring; moderately experienced divers may be taken to a reef frequented by giant groupers, with a sheer wall dropping to 35 metres. Advanced divers can visit the wreck of a World War II bomber shot down between Kaş and Kastellórizo, resting nearly intact in 60 metres of water. *Bougainville Travel*, Çukurbağlı Cad 10 (☎0242/836 3142, fax 836 1605), is one of the better-equipped outfitters, with a boat large enough to weather swells in comfort; their prices are approximately $63 for a full day's outing (two dives, with lunch), or $30 for a single dive (morning or afternoon, by choice); rates are slightly lower if you supply your own gear except tanks.

name of the tomb is derived from the four lifting bosses (projecting bits of masonry used to remove the Gothic-style lid from its base) in the shape of lions' heads, resting their chins on their paws.

The beaches

Considering that Kaş is a major Turkish resort, local **beaches** are surprisingly awful. The main, closest ones, **Küçük Çakıl** (Small Gravel) and **Büyük Çakıl** (Large Gravel) – the former 400m east of the harbour, the latter a kilometre east of town – are, as their names suggest, stretches of grubby shingle that few people would acknowledge as proper beaches. Leaving town along Hastane Caddesi, the Çukurbağ peninsula gives good views of the Greek island Kastellórizo, and is lapped by clear, aquamarine water, but again has no beaches to speak of. The nearest decent beach is **Kaputaş**, on the way to Kalkan (see p.411), a small stretch of pebbly sand which understandably gets crowded.

Boat tours and Kastellórizo

The local boatmen's cooperative, the *Kaş Deniz Taşıyıcıları Kooperatifi*, offers **standard full-day tours** (depart 10am, return 6pm) from the harbour to Kekova for $10 per person (plus $4 for buffet lunch), to Patara for about the same, and to the Greek island of Kastellórizo for $25. **Custom tours** start at $140 a day at the beginning of the season (April and May), reaching $230 by late season (Aug and Sept).

Trips to Greece are on a demand-only basis, not necessarily daily, although there is sometimes an extra, unpublicized Greek boat to Kastellórizo in the evening. The main catch is that you may not be allowed to stay the night on the island, since Kastellórizo is not yet an official port of entry to Greece – so neither the Greek nor Turkish boats can be depended upon as a one-way ferry. Returning to Kaş from Kastellórizo, no fresh visa fee is payable as long as you have ample time left on your existing visa and you come back the same day.

Kastellórizo (Meis)

The port of the Greek island **Kastellórizo**, Meis in Turkish, is just over three nautical miles off the Turkish coast; the distance between the island's northernmost cape and the Çukurbağ peninsula is rather less. It is among the smallest inhabited islands of the Dodecanese archipelago, once supported by trade with Kaş and Kalkan, which ceased completely after the occupation of Kastellórizo by Italy. The subsequent torching by unidentified arsonists of many houses in 1944 further upset the fortunes of the island, but recently its fine port has begun to attract yachtsmen, and it's a favourite place to nip across to in the event of expiration of a three-month Turkish tourist visa. You'll find complete coverage of the island in *The Rough Guide to Rhodes, the Dodecanese and the East Aegean* but it's worth saying here that there are at least two weekly onward boats to Rhodes most of the year, plus three to five weekly flights on a puddle-jumper; if you just miss a departure, a couple of days on the island will be time well spent.

Eating out

There is still a bare handful of good **restaurants** in Kaş, an increasingly important bit of intelligence now that relations between prices and portions are no longer controlled. Best avoided are a string of eateries in the pedestrian arcade – officially Orta Okul Sokağı – between the marketplace and the quay; the *Derya* in particular has generated complaints of price-gouging. There are few restaurants actually on the waterfront, other than the rip-off *Mercan Eriş* by the quay; currently the best of the inland crop of Turkish eateries is *Bahçe*, at the very top of Uzun Çarşı, with reasonably priced, fresh fare. Otherwise, try the *Çınar Restaurant* on Çukurbağlı Caddesi, where you can eat well on *meze* and *döner* for about $6 until midnight, or the sound-alike *Çınarlar* on the same street, which does good *börek*, *pide* and Italian pizza. For a worthwhile splurge, look no further than *Chez Evy*, Terzi Sok 2 (off Süleyman Topçu Sok), where French country recipes meet Turkish flavours; the result is happier and more generous than you'd expect, and Evy herself is one of the characters of Kaş. Booking for the garden seating (☎0836 1253) is necessary in season; otherwise wait for a table, or have a night-cap, in the rustic downstairs bar.

Nightlife

A varied, crowded, and often deafening **nightlife** is what makes Kaş for many visitors. Among the dozen-plus bars, *Redpoint*, which plays taped rock and blues on Süleyman Topçu Sokağı, reigns as the town's premier after-hours pub, packed solid after midnight. *Antique*, ironically near the *jandarma* post on Hükümet Caddesi, operates illegally around an ancient tomb, with live Turkish soft rock many nights; other outfits along the same street include *Cafe Nectar*, with live Turkish *sanaat* music and *Deja Vu*, the favourite early-evening bar, perfectly situated for the sunset. Just inland on Ilkokul Caddesi, the more tranquil *Genç Club* is better for a quiet drink and talk, with a rustic interior and fire going in the cooler months. On the harbour front, long-established *Mavi/Blue*, which until the mid-1980s was a coffeehouse where the fishermen played backgammon, is now loud and studenty. The *Sun Café*, west of the jetty, is a calmer bar-gallery, with cushions and low tables, which occasionally hosts Turkish musical evenings.

Shopping

The upmarket tourist industry in Kaş centres around Uzun Çarşı (Long Market) Caddesi, and that's exactly what it is – an uninterrupted bazaar of **crafts and designer clothing shops** with a selection (and prices, of course) that would fit right in at London's Covent Garden or San Francisco's Ghirardelli Square. While Naf Naf, Benetton or Quicksilver rags, mass-produced under licence, are easy to come by, there are also local designers tailoring to order from hand-woven fabrics produced in nearby villages. You can best view such raw cloth at the weekly Friday market held in the *pazar alanı*, while fine produce is offered every day in the lanes just south.

Among the **antique shops** on Uzun Çarşı, *Kybele* at no. 4 (assorted knick-knacks) and *Argentum* at no. 19 (silver items) are worth singling out. There's another enclave of more conventional **carpet shops**, such as the long-lived *Kaş and Carry*, on adjacent Orta Sokağı, or you might try one of *Magic Orient Carpets'* two premises, (Cumhuriyet Meydanı and Hükümet Cad 15), where staff are knowledgable and not pushy.

Listings

Books and magazines The *Merhaba Cafe* on Çukurbağlı Caddesi towards the PTT, in addition to gourmet cakes and coffee, sells foreign newspapers and books, as well as quality postcards; a nameless hole-in-the-wall at Süleyman Topçu 7/2 has a small stock of used books, as well as music cassettes.

Car rental No big chains here; take your chances with *Alim Tour*, Hastane Cad 1 (☎0242/836 1354), or *Kaş Rent-a-Car*, Cumhuriyet Meydanı (☎0242/836 1749).

Exchange *Yapı Kredi* autoteller on the waterfront, plus *Halkbank* and *İş Bankası* cashpoints on Elmalı Caddesi; the *Ziraat Bankası*, next to the PTT, has a foreign-note-changing machine.

Laundries Two along Süleyman Topçu Sokağı; also *Habesos*, around the corner on Antik Sokak.

Travel agency British/Turkish/Dutch-run *Bougainville Travel*, Çukurbağlı Cad 10 (☎0242/836 3142, fax 836 1605), is the foremost adventure travel agency in the area – this is where you go for dive tours, mountain treks, canyoning and kayaking, though they also offer more conventional excursions. *Simena* at Elmalı Caddesi (☎0242/836 1416) will more likely handle airport transfer and flight confirmation for package clients.

Water Delicious and potable, straight from the limestone mountains, available free at taps by the harbour mosque.

Above Kaş: Gömbe, Yeşil Göl and Akdağ

When sea-level pleasures at Kaş pall, especially in excessively hot weather, there's no closer escape than the cool fastnesses of the **Akdağ range**, which soars to over 3000 metres in the space of 20km. The standard jump-off point for excursions into the mountains, and one easily reached by public transport from Kaş, is **GÖMBE**, a small town 60km above Kaş, towards Elmalı. The ride up is mostly shaded by extensive cedar forests, which yield

---

THE TAHTACIS

The so-called *Tahtacılar* or "Board-Cutters" are a secretive and much-maligned group who are in fact Alevis, a sect closely related to Shiism and especially the Bektashi dervish order, descended from remnants of the army of Shia Shah Ismail, defeated by Sultan Selim I at the Battle of Çaldıran in 1514. Like all good heretics before and since, the stragglers retreated high into the mountains, out of reach of their enemies, and today occupy villages in a wide montane crescent, extending from Edremit to Adana, with a special concentration in the Toros ranges. Their present name commemorates the professions of logger and wood-carver which many of them have followed in recent centuries; such Tahtacıs are semi-nomadic, under summer contract to the Forest Service, with whole villages sent to fell trees in areas that change from year to year.

While the allied Bektashis have their spiritual centre at central Anatolian Hacıbektaş, the Tahtacıs still maintain a seminary at Narlıdere outside İzmir. In their beliefs, which they can be reluctant to discuss in detail with outsiders, they share most of the tenets of **Alevîsm**: the stress on inner purity of observance rather than the external ritual of daily prayers, or abstention from alcohol; interdenominational tolerance and disdain of materialism; and relatively equal status for women. They are abhorrent to orthodox Sunni Muslims, who in recent decades constructed mosques – often at gunpoint – in previously mosque-less Alevi villages; and their free-thinking has often brought them into (sometimes violent) conflict with the authorities. Their attitude to women has engendered the most scurrilous slanders, and for visitors, it is the boldness of the unveiled women – who are not shy about addressing strangers – that is the most reliable clue that you are in a Tahtacı area, and a welcome change after the po-faced sexual segregation of mainstream Turkish village society.

to vast apple orchards as you approach Gömbe. The place is famous for a festival of the local Tahtacıs which happens in June, and another farmers' fair during the latter half of August. There are simple but adequate **restaurants** around the main square, plus an equal number of *pansiyons*: fanciest of these is the *Toros* (①), though the *Akın*, a few hundred metres along the road to Kaş, is adequate and clean, with shared bathrooms (①).

Yeşil Göl and Akdağ

Most people come to Gömbe to visit **Yeşil Göl** (Green Lake), a short distance west and one of the few semi-permanent bodies of water in the generally arid, karstic Akdağ sierra. It's best to have your own wheels, but the following directions apply equally to those walking. Leave the square heading north and turn left immediately after crossing the river bridge, then take the second right and begin climbing. Zigzags will take you past a mosque, and over the runnel of an aqueduct; confirm directions by asking for the track to "Subaşı Yayla". Exactly 6500m above Gömbe, about half an hour's drive, you'll reach a widening in the track beside a stream. The track is by now very rough, and you certainly won't get much further in a two-wheel-drive car. Leave the main track, crossing the vigorous stream by a small bridge, and pick up the fairly clear trail on the opposite bank. Heading south over a low ridge, you should pass some rudimentary shepherds' huts and corrals, before emerging abruptly at the overlook for the lake.

The lake is claimed never to completely dry up but is at its best between April and June; the earlier in spring you show up, the finer the wildflower displays. The southern shore of the lake has enough space for a handful of tents, should you wish to camp the night – advisable if you plan to bag Akdağ (see below). Continuing twenty minutes in the same direction, you top another crest from which you can view the impressive **Uçarsu waterfalls** pouring off the flank of Akdağ summit – though these run only during May and June, essentially a melting snow phenomenon.

If you intend to **climb the peak** of Akdağ (3073m), retrace your steps to the main track and proceed west; after about ten minutes you pass a quadruple-spouted spring. After a few bends, and now high above the stream bed, you adopt the true right bank (facing the direction of flow) of the watercourse. When you reach a tributary coming from the south, turn to follow it, keeping to the true left bank. The summit ridge will be ahead, on your right; soon you should pick up a distinct, cairned path which will take you to all the way to the top, a two-hour hike one-way with a daypack, from the four-way spring. The summit cairn contains a "guestbook" to sign, and the views over the snow-flecked badlands are superb. An ice-axe is most useful until June or July (depending on the preceding winter), and you'll need an adequate water bottle at any season.

The Kekova region

Some of the most beautifully situated ruins on the south coast are in the area known as **Kekova**, after the eponymous offshore island: a stretch of rocky coastline littered with remains of Lycian settlements, some now submerged under the translucent waters that lap around these calm, shallow coves.

Üçağız

The central village – and most useful base for the region – is **ÜÇAĞIZ**, connected to Highway 400 by a surfaced, twenty-kilometre road. Thus its quiet days are numbered: already carpet and antique shops have sprouted, boat-trip touts swarm around you on arrival, and you've little hope of finding one of the eighty-odd beds in July or August. The fact that most of the surroundings have been designated as an archeological site should protect Üçağız from unseemly concrete expansion, limiting the number of new

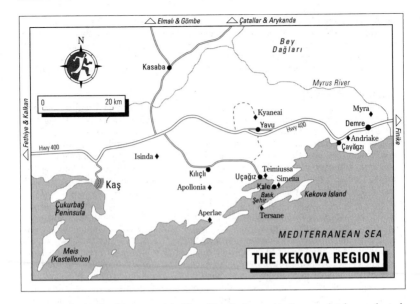

buildings. And indeed its essential village identity has yet to be completely supplanted – out of season the place is still idyllic.

Üçağız's **pansiyons** are simple but often fairly pricy considering the remote location and lack of a beach. Although fresh water has been piped in from the mountains around Gömbe, hot water showers are rare. The fanciest and most secluded is the *Ekin* (☎0242/874 2064; ③–④), at the far west end of the village, with a pleasant garden, clean, airy rooms and all-important insect screens; the price differential describes rates for the original bathless wing, and the new en-suite extension. Runners-up are the *Onur* (☎0242/874 2071; ②), the only establishment overlooking the water; the new *Koç* (☎0242/874 2080; ③), where all rooms are en suite and better value than the *Ekin*'s; and the inexpensive *Nergiz* (☎0242/874 2041; ②), partially en suite and run by the friendly Aliçavuşoğlu family – it's unmarked, but just opposite the primary school.

None of the four waterside **restaurants** represents fantastic value; about the most tolerable and durable is the *Liman Marina*, better known as *Ibo's*. On its own, five minutes' walk east of the village, the *Kalealtı*, run by the Kormel family, offers a novel setting: tombs around, castle overhead, one of two brackish shoreline springs flowing through its grounds; it's also marginally cheaper than the places around the harbour.

Around Üçağız

Until the road was built, the Lycian remains that surround Üçağız were visited by few apart from hardy goats and explorers. Teimiussa – and if you like walking, Simena and Aperlae – can be reached on foot from the village, but sooner or later you'll go on a **boat trip**, the main thing to do at beachless Üçağız. Destinations and prices are fairly standard: $8 per person to take in nearby Kale (Simena) and Kekova island; $12 to Andriake port or Aperlae ruins; $4 for a one-way shuttle to Kale (the walk back takes 45min–1hr over rocky terrain, preferably on a cool day).

SEA-KAYAKING AROUND KEKOVA

Bougainville Travel in Kaş offer organized **sea-kayaking day tours** in the Kekova area, a wonderful, low-impact way of appreciating the eerie seascapes here. They have the further advantage of allowing you to approach the shoreline, and the Batık Şehir in particular, much closer than the cruise boats do, and also of using narrow, shallow channels off-limits to larger craft – which are, incidentally, your main threat, as you must be wary of their wake. Since the ban on swimming in the vicinity of submerged antiquities, this is really the only method of getting a good look at them. With a suitable head covering and a water bottle secreted under your apron, you'll tolerate all but the hottest summer days, even wrapped inside a life vest. Trips often begin with a motorized tow from Üçağız to the starting point of your choice, for example Tersane; outings can be as long or short as stamina allows. Per-person rates, including a transfer from Kaş to Üçağız and a picnic lunch, are approximately $45 for a day's excursion; for current information contact Ufuk Güven, programme co-ordinator at *Bougainville Travel* (see p.416 for address).

Üçağız translates as "three mouths" in Turkish, and the old Greek name of Tristomo, meaning exactly the same thing, is still used. The three apertures in question are the straits at each end of the island opposite, plus the entry to the lake-like inlet, at whose rear the village is situated. **Kekova Island** itself boasts the area's only beach, plus the best of the ruins, most of which are submerged but visible below the sea. The ruins of the ancient town of **Aperlae** are found on the other side of a peninsula to the west of Üçağız, while at the east edge of the village stand the acropolis and tombs of the site of another small Lycian settlement – **Teimiussa**. A little way beyond lies the village of Kale and the castle of **Simena**, clearly visible on the horizon. Several small islands, quarried in ancient times to near sea level, dot the bay.

Kekova Island

The most romantically situated antiquities in the area are those submerged along the northern coast of **Kekova Island**, known as *Batık Şehir* (Sunken City) locally, and to date not identified with any ancient city. The underwater remains of stairs and pavements, house walls and a long quay wall can all be seen; however, snorkelling, and swimming in general, are banned to prevent the removal of antiquities from the area, and most boatmen won't approach the rocky shoreline. Near the southwest tip of the island, at the spot known as *Tersane* (Dockyard), looms the apse of a long-vanished church, in whose shadow bathers spread their towels; unhappily, much of it collapsed during a particularly violent storm in February 1996.

Teimiussa

Ancient **TEİMİUSSA** is easily reached from the *Kalealtı* restaurant immediately below it. Nothing is really known about the history of the settlement, but inscriptions indicate that it was occupied in the fourth century BC. The site, which suggests a settlement without walls and few or no public buildings, consists mainly of a good scattering of rock tombs; some of these have semicircular benches cut into their bases – convenient for pondering mortality as you stare out to sea. On the hill above squats a small fort or tower, about the size of a house, while far below at sea level you can try to hunt for the tiny, rock-cut landing stage.

Simena and Kale

The ruined castle of the Knights of St John at **Simena** – and the village of **KALE** below it – are a fifteen-minute boat ride, or a longer kayak-paddle or walk from Üçağız. The secluded village itself, an archeological protected zone, is the haunt of Rahmi Koç, scion of a wealthy Turkish industrialist family, who donated a school in conjunction with restoring an old house here as a holiday retreat. Even for lesser mortals Kale makes a lovely place to stay, though as at Üçağız, some rustic-looking **pansiyons** overlooking the sea (and a marooned sarcophagus) seem pricy for what you get; at the seven or eight **restaurants**, charging a set price (around $4) for a fill-your-plate *meze* buffet seems the norm.

The climb to the castle is steep and tiring, but worth it both for the views and the castle itself, whose castellated ramparts are in good condition, partly resting on ancient foundations. Inside the castle is a fifteen-metre-wide theatre – large enough for 300 people – and on the northern slopes of the hill, off the path, stand some well-preserved sarcophagi.

Aperlae

In the opposite direction, southwest of Üçağız, lies the site of **APERLAE**, an hour's boat ride followed by a 45-minute walk; it's also reachable by a ninety-minute walk from the village of Kılıçlı (formerly Sıçak), a few kilometres from Üçağız on the side road back to Highway 400. The difficulty of access means that the site is practically deserted, and it's possible to swim around the sunken ruins and take a good look, while being wary of sea urchins and sharp rocks. The remains of the **city walls**, which bisect the hillside and enclose a rectangular area, with the sea on its southernmost side, are fairly well preserved and easily identified. Submerged are the remnants of a **quay**, indented at fifteen-metre intervals for the mooring of ships, and the foundations of rows of **buildings**, divided by narrow streets.

Though it's not known for certain, the assumption is that Aperlae was a Lycian city – a theory borne out in part by the Lycian coins with inscriptions "APR" and "PRL" that have been found. What is known for sure is that in imperial Roman times Aperlae headed a league of four cities – the others being Simena, Apollonia (closer to Kılıçlı) and Isinda (near modern Belenli) – whose citizens were collectively termed "Aperlite".

Kyaneai (Cyaneae)

East of the turn-off to Üçağız, Highway 400 enters a stretch of wild, inhospitable countryside, whose bleak aspect seems fit only for the herds of sheep and goats that graze it. In antiquity, however, this part of the world was scattered with small settlements, the most interesting of which nowadays is **KYANEAİ** (Cyaneae), 23km from Kaş in the hills above the village of **Yavu**. From the centre of the village there's a signposted, two-kilometre path to the site; the hike up only takes about 45 minutes but the route is extremely steep. Rather easier is an unmarked, four-kilometre dirt road which takes off from the north side of Highway 400, precisely 1km west of the side road to Yavu; the last stretch of this track is extremely rough, but negotiable with care in an ordinary saloon car. It's possible to take a guide along, but not strictly necessary; they can be found (or will find you) in the village, or at the *Çeşme* restaurant (see below). They tend to demand $12 per party – settle for half that.

The name Kyaneai derives from the Greek word meaning "dark blue" – also the origin of the word cyanide – but it's not known why the city was given this name. Nowadays it is often called "the city of sarcophagi", a more obvious epitaph, since the rows of Lycian and Roman sarcophagi to be seen at the site are the most numerous of any city in the region, and the main reason to visit. Little is known about Kyaneai's history, apart from the fact that it was the most important settlement in the region between Myra and Antiphellos (modern Kaş), and linked by a direct road to the harbour of Teimiussa, 12km away as the crow flies. It prospered in Roman times, and was the seat of a bishopric in the Byzantine age.

On the left of the path up from the village are some of the oldest and most interesting of the **tombs** to be found at the site. These line either side of a passage that may have been part of the ancient road. The most impressive among the group is to the south of the road, a sarcophagus carved completely from the rock on which it stands. The Gothic-arch "lid", cut from the same piece of rock, has two lions' heads projecting from each side. Near the top of the path, keep an eye out for a subterranean shrine or tomb with six columns.

Below the city, fairly inaccessible on the south face of the hill, stands an impressive **temple tomb** whose porch has a single free-standing column, and, unusually, a recess above the pediment in which a sarcophagus has been installed. According to an inscription, the sarcophagus was reserved for the bodies of the head of the household and his wife, while the rest of the family were buried in the tomb.

The top of the hill, the **acropolis**, is surrounded on three sides by a wall, the south side being so precipitous that it didn't need protection. The buildings inside are in a ruined state and covered with vegetation, but several have been more or less tentatively identified, including a library, baths, and two Byzantine churches, one with a lengthy inscription by the door. Near the summit is a tomb with a relief of a charioteer driving a team of four horses. The city had no natural spring nearby, so vaulted cisterns and reservoirs square-cut from the living rock are ubiquitous.

To the west of the summit, on the far side of the area used for parking, stands a moderate-sized **theatre** with 23 rows of seats still visible, divided by a walkway. Its upper rows make ideal vantage points to survey the western walls of the acropolis, the Kekova inlet to the south, and a row of sarcophagi flanking an ancient path linking the theatre and the acropolis. Mainly Roman, these tombs tend to be very simple, with rounded lids and crests, but include a few lion-head bosses too.

Back on Highway 400, about 500m in the Antalya direction, the *Çeşme* is a welcoming **restaurant**, run by an extroverted Turkish woman, Gülay Akkuş. Besides the only decent (and reasonably priced) cooking for 20km to either side, there are four *pansiyon* **rooms** available (☎0242/871 5425; ①), with more being readied in an old house nearby.

A popular local **walk**, best in winter or spring, involves following the still-existing, rather broad, ancient path from here towards Teimiussa: an outing of just under three hours, with the last hour unfortunately spent trudging along the paved side road. People at the restaurant can point you to the start of the route.

Demre and around

Beyond Yavu and the turning for Kyaneai, Highway 400 swoops down in a well-graded arc towards the river-delta town of **Demre**, the location of some of the more intriguing sites in Lycia. It's worth pausing for a few hours here in order to see the ancient city of **Myra** just to the north, and perhaps the beach and ancient harbour of **Andriake** a little way south (which you pass on the way in from the west), not to mention the **Church of St Nicholas** in the town itself – best observed in peace and quiet before 9am or after 5pm, when Demre is practically empty of visitors.

Some history

Myra was one of the most prominent members of the Lycian Federation, and retained its importance throughout the Middle Ages because of its associations with the bishop Saint Nicholas (aka Santa Claus). An ancient tradition claims that the name of the city derives from the Greek word for myrrh, the gum resin used in the production of incense. Although no record of the manufacture of this unguent is recorded, the emperor Constantine Porphyrogenitus described the city as the "thrice blessed, myrrh-breathing city of the Lycians, where the mighty Nikolaos, servant of God, spouts forth myrrh in accordance with the city's name". There is also a tale that when the tomb of Saint Nicholas was opened by Italian grave robbers, they were overwhelmed by the smell of myrrh that emanated from it.

Despite Myra's importance in the Lycian Federation, there is no mention of the city in records before the first century BC. In 42 BC Myra distinguished itself with typically Lycian defiance by refusing to pay tribute money to Brutus; Brutus's lieutenant had to break the chain closing the mouth of the harbour at Andriake – the city's port – and force his way in. Subsequently, Myra had an uneventful if prosperous history, treated well by its imperial overlords and receiving its highest accolade when the Byzantine emperor Theodosius II made it capital of Lycia in the fifth century.

By then the fame of the city had been much enhanced by one of its citizens, namely **Saint Nicholas**, born in Patara in 300 AD and later bishop of Myra. Saint Nicholas is supposed to have slapped the face of the Alexandrian heretic Arius at the Council of Nicaea in 325 AD, although his Western identity as a genial old present-giver is perhaps more familiar, arising from the story of his kindness to the three daughters of a poor man who were left without a dowry. Nicholas is credited with throwing three purses of gold into the house one night, enabling them to find husbands instead of selling themselves into prostitution. Many posthumous miracles were attributed to the saint, but little is actually known about the man; it has been established that on his death he was buried in the church in Demre now dedicated to him, and it is also widely believed that in 1087 his bones were carried off to Italy by a group of devout raiders from Bari (although the Venetians and Russians lay dubious claim to a similar exploit).

Demre is still proud of its connection with Saint Nicholas, and every December 6 (the saint's feast day) a special mass is held in his church, attracting pilgrims from Greece, Italy and (lately) Russia.

Demre

DEMRE (officially called, and signposted as, Kale) is a rather scruffy little place, too far away from the coast to merit a "seaside" tag, and afforded more mid-day attention by tour parties than it can really handle. Tourism is still dwarfed by the main local business of growing oranges and tomatoes, whose greenhouses – spread below as you descend the escarpment to the west – make the town seem bigger than it really is.

The Church of St Nicholas

The **Church of St Nicholas** (daily 8am–7pm; winter & spring closes 5/6pm; $3) dominates the centre of Demre, situated on the right of Müze Caddesi as you head west. Despite the recent erection of a horrible synthetic protective canopy, the building is evocative of the life and times of its patron saint, even if the myths surrounding him are more romance than fact.

The beatification of Nicholas occurred when visitors to his tomb here made claims of miraculous events, and Myra soon became a popular place of pilgrimage. A monastery was built nearby during the eleventh century, and even after the Italian merchants stole the bones of the saint, the pilgrimages continued; indeed, it is thought that the monks simply designated another tomb as that of Saint Nicholas, and would pour oil through openings in the top and collect it at the bottom, to sell to pilgrims as holy secretions.

The contemporary church has little in common with the third-century original, which was first rebuilt by Constantine IX in 1043, probably after its destruction by occupying Saracens. Today's shrine is basically a three-aisled basilica in form, with a fourth added later. In 1862 Tsar Nicholas I had the church renovated, installing a vaulted ceiling instead of a cupola in the central nave, along with a belfry – both unheard of in early Byzantine architecture. Turkish archeologists have carried out more recent restoration in order to protect the building, such as the addition of the small stone domes in the narthex.

Perhaps the most typical Byzantine feature is the **synthronon** or bishop's throne in the apse, a relatively rare sight in Turkish medieval buildings since most were removed when such churches were converted into mosques. **Mosaic floor** panels, mainly comprising geometric designs, adorn the nave and south aisle (many regrettably off-limits), while among the pieces of masonry cluttering the courtyard at the back is one carved with an anchor – Nicholas is the patron saint of sailors as well as virgins, children, merchants, scholars, pawnbrokers and Holy Russia. His supposed **sarcophagus**, in the most southerly aisle as you face the bishop's throne, is worth a look, although it is not considered genuine; the tomb from which the saint's bones were stolen was said to be located under a stone pavement – and, more significantly, there are marble statues representing a man and a woman (obviously a couple) on the lid.

Practicalities

In the wake of the general Turkish tourism slump, and heightened customer expectations of amenities, **accommodation** options in Demre are dwindling by the year. Neither of the *pansiyon*s out of town on the way to ancient Myra – the *Kent* (☎0242/871 2042; ①), about 400m before the ruins, and the *Lykia* (☎0242/871 2579; ①), 100m before – currently show much sign of life. Central hotels include the en-suite *Şahin*, on Müze Caddesi (☎0242/871 2686; ②), and as a last resort, two pricier options – the *Topçu* (☎0242/871 2200; ③) and the *Kıyak* (☎0242/871 2092; ③) – which face each other at the south entrance to town on Finike Caddesi, on the corner with the main highway. The best **restaurant** downtown is the *İpek*, on the same side of Müze Caddesi as the church; the locals patronize it, and the bill for two with wine won't exceed $13.

Myra

The remains of ancient **MYRA** (daily 8am–7pm; $1) are a two-kilometre walk or drive north of Demre's town centre, and make up one of the most easily visited, and most beautiful, Lycian sites. The imagination is captured by the immediacy with which you can walk out of the twentieth century and into a Greco-Roman theatre or a Lycian rock tomb. Not surprisingly the place is crawling with people throughout the summer season, and the best times to visit are either early morning or after 5.30pm.

Apart from the highlights – a large theatre and some of the best examples of house-style rock tombs to be seen in Lycia – most of the city is still buried. The **theatre** was destroyed in an earthquake in AD 141 but rebuilt shortly afterwards; the rock face behind it being vertical and unable to support the cavea, the structure had to be built up with masonry on either side, although its back rests against the cliff. The theatre is flanked by two concentric galleries, covering the stairs (still intact) by which spectators entered the auditorium; lying around the orchestra are substantial chunks of carving that would once have decorated the stage building, including one depicting two theatrical masks (now toppled upside down).

The main concentration of **tombs** is to the west of the theatre, and only accessible by some uphill scrambling; the series of iron ladders up the cliffside have now rusted away. Most of the tombs are of the house type, supposed to imitate Lycian dwelling-places, even down to the wooden beams supporting the roofs. Some are decorated with reliefs, including warriors at the climax of a battle, a naked page handing a helmet to a warrior, and a funerary scene.

The second group of tombs, called the **river necropolis**, is around the side of the second long ridge on the right as you stand with your back to the theatre stage. To get there, leave the main site, turn left off the final access drive onto the main approach road, and continue inland for 1500m. Here a monument known as the **painted tomb** features the reclining figure of a bearded man and his family in the porch, and outside on the rock face what is presumed to be the same family, dressed in outdoor clothes.

The tomb retains some traces of red and blue paint. To the east of the theatre, below the acropolis hill, lie the remains of a brick building whose identity is unknown, although it preserves an inscription on a Doric column concerning a ferry service that operated between Myra and Limyra in imperial Roman times.

Andriake

The port of the ancient city, **ANDRİAKE** (now known as **Çayağzı**, "rivermouth"), lies well over 2km beyond Demre, and nearly 5km from Myra itself. To get there, head west out of Demre towards Kaş, and then bear left, following yellow signs, when the main highway begins tackling the grade on the right bank of the stream leading down to the sea. Andriake also offers a sandy **beach**, a **campsite** and a **restaurant**. The *Çalpan* restaurant, on the far side of a wooden pedestrian bridge over the stream, overlooks the beach, while *Ocakbaşı Camping*, 1500m before the beach on the east side of road, has a few rooms, and is close to some cold mineral springs which gush out from just below the highway. Andriake is still a working fishing port, with a boatyard, and it's possible to get a **boat** from here to the Kekova area, a 45-minute journey, followed by the standard tour of the underwater ruins at Kekova Island, but you'll need a boatload (15–20 people) – although some owners will take individuals for a fee of around $10.

The beach and the ruins

The main reason to come to Andriake is for a swim. The **beach** here is fairly short, but broad and duney – though also trash-strewn and prone to algae slicks, which, together with the Kaş–Demre highway passing just overhead, perhaps accounts for the minimal development here. However the beauty of the skyline to the west cannot be underestimated, where parallel ridges as in a Japanese print march down to Kekova.

Ancient Andriake, built on either bank of the ancient Androkos River, was the site of **Hadrian's granary**, used to store locally grown grain and vital not only to Myra but to the whole Roman world, since its contents were sent to Rome to be distributed around the empire. The substantial remains of the building can still be seen south of today's river, which runs parallel to the road between Demre and the beach. The granary – built on the orders of Hadrian between 119 and 139 AD, and very similar to the one at Patara – consists of eight rooms constructed of well-fitting square-cut blocks. The outer walls are still standing to their original height, giving a clear idea of the impressive overall size of this structure. Above the main central gate are busts of Hadrian and what is thought to be his wife, the empress Sabina. Another decorative relief on the front wall, near the second door from the west, depicts two deities of disputed identity, one of whom is flanked by a snake and a griffin, while the other reclines on a couch.

Finike and around

A twisty half-hour drive beyond Demre, the harbour town of **FİNİKE**, formerly Phoenicus, no longer preserves evidence of its historical past, and offers precious little to suggest an illustrious future either. Highway 400 has been a double-edged sword as far as Finike is concerned. Its completion in the early 1960s provided the town with a much-needed easy transport route to local citrus groves, the mainstay of the local economy; but the busy thoroughfare has also ruined Finike aesthetically by cutting its centre off from the beach and disturbing the peace of this once attractive place. The town used to be deserted in summer as its residents headed for the hills, particularly to the *ova* or plateau around Elmalı, but now ominous concrete constructions are beginning to obscure the view of the bay, and vastly overshadow the few remaining Ottoman houses, now mostly found inland. Frankly, the only reason to stay in Finike is for its easy access inland to a pair of nearby ancient cities – Arykanda and Limyra.

Finike's main **beach**, extending east of town for some kilometres, has little to recommend it other than sandiness and length: it's not terribly scenic, clean nor protected from wind and waves. For calmer **swimming**, there are a pair of prettier pebble coves – Çağıllı and Gökliman – between Finike and Demre.

Finike practicalities

Finike's otogar is centrally situated, just off Highway 400 and 300m along the road to Limyra, Arykanda and Elmalı. Tourism seems to be stalled or even going backwards here, so there's relatively little choice in terms of accommodation; the old standby *Kale Pansiyon* has closed, as have a few campsites along the beach, with the survivors run by and for Turkish organizations such as the local Red Crescent. Among the few remaining **hotels** and **pansiyons** in town, your best option, up a long flight of steps on the hill 150m south of the *otogar*, might be the *Paris Hotel and Pansiyon* (☎0242/855 1488; ②), a pleasant place with some plumbed rooms, and a terrace with a good view of Finike bay. The friendly family who manage the place speak French and English, and operate a rooftop restaurant in summer, as well as an auxiliary *pansiyon* 4km out along the beach. Otherwise, try the medium-sized, basic *Şendil* (☎0242/855 1660; ①), admirably well signposted at a quiet spot 300m inland from the shoreline park, or – if you require still greater comfort – the en-suite *Bahar Otel* (☎0242/856 2020; ③), right in the town centre. **Eating** options in Finike are similarly limited: besides the *Paris*, the *Deniz*, near the PTT, is an old standby, though portions tend to be small even by Turkish standards; patronize by preference the newish, better-value *Birlik* (near the *Bahar Otel* across from the *Ziraat Bankası*), which claims to be open around the clock.

Into the mountains: Limyra, Arykanda and Elmalı

The road inland from Finike to Elmalı is a two-hour drive along a precipitous mountain route, made especially terrifying by the cavalier attitude of the numerous lorry drivers who hurtle up and down it with timber or loads of produce from the local orchards. On the way up, especially under your own power, it's worth stopping to visit two beautiful mountain sites, Limyra and Arykanda.

Limyra

The site of LİMYRA is the less impressive of the two, but it's more easily accessible if you have just a cycle or a motorbike. It's about 10km outside Finike, 3km from the Finike–Elmalı Highway 635: turn off at the village of Turunçova and head east down a signposted road. If you don't have transport, get a dolmuş to drop you off here and walk or hitch the remaining distance. There's a car park and village of sorts at the site itself.

Limyra had a promising start: founded in the fifth century BC, the city was made capital of Lycia by local ruler Pericles in the fourth century. From then on its fortunes were broadly the same as other Lycian cities, and it didn't make much of an appearance in the history books until 4 AD, when Gaius Caesar, grandson and adopted heir of Augustus, died here on his way home from Armenia. During Byzantine times it became the seat of a bishop, but suffered badly during the Arab raids of the seventh to ninth centuries and was largely abandoned. A peculiar feature of the site, noted in antiquity, is the vigorous spring-fed river, typical of this kind of rock strata, that emerges suddenly at the base of Tocak Dağı.

The main settlement, and consequently most of its public buildings, lay at the foot of the hill, but now few traces of ancient buildings are visible on the flatlands among the branches of the river, and the ruins mostly consist of several hundred **tombs**. The southern slope of the mountain is covered by tombs cut into the rock face; above is a fortified **acropolis**. On the left of the road from Turunçova, the western **necropolis** includes an impressive two-storey tomb in a citrus grove. North of the road looms a **theatre** dating from the second century AD, behind which is a freestanding fourth-century sarcophagus with an inscription in Lycian announcing it as the tomb of Xatabura, thought to have been a relation of Pericles (the founder of the Lycian Federation). Among its abundant relief carvings are a funeral feast on the south side, and on the west a scene depicting the judgement of Xatabura, pictured as a naked youth.

At the top of Tocak Dağı, north of the site, stands the most interesting **tomb** of all, indicated as the "Heroon" from the theatre. It's about a forty-minute climb to get there, up the path leading from the back of the village, but worth the effort – swarms of village children will offer their unnecessary services as guides. This mausoleum is probably that of Pericles, who saved Lycia from the ambitions of Mausolus in the fourth century. The tomb divides into two parts: a lower grave chamber, and the upper chamber styled like a temple, with a row of four caryatids at front and back. The figures of the frieze, which show the hero mounting his chariot, indicate the blend of Greek and Persian influences on later Lycian art.

Arykanda

ARYKANDA lies 32km from Finike, on the right-hand side of the road; if you're coming directly from Kaş, you should certainly make use of the short cut between Kasaba and Çatallar, 4km below the ruins, which is paved despite pessimistic depictions on obsolete touring maps. Travelling by dolmuş, you should ask to be dropped off at the village of Arif, from where it's a one-kilometre signposted walk to the ruins along a side road passable to any car. At the end of the line you'll find toilets, water taps, and a double parking area, but as yet no ticket booth; the ruins are scattered and unlabelled, so if Ramazan, the knowledgable, English-speaking warden, is about, it's worth accepting his offer of a guided tour of the site.

Finds here date back to the fifth century BC, but the typically Lycian "-anda" suffix suggests that the city may have been founded a millennium earlier. Although Arykanda was a member of the Lycian Federation from the second century BC, its inhabitants were chiefly renowned for their sloth and profligacy: when Antiochus III tried to invade Lycia in 197 BC, they are said to have taken his side in the hope of reaping financial benefits to help them repay their debts. Christianity gained popularity here in the third century, as proved by a copy of a petition to the emperor Maximinius, in which the Arykandans request that the "illegal and abominable practices of the godless" be denounced and suppressed. The city continued in a much reduced form until the eleventh century, mainly confined to the area just to either side of today's main path.

Arykanda's setting is breathtaking, comparable to Delphi in Greece as it occupies a steep, south-facing hillside overlooking the major valley between the Akdağ and Bey mountain ranges. A pronounced ravine, and a series of power pylons, divide the site roughly in half. The first thing you'll see, beside the lower parking area, is a complex structure variously dubbed Naltepesi or **"lower acropolis"**; entered by a right-angled stairway, its function is not yet completely understood, but you can make out a small bath-house and presumed shops. North of the same parking area sprawls a large **basilica** with extensive mosaic flooring under tin-roof shelters, and a semicircular row of benches (probably a synthronon) in the apse. But the most impressive sight as you arrive, looming to the east, is the ten-metre-high facade of the **baths**, with numerous windows on two levels, and an apse at one end.

Other constructions worth seeking out include a small **temple** or tomb above the baths complex that was presumably adapted for Christian worship – on the east wall is the Greek inscription "Jesus Christ is Victorious" and a crude cross; there are more Roman or Byzantine mosaics in the tombs or temples immediately east of the Christianized one. West of the ravine and power lines, and above the agora – whose engaging odeion has lately been defaced by horrible new marble cladding – an impressive **theatre** retains some twenty rows of seats divided by six aisles, plus a well-preserved stage building.

Elmalı

The 1100-metre-high plain around Elmalı is the biggest stretch of arable land in upland Lycia, an important centre for apples and sugar beet. **ELMALI** (literally, "with apples"), dominated by nearby snowcapped Elmalı Dağı (2296m), is a town of 12,000 remarkable for its domestic architecture: a large number of houses are beautiful Ottoman timber-framed *konak*s, some in excellent condition. The air is cool and fresh even in summer, with a faint smell of wood smoke; and Gömbe (see p.418) is even easier to reach from here than from Kaş. There is a reasonable municipal **hotel** in town, the *Belediye Otel* (☎0242/618 3137; ②), whose comfortable pillows and hot water make it good value.

Elmalı has a fine Classical Ottoman mosque, the early seventeenth-century **Ömerpaşa Camii** (open only at prayer time), whose exterior is decorated with beautiful faïence panels and inscriptions; the mosque *medrese* now serves as a library. Further up the main street is all that remains of a Selçuk mosque, a stubby piece of masonry that was once the base of a minaret; to the west, in the street behind the former *medrese*, you'll find the sixteenth-century **Bey Hamamı**. The town comes alive for its notable **wrestling competition**, held in a purpose-built stadium during the first weekend of September.

The Olympos coast

East of Finike, the coast road barrels dead straight past the beach before turning ninety degrees to enter Kumluca, an unattractive market town that has mushroomed into low-rises in tandem with the growth of hothouse farming hereabouts. Beyond Kumluca, recently refurbished Highway 400 curls up into the **Beydağları National Park**, here a spectacular sequence of densely pine-forested ridges and precipitous bare cliffs. Hidden at the mouths of canyons plunging toward the sea are two of Lycia's more unspoiled beach resorts: **Adrasan** and **Olympos/Çıralı**. If you're heading towards either under your own power, forgo the main highway in favour of the narrow but paved side road which veers off at the east edge of Kumluca, signposted "Beykonak, Mavıkent". This scenic short cut rollercoasters through forested valleys before emerging at Çavuş, the nearest proper village to Adrasan and Olympos.

Adrasan

Some 8km beyond Kumluca on Highway 400, the first side road to Olympos (see below) provides an alternative route to Çavuş village (15km) and the bay of Adrasan. Whether you arrive at Çavuş from this direction, or from Mavıkent, you'll turn east onto the unmarked seaward road, following hotel placards for 4km more to emerge at the beautiful, relatively peaceful beach resort of **ADRASAN**: attractively lit at night, and attractively deserted in the daytime. You can get here directly by afternoon bus from Antalya, arriving in time to stay at one of the two dozen **pansiyons** and **hotels** dotted along the length of the beach, and also along the stream meeting the sea at the north end, under the shadow of pointy Musa Dağ. Adrasan falls within the confines of the national park, which as much as anything else has acted as a healthy brake on development here.

Most of the fancier hotels (though the term is only relative here), aimed at British package tourists, have been built at the south end of the strand, near the jetty. One of the better of these, with a pool and its own patch of beach, is the oddly named *Ford* (☎0242/883 5121, fax 883 5097; ④), which intends to cater only for independent tourists from 1997 onwards. At mid-beach, right where the southerly branch of the split access road meets the coastal promenade, stands the rather older *Hotel Atıcı* (☎0242/883 5107; ③); they also have an annexe *pansiyon* north along the beach. Beyond and slightly inland along the northerly access drive from Çavuş, you'll find the adjacent *pansiyon*s *Gelidonya* (☎0242/883 5190, fax 883 5275; ③), spartan but clean and en suite, and the *Özcan* (☎0242/833 5220; ③), part of a trout restaurant.

Indeed one of the best spots to **eat** locally is the enchanting watercourse where the *Özcan* and two other trout restaurants, the *Paradise* and the *River Garden*, stand: clients are seated by or even in the streambed, where families of ducks come to beg your spare bread. Price, and to some extent quality, ascend as you go upstream, but none are grotesquely expensive or greasy. Back on the south end of the beach, the *Oktapus* (near the *Atıcı*) and *Cengiz Haan* (close to the *Ford*) make the best choices. A popular **boat-trip** destination is **Ceneviz Limanı**, a cliff-girt bay beyond Musa Dağ that's inaccessible on foot. **Horses** can be rented for $9 per hour at *Korkmazer'in Yeri* restaurant.

Olympos and Çıralı

From Highway 400, two marked side roads lead down to the ruins of the ancient Lycian city of **OLYMPOS**. The southerly approach (marked "Olympos 11, Adrasan"), once you leave the asphalt towards Adrasan after 8km, becomes a rough, three-kilometre dirt track ending at a car park and inland ticket booth ($1). Just before are five "free" **campsites**, which double up as **restaurants** and also offer basic A-frame **lodging** in the pleasant river valley here – a popular alternative with Anglophone backpackers to the accommodation at Çıralı. *Kadir* (☎0242/892 1250; half-board ②), with three separate, evenly spaced premises and a much-imitated treehouse format, is the most popular, while closest to the sea, *Bayram*'s nestles in an orange grove and offers half-board and treehouse at rates similar to *Kadir*'s. Two or three times daily, shuttle bus service up to the main road is provided. The main drawback of basing yourself here is that you're still some way from the beach, and need to keep the present day's admission ticket with you every time you cross the Olympos archeological zone for a swim.

Back up on the main road, the northerly turning off Highway 400, 800m north of the southerly one and signposted "Çıralı 7, Yanartaş, Chimaera", leads down to the hamlet of **ÇIRALI** on the coast, which also has food and accommodation, and easy access to the ruins by a short stroll south along the beach from there.

Above the coastal plain of Çıralı, on the toes of nearby Tahtalı Dağ, burns a perpetual flame, fed by natural gases issuing from the ground. This has been known since antiquity as the Chimaera, a name it shares with a mythical fire-breathing monster supposed to have inhabited these mountains.

Some history

Nothing is known about the origins of **Olympos**, but the city presumably took its name from Mount Olympos, thought to be present-day Tahtalı Dağ, 16km to the north – one of over twenty mountains with the name Olympos in the classical world. The city first appeared in history in the second century BC, when it was striking its own coins in the manner of the Lycians. Strabo the historian wrote in 100 BC that Olympos was one of six cities in the Lycian Federation that had three votes, attesting to its importance.

The principal deity of Olympos was Hephaistos (Vulcan to the Romans), god of fire and of blacksmiths. He was considered a native of this region, and the remains of a temple dedicated to him can be found near the Chimaera; fines for damage to local tombs were payable to the temple treasury. In the first century BC, the importance of Hephaistos diminished when Cilician pirates led by Zenicetes overran both Olympos and nearby Phaselis and introduced the worship of Mithras, a god of Indo-European origin, whose rites were performed on Mount Olympos. Zenicetes made Olympos his headquarters, but in 78 BC he was defeated by the Roman governor of Cilicia, and again in 67 BC by Pompey, after which Olympos was declared public property. The fortunes of the city revived after it was absorbed into the Roman Empire in 43 AD, and Christianity became prominent. Olympos was used as a trading base by the Venetians and Genoese in the eleventh and twelfth centuries – thus Ceneviz Limanı or "Genoese Harbour" just to the south – but it was abandoned in the fifteenth century, in the wake of Turkish domination of the Mediterranean.

The site of Olympos

About fifteen minutes' walk south along the beach from Çıralı, the site of **Olympos** ($1 admission when booths staffed) is quite idyllic, located on the banks of an oleander- and fig-shaded stream running between high cliffs. Turtles, ducks and frogs swim in the stream, and it's a good place to spot rare birds and butterflies, all this compensating adequately for the scantiness of the ruins. The main site remnants line the banks of this river, which rarely dries up completely in summer, owing to three freshwater springs welling up on the north bank, quite close to the ocean.

The first thing you'll notice are extensive **Byzantine-Genoese fortifications** overlooking the beach from each creek bank, just twenty to thirty metres up the crags. At the base of the fort on the north bank are two recently revealed "**harbour tombs**", recognizably Lycian in form, with a touching epigraph on one translated for viewers. Further along on the south bank stands part of a quay wall and an arcaded **warehouse**; to the east on the same side lie the walls of a Byzantine church; in the river itself is a well-preserved pillar from a vanished bridge. Back in the undergrowth, there is a **theatre**, most of whose seats have vanished.

On the north bank of the river are the most striking ruins. On the hill to the east of the path to the beach looms a well-preserved marble **door frame** built into a wall of ashlar masonry. At the foot of the carved doorway is a statue base dedicated by an inscription to Marcus Aurelius, with the dates 172–175. East of the portal is hidden a Byzantine **villa** with mosaic floors, a mausoleum-style **tomb**, and a Byzantine aqueduct that carried water to the heart of the city. The **aqueduct** overlaps, logically enough, the outflow of one of the aforementioned springs; follow it upstream, past the mausoleum-tomb, to the villa. Though paths have recently been hacked through the jungly vegetation beyond the portal, the aqueduct trough remains your best bet for clear navigation.

The Chimaera

North of Olympos, in the foothills of Tahtalı Dağ, the eternal flame of the **Chimaera** is about an hour's stroll from Çıralı village; it's also possible to drive to the bottom of the ascent and walk from there (about 20min). Tracks to the trailhead are well signposted, and the path up well marked and well trodden. The climb is most rewarding (and coolest) as dusk falls, since the fire is best seen in the dark; some people make rag-torches and ignite them from the flames, using them to light the path on the way down. Kadir organizes recommended nocturnal visits from his treehouse lodging on the southerly approach to Olympos, with transfer by tractor-drawn carriages.

The Chimaera, a series of flames issuing out of cracks in the bare hillside, is one of the most unusual sites in the whole of Lycia. It's not known what causes the phenomenon; a survey carried out by oil prospectors in 1967 detected traces of methane in the gas but otherwise its make-up is unique to this spot. The flames can be extinguished temporarily if they are covered over, when a gaseous smell is noticeable, but will spontaneously re-ignite.

What is known, however, is that the fire has been burning since antiquity, and inspired the local worship of Hephaistos (Vulcan), generally celebrated in places where fire sprang from the earth. The mountain was also the haunt of a fire-breathing monster with a lion's head and forelegs, a goat's rear, and a snake for a tail: the Chimaera. Its silhouette, incidentally, has become the logo of the state-run *Petrol Ofisi* chain of Turkish filling stations.

Legend relates how a certain **Bellerophon** was ordered by the King of Lycia, Iobates, to kill the Chimaera in atonement for the supposed rape of his daughter Stheneboea. With the help of the winged horse Pegasus, Bellerophon succeeded in this mission, killing the beast from the air by dropping lead into its mouth. Bellerophon was later deemed to have been falsely accused and avenged himself on Stheneboea by persuading her to fly away with him on Pegasus and flinging her into the sea. He later got his own just desserts when he attempted to ascend to heaven on Pegasus, was flung from the horse's back and, lamed and blinded, forced to wander the earth as a beggar until his death.

Çıralı practicalities

There is a single daily direct **minibus** from Antalya to Çıralı, running Monday to Saturday in the late afternoon, returning the next day at 6.30am, as well as three **buses** a week from Kumluca. Whatever else you may be told, all other services merely pass by the two turn-offs up on the main road; when promised through services do not materialize, budget an extra dollar or two for a connecting dolmuş which may or may not trundle up from the beach area, or allow extra time to hitch the 7km of paved but steep side road down to Çıralı.

Since 1990, tourist development has taken off noticeably at Çıralı, with a few **hotels** and more than a dozen **pansiyons** – most quite primitive – springing up in the orange groves behind the beach (see also p.430 for alternatives along the southerly approach to Olympos). The best budget spots include the sympathetic *Flora Pension* (☎0242/825 7201; ②), run by the Kalıpçı family, who offer characterful rooms with shared bathrooms in an older house, as well as vegetarian suppers and a paperback trading library; and, on the same orchard track, the leafy *Barış Pansiyon* (☎0242/825 7080; ②), just behind the beach, with spartan but en-suite rooms and ample parking. The next notch up, reached along the same track but to its west, is the quiet *Olympos Yavuz* (☎0242/825 7021; ④), a two-storey motel set appealingly in a poplar grove. Much further east along the beach – continue along the same track system, following a concrete aqueduct – is the cul de sac ending at the *Argos Pension* (☎0242/825 7125; ③), where the Turkish turtle freaks stay, and the somewhat more conventional *Atalay Pension* adjacent (☎0242/825 7127; ③). Comfort and facilities-wise, there's little between these possibilities and the German-run, mostly German-patronized *Olympos Lodge* (☎0242/825 7171, fax 825 7173; ⑦), a complex of luxury cabins set in well-landscaped grounds next to the beach, but overpriced even considering that rates include half-board.

At the other extreme, rough camping – which has contributed appreciably to the often considerable seasonal litter on the sand and out to sea – is now actively discouraged, especially since the opening of a proper **campsite**, the well-maintained *Green Point*, at the north end of the beach. Moreover, it is one of the several factors which endangers the survival of the **loggerhead turtles** which use this formerly deserted bay to lay their eggs, as at Dalyan and Patara. The Turkish Society for the

Protection of Nature maintains an information centre in the former premises of the *Om* pudding shop beside the *Olympos Lodge*, dispensing an informative leaflet on the turtles.

Long-running disputes between the forestry and archeological services on the one hand, and local proprietors on the other, have resulted in beachfront **restaurants** being periodically demolished with little warning unless payoffs are forthcoming. At present the most durable exception is the *Olympos Yavuz* teahouse, one of three rivals serving light snacks on the right bank of the river as it meets the sea, strategically straddling the sandy path to the ruins. On the left bank, accessible by the coastal road paralleling the aqueduct, is *İkiz Show*, the best of a surprisingly mediocre bunch of full-service restaurants, with the most varied menu and selection of wines.

Ulupınar restaurants
Better food can be found very close to the northerly turning to Çıralı from the main road, at several **restaurants** in the tiny, wooded hill-hamlet of **ULUPINAR**. Here choose between the jointly-run *Yücel* and *Çınar*, downhill by the gushing spring and serving *güveç*, quail and locally farmed trout, or the *Ulupınar Prima* up on the main highway, where more professional management and a wider menu offset the road noise. For a blowout try the *Park Restaurant*, installed in a former watermill, where similar ingredients receive gourmet treatment – and prices.

On to Antalya

Heading north from Olympos, there is very little reason to stop before Antalya. The mainly overdeveloped and overpriced resorts along this stretch of coast leave a lot to be desired, and only the ruins of the ancient city of **Phaselis** might tempt you off the main road.

Tekirova

Apart from the eight mammoth hotel complexes completely blocking access to the beach, **TEKİROVA**, some 14km north of the Çıralı detours, consists of a single dead-end shopping street with signs advertising gold and furs in German and Russian. The place, conjured from scratch in the early 1980s, is at best a convenient base for visits to Phaselis – although many of its patrons probably never make it that far. If you're not on a German package tour, there is very little accommodation available, apart from way inland by the south entrance to the resort area at the *Marti Pansiyon* (☎0242/821 4163; ③), which offers nice clean rooms around a swimming pool.

Transport in and out of Tekirova is fairly regular, with half-hourly connections to Antalya in season, calling at Kemer and the junction for Phaselis on the way.

Phaselis

The ruins of ancient **PHASELİS** (summer daily 8am–7pm; winter daily 8am–5.30pm; $2), 3km north of Tekirova, are magnificently situated around three small bays, providing ample opportunity to contemplate antique architectural forms from a recumbent position on one of the beaches. The natural beauty of the site, the encroaching greenery, the clear water of the bays, and the seclusion, all make for a rewarding half-day outing – though you may wish to take a supply of food and drink, if you don't fancy patronizing the small café in the visitors' centre.

Some history

Phaselis was not always in Lycia; situated at the border with Pamphylia, the city at certain points in its history was decidedly independent. According to legend, Phaselis was founded in 690 BC by colonists from Rhodes, and until 300 BC inscriptions were written in a Rhodian variety of the Dorian dialect.

The Phaselitans were great traders; they are supposed to have bought the land on which the city was founded with dried fish, and a "Phaselitan sacrifice" became proverbial for a cheap offering. There is evidence that the city's trading links stretched as far as Egypt, and their coins commonly depicted the prow of a ship on one side and the stern on the other. They also earned themselves a reputation as venal scoundrels, perhaps because at one point, needing funds, they sold Phaselitan citizenship for a hundred drachmas, attracting undesirable elements from all over Asia Minor.

Along with most of the rest of Asia Minor, Phaselis was overrun by the Persians in the sixth century, and was not freed until 469 BC. By that time, they had begun to feel loyalty to their imperial overlord, and it was with some difficulty that the Athenian general Kimon liberated them, making the city part of the Athenian maritime confederacy along with Olympos.

In the fourth century, Phaselis demonstrated its autonomy (or perhaps its perversity) by providing help to Mausolus, the satrap – or principal governor – of Caria, in his attempt to subdue the Lycian kingdom. Further evidence of Phaselitan sycophancy in their approach to authority was their behaviour toward Alexander the Great in 333 BC: not content with just surrendering their city to him, they also proffered a golden crown.

Phaselis became part of the Lycian Federation during the second century BC, but was soon, like Olympos, overrun by Cilician pirates. Although it was accepted back into the Federation afterwards, the long occupation of the city reduced it to a mere shell, with a sparse, penniless population. After the *pax Romana* came into effect, Phaselis distinguished itself with yet more obsequiousness: when Emperor Hadrian visited in 129 AD during a tour of the empire, statues were erected, a forum was constructed, and a gateway dedicated to him.

The site

The paved, one-kilometre side road that leads to the city from Highway 400 passes a **fortified settlement** enclosed by a wall of Hellenistic masonry, the northernmost section of which has a tower and three archery slits. The most obvious landmark on reaching the main site are the substantial and elegant remains of a Roman **aqueduct**. Supposed to have been one of the longest such conduits in the ancient world, it took water from a spring within the northern fortifications almost as far as the south harbour.

Arranged around a 400-metre-long promontory on which most of the city is situated, Phaselis's three **harbours** are immediately obvious, and an ideal means by which to orientate yourself. They served the city's extensive mercantile activities, particularly the export of local timber and botanical oils. The **north harbour** was too exposed to be used commercially except in very favourable conditions, but it has the remains of an ancient quay on its south side. It offered an easy landing-point for aggressors, however, so the crest of the cliffs above were well fortified. This three-metre-wide wall now lies below the sea, but is still intact. The middle or **city harbour** has a strong sea wall, since it is exposed to the north and east, and the eighteen-metre-wide entrance could be closed off. Today it's a sheltered cove with an excellent beach and shallow water for swimming. The largest harbour, the **south harbour**, was protected by a 180-metre-long breakwater, most of which is now submerged. It provided docking for larger trading ships of up to a hundred tons.

Between the harbours the promontory is covered in the ruins of ancient houses, very overgrown, and of round cisterns. Important in the layout of the city is the paved avenue leading from the monumental **gateway** at the southern harbour, constructed in honour of Hadrian's visit, to the rectangular agora between the main hill and the middle harbour. The gateway, built of grey-white marble blocks, was erected in 129 or 131 AD and bears a dedication to the emperor.

The **theatre**, which could hold around 1500 people, lies to the southeast of the main thoroughfare. During the second century AD it occupied a central point in the fan-shaped layout of the city. There are three large doors above present ground level, which probably led onto the stage. Just visible below these are a row of four smaller doors that would have opened into the orchestra beneath the stage, and were possibly used to admit wild animals.

Kemer

Some 16km north of Tekirova along Highway 400, **KEMER** is one of the least appealing of the resorts on the Turquoise Coast, and indeed has far more in common with the tone of the Mediterranean east of Antalya – including universal (high) pricing in deutschmarks for a largely Germanophone clientele, leavened by wealthy Russians who come to gamble and shop for leather and jewellery. Unlike Tekirova, there was a pre-touristic village here, but you wouldn't know that looking at this white-concrete, government-designed holiday village that's dominated by a swanky yacht harbour and a beach overcrowded with tour parties. Even the staff at the tourist office admit that there's not a lot to do apart from sunbathe and swim, and if you're travelling independently you'd be well advised to bypass the place entirely.

Practicalities

The **tourist information office** in the town hall, near the harbour (daily 8.30am–6pm; ☎0242/814 1112), can provide a hotel price list and maps. The closest **campsite**, *Overland Camping*, 1km north with its own sand and stone beach in the Çınaryanı Mevkii district, rents both tents and bungalows (③) with hot water and breakfast. Villa-style **pansiyons** along the principal, partly pedestrianized Liman Caddesi include *Esmer* at no. 104/14 (☎0242/814 2506; ④) and *Erol* at no. 109, Sok 21 (☎0242/814 1755; ④). But Kemer is not really about roughing it in overpriced pansiyons; if you choose to come here, you'll probably want to book in advance at such as the five-star *Türkiz* by the marina (☎0242/814 4100, fax 814 2833; ⑦), moderately sized by the area's standards and with all creature comforts to hand; or the even smaller, four-star *Otem* nearby (☎0242/814 3181, fax 814 3190; ⑦), where the service is willing, if not completely devoid of rough edges, owing to its role as the training venue for students at the local tourism vocational academy. Exciting **food** isn't the order of the day here, but you might try the *Mimosa* on Hastane Caddesi near the PTT, or the *Sultan Sofrası* across from the high school, both acceptable for Turkish fare. A visit to the *Yörük Parkı*, on a small rise dividing the yacht harbour from the south beach, is justified mostly by the *gözleme* cooked there. Otherwise, its attempted re-creation of a nomadic tent village, complete with black goat-hair *yörük* tents and a bar installed in their midst, is rather tawdry and fake – even the staff, including waitresses dressed as "shepherd girls", appear mildly embarrassed by its existence.

The **PTT** on Atatürk Bulvarı changes money (Mon–Sat 8.30am–12.30pm & 1.30–6.30pm), though there are also *Yapı Kredi* and *Garanti* autotellers. There are **dolmuşes** to Tekirova and Phaselis from Kemer, and buses to Antalya's *otogar* every half an hour. It's also possible to rent a **boat** to Phaselis from Kemer harbour, which costs around $20 a day per person, including lunch; *Rosemary Charter* is one of the more reliable operators. It's worth knowing that certain **car rental** chains have bona fide offices in Kemer, so if a car picked up elsewhere is playing up, you could try swopping it here:

Avis, Atatürk Bul 8/G (☎0242/814 3936); *DeCar*, Yalı Cad 3 (☎0242/814 5608); and *Europcar*, Liman Cad 29/E (☎0242/814 2083). Another pit-stop, especially if you're yachting, camping or trekking, might be the *Migros* supermarket just off Highway 400 on the approach road – certainly the largest selection of food on view since Fethiye.

Beldibi

BELDİBİ, situated some 12km north of Kemer and 35km short of Antalya, is really just a beach, and not a very good one at that, consisting of watermelon-sized boulders rather than small pebbles; behind it runs the old highway of these parts, 6km of continuous and rather tatty development, whose main virtue is that the small, low-rise hotels at least allow some free access to the shoreline. If you're driving a caravan, head for the popular and well-equipped *Kındılçeşme* forestry **campsite** south of this strip. Two adequate **hotels** – best pre-booked if possible – are the three-star *Sport* (☎0242/824 8549, fax 824 8308; ⑥), in a garden setting at the south end of the strip, or the *Belpınar* (☎0242/824 8048; ⑥), at the very north end of the resort.

travel details

Buses and dolmuşes

Dalaman to: Antalya (2 daily in summer; 6hr); Bodrum (5 daily; 6hr); Denizli (2 daily; 5hr); Fethiye (2 an hour; 1hr 30min); İstanbul (2 daily; 13hr); İzmir (14 daily; 6hr); Kaş (4 daily; 4hr); Marmaris (12 daily; 2hr); Muğla (18 daily; 2hr); Ortaca (2 an hour; 20min).

Demre to: Ankara (2 daily; 9hr); Elmalı (3 daily; 2hr); Fethiye (6 daily; 5hr); Finike (hourly; 30min); İstanbul (2 daily; 11hr); Üçağız (1 daily; 45min).

Elmalı to: Antalya (9 daily; 3hr); Demre (6 daily; 2hr); Finike (2 an hour; 2hr); Kaş (3 daily; 3hr).

Fethiye to: Ankara (2 daily; 12hr); Antalya (8 daily; 4hr); Aydın (6 daily; 5hr); Bodrum (6 daily; 5hr); Denizli (5 daily; 4–7hr – ask for express route); İstanbul (3 daily; 14hr); İzmir (2 an hour; 7hr); Kaş (15 daily; 2hr 30min); Marmaris (hourly; 3hr); Muğla (10 daily; 3hr); Pamukkale (8 daily; 4–5hr); Patara (15 daily; 1hr 30min).

Finike to: Ankara (1 daily; 13hr); Antalya (2 an hour; 2hr 15min); Demre (hourly; 30min); Elmalı (2 an hour; 1hr 30min); Fethiye (13 daily; 4hr); İstanbul (1 daily; 15hr); Kalkan (2 daily; 2hr 30min); Kaş (7 daily; 1hr 30min).

Kalkan to: Ankara (1 daily; 12hr); Antalya (7 daily; 5hr); Bodrum (1 daily; 7hr); Fethiye (every 30min; 2hr); İstanbul (1 daily; 15hr); İzmir (3 daily; 9hr); Marmaris (2 daily; 5hr); Pamukkale (1 daily; 6hr).

Kaş to: Antalya (6 daily; 5hr); Bodrum (3 daily; 7hr); Fethiye (15 daily; 2hr 30min); Gömbe (3 daily;

1hr 45min); İstanbul (2 daily; 12hr); Marmaris (4 daily; 4hr 30min); Pamukkale (2 daily; 10hr); Üçağız (1 daily; 45min).

Kemer to: Antalya (2 an hour; 1hr 30min); Phaselis (2 an hour; 30min); Tekirova (2 an hour; 30min).

Ortaca to: Ankara (3 daily; 10hr); Antalya (2 daily; 6hr); Bodrum (5 daily; 4hr); Dalaman (2 an hour; 20min); Dalyan (25 daily; 20min); İstanbul (3 daily; 14hr); İzmir (10 daily; 5hr 30min); Kaş (5 daily; 5hr); Pamukkale (14 daily; 5–6hr).

Patara to: Antalya (8 daily; 4hr); Fethiye (8 daily; 1hr 30min); Kalkan (10 daily; 30min); Kaş (10 daily; 1hr).

Many of the above minimum frequencies are greatly enhanced in season by the 24-seat minibus services of *Kaş-Patara Koop*, which ply the coast between Fethiye and Finike.

International hydrofoils

Fethiye to: Rhodes (2–3 weekly in season; 1hr 30min).

Domestic flights

The following services are provided by either *THY* or *İstanbul Airlines*.

Dalaman to: Ankara (2 weekly in season; 1hr 15min); Antalya (2 weekly in season; 50min); İstanbul (at least 3 daily in season, 4 weekly out of season; 1hr 20min).

CHAPTER SIX

THE MEDITERRANEAN COAST AND THE HATAY

T he **Mediterranean coast** of Turkey, where the Toros (Taurus) mountain range sweeps down to meet the sea, offers some of the country's finest unspoiled shoreline. Dominated by the mountains, the landscape is more austere than that of the Aegean and Turquoise coasts, but it has the advantage of being quieter, and with a little effort it's always possible to escape the crowds and find a stretch of underpopulated beach or an undiscovered coastal village.

This coastal region broadly divides into three parts. The stretch from Antalya to Alanya is the most accessible part, with the looming presence of the Toros range separated from the sea by a narrow coastal strip. East of Alanya, the mountains meet the sea head-on, making for some of Turkey's most rugged stretches of coastline, where hairpin bends and mountain roads can at times make travel an agonizingly slow process. At the eastern end of the Mediterranean the mountains recede, giving way to the flat, monotonous landscape of the Ceyhan river delta.

Antalya is a bustling modern city whose international airport and comprehensive bus services make it a prime arrival and junction point. East of here the mountains slope gently down to sandy beaches and a fertile coastal strip supporting an economy based on cotton-growing and tourism. This area largely covers the ancient region of **Pamphylia**, settled by refugees from Troy in 1184 BC. The ruins of four cities – **Perge**, **Sillyon**, **Aspendos** and **Side** – testify to the sophisticated civilization that flourished here during the Hellenistic period. Perge and Aspendos are well-established day-trip destinations from Antalya, and the modern town of Side has become a mecca for package tourists, the yearly summer influx inevitably detracting somewhat from the appeal of its ancient architecture.

Seventy kilometres further along the coast, the former pirate refuge of **Alanya** is set on and around a spectacular headland topped by a stunning Selçuk citadel. Alanya, too, has recently grown into a bustling tourist centre, shaking off the sleepy feel of some of

---

ACCOMMODATION PRICE CODES

In this guide, motels and nearly all hotels and *pansiyon*s have been categorized according to the price codes outlined below, which are based on US$ because of the high domestic Turkish inflation rate. These categories represent the minimum you can expect to pay for a **double room in high season**. Rates for hostels and for the most basic hotels and *pansiyon*s, where guests are charged **per person**, are given in US$, instead of being indicated by price code. For further information, including a rough outline of what you might expect in each category, see p.37.

① under $12	② $12–17	③ $18–25
④ $26–35	⑤ $36–45	⑥ $46–55
⑦ $56–75	⑧ over $75	

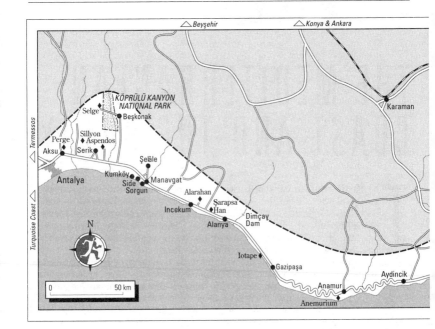

the smaller Mediterranean settlements. Beyond here the coast becomes wilder, the road reduced to a clifftop roller-coaster ride that descends occasionally into steep-sided valleys lush with banana plantations. Inaccessibility made this section of the coast a haven for pirates until the Romans mounted a clean-up operation during the first century BC, and in places it still has a desolate, untamed feel. The best locations to break your journey are **Anamur**, where a ruined Hellenistic city abuts some of this coast's best beaches, and **Kızkalesi**, whose huge Byzantine castle sits a hundred metres from the sandy shore of a bay. Kızkalesi also makes a good base from which to explore the ancient city of **Uzuncaburç**, a lonely ruin set high above the sea in the Toros mountains.

Beyond Kızkalesi is the fertile but dull alluvial delta known as the **Çukurova**, where the Ceyhan River spills down from the mountains and meanders sluggishly into the eastern Mediterranean, spawning a string of cities surrounded by medium-density concentrations of industry and manufacturing amid the low-lying cotton plantations. This end of the Mediterranean coast has less to recommend it. **Mersin** is a large, modern port only likely to be of interest to those en route to northern Cyprus, to which there are regular ferry connections; **Tarsus**, the birthplace of Saint Paul, has few surviving reminders of its long history; **Adana**, one of the country's largest urban centres, is a hectic transit point, and a staging post on journeys to the east.

East of Adana, you leave tourist Turkey behind. The travelling is harder and there are fewer resorts or places of established interest, with the consequence that visitors are much thinner on the ground. The area formed by the curve of the coast down towards Syria, the **Hatay**, has long been one where different civilizations and cultures have met and sometimes clashed. The towns here formed an eastern outpost of the Roman Empire and, after the fall of Rome, experienced successive waves of conquest and counter-conquest. Almost everybody seemed to pass through at one time or another: Arabs, Crusaders, Selçuks, Mongols and finally the victorious World War I allies.

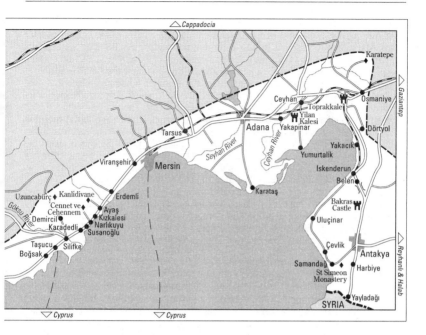

Today something of this frontier atmosphere persists, and you'll notice that in many towns ethnic Turks are in the minority. It's a sometimes volatile racial mix, exacerbated by fundamentalist pressures and the separatist sympathies of some of the population, not to mention the often heavy-handed tactics of the Turkish authorities. Travelling around is, however, no problem, at least in the western part of the region, with good bus links between all the major towns.

Antakya is the Hatay's main centre and the best starting point for exploring the region. Though little survives from the city's Seleucid and Roman past, it has enough attractions to make it worth at least a full day, notably an excellent archeological museum and an odd cave church from where Saint Peter is said to have preached. From Antakya there are frequent dolmuş connections to **Harbiye**, site of the Roman resort of Daphne, and the town of **Samandağ**, with its appealing though sadly polluted beach adjacent to what's left of the ancient Roman port of Seleucia ad Piera.

ANTALYA TO ALANYA

The western part of the Turkish Mediterranean coast – between Antalya and Alanya – is, not surprisingly, the most popular with tourists, with long stretches of sandy beach and a rapidly developing tourist infrastructure. The cotton-rich coastal margin covers what was the ancient region of **Pamphylia**, a loose federation of Hellenistic cities established by incomers from northern Anatolia. According to ancient Greek sources, Pamphylia was settled by a "mixed multitude" of peoples following the fall of Troy in 1184 BC. It played a relatively minor role in the history of Anatolia, never even attaining local military significance, and the Pamphylian cities were fought over for centuries by stronger neighbours like the Lydians and Persians. To an extent, the Pamphylians profited from this, playing off one would-be invader against the next while continuing to run their own affairs, regardless of who exercised ultimate control of the region. In later years, Mark Antony was sent to take control of the region, treating it as his personal domain until defeated by Octavius Caesar at the Battle of Actium in 31 BC, after which Pamphylia was formally absorbed into the Roman Empire under the *Pax Romana*.

You're most likely to start your explorations at **Antalya**, a booming place that over the last five years or so has turned into a fully-fledged resort – worth visiting for its restored old town and marvellous archeological museum. The four surviving ruined cities of Pamphylia rival the beaches as a tourist magnet, with **Perge** and **Aspendos** the best-preserved and most evocative sites. In between these two, the less intact remains of **Sillyon** are harder to reach. Further along the coast, **Side** is perhaps the Mediterranean coast's major resort, although sadly the striking ruins of its ancient city are fast being overshadowed by the rapidly growing tourist facilities. It remains, however, the ideal place if you're after beach action and holiday nightlife.

Alanya, the next major centre, has also seen an explosion of hotel building and tourism-related commerce over the last few years, but so far the town planners have managed to retain some sense of proportion as regards development. As for less well-trodden tourist paths, the **Köprülü Kanyon** national park and the ruins of ancient **Selge**, not far inland from Antalya and Side, make a delightfully untouched day excursion.

Antalya

Turkey's fastest growing city, **ANTALYA** is also the one metropolis besides İstanbul that's a major tourist mecca. Blessed with an ideal climate (except during the searing heat of July and August) and a stunning setting atop a limestone plateau – with the formidable Beydağları looming to the west and the Mediterranean rippling below – Antalya has seen the annual tourist influx grow to almost match its permanent population, which now stands at just under half a million. Over half of the vacationers are Germans, but, surprisingly, "new" Russians now make up the second largest group of foreign visitors. Despite the appearances of its grim concrete sprawl, Antalya is an agreeable enough city to live in, but the main area of interest for outsiders is confined to the relatively tiny and central old quarter. With the exception of the excellent **archeological museum**, most attractions – as well as the two bus terminals – are within walking distance of each other. Three or four days here – including half-day excursions to the nearby ruins of Termessos, Perge and Aspendos – should be sufficient.

Antalya was founded as late as the second century BC by Attalus II of Pergamon, and named **Attaleia** in his honour. The Romans did not consolidate their hold on the city and its hinterland until the imperial period, at the conclusion of successful campaigns against local pirates. Christianity and the Byzantines got a similarly slow start, though because of its strategic location and good anchorage Antalya was an important halt for the Crusaders. The Selçuks supplanted the Byzantines for good early in the thirteenth century, and to them are owed most of the medieval monuments visible today (albeit some built on Byzantine foundations). Ottoman Antalya figured little in world events until 1918, when the Italians made it the focus of their short-lived Turkish colony.

Arrival and information

Both **buses** and **dolmuşes** now use the **central otogar**, up at the top of Kazım Özalp Caddesi, a street still universally referred to by its old name of Sarampol, which runs for just under a kilometre down to the Saat Kulesi (Clocktower) and the intersection with Cumhuriyet Caddesi, on the fringe of Kaleiçi or the old town, a maze of short alleys just to the south of here. To the west along the waterfront, down Kenan Evren Bulvarı, later

Akdeniz Bulvarı which backs Konyaaltı beach, is the dock where **ferries** arrive from Venice – 5km from the centre of town but connected by dolmuş. Antalya's **airport** (☎0242/217 780) is around 10km northeast of the city centre, from where *THY* buses make the fifteen-minute trip into town; city centre-bound dolmuşes pass the start of the airport access road, 2km away. Failing that, take a taxi – about $7 during the day.

There are two central **tourist information offices**, one beside *THY* at Cumhuriyet Caddesi 91 (Mon–Fri 8am–5.30pm, Sat & Sun 9am–5pm; ☎0242/241 1747), the other in Kaleiçi next to the *Hotel Aspen* (Mon–Fri 8am–noon & 1.30–5.30pm; ☎0242/247 0541). Both hand out city maps but neither seems to have much in the way of accommodation listings.

Accommodation

In recent years a craze for restoring dilapidated houses in Kaleiçi as modest *pansiyon*s has gripped Antalya, and these days most travellers **stay** in this part of town. The old nucleus of hotels between the *otogar* and the bazaar now gets more of a Turkish commercial clientele; you'd only want to stay there if arriving very late or for a nap between buses. Ignore touts at the *otogar*, who work on commission.

Kaleiçi

In Kaleiçi, every street has *pansiyon*s, most offering competitive prices for en-suite rooms around characterful garden courtyards. The following is only a selection; there are dozens of similar options with equally attractive features. Note that the older restored houses often have a wide variety of different-sized rooms, with a corresponding range of prices; rates are normally negotiable even up to the end of June.

INEXPENSIVE AND MID-RANGE

Adler Pansiyon, Civelek Sok 16 (☎0242/242 6610). The least expensive of the old *pansiyon*s, without en-suite bathrooms and, unfortunately, slipping into neglect. ①.

Antique Pansiyon, Paşa Camii Sok 28 (☎0242/242 4656, fax 241 5890). Original wooden Anatolian building with a shady courtyard and more than agreeable rooms. Recommended. ③.

Bermuda Pansiyon, Hesapçı Sok 74 (☎0242/241 1965). Simple but clean modern rooms with baths; ideal for singles. ②.

Camel Pansiyon, Hesapçı Sok next to the *Hodja Pansiyon* (☎0242/242 6214). Only six rooms, but cheap and recommended. ②.

Dedekonak Pansiyon, Hıdırlık Sok 13 (☎0242/247 5170). Rooms are small but pleasant in this medium-sized establishment catering largely to Turkish tourists. ③.

Erken Pansiyon, Hıdırlık Sok 5 (☎0242/247 6092). Small but attractive rooms with fun platform beds for children. No single rooms. ②.

Ertan Pansiyon, Uzum Çarşı Sok 9 (☎0242/241 5535). A modern breeze block affair with acceptable rooms; fine views from rooftop doubles. ③.

Garden Pansiyon, Zafer Sok 16 (☎0242/247 1930). Clean and spartan rooms with en-suite bathrooms. A little overpriced. ③.

Hadrianus Pansiyon, Zeytin Sok 4\A (☎0242/241 2515). An ageing building with one of the choicest gardens around. ③.

Hodja Pansiyon, Hesapçı Sok 37 (☎0242/248 9486). Variable but clean and generally appealing tiled rooms with en-suite bathrooms, including good-value singles. ③.

Keskin Pansiyon, Hıdırlık Sok 35 (☎0242/241 2865). Variable but generally clean and passable rooms, with one of the best rooftop views in Kaleiçi. ③.

Sabah Pansiyon, Hesapçı Sok 60 (☎0242/247 5345, fax 247 5347). Friendly and well-run backpacker joint with informal information service, car rental and tours. Cheaper rooms come without bath, or you can sleep on the roof for a couple of dollars. Patron Ali Sabah speaks fluent English. The restaurant house special, *turlu* ,comes recommended. ①–③.

Senem Family Pansiyon, Zeytingeçidi Sok 9, near Hıdırlık Kulesi (☎0242/247 1753). Modern and clean rooms with flexible prices and a family touch, and morning views from a rooftop breakfast bar. ②.

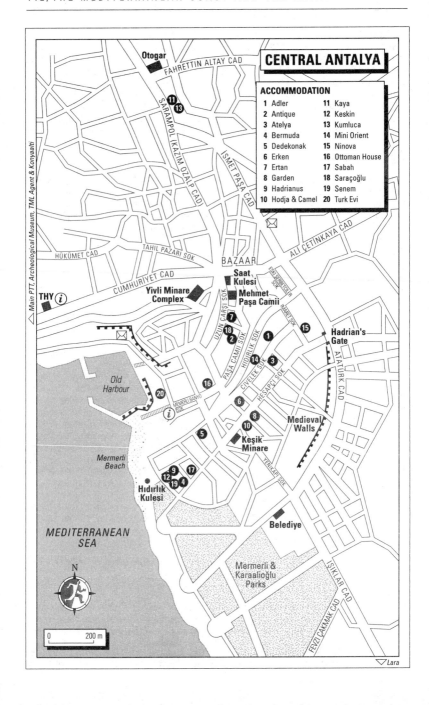

CENTRAL ANTALYA

ACCOMMODATION

1	Adler	11	Kaya
2	Antique	12	Keskin
3	Atelya	13	Kumluca
4	Bermuda	14	Mini Orient
5	Dedekonak	15	Ninova
6	Erken	16	Ottoman House
7	Ertan	17	Sabah
8	Garden	18	Saraçoğlu
9	Hadrianus	19	Senem
10	Hodja & Camel	20	Turk Evi

Otogar

FAHRETTİN ALTAY CAD

SARAMPOL (KAZIM ÖZALP) CAD

İSMET PAŞA CAD

Main PTT, Archeological Museum, TML Agent & Konyaaltı

HÜKÜMET CAD

TAHIL PAZARI SOK

ALİ ÇETİNKAYA CAD

BAZAAR

CUMHURİYET CAD

THY

Yivli Minare Complex

Saat Kulesi

Mehmet Paşa Camii

UZUN ÇARŞI SOK

PAŞA CAMII SOK

HIDIRLIK SOK

CİVELEK SOK

HESAPÇI SOK

İMARET SOK

Hadrian's Gate

ATATÜRK CAD

Old Harbour

MEMERLİ BANYO SOK

Medieval Walls

Keşik Minare

YENİKAPI SOK

Mermerli Beach

Hıdırlık Kulesi

Belediye

MEDITERRANEAN SEA

N

Mermerli & Karaalioğlu Parks

IŞIKLAR CAD

FEVZİ ÇAKMAK CAD

0   200 m

Lara

EXPENSIVE

Atelya Pansiyon, Civelek Sok 21 (☎0242/241 6416, fax 241 2848). Excellent restoration of two connected houses set around an attractive courtyard. ④.

Pansiyon Mini Orient, Civelek Sok 30 (☎0242/244 0015). Small and cosy restored house with only six rooms, slightly let down by mediocre bathrooms. ③.

Ninova Pension, Hamit Efendi Sok 9 (☎0242/248 6114, fax 352 0479). Very quiet, elegantly restored house with air-conditioned rooms and a pleasant garden. ④.

Ottoman House Hotel, Memerli Sok 8 (☎0242/247 5738, fax 247 6258). Dull rooms compensated for by the establishment's fine tilework, a plunge pool, and regular evenings of traditional music. ⑤.

Saraçoğlu Pansiyon, Karanlık Sok 12 (☎0242/241 5862, fax 242 5513). Clean, bright rooms and pleasing gardens, popular with Danish tour groups. ③.

Turk Evi Otel, Memerli Sok 2 (☎0242/248 6591, fax 241 9419). Top-of-the-range luxury hotel in a good location, with a pool and sauna facilities and a fine restaurant. ⑨.

Near the otogar

Kaya Oteli, 459 Sok 12 (☎0242/241 1391). Spartan but clean with en-suite bathrooms. ②.

Kumluca Oteli, 457 Sok 21 (☎0242/244 0001). Cheap rooms with washbasins and shared showers. ①.

Camping

Camping is not really advisable within the city limits. Only the *Camping Bambus*, 3km along the road to Lara (☎0242/321 5263), is operating: expensive and oriented toward caravanners, it does, however, boast its own beach and decent facilities.

The City

The intersection of Cumhuriyet Caddesi and Sarampol, better known as Kalekapısı (Castle Gate), is the most obvious place to begin a tour of Antalya, dominated by the **Yivli Minare** or "Fluted Minaret", erected during the thirteenth-century reign of the Selçuk sultan, Alâeddin Keykubad, and today something of a symbol of the city. The adjacent mosque – now the Fine Arts Gallery – is much later; the original foundation was built on top of a church. Part of the same complex, accessible by a stairway from Cumhuriyet Caddesi, are a **türbe** from 1377 and a dervish **tekke**, or gathering place.

It's hard to resist continuing downhill from the Yivli Minare to the **old harbour**, restored over a decade ending in 1988. Inevitably authenticity has been sacrificed – the only fishermen left among the yachts are the sort who have radar and solar-powered TVs on board – but on balance it was a successful venture, as reflected in the fact that half of Antalya appears to come out for their evening promenade on what was once a gravel foreshore. By contrast once-bustling Sarampol, and even the cafés up on Cumhuriyet Caddesi, are nocturnal deserts now that the centre of social gravity has shifted seaward.

Returning to Kalekapısı past souvenir and carpet shops and the eighteenth-century **Mehmet Paşa Camii**, and bearing onto Atatürk Caddesi, you'll pass the disappointing **bazaar** and soon draw even with the triple-arched **Hadrian's Gate**, recalling a visit by that emperor in 130 AD. Hesapçı Sokak, the quietest entry to Kaleiçi, begins here at a small park area; follow it through the old town, which, while interesting enough, is inevitably succumbing to tweeness as every house – virtually without exception – has been redone as a carpet shop, café or *pansiyon*. About halfway along Hesapçı Sokak stands the **Kesik Minare** (Broken Minaret), topping an even more ruinous structure with various pedigrees: ancient masonry is plainly visible in this converted fifth-century church.

Almost too suddenly you emerge onto the adjoining **Mermerli** and **Karaalıoğlu** parks, with a number of tea gardens, plus the **Hıdırlık Kulesi** at one corner. Of indisputable Roman vintage, the tower has been variously interpreted as a lighthouse, bastion and tomb. Below the tower, steps lead down past a waterfall to a series of tamped dirt terraces, and the sea. This area is the city's best venue for the often spectacular **sunsets** over the primordial, snow-capped mountains across the Gulf of Antalya.

The Archeological Museum

The one thing you shouldn't miss while in Antalya is the city's **Archeological Museum** (Tues–Sun 9am–6pm; $3.50), situated on the western edge of town at the far end of Kenan Evren Bulvarı. It's one of the top five archeological collections in the country, and is well worth an hour or two of your time. To get there from the city centre, take any dolmuş labelled "Konyaaltı/Liman", stopping at all "D" signs along Cumhuriyet Caddesi and its continuation Kenan Evren Bulvarı.

The well-lit galleries are arranged both chronologically and thematically. Standing out among the early items are a cache of Bronze Age **urn burials** from near Elmalı, and finds from an unusually southerly **Phrygian tumulus**, with the trademark Phrygian griffon head much in evidence. Several showcased silver or ivory Phrygian figurines, with droll yet dignified expressions, date from the eighth and seventh centuries BC and are among the museum's worthiest treasures.

It's quite a jump in time to the next gallery, which contains second-century AD statuary from Perge: a complete **pantheon** in unusually good condition has been assembled. Next, a catch-all room is filled with finds of different eras, materials and origins, including several versions of **Eros and Aphrodite**, followed by the so-called "Empire Room", crammed with more Perge statuary honouring the various demigods and priestesses of the Roman imperial cult; don't miss the graceful **dancer** somewhere in the middle. Best of the adjoining sarcophagus wing is an almost undamaged coffer depicting the **life of Hercules**. In the building's corner hall, **mosaics**, including one depicting Thetis dunking Achilles in the Styx, are in fair-to-good condition but crudely executed; a **gaming board** nearby, recovered from Perge, is more unusual.

A narrow room adjoining the mosaic hall is devoted to **icons** recovered from various churches in the Antalya area after 1922. They're mostly of recent date, and popular in style, but unusually interesting for their rarely depicted themes and personalities. At the centre of the collection is a reliquary containing what are purported to be the bones of **Saint Nicholas of Demre** (see p.424). The coin gallery, next up, displays several famous hoards found in the region – more interesting than it sounds.

The collection is rounded out by an **ethnography section**, a hotchpotch of İznik ceramics, kitsch glass lamps, smoking and writing implements, household implements, weapons, dress and embroidery, weights and locks, musical instruments and a fine Arabic map of the Middle East. A diorama of nomad life is appropriately followed by socks and carpets; there's also a display case telling where all those wooden spoons peddled on street corners come from.

Besides the collections, there's a **bookshop**, a **café** and a pleasant garden scattered with overspill works of art. Crossing the road from the museum reveals fine views of Konyaalti Bay and a path that leads down to the beach (see below).

The beaches and waterfalls

Despite earnest promotion in tourist bumph, Antalya's city beaches don't rate much consideration. **Konyaaltı**, 3km west of Kalekapısı, is divided into paying sections (clean) and free zones (filthy), but all are shadeless, pebbly and sullied by industrial pollution from the nearby harbour. **Lara**, 10km distant in the opposite direction and reached by dolmuşes running along Atatürk Caddesi, has fine sand but is enclosed in a forbidding fence and accessible only for a fee.

The lower **Düden waterfalls** reach the ocean at Lara, though to see them to full advantage you'll need to take a boat tour from the old harbour (see "Listings", p.446). The upper cascades, some 4km northeast of town, are frequently served by dolmuş from the central *otogar* or stops on Ali Çetinkaya Caddesi, but beware that the surrounding parkland is often mobbed – and the falls themselves are reduced to a trickle in late summer.

The **Kursunlu waterfalls** (daily 9am–8pm; $5), 18km from Antalya off the Alanya road, can also be reached by dolmuş from the central *otogar*. According to local stories, the falls were discovered by a shepherd less than twenty years ago, and their setting is certainly secluded. The set-up is still fairly uncommercialized despite the entrance fee, but the green pool into which the high falls cascade is forbidden to swimmers, so you wouldn't want to stay here long in the height of summer.

Eating, drinking and nightlife

Since the closure or gentrification of many old favourites, Antalya's range of **restaurants** is quite limited – and the pressure of tourism has inevitably driven prices up. For sipping a tea or something stronger, the situation is much better, with the various bistros and watering holes in Kaleiçi and around the yacht harbour pleasant and affordable for most wallets.

Cumhuriyet Caddesi is the location of a number of cafés and restaurants with terraces offering excellent views of the harbour – good for leisurely breakfasts. Southwest of the junction of Cumhuriyet Caddesi and Atatürk Caddesi, there's a covered pedestrian precinct, **Eski Şerbetçiler İçi Sokak**, crammed with tiny restaurants – and tourists having a feed. The local speciality is *tandır kebap*, clay-pot-roasted mutton, sold by weight and not particularly cheap. A 300-gramme portion – of which nearly half will be gristle and fat – runs to about $4. Check prices and portion sizes here before eating though – some stalls are less than scrupulous. For the best *lokum* in town, try the *Yenigün*, on the northern corner of Eski Şerbetçiler Sok.

Streets ahead in quality, but only marginally more expensive are the twin *Gaziantep 1 & 2* eateries, 200m apart at the edge of the bazaar; approach them through the *pasaj* at İsmet Paşa Caddesi 3, across from the branch PTT. Here *meze*s are presented to you on a tray and you choose your meat from spits lined up by the grill. Also close to the PTT and recommended are the *Nasreddin Hoca Sofrasi* and *Kafkas Etli Pide* on İsmet Paşa Caddesi, the latter positioned opposite the Cumhuriyet Hamam. A couple of hundred metres north of Cumhuriyet Meydanı lie a group of popular **late-night eateries**, with fine chicken soup a speciality; one to try is the *Gaziantep Ora*.

Out of the archeological museum at Kenan Evren Bulvarı 68/C, and the perfect spot for lunch after a visit, the *Develiler Kebapçisi* is considered the best carniverous chowdown in town; the bill for a meal shouldn't exceed $8. If you're determined to splash out – not difficult in Antalya – probably the most atmospheric place to do so is the *Hisar Restaurant*, installed, as the name suggests, in a rampart of the castle directly over the old port. The sea-view terraces fill up quickly; a fish-and-wine meal under one of the old stone arches should set you back about $12 apiece. The upmarket *Kale*, near the *Turk Evi Otel*, has similarly grand views of the old harbour. For a lighter meal, *Cafe Gül* just southeast of the Kesik Minare in Kaleiçi is a small snack bar featuring *mantı* and kebabs. *Tektat*, at Sarampol 84, has the best puddings in town, and a garden to shield you from the traffic.

For all intents and purposes **nightlife** is down at the yacht harbour, where the *Cafe İskele*, its tables grouped around a fountain, is pleasant and not absurdly priced, with more locals than tourists. Besides the full-on discos – of which the *Dedeman* on the way to Lara 3km from Antalya is the best – the highly priced *Club 29* is an upmarket restaurant, disco and bar with a terrace overlooking the harbour. *CC* at the harbour has live music and a good atmosphere.

Listings

Airlines *Air France*, Cumhuriyet Cad, 59 Sok 8; *İstanbul Airlines* in Özel İdare İşhanı, Cumhuriyet Cad (☎0242/243 3892); *THY*, Özel İdare İşhanı Altı, Cumhuriyet Cad, next to tourist information (☎0242/243 4384).

Airport departures The *Havaş* bus departs for the airport, 12km east of town, 75min before each *THY* flight – from the *Büyük Oteli*, 300m east of the *THY* office. Otherwise, eastbound dolmuşes pass the side road to the airport, but it's a hot, 2-km walk away and the gate guards will view you with extreme suspicion; far better to take a taxi (about $7 per car during the day, $10 at night).

Boat trips Boats by the harbour offer a variety of half- and full-day local tours, all of which take in the best views of the Düden waterfalls, plus a combination of local beaches (often Lara), swimming, cruises across the gulf and a barbecue lunch. Some also offer night-time entertainment in the shape of moonlit buffets and belly dancing. Prices vary according to the number of people, season and itinerary, but you can expect a half-day trip to cost from around $15 per person. Some yachts are open to charter.

Books The *Owl Bookshop* in the old town at Akar Çeşme Sok 21 off Hesapçı Sok is a second-hand, mainly English-language book exchange with an excellent selection. Limited English-language selection at *Ardıç Kitabevi*, Selekler Çarşı 67, and at *NET*, in the luxury *Dedeman Hotel*, 7km out on the road to Lara.

Car, bicycle and moped rental It seems every old building in Kaleiçi that's not a *pansiyon* or a rug shop is a car rental agency; most of the rest line Fevzi Çakmak Cad on the way to Lara beach. Among the more prominent one-offs or small chains are *Airtour*, Demircıkara Mah Çiçek Sitesi A Blok 3/4 (☎0242/322 1121); *Grand*, Fevzi Çakmak Cad 10/2 (☎0242/241 8822); *Kavas*, Paşacami Sok 32, Kaleiçi (☎0242/247 9457), which also rents bicycles, motorbikes and mopeds; *Metro*, Fevzi Çakmak Cad 27/E (☎0242/173 189); *Uno*, Lara Yolu Mezbaha Karşısı, Kurt Apt D1/2 (☎0242/182 550); and *Urent*, Kalekapısı İmaret Aralığı 5 (☎0242/242 4574). The biggies are *Avis*, Fevzi Çakmak Cad 2/B (☎0242/242 5642); *Budget*, Ağustos Cad, Atilgan Apt 7/2 (☎0242/242 6220); and *Europcar/InterRent*, Fevzi Çakmak Cad 14/A (☎0242/241 1260); all three have outlets at the airport.

Cinemas For Western releases try the *Oscar* in the heart of the old town, the *Kültür*, on Atatürk Cad, or the *Kent* just off Sarampol, south of the *otogar*.

Consulate *Britain* Pınltı Sitesi Katı, Dolaplıdere Cad, Kızılsaray Mah (☎0242/247 7000).

Exchange There are *döviz* offices throughout the city, and many jewellery shops now officially double as *döviz*, especially on Kazim Özalp Cad. Evenings and weekend exchange in the *Vakıfbank* booth at Kalekapısı (daily 9am–7pm); also at the central PTT (see below).

Ferry agent The *TML* office, for the fortnightly ferry to Venice, is at Kenan Evren Bul 40/19 (☎0242/241 1120).

Festivals The Altın Portakal ("Golden Orange") Film Festival takes place in the last week of September or the first week in October, usually back-to-back with the Akdeniz Song Festival; beware, hotel and *pansiyon* space is tight. Antalya is also crowded during the Aspendos Opera and Ballet Festival (see p.452).

Hamams In Kaleiçi, *Nazır* on Hamam Aralığı Sok behind the Mehmet Paşa mosque (daily men 6–10am; women 10am–5pm; mixed 5pm–midnight; $2.50 bath, $2.50 massage). The *Sefa Hamamı*, on Kocatepe Sok, opens daily for mixed bathing (6am–midnight; $5), while the *Cumhuriyet*, on 403 Sok (beginning at Sarampol 38), is open for men only continuously until 11.30pm.

Hospital Soğuksu Cad (☎0242/241 2010).

Laundry *Öz Ünallar*, Kiliçarslan Mah, Hesapçı Sok 43; $4 for a 5kg wash, more if dried and ironed. **Left luggage** At the *otogar*, open until midnight.

PTT The main office at Anafartalar Cad 9 is open daily 9am–9pm for exchange and letter service; phone division open 24hr. The more conveniently sited branch on İsmet Paşa Cad is smaller and keeps standard small-town hours, and there's another diminutive branch by the harbour catering to tourist needs.

Tourist police Emniyet Mündürlüğü, Yat Limani, Kaleiçi (☎0242/43 1061).

Travel agents Countless agents in Kaleiçi can book you on trips to the Pamphylian sites as well as rafting in Köprülü Kanyon. Try *Pamfilia Turizm*, Işıklar Cad, Göksoy Apt 57/8 (☎0242/241 1069), or *Express Turizm*, Konyaalti Cad 19/A (☎0242/241 1069).

Turkey Touring Association office (TTOK) Milli Egemenlik Cad, Dallar Yıldız Çarşısı 9 (☎0242/247 0699).

Termessos

After a couple of nights spent in Antalya you may well be in a hurry to move on, heading east or west along the coast in search of better – and quieter – beaches. But before you head off, consider staying in town for another night and having a look inland, where the ancient site of **TERMESSOS**, situated over a thousand metres above sea level, is one of Turkey's prime attractions. Indeed its dramatic setting and well-preserved ruins, tumbling from the summit of the mountain and enclosed within the boundaries of a national park – the **Güllük Dağ Milli Parkı** – merit a considerable journey.

Despite its close proximity to Lycia, Termessos was actually a Pisidian city, inhabited by the same warlike tribe of people who settled in the Anatolian Lakeland, around Isparta and Eğirdir, during the first millennium BC. The inhabitants of Termessos originally named themselves after the nearby mountain of Solymus – today's Güllük Dağ; their language, of which no surviving inscriptions remain, was a dialect of Pisidian, which Strabo called Solymian. The first mention of the Solymians comes in the ancient myth of Bellerophon and Pegasus, when Bellerophon, after defeating the monster of the Chimaera (see p.431), was sent to fight them. The first appearance of the Solymians in history proper was in 333 BC, when Alexander the Great made an attack on the city and was repelled. Fourteen years later, Termessos played an interesting part in the history of the region when Antigonus – one of Alexander's successors – was challenged by Alcatus for command of the region. The Pisidians supported Alcatus, and he took refuge in Termessos. The elders of the city, however, saw the possible dangers involved in defying Antigonus and laid a trap for Alcatus, preparing to take him captive. Alcatus committed suicide; his body was delivered to Antigonus, but after three days it was rescued and reburied in Termessos.

Unlike that of its Lycian neighbours, much of the history of Termessos is characterized more by attack than defence, and in the third and second centuries BC the Termessians first took on the Lycian Federation, then their neighbours in nearby Isinda. In the second century BC they formed an alliance with the Pisidian city of Adada – by which time, according to inscriptions, the city was being run on democratic lines. Later, in 70 BC, Termessos signed a treaty of friendship with Rome, under which they were exempted from the jurisdiction of the governor – an independence which they proudly expressed by never including the face or name of a Roman emperor on their coinage.

The site

Even if you don't have to walk the final 9km through the national park (see below), the approach to the **site** of Termessos (daily 7.30am–7.30pm; $1) can seem a stiff one. Walking shoes and a supply of water are advisable, as is a sensibly timed visit to avoid the midday sun. After checking the site map at the car park you'll need to climb a good twenty minutes before you reach the first remains of any interest, although on the way you'll pass a number of well-labelled ruins. These, however, are – like the aqueduct and cistern high on the cliff face to the left of the path – mainly inaccessible. The second-century AD **King's Road** was the main road up to the city, close to which the massive proportions of the lower and upper **city walls** testify to a substantial defence system. The central part of the city is beyond the second wall, to the left of the path. Its surviving buildings, formed of square-cut grey stone, are in an excellent state of repair, their walls standing high and retaining their original mouldings – something due in part to the inaccessibility of the site; it's difficult to imagine even the most desperate forager coming up here to pillage stone.

The first building you reach is the well-preserved **gymnasium**, with a baths complex alongside. This, however, is far overshadowed by the nearby **theatre**, one of the most magnificently situated in Turkey, with the mountain climbing behind and a steep gorge dropping to its right. Greek in style, it had seating space for 4200 spectators, and wild animals were released into the orchestra from a basement under the later, Roman-built, stage. Some of the seats are missing, but otherwise it's in a good state of preservation.

To the west of the theatre is the open grassy space of the **agora**, at the far end of which is a **mausoleum**, approached up a broad flight of steps, with a six-metre square platform – at the back of which a grave pit is sunk into the rock. Its unusual position on the marketplace suggests that the tomb belonged to an extremely eminent citizen, and it has even been suggested that this could be the tomb of Alcatus, the pretender to the governorship of Pisidia – though the example on the hill above (see below) is generally accepted as more likely. On the far side of the agora from the theatre stands a smaller theatre or **odeion**, which according to inscriptions was used for horse and foot races, races in armour, and – by far the most frequently held – wrestling. The walls of the building stand to almost ten metres, although the interior doesn't amount to much more than a heap of rubble. Surrounding the odeion are four **temples**, only one of which – that of Zeus Solymus, god of war and guardian of the city of Termessos – is in a decent state of repair, with walls standing to over five metres and a bench at the back for statues. Two of the other three temples on the southeast side of the odeion – the two with portals still standing – were dedicated to the goddess Artemis.

Following the trail up the hill from here brings you to a fork, the left-hand path of which continues on to the **necropolis**, where you'll see an incredible number of sarcophagi dating from the first to the third centuries AD. Most are simple structures on a base, though there are some more elaborate ones, with inscriptions describing penalties for their violation. Fines were normally made payable to Zeus Solymus, but a portion of the money – a half or a third – was often set aside for informers.

Returning downhill, take the left-hand fork for several hundred metres to the so-called **"tomb of Alcatus"** – widely accepted as the mausoleum of the general. The tomb itself is cave-like and undistinguished, but the carvings on its facade are remarkable, particularly one depicting a mounted soldier, with a suit of armour, a helmet, a shield and a sword – the armour of a foot soldier – depicted lower down to the right of the figure. The tomb and reliefs are consistent with the date of Alcatus's death, and the figure in the carving wears armour identical to that of Alexander the Great in a mosaic of the battle of Issus in the Naples archeological museum.

Practicalities

Antalya, 30km away, is the most obvious – and best – base for visiting Termessos, whether you're travelling by public transport or in your own vehicle. To **get there** by car, take the Burdur road out of Antalya, turning left after 11km towards Korkuteli. The turning to Termessos is marked off the Korkuteli road after about 14km, from where a track leads 9km up through the forested national park (entrance $0.25, $0.75 per car) to the site. Using public transport, you need to take a dolmuş headed for Korkuteli as far as the beginning of the forest track, from where – if you can't hitch a lift – it's a two-hour walk to the site. There is no accommodation near the site apart from a **campsite** close by the national park entrance.

The Pamphylian cities

The twelfth century BC saw a large wave of Greek migration from northern Anatolia to the Mediterranean coast, many of the incomers moving into the area immediately to the east of Antalya which came to be called **Pamphylia**, meaning "the land of the tribes", reflecting the mixed origins of the new arrivals. Pamphylia was a remote area, cut off from the main Anatolian trade routes by mountains on all sides; nevertheless four great cities grew up here – Perge, Sillyon, Aspendos and Side (see p.455).

The first recorded mention of the region dates from the sixth century BC, when Croesus, the last king of Lydia, absorbed Pamphylia into his realm. When Croesus was defeated by the Persians in 546 BC, the Persians assumed control of the area. This alarmed the Greeks, who attempted to gain control of Pamphylia, resulting in a series of wars, with the Pamphylians fighting on the side of the Persians. With the exception of Sillyon, Pamphylia eventually fell to Alexander the Great, after whose death the region became effectively independent, though nominally claimed by the various successor kingdoms that inherited Alexander's realm. During the first century BC the Romans, annoyed by the activities of the Cilician pirates operating from further along the Mediterranean, took control of the coast, ushering in three centuries of stability and prosperity, during which the Pamphylian cities flourished as never before.

Perge

About 15km east of Antalya, the ruins of **PERGE** can be reached by taking a dolmuş to the village of Aksu on the main eastbound road, from where it's a fifteen-minute walk to the site itself (you may be able to hitch a dolmuş ride if you don't want to walk). At the top of the hill is the site entrance (daily 9am–noon & 1.30–5pm; $3), the city opening up beyond its stadium – the largest in Asia Minor. It's an enticing spot, the ruins expansive and impressive, and you could easily spend a long afternoon looking around. Substantially more of the city survived until 1922, when, according to some accounts, the theatre was more or less intact. However, a 1920s construction boom in the nearby village of Murtunas led to the readily available supplies of stone at Perge being pillaged by local builders.

Some history

Perge was founded around 1000 BC and ranked as one of the great Pamphylian trading cities, despite the fact that it's nearly 20km inland – a deliberate defensive siting so as to avoid the unwanted attentions of the pirate bands and raiders who terrorized this stretch of the Mediterranean. Later, when Alexander the Great arrived in 333 BC, the citizens of Perge sent out guides to lead his army into the city. Alexander was followed by the Seleucids, under whom Perge's most celebrated ancient inhabitant, the mathematician Apollonius, lived and worked. A pupil of Archimedes, Apollonius wrote a series of eight books describing a family of curves known as conic sections, comprising the circle, ellipse, parabola and hyperbola – theories that were developed by Ptolemy and later by the German astronomer Kepler. Most of the city's surviving buildings date from the period of Roman rule which began in 188 BC. After the collapse of the Roman Empire, Perge remained inhabited until Selçuk times, before being gradually abandoned.

The theatre and stadium

Just beyond the site entrance, the **theatre** was originally constructed by the Greeks but substantially altered by the Romans in the second century AD. Built into the side of a hill, it could accommodate 14,000 people on 42 seating levels rising up from the arena, and was the venue not only for theatrical entertainment but also for gladiatorial displays. Look out for the fragmentary marble reliefs running around the stage area, mainly featuring Eros and Dionysus. From the top of the auditorium you can appreciate the size and scope of the rest of the city.

To the northeast of the theatre is Perge's massive horseshoe-shaped **stadium**, 234m by 34m, with a seating capacity of 12,000. Because the stadium was built on level ground it was necessary to provide massive supporting pillars and arches. The spaces between these arches were divided into about thirty huge rooms (housing shops and businesses), many of which are still intact, giving a good impression of the scale of the whole stadium complex.

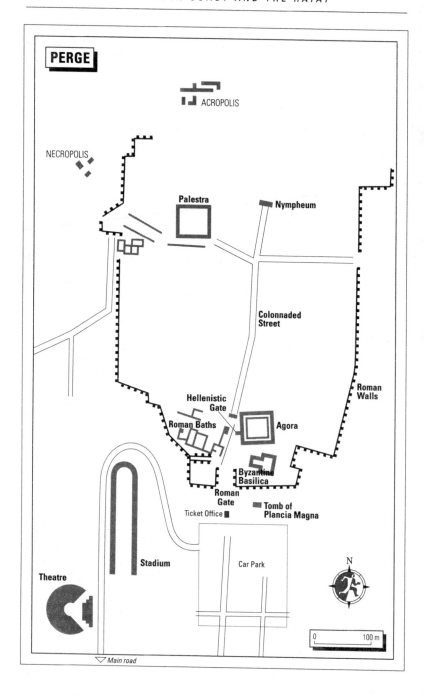

PERGE

ACROPOLIS

NECROPOLIS

Palestra

Nympheum

Colonnaded Street

Roman Walls

Hellenistic Gate

Roman Baths

Agora

Byzantine Basilica

Roman Gate

Ticket Office

Tomb of Plancia Magna

Stadium

Car Park

Theatre

N

0   100 m

▽ Main road

The walled city

To the east of the stadium is the entrance to the city proper, marked by a cluster of souvenir and soft drinks stands. In places, stretches of the Seleucid walls have survived, giving some indication of the extent and ground plan of the original city. Just in front of the outer gates is the **tomb of Plancia Magna**, a benefactress of the city, whose name appears later on a number of inscriptions. Passing through the first Roman **city gate**, you'll see a ruined **Byzantine basilica** on the right, beyond which lies the fourth-century AD **agora**, centred around a ruined temple. To the southwest of the agora are the excavated **Roman baths**, where a couple of the pools have been exposed; walking across the cracked surface of the inlaid marble floor, the original layout of frigidarium, tepidarium and caldarium can – with the help of a few signs – still be discerned. Also visible in places are the brick piles that once supported the floor of the baths, enabling warm air to circulate underneath.

At the northwest corner of the agora is Perge's **Hellenistic Gate**, with its two mighty circular towers, the only building to have survived from the Hellenistic period. Behind, the horseshoe-shaped court and ornamental archway were both erected at the behest of Plancia Magna, the former once adorned with statues – the bases of a number of which were found during excavations carried out during the mid-1950s. Beyond is the start of a 300-metre-long **colonnaded street**, with a water channel running down the middle and the shells of shops to either side. Walking along it, you'll be able to pick out the ruts made by carts and chariots in the stone slabs of the roadway. Also visible are a number of reliefs near the tops of the columns, just beneath the capitals, one of which depicts Apollo, while another shows a man in a toga, offering a libation at an altar. At the end of the street is the **nympheum**, an ornamental water outlet from where a stream splashes down into the water channel below. Above here is the **acropolis hill** – probably the site of the original defensive settlement, of which little has survived. To the west of a crossroads just before the nympheum is a **palestra**, dating from 50 AD, according to an inscription found on its south wall. West of here archeologists have found a **necropolis**, leading from one of the city gates, sarcophagi from which can now be seen in the Antalya museum.

Sillyon

About 7km east of Perge are the ruins of the ancient city of **SİLLYON**, also dating from about 1000 BC, although much less intact than Perge – and, without your own transport, somewhat difficult to reach.

Situated on top of a table-like hill, its strategic position enabled it to repulse an attack by Alexander the Great, who never succeeded in capturing it. These days it doesn't seem to attract as many visitors as some of the other Pamphylian sites, perhaps because of the 1969 landslide which swept about half of it away. To get there from Perge, head back to Aksu and follow the coastal road, taking a signposted left turn about 7km east of the village. From here a road leads 8km inland to the small modern settlement of Asar Köyü, from where an unsignposted dirt track leads to the site itself. It's possible that some of the villagers may offer to guide you around, which can be quite useful as they'll alert you to the presence of hazardous unfenced cisterns.

The site

You can climb up to the acropolis of Sillyon by way of a ramp leading from the **lower gate** up the western side of the hill. To the left of the gate are the foundations of a **gymnasium** used as a bishop's palace in Byzantine times, and now home only to sheep. At the top of the ramp you'll find a large and well-preserved **city gate** and, scattered around the rest of the hilltop, a number of buildings of indeterminate age and function.

The largest is a late **Hellenistic structure** with several arched windows in its upper storeys that later served the Selçuks as a fortress. Just to the south is a long hall-like building, possibly a former **gymnasium**, in which you can see the slots and holes used to hold wooden shutters in place in the window frames. East of here lies a building with a **37-line inscription** carved into its stone doorjamb – the only surviving written example (apart from a few coins) of Pamphylian, the Greek dialect spoken in this area until the first century AD.

The most interesting part of the acropolis is the area around the **ruined theatre**, which offers graphic visual evidence of nature's gradual erosion of the man-made past. Only the top eight rows of seats remain, the rest of the structure now lying scattered across the plain below – the huge blocks you can see were once part of the seating terraces. Further east are the foundations of a number of houses and part of a temple, which, judging by their precarious state, seem destined to follow the theatre terraces over the edge of the hill.

Aspendos

Returning to the main road, head east for **ASPENDOS**, whose theatre is probably the best preserved in Asia Minor. In summer, there are regular dolmuşes to Aspendos from Antalya and Side, but if you can't get there directly, ask to be dropped off at the signposted turning just before the humpbacked Selçuk bridge a few kilometres east of the village of Serik. From here you should be able to get a ride to the site, although it's only a three-kilometre walk. Just before Aspendos, the village of **Belkis** has a couple of **eating places**, including the pleasant riverside *Belkis Restoran*. About half a kilometre northeast of the village lies the car park and Aspendos site entrance (daily 8am–7pm; $3.50). The annual **Aspendos Opera and Ballet Festival** is held in the ampitheatre in June, featuring popular classics in a grand setting. Tickets (a reasonable $6), programmes and free shuttle buses are available in both Anatalya and Side.

Some history

Aspendos first came to prominence in 469 BC when the Persian Wars culminated in a huge and bloody naval battle at the mouth of the nearby Eurymedon river. The Greeks won and went on to defeat the Persians again in a land battle, when, heavily outnumbered, they outwitted their opponents by coming ashore disguised as Persians, using the element of surprise to stage a successful attack.

This wasn't the end of Persian influence in Pamphylia, since the locals, particularly the people of Aspendos, weren't any keener on the Greeks, eventually, in 389 BC, murdering an Athenian general sent to collect tribute, after which control of the area passed to Sparta. The Spartans proved to be ineffective rulers, and by 386 the Persians were back, staying until the arrival of Alexander the Great in 333 BC. On hearing of Alexander's approach, the rulers of Aspendos agreed to surrender but asked Alexander not to garrison soldiers in the city. Alexander accepted their terms on condition that they paid him a tribute of money and horses, and went off to lay seige to Sillyon. After his departure he was angered to learn that the citizens of Aspendos were busy fortifying the city, and he returned demanding a larger tribute and hostages. His demands were met, and Aspendos had to accept a Macedonian governor into the bargain.

After Alexander's death in 323 BC, Aspendos became part of the Seleucid kingdom and was later absorbed into the realm of the kings of Pergamon. In 133 BC, the city became part of the Roman province of Asia. Roman rule consisted mainly of a succession of consuls and governors demanding protection money and carting off the city's treasures; only with the establishment of the Roman Empire did the city prosper, growing into an important trade centre, its wealth based on salt from a nearby lake.

Aspendos remained important throughout the Byzantine era, although it suffered badly from the Arab raids of the seventh century. During the thirteenth century the Selçuks arrived, followed by the Ottomans a couple of hundred years later, who ruled here until the eighteenth century, when the settlement was abandoned.

The theatre

The Aspendos **theatre**, which is still used for the staging of various events, was built in the second century AD by the architect Zeno. He used a Roman rather than Greek design, with an elaborate stage behind which the scenery could be lowered, instead of allowing the natural landscape behind the stage to act as a backdrop, as had been the custom in Hellenistic times.

The stage, auditorium and arcade above are all intact, as is the several-storey-high stage building, and what you see today is pretty much what the spectators saw during the theatre's heyday – a state of preservation due in part to Atatürk, who after a visit declared that it should be preserved and used for performances rather than as a museum. A dubious legend relates that the theatre was built after the king of Aspendos announced that he would give the hand of his beautiful daughter to a man who built some great work for the benefit of the city. Two men rose to the challenge, one building the theatre, and the other an aqueduct, both finishing work simultaneously, with the result that the king offered to cut his daughter in two, giving a half to each man. The builder of the theatre declared that he would rather renounce his claim than see the princess dismembered, and he was of course immediately rewarded with the hand of the girl for his unselfishness. Later, the theatre was used as a Selçuk *kervansaray*, and restoration work from that period – plasterwork decorated with red zigzags – is visible over the stage. There's also a small museum to the left of the entrance, exhibiting pictures of theatre "entrance tickets" and coins.

The acropolis

After visiting the theatre many visitors leave Aspendos, not realizing that there is more to see on the hill above. From close by the theatre a path leads up to the **acropolis** – like that of Sillyon, built on a flat-topped hill. The site is a little overgrown, but a number of substantial buildings are still in place, foremost among them the **nympheum** and **basilica**, both 16m in height. To the north of the acropolis, on the plain below, stretches a Roman **aqueduct** originally 15km long, which brought water to Aspendos from the mountains above. This can also be reached by taking a left turn down a dirt track just outside Belkis, skirting around the western side of the hill.

Köprülü Kanyon national park and Selge

Inland of Aspendos, the **national park of the Köprülü River** and its Roman bridges, and the sparse ruins of Selge high in the mountains above, make a good half-day outing, provided that you have a sturdy car and something else in mind to do on the way there or back. There is little **public transport** to Selge or to the national park – one elusive afternoon dolmuş passes by each day between Serik on the coastal highway and the village of Zerk at the very top of the Köprülü valley.

The turn-off for both the national park ("Milli Parkı") and Selge is signposted 48km east of Antalya on Highway 400; the asphalt on the side road ends at Beşkonak, a straggly village 37km in. Five kilometres or so further on, you reach the *Kanyon Restaurant*, with treehouse-type seating in some giant plane trees overhanging the swift-flowing river. It's a spot as popular with Turks as coached-in foreigners, but the **trout** awaiting you in the tank under one of the several gazebos is expensive at \$4 a shot, and farm-raised. Ironically the Köprülü itself teems with brown trout, but it's illegal to catch them. Several **rafting** companies operate tame but enjoyable half-day trips down the river from here, stopping en route for a swim and lunch; contact a travel agent in Antalya for bookings (see p.446).

Just above the treehouse restaurant the road narrows; take the left fork, and inch across the first of two Roman spans, the **Oluk bridge**. From here it's 13km up to Selge, reached by taking the right fork just after the bridge, although you may want to bear left for the kilometre to the **bridge of Böğrüm**, which has a huge, popular picnic and swimming area just downstream from it. In all honesty the bridges are nothing special in themselves, little different from hundreds of others in Turkey, whether Roman, Byzantine or Selçuk, and it's only the setting that makes Köprülü any different.

The final stretch up to **SELGE** has recently been widened and improved, so it's now passable to most cars. As you climb to an eventual altitude of 900m, the panoramas become more sweeping, the thickly wooded countryside more savage, and the 2500-metre Kuyucuk range ahead more discernible and forbidding. At the scattered hamlet of **Zerk** (also known as Altınkaya), some 400m before the ruins, signs beckon you to park near the *Cafe Dallas*, which can provide cold drinks, food, a guide, information on walks in the mountains, and even a place to crash for the night – ask for Ismael or Davut. You may eventually be collared by the site attendant and asked to buy a ticket ($1).

The main track, now suitable only if you're travelling by jeep, continues toward the theatre which dominates Selge, but your guide will probably take you on a faint path left and south to the ancient agora and two hilltop temples. The **agora**, part of its paving still extant, will excite amateur archeologists with its submerged masonry and chunks of unexcavated inscriptions; the foundations of a **Byzantine church** sit up on a hill to the southeast and enjoy panoramic views down valley and up to snow-streaked peaks, while the jumbled remains of a **temple of Zeus** and a large water cistern lie to the northwest along the ridge. From here you can catch views to the ruined temple of Artemis and old city wall to the northwest and to the stoa in the valley below. Returning to the main track via some village farmyards, you'll pass the **stadium**, of which only the western ranks of seats are left; the sporting area itself is a wheat field. The **theatre**, partly cut into living rock, is impressive, but would be more so if the stage building hadn't been pulverized by lightning some decades ago, and if the highest tier of seats hadn't sustained rain damage in 1989. Three of the five doors giving access backstage still remain.

Little is known for certain of the origins of Selge; it only left the realm of mythological ancestry and anecdote to enter history – and the Roman Empire – in the first century AD. The city was famous for its storax gum, made from a local shrub, and was still inhabited until early Byzantine times. The site has always been arid – only recently did modern Zerk get a permanent spring – and the ancient town must have been abandoned when the aqueduct supplying it with water collapsed. The overwhelming impression you'll have is of the determination necessary to keep a city of 20,000 thriving in such a godforsaken wilderness.

Side and around

About 25km east of Aspendos, **SİDE**, a ruined Hellenistic port and one-time trysting place of Antony and Cleopatra, was perhaps the foremost of the Pamphylian cities. The ruins of the ancient port survive, but over the last few years Side has changed almost unrecognizably; today the resort has one of the highest tourist densities of any town in Turkey and many would say that it has been ruined by indiscriminate tourist development, its 24,000 hotel beds complemented by an endless array of cafés, restaurants, leather shops, jewellery shops and one-hour film processing laboratories. If it's sun, sand and surf you're after, you may want to spend some time here – the beaches are superb. If you're more interested in the ruins, try and visit out of season when you'll at least be able to move in the streets. Failing that, arrive early in the day and do your exploring before the crowds come out in force.

Side (meaning "pomegranate" in an ancient Anatolian dialect) was founded in the seventh century BC, its colonists attracted by the defensive potential of the rocky cape. It grew into a rich port with an estimated 60,000 inhabitants during its peak in the second century AD. Initially a significant proportion of Side's wealth rested on the slave trade, with the city authorities allowing pirates to run an illegal slave market inside the city walls, in which thousands of human beings were bought and sold every day. This trade was later outlawed, and after the collapse of the western Roman Empire, Side survived only until the Arab invasion during the seventh century AD. They put the place to the torch, driving out the last inhabitants, and Side was abandoned until the beginning of this century, when it was resettled by Greek Muslim fishermen from Crete, who built a village among the ruins. Despite later attempts by the Turkish government and various archeological agencies to evict them, these villagers stayed, and by the 1980s their descendants were starting to reap the rewards of Side's tourist boom.

Arrival and information

There are plenty of **buses and dolmuşes** running to Side from Antalya, but if you can't get one take any bus heading east and ask to be dropped off at the turning for Side, next to a petrol station and clearly signposted, from where it's easy to pick up a dolmuş into Side itself. The road into town is lined with hotels and signs advertising hotels, an ominous taste of what lies ahead. The **otogar** lies a five-minute walk north of the town's main ruins. If you can't face the walk, tractors drag wagons full of tourists to the entrance to the town at the top of the main street. If you're in a **car**, you can't enter the town from 2pm to 1am. The car park is opposite the ancient theatre and they charge a minimal daily fee – don't make the mistake of parking anywhere along the approach road as towing is vigorously carried out.

Side's **tourist information office** (Mon–Fri 8am–6pm; ☎0242/753 1265) is on the main road into town just before the first city gate, though like most Turkish tourist offices it won't overburden you with information. Banks and a PTT can be found on the square at the southern tip of the promontory.

Car rental outlets are nearly as ubiquitous here as in Alanya and Antalya, with the road approaching the main entrance lined with small local outlets, such as *Side Rent a car* near the car park (☎0242/753 1097). Also next to the car park are major companies like *Europcar* (☎0242/753 1764) and *Avis* (☎0242/753 1348).

Accommodation

Accommodation possibilities are endless, with hundreds of hotels and *pansiyon*s on just about every corner, many of them built against stretches of ancient masonry. Many, however, are block-booked by English or Scandinavian tour groups, which narrows the choice during high season; and finding a single room can be a real problem – you'll normally be asked to pay the same price as a double.

One of the most attractive options is the *Hanimeli Pansiyon*, on the **western side** of town at Turgut Reis Sok (☎0242/753 1789; ③), an immaculate place with details such as a double marble staircase and shuttered windows overlooking the breakfast garden. Opposite is the overpriced, but well-run and clean *Şen Pansiyon* (☎0242/753 1025; ③), which has a balcony from which to view Side's famous sunsets. For those with deeper pockets, the *Kleopatra Hotel* on the same street gives easy access to the town's western beach (☎0242/753 1033, fax 753 3738; ⑤). A downmarket option is the *Sergün Motel* (☎0242/753 2634; ③), on Limon Cad, where rooms are clean but can be noisy.

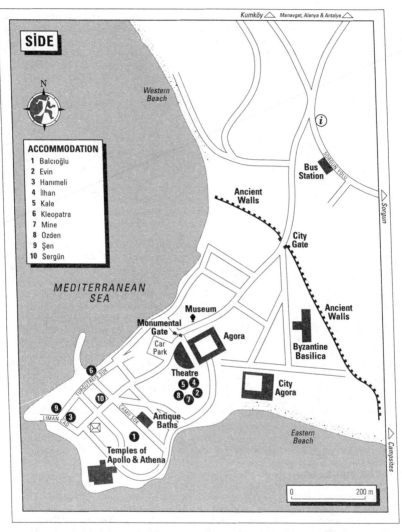

SİDE

N

Kumköy △ Manavgat, Alanya & Antalya △

Western
Beach

i

ACCOMMODATION

1 Balcıoğlu
2 Evin
3 Hanımeli
4 İlhan
5 Kale
6 Kleopatra
7 Mine
8 Ozden
9 Şen
10 Sergün

Bus
Station

SORGUN YOLU

△ Sorgun

Ancient
Walls

City
Gate

*MEDITERRANEAN
SEA*

Museum

Monumental
Gate

Car
Park

Agora

Ancient
Walls

Byzantine
Basilica

TURGUTREİS SOK

Theatre

⑤ ④
⑧ ⑦ ②

City
Agora

⑥
⑩
⑨ ③
LİMAN CAD
CAMİİ SOK

Antique
Baths

①

Eastern
Beach

△ Campsites

Temples of
Apollo & Athena

0   200 m

The **eastern side** of Side has the wider choice of places to stay. Best value is probably the *Evin Pansiyon* (☎0242/753 1074; ②), not far from the city agora with clean,
bright rooms giving easy access to the eastern beaches. Next door is the new and
slightly more upmarket *İlhan Hotel* (☎0242/753 1099, fax 753 1869; ③), half of which is
used by tour groups. Just around the corner, the basic *Kale* (☎0242/753 284; ③) represents better value for singles than doubles, though a nice courtyard compensates for
cramped rooms; contact the reception of the nearby *Erol Motel* for details. *Özden
Pansiyon*, Gül Hammam Sok 17 (☎0242/753 1337; ③), and the nearby *Mine Pansiyon*
(☎0242/753 2358; ②), offer the lion's share of their rooms to packaged groups, but are

both worth trying for their clean rooms arranged around pretty courtyards. The *Balcıoğlu Pansiyon* (☎0242/753 4098; ③), a couple of blocks south, is a small family-run place that caters solely to the independent traveller; rooms are better in the main house than in the chalet-like annexe.

Good **campsites** include the *Gürdal* (☎0242/753 1361), out of town on the west beach road past the Sorgun turnoff, and *Yeşil Park* (☎0242/756 9141), 3km along the road to Sorgun.

Ancient Side

Ancient Side has been almost overwhelmed by the modern town, but fortunately even the inroads of mass tourism have been unable to smother the grandeur of its buildings and monuments. The road into town actually passes through the **city gate**, although this is in such bad repair you could be forgiven for not noticing it. The **city walls** have fared better, the section running east from the city gate particularly well preserved, with a number of towers still in place.

The agora and museum

From the city gate a colonnaded street runs down to the **agora**, the site of Side's second-century slave market, and today fringed with the stumps of many of the agora's columns. It's a popular spot with the nomads who hang around trying to tempt people into taking camel rides. The circular foundation visible at the centre is all that remains of a **temple of Fortuna**, and in the northwest corner, next to the theatre, you can just about make out the outline of a semicircular building that once served as a public latrine, seating 24 people.

Opposite the agora is the site of the former **Roman baths**, now restored and home to a **museum** (daily 8am–noon & 1–5pm; $2.50). It retains its original floor plan and contains a cross-section of locally unearthed objects – mainly Roman statuary, reliefs and sarcophagi. If you find yourself wondering why many of the statues seem to be headless, it's because they were decapitated in an outbreak of religious zeal during the early days of Christianity.

The monumental gate and theatre

Just south of here, the still-intact **monumental gateway** now serves as an entrance to the modern resort. To the left of the gateway is an excavated monument to Vespasian, built in 74 AD, which takes the form of a fountain with a couple of water basins in front. Inside the gate is the entrance to Side's 20,000-seat **theatre**, the largest in Pamphylia, and different from those at Perge and Aspendos in that it was built as a freestanding structure supported by massive arched vaults, and not into a hillside. The effect is stunning, but unfortunately the site has been closed for the last two years due to structural instability – restoration work is under way, and already part of the stage-building has been reconstructed. The two-metre wall surrounding the orchestra was built to protect the audience from the wild animals used during gladiatorial shows.

Other ruins

From the gateway, modern Side's main street leads down to the old harbour and the **temples of Apollo and Athena**, both under restoration right now, although their location makes a good spot to watch the sunset. In the days when Side was an important port, the area to the immediate west of here was a harbour. Even in Roman times it was necessary to dredge continuously to clear silt deposited by the Manavgat River, and after the city went into decline it soon became clogged up. Elsewhere, you'll find a number of other buildings, including the **city agora**, on the eastern side of the peninsula just a stone's throw from the sea, and, a little inland from here, a ruined **Byzantine basilica**, gradually disappearing under the shifting sand of the dunes. Off Camii Sokak behind the *Çinçin Café-bar* and Nilgin market are the remains of **antique baths** where Cleopatra is supposed to have bathed. The remains are substantial including several separate rooms, baths and a garden, and even a marble seat with a dolphin armrest.

Beaches

Given Side's fine sandy **beaches**, it's not surprising the town has developed so rapidly. To the west the beach stretches for about 10km, lined by expensive hotels and beach clubs, and various points renting windsurfing boards for about $2.50 per hour; the crowds, however, can be heavy during the high season. To the east and best reached by road through pine forests, **Sorgun** beach is well maintained by the local authority. It's also quieter and less tacky than Side's beaches. To reach it you currently have to take a minibus from Manavgat as there is no transport from Side, even though it's only 3km away. In the other direction beyond the western beach, **Kumköy** is like an offshoot of Side with nearly as much in the way of beachside development, but again it's beaches aren't as crowded as Side's. Many of the buses that run between Antalya and Side now go via Kumköy.

Eating, drinking and nightlife

There's no shortage of places to **eat and drink** in Side, with what seem like hundreds of establishments up, down and around the main street catering to all tastes, particularly German ones. Try the *Toros Restaurant* down near the old harbour, where you can sample reasonably priced fish dishes on their terrace, or the nearby *Aphrodite*, which has excellent swordfish. The *Ayişiği*, reached from the main street by taking Camii Sok (the street with the mosque) until you can't go any further, is a garden restaurant with sea views from the terrace; it isn't cheap but service is good and the food above average.

The *Apollonik*, by the sea, reached by turning left at the end of the main street, is an excellent **bar**. Further east round the headland on the southeast side of Side, music-led bars such as the *Zeppelin*, *Stones Bar* and *Barracuda* offer fine views out onto the Mediterranean. To save money, cruise the **happy hours** that run staggered in different bars (between 6 and 9pm). There are also a few **discos** in town all of which conform more or less to the holiday stereotypes. Perhaps the least awful is the *Nimfeon*, on the way out to the eastern beach.

On towards Alanya: Manavgat, Alarahan and beyond

Fifteen minutes east of Side by dolmuş, the small town of **MANAVGAT** is not especially alluring, but it could be used as a cheap base from which to explore the surrounding coast – the hotels here are fewer but cheaper than those in Side. Attractions are few and far between: river boats run tours up to the rather overrated Şelâle or Manavgat Waterfalls nearby, and the local market on Monday explodes into life as hundreds of merchants head in from the surrounding countryside.The town centre is five minutes' walk west of the **otogar** (past the PTT and over a bridge), and is home to a few restaurants and a handful of cheap **hotels** – the eccentric *Konya Aile Pansiyon*, Lise Cad 11 (☎0242/746 3974; ①), the waterless *Hotel Şelâle*, a few doors further down (☎0242/746 1560; ①), and, pick of a poor bunch in the budget category, the *Yilmaz Pansiyon* (☎0242/746 3908; ①), with good rooms for the price. A huge leap in comfort takes you to the recommended *Hotel Nil*, Çayboyu Cad, on the banks of the river (☎0242/746

5289; ③), and the slightly cheaper *Otel Kernan* (☎0242/746 4400; ③), 200m upstream. The *Moonlight* and *Marina* **restaurants** on the river serve reasonable food, as does the *otogar* restaurant, concealed in the underpass that leads down from the main road.

Dolmuşes shuttle between Manavgat and Side every fifteen minutes, Antalya every half-hour and Sorgun every now and then. Alanya-bound dolmuşes depart from Manavgat more frequently than from Side, although it's usually no problem to catch a ride with a bus from the Side turnoff. The road hugs the Mediterranean and there are good beaches all the way, as a result of which small resorts are springing up all along this stretch of the coast.

Just under 30km east of Manavgat, a rough road spears off north to **ALARAHAN**, with its quirky thirteenth-century Selçuk *kervansaray* built for the benefit of traders operating between the Selçuk city of Konya and the port of Alanya. It was the creation of Sultan Alâeddin Keykubad – also responsible for the castle at Alanya – and is particularly impressive, nestling in the tranquil river valley. Further up the same road, ranged around a pyramidal hill, there are the ruins of an ancient **castle**, scarcely discernible against the stony backdrop but accessible by way of a tunnel fifteen minutes on from the *kervansaray*. Returning to the main road and continuing east there's another Selçuk *kervansaray*, the **Şarapsa Hanı** – now being used as a disco.

Alanya

Until a little over ten years ago **ALANYA** was just another sleepy coastal town with no more than a handful of flyblown hotels to its name. Now it has become one of the Mediterranean coast's major resorts, a booming and popular place which has fortunately managed to hold on to much of its original character, with none of the claustrophobic atmosphere of Side. These days it is, like Side, probably best appreciated out of season, though it is much less crowded than its rival, even in mid-summer. Most visitors come into town from the west, an approach that reveals Alanya at its best, the road passing through verdant banana plantations on the edge of town and suddenly revealing a rocky promontory, topped by a castle, rearing out of the Mediterranean.

Little is known about Alanya's early history, although it's thought that it was founded by Greek colonists, who named it Kalonoros or "beautiful mountain". Things were pretty quiet until the second century BC when Cilician pirates began using the town, known by now as Coracesium, as a base to terrorize the Pamphylian coast. Eventually the Romans decided to put an end to the activities of the pirates and sent in Pompey, who destroyed the pirate fleet in a sea battle off Alanya in 67 BC. In 44 BC Mark Antony gave the city to Cleopatra as a gift. Romantic as this might sound, there was a practical reason for his choice: the area around the city was an important timber-producing centre, and Cleopatra needed its resources to build up her navy. In 1221, the Byzantine city fell to the Selçuk sultan Alâeddin Keykubad, who gave it its present name and made it his summer residence; it's from this period that most buildings of historical importance date.

Arrival, information and accommodation

It's about a twenty-minute walk to the town centre from Alanya's **otogar**, but there are plenty of *servis* minibuses to shuttle bus passengers in; if you're coming to Alanya by dolmuş or on a through bus heading for Antalya, Adana or Mersin, you'll probably be able to get off in the centre of town anyway. The **tourist information office** is opposite the town museum at Çarşı Mahallesi, Kalearkası (Mon–Fri 9am–5.30pm; ☎0242/513 1240).

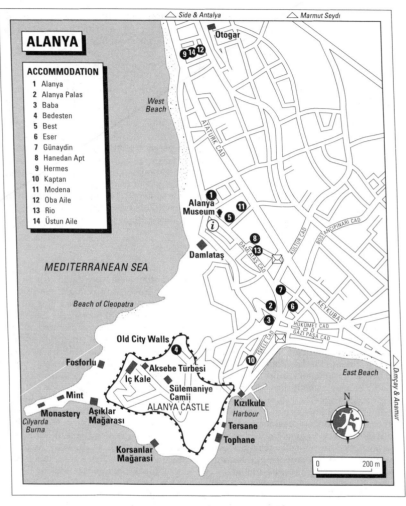

As in Side, **accommodation** possibilities are almost endless, taking in the full price range, though sadly the best places tend to be block-booked by tour groups from May until September. It is possible, however, to pick up some out-of-season bargains. **Budget** travellers should head for **Damlataş Caddesi** and İskele Caddesi. Just behind the museum, off Damlataş Cad on the fourth floor of an apartment block, is the *Pension Best*, Alaaddinoğlu Sok 23 (☎0242/511 0171, fax 513 0446), offering immaculately clean bed and breakfast rooms (③), or larger two-, four- or six-person apartments, complete with bathroom, living room and kitchen ($30–45). Just north of here, the *Pansiyon Alanya*, Nergis Sok 4, Güzelyalı Cad (☎0242/513 1897; ③), has clean modern rooms and a nice balcony. A hundred metres northeast of the *Best* is the comfortable two-star *Otel Modena*, Alaaddinoğlu Sok 9 (☎0242/512 3399; ④). Heading south along Damlataş Cad you will come to the modern and clean *Rio Hotel* at no. 54 (☎0242/512 4347; ③), with poor bathrooms but good-value singles. For less opulent but cheaper apartments than the *Best*, turn left down Akmanlar Sok to the friendly *Hanadan Appartment Hotel* at no. 10 (☎0242/512 5745; ④). Further down Damlataş is the styleless *Günaydin Hotel*, 26 Kültür Cad 26 (☎0242/513 1943; ②), where at least you will get breakfast in with the room.

There are a few budget hotels where Damlataş Caddesi becomes İskele Caddesi: the *Alanya Palas*, İskele Cad 6 (☎0242/513 1016; ①), which is the cheapest in town but often rented-out to long-term residents; the nearby *Baba Hotel* (☎0242/513 1032; ②), which has undergone a recent facelift but whose prices have been hiked up to pay for it; and the *Hotel Eser*, Bostancıpınarı Cad 10 (②), which is basic and noisy.

If you've come primarily for the beach scene then you might want to chose from one of the hotels **near the bus station**. The *Üstun Aile Pansiyon*, Meteorologi Sok 4 (☎0242/513 2262; ③), has clean and spacious rooms with a balcony and communal kitchen, a stone's throw from the beach. The nearby *Oba Aile Pansiyon* (☎0242/513 2675; ②) is cheaper and more modest but still pleasant. The Scandinavian-oriented *Hotel Hermes*, Meteorologi Sok 2 (☎0242/513 2135; ③), is closest to the beach, with a small pool and nice rooms.

Keykubat Caddesi, the extension of Atatürk Caddesi leading off to Mersin and backing the eastern beach, is Alanya's resort strip, lined with the **upmarket hotels** that have contributed more than anything to the character transformation of the city. If you're on a sun and beach trip, try the *Hotel Banana*, 2km out of town on Keykubat Cad (☎0242/514 1111; ⑤), which has simple rooms around garden pools and its own immaculate beach – but there are dozens of identical options. The *Hotel Kaptan*, İskele Cad 70 (☎0242/513 4900, fax 513 2000; ⑤), is comfortable and reasonably classy with its own pool and good views of the bay from the restaurant and front balconies. The choicest hotel in Alanya has to be the *Bedesten* (☎0242/512 1234, fax 513 7934; ⑤), a former thirteenth-century *kervansaray* near the Süleymaniye mosque on the winding road up to the citadel; its rooms lie around a courtyard and the more expensive suites are next to the pool.

There are a couple of good **campsites** west of Alanya on the Side road: the *Alanya-Motorcamp*, about 25km out just before a large hotel complex, newly built and with facilities including a restaurant and shops; and the the *BP-Kervansaray Motorcamp*, a little closer, where you get roughly the same deal.

Old Alanya

Most of **old Alanya** lies on the great rocky promontory that juts out into the sea, dominating the modern town. Dolmuşes from the west drop you off near the PTT on Atatürk Caddesi. From here, walk towards the harbour on the east side of the promontory, where stands the **Kızılkule** – "The Red Tower" – a 35-metre-high defensive tower of red stone built by Alâeddin Keykubad in 1226 and restored in 1951. Today it houses a pedestrian **ethnographic museum** (Tues–Sun 8am–noon & 1.30–5pm; $0.75), and has a roof terrace that overlooks the town's eastern harbour. Old wooden houses cling to the slopes above the tower, and you can follow the old coastal defensive wall along the water's edge to the **Tersane**, an Ottoman shipyard, consisting of five workshops linked by an arched roof. Beyond here is a small defensive tower, the **Tophane**.

Alanya castle

Reaching **Alanya castle** isn't quite so easy. If you have the time and inclination you can walk it; set off early in the day before it gets too hot, or better still do it in the late afternoon and catch the sunset from the top. It's a long, winding climb and will take about an hour, assuming you're averagely fit – there are lots of restaurants and little cafés to stop off at on the way up, if you get tired. Often these are little more than a table and an awning in someone's garden but there are good views all the way up. If you can't face the walk, catch the hourly bus (on the hour) from just outside the tourist office on the western side of the promontory.

The castle itself is a huge fortification system, with walls snaking right around the upper reaches of the promontory. A huge archway (bearing an inscription in Persian) leads into an area which demarcated the original limits of Alanya back in Selçuk times. In among the foliage off the road is an area known as **Ehmediye**, a small village with a few old Ottoman houses clustered around the dilapidated sixteenth-century **Süleymaniye Camii**, a *kervansaray* and the **Aksebe Türbesi**, a distinctive thirteenth-century tomb.

At the end of the road is the **İç Kale** ("Inner Fortress"; daily 8am–8pm; $2.50), built by Keykubad in 1226. Inside the gates local women sell lace, and the smell of lavender hangs on the air. The fortress is pretty much intact with the shell of a **Byzantine church**, decorated with fading frescoes, in the centre. Look out for the **cisterns** which supplied the fortress with water and to which it owed much of its apparent impregnability. In the northwestern corner of the fortress, a platform gives fine views of the western beaches and the mountains, though it originally served as a springboard from which prisoners were thrown to their deaths on the rocks below. These days tour guides assure their wards that it's customary to throw a rock from the platform, attempting to hit the sea rather than the rock below – an impossible feat supposed to have been set for prisoners as a chance to save their necks.

The modern town and beaches

Back down at sea level, apart from the hotels and restaurants, **modern Alanya** has very little to offer. On the western side of the promontory, the **Alanya Museum** (Tues–Sun 8am–noon & 1.30–5pm; $0.75) is filled with local archeological finds and ethnological ephemera, including finds from and photos of several small Pamphylian sites in the region. There's also a mock-up Ottoman living room complete with a beautiful carved ceiling, shutters and cupboards, and photos and explanations of select examples of late nineteenth-century Ottoman houses, though the best thing about it is probably the garden, a former Ottoman graveyard in which you can take refuge from the heat in summer. Don't be taken in by signposts pointing to a museum in the back streets away from the shore – they in fact lead to a house Atatürk stayed in for exactly three days in 1935 which is, frankly, not very interesting.

Alanya's beaches are extensive, stretching from the town centre for a good 3km west and 8km east. The sand is not the finest, and little effort is made to keep the beaches clean, so it's well worth heading out of town for 23km on the Side road to **Incekum** ("fine sand"), a three-kilometre stretch backed by pine forests which does live up to its name, even though it has been voraciously gobbled up by big hotel complexes in the last few years.

The caves

Not far away from the museum, accessible from behind the *Damlataş Restaurant*, you'll find the **Damlataş** or "Cave of Dripping Stones" (daily 10am–sunset; $0.75), a stalactite- and stalagmite-filled underground cavern with a moist, warm atmosphere said to benefit asthma sufferers. There are other caves, dotted around the waterline at the base of the promontory, and various local nautical entrepreneurs offer **boat trips** around them, charging about $13 per boatload for a one-hour trip and $25 for the full two-and-a-half hours, happily cramming on board as many passengers as possible. You can also hire out a boat for a day for a posted rate of $15 per person including lunch, though you'll probably need a group of at least five to get this price.The first stop is usually the **Fosforlu** (Phosphorus Cave), where the water shimmers green; then it's on round the **Cilyarda Burnu**, a long spit of land that is home to a ruined monastery and former mint. It's not actually possible to go ashore, but on the other side of the skinny peninsula is the **Aşıklar Mağarası** (Lovers' Cave), in which, according to a bizarre local story, a German woman and her Turkish boyfriend were stranded for three months in 1965 while the police and army mounted searches for them. A little further round is the **Korsanlar Mağarası**, which according to more believable stories is where the pirates of yesteryear used to hide out. You will also be taken to the **Beach of Cleopatra** where the legends claim the queen used to descend to bathe, while staying here with Mark Antony.

Eating and drinking

You won't starve to death in Alanya. The small streets running between Gazipaşa and Hükümet *caddesi*s are lined with *pide* and kebab places where you'll be able to fill up for $5 or thereabouts; *Gaziantep* at Eskihal Cad 19 serves good stews with flat bread. The *Imren Lokantasi*, on a side street off Hayatehanım Caddesi near the *Günaydin Hotel*, comes recommended though it can be tricky to find. Otherwise, try the *Derya* or *Konak* on Atatürk Caddesi a few hundred metres north of the PTT. There are plenty of cheap touristy restaurants and café-bars along Damlataş Caddesi where you can also get a meal for $5 without too much difficulty. For something quite different, head for the appetizing *Vitamin Station* on Damlataş Caddesi, which does freshly squeezed fruit juices, milkshakes and passable hamburgers. There are also two very good ice cream parlours, the *Mavi Koşe* and the *Çamlıca*, both near the *Alanya Palas* hotel.

There are better, more expensive restaurants along the seafront, on the street parallel to Gazipaşa Caddesi, most of them serving fish – try the *Malperi MS Sultan*, the *Yöret* and the *Janus*, although expect to pay at least $7 a head.

Listings

Bicycle and motorbike rental Bikes cost $4 per day, mopeds $12 and Czech-built Jawa 250cc motorbikes $30, available from countless outlets around town.

Car rental *Airtours*, İskele Cad 52/B (☎0242/25 939); *Akdem*, Bostancıpınarı Cad, Kuyularönü Camii 2/A (☎0242/27 607), who have Chevrolets, Suzuki jeeps and minibuses; *Avis*, Atatürk Cad 13 (☎0242/513 3513); *Budget*, İskele Cad 68/5 (☎0242/4400); *Europcar*, Keykubat Cad 21/A (☎0242/513 1929).

Excursions Try *Panel*, Kalearkası Cad 37 (☎0242/4151), for trips to Cappadocia, Pamukkale, the Pamphylian cities and boat excursions around Alanya.

Health centre On İskele Cad, next to the police station (☎0242/15 629).

Laundry *Viola*, Saray Mah, Zoğlu Sok, next to the *Modena Hotel* off Damlataş Cad (daily 8am–midnight); *Jet 2*, Taşçiali Sok.

Market For provisions, there is a small fruit-and-veg market on Gazipaşa Cad.

Music Cassettes from *Playback*, İskele Cad 34/A, and nearby *Saturn* and *Tezcan*, or *Odeon Music Shop*, Hayatehanım Cad 15/C.

PTT Atatürk Cad, opposite Kültür Cad (daily 8am–midnight); card phones. There are also PTT caravans scattered about the place during the summer.

Shopping Touristy silverware and carpets on sale in İskele Cad, more carpets on the side streets between Gazipaşa Cad and Hükümet Cad.

THY Flight bookings from *Ari Tourism*, İskele Cad 46 (☎0242/513 1194).

Watersports Jet skis $25 for 15min, parasailing $25 for 15min, waterskiing $19 per half-hour, banana boat ride $6, from several outlets on the West Beach. There are a few scuba diving schools located by the harbour. Windsurfing boards come out when seas are calm, and you can even go bungee jumping in the bay around from the harbour.

Around Alanya

Alanya's tourist information office distinguishes itself by its dearth of information about sites in the region, and even archeological sites are not signposted from the road, so lopsided is tourism development here. Private tour operators are helping to fill the gap with trips to Alanya's nearby mountain villages and to the Dimçay River, but otherwise you'll need a good map and a car to see most of the following.

The Dimçay River

The **Dimçay** is 6km from the centre of Alanya, but still within the boundaries of the modern city. Take a "Banana dolmuş" out of town from along Keykubut Caddesi to the bridge signposted "Dimçay". The river banks, especially the western side, are lined with restaurants offering fresh trout or kebabs at tables actually in the shallow river, so you can cool your feet as you eat. Further up, as you near the Toros mountains, the scenery becomes more spectacular, and the most impressive location is that of the *Duru* restaurant about 8km from the bridge. The river deepens here into a beautiul green pool where you can swim in freezing mountain spring water. Further up the Dimçay is a dam creating a deeper pool, but unfortunately this region is more commercial with parking fees, crowds and higher-priced restaurants.

Mahmut Seydi

Alanya's principle *yayla* or summer mountain retreat is **MAHMUT SEYDI**, an attractive village 25 tortuous kilometres out of town. Minibuses aren't designed to meet the needs of tourists, the bus arriving in the evening and leaving the following morning, and there's no accommodation. To get there, take Yayla Caddesi off Atatürk Caddesi and head for the hills. Once out of town you may be able to pick up a lift in that direction.

It's worth the effort of hitching or renting means of transport partly to escape from Alanya's oppressive summertime heat, but also to visit the town's thirteenth-century **mosque**. The exterior of the building is modern but most of the interior fittings, including the woodwork of the ceilings, doors, cupboards and galleries, are original. Unfortunately, the woodwork was painted in recent restorations, but its former glory can still be appreciated, especially in the fine work of the ceiling. In the courtyard is part of the original fountain and a 650-year-old fir tree. From viewing platforms next to the tree and the mosque, the valley, its surrounding mountains and village houses are visible, as well as the distant beach of Incekum. Also visible is the town's real pride and joy – a two-storey **public toilet**.

Opposite the mosque on the other side of the street, Mehmet Gürses keeps a grocer's shop and provides hospitality for visitors in a little shed affair full of paraphernalia new and old; an Ottoman chimney piece is adorned with a 1950s alarm clock and, if you're lucky, he'll bring out a Selçuk sword with silver inscriptions. *Toros Piknik*, a romantically situated **restaurant** 3km below the village, will serve up a good spread while you admire the mountainside views.

ALANYA TO ADANA

The region between Alanya and Adana formed ancient **Cilicia**, settled by refugees from Troy at the same time as Pamphylia further west, but its remoteness meant that it was never as developed, and, although it had a couple of significant centres, the region seems to have been largely wild and lawless. In ancient times it was divided between

Cilicia Tracheia (Rough Cilicia) – Alanya to the western edge of the Çukurova – and *Cilicia Campestris* (Smooth Cilicia), comprising the dull flatlands of the Ceyhan delta.

Cilicia Tracheia, with its rugged, densely wooded coastline, was a haven for pirates, whose increasingly outrageous exploits finally spurred the Romans into absorbing Cilicia into the empire in the first century BC. Today, it retains a wild appearance, and travel through it involves some frighteningly daring bus rides along winding, mountain roads which hug the craggy coastline, traversing the rocky coves that once served as pirate hangouts. All this is to the good if you're trying to escape the crowds further west, since far fewer people make it along here. There are some decent stretches of beach around **Anamur**, overlooked by an Armenian settlement and a partially excavated Greek settlement; at **Kızkalesi**, there are more good beaches and weird ruins, while in the mountains above **Silifke** – the next major town – the abandoned city of **Uzuncaburç** is perhaps the most extensive of the coast's ancient sites, though there are numerous more, most of them untended, between here and **Mersin**. This marks the beginning of what was Cilicia Campestris, and the end of the area's real touristic interest, with ferries to northern Cyprus but little else to stop for. Similarly, **Tarsus**, a little further on, has little to betray its former historical importance these days; and **Adana**, Turkey's fourth largest city, contains few remains of any era, despite a long and venerable history. Indeed, the time most travellers spend here waiting between bus connections is normally more than enough to exhaust the city's possibilities.

Alanya to Silifke

The first significant settlement after Alanya is **GAZİPAŞA**, about 50km to the east – nothing special (though it has been designated as the site for a new airport) but offering access to reasonable stretches of beach, slightly less populated than those at Alanya. The beach, 3km from the town centre, is sand and pebble and is most easily accessible for guests of the *Selinus Holiday Village*, a simple campsite with cheap chalets.

The only site of real interest in this area is **IOTAPE**, about 10km back on the Alanya road. Oddly situated on a rocky promontory between the road and the sea, this ancient site was named after the wife of the Commagenian king Antiochus IV (38–72 AD), and struck its own coins from the reign of Emperor Trajan until that of Emperor Valerian.

The ruins are mainly very tumbledown apart from a fairly impressive triple-arched bathhouse which can be clearly seen from the road. Closer inspection uncovers drainage and heating systems. The acropolis is on the promontory out to sea and a colonnaded street runs east–west along the valley linking the promontory to the mainland. Also visible from the road are statue bases giving information about successful athletes and philanthropists of the city, and there are frescoes to be seen inside the niches of a small, single-aisled church. The beach below Iotape is idyllic: very clean and if you're lucky you might get it to yourself.

Beyond here the road cuts through the mountains, traversing occasional valleys planted with bananas but rarely losing sight of the sea. On the way you'll pass the odd little wayside restaurant and campsite – at **ŞEHİR** for example – and sheltered but difficult-to-reach sandy bays, which even at the height of summer are guaranteed to be almost empty.

Anamur, İskele and around

Apart from the *otogar* – site of the local **tourist information office** (☎0324/814 3529) – there's little of interest in **ANAMUR** itself. Its small harbour **İSKELE**, about 5km away and accessible by dolmuş from the centre of Anamur, is, however, picking up as a resort – though it's still quiet compared to Alanya.

There are quite a few reasonable restaurants and **hotels** in İskele. If you arrive late at the bus station try the nearby *Dedehan Pansiyon* (☎0324/816 4348; ①). Top recommendation, however, is *Eser Pansiyon*, a block back from the sea (☎0324/814 2322; ②), which offers clean rooms, a nice terrace and a relaxed atmosphere. Cheaper options include the clean and simple *Pension Kafka* (☎0324/814 2916; ①) with a popular rooftop bar; the *Star Pansiyon* (☎0324/816 4605; ①), generally neglected but with nice corner rooms; and the *Sen Aile Pansiyon* (☎0324/814 2330; ①), a sleepy family-run block just off the beach at the other end of town. The *Cap Anamur* (☎0324/814 2374; ②) has small but comfortable rooms just off the central square and possibly the best **restaurant** in town. Equally comfortable is the new *Sezgin Hotel* (☎0324/816 6664; ②), but the best in town is the *Hermes* (☎0324/814 3950, fax 814 3995; ⑤), with a swimming pool, air-conditioning, sea views and a thumping top-floor disco.

There are **camping** facilities just west of İskele at the *Yalı Motorkamp*, where you can also rent small bungalows for $8–12, though it gets full in the summer. There are also a few very basic campsites in İskele itself where you'll pay less than $2 per night for an all-in deal.

Anemurium

Six kilometres southwest of modern Anamur is **Anemurium** (dawn–dusk; $1), on the eastern side of a headland formed where the Toros mountains jut out into the sea. An access road leads down to the partially excavated site from the main road (look out for the yellow sign). Anemurium was at its peak during the third century AD, and most of what remains dates from this period. As you approach the site you'll see two parallel **aqueducts** running north to south along the hillside to the right. Below these a sun-baked **necropolis** contains numerous freestanding tombs whose cool interiors harbour murals of mythological scenes on the walls. The most notable of these lies near the lower aqueduct, its vault painted with scenes representing the four seasons, while on one of the walls Hermes is shown in his role as Psychopompos, conductor of the souls of the dead – though you'll really need the site guardian to help you locate the tomb. To the right of the road are the hollow ruins of three **Byzantine churches**, set starkly against the blue backdrop of the Mediterranean.

Further down towards the beach you'll see the crumbling remains of a **bath complex** and a desolate **palestra** or parade ground. Southwest of here is a ruined but still identifiable **theatre** set into the hillside of the headland. Above the theatre on the slope, between the lower and upper aqueduct, are the remains of a number of houses, some of which have intact vaulted roofs. East of the theatre is the shell of a building containing six rows of seating, thought to have been either a **council chamber** or **concert hall** (possibly both). Beyond here some steps lead down to a courtyard, the centre of a small workshop complex. Returning towards the theatre and heading south, you'll come across another **baths complex**, a two-storey vaulted structure that is probably the best preserved building in Anemurium, with easily discernible traces of decoration and tile-work on the interior walls.

With time, you might want to clamber up the scrubby slopes of the headland to what was once Anemurium **acropolis**. There isn't a lot to see here but the promontory is Turkey's southernmost point, and on a clear day gives views of the mountains of Cyprus 80km to the south.

Mamure Kalesi

In the opposite direction from Anamur, a couple of kilometres east of İskele, is **Mamure Kalesi** (daily 9am–5pm; $1), a forbidding castle built by the rulers of the Cilician kingdom of Armenia on the site of a Byzantine fort. It was later occupied by Crusaders, who had established a short-lived kingdom in Cyprus and used Mamure Kalesi as a kind of bridgehead in Asia. Used by successive rulers of the area to protect the coastal strip, it was most recently garrisoned by the Ottomans, who reinforced it after the British occupied Cyprus in 1878, maintaining a strong presence here during World War I. Constructed directly above the sea, its stark facade of crenellated outer walls and watchtowers are certainly impressive, and they hide an interior of languorously decaying buildings that is quietly atmospheric – worth an hour or so's idling if you've time on your hands. Opposite is a small, family-run fish **restaurant**; a few kilometres east, there's a good forested **campsite**, the *Pullu Mocamp*, which also has an excellent restaurant.

Aydıncık, Boğsak, Taşucu – and on to Cyprus

Beyond Anamur the road continues on its twisting mountainous course, about 10km east of İskele passing **Softa Kalesi** – another ruined castle, again Armenian. About fifty winding kilometres beyond here the settlement of **AYDINCIK** stretches along the road for a few kilometres, offering a few cheap *pansiyon*s and one or two stretches of sandy beach. You could stop here for a look at relatively tourist-free Turkey, but bear in mind that people here are not as used to visitors as their neighbours to the west, and the topless bathing you might have got away with in Alanya is not advisable here. At **BOĞSAK**, about 50km further east, there are some fine sandy beaches with camping facilities, a few small motels, and a big beach club complex, as well as another medieval **fortress**, Liman Kalesi, built by the Knights of Saint John. Moving on, there are a couple of quiet bays with sandy beaches, but most people push straight on to **TAŞUCU**, from where there are frequent **ferry** and **hydrofoil services to Cyprus**. If you want to spend the night, you could try the central *Ali Baba Otel* on Atatürk Caddesi near the harbour (✆0324/741 4026; ①), or the much better *Hotel Fatih* (✆0324/741 4125; ②), just beyond the ferry offices. Best in town is the *Lades Motel*, Atatürk Cad 89 (✆0324/741 4008; ④), with a swimming pool and fine sea view. The main **beach** lies on the eastern side of the harbour and here you can find several cheap places, including the quiet *Baris Pansiyon* (✆0324/741 4381; ②).

On to Cyprus: ferries and hydrofoils

Hydrofoils depart from Taşucu to Gırne (Kyrenia) in the "Turkish Republic of Northern Cyprus" (TRNC) every day at 11am and 4pm. Agents are *Fergün Deniz Otobüsü* (✆0324/741 3731). The journey lasts 2hr 30min and costs $12 one-way, $22 return. **Ferries** currently depart from Sunday to Thursday at midnight, take 6 hours, and cost $10 one-way, $18 return; agents are *Fergün* (✆0324/741 2323), *Ertürk* (✆0324/741 4325) and *TML* (✆0324/741 5553). You'll also be stung for a "harbour tax", quoted as $4.50 one-way, $7 return. Tickets can also be booked at Silifke *otogar* (see below) and in Mersin. At the moment, EC (including British), US, Canadian and Australasian citizens require only a valid passport for entry into the TRNC – three-month tourist visas are routinely issued on arrival. Bear in mind that it's not possible to enter southern (ie Greek-speaking) Cyprus from the TRNC.

Silifke

About 10km east of Taşucu, **SİLİFKE** was ancient Seleucia, founded by Seleucus, one of Alexander the Great's generals, in the third century BC. Nowadays it's a quiet, fairly undistinguished town, relatively untouched by tourists – who, if they come here at all, do so only on their way to the ruins at Uzuncaburç and points north. Nevertheless, the very ordinariness of Silifke has its own appeal, especially after the crowds of the resorts. Many local men wear traditional baggy trousers and the streets are full of three-wheeled motorcycles, which seem to be the main means of transport. You may also notice that the food here starts getting spicier, hinting at even hotter things to come in the east of the country.

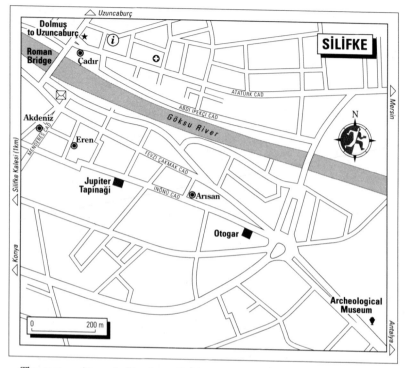

The centre of town is Menderes Caddesi, around fifteen minutes' walk from the **otogar** along İnönü Caddesi. There are very few sights of note in and around the town. Signs lead up to **Silifke Kalesi**, a Byzantine castle which dominates the local skyline but looks a lot less spectacular close up. At the top there's a café and a great view of the town. On the way up you'll pass an old **cistern** – the so-called *tekir amban* or "striped depot" – which kept Byzantine Silifke supplied with water.

Other sights include the second-century AD **Jupiter Tapınağı** (Temple of Jupiter) on İnönü Caddesi, which comprises little more than a pile of stones and a few pillars. On the Antalya Asfaltı on the way out of town there's an **archeological museum** (Tues–Sat 8am–noon & 1–5pm; $1), containing some locally unearthed bits and pieces.

Incidentally it was near Silifke that **Frederick Barbarossa**, the Holy Roman Emperor, met his end – he drowned while fording the Calycadnus (now Göksu) River about 9km north of town, en route to Palestine with the Third Crusade; today a plaque marks the spot. Four kilometres west of Silifke and then one kilometre north takes you to Meyemlık and the early Christian site of **Aya Tekla**. There's little to see except the underground chapel (bring a torch) used in secret by Tecla, the first female Christian teacher, and the early Christians after her.

The Göksü delta, the area southeast of Silifke towards the coast, forms the **Kuşcenneti** bird reservation, at its best between March 1 and April 21 when hundreds of species call in on their migration from Africa to Europe. To reach Kuşcenneti, take a dolmus from the PTT in Silifke to Kurtulus Köy; the Silifke tourist office may be able to help find a guide.

The town's international **music and folklore festival** takes place between May 20 and 26.

Practicalities

Silifke's helpful **tourist information office** is at Veli Gürten Bozbey Cad 6 (Mon–Fri 8.30am–5.30pm; ☎0324/714 1151), reached by way of the Roman bridge spanning the Göksu River.

Hotel possibilities are limited. Two cheap but basic options in the centre are the depressing *Hotel Akdeniz*, Menderes Cad 76 (☎0324/714 1285; ①), and the better *Hotel Eren*, Ziraat Bankası Arkası (☎0324/714 1289; ①). The best budget choice, however, is the new *Arisan Pansiyon* on İnönü Cad, not far from the *otogar* (☎0324/714 3331; ①), with clean bright rooms and sparkling en-suite bathrooms. Best hotel in town is the presentable but overpriced *Çadır Oteli*, Atatürk Cad 16 (☎0324/714 2449, fax 714 1244; ③).

There are lots of basic places to **eat and drink** but after dark most close, leaving you with only a few options. Best bet is the *Babu Oğlu*, opposite the *otogar*, which has medium-priced grills but expensive fish; otherwise try one of the several cheap *pide* places nearby.

Inland: the road to Uzuncaburç

Dolmuşes bound for the ancient city of Uzuncaburç depart from Silifke *otogar* and from near the tourist office. If there aren't any dolmuşes around, a taxi costs about $20 for the return trip, though this is highly negotiable.

The ride to Uzuncaburç is spectacular, taking you through a jagged gorge and a couple of villages that time seems to have forgotten. If you have your own transport, or don't mind doing a spot of hitching, you might care to stop off in the village of **DEMİRCİLİ**, known in ancient times as Imbriogon, where there are six **Greco-Roman tombs**, spread out on either side of the road among the olive trees. Visiting these is a rather strange experience: looking more like long-vacated houses than tombs, they are unattended and unrestored, and it's hard to believe that they have survived the depredations of time and stone plunderers. The first is a simple one-storey affair just to the right of the road; a little further along there's a larger two-storey structure. To the west of the road is the **Çıfte Anıt Mezarları** or "double mausoleum", consisting of two linked tombs, the right-hand one of which contains three sarcophagi with various decorative features – one with a relief of a lion, another featuring a man's head, the nude figures of two women and the heads of two women.

Uzuncaburç

From Demircili the road continues uphill and then turns off to the right towards the ruins of **UZUNCABURÇ**, originally a Hittite settlement that was known to the Greeks as Olba and to the Romans as Diocaesarea. A small modern settlement has grown up in haphazard fashion around the ruins, but few concessions have been made to tourism; in fact the village wasn't even connected to the electricity grid until a couple of years ago. These days it's famous for handmade rugs known as *çul*, and leather bags, examples of which you may find on sale at makeshift stalls. Local culinary specialities include *kenger kahvesi* (coffee made from acanthus) and *pekmez* (grape molasses). The *Burç Restaurant* offers simple **meals** and soft drinks, but there isn't anywhere to stay.

The main site

The main site of Uzuncaburç (no gates; $1 when the site guardian is around) lacks the size and scale of Perge and Aspendos, but is atmospheric enough in its own way, if only because of the relatively neglected state of most of it. Although the area was first settled by Hittite peoples, they left little behind in the way of souvenirs, and the most impressive ruins that survive date from Hellenistic times. The large site is intertwined with a modern settlement, but its core, including the centrepiece temple of Zeus Olbios, is relatively small.

The usual drop-off point is near an overgrown Roman **theatre**, overlooked by a couple of beautiful houses whose walls are chock-a-block with classical masonry. From here, pass through an enormous five-columned **monumental gateway**, beyond which a colonnaded street, once the city's main thoroughfare, runs east to west: keep your eyes open for what look like small stone shelves on the columns, which once supported statues and busts. On the northern side of the street is a **nympheum**, now dried up, which once formed part of the city's water supply system. This was part of a large network of pipes and tunnels, built by the Romans nearly two thousand years ago, that still supplies water to the modern village and others around.

To the south, the **temple of Zeus Olbios** is one of the earliest examples of the Corinthian order, erected during the third century BC by Seleucus I, of which only the fluted columns now remain intact. Look out for the fine sarcophagus carved with three Medusa heads and a sarcophagus lid depicting three reclining figures. At the western end of the colonnaded street is the **temple of Tyche**, dedicated to the goddess of chance, reckoned to date from the second half of the first century AD. Five marble columns still stand, joined by an architrave bearing an inscription stating that the temple was the gift of a certain Oppius and his wife Kyria. From here a right turn leads to a large three-arched **city gate**, which according to an inscription dates from the fifth century AD.

Other ruins

Most of the rest of Uzuncaburç's attractions lie to the north of these ruins. Walk from the drop-off point as far as the *Burç* restaurant, and turn right for the **High Tower**, a 22-metre-high, five-storey Hellenistic structure that once formed part of the city wall and which today gives its name to the modern town. An ancient Greek inscription above the entrance gives details of repair work carried out during the third century AD. It is believed that in addition to playing a defensive role this tower was also part of an ancient signalling network, whereby messages were relayed by flashing sunlight off polished shields. Today it looks in danger of imminent collapse.

Just outside the modern village, past the *Burç* restaurant as far as the Atatürk bust (heed the signs for the "Antık Mezar" and follow the curve to the right), is a **necropolis** used by Greek, Roman and Byzantine inhabitants of the area. It has three basic types of resting place – sarcophagi, graves carved into the rock, and cave tombs housing whole families. Most of these are clearly visible, and it's even possible to enter some of the cave tombs, though they have long since been cleaned out by grave robbers.

About 1km south of Uzuncaburç, 500m west of the main road, is another **mausoleum**, this time with an eye-catching pyramid-shaped roof, dating from Hellenistic times. Inside, the tombs were hidden under the floor and outside the rim of the roof was lined with statues of the deceased.

Another possible excursion from Uzuncaburç is to the ruins of **OLBA** (present-day **URA**), a similar but less impressive ancient city 5km to the east, which was the third-century BC capital of a temple state run by a powerful priest caste. At the village crossroads you will find a nympheum, cistern and theatre nestling at the base of an acropolis; 500m further northeast you can see the aqueduct built to feed the nympheum, and the watchtowers built to protect the aqueduct.

East from Silifke

About 7km east of Silifke, **KARADEDELİ**, a small village settled by former tent-dwelling Turcoman nomads, makes a good starting point for a walking tour of some ruined sites to the north. A series of pathways connects these sites, and it's possible to rent a donkey in the village to make the trek (enquire at the village café). The sites themselves are hardly breathtaking, but make an interesting enough target for some gentle hill-walking. First stop, 2km north of the village, is **YALAK TAŞ**, where there are some Greco-Roman foundations, and the ruins of a cistern together with what's thought to be an olive oil factory. Another 2km to the north brings you to **DİLEK TAŞ** and a few more ancient cisterns. The largest ruins are at **KARAKABAKLI**, where there are a few Greco-Roman houses, some of them two storeys high. Anyone with a special interest in exploring more ruins off the beaten track should buy Celâl Taşkiran's *Silifke and Environs*, an exhaustive guide to all the sites between Anamur and Mersin, available at many of these sites for about $10.

About 5km east of Karadedeli is **SUSANOĞLU**, the site of the ancient port of Corasium, and today a small resort with a good beach. A number of Roman remains are scattered through a valley running north from the beach, which is actually a silted-up Roman harbour. About half a kilometre east of the village itself is **Yapraklı Esik** ("the cove with leaves"), a quiet inlet whose waters are claimed to have curative properties.

Inland from here – reachable if you have your own transport – the ruins of another ancient settlement signal a two-kilometre diversion to the east down a dirt road to the third-century **Mezgit Kalesi** or "mausoleum of the fearless satrap". This is similar in appearance to those at Demircili, but a carving of a phallus adorns the exterior. The phallus represents Priapus, the well-endowed son of Dionysus and Aphrodite, and is supposed to signify that the occupant of the tomb was courageous and valiant, as well as being hung like a horse.

Heading eastwards along the coast from Susanoğlu you'll come across a number of bays with beaches, including, just a short distance past the village of Atakent, a swanky looking *Altinorfoz Banana/Ertur* development. You'll probably neither want nor be able to afford to stay here, but their beach is worth checking out.

Narlıkuyu and Akkum

A little way beyond Atakent, **NARLIKUYU** lies on the fringes of an exquisite bay with restaurants and a couple of basic *pansiyon*s. There's a small car park in the centre of the village, next to which are the remains of a Roman bathhouse ($1), known after its founder as the **Bath of Poimenius**. Inside, there's a dusty mosaic depiction of the well-rounded nude forms of the Three Graces, the daughters of Zeus and companions of the Muses. The bath was fed from the limestone caves above by an ancient Roman spring which supplied a celebrated fountain, the waters of which were supposed to confer wisdom on those who drank from them. A kilometre or so further down the road is the village of **AKKUM**, again with a few *pansiyon*s and a good stretch of beach. One *pansiyon* well worth checking out is the *Kökler*, not far from the beach (☎0324/723 3214; ②), which is clean and friendly and has an English-speaking proprietor.

The Caves of Heaven and Hell

From Narlıkuyu a narrow paved road winds 3km northwards into the hills through groves of olive trees to **Cennet ve Cehennem** or the Caves of Heaven and Hell (daylight; $1) – some of the most impressive of the many limestone caverns scattered along this coast. At the end of the road there's a car park, and a cluster of tea shops and souvenir stands.

There is in fact a series of three caves, and the local kids are usually quick to offer their services as guides, though their assistance isn't really necessary. The largest and most impressive cave is **Cennet Deresi** (the Cave of Heaven), immediately adjacent to the parking space – actually a seventy-metre-deep gorge, formed when the roof of an underground canyon collapsed. It's entered via 452 steps cut into the rock on the eastern side of the canyon. On reaching the bottom, head south towards the entrance to the **Cave of Typhon**, a bona fide cave of some depth, at the end of which runs a stream of drinkable water from the same source as the spring water in Narlıkuyu. As you go further in, it gets progressively more difficult to breathe and it's best not to hang around too long, a fact recorded by Strabo, the ancient geographer, leading some historians to believe that this cave may have been considered one of the mythical entrances to Hades. According to the legend, Typhon, after whom the cave is named, was an immense hundred-headed fire-breathing lizard, the father of Cerberus – the three-headed dog who guarded the entrance to Hades on the banks of the river Styx, allowing only the souls of the dead to enter and refusing to let them out. At the entrance to the cave is the **Chapel of the Virgin Mary**, a well-preserved Byzantine church built over the former Temple of Zeus and still containing a few frescoes.

About 100m to the north of "Heaven", the **Cehennem Deresi** (the Cave of Hell) is similar in formation but impossible to enter, as its sides are practically vertical and there's no clear way down. According to legend Zeus imprisoned Typhon here, before banishing him forever to the depths of the earth or, as one legend goes, trapping him underneath Mount Etna in Sicily. This gorge is supposed to be another of the entrances to Hades, and local people used to tie rags to surrounding trees to placate evil spirits.

About 500m west of "Heaven" is fourth cave, the **Dilek Mağarası** (the Wishing Cave), the opening of which has been specially widened and a spiral staircase provided for ease of access. Down below, solid pathways connect a number of subterranean halls, with a total length of about 200m. The main chamber is filled with stalactites and stalagmites, and the air down below is supposed to be beneficial for asthma sufferers.

Kızkalesi

A few kilometres east of Narlikuyu, **KIZKALESİ** ("Maiden's Castle") is the biggest resort along this stretch of coastline. It has scores of hotels, *pansiyons* and restaurants and, if you can find somewhere to stay – which is not always easy in high season – it makes a very relaxing place to spend a few days taking in the local sights and the beach.

Kızkalesi, known as Corycus in ancient times, changed hands frequently until the arrival of the Romans in 72 BC, after which it prospered, becoming one of the most important ports along the coast. It continued to thrive during the Byzantine era despite occasional Arab attacks – against which the town's defences were strengthened with two castles constructed during the twelfth and thirteenth centuries – before falling to the Ottomans in 1482.

The castles

Kızkalesi's most compelling feature is the thirteenth-century **sea castle** (daily dawn–dusk) on an island lying about 200m offshore, where the legend of the so-called Maiden's Castle – examples of which are found all over Turkey – is said to have originated. The story goes that one of the Armenian kings who ruled the region in medieval times had a beautiful daughter. After it was prophesied that she would die as the result of a poisonous snakebite, the king had the castle built and moved the girl out to it, imagining that she would be safe there. One day one of the king's advisers sent a basket of fruit out to the island for her, out of which slid a snake that killed the girl. According to local stories, the snake still lives on the island, and the only people who venture out to it are tourists, for whose benefit various cheap boat services operate. The unadorned walls and sturdy towers still stand, but apart from masonry fragments and weeds there's little to see within.

Opposite the sea castle, the overgrown ruins of the mighty **land castle** at the eastern end of the beach ($0.75 if there's anyone around to collect it) are easily explored and its battlements make a good venue for some sunset watching if you can stand the mosquitoes. Look out for the main gate, constructed from ancient stones bearing various Greek inscriptions. The western gate was originally a Roman structure, built during the third century AD and later incorporated into the castle.

Practicalities

Every second building in Kızkalesi is either a **hotel** or **pansiyon**, and most of them are very good value – though not for single travellers, who usually have to pay for a double room. Among the cheapest places are the friendly, family-run *Hülya Pansiyon* (☎0324/523 2067; ①); the clean and bright *Motel Gold* (☎0324/523 2322; ①), in the centre of the town's limited action; the nearby *Nisan Motel* (☎0324/523 2271; ①); and the plain but spacious rooms of the *Hotel Ferah* (☎0324/523 2218; ②). For a slightly more civilized place on the beach, it's well worth trying the German-dominated *Hotel Peyda* (☎0324/523 2607; ③) or, failing that, the *Hotel Hantur,* a couple of hundred metres west along the beach (☎0324/523 2367; ③). Top-range places with air conditioning and swimming pools include the three-star *Hotel Eylem* (☎0324/523 2416, fax 523 2395; ③) and *Club Barbarossa* (☎0324/523 2364; ⑤). The best local **campsite** is the *Kızkalesi Aile Plaja* (about $2.40 for a car, tent and two people), in the shadow of the land castle, which also has a good restaurant and some very basic rooms. **Eating and drinking** possibilities are almost endless, and mostly fairly reasonable.

Around Kızkalesi

The area **around Kızkalesi** offers a few points of interest, closest of which, immediately northeast of the village across the main road from the land castle, is a **necropolis**, dating from the fourth century AD and containing hundreds of tombs and sarcophagi, some of them beautifully carved. Many of the epitaphs give the jobs of the occupants – weavers, cobblers, goldsmiths, vintners, olive-oil manufacturers, ship owners and midwives, who all had their last resting places here. Also scattered around this area are the remains of a number of Byzantine churches and cisterns.

Perhaps more intriguing is the series of **rock reliefs** in a valley about 6km north of the village (the turning is near the PTT), marked by a sign bearing the legend *Adam Kaylar* or "People's Reliefs". Follow the path indicated from here for about a kilometre until it starts to dip down into a valley, where steps cut into the rock lead down to a kind of platform from which you can view a series of Roman men, women and children carved into niches in the wall. There are seventeen human figures and a mountain goat. Unfortunately extensive damage has recently been caused to one of the figures by treasure hunters who used dynamite in the hope of finding booty supposedly secreted inside the statue. It's not clear who the figures are, or why they might have been constructed, and the fragmentary inscriptions below most of them offer few clues.

East from Kızkalesi

East of Kızkalesi, on both sides of the road, are more ruins, stretching as far as the village of **AYAŞ**, 3km away, the site of the settlement of Elaioussa Sebaste, which in the time of Augustus was important enough to coin its own money. Passing through the village, the remains of an ancient canal, a sixteenth-century Selçuk tomb and some columns on the site of a Roman temple are visible north of the road, though most is unrestored and largely unrecognizable. Beyond the remains, an aqueduct leads to a massive underground cistern, near which you'll find a ruined theatre. Scattered around the area are numerous tombs, many of them richly decorated with reliefs.

Kanlıdivane

About 7km east of Kızkalesi, a signposted turnoff leads 3km north to the village of **KANLIDİVANE**, literally "place of blood" owing to its being the site of the ancient city of Kanytelis, where locals used to believe condemned criminals were executed by being thrown into a huge chasm and devoured by wild animals. You can visit the site, which contains some significant Roman and Byzantine remains – a car park and ticket sellers' hut mark the entrance (daily 8am–5.30pm; $1).

The **chasm** in question is certainly large and frightening enough to have given rise to the legends, 90m long by 70m wide and 60m deep, and forms the core of the ancient city. Visitors can descend into it by way of a partly eroded staircase. On the southern and western sides of the chasm there are a number of carvings in niches, one a portrait of a family of six and one of a Roman soldier. On its southwestern edge, near the car park, is a seventeen-metre-high tower dating from Hellenistic times, with an inscription on the southwestern corner next to a three-pronged triskele, a symbol that links the region to the nearby state of Olba. Near the tower are a number of Byzantine basilicas in various states of collapse, of which the best preserved is the Papylas Church. There's another big cluster of tombs northeast of the chasm with numerous sarcophagi and tombs.

Back on the main road, heading east towards Mersin, you can see the remains of a number of aqueducts which brought water to the various coastal and inland settlements during Roman times. The next major stop is **ERDEMLİ** – an unexciting town on the whole, with a rudimentary **campsite** called *Erdemli Çamlaği*.

Viranşehir

Twenty-three kilometres east of Erdemli lies **VİRANŞEHİR**, site of the ancient Pompeiopolis, an important Roman city, the site of which is signalled by a yellow sign directing you down a side road towards the sea. From the road, the first signs of previous occupation are a number of ancient canals and aqueducts on the left-hand side. About 1500m from the main road, a second-century AD **colonnaded street**, with about 40 of its 200 columns remaining, leads to the ruined ancient **harbour** where two walls project into the sea.

Viranşehir is also a popular spot with people from Mersin who come to swim and picnic on the sandy beach, and stay in the town's few cheap *pansiyon*s. Whether it's worth joining them or not is debatable: the beach is drab and the proximity of Mersin casts some doubt on the cleanliness of the water.

Mersin

The largest Mediterranean port in Turkey, **MERSİN** is the first of the three large cities that gird the Ceyhan delta, a modern harbour city that – aside from its regular ferry connections to Cyprus – is almost entirely without interest. Though inhabited since Hittite times, the settlement was, until the beginning of the twentieth century, little more than a squalid fishing hamlet. Over the last eighty years or so, however, rapid growth and industrialization, coupled with Mersin's role as a free trade zone – which has greatly increased the city's role in international trade, especially with the Middle East – have turned it into a model, if soulless, example of contemporary Turkish urban planning.

If you do find yourself with time on your hands, the local **museum** (Tues–Sun 9am–5pm; $1) offers a small but well-presented collection of local archeological finds and ethnographical knick-knacks, though you may find the confusion of stone carvings strewn about the garden more inspiring.

Practicalities

The city's orientation is slightly awkward; the **otogar** is some way out of town and you'll need to take a dolmuş into the centre. Unfortunately these don't pass directly in front of the *otogar*, and it's a five-minute walk (under the huge overhead sign saying "Ormansiz yurt bir memleket değildir") to the dolmuş stop. If you're arriving by bus late at night, head for the street one block west of the *otogar*, lined with dozens of hotels. There's a small **tourist information office** at the *otogar*, but the main branch is by the harbour on İnönü Bulvarı, Liman Giriş Sahası (Mon–Fri 9am–5.30pm; ☎0324/238 3271).

As an important port, Mersin supports plenty of **hotels**, but **budget** choices are limited. The *Hotel Ocak*, İstiklâl Cad 48 (☎0324/237 0489; ②), once a good option, is now

spiralling into terminal decline – catch it before it sinks much lower and you'll get a noisy but passable room with en-suite bathroom. The *Otel Emek*, İstiklâl Cad 81 Sok 5 (☎0324/232 5370; ①), is clean and acceptable, but a better choice is the *Otel Hayat*, İstiklâl Cad 88 (☎0324/231 1076; ①), with excellent-value rooms and en-suite bathrooms.

A good **mid-range** place is the well-located *Toros Hotel*, Atatürk Cad 33 (☎0324/231 2201, fax 237 8554; ③), with simple but clean and quiet rooms. The *Aktaş Hotel*, back on İstiklâl Cad at no. 152 (☎0324/233 7007, fax 232 3168; ③), is more expensive, but has an English-speaking manager, rooms with TV and minibar, and breakfast included in the price. For air-conditioned comfort head for the *Hotel Gökhan*, Soğuksu Cad 20 (☎0324/231 6256, fax 237 4462; ④), or the three-star *Hotel Derman*, İstiklâl Cad, İleri İlkokulu Yani 15/37 (☎0324/237 5028, fax 233 3824; ④). **Top-of-the-range** business hotels include the *Mersin Hotel*, in the centre of town on Gümrük Meydanı (☎0324/238 1040, fax 231 2625; ⑤), and the towering *Mersin Merit* at Kuvayi Milliye Cad 165 (formerly the *Ramada*; ☎0324/336 1010, fax 336 0722; ⑦), easily visible to the north.

There are various possibilities for **food** in Mersin. The *Balik Pazari* off Uray Cad is the best option in town for cheap fish, and opposite, off Silifke Cad, the *Mavi Köşe Ocak Başi* is a tiny outlet serving up filling *durum* (meat-filled pastry) and *güveç*. The *Ali Baba* fish restaurant, off Atatürk Cad at Çankaya Mah 93 Sok 7, is well known locally for its fish dishes and *meze*s, and has a reasonably pleasant interior. The young crowd meet out near the museum at *Pizzeria Ocim*, Bahri Ok Işhani B39, off Atatürk Cad, where they serve pizzas, spaghetti, and fried chicken, in an air-conditioned café where young people can actually hold hands without incurring the wrath of their elders.

On İnönü Bulvarı opposite the tourist office are *Olcartur*, selling *THY* **air tickets**, and *İstanbul Airlines*, who also have flights from Adana. The *THY* office itself can be found on İstiklâl Cad 27 (☎0324/233 9858). **Car rental** companies include *Esin*, Uray Cad, Güvenç İş Merkezi, *Flash Rent a Car*, İsmet İnönü Bulvarı Vysal Apyt 100/C, *Avis* next door (☎0324/232 3450), and *Europcar*, Uray Cad, Güvenç Iş Merkezi, B Block (☎0324/232 0017).

On to Cyprus

TML operate a **ferry service** to Mağosa/Famagusta in northern Cyprus, departing Monday and Wednesday at 10pm and Thursday at noon (journey time 10hr); on Fridays in summer the ferry goes on to Syria; at other times it returns the following day. **Tickets** are available at the harbour from *Turkiye Denizlik İşletmeleri Deniz Yollari İşletmesi* (*TML*), Liman Giriş Sahası on the first floor (☎0324/233 9858); one-way fares are around $20 with luggage, $16 without, for a pullman seat, return fares twice that, with a ten-percent reduction for students on production of an ISIC card. Cars cost around $50.

At the moment, EC (including British), US, Canadian and Australasian citizens require only a valid passport for entry into the "Turkish Republic of North Cyprus" (TRNC) – three-month tourist visas are routinely issued on arrival. Bear in mind that it's not possible to enter southern (ie Greek-speaking) Cyprus from the TRNC.

In Mersin the **TRNC Consulate** is at Hamidiye Mahalle Karadeniz Apt (☎0324/237 2482). You can also buy tickets for the **Taşucu–Kyrenia ferry and hydrofoil** – a much faster and cheaper crossing – in Mersin from *Fergün Denizcilik Şinketi*, on İnönü Bulvarı (☎0324/231 7921); they also run a service bus to Taşucu ($2).

Tarsus

About thirty kilometres east of Mersin, across an uneventful plain dotted with occasional factories, lies **TARSUS**, birthplace of Saint Paul, and the city where Cleopatra met Mark Antony and turned him into "strumpet's fool". Saint Paul was born as Saul in Tarsus about 46 years after the meeting between Cleopatra and Antony. He returned after his conversion on the road to Damascus, fleeing persecution in Palestine. He seems to have been proud of his roots and is described as having told the Roman commandant of Jerusalem: "I am a Jew, a Tarsian from Cilicia, a citizen of no mean city". Nowadays, however, few reminders of the town's illustrious past remain. Architecturally the overriding impression is one of down-at-heel uniformity, and the majority of modern Tarsians work in the textile mills that process the locally grown cotton.

Near the main bus drop-off point is the **Kancık Kapısı** ("the gate of the bitch"), a Roman city gate also known as Cleopatra's Gate. Although the gate doesn't actually have any factual connection with the Egyptian queen, she is thought to have come ashore for her first meeting with Mark Antony somewhere in the vicinity (at that time Tarsus was linked to the sea by a lagoon which has since silted up).

From Cleopatra's Gate, head north to a major junction and follow the signs to **St Paul's Well** (left turn and then a right turn), a walk of ten minutes through the city's ramshackle – and in spring, flower-bedecked – backstreets. There's little to see, just a borehole in the ground covered by a removable lid; it's said to be on the site of Saint Paul's house, however, and therefore attracts a steady stream of visitors. Signs tell you not to tip the attendant but after he's hauled a bucket of water up from the depths for you to drink from you might feel inclined to offer him a few lira. From the well, make your way back to the yellow sign and turn left. This leads to the old **mosque**, **Roman baths** and a fairly mundane **museum** (Mon–Fri 8.30am–noon & 1–5.30pm; $0.50), with an unexplained mummified lower arm of a woman and the odd case of jewellery exhibits.

Buses on to Adana leave from near the old mosque. There's a dearth of **hotels** in Tarsus, and in any case there's no reason to stay. If you get stuck, in the town centre there's the *İpekoğlu Oteli*, Adana Cad 90 (①), which is very basic but okay. The nearby *Hotel Zorbaz* is modern and clean (②), as is the *Cihan Palas Oteli* (①), 400m to the south.

Adana and around

East of Tarsus sprawls **ADANA**, Turkey's fourth largest city with 1.2 million inhabitants, a modern place which has grown rapidly since the 1918–20 French occupation. Today, as in the past, Adana owes much of its wealth to the fertile surrounding countryside of the Çukurova, with a textiles industry that has grown up on the back of the local cotton fields. It is also an important centre for the trade in gold.

Despite its contemporary metropolitan feel, Adana has historical roots going back to 1000 BC. The arrival of the Greeks precipitated an on-off power struggle between them and the powerful Persian Empire to the east that was to last for a thousand years, ending only with the arrival of the Romans during the first century BC. Under the Romans the city became an important trading centre, afterwards passing through various hands before falling to the Ottomans during the sixteenth century.

The City

The rather schizophrenic city is divided by the E5 Highway into the swanky north, with its cinemas and designer malls, and the kinetic south with the markets, mosques and hotels of the old town. The city's most substantial ancient monument is the **Taş Köprü**, a sixteen-arched Roman bridge built by Hadrian to span the Seyhan River, just east of the city centre. Not far from the bridge in the city centre, the **Ulu Cami**, on Abidin Paşa Caddesi, was built in the Syrian style out of white and black marble in 1507, the sole legacy of Halil Bey, Emir of the Ramazanoğlu Turks, who ruled Adana before the Ottoman conquest. Inside the mosque, Halil Bey's tomb has some fine tilework and beautiful mosaics.

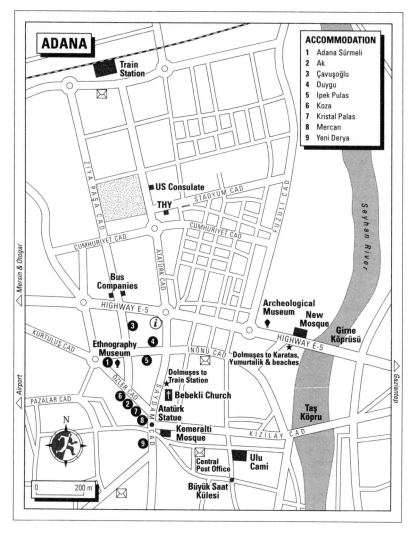

Another mosque, just off İnönü Caddesi, houses the **Ethnography Museum** (Tues–Sun 9am–6pm; $0.75), full of carpets and weaponry, with a nomad tent and contents as an added attraction. Adana's other main museum is the **Adana Archeological Museum** (Tues–Sun 8.30am–noon & 1.30–5.30pm; $1), well arranged and containing predominantly Hellenistic and Roman statuary, plus some fine sarcophagi and Hittite statues. Currently under construction is the Merkez Camii next door, testifying to the continued strength of Islam in the southeast. It will boast the highest dome in Turkey and house 28,500 people.

Practicalities

Adana's **otogar** is located about 5km out of town on the E5. Frequent dolmuşes go from here to the town centre and your bus company will probably have a *servis* minibus to their office in the centre. Conversely when you want to leave town, buy a ticket from one of these offices, which are concentrated on the E5 between Ziya Paşa and Atatürk *caddesi*s, and a *servis* bus will take you to the *otogar*. The city's **train station** is at the northern end of Ziya Paşa Caddesi, about twenty minutes' walk north of the town centre. The local **tourist information office** is at Atatürk Cad 13 (Mon–Fri 8am–5pm; ☎0322/359 1994). Adana is one of the few towns where the **airport** is closer to the centre than the bus station. To get into town from the airport, don't take a cab from outside the door unless you want to pay double; instead, walk another 50m onto the street and either get a dolmuş into the centre or a normal cab.

Adana has several **youth hostels**, each charging $5 a head per night – you'll need an IYHF, IYC or ISIC card, and it's wise to book well in advance. There's a women's hostel at Kurtulus Mah, Cumhuriyet Cad 76 (☎0322/453 1069), and a men's hostel at Çukurova Üni Meslek Y.O. Kampüsü at Ceyhan (dolmuşes from Girne Köprüsü; ☎0322/612 2451). The Fevzi Çakmak Yurdu at Çukurova Üniversitesi, Balçali Kampüsü (☎0322/338 6158), is mixed.

On and around Saydam Caddesi and Özler Caddesi, you'll find some **cheap hotels**. The *Hotel Mercan*, Ocak Meydanı 5, 39 Sok 29 (☎0322/351 2603; ①), is really good for the price, with mosquito netting and fans in all the rooms; to find it look down the side street due west of the central Atatürk statue. Just south of here is the *Yeni Derya Oteli*, Saydam Cad 46/1 Sok 3 (☎0322/351 6884; ①), a rock-bottom place bearable for one night. Heading up Özler Cadessi you'll come to the *Kristal Palas Oteli* at no. 19 (☎0322/352 2293; ①), whose grandiose reception conceals a less salubrious interior, and the similar *Ak Hotel* at no. 43 (☎0322/351 4208; ①). On İnönü Caddesi there are several old-fashioned **mid-range options**, including the overpriced but air-conditioned *Otel Duygu*, İnönü Cad 14/1 (☎0322/359 3916; ③), and the somewhat drab *İpek Palas*, İnönü Cad 103 (☎0322/351 8741; ③). For a really decent room you will have to go **upmarket** to the new, and again overpriced, *Turistik Hotel Koza*, Özler Cad 103 (☎0322/352 5857, fax 359 8571; ⑥), the better-value *Otel Çavuşoğlu*, Ziyapaşa Cad 115 (☎0322/351 1350; ④), or top-of-the-range *Adana Sürmeli Oteli*, İnönü Cad 151 (☎0322/351 7321, fax 351 8973; ⑧).

Adana's single **campsite**, on the eastern edge of town just off the main eastbound road, is the *Raşit Emer Camping*, Girne Bulvarı, İskenderum Yolu. To get there, take the Inciler dolmuş from the roundabout next to Çetinkaya shopping arcade, at the junction of Kurtuluş and İnönü *caddesi*s. The site is on the small side and noisy, but the facilities, including a restaurant and pool, are reasonably priced.

In the centre of Adana there are plenty of places to **eat and drink**. The local speciality is the spicy *Adana kebap* – minced lamb and pepper wrapped around a skewer and grilled – and one of the best places to try it is the *Onbaşılar Restorant* on Atatürk Caddesi opposite the tourist office, where you'll get the works for about $3. There are plenty of other possibilities up and down İnönü Caddesi, not least the *Yudum Kafeterya* on the corner of Atatürk and İnönü. The *Café Rose* at the western end of İnönü Caddesi is a good-value bar with food available. There are also numerous hole-in-the-wall *börek* and kebab places near the central PTT.

Listings

Car rental *Talay Turizm*, Gazipaşa Bul 48/C (daily 8am–7pm; ☎0322/454 4891); *Budget*, Gazipaşa Bul 274 Sok 33/2 (☎0322/457 0754); *Europcar*, Ziyapaşa Bul 37/B (☎0322/453 4775).

Cinemas Try the *Metro*, a couple of blocks south of the *otogar*, or the *Galleria Cinema* in the shopping complex of the same name on Fuzulı Cad.

Consulate *United States*, Atatürk Cad, Vali Yolu (☎0322/453 9106), here mainly to keep an eye on the huge air force base outside Adana.

Exchange *Turkiye Vakiflan Bankasi*, Atatürk Cad, take travellers' cheques. There are also several *döviz* offices around Saydam Cad and Özler Cad.

Hamams *Çarşi Hamam*, Büyük Saat Civari (9.30am–4pm; women only); another near the Atatürk statue (9am–4pm; men only).

Magazines *Yolgeçen Kitabevi*, 64 Atatürk Cad, for *Time*, *Newsweek* etc.

PTT The main office is on Ulu Camii Cad, the street running parallel to Kizilay Cad, for phone cards and *jeton*s.

Shopping For foodstuffs, clothing, toiletries etc, Çetinkaya shopping arcade is at the roundabout at the western end of İnönü Cad. Also try the huge Galeria (Ix 'ell') Shopping Mall on Fuzulı Cad.

THY Stadyum Cad 32 (☎0322/454 2393).

Travel agents *Aytok*, Çakmak Cad 109, and *Adana Turizm*, İnönü Cad 44, both handle national and international flights; *Cyprus Turkish Airlines*, Atatürk Cad, Arabacioğlu Işhani 5, ground floor, have 3 flights a week.

Around Adana

South of Adana lies the rich agricultural land of the **Çukurova**, a broad delta formed by silt deposits from the Ceyhan River. It's an area of extensive cotton plantations, on which much of the local economy depends, and with many Arabic-speaking pockets, a foretaste of the heavy Arab influence to be found further east. About 50km south of the city sits the small resort of **KARATAŞ**, on the southernmost tip of the delta, with a pleasant stretch of beach. Easily reached by bus or dolmuş from Adana *otogar*, it doesn't see many visitors outside of bank holidays – it's nothing special but would make an alternative to Adana if you're in the area. A recommended local **hotel** is the *Hotel Sidi* (①), and there are a couple of decent fish **restaurants**.

In the opposite direction, about 5km north of Adana, is the **Seyhan Barajı**, a huge artificial lake along whose shores bathing (though not at the southern end due to strong currents) and sailing are permitted. It's a popular weekend retreat for overheated city dwellers, who come to picnic or enjoy the many fine lakeshore restaurants and bars. The reservoir supplies the area with fresh water, and there's a bird sanctuary immediately to the west.

Towards İskenderun

Heading east from Adana, towards İskenderun and Antakya (referred to as "Hatay" at the *otogar*), the first town you reach is **YAKAPINAR** (also known as Misis), just south of the main road, where there's a small **Mosaic Museum** (Tues–Sun 9am–5pm; $0.50), worth a quick look for its examples of locally unearthed Roman mosaics. Beyond here you'll see an Armenian castle on top of a mountain, 3km to the south of the main road – the **Yılan Kalesi** or "Snake Castle" ($0.25). If you're travelling with your own car, you can drive up to the top and admire the view of the meandering Ceyhan River.

About 12km further on is **CEYHAN**, which, despite the colourful-looking old houses in the town centre, doesn't rate more than a cursory look. South of here at the end of a winding and at times hilly road is the resort of **YUMURTALIK** – a better destination than Karataş if you're after a bit of beach action. There's a small ruined castle here, built by the Knights of St John, and the place is something of a weekend destination for the people of Adana. The best **hotel** in town is the *Hotel Öztur*, and there are primitive **camping facilities** on the beach.

About 40km east of Ceyhan the road forks. Due east leads to Gaziantep and beyond, while the southern fork heads towards Antakya. The castle you can see towering above the road junction is **Toprakkale**, much fought over by the Armenians and Crusaders during medieval times but abandoned since about 1337. You can visit Toprakkale, but be careful – much of it is very unstable and there are numerous concealed cisterns waiting for unwary people to fall into them.

Karatepe Arslantaş National Park

If you have your own transport you might want to consider a seventy-kilometre detour to the **Karatepe Arslantaş National Park**, with its fine neo-Hittite stone carvings. To get there drive east for 10km to Osmaniye and then turn north, crossing the Ceyhan River and passing the columned Hellenistic ruins of Hierapolis Castabala, before following signs up to the green pines and turquoise waters of the park – the Arslantaş Dam that surrounds Karatepe's stranded site provides the perfect venue for a picnic or a barbecue. Park your car at the entrance ($0.50) and walk up to the gatehouse where you will be sold a ticket (Tues–Sun 8.30am–12.30pm & 2–5.30pm; $1) and escorted on a tour of the site.

Karatepe is thought to have been a frontier castle or summer palace of the neo-Hittite King Asitawanda, whose capital at Pahri near modern Yakapinar reached its peak around the ninth century BC before finally being sacked by the Assyrians. Little of the building complex remains, but the real reason to come is to see the eloquent **stone carvings** arranged around the two entrance gates of the former palace. Designs at the first gate depict sacrificial, hunting and feasting scenes, all guarded by sphinxes, horses and lions tattooed in hieroglyphics. The second gate has similar statues of winged sphinxes, one with eyes of ivory, and other fine carvings. Look out for a mini-pantheon of Hittite gods including Beş the Monkey God and a Hittite sun god which shows similarities to the Egyptian god Horus and the Persian Ahuramazda. There is also a spread of more personal carvings in an almost cartoon style, including one of a woman suckling her child under a date tree.

Dörtyol and Yakacık

South of Toprakkale, the Antakya road is rather nondescript, and the first major town, **DÖRTYOL** ("crossroads"), does little to break the monotony. It was about 10km north of Dörtyol that Alexander the Great defeated the Persian king Darius at the **Battle of Issus** in 333 BC. Alexander's army of about 35,000 took on a Persian force of over 100,000, but despite these unfavourable odds Alexander carried the day by personally leading an attack against Darius and his entourage. Darius panicked and fled, only narrowly avoiding capture (though he was forced to leave his wife and three children behind), and the route south was opened up for Alexander and his army. Today the exact site of the engagement is uncertain, and the task of identifying it from contemporary accounts has been made harder by the fact that, due to earthquakes, the physical appearance of the landscape has changed over the intervening two thousand years.

At **YAKACIK** (Payas) about 10km south, the little-visited sixteenth-century **Sokullu Mehmet Paşa** complex incorporates a *kervansaray*, hamam, *medrese*, bazaar and two former Genoese fortresses, all well preserved and well worth the one-kilometre detour from the main road; the site guardian is most likely to be found in the bazaar arcade opposite the hamam. A few kilometres south of here lie the classical Pillars of Jonah, the site where, according to legend, Jonah was cast from the whale. Beyond here, wayside industry and pollution prepare you for the unpleasantness of İskenderun.

THE HATAY

The **Hatay**, which extends like a stumpy finger into Syria, is an Arab enclave and has closer cultural links with the Arab world than with the Turkish hinterland. There has been some separatist tension in the area but fortunately these problems are unlikely to affect visitors, and indeed the Hatay's multi-ethnic identity gives it an extra edge of interest. **Antakya**, the largest town, is set in the valley of the Asi River separating the Nur and Ziyaret mountain ranges. The city, which dates back to Seleucid times, was an important centre under the Romans, and although little has survived from the past, Antakya's Arab atmosphere, its excellent museum and the proximity of places like **Harbiye** – the ancient resort of Daphne – and **Samandağ**, a quiet coastal town, make it worth a day or two on anyone's itinerary. The Hatay's other main centre is **İskenderun**, a heavily industrialized port of minimal interest.

Some history

The Hatay only became part of modern Turkey in 1939, having been apportioned to the French Protectorate of Syria since the dismemberment of the Ottoman Empire. It was handed over to Turkey after a plebiscite, in a move calculated to buy Turkish support, or at least neutrality, in the imminent World War. The majority of people here speak Arabic as their first language and there's some backing for union with Syria, which in 1983 led to serious unrest in Antakya. For its part, Syria is keen to see the Hatay returned, reflected in continuing border tension. The most recent outbreak was in October 1989, when the Syrian air force shot down an unarmed Turkish survey plane.

In fact, Arab influence in the Hatay goes back to the seventh century AD, when Arab raiders began hacking at the edges of the collapsing Byzantine Empire. Although they were never able to secure long-lasting political control over the region, the Arabs were able to establish themselves as permanent settlers, remaining even when the Hatay passed into Ottoman hands. Prior to the arrival of the Arabs, the area had been held by the Romans and before that the Seleucids, who prized its position straddling trading routes into Syria.

İskenderun and around

İSKENDERUN was founded by Alexander the Great to commemorate his victory over the Persians at the nearby Battle of Issus (see p.481) and, as Alexandria ad Issum, became a major trade nexus during Roman times. Under the Ottomans İskenderun became the main port for Halab (Aleppo), now in Syria, from where trade routes fanned out to Persia and the Arabian peninsula. Today there's nothing of historical interest to see here, indeed there's not much of any interest at all – modern İskenderun is basically an industrial centre and military and commercial harbour.

The local **tourist information office**, Atatürk Bul 49/B (Mon–Fri 8am–noon & 1.30–5.30pm, Sat & Sun 9am–noon & 1.30–6pm; winter closed weekends; ☎0326/614 1620), is on the waterfront 300m south of the town pier, in an area that's home to most of the town's cheaper **pansiyons and hotels**. The best of the inexpensive places is the *Hotel Açikalin*, Şehit Pamir Cad 13 (☎0326/617 3732; ①), with reasonable comfort and good-value singles. Slightly upmarket is the *Altındişler Oteli* (☎0326/617 1011; ③), practically next door to the above on Şehit Pamir Cad, and similar but with primitive air-conditioning. For real comfort, good service and pleasant surroundings, try the *Hotel Cabir* at Ulucami Cad 16 (☎0326/612 3391, fax 612 3393; ④), with an American bar, lobby and disco. Cheaper air-conditioned comfort can be found at the *Hotel İmrenay*, Şehit Pamir Cad 5 (☎0326/613 2117; ③), and the waterfront *Kıyı Otel*, just south of the tourist information office (☎0326/617 3680; ④), though you'll pay more here for the sea view than the quality of the rooms. The *Belediye* **campsite** is out to the southwest of town, reached by dolmuş ("49 Evler/Sahil Evler" on the front of the dolmuş) from Şehit Pamir Cad.

For **food**, the *Hasan Baba* at Ulucami Cad 43/E has excellent *İskender kebap*, and for afters, round the corner at Kanatlı Cad 45/B, the *Victoria Patisserie* serves excellent *karışık dondurma* (mixed ice cream), decorated with loads of fruit at ridiculously cheap prices.

Buses to all major towns including Adana and Mersin can be picked up at İnönü Meydanı on Muanner Aksoy Cad, near the *Ontur Hotel*.

Uluçınar and south of İskenderun

Dolmuşes run from Atatürk Bulvarı in İskenderun to the small resort and fishing town of **ULUÇINAR** about 40km to the southwest, where there are some decent stretches of beach (though often charging for entry) – very popular with Syrian tourists and people from İskenderun. Of a number of **hotels** and **pansiyons** in the town, best is probably the *Motel Yunus*, Akdeniz Caddesi, opposite the post office, where you'll be able to get a three-bed room for about $15. Another recommended place is the three-star *Arsuz Turistik Hotel* (☎0326/643 2444). The best **place to eat** is the waterfront *Plaj Restaurant*, which does good fish and seafood dishes. Beyond Uluçınar the coastal road exists more on maps than in reality, although if you can be bothered to follow it for a few kilometres you'll come across some more undiscovered **beaches**.

The road southeast from İskenderun rises up into the mountains, passing through the small hill town of **BELEN**, where a pair of cafés make a good place to break a long journey. It's a quiet, unspoilt place, with a few springs gushing curative water. From here the road strains and curves through the **Belen Pass** – of great strategic importance during Roman times, when it was known as the *Pylae Syriae*, the "Gates of Syria". The pass is perhaps not quite as dramatic as the name suggests, mainly bare hillside and scree slopes with few distinctive features, from where the road descends gradually into the lush Amık plain below.

About 5km beyond the Belen Pass you'll come to a major road junction, from where a right turn leads towards Antakya. After a few kilometres a sign marks the road to **Bakras Kalesi**, an imposing medieval castle about 4km off the main road and a fifteen-minute climb from the village below. The first castle to be built on this site was erected by the Arabs during the seventh century and destroyed during the First Crusade. Later the Knights Templar built a new fortress, which became an important link in their defensive system, forming the basis of what you see today. It was much fought over, and in 1156 a bloody battle took place here between the Templars and the soldiers of Thoros, ruler of Cilician Armenia. In 1188 the castle fell to Arabs but possession was fiercely contested until the Ottomans took over during the sixteenth century.

Antakya

ANTAKYA, 25km south of Bakras castle, stands on the site of ancient Antioch, and although there's little sense of historical continuity, the city's laid-back pace and heavily Arab atmosphere make it unique in Turkey. Flanked by mountains to the north and south, it sits in the bed of a broad river valley planted with olive trees – a welcome visual relief after travelling from the drab flatlands surrounding Adana.

The city was founded as Antioch on the Orontes in the fourth century BC by Seleucos Nicator, one of the four generals among whom the empire of Alexander the Great was divided. It soon grew into an important commercial centre, and by the second century BC had developed into a multi-ethnic metropolis of half a million – one of

the largest cities in the ancient world, a major staging post on the newly opened Silk Road trade routes from the Mediterranean to Asia, and a centre of scholarship and learning. It also acquired a reputation as a centre for all kinds of moral excess, causing **Saint Peter** to choose it as the location of one of the world's first Christian communities in the hope that the new religion would exercise a restraining influence.

Despite being razed by a series of earthquakes during the sixth century AD, Antioch was able to maintain its prosperity after the Roman era, and only with the rise of Constantinople did the city begin to decline. In 1098 the Crusader kings Bohemond and Raymond took the city in the name of Christianity after a vicious eight-month siege and a savage massacre of Turks, implanting a Christian rule in Antioch which lasted until the city fell to the Mamelukes of Egypt, who sacked it in 1268. By the time the Ottomans, under Selim the Grim, took over in 1516 Antioch had long since vanished from the main stage of world history, and by the turn of the last century the city was little more than a village, squatting amid the ruins of the ancient metropolis. After World War I, Antakya, along with most of the rest of the Hatay, passed into the hands of the French, who laid the foundations of the modern city.

The City

Antakya is cut in two by the Asi River, known in ancient times as the Orontes. At the heart of the city, spanning the river, is the much-renovated **Rana Köprüsü** or "Old Bridge" which dates from the third century AD. The eastern bank is home to **old Antakya** – a maze of narrow streets, backed by the rocky cliffs of the Ziyaret Dağı range (ancient Mount Sipylus). In addition to seeing the fabulous mosaics at the Archeological Museum and the Sen Piyer Kilisesi, it's well worth spending an hour or two wandering around the bazaar and market areas north of Kemal Paşa Caddesi (running from west to east just north of the Rana Köprüsü). At the eastern end of Kemal Paşa Caddesi, on the junction with Kurtuluş Caddesi, is the **Habibi Naccar Camii**, a mosque incorporated into the shell of a former Byzantine church, which was in turn built on the site of an ancient temple. The distinctive pointed minaret was added during the seventeenth century and is not – as you might be tempted to imagine – a former church tower. Some way to the east of here is the **Habibi Neccar Cave**, a minor muslim holy place that was once home to a solitary prophet. Among other lesser sights is the **Aqueduct of Trajan**, at the southeast edge of town near the hospital, a surviving fragment of the city's Roman water supply system.

The Archeological Museum

From the Rana Köprüsü, it's a quick hop across to the western side of the river and the **Archeological Museum** (Mon 1.30–5.30pm, Tues–Sun 8am–noon & 1.30–5.30pm; $2), whose collection of locally unearthed Roman **mosaics** ranks among the best of its kind in the world. Imaginatively lit and well laid-out in the first four rooms of the museum, they are in a state of near-immaculate preservation – bar the odd bare patch where the tiles have fallen off – and mostly depict scenes from Roman mythology.

The majority were unearthed at the suburb of Daphne (now Harbiye), which was Antioch's main holiday resort in Roman times, and this is reflected in the sense of leisured decadence that pervades many of the scenes, whether taken from everyday life or from the myths. A good example of the latter is the charming **Narcissus and Echo** (room 2, no. 3), which depicts Narcissus gazing admiringly into a pool of water, in love with his own reflection, as an unrequited Echo looks on in sadness. One of the finest in terms of size and scope is the so-called **Buffet Mosaic** (no. 4), a vivid depiction of the rape of Ganymede, abducted by Zeus in the form of an eagle, and a banquet scene showing different courses of fish, ham, eggs and artichokes. Memorable images in room 3 include bouncing baby **Hercules** strangling the serpents sent to kill him by jealous Hera (no. 4), and a fascinating depiction of the **Evil Eye** – a superstition that still has remarkable resonance in modern Turkey – being attacked by a raven, dog, scorpion, snake, centipede, panther, sword and trident as a horned goblin looks away (no. 6). Room 4 continues with an inebriated Dionysus, too drunk to stand (no. 12), Apollo capturing Daphne as her clothes conveniently fall off (no. 14), Orpheus surrounded by animals entranced by the beauty of his music (no. 23), and a fine portrait of **Thetis and Oceanus** (no. 24), the latter recognizable by the lobster claws protruding from his wet hair, one of many water-inspired motifs that decorated the floors of public and private baths.

After the mosaics, the rest of the museum seems a little more mundane, with only a couple of first-century AD **statues of Venus** in the entrance hall, a fine statue of **Hades and Cerberus** in the penultimate hall, and some Hittite and Assyrian reliefs and idols recovered from funeral mounds on the Amık plain, to write home about. Among the latter, look out for the two **stone lions**, which were used as column pediments during the eighth century BC.

Sen Piyer Kilisesi

At the northeastern edge of Antakya is the **Sen Piyer Kilisesi** (Tues–Sun 8am–noon & 1.30–6pm; $0.50), the famous cave church of Saint Peter, from which it's said that the apostle preached to the Christian population of Antioch. It's reached by following Kurtuluş Caddesi in a northeasterly direction for about 2km until you come to a signposted right turn. Follow a dirt track towards the mountains and after about ten minutes you come to the church, set into the hillside just above the track.

Whether Saint Peter really did preach from the Sen Piyer Kilisesi is – like the exact dates of his stay in the city – open to question. All that theologians seem to be able to agree on is that he spent some time in Antioch between AD 47 and 54, founding one of the world's first Christian communities with Paul and Barnabas. Indeed the church must have been one of the first ever built and quite possibly the place where the term "Christian" was first heard (in other parts of the Middle East Christians were known as "Nazarenes"). The slightly kitsch-looking facade of the church was built by Crusaders during the twelfth century. Inside water drips down the cave walls and the cool atmosphere provides a welcome break from the heat of summer. Beneath your feet you'll be able to discern traces of mosaic thought to date from the fifth century AD, while to the right of the altar is a kind of font set in the floor and fed by a spring with reputed curative properties. Left of the altar is a blocked tunnel down which the early Christians could flee in the event of a raid. A special service is held here on June 29 to mark the anniversary of Saint Peter's death, attended by members of Antakya's small Christian community, and Sunday afternoon mass is held here every week (more frequent masses are celebrated in a nineteenth-century church just off Kurtuluş Caddesi).

Scattered around the vicinity of the church are a few sarcophagi, and if you follow the path around to the left of the church for 200m and then clamber up the hillside, you'll find a relief thought by some to be of Charon, ferryman of the River Styx at the entrance to the Underworld – though the portrait is more likely the face of a veiled woman, with a tiny man (probably the second-century BC Seleucid emperor Antiochus Epiphanes IV) perched on her shoulder. With your own transport it's possible to drive the 15km – along Kurtuluş Caddesi and around the back of Mount Sipylus – up to the ruined *kale*, from where there are fine views over the city.

Practicalities

From the **otogar** it's a ten-to-fifteen-minute walk south to the town centre. Antakya's **tourist office** is in the new town on Vali Ürgen Meydanı (Mon–Fri 8am–noon & 1.30–5.30pm). Antakya has a good range of **hotels** in every price range. Best budget choice is the *Jasmin Hotel*, İstiklâl Cad 14 (☎0326/212 7171; ①), where rooms and communal showers are spotless, and you get access to the communal kitchen and all the hot water or tea you can drink. The only drawbacks are that the artificially lit rooms are waterless and can be noisy; those on the second floor away from the lobby television and set off from the main road are much quieter. Uninspiring cheapies include the *Hotel Güney* behind İstiklâl Cad on İstiklâl Sok 28 (☎0326/214 9113; ①), and the *Divan Hoteli*, İstiklâl Cad 62 (☎0326/215 1518; ②), both with en-suite bathrooms. A giant step up in comfort leads to the *Hotel Saray*, Hürriyet Cad 3 (☎0326/214 9001, fax 214 9002; ②), the best-value deal in Antakya with spotlessly clean rooms and breakfast thrown in with the price. For similar comfort plus air conditioning, but at around twice the price, there's the *Atahan Hotel*, Hürriyet Cad 28 (☎0326/214 2140, fax 215 8060; ③), or the long, narrow rooms of the new and characterless *Hotel Orontes*, near the *Divan Hoteli* at İstiklâl Cad 58 (☎0326/214 5931, fax 214 5933; ④). Flashiest hotel in town is the four-star *Büyuk Antakya Oteli*, Atatürk Cad 8 (☎0326/213 5860, fax 213 5869; ⑤), equipped with most of the facilities you could ever wish for.

The best places to **eat and drink** are on Hürriyet Caddesi, notably the excellent and cheap *Saray Restaurant* at no. 3, and the *Han* a few doors down at no. 19/1, which has an unprepossessing exterior but a walled garden courtyard where excellent *meze*s and *ızgara* are serverd. Local delicacies and specialities worth sampling include the ubiquitous *künefe*, a sweet crepe-like dessert made with cheese; crystallized squashes sold by weight in many of the *pastane*s; and *içli köfte*, meat wrapped in a bulgur pastry.

For **English-language papers**, magazines and a few novels, try *Ferah Koll*, Hürriyet Cad 17. The *Konak Sinemasi*, 100m east of the Rana Köprüsü behind the PTT, shows first-run Western **movies**. There are several **banks** on Istiklâl and Ataturk *caddesi*s, and you can change money at the weekends at the *Büyük Antakya Oteli* on Atatürk Cad. Under the *Büyük Antakya* is a *THY* agent.

Saint Simeon monastery, Samandağ and Çevlik

One of the more bizarre aspects of early Christianity was the craze for pillar sitting, which developed in Antioch during the fourth century. The trend was started by Simeon Stylites the Elder, whose basilica still stands at Qala'at Samaan near Halab in Syria, and was perfected by **Simeon Stylites the Younger**, whose **monastery**, perches on a high ridge southwest of Antakya, 7km south of the road to Samandağ. Simeon the Younger first chained himself to a rock in the wilderness in an act of ascetic retreat and then ascended progressively higher pillars before reaching a final height of some thirteen metres. He lived chained to the top of this **pillar** for 25 years, meditating and making sporadic pronouncements castigating the citizens of Antioch for their moral turpitude. The base of the pillar still remains, surrounded by the complex octagonal layout of the monastery that grew up around Simeon as he began to attract growing numbers of curious pilgrims eager to share in his enlightenment – about 250 followers mounted pillars of their own throughout the Middle East. Just south of the pillar you can still see the steps that pilgrims would climb to gain audience with the holy man. It's possible to climb on top of the diminutive pillar, which is just wide enough to lay down on and reap the same views of the Orontes Valley and of Mount Cassius looming out of the Mediterranean that Simeon must have enjoyed over fifteen centuries ago.

To reach the monastery turn south off the main Antakya–Samandağ road at **Uzunbağ**, just past Karaçay, and continue uphill along a good road for about 4km, before branching off to the right, by a white muslim shrine, and following a bad dirt track for another couple of kilometres. There is no public transport to the monastery, but you should be able to find a taxi in Karaçay willing to take you.

Samandağ

About 25km southwest of Antakya, **SAMANDAĞ** is an Arabic-speaking resort town of about 30,000 people (though it feels smaller), decaying genteelly on a sloping plain between the hills and the Mediterranean. It's a popular place, especially with Syrians and other Arab visitors, served by regular dolmuşes from Antakya *otogar* which will deposit you in the town's unprepossessing centre, a couple of kilometres inland. Here you'll find a few shops and restaurants and a couple of banks.

To get to **the beach**, take any dolmuş heading for "*Deniz*" ("the sea") – although swimming here is not really recommended because of pollution from İskenderun, 50km or so up the coast. There are a couple of **hotels** close to the beach, best of which is the colonial-style *Dervişan Tesisleri* (☎0326/512 1656; ②). The hotel also has a **restaurant** which does good food and acts as a social focus for the area. Next door is the *Dönmez Hotel Restaurant* (☎0326/512 1841), where the emphasis is more on the restaurant side of the operation, but they have six very basic rooms up on the roof.

Çevlik (Seleucia ad Piera)

A few kilometres north of Samandağ is the village of **ÇEVLİK**, easily reached along the beach – although the path is marred by a stinking refuse tip midway between the villages. You can also reach Çevlik by dolmuş from Samandağ town centre. The village has a few **pansiyons** and a **campsite**, and you can also camp on the beach, although strictly speaking this is illegal and you might get moved on. In ancient times Çevlik was the port of **Seleucia ad Piera**, serving Antioch, and it is from here that Paul and Barnabus are thought to have set off on their first evangelical mission to Cyprus. There are still a few ruins scattered around, including the 130-metre-long **Titus ve Vespasiyanus Tüneli** (dawn–dusk; $1), a huge channel carved out of the hillside to prevent flooding and silting of the harbour. Two inscriptions at the upper end give details of its construction. Also scattered around you'll see foundations, sections of ruined wall and Roman tombs. Again, swimming is probably unwise, although the village beach is popular with local fishermen.

South of Antakya: Harbiye and the road to Syria

About 10km south of Antakya is **HARBİYE**, the ancient and celebrated suburb of Daphne, a beautiful gorge to which revellers and holidaymakers flocked in Roman times, drawn by shady cypress and laurel groves dotted with waterfalls and pools. Those who could afford to built villas here, while lesser mortals had to content themselves with a day trip. Today Antakya's modern citizens follow their example and Arab tourists have their summer residences in the village; and there is a regular **dolmuş** service from just north of the city *otogar*. From the dolmuş drop-off point follow a road uphill past modern houses until you come to a waterfall. From here follow the path down into the gorge, where a number of shady tea gardens (but not much else) await amid a landscape that can have hardly altered since Roman times. Several resort **hotels** ring the gorge, including the comfortable *Çağleyan* (☎0326/231 4011; ③), and the cheaper *Hotel Çinar* (②), though there's little reason to stay here now.

The Romans built a temple to Apollo here, since it was generally held to be the setting for the god's pursuit of Daphne. According to the myth, Daphne, when seized by amorous Apollo, prayed for deliverance; in answer to her prayers, Peneus transformed her into a laurel tree. Another legend relates that the resort was the venue of Paris's gift of the golden apple to Aphrodite, indirectly precipitating the Trojan War. Later, and with possibly more basis in fact, Mark Antony and Cleopatra are said to have been married here. Harbiye was also home of the Antioch Games, which were in their day more spectacular than the ancient Olympics, and a haven for escaped slaves and prostitutes, who ran a brisk trade among the laurels. In later years local Christians pulled down the temple of Apollo, and used its stone to build their churches. With the departure of the Romans the place went into decline, a process compounded by the destructive attacks of the Persians and Arabs during the sixth and seventh centuries. Now Harbiye is famous for Defue soap, made from the fruit of the laurel tree and doubling as shampoo. Another local speciality are wolf and fox pelts, hunted from the surrounding hills and sold in gift shops.

About 8km south of Harbiye lies **Qalat az Zaw**, a ruined fortress originally built to defend the southern approaches to Antioch and much fought over by Crusaders, Arabs and Mamelukes. Twenty-odd kilometres further on, close to the Syrian border, is the village of **YAYLADAĞI**, a quiet spot that has a pleasant **picnic area**, set in mountain woods down towards the frontier – a good point for a break if you're en route to the border itself.

Near Yayladağı is the 1759-metre **Djebel Akra**, the ancient Mount Cassius, a sacred summit since Hittite times and the site of an ancient temple of Zeus, to whom Seleucus made sacrifices before choosing the site of Antioch's port. If you want to explore the mountain you need permission from the local civil and military authorities, and you have to hire a guide – enquire at Antakya tourist office.

travel details

Trains

Adana to: Ankara (daily overnight; 14hr); Gaziantep (4 weekly; 3hr); Mersin (6 daily; 1hr 15min).

Mersin to: Adana (6 daily; 1hr 15min).

Buses and dolmuşes

Adana to: Adıyaman (7 daily; 6hr); Alanya (8 daily; 10hr); Ankara (hourly; 10hr); Antalya (3 daily; 12hr); Diyarbakır (3 daily; 10hr); Gaziantep (5 daily; 4hr); Kâhta (2 daily; 7hr); Kayseri (3 daily; 7hr); Konya (hourly; 7hr); Malatya (3 daily; 8hr); Şanlıurfa (4 daily; 6hr); Van (1 daily; 18hr).

Alanya to: Adana (8 daily; 10hr); Ankara (8 daily; 10hr); Antalya (every 30min; 2hr); İstanbul (4 daily; 18hr); Konya (3 daily; 8hr); Mersin (8 daily; 9hr); Samsun (1 daily; 24hr); Silifke via Taşucu (8 daily; 7hr).

Antakya to: Adana (hourly; 3hr); Aleppo (4 daily; 4hr); Gaziantep (8 daily; 5hr); İskenderun (hourly;1hr); Samandağ (hourly; 1hr); Şanlıurfa (daily; 8hr).

Antalya (central *otogar*) to: Adana (several daily; 11hr); Afyon (almost around the clock; 5hr); Alanya (hourly; 2hr); Ankara (almost around the clock; 10hr); Denizli (6 daily; 5hr 30min); Fethiye, by inland route (3 daily; 4hr); Isparta (hourly; 2hr 30min); İzmir (6 daily; 9hr 30min); Kaş (7 daily; 4hr 30min); Kemer (every 30min; 45min); Konya (6 daily; 6hr 30min).

Silifke to: Adana (every 15–20min; 2hr); Alanya (8 daily; 7hr); Antalya (8 daily; 9hr); Konya (12 daily; 5hr); Mersin (every 20min; 2hr).

Ferries

Antalya to: Venice (1 fortnightly; 71hr).

Mersin to: Mağosa (Famagusta, north Cyprus; 3 weekly; 10hr), with an onward service to Syria during summer.

Taşucu to: Girne (Kyrenia, north Cyprus; 2 daily except Fri & Sat; 6hr).

Hydrofoils

Taşucu to: Girne (Kyrenia, north Cyprus; 2 daily; 2hr 30min).

Planes

Adana to: Ankara (2 daily; 1hr); İstanbul (4 daily; 1hr 15min); İzmir (3 weekly; 1hr 30min); Lefkoşa (Nicosia, north Cyprus; 3 weekly; 1hr).

Antalya to: Ankara (1 daily on *THY*; 1hr); İstanbul (6 daily; most on *THY* but some on *İstanbul Hava Yolları*; 1hr 5min).

CHAPTER SEVEN

SOUTH CENTRAL ANATOLIA

Whatever your plans, the central Anatolian plateau seems at first sight to be an unpromising prospect. A large area around the lake of Tuz Gölü is virtual desert, and much more of the central plateau is steppe, suitable only for the grazing of livestock. During summer water is scarce except in the river valleys and in areas which have been artificially irrigated, and in winter the region is blitzed by cold and heavy snowfall. Gertrude Bell recorded the impressions of a European traveller approaching the central plateau in 1909:

> *Before him stretch wide plains, corn-growing where rainfall and springs permit, often enough barren save for a dry scrub of aromatic herbs, or flecked with shining miles of saline deposit; naked ranges of mountains stand sentinel over this featureless expanse; the sparse villages, unsheltered from wind or sun, lie along the skirts of the hills, catching thirstily at the snow-fed streams that are barely enough for the patch of cultivated ground below; the weary road deep in dust or mud according to the season, drags its intolerable length to the horizon. It is Asia, with all its vastness, with all its brutal disregard for life and comfort and the amenities of existence; it is the Ancient East, returned after so many millenniums of human endeavour to its natural desolation.*

The "shining miles of saline deposit" constitute part of the Turkish **Lakeland**, the region south of **Afyon** and west of **Konya**, largely ignored by the Turkish tourist industry. These stretches of azure or silver waters stand out against the grey plateau, or appear suddenly between mountains to startling effect. Many of them, like **Çavuşçu Göl** or **Acı Göl**, have a high salt content which discourages aquatic life and human settlement alike; others are avoided as their flat shores are liable to flood. Only the residents of **Eğirdir** and the small community on the banks of **Akşehir Gölü** manage to make a tenuous living out of fishing their respective lakes, and Eğirdir is an increasingly popular stop-over for passing tour parties and backpackers.

To the east of the lakes, the plateau rises gradually towards the highlands. **Tuz Gölü** to the north is little more than a vast salt-producing basin, and aridity in the region is increased by the underground dissipation of water. To make matters worse, the light

---

ACCOMMODATION PRICE CODES

In this guide, motels and nearly all hotels and *pansiyon*s have been categorized according to the price codes outlined below, which are based on US$ because of the high domestic Turkish inflation rate. These categories represent the minimum you can expect to pay for a **double room in high season**. Rates for hostels and for the most basic hotels and *pansiyon*s, where guests are charged **per person**, are given in US$, instead of being indicated by price code. For further information, including a rough outline of what you might expect in each category, see p.37.

① under $12	② $12–17	③ $18–25
④ $26–35	⑤ $36–45	⑥ $46–55
⑦ $56–75	⑧ over $75	

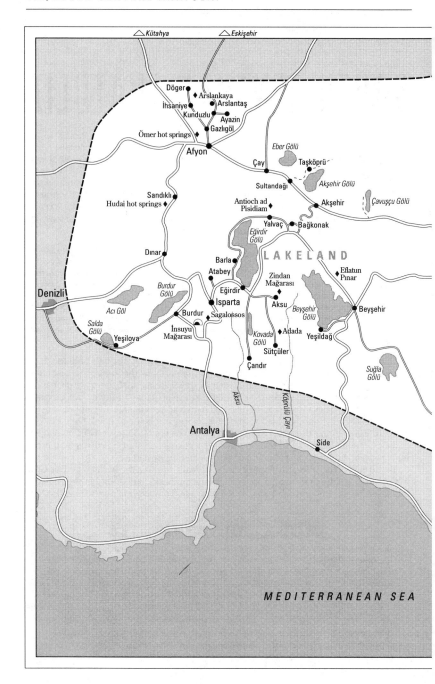

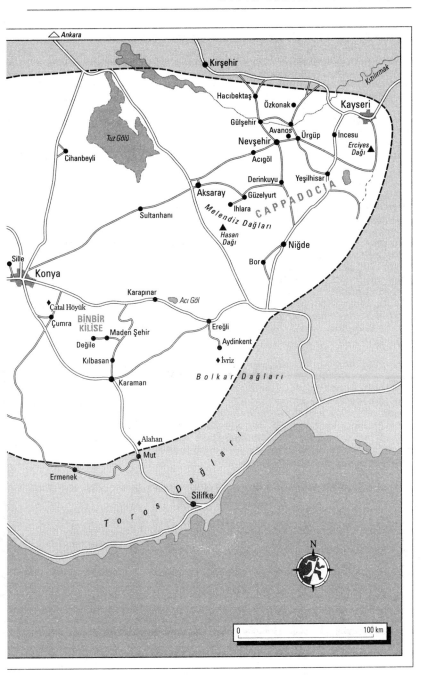

forest that once covered this land was destroyed between 5000 and 1000 BC by herds of livestock that grazed the steppe.

Despite the inhospitable nature of this region, it has been populated as long as anywhere in Anatolia. From the early Paleolithic Age man was drawn to the lakes, which provided a livelihood for primitive hunters and fishermen, and during the Bronze Age the **Hittites**, a race who once rivalled the Egyptians, chose the plateau as their homeland. By the early historical period, northern Lakeland had been settled by the **Pisidians**, mountain people with a reputation for fierce independence who worked as mercenaries throughout the eastern Mediterranean. Their strategically situated settlements were difficult to subdue, and Xenophon described them as obstinate troublemakers, who managed to keep their towns independent despite the encroachments of the Persian Empire.

Further east, the area between the extinct volcanoes of **Erciyes Dağ** and the Melendiz range is **Cappadocia**, whose legacy of compacted lava-ash soil is favourable to vine-growing and horse-breeding. Water and wind have created a land of fantastic forms from the soft rock known as tuff, including forests of cones, table mountains, canyon-like valleys and castle-rocks, all further hewn and shaped by civilizations which have found the region particularly sympathetic to their needs. Rainfall is low, but Cappadocia is nevertheless extremely fertile compared to the rest of South Central Anatolia, and it became an important crossroads and home to a politically autonomous state between the third and first centuries BC. From the seventh to the eleventh centuries AD, it was a place of refuge during Arab and Turkish invasions into the steppe. Today its churches and dwellings carved from the rock, particularly by monastic communities, and its unearthly landscapes make an irresistible tourist draw, and Cappadocia is certainly likely to prove the highlight of any travels in this region.

LAKELAND

One of the country's least visited, most underexploited areas, the Turkish **Lakeland** seems just waiting to be discovered by tourism. Until it is, facilities may not be five-star, but the various eye-catching lakes, as well as **natural attractions** around Eğirdir, remains of Pisidian cities, the monuments of the Selçuks and later local emirates, plus largely unspoilt provincial towns, together make it ideal for quiet, unhurried holidays away from the seething coastal resorts.

THE LAKES

There are three types of lakes in the Lakeland region: the usually mild-to-strong alkaline ones in narrow sunken basins with shores fixed by mountain borders, like Burdur Gölü; others which are residual sheets of once much larger lakes and now resemble marshes, with an even higher salt content that varies according to the surface evaporation (that of Acı Göl is 101 grammes per litre); then there are those filling depressions in karstic plains, caused by the clogging of underground outlets by the clay which is produced when limestone dissolves. These include relatively shallow stretches of fresh water like the lakes of Beyşehir, Eğirdir and Akşehir, the last of which is so reed-fringed and shallow that it sometimes dries out completely. Although animal life is sparse, most of the less salty lakes contain fish of some kind – even if it's just one species – and have supported small human communities since they were first fished in the early Paleolithic Age.

Afyon

Dominated by a tall and imposing rock on which stands a powerful ancient citadel, **AFYON**'s skyline certainly leaves a vivid impression. The town remains impressive on closer inspection: it is clean and relaxed, retaining much interesting Ottoman architecture as well as a number of attractive mosques. In addition, a few reasonably priced hotels and their restaurants make it a good choice for a night's stop-over.

In honour of the fortress, and the 200-metre-high **dark rock** on which it's built, the city until recently bore the resounding name of Afyon Karahisar (**Opium Black Fortress**). The rock is believed to have first been fortified by the Hittite king Mursil II, and remains have also been found dating to the Phrygian era. The Romans and Byzantines – who called the city Akronium or "High Hill" – also occupied the city, the Byzantines building the greater part of the present-day fortress, which was subsequently used as an imperial treasury by both Selçuks and Ottomans.

For three weeks leading up to August 26, 1922, Afyon was Atatürk's headquarters, prior to the last, decisive battle of the independence war, fought against the Greeks at nearby Dumlupınar. The town's statue commemorating the Turkish victory – depicting one naked man towering over another in an attitude of victory – is one of the most moving memorials to Atatürk.

Today Afyon is a relative backwater, noted for its production of *sucuk* (sausage), *pastırma* (pastrami) and *kaymak* (clotted cream) – and its role as a stronghold of fundamentalists and right-wing nationalists. When Elia Kazan, the noted American filmmaker of Anatolian Greek descent, was looking for a location in western Asia Minor in the mid-1980s to shoot a historical extravaganza, he approached the city fathers for permission to use Afyon's exquisite old town as the setting – and was told in no uncertain terms to go elsewhere.

The Town

Arrival in Afyon is pretty straightforward. The **train station** is at the far end of Ordu Bulvarı, about 500m from the centre, while the **otogar** is about the same distance east of town on the *çevre yolu* (ring road). Both terminals are linked with the middle of town by a dolmuş service marked "Sanayi/PTT" which provides an initially not very enticing introduction to the city. Towards the end of its run it does, however, pass close by all the city's best hotels, coming to rest at a terminal on Ambaryolu, two blocks behind the main PTT (which stands on the main north–south street, Milli Egemenlik Caddesi). The **tourist information office** (Mon–Fri 8am–noon & 1.30–5.30pm; ☎0272/214 1221) is on the ground floor of the Hükümet Konağı, Hükümet Konağı Meydanı, opposite the Belediye Parkı, off Milli Egemenlik Caddesi.

The best way of establishing what's where on arrival is to head for the highest point in town: the **fortress** on its 226-metre-high black monolith, which you have to climb some 700 steps on the southern face of the rock to reach. On the way up look out for hoopoes among the varied birdlife, and at the top for votive rags, representing wishes, tied to trees by petitioners. If you ascend at prayer time, the calls to prayer from as many as eighty minarets resound and echo off the rock to dramatic effect.

The fortress itself is thought to stand on the site of the Hittite fortress of Khapanouwa, built around the middle of the second millennium BC. The rock was subsequently fortified by the Phrygians, the Byzantines and the Turks, but all that remains now are a few crenellated walls and towers to be clambered on mainly for the views they offer; as you look out, a fair amount of light industry is evident on the outskirts of the city but the centre remains well planned and attractive.

OPIUM

A town called **"Opium"** (the translation of *Afyon*) could hardly be accused of reticence concerning its most controversial claim to fame. This region produces 25 percent of the world's legal opiates: it used to be almost half, but in 1971 the United States forced Turkey to impose a ban on production because of the extent of illegal drug trafficking. This had reached a height in the late 1960s, when control was so slack that everyone from small-time users to international marketeers were converging on the area to reap the harvest for themselves. Nowadays, although poppy seeds are sprinkled liberally on bread loaves and the leaves of the plant are used in salads, all of the 20,000 tonnes of capsules processed around Afyon must arrive at the factory intact, and the poppy fields are regularly patrolled by government officials. If you want to take a look at the crop, head out of town in June on the Sandıklı road for around 5km, and the open fields of poppies are clearly visible from the road.

While the authorities may be circumspect about touting the city's eponymous enterprise as a tourist attraction, there are still telltale signs of civic pride in the traditional industry: a close look at the fountain in the town square reveals that it is a graceful bronze sculpture of poppy seed-pods.

Immediately surrounding the fortress rock is the **old town**, a warren of tiny streets frequented by gangs of street urchins speaking Turkish in the peculiar local dialect and a few words of English. Afyon's domestic **Ottoman architecture** is renowned in Turkey; the half-timbered houses here all support overhanging upper storeys, some even complete with a *kafes*, the wooden latticework on the windows designed to protect the chastity of a household's womenfolk. Some showcase pieces in the streets bordering Ulu Cami have undergone restoration, but in most cases it is still sorely needed.

There are a number of impressively old and well-preserved mosques near the citadel, with many more somewhat less distinguished ones in the bazaar proper. Opposite the base of the steps leading up the side of the rock stands Afyon's most ancient mosque, the **Ulu Cami** (outside of prayer time wait for the caretaking *bekçi* to let you in; small donation). This typically square Selçuk construction, built between 1272 and 1277, has been restored, so its originally flat roof is now pitched, but it retains forty original carved wooden columns with stalactite capitals and beams supporting a fine geometric ceiling.

Slightly downhill from the Ulu Cami, the **Mevlevi Camii** is a double-domed mosque noticeable for its pyramid-roofed *son cemaat yeri*, a porch in which latecomers pray – literally the "place of last congregation". The adjoining *semahane* or ceremonial hall has a walnut-wood floor on which Mevlevi dervishes once performed their whirling ceremony. The building has now been converted into a **museum of the Mevlevi** (open at prayer times or on request to the *imam*), with exhibits of musical instruments and the ceremonial costumes of the dervishes. Afyon became the second largest centre of the Mevlevi order after this branch of Islamic mysticism was introduced to the city from Konya by the son of the Mevlâna, Sultan Veled.

The **Archeological Museum** (closed indefinitely due to an incident of vandalism), 1km east of the centre on Kurtuluş Caddesi, is labelled only in Turkish but is worth a visit, if it has reopened: the collection is housed in a light, airy building and the objects are nicely displayed. The most interesting are Roman, excavated at nearby Çardalı and Kovalık Höyük, dating from the third and fourth centuries AD. Exhibits from this period include a small marble statue of Diana and a price list from an agora, outside in the covered gallery.

Also on Kurtuluş Caddesi but nearer the centre in its own patch of parkland, the **Gedik Ahmet Paşa Külliyesi** was built for one of the viziers of Mehmet the Conqueror in 1477. Adjoining it are a stone *medrese* and a functioning hamam – the original marble floors are in good condition, but it's otherwise in a bad state of repair, smelly and dirty.

The complex's mosque, identified as the İmaret Camii, has a fluted minaret dashed with zigzagging blue İznik tiles. The *medrese* of the mosque complex houses the local ethnographical museum (Tues–Sun 8am–noon & 1.30–5pm; $0.50), whose exhibits, though labelled solely in Turkish, are well lit and organized. The main emphasis is on locally produced felt, including a Turkmen *topakev* (nomad's tent) and a shepherd's cloak. Among other exhibits are faithful reconstructions of a local feltworks and a cobbler's shop.

Atatürk's brief stay in Afyon is commemorated in a museum, the **Zafer Müzesi** (daily 9am–5pm; free), opposite the tourist information office on Milli Egemenlik Caddesi. This is the building in which he planned his victory at Dumlupınar: his office has been preserved, and weapons and other paraphernalia from the war, as well as old photos of Atatürk and Afyon, are on show.

Practicalities

There are three extremely comfortable luxury-class **hotels** in town: the *Hotel Soydan* on Milli Egemenlik Caddesi (☎0272/215 6070; ③), a friendly and modern place which is currently best value in town; the *Oruçoğlu* also on Milli Egemenlik Caddesi (☎0272/212 0120; ④); and the *Ece* on Ordu Bulvarı (☎0272/215 7871, fax 215 6265; ④). The *Oruçoğlu* has a good restaurant with views of the castle and a fixed menu at around $9 a head. Cheaper options for a bed include the dusty, rather rundown *Otel Mesut*, by the PTT at Dumlupınar Cad 5 (☎0272/212 0429; ②); and the slightly better-value but similarly old-fashioned *Sinada* at Ambaryolu 25 (☎0272/215 6350; ②), where some rooms have views of the citadel.

The *Otel Naman* (☎0272/212 0948; ③), close to the train station and the Devlet Hastanesi (State Hospital) on the Ankara–İzmir road, represents excellent value, and has a pleasant terraced **restaurant** on the top floor, where you'll be plied with a good selection of *meze*s and meat dishes; they also serve up the regional speciality of *kaymak* on demand. The old-fashioned *İkbal Lokantası*, on Uzun Çarşı (the other side of Milli Egemenlik Cad from the *Oruçoğlu*), ranks as the most famous restaurant in town, with such arcane specialities as bull's bollocks (*billur*, "crystal", is the menu euphemism). Judging by its canopied exterior and well-furnished interior, the *Adem Usta*, on Ordu Bulvarı, looks pricy, but in fact it's excellent value for filling *ezo gelin* soup, *izgara*, and a selection of ice creams to follow: a three-course meal for two will come to around $7.

Around Afyon

The most interesting side-trip from Afyon is to see a series of sixth-century Phrygian sites, notable for their stone carvings, in the vicinity of **İHSANİYE**. The trip is best done with your own transport, but there are three convenient daytime **trains** from Afyon to İhsaniye, as well as **dolmuşes** that leave from a garage at Ordu Bulvarı 11a opposite the tourist office. It's about a forty-minute journey, and beyond İhsaniye it's necessary to hitch, walk or rent a dolmuş to take you to Döğer (about 10km north of İhsaniye) or Ayazin (about 15km east of İhsaniye, 30km from Afyon). You can also get a bus straight to the village of Kunduzlu, near Ayazin, from Voyvoda Gazlıgöl Caddesi, opposite the *Belediye* building in town.

Best of all are the remains of a Phrygian town located in the modern-day village of **AYAZİN**, reached via a right turn off the minor Afyon–Eskişehir road at Kunduzlu. **Cave houses** and a well-preserved ninth-century **Byzantine church** are visible across fields of opium poppies on the road to the village. Closer observation reveals lion reliefs, and the scars from excavations by locals and archeologists, who have found coins and other objects in the rooms.

The rock-cut tomb of **Arslantaş** (Lion Stone), near the village of **KAYA** (formerly Hayranveli), is flanked by another relief of lions, two enormous beasts snarling at each other with bared teeth. This should not be confused with another Phrygian cult monument called **Arslankaya** (Lion Rock), featuring a high relief of the goddess Cybele flanked by two more enormous lions. Arslankaya is near Lake Emre in the village of **DÖĞER**, where the remains of a fifteenth-century Ottoman *kervansaray* can also be found.

Some spas

The Afyon region is also well known for its **hot springs**, whose waters bubble up at temperatures between 60 and 80°C and have a high content of fluoride, bromide and calcium salts. Mineral water from this region is bottled and sold all over Turkey. Visits to the closest spa, **Ömer**, 15km from town on the Kütahya road, and to **Heybelli**, 25km east of Afyon on the Sultandağı road, can be made by dolmuş, leaving from in front of the *Belediye* building.

Hudai Kaplıcıları, beyond Sandıklı off the Denizli road, is the most organized of the spa resorts and worth a visit if only for a wallow in its deep mud baths. It's hard to get there without your own transport, however, as there's a further six-kilometre hike from the turning 6km beyond Sandıklı. The *Sandıklı Termal* **hotel** at Hudai (☎0272/535 7320; ⑤; baths daily 8am–5pm, $4) has a neighbouring **campsite**, mud baths, a hot spring hamam and an outdoor pool. The spring water here contains high levels of sodium, chloride, magnesium and calcium salts, and is principally a curative for rheumatic diseases – though it's claimed to cure any number of ailments, including kidney stones, neuralgia and chronic period pains. The mud baths are supposed to heal joint and spine calcification.

Sultandağı and Akşehir

Sixty-seven kilometres out of Afyon on the Konya road, **SULTANDAĞI** is a reasonably large cherry- and apple-processing town with only a badly ruined Selçuk *kervansaray* and access to the marshy lakes of **Eber Gölü** and **Akşehir Gölü** to recommend it. The town is basically a dump; if you're forced to **stay overnight**, there's only the rather spartan *Hotel Mehtap* (☎0272/656 2665).

The small provincial town of **AKŞEHİR**, about halfway between Konya and Afyon, has scarcely any more to offer visitors. If you're compelled to **stay**, the *Otel Yaşar*, between the *otogar* and bazaar, has acceptable rooms with baths, while you can **eat** at the nearby *Şehir Lokantası*, actually a licensed *meze*-grill. More likely, you'll just end up with an hour to waste here awaiting a train (the **station** is 2km northeast of town on the main highway) or a bus connection south towards Eğirdir, in which case it's worth dashing out for a visit to the **türbe of Nasrettin Hoca**, situated in a beautiful park five minutes from the *otogar*. The tomb, located in a green pavilion open on three sides but with a locked gate on the fourth, honours the fourteenth-century folk hero and Akşehir native Nasrettin Hoca. A vast body of satirical tales and jokes are attributed to this comic figure, but even in translation they're lost on modern, English-speaking sensibilities, as many souvenir-book purchasers have learned to their cost. The beturbanned *hoca* is often pictured seated on his equally famous donkey, and his descendants still jog about the surrounding countryside on the beasts, which predominate until the Aegean valleys and their horse-culture are reached.

Isparta and around

The road between Akşehir and Bağkonak, the most direct route to the heart of Lakeland, climbs and winds through beautiful mountainous scenery; beyond Bağkonak it plunges down towards Eğirdir and its eponymous lake, eventually following the shore round into town. However, public transport along this route is exceedingly sparse, so you'll most likely be approaching the lakes from Afyon, via Isparta.

Isparta

ISPARTA doesn't have anything like the attractions of neighbouring Eğirdir, being a mostly modern town whose only suggestion of romantic appeal lies in its chief industries: **rosewater**, distilled here for over a century, and **carpets**. Otherwise there's good transport in and out – and some comfortable hotels which are better equipped to deal with Anatolian winters, though not better value, than those in the holiday town of Eğirdir (see below).

Some history

Isparta has long been an important city. In its early years it was occupied by Hittites and Lydians before being ruled briefly by the Macedonians. After Selçuk occupation in 1203, Isparta, like Eğirdir, was one of the cities which came under the control of the Hamidoğlu emirates towards the end of the thirteenth century, and was capital of a territory delimited by the four great lakes of Beyşehir, Burdur, Akşehir and Eğirdir. In the face of Ottoman expansion the Hamidoğlu emir cut his losses and sold the kingdom to the Ottoman sultan Murat I in 1381, and thereafter its star waned. Only when Eğirdir lost its importance did Isparta and neighbouring Burdur regain significance as market towns in their respective areas. This process gained impetus towards the end of the last century, when large numbers of Muslim refugees from the Balkans settled in the area, particularly Bulgarians who brought their rosewater-distilling skills with them. The local carpet industry dates from approximately the same era.

The Town

As for spending time here, there's not a whole lot to see or do, but enough to stop you from going crazy between buses. There's a simple, clean **hamam**, *Yeni Hamam* (men only), in the town centre, opposite the Müftülüğü on the corner of Zübeyde Hanım Caddesi and Eski Tabakhane Caddesi.

The **Ulu (Kutlubey) Cami** nearby dates from 1417, its size and grandeur attesting to the importance of the town in Ottoman times; but the terrible late-Ottoman restoration with arabesque painting and light green walls doesn't do it justice. A better monumental destination is the **old residential quarter**, above and behind the *Büyük Isparta Otel*. The town's **Archeological Museum** (daily 8.30am–noon & 1.30–6pm; $0.50), on Kenan Evren Caddesi 500m northeast of the *Belediye* building, has a few interesting remains from the early Bronze Age, Roman and Byzantine periods, shakily labelled in English, and the rest is devoted to ethnography, with Isparta carpets exhibited upstairs.

Many of those **carpets** are machine-woven and thus not really refined collector's items; they're instead meant to cover large floor areas decoratively but economically. You can see and buy them best in the **Halı Sarayı**, a wholesale and retail bazaar just behind the *Belediye* building.

Practicalities

Isparta's regional **Directorate of Tourism** (*Turizm Müdürlüğü*) is on the third floor of the massive Vallikonağı (town hall), on Hükümet Meydanı, next to the main square Kaymakkapı Meydanı (Mon–Fri 8am–5pm). The **train station** is at the far end of Hükümet Caddesi from the town centre, a half-kilometre walk, and the **otogar** is 5km out of town on Mimar Sinan Caddesi – take a bus marked "Otogar–Yedişehitler–Mimar Sinan" into town. *Gürman* buses from Ankara, İzmir, İstanbul, Bursa, Edirne and Gaziantep arrive at a small car park on the other side of Ulu Cami from the Vallikonağı.

The best of the mid-range **hotel** options is the three-star *Hotel Artan*, located in a quiet backstreet off the main drag at Cengiz Topel Cad 12/B (☎0246/232 5700, fax 218 6629; ④), with well-kept, well-furnished and centrally heated rooms with TVs. The most prominent comfortable hotel in town is the *Büyük Isparta* on Kaymakkapı Meydanı (☎0246/232 7001, fax 232 4086; ⑤); with a similar degree of comfort, but slightly more expensive, is the *Hotel Bolat* off Kaymakkapı Meydanı at Demirel Bul 67 (☎0246/223 9001, fax 218 5506; ⑤). In both these hotels rooms are centrally heated and equipped with televisions; the rooftop restaurant of the *Bolat* is more reasonable than that of the *Isparta*. A good cheap option is the *Hotel Altuğ*, off Mimar Sinan Caddesi on 1738 Sokak (☎0246/232 2624; ②), where the only disadvantage is that the rooms – with bathrooms – are on the small side. The nearby *Selçuk Otel*, Cami Sok 10 (☎0246/218 4724; ③), has better rooms but isn't really worth the jump in price.

A good cheap **restaurant** is the *Haci Mehmet Et Lokantası* opposite the Firdersbey Camii on Mimar Sinan Caddesi, where they serve a wide selection of fresh *pide*, steam-tray stews, *izgara*, and soup.

Money exchange is best done at any of the change offices on Mimar Sinan Caddesi; otherwise, the *Büyük Isparta* changes money for a commission. The **PTT** is near the Vallikonağı on Hükümet Caddesi, the road which runs perpendicular to Mimar Sinan at its south end.

West and south of Isparta

If the town itself isn't that exciting, Isparta does make a good base from which to explore the lakes to the west, and a spectacular cave and the remains of an ancient city to the south. **Gölcük**, the closest attraction 13km southwest, is a tiny crater lake surrounded by trees, with a picnic area nearby in a clearing. You'll need your own transport to get there through fields of cultivated roses: take İsmet Paşa Caddesi out of town. On the way, to the right of the road, you'll pass the Milas picnic spot with a little artificial lake and tables beneath the trees. The management can offer a barbecue (*mangal*) and *şiş kebap*.

Burdur

BURDUR may look promising on the map, but in fact it's situated some way from its lake, and there's little reason to spend time in the town itself. It's known to Turks mostly as the location of an army camp where privileged youths with the money and connections to buy out of most of their military service do a token, two-month stint. Despite its status as a provincial capital, flat-roofed village houses are in evidence, and the only impressive monument is a fourteenth-century mosque, the **Ulu Cami**, a relic of the Hamidoğlu dynasty.

If you get stranded here, the *Burdur Oteli* (③) right in the middle of town has **rooms** with showers, as well as a decent **restaurant**; at lunchtime the *Emniyet Lokantası* at Cümbüzlü Cad 9 is recommended for steamtray food. Frequent **dolmuşes** cover the scenic hour's drive from Isparta to Burdur, and there are regular onward services towards the lake.

The **lake**, situated to the northwest of town, is most easily reached along Highway 330 to Denizli and Acıpayam. Dolmuşes will drop you 5km from Burdur at its most popular bathing area, the five-kilometre-long **Çendik Beach**, location of the *Çendik Touristik Motel* (☎0248/242 8088; ③). The 200-square-kilometre lake is extremely saline (21 grammes of salt per litre) and surrounded by desert-like **badlands** developing in the surrounding clay and sand.

Salda Gölü

Continuing 70km west from Burdur, **Salda Gölü** lies about halfway to Denizli, 6km from Yeşilova, where you'll have to change dolmuş. The westernmost of the lakes, Salda Gölü is a crystal-green expanse, its water lightly alkaline but pleasant to swim in.

A succession of campsites, restaurants, the *Hotel Şahman* (☎0248/618 0480; ④) and a forest service picnic area line the south shore road, with the scenery becoming more appetizing and pine-fringed as you proceed from east to west.

İnsuyu Mağarası

The 600-metre-long **İnsuyu Mağarası** is well signposted off the Burdur–Antalya road, 14km from Burdur, and easily reached on any Antalya-bound bus. The cave (daily 8.30am–6pm; $0.50) is well organized with lighting and footpaths. It's nothing like as much of an adventure to explore as the Zindan Mağarası (see p.505), but it does have a series of seven beautiful underwater lakes, the largest of which, Büyük Göl, measures 150m by 30m and can attain a seasonal depth of 15m. Its mineral-rich water is phosphorescent blue, warm, and supposedly therapeutic for diabetics. Be warned that especially in late summer the lakes are prone to dry up, in which case the caves will be much less impressive.

Sagalossos

One of the more impressive ancient sites in the region is the city of **SAGALOSSOS**, the second most prominent Pisidian settlement after Antioch (see p.504), and also one of the oldest. Its people were mentioned in 1224 BC as being among "the people of the sea" who attacked the Egyptian coast, and according to Livy its inhabitants were "by far the most warlike in the country".

The remains, still being excavated, lie due south of Isparta, some 40km distant by a rather roundabout road. It's probably not worth being stranded here between public transport connections – best to visit in your own vehicle or with a tour bus from Eğirdir (see below). Buses running between Isparta and Antalya will drop you by the modern village of Ağlasun, but without hiring an onward taxi you face a steep, unshaded climb up more than 7km of asphalt road to the site (unfenced; small fee when guard present).

The strategic position of Sagalossos, set 1400m above sea level on a bare plateau against a steep, impressive, 2000-metre rocky escarpment, compelled passing conquerors to take it; among them, both Alexander the Great and the Roman consul Manlius stopped here on their way to Termessos. Today the rather scattered ruins blend in with the grey limestone of the cliff from which their stones originated. The **theatre**, above the access track to the northeast, had a 320-foot cavea, the eastern half of which rested on rock, while the western half was supported by masonry. Just below lies what may be a **nympheum** or fountain-house, currently being excavated.

Other discernible remains include a prominently positioned **Corinthian temple** (jumbled rubble now) dedicated to Antonius Pius, in the far south of the site and, west of the higher of two paved **agoras**, a first-century BC **Doric temple** with two standing walls. The original frieze from this temple, depicting Apollo playing a zither, attended by Muses, has been removed for safekeeping.

Cut into the cliff to the west of the city, just above remnants of an ancient road and possibly a gatehouse, are some small **rock tombs**, rather like statue niches or hand basins, which held cremated bodies. All told, though, there isn't much intact and impressive above ground – the setting, with its stupendous views 50km south, is the thing.

Eğirdir (Eğridir)

EĞİRDİR, thirty minutes' drive from Isparta, is a seaside town without the sea (though the lake is the second largest body of fresh water in Turkey), with the forgotten air of a British resort out of season and a climate to match. But the setting is astonishingly beautiful, clinging to the little flat land allowed by the Toros (Taurus) mountain range, which appears to have squeezed half of the town onto two tiny islands in the lake beyond.

Eğirdir suffers from its convenience as a lunchtime stop for tour parties, when large groups descend on and swamp the town, only to leave it feeling all the more desolate when they take off an hour later. Most of the people who do stay overnight here are an international mix of overlanders resting up from the rigours of Anatolian travel at the numerous *pansiyon*s on the island of Yeşilada. There is certainly enough to see in the region to make it worth spending a couple of days here; *pansiyon* proprietors are full of worthwhile tips on how to pass your time. In April the lake basin's numerous apple orchards are in bloom; during the summer you can swim in the lake; and in September/October, said apples are harvested.

Some history

Founded by the Hittites, Eğirdir was taken by the Phrygians in 1200 BC, but it was not until Lydian times, when it straddled the so-called King's Way from Ephesus to Babylon, that the town became famous for its recreational and accommodation facilities.

Early in the thirteenth century the town came under the control of the Konya-based Selçuks, who refortified it in its role as a gateway to Pisidia. Shortly thereafter the city reached the height of its fortunes as capital of the **Emirate of Felekeddin Dündar**, remaining prominent during the reign of the Hamidoğlu clan. In 1331 the geographer Ibn Battutah could still describe Eğirdir as a rich and powerful city; when the Ottomans took over fifty years later, however, its strategic significance – and opulence – disappeared.

The Byzantines knew the place as **Akrotiri** ("promontory" in Greek) after the obvious geographical feature just behind; this name was originally corrupted in Ottoman times to **Eğridir** (meaning "it's bent"), but was changed again in the mid-1980s to **Eğirdir**, meaning "s/he's spinning", which officialdom apparently thought more dignified.

Arrival, information and accommodation

The **train station** is 3km out of town on the Isparta road; to get into town from here, take a blue "Altınkum" bus, or a white "Yazla–Nizamiye–İstasyon–Plaj" dolmuş. The **otogar** is right in the town centre, and from here there are eight daily buses (five in low season) to Yeşilada, the last one at 9pm. The **tourist information office** at 2 Sahil Yolu 13 (daily 8.30am–noon & 1.30–6pm; ☎0246/311 4388) is by the lakeside, five minutes' walk out of town on the Isparta road, and can suggest fancier hotels and excursions; touts for some of the thirty-odd more modest *pansiyon*s (not necessarily the best) will have met you alighting your bus long before you get to the tourist office.

Most of the town's cheap and charming **pansiyons** are on **Yeşilada**, and while the backpackers' scene on the islet may not be to everyone's taste, it is at least quiet out there, with all your needs (namely meals and excursions) well catered to. **Access** is by means of the causeway built in 1974, a date which not coincidentally also marked the start of the systematic destruction of the islet's architectural heritage.

Room prices are low, partly because of cut-throat competition, partly through *Belediye* control. Top billing goes to *Ali's Pension* (0246/312 2547; ②) on the sunset-facing seaward shore, where very clean, newly renovated rooms feature guaranteed hot water, central heating and bare wooden floors. Ali takes tourists out in his boat at 7am, to fish for bass, crayfish and carp. Another excellent choice on this side of the island is the friendly, new *Paris Pansiyon*, with its own fish restaurant downstairs (☎0246/311 5509; ②), where pleasant rooms with bathrooms give onto balconies facing the lake and sunset. On the east side of the island, the excellent *Göl Pansiyon* (☎0246/312 2370; ②) has extremely well-kept rooms with balconies, the room on the terrace having the best view of all; breakfast is served beside the lake. The *Halley Pension* (☎0246/312 3265; ②), on the east shore, is a popular option with European backpackers – the rooms with baths are nothing special, but it's run by a friendly family and located next to the best beach on the island. Nearby, the first hotel you come to at the island end of the cause-way is slightly upmarket of most of the *pansiyons* on the island: the *Adac* (☎0246/312 3074; ③) has spotless rooms with en-suite bathrooms and wonderful views, and they offer free use of their rowing boat.

The hotels in the **centre of town** are excellent value, standards being high because of competition from *pansiyons* on Yeşilada. Easily accessible from the *otogar*, the three-star *Eğirdir Hotel* on Poyraz Sahil Yolu (☎0246/311 4992; ③) consists of comfortable, centrally heated rooms with TVs, while the *Otel Apostel*, on the lakeside opposite the *Kervansaray Restaurant* at Atayolu 7 (☎0246/311 5451; ④), has balconied modern rooms with TVs and a pleasant rooftop terrace. The *Hotel Ünal* (☎0246/311 5813; ②), opposite the *otogar* on Lodos Sahil Yolu, is run-down but acceptable if you can't make it out to Yeşilada or Yazla Mahalle; ask for a room with a lake view.

In **Yazla Mahalle**, by the lakeside, the attractive *Yalı Pansiyon* (☎0246/312 4773; ②) offers three rooms with kitchen facilities, and a lakeside garden where you can **camp** (rental tents available). The *Köşk Pansiyon* at Yazla Mah 37 (☎0246/311 6350; ②) has simple rooms with en-suite facilities and wonderful views of the lake from the terrace; the friendly patron provides a car service between the *pansiyon* and the *otogar*. Otherwise, to get to Yazla Mahalle, take a blue "Altınkum" bus, or a white "Yazla-Nizamiye-Istasyon-Plaj" dolmuş from 2 Sahil Yolu or from the train station. These will also take you to the town's most convenient **campsite**, the *And Camping*, located beyond Yazla (about 1500m from the town centre) on the lakeside.

The town and beaches

Considering Eğirdir's historical importance, monumental architecture is surprisingly scarce, but anything of significance has been proudly preserved and is eagerly dis-played to visitors. On a preliminary wander the most obvious remains are the nicely restored **Dündar Bey Medresesi**, which began life in 1218 as an inn, was converted into a *medrese* by Felekeddin Dündar in 1281 and now serves as a shopping precinct; and the adjoining **Hızırbey Camii**, whose roof is supported by Selçuk-style wooden pil-lars and which has an ornately carved door, wooden porch and İznik-tiled *mihrab* (a thirteenth-century hamam – daily 8am–11pm – with separate sections for men and women, belongs to the same mosque complex). The Thursday **street market** is more exciting than the extraordinarily ordinary wares in the *medrese*.

Nearby, overlooking the approach to the islands, are the ramparts of a Byzantine and Selçuk **citadel** (*kale*) on which an imposing cannon is still perched as a reminder of the importance of the trading interests that were once protected. The twelfth-century Byzantine church of **Ayios Stefanos** on Yeşilada is disappointingly dilapidated, and has been closed for years pending "restoration". It is the most tangible reminder of the 1000-strong community of Anatolian Greeks who lived here before 1923.

Belediye Plaji, 750m from the town centre in the Yazla district, is the least attractive of the town's sandy **beaches**. **Altınkum** is a more promising stretch, but with few facil-ities, located 3km out of town on the Isparta road, below the train station. **Bedre Köyü**, 8km out on the road to Barla, leafier, longer and more rural, is even more inspiring, and with its restaurant and "mocamp" would make an excellent base for caravanners. During the summer swimming season, both Altınkum and Bedre are accessible by bus from beside the Hızırbey Camii – or Bedre makes a good destination for a pedal on a bicycle.

Eating and drinking

Not surprisingly, **lake fish** – especially bass, carp and crayfish – figure prominently on local restaurant menus. On the island, many *pansiyon* owners double as fishermen and offer fresh-caught lake fish deliciously presented either as batter-fried fillets or *bulama soslu* (poached in tomato sauce); especially recommended are the restaurants of the *Paris* and *Adac pansiyon*s. If you prefer a conventional **restaurant**, head for the *Melodi* at the southeastern tip of the island, which sells reasonably priced bass, crayfish and seafood, and has a licence to serve alcohol. The poshest restaurant in town is the *Kervansaray*, on Atayolu near the island causeway, where generous portions of a range of fish and seafood are surprisingly reasonable, given the pleasant waterside terrace and smart white-tablecloth interior. In the town centre at Posthane Cad 9, the *Halil İbrahim Sofrası* is a good-value *lokanta* with specialities of stews baked in clay pots (*güveç*), and spit-roast chicken; they also offer good desserts.

Excursions from Eğirdir

Many of the *pansiyon*s in Eğirdir offer **boat trips** out on the lake and – possibly of more interest – **minibus or taxi excursions** to points of interest within a few hours' journey of the town. Unless you have a car, it's worth signing on for these, as you'd never find or get to many of these spots, which are described below. Rather unusually in Turkey, *pansiyon* proprietors often cooperate, pooling signed-up clients to fill vehicles.

Barla, Atabey and Antioch

Virtually the only other settlement of any size near the lakeshore, the old village of **BARLA**, 25km northwest of town, spills down a hillside about 200m above the water level. That said, there isn't any specific monumental attraction here; in fact, you're better off persuading a tour-taxi to head for **ATABEY**, 25km from Eğirdir or Isparta, and accessible by dolmuş from the latter. Next to the fine, wooden-porched mosque here stands a Selçuk *medrese* with an elaborately carved portal.

Almost equidistant (75–80km) from Eğirdir whether you travel via the east shore road past apple orchards, or make the complete circuit of the lake via Barla, the ancient city of **ANTIOCH AD PISIDIAM** lies about 2km northeast of the modern town of Yalvaç, itself at the head of a valley draining southwest into the lake. The town was a Hellenistic foundation of the late third century BC, but thrived much later as the capital of Pisidia under the patronage of the Roman emperors, and remained important well into Byzantine times. The apostles Paul and Barnabas both spent considerable time here during their evangelization journeys through Anatolia.

During the 1950s, American archeologists uncovered a number of buildings and areas which can still be seen. On the presumed acropolis stands the *propylaea* (gateway) with a **triple archway**, flanked by two wide, **paved plazas**, the easterly one limited by a **colonnade** and, a bit northwest, the foundations of a fourth-century **basilica** with a mosaic pavement. Back in **YALVAÇ**, a lively market town, a small **museum** houses finds from the site.

Kovada national park and the Kral Yolu

Thirty-five kilometres south of Eğirdir, the beautiful forests surrounding **Kovada Gölü** form a carefully tended and hardly visited national park. Animals found in the reserve supposedly include wolves and bears, more certainly wild boar and snakes – and swarms of butterflies, which attract aficionados in springtime.

The lake itself, teeming with fish, receives the outflow of Eğirdir Gölü, but its harsh limestone shore is not particularly good for swimming. There's an excellent fish **restaurant** with **camping** facilities, the *Çadır*, at the neck of the isthmus jutting into the lake, offering free use of a rowing boat to customers. Most tours continue another 30km towards **Çandır** – along a rough road not recommended for low-clearance rental cars – and a series of icy but scenic pools and waterfalls, crisscrossed by bridges and best sampled at the height of summer. Here too are identifiable, well-preserved stretches of the **Kral Yolu** or "King's Way", an ancient road which threaded through Pisidia on its way from Ephesus to Babylon.

The countryside around Çandır and Kovada is pastureland for Yörük nomads, and their goat-hair tents are frequently in evidence during the summer months. You may be lucky enough to witness *tandır* baking of *köy ekmeği* (village bread), or wool being spun on the simplest of wooden spindles.

Adada and the Zindan Mağarası

Signposted off the road just above Sütçüler, 65km from Eğirdir, **ADADA** is another ancient town cut from grey stone. History books are strangely silent on the place, even to the extent of its original name, but judging from coins found in the area, the place was thriving during imperial Roman times like the rest of Pisidia. Visible remains include a particularly well-preserved **Corinthian temple**, a forum, and Hellenistic buildings with inscriptions. An impressively preserved stretch of the **Kral Yolu** descends through much of the site.

Off the same road 27km from Eğirdir, and easily visited on the same tour, is the **Zindan Mağarası**, beyond the villages of Yılanlı and Aksu. Go straight up Cumhuriyet Caddesi in Aksu until you come to the river, crossed by an attractive Roman bridge: the entrance to the cave is in the rock face opposite. Inside, the cave has everything from bat colonies and guano stench to stalactites and stalagmites. It's ideal for commando-type adventuring, but a lamp and old clothes are essential if you intend to plumb all 2500m of the cave's depths; the first kilometre is the best.

Beyşehir

Leaving Eğirdir in the direction of Konya, the next major lake is **Beyşehir Gölü**. The town of **BEYŞEHİR** sees a lot of through traffic heading in this direction, and its attractive lakeside position and historical legacy make it a good prospect for at least a day trip.

Judging by the Neolithic remains found in the region, there has been human settlement here since the sixth or seventh millennium BC. There is also extensive evidence of Hittite settlement around the lake. The town itself was originally Byzantine, known as Karallia, and in Selçuk times was surrounded by walls, as well as acquiring a citadel, mosques and hamams. The local golden age, though, came under the Eşrefoğlu dynasty (1277–1326), and its best building dates from that time.

Beyşehir's assets are not immediately obvious at first glance. It's a scattered, rather vague-looking place, where baggy *şalvar* trousers and other traditional clothing, long since superseded in more westernized cities, are much in evidence on the dusty streets. Once you start to explore, though, you'll find a number of attractive monuments in the town, and a lovely Ottoman weir-bridge, built in 1902 across the lake's outlet, from which you can watch locals throwing their nets out for the evening catch of *sazan* (carp) in defiance of "No fishing" signs.

The Town

The most important – and beautiful – monument in Beyşehir itself is the **Eşrefoğlu Camii**, built by Eşrefoğlu Seyfeddin Süleyman between 1297 and 1299. Standing across the weir-bridge northwest of town, this large, flat-roofed stone building surmounted by a typical Selçuk flat-sided cone is an exceptional piece of medieval Turkish architecture, the best surviving example of a wooden *beylik* mosque – the *beylik*s being the minor Turkish principalities which ruled Anatolia before the Ottomans gained supremacy. Restoration carried out in the 1950s explains the ugly concrete blocks at the base of the minaret, but otherwise the mosque is in a remarkable state of preservation, especially the beautifully carved **main north portal**, typically Selçuk in its geometric ornateness though currently swathed in scaffolding.

The effect inside (most reliably open at prayer time) is incredibly forest-like: not only are the columns and capitals wooden, but also the rafters, the galleries, the furniture and the balustrades. Adding to the sylvan effect, light plays on the columns from a central aperture, now glassed over, and from high-set windows. The *mihrab* is decorated in typical Selçuk style, its turquoise, black and white tiles being almost the last surviving of their type, and the *mimber* is also a lovely period-piece of woodcarving, echoing the star motif apparent throughout the mosque. Although the three original Selçuk carpets have now been removed to Konya, there are still some interesting and beautiful examples of later kilims covering the floor.

The **Eşrefoğlu Türbesi**, the conically roofed building attached to the east side of the mosque, dates from 1302, and was also built for Eşrefoğlu Seyfeddin Süleyman who died in that year. It's worth asking the *imam* if he'll open it up for a look at its beautifully tiled interior, one of the most ornate surviving examples of its type.

Behind the mosque, to the south, stands a small **medrese** with an almost equally ornate portal. To the north of the mosque there's the late thirteenth-century **Dokumacılar Hanı** (Cloth Hall), also originally built during the Eşrefoğlu period, with six domes recently restored in brick; again, you'll need to ask permission to see it. It's one of the earliest remaining domed bazaars; unlike the Byzantines, and the Ottomans after them, the Selçuks tended to use domes in secular business buildings rather than in their monumental religious architecture. To the northwest of the hall there's a double **hamam**, dating from 1260, usually open. Although the building is in a fairly good state of repair, the pipes which heated the interior – using the same principle still employed in modern Turkish apartment buildings – have become exposed in the main room. Outside, at the door, there's another pipe which is said to have supplied milk for bathing purposes.

Practicalities

Beyşehir's only decent central **hotel** is the *Beyaz Park* (☎0332/512 3865; ②), in an imposing stone building overlooking the weir at Atatürk Cad 1. Rooms are basic but pleasantly furnished; ask for lakeside as the roadside is noisy. There are cheaper options in the town centre but they're seriously unpleasant. On the Yeşildağ road, 3km out of town, the *Martı Camping/Motel* (☎0332/512 1012; ②) used to be by the lakeside before the lake retreated, leaving behind vast stretches of reeds; it offers rooms with baths, a good selection of *mezes* in the restaurant, and a **campsite**, but isn't particularly friendly. If you approach the town from Eğirdir you'll pass the *Martı* on the way; otherwise, you'll need to take a cab out there.

The best **restaurant** in town is at the *Beyaz Park*, with reasonable food (including lake fish) and drinks, served in the riverside garden, weather permitting. Opposite is a shop worth mentioning: a carpet and antique dealer's called *Ceylanlar Ticaret*, which sells a good selection of kilims, copperware, Ottoman handguns and old jewellery. The **otogar** is supposed to be moving from next to the Eşrefoğlu complex to a new terminal 2km northeast of town, but this has been "imminent" for the past three years.

Around the lake

The most obvious lure of Beyşehir probably remains the shallow freshwater **lake**; although Turkey's largest in surface area, its 650 square kilometres average a mere ten metres in depth. The number of islands appears to be a hotly disputed topic among the locals, which may be explained by the fact that smaller ones appear and disappear according to the water level (presently very low), but the named ones – many with ruined Byzantine monasteries upon them – number about twenty. The best **beach** on the lake is **Karaburnu**, 18km from Beyşehir on the Yeşildağ road, then signposted 500m off to the right. It's possible to rent a boat from Burdur and explore the islands and the lakeshore.

Hiring a boat will certainly be more relaxing than attempting to circumnavigate the lake **by car**, a tiring, fuel-wasting exercise on bad roads which will also consume the better part of three hours. People in the forgotten villages of the west shore will want to know what you're up to, a not unreasonable question, since few outsiders venture there.

The only destination with rewards in proportion to the effort spent getting there is easily accessible on the main, east-shore road towards Eğirdir. This is the **Eflatun Pınar** (Violet Spring), a thirteenth-century BC Hittite shrine initially signposted 15km northwest of town, just before a petrol station. Turn right, following a paved side road for 5km, then bear left for 2km more along a dirt track to the eponymous village.

At the outskirts, a large, walled pond filling a natural depression in the hummocky countryside receives the flow of vigorous springs; at one corner stand huge carved blocks bearing **four relief figures** with winged sun discs (symbols of royalty) carried by semi-human monsters. To either side at water level are statues of seated divinities; you won't be able to make out much detail without wading boots or binoculars, since the figures face the water and the pond is surprisingly large.

Konya

Focus of Sufic mystical practice and teaching for the Middle East, **KONYA** is a place of pilgrimage for the whole of the Muslim world. As such, this initially unattractive city on the edge of the Anatolian plateau is often spoken of by Turks with more pride than the better-known tourist resorts. This was the adopted home of Celâleddin Rumi, better known as the **Mevlâna** (Our Master), the Sufic mystic who founded the **Whirling Dervish sect**, the Mevlevi; his writings helped reshape Islamic thought and modified the popular Islamic culture of Turkey.

In western Turkey, Konya has a reputation as one of the country's most religious and conservative cities, and while the teachings of Sufic mystics like the Mevlâna and of Hacı Bektaş are still important in Konya, it is also a Refah Partisi (Islamic Welfare Party) stronghold, suggesting a strong current of mainstream Islamic thought. An episode stuck in the minds of western Turks is that of a local severely beaten for smoking in the street during Ramadan during the 1980s; foreigners, however, are treated with more forbearance. In their defence, the citizens of Konya point out that while the place may appear underdeveloped, with poorly equipped schools and people more dour and less sophisticated than those nearer the Aegean, this is partly because they are not allocated their fair share of resources by Ankara. Even the city's obligatory Atatürk statue faces north – towards Ankara and away from the city centre – which locals claim is symbolic of the fact that they have been ignored since the establishment of the Turkish Republic.

The "backwardness" in fact goes some way to creating what for many visitors is Konya's charm. This may be Turkey's eighth largest city – with a population of over half a million – but there are relatively few private cars on the road and bikes have a higher profile than in İstanbul and Ankara. Despite their numbers, foreigners are still usually treated according to Islamic precepts of hospitality, though there are occasional outbursts of printed anti-Western hostility emblazoning certain mosques.

Some history

Konya boasts a history as long and spectacular as any Turkish city's. The earliest remains discovered here date from the seventh millennium BC and the acropolis (now the Alâeddin Tepesi) was inhabited successively by Hittites, Phrygians, Romans and Greeks. Saint Paul and Saint Barnabas both delivered sermons here after they had been expelled from Antioch, and in 235 AD one of the earliest church councils was convened in the city – known then, under the Byzantines, as Ikonium.

It also took a central role during the era of the western **Selçuks**, becoming the seat of the **Sultanate of Rum**. After they had defeated the Byzantine army at the Battle of Manzikert in 1071, the Selçuks attempted to set up a court in İznik, just across the Sea of Marmara from İstanbul. They were expelled from there by the combined Byzantine and Crusader armies, but still ruled most of eastern and central Asia Minor until the early fourteenth century.

While the concept of a fixed capital was initially somewhat alien to the nomadic Selçuks, Konya became the home of their sultans from the time of Süleyman Ibn Kutulmus, successor to Alparslan, the victor at Manzikert. Alâeddin Keykubad, the most distinguished of all Selçuk sultans, established a court of **artists and scholars** in Konya early in the thirteenth century, and his patronage was highly beneficial to the development of the arts and philosophy during the Selçuk dynasty. Many of the buildings constructed at this time are still standing, and examples of their highly distinctive tile work, woodcarving, carpet-making and masonry are on display in Konya's museums. All of these art forms later served as the basis of their Ottoman counterparts.

Arrival, orientation and information

Konya's **otogar** is 2km out on Ankara Caddesi; take the "Konak–Otogar" dolmuş ($0.25) into town, or the tramway to Alâeddin Parkı. The **train station** is slightly closer, at the far end of Ferit Paşa Caddesi, connected to the centre by #71 municipal buses every half hour, or by taxi (around $2).

Orientation in Konya should not present serious difficulties, despite the absence of detailed, accurate maps. The town centre consists of a large roundabout – encircling the hillock of **Alâeddin Parkı** – and one main street, first called **Alâeddin**, and later **Mevlâna Caddesi**, leading southeast from the park to the Mevlâna museum. The city's preferred hotels and restaurants are all situated in this central area, as are most of the monuments and other attractions.

The **tourist information office** (Mon–Fri 8am–5.30pm; May–Sept discretionary weekend hours; ☎0332/351 1074, fax 350 6461) is at Mevlâna Cad 21, handing out terrible maps, and also handling bookings for the December dervish festival (see p.512) – for which you should contact them well in advance, as seats for the ceremonies sell out. *Konya Döviz* on Hükümet Alanı changes currency, and there's a tour company with car rental, *Rüya Turizm* (☎0332/352 7228), at Şerafeddin Caddesi, Şükran Han 42.

Accommodation and eating

Buses arriving at the *otogar* – not to mention tourists strolling the main street – will probably be met by hotel **touts**, carpet-shop hustlers and self-styled guides, many having only a hazy idea of the location and history of Konya's monuments. If you'd rather look yourself, most of Konya's **hotels** are located on or just off Alâeddin/Mevlâna Caddesi. Finding a room shouldn't be a problem, except during the December festival, when Konya fills up and an advance booking is an absolute necessity. There's a good if expensive hotel located in the bus station: the *Özkaymak Park Hotel* (☎0332/233 3730; ⑤) has satellite TV in all rooms and minibars in most of them.

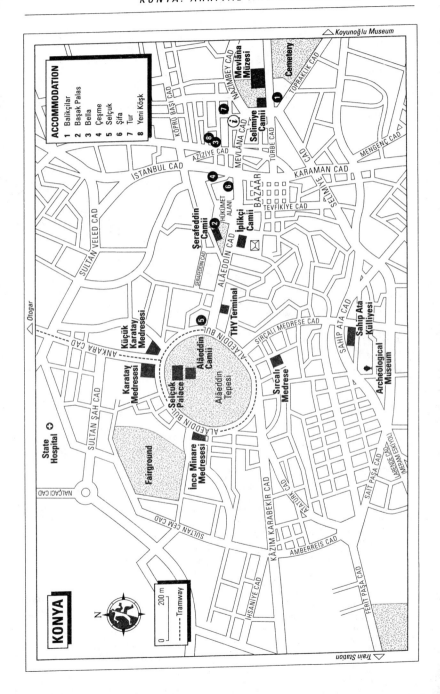

You'll find more reasonable options tucked in quiet streets to the north of Mevlâna Caddesi. *Otel Tur* (☎0332/351 9825; ②), on Esarizade Sokak, is quiet, comfortable, and cheap considering its proximity to the Mevlâna Museum. The equally quiet and well-maintained *Yeni Köşk*, off Aziziye Caddesi at Kadılar Sok 28 (☎0332/352 0671; ③), gets uniformly positive reviews for its clean basic rooms with TVs and baths (make sure you ask for the *Yeni Köşk*, as the *Mavi Köşk* and the *Köşk* are nowhere near as good). Nearby, the more expensive *Bella Hotel*, Aziziye Cad 19 (☎0332/351 4070; $24, breakfast $3 extra), has better-furnished rooms, but can be noisy at the back. The new, fairly plain but clean and comfortable *Otel Çeşme* (☎0332/351 2426; ③), Akıfpaşa Sok 35 off İstanbul Cad, is situated in a quiet side street, and is worth considering especially if it maintains this reasonable price.

Closer to the main boulevard, the conspicuous *Başak Palas*, Hükümet Alanı 3 (☎0332/351 1338; ④), is old, run-down and overpriced. For slightly more, the newly refurbished rooms in the *Şifa Otel*, Mevlâna Cad 11, represent good value (☎0332/350 4290; ④). Finally, if money's no object, a couple of good places to spend it are the new, luxury *Balıkçılar Hotel* (☎0332/350 9470, fax 351 3259; ⑧) at Mevlâna Alanı 1, with air conditioning, satellite TV, and balconies overlooking the Mevlâna Museum, and the *Selçuk Otel*, with plush rooms just off the west end of Alâeddin Caddesi (☎0332/353 2525; ⑦).

Whether or not you end up in a fairly basic, unlisted bazaar hotel, you may want to patronize the pleasant **hamam** behind the Şerafeddin Camii on Hükümet Alanı. It's everything you could ask of a Turkish bath: white stone and marble with traditional tiny round skylights striping the steam with rays of sunlight. It has separate wings for men and women, and the masseurs are skilled and thorough.

The City

Konya may be surrounded by some of Turkey's most fertile countryside (the region is known locally as "the breadbasket of Turkey"), but except for the parks on Alâeddin Tepesi and around the Mevlâna shrine there's hardly any greenery in the city itself. Extremes of temperature combine with the ubiquitous light-coloured stone to create an effect of bleakness in winter and sun-bleached desiccation in summer. If it's your first, or only, extended visit to the Anatolian interior, you'll find this the rule rather than the exception for Turkish inland towns, and particularly appropriate to Konya's substantial Selçuk remains, reminiscent as they are of nomadic tents standing out on an arid steppe.

The Mevlâna Müzesi

A visit to the **Mevlâna Müzesi** (summer Mon 10am–6pm, Tues–Sun 9am–6pm; winter Tues–Sun 9am–5.30pm; tickets sold until twenty minutes before closing time; $2) is among Turkey's most rewarding experiences. It's housed in a former *tekke*, the first lodge of the Mevlevi dervish sect, at the eastern end of Mevlâna Caddesi, and can most easily be found by locating the distinctive fluted turquoise dome which rises directly above Celâleddin Rumi's tomb.

The teachings of the Mevlâna were an exciting departure from Islamic orthodoxy, and they're still one of the most attractive aspects of the religion to Westerners and liberal Muslims alike. Although his ideas have never been fully accepted as Islamic orthodoxy, it's reassuring that a man who was expressly opposed to religious bigotry, while advocating song, dance and humility as a means to divine union, should still have a dedicated following among devout Muslims.

The site of the *tekke* is thought to have been presented as a gift to the Mevlâna's father, Bahaeddin Veled, by the Selçuk sultans. Bahaeddin Veled was certainly buried here in 1232, and his tomb stands upended beside that of his son. According to popu-

THE LIFE AND TEACHINGS OF THE MEVLÂNA

Celâleddin Rumi, later known as the **Mevlâna**, was born in Balkh, a central Asian city, in 1207. Various prodigies attended his infancy, and a wandering dervish prophesied that the boy was destined for greatness. At the age of twenty, vouchsafed a warning vision, the young man convinced his father to flee Balkh with him for western Asia, which they did just in time to avoid being massacred with the rest of the town by marauding Mongols.

They settled in Konya, where the reigning sultan Alâeddin Keykubad received them cordially. Poised on the marches between Byzantium and the young Turkish principalities, the city had a cosmopolitan population, whose beliefs were not lost on the young man; it was almost inevitable that he should emerge as a leading heterodox mystic or Sufi. In 1244 came a fateful meeting with **Shams-i-Tabriz**, a wandering dervish from Iran whom Rumi immediately recognized as a spiritual mentor. For several years the two men kept near-constant company until some of Rumi's followers, jealous of the interloper's hold on their teacher, plotted to have Shams murdered.

Until the 1250s, Rumi remained inconsolable, and apparently only reconciled himself to his companion's death in the process of composing a masterpiece of Persian devotional poetry, the **Mathnawi**. A massive work covering several volumes (see "Books" in *Contexts* for a recommended translation of excerpts), it concerns the soul's separation from God – characterized as the Friend – as a consequence of earthly existence, and the power of a mutual yearning to bring about a reunion, either before or after bodily death. The Mevlâna – as Rumi was by now widely known – himself died on December 17, 1273, a date subsequently referred to by his followers as the Wedding Night.

On a practical level, the Mevlâna instructed his disciples to pursue all manifestations of truth and beauty, while avoiding ostentation, and to practise infinite tolerance, love and charity. He condemned slavery, advocating monogamy and a higher prominence for women in religious and public life. The Mevlâna did not advocate complete monastic seclusion – the Mevlevis held jobs in normal society and could marry – but believed that the contemplative and mystical practices of the dervish would free them from worldly anxieties.

lar myth, Veled's tomb rose until it stood upright when the Mevlâna was buried alongside in 1273, a measure of the unusual respect held by the father towards his son. (Conversely, the custom of a son rising to his feet when his father enters a room is still prevalent in Turkey.)

The structures adjacent to the tomb were subsequently enlarged by the *çelebi*s (literally "nobility"), the disciples of the Mevlâna who took over leadership of the order after his death. They served as a place of mystical teaching, meditation and ceremonial dance (*sema*), from shortly after Rumi's death in 1273 until 1925, when Atatürk banned all Sufic orders; over the centuries the various dervish orders had become highly influential in political life and thus could pose a threat to his secular reforms.

Most of the buildings in the compound, including the *tekke* and *semahane*, were built late in the fifteenth and early in the sixteenth centuries by the sultans Beyazit II and Selim I. Opposite the entrance a *şadırvan*, or fountain for ritual ablutions, still plays. Along the south and east sides of the courtyard are the **cells** where the dervishes prayed and meditated, today containing waxwork figures dressed in the costume worn during the whirling ceremony. Before they were allowed the privilege of seclusion in the cells, the novices had to spend a period of a thousand and one days in manual labour in the soup kitchens, which are also open to the public. After the novitiate they could return to the community and take jobs, even marry, while retaining membership of the order. Next to the *şeyh*'s quarters, now the museum office, is a **library** of five thousand volumes on the Mevlevi and Sufic mysticism.

Across the courtyard in the main building of the museum is the **mausoleum** containing the tombs of the Mevlâna, his father and other notables of the order. You should leave your shoes at the door and shuffle along in a queue of pilgrims, for whom this is the primary purpose of their visit. Women must cover their heads, and if you're wearing shorts you'll be given a skirt-like affair to cover your legs, regardless of sex. The measure of devotion still felt toward the Mevlâna is evident in the weeping and impassioned prayer which take place in front of his tomb, but non-Muslim visitors are treated with respect and even welcomed. This is in strict accordance with Rumi's own dictates on religious tolerance:

Come, come whoever you are, whether you be fire-worshippers, idolaters or pagans. Ours is not the dwelling-place of despair. All who enter will receive a welcome here.

If you're a lone *gâvur* (infidel) in a centre of Islamic pilgrimage this sentiment is surely one to be cherished.

THE SEMAHANE

In the adjoining room, the original **semahane** (the circular hall in which the *sema* was performed, considered the finest in Turkey), exhibits include some of the musical instruments of the original dervishes, including the *ney* (reed flute). Novice dervish-musicians did not, and still do not, buy a *ney*, but are given one by their *murşid* or spir-

---

THE SEMA OR MEVLEVI CEREMONY

Since Konya is the spiritual and temporal home of the Whirling Dervishes, the city plays host to the annual **Dervish Festival** every December 10–17, during the week prior to the anniversary of the Mevlâna's death. Unfortunately this is not the best place or season to witness a dervish rite: with sub-zero temperatures, doubled hotel rates and shops full of Whirling Dervish lampstands and other kitsch, Konya is probably at its worst.

Moreover, the troupe which performs the ritual in an indoor basketball court do not profess to live as Mevlevis; before you fork out for the ticket (also pricy) it's worth remembering that the best place to witness a ceremony is probably in the restored *semahane* in Galatasaray in İstanbul. The group who turn there have official recognition as a dance troupe, but its members are also practising dervishes who have undergone the novitiate and live according to the teachings of the Mevlâna on a daily basis.

Contrary to the main body of Islamic belief, the Mevlâna extolled the virtues of music and dance, and the **whirling ceremony** – more properly the *sema* – for which the Mevlevi dervishes are renowned is a means of freedom from earthly bondage and abandonment to God's love. Its ultimate purpose is to effect a union with God.

The **clothes** worn by the Mevlevis during the observance have symbolic significance. The camelhair hat represents a tombstone, the black cloak is the tomb itself and the white skirt the funerary shroud. During the ceremony the cloak is cast aside, denoting that the dervishes have escaped from their tombs and from all other earthly ties. The **music** reproduces that of the spheres, and the turning dervishes represent the heavenly bodies themselves. Every movement and sound made during the ceremony has an additional significance, and is strictly regulated by detailed and specific directions. As an example, the right arms of the dancers are extended up to heaven and the left are pointing to the floor, denoting that grace is received from God and distributed to humanity, without anything being retained by the dervishes themselves.

The three **stages of the dance** are: knowledge of God, awareness of God's presence, and union with God. As the dancers turn they repeat a *zikir* or "chant of remembrance" under their breath, while the musicians sing a hymn expressing the desire for mystic union. In the final part of the ceremony, the *şeyh* or current head of the order, the incarnation of the Mevlâna, joins the dancers and whirls with them.

itual (and music) teacher, who fashions it for them. The reeds for these flutes are still grown throughout southeastern Turkey; it is said that the sound they make is a cry for their nursery reedbed. An analogous but more esoteric explanation in the *Mathnawi* describes it as the lament of the human soul for reunion with the One Friend, the dervish epithet for the Godhead. The instrument indeed has the same range as a human voice, and in the hands of a virtuoso the sound is extremely poignant. A tape of dervish music plays continually in the museum, and the "voice" of the *ney* is clearly distinct above the other instruments.

Other exhibits include the original illuminated *Mathnawi* – the long devotional poem of the Mevlâna now translated into twelve languages, and silk and woollen carpets, some of which form part of the great body of gifts received by Celâleddin Rumi from sultans and princes. One 500-year-old silk carpet from Selçuk Persia is supposed to be the finest ever woven, with 144 knots to the square centimetre; it took five years to complete. The Selçuk rugs on display here give credence to the theory that their skills were adopted by the Ottomans, since many of the patterns and motifs, previously unique to Selçuk works, recur in subsequent carpet work throughout Asia Minor, and some of the same knots are used in Selçuk, and later, Ottoman examples.

The latticed gallery above the *semahane* was for women spectators, a modification introduced by the followers of the Mevlâna after his death. The heavy chain suspended from the ceiling and the concentric balls hanging from it have been carved from a single piece of marble. In the adjoining room, a casket containing hairs from the beard of the Prophet Mohammed is displayed alongside some finely illuminated medieval Korans.

The Alâeddin Tepesi

The **Alâeddin Tepesi** stands at the opposite end of Mevlâna/Alâeddin Caddesi from the Mevlâna Müzesi, and as traffic islands go it's a nice place to stroll; there are also a few outdoor cafés to sit at. The site of the original acropolis, the *tepe*, has yielded finds dating back to 7000 BC as well as evidence of Hittite, Phrygian, Roman and Greek settlers, most of which are now in the museum in Ankara. At the foot of the hill to the north are the scant remains of a **Selçuk palace**: two pieces of stone wall incongruously surmounted by an ugly concrete canopy.

The only other surviving building to bear witness to any of the long history of this mound is the imposing **Alâeddin Camii**, begun by Sultan Mesut I in 1130 and completed by Alâeddin Keykubad in 1221. External features worthy of note are the irregularity of its form – probably a result of the time taken over its construction – and the use of masonry on the northeast facade from an earlier, unidentified classical construction. This masonry comprises a row of classical marble columns whose varying sizes have been cleverly compensated for in the surrounding stonework and whose diminishing heights echo the slope of the hill. The original building probably consisted of the fan-shaped hall, whose flat mud roof is supported on six more rows of Roman columns.

Despite ongoing restoration work, still in progress after nearly ten years, the mosque is now open to the public. Its typical Selçuk interior contains 42 ancient columns with Roman capitals supporting a flat roof, with a small domed area over the *mihrab*. The beautiful carved ebony *mimber*, dated 1155, is the oldest inscribed and dated Selçuk work of art in existence. A hoard of Selçuk carpets discovered here when the mosque was renovated at the beginning of this century has been relocated to the Mevlâna Müzesi, but the remains of eight Selçuk sultans, including the warrior Alparslan and Alâeddin Keykubad, are still enshrined in a *türbe* located in a separate hall of the mosque interior.

The Karatay Medresesi

The nearby **Karatay Medresesi** on Ankara Caddesi (Mon–Sat 8.30am–noon & 1.30–5.30pm; $1) is another important Selçuk monument. Built in 1251, the *medrese*, or school of Islamic studies, now houses a museum of ceramics, but the building itself provides greater interest. The main **portal** is a fine example of Islamic art at its most decorative, combining elements such as Arabic striped stonework and Greek Corinthian columns with a structure which is distinctly Selçuk: a tall doorway surmounted by a pointed, stalactite arch, reminiscent of the entrance of a tent. The features that distinguish Konya's two important Selçuk portals – this and the even more decorative example at the entrance of the İnce Minare Medresesi – from other examples of Selçuk masonry are the use of Koranic script and interlacing, geometric patterns in the decoration.

Inside the *medrese* the most attractive exhibit is again part of the building itself. The symmetrical tiling of the famed **dome of stars** is a stylized representation of the heavens in gold, blue and black monochrome tiles. Painted Ottoman tiles from İznik and Kütahya appear clumsy in contrast with those of this delicate mosaic. Selçuk **ceramics** on display in the galleries bear witness to the fact that pious concerns were overruled by secular taste – not to mention the contributions of conquered Christian and pagan subjects – even in medieval times; the striking images of birds, animals and even angels would have been strictly forbidden in more orthodox Islamic societies.

The İnce Minare Medresesi

Behind its fine Selçuk portal the **İnce Minare Medresesi** or "Academy of the Slender Minaret" (Tues–Sun 9am–noon & 1.30–5.30pm; $0.50), on the west side of Alâeddin Tepesi by the tramway stop, is now being used as a lapidary and woodcarving museum. The minaret from which it takes its name was severely truncated by lightning in 1901; today the most exquisite feature is the **portal**, even more ornate than that at the Karatay Medresesi.

Most of the exhibits in the museum, like the ceramics in the Karatay Medresesi, came from the ruined Selçuk palace across the way. The finest individual items on display are the Selçuk stone reliefs, explicitly showing the influence of Byzantium; most prominent are winged angels, bestiary pediments and a two-headed eagle relief, said to be from the vanished walls of the medieval city and now the official logo of the modern town.

Other museums and monuments

A short walk southeast of Alâeddin Parkı along Ressam Sami Sokak, the thirteenth-century **Sırçalı Medrese** now houses government offices (Mon–Fri 8.30am–5.30pm; free). Highlights of the building, mostly restored in harsh brick, are the fine blue-glazed tilework in the rear porch, all that remains of what was once a completely ornamented interior, and the handsome portal – all visible even if the gate is locked.

Continuing in the same direction, you'll reach the **archeological museum** (Tues–Sun 9am–noon & 1.30–5.30pm; $1), containing the only pre-Selçuk remains in the city. These include the few Hittite artefacts from the nearby site of Çatal Höyük (see opposite) that have not been relocated in Ankara, and three well-preserved Roman sarcophagi from Pamphylia, one of which depicts Hercules at his Twelve Labours. Just northeast of the museum, the thirteenth-century **Sahip Ata Külliyesi** is semi-ruined but retains its beautiful brick-and-stone entrance portal, plus a tiled *mihrab*.

On Hükümet Alanı, the north edge of Konya's workaday bazaar is marked by the three-domed **İplikçi Camii**, Konya's oldest (1230) mosque to survive intact and still be in use; legend claims that the Mevlâna preached and meditated here.

On the southeast side of the centre, the **Koyunoğlu Müzesi**, at Kerimdede Cad 25 (Mon–Sat 8am–5.30pm; $0.50), is an eclectic private collection donated to the city by the Koyunoğlu family. Downstairs are black and white pictures of old Konya, but the museum is mainly interesting for its ethnographic section upstairs, which consists of a rich collection of embroidered textiles, some Selçuk and Ottoman ceramics, and objects from nineteenth-century everyday life, such as bath clogs and musical instruments. There's also a fine collection of antique carpets which enthusiasts shouldn't miss, including examples from Niğde, Konya and Karaman.

Eating

Eating in Konya is generally fairly undistinguished, with **alcohol** fairly hard to come by in this religious town – or at least well concealed out of sight of the disapproving. One fairly forgettable **local speciality** is *fırın kebap*, pretty much the same grease-and-gristle cut as in Antalya; the local thin-crusted variant of *pide*, an apparent hybrid of *pide* and *lahmacun*, is more savoury and makes a wonderful breakfast.

The best **restaurant** is attached to the *Şifa Otel* on Mevlâna Caddesi, with a wide variety of hot oven-tray and cold *zeytin yağlı* food, plus desserts. The *Villa Restaurant*, on Meram Caddesi (the continuation of Kâzim Karabekir Caddesi), serves excellent, unusual varieties of kebabs with alcoholic beverages in a large dining area, but closes early, at around 9pm. Kebabs, *pide* and steamtray dishes are served at *Hanedan Et Lokantası*, near Aziziye Caddesi on Alâeddin Caddesi.

Tuba Pastanesi, Alâeddin Cad 22, serves excellent breakfasts, a good option if you're staying in one of the hotels where breakfast is an overpriced extra. The best-stocked bar in town is that of the *Damla Restaurant*, in a passageway off Mevlâna Caddesi near the *Şahin Hotel*. They also serve a good pot-roasted chicken, but the TV can be annoying especially if there's a match on.

Around Konya

In the environs of Konya are a number of attractions most easily visited in your own car: Byzantine churches in various numbers and states of repair, and – of mainly specialist interest – the location of what may be Anatolia's earliest settlement.

Sille

A tumbledown village hidden in a canyon 8km northwest of Konya, **SİLLE** is accessible by #64 city bus. With your own vehicle, thread through the village, following the canal spanned by tiny old bridges, until arriving at the bus's final stop, labelled "Son Durak". It's best to show up while school is in session – otherwise the village children can be unusually annoying.

A **Byzantine church** (daily except Mon 9am–4pm), more impressive than handsome, stands visible just to the southwest. The brickwork of the drum dome surmounting the vast, boxy structure is obviously medieval; inside, however, the naive nineteenth-century decor, collapsed icon screen and fairly well-preserved ceiling murals show that the church was in use until 1923. In the surrounding cliffs you can glimpse some hermitages.

Çatal Höyük

Excavations at the important Neolithic site of **Çatal Höyük** have been so thorough that there's practically nothing left to see, but if prehistoric tumuli excite you, or if you have a lively imagination, it's fairly easy to get to from Konya. Take a dolmuş from Konya to Çumra, from where you will need to take a taxi to the site itself, 10km north of the town.

With your own transport, leave Konya on the Karaman/Mersin road, Highway 715, and take a left to Çumra 2km before İçeri Çumra. The road to the site is marked in the town. Discovered by the British archeologist James Mellaart in 1958, **the site** consists of twin flattened hills which are supposed to resemble the shape of a fork, hence the name Çatal Höyük or "Fork Tumulus". A number of exciting discoveries made here gave significant clues about one of the world's oldest civilizations. Thirteen strata have been identified, the earliest dating from 6800 BC, the latest from 5500 BC. Evidence pointed to entire complexes of houses, crammed together without streets to separate them, and entered through holes in the roof. Also found were murals of men being eaten by vultures, animal-head trophies stuffed with squeezed clay, and human bones wrapped in straw matting and placed under the seats in a burial chamber.

Most famous of all the discoveries are statuettes of the **mother goddess**, supposed to be related to the Phrygian goddess Cybele and her successor Artemis. The baked earthenware or stone figures are 5–10cm tall and show a large-breasted, broad-hipped woman crouching to give birth. The most interesting pieces are now in Ankara's Museum of Anatolian Civilizations.

Binbir Kilise

Binbir Kilise or "A Thousand and One Churches" is the name given to a remote region directly north of Karaman, not easily reached from Çatal Höyük. Scattered across the base of the extinct volcano Kara Dağ are indeed close to that number of ruined churches and monasteries, mostly dating from the ninth to the eleventh centuries, when the region was a refuge for persecuted Christians.

To get there, travel on the paved road 21km north from Karaman via Kılbasan, and then turn left or northwest on a rougher dirt track for 10km more towards the village of **MADEN ŞEHİR**, in the middle of one of the main concentrations of basalt-built chapels. These, many in good condition, are all that's left of a substantial, unidentified town which flourished from Hellenistic to Byzantine times. If you're intrigued, and have a tough car, there's yet another abandoned town with a cluster of churches at the hamlet known variously as **DEĞİLE** or **DEĞLER**, about 8km to the west. Villagers at Maden Şehir may well offer guiding services, and it's probably a good idea to take them up on it.

Alahan

Beyond Karaman, Highway 715 begins climbing up into the forested Toros, on its way to Silifke on the Mediterranean coast. It takes some elasticity of geography to include **ALAHAN**, 175km from Konya, as falling in its surroundings, but the extensive Byzantine monastic complex here belongs to roughly the same era – and impulse – as those at Binbir Kilise.

Intact buildings at the site, well signposted 2km to the east of the road, include two late fifth- and early sixth-century **basilicas**, one sporting elaborate relief sculptures of the Evangelists and the two archangels, and a **baptistry**. If you're headed this way it's well worth the slight detour, since otherwise you won't see anything like this outside of eastern Turkey.

Towards Cappadocia

Heading east from Konya towards Cappadocia, very little breaks the monotony of rolling wheatfields for some 150km: the Konya plain is flat, fertile and relentless. Sights en route are sparse, and in the case of İvriz add up to nearly a full day's detour.

Acı Göl and İvriz

Just off Highway 330 – also accessible from Karaman if you've been to Binbir Kilise or Alahan – there's a very beautiful crater lake just east of Karapınar. The lake, **Acı Göl**, is hidden from the road, and the turn-off is merely a narrow, unsignposted, white-dirt track a bit east of a *Türkpetrol* truckstop on a knoll, about 11km after the turn-off to Karapınar. You could camp and perhaps swim here, as you're far enough from the road to ensure some privacy, but as the name (Bitter Lake) implies, the water is undrinkable.

There are no such potability problems at **İvriz**, a remote Assyro-Hittite site south of Ereğli, in the very foothills of the Bolkar Toros range. Highway junction signs are misleading inasmuch as a 21-kilometre drive from Ereğli only brings you to Aydınkent, the village closest to İvriz; from there you face at least a two-hour hike up a spectacular canyon to an eighth-century **rock relief**, which shows a deity, Tarhunzas, presenting a bunch of grapes and an ear of corn to the ruler of the nearby Hittite kingdom of Tuvanuva (near present-day Niğde). Like many such Hittite cliff shrines, it seems intended to bestow fertility on the river flood-plain below the gorge – still heavily cultivated today with the aid of the stream below.

The path up the canyon, not always totally clear, begins from the bridge over the stream – incidentally the last reliable water – which erupts suddenly at the top of the village. You must be reasonably self-sufficient, since Aydınkent can only offer a simple store, a single phone, and a *köy konağı* or guest room where you might pass the night. However, the trip, which appears on the itineraries of the more imaginative adventure tour companies, is well worth the effort.

Sultanhanı Kervansaray

The **Sultanhanı Kervansaray** (daily 7am–7pm; $1), 108km of dull driving from Konya on the Aksaray road, was one of the many public inns built by the Selçuks during the reign of Alâeddin Keykubad, testifying to the importance placed on trade and social welfare by this highly cultured society. The buildings date from 1229, but have been substantially restored, first by Mehmet the Conqueror, evidence of the continued importance of this east–west trading route in the Ottoman period, and more recently by Turkish Radio and Television, who used the *kervansaray* as the location for a historical drama. The results – while employing too much modern building material – are still impressive, especially compared to the much smaller Ağzıkarahan Kervansaray east of Aksaray.

The emphasis placed on security is clear from the high walls surrounding the compound, and from the size of the portal, truly massive and impressively ornate. Inside, the most prominent building is the small mosque, which takes a central position raised high above the courtyard on four pillars, away from the dangers of stray pack-animals. Animals were stabled opposite the entrance, in the enormous hall with five cradle-vaulted naves divided by huge pillars. The height of this room suggests accommodation for elephants rather than camels and mules, but it was meant to convey an impression of might and vigour to the foreign merchants who stayed in these provincial *hans* for up to three days completely free of charge. To either side of the entrance were private rooms and dormitories for servants, a hamam, workshops, a smithy and storerooms.

The large village which has grown up around the *kervansaray* specializes in raga-muffin children selling knitted socks, and boasts several **pansiyons** with camping facilities. At the southeast edge of town, the *Kervan* (☎0382/242 2325; ②), run by a friendly, welcoming family, has comfortable en-suite rooms, plus attractive camping facilities on their lawn. Mother cooks a good evening meal, often eaten out in the garden. The *Sultanhanı Pansiyon* (☎0382/242 2008; ②) is more central, but the facilities aren't as good.

CAPPADOCIA

A land created by the complex interaction of natural and human forces over vast spans of time, Cappadocia is unique to Turkey and should be visited and revisited. Its complexities cannot be understood in the time it takes a tour party to polish off a few frescoes on a photo stop between hotel and carpet shop.

Initially, the great expanses of bizzarely eroded, carved and shaped volcanic matter can be disturbing. The still dryness and omnipresent dust give an impression of barrenness, and the light changes with dramatic effect to further startle and alienate the observer. Only with time comes the realization that the volcanic **tuff** that forms the land is exceedingly fertile, and that these weird formations of soft, dusty rock have accommodated and been adapted over millennia to many varying cultures and ways of life. While the invading armies of great empires have generally disregarded Cappadocia, indigenous peoples have always exploited the region's potential, living in conditions of comparative cultural and material wealth. The most fascinating aspect of a visit to the area is the impression of continuity: rock caves are still inhabited; the fields are still fertilised with guano collected in rock-cut pigeon houses; and pottery is still made from the clay of the main river, the Kızılırmak. **Wine** is produced locally as it has been since Hittite times, and the **horses** from which the region takes its name (Cappadocia translates from the Hittite as "land of well-bred horses") are still bred and widely used in the region, along with mules and donkeys, in transport and agriculture.

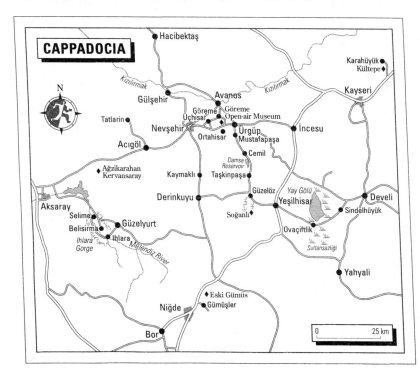

THE GEOLOGICAL FORMATION OF CAPPADOCIA

The peaks of three volcanoes – **Erciyes, Hasan** and **Melendiz Dağları** – dominate Cappadocia. It was their eruptions some thirty million years ago, covering the former plateau of Ürgüp in ashes and mud, that provided the region's raw material: **tuff**. This soft stone formed by compressed volcanic ash has been worked on ever since by processes of erosion to form the valleys and curious **fairy chimney** rock formations for which the region is so famous.

The original eruptions created a vast erosion basin, dipping slightly towards the Kızılırmak River, which marks an abrupt division between the fantasy landscape of rocky Cappadocia and the green farmland around Kayseri. In the south especially, the plateau is formed of a very pure, homogenous tuff and rivers have carved out a number of straight-sided valleys. Elsewhere, where the tuff is mixed with rock, the erosion process has resulted in various formations collectively known as fairy chimneys. The stages in the creation of these extraordinary scenes can be clearly seen in many places: a block of hard rock which resists erosion, usually basalt, is left standing alone as the tuff around is worn away, until it stands at the top of a large cone. Eventually the underpart is eaten away to such an extent that it can no longer hold its capital: the whole thing collapses and the process starts again.

In the Cemil Valley, near Mustafapaşa, the cones give way to tabular formations – **table mountains** – caused by the deep grooves made by rivers in the harder geological layers. The area is characterized by increased amounts of water and high cliff banks surmounted by vertical rocks.

Another important region lies to the northwest of the Melendiz mountain range, the valley of the Melendiz Suyu or **Ihlara valley**. The most individual feature of this region is the red canyon through which the river flows, probably the most beautiful of all the Cappadocian landscapes.

The increase in the number of tour companies who pass through the area may have given rise to some large and ugly hotels, to the omnipresent carpet mafiosi and to seasonally packed museums, but these crowds are confined to a few designated areas, and tour guides ensure they don't stray too far. The essential Cappadocia is still there, waiting to be explored by travellers with time to appreciate changing forms and light, and to learn a little about how such an environment has been affected by – and has affected – the peoples who have settled there.

The best-known sites of Cappadocia, those most frequented by tour groups, are located within the triangle delimited by the roads connecting Nevşehir, Avanos and Ürgüp. Within this region are the greater part of the valleys of **fairy chimneys**; the **rock-cut churches** of the Göreme open-air museum, with their amazing selection of frescoes; and the **Zelve monastery**, a fascinating warren of troglodyte dwellings and churches. **Nevşehir** itself isn't up to much as a town, but is an important centre for travel in the region, while **Ürgüp** and its neighbouring villages, **Göreme, Çavuşin, Üçhisar** and **Ortahisar**, all make attractive bases from which to tour the surrounding valleys, but aren't well served by public transport. **Avanos**, beautifully situated on the Kızılırmak, is a centre of the local pottery industry. Outside the triangle heading south, but still fairly well frequented by tour groups en route to the Mediterranean, are the underground cities of **Derinkuyu** and **Kaymaklı**, fascinating warrens attesting to the ingenuity of the ancient inhabitants. Less well-known sites are located further to the south, to the east and west. The **Ihlara valley** near **Aksaray**, a red canyon riddled with churches cut into its sides, is the most spectacular sight yet to feel the full force of tourism. **Kayseri** has been dropped from itineraries as a result of the development of tourism elsewhere in the region, and is now a quiet provincial capital recommended for

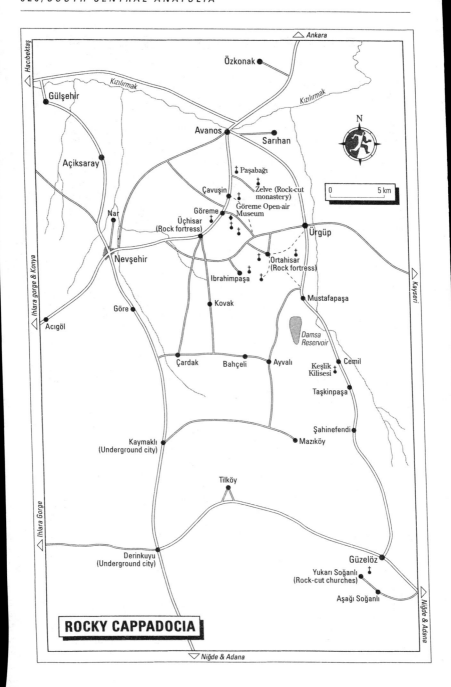

ROCKY CAPPADOCIA

its Selçuk architecture and the ski resort on Erciyes Dağı. To the south, attractions around the town of **Niğde** include the Sultansazlığı bird sanctuary and the nearby Eski Gümüşler monastery, whose frescoes rival the more famous examples in Göreme.

The history of the region

The earliest known settlers in the Cappadocia region were the **Hatti**, whose capital, Hattuşa, was located to the north of Nevşehir. The growth of the Hattic civilization, which was undergoing an early Bronze Age at the time, was interrupted by the arrival of large groups of Indo-European immigrants from western Europe, the **Hittites**. By 2000 BC these immigrants had imposed their rule on the region, mixing their own language and culture with that of the Hatti. The result was a rich and varied culture, and a body of laws that was remarkably humane for its time. Torture and mutilation of political prisoners, common practices of the time, were unknown to the Hittites, incest was forbidden by law, and the Hittite King was "first among equals" rather than an absolutist monarch. In the Hittite laws it was written concerning the power of the monarch: "Whoever commits evil against his brothers and sisters answers for it with the royal head. Call the assembly, and if the things come to a decision he shall pay with his head."

After the fall of the Hittite Empire around 1200 BC the region was controlled to varying degrees and at different times by its neighbouring kingdoms, Lydia and Phrygia in the west, Urartu in the east. This situation continued until the middle of the sixth century BC, when the Lydian king Croesus was defeated by the **Persians** under Cyrus the Great.

Cappadocia was saved from Persian rule by the arrival of **Alexander the Great** in 333 BC, and subsequently enjoyed independence for 350 years, until it became a Roman province with Kayseri as its capital. Despite this nominal annexation, effective independence was ensured in the following centuries by the relative disinterest of the Roman and Byzantine rulers, whose only real concerns were to control the roads and thereby keep open eastern trading routes; to make the best use of the local manpower for their armies; and to extort tributes of local produce. Meanwhile the locals existed in much the same way as they do now, living in rock-hewn dwellings or building houses out of local stone, and relying economically on agriculture, viniculture and livestock breeding.

This neglect, combined with the influence of an important east–west trading route, meant that a number of faiths, creeds and philosophies were allowed to flourish here. One of these was **Christianity**, introduced in the first century by Saint Paul. Taking refuge from increasingly frequent attacks by Arab raiders, the new Christian communities took to the hills, and there they literally carved out dwelling places, churches and monasteries for entire communities.

In the eleventh century the **Selçuk Turks** arrived, quickly establishing good relations with the local communities. They too were interested primarily in trading routes, and their energies went into improving road systems and building the *kervansaray*s which are strung along these roads to this day. The Selçuk Empire was defeated by the Mongols in the middle of the thirteenth century, and Cappadocia was controlled by the Karaman dynasty, based in Konya, before being incorporated into the Ottoman Empire in the fourteenth century. The last of the Christian Greeks left the area in the 1920s during the exchange of populations by the Greek and Turkish governments.

Nevşehir and around

Said to be home to Turkey's richest community, **NEVŞEHİR**, at the very heart of Cappadocia, can hardly be accused of an ostentatious display of wealth: the town consists of a couple of scruffy streets, with no apparent centre or monumental architecture. If you were hoping for a pleasant and comfortable town with decent amenities from which to set out on your excursions into the region, you won't find it here.

Nevşehir is an important transport node, particularly for buses arriving from other regions of Turkey, though many tourists arrive here by default, having bought a ticket to Göreme in good faith, and then being deposited at Nevşehir *otogar*. If you arrive late and are not disposed to hitch to Göreme or Ürgüp, you may as well make the most of your time here. Fortunately, the longer you have to spend in the town, the more attractive it becomes, and a stroll up to the castle or a minibus ride to Nar is all you really need to convince you that the area has merits beyond modern commerce.

Arrival, orientation and information

Orientation is a simple matter in Nevşehir: the castle, which stands at the heart of the old city – to the southwest of the modern centre – is a continual landmark. The new city below is divided by two main streets: **Atatürk Bulvarı**, on which are situated most of the hotels and restaurants, and **Lale Caddesi**, turning into Gülşehir Caddesi to the north, where the **otogar** is located.

Nevşehir's *otogar*, however, does not make a pleasant point of **arrival** to the region, especially not at night, when there are no connections on to central Cappadocia. To save the 1500-metre walk to the centre, or the kilometre-plus to the nearest hotel, the *Nevkur* company runs dolmuşes from the *otogar* into town until 11pm. You may be met at the *otogar* by unscrupulous unofficial tour operators who try to persuade you that there are no minibuses to the rest of Cappadocia, or that the hotels in Göreme or Ürgüp are all full or closed. Ignore them: there are dolmuşes to Ürgüp, though they stop at 6pm in winter, 7pm in summer, and to Göreme (stopping at 8pm in summer, 6pm in winter); after these times, some Göreme *pansiyon* owners will pick you up from Nevşehir *otogar* if you have a prior booking with them.

The only company who operate buses to Göreme village at present are *Nevtur/Göreme* (the same company operating under two names), and even they have been known to let passengers off at Nevşehir if there are not enough people making the journey to Göreme. Worse still, other companies – particularly those operating buses from Pamukkale, Eğirdir, Selçuk and the Mediterranean resorts – have been simply dropping clients by the roadside, leaving them stranded in Aksaray or even on one or other of the main highways. If your ticket says Göreme, don't get off the bus until you see fairy chimneys and the small village of Göreme with its central bus garage. Show your ticket to fellow passengers if need be.

There are two **tourist information offices**: the main office on Atatürk Bulvarı on the right as you head downhill towards Ürgüp (daily 8am–6pm; ☎0384/213 9604 or 213 3659); the other in the bus station (May–Oct daily 6am–8pm; ☎0384/213 4025). The staff of both are friendly and helpful, and they can arm you with a hotel price list, a map of Nevşehir and surroundings, and advice on transport in and out of the city.

Minibuses to most locations around Cappadocia leave from the *otogar*, and stop near the hospital at the top of Yeni Kayseri Caddesi. The exception to this is the Aksaray dolmuş, which leaves from the old bus station at the top of Atatürk Bulvarı. Long-haul buses, for example to Ankara and İstanbul, stop after leaving the bus station at the *Nevtur* office on Lâle Caddesi, where tickets can be purchased; the Ankara bus also stops at Aksaray.

The two competing official **tour companies** in Nevşehir are *Tui*, located at Lâle Cad 154, on the fourth floor of the Çekirdekçiler İşhanı (☎0384/212 2100); and *Red Valley* (☎0384/213 9792) in the *otogar*, who also have **rental cars**.

Accommodation

Accommodation in Nevşehir is nowhere near as easily found, as cheap or as good as elsewhere in Cappadocia. Tourism facilities have seen a decline here in recent years, and many of the better accommodation options have closed down.

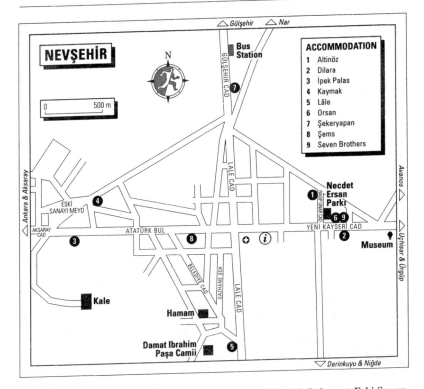

Among **budget hotels**, the *Kaymak*, near the top of Atatürk Bulvarı at Eski Sanayı Meydanı 11 (☎0384/213 5427; ②), is reasonably priced but old, with shared bathrooms. More comfortable and friendly is the *Hotel Şems* (☎0384/213 3597; ②), on Atatürk Bulvarı above the *Aspava Restaurant*. Rooms have en-suite bathrooms and guaranteed hot water, but are dingily furnished; the main problem, however, is traffic noise, so ask for a room at the back, where the views are better too. The *İpek Palas* (☎0384/213 1478; ①), further west on the same street, has only shared bathrooms and suffers the same problem of traffic noise. The *Lâle Hotel*, Belediye Caddesi, next to the *Belediye* building (☎0384 213 1797; ③), is in a quieter more atmospheric part of town on the way to Ibrahim Paşa Camii. Rooms are old but comfortable, with TVs and bathrooms.

Going **upmarket** you'll be better served, as Nevşehir is a popular choice for tour companies with an eye for a good hotel. The easiest to reach from the *otogar* is the pleasant *Şekeryapan*, Gülşehir Cad 8 (☎0384/213 4253; ③), comfortable and nicely furnished, with its own hamam and sauna. The *Hotel Altınöz* (☎0384/213 5305, fax 213 2817; ⑧), with zany hi-tech glass lifts, air conditioning, satellite TV and minibars in the rooms, good service and an excellent restaurant, is situated off Yeni Kayseri Caddesi, at Ragip Ünar Cad 23. Three hotels which have lowered their prices considerably in face of competition from the above and a decrease in demand, are the two-star *Dilara* (☎0384/213 5441; ③), Yeni Kayseri Cad 2, which is basic but reasonably priced; the more comfortable *Seven Brothers* (☎0384/213 4979, fax 213 0454; ③), off Yeni Kayseri Caddesi at Tusan Sok 23; and the three-star *Orsan* (☎0384/213 5329; ⑤), Yeni Kayseri Cad 15, which has a fair-size swimming pool, a pleasant garden and large, well-furnished rooms.

The nicest of the **campsites** in the Cappadocia region, the *Koru Mocamp* (☎0384/212 2157 or 212 1190), is 8km east of Nevşehir, signposted off to the right as you turn off the Ürgüp road to go to Üçhisar. It's quiet and green with lots of space to pitch tents under pine trees, and a good swimming pool.

The Town

The long walk up to the castle becomes more pleasant the closer you get: the streets turn gradually steeper and narrower, and of a summer evening the atmosphere is increasingly dominated by women working at the local handicraft of lacemaking. The remains of the Ottoman **citadel** are no big deal in themselves, being just a few crenellated walls at the top of the hill, but from this vantage point you are provided with a graphic overview of the historical development of the city.

To the southeast is the small shanty town of **Muşkara**, a village of eighty houses and some three hundred people. It was lucky enough to produce a Dick Whittington-type figure who left home and went to seek his fortune in İstanbul. He found work in the Topkapı Sarayı, married a daughter of the sultan, and eventually became Grand Vizier **Damat İbrahim Paşa**, who profoundly affected the reign of Ahmet III, particularly in terms of its architecture. Like all good heroes he never forgot his roots, and he returned to Muşkara to found a "new town" (the meaning of Nevşehir), based around his own mosque complex, which included *medrese*, *imaret* and hamam. The town was planned with wide, Western-style boulevards – for which the buildings are nowhere near grand enough – and with a long, broad piazza between the market and the mosque.

The **Damat İbrahim Paşa mosque complex** (1726) is still the most imposing building in Nevşehir, situated on the side of the citadel hill with its *medrese* and library above it, and a tea garden directly below. It is set in a large precinct made all the more impressive by the cramped streets of the surrounding residential centre. The stone of the building is a pleasant, unadorned yellow, and its internal painting, especially under the sultan's loge and around the casements, is lovely. The cool, dark interior is further enhanced by small details like the fan-shaped decoration on the marble capitals, and the original carved wooden *kafes*, the screens which separated the women's balcony from the main hall. Opposite the mosque, the **Damat İbrahim Paşa Hamamı** (daily 7.30am–9pm, open to couples after 6pm as long as you give prior warning; Saturdays women only, all other days men only; $4 with massage and towel) is also in good working order and well run.

The museum
Nevşehir Museum, on Yeni Kayseri Caddesi (Tues–Sun 8am–noon & 1–5pm; $1), is well worth the walk out from the tourist information office. The whole museum is well laid out, and labelled in an unusually comprehensive manner. Its exhibits include three terracotta sarcophagi, dating from the third to fourth century AD, which resemble abstract mummy cases with little doors inserted at face and knee level. Finds from the Phrygian and Byzantine periods include mirrors, pins, spoons, terracotta pots and the like; upstairs is an exhibition of Turkish carpets and kilims and the looms on which they were made, as well as lovely old heavy silver Ottoman jewellery.

Eating and drinking

The best **food and drink** in town is to be found in the restaurants and bars of the hotels. Otherwise, the *Restaurant Lâle*, round the corner from the hotel of the same name on Gazhane Sokak, has a good choice of *meze* and kebabs. The *Aspava Restaurant*, at Atatürk Cad 100, serves well-prepared, cheap *lokanta* food and kebabs, and almost opposite but further up the hill is the slightly more expensive *Park*

Restaurant, situated off the road in pleasant gardens. Nevşehir's **market** is important to the region and consequently runs from Sunday morning to Monday night, taking over a large area below Eski Sanayı Meydanı. The best *döviz* office for **changing foreign currency** is *Üzer* opposite the main PTT, which gives a good rate of exchange and takes traveller's cheques.

Nar and Açıksaray

The tiny troglodyte village of **NAR**, 2km north of Nevşehir, is one of the prettiest in the Cappadocia region, and has been left off tour itineraries, possibly because it doesn't lay claim to any rock-cut churches. There are no eateries and only the ugly and exorbitant *Peri Motel* (☎0384/212 8816; ⑨) to stay in, but the villagers are friendly and don't mind if you wander up cobbled streets admiring their picturesque old houses, some of which have cave sections at the back. Further up the steep hillside on which the village is located, caves are used for storage, and at the top there's a cemetery with a number of Ottoman gravestones. Transport to Nar from Nevşehir is by frequent **dolmuş** from the corner of Lâle Caddesi and the Nar road, or from anywhere along Lâle Caddesi.

About 19km north of Nevşehir, the **Açıksaray** – reached by frequent Gülşehir dolmuşes from Nevşehir's *otogar* – is a sixth-to-seventh-century monastic complex, with chapels, refectories, dormitories and a kitchen, all cut into fairy chimneys in double and triple tiers, their facades decorated with false arcades. Nearby, a similar arrangement served as a convent. Two kilometres further on the same road towards Gülşehir, the Church of St John is at the time of writing being restored, with beautiful frescoes appearing as its blackened walls are cleaned. Check with Nevşehir tourist information office to find out whether the church has yet been opened to visitors.

Hacıbektaş

The **Museum of Hacıbektaş** (Tues–Sun 8am–noon & 1–5pm; $1), dedicated to one of the greatest medieval Sufic philosophers – Hacı Bektaş Veli – is located in the village of the same name, about 50km north of Nevşehir and accessible by four daily Ankara-bound buses from Nevşehir or frequent dolmuş from Gülşehir.

The village of **HACIBEKTAŞ** was chosen by the dervish as the location of a centre of scientific study, founded there in his lifetime, and the village was renamed in his honour after his death. The tomb of Hacı Bektaş Veli is located within the monastery complex, but the main part of the complex dates from the Ottoman period, when it was the headquarters of a large community of Bektaşi dervishes.

The teachings of Hacı Bektaş Veli had reverberations throughout the Muslim world, and different sects, including the Bektaşi, the Alevi and the Tahtacı, still follow traditions that originated in his doctrines. These sects are now the main counterbalancing force to Islamic fundamentalism in Turkey.

Little is known about his life, but he is believed to have lived from 1208 to 1270. Like other Turkish intellectuals of the time he was educated in Khorasan, where he became well versed in religion and mysticism. After journeying with his brother, who was later killed in battle, he returned to Anatolia and lived in Kayseri, Kırşehir and Sivas. Eventually he settled in a hamlet of seven houses, Suluca Karahöyük, the present location of the monastery.

As a religious leader and ethical teacher Hacı Bektaş prepared the way for the Ottoman Empire in Asia Minor: he was the recognized spiritual leader of soldiers and peasants, promoting the Turkish language and literature among them, and helping to popularize the Islamic faith in pre-Ottoman Turkey. The Bektaşi sect grew rapidly in Anatolia after the founder's death, largely because of the demoralization and impoverishment of monastic foundations and the similarity of many of the Bektaşi rites to

THE TEACHINGS OF HACI BEKTAŞ VELI

While the life of Hacı Bektaş Veli may be a subject for speculation, his teachings are well known, especially his great work the **Makalât**, which gives a valuable account of his mystical thought and philosophy.

According to Hacı Bektaş, the way to enlightenment has four stages, which he called "the Four Doors". The first is the ability to judge between clean and dirty, right and wrong, as taught by the laws of religion. Second is the duty of the dervish to pray night and day, and to call on God's name – a striving towards a future life. The third stage he called *Marifet* or "enlightenment", claiming that enlightened mystics are like water, making other things clean, and that they are beloved of God. The last stage, *Hakikat* or "reality", is achieved by those who practise modesty, resignation and submission; those who have effaced themselves in the presence of God and attained a level of constant contemplation and prayer.

The faults which grieved Hacı Bektaş most were those of ostentation, hypocrisy and inconsistency: "it is of no avail to be clean outside if there is evil within your soul". This could be the origin of the unorthodox customs of later followers of the Bektaşi sect, which included drinking wine, smoking hashish, eating during Ramadan, and – for women – uncovering the head outside the home. Hacı Bektaş's own dictum on women was unequivocal, and it is one of the most popularly quoted of all his sayings: "a nation which does not educate its women cannot progress".

Christian ones, including sprinkling a congregation with water in a ceremony resembling the baptism. The Bektaşi sect was closely linked to the janissary corps, known as the sons of Hacı Bektaş, and the two were abolished at the same time.

The town of Hacıbektaş is also well known for its **onyx**, which is by far the cheapest in the region – the shops are found in the street leading up to the Hacıbektaş Museum.

The monastery complex

Construction of the **complex** itself was begun during the reign of Sultan Orhan in the fourteenth century, and it was finally opened to the public as a museum in 1964, after extensive restoration. It comprises three courtyards, the second of which contains the attractive Aslanlı Çeşmesi, the **lion fountain**, named after a lion statue which was brought from Egypt in 1853. The sacred *karakazan* or **black kettle** (actually a cauldron) can be seen in the kitchen to the right of the courtyard. Important to both the Bektaşi sect and the janissaries, the black kettle originally symbolized communality, with possible reference to the Last Supper of the Christian faith. Subsequently, as the janissaries gained power, the symbolic significance of the kettle changed: by overturning it, the janissaries showed their displeasure with the sultan, and this could end in his deposition, as was the case when Selim III tried to replace the sect with his New Model Army. To the left of the courtyard is the **Meydan Evi**, bearing the earliest inscription in the complex, dated 1367. The timber roof of the Meydan Evi – where formal initiation ceremonies and acts of confession took place – has been beautifully restored, showing an ancient construction technique still in use in rural houses in central and eastern Anatolia. It's now an exhibition hall containing objects of significance to the order, including musical instruments and a late portrait of Hacı Bektaş, apparently deep in mystical reverie, with a hart in his lap and a lion by his side.

The third courtyard is the location of a **rose garden** and a well-kept graveyard, where the tombs bear the distinctive headware of the Bektaşi order. The tomb of the prophet is also located in the third courtyard, entered through the Akkapi, a white marble entranceway decorated with typical Selçuk motifs including a double-headed eagle. Off the corridor leading to the tomb is a small room which is said to have been the cell of Hacı Bektaş himself.

Derinkuyu and Kaymaklı

Among the most extraordinary phenomena of the Cappadocia region are the remains of underground settlements, some of them large enough to have accommodated up to 30,000 people. A total of 40 such settlements, from villages to vast cities, have been discovered, but only a few have so far been opened to the public. The best known are Derinkuyu and Kaymaklı, on the road from Nevşehir to Niğde. There are no fairy chimneys here, but the ground consists of the same volcanic tuff, out of which the beleaguered, ever-resourceful Cappadocians created vast cities that are almost completely unnoticeable from ground level.

In origin, the cities are thought to date back to **Hittite** times at least (1900–1200 BC). Hittite-style seals have been found during excavations and other Hittite remains, such as a lion statue, have turned up in the area. It is possible that the underground rooms were used as shelters during the attacks of 1200 BC, when the Hittite Empire was destroyed by invaders from Thrace. Later the complexes were enlarged by other civilizations, and the presence of missionary schools, churches and wine cellars would seem to indicate that they were used by **Christian communities**. There were certainly pre-Christian underground cities in the area as early as 401 BC: they are referred to by **Xenophon**, a Greek mercenary who took charge of the Ten Thousand after the death of Cyrus, marching across Cappadocia with them:

The houses here were built underground; the entrances were like wells but they broadened out lower down. There were tunnels dug in the ground for the animals while the men went down by ladder. Inside the houses there were goats, sheep, cows and poultry with their young . . . There was also wheat, beans, and barley wine in great bowls . . . When one was thirsty, one was meant to take a reed and suck the wine into one's mouth. This barley wine is exceedingly strong and is best mixed with water; but any man who is accustomed to it and drinks it undiluted enjoys its flavour to the full.

The most thoroughly excavated of the underground cities is located in the village of **DERİNKUYU**, 29km from Nevşehir. There's a daily **bus** here from Aksaray and half-hourly **dolmuşes** from Nevşehir.

The **underground city** of Derinkuyu, which means "deep well" (May–June daily 8am–6pm; July–Sept daily 8am–7pm; Oct–April daily 8am–5pm; $2), is signposted off to the left as you approach from Nevşehir. It's advisable to get there before 11am, when the tour groups arrive. The city is well lit and the original ventilation system still functions remarkably well, but some of the passages are small and cramped, and can be overcrowded if your visit coincides with that of a tour group. The size of this rock-cut warren is difficult to comprehend even on a thorough exploration, since only part of what has been excavated is open to the public, and even the excavated part is thought to comprise only a quarter of the original city.

The area cleared to date occupies 1500 square metres and consists of a total of eight floors reaching to a depth of 55 metres. What you'll see includes, on the first two floors, stables, wine presses and a dining hall or school with two long, rock-cut tables; living quarters, churches, armouries and tunnels on the third and fourth floors; and a crucifix-shaped church, a meeting hall with three supporting columns, a dungeon and a grave on the lower levels. In a room off the meeting hall is a circular passageway which is believed to have been a **confessional**. The **wine press** on the first floor would have had an opening to the ground above. Grapes thrown into the press would have been trampled and their juice collected in vats below. Dropping between 70 and 85 metres to far below the lowest floor level were 52 large **ventilation shafts** and the **deep wells** from which the city takes its name, and the whole complex is riddled with small ventilation ducts – 15,000 on the first level alone. There are also a number of escape routes from one floor to another, and passages leading beyond the city, one of which is thought to have gone all the way to Kaymaklı, 9km away. The walls of the rooms are completely undecorated, but chisel marks are clearly visible and give some idea of the work that must have gone into the creation of this extraordinary place. Most evocative of the lifestyle of former inhabitants are the huge **circular doors** that could be used to seal one level from another. The doors, which were virtually impregnable from the outside, would have been closed with a pole through the circular hole in their centre, and through this hole arrows could have been shot once the door was secure.

Nine kilometres north of Derinkuyu, the Nevşehir–Niğde highway passes **KAY-MAKLI** (March–Sept daily 8am–7.30pm; Oct–Feb daily 8am–5pm; $2). Smaller and consequently less popular than Derinkuyu, only five of this city's levels have been excavated to date. Should you arrive without a guide, a helpful plan of the city ($1) is on sale outside the door. The layout is very similar: networks of streets with small living spaces leading off them open into underground plazas with various functions, the more obvious of which are stables, smoke-blackened kitchens, storage space and wine presses.

Üçhisar

ÜÇHİSAR, 7km east of Nevşehir on the Nevşehir–Ürgüp and Nevşehir–Göreme dolmuş runs, is the first truly Cappadocian village en route to the centre of the region from Nevşehir. It's a good place to base yourself if you have your own transport, as accommodation possibilities include some of the best *pansiyon*s in the region, and the atmosphere is less frenetic than in Göreme. It makes sense to stop here anyway, if only to take your bearings from the vantage point of the sixty-metre-high rock that dominates the village. Riddled with the cave homes of villagers who lived here until it became too dangerous, the rock is now open to visitors (daily 8am–8.30pm; $1). The best time for a visit is at sunset, when the views of the surrounding countryside, including Erciyes Dağı to the east and Melendiz and Hasan Dağları to the southwest, are particularly alluring. It's an excellent place to get a first impression of Cappadocia's extraordinary geology.

If you're looking for scenery and solitude, head out of town on the old Göreme road, which hugs a very steep hill below the fortress affording good views of the surrounding scenery. To the right about 200m out of town you'll find a group of small **pansiyons**, including the excellent *Kaya Pansiyon* (☎0384/219 2441, fax 219 2079; ②), which is clean and attractively furnished, with a pleasant terrace restaurant affording fantastic views; an excellent buffet-style breakfast is included in the price and evening meals are inexpensive. Another good bet in the same area is *La Maison du Rêve* (☎0384/219 2199, fax 219 2775; ②), with some large, well-appointed rooms (waterless) and good views of the fairy-chimney landscapes from the balconies. The *Garden of 1001 Nights*, on the new Göreme–Üçhisar road as you leave the village (☎0384/219 2293; ③), occupies a series of caves cut into fairy chimneys, some even en suite, combining the quirkiness of a rock-cut *pansiyon* with the facilities of a hotel and magnificent views from its balconies.

Göreme and around

The small town of **GÖREME** – just 3km east of Üçhisar – is of central importance to Cappadocian tourism partly because of its museum, located a couple of kilometres away on the Ürgüp road, but most importantly because it is the most famous of the few remaining Cappadocian villages whose rock-cut houses and fairy chimneys are still inhabited. The village is presently reeling a little from the effects of tourism, which has expanded quite remarkably in the last decade or so: its main street is given over almost entirely to servicing visitors – carpet shops, tour companies, restaurants – and seemingly every small dwelling now has rooms to let and proudly proclaims itself a *pansiyon*, regardless of the facilities on offer.

Despite the commercialization, the place has managed to hold on to a degree of authentic charm, and a short stroll will still take you up into tuff landscapes, vineyards which the locals cultivate for the production of *pekmez* (a breakfast syrup made from grape seeds), and the occasional rock-cut church, unknown to the hordes who frequent the nearby museum. Transport to Göreme, however, can be a problem, with only the *Nevtur/Göreme* company offering long-distance bus services here (see p.522 for the full story). Once you get to Göreme, public transport around the region is adequate and hitching relatively easy, so it's not a bad place from which to base your explorations.

The Town

Modern development in the town, including shops, houses and shopping precinct, is the biggest threat to its future, since ancient dwellings have been destroyed in the process. In opposition to the destructive and often illegal building, the "Save Göreme" committee – with the help of organizations like the Supreme Board for Monuments – are aiming to prevent local development while persuading the authorities to renovate existing buildings and invest money in modern techniques to halt erosion. They have highlighted the destruction of frescoes in fairy chimneys on *pansiyon* premises, and have helped to halt the building of an ugly annexe to the *Ataman Hotel*, but as so often in Turkey, money talks, and the penalties are not enough to prevent transgression where big business is concerned.

The village's long history and the variety of its cultures are evidenced in the fact that Göreme is the fourth known name bestowed on the village. The Byzantines called it Matiana, the Armenian Christians Macan, and the Turks originally called it Avcılar, only giving it the name Göreme ("unseen"), in honour of its valley of churches of the same name, in the last decade.

After you've drunk your quota of apple tea you may be pleased to escape to the more rarefied climes of the tuff hills above town, where people perpetuate the traditions of centuries despite the recent changes in the village below. Pigeon droppings are still collected and used to fertilize the crops, the main form of transport is the donkey, and fields are irrigated with water stored in nearby caves.

There are two **churches** located in these hills near the *Ataman* hotel, signposted from the road leading straight off the main street to the hotel. The **Kadir Durmuş Kilisesi** (named after the man who owns the neighbouring fields, and signposted) has a cave house with rock-cut steps next door to it, clearly visible from the path across a vineyard. It's not painted but has an impressive and unusual upstairs gallery, and cradle-shaped tombs outside. Thought to date to the seventh century, it could have been a parish church. The second church, the eleventh-century **Yusuf Koç Kilisesi**, is also known as "the church with five pillars"; its sixth was never carved. There are two domes, one of which has been damaged in the past to accommodate a pigeon coop, and frescoes in very good condition. Among them are the Annunciation, to the left; saints George and Theodore slaying the dragon, to the right; and Helena and Constantine depicted with the True Cross beside the door. In the dome above the altar are the Madonna and Child, and below, beside the altar, are the four evangelists, the only paintings in the church to have suffered substantial damage.

The best-known, most rewarding **walk** in the Göreme region is along a path starting from just above the *Ataman Hotel* to Üçhisar, through the Uzundere valley, passing through rock-cut tunnels into the heart of the Cappadocian coutryside. Good shoes are a necessity, and the final descent into Üçhisar is precipitous, with fairly narrow stretches of path. It's better to go in a group from a *pansiyon* (the *Köse Pansiyon* owner knows the route well), or with a local guide.

The wealth enjoyed by the village in Ottoman times is reflected in the structures surviving from that period, including one that is periodically open as a restaurant, the **Konak**

Türk Evi, also known as the *Mehmet Paşa House*, after its original owner, an Ottoman dignitary. The palatial building has been restored by Dutch architect Nico Leyssen, and is notable for the frescoes in the two main rooms, the *haremlik* and the *selâmlik*, originally painted by the artist of the Ahmet III dining room in Topkapı Palace. To get there from the bus station, cross the canal by the bridge and take a right and another right before the Gaferli Camii, and it's up behind the *Phoenix Pansiyon* (see below).

Practicalities

The PTT is the best place in town to **change money**, including traveller's cheques. *Zemi Tours* (☎0384/271 2576) on the main street near the PTT also changes money and is the only **tour company** in Cappadocia presently offering camping tours to the Ihlara valley. **Rental cars** are available at *Rose Tours* on the Nevşehir road (☎0384/271 2059), and *Şovalye* at the *otogar* (☎0384 271 2622), which also has **bicycles** ($6 a day). *Hiro Tours* at the *otogar* (☎0384/271 2542) rents mopeds for $18 a day, and the *Rainbow Ranch*, on the road leading uphill behind the *Blue Moon* (☎0384/271 2413), lays on **horse** tours to the surrounding valleys. There's a **laundry**, the *Çamışırhane* (daily 8am–8pm), next to the *Escape Bar*.

Accommodation

Göreme's **pansiyons** have long been a favourite with young travellers looking for cheap lodgings with a relaxed, easy-going atmosphere. Because of this the villagers are well used to foreigners and their wayward ways, although women travelling alone or in pairs have complained of much unwanted attention, and have preferred to stay elsewhere in Cappadocia. *Pansiyons* spring up every year, and competition is fierce: tourists are waylaid at the bus station, and prices are so low that the better ones are finding it hard to maintain standards, despite collective price control which was supposed to make the atmosphere healthier. *Pansiyon* **prices** are fixed, at $14 a double with bathroom, $10 a double without, but because it's now difficult for *pansiyon* owners to make a living, they're going into other businesses, establishing partnerships in carpet firms, running tour companies, or setting up restaurants on their premises. In this way they compensate for the loss of revenue that fixed prices entail, but guests may feel pressured by their *pansiyon* owner and uncomfortable about patronizing rival establishments. It also means that a formerly tight-knit community is riven by competition and jealousy.

Nevertheless, there are a number of excellent establishments in the village – too many to list comprehensively – at all levels of comfort. Many are now run by Turkish–European/Australasian partnerships, and those that aren't will have fluent English speakers at hand. For the better establishments, listed here, the fixed prices are ridiculously low.

The English-run *Blue Moon* (☎0384/271 2433), reached from the *otogar* by crossing the bridge over the canal, has a terrace overlooking the town, and four restored stone-built rooms, with traditional arched ceilings. The place is immaculate, with continuous hot water in en-suite bathrooms, and is a good bet in winter for its central heating and double glazing. Crossing the bridge from the *otogar* and walking in the other direction from the *Blue Moon*, then taking the first right off the main street before the Gaferli Camii, will bring you to the Kiwi-run *Phoenix Pansiyon* (☎0384/271 2561), a well-furnished renovated Ottoman house with carpeted rooms, around a central vine-covered courtyard, where converted stables have en-suite bathrooms. It's busy in winter because of central heating and duvets. Next to it, the *Tuna* (☎0384/271 2051) is all cave rooms, some cut into fairy chimneys approached by a ladder; even the original kitchen, with *tandır*, smoke-blackened walls and chimney, is in use as a bedroom. On the road running parallel to the Nevşehir road out of town, *L'Elysée* (☎0384/271 2244) is run by a charming French woman who keeps a tastefully furnished, immaculate old village house, with a garden courtyard, washing machine and night-time trout barbecues. The *Köse Pansiyon* (☎0384/271 2294), with a pleasant garden behind the PTT on the Avanos road out of town, is comfortable and friendly, presenting a choice of cheaper dormitories, doubles with and without bathrooms, and singles; the Turkish and Scottish owners will pick up stranded clients from Nevşehir. On the road to Göreme Open-Air Museum, the *Paradise Pansiyon* (☎0384/271 2248) has a well-deserved reputation for hospitality, friendliness and excellent cooking; here you can stay in a centrally heated cave with en suite bathroom. Next door, the *Peri Pansiyon* (☎0384/271 2136) has immaculate cave rooms in fairy chimneys around a lovely garden courtyard.

The choicest views, and some of the best *pansiyons*, are on the hills above the town. To get to the popular *Kelebek* (☎0384/271 2531; rooms with or without bathrooms), carry on uphill from the *Tuna*; here you can choose between sixth-century fairy chimney caves and a renovated Ottoman house. The nearby *SOS Motel Pansiyon* (☎0384/271 2134) offers caves with views and even balconies (with or without bathrooms), and the owner will pick up from Nevşehir.

For a little more class and comfort, there are a number of attractive **hotels** in Göreme, whose prices are not controlled. The most luxurious is the *Ataman* opposite the SOS Motel Pansiyon on the hill above town (☎0384/271 2319; ⑧), whose corridors are rock-cut and whose rooms are built in Ottoman style, beautifully furnished with antiques, old lace and kilims. The Australian-run *Ottoman House* (☎0384/271 2616; ③), next to the canal on the Üçhisar road out of town, is a comfortable new house built in the old style, en suite throughout.

There are several **campsites** on the fringes of Göreme, including *Berlin Camping* (☎0384/271 2249), on the Ürgüp road near the *Peri Pansiyon*, with good facilities and lots of shade, and *Dilek Camping* (☎0384/271 2396) next door, with its own water supply, a nice little restaurant and a swimming pool. The *Panorama* (☎0384/271 2352), 1km out on the Üçhisar road, has hot water and good facilities, plus panoramic views of the fairy chimneys, but it's a bit exposed to the road and has no trees to speak of.

Eating and drinking

The best **restaurant** in Göreme, indeed among the best in Cappadocia, is at the *Ataman* hotel (☎0384/271 2310). It's pricy for the village, but everything is immaculately prepared and served, from local specialities like Kayseri *pastırma* (cured meat) baked in paper, to French soufflés and flambées. Expect to pay between $8 and $20 a head.

Cheaper options include the highly recommended *Orient Restaurant*, with a garden where they offer excellent *menemen* (Turkish-style scrambled egg) breakfasts, and a varied, reasonably priced daytime menu. The *Sultan Restaurant* opposite the *otogar* is more sophisticated, with excellent *meze* and tender kebabs, and efficient, friendly service; they have a terrace upstairs and a pleasant restaurant downstairs. Opposite the bus station on the *Blue Moon* side, the *Rose Kebab House* does a filling, cheap chicken kebab sandwich, and between here and the *Paradise* carpet shop, there's a new, as yet unnamed restaurant with a garden out front, which serves up delicious regional soups and stews from earthenware pots. The *Escape Bar* on the road to the Gaferli Camii is the current favourite **watering hole** and disco.

Göreme Open-Air Museum

The **Göreme Open-Air Museum** (daily 8am–7pm; winter closes 5pm; $3.50), 2km from the village up a steep hill on the road to Ürgüp, is the best known and most visited of all the monastic settlements in the Cappadocia region. It's also the largest of the religious complexes, and its churches, of which there are over thirty, contain some of the most fascinating of all the frescoes in Cappadocia. Apart from a small sixth- to seventh-century chapel, which has almost collapsed, all the churches in Göreme date from the period after the Iconoclastic controversy, and mainly from the second half of the ninth to the end of the eleventh century.

The best preserved and most fascinating of all the churches is the **Tokalı Kilise**, "the Church with the Buckle", located away from the others on the opposite side of the road about 50m back towards the village. If it's closed, ask the curator at the ticket office to open it for you. The church is different in plan to others in the area, having a transverse nave and an atrium hewn out of an earlier church, known as the "Old Church". Most striking as you enter is the bright blue colour used in the background to the paintings. The frescoes of the **Old Church**, dating from the second decade of the tenth century, depict various scenes from the life of Christ. They are classic examples of the archaic period of Cappadocian painting, which was characterized by a return to the forms of the best work of the fourth to sixth centuries: the style is linear, but like the mosaics of Aya Sofya in İstanbul, the faces are modelled by the use of different intensities of colour and by the depiction of shadow.

The paintings in the **New Church** are some of the finest examples of tenth-century Byzantine art. Again they represent a return to archaic models, depicting a series of tall and elegant figures, the niches in the walls of the nave serving to give a sense of depth and substance to the paintings. The pictures represent more scenes from the life of Christ and reflect an interpretation of the apse as the sepulchre of Christ and the altar as his tomb. The crucifix is in the conch of the apse, and the semicircular wall is used for the four scenes of the Passion and Resurrection: the Descent from the Cross, the Entombment, the Holy Women at the Sepulchre and the Resurrection.

The best known of the churches in the main complex of Göreme are the three **columned churches**: the **Elmalı Kilise** (Church of the Apple, presently closed to the public, and not likely to reopen in the foreseeable future), the **Karanlık Kilise** (Dark Church, also closed for restoration, but may be reopened soon with an additional entrance fee) and the **Çarıklı Kilise**, the "Church of the Sandals". These eleventh-century churches were heavily influenced by classical Byzantine forms: constructed to an inscribed cross plan, the central dome, supported on columns, contains the Pantocrator above head-and-shoulders depictions of the Archangels and seraphim. The painting of the churches, particularly Elmalı Kilise, is notable for the skill with which the form and movement of the figures correspond to the surfaces they cover. They are clad in drapery which closely follows the contours of their bodies, and their features are smoothly modelled, with carefully outlined eyes. The facade of the Karanlık Kilise is intricately carved to give more of an impression of a freestanding building than elsewhere in Göreme. The expensive blue colour obtained from the mineral azurite is everywhere in the church, whereas in the Elmalı Kilise grey is the predominant tone.

A number of other late eleventh-century single-aisle churches in the museum are covered in much cruder geometric patterns and linear pictures, painted straight onto the rock (unlike the frescoes of the three columned churches, which were preceded by a layer of plaster). In the Tokalı Kilise, this kind of painting can be seen appearing from beneath the plaster, but in churches where it was not plastered over, the painting is extensive. The predominant colour of this style was red ochre and the ubiquitous symbol was the cross, which indicated that the church had been consecrated.

In this style is the **Church of St Barbara**, named after a depiction of the saint on the north wall. Christ is represented on a throne in the apse. The strange insect-figure for which the church is also known must have had symbolic or magical significance which is now lost.

The **Yılanlı Kilise** (Church of the Snake), also in this group, is most famous for the depiction of Saint Onophrius on the west wall of the nave. Saint Onophrius was a hermit who lived in the Egyptian desert in the fourth and fifth centuries, eating only dates, with a foliage loincloth for cover. According to Cappadocian guides and literature, the

CHRISTIANITY IN CAPPADOCIA

For many centuries Anatolia was the most vital centre of Christianity in the Mediterranean region. The great ecumenical councils which established the elemental doctrines of the faith were all held in Anatolia, and the region was home to some of the greatest early ecclesiastical writers. Most famously, these included the fourth-century **Cappadocian Fathers**: Basil the Great, Gregory of Nazianzuz and Gregory of Nyssa. The religious authority of the capital of Cappadocia, Caesarea – present-day Kayseri – extended over the whole of southeast Anatolia, and it was also the birthplace of Gregory the Illuminator, the evangelizer of Armenia. The unique, creative art forms in the region are attributable to a long and complex history. Before becoming a Roman province in 18 AD the kingdom had enjoyed a 300-year period of independence, during which time small states, centred on a sanctuary and controlled by priests, had been the predominant units of power. Cappadocia's religion until the arrival of Christianity had been Semitic- and Iranian-influenced, and its own language did not die out until the fourth century. Caesarea came under the Patriarchate of Constantinople in 381 BC, and from then on was influenced more and more by religious ideas from the capital.

TURBULENT YEARS

Most disruptive was the **Iconoclastic controversy** of 726–843, which had a profound effect on the creative life of Cappadocia. By the beginning of the eighth century, the cult of images had become extravagant, particularly noticeable in contrast to Muslim and Jewish hostility to the worship of images. In addition, the political power of the monks, whose numbers had increased considerably during the seventh century, began to cause concern. The Iconoclastic movement was accompanied by the closure of monasteries and confiscation of their property. The worst period of repressive activity occurred during the reign of Constantine V, marked by the Iconoclastic Council of 754. All sacred images except the cross were forbidden, but at the same time the destruction of any religious building and its furnishings, whether or not they were decorated with idolatrous images, was prohibited.

From the middle of the sixth century the region had also been suffering a 300-year period of turbulence as the battleground of the Byzantines and the Arabs, and was subjected to continual Arab raids, characterized by widespread plunder and destruction. The inhabitants responded with ingenuity: in the plains they went to ground, creating underground cities (or extended existing complexes); and in rocky Cappadocia they took to the hills, carving monastery complexes at precarious heights in the tuff cliff faces.

After the restoration of the cult of images in 843, there was a renewed vigour in the religious activity of Cappadocia. During this period, the wealth of the church increased to such an extent that in 964 monastery building was prohibited, an edict only withdrawn in 1003. Meanwhile the religious communities were brought to heel, becoming controlled to a greater extent by the ecclesiastical hierarchy. Even though Cappadocia continued to be a centre of religious activity well into the Ottoman period, it had lost the artistic momentum which had produced the most extraordinary works of earlier centuries.

REMAINING CHURCHES

Today, the number of churches in the Cappadocia region is estimated at considerably more than a thousand, dating from the earliest days of Christianity to the thirteenth century. About 150 of these are decorated. Religious complexes are scattered all over Cappadocia, and despite the damage caused by time and human agencies, some of them are exceptionally well preserved. The technique of excavation, still used today, is evident in the fresh-looking pick marks on walls and ceilings. Most of the architecture is barely discernible from the outside, apart from a few small holes serving as doors, windows or air and light shafts. Inwardly, however, the churches recreate many of the features of Byzantine buildings, especially as imperial influence increased in the region. Later churches have domes, barrel-vaulted ceilings and inscribed cross plans supported by totally irrelevant pillars, capitals and pendentives which have no structural significance whatsoever.

saint was originally a woman, and a bit of a temptress at that. When eventually she repented her wicked ways and asked to be delivered from the desires of men, she was granted her wish, and received a beard, like that of the figure in the fresco. The story probably derives from the emphasized breasts of the figure in the picture, and from the desert foliage which the saint uses as a loincloth.

Opposite Saint Onophrius, Constantine the Great and his mother Saint Helena are depicted holding the True Cross. After a vision in which she saw the True Cross, Saint Helena travelled to Jerusalem at the age of eighty to find it. She unearthed three crosses and to test which of them was genuine she laid them in turn on the coffin of a dead youth, who revived at the appropriate moment. Next to this painting, two of the "Soldier Saints", George and Theodore, are seen trampling a serpent. Saint Theodore was a Roman soldier who refused to enter into pagan worship and set fire to the temple of the mother goddess in Amasea (Amasya), Pontus: he was tortured and thrown into a furnace. Between the Yilanlı and the Karanlık churches is a **refectory** with a rock-cut table designed to take about fifty diners.

Outside the museum, there are a few more churches on the road back to Göreme village. All of them, however, are presently closed to the public, and permission is needed from the Ministry of Culture in Ankara to enter them. They include the twelfth-century **Church of St Eustace**, reached by an iron staircase, with red and green paintings thought to have been the work of Armenian Christians. Also to the left of the road is the four-columned **Kılıçlar Kilise** (Church of the Swords), and on the right beyond Tokalı Kilise is the **St Daniel Chapel**, with a picture of Daniel in the lion's den. The **Saklı Kilise** (Hidden Church), about halfway between the museum and the village, uses Cappadocian landscapes complete with fairy chimneys as a background for biblical scenes.

Çavuşin

Six kilometres from Göreme off the road to Avanos, **ÇAVUŞİN** is a small village with a good hotel and a few nice *pansiyon*s, as well as a really beautiful church located in the hills nearby. The best approach to the village is to walk – through fabulous tuff landscapes – on a path beginning just beside *Kaya Camping* on the road from Ürgüp to Göreme. Follow the path for about half an hour, and where it takes a helter-skelter type bend through a tuff tunnel to the left, follow the precipitous path to the right, heading down into the Kızılçukur valley: this will lead you to Çavuşin, in the same general direction you came from, in another half hour or so.

The villagers have gradually moved out of their cave dwellings as a result of rock falls, but the old caves, in the hills above the village, can be explored if some care is taken; it's best to take a guide from the *Çinar Cafe*. In their midst is the **Church of St John the Baptist** (free entry at all times), a large basilica thought to have been a centre of pilgrimage and an important religious centre for the whole region. Its position up on the cliff face, combined with the imposing aspect of its colonnaded and moulded facade, gives it prominence over the whole valley. The church, most probably constructed in the fifth century, contains a votive pit, the only one in Cappadocia, which is thought to have contained the hand of Saint Hieron, a local saint born a few kilometres away. The walls are covered with paintings ranging in date from the sixth to the eighth century, probably *ex votos* from grateful pilgrims.

A short distance away, located in a tower of rock in the same valley, the church known as the **"Pigeon House"** has frescoes commemorating the passage of Nicephoras Phocas through Cappadocia in 964–965, during his military campaign against Cilicia. The frescoes probably commemorate a pilgrimage to the Church of Saint John the Baptist by the Byzantine emperor, who is known to have hankered after the monastic life and dreamed of retiring to Mount Athos with his spiritual father.

In the village itself, on the left as you descend to the main road, the *İn* (☎0384/532 7070; ①) is a simple but comfortable **pansiyon**, with shared bathroom (containing a real bath). Across the road, the *Green Motel* (☎0384/532 7050, fax 532 7032; ②) is an extremely attractive en-suite establishment in a pleasant garden which doubles up as a **campsite**. A new venture in Cappadocia is **hot-air ballooning**, offered by the *Green Motel* ($170 per person). The balloon leaves at sunrise for its four-hour trip, though the exact itinerary depends on the day's wind and air currents. Down on the main Ürgüp–Avanos road are a couple of good **onyx shops** which seem fairly priced: the *Fabrique d'Onyx* and the *Çavuşin Onyx Factory and Silver Shop*.

Zelve

The deserted **monastery complex** located in the three valleys of **Zelve** (daily 8am–7pm; winter closes 5pm; $2.50), 3km off the Avanos–Çavuşin road, is one of the most fascinating remnants of Cappadocia's troglodyte past. It's accessible by hourly dolmuşes which run between Ürgüp and Avanos, and drop at Zelve on request. The churches in Zelve date back to the pre-Iconoclastic age (that is before the ninth century) but the valley was inhabited by Turkish Muslims until 1952, when rock falls, which still occur, made the area too dangerous to inhabit.

For the most part, the structure of the complex is dictated by the form of the tuff rock-faces into which it is carved: the inhabitants simply hacked out their dwellings, making few attempts – apart from the odd dividing wall – to diversify the structure with architectural features. On the left-hand side of the first valley (now accessed via the middle valley because of a rock fall which has cut off the entrance), are the remains of a small Ottoman mosque, the prayer hall and *mihrab* of which are partly hewn from the rock, showing a continuance of this ancient architectural tradition.

An exploration of the complex really requires a torch and old clothes, along with a considerable sense of adventure. At the top of the right-hand valley, on the right as you go up, a honeycomb of rooms are approached up metal staircases. Once you're up on the rock face the problems start: some of the rooms are entered by means of precarious steps, others by swinging up through large holes in their floors (look out for ancient hand and foot holes); and on occasions, massive leaps to a lower floor are required. Another daunting challenge is the walk through the tunnel which leads between the two valleys on the right (as you face them from the car park) – impossible without a torch and nerves of steel. None of this is recommended for the infirm or claustrophobic, but it's good fun if you're reasonably energetic and have a head for heights.

A large number of chapels and medieval oratories are scattered up and down the valleys, many of them decorated with carved **crosses**. This preponderance of crosses, combined with the relatively small number of frescoes in the valleys, is thought to demonstrate a pre-Iconoclastic opposition to the cult of images. The few **painted images** found in Zelve are in the churches of the third valley, on the far right. The twin-aisled Üzümlu Kilise has pre-Iconoclastic grapevines painted in red and green on the walls, and a cross carved into the ceiling.

The most picturesque of all the Cappadocian valleys, **Paşabağı**, located 2km from the Zelve turn-off on the Avanos road, is possibly also the most photographed. Previously the area was known as "Valley of the Monks", because it was a favourite place of retreat for stylite hermits who lodged in the fairy chimneys – which, with their black basalt caps, are double- or even triple-coned here. In one of the triple-coned chimneys is a chapel dedicated to Saint Simeon Stylites, hollowed out at three levels, with a monk's cell at the top. A hundred metres east of the chapel is a cell, bearing the inscription "Receive me, O grave, as you received the Stylite".

Ortahisar

A friendly little village located a little off the road between Göreme and Ürgüp, **ORTAHİSAR** sees none of the hordes that are affecting Göreme village so profoundly. Despite being surrounded by the storehouses of Turkey's lemon mafiosi (the rock-cut caves in the region are particularly congenial to the storage of the fruit), the village itself has retained a degree of charm and innocence. After a few hours here you feel as if you know the whole populace – and they will certainly know you.

One of the chief attractions of Ortahisar is the fortress-like, 86-metre-high **rock** which, as at Üçhisar, once housed the entire village. It can now be explored and climbed (daily 7.30am–8.30pm; $1.50) for excellent views of the surrounding valleys. The village itself is clustered around two squares, the first of them dominated by the bus station, the second, Cumhuriyet Meydanı, crouched beneath the village rock.

There's plenty to explore in the valleys around Ortahisar, so if you don't have your own transport and you want to spend time in the area it makes sense to **stay** the night. The *Hotel Gümüş* (☎0384/343 3127; ①), next to the PTT on the road into town, has plain but comfortable rooms with bathrooms, and fabulous views from the terrace, at the back of which there are more attic-style rooms with sloping roofs. Mainly catering to groups but also welcoming to individuals, the *Saray 3* **restaurant**, on Cumhuriyet Meydanı, dishes up exceptionally good Anatolian cuisine cooked on a charcoal fire, served with warm *pide*. The *Sinbad* **nightclub** (☎0384/343 3814), located in a former lemon storage cellar, is less expensive than the competition in Ürgüp and Avanos, and is aimed at a lefty, more intellectual audience.

There are also a few good **junk shops**, the best being *Ahmet Yönemli's* and *Crazy Ali's Curiosity Shop*, both selling old silver and copperware on the second village square, and an onyx factory, *Hisar Onyx*, where you can watch the production process from scratch.

Churches around Ortahisar

The village **guide** is a deaf mute, Ercan, who seems to know the area better than anyone. Enquire in *Hisar Onyx*: it would be almost impossible to find some of the churches in the surrounding valleys without him.

Taking the road marked "Pancarlık Kilise" off the second square, you'll come to the valley of the Üzenge Çay, the opposite side of which is covered in pigeon coops. If you walked down this valley to the left for a little over 2km you'd arrive in Ürgüp, but straight ahead a rough track leads across the valley to the **Pancarlık church and monastery complex**, 3km from Ortahisar. Hardly visited because of the difficulty of access, the church ($0.50) has some excellent frescoes in good condition – even their faces are intact. They include the Baptism of Christ and the Annunciation, and to the left of the altar what looks like the Virgin taking a bath.

Heading the other way out of Ortahisar, down Hüseyin Bey Camii Sokak and into the Ortahisar ravine, there's a group of churches which includes the **Balkanlar Kilise**, said to contain some of the oldest frescoes in Cappadocia, and the **Sarıca Kilise**, which has a dome and two freestanding pillars, as well as frescoes of the Annunciation and, on the pendentives, angels. Another church in this valley has a carving typical of the symbolism of the Early Christian period: it shows a palm, representing the Tree of Paradise, above a cross enclosed within a crown.

Another interesting rock-cut complex which is hardly known to the public is the **Hallaç Hospital Monastery**, so called because it's thought once to have been an infirmary. It's reached by following the road leading to *Öz Ay* carpet shop and continuing past the shop for about twenty minutes. The complex is carved and painted inside and out, the facade decorated with mock doors, windows and pillars, painted in green, black and red.

Ürgüp and around

Above all else, **ÜRGÜP** is tourist-friendly: if you're looking for good facilities, nightlife and shopping in a pleasant environment then Ürgüp was made for you. But unlike many resorts of this size, the place has also had the resilience and composure to accommodate its visitors without too many compromises. Before the exchange of populations in 1923, Ürgüp had a largely Greek population, and there are still many distinctive and beautiful houses of Greek (and Ottoman) origin scattered around the town, many used as government buildings or hotels, while others remain domestic residences. The tuff cliffs above the town are riddled with man-made cave dwellings, now put to use as storage space and stabling for the donkeys whose braying takes the place of a dawn chorus all over Cappadocia. Tourism has meant that the younger generation has moved out of the family caves and opened shops and hotels in the town below, but at least for the season they are still in Ürgüp, and as long as they remain they will safeguard the traditions and memories of the community.

Arrival, information and accommodation

Arriving in Ürgüp the first surprise is that the **otogar** is in the centre of town. What's more, the tourist office, post office, museum and shops are all within walking distance, while the best hotels are at most a cheap taxi ride away.

To reach most of Ürgüp's shops and facilities, find the steps leading up from the bus station, beside *Murat's Bar*, to Cumhuriyet Meydanı. Kayseri Caddesi, the street leading downhill to the tourist information office and museum, is also the main shopping street. The **tourist information office** (May–Sept daily 8.30am–8pm; Oct–April daily 8.30am–noon & 1.30–5.30pm; ☎0384/341 4059) is at Kayseri Cad 37, pleasantly located next to the museum in a park, complete with tea garden, where you can peruse their maps and hotel price list.

Accommodation shouldn't be a problem in or out of season, since Ürgüp is full of hotels and *pansiyon*s. There are several attractive, well-run hotels **northwest of the centre**, on the roads leading in and out of Ürgüp in the Nevşehir/Göreme direction. *Hotel Konak* on Ahmet Refik Caddesi (☎0384/341 4667; ②) is immaculately kept and a good choice for families, as children will enjoy beds up on wooden platforms. The balconied rooms have large windows affording views of the rock-cut houses and pigeon coops opposite. The *Hotel Surban* (☎0384/341 4603; ③), on the same road beyond the *Hanedan* restaurant, is well decorated, modern and comfortable. Beyond the characterless *Hotel Turban* is the area known as Esbelli, where troglodyte dwellings are cut into the hillside. The *Esbelli Ev* here is one of the most effectively restored buildings in Cappadocia (☎0384/341 3395; ⑦). Original features of this collection of village houses have been retained, and the rock-cut rooms are tastefully furnished with period furniture, and heated by wood-burning fires in winter. The atmosphere is less that of a hotel than a guesthouse: you're invited to help yourself from the fridge in the kitchen, cook a meal, and sit in a communal sitting room, listening to classical and jazz CDs. Guests can use the *Turban*'s pool.

On the **west side of the town centre**, *Hotel Hitit*, İstiklâl Cad 46 (☎0384/341 4481, fax 341 2206; ④), is a fascinating 600-year-old house, run as a *pansiyon* by the charming family who have lived here for years. At the back of their abundant vegetable garden, there's a cave with a circular stone door of the type found in the underground cities, prompting speculation about an unexcavated refuge for the citizens of Ürgüp. The rooms, looking onto a bright, pleasant courtyard, have attractive vaulted ceilings and Kayseri rugs, but otherwise furniture and fittings, which include central heating, are everyday and practical. At İstiklâl Cad 38 (the entrance to town on the one-way system), the *Hotel Asia Minor* (☎0384/341 4645 or 341 4721; ③) occupies one of Ürgüp's oldest and loveliest buildings, with an attractive garden courtyard; the new management plans to improve the rather spartan interior, so it may be worth checking out. Opposite on İstiklâl Caddesi, the *Cappadoce Hotel* (☎0384/341 4714; $10) occupies an old Greek monastery building – now somewhat rundown though heated in winter – with a garden courtyard and a range of accommodation from four-person rooms to doubles with bathrooms. Facing the *Cappadoce*, in a similarly elevated position above the town's hamam, the *Sun Pansiyon* (☎0384/341 4493; ③) is a ramshackle affair with a pleasant terrace and a welcoming owner; some rooms are caves, and others have en-suite bathrooms.

On the **east side of the centre**, *Göreme Şato Otel* (☎0384/341 4022; ②) is a cheaper option, set in an old, fairly rundown building that has a lot of character, with double rooms (some with baths) and camping space in the garden. Nearby on Kayseri Caddesi, the *Hotel Anatolia* (☎0384/341 4487; ②) and the *Yildiz* directly opposite (☎0384/341 4487; ③) are both simple, clean, family-run affairs, the *Yildiz* having the edge in terms of service and furnishings (reflected in the price difference). In both it's better to ask for rooms at the back as the front can be noisy. The *Hotel Feza*, Elgin Sok 11 (☎0384/341 2184; ③), is a similar simple, family-run affair, where clean basic rooms have balconies (but no views).

The *Çamlık* **campsite** (☎0384/341 1146 or 341 1022), across the Damsa stream on the Kayseri road about 1km out of town, has excellent facilities and plenty of shade. There's also a camping site and swimming pool at the back of the *Pınar Hotel* (☎0384/341 4054) at Kayseri Cad 24.

The Town

Ürgüp may be carefully trimmed with fancy street lighting and cobbles, but before tourism awakens of a morning it is once again a rural village, its streets taken over by men and women in traditional costume, leading horse-drawn vehicles and donkeys out to the vineyards, orchards and vegetable gardens roundabout. This is the time to explore the **old village**, whose buildings appear to be slowly emerging from the rocky hills into which they have been carved, some with stylish pillared and decorated facades of the same stone, others simple caves with doors and windows cut into the cliffs themselves.

Walk up to the Temmeni "wishpoint", beginning with a flight of steps opposite the thirteenth-century **Kebir Camii**. Local children hang around outside the mosque and may offer to act as guide on the way up. It's worth taking up the offer, as they'll guide you through a 700-metre-long tunnel (original purpose unknown), which leads through the hill to a door and "balcony" on the other side, furnishing panoramic views of the town and surrounding countryside. Continuing uphill, past the former troglodyte town dwellings (now mainly used for storage or abandoned altogether), brings you to a park known as **Temmeni** ("Hill of Wishes"; daily 8.30am–6pm; $1), where the Selçuk tomb of Kılıçarslan IV, dating from 1268, and a small renovated *medrese* from the same period, now used as a café, are open to visitors.

Viticulture and apple-farming along the banks of the Damsa River constitute an important part of the local economy, but Ürgüp's recent wealth is largely a result of tourism – though this is now on the decline, in the face of stiff competition from Göreme. The town's traditional village shops have been replaced by banks, tour companies and other tourist-related businesses, but if the decline continues, they may either revert to their former uses or close down altogether.

The town's **museum** (Tues–Sun 8am–5.30pm; $0.50) is tiny and not particularly well labelled, but the staff are extremely helpful and prepared to explain the exhibits. These include a selection of prehistoric ceramics, figurines, lamps, stelae, statues and ornaments found during excavations in the area.

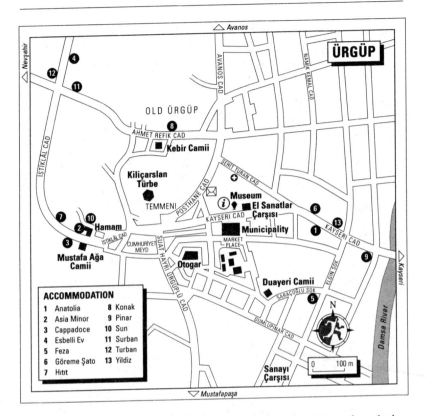

The town's main **shopping** strip, starting at Cumhuriyet Meydanı and continuing down Kayseri Caddesi, has some of the best carpets, jewellery and antiquities in the whole of Turkey. They're not necessarily a lot cheaper here than in İstanbul, but Turkish traders from the east generally make the trip to Ürgüp before starting the journey up to İstanbul, so Ürgüp's shops have first pick of the merchandise. Muammer Sak of *Aksa*, opposite the tourist information office on Kayseri Caddesi, stocks a range of some of the finest antique **carpets and kilims** to be found in Turkey – among his customers are the Royal Scottish Museum and Liberty's – and is a mine of information on ancient designs and motifs. Other well-stocked outlets in the area include *Le Bazaar d'Orient*, Kayseri Cad 32, run by the Güzelgöz, one of Ürgüp's oldest families; *Galerie Öz* at Cumhuriyet Meydanı 12, or in the *El Sanatlar Çarşısı* (the handicrafts market) on Kayseri Caddesi; and *Sultan Mehmet*, which also stocks leather, ceramics and hookahs at fixed but reasonable prices. This list is by no means comprehensive: whatever kind of carpet you are looking for – bar Axminster – you should be able to find it somewhere in this street.

Antiques, especially silver, are also readily available in Ürgüp, collected from nomad villages in the east of Turkey by Aziz Güzelgöz (also an accomplished *saz* player) of *Antikite Aziz Baba*, Kayseri Cad 28, and by Veli Kırcı of *Antikite Veli Baba*, Kayseri Cad 14 (☎0384/341 1042). A comprehensive collection of **local wine** is available from *Mahzen Şarap Evi* on Cumhuriyet Meydanı. Wine tasting is possible at any of Ürgüp's six wineries, but the best local wines are widely acknowledged to be those produced by the *Turasan* house, near the *Turban Hotel* on the Nevşehir road out of Ürgüp, and by the welcoming *Taşkobirlik* cooperative in a former *kervansaray*. It's worth remembering that white Cappadocian wines are much better than red; the reds are mixed with wines from other regions, and dyes are added.

Eating and nightlife

Ürgüp's best **restaurant** is the *Sömine* on a terrace above the main square, Cumhuriyet Meydanı (☎0384/341 8442); the service is friendly, decor pleasant and the well-prepared food good value. Local specialities include *osbar* (haricot beans with pastrami) and *testi kebap* (a lamb and vegetable stew cooked slowly in the oven with no water). The *Hanedan* (daily noon–3pm & 7pm–2am; ☎0384/341 1266 or 341 1366), opposite the *Türkerler Motel* on Ahmet Refik Caddesi, has a French-influenced evening menu including quail, snail bourguignon and octopus stew. Their prices are nearer to the European too. Cheaper options include the excellent *Han Çirağan* on Cumhuriyet Meydanı, serving simple regional food, like *düğün çorbası* (wedding soup), *saç tava* (lamb, tomatoes and onions cooked and served on a wok), and *mantı* (Turkish ravioli). The *Kardeşler Pizza Restaurant*, Dumlupınar Cad 9, serves excellent crusty *pide* and beer, at around $5 for two people. Next door the *Kent Restaurant* serves *saç kavurma* and oven-baked kebabs, also at reasonable prices.

Ürgüp's **nightlife** is excellent when you consider that this is central Anatolia and there's not a beach in sight. Entertainment combined with unlimited alcohol and an à la carte menu ($12 inclusive) can be found at the *Garden Coupole* (☎0384/341 1520) on İstiklâl Caddesi, where the folk-dancing programme includes a traditional Turkish wedding ceremony (preliminaries including the shaving of the groom) and dances celebrating courtship and harvest-time, accompanied by good lively music, audible for miles around. The *Dionysos* (also known as *Asimin Yeri*; daily 9pm–4am; admission $6), behind the *Turban Hotel* in Esbelli, is a cave-cut bar serving up limitless amounts of good local wine, and live Turkish music. The *Barium Bar*, opposite the *Hitit Hotel* at İstiklâl Cad 31, has occasional live bands and a good atmosphere. *Murat's Bar*, next to the *Magic Valley* tour company at the *otogar*, is cheap and sometimes cheerful.

The town's **discos** are the *Harem* on Suat Hayrı Ürgüplü Caddesi, and the *Armağan*, at the top of Kayseri Caddesi, the latter larger with a cosy log fire (both close Jan 1–Mar 30). Both give free entry but drinks are $2 each.

Listings

Car rental *Avis*, İstiklâl Cad, Belediye Pasajı (☎0384/341 2177); *Eretna Tour* in the *otogar* (☎0384/341 3599; also minibuses); *Europcar*, İstiklâl Cad 10 (☎0384/341 4315); *Tonnerre Travel Agency*, İstiklâl Cad, Belediye Pasajı, (☎0384/341 4879).

English-language newspapers *Niyazi Kuruyemiş* on Kayseri Cad near Cumhuriyet Meydanı.

Exchange The *Vakıf Bank* (summer daily 8.30am–noon & 1.30–9.30pm in summer; normal banking hours in winter), opposite the tourist information office at Kayseri Cad 38, has a cash machine for major international credit cards.

Hamam İstiklâl Cad (mixed; daily 9am–8pm).

Hospital Posthane Cad (☎0384/341 4031).

Motorbike rental *Hepa* (☎0384 341 4543) in the *otogar*; mopeds from $18 a day.

Pharmacy *Hulya Eczaneşi*, Açikpazar Yeri 41 behind the bus station, is friendly with some English spoken.

Post office Posthane Sokak; daily 8.30am–11pm to sell phone tokens and cards, 9am–5pm for ordinary business.

THY agent *Argeus*, İstiklâl Cad 13 (☎0384/341 4688).

Tours The best company is *Argeus* (see above), with horse, bike and walking tours throughout Cappadocia; also tours to the Ihlara valley, trekking tours to the Kaçkar mountains, and in winter, skiing tours to Erciyes Dağı. They're slightly more expensive than the competition, which is mainly located at the *otogar*. Alan Turizm (☎0384/341 4667, fax 341 2025), with offices in the *Surban Hotel* on the road to Nevşehir, offer walking tours in Cappadocia and trekking in the Kaçkar and Toros mountains, and are fast gaining an excellent reputation. *Trekking in Turkey* at Dağıstanlı Sok 10 (☎0384/341 4352) organize cycle tours in Cappadocia, and trekking or skiing in the Toros and Kaçkar mountains.

Mustafapaşa to Soğanlı

The small village of **MUSTAFAPAŞA** is a pleasant bike ride from Ürgüp. The charm of the place lies in the concentration of attractive carved facades dating back to the end of the last century, when it was home to a thriving Greek community known as Sinasos; it is also central to a cluster of little-visited churches. Unfortunately Mustafapaşa makes an awkward base unless you have some way of getting about: there are a couple of municipality **buses** to and from Ürgüp, but nothing beyond that in the Cemil/Soğanlı direction.

The nicest **hotel** in Mustafapaşa is the *Lamia* (☎0384/353 5413; prices not decided at the time of writing, but probably ③). To find it, go through the village past the over-priced *Sinassos Hotel* and *Kervansaray* carpet shop, and after the main square take the first right and follow the road round, past a fountain. It's an old Greek stone house recently converted and furnished with great attention to detail, the four bedrooms arranged around a garden courtyard; bathrooms are sparkling and modern. Another popular *pansiyon*, the *Monastery* (☎0384/353 5005; ②), just after the turn-off to the *Lamia*, before the bridge, derives its name from its original function; it's clean, pleasant and cheap, with bunk beds or mattresses on the floor. The *Pacha Hotel* (☎0384/353 5331; ③), a former mansion house with a typical broad loggia opposite the *Sinassos Hotel*, has clean basic rooms and a friendly owner, who speaks fluent French. **Camping** is an attractive option at the attached *Pacha* campsite above the Uzengi Dere ravine – $2 per person with your tent, $3 with theirs. Turkish village food is served, and there's also a well-equipped kitchen for preparing your own.

In the centre of Mustafapaşa an attractively renovated *medrese* has been converted into a **carpet workshop** and salesroom, the *Kervansaray*. Here you can watch women weaving beautiful silk carpets, but in this instance beware of the word "cooperative". The women are low-waged, the work is damaging to their sight, and the carpets are overpriced.

The church of **Ayos Vasilios** is located to the north of the village, beyond the *Pacha*; pick up the key from the makeshift **tourist information office** (opening hours variable), next to the *Kervansaray* carpet shop, before setting out. The church has well-preserved frescoes, although the faces are damaged, and four rock-cut pillars. Another church below in the Uzengi Dere ravine is the Holy Cross, partly rock-cut and partly masonry built, with pre-Iconoclastic and tenth-century paintings including a most attractive Christ of the Second Coming. On the other side of the village, passing through streets of houses cut by former Greek occupants into the tuff cliffs, is a **monastery** complex including the churches of Aya Nicola and Ayos Stefanos.

Following the Soğanlı road from Mustafapaşa – either hitching or in your own vehicle as there's no public transport – the fairy chimneys give way to a **table mountain** formation which is no less fantastic and surreal than preceding landscapes: the red canyon ridge which the road follows could be a backdrop for *Roadrunner*. About 3km from Mustafapaşa, watch out on your left for a sign advertising *Tesisleri alabalık* which points to a precipitous dirt track off to the left. The track leads to a tiny **fish farm** and restaurant where fresh trout are oven baked. To the right of the Soğanlı road, 5km from

Mustafapaşa, lies the **Damsa Dam**, which is responsible for the fresh, green appearance of the well-irrigated fields in this area. Access to a small beach, which gets crowded on summer weekends, is beside an obvious ticket gate.

Cemil and Taşkınpaşa

The next village along this road is **CEMİL**, a picturesque hamlet of tuff houses piled up against the cliffside. One-and-a-half kilometres beyond the village, just off the road, lies the **Keşlik monastery complex** – three churches, a wine press and a refectory. This is believed to be one of the earliest communal monastic establishments in the region. The watchman, who speaks some English, gives a worthwhile tour of the frescoes in the churches: the first, named after a prominent picture of the Angel Gabriel, includes depictions of the Last Supper, the Annunciation and the Flight to Egypt, all badly damaged and soot-blackened (a flashlight is essential); the Church of Saint Michael has a wine cellar downstairs; while the Church of Saint Stephen (seventh or eighth century) is the most beautiful of all, elaborately and unusually decorated. Non-figurative ornament includes stylized foliage and interlaced patterns reminiscent of Turkish kilims, and figurative designs include depictions of various fruits and animals, and three peacocks eating grapes.

Four kilometres further along the same road is the village of **TAŞKINPAŞA**. Here a fourteenth-century Selçuk mosque, the **Taşkınpaşa Camii**, is flanked by two hexagonal tombs. The original marble pillars and their disparate capitals are still in place, supporting the twin domes of the mosque, and the old Selçuk minaret can be reached by a set of steps, but the intricately carved *mihrab* and *mimber* for which the building was originally famed have now been removed to Ankara, and only photographs are left in the mosque itself. To the left just beyond the village you can see the remains of another Selçuk building believed to have been a **medrese**, with an attractively carved stone portal.

Soğanlı valleys

One of the most spectacular sights this side of Ürgüp are the **Soğanlı valleys** (daily 8am–5/6pm; $1.50), 5km off the road from Taşkınpaşa to Yeşilhisar, and less than 20km from either. **SOĞANLI** itself is an attractive village in two parts, Yukarı (upper) and Aşağı (lower) Soğanlı, set into the side of a table-top mountain. Part of the place's charm derives from its inaccessibility. It is off the tour route of all but small local companies – there are just a couple of simple restaurants, and a few stalls selling the village-made rag dolls. This isolation also means that there's no public transport, and in winter the village is often completely cut off by snow drifts.

The Soğanlı valleys were continuously occupied from early Byzantine times to the thirteenth century and are remarkable for the architecture of their churches and the beauty of the ninth- to thirteenth-century frescoes they contain. The name is supposed to derive from the Turkish *sona kaldı* (meaning "left to the end"), rather than "with onion", the literal meaning of *soğanlı*. This could be a reference to the fact that this was the last village to be taken during the Arab invasion of Cappadocia led by Battal Gazi in the sixth century.

The most interesting of the churches and monasteries are located in the right-hand valley (as you face Yukarı Soğanlı) and are all accessible with a modicum of effort. To reach the two-storeyed **Kubbeli Kilise**, "the Church with the Dome", follow the footpath across a stream bed from the village square, and proceed uphill through the village and along the side of the valley. This has perhaps the most interesting exterior of all the Cappadocian rock churches, its form – a conical dome which is the tip of a fairy chimney resting on a circular drum – being an imitation of a masonry structure. The

Saklı (Hidden) Kilise, with frescoes of the apostles, is 100m before the Kubbeli Kilise, its door facing into the valley.

Descending to the road and then up the other side of the valley, the **Meryem Ana Kilisesi** (Church of the Virgin) has four apsidal chapels with frescoes and Iconoclastic decoration. The **Yılanlı Kilise** (Church of the Snake) is best seen using a torch, as it is blackened and damaged by Greek and Armenian graffiti from the turn of the century. It derives its name from an eleventh-century painting of Saint George slaying the Dragon, to the left of the entrance. Returning towards the village, the **Karabaş Kilise** (Church of the Black Head) has two adjoining apsidal chapels, the first of which has well-preserved tenth- and eleventh-century frescoes depicting scenes from the life of Christ.

In the second Soğanlı valley, reached by passing the restaurants of Yukarı Soğanlı, the **Geyikli Kilise** (Church with the Deer) has two aisles which were decorated in the eleventh century, and derives its name from a damaged depiction of Saint Eustace with a poorly defined deer. Further up the valley the **Barbara Kilise**, a single-aisled basilica divided into two by a transverse arch, has an inscription dating it to the early tenth century.

Avanos and around

The old city of **AVANOS** clambers up hills overlooking the longest river in Turkey, the Kızılırmak. A magnificently "Red River" with a temper to match, the Kızılırmak appears after a good rainfall to be on the verge of bursting its banks. Avanos itself is a town of some character, separated from the rest of Cappadocia by the river and distinguished from all other towns in Turkey by the distinctive earthenware pottery made here. The same red clay that colours the river has been worked here for many centuries, and techniques dating right back to Hittite times are still in use. Strolling through the cobbled backstreets of the old town there are superb views out across the river – only slightly marred by the new housing development all too evident on the south bank. Exploration of the fields and hills around the town reveals further attractions: calcium pools and thermal springs, a tiny *kervansaray*, and even an underground city, 14km away at Özkonak. Transportation is good, with half-hourly **dolmuşes** to Avanos from Ürgüp, Göreme and Nevşehir.

Information, accommodation and tours

The **tourist information office** (summer Mon–Fri 8am–noon & 1.30–7.30pm; winter Mon–Fri 8am–noon & 1.30–5.30pm; ☎0384/511 1360) is at the *otogar* before the bridge into town. The PTT is more sensibly located just beyond the pottery monument on the main street, next to the public toilets.

It's easy enough to find **accommodation**, with a selection of hotels and *pansiyon*s catering to most tastes and requirements. The *Sofa Hotel* (☎0384/511 4489; ③) is just after the bridge next to the Haci Nuri Bey Konağı (an imposing Ottoman mansion highly visible as you cross the bridge). The hotel has been put together from twenty redesigned Ottoman houses, with immaculate rooms (all with bathrooms), a garden courtyard and a restaurant. In Yukarı Mahalle, reached from the road that leads uphill behind *Chez Galip* pottery, the *Hittite Pansiyon* (☎0384/511 4984; ②) is a friendly affair run by the Arikan brothers; it offers clean, comfortable rooms with a bathroom down the corridor, and evening meals, possibly accompanied by a brother playing *saz*. The *Tafana Pansiyon* (☎0384/511 5383; ②) in the same area is run by the *Chez Galip* pottery (ask there for directions). Downstairs is the family home, while upstairs are well-kept *pansiyon* rooms off a pleasant terrace, with a kitchen for guests. The newly renovated *Kirkit Hotel* (☎0384/511 3148; ①–②), off Atatürk Caddesi (take a right after the bridge, then a left 200m later), belonging to the tour company of the same name, is another series of beautifully converted sandstone houses, decorated with kilims, where rooms have either full bathrooms or just a shower. Moving **upmarket**, the *Irmak Hotel* (☎0384/511 4317; ⑦) is well designed to make the most of its secluded setting in extensive gardens on the banks of the river. It caters mainly to groups so prices are high.

Mesut **camping** ($2 a head), on the banks of the Kızılırmak near the footbridge, has a restaurant with a *pide tandır* (an oven cut into the ground) on which the proprietor's wife cooks excellent *bazlama*, a kind of sandwich.

If you have any equestrian leanings at all, you should see the countryside here from horseback – and, fortunately, the best stable in the region is located in Avanos. They have twenty locally bred **horses**, a couple of which are quite sprightly (read "terrifying" if you're not of a horsey inclination), though most are gentle and ideal for trekking. Costs are $30 for one day, $18 for a half-day, $6 hourly; enquire at *Chez Galip* pottery (☎0384/511 4240, fax 511 4543) for details. *Kirkit Voyage*, Atatürk Cad 50 (☎0384/511 3259), is an excellent **tour company** which also runs horseback trips, as well as bike and even snowshoe tours all over Cappadocia.

The Town

Though the quaint, cobbled back streets and rustic, tumbledown buildings are enjoyable, Avanos's real tourist attraction is **pottery**. The potters' square and the streets that surround it – carry on past the clay sculpture which is a memorial to this and the other local craft of weaving – contain numerous tiny workshops where the Cappadocian potter's techniques can still be observed or even attempted.

Perhaps the most famous of all the Avanos potteries is *Chez Galip,* belonging to master potter **Galip**. It's generally thronged with groups, but if you arrive at a quiet time you may be shown into one of the back rooms where Galip stores hair collected from his female visitors over the past ten years or more – countless locks trail from the ceiling and walls of a musty cave. The sinister aspects of the custom are partially diminished by the fact that every year Galip draws the names of ten of his hair-donors from a hat and gives them fifteen days' holiday in Avanos at his expense.

A tour of the workshop reveals a cellar where some fifty to sixty tonnes of local red earth, collected from dried-up beds of the Kızılırmak, is stored awaiting the water which will transform it into malleable clay. The clay is worked on a wheel, turned by the foot of the potter, in natural light from the open doorway. Afterwards, the polished finish on the pots is achieved by a laborious process using the rounded end of a piece of metal, a technique thought to date back to Hittite times. The pots dry slowly in a storeroom upstairs, above the workshop, and later more quickly out in the open air. They are then fired in a wood-fired furnace at 950–1200°C for ten hours, and sometimes the firing is repeated to produce the distinctive blackened colour of some of the pots.

Galip is also involved in a movement to revive the production of fine **ceramics** in Turkey. His workshops, where young people are learning to throw, fire and decorate a range of designs, are called *Çeç*, and are located near the *Motif Restaurant*; if you are interested in seeing the process, inquire at the main pottery. *Chez Galip* also run **pottery and weaving courses** through the winter, with participants lodged in typical village houses and taught by local craftspeople. It's an excellent way of becoming acquainted with the Cappadocian lifestyle, and Galip and his wife are very welcoming.

Chez Güray, opposite Alâeddin Camii and the Atatürk statue, and *Chez Ömurlü*, adjacent to *Chez Galip*, have a mixture of avant-garde and traditional pottery, the best , such as waist-high water coolers, being too difficult to take home.

Another local craft which deserves a mention is **knitting**. The shops in Uğur Mumcu Caddesi, the main street running alongside the river, are full of beautiful, brightly coloured hand-knitted sweaters as well as a good selection of *şalvar* (harem pants), silver and carpets. The best selection of sweaters is at no. 66, at the *Butik Famex*, while silver, *şalvar* and semiprecious stones can be found further along towards the bridge at *Chez Efe*.

Eating and nightlife

Sofra, on the main street near the PTT, is a reasonably priced **restaurant**, serving *döner* and steamtray food in a friendly atmosphere. The *Tafana Pide Salonu*, Kenan Evren Cad 47 (☎0384/511 1862), is also cheap, and serves a local speciality called *kiremit*, a kind of lamb stew, as well as excellent *pide*. The *Tuvanna* on the same street is a slightly more expensive place that caters mostly for groups, but it's worth asking them for their *günün yemeği* (daily menu) at lunchtimes ($1.50); the *mezes* are also well prepared and interesting. The *Şato Restaurant*, and the *Çeç Bar* above it, are pleasantly located on the river near the road bridge, but again they're aimed mainly at groups rather than passing trade.

One of the best **nightclubs** in the region, the *Dragon* (☎0384/511 4486), is located in the area called Bezirhane, well signposted off the Gülşehir road. The caves here have been painstakingly carved out of tuff by another famous local potter, Mehmet İpekdere. The evening's programme is a familiar one, consisting of Turkish folk dancing and oriental (belly) dancing, followed by a disco, but *Dragon*'s folk dancers are possibly Cappadocia's most accomplished and the management takes pains to rent the best available oriental dancers. The caves are huge but popular with groups, so it's worth booking in advance. An evening at *Dragon* can be combined with a visit to Mehmet's large and impressive pottery next door, where you can sup local wine from tiny clay vessels and watch Mehmet deftly throw another pot.

If oriental dancing is not your thing, the *Motif Restaurant* on the other side of the river, signposted off the Nevşehir road beyond the *Irmak Hotel* at Hasan Kalesi Mevkii (☎0384/511 2048), has a well-established reputation for its folk dancing programme and good food: $24 for meal and entertainment in a pleasantly relaxed atmosphere. For a less organized evening, the *Kervanhan Disco-Bar* off the main square is open every night, and the *Bambu Bar* at Atatürk Cad 78 has live *saz* music most evenings, and a well-stocked bar.

Özkonak

ÖZKONAK (summer daily 8am–7pm; winter daily 8am–5pm; $1), 14km from Avanos off the Kayseri road, is one of the least-known and -excavated underground cities in the Cappadocia region. Dolmuşes from Avanos leave hourly from beside the PTT.

In its present state it's not as interesting as Derinkuyu or Kaymaklı, but by the same token it's not as crowded. The city was discovered in 1972 by muezzin Latif Acar, who was trying to find out where the water disappeared to when he watered his crops. He discovered an underground room which, later excavation revealed, belonged to a city with a capacity for sixty thousand people to exist underground for three months, with ten floors to a depth of 40m. At present only four floors are open (to 15m), but throughout the village can be seen parts of rooms belonging to the first and second levels. These first two levels were used for food storage and wine fermentation, and a press and reservoir are labelled, as are mangers for stabled animals. Another typical feature is the stone doors, moved by wooden levers; above them was a small hole, through which boiling oil would have been poured on an enemy trying to break the soft sandstone door.

Southern Cappadocia: Niğde, Aksaray and the Ihlara valley

The majority of Cappadocia's visitors never get beyond the well-worn Nevşehir–Avanos–Ürgüp triangle, leaving southern Cappadocia far less charted and trampled. Although there's a consequent feeling of excitement about explorations made in this area, there's also less to be explored. The two major towns, Aksaray and Niğde, leave a lot to be desired as tourist centres, and the scenery is generally scrubby, barren steppe, more prone to cause depression than to recharge your holiday spirits.

The area does have its peculiarities and fascinations, however, and these are worth a degree of discomfort to experience. On the way to Niğde you can stop off at the underground cities of Derinkuyu and Kaymaklı (see p.523), located in a rain-washed basin between the central Anatolian plateau and the valleys of cones. More worthwhile is the **Ihlara valley**. Here the **Melendiz River**, running between Aksaray and Niğde alongside the Melendiz mountain range, has created perhaps the most beautiful of all Cappadocian landscapes, a narrow ravine with almost vertical walls being cut ever deeper by the river that runs through it. Easily accessible from Niğde, too, are a small enclave of beautifully painted rock-cut churches belonging to the **Eski Gümüşler monastery**, and the Sultansazlığı bird sanctuary (see p.557).

Niğde

NİĞDE is a small provincial town which, despite a long history spent guarding the important mountain pass from Cappadocia to Cilicia, has few remaining monuments of any great interest. Apart from a Selçuk fortress perched above the main street on a hill of tuff, and a couple of medieval mosques, the town looks as if it has been thrown together by people who were more interested in nomadic wandering than town planning. Nearby, however, is the Eski Gümüşler monastery complex, which will no doubt become part of the regular Cappadocia itinerary in time. For the time being it's hardly known to the tourists who flood to Göreme Open-Air Museum, even though its frescoes are in a much better state of preservation.

Niğde's history really began in the tenth century, when Tyana, the town which formerly controlled the pass between the Melendiz mountains to the west and the Toros mountains to the east, was ruined by Arab incursions. From then on Niğde, a town which had been mentioned as early as Hittite times by the name of Nakida, took on the defensive role. Conquered by the Selçuks towards the end of the eleventh century, it was endowed with some attractive buildings during the reign of Alâeddin Keykubad. When the Arabian geographer Ibn Battutah visited the town in 1333, it was in ruins, probably as a result of the wars between the Mongols and the Karamanoğlu, the great rivals of the Ottoman dynasty. The Ottomans finally moved in in 1467, since when the town has been little more than a landmark on the Kayseri–Adana road.

Practicalities

The **otogar** is 1km from the centre off the Nevşehir–Adana highway on Emin Eşirgil Caddesi, and there are frequent dolmuşes into town. The **train station** is right on the highway, within sight of the citadel's clocktower, a convenient marker for the centre. To get into town from here, cross the highway and take İstasyon Caddesi into the centre, a walk of ten minutes or so. İstasyon Caddesi is the location of a comfortable **hotel**, the *Murat* at no. 46 (☎0388/212 33978; ③), with en-suite bathrooms. Slightly cheaper is the *Otel Evim* (☎0388/232 0869; ③), on Hükümet Meydanı, at the top of İstasyon Caddesi, after it circumvents the citadel; the pleasant balconied rooms all have bathrooms. The *Hotel Stad* (☎0388/213 7866; ①), next to the *otogar* on Faik Şahenk Bulvarı, is spartan but clean, with bathrooms down the corridor.

The **tourist information office** (Mon–Sat 8.30am–noon & 1.30–5.30pm) is at Hükümet Meydanı 16, on the first floor.

The Town

The **citadel** on its tuff hill was originally founded by the Selçuk sultan Alâeddin at the end of the eleventh century, but was restored by Işak Paşa in 1470, and the keep, all that remains today, probably dates from that time. On a mound to the south of the castle stands the **Alâeddin Camii**, dating from 1203 and later restored by Sultan Alâeddin. The facade is striped grey and yellow and there is a beautiful portal to the east, richly decorated with arabesques and sculpted designs. Below the mosque is the eighty-metre-long **bedesten**, a covered market street dating from the sixteenth and seventeenth centuries, and opposite this, on Nalbantlar Önüat at the foot of the citadel hill, is the fourteenth-century **Sungur Bey Camii**. Its portal is framed by geometrical mouldings, and above the door to the east of the prayer hall a rose window gives the mosque a Gothic look. At the other end of this street, approaching Vali Konağı Caddesi, is the **Akmedrese**, built in the Selçuk open-courtyard style with a white marble portal. It now serves as the town's **museum** (Tues–Sun 8.30am–5pm; $1), most famous for the Byzantine mummy of a nun which is exhibited in a glass case to full hideous effect.

Eski Gümüşler monastery

The real reason for coming to Niğde is the **Eski Gümüşler monastery** (summer daily 9am–noon & 1.30–6.30pm; winter daily 8am–12.30pm & 1.30–5.30pm; $1), 6km from town off the Yeşilhisar road. To get there, take the white *belediye* bus which leaves the Niğde *otogar* every 45 minutes for the village of Gümüşler. Signposted off to the right about 1km out of Niğde, Gümüşler is attractively set in a valley surrounded by cherry orchards, but for the monastery you stay on the bus past it.

The monastery, rediscovered in 1963, has a deserved reputation for the excellent state of preservation of its paintings, which seem to have escaped Iconoclastic and other vandalism through the ages. Even the faces are intact, providing some of the finest examples of Byzantine painting yet to be discovered in Cappadocia.

The **main church**, with its tall, elegant pillars, is entered through an almost circular arched doorway opposite the entrance to the courtyard. Decorated with black-and-white geometric designs, the church contains beautiful **frescoes** in the most delicate greens, browns and blues. They include a nativity scene complete with tiny animal heads peering in at the swaddled Jesus and the Magi, off to the left; and a tall, serene Madonna, framed in a rock-cut niche. The linear stylization of the figures is marked, the features are drawn boldly and simply, and the light and shade of draperies is reduced to monochrome.

The upstairs **bedroom** was formerly reached by means of niches cut into the side of a shaft; now a metal ladder has been provided. The walls of the bedroom, which is complete with rock-cut beds, are decorated with a wolf, a deer, a lion, and a flamingo, being hunted by men with bows and arrows; there's also a depiction of a Roman soldier.

Connected to the church is a **wine press**, complete with metre-wide wine vats, and outside in the central courtyard there's a skeleton in its grave, protected under glass. Next to the graves are round holes in which precious belongings would have been buried. Other rooms excavated to date include a kitchen and underground baths reached down a set of steps; below ground level are newly excavated chambers and a water reservoir.

Aksaray

Huddled in an oasis on the Melendiz River, on the far side of the Melendiz mountain range from Niğde, **AKSARAY** is a market town with no real interest except as a base for reaching the Ihlara valley. Although no trace of the ancient city survives, Aksaray probably occupies the site of the Byzantine town **Archelais**. It was captured by the Selçuks in the eleventh century, then passed to the Mongols in the middle of the thirteenth century, but when the power of the Mongols began to wane the Karamanoğlu took possession in the fourteenth century. After the fall of Constantinople in 1453, part of the population of Aksaray was transferred to the capital, a repopulation programme that was a measure of how weak the Byzantine city had become before the final collapse of its empire. The displaced people named the district of İstanbul in which they settled after their hometown, a name which that shabby, lively suburb still retains. The main square, with its Atatürk statue and restored public buildings, is the only really impressive sight in town, the rest a mere sprawl of apartment buildings with some evidence of local wealth.

Practicalities

The **tourist information office** (Mon–Sat 8am–noon & 1.30–5.30pm; ☎0388/213 2474) is at Ankara Cad, Dinçer Apt 2, on the second floor. The best **hotel** in town is the *Otel Yuvam* (☎0382/212 0024; ③), in a renovated old town house next to the Kurşunlu Camii at Eski Sanayı Caddesi; rooms are attractively furnished and clean, with modern bathrooms. Cheaper hotels are all located behind the *Vilayet* building off Hükümet Meydanı, including (both en-suite) the *Otel Çakir Ipek* on Kizilay Caddesi (☎0382/213 7053; ②), and the nearby, clean *Hotel Yoğuran* at Nolu Hükümet Cad 3 (☎0382/213 5490; ③).

The Ihlara Valley

A fertile gorge cut by a deep green river between red cliffs, the **Ihlara valley** is as beautiful a place as you could conceive. If you add some of the most attractive and interesting churches and rock-carved villages in the Cappadocia region, it's hard to believe that the valley hasn't been touristed off the map. It may be that the end of paradise is already in sight: telltale litter is starting to appear on the river banks, and frescoes have suffered terrible damage in recent years. Restraint and common sense may prevail, but if you want to be sure of seeing the place before things get out of hand, try to visit now.

Minibuses to Ihlara village leave from Aksaray *otogar* three times daily, passing Selime and the turn-off to Belisırma, and returning the same day. A **taxi** to Ihlara is $15, and the round trip $25 – they'll pick you up in Belisırma. There are also six dolmuşes daily from Aksaray to Güzelyurt, and frequent dolmuş connections between Güzelyurt and Ihlara. A large enough group could rent a whole minibus either from the drivers in Aksaray *otogar* or from Ürgüp (you'll need about 10 people to make it viable).

If you have time, it's satisfying to do the trip independently, taking a dolmuş to Selime and walking the 6km to Belisırma for an overnight stop, then completing the 10km to Ihlara village via the majority of churches the following day, and catching the dolmuş back to Aksaray from Ihlara. If you're returning to central Cappadocia, you could try asking a private tour bus from there for a lift back, for which they should ask only a small fee.

Most local companies offer **tours** to the valley (around $20 for a day trip). The best of these include *Zemi Tours* (☎0384/271 2576) in Göreme, who can organize two-day camping tours to the region, and *Argeus* (☎0384/341 4688) in Ürgüp, who will walk the

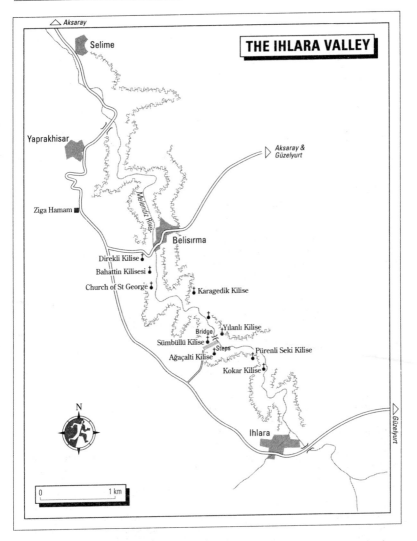

length of the valley with those who want to, transporting the rest of the group back to central Cappadocia by minibus. *Alan Turizm* (☎0384/341 4667) in Ürgüp are also a good bet for a well-informed guide and a pace that's leisurely enough to take in the sights. If you decide to make a visit on a day trip with less reputable, cheaper companies not listed here, insist on at least a half-day in the area, preferably entering the valley via the **main entrance** – about halfway between Belisırma and Ihlara and location of the greatest concentration of churches – or walking to this point from either Belisırma or Ihlara.

Selime

One of the most beautiful parts of the whole valley, the troglodyte village of **SELİME** has previously been passed over in favour of the better-known, more frequented Ihlara village area. It's the first village you pass on the way to Ihlara or to the official entry to the valley, and it's worth at least a couple of hours' visit, if not a stop-over in one of the valley's best hotels. The *Piri Motel and Camping* (☎0382/454 5114; ③) offers spotless comfortable rooms with luxurious bathrooms and breakfast, and its owner Mustafa is willing to act as a guide to the surrounding churches.

A number of massive, rather squat fairy chimneys dot the valley at Selime, many of which contain churches, and there's even a rock-cut cathedral, divided into three aisles by irregularly shaped pillars. The village takes its name from a Selçuk mausoleum with a pyramidical roof in the village cemetery inscribed "Selime Sultan", a dedication of unknown origins.

Belisırma

The troglodyte village of **BELİSIRMA** blends in with the tawny rockface from which it was carved to such an extent that in a bad light it can all but disappear from view. Its tranquil riverside location provides the opportunity to rest at a table in the water at one of the simple tree-shaded restaurants on the west bank.

Access to Belisırma from the Ihlara–Selime road is complicated by the fact that the sign is frequently removed: just over a kilometre south of Yaprakhisar, turn off to the left down a two-kilometre-long dirt track. The most rewarding way to reach Belisırma, however, is to walk along the valley, either from Selime, as noted above, or from Ihlara – about a two-hour hike, during which you can take in the majority of the valley churches (see the note below about entrance charges).

The village is home to two primitive **campsites**: *Valley Anatolia* (☎0382/451 2433), which has tents for hire and an excellent **restaurant** where you can eat trout or *saç kavurma* very cheaply, and the *Aslan* (☎0382/451 2425), which also has a riverside restaurant. For rooms, ask at the *Valley Anatolia* and they'll take you to one of two house **pansiyons** in the village; the nicer of these, the *Lüx Pansiyon* (☎0382/451 2564; ②), has comfortable rooms with en-suite bathrooms. From Belisırma, it's another 2.5km to the village of Ziga, where hot springs feed a hamam (8am–10pm; $1).

Around Belisırma, the eleventh-century **Direkli Kilise** (Church with the Columns) has fine examples of Byzantine frescoes including a beautiful long-fingered Madonna and Child on one of the columns from which the church takes its name, and a picture of Saint George fighting a three-headed dragon.

The **Church of Saint George**, 50m up the cliffside, a half-kilometre south of Belisırma and 3km from the stairs at the main entrance, was dedicated to the saint by a thirteenth-century Christian emir, Basil Giagoupes, who was in the army of Mesut II. It bears an inscription expressing Christian gratitude for the religious tolerance of the Selçuk Turks. St George is depicted in armour and cloak, holding a triangular shield and flanked by the donor and his wife Tamara, who is handing a model of the church to the saint. To the right of this oblation scene, St George can be seen in action, killing a three-headed serpent, with an inscription above that reads "Cleanse my soul of sins".

Ihlara village

Best known of the quaint villages in the valley bottom, **IHLARA** is slightly more developed than its rivals. However, its few *pansiyons* are still devoted to the kind of backpacking tourists who have scant regard for such luxuries of life as hot water, towels and carpeted rooms – an asceticism that keeps the large commercial tour parties away, at least after dark.

One of the better **pansiyons** in the area is the *Star Motel* (☎0382/453 7429; ②), right in the valley with beautiful views from the balconies; spartan but clean, it's open all year round. It also has a good **restaurant**, where you can eat *saç kavurma* (lamb stew, supposed to be still bubbling when it reaches your table) beside the river. Above the valley, on the road to the main entrance, the *Anatolia Pansiyon* (☎0382/453 7128; closed in winter; ②) is also quite comfortable and friendly, and offers the luxury of en-suite bathrooms. The *Akar Pansiyon* (☎0382/453 7018, ②), just off the road to the main valley entrance, is clean and quiet, with comfortable doubles; the owner will pick customers up from Aksaray for the price of the petrol if you have any problems getting here. The **hamam** (daily 10am–10pm; $0.50), reached down a set of steps behind the mosque on the road out of the village, is served by natural hot springs.

The main churches

The monastic occupation of the Ihlara valley, or **Peristrema** as it was originally known, seems to have been continuous from medieval times until the fourteenth century, a long period of use reflected in the numerous adaptations and restorations of the churches. It would seem from the decoration of the churches, whose development can be traced through pre- and post-Iconoclastic periods, that the valley was little affected by the religious disputes of the period. Paintings show both eastern and western influence, so that some figures wear Arab striped robes, whereas others resemble those in Byzantine frescoes in Europe.

The **official entrance** to the valley is located midway between Ihlara and Belisırma (daily sunrise–sunset; $2) off the road in from Aksaray. Descending from here, down several hundred steps to the valley floor 150m below, is precipitous, but manageable even for sufferers of vertigo. The most interesting of the churches are located near the small bridge midway between Ihlara and Belisırma at the bottom of the flight of stairs. It's also possible to walk from Ihlara village along the southwest bank of the river to the bridge, or from Belisırma to the northwest keeping to the same side of the river; you now have to pay the same entrance fee coming from Ihlara village, though not yet from Belisırma (ticket booths are under construction in the village at the time of writing). Walking from either village to this point takes about an hour and a half, a fairly straightforward hike that's well worthwhile for the tremendous sense of solitude away from the main tourist centre.

At the bottom of the steps is a plan showing all the accessible churches, most of which are easy enough to find. To the right of the bridge, on the same side as the steps, is the **Ağaçaltı Kilise**, "the Church under the Tree". Cross-shaped with a central dome, the church originally had three levels, but two of them have collapsed, as has the entrance hall. The most impressive of the well-preserved frescoes inside depict the Magi presenting gifts at the Nativity, Daniel with the lions (opposite the entrance in the west arm) and, in the central dome, the Ascension. The colours are red, blue and grey, and the pictures, naive in their execution, suggest influence from Sassanid Iran, particularly in the frieze of winged griffins. Unfortunately in recent years these frescoes have suffered serious damage.

The **Pürenli Seki Kilise** lies 500m beyond this, also on the south bank, and can be seen clearly from the river, 30m up the cliffside. The badly damaged frescoes here mainly depict scenes from the life of Christ. Another 50m towards Ihlara, the **Kokar Kilise** is relatively easy to reach up a set of steps. Scenes from the Bible in the main hall include the Annunciation, the Nativity, the Flight into Egypt and the Last Supper. In the centre of the dome, a picture of a hand represents the Trinity and the sanctification.

One of the most fascinating of all the churches in the valley is located across the wooden footbridge, about 100m from the stairs. The **Yılanlı Kilise** (Church of the Snakes) contains strikingly unusual depictions of sinners suffering in hell. Four female sinners are being bitten by snakes: one of them on the nipples as a punishment for not breast-feeding her young; another is covered in eight snakes; and the other two are being punished for slander and for not heeding good advice. At the centre of the scene a three-headed snake is positioned behind one of the few Cappadocian depictions of

Satan; in each of the snake's mouths is a soul destined for hell. Another church worth exploring is **Sümbüllü** (Church of the Hyacinths), just 200m from the entrance stairs. The church shows Greek influence in its badly-damaged frescoes and has an attractive facade decorated with blind horseshoe niches.

Güzelyurt

GÜZELYURT, the nearest small town to the Ihlara valley, provides an opportunity to catch a glimpse of the old, untouched Cappadocia, and to stay in the best hotel in the region; if that isn't enough incentive, there are good dolmuş connections with Aksaray and Ihlara, and plenty of sites worth visiting in the town and within easy walking distance. The excellent *Kirkit Voyage* tour company in Avanos (☎0384/511 3259) run horse trekking and mountain-bike tours in the Güzelyurt region.

The beautiful *Karballa* **hotel** on the main square (☎0382/451 2103, fax 451 2107; ③, or $18 per person for half-board) occupies a nineteenth-century Greek monastery. Monks' cells are bedrooms, with central heating and individual bathrooms now added, and the refectory has become an excellent restaurant, but the former character of the building has been largely retained.

The important religious community of Güzelyurt was established by **St Gregory of Nazianze** in the fourth century, and a **church** dedicated to him, called Cami Kilise by locals, is located a short walk from the main street, past the PTT and mosque, on Kör Sokak. Renovated several times by the town's Greek community, the church is now in line for further work, with plans to turn it into a museum. A golden bell given to the church by a Russian Orthodox community in Odessa is now in Afyon museum, but other items of interior decor, such as a carved wooden iconostasis and chair, gifts from Tsar Nicholas I in the eighteenth century, can still be seen in situ. In place of the bell tower now stands a brick minaret, dating from the church's conversion to a mosque after the departure of the Greeks in 1924. Elsewhere on Kör Sokak and in the old town around it are still-inhabited troglodyte dwellings and old Greek houses with beautifully carved facades.

The most impressive sight in the Güzelyurt area, however, has to be "Monastery Valley" below the town to the northeast, approached by taking a right turn out of the village after the church of St Gregory of Nazianze. The valley is riddled with over fifty rock-cut churches and monastery complexes – some dating from the Byzantine era – of which the most attractive is the nineteenth-century **Yüksek Kilise** (High Church), dramatically located on a high rock. A walk up the 4.5-kilometre-long valley takes about two and a half hours, and brings you to the village of Sivrihisar. From there, a signposted fifteen-minute walk south will bring you to a free-standing church of note, the sixth-to-seventh-century **Kızıl Kilise** (Red Church), one of the few remaining churches containing masonry in the whole of Cappadocia.

Kayseri and around

Green fields and wooded hills, a snow-capped volcano and a solid-looking city built of black stone and concrete, **KAYSERİ** and its surroundings feel refreshingly familiar after the spookiness of Cappadocia's better-known landscapes. Tourism developed here long before the villages around Ürgüp realized the potential of the industry, and for some time it used to be the only place you could find a reasonable hotel in Cappadocia. Now there are fewer visitors, but the old-fashioned, rather jaded **hotels** still hold good, and despite a reputation for **religious conservatism** there's a gentle acceptance of the waywardness of foreigners which has yet to mature in, say, Nevşehir or Niğde. In place of visitors the town has fallen back on traditional commerce, particularly raw textiles and carpets, and there is a reassuring feeling that nothing was compromised by tourism and so its decline is no great loss.

The long history and strategic importance of the town have left it with a littering of impressive **monuments**, another factor contributing to its desirability as a base from which to explore the surrounding countryside. Two of the more obvious nearby attractions are **Sultansazlığı bird sanctuary** and **Mount Erciyes**, ideal for picnics in summer and skiing in winter.

Ancient civilization in the region dates back to the fourth millennium BC and a Chalcolithic site at **Kültepe**, 21km from Kayseri on the road to Sivas. During the early Hittite period the site was composed of two settlements: **Kanesh**, the capital of the kingdom of the same name, probably the most powerful in Anatolia in its time; and **Karum**, which was established by Assyrian merchants as a bazaar, one of the oldest in the world.

The site of present-day Kayseri was originally called Mazaka. Its origins are unknown, but the city gained importance under the rule of the Phrygians. In 17–18 AD it was named **Caesarea** in honour of the Emperor Tiberius, and at the same time became the capital of the Roman province of Cappadocia. Captured by the Persians after the Battle of Edessa (Urfa), it was quickly regained by the Romans. As part of the Byzantine Empire, Caesarea was relocated 2km to the north of the ancient acropolis, allegedly around a church and monastery which had been built by Saint Basil, the founder of eastern monasticism and a bishop of Caesarea in the fourth century. The position was strategic in terms of both trade and defence, and it soon became a leading cultural and artistic centre, though always vulnerable to attack from the east. The Arab invasions of the seventh and eighth centuries were particularly threatening, and in 1067 it finally fell to the great Selçuk leader Kılıç Aslan II. The town became capital of a powerful Danişmend emirate which included Cappadocia, Sivas and Amasya. In 1097 the Crusaders were in brief possession and it was ruled equally briefly by the Mongols in 1243. Passing through the hands of various Turkish chiefs it came into the possession of Beyazit I in 1397, but when he was defeated by Tamerlane at the Battle of Angora the city was occupied by the Karamanoğlu and then the Mameluks before finally becoming part of the Ottoman Empire in 1515, under Selim the Grim.

The City

Part of the delight of Kayseri is that it centres around its most beautiful old buildings, and that these still play an important part in the everyday life of the place. The nature of the buildings that have survived bears witness to the social conscience of the early Muslims, particularly of the Selçuks. Koranic teaching forbade excessive concern with private houses, and very few of them have survived. Instead the buildings of real note in the city are those which served public welfare and communal activites, especially exemplified in mosque complexes that included schools, soup kitchens and hamams.

Other buildings still integral to Kayseri's life are the **covered markets**, where commercial activity – as conspicuous now as it was for the first Assyrian settlement – is most obvious. The prominence of commerce can be ascertained by the fact that there are three covered markets in the town centre, all dating from different periods. The **Bedesten**, built in 1497, was originally used by cloth sellers but is now a carpet market; the **Vezir Hanı**, built by Damat İbrahim Paşa in 1727, is where raw cotton, wool and Kayseri carpets are sold, and leather is prepared for wholesale; while the recently restored **covered bazaar** in the same area, built in 1859 by natives of Kayseri, has five hundred individual shops. If you do shop here, you'll have to bargain hard: stories can be heard all over Turkey about how hard-nosed the businessmen of Kayseri can be.*

---

*The one about a Kayseri man stealing a donkey, painting it and selling it back to its owner has become even more hostile in recent years: the man now abducts his mother, paints her up and sells her back to his father.

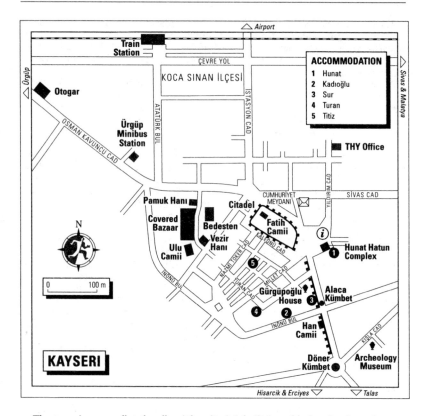

The towering crenellated walls of the **citadel**, built from black volcanic rock, are a good place to start exploring, since the life of the town seems to centre on this point. A sixth-century fortress erected in the reign of the emperor Justinian once stood here, but the citadel you see was built in 1224 by the Selçuk sultan Keykubad, and has been much restored since, particularly by Mehmet II, who also built the **Fatih Camii**, the small mosque near the southwest gate. The fact that the city walls have all but disappeared serves only to confirm the importance of this fortified nerve centre: it was preserved at all costs even after the walls had lost their importance. Not surprisingly for Kayseri, there is now a modern **shopping precinct** located within the walls of the citadel.

Beyond the market area is the first of several ancient mosques in the city, the **Ulu Cami** or Great Mosque. Constructed under the Danişmend Turkish emirs in the first half of the thirteenth century, the mosque, which can be entered from three sides, is still in remarkably good condition. Its roof is supported by four rows of stone pillars with varied marble capitals, some of them taken from other buildings, and it retains its original carved wooden *mimber*, although the central dome is modern.

Kayseri has been described as the **city of mausoleums** because of its large number of tombs: curious, squat, beautifully carved bits of masonry known as *kümbet*s, dating from the twelfth to fourteenth centuries, which can be found scattered about in the most unlikely places – a couple of them are on traffic islands on the main highway to Mount Erciyes. They are graceful constructions that seem out of place in such a modern environment. Examples can be found all over Persia and Turkey, an architectural form for which the Selçuk Turks were responsible: they were generally two-storeyed, with the burial chamber and sumptuous coffin located in the upper storey. It is supposed that the design was modelled on the *yurd*, a conical tent inhabited by various tribes of the region, including the Selçuk Turks. The best known of them in Kayseri is the **Döner Kümbet**, a typical example probably dating to around 1275, built for Sah Cihan Hatun. Mysteriously the name of the monument means "turning tomb", although it doesn't turn and never has done. The tomb is decorated with arabesques and palmettes, and a tree of life with twin-headed eagles and lions beneath.

The museums

Near the citadel in the town centre, the **külliye of Hunat Hatun** was the first mosque complex to be built by the Selçuks in Anatolia. It consists of a mosque (1237–38), and one of the most beautiful examples of Selçuk architecture in Turkey, the thirteenth-century *medrese*. This former theological college has an open courtyard and two *eyvan*s (vaulted chambers open at the front) and nowadays houses the city's **ethnographic museum** (summer Tues–Sun 8.30am–5.30pm; winter Tues–Sun 8am–5pm; $1), with displays reflecting folk traditions of the Kayseri region. Exhibits include beautiful Selçuk tiles from the Hunat Hatun complex, depicting women's faces and birds, unlabelled carpets and kilims, and a *topak ev*, or nomad's tent, located in the main classroom of the *medrese*. The main exhibit is the octogonal Hatun Türbesi, the tomb of Mahperi Hunat Hatun, Greek wife of Sultan Keykubad.

The **archeological museum** on Kışla Caddesi (Tues–Sun 8.30am–5.30pm; $1) is certainly the best museum in the region, containing some of the most interesting artefacts to be found in Cappadocia, extremely well labelled and explained in English. The first room deals with the **Hittites**, their cuneiform writing and hieroglyphics, and includes a fascinating Hittite rock relief from Develi and the head of a sphinx. The rest of the museum is mainly dedicated to finds from the excavations of **Kültepe**. They include early Bronze Age depictions of the mother goddess, Assyrian bowls and jugs in the shape of animals, dating from the second millennium BC, and a collection of clay tablets in their clay envelopes – essentially small cheques – from the same period.

In the second room are finds from around Kayseri itself, including Hellenistic and Roman jewellery, and grave gifts from a Roman tumulus, among them highly worked pieces in gold and silver. In the garden can be found a pair of lovely seventh-century BC **Hittite lions**, with all their own teeth, from Göllüdağ near Niğde.

The **Gürgüpoğlu House**, just inside the city walls off Turan Caddesi (daily 8.30am–noon & 1.30–5.30pm; $0.75), is a restored Ottoman family home dating from the fifteenth century. It's been arranged as a museum of ethnography, complete with tableaux of wax dummies, but these don't distract from the beauty of the semi-timbered building, which is one of the few examples of this kind of vernacular architecture to be opened to the public. The first room is a typical Turkish salon, its walls intricately painted using natural dyes, with models seated on low divans, holding musical instruments. The guest room upstairs has a beautiful carved and painted wooden ceiling; you'll also be escorted round a bride's room (labelled in Turkish but the scene is fairly self-explanatory) and the kitchen.

Practicalities

To get into town from the **otogar**, take the "Terminal" dolmuş from the opposite side of Osman Kavuncu Caddesi. The **train station** is 1km out of town at the end of Atatürk Bulvarı: "Terminal" dolmuşes into town – and to the *otogar* in the other direction – pass frequently. **Turkish Airlines** have an office at Yıldırım Cad 1 (☎0352/222 3858), with a service bus to and from the **airport** ($0.75), which, for departures, leaves 45 minutes before check-in time; an *Argeus* tour agency minibus also meets flights and will deposit you in the village of your choice in Cappadocia. The **tourist information office** (summer daily 8.30am–noon & 1–5.30pm; winter daily 8am–noon & 1–5pm; ☎0452/222 3903) is right at the centre of things, next to the Hunat Hatun complex. They have all kinds of useful information, including train, plane and bus times, hotel and restaurant lists, and the latest on the Mount Erciyes ski resort. The main **banks** are on and around Nazmi Toker (Bankalar) Caddesi, running parallel to Millet Caddesi.

Accommodation

There are several good **hotels** to choose from in Kayseri. A central, reasonably priced and well-run option is the *Hotel Sur* (☎0352/222 4367; ③) at Talas Cad 12, taking its name from the city walls which it overlooks. Rooms with TVs and bathrooms are basically furnished and on the small side, leading off landings arranged like those of an old-style prison; choose a room at the back, away from the busy road. The *Turan Oteli*, Turan Cad 8 (☎0352/222 5537; ③), is owned by a charming but hard-nosed Kayseri carpet dealer, with a warehouse in the basement where if you're lucky you'll get away without paying for the apple tea. The hotel is in need of refurbishment, though it has a couple of decent-sized rooms on the first floor. The *Kadıoğlu Oteli* on İnönü Bulvarı (☎0352/231 6320, fax 222 8296; ③) is not as friendly, but slightly better looked after. The *Hotel Titiz*, Maarif Cad 7 (☎0352/222 5040; ③), has small, nicely furnished rooms, with TVs, fridges and tiny bathrooms. Of the cheaper options, the *Hunat Otel* behind the Hunat Cami (☎0352/232 4319; ①, bath and heating extra) is the quietest and most convenient, where clean rooms share bathrooms, but provide pleasant views of the mosque. The *Terminal Oteli* in the *otogar* is comfortable but suffers badly from traffic noise (☎0352/232 4319; ③).

Eating and drinking

Kayseri's **restaurants** are disappointing, and this is one place where self-catering seems like a feasible option, with the local *pastırma* (pastrami) and *sucuk* (spicy sausage) for which Kayseri is famous, readily available – though beware that the smell of *pastırma* will exude from your pores for days after eating it. Some cheap eateries you may like to try include the *Kayseri Sofrası* on Talas Caddesi, which is better value though less exciting than its posh exterior suggests: they only serve *izgara*. The *Bebek Et Lokantası* at Nazmi Töker (Bankalar) Cad 9 is a modern well-furnished upmarket option, very popular with locals, with the widest variety of dishes in town. The *günün yemeği* (speciality of the day) is reasonable value at $1.50, but portions are small. Otherwise an old favourite is the *Iskender Kebab Salonu* at Millet Cad 5, across from the Hunat Hatun complex. The air-conditioned *Divan Pasthanesi* on Millet Caddesi is the place to eat ice cream and cakes.

Mount Erciyes

Erciyes Dağı, the 3916-metre-high extinct volcano dominating the city to the southwest, is one of the greatest pleasures the area offers. If you have **transport**, take a packed lunch and head for the foothills of Erciyes, a twenty-minute drive out of town. For those relying on public transport, there's a bus to **Hisarcık** about every half-hour, leaving from Talas Caddesi 500m from the tourist information office. From Hisarcık, you have to walk or take a taxi ($12) a further 16km to the *Kayak Evi*, the **ski lodge** run by Kayseri council (☎0352/342 2031; beds $7 per person, full board $35, closed out of season) at Tekir Yaylası, a plateau 26km south of Kayseri at an altitude of 2150m. The skiing season runs from December to May, and there's a chair lift from the *Kayak Evi* to the slopes. **Ski rental** is under $10 per day (ski clothes also available).

Once you get beyond the foothills Erciyes is a harsh mountain, with little vegetation to soften its contours. More important for hikers is the lack of spring water, making it a tough place to climb in the height of summer. The most reasonable hike starts at the *Kayak Evi* and goes west. A guide, and sundry essential equipment such as crampons and ice axes, are recommended: both should be available from the *Kayak Evi* on demand.

Sultansazlığı

Beyond Mount Erciyes the countryside around the Kayseri–Niğde road becomes flat, dull steppe which you might well assume was as barren of bird or plant life as the fairy chimneys of Cappadocia. Consequently, the oasis of the **Sultansazlığı bird sanctuary** is easy to miss in the small back lanes which wind around the tiny lakes in the region, but it's worth the effort of hunting out.

The complex of wetlands at the bottom of a closed basin comprises two main lakes – Yay Gölü and the smaller Çöl Gölü – and about two thousand hectares of surrounding marshes, covered in reed and cane. The lakes are saline, while the marshland is entirely fresh water, and this particular combination of lakes, marshland, mud flats and steppe makes for an enormous variety of ecosystems. This, allied with the fact that the area is positioned right at the crossroads of two large bird migration routes, make Sultansazlığı an extremely important wetland for breeding migrant and wintering birds.

Although no really detailed ornithological research has so far been carried out, at least 250 species have been recorded, 69 of which breed in the area. Most excitingly for the lay bird-watcher, visiting species include flamingos (particularly in the Yay Gölü region), pelicans, storks, golden eagles from the surrounding steppes, herons, spoonbills and cranes.

There's a **watchtower** in Ovaçiftlik, which can provide very good viewing as long as the water isn't too low (as it may well be in the height of summer), and a little thatched **museum** exhibiting examples of the many feathered species found in the region. There are also various good bird-watching opportunities to the northeast of Ovaçiftlik, near the small village of Soysallı.

The Sultan marshes were surprisingly only afforded Protected Area status in 1988. Up till then, various factors threatened them, and some of these – including the drainage of the marshes for agricultural purposes, and hunting – have still not been completely eradicated.

Practicalities

The marshes, also known as **Kuş Cenneti** (Bird Paradise), are easily accessible from Kayseri: take the Yahyalı **bus** (8 daily until 5pm from the *otogar*) and get off at Ovaçiftlik, from where it's a one-kilometre walk to the water.

The best time to birdwatch is at dawn, so it's worth staying in one of Ovaçiftlik's two **pansiyons** with camping facilities. *Sultan Pansiyon and Camping Restaurant* (☎0352/658 5549; $6 per person) can offer dormitories with bunkbeds, with hot showers outside, and plates of *saç tava* (wok-fried lamb). They run **boat trips** for $20 (maximum 4 people), and organize tours around Yay Gölü. *Atilla Pansiyon* next door (☎0352/658 5576; $6 per person) has similar dormitory-style rooms and a boat for hire.

Kültepe

Northeast of Kayseri at a distance of 22km, the important archeological site at what is now known as **Kültepe** was, before excavation, the largest artificial mound in Turkey. The primary importance of this site, however, derives from the fact that the earliest written documents of Anatolia were found here, in the ancient city called Kanesh. Nearby is the **Karum of Kanesh**, a sort of chamber of commerce, where a colony of Assyrian traders lived and worked controlling commerce between Assyria and Anatolia. Both sites are well signposted and labelled, but should you need further assistance, the charming site watchman will appear on his bicycle to show you around. There's no entrance fee or opening times, but you may like to tip him for his efforts.

Some 15,000 clay tablets and a well-preserved selection of household furnishings, including human and animal statuettes, have been discovered here. Most of these are now scattered throughout the various museums of Turkey, with particularly good collections in Kayseri and Ankara, but the site at which they were originally found has been impressively and efficiently excavated to give some idea of building plans and street layouts, as well as construction techniques which are still prevalent in Anatolia.

Some history

The walled city of Kanesh was inhabited continuously from the fourth millennium BC to the Roman era, but it's golden age was in the second millennium BC. At that time, the Karum of Kanesh, the most important of nine Assyrian *karum*s (trade centres) in Anatolia, importing tin, fine garments and other textiles in exchange for cattle, silver, copper and skins, was inhabited by the Assyrian trading colony and the lower classes, while Kanesh itself was reserved for royalty of Anatolian stock. The thin layer of ash covering the site (the origin of the name Kültepe, "ash hill") dates from two massive conflagrations, the first in around 1850 BC, when the *karum* was also destroyed, and the second between 1200 and 1180 BC. After the first, the *karum* was rebuilt and continued to trade until 1780 BC, when, it would appear, the traders departed in a hurry, leaving behind numerous personal belongings, including large quantities of earthenware vessels, many with graceful or comical animal forms. The city lost its importance during the Hittite age, but was still settled during the Hellenistic and Roman periods (a square building with towers at the corners was probably a Roman temple). Large quantities of ceramics from these later periods have been unearthed, and are now in museums, including that of Kayseri.

The sites

Excavations labelled "level II", from the second millennium BC, dominate the upper site, especially the **Large Palace**, which covered an area of 3000 square metres and included a paved central courtyard, and the **Palace of Warsana**, king of Kanesh. Walls were generally of large mud bricks with stone foundations, though the Large Palace had long storage rooms with stone walls.

The **Karum** is a five-minute walk further down the country lane which leads past the entrance to Kanesh. Here excavations have revealed the foundations of shops, offices, archives and store rooms, all packed closely together inside a defensive wall. **Houses** from this period had one or two storeys built of mud bricks resting on stone foundations, like the palaces of Kanesh. The dead were buried together with precious gifts under the floors of their own houses in stone cist graves, some of which can be seen on site. Upstairs were the living quarters, while downstairs were workrooms, stores and, in some houses, ovens for baking tiny **clay tablets**, the records of all business trans-actions at Kanesh. In one archive alone, 1500 of these tablets were stored, recording the import of lead, cloth and garments, and the export of metals, mainly copper, to Assyria. The tablets also reveal that the Assyrians and Anatolians had friendly relations, and even intermarried.

travel details

Trains

Afyon to: Denizli (2 daily; 5hr); Gaziantep (3 weekly; 19hr); Isparta (2 daily; 5hr); İstanbul (4/5 daily; 8hr 30min); Konya (4/5 daily; 5–6hr).

Eğirdir to: Afyon (1 daily; 6hr); Isparta (4 daily; 1hr 10min).

Isparta to: Afyon (2 daily; 5hr); Denizli (1 daily; 5hr); Eğirdir (2 daily; 1hr 10min); İstanbul (1 daily; 13hr); Konya (3 daily; 1hr 10min).

Kayseri to: Adana (2 daily; 7hr); Ankara (1 hourly; 8hr 30min); Diyarbakır (4 weekly; 20hr); İstanbul (2 daily; 12hr); Kars (1 daily; 24hr); Van (3 weekly; 22hr).

Konya to: Adana (3 weekly; 8hr); Afyon (4/5 daily; 5–6hr); Gaziantep (3 weekly; 13hr); Isparta (3 daily; 1hr 10 min); İstanbul (2 daily; 14hr).

Buses

Afyon to: Adana (3 daily; 10hr); Alanya (5 daily; 6hr 30min); Ankara (5 daily; 4hr); Antalya (13 daily; 5hr); Aydın (15 daily; 5hr); Bursa (3 daily; 5hr); Fethiye (2 daily; 7hr); Isparta (3 daily; 2hr); İstanbul (4 daily; 8hr); İzmir (4 daily; 6hr); Konya (3 daily; 3hr); Kuşadası (2 daily; 7hr); Kutahya (5 daily; 1hr 30min); Marmaris (1 daily; 9hr).

Beyşehir to: Alanya (6 daily; 4hr); Ankara (4 daily; 5hr); Antalya (14 daily; 4hr); Eğirdir (6 daily; 1hr 30min); Isparta (6 daily; 2hr 30min); İstanbul (3 daily; 10hr); İzmir (5 daily; 8hr); Konya (every 30min; 1hr 15min).

Eğirdir to: Ankara (5 daily; 7hr); Antalya (hourly; 3hr); Beyşehir (6 daily; 1hr 30min); Denizli (8 daily; 3hr); Göreme (5 daily; 7hr); İstanbul (1 daily; 10hr); Konya (every 30min; 4hr).

Göreme to: Alanya (1 daily; 12hr); Ankara (5 daily; 4hr); Antalya (1 daily; 10hr); Denizli (2 daily; 10hr); Eğirdir (3 daily; 8hr); İstanbul (3 daily; 11hr); İzmir (1 daily; 11hr 30min); Kayseri (6 daily; 2hr); Konya (3 daily; 3hr); Marmaris (2 daily; 15hr); Side (1 daily; 11hr).

Kayseri to: Adana (10 daily; 5hr 30min); Adiyaman (for Doğubeyazit; 1 daily; 8hr); Afyon (6 daily; 9hr); Ankara (hourly; 4hr 30min); Antalya (4 daily; 12hr); Bursa (4 daily; 11hr); Isparta (3 daily; 9hr); İstanbul (7 daily; 12hr); İzmir (3 daily; 12hr); Konya (8 daily; 4hr); Niğde (hourly; 1hr 30min); Ürgüp (7 daily; 1hr 30min).

Konya to: Afyon (2 daily; 3hr); Alanya (2 daily; 7hr); Ankara (hourly; 3hr); Antalya (4 daily; 5–6hr); Beyşehir (every 30min; 1hr 15min); Bursa (1 daily; 10hr); Göreme (3 daily; 3hr); Isparta (2 daily; 4hr); Kayseri (8 daily; 4hr); Silifke (5 daily; 4hr).

Nevşehir to: Adana (1 daily; 5hr); Ankara (4 daily; 4hr); Antalya (3 daily; 11hr); Fethiye (1 daily; 12hr); İstanbul (3 daily; 10hr); Kayseri (8 daily; 2hr); Konya (4 daily; 3hr); Mersin (2 daily; 5hr).

Niğde to: Aksaray (7 daily; 1hr 30min); Alanya (1 daily; 12hr); Ankara (8 daily; 4hr 30min); Antalya (2 daily; 10–12hr); Derinkuyu (hourly; 45min); İstanbul (3 daily; 12hr); Kayseri (12 daily; 1hr 30min); Konya (5 daily; 3hr 30min); Mersin (5 daily; 4hr); Nevşehir (hourly; 1hr 30min); Samsun (1 daily; 8hr); Sivas (2 daily; 6hr).

Ürgüp to: Adana (2 daily; 5hr); Alanya (2 daily; 14hr); Ankara (4 daily; 5hr); Antalya (2 daily; 11hr); Denizli (2 daily; 12hr); Göreme (every 30min; 20min); İstanbul (1 daily; 13hr); Kayseri (hourly; 2hr); Konya (4 daily; 3hr); Marmaris (2 daily; 15hr); Mersin (3 daily; 5hr); Nevşehir (every 30min; 30min); Side (2 daily; 13hr).

Planes

Kayseri to: İstanbul (1 daily; 1hr 20min).

CHAPTER EIGHT

NORTH CENTRAL ANATOLIA

When the first Turkish nomads arrived in Anatolia during the tenth and eleventh centuries, the landscape must have been strongly reminiscent of their Central Asian homeland. The terrain that so pleased the tent-dwelling herdsmen of a thousand years ago, however, has few attractions for modern visitors: monotonous, rolling vistas of stone-strewn grassland, dotted with rocky outcrops, hospitable only to sheep. In winter it can be numbingly cold here, while in summer temperatures rise to almost unbearable levels.

It seems appropriate that the heart of original Turkish settlement should be home to the political and social centre of modern Turkey, **Ankara**, a modern European-style capital rising out of a stark landscape, symbol of Atatürk's dream of a secular Turkish republic. Though it's a far less exciting city than İstanbul, Ankara does make a good starting point for travels through Anatolia. And even if it's a city more important for its social and political status than for any great architectural or aesthetic merit, it does have its moments: certainly a visit to the Anatolian Civilizations Museum is essential if you want to gain some impression of how Anatolia has developed since it was first settled during Neolithic times.

North Central Anatolia also boasts the remains of one of the earliest known cities in Turkey – **Hattuşaş**, the capital of the Hittite Empire, near the village of **Boğazkale**. East of here, at **Amasya**, **Tokat** and **Sivas**, later cultures and civilizations have left their successive marks. At Amasya, the rock-cut tombs of the pre-Roman Pontic kings tower over a haphazard riverside settlement of Ottoman wooden houses; Tokat boasts a fine Selçuk seminary housing a museum and some well-preserved Ottoman houses, while Sivas has some of the finest Selçuk architecture in Turkey. Hidden away in the mountains to the north of Ankara you'll find **Safranbolu**, an almost completely intact Ottoman town of wooden houses tucked into a narrow gorge, where the traditions of a century or two ago

---

ACCOMMODATION PRICE CODES

In this guide, motels and nearly all hotels and *pansiyon*s have been categorized according to the price codes outlined below, which are based on US$ because of the high domestic Turkish inflation rate. These categories represent the minimum you can expect to pay for a **double room in high season**. Rates for hostels and for the most basic hotels and *pansiyon*s, where guests are charged **per person**, are given in US$, instead of being indicated by price code. For further information, including a rough outline of what you might expect in each category, see p.37.

① under $12	② $12–17	③ $18–25
④ $26–35	⑤ $36–45	⑥ $46–55
⑦ $56–75	⑧ over $75	

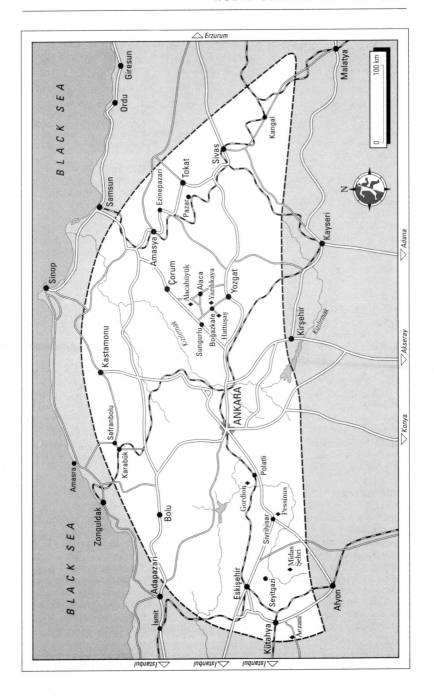

are still current. North of Ankara also is **Kastamonu**, home to a couple of interesting mosques which are in turn overshadowed by the town's huge citadel.

Attractions in the west of the region are sparse and less accessible. High points are the remains of the Phrygian capital of **Gordion** and the Roman temple site of **Aezani**. In between, the Phrygian temple-city of **Pessinus** and the sacred site at **Midaş Şehri** are worth visiting if you have your own transport. En route you'll inevitably pass through **Sivrihisar** with its appealing Selçuk Ulu Cami and **Seyitgazi** with its Dervish monastery built around the tomb of a legendary Arab warrior. **Eskişehir**, the largest city hereabouts, is of little interest other than as a staging post on the way to places like Bursa, Bandırma and the Sea of Marmara, or to **Kütahya**, from where there's access to Aezani.

Oases like these, set amid the forbidding landscape of the region, bear witness to nearly 10,000 years of human settlement, and a complex and turbulent history punctuated by war and waves of conquest. Anatolia was the Roman frontline against the Persians, and in a sense it's still an arena where conflicting currents in Turkish society are played off against each other; the clash of traditional and more modern ways of life in modern Turkey is immediately apparent in cities like Ankara, where sizeable European-oriented middle class populations live side by side with newcomers from the countryside who only a decade or two ago were living a centuries-old peasant existence.

ANKARA

Modern **ANKARA** is really two cities, each seeming to exist separately and within its own time zone. It owes this double identity to the breakneck pace at which it has developed since being declared capital of the Turkish Republic in 1923.

Until then Ankara – known as **Angora** – had been a small provincial city, almost lost in the midst of the steppelands, known chiefly for the production of angora, soft goat's wool. This city still exists, in and around the old citadel which was the site of the original settlement. The other Ankara is the modern metropolis, Atatürk's capital, which has grown up around the old one, surrounding and almost swamping it. This city is a carefully planned attempt to create a seat of government worthy of a modern, Westernized state.

For visitors, Ankara is never going to be as attractive a destination as İstanbul, and the couple of excellent museums and handful of other sights that the city can offer are unlikely to detain you for more than a day or two (note that most of the museums are closed on Mondays). Even so it's worth the trip to find somewhere as refreshingly forward-looking as Turkey's administrative and diplomatic centre.

Some history

It was the Hittites who founded Ankara, naming it Ankuwash, around 1200 BC. Under them the town grew and prospered thanks to its position on the royal road running from Sardis to their capital at Hattuşaş. The Hittites were succeeded by the Phrygians who called the city Ankyra (and left a significant reminder of their presence in the shape of a huge necropolis uncovered near the railway station in 1925). The Lydians followed and after their defeat at the hand of the Persians, the town became a staging post on the Persian royal road from Susa to Sardis. Alexander the Great passed through on his way east and his successors squabbled over Ankara just as they squabbled over the rest of Anatolia. In the third century BC, invading Galatians (Gauls) held sway for a while, renaming the city Galatia. Throughout all this coming and going, Ankara retained its importance overlooking the east–west trading routes, which by now extended into Persia and beyond.

By the beginning of the first century BC, the Romans had made substantial inroads into Asia Minor, and in 74 BC their fourteen-year campaign against the kingdom of

Pontus ended when Mithridates the Great was defeated just northeast of Ankara by the Roman general Pompey. This event opened up central Anatolia to Roman control and in 24 BC Ankara was officially absorbed into the Empire under Augustus and renamed Sebaste (Greek for Augustus).

Ankara prospered under the Romans, thanks to its position astride major trade routes, developing into a thriving city of 200,000 inhabitants by the third century AD. The Byzantine era signalled the end of prosperity and stability for Ankara, ushering in a period of decline and sporadic attack at the hands of whoever happened to be waging war in the area. Arabs, Persians, Crusaders and Mongols stormed the city en route to greater prizes but only the Selçuks were to settle, taking control of the city in 1071.

By 1361 Ankara had been incorporated into the burgeoning Ottoman state, briefly occupying centre stage when the Mongol ruler Tamerlane defeated the army of Beyazit Yıldırım 30km north of the modern city in 1402. Though Tamerlane died three years later and this final wave of Mongol conquest soon ebbed, the defeat precipitated several years of dynastic in-fighting among the Ottomans as Beyazit's sons fought it out among themselves for the succession. It also slowed the pace of the Ottoman advance, giving the Byzantine Empire a fifty-year stay of execution. With the restoration of Ottoman rule Ankara went into something of a decline, with only its famous wool to prevent it from disappearing altogether.

After Atatürk's final victory, it was decided to make Ankara the official capital of the Turkish Republic, a decision that was ratified by parliament on October 13, 1923. This move marked the beginning of modern Ankara, though at this stage the city was still little more than a backward provincial centre, the majority of its population living in mudbrick buildings where electricity and running water were almost unheard-of luxuries. Turkey's vociferous pro-İstanbul lobby was dismayed by the choice of Ankara as capital and many foreign governments, too, baulked at the idea of establishing embassies here, though this was as much out of hostility to the new government as reluctance to endure the primitive conditions in the city. Gradually however, the lure of free land for the building of embassies and a softening of opposition to Atatürk's republic lured in the diplomatic corps, with the British, who had been among the most vocal denigrators of the new capital, snapping up one of the best sites.

The government recruited German and Austrian town planners to transform the city and Ankara soon overspilled its original boundaries in a network of new streets, public buildings and parks, conforming to Atatürk's vision of a modern, westward-looking capital. Rapid development resulted in a corresponding population explosion with tens of thousands of people drawn to the city from the Anatolian countryside each year in search of work and a higher standard of living. The planners reckoned on the population of the city swelling from 30,000 to about 800,000, but the influx far exceeded their expectations and the total number of inhabitants now stands at well over three times that figure.

One of the most socially significant and visible results of this has been the growth of *gecekondu* squatter settlements that now ring the city. Incomers took advantage of an old Ottoman law stating that anyone who could build a house in a single night on an unused plot had the right to legal ownership, and over the decades what were originally shanty towns have become established as legitimate communities.

As the century draws to a close the city authorities are working hard at expanding Ankara's infrastructure to integrate the planned and unplanned parts of the city. Various public transport projects, including an underground railway system, are under construction and there have been concerted efforts to woo in foreign investment. Ultimately, it would seem, the aim is to turn the city into a credible Middle Eastern regional centre, taking maximum advantage of its traditional east–west links in the redefined post-Cold War world.

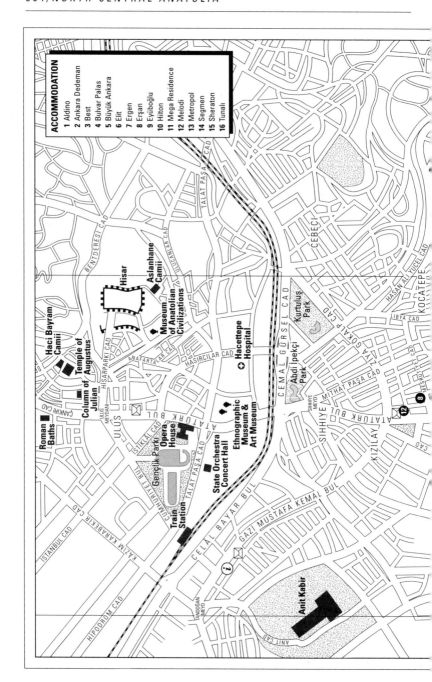

ACCOMMODATION

1 Aldino
2 Ankara Dedeman
3 Best
4 Bulvar Palas
5 Büyük Ankara
6 Elit
7 Ergen
8 Erşan
9 Eyüboğlu
10 Hilton
11 Mega Residence
12 Melodi
13 Metropol
14 Segmen
15 Sheraton
16 Tunalı

Otogar (5km)

ANKARA

see 'Central Ankara' map

Kocatepe Camii

Parliament

US Embassy

German Embassy

Bulgarian Embassy

Yugoslav/Serbian Embassy

Karum Shopping Centre

Iranian Embassy

Pakistani Embassy

Iraqi Embassy

Indian Embassy

Australian Embassy

Russian Embassy

Canadian Embassy

British Embassy

Presidential Palace

Atakule & Simon Bolívar Cad

GAZİOSMANPAŞA

ÇANKAYA

KAVAKLIDERE

AŞAĞAYRANCI

BAKANLIKLAR

İSMET İNÖNÜ BUL

MÜDAFAA

AKAY CAD

BESTEKAR CAD

TUNUS CAD

PARİS CAD

A T A T Ü R K   B U L

DİKMEN CAD

TANYERİ CAD

HOŞDERE CAD

CİNNAH CAD

GÜVENLİK CAD

GÜNEŞ SOK

ARAB SOK

GALİP DEDE SOK

BÜKREŞ CAD

CANKAYI CAD

İRAN CAD

ARJANTİN CAD

BOGAZ SOK

KIRANGIÇ SOK

NENEHATUN CAD

REŞİT GALİP CAD

FİLİSTİN SOK

HOSRAVAN SOK

VÜKELÜS SOK

KÜLLÜBE SOK

GÜNİZ SOK

BÜYÜKÇELİK SOK

İNÖNÜ HİLMİ CAD

TAMBALI CAD

Kurtlu Park

THY

500 m

0

Arrival, orientation and city transport

Finding your way around Ankara is fairly easy. The city is neatly bisected along its north-to-south axis by **Atatürk Bulvarı**. Everything you need will be in easy reach of this broad and busy street. At the northern end is **Ulus Meydanı** (usually known simply as Ulus), a large square and an important traffic intersection, marked by a huge equestrian Atatürk statue, which has lent its name, Ulus (meaning "Nation"), to the surrounding area. Ulus is the point to which you'll probably gravitate on arriving in Ankara, as it's the home of the cheap hotels and and well positioned for both sightseeing and city transportation. About 1km east of here, down Hisarparkı Caddesi, stands the **Hisar**, Ankara's old fortress and citadel, not far from the famous **Museum of Anatolian Civilizations**.

Heading south down Atatürk Bulvarı from Ulus brings you to the main west–east railway line, beyond which lies Sıhhıye Meydanı, an important junction marking the beginning of **Yenişehir** (New City). A ten-minute walk south of Sıhhıye brings you to **Kızılay**, the busy square which is the main transport hub of the modern city, and which has lent its name to the surrounding shopping and restaurant district. Keep going south and you'll pass the parliament building on the right, before moving into the Kavaklıdere district, home of various major embassies. At the bottom of Atatürk Bulvarı is Çankaya, Ankara's most exclusive suburb and location of the **Presidential Palace**.

There are **tourist information offices** at the airport, and more reliably, at Gazi Mustafa Kemal Bul 121, Tandoğan (☎0312/231 5572; daily 8.30am–5.30pm). Neither of these is especially helpful but they will be able to provide you with a city plan.

Arrival

Ankara's Esenboğa **airport**, with several places to change money, is 33km north of town, and buses into town ($3) tend to depart about half an hour after flights land, dropping you off at the *THY* terminal by the train station (see below). Alternatively, a taxi into the centre of Ankara from the airport will set you back about $15. If you arrive at the **city otogar** in the western suburbs ask your bus company about a service minibus into the centre. Alternatively, cross the access bridge to the main road and hail a dolmuş to Ulus or, less likely, to Kızılay; city bus #623 also goes to Kızılay. The **train station** is close to the heart of things on Hipodrom Caddesi, with frequent buses to Ulus, Kızılay and and Maltepe; check the signs on the front of the bus.

City transport

Getting around Ankara is no problem, with plentiful **city buses** running the length of Atatürk Bulvarı. Buses from Ulus run to Kızılay and then branch off to Maltepe or continue to Çankaya (#613). Bus #265 runs to Anıtepe and #447 serves the train station. Bus tickets cost $0.25 and are bought in advance from kiosks next to the main bus stops, though some private buses require payment on board. There are plenty of **taxis**, too, with $0.80 ($1 at night) as a minimum fare and the average trip working out at about $3.

Accommodation

There's no shortage of **hotels** in Ankara, covering the full price and quality spectrum, and finding a room will rarely be a problem, given the relative absence of tourists. Not surprisingly, prices tend to be slightly higher than in smaller towns, but there are plenty of decent possibilities offering doubles in the $12–$17 range.

Most of the cheaper hotels are in **Ulus**, in the streets east of Atatürk Bulvarı between Ulus Meydanı and Opera Meydanı. Moving down into **Sıhhıye** and **Kızılay** will take you up another notch or two with prices and standards increasing steadily as you move south into **Kavaklıdere**, home to top-of-the-range places like the *Hilton* and *Sheraton*. In the highly unlikely event that you draw a blank in these areas head for **Maltepe** where Gazi Mustafa Kemal Bulvarı (running northwest from Kızılay) and the surrounding streets offer everything from fleapits to decent, mid-range places.

Bear in mind that a little haggling can go a long way, even at the more expensive places (perhaps not the *Hilton*), particularly if it's out of season when you visit. At the very least you can try to get the KDV (or local sales tax) knocked off your bill.

Hotels in Ulus, Sıhhıye and Maltepe are marked on our "Central Ankara" map (see p.570), those in Kızılay and Kavaklıdere on our main "Ankara" map (see p.564).

Ulus

Ulus is the place to head for a wide range of low-priced hotels – try the area bordered by Ulus Meydanı and Opera Meydanı, near the Museum of Anatolian Civilizations and the castle. More salubrious places tend to lie on and around Çankırı Caddesi. It's worth bearing in mind that the cheapest hotels often charge a couple of dollars for the use of communal bath which can make the total cost comparable to a room with bathroom at a far nicer establishment.

Budget

Otel Avrupa, Posta Cad, Susam Sok 9 (☎0312/311 4300). Very basic but bearable for one night. ①.

Farabi Oteli, Denizciler Cad 46 (☎0312/312 7595). Plain rooms with showers but good value for singles. ②.

Otel Fuar, Opera Meydanı, Kosova Sok 11 (☎0312/312 3288). Bare but quiet rooms with washbasins. ①.

Hisar Oteli, Hisarparkı Cad 6 (☎0312/311 9889). Washbasins only, but the rooms are clean and presentable. ①.

Otel Kösk, Denizciler Cad 56, near Opera Meydanı (☎0312/324 5228). Formerly mid-range now in rapid decline – you can do better. ①.

Marmara Oteli, Denizciler Cad 17 (☎0312/324 2740). Plain, waterless rooms which aren't too bad. ①.

Olimpiyat Hotel, Rüzgarlı Eşdost Sok 18 (☎0312/324 3331). Good rooms at a reasonable price in this one-star place. ②.

Otel Selçuk, Çankırı Cad, Beşik Sok 4 (☎0312/311 8384). Acceptable cheap hotel. ②.

Şan Otel, Anafartlar Cad, Şan Sok 8/C (☎0312/311 0943). Clean budget option close to the Museum of Anatolian Civilizations. Cheaper rooms come without showers. ②.

Otel Sıpahı, Opera Meydanı, Kosova Sok 1 (☎0312/324 0235). Clean, bright rooms with some great tourism posters from the 1960s. One of the better budget choices. ②.

Otel Turan Palas, Çankırı Cad, Beşik Sok 4 (☎0312/312 5225). Cheap but dark and damp. ①.

Mid-range

Otel Akman, Opera Meydanı, Tavus Sok 6 (☎0312/324 4140). Clean and bright rooms with nice bathrooms. ②.

Buhara Oteli, Sanayi Cad 13 (☎0312/324 3327). Recently renovated hotel with small but immaculately clean rooms. One of the better mid-range choices. ②.

Otel Bulduk, Sanayi Cad 26 (☎0312/310 4915). Big, modern place. ③.

Otel Devran, Opera Meydanı, near Gazi Lisesi (☎0312/311 0485). Well-run, friendly place with decent, though small rooms. ②.

Otel Erden, Opera Meydanı, near Gazi Lisesi (☎0312/309 3595). Acceptable place, cheaper if you're willing to forgo the luxury of en-suite bathroom. ②.

Otel Güleryüz, Opera Meydanı, Sanayi Cad (☎0312/310 4910). Comfortable two-star place but perhaps overpriced. ③.

Otel Mithat, Opera Meydanı, Tavus Sok 2 (☎0312/311 5410). Decent rooms with bathrooms. ②.

Otel Safir, Denizciler Cad 34 (☎0312/324 1194). Clean, spacious rooms with bathrooms – a good choice. ②.

Hotel Suna, Çankırı Cad, Soğukkuyu Sok 6 (☎0312/324 3250). Quiet and gloomy but the rooms are reasonable. ②.

Expensive

Canbek Hotel, Soğukkuyu Sok 8 (☎0312/324 3320, fax 311 1373). Fancy two-star down a side street off Çankırı Cad. ③.

Otel Çevikoğlu, Çankırı Sok 2, Beşik Sok 7 (☎0312/310 4535). Spotless two-star option just north of Ulus. ④.

Hitit Hotel, Hisarparkı Cad, Firuz Ağa Sok 12 (☎0312/310 8617). Well located near the foot of the citadel. ④.

Otel Karyağdi, Sanayi Cad, Kuruçeşme Sok 4 (☎0312/310 2440, fax 312 6712). A spotless modern hotel, highly recommended for its comfortable rooms and professional, courteous staff. ④.

Hotel Selvi, Çankırı Cad 16 (☎0312/310 3500, fax 312 2692). Presentable semi-luxury possibility just above Ulus. Rooms at the front can get noisy. ④.

Turist Hotel, Çankırı Cad 37 (☎0312/310 3980, fax 311 8345). Doesn't really deserve its three stars, but facilities are reasonable; frequented by package-tour groups. ④.

Sıhhıye and Maltepe

Hotel Acar, Gazi Mustafa Kemal Bul 66 (☎0312/231 3522, fax 231 8694). Plush rooms in a chic reincarnation of the old *Babil Otel*. ④.

Büyük Sürmeli Hotel, Cihan Sok 6, Sihhiye (☎0312/231 7660, fax 229 5176). The works, as you'd expect for the price, including a pool and casino. ⑧.

Otel Örnek, Gülseren Sok 4 (☎0312/231 8170, fax 229 0353). Down a side street just of Gazi Mustafa Kemal Bul, this is fine but a little overpriced. ⑤.

Yeni Otel, Sanayi Cad 5/B (☎0312/310 4720, fax 311 8439). Nice, spacious rooms off Sıhhıye Meyd, but often full. ③.

Kızılay

Otel Elit, Olgunlar Sok 10 (☎0312/417 4695, fax 417 4697). Comfortable and quiet. ④.

Hotel Ergen, Karanfil Sok 48 (☎0312/417 5906, fax 425 7819). Standard-issue mid-range hotel. ④.

Hotel Erşan, Meşrütiyet Cad 13 (☎0312/418 9875, fax 417 4943). Small and smoky rooms. A good location but with an outdated, exhausted feel. ④.

Eyüboğlu Hotel, Karanfil Sok 73 (☎0312/417 6400, fax 417 8125). Expensive but pleasantly located at the quieter end of the street. ⑦.

Otel Melodi, Karanfil Sok 10 (☎0312/417 6414, fax 418 7858). Very central with all the usual comforts. ⑥.

Hotel Metropol, Olgunlar Sok 5 (☎0312/417 3060, fax 417 6990). Sterile luxury option with a good location. ⑦.

Kavaklıdere

Otel Aldino, Tunalı Hilmi Cad, Bülten Sok 22 (☎0312/468 6510, fax 468 6517). Prime location for dedicated shoppers, with a nightclub and Turkish bath to boot. ⑨.

Hotel Ankara Dedeman, Büklüm Sok 1 (☎312/417 6200, fax 417 6214). A luxury place where you may be able to negotiate a worthwhile discount. ⑦.

Hotel Best, Atatürk Bul 195 (☎312/467 0880, fax 467 0885). Plush enough but you'll find quieter options in the streets further east. ⑦.

Hotel Bulvar Palas, Atatürk Bul 141 (☎312/417 5020). The journalists' hotel and very nice it is too. ⑦.
Büyük Ankara Oteli, Atatürk Bul 183 (☎312/425 6655, fax 425 5070). The city's second-best luxury hotel (after the *Hilton*), near the parliament building. ⑧.
Hilton International Hotel, Tahran Cad 12 (☎312/468 2888, fax 468 0909). You might want to stay here if you're on a generous expense account. ⑧.
Mega Residence Ankara, Tahran Cad 5 (☎312/468 5400). An alternative to the nearby *Hilton* and *Sheraton* if your wallet extends to $200 a night. ⑧.
Seğmen Hotel, Büklüm Sok 13 (☎312/417 5374, fax 417 2859). Edging up towards the $100 a night mark. You're paying for the location as much as anything else. ⑧.
Sheraton, Noktalı Sok (☎312/468 5454, fax 467 1136). Enjoy a pampered existence among the business travellers for $240 a night with casino and pool to hand. ⑧.
Otel Tunalı, Tunalı Hilmi Cad 119 (☎312/467 4440, fax 427 4082). Good upper mid-range option. ⑦.

The City

For most visitors, the first taste of Ankara is **Ulus Meydanı**, home of the cheap hotels, and it's none too enticing. Ulus marked the westernmost limits of pre-Republican Ankara which occupied the area between here and the citadel, but now the streets are mostly lined by drab, concrete stacks with only the occasional Ottoman-era survivor breaking the monotony. Unpromising as it looks, the area does hide a couple of Roman monuments, offering a hint at the depth of history beneath the prevailing modernity.

A towering equestrian **statue of Atatürk** – flanked by threatening bronze soldiers in German-style coal-scuttle helmets – gazes out over the busy intersection of Cumhuriyet and Atatürk *bulvarı*s at Ulus Meydanı. The former president gazes towards the building which housed the Turkish Grand National Assembly, the provisional parliament convened by Atatürk and his Nationalist supporters on April 23, 1920; this modest, late-Ottoman schoolhouse building is where the Turkish Republic was declared on 29 October 1923, with Atatürk as president and his long-time supporter and close friend Ismet İnönü as prime minister, and served as parliament until 1925. Today it houses the **Museum of the War of Independence** (see p.580), devoted to the military struggle that preceded the foundation of the modern republic. Opposite the museum stands Ankara's first hotel, the *Ankara Palas*, once again serving as a guesthouse for visiting dignitaries.

From Ulus, Hisarparkı Caddesi leads east to the Hisar: on the way a quick diversion south down Susam Caddesi, followed by a fork to the left, brings you to the **Yeni Hallar**, the city's premier fruit and veg market. Just behind here on Konya Caddesi is the **Vakıf Sultan Çarşısı**, a restored *han*, now home to multitudes of cheap clothing shops.

Roman Ankara

What's left of Roman Ankara lies just north of Hisarparkı Caddesi. Following Hükümet Caddesi and taking the first right fork leads to the remains of the **Temple of Augustus and Rome**, Ankara's most important ancient monument. Built in honour of Augustus between 25 and 20 BC after Ankara was made the provincial capital of Galatia, its main claim to fame is the inscription detailing the *Res Gestae Divi Augusti* (Deeds of the Divine Augustus) on the outer wall: this was the emperor's political testament which was carved on the walls of every temple of Augustus in the Roman world after his death. The Ankara version is the only one that survives in its entirety. The temple, whose walls alone have endured, was converted into a Christian church around the fifth century AD, and during the fifteenth century it became the *medrese* of the **Hacı**

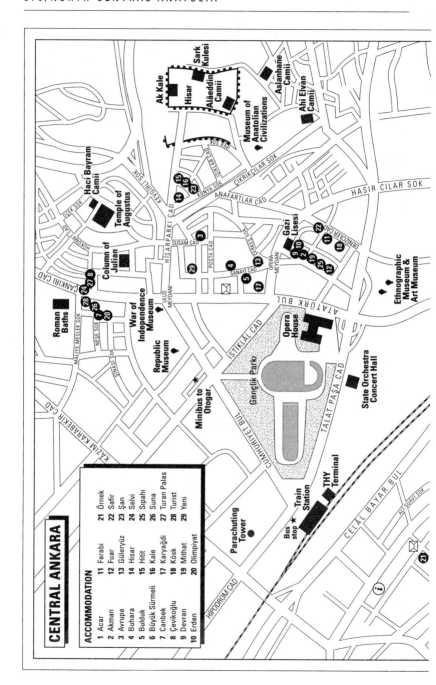

CENTRAL ANKARA

ACCOMMODATION

1 Acar	11 Farabi	21 Örnek
2 Akman	12 Fuar	22 Safir
3 Avrupa	13 Güleryüz	23 Şan
4 Buhara	14 Hisar	24 Selvi
5 Bulduk	15 Hitit	25 Sipahi
6 Büyük Sürmeli	16 Kale	26 Suna
7 Canbek	17 Karyağdi	27 Turan Palas
8 Çevikoğlu	18 Kösk	28 Turist
9 Devran	19 Mithat	29 Yeni
10 Erden	20 Olimpiyat	

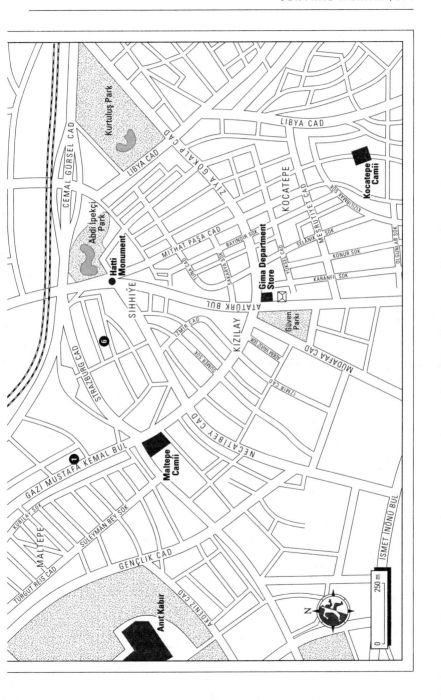

Bayram Camii, named after Bayram Veli, founder of the Bayrami order of dervishes and Ankara's most celebrated Muslim saint, who is buried in the *türbe* in front of the building.

A couple of hundred metres to the southwest on Hükümet Meydanı is the **Jülyanüs Sütunu** (Column of Julian) commemorating a visit to Ankara by the Byzantine emperor Julian the Apostate, chiefly remembered for his shortlived attempt to revive worship of the old Roman gods in the fourth century. The stonework of his column has a strange layered effect rather like a long, cylindrical kebab. After memories of the Byzantine Empire had faded, the locals took to calling the column Belkız Minaresi, "the Queen of Sheba's Minaret".

Ankara's other main Roman monument, the **Roma Hamamları** or **Roman Baths** (daily 8.30am–12.30pm & 1.30–5.30pm; $0.50), are about ten minutes' walk north of here on the western side of Çankırı Caddesi. They are set in a large *palaestra* (exercise field) scattered with truncated columns and fragments of cracked masonry. Of the baths themselves, which date back to the third century AD, only the brick pillars that supported the floors and allowed warm air to circulate and heat the rooms above survive.

The citadel and old town

From Inönü Park, at the eastern end of Hisarparkı Caddesi, a sharp right turn leads to the **Museum of Anatolian Civilizations**, an outstanding archeological collection documenting the peoples and cultures of Anatolia from the late Stone Age through to classical times. Housed in a restored fifteenth-century *bedesten*, this unmissable museum is, for most visitors, the highpoint of a visit to Ankara (see p.570).

A pathway leads up through Inönü Park between the inner and outer walls of the **Hisar**, the Byzantine citadel whose walls enclose the oldest part of the city, an Ottoman-era village of cobbled streets and ramshackle wooden houses that, of all Ankara's districts, most fully rewards a relaxed and aimless stroll. Most of the area is defiantly unrestored, not to say verging on the squalid, and at times the old-world atmosphere is pungently authentic with the stench of rotting rubbish and bad drains hanging heavy on the air. All this is starting to change, though, and a number of grand Ottoman mansions have been renovated, decked out with carpets and antiques, and transformed into restaurants geared towards the tourist trade. Some succeed in recapturing the atmosphere of times past, while others seem as hopelessly kitsch as upmarket hotel restaurants (see "Eating and drinking", p.581).

Ankara's first **city walls** were probably constructed by the Hittites who recognized the defensive potential of the citadel outcrop over three thousand years ago. The walls that can be seen today are much more recent, built on the orders of the Byzantine Emperor Michael III (remembered as "Michael the Sot") in 859, who updated defences built by the Roman emperor Heraclius (who in turn had used earlier Gaulish fortifications as a foundation).

At the northern end of the citadel is the **Ak Kale** (White Fortress) with tremendous views of Ankara old and modern. The northeastern edge of the city, just about visible from here, is the approximate site of the battlefield where Pompey defeated the Pontic king Mithridates the Great in 74 BC. **Şark Kulesi**, a ruined tower rising out of the eastern walls, which is a favourite kite-flying spot with local children, also offers panoramic views. It's from here that you can best appreciate the impact of the *gecekondu* squatter settlements that have grown up around modern Ankara.

At the southern end of the citadel is the **South Gate**, with two vast towers flanking a twin portal. Embedded in the wall connecting the towers are various fragments of Roman masonry, including altars supported by recumbent statues of Priapus. Just inside the gate is the **Alâeddin Camii**, a twelfth-century mosque, much restored in later years, whose unexceptional exterior conceals a painstaking-ly carved Selçuk *mimber*.

An unadulterated example of Selçuk architecture can be found a few streets to the southeast in the shape of the **Aslanhane Camii** (Lion-House Mosque), Ankara's oldest, largest and most impressive mosque. The Aslanhane Camii is a "forest mosque", so called because of the 24 wooden columns (arranged in four rows of six) that support the intricately carved wooden ceiling. The astonishingly detailed wal-nut *mimber* dates back to 1209 and is one of the last examples of Selçuk decorative carving. It's well complemented by the stucco and tile *mihrab*, another exceptional piece of work. Ahi Şerafattin, the founder of the Aslanhane Camii, is buried opposite the mosque in Ankara's sole surviving Selçuk **tomb**, with its distinctive octagonal plan and pointed roof.

There's another forest mosque, the **Ahi Elvan Camii**, a few minutes' walk south-west of here. It's an Ottoman example of the style, dating from the late thirteenth cen-tury and, though not as impressive as the Aslanhane Camii, worth looking in on. This particular mosque was founded by the Ahi brotherhood, a medieval guild associated with the dervish orders. The carved *mimber*, though overshadowed by the example up the road is, none the less, a fine piece of work.

Kızılay and around

The bus ride from Ulus to Kızılay is not an especially thrilling experience. Immediately south of Ulus you pass Ankara's main PTT, on the east side of Atatürk Bulvarı, and there-after comes a succession of banks. Look out for the entrance to **Gençlik Parkı** (Youth Park) on the right after the roundabout. The park was built on the orders of Atatürk to provide a worthy recreational spot for the hard-toiling citizens of his model metropolis. On most summer evenings, it's packed with promenading families strolling around the artificial lake and enjoying the numerous cafés. Occasional outdoor concerts are held here and there's also a *Luna Park* funfair full of antiquated rides. The **Opera House**, looking like a dark-pink Art Deco underground station, stands near the entrance, and was built at Atatürk's behest – he developed a taste for opera while serving as military attaché in Sofia in 1905, and decided that Ankara, as a great modern city, needed an opera house; today the opera is thriving and affordable (see "Nightlife", p.584).

Heading on down Atatürk Bulvarı you pass the **Ethnographic Museum** (see p.580), a grandiose white marble building on the eastern side of the street, the original resting place of Atatürk before the construction of the Anıt Kabir mausoleum. To the west is what appears to be an industrial wasteland, but beyond the rail and road bridges which span the road a little further south things start to improve, as modern Ankara sudden-ly begins. To the immediate east is another park, the **Abdi İpekçi Parkı**, with a small lake and teahouses, and just to the south is the **Sıhhıye Meydanı**, at the centre of which stands the Hatti Monument, with a statue based on the Bronze Age Anatolian stag symbol. Here the road branches in three directions. Along Atatürk Bulvarı the pace of streetlife picks up rapidly as you approach **Kızılay**, the centre of modern Ankara, which turns out to be yet another immense traffic junction with a small park and mighty Atatürk statue.

At the southeastern corner of this huge junction, on the eastern side of Atatürk Bulvarı, is the *Gima* department store – where the merchandise smacks of the bargain basement – and a post office. Moving south from the square are numerous fancy clothes shops, which although very expensive by Turkish standards, actually work out quite cheap in western European terms. To the east of Atatürk Bulvarı a restaurant and café culture permeates the parallel pedestrian precincts and hides some of the city's best cinemas and music and bookshops.

ATATÜRK

Modern Turkey is largely the creation of one man, **Mustafa Kemal Atatürk**. A complex and often contradictory figure driven by both fervent patriotism and blinding ambition, he salvaged the Turkish state from the wreckage of the Ottoman Empire and defined it as a modern, secular nation. The omnipresent public statues and portraits are not merely symbols of the personality cult that has been built up around him; they reflect the widely held conviction that without him Turkey in its present form simply would not exist.

Born in Salonica on the fringes of the declining Ottoman Empire in 1881, Atatürk set his sights on a military career from an early age. After the death of his father, a minor civil servant and unsuccessful businessman, he persuaded his reluctant mother to let him attend military school where he proved to be an excellent pupil.

EARLY CAREER

In 1902 his military education took him to the Staff College in İstanbul. By now, popular feeling thought that it was time to replace the decay of the old regime with a democratic structure. Atatürk was soon involved in anti-government political activities which continued after his commission into the regular army, and in 1906 he helped form a revolutionary patriotic society called *Vatan* (Fatherland), which in the following year became part of the **Committee of Union and Progress** (CUP), a radical political organization set up by supporters of the Young Turk revolutionary movement.

In April 1909, Atatürk played a key role in the CUP coup that deposed Sultan Abdulhamid, leading the "Army of Liberation" into İstanbul and securing the city for the revolutionaries. Despite his prominent role in these events, political and personal differences with the increasingly authoritarian CUP leadership led to his political sidelining (and a couple of unsuccessful assassination attempts). Appointments in distant parts of the empire, followed by a posting to Sofia as military attaché, served to keep him out of the way until the outbreak of World War I.

GALLIPOLI VICTORY

In February 1915, Atatürk was sent to **Gallipoli**, where an Allied landing was imminent. It was to prove a highly significant posting in terms of both Atatürk's own career and the Turkish war effort. When the Allied assault came in April he organized a daring counterattack preventing the Allies from breaking out of the Arıburnu (Anzac Cove) bridgehead. His skill as a commander, coupled with his willingness to put his own life at risk in the front line, galvanized the Turkish troops into fierce and heroic defence, and he was rewarded with promotion to colonel and command of the army corps controlling the strategically vital Anafarta ridge. In this role he was successful in repulsing a second major attack in August, and was himself wounded. The Allied attempt to push through Gallipoli towards İstanbul was now finished and they withdrew in January 1916. Atatürk's key role in the defence of Gallipoli had established his military reputation and, more significantly, brought him a nationwide respect that he would put to good use after the 1918 armistice.

As a result of his Gallipoli successes, Atatürk was promoted to general. There was little he could do to turn the wider tide of defeat about to engulf the Ottoman Empire and he spent the remainder of the war taking part in rearguard actions on the southern fringes of the empire. When the armistice was signed on October 30, 1918, he began the task of trying to preserve the demoralized army, knowing there were further battles to come.

BATTLE FOR INDEPENDENCE

Recognizing that the victorious World War I Allies were about to carve up the empire, and that Sultan Mehmet VI's government wasn't going to do anything about it, Atatürk decided to organize **Turkish resistance** from Anatolia where nationalist guerilla bands were already active. In May 1919, he managed to secure a posting to Samsun, ostensibly to restore order in the region. His arrival there can be seen as the beginning of the Turkish struggle for independence. In the words of Atatürk's biographer Patrick Kinross, he had "set up his standard of liberation on the shores of the Black Sea".

He came out into the open on June 21 in the town of Amasya, delivering a speech calling for national resistance to outside attempts to dismember Turkey, which as the recent Greek occupation of İzmir had shown were now well under way. Atatürk and his followers were now in open rebellion against the government. He went on to preside over Nationalist congresses at Erzurum and Sivas, which drafted and confirmed a political manifesto known as the **National Pact** calling for the preservation of Turkey's existing frontiers and the establishment of a provisional government.

With growing support for the Nationalists, the Allies occupied İstanbul and, a month later, the Sultan suspended parliament. The time was right for Atatürk to put into effect his plan to create an alternative Anatolian-based government, and on April 23, 1920, the first session of the **Grand National Assembly** opened with him as president. A month later the Sultan's goverment condemned Atatürk and some of his followers to death. Turkey was now split in two and Atatürk was undisputed figurehead of the Nationalist cause.

BIRTH OF THE REPUBLIC

In this role of Nationalist leader, he oversaw a series of complex political and military manoeuvrings, most significant of which was the repulse of the Greek invasion of Anatolia in 1921. This culminated in the epic **Battle of Sakarya** which took place 100km west of Ankara between August 23 and September 13. Atatürk took personal command in the field, reprising his Gallipoli role, and smashed the Greek advance. The following summer he directed a lightning offensive that drove the Greeks from Anatolia, culminating in the sacking and burning of İzmir. On October 11, 1922 an armistice agreement was signed with the Allies and on November 1 the Nationalists abolished the Sultanate.

1923 saw the consolidation of Atatürk's gains. The Treaty of Lausanne signed on July 24 established Turkey's borders and in October the Allies withdrew from İstanbul allowing the Nationalist troops to occupy the city. In the same month Ankara was officially made capital, and on October 29, Turkey was declared a **republic** with Kemal as president.

REFORMS

Having achieved wider political and military objectives, Atatürk now turned his attention to **internal reform**. His main aim was to transform Turkey into a modern, Western-oriented society, and between 1923 and 1934 he developed a series of dramatic reforms that touched every aspect of Turkish life. Among the most significant of these were the separation of religion and state with the abolition of the Caliphate in 1924, the adoption of Latin script in 1924, and the establishment of full suffrage for women in 1934. In the same year, it was decreed that all Turks should adopt surnames. Atatürk's own name, meaning "**Father Turk**" dates from then – previously he had been known only as Mustafa Kemal.

Despite these reforms Atatürk's style of rule is best described as **benign despotism**; he used a Kurdish revolt in 1925 as a pretext to ban Turkey's sole opposition party and institute censorship of the press. The revolt itself was suppressed with mass hangings of the ringleaders in Diyarbakır. The following year an amateurish plot against Atatürk's life was uncovered, an event which was blown up into a full-scale conspiracy and provided a convenient excuse for hanging several members of the former CUP leadership who had been vocal opponents of Atatürk. The 1926 purge served its purpose in muting the opposition and was not repeated.

Atatürk and associates pursued a policy designed to create a self-sufficient industrial base for Turkey, along the lines of fascist Italy; it was a failure, as massive subsidies crippled the rest of the economy. Atatürk's foreign policy dealings were more successful, and his resolute non-interventionism kept Turkey out of the impending European conflict.

By the mid-1930s, it was evident that his greatest achievements were behind him and his **final years** present a sad picture of decline. Bad health accelerated by heavy drinking made him increasingly unpredictable and irascible. By the winter of 1937 it was evident that he was seriously ill. He survived long enough to oversee the first stages of the transfer of the Hatay from France to Turkey, the last political action in which he took a personal hand. He died of cirrhosis at İstanbul's Dolmabahçe Palace on November 10, 1938, and was succeeded the following day by Ismet İnönü.

South of Kızılay

For many visitors explorations of modern Ankara terminate around Kızılay. It is, however, worth pressing on by foot or bus down Atatürk Bulvarı, where surrounding real estate values increase exponentially as you move south towards Çankaya. A few blocks east of the main thoroughfare, the minarets of the massive **Kocatepe Camii** tower above the surrounding streets. This neo-Ottoman structure, finished in 1989 complete with shopping centre and car park underneath, is Ankara's largest mosque and, indeed, one of the biggest in the world.

Half a kilometre or so beyond Kızılay is the **Grand National Assembly**, Turkey's functional modern parliament building, prelude to a strip of well-appointed embassy buildings and glossy hotels that stretches all the way to the Presidential Palace. About halfway along is the innocuous little **Kuğulu Parkı**, so packed with trysting couples you'll feel like a voyeur as you stroll through it. At the eastern side of the park is the gleaming **Karum shopping centre**, which, with its air conditioning and mall kids, comes as something of a culture shock after the crowded streets of Ulus and Kızılay. You're now in **Kavaklıdere**, one of the capital's smartest suburbs and also one of the liveliest. This is the place to come for Western-style nightlife and designer stores, both of which you'll find in abundance along **Tunalı Hilmi Caddesi**, running north from the Kuğulu Parkı roundabout.

At the end of Atatürk Bulvarı is Çankaya Caddesi, beyond which lies the modern **Presidential Palace** (Çankaya Köşkü), Atatürk's Ankara residence (Sun 1.30–5.30pm). To visit, you must check in at the guardhouse and surrender your passport before joining a group tour. The house itself is a reasonably modest affair, a largish two storey villa set in formal grounds, but by no means a palace. Atatürk moved here in 1921, and the venue saw much political plotting among the president and his cronies to ensure that he and his ideas would be dominant in the new Turkey. The ground floor is furnished in a style best described as Ottoman Baroque with much heavily carved and inlaid dark wood furniture in evidence; upstairs in Atatürk's living quarters the decor is a little more relaxed with personal touches like a billiard table on display.

Back on Çankaya Caddesi, heading southwest for ten minutes or so leads to **Atakule**, a vast mushroom of a tower in reinforced concrete and mirror glass with another smart shopping centre at its foot. It's worth shelling out a dollar for the lift ride up the tower to enjoy an unbeatable view of the city and an expensive drink in the bar.

Anıt Kabir

Anıt Kabir, Atatürk's mausoleum, is a national shrine to the memory of the man who shaped modern Turkey (daily 9am–5pm; winter closes 4pm; bus #265 from Ulus). The main entrance to the mausoleum is reached by travelling up Anıt Caddesi from Tandoğan Meydanı (at the northwestern end of Gazi Mustafa Kemal Bulvarı), and it's this approach that reveals the place at its most impressive (you can also enter the grounds of the mausoleum from a rear entrance on Akdeniz Caddesi).

The Anıt Caddesi approach takes you through the immaculately kept grounds of the mausoleum to a car park. A flight of steps leads up to a colonnade, guarded by Hittite-style stone lions, which in turn leads to the central courtyard of the mausoleum. The entrance to the colonnade is flanked by two towers, the **Independence Tower** on the left and the **Freedom Tower** on the right. Inside the towers you'll find a scale model of the Anıt Kabir complex, a selection of before-and-after aerial shots of its construction from 1944 to 1953, and some intriguing runner-up designs that never quite made it off the page.

At the head of the vast courtyard that opens up at the end of the colonnade is the **mausoleum** itself, a squared-off Neoclassical temple with huge bronze doors. Visitors wearing hats must remove them as they enter and soldiers stand guard to ensure that everyone evinces the appropriate degree of respect. The mausoleum interior is almost completely bare – the only decoration some discreet mosaic work – so that all attention is focused on the plain sarcophagus. Atatürk's body was brought here in 1953 from its original resting place in what is now the Ethnological Museum.

At the opposite side of the courtyard is the **tomb of Ismet Inönü** (1884–1973), Atatürk's old comrade and long-time supporter, who served as first prime minister of the Turkish Republic and became president after Atatürk's death. Three large halls are positioned around the courtyard. The largest of these, on the southern side, contains the **Atatürk Museum** (daily 9.30am–12.30pm & 1.30–5pm) where you'll find everything from Atatürk's evening dress to the rowing machine he used for exercise. Among the most eye-catching exhibits are a gun disguised as a walking stick that Ian Fleming would have been proud of, and the gifts of a diamond-encrusted sword from the Shah of Iran and an elegant toilet set from the king of Afghanistan. An adjacent hall houses Atatürk's cars, a couple of Lincoln limousines used for official business and an imposing black Cadillac (reputedly still in working order) used as personal transport. In the nearby information centre there's not much in the way of information but fans of esoteric souvenirs will appreciate the selection of Atatürk key rings, ashtrays and wall-clocks that propel the Atatürk personality cult into the same league as Lenin or Chairman Mao.

Ankara's museums

Ankara has one of the most prestigious museums in Turkey in the shape of the unmissable Museum of Anatolian Civilizations. The city's remaining museums are left in the shade by comparison but those listed below are all worth a visit. If time is limited the Ethnographic Museum, with its collection of folk costumes and Anatolian art and artefacts, and the Republic Museum, housed in the former Grand National Assembly building and detailing the foundation of modern Turkey, are the most rewarding.

Museum of Anatolian Civilizations (Anadolu Medeniyetleri Müzesi)

The Museum of Anatolian Civilizations (Tues–Sun 9am–5.30pm; $2.50) chronicles the development of civilization in Anatolia from the first isolated settlements of the Late Stone Age through to the Classical era. Housed in an old *bedesten* it contains a vast treasure hoard of artefacts laid out in chronological order, most well-labelled in English and German; as you enter you may well be importuned by an official guide offering to accompany you on your tour. If you have $15 or so to spare and like the look of whoever approaches you, this can be worth doing – many of the guides are moonlighting academics and correspondingly well informed.

● **Paleolithic (Old Stone Age) section**. By the museum entrance, this acts as a kind of prelude to the museum proper. An assortment of bone fragments and primitive stone tools and weapons from a cave-site at Karain, 30km northwest of Antalya, bear witness to the two-million-year hunter-gatherer period of development that ended about 10,000 years ago. Later finds from Karain include more sophisticated bone awls, needles and ornaments that are a foretaste of the more complex artefacts found in the following section.

● **Neolithic section (7000–5500 BC)**. This is based mainly around objects found at Çatal Höyük, a settlement of New Stone Age mud-brick houses 52km north of Konya, which has yielded important evidence about the period in which the seeds of our civilization were sown. This was the era when settled agriculture began, accompanied by the refinement of tool-making techniques and the appearance of hand-made pottery. One of the most interesting features here is the re-creation of a room from a Çatal Höyük dwelling, complete with characteristic bull's-head emblem and wall-paintings. The importance of agriculture in this period perhaps accounts for the abundance of fertility goddess figures – represented by baked clay female forms of ample proportions – that reappear in various forms throughout the museum. Later on in this period evidence of a more sophisticated lifestyle emerges in finds dating back to 5700–5600 BC from a settlement at Hacılar in southwest Anatolia. Vessels in the shape of animals and a red cup in the shape of a stylized female form reveal improvements in pottery-making methods. Other objects on display include simple bead jewellery and tools and weapons made from obsidian and flint.

● **Chalcolithic section (5400–3000 BC)**. Further finds from Hacılar can be found here, including simple copper implements, the first use of metal in Anatolia. The pottery is decorated with geometric designs that become more complex as the centuries go by. Stone seals suggesting formal property ownership bear witness to an increasingly well-organized society.

● **Bronze Age section (3000–2000 BC)**. Hammering and casting techniques had been greatly refined and were used to work not only bronze but also gold, silver and electron (an alloy of gold and silver). This era was characterized by large settlements of mud-brick houses built on stone foundations and surrounded by defensive walls. Most of the objects here come from Alaca Höyük; among the most striking exhibits are the pieces of gold jewellery unearthed in the royal tombs. Other memorable objects are cult symbols featuring stags, bulls and the sun. The pottery is plainer than that of the Chalcolithic period but better made with obvious spouts and handles. This was an era when Anatolia reached an advanced level of civilization with well-established trade links between the various settlements. One symbol of continuity, the mother goddess figure, has now slimmed down or been transformed into a distinctive violin shape.

● **Assyrian Trading Colony section (1950–1750 BC)**. This section includes some well-preserved examples of the earliest written records in Anatolia in the shape of cuneiform tablets produced by the Assyrians. Also striking are the libation vases in the form of birds and animals, and vases made of obsidian and rock crystal. This period saw Assyrian traders from northern Mesopotamia establishing a trading network that covered most of Anatolia, importing tin, goat-hair felt, cloth, garments, ornaments and perfumes, and establishing markets called *karum*s outside their cities. The central *karum* was at Kaniş, outside Kültepe, and it's from there that most of the objects on display in this section are drawn.

● **Old Hittite section (1700–1450 BC)**. The Hittites left behind spectacular sites at Boğazköy and nearby Yazılıkaya east of Ankara; most of the objects on display are from Boğazköy and Alaca Höyük. Hittite pottery is similar to that found in the Assyrian Trading Colony period, the most sophisticated example here being a vase with a relief depicting a lively wedding procession. There's also some well-executed metalwork, including statues of gods and goddesses in bronze. Also in this section are a number of stelae carved with hieroglyphics that have proved a valuable source of information about the Old Hittite Kingdom.

● **Hittite Empire section (1450–1200 BC)**. This was a period of expansionism and warfare, particularly against the Egyptians, and it represents the zenith of Hittite power. The large and elaborate reliefs from Alaca Höyük in the central hall bear witness to the sophistication of Hittite culture during this time. Most depict religious themes: a king and queen offering libations to a bull, and an elaborate festival scene with a juggler,

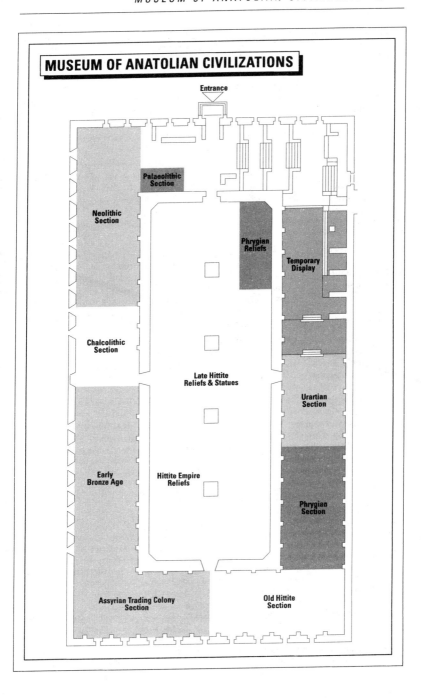

MUSEUM OF ANATOLIAN CIVILIZATIONS

Entrance

Palaeolithic Section

Neolithic Section

Phrygian Reliefs

Temporary Display

Chalcolithic Section

Late Hittite Reliefs & Statues

Urartian Section

Early Bronze Age

Hittite Empire Reliefs

Phrygian Section

Assyrian Trading Colony Section

Old Hittite Section

acrobat and musician stand out in particular. If you're planning to visit Hattuşaş look out for the lion and sphinx figures from the city gates there, and the bearded, hook-nosed figure of the weather god Teshuba. These are the originals, replaced with replicas at the site itself.

● **Late Hittite section (1200–700 BC)**. The main Late Hittite sites were at Kargamiş, Karatepe and Malatya-Aslantepe. A number of well-preserved and detailed reliefs from this period are in the central hall, one of the most vivid being a battle scene showing a chariot carrying an archer running over a dead man. Others show the children of the Hittite king Araras at play, a procession of three women in mourning, and the Hittite mother goddess Kubaba in various poses.

● **Phrygian section (1200–700 BC)**. Most of the objects here were recovered from the royal tumulus at Gordion, capital of Phrygian Anatolia after the fall of the Hittites. The timber-framed chamber at the heart of the tumulus has been re-created and objects from it are on show nearby. Most impressive are a wooden table of intricate design, and skilfully wrought bronze vessels. Other exhibits attest to their culture's sophistication: pottery with stylized animal reliefs and a translucent glass bowl, one of the earliest known examples of glasswork.

● **Urartian section (1200–700 BC)**. Main rivals of the Phrygians and descendants of the Hurrians, the Urartians established a vast empire centred on Van and extending from Sivas and Erzincan to Iran, held together by a series of fortified citadels. Most of what is known about the Urartians derives from clay tablets listing military successes. On the evidence of the artefacts on display here their culture was less sophisticated than that of the Phrygians, though the large bronze cauldron resting on a tripod with cloven bronze feet is austerely beautiful.

The collection concludes with a look at the most **recent excavations**, carried out in Ulus, Külhöyuk and Kultepe in the last five years, and then spills Greek and Roman statuary over into the **café** and outdoor garden. The museum **bookshop** offers a fine catalogue and some useful introductory history books and postcards.

Other museums

Ethnographic Museum (Etnografya Müzesi), Talat Paşa Caddesi, off Atatürk Bulvarı (Tues–Sun 8.30am–12.30pm & 1.30–5.30pm; $1). Housed in a white marble building with an equestrian statue of Atatürk out front, this extensive collection of folk costumes and artefacts from Selçuk times onwards is well worth an hour or two. Packed with carpets, furniture and domestic utensils, with a number of re-created Ottoman household interiors, it gives an excellent overview of Anatolian folk art. Amid all the carpets and costumes there are also some fine examples of Selçuk wood carving, including a *mihrab* from a village mosque near Urgüp that must represent thousands of hours of carving. Before becoming a museum, the building was used as a resting place for Atatürk's body from his death in 1938 until removal to Anıt Kabir in 1953.

Museum of the War of Independence (Kürtülüş Savaş Müzesi), Cumhuriyet Bulvarı/Ulus Meydanı (Tues–Sun 8.30am–12.30pm & 1.30–5pm; $0.50). The display here covers the struggle to preserve Turkish independence waged between 1919 and 1923. An extensive collection of photographs, documents and ephemera covers every detail of the various military campaigns and concurrent political events. Captions are all in Turkish, but fortunately much of the material speaks for itself. The museum is housed in the first Grand National Assembly building, and visitors can view the chamber where delegates sat in small school desks by candle- and oil-light with Atatürk overseeing from the vantage point of a raised platform.

Painting and Sculpture Museum (Resim ve Heykel Müzesi), next door to the Ethnographic Museum (Tues–Sun 8.30am–12.30pm & 1.30–5.30pm; $0.50). An unusual mix of European and traditional Turkish styles is displayed in the work of native artists.

Railway Museum (Demiryollari Müzesi), Ankara railway station (Tues–Sun 8.30am–noon & 1–5.30pm). Not invariably found to be open during these times, and really of interest only to railway fans. The museum is located near Atatürk's personal railway coach, which is on display just off the concourse.

Republic Museum (Cumhuriyet Müzesi), Cumhuriyet Meydanı (Tues–Sun 9am–noon & 1.30–5pm; free). The emphasis here is on the achievements of the Turkish Republic, but Turkish-only captions make it all fairly impenetrable for non-linguists. The museum is housed in the post-1925 headquarters of the Grand National Assembly and you can take a look at the delegates' chamber which looks like a lecture hall – a natural progression perhaps from the schoolroom layout of the original building.

Eating and drinking

Although there's no shortage of standard kebab and *pide* places in Ankara, and an abundance of good sweet and cake shops, locals complain that there's very little else. In fact there are decent **restaurants** in Ankara, they just take a little finding; as with hotels, the further south you move the more expensive places tend to become.

For **drinking** the *pinik*s (polite *meyhane*s) on and around Bayındır, Iniklap, Karanfil and Selânik *sokak*s in Kızılay make a good starting point. Though these are largely male-dominated, female visitors shouldn't attract too much unwelcome attention. For something more upmarket head for the bars of Kavaklıdere, particularly Tunalı Hilmi Caddesi which is the city's main see-and-be-seen strip.

Restaurants

Ulus is your best bet for cheap eats, while Kızılay has most of the mid-range places (particularly on and around Karanfil and Selânik *sokak*s), and the more classy restaurants can be found in Kavaklıdere and Çankaya. An exception to this general rule are the restaurants that have opened up in restored Ottoman houses in the citadel over the last few years.

Ulus and around
Akman Boza ve Pasta Salonu, Atatürk Bul 3. In a shopping plaza just south of the Atatürk statue, serving light meals, pastries and *boza*, a refreshing millet-based drink.

Bosna Işkembecisi ve Lokantasi, Çankırı Cad 11. Excellent *iskender kebap, sutlaç* and other trusty favourites make this a popular and convenient dinner or lunch stop. Open 24hr.

Boyacızade Konağı (Kale Restaurant), Berrak Sok 9. One of the best of the citadel restaurants. Spread across several floors of a rambling old mansion house, imaginatively decorated with carpets and bric-a-brac, it specializes in traditional Turkish cuisine including *manti* (Turkish-style ravioli). There's a good wine list and prices are surprisingly reasonable. The separate fish restaurant on the second floor is a little lacking in atmosphere, though the dishes are good.

Çiçek Lokantası, Çankırı Cad 12/A. On the eastern side of the street, a few hundred metres past the intersection. A pricy, white-tablecloth, sit-down place serving traditional dishes.

Dadaşlar, Denizciler Cad. Value-for-money restaurant on the way up to (or down from) the citadel that makes an excellent place to break for lunch during your wanderings. The range of kebabs and chops on the menu spring few surprises, but a meal for two will leave you with change from $10 and you can get a drink into the bargain. Outdoor seating in a garden set back from the street in summer.

Hacıbey, Denizciler Caddesi (across Atatürk Bulvarı from the Opera House). Unpretentious kebab restaurant that's a good bet for a lunchtime fill-up.

Hacı Mehmet Özlek, Sanayi Cad 7. A pleasant, friendly place with a decently priced menu. Ask to be seated upstairs.

Kebabıstan, Sanayi Cad, directly above the *Akman*. Another branch of the Kızılay restaurant, not quite as pleasant.

Kınacılar Evi, Kale Kapısı 28. A moderately priced restaurant in a restored mansion near the main gate of the citadel. There's an excellent selection of appetizers plus the usual meat dishes, and live music most evenings.

Rema Lokantası, Posta Cad/Sanayi Cad. Dirt-cheap, basic *lokanta* for just about the best bargain eats in the area.

Uğrak Piknik and **Uğrak Lokantası**, Çankırı Cad. Two for the price of one, a cafeteria with fixed meals for about $2.50, and a proper restaurant; after the first turning on the western side of the street. Single women may well feel uncomfortable in the *rakı*-induced haze of the ground floor.

Zenger Paşa Konağı, Doyran Sok 13, Kaleiçi. Another excellent citadel restaurant in a well-restored mansion packed with Ottoman-era ephemera. *Kuzu kapama* (a lamb dish) and *manti* are recommended. They also do enormously long *pide*. Open until lam.

Kızılay

Altin Şiş, Karanfil Sok 17. Reasonably priced kebab place with good puddings.

Canlı Balık, Sakarya Sok 8/C. Lunchtime fish restaurant tucked into the second floor of an office block.

Gondol, Bayındır Sok 23. Cheap, licensed fish restaurant.

Hosta, Sakarya/Selânik Sok. Take-away with busy *sandviç* and *ayran* trade at lunchtimes.

Hunkar Iskender Kebap, Selânik Sok 16. Excellent *iskender kebap*, lunchtime only.

Içkele, Tuna Cad 28. A recommended seafood place with good red mullet and sardines.

Iskele, Bayındır Sok 14/A. A fancy fish restaurant, licensed and open in the evening.

Karanfil, Karanfil Sok 15. Moderately priced sit-down place, good for kebabs and light snacks.

Kebabıstan, Karanfil Sok/Yüksel Cad. Plush restaurant, offering all kinds of kebab including excellent mushroom *şiş*. Main course with pudding and soft drink costs about $4.

Körfez, Bayındır Sok 24. Possibly the best place in town, serving good portions of excellent kebabs, grills and fish. The bill for two people with wine should come to about $18.

Köşk, Tuna Cad, İnkılap Sok 2. The best *iskender kebap* and *inegöl köfte* in town.

Mudurnu Piliç, Selânik Sok 14. Specializes in spit-roast chicken.

Pizzeria, Meşrutiyet Cad 7. A very popular pizza/pasta place. Authentic Italian atmosphere and reasonable prices. Pizzas are generally a safer bet than pasta which occasionally misses the mark slightly.

Rumeli İskembecisi, Bayındır Sok 25/A. Soups and grills but no booze. You'll pay about $3.50 for average food but it is open 24hr.

Kavaklıdere

Hacı Arif Bey, Güniz Sok 48/1. One of the oldest and best-established restaurants. For succulent kebabs in *bona fide* restaurant surroundings (rather than the usual canteen ambience) head here. Closes 11pm.

Kebab 49, Bestekâr Sok 13/A. Standard kebab place in an upmarket part of town.

Kıtır Piliç, Tunalı Hilmi Cad 114/K. The roast chicken and baked potato dishes here make a welcome break from standard restaurant fare. Closes 10.30pm.

Mutfak Manti, on the corner of Tunalı Hilmi and Bestekâr Sok. A small café specializing in Central Asian ravioli.

Öz Annem, Tunalı Hilmi Cad 66/2, Kavaklıdere. Open-air seating beneath the trees makes this kebab and *pide* restaurant the place to head for on warm evenings. They also do chicken dishes and puddings. A meal for two should leave you with change from $10.

Pizza Pino, Tunalı Hilmi Cad 111/B. The pizzas taste authentic enough but you may find them cheaper elsewhere.

Silk Road, Bestekâr Sok 88/B. A small Chinese restaurant serving Cantonese cuisine. Set menus start at $5. Closed Sun.

Villa, Boğaz Sok 13. Pizza and steaks though it's best to stick to the former for the sake of both pocket and palate. A meal for two with wine should work out at around $20.

Wine House, Boğaz Sok 28. Chalet-style decor with slightly unreliable food. Nevertheless attracts a youngish clientele who perhaps feel that weighty bills represent quality.

Yeni Hamsiköy, Bestekâr Sok 13. Reasonable fish place with emphasis on anchovies.

Elsewhere in Ankara

Ankara Sofrası, Hoşdere Cad 76. Classic traditional Turkish cuisine in pleasant surroundings. Recommended are the *börek* and *yaprak sarma* (vine leaves stuffed with rice and minced meat).

India & China Town, Nenehatun Cad (near the junction with Çankaya Cad). A bizarre place serving, as might be inferred from the name, a mix of Indian and Chinese dishes. Prices are reasonable but the service is surly and there's no atmosphere. Very popular with the expat community.

Pasta Villa, Güneş Sok 1/B, Çankaya. Affordable pizza and pasta.

Pineapple, Koroğlu Cad 64/B, Gaziosmanpaşa. "International" cuisine which tends to mean steak-and-chips variations. It's not too pricy and the portions are generous.

Tadım Pizza, Simon Bolivar Cad 85 (an extension south of Cinnah Cad), Çankaya. Decent pizza place though it's probably best to steer clear of the salad bar.

Yunus's, Cemal Nadir Sok 18, Çankaya. Interesting mix of Italian and Turkish dishes on the menu, as well as seafood and vegetarian dishes. There's also a bar. The only catch is the prices.

Bars and cafés

Head for Bayındır, Iniklap, Karanfil and Selânik *sokak*s in Kızılay for bars in abundance, the more ritzy Kavaklıdere for more glamorous surroundings (and prices to match).

Bizon, Cinnah Cad 110/A, Çankaya. Flashy, pricy bar (reckon on paying about $3 for a beer, $5 for a cocktail) that's very popular with students from the private Bilkent University.

Büyük Ekspress, Bayındır Sok 11/D, Kızılay. Expat and student haunt. It looks a bit rough and ready but it's a good place for a beer. Greasy snacks (burgers and kebabs) complement the serious drinking atmosphere.

Cabaret, Atakule 435, Çankaya. Another hangout popular with Bilkent students. Come here to meet the Levis- and Timberland-wearing gilded youth of Ankara.

Cafés des Cafés, 81 Tunalı Hilmi Cad. Although the bar serves food this joint primarily provides an ideal resting place for a caffeine and nicotine fix.

Café Seven, Reşit Galip Cad 57/A, Gaziosmanpaşa. Café-bar serving snack dishes that's popular with the student crowd. There's outside seating in the garden during summer and in winter they warm things up inside with a log fire.

Eylul, Noktalı Sok 3/2, Çankaya. Upmarket bar opposite the *Sheraton* that attracts a young, fashionable crowd.

Galeri Nev, Horasan Sok 14, Gaziosmanpaşa. Art gallery café with summer garden that pulls in a fashionable, arty crowd. Come here carrying a Sartre title and wearing a serious expression if you want to fit in.

Gitanes, Tunalı Hilmi Cad, Bilir Sok 4/3, Kavaklıdere. An intimate, candlelit bar with regular live music. As good a starting point as any for your in-depth exploration of the Tunalı Hilmi scene. Open until 2am.

Hicaz Bar, Kale Sok 1. A small bar hanging on the coat tails of the new restaurants in the citadel. The terrace has excellent views of the city and is a good place to break your explorations of the area with a cool beer. They also do snack dishes and soup. Open 24hr.

Jazz Time, Tunalı Hilmi Cad, Bilir Sok 4/1, Kavaklıdere. A friendly bar, with live music (usually Turkish pop), that's always packed to the gills.

Karpiç, Güvenlik Cad 97, Çankaya. A little off the beaten track but worth seeking out. Run by Alpay, a famous Turkish singer who occasionally performs. Closes 10pm.

Marilyn Monroe's, Tunalı Hilmi Cad, Büklüm Sok 54/A, Kavaklıdere. Rather tacky, as the name suggests, but immensely popular with expats, mostly engineers. You can play darts here should you so desire.

Pabsi Bar, Tunalı Hilmi Cad 68/C, Kavaklıdere. Another hangout popular with expats. It can get very busy but the beer is reasonably cheap.

PM, Cinnah Cad 29/A, Çankaya. This is where the Bilkent kids come when they've grown up and got well-paid jobs. Dress smart but not too smart to blend in – it's a jeans and blazer kind of place. Live music.

Timeout, Simon Bolivar Cad 28, Kavaklıdere. Trendy bar that's livelier than most thanks to the big dance floor.

Villa, Boğaz Sok 13, Çankaya. Smart bar for those with money to burn. They do food here too – the pizzas are okay but the rest of the menu isn't so hot.

Z Bar, Selânik Cad. Similar clientele to *Büyük Ekspress*, though this place is a little more upmarket, with live music (mostly guitarists playing a mix of Turkish and Western standards).

Nightlife and entertainment

Nightlife in Ankara is extremely limited, and the only thing that seems to be open late are a series of seedy *gazino*-type places along Gazi Mustafa Kemal Bulvarı in Maltepe, and a few tacky **discos** in Kavaklıdere and Çankaya. There are some studenty late-night venues hidden away in the backstreets of the university district, Cebeci, but you really need to find a local to guide you to them.

Discos
The following discos, catering mainly to Ankara's gilded youth and students, are the places where foreign visitors are most likely to feel at home. Music is influenced by the current MTV playlist. Entrance is $10–15 (often includes first drink).

Airport, Paris Cad 49/6, Şili Meydanı (near Kuğulu Parkı), Kavaklıdere.

Graffiti, Farabi Sok, Çankaya.

Paradise, Farabi Sok 34, Çankaya.

Opera
A visit to Ankara's Opera House on Atatürk Bulvarı (just south of the entrance to Gençlik Parkı; ☎312/324 2210) is a unique experience, although the main season starts in earnest in the autumn. Repertory performances of *Tosca, La Bohème, Madame Butterfly* are lively and well attended, and there are occasional piano recitals and classical concerts. The atmosphere is refreshingly informal and tickets will cost no more than $2–4 (available from the box office).

Cinema
The following cinemas all show recent international releases (foreign films are usually subtitled) and tickets will cost about $3. The tourist information office can supply details of Ankara's film festival in March.

Akun, Atatürk Bul 227, Kavaklıdere (☎0312/427 07656).

Batı, Atatürk Bul 151/1, Bakanlıkar (☎0312/418 8323).

Derya, Necatibey Cad 57, Kızılay (☎0312/229 9618).

Kavaklıdere, Tunalı Hilmi Cad 105 (☎0312/426 7379).

Kızılırmak, Kızılırmak Sok 21/A, Kızılay (☎0312/425 5393).

Megapol, Konur Sok 33, Kızılay (☎0312/419 4492).

Metropol, Selânik Cad 76, Kızılay (☎0312/425 7478). Also special showings of classic movies.

Listings

Airlines *Aeroflot*, Cinnah Cad 114/2, Çankaya (☎0312/440 9874); *Air France*, Atatürk Bul 231/7, Kavaklıdere (☎312/467 4400); *British Airways*, Atatürk Bul 237/1, Kavaklıdere (☎312/467 5557); *Delta*, Tunalı Hilmi Cad 112/1, Kavaklıdere (☎312/468 7805); *Istanbul Airlines*, Atatürk Bul 61/1 (☎312/432 2234); *KLM*, Cinnah Cad 43/8, Çenkaya, Bakanlıklar (☎312/417 5616); *Lufthansa*, Iran Cad 2, Kavaklıdere (☎312/467 5510); *Middle East Airlines*, Cinnah Cad 7/D, Kavaklıdere

(☎312/426 5899); *THT*, Atatürk Bul 125/2 (☎312/419 1492); *THY*, Atatürk Bul 231/A, Kavaklıdere (☎312/468 7330).

Antiques *Anatolia*, Tunalı Hilmi Cad, Ertuğ Pasajı 88/79, Kavaklıdere, has a good selection of old and new copper and brass, kilims and rugs, though not particularly cheap; *Gul Özer*, Cinnah Cad 30, Çankaya, has general antiques and bric-a-brac marginally cheaper than you might expect to find at home.

Books Try *ABC*, Selânik Cad 1/A, Kızılay, for foreign-language titles and a range of guidebooks. *Tahran*, Selânik Cad 19/B, Kızılay, has a good selection of books in English, French and German. *Dost Kitabevi*, Karanfil Sok 11/A, Kızılay, has cheap novels and a good selection of pricier books.

Buses Ankara's new bus station, 5km west of Kızılay, is a monster housing over 100 bus companies, with transport running to almost every conceivable destination, even as far away as Moscow (72hr, $75). Buses and minibuses marked "Yeni Garaj", "Terminal" or "AŞTI" leave for the station from the minibus terminal 300m southwest of Ulus; bus #623 runs from Kızılay. Bus companies will normally give you a lift there in their own *servis* buses if you buy your ticket in their town offices, which are mostly situated on Gazi Mustafa Kemal Bul or Ziya Gökalp Cad. There's a bewildering choice of companies to choose from but for popular destinations (eg Istanbul) try the larger companies such as *Varan* (booth 12), *Ulusoy* (13), *Pammukale* (58) and *Kamil Koç* (18). Other specific destinations include: Adıyaman (36), Amasya (60, 6), Bursa (45), Erzurum (80, 68), Hatay (67, 55), Kastamonu (25, 65), Konya (39, 74, 54, 42), Kütahya (14, 18), Nevşehir (50), Polatli (28), Safranbolu (15, 4), Sivas (27), Tokat (60, 6).

Car rental *Atak*, Arjantin Cad 25, Gaziosmanpaşa (☎312/467 1394); *Avis*, Tunus Cad 68/2, Kavaklıdere (☎312/467 2314); *Best*, Büyükelçilik Sok 17, Kavaklıdere (☎312/467 0008); *Budget*, Tunus Cad 39, Kavaklıdere (☎312/417 5952); *Europcar*, Akay Cad 25/C, Küçükesat (☎312/418 3877); *Hertz*, Kavaklıdere Sok 23, Şili Meyd, Kavaklıdere (☎312/426 9459); *Thrifty*, Köroğlu Cad 65/B, Gaziosmanpaşa (☎312/436 0505).

Car repair *Ford*, Söğütlük Sok 3/B, Büyük Sanayi (☎312/341 4474); *Lada*, Ali Suavi Sok 6, Maltepe; *Volkswagen/Audi*, Meçulasker Sok, Tandoğan (☎312/213 3002).

Cultural centres *British Council*, Kırlangıç Sok 9, Çankaya (☎312/468 6192); *French Cultural Association*, Ziya Gökalp Cad 15, Kızılay (☎312/431 1458); *German Cultural Centre*, Atatürk Bul 131, Bakanlıklar (☎312/425 1436); *Turkish American Association*, Cinnah Cad 20, Kavaklıdere (☎312/426 2648).

Embassies *Australia*, Nenehatun Cad 83, Gaziosmanpaşa (☎312/446 1180); *Azerbaijan*, Cemal Nadir Sok 20, Çelikler Apt, Çankaya (☎312/441 2620); *Belgium*, Nenehatun Cad 109, Gaziosmanpaşa (☎312/446 8247); *Britain*, Şehit Ersan Cad 46/A, Çankaya (☎312/468 6230); *Bulgaria*, Atatürk Bul 124, Kavaklıdere (☎312/426 7455); *Canada*, Nenehatun Cad 75, Gaziosmanpaşa (☎312/436 1275); *Denmark*, Kırlangıç Sok 42, Gaziosmanpaşa (☎312/468 7760); *Finland*, Galip Dede Sok 1/19, Kavaklıdere (☎312/426 4964); *France*, Paris Cad 70, Kavaklıdere (☎312/468 1154); *Georgia*, Ulubey Sok 28, Gaziosmanpaşa (☎312/447 1720); *Germany*, Atatürk Bul 114, Kavaklıdere (☎312/426 5465); *Hungary*, Gazi Mustafa Kemal Bul 10, Kızılay (☎312/418 6257); *Iran*, Tahran Cad 10, Kavaklıdere (☎312/427 4320); *Iraq*, Turan Emeksiz Sok 11, Gaziosmanpaşa (☎312/468 7421); *Kazakhstan*, Ebüzzia Tevfik Sok 6, Çankaya (☎312/441 2301); *Lebanon*, Kızkulesi Sok 44, Gaziosmanpaşa (☎312/446 7485); *Netherlands*, Köroğlu Sok 5, Çankaya (☎312/446 0470); *New Zealand*, Iran Cad 13 Kat 4, Kavaklıdere (☎312/467 9056); *Pakistan*, Iran Cad 37, Gaziosmanpaşa (☎312/427 1410); *Romania*, Bukreş Cad 4, Çankaya (☎312/427 1241); *Russia*, Karyağdi Sok 5, Çankaya (☎312/439 2122); *South Africa*, Filistin Sok 27, Gaziosmanpaşa (☎312/446 4056); *Syria*, Abdullah Cevdet Sok 7, Çankaya (☎312/440 9657); *Ukraine*, Cemal Nadir Sok 9, Çankaya (☎312/440 5289); *USA*, Atatürk Bul 110, Çankaya (☎312/468 6110); *Uzbekistan*, Ahmet Rasim Sok 14, Çankaya (☎312/439 2740).

Emergency services Police ☎155; Ambulance ☎112; Fire ☎110.

Exchange Outside banking hours you can exchange cash (not travellers' cheques) at PTT branches. The railway PTT is open 7am–11pm and the main PTT is open 24hr. For travellers' cheques try the cashiers at the big hotels though they are often reluctant to cash cheques for non-residents.

Football Local teams Ankaragücü and Geçerbitliği play on Sat or Sun afternoons at the 35,000 capacity 19 Mayıs stadium behind Gençlik Parkı.

Hamams *Ankara Erkekler Hamamı*, Talat Paşa Bul 166 (men only; 6am–9pm); *Küçükesat Hamam*, Esat Cad 81/A, corner of Tunak Hilmi Cad, Küçükesat (men daily except Tues 7am–10pm; women Tues 7.30am–6pm); *Yenişehir Hamam*, Sumer Sok 16/A, Maltepe (men only; 6am–10.30pm).

Hospitals If you need medical treatment head for the *Hacettepe Hastanesı*, just west of Hasırcılar Sokak in Şihhiye, where there should be an English-speaking doctor available. You may be treated quicker at one of Ankara's private hospitals: the *Acil Kavaklıdere Tıp Merkezi*, Şimşek Sok 6, is the most central.

Ice skating *Belpa Ice Skating Palace*, Bahçelievler (near the train station). A smallish rink with café and restaurant; $4 per session. Bus #317 or #132 from Kızılay.

Left luggage The train station facility is open 7.30am–10pm; the fee is $1–2 depending on the declared value of your bag.

Music Western and Turkish cassettes and CDs from *Dost Kitabevi*, Karanfil Sok, 11A, Kızılay, and adjacent shops.

Pharmacies There are plenty of pharmacies in Ankara where you can obtain medication for most minor ailments. Central options include: *Bulvar*, Atatürk Bul 71/B, Kızılay; and *Ülkü*, Meşrutiyet Cad 23/A, Kızılay.

PTT Ankara's main post office is on Atatürk Bul, Ulus (24hr). Come here to make international calls and buy stamps, phonecards, *jetons* etc. You can also place transfer charge calls here.

Shopping centres *Atakule*, Cinnah Cad/Çankaya Cad, Çankaya; *Beğenik*, Kocatepe (beneath Kocatepe Camii); *Karum* , İran Cad, Kavaklıdere.

Swimming Some of the big hotels open up their pools to non-residents. The cheapest option is the *Büyük Sürmeli* (Mon–Sat 10am–9pm; $10 weekdays, $12 Sat). Swimming at the *Hilton* (daily 6.30am–8.30pm; weekdays $12, weekends $15) works out a little more expensive. There's also an open-air pool, *Tursan*, at Karakusunlar Mevkii 14/1, Balgat, in the western suburbs (June–Sept only; $6; bus #132 from Kızılay).

Tourist police ☎312/384 0606.

Turkish Maritime Lines Şehit Adem Yavuz Sok 3/2, Kızılay (☎312/417 1161).

WEST OF ANKARA

Attractions west of Ankara are few and far between, and with one exception, probably best treated as stop-off points on the way to or from the Aegean coast. The exception is the Phrygian capital of **Gordion**, which lies 90km or so outside the capital, making it a feasible day-trip destination. Beyond Gordion are a number of less accessible sites probably only worth tackling if you have your own transport; these include **Sivrihisar** with a fine Selçuk **Ulu Camii**, and the nearby temple city of **Pessinus**. Even further off the beaten track, towards Eskişehir in the west of the region, are the small town of **Seyitgazi** with its atmospheric dervish monastery and the important Phrygian centre of **Midas Şehri**. **Eskişehir** itself is primarily an industrial centre with little to offer other than meerschaum souvenirs. Better to press on in the direction of **Kütahya**, a relaxed city famed for its ceramic tiles that makes a good base for excursions to the Roman site of **Aezani** with its eerie temple ruins.

Gordion

After the collapse of the Hittite Empire the Phrygians briefly dominated Anatolia, and their capital **GORDION** is one of western Anatolia's most important archeological sites. The first things you'll see as you approach are the immense royal tumuli scattered across the drab, steppe-like landscape. Inside them archeologists found a wealth of stunning artefacts bearing witness to the sophisticated nature of Phrygian culture. Nearby the foundations of the Gordion acropolis have been uncovered.

There are **buses** every half-hour from Ankara's *otogar* to the town of **Polatli**, 15km southwest of Gordion. From Polatli *otogar,* take a *servis* minibus into town and seek out one of the infrequent dolmuşes to the village of **Yassihüyük**, just short of the site itself. A taxi to and from the site will cost around $20.

Some history

The original settlement at Gordion dates back to the Bronze Age and the site was certainly occupied during the Hittite period. The Phrygians probably took up residence during the middle of the ninth century BC and a hundred years later the settlement became capital of the empire founded by the Phrygian king Gordios. The history of Gordion under the Phrygians mirrors the history of the Phrygian Empire itself, a brief flowering followed by destruction and protracted decline.

Phrygian prosperity stemmed from the abundant natural resources of the region and the fact that their empire straddled major east–west trade routes. Ironically it was another set of invaders, the Cimmerians, who laid waste to the Phrygian Empire, destroying Gordion, and though the Phrygians made a comeback and rebuilt their capital, their power had been irreversibly reduced. In 650 BC the city was occupied by the Lydians, falling to the Persians just over a century later. In 333 BC, Alexander the Great wintered here during his great march east, managing to sever the Gordian Knot (see box overleaf) during his stay. The arrival of the Galatians (Gauls) in Asia Minor in 278 BC was the final act in the long decline of Gordion, precipitating the flight of the city's population.

THE ACROPOLIS

From the dolmuş drop-off point in the village it makes sense to head first for the eighth-century BC **acropolis**. This raised area was the heart of the city, location of the royal palace, temples and administrative buildings, the foundations of which have been revealed by excavations. Substantial remains of the huge Phrygian-era **town gate** survive on the southeastern side of the acropolis. This must have been a formidable structure in its day: even in its present truncated state it's over ten metres high, making it one of the largest surviving pre-classical buildings in Anatolia. The outer portal was flanked by twin towers from which defenders would have been able to inflict heavy casualties on attackers in front of the gate. The foundations of what are thought to have been storage rooms stand on either side of the inner portals – the remains of *pithoi* or stone storage jars were found in the right hand one when it was excavated.

The **palace** at the heart of the acropolis consisted of four *megara* or large halls with vestibules. The second of these is the most impressive, with the remains of red, white and blue mosaics forming geometrical patterns still visible on the floor. When it was excavated, charred fragments of wooden furniture inlaid with ivory were found in the rubble, suggesting that this could have been the central hall of the palace. The fourth *megaron* was probably a temple to Cybele, the Phrygian incarnation of the mother goddess. If this is the case, then it's here that Alexander the Great cut the Gordian Knot. Behind the palace are the foundations of eight more large *megara*, thought to have been the quarters of palace servants.

THE ROYAL TOMBS

The main concentration of the huge and inscrutable **tumulus tombs** of the Phrygian kings is at the eastern end of Yassıhüyük, but just southeast of the acropolis is the **Küçük Hüyük**, a clay mound that's actually higher than the citadel itself. The Küçük Hüyük was originally a fortified suburb of Gordion, which was destroyed when the Persian army of Cyrus marched through the region en route to Sardis and was later turned into a tomb for the defeated ruler of Gordion.

The largest of the tumuli, the **Büyük Hüyük** is at the eastern end of the village. It's worth dropping in on the small **museum** (Tues–Sun 8am–12.30pm & 1.30–5pm; $1.50), which contains some of the items recovered from the tombs, though inevitably the best of the finds are in Ankara's Museum of Anatolian Civilizations. At over 50m high and 300m in diameter (reduced by erosion from its original height of around 80m), the Büyük Hüyük dominates the vicinity, and with these dimensions it's easy to

MIDAS

The name **Midas** is inextricably associated with Gordion. A number of Phrygian kings bore this name, and over the centuries a kind of composite mythical figure has emerged around whom a number of legends have grown up. The best known of these is that of Midas and the golden touch. According to the story Midas captured the water daemon Silenus after making him drunk by pouring wine into his spring. In ransom for Silenus, Midas demanded of Dionysus the ability to turn all he touched into gold. Dionysus granted this wish but Midas was dismayed to find his demand had been taken quite literally, and his food and even his own daughter were transformed. He begged Dionysus for release from the curse and was ordered to wash his hands in the River Pactolus. The cure worked, and thereafter the river ran with gold.

Another tale tells of how Midas was called upon to judge a musical contest between Apollo and the satyr Marsyas. Midas decided in favour of Marsyas and in revenge Apollo caused him to grow ass's ears (Marsyas came off even worse – the god skinned him alive). To hide his new appendages, Midas wore a special hat, revealing them only to his barber who was sworn to secrecy on pain of death. Desperate to tell someone the king's secret, the barber passed it on to the reeds of the river who ever after whispered "Midas has ass's ears".

These legends are thought to relate to the successor of Gordios, about whom another story that may have some basis in reality exists. It tells how, during the reign of Gordios, an oracle foretold that a poor man who would enter Gordion by ox cart would one day rule over the Phrygians. As the king and nobles were discussing this prediction, a farmer named Midas arrived at the city in his cart. Gordios, who had no heirs, saw this as the fulfilment of the prophecy and named Midas his successor. Subsequently Midas had his cart placed in the temple of Cybele on the Gordion acropolis, where it was to stand for half a millennium. Somehow the belief arose that whoever untied the knot that fixed the cart to its yoke would become master of Asia. During his stay in the city **Alexander the Great** took it upon himself to undo the knot, severing it with his sword.

The final king of the Phrygian Empire was also called Midas, and some concrete information about his reign survives. He is referred to in Assyrian records as Mitas of Mushki, who paid tribute to the Assyrians after being defeated in battle by them. He is thought to have reigned from 725 BC to 696 BC and the Greek historian Herodotus describes how he dedicated his throne at the Delphic shrine of Apollo and married the daughter of one of the Ionian kings.

see why it was originally thought to house the remains of either Gordios or Midas. However, material found in the burial chamber by archeologists dates the tomb at somewhere between 750 and 725 BC, too late for Gordios or his successor and too early for the last king Midas.

The tumulus was excavated by American archeologists during the early 1950s, who bored a sixty-metre tunnel through to its centre. Here they found an intact wooden chamber containing the skeleton of a man in his sixties on a wooden couch surrounded by grave objects. Among these were three exquisitely crafted wooden tables, inlaid wooden screens, large numbers of bronze clasps for garments, and 178 bronze vessels of all sizes, including three large cauldrons.

Sivrihisar and Pessinus

About 60km to the west of Polatlı along the E90 highway is the town of Sivrihisar, Byzantine Justiniapolis, with a fine Selçuk forest mosque and access to the Phrygian temple city of Pessinus. These two destinations only really make sense if you have your own transport and are looking for a place to break your journey – you'd have to be a devotee of Selçuk architecture or the history of the Cybele cult to try and undertake them by public transport. Should this be the case, you can reach Sivrihisar by asking to be let off through buses at the turn-off for the town and then walking, hitching or picking up a local dolmuş into the centre. For Pessinus there's an infrequent dolmuş service from Sivrihisar to the modern town of Balihisar adjacent to the site.

SİVRİHİSAR itself is a torpid little place which is overlooked by a ruined Byzantine fortress, perched on a crag high above. In such an ordinary town, the interior finery of the **Ulu Cami**, built by the Selçuks in 1274, seems to belong to another world. There are 67 painstakingly carved wooden columns supporting a timber ceiling, and the walls are decorated with colourful Turkoman motifs. A typically Selçuk feature is the incorporation of stone capitals from ancient columns into the structure of the building.

The ancient temple city of **PESSINUS** is in the modern village of Balihisar, about 13km southeast of Sivrihisar down a rutted, winding road. The temple was founded by the Phrygians in honour of the earth goddess Cybele. The priests of the cult were eunuchs and the orgiastic rites associated with worship sometimes culminated in self-castration by over-enthusiastic adherents. Though the site fell to the Galatians after their invasion of Anatolia, the temple was maintained and a steady stream of pilgrims ensured that the town prospered. The main symbol of the cult at this site was the Baitylos, a black meteorite which was transported to Rome in 205 BC at the behest of King Attalus I of Pergamon, who had formed an alliance with the priests of Pessinus. As a result, when the Romans defeated the Galatians, Pessinus became part of Pergamon, and it's from this period that the buildings near the temple date. The **temple** site was excavated during the 1970s to reveal extensive foundations, and features a perfectly square inner sanctum with 7.5-metre-long walls. Nearby are the remains of the town **odeion**.

Seyitgazi

SEYİTGAZİ sits in a fertile valley set incongruously amid the rolling Anatolian steppe. To get there turn off the E90 at the signpost for Hamidiye around 60km west of Sivrihisar and take the first right which will bring you to your destination after 25km. The town takes its name from Şehit Battal Gazi, the commander of one of the Arab armies that forayed into Anatolia during the eighth century, around whom an unlikely legend has grown up. The story has it that he was killed during the siege of Afyon and buried with a Byzantine princess who had pined away through love for him. The site of their resting place was revealed to the mother of the Selçuk sultan Alâeddin Keykubad who promptly built a *türbe* for the Gazi. It became a popular place of pilgrimage and during the thirteenth century Hacı Bektaş Veli, founder of the Bektaşi dervish order, established a *tekke* or monastery here. During the sixteenth century, the complex was thoroughly restored on the orders of Selim I, a ruler who numbered among his other contributions to religious life in Anatolia the massacre of 40,000 Shi'ites.

The *türbe/tekke* **complex**, on the slopes of the valley above the town, seems nothing more than an agglomeration of sandy walls topped by grey-white domes when seen from the distance. The ground plan is roughly horseshoe-shaped, open towards the valley slope with a Byzantine church and a Selçuk mosque by the entrance. The former is a reminder that a Christian convent originally stood on the site, while the latter contains the outsize sarcophagus of Şehit Battal which measures in at just under 7m in length. Next to it is the more modest sarcophagus of his princess. To the rear of the complex is an Ottoman mosque dating from Selim's restoration with adjacent dormitories and ancillary buildings for the monastery.

Midas Şehri

MİDAS ŞEHRİ is a major Phrygian site about 30km due south of Seyitgazi. To reach it, head in the direction of Afyon and take the first left turn towards the village of Yazilikaya (not to be confused with the Hittite site east of Ankara). The unmetalled road is pretty abysmal but the landscape, with its eerie rock formations, makes up for the discomfort. This whole area is dotted with Phrygian tombs, temples and fortifications, but those at Midas Şehri are by far the most accessible and substantial.

The **site** itself comprises the sketchy ruins of a Phrygian city set on top of a thirty-metre-high plateau whose steep rock sides have been carved with elaborate decorative facades. Despite the fact that Midas Şehri means "City of Midas" in Turkish, there's no specific Midas connection, though it was for a while supposed that one of the Phrygian kings of that name was buried here.

The carved facade on the northwestern face of the plateau has come to be known as the **Midas tomb**. From a distance this huge expanse of tufa, measuring about 15 by 17m, resembles the interior wall of a house that has had a large fireplace cut into it a few metres above ground level. Closer up it can be seen that rectilinear bands in raised relief criss-cross the facade, topped by a decorative pediment. An early Western visitor to the site in 1800, one Captain Leake, concluded that the "fireplace" niche had to let onto a concealed entrance to a tomb. Attempting to decipher the Phrygian inscription on the monument, he mistranslated one word to read Midas and assumed it was a royal tomb. It's now known however that the word Leake took to mean Midas actually reads Mida, another name for Cybele, and it's probable that the niche housed a cult statue of the goddess. Following the plateau sides round to the west from here leads to more niches carved in the rock, a number of rock tombs and an incomplete relief.

Access to the upper part of the plateau and the remains of the Phrygian **citadel** is via a flight of steps on the eastern side. Near the top of the steps are a number of altars and tombs, some of which bear inscriptions and decorative reliefs. In the southwestern part of the citadel is a **rock throne**, a kind of stepped altar on which the figure of a deity would have been placed. The upper part of this throne has a clear **inscription** and crude decorative scratchings. Elsewhere a few fragments of the citadel's defensive wall survive.

Eskişehir

ESKİŞEHİR gives the impression of being little more than a modern industrial city, and indeed it's true that nowadays the place is primarily given over to the construction of railway locomotives, the textile industry and cement manufacture. It's also the centre of the Turkish meerschaum industry, a good place for souvenir hunters to stock up on pipes, walking sticks and the like, which you won't find cheaper anywhere. The locally mined mineral is worked in a number of shops around town and with a little haggling it should be possible to pick up some bargains. Eskişehir's most famous pipe shop is *Işik Pipo*, Sakarya Cad, Konya İşhani 12/6, where you can watch the craftsmen at work.

Despite appearances, Eskişehir has a long history, the modern town having been grafted onto an ancient settlement during the postwar period of rapid industrialization. Its origins go back at least to Greek times, when it was known as Dorylaeum. Some relics of this old city can be seen in the local **archeological museum**, or for a taste of the more recent past head for the old quarter of **Yenişehir** in the northwestern corner of town, centred around a Selçuk castle. On the opposite, eastern edge of the city stands the **Kurşunlu mosque**, attributed to Sinan.

Practicalities

Eskişehir's sights do not amount to a great deal, and it's not a place you'd want to hang around in for more than a few hours. Fortunately there are good road and rail connections, with trains running to Ankara, İzmir and İstanbul, and frequent buses and dolmuşes on the same routes. The **otogar** is on Yunus Emre Caddesi, near the river, and the **train station** is on the northwestern edge of the city centre. Both are within walking distance of the not very useful **tourist information office** at Iki Eylül Cad 175a. The best local **hotel** is the *Sale Oteli*, İnönü Cad 17/1 (☎0221/221 4144; ④)

Kütahya

Dominated by an Ottoman fortress, **KÜTAHYA** is famous above all for its fine tiles, which are manufactured in the city and sold from shops on virtually every street. **Kütahya tiles** are used throughout Turkey, especially in restoration work on Ottoman mosques, replacing the İznik originals just as Kütahya has replaced İznik as the country's leading tile-producing centre. Many modern local buildings, including the *otogar*, are entirely covered in tiles.

Some history

Kütahya's earliest recorded inhabitants were the Phrygians and thereafter the city endured the usual Anatolian round of conquest and occupation, coming to the fore briefly when Alexander the Great established his headquarters here en route to Gordion. The town was occupied by the Selçuks after the Battle of Manzikert in 1071, but then lost to the army of the First Crusade. The Selçuks returned in 1182 and a century or so later the city became capital of the Germiyanid, a Kurdo-Turkish tribe who had been brought into the area from the east. They were ousted by the Ottomans only to make a brief comeback after Beyazit Yıldırım's defeat at the hands of the Mongol ruler Tamerlane. The Germiyanid emirate survived until 1428, when Kütahya fell permanently into Ottoman hands.

It was under the Ottomans that Kütahya enjoyed its golden age as a tile-making centre. Sultan Selim I forcibly resettled tile workers from Tabriz here after defeating the Persians at Çaldıran in 1514. He dispatched some of their colleagues to İznik, instigating a two-hundred-year rivalry between the two cities that only ended when the İznik industry was transferred to İstanbul. Contemporary Kütahya tiles, however, look a little garish and crude when compared to Ottoman-era examples – the secret of the pigment blends that gave the original Kütahya tiles their subtle and delicate lustre has been lost with the centuries.

During the War of Independence, the Greek army occupied the city during their advance on Ankara. The invaders were defeated twice in battles at the defile of Inönü northeast of Kütahya in January and April 1921. They managed to break out in the summer of the same year capturing Eskişehir and Afyon and launching an offensive that took them to within striking distance of Ankara. The following year the Turkish offensive that was to throw the Greeks out of Anatolia once and for all began at Dumlupınar, midway between Kütahya and Afyon.

The Town

If you're coming in by bus from Eskişehir you'll be dropped off at Kütahya **otogar** (known as Çinigar or "Tile Station") on Atatürk Bulvarı, just to the northeast of the centre. From the *otogar* it's a short walk down Atatürk Bulvarı to **Belediye Meydanı**, the town's main square, distinguished by a fountain with a huge ceramic vase as its centrepiece.

A number of well-preserved Ottoman-era houses in the immediate vicinity of Belediye Meydanı set the tone for Kütahya. The rest of the city's attractions, however, lie at the end of Cumhuriyet Bulvarı which runs west from Belediye Meydanı. After about 500m, at the point where the road splits off in several directions, you'll find the **Ulu Cami**, an attractive but unexceptional fifteenth-century mosque. Its construction was begun by Sultan Beyazit I, but interrupted by his defeat at the hands of Tamerlane. Work resumed under his son Mehmet I and was finally completed mid-century by Mehmet II; the building was later given a restorative reworking by Sinan. The mosque stands in the midst of Kütahya's lively bazaar area which extends over several streets in the vicinity.

Just next to the Ulu Cami is the town **museum** (Tues–Sun 8.30–noon & 1–5.30 pm; $1), with a collection of archeological finds from the area, including a beautiful sarcophogus found at Aezani depicting a heroic battle between the Greeks and Amazons. The contents of the museum are considerably less interesting than the building which houses them, the **Vacidiye Medresesi**, a fourteenth-century *medrese* built by the Germiyanid emir Bey Bin Savcı as an astronomical observatory and school of science and mathematics. The highpoint of the interior is the central marble pool beneath a dome with glass skylights.

Beyond the Ulu Cami and museum, signs point out the way to the **Kossuth Evi**, a few minutes' walk to the west (Tues–Sun 8.30am–noon & 1.30–5.30pm: $0.50). This is the house that was occupied by Lajos Kossuth (1802–94), the Hungarian patriot who fled to Turkey after the failure of the 1848 uprising against Hapsburg rule. The immaculate house has been preserved much as it must have been when he lived in it in 1850–51, though it's the nineteenth-century Ottoman ambience of the rooms rather than the Kossuth connection which will be of interest to most visitors. There are many other fine but unrestored houses scattered to the north and east of the Ulu Cami, and it is these backstreets and the surrounding bazaar district that give Kütahya much of its charm.

Kütahya's **kale** towers above the Kossuth house and signposts point you in the right direction should you wish to wander up to the summit, from where there are predictably impressive views of the city below. The fortress was originally built by the Byzantines and extended by their successors, but these days only the western walls survive in anything like their original state.

Practicalities

Kütahya's **tourist information office** (☎0274/223 1962) is conveniently located in the *vilâyet* building on Konak Meydanı; there's also a summer-only information kiosk just to the east on Azerbaican Meydanı.

Pick of the budget **hotel** options is the *Hotel Yüksel 2*, Belediye Meyd 1 (☎0274/212 0111; ①), which is plain but clean and about as central as you could hope for. The *Otel Kösk*, Lise Cad 1 (☎0274/216 2024; ①), has clean, spacious doubles with a less-than-salubrious shared bath. Less appealing but even cheaper are the rooms with private bathrooms at the *Park Hotel* (☎0274/216 2310; ①), a few doors down from the *Yüksel*. Kütahya suffers from a dearth of mid-range options: there's only the *Gönen Otel* (☎0274/224 7799; ④), offering overpriced rooms on the southern side of Belediye Meydanı. For just a few dollars more, however, you can enjoy the tiled comfort of the *Hotel Gül Palas* (☎0274/216 1759, fax 216 2135; ⑤) or the *Hotel Erbaylar*, Afyon Cad 14 (☎0274/223 6960, fax 216 1046; ⑤), both just off the main square. If you arrive late at the bus station you may want to consider the comfortable *Hotel Bakirsözer* (☎0274/224 8146; ④) or the slightly plusher *Otel Tahya* (☎0274/224 3070; ⑤), both next to the *çinigar*.

For **eating and drinking** try the *Çınar Köfte*, Lise Cad 7, where you'll get a couple of courses for next to nothing. Across the road from the *Hotel Yüksel 2*, the *Kervan* serves a good range of cheap food, as does the smarter *Cumhuriyet*, under the *Otel Kösk*. For something a little more refined head for the *Pehlıvan Anın* or *Beyaz Saray*, both on Afyon Cad, though watch out for the water charge in the former. There are several sprawling teahouses on the main square and about 200m east of here, where Kütahya's youth go to cast a watchful eye on each other.

Aezani

Easily reachable, 60km or so southwest of Kütahya, is the site of Roman **AEZANİ**, famous for its atmospheric and well-preserved Temple of Zeus. To get there, take a Gediz-, Sımav- or Emet-bound **bus** from Kütahya *otogar* or, more conveniently, from the ticket office on Afyon Cad (journey time approximately 1hr) and ask to be let out at **Çavdarhisar** – the site lies just 1km north of this tranquil village. The most convenient buses leave Kütahya at 9.30am and return at 1pm.

The site
The **Temple of Zeus**, built by Hadrian in 125 AD and occupying a commanding position on top of a large, rectangular terrace, is one of Anatolia's best-preserved Roman buildings. To reach it walk up the side road that leads from the main road in Çavdarhisar in the direction of Emet, and cross the Koca Çay over the Roman bridge, with its marble frieze commemorating the successful sea passage of its sponsor, Marcus Eurykles. On the north and west sides of the main temple building double rows of columns topped by a pediment survive, but elsewhere the columns have largely collapsed and their broken fragments are scattered on the ground nearby; three on the eastern side were repositioned after falling in the Gedız earthquake of 1970. At the heart of the temple is the **inner sanctum** once dominated by a magnificent statue of Zeus. Its walls, made of rectangular stone blocks, are largely intact but the roof has long since caved in. Beneath there's a subterranean **sanctuary** dedicated to Cybele, which the affable site attendant will open up on request. Back outside just northeast of the building, a fallen but well-preserved bust of Cybele – not, as locals will tell you, Medusa – surveys the landscape.

From the temple, you can walk north past the baths to the remains of the uniquely combined **stadium/theatre**. Paths lead up from the fine inscriptions of the southern gate between ruined stadium seats to the backdrop wall of the theatre and the fallen remains of its marble facade.East of the temple stand the arches of the ruined **agora**, and from here the old ceremonial road leads south over a second Roman bridge to the enigmatic **macellum** (market place), whose walls carry a fourth-century decree from Emperor Diocletian fixing market prices in an attempt to stop rampant inflation. Complete your circular tour by heading back to the first Roman bridge, and, if you have time, ask the site guardian to open up the nearby second set of **baths**, with their satyr mosaic and statue of Hygeia, goddess of the baths.

NORTH OF ANKARA

The mountain ranges that lie between Ankara and the Black Sea are rugged and pine-clad, forming a landscape that at times becomes almost Alpine in flavour. They are undeniably appealing yet, scenery aside, there is little to attract the traveller. Only **Safranbolu**, with its Ottoman mansions of timber construction, set in a steep-sided gorge, rates a visit on its own merits. Other places in this direction – notably **Bolu** and **Kastamonu** – are no more than attractive potential stop-overs en route to other destinations.

Bolu

The only reason you're likely to visit **BOLU** is as a stop-over between Ankara and İstanbul. It has a massive town centre **Ulu Cami** and a couple of **hotels** on the main street, but not much else. The *Otel Turist* (②) is the cheapest place to stay, while the *Otel Menekşe* (⑤) offers a little more luxury a few doors down. Most **buses** seem to avoid the town centre so you'll probably be dropped on the main road, just to the north. From here it's a fifteen-minute walk into town, or you can take a taxi for about $1.50. To leave you'll have to get back to this main road and wait for a bus.

If Bolu itself is unattractive, the countryside roundabout goes some way to compensating – gently mountainous, with extensive deciduous forests dotted with lakes. There's an almost central European feel to this region, especially around **Aladağ** and **Kartalkaya** to the south, where there are skiing facilities. To the southwest lies **Abant Gölu**, a lake a mile above sea level, well stocked with trout. To the north, **Yedigöller national park** would appear to be the most attractive option of all. In practice, however, it's more trouble than it's worth, reached by an atrocious dirt road with no public transport, and it turns out to be a series of muddy ponds used as trout farms, disfigured by numerous dams and weirs.

Safranbolu

SAFRANBOLU is a stunning town of half-timbered houses some 220km north of Ankara, approached via **Karabük**, which is overshadowed by a vast steelworks and perpetually shrouded in a film of industrial grime. Fortunately, many buses from Ankara now go all the way through to Safranbolu; the alternative is to cover the last 10km in a dolmuş from the *otogar* on the edge of Karabük. After passing through a suffering landscape of rocks and stunted trees, and **Kiranköy**, the modern section of Safranbolu, the road descends into a steep-sided valley, snakes up the other side and finally drops again into

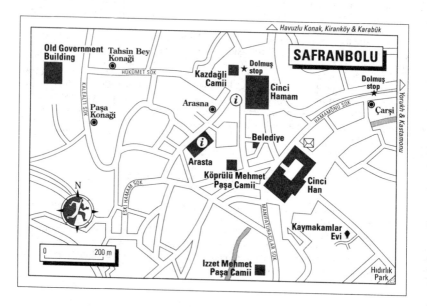

the ravine where you'll find **Eski Safranbolu** (also known as Çarşi) – Old Safranbolu – a town as far removed from its modern counterpart as it's possible to imagine.

Eski Safranbolu

Ancient houses rise up the slopes of the ravine as you descend into town, a smudge of dirty pastel-coloured timber and red-tiled roofs; although tourism has definitely arrived – Safranbolu is already established as a summer coach-trip destination for Turks – the old way of life remains remarkably intact. Apart from a bazaar of souvenir shops, few concessions have been made to the twentieth century: come here out of season and you might well be the only visitor in town. Various restoration and prettification projects have been discussed, but for the time being the town remains slightly run-down, and all the better for it. Wandering the narrow streets and soaking up the unique atmosphere are still the most rewarding activities.

The dolmuş drop-off point is on the sloping square next to the **Kazdağli Camii**. Behind is the **Cinci Hamam** – well worth a visit if you have time – adjoining the town square. Its seventeenth-century Ottoman baths are fully restored so that you can relax in comfort in their marble splendour (separate men's and women's sections; daily 6am–11pm; $2). Past the hamam, old streets lead towards the **Cinci Han**, a huge, crumbling *kervansaray* dominating the town centre. At the time of writing, this was being restored with the eventual aim of turning it into a hotel.

Roughly northwest of the Cinci Han is the unexceptional seventeenth-century **Köprülü Mehmet Paşa Camii**, whose courtyard leads to its restored **arasta** (bazaar). This is where the day-trippers are brought to browse at the well-stocked souvenir and antique shops. South of the *arasta* lies the old bazaar district where traditional stalls of blacksmiths, cobblers, leatherworkers, tanners and saddlemakers once serviced the needs of Black Sea traders and which still lead the way to the **İzzet Mehmet Paşa Camii**, an elaborate, late-eighteenth-century mosque. Beyond, the town slides into dilapidation, and the stream which runs through it cuts a deep fissure into the base of the ravine, now used as a household dump. Further downstream women wash clothes in the water. If you walk down, there's a stunning view back towards the İzzet Mehmet Paşa Camii, whose domes and minarets seem to hover above the surrounding houses.

Back in town, immediately beneath the southeastern walls of the Cinci Han, there's an open-air market, from where a narrow street to the immediate left of the *Ziraat Bankası* leads up the side of the valley to the **Kaymakamlar Evi**, the "Governor's House", a restored Ottoman mansion or *konak* typical of many around the town (Tues–Sun 8.30am–12.30pm & 1.30–5.30pm; $0.50). A traditional conservatism dominates the *konak* design: the ground floor, devoid of external windows, would have been used as a stable, while on the upper floors the *selâmlik* (male guest rooms), overlooking the street, would have been divided from harem quarters, with a separate entrance and lattice windows looking only onto interior courtyards. Each room has a distinctively carved wooden ceiling and furniture is sparse – personal items would have been stored in decorative wall niches, bedding in cupboards doubling as bathrooms – but carpets still cover the floors, and you'll be asked to suffer the indignity of wearing shower caps on your feet to protect them as you're conducted on your tour.

Making your way from here to the hilltop **Hıdırlık Park**, vantage points let you look down over the whole town, which looks at its best in the late afternoon light. The palatial-looking edifice above the town on the opposite side of the ravine is an old government building, long since derelict.

Practicalities

The main **tourist information office** (Mon–Sat 9am–noon & 1.30–5pm; ☎0372/712 3863), in the *arasta*, sells excellent maps of the town ($1.50) and a locally produced book detailing the town's Ottoman architechture.

The most expensive **accommodation** in **Eski Safranbolu** is the *Havuzlu Konak*, on Mescit Sok on the north side of town (☎0372/725 2883, fax 712 3824; ⑤), with eleven immaculately restored rooms, a basement restaurant and a fine tearoom arranged around a central pool. Closer to the centre of the old town you'll find the *Otel Tahsin Bey Konaği* and the affiliated *Paşa Konaği*, Hükümet Sok (☎0372/712 6062; ⑤), two charming and individual old houses with fine views of the old town and authentic touches such as bathrooms housed in step-in cupboards. Those who like their style a little cheaper should try the *Arasna Pansiyon*, just next to the Cinci Hamam (☎0372/712 4170; ③), though be aware that the creaky original floorboards struggle to screen out noise from the thumping bar below. The only budget option in the old town is the modern, bright and clean *Çarşi Pansiyon*, Bozkurt Sok (☎0372/725 1079; ②), which has rooms with basic private bath (upstairs) or nice communal bath (downstairs) for the same price.

There's little reason to stay in **Kiranköy** to suffer the small and vastly overpriced rooms of the *Hotel Uz* (☎0372/712 1086; ⑥) or the unrestored squalor of the *Gülen* (☎0372/725 1082; ②); a far better option if you can't find a room in Eski Safranbolu is the *Konak Pansiyon*, Kaya Erdem Cad, Sağlik Sok (☎0372/725 2485; ③), which offers cool and clean rooms in a family house with shared bathroom.

There's a limited choice of places to **eat and drink** in Çarşi. The pleasant *Boncuk Café* in the *arasta* does tea, coffee, soft drinks and snacks, including burgers, while the *Merkez Lokantasi* next door to the Cinci Hamam does basic dishes. The *Kadioğlu Şehzade Sofrasi* by the *Arasna Pansiyon* is classy but cheap, and the *Beyaz Evi*, on the south side of the Cinci Han, is the best place to grab a beer. Otherwise there are a few cheap *lokanta* places on the main drag in the new town, and the *Hotel Uz* has a reasonable restaurant that serves alcohol. Sanfranbolu is famous for its *lokum* and *helva* **sweets**, which you can sample in the *Arasta* or *Safran Tat* shops in the new and old towns.

Kastamonu

It was in **KASTAMONU** that Atatürk made his first speech attacking the fez in 1925. Little has happened here since. Today, a couple of venerable mosques, some fine old Ottoman houses and a crumbling *kale* make the place worth an afternoon or morning visit on the way to somewhere else, but not much more.

The **otogar** is about a ten-minute walk north of the centre (if your bus is coming in from the south, save yourself a walk by asking to be let out at the town centre), on the eastern bank of the river that cuts the town in two from north to south. Kastamonu's main street, Cumhuriyet Caddesi, runs south from the *otogar*, parallel with the river.

Near the *otogar* on the western side of the river is the **İsmailbey Camii**, a fine, twin-domed medieval mosque set atop a plug of rock, adjacent to a small park. Heading south into town, take a right turn about five minutes after the *Otel İdrisoğlu* onto the town's main square, where you'll find the **Nasrullah Kadi Camii**, one of Kastamonu's larger and more distinguished mosques. At the western end of the square, the **Asirefendi Han** is still used for commercial purposes, and behind it there's an old and decrepit-looking hamam. From here a street runs south up to the **Yavapağa Camii**, a modern building screened by the ruins of a larger, much older mosque complex. The same street now curves off up to the west, in the direction of the *kale*. Along the way you'll pass the **Atabey Camii**, a rectangular stone building with a very low interior, built in 1273 but much repaired and restored in the intervening years.

Just above is the **kale**, unsignposted but hard to miss. It was built by Tamerlane, more famous for destruction than construction, and time hasn't been kind to it. Only the massive walls and main gateway are wholly intact, but its grassy grounds are now a favourite spot with people indulging in Turkish-style contemplation and relaxation.

The town **museum** (Tues–Sun 8.30am–5pm; $1) is about ten minutes' walk south of the *Otel İdrisoğlu*, with the usual collection of local miscellanea.

Practicalities

Should you want to stay in Kastamonu there are quite a few **hotels**. For the budget-minded, the *Otel Ilgaz*, Belediye Cad 4, offers basic waterless rooms (①). Slightly better options include the *Otel Hâdi*, Belediye Cad 8 (☎0366/212 1696; ①), and the *Otel Selvi*, Banka Sok 10 (☎0366/214 1763; ①). Nearby and slightly more expensive, though not significantly better than the *Hâdi* or the *Selvi*, is the *Otel İdrisoğlu*, Cumhuriyet Cad 25 (☎0366/214 1757; ②). Next door is the passable *Rugancı Otel*, Cumhuriyet Cad 27 (☎0366/214 9500; ②), but the best place in town is the new two-star *Otel Mütevelli*, Cumhuriyet Cad 10 (☎0366/212 2020, fax 212 2017; ④), with clean and modern rooms overlooking the main square.

There aren't too many places to **eat** in town after dark; your best bet is probably the *Uludağ Pide ve Kebap Salonu* at the corner of Belediye and Cumhuriyet *caddesi*s, a white-tablecloth place that does excellent *pide*. For dangerously addictive chocolate mousse simply move next door.

If you're heading on to Ankara or İstanbul, note that *Kastamonu Özlem* has a convenient ticket office and pick-up point opposite the *Otel Mütevelli*, on the central square.

EAST OF ANKARA

East of Ankara, prospects improve considerably, with numerous places worth going out of your way for. Just three hours away lies the ancient Hittite capital of **Hattuşaş**, near the modern village of Boğazkale. The scale of the place is perhaps more astonishing than the ruins themselves, and it's this sheer size, rather than any artistic finesse, that makes Hattuşaş and the surrounding sites so impressive.

Northeast of the Hittite capital is the ancient city of **Amasya**, with its Pontic rock tombs and riverside quarter of Ottoman houses. If you visit only one place outside of Ankara in North Central Anatolia, this should be it. Southeast of Amasya, **Tokat** has a couple of interesting buildings, including the striking Gök Medrese, but not enough to make it worth a long stay. **Sivas**, too, is a place to visit in passing, despite what virtually amounts to a theme park of amazing Selçuk architecture.

Sungurlu, Boğazkale and the Hittite sites

The Hittite sites centred around the village of Boğazkale are the most impressive and significant in the whole of Anatolia. This area was once the heart of the Hittite Empire, whose capital was at **Hattuşaş**, spread over several square kilometres to the south of the modern village. A few kilometres to the east is the temple site of **Yazılıkaya**, with reliefs much featured on postcards but badly worn by time. **Alacahöyük**, a smaller Hittite settlement dating back to 4000 BC, 25km north of Boğazkale, is further off the beaten track, but worth the trip if you have your own transport. Many of the objects unearthed here after excavation began in earnest in 1905 are now in the Museum of Anatolian Civilizations in the capital. If you've already seen the museum, a visit to the original excavations will be doubly interesting.

How best to go about visiting the sites needs some consideration. Theoretically Hattuşaş and Yazılıkaya can be covered **on foot** from Boğazkale if you're reasonably fit. However, it gets very hot here in summer and there are some steep hills to be climbed.

You might therefore want to take a tour round the sites **by taxi**: various characters in Boğazkale will offer all-in deals, and in the unlikely event that they don't seek you out you'll probably be able to find them at the *Aşıkoğlu* hotel. A typical offer is $15 to visit Hattuşaş and Yazılıkaya. If you don't want to spend the night in either Boğazkale or Sungurlu, then you might want to take a taxi round all three sites from Sungurlu, getting back in time for an onward bus. This will set you back about $20. It's also possible to hire a minibus to make the trip for about $25–50 (all prices are negotiable, and there's a good chance you'll be able to knock a fair bit off if business is slack).

Sungurlu

SUNGURLU is a small town lying just off the main Ankara–Samsun road. You'll have to pass through it if you're heading for the Hittite sites, but there's really no other reason for stopping here. Sungurlu-bound buses depart roughly every hour from Ankara's *otogar* on a three-hour journey across the treeless, rolling landscape of central Anatolia.

Sungurlu doesn't have an *otogar*. Through buses will drop you off by the main road about 1km west of town, and direct services will take you into the town centre. The departure point for Boğazkale-bound dolmuşes is the main square in Sungurlu, though you may be able to pick one up from the main road if you're dropped off by a through bus. The journey to Boğazkale takes about one hour and costs around $1, with the last departure at 5pm (last return from Boğazkale to Sungurlu is at about 6pm). The aforementioned taxi drivers are usually hanging around the square in Sungurlu and at the bus drop-off point looking for tourists. They'll ask $10 to take you to Boğazkale, although you should be able to beat them down to about half that.

If you miss the last Boğazkale-bound dolmuş you might need to stay overnight in Sungurlu. The cheapest of the **hotels** here are the very basic *Masatlı Oteli* (①) and the nearby *Ferhat* (①), both 100m east of the clocktower. Otherwise, try the *Hittit Motel* (☎0364/311 8409, fax 311 3873; ④) on the main road 1km east of town, which claims to have put Prince Charles up while on a private visit here.

Boğazkale

BOĞAZKALE, 5km east and then 20km south of Sungurlu, at the end of a metalled, but at times badly potholed road cutting across rough pastureland, is a fairly uneventful modern village, with the ancient Hittite capital of Hattuşaş fanning out from its southern rim. Finding your way around is fairly straightforward; it's basically a one-street place, running about half a kilometre from a welcome arch, up a hill, to the main square. The only attraction in the village itself is a small **museum** (Tues–Sun 8am–noon & 1.30–5.30pm; $1) on the left-hand side of the main street on the way up to the village square. It has a small collection of objects (mainly cuneiform tablets and pottery) from the Hattuşaş site, some useful books for sale and a large-scale map that sets the scene for what's to come.

There are several **hotels**, often block-booked by tour groups. Pick of the bunch is the *Başkent Touris Restoran, Motel ve Camping*, Yazılıkaya Yolu Üzeri (☎0364/452 2037, fax 452 2567; ②), on the road leading from Boğazkale to Yazılıkaya. They also have space for **camping** and tents for rental. The restaurant, with a view of the ruins of the Great Temple, is good value. The *Kale* further up the hill (☎0364/452 2189; ②) is a similar operation with less impressive facilities. Alternatively, the *Aşıkoğlu Motel* (☎0364/452 2004; ③) lies right at the entrance to the village, offering basic, overpriced rooms with showers (outside of summer the rooms are freezing and very damp), and a busy restaurant which can be swamped with tour groups. Five hundred metres or so beyond the *Aşıkoğlu* on the village square, the *Hattuşaş Pansiyon* (☎0364/452 2013; ①) is the best budget option; most rooms come without bathroom but are clean and spacious, and the friendly English-speaking management understands backpacker needs.

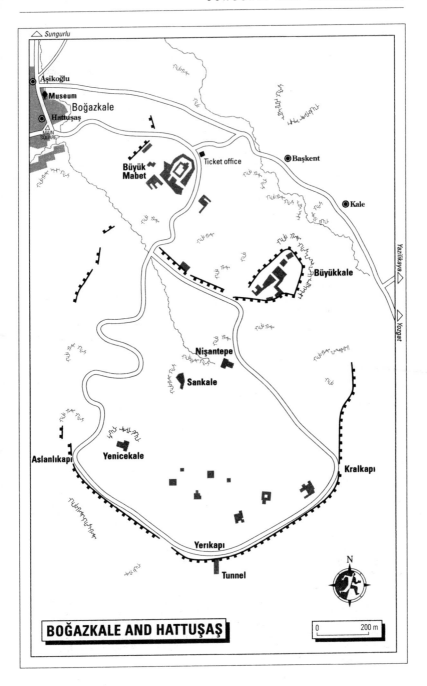

BOĞAZKALE AND HATTUŞAŞ

Hattuşaş

Enclosed by six-kilometre-long walls, **HATTUŞAŞ** was by the standards of the time an immense city, and its scale is still awe-inspiring today. The site was originally occupied by the Hatti, who established a settlement here around 2500 BC. The Hittites moved in after their conquest of central Anatolia, making it their capital from about 1375 BC onwards during the period when their empire reached its greatest extent. By 1200 the influence of the Sea Peoples had put an end to Hittite dominance of the region; Hattuşaş was destroyed and later the Phrygians built a large city on the site.

The Hittite city, unearthed by archeologists during the first half of this century, occupied a steeply sloping expanse, dotted with rocky outcrops to the southwest of modern Boğazkale. Of numerous buildings scattered over a wide area only the limestone foundation blocks have survived, the upper parts – timber frames supporting clay brick walls – having long since vanished. The main points of interest, all conveniently linked by a metalled road, are the **Büyük Mabet** (Great Temple), just outside the modern village; the section of **wall** with three **gateways** at the southern extremity of the site; and the **Büyük Kale** (Great Fortress). Approaching the site from the direction of the village square leads to a ticket office (daily 8am–5.30pm; $1.50 joint ticket for Hattuşaş and Yazılıkaya).

The Büyük Mabet

Beyond the ticket office is the **Büyük Mabet** or "Great Temple", also known as Temple I, one of an original seventy on the site. The largest and best-preserved Hittite temple in existence, it was built around the fourteenth or thirteenth century BC and dedicated to the storm god Teshuba and the sun goddess Hebut. It consisted of a central temple building surrounded by around seventy-eight storage rooms laid out to an irregular plan.

Today the temple site comprises little more than an expanse of stone foundations and it's quite difficult to work out what was where. As you enter the site through the main gate, you'll be assailed by local men masquerading unconvincingly as archeologists, who will offer to guide you through the ruins and try to sell you little carved figures. They're pretty persistent and the only hope you have of shaking them off is to say that a big tour bus is on the way up from the village. You'll probably meet them again later as they're in the habit of pursuing tour groups around the rest of Hattuşaş by motorbike.

After running the gauntlet of would-be guides, you pass between two large stone blocks, remnants of the **ceremonial gateway** that let on to the temple precincts. Nearby is a stone lion that originally formed part of a cistern. In Hittite times the king and queen, in their roles as high priest and priestess, would have led processions through here on holy days. Today most visitors end up following the route they took, along a clearly defined processional way of uneven slabs. The thoroughfare is flanked by the foundations of many storerooms and after about 30m swings round to the right, opening up on the temple proper.

The **temple** consisted of about twelve small chambers around a central courtyard with the rooms that would have contained the cult statues of Teshuba and Hebut at the northeastern end, the god on the left and the goddess on the right. In the latter room is a small stone slab which may well have supported the statue of Hebut. In some of the storerooms adjacent to the temple you can see *pithoi* or earthenware storage vessels that have been exposed. Some are complete, pieced together by archeologists, with distinctive zig-zag markings running round them. In other cases only jagged shards remain sticking out of the ground. Just below the Büyük Mabet archeologists have identified an early Assyrian merchant quarter which held the Hittite equivalent of the Rosetta Stone, a parallel Hittite hieroglyphic and Akkadian inscription which led to the final cracking of the hieroglyphic code.

The Yenicekale and the Aslanlıkapı

About 350m beyond the Great Temple, on the site of the original Hattic city, the road forks. Taking the right-hand branch leads up a steep hill. After about 800m (this is the worst foot-slogging section if you're walking), the **Yenicekale**, a ruined fortress, is visible about 50m to the left of the road. Although little remains, its construction was clearly a considerable achievement; Hittite engineers had to create an artificial platform out of the uneven and rocky terrain before they could start building.

A little higher up is the **Aslanlıkapı** or "Lion Gate", one of the three gateways that studded the southern section of the city wall. The Aslanlıkapı takes its name from the two stone lions that flank the outer entrance, symbolically guarding Hattuşaş from attackers and evil spirits. The lions you'll see are actually fairly convincing copies of the originals, which now reside in the Museum of Anatolian Civilizations in Ankara. The Aslanlıkapı marks the beginning of the surviving section of dry-stone **city wall**, which runs along the top of a massive sloping embankment ten metres in height and surfaced with irregular limestone slabs. Rectangular towers were placed along it at regular intervals and the foundations of some of these are still visible.

The Yerıkapı

The road follows the embankment to the **Yerıkapı** or "Earth Gate", more popularly known as the Sphinx Gate after the two huge sphinxes who once guarded its inner portal but which now live in museums in İstanbul and Berlin. The most striking feature of the Sphinx Gate is the seventy-metre **tunnel** that cuts through from the city side of the walls to the exterior. The tunnel was built using the corbel arch technique, a series of flat stones leaning towards each other creating its triangular profile. One theory as to its purpose is that it served to let the defenders of the city make surprise attacks on besieging enemies. However, its obvious visibility from the outside and the presence of two sets of monumental steps leading up the embankment on either side of the outer portal cast doubt on this, and a more ceremonial function has been suggested.

It's possible to walk through the tunnel to the outer side of the city walls from where you can scramble up the embankment to examine the scant remains of the Sphinx Gate and enjoy the view of the rest of Hattuşaş. The sphinxes that stood on the inner side of the gate were found in fragments, but archeologists were able to piece them back together to reveal imposing leonine figures complete with wings. The outer side of the gate was also flanked by sphinxes – one survives but so eroded by the elements as to be virtually unrecognizable. The scattered foundations visible on the far side of the road immediately to the north of the Sphinx Gate are the remains of seven large temples.

The Kralkapı, the Nimantepe and the Sarıkale

Following the road east from the Sphinx Gate leads to the **Kralkapı**, or "King's Gate", named after the regal-looking figure carved in relief on the left-hand pillar of the inner gateway. This actually represents the god Teshuba and shows him sporting a conical hat while raising his left fist in the air as though holding an invisible sword. Again, what you see is a copy – the original is in Ankara's Museum of Anatolian Civilizations.

Further down the hill lies the **Nişantepe**, a rocky outcrop with a ten-line Hittite inscription carved into its eastern face. The thirty-centimetre hieroglyphs are badly weathered but enough has been deciphered to suggest that it's a memorial to King Suppiluliuma II, last of the Hittite kings. To the immediate southwest of the Nişantepe is the **Sarıkale**, the foundations of a Phrygian fort built on the site of an earlier Hittite structure.

The Büyük Kale

From the Nişantepe the road leads down to the **Büyük Kale**, or "Great Fortress", which served the Hittite monarchs as a fortified palace during the fourteenth and thirteenth centuries. The Büyük Kale consisted of three courtyards, each higher than the previous one, meaning that any attacker would have had to capture it piecemeal. The lower and middle courtyards are thought to have been given over to servants and aides of the royal family while the upper courtyard was the palace proper. It's easy to see why they chose this wild and windswept location on the very eastern edge of Hattuzaz as their residence. In effect it was a citadel within the city, protected on all sides by steep drops. On the outer side to the east these are natural, but the inner side was originally a man-made construction with a series of terraces supported by retaining walls made of vast limestone blocks.

Access today is via a flight of steps leading up to what was the southeastern gate of the palace. On the site of a building near this entrance archeologists found three thousand **cuneiform tablets** which, when deciphered, yielded important clues about the nature of Hittite society. Among them was the Treaty of Kadesh, signed in around 1270 BC by the Hittite king Hattuziliz II and Ramses II of Egypt, the earliest surviving written treaty between two nations. These days walkways, the lower parts of walls, and masonry fragments, are all that survive of the Büyük Kale, offering few clues as to the original layout. But it's worth coming up here to wander among the weather-battered remnants and take in the stunning, plan-like view of the Great Temple. The eastern end of the site, where the ground falls away sharply into a ravine below, is particularly atmospheric.

THE HITTITES

The **Hittites** appear to have been an Indo-European people who moved into Anatolia around 2000 BC. Where exactly they came from remains unclear, though the Caucasus and the Balkans have been suggested. They moved into the territories of the **Hatti**, an indigenous people, and though no records survive of how their rise to dominance was effected, archeologists have found layers of burnt material in most Hatti settlements that can be dated to around 2000 BC, suggesting that in part at least it was achieved by violence. However, the fact that the Hittites also absorbed important elements of Hatti culture suggests that a more complex interaction may have taken place.

Initially the Hittites set up a number of city-states. These were drawn together during the mid-eighteenth century under King Anitta. According to cuneiform tablets found at Hattuzaz, he transferred his capital from the city of Kushara (possibly modern Alizar) to Nesha (Kültepe), and destroyed Hattuzaz, cursing any Hittite king who might attempt to rebuild the place. A century or so later his successor Labarna returned to Hattuzaz and did just that. The Hittites came to regard Labarna and his wife Tawannanna as founders of the Hittite kingdom and their names were adopted as titles by subsequent monarchs. Labarna's son Labarna II took the name Hattuzaz and launched a number of military campaigns against his neighbours, extending Hittite territory into modern-day Syria and western Anatolia.

Hittite **expansion** was not a uniform process and over the centuries the boundaries of their territories ebbed and flowed across Anatolia. In 1595 BC, Mursili I succeeded in capturing distant Babylon, but his successor Hantili (who gained power by assasinating Mursili) lost many gains. This early period, known to historians as the Old Hittite Kingdom, ended with a descent into succession-related strife. Stability was restored under Tudhaliyas II around 1430 BC, and he re-established the Hittite state as an empire. An important period of expansion followed under King Suppiluliuma (1380–1315 BC), who secured the northern borders of the empire and conquered the Hurrian kingdom of Mitanni, which had exerted an important cultural influence on the Hittites. This achievement raised the Hittites to superpower status, equal with Egypt, Assyria and Babylon. The Egyptians even asked Suppiluliuma to send one of his sons to marry the widow of Tutankhamun (the union didn't happen as the boy was murdered en route). After

Yazılıkaya

From the Hattuzaz ticket office signs point to the temple site of **Yazılıkaya** with its famous reliefs, about 3km to the east. The route there, which more or less follows the Hittite processional route from city to temple, dips down into a river valley then up towards the *Baxkent* hotel, from where further signs point the way onwards and then left (the road right continues to Yozgat). When you arrive you'll have to fight your way through the inevitable crowd of would-be guides and souvenir sellers to the ticket kiosk (normally unmanned as joint tickets are now sold at Hattuzaz).

Archeological evidence suggests that a temple of some sort existed on the site as early as 1500 BC, but it wasn't until the thirteenth century BC that the two small ravines that cut into a rocky outcrop at the rear of the site were decorated with reliefs (hence Yazılıkaya, Turkish for "inscribed rock"). At roughly the same time a **gateway** and **temple buildings** were constructed. Today a few sketchy foundations are all that remain of these ancient structures and all attention is focused on the two "galleries" of reliefs depicting nearly a hundred figures, mostly gods from the vast array of Hittite deities.

The reliefs

The entrance to the **larger ravine** of the two is on the left behind the temple foundations. The left-hand wall is lined with images of gods moving left to right and the right-

Suppiluliuma's death, Hittite expansion continued and in 1286, during the reign of Muwatalli II, a Hittite army defeated the Egyptians at the Battle of Kadesh, an empire-shaking event that was carved into the columns of Luxor.

Following the conflict, peace between the two empires was established, cemented by the marriage of one of the daughters of Ramses II to Hattuziliz III. However, the Hittite Empire had less than a century left. The arrival of the Sea Peoples in Anatolia ushered in a period of instability that was to erode Hittite power, culminating in the **destruction of Hattuzaz** around 1200 BC, roughly the same time as the fall of Troy. The Phrygians replaced the Hittites as the dominant power in central Anatolia, taking over the ruins of Hattuzaz and other Hittite cities.

Hittite culture survived in a number of small successor kingdoms established in south-eastern Anatolia and northern Syria, most notably around Carcemish (Kargamiz), Malatya and Karatepe. These Neohittites are mentioned in the Bible in conjuction with Abraham and David and endured until around 700 BC when they were finished off by Assyrians, after which the Hittites disappeared from history completely until their rediscovery this century.

While it lasted, Hittite civilization was highly advanced with a complex **social system**. The Hittite kings were absolute rulers but there was an assembly called the *panku*, which at times seems to have wielded considerable influence. The major division in Hittite society was between free citizens and slaves: the former included farmers, artisans and bureaucrats, while the latter, although they could be bought and sold, are thought to have had the right to own property and marry. Society was regulated by a legal code of two hundred laws under which defiance of the state, rape and bestiality were all punishable by death. Murder and assault, on the other hand, were punished by fines which varied according to whether the victim was free or a slave. For property offences there was a compensatory system of fines.

Hittite **religion** seems to have been adopted from the Hatti, with the weather god Teshuba and the sun goddess Hebut as the two most important deities. Up to a thousand lesser gods also played a role in the religious belief of the Hittites, who were in the habit of incorporating the gods of conquered peoples into their own pantheon. Evidence for all this comes from large numbers of cuneiform tablets found by archeologists. These were kept in chambers maintained specifically for that purpose and subsequently unearthed at various sites.

hand one with images of goddesses wearing identical long, pleated dresses and conical headgear. A number of the figures on the male side of the ravine stand out, in particular the group of twelve war gods bringing up the rear of the procession. Further along are two figures with human bodies and bulls' heads. The deities seem to rise in rank as the procession progresses, and towards the front are the conspicuous figures of the moon god Kusuh, with a crescent moon, and the sun god, seemingly balancing a winged sun symbol on his head.

The two lines of deities meet on the far wall of the ravine. The scene carved here depicts Teshuba astride a couple of mountain peaks facing Hebut, who is standing on a panther. Behind her is their son Sharruma, also standing on a panther, with two lesser goddesses nearby. All are identified by hieroglyphs written above an uplifted hand. Just behind the procession of goddesses near the ravine entrance is a well-preserved image of a male figure. This represents Tudhaliyas IV (1250–1220 BC) who is thought to have built the temple. He is holding a standard in his left hand and a winged sun-disc in his right. Hittite accounts of religious rituals seem to suggest that this gallery was used for new year celebrations which probably coincided with the beginning of spring.

The **smaller ravine** lies over to the right and can be reached via the short flight of steps that leads up to a cleft in the rock. The entrance to the ravine is guarded by two sphinx reliefs, and a group of twelve figures armed with swords lines the left-hand wall. These are similar to the warrior-god figures seen in the first ravine but are much better preserved. Opposite this group are two separate reliefs. One shows an unusual figure that has come to be known as the "Sword God", a blade with a human torso and head where the handle should be. To add to the already strange effect, lions' heads, instead of arms, sprout from the torso shoulders. This vaguely disturbing image is thought to depict Neargal, the Hittite god of the underworld. Next to it is a relief depicting the god Sharruma embracing Tudhaliyas IV. The god is shown as a giant figure in a conical headdress holding the slightly built king in what looks almost like a headlock. The discovery of the remnants of cremations in niches in the rock, next to the gods armed with swords, suggests this part of the temple may have been used for the funerals of Hittite kings.

Alacahöyük

After Hattuşaş, **ALACAHÖYÜK**, 25km north of Boğazkale, is the most important Hittite site in existence. Originally a major Hattian settlement, it was taken over by the Hittites during the early stages of the second millennium BC; as at Hattuşaş, the Phrygians in turn seem to have taken over the site for a while after the demise of the Hittites. The ruins that remain are mainly Hittite, but a number of extensive archeological digs throughout the century have unearthed a vast array of Hatti artefacts, including standards featuring stags, bulls, sun-discs and statues of the earth goddess, from a number of tombs on the site.

Unfortunately, **getting there** presents a few difficulties if you don't have your own transport. If you are travelling under your own steam, from Boğazkale head back in the direction of Sungurlu and turn right at the road signposted for Alacahöyük. After about 11km take a signposted left turn for the remaining 12km to the site. If you don't have your own transport, you should be able to pick up a dolmuş to the village of Alaca about 10km southeast of the site, but from there you'll have to hitch. The only other alternative is to take a taxi from Boğazkale or Sungurlu which will set you back at least $10. The hamlet of **HÖYÜK** next to the site is small but it does have a few basic shops and a PTT. In theory there's also a *pansiyon* with a restaurant, the *Kaplan Restaurant ve Hotel* (②), but don't bank on it being open.

The site

Next to the **site** (daily 8am–noon & 1.30–5.30pm; $1) is a small **museum** (same hours, but closed Mon). For once, the museum is well worth investigating, as it includes some striking Hatti standards and pottery with elegant designs. There's a less inspiring ethnographic section downstairs devoted mostly to farm implements.

The site itself is entered via the southern **Sphinx Gate**, named after the large sphinxes that guard it. These eerily impressive figures, stained ochre by lichen, have blunted faces with empty eye sockets, and sweeping headdresses. There's a double-headed eagle at the right-hand base of the gate, a symbol that appears on seals found at the Assyrian trading colony at Kültepe. Either side of the gate are **reliefs** (copies of originals now in Ankara), depicting religious ceremonies. The left-hand section is the more lively of the two, showing a procession moving towards the god Teshuba – shown here as a slightly comical-looking bull with outsize sex organs. Approaching him are a king and queen followed by sacrificial animals and priests, with a group of what look like acrobats bringing up the rear.

The Sphinx Gate opens onto a pathway, on either side of which are excavated areas, all well signposted in English. Immediately behind the gate are vast irregular blocks, the remnants of the city walls, followed by the foundations of storage buildings. Beyond the storage areas, a few metres below ground level to the left of the path, are thirteen **tombs**. These date from the Hatti period and yielded much of the vast hoard of archeological treasure now in the Bronze Age section of the Museum of Anatolian Civilizations in Ankara. Judging by the opulence of the grave goods found in them, these were the tombs of Hatti monarchs. The two largest ones are set on raised platforms and the timber cladding that covered them has been re-created.

To the right of the pathway are the foundations of what may have been palace buildings, while the tumble of ruins at the head of the pathway was almost certainly a temple. Beyond the tombs are a series of irregular mounds identified only as "Hittite building levels". The foundations of the west gate of the settlement entrance survive, as do the beginnings of a tunnel system, similar to the one under the Sphinx Gate at Hattuşaş.

Amasya

The approach to **AMASYA** does little to prepare you for the charm of the place. Along the E80 highway (the main approach road if you're coming in by coach from points west), the landscape is thoroughly uninspiring until just a few kilometres before the town itself, when you suddenly find yourself amid the lush farmland and orchards of the Yeşilırmak valley. Even arriving at the *otogar* or train station, both well outside the town centre, Amasya doesn't seem especially impressive.

Once you've made the dolmuş trip into town, however, Amasya turns out to be one of the high points of North Central Anatolia. It occupies a point in the river valley so narrow that it's almost a gorge, and is blessed with a superabundant historical legacy. Most people come here to see the rock tombs hewn into the cliffs above the town by the kings of Pontus over 2000 years ago, but Amasya also harbours some truly beautiful Selçuk and Ottoman architecture, and a multitude of colourful nineteenth-century wooden houses.

Some history

Amasya may seem tranquil now, but in the past it was the scene of battle and conquest. According to some accounts, including that of the locally born geographer and historian **Strabo** (64 BC–25 AD), Amasya was founded by the Amazon queen Amasis. In reality it's more likely that the town began life as a Hittite settlement, later falling to Alexander the Great. The decades of upheaval that engulfed Anatolia after the death of Alexander resulted in the creation of a number of small kingdoms. One of these was **Pontus**, established by Mithridates, a refugee-adventurer from Cius (a Greek city state on the shores of the Sea of Marmara – modern Gemlik), who fled east after his city fell to Antigonus. Mithridates arrived in Amaseia (as the town was then known) in 302 BC, setting himself up in the local castle and in time establishing a kingdom. Pontus survived for two hundred years and, at its height, occupied a mountainous region roughly bounded by the Kızılırmak and the Yeşilırmak rivers. The downfall of Pontus began when Mithridates VI Eupator reputedly ordered the massacre of 80,000 Romans in one day and plunged his kingdom into a series of wars which culminated in it being absorbed by Pompey into the Roman Empire around 70 BC.

The best description of Amasya during ancient times comes from the writings of Strabo, who compiled a description of the then-known world in seventeen volumes called the *Oikomene*. Of his own town he wrote:

My native city is located in a deep and large valley through which flows the River Iris. It has been endowed in a surprising manner by art and nature for serving the purpose of a city and fortress. For there is a lofty and perpendicular rock, which overhangs the river, having on one side a wall erected close to the bank where the town has been built, while on the other it runs up on either side to the summits of the hill. These two are connected to each other and well fortified with towers. Within this enclosure are the royal residence and the tombs of the kings.

Under the Romans and through the succeeding centuries of Byzantine rule the town prospered, and it continued to do so after falling to the Selçuks – who left their distinctive architectural signature on the town – in 1071. In the mid-thirteenth century, Amasya was caught up in the first Mongol invasion of Anatolia, part of the catastrophic irruption begun by Genghis Khan – the self-styled "scourge of god" – and continued by his successors. The Selçuk realm was reduced to a Mongol vassal state and Amasya apportioned to the Il-khan Empire, one of the several huge *khanate*s into which the Mongol Empire split after the death of the Great Khan Möngke in 1259.

With the waning of Mongol power in the late thirteenth century, the Ottomans emerged as a force to be reckoned with in Anatolia, and Amasya soon became part of their burgeoning state. During the brief but violent return of the Mongols under Tamerlane after the defeat of Beyazit I at Ankara in 1402, the latter's son Mehmet (later to restore the Ottoman state as Mehmet I) took refuge in Amasya *kale*. When Ottoman rule over Anatolia was re-established in 1413, Amasya became (like Manisa) a training ground for crown princes, who would serve as governors of the province to prepare them for the rigours of statesmanship at the Sublime Port.

Under the Ottomans during the Middle Ages, Amasya enjoyed great prosperity, and it's from this period that the some of the town's most imposing monuments date. It also developed as a theological centre, boasting eighteen *medrese*s with up to two thousand students by the eighteenth century.

Like most prosperous towns of the period, Amasya had a wealthy Armenian trading class until World War I. Most of its members disappeared in one way or another after the pogroms of 1915. A few years after these tragic events, Amasya became a vital staging post en route to the creation of modern Turkey. On June 21, 1919, Atatürk delivered a speech at Amasya that was in effect a call to arms for the coming War of Independence. Afterwards he and a group of supporters drafted a Declaration of Independence, a document that presaged the establishment of the provisional government in Ankara, and ultimately the Turkish Republic itself. Since then – apart from a severe earthquake in 1939 and a number of bad floods – things have been quiet.

The Town

At the centre of Amasya, the riverfront Atatürk Square commemorates Atatürk's 1919 visit with yet another equestrian statue of the hero surrounded by admirers. At the eastern end of the square, the creamy yellow **Gümüşlü Cami**, or "Silvery Mosque", was originally built in 1326, but has been reconstructed at various intervals since. Its almost pavilion-like oriental exterior and carved wooden porch overlook the river, and there's an unusual tall, brick minaret.

There's another architectural oddity on the southern side of the square in the shape of the **Pir Mehmet Çelebi Camii**, which dates from 1507. It's an extremely small example of a *mescit*, or mosque without a minaret, the Islamic equivalent of a Christian chapel. The carved facade of this particular example has been decorated with ochre paint, and it's improbably small, almost as though it were a play mosque built for children.

West along Atatürk Caddesi

West of the square, Atatürk Caddesi runs off through the town. A hundred metres or so along, on the southern side, is the **Kileri Süleyman Ağa Camii**, an imposing but conventionally designed Ottoman mosque, built in 1489. Behind it stands the eighteenth-century **Taş Han**, a crumbling old brick and stone structure that is now home to a metal workshop. To the rear of the Taş Han is the **Burmalı Minare Camii** (Twisted Minaret Mosque). Named after the spiral effect of the stonework of its minaret, this compact building was erected in 1242 but heavily restored in the eighteenth century following a fire. Inside, wooden galleries run around the walls facing the *mihrab*.

Back on Atatürk Caddesi, a twin-domed *bedesten* in grey stone stands opposite the Kileri Süleyman Ağa Camii, still home to various shops and businesses. Continuing west for about ten minutes brings you to the **Sultan Beyazit II Camii**, set in a spacious rose garden on the northern side of the street. Built in 1486, this is Amasya's largest mosque, laid out on a symmetrical plan with two large central domes flanked by four smaller cupolas and two slightly mismatched minarets. Though some of Amasya's other mosques beat it for sheer whimsicality, none of them can quite match it for structural harmony. The front of the mosque faces the river, and it's from this side that the whole is best appreciated. The five-domed porch runs along the facade protecting a minutely carved entrance portal. Either side of this are two marble columns, which though they appear to be fixed are in fact free to rotate. Any shift in their position (after an earthquake for example) gives warning about the mosque's structural state. Adjoining the mosque are a multi-domed *medrese* and a library housing around 20,000 volumes, including ancient manuscript copies of the Koran.

A little to the west of the Sultan Beyazit Camii on the other side of Atatürk Caddesi is Amasya's **archeological and ethnographic museum** (Tues–Sun 8.30am–noon & 1.30–5.30pm; $1), a pearl among Turkish municipal museums. Centre of attraction is the door of the Selçuk Gök Medrese (see below) on the **ground floor**, a riot of *girikh* and arabesque geometrical patterns enclosing lattice-reliefs. The rest of this level is devoted to more standard fare, though somehow the Roman clay bathtubs and sarcophagi on display seem more substantial than those in other museums. There are also some excellent carpets (a subtly vivid nineteenth-century prayer rug from Avanos stands out in particular), and a number of studded wooden cupboard doors from Ottoman-era homes.

The **upper floor** is home to archeological finds dating back as far as the Bronze Age, which is represented by some practical-looking pottery and a caseful of rather unwieldy tools. Hittite relics include beak-spouted jugs, some with what look like built-in filters, and a statue of the storm god Teshuba. From here things jump forward to ornate Roman glassware and coins recovered from burial sites complete with clay con-

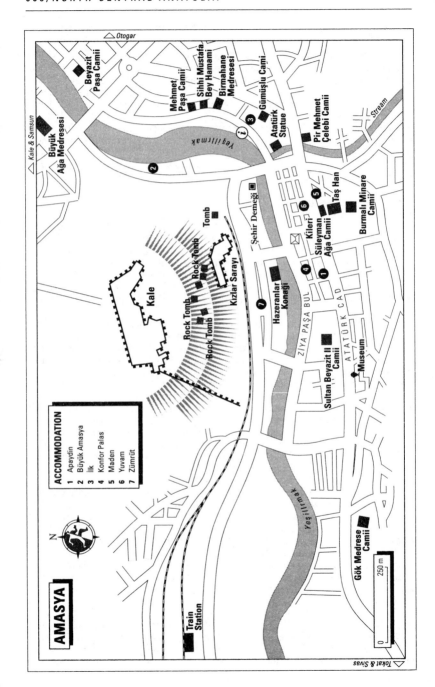

tainers. The rest of the floor is devoted to Ottoman times with a comprehensive selection of costumes, weapons, astronomical instruments and mother-of-pearl inlaid wooden items, including some fetching hamam clogs. A curiosity is the **türbe** in the museum grounds labelled "Mummies", containing five desiccated human husks which were found underneath the Burmalı Minare Camii. These are identified as the remains of two Mongol governors, a "concubine", and the children of a Selçuk family.

A five-to-ten-minute walk west of the museum is the **Gök Medrese Camii**, the thirteenth-century Selçuk "Mosque of the Blue Seminary", with a particularly intricate carved doorway (the actual door is in the museum). This doorway was once covered in blue tiles – hence the name – but time seems to have taken its toll, and today there's little trace of them. The **türbe** beside the mosque, with traces of turquoise tiles on its octagonal turret, is that of the Emir Torumtay, a Selçuk governor of the town. The tomb is supposedly haunted by the ghost of the Selçuk sultan Kiliç Aslan, who appears on horseback holding a sword that drips blood.

North of Atatürk Square

Returning to Atatürk Square and heading north parallel to the river will bring you to the rest of Amasya's historic buildings. The **Bırmahane Medresesi** was built by the Mongols in 1308 as a lunatic asylum. The popular image of the Mongols as a brutal, destructive people makes the presence of this abiding monument to their occupation of Amasya something of a surprise. But the heirs of Genghis Khan were more settled than their forebears, and the Bırmahane Medresesi is a typical example of the way in which they adapted the architectural styles of their subjects, with heavy Selçuk influences in its design. Only the outer walls are still standing, but it remains a typical Mongol building, reflecting the architectural styles encountered and adapted by the Mongols in the various lands they ravaged.

Further on is the **Sıhhı Mustafa Bey Hamamı**, very old but very much in use, as the wreaths of vapour emerging from its chimneys testify. Next comes the **Mehmet Paşa Camii**, constructed in 1486 by Mehmet Paşa, who was the tutor of Prince Ahmet, son of Sultan Beyazit. It's a sizeable place with a guest house, soup kitchen and *medrese*, and boasts a finely decorated marble pulpit.

A little further along is the **Şiranli Camii**, built little over a hundred years ago though it looks far older. According to a sign outside, it was constructed using money which had been raised by Azeri Turks, although it's not too clear why they should have paid to build a mosque in Amasya. The final mosque of any importance is the early fifteenth-century **Beyazit Paşa Camii**, whose leafy riverbank location enhances the quiet beauty of its architecture.

From here a bridge crosses the river to the **Büyük Ağa Medresesi**, a seminary/university founded in 1488 by the Chief White Eunuch of Beyazit II. This roughly octagonal structure of stone and brick is nowadays a Koran school. Although it's not open to the public, no one seems to mind if you take a look inside the courtyard where the boys who study here play football between lessons.

The rock tombs

The massive **rock tombs** of the Pontic kings are carved into the cliff face on the northern bank of the Yeşilırmak. To reach them follow Ziya Paşa Bulvarı west along the river bank from Atatürk Square. After about five minutes you'll come to a footbridge. Cross this and follow the signs bearing the words "Kral Kaya Mezarları", under a railway line and through narrow streets of yellow walls, wooden beams and terracotta tiles, to the **Kızlar Sarayı**, or "Palace of the Maidens". This erstwhile Ottoman palace is named after the harem once housed within its walls, but today little more than a few ruined walls, a ruined bathhouse and a crumbling tower remain.

There are two main clusters of **tombs**, and bearing right from the Kızlar Sarayı will bring you to the most accessible group, as well as a café and toilet. You can clamber up inside some of the tombs through the raised stone doorways, though whether you'll want to is another matter, as people seem to be in the habit of using them as impromptu urinals. Passages cut out of the rock run behind two of these tombs and you can only marvel at the work that must have been involved in excavating them. Bearing left will bring you to two larger tombs; beside the entrance to one of them is the mouth of a tunnel which is thought to lead to the river. Further tombs can be found with a bit of effort, but none as impressive as these. At night, the rock tombs are lit up to give the city a spectacular backdrop.

Ottoman houses

Below the rock tombs, on the narrow strip of land between railway line and river, is Amasya's other big attraction, the half-timbered **Ottoman houses** that do so much for the atmosphere of the town. They give the impression of being about to slide into the river and, in fact, many of them are – their parlous state of disrepair has seen several succumb to the elements or flooding over the last couple of decades, and many more have been deliberately demolished, including the majority of those on the southern bank. The fact is that, appealing as they may be to the tourist, these houses are very expensive to maintain; many owners prefer to live in prefabricated concrete apartments, which are a great deal easier to look after. Fortunately, the status of the survivors as a tourist attraction will probably preserve the examples on the north bank.

A good starting point for explorations of this area is the ninteenth-century **Hazeranlar Konağı**, an imposing mansion at the river's edge that has been turned into an **ethnology museum and gallery** (Tues–Sun 8.30am–noon & 1.30–5.30pm; $0.50). The heavily restored interior has been turned into a convincing re-creation of a nineteenth-century family home, liberally decked out with carpets, period furniture and household artefacts. It incorporates typical features of the time: wall niches for oil lamps, bathrooms secreted away behind cupboard doors, and divan seating running along the walls, all of which reflect the nomadic distaste for cumbersome furniture. Dummies in period costume have been placed in some of the rooms. In the basement of the house, there's a small gallery that plays host to changing exhibitions. Following the street west from the Hazeranlar Konağı as far as the footbridge leading across to the Sultan Beyazit Camii takes you through the heart of the old house district.

The kale

In the crags high above the rock tombs is Amasya's sprawling **citadel** (*kale*), a structure that dates back to Pontic times – though the surviving ruins are of Ottoman vintage. The *kale* is difficult to reach but well worth the effort for the stupendous views of the town in the gorge below. There is supposedly a path leading up to the *kale* through the rocks above the tombs but, if it exists, it must be fairly precipitous. A far easier way to get there is to follow the Samsun road out of town from near the Büyük Ağa Medresesi until you spot the "Kale" sign hidden in a backstreet to the left. From here a steep dirt road winds its way up to the summit for about 2km. If you're on foot it's quite a climb: reckon on an hour or two to complete it and avoid attempting it in the midday heat. If you're not up to the climb, it's worth renting a taxi as the panorama of the town from the *kale* summit is an essential complement to sightseeing wanderings below.

At the top, the outer walls of the *kale* have been rebuilt in bright, modern stone, but beyond you'll find the crumbling remains of the Ottoman-era fortress. Nothing is signposted and there are no clear paths through the ruins, so much of the time you'll find yourself scrambling over rocks and rubble and through undergrowth. At the southeastern extremity of the ruins, you'll find a rough breeze-block shed housing an old cannon that's discharged to thunderous effect at sundown during Ramadan. Beware of a large unfenced hole hidden in the undergrowth nearby. The best views are to be had from the western end of the *kale*, where the Turkish flag flies.

Practicalities

Amasya's **otogar** lies well to the east of the town proper and you'll need to take a dolmuş into the centre (when leaving town you can buy your ticket from the bus offices on Atatürk Cad). The **train station** is about 1km to the west, also served by dolmuşes. The **tourist information kiosk** (Mon–Fri 9.30am–noon & 1–5pm; ☎0358/218 7428) stands on Mustafa Kemal Bulvarı, by the river bank, just north of Atatürk Square.

As for **accommodation**, there's a sprinkling of pretty basic hotels, plus two expensive "tourist" hotels and one excellent *pansiyon*. This, the *İlk Pansiyon*, Hittit Sok 1 (☎0358/218 1689, fax 218 6277; ②–④), is down a narrow street more or less opposite the tourist kiosk. It's an eighteenth-century Armenian mansion which has been faultlessly restored by architect Ali Yalçım, retaining much of the original atmosphere and decor. As pleasant a place to stay as any in Turkey, it has just six rooms, each priced differently, and they're often booked ahead during the season, making reservations advisable. The *Yuvam Pansiyon*, Atatürk Cad 24/1 (☎0358/218 1342; ②), above a pharmacy on the town's main street, is reasonable value, though the rooms – either with or without bathroom – are a little on the plain side. The owners of the *Yuvam* also have another *pansiyon* south of Atatürk Caddesi. Prices are the same but it's quieter and more homely, with a pleasant garden. For both places ring the bell or enquire at the pharmacy.

Amasya's other budget options are fairly unprepossessing. Best of a bad bunch are the *Otel Apaydın*, Atatürk Cad 58 (☎0358/218 1184; ①), and the cheaper *Konfor Palas*, Ziya Paşa Bul 4 (☎0358/218 1260; ①), overlooking the river. The clean *Zümrüt Pansiyon* has a fine location in the heart of the old town, 100m east of the Hazeranlar Konaği, but the rooms are waterless and slightly overpriced (☎0358/218 1769; ②).

At the other end of the price spectrum, there's the *Hotel Maden*, Atatürk Cad 5 (☎0358/218 6050, fax 218 6017; ④), a nice, modern affair with some quiet rooms away from the main road, and the *Büyük Amasya Hotel*, Herkiz Mahallesi, Elmasiye Cad 20 (☎0358/218 4054, fax 218 4056; ④), a soulless two-star place on the north bank of the river (cross via the bridge near Atatürk Square and follow the road round past the *Belediye* park and teahouses).

The best **restaurant** in town is the *Şehir Derneği* in the Öğretmen Evi (House of Teachers), just across the bridge from the main square, accessed from the side. This is actually a local civil service club, but its restaurant seems to be open to whoever wants to try out the exceptionally good food. Also worth trying are the *Ocak Başı Aile Kebap Salonu* and the *Ali Kaya Restoran*, both near the *Konfor Palas Hotel*, or the precooked food of the *Vebbes Restaurant*, Atatürk Cad 22.

Tokat

TOKAT clusters at the foot of a jagged crag with a ruined Pontic fortress on top. Despite its undeniably dramatic setting, it comes as something of an anti-climax after Amasya, with none of the soothing riverside atmosphere and much less to see.

The journey from Amasya takes about an hour and a half, and en route are a couple of ruined **kervansarays**. The first is at **Ezinepazari**; in the days of the great caravans, this place was a day's ride by camel from the town you left half an hour ago. If you have your own transport or are willing to do a bit of hitching, it's worth making a six-kilometre detour to the signposted village of Pazar about 26km short of Tokat. Here you'll find the **Hatun Hanı**, a well-preserved Selçuk *kervansaray* that would have been the next night's stop.

Tokat itself has two main claims to fame and only one of these carries much weight outside Turkey, or indeed outside Tokat. The internationally known one – which is no reason to stop here – is that Julius Caesar uttered the famous words "Veni, vidi, vici" (I came, I saw, I conquered) near the town in 47 BC, after he defeated Pharnaces, son of the Pontic king Mithridates Eupator, who had taken advantage of a period of civil war in Rome to attempt to re-establish the Pontic kingdom as an independent state. The local claim to fame is the **Gök Medrese**, another Selçuk "Blue Seminary", now used as a museum. This is more of a reason to pause, although not necessarily for long. Tokat makes a good stop-off when travelling between Amasya and Sivas (or vice versa) – leave Amasya in the morning, stop off for something to eat and a look round in Tokat, and aim to be in Sivas by late afternoon or early evening (you'll need to check bus times at the *otogar* before setting off into Tokat).

Some history

Tokat first came to prominence as a staging post on the Persian trans-Anatolian royal road, running from Sardis to Persepolis. Later it fell to Alexander the Great and then to Mithridates and his successors. In 47 BC, Julius Caesar extinguished Pontus once and for all in a five-hour battle at Zile, just outside Tokat, prompting his immortal line.

Under Byzantine rule, Tokat became a frontline city in perpetual danger of Arab attack, a state of affairs that continued until the Danişmend Turks took control of the city after the Battle of Manzikert in 1071. Less than one hundred years later the İlhanid Mongols arrived, ushering in a period of war and uncertainty which finally ended in 1392 when the citizens of Tokat, tired of the endless strife, petitioned Sultan Beyazit Yıldırım to be admitted to the Ottoman Empire. Their request was granted and peace returned until the arrival of the second great Mongol wave under Tamerlane. On this occasion the town was sacked but the castle survived a lengthy siege.

With the departure of the Mongols and return of the Ottomans, life returned to normal and a period of prosperity ensued. In time, though, trade patterns shifted, the east–west routes to Persia lost their importance, and Tokat became the backwater it remains today.

The Town

Tokat's **otogar** is a little way outside town on the main road. It takes about fifteen minutes to walk to the centre – head for the roundabout near a bridge flanked by cannon and turn left down Gazi Osman Paşa Bulvarı. On the way you'll pass a couple of distinctive tombs. The Mongol-built **Nurettin Bini Sentimur Türbesi**, with its hat-like pointed roof and Selçuk-influenced portal, is the more interesting; the **Sümbül Baba Türbesi**, further along the street, is a Selçuk work now incorporated into the side of a more recent, crumbling building.

The first real reason to stop is the **Gök Medrese**, a squat, rectangular building with a portal, whose recessed arch resembles a picturesque cluster of stalactites. Built in 1275 by the Selçuk emir Mu'in al-Din Süleyman (also known as Pervane or "Butterfly", an epithet given to advisors of the Selçuk sultans), the *medrese* was named for the turquoise tiles that once covered its entire exterior. Most of these have unfortunately vanished but a few still manage to remain tenaciously gripping the walls of the inner courtyard.

Today the Gök Medrese is home to the town's **museum** (Tues–Sun 8.30am–noon & 1–5pm; $1), a repository for local archeological finds and various unusual relics collected from the churches which served the town's sizeable Greek and Armenian communities before World War I. Typical of these is a wax effigy of Christina, a Christian martyred during the rule of the Roman emperor Diocletian. The ethnographic section features examples of local *yazma*-making – printing on cloth by means of wooden blocks to produce colourful patterned handkerchiefs, scarves and tablecloths.

Keep walking down Gazi Osman Paşa Bulvarı past the *Belediye Oteli* and you'll come to the **Taş Han**, originally called the Voyvoda Han, built in 1631 by Armenian merchants. A large, rectangular building of two storeys, it houses a collection of shabby shops centred around a weed-infested courtyard. On the other side of the street is a market area, and on the street behind is the **Hatuniye Camii**, an impressive Ottoman mosque with an adjoining *medrese*, built in 1485 during the reign of Sultan Beyazit II.

Pressing on straight down the main street eventually brings you to busy **Cumhuriyet Alanı**, the town's central square, location of the **PTT** and an underground shopping mall. More interesting is the venerable **Ali Paşa Hamamı** on the left-hand side with its distinctive nipple-like domes studded with coloured glass. Opposite the hamam on the square itself stands the black-domed **Ali Paşa Camii**, with the *türbe* of its founder in the garden.

A number of Ottoman-era half-timbered houses survive in the side streets of Tokat, though most are in states of advanced decrepitude; one exception is the **Madimağın Celal'ın Evi** just east of the Ali Paşa Hamamı, with a lavishly decorated interior that includes unusual painted panels featuring floral motifs and views of İstanbul. Sadly it's not open to the public. A more accessible example is the **Latifoğlu Konağı** (Tues–Sun 9am–noon & 1.30–5pm; $0.50) on Gazi Osman Paşa Bulvarı, a couple of hundred metres past Cumhuriyet Alanı, which has been turned into a museum. Heavily restored, it stands out a mile from the surrounding modern buildings with its plain white walls, brown-stained woodwork and low-pitched roof. The interior is opulent almost to the point of tastelessness, but gives a good impression of how a wealthy nineteenth-century family would have lived. High points are the **Pasha's Room** upstairs, with its exquisitely carved ceiling and elaborately decorated fireplace, and the **Women's Room** with garish floral motifs on the walls and windows incorporating Star of David designs.

Tokat's **kale**, dominating the town from its jagged eminence northwest of Cumhuriyet Alanı, was originally a Pontic fortress (although its original construction date is unknown) and was later used by the Selçuks and Ottomans who added to the existing defences. It's fairly inaccessible though you might be able to find a way up to the top if you want to view the town from on high. The surviving walls enclose only rubble.

Practicalities

The best source of information is the locally run **tourist office** (summer daily 8.30am–6pm; ☎0356/214 8252) in the Taş Han; if you have trouble finding it ask for "Taş Han Turizim Sitesi". In theory, there's also a government-run office in the *Vilâyet* building on Cumhuriyet Alanı, but as they'll only direct you to the Taş Han, there's little point in going there.

Finding a **place to stay** should present few problems. The best budget option is the new, friendly, modern and clean *Hotel Çağri*, Gazi Osman Paşa Bul 92 (☎0356/212 1028; ①), which offers a spread of rooms with or without shower. On either side of the *Çağri* lie the run-down *Taç* (☎0356/214 1331; ①) and the wildly variable doubles and depressing single rooms of the *Çamlica* at no. 92 (☎0356/214 1269; ②). Moving upmarket slightly you'll find the *Plevne Otel* across the road at Gazi Osman Paşa Bul 83 (☎0356/214 2207; ②), though a better choice for the same money is the *Hotel Gündüz* (☎0356/214 1278; ②), a few minutes' walk north at Gazi Osman Paşa 200, with well-furnished, spacious rooms and a nice restaurant. The old-fashioned *Turist Otel* is central enough at Cumhuriyet Alanı 10 (☎0356/214 1610; ②), but the faded decor has seen grander days. Best value in the moderate range is the two-star *Hotel Burcu*, Gazi Osman Paşa Bul 48 (☎0356/212 8494, fax 212 7891; ③), whose comfortable, nicely furnished rooms and clean bathrooms are set off from the main street a couple of hundred metres south of the square. For four-star semi-luxury you must head a couple of kilometres northwest of the town centre to the *Büyük Tokat Oteli* (☎0356/228 1661, fax 228 1660; ④), site of the **THY office**. The hotel's impressive reception hides less impressive rooms but a swimming pool goes some way to compensate.

There are cheap **places to eat** on virtually every street in town. If the weather's good head for the *Park Restaurant*, in the park next to the *Belediye* building on Cumhuriyet Alanı. Also recommended are the *Belediye Lokantası* on the ground floor of the hotel of the same name, and the *Sofra Restaurant*, Gazi Osman Paşa Bul 8 (just south of Cumhuriyet Alanı). A local speciality is *Tokat kebap*, a mouth-watering and very filling combination of roast lamb, potatoes, aubergine, tomato and peppers; portions tend to be gargantuan.

Sivas

At first sight **SİVAS** is grim, even intimidating. Both main arrival points, the **otogar** and **train station**, are located well outside the town centre and surrounded by new concrete blocks. Indeed this city of 200,000 people wouldn't figure on anybody's itinerary were it not for a concentration of Selçuk buildings – among the finest in Turkey – conveniently located in a town centre park.

Sivas has been settled since Hittite times and according to local sources was later a key centre of the **Sivas Frig Empire** (1200 BC), an unfortunately named realm which seems to have been consigned to historical oblivion. With more certainty it can be said that under the Romans Sivas was known as Megalopolis and then Sebastaea, which in later years was corrupted to Sivas.

The town's real flowering came during Selçuk times, after the Battle of Manzikert, and ample architectural evidence of this remains. Sivas intermittently served as the **Selçuk capital** during the Sultanate of Rum, before passing into the hands of İlhanid Mongols during the late thirteenth century. The Ottomans took over in 1396 only to be ousted by the Mongols four years later under Tamerlane, who razed much of the city after an eighteen-day siege and put its Christian inhabitants to the sword. The Ottomans returned in 1408 and Sivas pretty much faded out of history until the twentieth century.

On September 4, 1919, the **Congress of Sivas** was convened here when Atatürk arrived from Amasya, on his mission to rally resistance against Allied attempts to carve up the Ottoman Empire. Delegates from all over the country came to Sivas, and the congress was a milestone on the way to establishing modern republican Turkey.

The Town

The centre of Sivas is **Konak Meydanı**, location of the main municipal buildings and **PTT**. You'll find a good strip of reasonably priced, but not always reasonably appointed, hotels on Atatürk Caddesi, which runs southeast out of town past the old **otogar** to hit the main Ankara–Erzurum road, and the new **long-distance bus station**. Unfortunately there's no dolmuş service between either old or new *otogar* and Konak Meydanı so you end up having to take a taxi which will set you back about $2 and $5 respectively; on long-distance routes your bus company may well lay on a *servis* minibus from the new otogar to the centre of town. You're better catered for if you arrive by train, as buses run down İstasiyon Caddesi (İnönü Bulvarı) from the **train station** to Konak Meydanı.

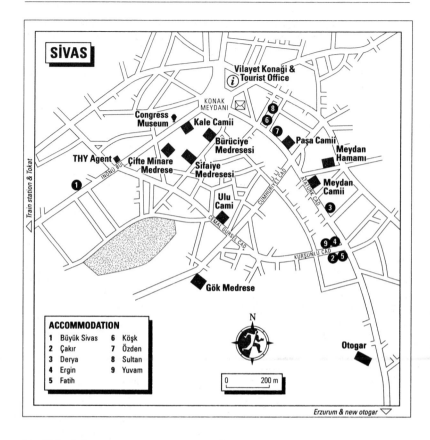

The Selçuk legacy

Most of Sivas's Selçuk monuments were built during the Sultanate of Rum and in the period of Mongol suzerainty that followed under the İlhanids. With their highly decorative facades and elaborately carved portals, the buildings epitomize Selçuk architectural styles, and nearly all are conveniently grouped together in and around a small park just off Konak Meydanı.

Closest to the *meydan* is the **Bürüciye Medresesi**, founded in 1271 by the İlhanid emir Muzaffer Bürücirdi. The building consists of a series of square rooms laid out to a symmetrical ground plan around a central courtyard. Passing through the entrance the *türbe* of the emir and his children is to the left. The *medrese* ostensibly houses an archeological collection, which in fact consists of three lonely pieces of stonework; more worthy of attention are the carpet sellers, who hang their wares from the walls, a small bookshop and a café that's spilled out into the open. Nearby is the **Kale Camii**, an oddity in this area as it's a straightforward Ottoman mosque, built in 1580 at the behest of Mahmut Paşa, a grand vizier of Sultan Murat III.

South of here is the stunning **Çifte Minare Medrese** (Twin Minaret Seminary), also built in 1271. The facade alone survives, adorned with tightly curled relief filigrees, topped by two brick minarets which are adorned here and there with pale blue tiles.

Behind, only the well-defined foundations of student cells and lecture halls survive. Directly opposite is the **Şifaiye Medresesi** (1217), a hospital and medical school built on the orders of the Selçuk sultan Keykâvus I. Inside are a bazaar, selling everything from kilims to hats, and a delightful tea garden bedecked in traditional rugs and kilims. Easily overlooked amid all the commercial activity is the tomb of Keykâvus to the right of the entrance. A number of glazed tiles with eight-pointed star motifs cling to the brickwork and the sarcophagi within are also tiled. In its heyday, the Şifaiye Medresesi was a centre for the treatment of psychological disorders and apparently music therapy and hypnosis were among the healing techniques employed.

The rest of the town's Selçuk monuments are outside the park. If you turn on to Cemal Gürsel Caddesi (just south of the park), you'll find the **Ulu Cami**, the oldest mosque in Sivas, built in 1197. This is a low, unattractive building, topped by an ugly corrugated-iron roof punctuated with equally ugly chimneys; but if you step inside the northern entrance you will enter the subterranean cool of a hypostyle mosque, supported by fifty wooden pillars, and a peaceful silence broken only by the murmur of boys reading from the Koran.

A right turn from Gürsel Caddesi will take you onto Cumhuriyet Caddesi where, on the left after a couple of hundred metres, you'll find the **Gök Medrese**, with its ornate tile-studded minarets. This could well be the most attractive "Blue Seminary" you've yet seen, particularly if you catch it during the afternoon when the absence of shadows reveals at their best the brickwork, carving (tree of life and star symbols are recurring motifs) and tiles which embellish its stunning facade. It was built in 1271 by the Selçuk grand vizier Sahip Ata Fahrettin Ali, who was also responsible for buildings in Kayseri and Konya. Until 1969 the building served as a museum, but recent restoration work has turned the *medrese* into a mess and hidden away the *mescit* (prayer chapel) and two *eyvan*s (three-sided niche-like rooms), which have some beautiful mosaic work.

Other monuments in Sivas

Sivas has a few other things you may want to investigate if you have time, though there's no need to feel too guilty if you neglect them. Just southwest of Konak Meydanı is the **Sivas Congress Museum** (Tues–Sun 8.30am–5pm; $0.50), with lots of Turkish-captioned photographs and documents commemorating the Sivas Congress. Heading east from Konak Meydanı brings you to the **Paşa Camii**, a big, yellow Ottoman pile which seems to have been squeezed into a space far too small for it by the encroachments of modern urban development. Further along Atatürk Caddesi, set below the street and reached by a flight of steps, is the **Meydan Camii**, built in 1554 but looking much older thanks to its austere and angular style of construction. Nearby, up a side street leading off Atatürk Caddesi, stands the **Meydan Hamamı**, which has been hissing and steaming for over four centuries and is still going strong.

Practicalities

The local **tourist office** is housed in the Vilayet Konaği, on the north side of Konak Meydanı (Mon–Fri 9am–5pm; ☎0346/221 3535) – go in and throw the German-speaking staff into panic by asking for some information. Sivas has a small **airport** with flights to Ankara every Wednesday and Friday. For more information enquire at the *THY* agent *Sivas Seyahat*, İstasyon Cad 50 Yıl Sıtesi 7–8, off İnönü Bulevar (☎0346/224 4624). An airport bus, costing $1, departs from outside the office about two hours before departure.

Hotels are plentiful but unfortunately most are pretty dismal. The *Hotel Koşk*, Atatürk Cad 7 (☎0346/221 1150; ③), just under 200m east of Konak Meydanı, is one of the more comfortable options. Cheaper alternatives in the centre include the gloomy

Otel Özden, Atatürk Cad 21 (☎0346/221 1254; ①), and the *Hotel Sultan*, just off the main road on Eski Belediye Sok 18 (☎0346/221 2986; ①), where prices include breakfast. The best rock-bottom option is the basic but acceptable *Otel Ergin*, Atatürk Cad 80 (☎0346/221 2301; ①), approximately 1km southeast of the main square; for a hot shower get the key off reception. If this is full try the similar *Yuvam Oteli* next door (☎0346/221 3349; ①). If these are too basic for you cross the road to the *Otel Fatih* at Kurşunlu Cad 15 (☎0346/223 4313; ②), where rooms come with television and shower. The *Çakır* next door is nicer still (②). Slightly closer to the centre is the friendly but basic *Otel Derya* (☎0346/221 3335; ①), with small rooms and shared bathrooms. The best hotel in town is the new four-star *Büyük Sivas Oteli* on İstasyon Caddesi (İnönü Bul), a few hundred metres west of Konak Meydanı (☎0346/225 4762, fax 225 2323; ④).

Finding a **place to eat** presents few problems. There are many cheap kebab places lining the road behind the PTT. The *Şehir Lokantaşi*, just around the corner from the Meydan Camii, does good, cheap *pide* and kebabs. For slightly classier atmosphere and marginally higher prices head for the *Cumhuriyet Lokantaşi* on Atatürk Caddesi near the *Hotel Köşk*. Sivas also has plenty of good sweet and pastry shops: try the *Seyidoğlu Baklava ve Pasta Salonu* on Atatürk Caddesi, opposite the Meydan Camii.

Kangal

The journey south from Sivas is fairly uneventful, although the further south you travel the more hilly and denuded the landscape becomes. Most Malatya-bound dolmuşes call at **KANGAL**, an inauspicious-looking, one-horse town, famous for its breed of ferocious sheep dogs which terrorize travellers the length and breadth of Eastern Turkey. There's nothing you'd want to see in Kangal itself, but from here you can pick up dolmuşes to a number of **thermal bath** establishments in the area. The **Balıklı Çermik** (13km from Kangal), in particular, has become a place of pilgrimage for sufferers of psoriasis and other skin ailments. Small fish eat away the affected skin as you wallow in outdoor pools. For people wanting to take the cure, the *Kaplıca Oteli* in Kangal (②) is the least pricy local accommodation possibility. There are also **camping** facilities in this area: check current details with the Sivas tourist office.

travel details

Buses

Amasya to: Ankara (hourly; 6hr); İstanbul (12 daily; 12hr); Kayseri (3 daily; 8hr); Malatya (5 daily; 9hr); Samsun (10 daily; 3hr); Sivas (6 daily; 4hr); Tokat (9 daily; 2hr).

Ankara to: Adana (12 daily; 10hr); Adiyaman (hourly;13hr); Amasya (hourly; 6hr); Antalya (12 daily; 10hr); Bodrum (10 daily; 12hr); Bursa (hourly; 7hr); Diyarbakır (5 daily; 13hr); Erzurum (4 daily; 15hr); Eskişehir (4 daily; 6hr); Gaziantep (12 daily; 12hr); İstanbul (every 30min; 8hr); İzmir (hourly; 9hr); Karabük (6 daily; 5hr); Kastamonu (3 daily; 5hr); Kayseri (14 daily; 5hr); Konya (14 daily; 3hr 30min); Kütahya (5 daily; 7hr); Mardin (3 daily; 16hr); Nevşehir (12 daily; 4hr 30min); Polatli (every half-hour; 1hr); Safranbolu (9 daily; 5hr); Samsun (10 daily; 8hr); Sivas (hourly; 8hr); Sungurlu (hourly; 3hr); Şanlıurfa (4 daily; 15hr); Trabzon (4 daily; 12 hr).

Eskişehir to: Ankara (4 daily; 6hr); Bursa (6 daily; 1hr); İstanbul (4 daily; 4hr); Kütahya (12 daily; 1hr).

Kastamonu to: Ankara (3 daily; 5hr); İnebolu (6 daily; 2hr); Safranbolu (hourly; 4hr); Samsun (3 daily; 6hr).

Kütahya to: Afyon (14 daily; 1hr 45min); Antalya (3 daily; 5hr); Balikeşir (4 daily; 5hr); Bursa (12 daily; 3hr); Eskişehir (10 daily; 1hr); İstanbul (14 daily; 6hr); İzmir (12 daily; 6hr); Uşak (5 daily; 1hr 15min).

Sivas to: Amasya (4 daily; 4hr); Ankara (12 daily; 8hr); Diviği (1 daily; 3hr); Diyarbakır (4 daily; 10hr); Erzurum (3 daily; 9hr); Malatya (3 daily; 5hr); Tokat (10 daily; 2hr).

Tokat to: Amasya (12 daily; 2hr); Ankara (12 daily; 8hr); Erzurum (1 daily; 11hr); Sivas (10 daily; 2hr).

Trains

Ankara to: Adana – *Çukurova Ekspressi* dep 8.10pm, arr 8am; İstanbul – *Boğazici Ekspressi* dep 6.15am, arr 2.40pm; *Başkent Ekspressi* dep 11.55am, arr 7.15pm; *Mavi Tren* dep 1pm, arr 9.20pm; *Anadolou Ekspressi* dep 10pm, arr 7.18am; *Ankara Ekspressi* dep 10.30pm, arr 7.35am; *Fatih Ekspressi* dep 11.30pm, arr 7.10am; İzmir – *İzmir Ekspressi* dep 6pm, arr 8.45am; *Mavi Tren* dep 9.15pm, arr 8.50am; Sivas, Erzurum & Kars – *Doğu Ekspressi* dep 10.40am, arr 5.55pm;

Sivas, Malatya & Diyarbakır (Mon, Wed, Fri, Sat) – *Güney Ekspressi* dep 6.50am, arr 1.20pm; Van (Tues, Thurs, Sun) – *Vangölu Ekspressi* dep 6.50am, arr 1.45pm; Zongulak – *Karaelmas Ekspressi* dep 8.10am, arr 8.25pm.

Sivas to: Diviği (daily, dep 5.55pm); Diyarbakır – *Güney Ekspressi* (4 weekly, dep 8pm); Erzurum – *Doğu Ekspressi* (daily, dep midnight); Samsun (8 weekly, dep either at 8.30am or 7.15pm).

Flights

Ankara to: Adana (daily; 1hr); Antalya (daily; 1hr); Diyarbakır (2 daily; 1hr 30min); Erzurum (daily; 1hr 45min); Gaziantep (1 daily; 1hr); İstanbul (14 daily; 1hr); İzmir (3 daily; 1hr 30min); Kars (daily; 1hr 40min); Malatya (daily; 1hr 40min); Sivas (2 weekly; 45min); Şanliurfa (5 weekly; 1hr 30min); Trabzon (daily; 1hr); Van (2 daily; 2hr).

Sivas to: Ankara (2 weekly; 1hr).

CHAPTER NINE

THE BLACK SEA COAST

E xtending from just east of İstanbul to the frontier with Georgia, the **Black Sea region** of Turkey is an anomaly, guaranteed to smash all stereotypes previously held about the country. The combined action of damp northerly and westerly winds and an almost uninterrupted wall of mountains south of the shore has resulted in a relentlessly rainy and riotously green realm, not unlike North America's, or Spain's, northwest coast. The peaks force the clouds to disgorge themselves on the ocean side of the watershed, leaving central Anatolia beyond the passes in a permanent rain shadow.

The Black Sea climate and resulting short summer season means there is little foreign tourism, and no overseas charters or package operators serve the area – but when the semitropical heat is on in July and August, you'll certainly want to swim. The sea is as peculiar as the weather: fed huge volumes of fresh water by the Don, Dnieper and Danube rivers to the north, and diminished not by evaporation but by strong currents through the Bosphorus and the Dardanelles, its upper layer is of such low salinity that you can almost drink it; however, you'd be ill-advised to do so, as in recent decades the Black Sea has been blighted by pollution – much of it carried down the Danube from as far afield as Germany and Austria. Each year huge quantities of phosphates and around 50,000 tonnes of oil are discharged into its waters. All of this has had a predictably devastating effect on the region's aquatic life. Attempts to formulate a coherent and effective environmental policy for the region are being hampered by the sheer number of countries involved, and chaotic conditions in the former Soviet Union.

The coastal ranges, beginning as mere humps north of Ankara but attaining world-class grandeur by the time the former Soviet border is reached, have always served to keep the region isolated as well as damp. Until recently they made land access all but impossible, and provided redoubts for a crazy quilt of tribes and ethnic subgroups. Many of these are still there, making the Black Sea one of Turkey's most anthropologically interesting regions.

Travelling around the region consists in large part of soaking up the atmosphere – you rarely need worry about missing important sights, as there really aren't many. A particularly relaxing, not to say stylish way of touring the coast is to take the *Turkish*

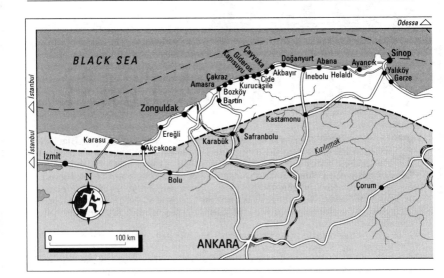

Maritime Lines' **ferry boat**, which cruises from İstanbul to Rize and back in a week, between mid-April and mid-September, calling in at Sinop, Samsun, Giresun and Trabzon on the way (see "Travel details" at the end of the chapter). The Black Sea region divides neatly into western and eastern halves, with the west comparatively lacking in character. Everything between the coal-mining town of **Zonguldak** and İstanbul is essentially a beach suburb of the latter. Between Zonguldak and **Samsun**, the largest and most featureless city of the region, only the Byzantine-Genoese harbour of **Amasra** and the historic, evocatively located town of **Sinop** reward a special trip. The **beaches** between Amasra and Sinop are admittedly magnificent, but the road on this stretch is substandard, with poor bus and dolmuş links, and travelling by car, or even cycle-touring (as long as you've plenty of stamina), is likely to be more rewarding than bus rides.

East of Samsun the prospects improve along with the road; buses emerge from their inland detours, and good **beaches** continue to crop up between potentially pleasant stop-overs in the old mercantile towns of **Ünye**, **Giresun** or **Tirebolu**. Beyond **Trabzon** (Trebizond) – along with the nearby **monastery of Sumela**, the only established tourist destination on the Black Sea – beaches diminish as the scenery inland gets more imposing. Other than the **Hemşin valleys**, though, there are few specific destinations to point to.

Some history

With much trepidation, the ancient Greeks ventured onto the Pontos Euxine (as they called the Black Sea) at the start of the first millennium BC, tilting with the local "barbarians" and occasionally – as in the semi-legendary tale of Jason and the Argonauts – getting the best of them. Between the seventh and fourth centuries numerous colonies of the Aegean cities were founded at the seaward ends of the trade routes through the Pontic mountains; these became the ancestors of virtually every modern Black Sea town. The region had its first brief appearance on the world stage when one of the home-grown Pontic kings, **Mithridates IV Eupator**, came within a whisker of expelling the Romans from Anatolia. Even after the suppression of the several

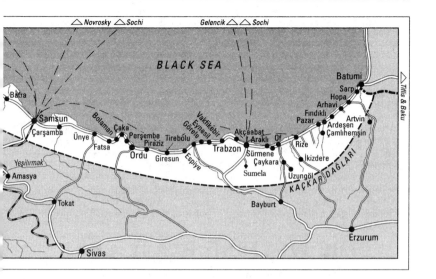

Mithridatic rebellions, the Romans concentrated on the western portion of the Black Sea and its hinterland, leaving the portion from Trabzon east in the hands of vassals. This, and the climate's heavy toll on all but the stoutest structures, accounts in part for the near absence of ancient ruins here.

With the arrival of Christianity, relations between natives and imperial overlords hardly changed at all. Only the Byzantine urban centres by the sea became thoroughly Hellenized, while subjects with grievances embroiled the Byzantine Empire in continual wars by appealing for aid to the neigbouring Armenian and Persian empires. The Byzantine defeat at Manzikert in 1071 initially meant little to the Black Sea, safe behind its wall of mountains; the fall of Constantinople to the Fourth Crusade in 1204 had far greater immediate effects, prompting the Black Sea's second spell of historical prominence. The empire-in-exile of the Comneni dynasty, centred around **Trebizond** (today's Trabzon), exercised influence grossly disproportionate to its size for two-and-a-half cultured (and ultimately decadent) centuries.

After Manzikert, Turkish chieftains had in fact begun to encroach on the coast, especially at the gap in the barrier ranges near Sinop and Samsun; the Trapezuntine dynasty even concluded alliances with them, doubtless to act as a counter to the power of the Genoese and Venetians who also set up shop hereabouts. Most of this factionalism was put to an end under the **Ottomans**, though even they entrusted semi-autonomous administration of the Pontic foothills to feudal *derebeys* (valley lords) until the early nineteenth century. This delegation of authority, and the fact that the usual replacement of Christian populations by Muslims took place only in the vicinity of Trabzon, meant that the region remained remarkably poor in Ottoman monuments – and that until early this century many towns were almost half Greek or Armenian.

This equilibrium was upset when the Black Sea entered the history books for the third time as a theatre of war between imperial Turkey and Russia. The two clashed four times between 1828 and 1915, with the Czarist regime giving active aid and comfort to various separatist movements in the area after 1877. Between 1918 and 1922, Greeks attempting to create a Pontic state fought it out with guerrillas loyal to Atatürk's Nationalists; with the victory of **the Republic** the Greek merchant class was expelled along with the rest of Turkey's Greek Orthodox population, and the Black Sea went into temporary economic eclipse, verging on famine during the 1930s.

Most of the credit for the recent **recovery** must go to the *hamsi*s, as the locals are nicknamed after the Black Sea anchovy caught in large numbers during winter. Enterprising, voluble and occasionally scandalous, they have set up mafias in the shipping, property and construction industries throughout the country, much of it funded by remittances from industrious *hamsi*s overseas.

All the above goes some way towards explaining why most Black Sea towns are so hideous. In the old days the shore was the province of Christian businessmen, who were largely responsible for what little attractive architecture has survived war and development. The norm for inland villages was, and is, scattered dwellings connected only tenuously to a single store and mosque; the idiosyncratic and independently minded hill people were freed of any constraint to cluster by abundant water and arable fields. In short, there was little indigenous tradition of town planning, so when the boom hit, concrete blight was the result as everyone did as they pleased. The reopening of the former Soviet border – which seems set to end the region's backwater status – may eventually trigger a new spasm of urbanization and a possible widening of the coast highway.

THE WESTERN BLACK SEA

The coast from Samsun west to Zonguldak is perhaps the least visited of the entire Turkish shoreline. This neglect is a joint result of poor communications and the relative lack of tourist facilities and specific attractions. While it's true that there's no pressing reason to make a special detour here, it's well worth fitting in some of this stretch if you're heading overland to the eastern Black Sea.

Samsun makes a dreary and discouraging gateway to the region, but matters improve as you head northwest to **Sinop**, a more interesting place than any other Black Sea town except Trabzon. Beyond Sinop the coast road west is tortuous and slow, but spectacular scenery, scattered, unspoiled beaches and small ports do something to compensate. The only place that gets much custom is **Amasra**, an old medieval stronghold at the western end of this beautiful stretch. **Zonguldak** has little to detain you, and with its good transport connections is of most use to travellers as an alternative entry and exit point to the region.

As a rule the **beaches** are cleaner and the weather drier along this section of the Black Sea than further east; figs and olives are seen, attesting to the mild climate, and if you just want to laze on the sand without any other stimulation, then you'll find plen-

---

BLACK SEA BUSINESS TRAVELLERS

Since the collapse of the Soviet Union and the opening of Turkey's eastern border, large numbers of Caucasians and Russians now regularly visit the region. Every town of any size has its *Rus Pazar* (Russian Bazaar), where traders sell everything from cigarettes to car parts and ceramics, raising hard currency to buy clothing and leather goods for later resale back home. Convoys of battered buses and arthritic cars stream along Black Sea roads heading to and from these symbols of long-severed trade routes in revival. Markets in larger cities are well-organized affairs overseen by the *Belediye Zabitasi* or market police but in smaller towns they resemble roadside car boot sales. An equally important aspect of cross-border economic activity has been a boom in prostitution with so-called *Natashas* plying their trade in many local hotels. This can cause problems for women travellers in the region as local men tend to assume all foreign women are here on "business". To minimize the likelihood of hassle try to check out which hotels are currently okay with local tourist offices where possible.

ty of opportunity. Sparse **bus** and **dolmuş** schedules are the only drawbacks; check frequencies to avoid getting stranded, or avoid them altogether with your own four- or two-wheeled transport.

Samsun

Despite a long and turbulent history – or perhaps because of it – **SAMSUN** has absolutely no remaining historical or scenic attractions, and you won't want to stay here longer than it takes to pass through. It's a thoroughly modern city of 250,000 people, laid out on a grid plan, and the centre of Turkey's tobacco industry; most of the locals work directly or indirectly for the state-run *Tekel* ("monopoly") cigarette factory.

For the record, Samsun – like several of its neighbours – began life as a colony of Miletus in the seventh century BC. Because of its strategic location, the place changed hands frequently over the centuries; besieged, captured (and usually sacked) by the Pontic kings, Romans, Byzantines and several tribes of Turks. The final insult came in 1425, when the Genoese – who had a major trading station here – torched the town rather than hand it over to Ottoman control.

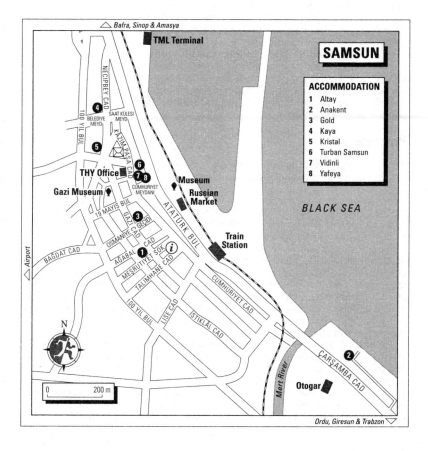

With the advent of the railway, which facilitated the transport of tobacco to Ankara and beyond, Samsun's flagging fortunes revived, and by 1910 it was a thriving city of 40,000 inhabitants. Atatürk's arrival here on May 19, 1919, after fleeing İstanbul, further boosted the town's prominence, and can be said to have marked the start of the war of independence. Rather than disbanding the groups of Turkish guerrillas who had been attacking Greeks in the area, as he had been ordered to do, he began organizing them into a cohesive national resistance army.

Today, Samsun is a busy port and centre for the processing of local agricultural produce, where any spare time you have is likely to weigh heavy on your hands. At the town centre lies **Cumhuriyet Meydanı**, with a statue of Atatürk on horseback and some wilting foliage, beneath which you'll find an uninspiring undergound shopping arcade. The rest of the town is largely concrete, though there are a couple of unremarkable fourteenth-century mosques, Hacı Hatun Camii and Pazar Camii.

Well labelled in English, the **Archeological Museum** next to the harbour off Atatürk Bulvarı (daily 8am–noon & 1.30–5.30pm; $1) is probably the best place to fill time. The main exhibit is a **Roman mosaic** found in Karasamsun, site of the ancient acropolis (now a military area), jutting out to sea 3km to the west of Samsun. Thought to have been repaired by the Byzantines, the mosaic is almost complete, and depicts the four seasons, and a struggle between Triton and Nereids; it's not well lit, but you can approach fairly closely to examine it. Other finds are from an early Bronze Age settlement, İkiztepe, 55km northwest of Samsun, including a skull that bears witness to the performance of cranial surgery there in the third millennium BC.

Next door, the **Atatürk Museum** (same opening hours; $1) has a large collection of weapons, clothes and photographs of Turkey's most famous citizen. The **Gazi Museum** on İstiklâl Cad (Tues–Sun 9am–5pm; free) is the former *Mintika Hotel*, where Atatürk stayed on his visit to the city in May 1919. Now a second museum to Atatürk's memory, his bedroom, study, and the hotel's conference room have all been preserved as he left them.

Practicalities

Samsun's **tourist information office** (daily 8am–noon & 1.30–5.30pm; ☎0362/431 2988), is hardly prominent at Talimhane Sok, off Cumhuriyet Cad, but the staff seem happy with the resultant anonymity. The **otogar** lies 2km east of the city centre on the main road out of town, the **train station** halfway towards the centre; buses #2 and #10, as well as dolmuşes marked "Garaj", link both with Cumhuriyet Meydanı, the town's hub. Tourists unable to get seats to Trabzon often fly in; the **airport** is 8km out of town, on the road to Amasya, linked to the town centre by a service bus ($0.20).

For a town with so little to see or do, Samsun has a great deal to offer in terms of food and lodgings. The number of **hotels** is a result of the tobacco trade rather than either tourism or prostitution, and Samsun's hoteliers go to some lengths to keep their town "respectable", so if you're in a couple, don't be surprised if you're grilled on your marital status before being given your room key. You may not be able to get a room without an advance booking in July, when Samsun hosts an international trade fair lasting the whole month, and possibly during the national folk dance festival in the last week of March.

The best-value hotel in Samsun is the *Anakent Sosyal Tesisleri* (☎0362/228 1470; ③), reached on foot by crossing Atatürk Bulvarı from the *otogar* (in your own vehicle go past the *otogar* as if to go out of town and at the first roundabout turn back towards the centre on a small unmarked road on the shoreside of the main road). The welcoming hotel, set well back from the main road, with restaurant, tennis courts and fancy lighting, looks more expensive than it is: it's owned and run by the local *belediye* who control the prices. Rooms are quiet and comfortable, most overlooking the sea, with balconies and good en-suite bathrooms. More central mid-range alternatives are the new, very comfortable *Otel Kaya* at Şeyhhamza Sok 9 (☎0362/432 4664; ④), where centrally heated, well-furnished rooms (with minibars and TVs) are heading for two-star status and possibly a price-hike; the *Gold Hotel*, Osmaniye Geçidi, off Cumhuriyet Cad (☎0362/431 1959; ③), with small, acceptable rooms but unpleasant staff; and the *Kristal Otel*, Gaziler Meydanı, Hastane Sok 5 (☎0362/431 1713; ③), where small rooms, some with en-suite bathrooms, are basically furnished. Budget options include the *Altay*, Meşrutiyet Sok 5 (☎0362/431 6877; ①), a friendly place with fairly comfortable, clean rooms and hot showers down the corridor.

Going **upmarket**, the *Otel Yafeya* on Cumhuriyet Meydanı (☎0362/315 1132; ④) has large, comfortable rooms, but the nearby three-star *Vidinli Hotel* (☎0362/431 6050; ④) has the edge if you're after luxury extras, offering satellite TV, a restaurant and a terrace bar. The town even has a four-star option, the *Turban Samsun Oteli* on Atatürk Bulvarı (☎0362/435 8079; ⑥), with outdoor pool and "American" bar, though relatively mediocre rooms.

For **food and drink** head for the area around Saat Külesi Meydanı, the clocktower square, where there are a number of reasonably priced possibilities. The *Oskar Restaurant* near the *belediye* building on Belediye Meydanı is highly recommended for surroundings, service, and food – *meze*, a variety of meat and fish dishes, and sweets to follow. On Saat Külesi Meydanı, the *Vivana Lokantası* serves *pide* and *İskender kebap* at reasonable prices; the *Cumhuriyet Restaurant*, next to the *Vivana* at Şeyhhamza Sok 3, has a very good reputation locally for fish, meat and *meze*.

To complete Samsun's list of amenities, the **THY** office is at Kâzım Paşa Cad 11/A (☎0362/431 5065), with flights to İstanbul and İzmir, and a service bus to the airport ($0.20). There are a few local **car rental** outlets, including *Yaşar*, at Lise Cad 24/B (☎0362/233 3288), and *Yavuztur Travel*, İstiklâl Cad 112 (☎ and fax 0362/233 9614), who also run trekking and birdwatching tours in the area. The **TML agency** is down at the harbour, Denizcilik Koll Şti 19 (☎0362/431 4614 or 445 1605). *Karden*, who run twice-weekly **catamarans to Sochi** in Russia (7hr; $55 one-way), also have offices by the harbour (☎0362/432 2387, fax 432 2382). *Cosmos Ro-Ro* (☎0362/445 2531) run ferries to Odessa in the Ukraine and to Novrosky in Russia, but they're primarily for lorry drivers (they don't take foot passengers) and expensive, at $400 one-way per vehicle to Odessa, $300 one-way to Novrosky. You'll need a visa, obtained from your own country, to board any of these.

Sinop

Most tourists will choose to leave Samsun as soon as possible: heading west, the coast road cuts inland through extensive tobacco fields and the market town of **BAFRA**, in the middle of the Kızılırmak delta, which can offer a reasonably priced and comfortable hotel, the *Mis* (☎0362/543 7350; ③), and cheap restaurants in the town centre. The road returns to the sea, passing some stunning sandy beaches and pastoral scenery a few kilometres before **GERZE**, a pretty village with many handsome old buildings in reasonable state of repair. Its handful of hotels – pick of them the *Ermiş* (③) overlooking the harbour – and eateries are flanked by stony, not too crowded beaches. In the third week of July, the Gerze Festival of Culture and Arts is a mass circumcision of local boys, who are distracted by international folk groups, the nomination of a local beauty queen and round-the-clock festivities. Outside of festival time, most people will press straight on to Sinop, 26km further west.

Blessed with the finest natural harbour on the Black Sea, **SİNOP** straddles an isthmus at the foot of an exposed headland. For once the town does some justice to a fine setting, with a clutch of monuments bestowing a real authority on the place. The port,

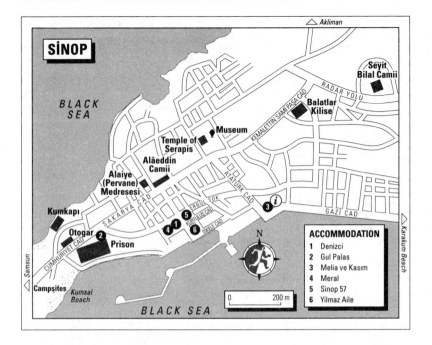

long outstripped by the those of Samsun, Trabzon and Zonguldak, is now dominated by fishing, which along with tourism provides most of the local income. Until recently this was the location of a NATO listening post: the Sinop peninsula is just about the northernmost point of Anatolia, less than 200 nautical miles from the Crimea, and this formerly US-run base played a front-line role in the Cold War.

Sinop takes its name from the mythical **Sinope**, an Amazon queen and daughter of a minor river god. She attracted the attention of Zeus, who promised her anything she desired in return for her favours. Her request was for eternal virginity; Zeus played the gentleman and complied.

The site's natural endowments prompted Bronze Age settlement long before the city was founded as an Ionian colony during the eighth century BC. The first famous native son was **Diogenes the Cynic**: Alexander the Great is said to have visited the barrel in which he lived and been sufficiently impressed to claim, "If I were not Alexander, I would rather be Diogenes". (He had earlier asked if there was anything he could do for Diogenes, to which the cynic replied, "Yes, stand aside, you're blocking my light").

In 183 BC the indigenous Pontic kings made Sinop one of their main cities, and later that century Mithridates Eupator, the terror of the Roman republic, was born here. After making the city his capital, he adorned it with splendid monuments, but of these, and of the Roman structures built after the general Lucullus captured the place in 63 BC, virtually no trace remains.

Sinop declined during the Byzantine period, and sixth- and seventh-century attempts to revive the town's fortunes were thwarted by Persian and Arab raids. The Selçuks took the town in October 1214, converting a number of churches into mosques and erecting a *medrese*, but after the Mongols smashed the short-lived Selçuk state, Sinop passed into the hands of the İsfendiyaroğlu emirs of Kastamonu until Ottoman annexation in 1458. Thereafter the town was rarely heard of, except on November 30, 1853, when the Russians destroyed both Sinop and an Ottoman fleet anchored here, thus triggering the Crimean War, and again on May 18, 1919, when Atatürk passed through en route to Samsun.

Arrival, information and accommodation

Sinop's **otogar** is adjacent to the prison, at the end of Sakarya Caddesi on the western edge of the town centre. Take the "Karakum" dolmuş to the centre (the stop in town is behind the *Melia ve Kasim*), or all the way to Karakum beach 2km out of town. There's a **tourist information office** (☎0368/261 5298; daily in season 8am–noon & 1–6pm) down at the harbour behind the *Hotel Melia ve Kasım*. The **TML agent** (☎0368/261 1424) is at the southeast harbour.

Sinop has a reasonable selection of **hotels**, most in the streets behind the harbour, but they tend to fill up in summer. *Otel Sinop 57* at Kurtuluş Cad 29 (☎0368/261 5462; ③) is currently best value in town for brand-new, very comfortable rooms with balconies and clean en-suite bathrooms. The *Otel Denizci*, Kurtuluş Cad 13, opposite the *Ziraat Bankası* (☎0368/261 2878; ③), is not as nice, but reasonably good value for rooms with showers. The *Otel Meral*, Kurtuluş Cad 1 (☎0368/261 3100; ②), offers rooms with no showers, and twenty-percent student reductions. Cheapest in town is the very basic *Yılmaz Aile Pansiyon* (☎0368/261 5752; ①). The clean and presentable *Gül Palas Oteli*, next to the prison at Cumhuriyet Cad 13 (☎0368/261 1737; ①), also has dorm rooms sleeping four ($4 per person). Overlooking the sea to the east of the harbour, the prominent *Hotel Melia ve Kasım*, Gazi Cad 49 (☎0368/261 4210; ③), has old, ill-kept rooms, some with en-suite baths and TV, suffering from the noise of the tacky *gazino* (nightclub) downstairs.

To the east of the town centre, at **Karakum beach**, the *Karakum Holiday Village* (☎0368/261 2693) has a near-monopoly on accommodation possibilities, with camping facilities, bungalows for two (③), *pansiyon* accommodation in rooms without bathrooms (①), and a hotel, the *Ada*, up on the cliff, where comfortable rooms have sea views and en-suite facilities (③). Their sheltered, sandy private beach, open to all customers, is about the best in the region. The family-run *Karakum Aile Pansiyon* (☎0368/265 6870; ③) on the opposite side of the road to the sea, well signposted off the beach approach road, offers clean simple rooms, with bathrooms and WCs down the hall, and use of a well-equipped kitchen.

There are also **camping** facilities at **Kumsal beach**, about five minutes' walk from the *otogar*. *Öztürkler Kamping* and nearby *Yuvam Dinlenme Tesisleri* (☎0368/261 7414), which has a basic restaurant.

The Town

Sinop is a sleepy place, where development has not caught up with the town's potential as a holiday resort, despite the best efforts of the local tourism office to promote it.

The first thing you'll notice on entering the town is a small **prison** out near the *otogar* on Sakarya Caddesi. The building was put to this use in 1877; before that it was a bastion of the citadel, and local tourism officers assure visitors that this means its walls are unscalable. Carrying on into town the **city walls** are still highly prominent, and although time has inevitably taken its toll, they remain by far the most atmospheric thing about Sinop. The first defences were probably built here by the original colonists back in the seventh century BC; during the Pontic kingdom more fortifications straddling the isthmus were added, and every subsequent occupier enlarged, strengthened and adapted the whole, until they reached a length of over 2km under the Byzantines. Most of the present structure dates from Byzantine/Genoese times, with Selçuk modifications. Considerable chunks are now missing but much is still intact, in particular the **Kumkapı**, which juts out bastion-like into the sea on the northern shore. Down near the harbour, a hefty square tower offers good views out to sea (and of the development swarming up onto the headland), and you can stroll along nearby sections of wall; watch out, though, for the vicious ravens who seem to regard this as their personal territory and can swoop down and deliver a swift peck on the back of the head to unwary visitors. Heading east from Kumkapı, Sakarya Caddesi leads to the **Alâeddin Camii**, a mid-thirteenth-century Selçuk mosque that's the oldest in town. Entry is via the tree-shaded courtyard with a central *şadırvan*, where a blue-painted porch lets onto a plain interior enlivened by a fine *mimber*. Behind the mosque is the **Alaiye Medresesi**, which also dates from the 1260s. The most notable feature is a marble-decorated entrance portal, relatively restrained by Selçuk standards. It's also known as the Pervane Medresesi after its founder, Mu'in al-Din Süleyman. The Selçuk sultans conferred the title of Pervane ("butterfly") on their viziers, and this particular chief minister became so powerful that he did away with his sovereign in 1264, ruling as virtual autocrat of this area until dispatched in turn by the Mongols in 1278.

Heading north down one of the side streets at the end of Sakarya Caddesi leads to Sinop's **museum** (Mon noon–5.30pm, Tues–Fri 8am–5.30pm, Sat & Sun 9am–5pm; $1), which has the expected array of objects from the Bronze Age onwards. Many of the oldest exhibits were unearthed at Kocagöz, an archeological site a few kilometres southwest of Sinop. Look out also for the Roman amphoras (there are more of these in the museum gardens), a reminder of the days when Sinop was an important trading centre, with ships unloading and loading wine and olive oil. All this, however, is fairly predictable stuff, and only the upper-storey **icon display** constitutes a departure from the usual Turkish small-town museum fare. Most of the icons are painted in Byzantine style, but actually date from the nineteenth century; scanty labelling makes their exact provenance uncertain, but it's a safe bet that they come from local Greek churches abandoned after 1923, including the Balatlar Kilise (see below). In the museum grounds are the sparse remains of the Hellenistic **Temple of Serapis**, excavated in 1951. A number of objects dug up on the site – including a fourth-century clay mask of the god (Serapis was the Egyptian form of Apollo) complete with long hair and beard – are now in the museum.

Following Kemalettin Sami Paşa Caddesi onto the headland will bring you to the forlorn **Balatlar Kilise**, a ruined seventh-century Byzantine church with a few faint traces of frescoes inside. There are a few mosques out here too, flanked by tombs, though only the hilltop **Seyit Bilal Camii**, with its decorative tiles, is worth seeking out.

Sinop's main **beaches** are Kumsal, under a kilometre southwest of the bus station, and a pay beach called Karakum (meaning "black sand", which is a fairly honest description), 2km southeast of town. They are connected with each other, via the *otogar* and the town centre, by twice-hourly dolmuşes. Kumsal beach is smaller, and backed by untidy campsites, but the sand is lighter, and the sea rather more enticing than at Karakum beach. The best beach on the northern side of the peninsula is Akliman, where a fine stretch of white sand is backed by pine forests and picnic areas, but it's less frequented than the other beaches as unpredictable currents make swimming dangerous.

Eating and drinking

For **food and drink**, there are plenty of options down by the harbour on İskele Caddesi: teahouses – the best known is the picturesque wooden *Yalı Kahvesi* – have chairs on the waterfront, and there are plenty of fish restaurants and fast-food places. Good possibilities include the *Saray Restaurant*, with fish *şiş, midye tava* (fried mussels) and salmon served out on a little floating pier; in the same area the *Yeni Sahil Restaurant* serves fish, *midye tava* and meat right on the waterfront, and the *Barınak*

Café has steak, egg and chips for homesick Brits. Also worth a try on İskele Caddesi is *Uzun Mehmet's*, the interior of which is a museum of old Turkish tools, where oven-baked lamb (*kuzu tandır*) is the speciality. One street back from the waterfront the *Akvaryum Canlı Balık Restaurant* between the *Meral* and *Denizci* hotels also does excellent fish – try the red gurnard with piquant yoghurt and black pepper sauce. For a taste of local **bar** life, head for the *Hasir Alti*, behind the *Melia ve Kasım Hotel*, a tiny makeshift place with a reed matting roof which gets very crowded at weekends.

West of Sinop: the coast to Amasra

Most public transport leaves Sinop for either Samsun or Kastamonu, but under your own steam it's quite rewarding to follow the little-travelled coast west to Amasra. Mountains, low but extending far inland, hedge the sea and force the recently paved road to wind around their knees. The region has always been a backwater, home in ancient times to the "barbarian" Paphlagonians and only lightly garrisoned by the Romans. It's still thinly populated, with many residents working overseas ten months of the year.

The coast road and the scenic but narrow inland alternative converge just south of Ayancik, reaching the coast again only at **HELALDİ**, a pleasant fishing port with a decent beach and a couple of *pansiyon*s. **ABANA**, a small resort 40km west, is the next place you might consider breaking the journey; a somnolent town with a decent, albeit shingly, beach.

Most, however, will press on to nearby **İNEBOLU**, the biggest place between Sinop and Amasra, but still mustering only 7000 inhabitants. A few isolated Ottoman houses grace the web of narrow streets, which is bisected by a river and wedged between the hills and the sea, with a long, empty shingle beach. The town's priciest **hotel** is the seafront *Hotel Deniz*, Zafer Yolu Cad 18 (②), where shabby rooms are not markedly better than those of cheaper options such as the *Otel Özlü*, Cumhuriyet Cad 42 (☎0366/811 4198; ①), or the *Otel Altınöz* at Cumhuriyet Cad 47 (☎0366/811 4502; $9), both with basic en-suite rooms on a street running inland from the waterfront just west of the *Deniz*. There's a **campsite** between the coast road and the sea. As for **eating and drinking**, head for the *Şehir Lokantası* set back slightly from the waterfront a little to the west of the *Deniz*; or the *Deniz*'s own restaurant, which will dish up fish, salad and a beer and leave you with change from $10; or the *Çiçek Lokantası*, in the street to the immediate east of Cumhuriyet Caddesi, which does good fish for a bit less money.

West of İnebolu, the clifftop road winds its way through a succession of sleepy little havens like Doğanyurt, Akbayir and Çayyaka, where you might want to break your journey for an hour or so if you're driving or cycling. Doğanyurt, just north of the road, is well off the beaten track and worth a look for precisely that reason; there's a friendly restaurant here. The constant curves mean that it takes a good two hours to drive to **CİDE**, where the town centre is actually a couple of kilometres inland, basically a one-street place with a **PTT**, **bank** and tiny **otogar**. The *Alkan Otel* at Fatimbey Cad 7 to the south of the *otogar* represents the best value in town, for very clean, well-furnished doubles with or without bathrooms (☎0366/866 1279; ①–②); but most arrivals take the "Sahil" bus to the harbour at the east of the shorefront esplanade and stay at the *Yalı Hotel* (☎0366/866 2087; ③–④). There's a choice between standard accommodation with baths and better-furnished rooms with fridges, TVs and balconies; a basic restaurant downstairs overlooks the quiet little harbour. The nearby **beach** here is pebbly, but extends for nearly ten, uncrowded kilometres to the west of the harbour.

GİDEROS, 15km west of Cide, is a small cluster of houses surrounded by green cliffs, where a friendly harbourside fish restaurant serves fried red mullet (*barbunya*) and offers lodgings for the night. Swimming is a possibility from rocks next to the pretty harbour, overlooked by a ruined medieval castle.

The road continues up a few steep grades and through a number of small villages with boatyards. The next popular stop is the village of **KAPISUYU**, an idyllic place where a mountain stream enters the Black Sea. The river's bank is shaded by trees, and at its mouth a fine stretch of sand has accumulated. It's a quiet place with just a single small *pansiyon* and restaurant, but many people camp along the beach.

If you need more facilities, **KURUCAŞİLE** lies just a few kilometres ahead. Long renowned as a boat-building centre, its shipwrights have lately applied their skills to crafting pleasure boats for customers from all over Turkey and northern Europe, after centuries of turning out oak-timbered fishing and cargo boats. The town's *Hotel A*, pleasantly located at İskele Cad 18 on the harbour (0378/518 1463; ②), is the biggest outfit between Cide and Amasra.

A final, agonizingly slow series of switchbacks brings you to **ÇAKRAZ**, whose good beaches and scattering of *pansiyon*s do little to disturb a splendid torpor. The best local strand is at **BOZKÖY**, nestled at the bottom of cliffs out of sight of the road, a couple of kilometres west. It can get crowded at holiday time, when perversely infrequent dolmuşes on the Kurucaşile–Amasra run are jammed to sardine-can density.

Amasra

AMASRA brazenly flaunts its charms to new arrivals. Approached from any direction, the town suddenly appears below you, swarming up onto a rocky headland sheltering two bays. Its original name was **Sesamus** – mentioned in Homer's *Iliad* – which was colonized by Miletus in the sixth century BC. The name Amasra derived from Queen Amastris, a lady of the court of Alexander the Great, who, after the death of her husband, acted as regent for her young son, only to be repaid with murder at his hands. The city then passed rapidly through the grip of a succession of rulers, until avid letter-writer Pliny the Younger was appointed Rome's special commissioner of the region in AD 110. From the ninth century, after a barbarian attack, the town declined in importance, although the Byzantines maintained a garrison here. The Genoese took over when Byzantine strength began to decline, and held the city until the Ottomans took it in 1460.

The Town

Amasra's setting and sleepy atmosphere make it worth at least an overnight stop. It's thoroughly relaxing, a quiet place with a small population only slightly swelled by tourism, full of shady corners to sit and contemplate.

The modern town occupies a headland; a narrow isthmus links the main town to Boztepe further out. Both parts are scattered with stretches of ancient fortifications from two Byzantine-Genoese castles. One of these is situated in the modern town above Büyük Liman (Big Harbour), and a short walk in this area, above the *Amasra Oteli*, reveals old cobbled streets straddled by Byzantine gateways. The other castle is reached by following Küçük Liman Caddesi across the isthmus to Boztepe, where a ruined watchtower on a piece of land jutting out into the harbour is still visible. Boztepe's heavy-duty walls, pierced by several gates, are still largely intact. The **inner citadel** is studded with towers and the Genoese coat of arms; of the two **Byzantine churches** which you can hunt down in the maze of alleys on Boztepe, the larger was converted to a mosque after the Ottoman conquest, while the ruined smaller one was apparently still used until 1923.

Amasra also boasts a good **museum** overlooking the Küçük Liman or "small harbour" (Tues–Sun 8am–5.30pm; $1), containing locally unearthed archeological finds, mainly from the Roman period. Pride of place is given to the torso of an emperor, with Romulus and Remus carved on his tunic, discovered in the citadel area in 1995.

Eighteenth- and nineteenth-century **woodcarvings** demonstrate a quality of craftsmanship sorely lacking nowadays; throughout town, you'll come across the hopelessly kitsch objects – goblets, ashtrays and back-scratchers, as well as more useful kitchen utensils – which local workshops now churn out by the thousand for the tourist market.

The ancient mole of the Küçük Liman across the isthmus, near the ancient watchtower, is the most likely spot for a quick **swim** if the jellyfish aren't too numerous; anywhere else the water is seriously polluted, particularly at the deceptively attractive town beach fronting the eastern fishing port – and the even busier industrial quays. It's best to regard Amasra as a base for forays to better beaches further east, and not the all-in resort which the city fathers would like to promote.

Practicalities

The **dolmuş and coach terminal** is on the small Atatürk Meydanı, near the middle of the main part of the headland. From here everything is in easy reach, including a small **tourist information office**, on Büyük Liman Caddesi, which is open when they can find someone to staff it.

Accommodation possibilities are all moderate in price and fairly well appointed. On Çamlı Sokak, in a quiet neighbourhood near the museum, the family-run *Paşa Kaptan Oteli* (☎0378/315 1011; ②) has some en-suite rooms with balconies. Next door, the *Nur Turistik Pansiyon* (☎0378/315 1015; ③) has similarly comfortable, quiet rooms. Just to the northwest of the main square, the *Çınar Restaurant-Pansıyon*, Küçük Liman Cad 1 (☎0378/315 1018; ②), is basic but clean, with showers down the hall. The *Belvü*, further along the same street (☎0378/315 1237; ①), gives off a slightly shabby Belle Epoque aura, though its rooms are clean enough (shared bathrooms). In summer you can **camp** on the harbour front near the Bartın road, but prepare yourself for traffic noise.

Overlooking the eastern beach on the Büyük Liman side of town, reached from Atatürk Meydanı by taking Büyük Liman Caddesi, the cheapest option is the *Hüzür Pansiyon* (no phone; ①), a family-run place with simple rooms and shared bathrooms. One block back from the eastern beach at Büyük Liman İskele Cad 59, the *Amasra Oteli* (☎0378/315 1007, fax 315 3025; ②) has some rooms with sea views, all with bathrooms and 24-hour hot water. The nearby *Otel Timur*, Çekiciler Cad 57 (☎0378/315 2589; ③), is deservedly popular (and often full) on account of its comfortable rooms, professional management and restaurant serving breakfast (included in the price).

For **food and drink**, check out the *Mustafa Amca'nin Lokantası* fish restaurant, on the water side of Küçük Liman Caddesi, easily Amasra's most colourful establishment, with booze and *istavrit* (Black Sea mackerel) dished up in abundance by a suitably piratical-looking "Uncle" Mustafa. Drop in at the *Seker Bar* next door for more drinking, in their waterside garden. For cheaper eats, try the *Kumsal Pide Salonu* above Küçük Liman, serving an excellent *karışık* (mixed) *pide*. On the eastern beach, near Büyük Liman, there are two excellent restaurants, one on the second floor of the *Öğretmenevi* (Teacher's House) next to the *Hüzür Pansiyon*, which serves succulent kebabs and salads; and the smartest place in town, the *Liman Restaurant* right on the harbour, with an impressively long fish menu including salmon (*saumon*), turbot (*kalkan*) and crayfish (*istakoz*), plus a bar stocked up with champagne and scotch whisky.

Beyond Amasra

Southwest of Amasra, Highway 010 leaves the coast, dipping inland to **BARTIN**, a large town of Ottoman wooden houses (most of which are sorely in need of restoration), with superior bus connections to Safranbolu and Ankara. If you want to continue along the coast, or demand sleeper-train comfort for travelling to Ankara, you'll have to make for the provincial capital of **ZONGULDAK**, nearly 100km away. Bang in the heart of

Turkey's main coal district, it's a surprisingly attractive city, approached from the south through a steep, tree-lined gorge, where towering pitheads seem to complement the dramatic valley scenery. If you spend much time in the city however, you may find your eyes stinging from the almost palpable pollution in the air; downtown Zonguldak is fittingly marked by a lump of metal from which figures representing coal miners are hacking their exit. On Gazipaşa Caddesi, the main drag, the *Grand Hotel Ay* at no. 61 (☎0372/251 1310; ③) has decent, though characterless, rooms with TVs, its inflated prices reflecting Zonguldak's importance for travelling businessmen.

EREĞLİ, still further west, is rather more unpleasant: the largest steelworks in the Middle East dominates the town, and hotels are even more overpriced than in Zonguldak. **AKÇAKOCA**, well on the way to İstanbul, has one last Genoese fortress, a seven-kilometre-long sandy beach – and hotels jammed with clients from the nearby metropolis. The town has grown recently into a glitzy Mediterranean-style resort, with disco-bars and three-star hotels, but no history to lend any substance or character. The *Sezgin Pansiyon* at Atatürk Cad 44 (☎0374/611 4162; ②) is the best-value **accommodation** in town; **campsites**, including the *Günbatımı* and *Nejat*, are to the west of town, on the road to the Genoese castle.

A thirty-kilometre drive throught hazelnut groves to the west, Kocaali has more sandy strands, but no shade. Beyond Kocaali, there's so much sand on the stretch of road to **KARASU** that the fields bordering the dunes are desert-like, only used as campsites by groups of nomads. Karasu itself is a drab town set back from the sea; the beach is sun brollies as far as the eye can see, with a massive campsite, the *Öz-su*, that also offers bungalow-style rooms. West of Karasu, it's best to ignore Kandira in favour of Ağva or Şile (see p.158), both attractive resorts with a number of accommodation possibilities.

THE EASTERN BLACK SEA

The eastern Black Sea sees far more visitors than the western half, partly because there's more of interest here, partly because it's easier to get to. **Trabzon**, with its romantic associations and medieval monuments, is very much the main event and, located as it is at the end of plane, ferry and bus services, makes a logical introduction to the region. It's also the usual base for visits to **Sumela monastery**, the only place in this chapter that you could describe as overwhelmed by tourists. Other forays inland, however, are just as rewarding if not more so – particularly the superlatively scenic **Hemşin valleys**, home to a welcoming, unusual people and the northern gateway to the lofty **Kaçkar Dağları**, covered fully in the "Northeastern Anatolia" chapter.

Other than Trabzon, the coast itself between the frontier and Samsun offers little apart from fine scenery and swimming, **Tirebolu**, **Giresun** and **Ünye** being the most attractive and feasible bases for exploration. All this is best appreciated with your own transport, but even without you'll face few problems – towns are spaced close together and served by seemingly endless relays of dolmuşes which replace the standard long-distance coach as the means of getting around here. Just about every journey is covered, and you can safely ask to be set down at an isolated beach in the near certainty that another minibus will be along to pick you up when necessary.

East of Samsun: the coast to Trabzon

Just east of Samsun, the Black Sea coastal plain, watered by the **delta of the Yeşilırmak**, widens to its broadest extent. The area was once thought to be the land of the **Amazons**, a mythical tribe of men-hating women who cauterized their right breasts to facilitate spear throwing and arrow shooting, and who only coupled with men – their neighbours the Gagarians – during two months of the year, sending male babies to the Gagarians to rear. Nowadays the delta is home to rather more conventional Black Sea Muslims, who are welcoming enough to members of either sex.

The road, slightly elevated to avoid flooding, heads well inland, across one of the most fertile patches along the coast. South of the highway, tobacco is the main crop. North of the asphalt the landscape is a morass of channels, copses and lagoons, teeming with wildlife pursued by the local fishermen and hunters; if you're interested in exploring, a canoe might be of more use than a car or local bus. Çarsamba, halfway across the delta, is a working town serving local agriculture: there are hotels near the bypass and restaurants on the river, but no real reason to stop.

Ünye

ÜNYE, a small, friendly town just over 100km east of Samsun, makes a good target if you need a place to stay overnight. Inland from the busy shore highway, the town has a few grand buildings dating from Byzantine times and its eighteenth-century heyday as a regional port, including a former Byzantine church that now serves as a hamam (men only) on the main square, Cumhuriyet Meydanı. The renovation craze has not yet hit Ünye; its fine buildings, many of them on Kadılar Yokusu, leading uphill from Cumhuriyet Meydanı, are rotting, most are squatted. Also worth exploring, if you're around at the time, is the massive and abundant Wednesday market, where you'll see gold-toothed farm women selling their own hazelnuts (harvested in August) and unusual edible plants (described under the umbrella term of *salata*), alongside churns full of farm-produced milk and cheese.

Ünye also profits from its status as a **beach resort**. You'd see the best strands approaching from the west, where the highway is lined by ranks of motels and *pansiyon*s of a sort not seen since the Aegean or the Marmara regions. The only specific sight is the medieval **fortress of Çaleoğlu**, 7km inland, built on much older foundations and flanked by a **rock-cut tomb** of Roman or Pontic kingdom vintage, suggesting that one or the other fortified the site. The steep climb from the road rewards you with a view south over an exceptionally lush valley, and north to the Ünye coast, but otherwise the trip is really hardly worth the effort.

Practicalities

Ünye's minuscule **otogar** is at the eastern edge of town, by the road to Niksar; a **tourist information office** (June–Aug daily 8am–6pm; Sept–May Mon–Fri 8am–noon & 1–5pm) is located next to the floodlit football pitch on the shorefront esplanade, just after the turn-off to Niksar as you come into town from the *otogar*.

If you want to **stay** in town and savour the bourgeois atmosphere, the family-run *Otel Güney* (☎0452/323 8406; ①–②) offers comfortable if uninspiring rooms with or without bathrooms, and a roof terrace looking out to sea. Behind the *belediye* building at Belediye Cad 4, the *Otel Burak* (☎0452/312 0186; ②) is a similar deal, where rooms have TVs and very small bathrooms.

If you're determined to stay near the water, best do it west of town out on the Samsun road; green and white dolmuşes marked "Curuderesi", leave every few minutes from the town centre. The *Belediye Çamlık Moteli* (☎0452/323 1333; ④), located in a little pine forest 2km from town, can lay on simply furnished rooms, a reasonably priced restaurant and good beach. A couple of kilometres further out, the two-star *Hotel Talip* (☎0452/323 2238; ⑥) was not yet open at the time of writing, but it looks like it will be the most comfortable establishment in town, with tastefully furnished, well-equipped rooms, a roof bar and an immaculate beach. A little further out at Gölevi, the *Pinar Pansiyon* (☎0452/323 3496; ②) boasts immaculate rooms (remove your shoes as you enter the *pansiyon*), with balconies and wooden floors spread with kilims, and a flower garden running with hens, whose eggs you will be served for breakfast. Guests can use the kitchen, including a fridge stocked with soft drinks, and there's easy access to the beach across the road.

The best **campsite** in the region is the wooded *Çınarsuyu* (☎0452/323 7346, fax 323 1009), 15km out of town with its own restaurant; their well-equipped bungalows are ample for four but will take seven ($38 per bungalow; book ahead in summer). The *Araplar Camping* (☎0452/323 2060), near the *Hotel Talip*, is not as well run, but can offer a good beach and barbecue grills for you to cook your own food on; they also serve *pide*.

Other **food** options – besides *Araplar Camping* and the *Belediye Çamlık Moteli* – include the seafront *Park* in the town centre which, with its white-tablecloth dining room and good service, is the most obvious option for fish, *meze* or *izgara*. Just past the *Çamlık* on the Samsun road, a road leads inland to the *Çakırtepe Picnic* restaurant, where *pide* is served in pleasant rural surroundings.

Fatsa and Bolaman

FATSA, 21km east of Ünye, is a shabby mess with polluted beaches and a sad recent history. Like nearby Bolaman, it is populated by Alevîs, a sect closely allied to Shiism and the Bektaşi Sufi order, and during the late 1970s the inhabitants took the opportunity to put the radical political beliefs which often accompany this affiliation into action by electing a Marxist city council. A Paris-style commune, the mayor a tailor popularly known as Terzi Selim, was established; as a run-up to the coup of September 1980, the army sent in tanks to close down the experiment. Locals erected barricades to no avail: an undetermined number of activists were killed or imprisoned, and Terzi Selim subsequently died in jail. Today the place is subdued as well as unattractive, with locals still reluctant to discuss these traumatic events.

If you're ready for a break, there's a good **restaurant** a kilometre or so west of Fatsa on the Ünye road, the *Mavi Deniz*, distinguished by its service and seafront setting, as well as its food (fish or meat). Just beyond the *Mavi Deniz* at the entrance to Fatsa, the *Dolunay* (☎0452/423 1528, fax 423 1633; ④) is a fairly luxurious **hotel**, whose centrally heated rooms with TVs, right on the sea and away from the main road, represent excellent value; there's no beach, but you can swim from concrete slabs beside the hotel.

At **BOLAMAN**, 9km east on the same bay, the so-called **"castle" of the Haznedaroğlu clan** that overlooks the harbour is perched atop a Byzantine substructure. The clan, de facto rulers of the area during the eighteenth and nineteenth centuries, called themselves the governors of Trabzon, in defiance of the Ottomans. Tiny Bolaman is worth a stop if you're in your own vehicle: alongside the castle, there's a pretty harbour ringed by Ottoman houses, a couple of restaurants and a tea garden.

The coast highway winds on northeastwards, past more sandy coves, to an inconspicuous sign at Yalıköy pointing towards **"Yason"**, a cape where mariners once sacrificed at a temple of Jason (the Argonaut) before venturing further onto the temperamental waters of the Black Sea. This was replaced in due course by a **medieval church** 500m off the road, still well preserved except for a chunk missing out of the dome.

Çaka, Perşembe and Ordu

Once past Yason, the scenery regains the drama of the stretch between Sinop and Amasra, as the hills tumble down directly into the water. **ÇAKA** has one of the prettiest white-sand beaches of the eastern Black Sea, but there's no place to overnight indoors – only Turkish-style *kamping*s next to restaurants hiding under the mulberry trees. Just the other side of Çam Burnu sprawls **PERŞEMBE**, the first substantial place since Fatsa, a pretty fishing port where the *Hotel Vona* (☎0452/517 1755; ⑤) fronts a small beach just east of town. With fair-sized, well-furnished rooms, all with balconies and sea views, and its own pool and playground, it's a surprisingly upmarket establishment for a town so small.

Called Kotorya by the ancients, **ORDU** is now an undistinguished city with just a few older houses scaling the green slopes to the west, above an abandoned nineteenth-century Greek church 600m before the **TML terminal**. The **otogar** is at the opposite, eastern edge of town on the Samsun–Trabzon highway, while the **tourist information office** (summer Mon–Sat 8am–noon & 1–5pm; winter Mon–Fri 8am–noon & 1–5pm; ☎0452/223 1606) is located in the *belediye* building a little to the east of the Atatürk statue, also on the main highway (here called Atatürk Bulvarı). The only other bits of history are at the **museum** in the Paşaoğlu Konağı (daily 8am–5pm; $1), signposted off Hükümet Caddesi, past the main PTT. Once home to a leader of the Muslim immigrants fleeing the Caucasus in 1877–78, this typical example of nineteenth-century Black Sea architecture is well worth a look if you have the time. Downstairs there's a fairly standard museum of ethnography, but upstairs the two bedrooms and their original furnishings have been beautifully restored.

There are a couple of good **hotels** in or around Ordu. The two-star *Turist Otel*, Atatürk Bul 134 (☎0452/225 3140; ④), has some good-sized rooms with sea views, balconies and TV. Over a kilometre to the east of town, the *Belde Hotel* (☎0452/214 3987, fax 214 9398; ④) is modern and more comfortable, with three-star trimmings including a pool, satellite TV, restaurant, Turkish bath and sauna. For those on a tighter budget, the *Hotel Kervansaray*, at Kazım Karabekir Cad 1 in town (☎0452/214 1330; ②), is gloomy and spartan, but passable.

For reasonably priced **food**, try the restaurant of the *Turist Hotel*. The *Midi*, however, sitting on a pier at Sahil Caddesi, İskele Üstü, is the best option for fish, including salmon, trout and *mezgit* (whitebait). Cheaper eats such as chicken şiş, hamburgers and Italian pizzas can be had in congenial, clean surroundings at *Cafe Bulvar Fastfood*, Atatürk Bul 98. Ordu is most famous for its hazelnut-in-chocolate products produced by *Sağra*, and there's a whole shop full of the stuff, called *Sağra Nuthouse,* at Süleyman Felek Cad 95, which runs parallel to Atatürk Bulvarı and perpendicular to Hükümet Caddesi.

Continuing east towards Giresun, there are no more appealing **beaches** until just before Piraziz, 14–16km out of Ordu; the best ones are marked at weekends by knots of parked cars.

Giresun

Tucked on both sides of a steep, fortified bluff 31km east of Ordu, **GİRESUN**, with its mix of old and new buildings and converted churches, must be a nice place to live – but you wouldn't necessarily visit unless you're intent on catching the *TML* ferry here, as there's precious little in the way of sights. The town entered history as Pharnacia, a second-century BC foundation of the Pontic king Pharnace, but the name was soon changed to Cerasus, the root of the word "cherry" in virtually all Western languages. It was from here in 69 BC that the Romans first introduced the fruit to Europe, and cherry orchards still flourish all around.

The grounds of the **castle** on the bluff, nucleus of the earliest settlement, are today the main city **park**. Partly overgrown, they're wild and satisfying in a way that normal, more regimented Turkish parks rarely manage. The locals picnic here en masse at weekends, and it's a good place to wait for an evening ferry. At the foot of the ramparts on Sokakbaşı Caddesi, an eighteenth-century **Greek church** has been recently pressed into service as an ethnographic museum (daily 8am–5pm, $1), containing a number of ancient wine and olive oil amphoras from ships that sunk off the Black Sea coast. To complete the rather threadbare picture, there's a Turkish wooden printing press, some heavy *bindalli* embroidery on velvet traditional costumes and a corner of fine kilims.

Further east, a nautical mile or so offshore, lies **Giresun Adası**, the only major island in the Black Sea. In pre-Christian times it was called Aretias, and was sacred to the Amazons who dedicated a temple to the war god Ares on it. Jason and his Argonauts supposedly stopped here to offer sacrifice, and the islet is still the venue for **fertility rites** (May 20–22), dating back four thousand years to celebration of Cybele, the mother goddess, and described by the tourist office as a festival of "abundance and male procreative power". Any village woman who doesn't have babies yet is ritually passed through a trivet (a hoop-like affair on legs); this is followed by a boat tour of the island for a large part of the population of Giresun, and finally pebbles (representing troubles and misfortunes) are cast into the sea. At other times of year, a small passenger ferry visits the island twice daily from Ali Riza Park jetty, to the east of the town centre on the way to the church museum; but there's nothing in particular to see except the scant ruins of a Byzantine monastery.

Practicalities

Giresun's **otogar**, with frequent services east to Tirebolu and Trabzon and west to Ordu, is inconveniently placed over 3km west of the centre. If you're coming in from the east, have your bus drop you on the west flank of the castle bluff at the central dolmuş drop-off point on Atapark; if you're coming from the west, there's a dolmuş between the *otogar* and Atapark, marked "Beyaz Baş". The **tourist information office** (summer daily 8.30am–7pm; winter Mon–Fri 9am–5pm; ☎0454/211 3560) is in a booth in the park. The *Ulusoy* company, running hourly minibuses to Trabzon, are just west of the nearby pedestrian flyover linking the Atapark and the **TML quay** (☎0454/216 2382) with the main hotel district. **Car rental** is available from *Asya*, Atatürk Bul 75B (☎0454/216 9661).

It's a good idea to book a room in advance in Giresun, as demand can exceed supply. One of the cheapest **hotels** is the *Bozbağ*, a barn of a place at the junction of Eskiyağcılar Sokak and Arif Bey Caddesi (head up Gazi Caddesi from the waterfront and take the second left), where you'll probably get a room late at night if you're desperate (☎0454/211 2468; ①–②). It's run-down and dingy, but rooms, with or without bathrooms, are more or less clean. Considerably more salubrious is the *Çarıkçı*, an immaculately restored old place round the corner at Osman Ağa Cad 9 (☎0454/211 1026; ④); however, it's used by tour groups so it can be difficult to find a room. You may have more luck at the new *Er-Tur Hotel* (☎0454/216 1757; ③) off Osmanağa Caddesi at Çapulacılar Sok 8, a modern, clean and comfortable affair, though this too fills up fast. Near the ferry dock and the pedestrian flyover, the two-star *Giresun Oteli*, Atatürk Bul 103 (☎0454/216 3017; ③), isn't particularly atmospheric and suffers from traffic noise, but the staff are friendly and it's reasonably priced for what you get. The swishest place in town is the three-star *Kit-tur Otel* at Anifbey Cad 2 off Gazi Caddesi (☎0454/212 0245; ⑤), which despite sauna and gym is overpriced for what you get in their standard rooms.

You certainly won't starve in Giresun, since the area around the *Bozbağ* and the *Çarıkçı* swarms with decent **restaurants**; nor is it that difficult to get a "wee drop" with your food, the town not being a fundamentalist stronghold. The *Deniz Lokantası*, on Alpaslan Caddesi, at the far side of Atapark from the sea and next to the *belediye* building, is the locals' favourite for steamtray food, while the *Kahramanmaras Pide Salonu*, around the corner from the *belediye* building on Köprülü Han Sokak, serves possibly the best *pide* on the entire coast. The *Kale Restaurant/Gazino* specializes in fish and *izgara* and is situated in a lovely wooded park up in the citadel, with good views of the town, its island and the church; there's also a beer garden up here. The town's best beach, the small but immaculate *Haci'nin Yeri* just beyond the *otogar*, is backed with a **disco-bar**, open till 5am.

Tirebolu and around

TİREBOLU, curled above a bay enclosed by two headlands, is an attractive spot. A Greek Orthodox community until 1923, it's virtually unique hereabouts in not having been entirely overrun by concrete atrocities. On the easterly promontory stands the intact **castle of St John**, built for a fourteenth-century Genoese garrison. However, there are few amenities and, all in all, there's not really enough here to make it worth an overnight stop.

Above the coast road, the main inland street, Gazipaşa Caddesi, is home to the **PTT** and the town's three **hotels**. Most central and best of these is the clean but rather plain *Huzur*, Gazipaşa Cad 15 (①), near the town's largest mosque, with baths in the halls. **Eating** is problematic: there are no waterfront fish restaurants, so you'll have to make do with the reasonable *Tütüncuoğlu* on Gazipaşa Caddesi, or the very basic *Rihtim* by the *otogar*. You can get a beer and *çerez* at *Yosun Fıçı Bira* by the fishing port, and a nocturnal **tea garden** operates on the lawn inside the castle – pleasant except for the blaring *arabesk*, and your only chance to see the fort's interior.

Tirebolu lies at the heart of the *fındık* or **hazelnut** growing area, which extends roughly from Samsun east to the ex-Soviet frontier. During late July and August you'll see vast mats of them, still in their husks, raked out to dry. Impatient locals perversely insist on eating them slightly green, when the taste resembles that of acorns. There are decent beaches between Tirebolu and **ESPİYE**, 12km back towards Giresun; here the standard-issue archeological service sign points inland to "Cağlayan Köyü, Gebe Kilisesi", but it's 40km to Cağlayan, 25 of them on a bad dirt road, and the historic church of Gebe is very difficult to find. Locating **Andoz Kalesi**, the westernmost of the three Genoese strongholds in the area, is far easier – a sign just west of Espiye points to the hill, less than a dirt-track kilometre inland – but it's so badly overgrown and crumbled that the climb is hardly worth the effort.

Beyond Tirebolu: castles, old houses and beaches

Beyond Tirebolu you'll see more of the numerous **castles** built, mostly by the Genoese but occasionally by the Byzantines, during the thirteenth and fourteenth centuries to protect the sea approaches to Trabzon. One well-preserved stronghold lurks 15km inland, up the Harşit River at Bedrama; the river, just east of Tirebolu, marks the furthest line of advance by the Czarist army in 1916. Nearby **GÖRELE** boasts a fine collection of Black Sea houses, more apparent than Akçaabat's (see below), but only really worth the effort for buffs of vernacular architecture with their own cars. The town's name is an obvious corruption of nearby **Coralla** citadel, just before Eynesil. Four kilometres after Eynesil, the modern, three-star *Hotel Bestt* (☎0462/871 3944; ③) is a lot better than anything in Tirebolu, with comfortable, centrally heated rooms and clean, tiled bathrooms with tubs. Another Byzantine castle at **AKÇAKALE**, close to the road, is the best preserved between Tirebolu and Trabzon; the fortress on **Fener Burnu** is less obvious. In addition to fortresses, there's a final flurry of wide **beaches** – especially just east of Tirebolu or between Vakfıkebir and Fener Burnu – but they're generally unshaded, functional and lacking in charm.

If you're depressed by the relentless drabness of Black Sea coastal architecture, then **AKÇAABAT**, 17km west of Trabzon, may serve as a partial antidote. From the looks of the shore districts it would seem to be more of the same, but **Ortamahalle** neighbourhood, on the central of the three ridges behind the modern town, features a dense concentration of the wood-and-stucco houses once prevalent throughout the region. Russian shelling in 1916 devastated much of Akçaabat, however, and only one medieval church out of three dozen survived the war. You can reach Akçaabat easily by red-and-white *belediye* **buses** plying frequently to and from Trabzon. It's also worth knowing about the *Saray*, a one-star **hotel** here, in case all of Trabzon's better accommodation is full – not inconceivable in high summer.

Trabzon and around

No other Turkish city except İstanbul has exercised such a hold on the Western imagination as **TRABZON** (ancient **TREBIZOND**). Traveller-writers from Marco Polo to Rose Macaulay have been enthralled by the fabulous image of this quasi-mythical metropolis, long synonymous with intrigue, luxury, exotic customs and fairy-tale architecture. Today the celebrated gilded roofs and cosmopolitan texture of Trebizond are long gone, replaced by the blunt reality of an initially disappointing Turkish provincial capital. But a little poking around the cobbled alleyways will still turn up tangible evidence of its former splendour – not least the monastic church of **Aya Sofya**, home to some of the most outstanding Byzantine frescoes in the world.

Some history

The city was founded during the eighth century BC by colonists from Sinope and Miletus, who settled on the easily defensible bluff isolated by today's Kuzgun and Tabakhane ravines. From the promontory's flat summit – *trapeza* or "table" in ancient Greek – came the new town's original name, Trapezus, and all subsequent variations. Under the Romans and Byzantines the city continued to prosper, thanks to extensive patronage by Hadrian and Justinian and its location at the northeast end of a branch of the Silk Route.

But Trabzon's romantic allure is derived almost totally from a brief, though luminous, **golden age** during the thirteenth and fourteenth centuries. A scion of the royal Comnenus line, Alexius, managed to escape the Crusaders' sacking of Constantinople in 1204; shortly after, he landed at Trebizond in command of a Georgian army, and proclaimed himself the legitimate Byzantine emperor. Despite the fact that there were two other pretenders, one in Epirus and the other at Nicaea (it was the latter's descendants who eventually retook Constantinople), it was the pint-sized Trapezuntine empire that was arguably the most successful.

The Trebizond kingdom owed its unlikely longevity to a number of factors. Mongol raiders of the mid-thirteenth century swept across the Middle East, accentuating the city's importance by forcing the main Silk Route to divert northward through Tabriz, Erzurum and ultimately Trebizond. The empire's diplomats, hampered by few scruples and with the survival of the state as their only aim, arranged short- and long-term alliances with assorted Turcoman and Mongol chieftains manoeuvring at the borders. In this they were aided by the preternatural beauty of the Comneni princesses, who were given in marriage to any expedient suitor, whether Christian or Muslim; garbled tales of Christian princesses languishing in the grasp of the infidel reached Western Europe and, among other literature, apparently inspired Don Quixote's quest for Dulcinea.

Someone had to transport all the goods accumulated at Trebizond's docks, and this turned out to be the **Genoese** – and soon after the Venetians as well – who each demanded and got the same maritime trading privileges from the Trapezuntine Empire as they did from the re-established empire at Constantinople. Western ideas and personalities arrived continually with the Latins' boats, making Trebizond an unexpected island of art and erudition in a sea of Turkish nomadism, and a cultural rival to the Italian Renaissance city-states of the same era.

Unfortunately the empire's factional politicking was excessive even by the standards of the age. In this respect they managed to outdo even the Medicis, lending extreme meaning to the disparaging adjective "Byzantine". The native aristocracy fought frequent pitched battles with the transplanted courtiers from Constantinople, and the Italian contingents rarely hesitated to make it a three- or even four-sided fray. One such civil war in 1341 completely destroyed the city and sent the empire into its final decline.

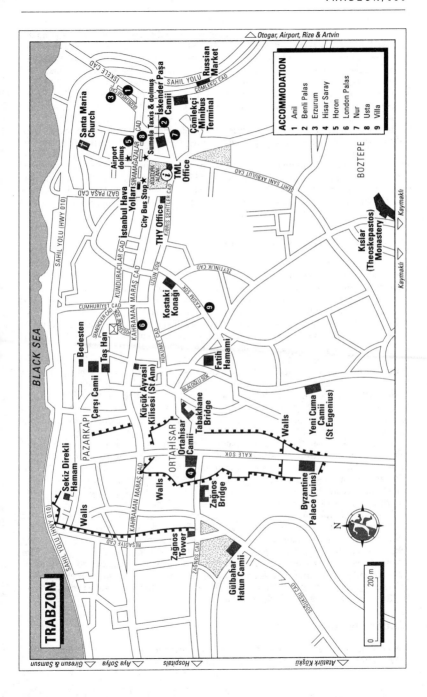

It was Mehmet the Conqueror, in a campaign along the Black Sea shore, who finally put paid to the self-styled empire; in 1461 the last emperor David, true to Trapezuntine form, negotiated a more or less bloodless surrender to the sultan. Under the **Ottomans** the city became an important training ground for future rulers: Selim the Grim, while still a prince, served as provincial governor here between 1490 and 1512, and his son Süleyman the Magnificent was born and reared here until his accession in 1520. Given these early imperial associations and the sultans' vigorous local Turkification programme, Trabzon, as it was renamed, was and still is a relatively devout place.

In late Ottoman times the city's Christian element enjoyed a resurgence of both population and influence; the presence of a rich merchant class justified the foundation of numerous western consulates in Trabzon and a spate of sumptuous civic and domestic buildings. But it was a mere echo of a distant past, soon ended by a decade of world and civil war and the foundation of the Republic. Shipping dwindled after the construction of the railway between Ankara and Erzurum and roads beyond into Iran. Today the outlook is still uncertain: though there was a brief boom during the Iran-Iraq war, both port and town have been overtaken by Samsun to the west.

Arrival, orientation and information

Trabzon's **airport** is some 8km away at the eastern edge of town, connected by frequent dolmuşes to the town centre; the *otogar* is closer, 3km out near the junction of coastal Highway 010 with Route 885 heading towards Sumela and Erzurum. If you ask, most dolmuşes or large buses coming from the west will let you alight at the far more convenient **Çömlekçi terminal**, near the Russian Bazaar at the foot of the bluff on which the downtown area is built. Local dolmuşes, including those to Rize, use this terminal. The **TML ferry port** is similarly handy, huddled at the base of the medieval shore bastion pierced by the coast highway tunnel.

Whether you take a dolmuş marked "Meydanı" in from the *otogar*, follow **Çömlekçi Caddesi** from Çömlekçi terminal, or climb **İskele Caddesi** from the port, all roads seem to converge on **Atatürk Alanı**, a tree-shaded square that's the hub of Trabzon's social life and frantic, endless dolmuş traffic. Bus company ticket offices, like those of *Ulutur* and *Aş*, also congregate at the corners of the square. Most of Trabzon's sights are within walking distance of Atatürk Alanı, though you'll need a dolmuş to get to Aya Sofya, and a bus or taxi to reach the Kaymaklı monastery behind Boztepe.

From Atatürk Alanı the city's two major longitudinal avenues lead west towards the old town: **Kıbrıs Şehitler Caddesi,** becoming **Uzun Sokak**, the pre-Republican high street, cobbled and narrow, heads off from the southwest corner; **Kahraman Maraş Caddesi** (shortened in addresses to Maraş Caddesi), the modern boulevard carrying most traffic, from the northwest corner. **Şehit Sani Akbulut Caddesi** leads from the southeast angle up toward **Boztepe**, the hill dominating Trabzon.

The **tourist information office** (March–Nov daily 8am–7pm; Dec–Feb Mon–Sat 8am–5pm) is located at the southeast edge of Atatürk Alanı. Now that Trabzon's tourism is fairly well-established, the staff are less than helpful on all fronts, but may see their way to storing luggage if you persuade them that you're desperate. They give away an absolutely useless map, and will provide information when grilled relentlessly. Most usefully, they can fill you in on the latest information about which hotels have slid down the slippery slope to brotheldom. More helpful, the **Turkish Maritime Line office** next door provide schedules for the Black Sea cruise ship.

Accommodation

Given Trabzon's status as the first major stop-off after the ex-Soviet border, many of the city's **hotels** double as brothels. T'.e red-light district is along İskele Caddesi and the streets immediately off it right down to the port, though not all the hotels in this area should be discounted. Those mentioned below are perfectly fine and are unlikely to deteriorate unless they change owners, but if you want to avoid walking through the area at night (particularly inadvisable for lone women), it might be sensible to choose a hotel in a more salubrious area.

The nicest of the **budget** places, located away from the red-light district in its own flowery garden off Uzun Sokak, is the *Villa Pansiyon* at Kasım Sok 23 (☎0462/321 7788; ①), where rooms have makeshift showers and share toilets, but are thoroughly clean and quiet. The cheapest of all the central options is the clean *Hotel Benli Palas* (☎0462/321 1022; ①–②), above the car park next to İskender Paşa Camii, with some en-suite bathrooms and good views; however, the plumbing's not particularly good so you might prefer to avoid the en-suites. The nearby *Nur Oteli* (☎0462/321 2798; ②–③), behind the mosque at Cami Sok 4, is also fairly comfortable if a bit old and shabby, with a good-natured management and a choice of shared or en-suite bathroom. Up a notch, but heading into the red-light district, the *Otel Anıl* (☎0462/321 9566; ③), off İskele Caddesi at Güzelhısar Cad 10, offers clean en-suites, but suffers from traffic noise on both sides. It's substantially better than the cheaper *Erzurum Oteli* (☎0426/322 5427; ①), opposite at Güzelhısar Cad 15, where rooms with showers are fairly clean but poorly furnished. The *Hotel London Palas* (☎0462/326 5426; ③), well out of the red-light district at Maraş Cad 71, is much better value at present than the *Anıl*, especially if you get one of their larger rooms at the back. They have their own marble Turkish bath, and free transport to and from the airport and *otogar*. However, prices will almost definitely go up as the hotel's reputation takes off.

Anything with a degree of **upmarket** comfort in Trabzon costs substantially more and may be booked up by tour groups. At the *Horon Oteli*, Sıramağazalar Cad 125 (☎0462/326 6455; ⑥), rooms are furnished in some style, with good firm beds, TVs, air conditioning and minibars, and there's a sauna downstairs. Also quite comfortable, but overpriced, is the older rather formal *Hotel Usta*, nearby at Teleğrafhane Sok 1, just south of İskele Caddesi (☎0462/326 5700; ⑦). The other possibility is the *Hisar Saray Pansiyon* (☎0462/326 3162; ⑤, prices negotiable), behind the Ortahisar Camii in the old town at Zaganos Cad 22, a large old Ottoman house with many original features (carved wooden ceilings and cupboards, for example) and great views from rooms at the back. It's located in a quiet, atmospheric neighbourhood, and is the best place to get away from the hectic action of central Trabzon.

It's also worth bearing in mind that there's an excellent *pansiyon*, the *Coşandere* (see p.649), on the way to Sumela monastery, 5km beyond Maçka and accessible by dolmuş from Trabzon.

The City

Trabzon straggles along the coast and penetrates inland for several kilometres, presenting you with the choice of short rides or substantial walks to get to many points of interest – a characteristic aggravated by the modern city centre's being a full kilometre from the ancient and medieval focus of settlement. On foot, you can see most of the in-town sights in a day; the suburban monuments require both extra time and use of public transport for access. If time is limited, concentrate on the two remote monasteries of Aya Sofya and Kaymaklı.

Around Atatürk Alanı and Uzun Sokak

An east-to-west walk along the seaward portion of town begins unpromisingly: the **Genoese bastion** straddling the coast highway tunnel, approached along Güzelhısar Caddesi, is an officers' club, off-limits to the public; detour slightly left instead, to the fly-over taking you to a tea garden and small park on the west flank of the castle. This seems to be Trabzon's sole acknowledgment of its seaside location, since – apart from the Russian market – the shoreline in general is amazingly dead, with the city introverted up on its plateau. The usually locked Catholic church of **Santa Maria**, a few alleys west of the ramparts, is the last surviving reminder of the Italians' former pivotal role here.

If you visit one **Russian Market** on the Black Sea it should be that of Trabzon, which occupies a long covered area next to the Çömlekçi minibus terminal. The nominal entrance fee will be waived if they realize you're not Turkish: hard currency is always welcome. Stalls display an amazing array of Eastern European memorabilia, from Russian dolls to 45s of balalaika maestros of our time (sadly, vodka has recently been forbidden for sale in the Russian markets).

Shifting northwest of Atatürk Alanı, pedestrianized **Kunduracılar Caddesi** (Shoemakers' Street) is the usual entry to Trabzon's **bazaar**. Ironically just about everything *except* shoes can be found on this avenue, with a special emphasis first on pharmacies and doctors, then on gold jewellery. Once past Posthane Sokak, Kunduracılar veers right to become **Semerciler Caddesi** (Saddlers' Street), devoted to a mix of factory-made clothing and the electrically striped *keşan*s (shawls) and *peştemal*s (waistbands) that are standard issue for so many Black Sea women. Copper merchants and tin-platers cluster on and just off **Yalahan Sokak**, which leads downhill from Semerciler to the water.

Sooner or later you'll stumble upon the monumental heart of the bazaar, where the **Çarşı Camii**, largest mosque in town, is handsome on the outside but late-Ottoman garish inside. Just behind it, the sixteenth-century **Taş Han** is a rather standard tradesmen's hall, still the location of retail outlets and workshops. The **Bedesten**, below the mosque, is more interesting despite its semi-ruined condition. Built by the Genoese in the fourteenth century, and revamped by the Ottomans, its shrub-tufted exterior seems square, but the interior, reached through the north portal, turns out to be octagonal. Once there were 48 shops on two storeys, but four square pillars were evidently insufficient to support the dome which has long since fallen in. Today the *bedesten* is used as a lumber mill, whose workers are amused by all the attention the structure gets.

Leave the bazaar going uphill, cross Kahraman Maraş Caddesi, and you can't miss the ninth-century Byzantine church of **Küçük Ayvasil** just the other side. Also known as St Ann's, the diminutive shrine is permanently locked; its frescoes were anyway obliterated sometime in the last seventy years. A stroll along **Uzun Sokak**, to the southeast and dotted with imposing Belle Epoque mansions, may be more satisfying. There's no real concentration of old houses in Trabzon; the appeal of leisurely strolling lies partly in the unexpected confrontation with a creaking masterpiece on an otherwise unremarkable block. One of the best examples of this is the **Kostaki Konağı**, just south of Uzun Sok on Kasım Sok, whose opening as a museum appears to have been delayed indefinitely.

The old town

Following Uzun Sokak west soon brings you to the **Tabakhane Deresi** (Stream) and the namesake bridge spanning it. On the other side sprawls the fortified old town on its "table", but before crossing you should make a detour left along the east bank of the ravine, being careful to bear onto **Bilaloğlu Sokak** (from the bridge, follow the hamam sign and then take a sharp right at the first turning – there is a street sign but it's hard to spot), away from markers pointing to the Fatih Hamamı. After about 350m you'll come to the thirteenth-century **Yeni Cuma Camii**, formerly the church of Saint Eugenius, patron saint of Trabzon. There may have been a shrine of sorts here as early as the third century, when Eugenius disrupted the cult of Mithra at Boztepe and was martyred by Diocletian for his pains. As so often happened in these cases, his skull was found on the spot within a few years of the arrival of a new ruler, Alexius Comnenus, and the present church was erected to house the holy relic. The saint's intervention supposedly spared the city from the Selçuks in 1222, but he let the side down in 1461; Mehmet the Conqueror offered up his first Friday prayers here after capturing Trabzon, and immediately reconsecrated the church and added its minaret. You'll need to time your visit to the plain but relatively undisturbed interior around the daily cycle of prayers.

Crossing the Tabakhane bridge you arrive in the **Ortahisar** (Middle Castle) district of the old town; further upstream, at the steepest point of the gullies flanking it, is the upper citadel, while below, tumbling off the tableland, sprawls the less defensible lower town, huddled behind a third circuit of walls which reach the sea. The **walls** are in variable condition but at their crenellated and vine-shrouded best give some idea of Trabzon's skyline in its heyday.

The highlight of Ortahisar is the former church of Panayia Khrisokefalos, now the **Ortahisar Camii** and also referred to as the Fatih Camii. As in the case of the Yeni Cuma Camii, there was almost certainly a church on this site from the third century, but the present building dates mostly from the thirteenth century, with massive renovation after a fire in the midst of the 1341 civil war. This was the main cathedral of the Trapezuntine Empire, and most royal weddings, funerals and coronations took place here; the epithet *Khrisokefalos* or "Golden-Headed" recalls the zenith of the dynasty, when the Comneni could afford to plate the dome with gold. This is of course long vanished, and the Byzantine frescoes inside, smothered under layers of Islamic whitewash, and a thirteenth-century mosaic floor, recently cemented over, are equally unavailable for viewing. Today it's the volume of the barn-like basilica, with its massive interior columns, that impresses, though as at Yeni Cuma you'll have to coincide with the conclusion of prayers or hunt down the key-keeper to get in. A handful of atmospheric teahouses and simple restaurants around the mosque help to ease any necessary wait.

From the apse end of the former church you can bear south, uphill, about 400m along **Kale Sokağı**, through a gateway astride the street, to enter the **upper citadel**. Of the glittering Comneni palace, in the southwest corner of the highest terrace overlooking the Kuzgun Deresi, nothing is left but battered masonry. From the eastern ramparts, dominating the Tabakhane Deresi, there's a fine view across to the Yeni Cuma Camii; careful navigating could get you through the maze of shacks and market gardens in the ravine bottom and up the other side.

Heading west from Ortahisar Camii, the **Zağnos bridge**, built by a Greek convert who was one of Mehmet the Conqueror's chief generals, leaves Ortahisar over the Kuzgun ravine where dilapidated Greek mansions are slowly losing ground to contemporary tenements. On the far side, the **Zağnos tower**, the southernmost dungeon in the outer enceinte of walls, has been lately restored as the *Zindan Restaurant* (see p.646).

Across a busy boulevard and a swathe of parkland from the tower squats the **Gülbahar Hatun Camii**, the most important Ottoman monument in Trabzon – though its background is more fascinating than the run-of-the-mill mosque you see now. The mother of Selim I and wife of Beyazit II – known in later life as Gülbahar or "Spring Rose" – was originally a Comneni princess famous for her piety and good works among Christians and Muslims alike. She died in 1512, the first year of Selim's reign, and he completed the mosque and her adjoining *türbe* by 1514.

From just in front of the Gülbahar Hatun complex, Soğuksu Caddesi heads up toward the finest surviving example of the palatial bourgeois follies that sprouted locally at the turn of the century.

The Atatürk Köşkü

Set in immaculately maintained gardens, the **Atatürk Köşkü** (daily 8am–7pm; winter closes 5.30pm; $0.50) began life in 1903 as the property of the Greek banker Karayannidhis, who was obliged to abandon it two decades later. Atatürk stayed here on the first of three occasions in 1924, and the city formally presented it to him a year before his death. As an example of patrician Black Sea architecture, the mansion, though in need of a lick of paint, is more compelling than the contents – which include a bevy of photos of Atatürk, plus a map bearing his strategic scribbles during the Kurdish Dersim revolt of 1937.

Both dolmuşes to the "Köşk" stop and red-and-white city buses marked "Park–Köşk" serve the site – which is 6.5km southwest of Atatürk Alanı. so you wouldn't want to walk. You can also catch the bus as it passes Gülbahar Hatun.

Aya Sofya (Haghia Sophia)

Alone on a park-like bluff overlooking the Black Sea, the monastery church of **Aya Sofya** is one of the most romantically set of Byzantine remains, and even the fact that Trabzon's suburbs have now overtaken it does little to detract from the appeal. It seems certain that there was a pagan temple here, and then an early Byzantine chapel, long before Manuel I Comnenus commissioned the present structure between 1238 and 1263. The ground plan and overall conception were revolutionary at the time, successfully assimilating most of the architectural trends, Christian and Muslim, prevalent in contemporary Anatolia. Aya Sofya's role as a model for many later Byzantine churches will be evident if you've already seen St Saviour in Hora (Kariye Camii) or the Pammakaristos church (Fethiye Camii) in İstanbul. Converted to a mosque after 1461, Aya Sofya subsequently endured some even leaner and more ignominious times as an ammunition store and then as a hospital. Between 1957 and 1964, technicians working under the supervision of David Talbot Rice and David Winfield rescued the building from certain oblivion, in particular restoring dozens of **frescoes** to their former glory. Well lit and accurately labelled in English, these are compulsory viewing even if you've only a passing interest in religious art.

The site

From Atatürk Alanı infrequent dolmuşes labelled "Aya Sofya" cover the 3km to the monument, or more regular ones marked "BLK Sigorta" will drop you 300m south of Aya Sofya, with the way onwards fairly well signed.

The **church** (April–Oct daily 8am–6pm; Nov–Feb Tues–Sun 8am–4pm; March Tues–Sun 8am–5pm; $1) is laid out along a greatly modified cross-in-square scheme, with a dome supported by four columns and three apses at the east end of what in effect is a triple nave. At the west end of the building a narthex extends across the full width of the nave; barrel-vaulted porticos adorn the north, west and south sides of the exterior. Before rushing in to view the famous frescoes, take a moment to study the finely sculpted, albeit weatherworn, **frieze** illustrating Adam and Eve in the Garden, which surrounds the south portal, the only one of the three not tampered with by the Turks when they reconsecrated the church. This relief work is the most obvious evidence of the strong Armenian, Georgian and even Syrian influence on the craftsmen – who left, in lieu of signature, the single-headed eagle of the Comneni dynasty over the biblical work of art.

Aya Sofya's **frescoes**, in their fluidity, warmth and expressiveness, represented a drastic break with the rigidity of prior painting, and compare well with the best work of their century and the next in Serbia and Macedonia as well as in Constantinople itself. If you're pressed for time, the most important compositions are in the apse and the narthex, as well as in the north porch – which many people miss.

In the central **apse** a serene *Ascension* hovers over *The Virgin Enthroned* between the two Archangels. The *Pantocrator* in the **dome** was unhappily beyond repair, but a host of angels swirls around Him, just above the Apostles. The **narthex**, whose ceiling is divided into three sections by stone ribs, is almost wholly devoted to scenes from the life of Christ. The central zone exploits its complicated quadruple vaulting by depicting each of the Tetramorphs, symbols of the Evangelists, accompanied by seraphim. Alongside, such miraculous episodes as *The Wedding at Cana*, a decidedly adolescent *Child Jesus Teaching in the Temple* and *Healing the Canaanite's Daughter* (complete with vomited demon), fill the south vault, while *Feeding the Five Thousand* and *Calming the Storm on the Lake of Galilee* can be seen to the north. The **north portico** is taken up mostly by Old Testament scenes, including *The Sufferings of Job*.

Just north of the church an ensemble of sunken masonry was once perhaps the **baptismal font**; the square **belfry** to the west is a 1443 afterthought, indicative of the strong Italian flavour of the waning empire. If the tower is open – a rare event – the frescoes within are not nearly of the same quality as those in the church proper. The southeast apse is thought to have once been the location of **Manuel I's tomb**.

Behind the Aya Sofya ticket office is the entry to a small **museum** (Mon–Fri, same hours as Aya Sofya; $1), consisting of a village house built and furnished in typical Black Sea style, and a seventy-year-old barn on stilts, with wooden disks at the top of the stilts, to prevent mice attacking the stored grain. A café in the garden offers breakfasts and drinks.

Boztepe

Boztepe, the hill dominating Trabzon to the southeast, has always been held in religious esteem; in olden days it was the site of the amalgamated cults of the Persian sungod Mithra and the Hellenic deity Apollo – an ironic dedication when you consider how little unfiltered sun the coast receives. This reverence persisted into Christian times, when the hill was studded with churches and monasteries. Two of the latter still stand – after a fashion – and one at least is well worth the effort to visit.

The ruined former **Convent of the Panayia Theoskepastos** or "God-protected Virgin" (in Turkish, Kızlar Manastırı) backs into the rocky slope 1.5km from Atatürk Alanı, reached by following Şehit Sani Akbulut Caddesi south and then bearing left when you see the shell of the building on the hillside. Dolmuşes to Boztepe, marked "Boztepe", leave from in front of the tourist information office on Atatürk Alanı. Though founded in the fourteenth century, and in continuous use by the Greek Orthodox church until 1923, few internal frescoes or other artistic details remain, and in any case the place has been securely locked for several years while the Ministry of Culture deliberates how or whether to restore it. Just above the convent an appealing picnickers' park and grillhouse shares the view over the city with a military watchtower and the mosque and tomb of **Ahi Evren**, a target of pilgrimage among Trabzon's faithful.

The former Armenian monastery of **Kaymaklı**, 3.5km beyond the turn-off for Theoskepastos, is in an altogether higher league, containing as it does the finest frescoes in the region after those of Aya Sofya and Sumela. It's too far to walk, so take a taxi, or a bus marked "Kemik Hastane" from Atatürk Alanı. The bus will drop you at the Mısırlı Cami, out by the local prison on the flat summit of Boztepe: 100m past the mosque, turn left (east) and down onto an unsigned dirt track; proceed 800m along this, bearing right at all forks, until you reach an informal car park next to an ugly, green-and-white house with a garage underneath. When the weather is dry you can get this far by car or taxi – from here it's another 250m to the monastery. After rain, the track is impassable so you'll have to walk the full distance from the main road however you arrive.

What's left of Kaymaklı studs a green plateau overlooking the highway to Erzurum; today the monastery grounds are a farm, and the resident family is used to showing visitors around. Much of the place dates from the mid-fifteenth century, though the current tenants have wedged a concrete dwelling into the former cells on the east edge of the courtyard. The chapel or baptistry is bare, but the main **katholikon** is a marvel, its interior protected until now by its use as a hay-barn.

Off-season visits will be somewhat easier, since in summer the bales hide the walls to human height and above, but at any time the best-preserved images are usually exposed, and the family is quite willing to help you dig down to get a look at the lower tier. The **south wall** bears a Bosch-like conception of Hell and the Apocalypse, complete with a *Four-Headed Cerberus* and *The Whore of Babylon Riding the Beast of the Apocalypse*; adjacent hagiographies and admiring angels are less lurid. In the **apse**, more frequently exposed and thus badly damaged, you can still make out a *Dormition* and *The Entry of Christ into Jerusalem*, with the Saviour most definitely riding a horse rather than an ass. None of the frescoes date from earlier than the seventeenth century, and are far more sophisticated in concept and execution than you'd expect for such comparatively recent work.

Eating and drinking

There are plenty of places to eat in central Trabzon, but few of them are really outstanding. Chicken and fish are the staple main courses, with red meat being scarce.

The almost uninterrupted line of **restaurants** on the north side of Atatürk Alanı gets most of the tourist custom, though not all of them deserve to. A couple of booths, including *Murat Balık Salonu*, serve up *hamsi* (anchovy), the Black Sea's most famous fish, and *uskumru* (mackerel), to be eaten in a slab of bread. They have been known to rip tourists off though, so check your change. Establishments on the south side of the square, while costing perhaps ten or fifteen percent more, are far more salubrious. They don't come more obvious than the excellent-value *İnan Kebap Salonu*, with a range of tasty offerings right across from the tourist information office. If you prefer alcohol with your meal, head for the welcoming *Kıbrıs Restaurant Meyhane* on the east side of Atatürk Alanı, where you can eat a selection of *meze* overlooking the busy square below, on their tiny balcony. At the *Çardak Pide Salonu*, on the corner of Uzun Sok and Atatürk Alanı, you can eat excellent, very cheap *pide* outdoors under an arbour, away from traffic. The restaurant of the *Otel Üzgür*, on the south side of Atatürk Alanı, a few doors down from the *İnan*, is about as upmarket as the town has to offer, serving enticing (and expensive) fish and meat dishes in a garden courtyard out back.

Away from the square, the *Seymen Lokantası* on Uzun Sokak is spotless, with freshly prepared appetizing dishes throughout the day, served with *komposto*, the local fruit juice (sweet, with the fruit still in the bottom). The *Şişman*, Kahraman Maraş Cad 5, looks enticing with its rooftop terrace, but the tablecloths are grubby and the portions would do weightwatchers justice. *Derya Restaurant* on İskele Caddesi has good-value steamtray food served with mashed potato (a bit of a treat in Turkey) or kebabs with *baklava* to follow. The most touristy but atmospheric place in town is the *Zindan Restaurant*, located in the Zağnos tower of the city walls. It's pricy compared to the rest of the city, but the service is good, and the medieval feel of this former dungeon is enhanced by candlelight. After your meal, you can take a drink at the terrace bar and enjoy the fine views of the old town and the modern city.

If you just want a **drink**, the most obvious possibility for men is *Reis'in Yeri*, İskele Cad 14, down towards *InterRent* car rental; here you'll sit outside with the boys, washing down *çerez* (nibble-snacks). Apart from the bars of the big hotels and the *Zindan* and *Kibris* restaurants, women will have difficulty finding anywhere to drink comfortably in the evening.

In terms of **desserts**, everybody has at least some puddings or sweets – the confectioners of Hemşin (see p.656) aren't far away. Try *Ren Patisserie* off Uzun Sokak at Zeytinli Cad 8, run by homesick Hemşinli bakers. The *pasthanes* on and off İskele Caddesi (particularly the *Burcu* on Güzelhısar Cad) have become late-night pick-up joints for prostitutes and their clients.

Listings

Airlines *THY* from *Ulutur* (see "Tour companies" below); *İstanbul Hava Yolları* at Kahraman Maraş Cad, Kazazoğlu Sok, Sonat İşhanı 9 (☎0462/322 3806); *Azerbaijan Airlines*, Kahraman Maraş Cad 15, third floor (☎0462/326 2497).

Airport bus There are frequent dolmuşes marked "Havaalanı" from a stop one block north of the Atatürk Alanı near the *Horon Hotel* on Sıramağazalar Cad.

Car rental Independent companies include *Uğur Oto Kiralama*, Kahraman Maraş Cad, Onbaşı İşhanı 39 (☎0462/326 5780); and *Rent-A-Car VIP*, Uzun Sok, Zafer Çarşısı 45 (☎0462/321 2551). The international operators are *Avis*, Gazi Paşa Cad 20/B (☎0462/322 3740); *Europcar/InterRent*, Gazi Paşa Cad, Razi Aksu İşhanı, ground floor (☎0462/322 4164); and *Hertz*, İskele Cad 39/A (☎0462/322 4437); all three also have booths at the airport.

Consulates *Georgia*, Gazipaşa Cad 20 (☎0462/326 2226); *Russia*, opposite Ortahisar Camii (☎0462/326 2600).

Exchange For after-hours encashment of travellers' cheques, try the *Hotel Usta*; the PTT may also oblige. There are *döviz* offices all over the centre, particularly on Atatürk Alanı and on Kahraman Maraş Cad.

Hamams Much the best on offer is the fairly ancient but newly restored *Sekiz Direkli Hamam*, Pazarkapı 8, Direkli Hamam Sok 1 (daily 6am–11.30pm; women only on Thurs, men only all other

---

CROSSING TO THE FORMER SOVIET UNION

At present, all non-Turkish travellers need to buy a **visa for Russia** in their country of origin in order to go from Turkey into Russia. In exceptional circumstances, a visa may be granted in İstanbul or Ankara, but you'll need good Turkish contacts for this. **Visas for Georgia** are obtainable from the Georgian consulate, Gazi Paşa Cad 20, Trabzon (☎0462/326 2226; Mon–Fri 9am–5pm), or in Ankara (see p.585); they cost $30 for a transit visa, $50 for a single-entry visa (valid for 15 days), and $60 (valid for 30 days) or $150 (valid for 3 months) for a multiple-entry visa. **Visas for Azerbaijan** are available on a discretionary basis from consulates in İstanbul (Yeniçarşı Cad 20, Beyoğlu; ☎0212/293 2123) and Ankara. You'll need a letter of invitation from an Azerbaijan tourist agency, or proof of a confirmed hotel reservation. Single-entry visas issued within 3–4 working days cost $40, multiple-entry visas issued within 7 working days $180.

From Trabzon, *Karden Line Ferries* (☎0462/322 1167), at Atatürk Alanı, Merdivenli Sok, opposite the *THY* office, operate a twice-weekly **ferry to Sochi**, in Russia. *Avrasya* (twice-weekly ferries to Sochi) and *Kometa* (daily catamarans) operate through a number of agencies including *Afacan* and *Papillon Tour* (see Trabzon "Listings" for addresses), and *Gürgen Tur*, İskele Cad 61 (☎0462/321 4439, fax 322 1167). *Afacan* also operate a weekly **ferry to Gelencik** in Russia.

Azerbaijan Airlines, at Kahraman Maraş Cad 15, third floor (☎0462/326 2497), run twice-weekly **flights to Baku** in Azerbaijan. *Aeroflot* have recently closed their Trabzon office down.

Daily **buses**, run by the *Mahmutoğlu* bus company, go to **Batumi** (Batum) and **Tbilisi** (Tiflis) in Georgia (Gurcistan), leaving from the main *otogar*. The frontier is crossed at **Sarp**, a far more dependable option than the other Turkish–Georgian land crossing at Posof, which is open only for local traffic. It's quite easy to do the trip to Georgia in bits, taking a dolmuş or taxi from Sarp to the border and then arranging local transport on to Batumi on the Georgian side.

Other options for leaving Turkey from the Black Sea region include buses from Rize to Georgia and to Erivan in Armenia (see p.652), from Samsun to Tbilisi (see "Travel details"), and boats and catamarans from Samsun to Russia and the Ukraine (see p.625). Occasional direct buses run to Tbilisi from Erzurum and Artvin, via Sarp (see the "Northeastern Anatolia" chapter).

days; $3). Second choices would include *Fatih*, three blocks south of Uzun Sok a little to the east of the Tabakhane bridge (daily 5.30am–10pm; women on Wed; $1.80), and the *Meydan*, located just off Atatürk Alanı on Kahraman Maraş Cad (daily 6am–10pm; women on Sat; $1.80).

Hospitals The *Özel Karadeniz* (private) on Reşadiye Cad (☎0462/229 7070), and *SSK* (state) on İnönü Sok (☎0462/229 7070) are both out near Aya Sofya.

Laundry *Pak Çiti*, Zeytinlik Cad, off Kıbrıs Şehitler (daily 8.30am–9.30pm). Dry cleaning at *Galip*, Uzun Sok 30.

Left luggage At the *otogar*, or by arrangement at the tourist information office.

Newspapers A booth to the north of Atatürk Alanı and *Büfe Güzel*, at Güzelhisar Cad, stock the *Turkish Daily News*.

PTT Posthane Sok: phones 24hr; post and exchange daily 8am–7pm.

TML agent Right next door to the tourist office on Atatürk Alanı (Mon–Fri 8am–5pm; ☎0462/321 2018).

Tour companies Reputable agencies are *Afacan*, İskele Cad 40/C (☎0462/321 5804, fax 321 7001); *Ulutur*, Gazi Paşa Cad, Ulusoy Apt 2, at the southwest corner of Atatürk Alanı (☎0462/321 1680); and *Papillon Tour*, Uzun Sokak, Ipek Apt first floor (☎ & fax 0462/321 7254). They take tours to Sumela and can organize bus, plane and boat tickets to Georgia and Russia. *Afacan* also take tours to Ayder and Uzungöl, and *Ulutur* are the *THY* agents.

Tourism police On the east side of Atatürk Alanı, open daily 9am–7pm (☎0462/322 4601).

The monastery of Sumela

At the beginning of the Byzantine era a large number of monasteries sprung up in the mountains behind Trabzon; this tendency was reinforced during the life of the Trapezuntine Empire, when many of them also played a military role near the tiny realm's southern frontier. The most important and prestigious monastery – and today the best preserved – was **Sumela**, clinging to a cliff face nearly a thousand feet above the Altındere valley, the sort of setting which has always appealed to Greek Orthodox monasticism. Despite the habitual crowds – and the poor condition of the premises – Sumela has to rate as one of the mandatory excursions along the Black Sea.

The name Sumela is a Pontic Greek shortening and corruption of *Panayia tou Melas* or "Virgin of the Black (Rock)", though some render it – taking a few more grammatical liberties – as "of the Black Virgin". She has been venerated on this site since at least the year 385, when the Athenian monk Barnabas, acting on a revelation from the Mother of God, showed up here with an **icon** said to have been painted by Saint Luke. He and his nephew discovered a site which matched that of his vision – a cave on a narrow ledge part of the way up the nearly sheer palisade – and installed the icon in a shrine inside.

A **monastery** supposedly grew around the image as early as the sixth century, but most of what's visible today dates from the thirteenth and fourteenth centuries, when Sumela was intimately linked with Trebizond's Comneni dynasty, several of whose rulers conducted their coronations at Sumela rather than in the imperial capital. Over the centuries the icon was responsible for numerous miracles, and the institution housing it shared its reputation, prompting even Turkish sultans to make pilgrimages and leave offerings.

Sumela was hastily evacuated in 1923 along with all other Greek Orthodox foundations in the Pontus; six years later it was gutted by fire, possibly set by careless squatters. In 1931 one of the monks returned secretly and exhumed a number of treasures, including the revered icon, from their hiding place. The Virgin can now be seen in the Benaki Museum in Athens; unfortunately when the other reliquaries were opened on arrival in Greece, precious illuminated manuscripts from the Byzantine era were found to have rotted away during their eight years underground.

At the time of writing, the monastery of Sumela was undergoing extensive restoration work. The aim is to secure what survives and rebuild the rest, though on the basis of work completed so far, there's some risk that the rebuilt sections are going to turn out to be an oversanitized version of the original, more or less correct in detail but lacking in atmosphere.

Practicalities

Without your own transport, you have three ways of **getting to Sumela** from Trabzon. **Taxis** from a rank signposted "Meryemana" (Mother Mary), on the east side of Atatürk Alanı, charge $36 round trip for a carload of four people. Or you can take a **minibus** to Sumela, from next to the taxi rank, for $6 per person round trip. Cheaper are the **organized tours** run at 10am daily by the *Afacan*, *Ulutur* and *Papillon* travel agencies (see "Listings" above for addresses); cost per person is $3 for a return minibus seat (you pay the admission fee), with a stop for tea thrown in en route. However you arrive, you should make it clear that you're interested in a very full half-day out, since the state of the roads and the final walk in dictates two hours thirty minutes for the return trip, and you'll want an equal amount of time at the ruins.

It's 54km in all from Trabzon to Sumela; after 31km you turn off the chewed-up Highway 885 at Maçka. Two kilometres beyond Maçka towards Sumela there's a **campsite**, *Sumela Camping*, and 3km beyond that is the excellent *Coşandere* **restaurant** and **pansiyon** (☎0462/531 1190; ①), which competes with the best in Trabzon for comfort and value for money, though it's sometimes booked up by tour companies. Perched on the valley side with excellent views of the surrounding pine-clad hills, the wooden chalet is divided into large, immaculate and well furnished rooms, some with extra double beds on wooden platforms, costing a couple of dollars more, which would be ideal for families or two couples on a budget. Very clean hot showers and WCs are outside the rooms. Filling fare at the excellent restaurant in the valley bottom includes Black Sea specialities like *hamsili kaygana*, a kind of savoury cake made from anchovies, *lahana dolması* (stuffed cabbage leaves) and *mısır çorbası* (corn soup). They also do a great oven-baked *sütlaç* (a genuine rice pudding) for afters.

The 23-kilometre side road up the Altındere past the *Coşandere* is a stunning approach to the monastery, through breathtaking pine-clad scenery. As you climb, the habitual cloud ceiling of these parts drifts down from the equally dense fir forest to meet you; in exceptional circumstances you may catch an advance glimpse of the monastery's faded, whitewashed flank soaring above the trees at the top of the valley, at an altitude of 1200m. Note, however, that traffic is frequently delayed on this stretch of road for dynamiting and bulldozing of landslides.

The environs of Sumela have been designated a **national park**, which means a trout farm, a picnic area and relatively expensive teahouses and kebab stalls; you may or may not have to fork over an additional $1 per vehicle at the park entrance booth, depending on prior arrangements with your driver. The monastery proper is linked to the valley bottom by a half-hour, often slippery woodland trail. **Visiting hours** change with daylight: June–Sept 8.30am–6pm, Nov–Feb 9am–3pm, March–May and Oct 9am–4pm. Full **admission charges** – collected at the top – are $5, half that for students.

The buildings

Sumela actually occupies a far smaller patch of level ground than its five-storeyed facade would suggest. A climb up the original entry stairs, and an equal drop on the far side of the gate, deposits you in the central courtyard, with the monks' cells and guest quarters on your right overlooking the brink, and the chapel and cave sanctuary to the left. Most of the former living areas are off-limits, undergoing restoration – scheduled for completion mid-1997, but likely to drag on longer – and the rest of the interior is full of scaffolding. The degree of vandalism and decay is appalling: sophisticated art thieves were caught levering away large slabs of the famous frescoes in 1983, and any within arm's reach have been obliterated by graffiti-scrawlers – much of the graffiti is pre-1923 vintage Greek, but Turkish, European and North American visitors have also left their marks.

The main grotto-shrine is closed off on the courtyard side by a wall, from which protrudes the apse of a smaller chapel. A myriad of **frescoes** in varying styles cover every surface, the earliest and best ones dating from the fourteenth century, with progressively less worthwhile additions and retouchings done in 1710, 1740 and 1860. The highest cave paintings are in good condition – ceilings being harder to vandalize – though the irregular surface makes for some odd departures from Orthodox iconographic conventions. The Pantocrator, the Mother of God, and various apostles seem to float overhead in space; on the south (left) wall is *The Virgin Enthroned*, while *Jonah in the Whale* can be seen at the top right.

Outside on the divider wall, most of the scenes from the life of Christ are hopelessly scarred. Among the more distinct are a fine *Transfiguration* about ten feet up on the right; just above sits *Christ in Glory*, an oft-repeated theme with at least three renditions nearby. At the top left is *Christ Redeeming Adam and Eve*. On the apse of the tiny chapel, *The Raising of Lazarus* is the most intact image; next to it is *The Entry into Jerusalem*, with *The Deposition from the Cross* on the extreme right. When craning your neck to ogle the surviving art gets too tiring, there is (mist permitting) always the spectacular view over the valley – and the process of imagining what monastic life, or a stay in the wayfarers' quarters, must have been like here in Sumela's prime.

The monasteries of Vazelon and Peristera

So many monasteries are crumbling away in the Pontic foothills that some may never be documented before they disappear forever. Two of the more famous ones, relatively close to Sumela, are best visited with your own transport – but in all honesty they will appeal only to specialists.

To reach the cloister of **Vazelon**, dedicated to Saint John the Baptist, proceed 10km south of Maçka on the road to Erzurum; 300m past two adjacent teahouses in the unmarked village of Kiremitli, bear right down a dirt road at a left curve in the main asphalt. Descend south to the river and the future main highway, crossing at a ford, and climb north up the far bank to the Ortamahalle district of Kiremitli. Continue along what's now a narrow forest road, bearing right at the only fork, until a huge landslide prevents further progress. From here you've a forty-minute walk west to the monastery, visible in the final stretch like a mini-Sumela on the cliff-face ahead.

In fact Vazelon once ranked second to Sumela in wealth and ecclesiastical clout, but its deterioration in recent years has accelerated alarmingly. Frescoes exclaimed over in the past have vanished under the ministrations of rain, campfire smoke and vandals, and within a few more years all will have disintegrated. For the moment, the side chapel outside the walls contains a *Dormition*, a *Raising of Lazarus* and a row of angels, all dating from the sixteenth century and in fair-to-poor condition. The *katholikon* or main sanctuary, reached by much crawling through rubble and nettles, has recently collapsed; only the northern exterior wall bears bits of a naive, eighteenth- or nineteenth-century *Last Judgement*.

The monastery of **Peristera** (in Turkish, Hızır İlyas Manastırı) is somewhat easier to get to but in no better condition. From Esiroğlu, 17km south of Trabzon, a rough fifteen-kilometre drive east leads first to Libova, thence to the village of Şimşirli, formerly Küstül. More nettles await the intrepid scaler of the nearby crag on which perch the monastery walls. No art remains; the view is the main thing.

East of Trabzon: towards the Georgian border

The shore east of Trabzon gets progressively more extreme as you approach the former Soviet frontier. If the Black Sea coast as a whole is wet, here it's positively soggy; mountains increasingly impinge on the sea and soar ever steeper upward; and the people match the landscape in their larger-than-life qualities.

Natives of this area have long exercised a disproportionate influence in national politics, the best current example being Rize's **Mesut Yılmaz**, once foreign minister, whose patronage of local prestige projects has become the second biggest growth industry after tea (see below). If a road is being improved or some other conspicuous public work is under way, it's probably due to his intervention; grateful supporters festoon boulevards with laudatory hoardings and generally accord him a status just inferior to deity.

Civics and commerce aside, however, the coast route has remarkably little to offer travellers. Visually the only colour is lent by the uniformly red-black-and-white-striped **keşans** (shawls) and multicoloured **peştemals** (waistbands) worn by women between a point just west of Trabzon and Çayeli. Another exotic touch is lent by occasional roadside signs in Georgian and Russian, aimed at visitors from the ex-USSR – probably the first time either language has appeared publicly in print in Turkey since 1923. Sounds may be better: if you happen upon a summertime knees-up, the **music** will be that of the *kemençe*, the Pontic three-string spike fiddle, and the *tulum*, the slightly more versatile local goatskin bagpipe.

Beaches

If you just want a swim and a half-day out from Trabzon, the first decent, unpolluted **beaches** are found between **ARAKLI** and **SÜRMENE**. The towns themselves are nothing to write home about, and the only point of cultural interest hereabouts is the late eighteenth-century mansion of the Yakupoğlu clan, *derebeys* or feudal overlords of these parts. Otherwise known as the **Kastel**, this squats above the west bank of the Kastel Çayı, 4km east of Sürmene, opposite a seashore teahouse, the *Kastel Restaurant*. Abandoned in 1978 by the Yakupoğlus – whose ranks include one of the richest men in the country, Cevher Özden – it's locked and beginning to decay, but is still impressive.

TEA

East of Trabzon, thanks to a climate ideal for its cultivation, **tea** is king. The tightly trimmed bushes are planted everywhere between sea level and about 600m, to the exclusion of almost all other crops. Picking the tender leaves is considered women's work, and during the six warmer months of the year they can be seen humping enormous loads of leaves in back-strap baskets to the nearest consolidation station. The tea, nearly a million raw tons of it annually, is sent more or less immediately to the fermenting and drying plants whose stacks are recurring landmarks in the region.

Oddly, tea is a very recent introduction to the Black Sea, the pet project of one Asim Zihni Derin, who imported the first plants just before World War II to a region badly depressed in the wake of the departure of its substantial Christian population in 1923. Within a decade or so tea became the mainstay of the local economy, overseen by Çaykur, the state tea monopoly. Despite the emergence of private competitors since 1985, and the Chernobyl accident which caused condemnation of the 1986 crop, Çaykur is still the major player in the domestic market. Export, however, seems unlikely until Chernobyl has faded from the collective consciousness of potential markets.

Four stone bulwarks guard the tapered centre of the ground plan; the lightness of the wood-and-stucco work on the upper storey, and the whimsical toadstool roof, seems incongruously wedded to the forbidding lower level.

It would only really be worth stopping at these places if you had your own car, and the same goes for the boatyards with their colourful, top-heavy *taka* fishing boats at ÇAMBURNU, 3km east. A much-touted pay beach is tucked at the base of the cliff just beyond the port, but equally good or better free **beaches** line the road to **OF** (pronounced "oaf"). If for some bizarre reason you got stranded in Of, there's a tourist-standard, one-star **hotel**, the *Çaykent*.

Rize

A modern Turkish city in a grand setting, **RİZE**'s name at least will be familiar to every tourist who's bought a souvenir box of "Rize Turist Çay". Of its ancient history as Rhizus nothing survives, and of its role as the easternmost outpost of the Trapezuntine Empire hardly more than a tiny castle. If you do pause it would be to visit the **Tea Institute**, a combined think-tank, botanical garden and tasting/sales outlet on a hill overlooking the town; follow the signs to the "Çay Enstitüsü". On the town square, Atatürk Meydanı, the **PTT** has been smartened up with wooden trimmings, to complement the two nineteenth-century restored wooden houses and the barn on stilts that are highly visible on the hill behind the square. The **otogar** is 800m to the west of town, with service buses to bring you to the town centre. Between the two main streets – Atatürk Caddesi and Cumhuriyet Caddesi, to the east of Atatürk Meydanı – is the town's major tea garden, not surprisingly the focus of the town's social whirl. The surrounding shops sell Rize tea in every conceivable packaging, plus the unlikely spin-off product of tea cologne.

The main body of **hotels** is on and off Atatürk Caddesi and Cumhuriyet Caddesi. A good exception is the *Otel Akarsu* behind the Hükümet Konağı off Atatürk Meydanı (☎0464/217 1779; ①), which has plain but clean rooms, with or without bathroom, in a quiet neighbourhood. The *Turist Hotel* on Cumhuriyet Cad (☎0464/217 2009; ③) is old-fashioned and a little the worse for wear, but some rooms have sea views and balconies and all have bathrooms and TVs; it's a particularly good option for unmarried couples, as you shouldn't be interrogated about your marital status, as may happen elsewhere in Rize. The two-star *Otel Keleş*, off Cumhuriyet Caddesi at Palandöken Cad 2 (☎0464/217 4612, fax 217 1895; ③), isn't as genteel as the *Turist* but has fairly comfortable rooms with fridges and TVs. For **food**, the *Kuğu 2 Kebab Salonu*, Cumhuriyet Cad 229, and the co-managed *Kuğu I* under the *Turist Hotel*, are both highly recommended: they're clean and cheap with friendly service, and wide-ranging menus of soups, fish (including grilled trout), chicken and kebabs.

Otherwise, **moving on** is quickly arranged. The two main bus companies operating from Rize are *Show Turizm* and *Ulusoy*, with buses daily to Batumi (4hr) and Tbilisi (10hr) in Georgia, and twice daily to Erevan in Armenia (10hr; Armenian visas must be obtained in your own country before departure), and *Ulusoy*; both have offices on Cumhuriyet Caddesi. Minibuses east and west leave from the main highway, the shore road.

Rize to Hopa: Lazland

Forty or fifty kilometres beyond Rize you pass the invisible former eastern limit of the Comneni holdings and enter the territory of the **Laz**, the Black Sea's most celebrated minority group – erroneously so much of the time, since other Turks have an annoying habit of stereotypically classing anyone from east of Trabzon as "Laz". Strictly speaking the Laz are a Caucasian people speaking a language related to Georgian, 200,000 of whom inhabit Pazar, Ardeşen, Fındıklı, Arhavı and Hopa, plus certain inland enclaves. The men, with their aquiline features and often reddish hair, particularly stand out; they also distinguish themselves by an extroversion unusual even for the Black Sea, a bent for jokes – practical and verbal – and an extraordinary business acumen that's the envy of slower-witted Turks and the source of so much of the Laz-baiting and misidentification further west. A fair chunk of Turkey's shipping is owned and operated by Laz, who recruit crews from improbably small villages. The wealth so generated makes them relatively progressive in outlook; the women are out and about in western garb from Fındıklı east, and the men too seem better dressed in the latest styles, though "progress" has also been translated into making the five municipalities listed some of the ugliest on the Black Sea – which is saying a lot.

From Ardeşen east the coast has absolutely no plain; imposing mountains, shaggy with tea and hazelnuts, drop directly into the sea. These natural defences have helped the Laz maintain a semblance of independence throughout their **history**. It seems most likely that they're descendants of the ancient Colchians (from whom Jason supposedly stole the Golden Fleece). The Laz accepted Christianity in the sixth century and almost immediately got embroiled in a series of protracted wars with the Byzantines, whose governors had managed to offend them – not hard to do. No power managed to fully subdue them until the Ottomans induced conversion to Islam in the early sixteenth century. Like their neighbours the Hemşinli (see p.656) they don't lose too much sleep over their religious affiliation, though with their peripatetic habits and far-flung enterprises the Laz are now well integrated into the national fabric.

Hopa and on to the Georgian border

HOPA, which used to be the end of the line until the nearby frontier was opened and the road to it was declassified militarily, is a grim industrial port, devoted to shipment of the copper mined slightly inland. The **minibus terminal** is just on the east bank of the stream which laps the west side of the town. If you have to stay here – and this would only happen if you were en route to the former USSR and arrived too late to cross the border – there are two reasonable **hotels** on the waterfront: the two-star *Papila* (☎0466/351 3641; ③), which offers comfortable rooms with central heating, minibars and satellite TVs, as well as a marine sunset from the balcony; and the newer, very clean *Cihan*, Ortahopa Cad 7 (☎0466/351 4897; ③). If your wallet's not up to these rates, there are a few less salubrious establishments near the central cluster of **restaurants**, **banks** and the **PTT**, between the *Papila* and the bus terminal.

Ten cliff-hemmed, twisty kilometres northeast of Hopa, **KEMALPAŞA** is the next-to-last Turkish village on the Black Sea, with a huge pebble **beach** and a couple of makeshift **campsites** a healthy distance away from the tea factory. There's no other accommodation, but you won't starve thanks to a handful of **restaurants** by the campsites.

Minibuses cover the entire 20km from Hopa to the **Turkish–Georgian frontier**, set by the Turkish and Soviet revolutionary governments in 1921 at the stream dividing the previously insignificant village of **SARP**, rather than more logically at the Çoruh River by Batumi. The crossing was virtually inactive between 1935 and 1988, a casualty of Stalinist, then Cold War, paranoia, but since the gates have opened, Turkish Sarp has become a busy 24-hour way-station for convoys of Georgians, Armenians and Russians heading for the markets of Turkey's Black Sea cities and towns. If you intend to do more than just ogle the colourful spectacle, show up with your **Georgian visa** (obtainable in Trabzon, İstanbul or Ankara). **Minibuses to Batumi** leave early evenings from Sarp.

Inland: the foothills from Trabzon to Rize

While Sumela is a hard act to follow, there are a number of other possible destinations in the hills southeast of Trabzon. The valleys leading to and past them are also useful alternative routes toward Erzurum, avoiding some or all of the often congested E390/885/915 highway.

Çaykara to Uzungöl

The starting point for excursions up the valley of the Solaklı Çayı is Of. Both Of and **ÇAYKARA**, the unexciting main town of the lower valley, are renowned for their devoutness, with the highest ratio of *kuran kursus* (Koran schools for children) per capita in the country, and phalanxes of bearded and skull-capped *hoca*s and *hacı*s striding about in the shadow of huge mosques. A further peculiarity is that anyone over forty speaks as their first language the Pontic dialect of Greek. It seems probable that the tribes of this valley were Hellenized (along with others such as those around Maçka) at some point during Byzantine rule, though they never lost their reputation as fierce brigands. Upon conversion to Islam at the end of the seventeenth century, their ferocity was transmuted into piety; as the saying goes, when the devil grows old he becomes a monk. It should come as no surprise, then, that you haven't a prayer of anything stronger than a fruit juice between Of and Uzungöl.

Sixteen kilometres inland, you might persuade your dolmuş to stop at the **covered wooden bridge of Hapsiyaş** (Kiremitli), photogenically romantic despite its prosaic setting. The present structure dates from only 1935, but it seems likely there's been a span here for several centuries.

Uzungöl and around

Twenty-five kilometres on from Çaykara, the tarmac ends and an appalling side road climbs twenty more kilometres to **Uzungöl** (Long Lake), the main attraction of this area. Especially at weekends, frequent dolmuşes make the ninety-minute trip up from Of. The lake, at 1100m, is only averagely scenic, with a bazaar district clustered around its outlet; the wooden houses of the namesake village, clustered on the slope above, are more picturesque.

The sole place to **stay** is the *İnan Kardeşler Tesisleri*, at the high end of the lake where most minibuses end their run. This is a combination trout farm/restaurant/campsite/motel managed by Hüseyin and Dursun İnan, one or other of whom will try and wait on you personally, even at weekends when the diner is mobbed. The food is simple, tasty and reasonable – under $6 for a medium-sized trout, salad and pudding.

Uzungöl is an ideal base for rambles up to the nearby peaks of **Ziyaret** (3111m) and **Halizden** (3193m), with a chain of glacier lakes at the base of the latter. It's a very long day's hike there and back – though you can go part way by car to save time – so take a tent and food for two days if at all possible.

The right-hand turning above Çaykara leads after 3.5km to **ATAKÖY**, one of the better preserved of the Black Sea foothill villages. Don't expect a museum piece like Safranbolu, but there are scattered clusters of half-timbered farmsteads above the main high street. The municipality runs its own occasional bus between here and Of. If you have your own vehicle the 70km from here to Bayburt via the 2300-metre Soğanli Pass make a very scenic and reasonably easy drive.

The İkizdere valley

The next major valley east of Uzungöl, the İkizdere valley, holds no special attraction to stop for, but the scenery along the way is memorable and the road eventually winds up to the highest driveable pass in the Pontic ranges – one of the three highest in all Turkey. The place is mostly worth knowing about as an alternative route to Erzurum or as an approach to the Kaçkar range (see the "Northeastern Anatolia" chapter).

İKİZDERE, with frequent minibuses from Rize, is logically enough the main town, and the transfer point for the 27-kilometre trip up the Yetimhoca valley to Başköy, the westernmost trailhead for the Kaçkar Dağları. Watch out though: there are at least three other Başköys or Başyaylas in a thirty-kilometre radius, so don't let yourself or your driver get confused. A better alternative, if possible, is to arrange transfer to Saler, the highest village in the valley with road access.

Beyond İkizdere, the main road soon finds itself between jagged peaks and the *yaylas* gathered at the 2600-metre **Ovitdağı Pass**, far more alpine than the overrated Zigana Pass to the west. The col marks the limits of Rize province and, presumably, Mesut Yılmaz's patronage, since the road deteriorates markedly soon after.

The Hemşin valleys

The most scenic and interesting of the foothill regions east of Trabzon is around the river of **Fırtına Çayı** and its tributaries, which tumble off the steepest slopes of the Pontic ranges, here known as the Kaçkar Dağları. Between the mountains and the sea lie a few hundred square kilometres of rugged, isolated territory that have been imperfectly controlled at best by the prevailing imperial, or regional, powers of every era.

For the less geographically minded the area is known simply as **Hemşin**, a word whose etymology encapsulates local history: "-eşen" is a local dialect suffix, derived from Armenian, meaning "population" or "settlement", as in "Hamameşen" or "the settlement around the baths" (the hot springs at today's Ayder). Over time this was abbreviated to Hemşin, and came to describe the triangular zone with its base against the mountains and its apex at Pazar, and by extension the people in it.

Çamlıhemşin and around

ÇAMLIHEMŞİN, 24km upstream from the mouth of the Fırtına Çayı, is still too low at 300m to give you a real feel for the Hemşin country. Nonetheless it's the last proper town before the mountains, utilitarian and busy, with a constant chaos of minibuses and shoppers clogging its single high street. There's a **bank**, a **PTT**, stores for last-minute hiking supplies, two or three **restaurants** and a lone **hotel** (the *Hoşdere*), but it's not a place to linger when so many better things await further up.

Above Çamlıhemşin, along both the main stream and the tributary flowing down from Ayder, you begin to see some of the many graceful **bridges** which are a regional speciality. Their age and attribution are both subject to debate, but many have been dated to the seventeenth century and credited to Armenian craftsmen. Just before the first of these bridges at Yolkiyi Köyü is the *Otel Doğa* (☎0464/651 7455; $6 per person), which offers spotless dormitory-style rooms with river views, as well as breakfast and evening meals. Owner İdris Duinan is a mine of information about the area and his hotel makes a good point from which to launch your explorations.

Two of the most gravity-defying bridges span the Fırtına Çayı at **ŞENYUVA**, a typically dispersed community of occasionally impressive dwellings 8–10km above Çamlıhemşin. If your level of commitment isn't up to camping out in the high moun-

THE HEMŞİN PEOPLE

The **Hemşinlis** are, according to competing theories, either a very old Turkish tribe, stragglers from the original tenth-century migrations who got stuck here; or, more likely, natives descended from the Heptacomete tribesmen of old, who spoke a dialect of Armenian and were nominally Christian or pagan until about a century-and-a-half ago. In support of the latter notion, there exists a group of Islamic Armenian-speakers south of Hopa who call their dialect Hemşince and claim origins in Hemşin proper.

Certainly the main body of Hemşinlis, with their strong-featured and fair-complexioned women and (literally) Caucasian-looking men, appear anything but mainstream Turkish, and these outgoing, merry, occasionally outrageous people are diametrically opposite in behaviour to the more serious central Anatolians. Quite a bit of this has to do with wearing their Islam lightly; there's none of the overt piety of the Çaykara valley, and you're unlikely to be blasted out of bed at dawn by a *muezzin* for the simple reason that most communities are too small to support a mosque. Despite stern little signs in the country stores warning that "alcohol is the mother of all ills", the men in fact are prodigious drinkers, a tendency aggravated by the **environment**. This is by far the dampest and mistiest part of Turkey, with the sun in hiding two days out of three and up to 200 annual inches of rain in some spots. It doesn't take a genius to predict cloud forest vegetation, with everything from moss-fringed fir and alders down to marsh species and creeping vines clinging to the slopes, as well as moods swinging wildly between moroseness and euphoria among the inhabitants.

Like the nearby Laz, whom they dislike being mistaken for, the Hemşinlis are intrepid and independent. They also have a special genius for the profession of pastry chef and pudding maker: the top **sweet shops** of major Turkish cities are usually owned and/or staffed by natives of these valleys. The number of Hemşinlis living in diaspora, a process begun under Russian rule last century, is far larger than the 15,000 permanently inhabiting this rather compact domain.

You know you've left the Laz zone when, a little way inland from Pazar or Ardeşen, you begin to see the brilliant yellow, black and red **scarves** (called *puşi*) of the Hemşin women, skillfully worn as turbans and contrasting with the drabness of the men's garb. Curiously, the scarves are not local but imported from India, perhaps a relic of the days when Trabzon was a terminus of the Silk Route.

As in attire, so in **housing**: a mix of vernacular and borrowed styles and materials, reflecting wealth earned outside. Some positively baronial residences preside over tea terraces and cornfields at lower elevations (Hemşin, incidentally, is one of the few places in Turkey where corn is made into food for human consumption rather than fed solely to animals). But to fully understand the Hemşin mentality you need to visit at least one **yayla**, or summer pastoral hamlet.

*Yayla*s are found throughout Turkey in the uplands, but in Hemşin they are at their best. These tightly bunched groups of dwellings, usually stone-built to waist height and chalet-style in timber thereafter, begin just at treeline and recur at intervals up to 2700m. They're inhabited only between late May and early September, when their tenants may come from as far away as Holland or Germany to renew attachments to what they consider their true spiritual homeland. Sanitary mod cons don't come to mind – shrouded in acrid smoke, awash in mud and nettles, *yayla*s seem more part of, say, Nepal than a country with EC candidacy – but if you're invited into a cabin the hospitality will be overwhelming even by Turkish standards, and that's saying a lot.

tains, head instead for the *yayla* of **POKUT**, where after several hours on the trail southeast from Şenyuva you can stay at the Akay family lodge. The following day you can strike out as far as Polovit *yayla* at 2300m, via Hazıntak (see below) and Amlakıt, returning the same evening to Pokut, with no need to carry any equipment heavier than a daypack and raingear. Pokut itself is fairly representative of the more substantial Black Sea *yayla*s, with handsome woodwork capped by mixed tin-and-timber roofs rising from stone foundations.

The upper Fırtına valley

Above Şenyuva along the main branch of the Fırtına, the road steadily worsens while the scenery just as relentlessly becomes more spectacular. Below, the water roils in chasms and whirlpools that are irresistible to the lunatic fringe of the rubber-rafting fraternity. Roughly 12km along, the single-towered castle of **Zılkale**, improbably sited by either the Armenians or the Genoese to control a minor trade route, appears at a bend in the track. The tree-tufted ruin, more often than not garnished with wisps of mist, today dominates nothing more than one of the most evocative settings in the Pontus. No such lonely castle would be complete without its resident ghosts, and the locals claim that after dark it's haunted by the shades of its former garrison and their horses – so don't get left behind if your minibus pauses to let you snap a picture.

Çat and around

After another 12km or so of violent abuse to your vehicle's suspension, you'll arrive at **ÇAT**, 1250m up. This is another classic base for rambles in the western Kaçkar, and though there seems not to be much to the village beyond a few scattered buildings, there's a surprisingly good **hotel/store/restaurant**, the *Otel Cancık* (①), with clean rooms upstairs; there's a hot shower on demand down the hall. If it's full, as may happen when a trek group's about, an alternative *pansiyon* can be found 1km downstream.

At Çat the upper reaches of the Fırtına divide. A road running parallel to the main fork heads 30km due south to Ortaköy, passing Zilkale's sister fort of Varoş at Kaleköy, where yet another side road winds up to an alternative **trailhead for the western Kaçkar mountains** at Kale Yayla. Don't try to walk any more of these tracks than you have to – between Kale Yayla and Çat, for example, you've a very boring three-to-four-hour slog in either direction – but wait for the one daily minibus at the junction in Çat.

The other turning above Çat bears almost due east, and is all but undriveable once past a final, exquisite bridge leading seemingly nowhere. The road eventually expires 9km later in **ELEVİT** (1800m). Somehow a Thursday-and-Friday-only **minibus** wrestles itself down from here to Pazar, descending at 8am and returning at about noon. There are actually more **shops** in Elevit than in Çat, as well as a single, crude **lodge** which should charge about the same as Çat's. Elevit, like its nearest neighbour Tirevit ninety minutes' walk east, is a Laz *yayla*, an enclave of sorts in Hemşin territory.

If you're lightly equipped, there are several possible day hikes from Elevit, most rewardingly three hours up to Yildizli Gölü at the top of the vale opening to the south of Elevit. Alternatively, with an early start, you could make a one-way dash to the safety of the lodge in Pokut (see above), via Tirevit, Polovit, Amlakıt and Hazıntak; for more information on these places consult "The Kaçkar Dağları" in the "Northeastern Anatolia" chapter, or *Trekking in Turkey* (see "Books" in *Contexts*).

Ayder

The busiest road above Çamlıhemşin ends after 17km at **AYDER** (1300m), the highest permanently inhabited settlement in the Hemşin valley system, poised somewhere between village and *yayla*. Concrete tattiness now overwhelms the indigenous wood cabins, but it doesn't matter too much as the surrounding scenery was always the main attraction. In recent years Ayder has become a resort of some note, partly because of its thermal baths but more for its role as a favourite jump-off point for hikes in the central Kaçkar Dağları. Accommodation is still uniformly basic, but that will doubtless change following the imminent completion of improvements to the access road. A new and predictably ugly spa complex is located in the upper village, but there's no bank, only a rudimentary PTT booth.

Arrival

In season, hourly **minibuses** depart Pazar for the one-hour-plus trip to Ayder between the hours of 10am and 6pm; you may have to change vehicles in Çamlıhemşin. Going down to the coast from Ayder, there are hourly departures to Pazar, three daily to Rize and one to Trabzon. In theory you can descend from Ayder to pick up the single daily minibus going up the main Fırtına valley toward Çat without having to return all the way to Pazar, but you'll need to be in Çamlıhemşin by 10am.

Accommodation

Among the half-dozen or so simple **hotels**, the *Otel Cağlayan* (no phone; ①), in the upper half of the village – the oldest traditional wooden lodge in Ayder – has the most character, and the staff do simple but typical Hemşin dishes such as *mühlama* (a fry-up of butter, cornmeal and cheese). It's also the most used to trekkers, since Kadir Sarı, co-manager and grandson of the original owner, is an experienced local mountain guide (another good local guide is Mehmet Okumuş: PO Box 15, Hemşin, 53550 Pazar, Rize). The *Ayder Hilton* (☎0464/657 2024; ②), a four-storey breeze-block structure in the village centre, rates itself as four-star but has spartan rooms. If you prefer traditional style (though maybe a bit less comfort), and the *Cağlayan* is full, try the *Otel Saray* (☎0464/657 2001; ①).

Hiking

Much the best day out of Ayder is the strenuous but rewarding **loop hike** via Hazıntak, Samistal and Aşağı Kavron *yayla*s. This isn't to be undertaken lightly – elevation changes are 3000 metres in total – but you can do it in eight hours of walking, excluding rest stops. The trail, beginning immediately behind the lower baths, first takes you southwest through maritime cloud forest to Hazıntak, a handsome cluster just above treeline, and then briefly follows a majestic river canyon on a corniche route south before veering up and southeast to the primitive rock-and-sod cottages of Samistal. From the ridge above this second *yayla*, weather permitting, you'll have spectacular views of the main Kaçkar summit ridge; then you face a stiff, zigzag descent east to Aşaği Kavron and the end of the forest road heading north back down to Ayder.

Again, for details on the rest of the Kaçkar, refer to the "Northeastern Anatolia" chapter.

Eating, drinking and bathing

In terms of **eating and drinking** in Ayder, the *Nazlı Çiçek* (the "Coy Flower") is the big evening hangout; there's brook trout on their menu as well as local dishes like *mühlama*. Local women, wearing traditional *puşi* headgear, also frequent the place, and the weekend's entertainment is to dance the *horon*, the Black Sea folk dance in which frenetic limb movements represent the movements of waves, boats and *hamsi* fish, accompanied by the *tulum*, the goatskin bagpipe native to these parts. Other restaurants with trout on offer are the *Şehir* and the *Viyana*, both slightly down-valley. Drinking holes (where both sexes can feel relaxed) are relatively easy to find in the village, although the *Nazlı Çiçek* doesn't serve alcohol. If you carry on past the *Otel Çağlayan* uphill on the road to Hoşdere, at the highest point of the village there are two unnamed bars on the hillside, both fairly well stocked, with makeshift protection from the rain. Hoşdere, about a kilometre above Ayder, is a beautiful plateau in the mountains where the village and visitors from the surrounding area congregate at weekends; a number of stands sell kebabs and the *horon* dance continues seemingly from where it left off the night before at the *Nazlı Çiçek*.

Few of Ayder's hotels have baths on the premises, let alone en suite, since it's expected that you'll patronize one of the village's two **hot springs**. The downstream **hamam** (men 6–9am & 5–7pm, women 9am–5pm; last admission 30min before changeover; $2) is accessible via a wobbly bridge to the far bank of the river. The scalding (close to 135°F) water is directed into a single round pool; descending trekkers will be glad to know that clothes laundering is possible. Not so at the upper **bath complex** (separate sections for men and women, 7am–8pm; $2), where washing of all sorts is discouraged, and even hotter water fills rectangular, tiled basking pools in each section.

travel details

Trains

Samsun to: Amasya (1 daily; 4hr 30min); Kayseri (4 weekly; 19hr); Sivas (1 daily; 12hr).

Zonguldak to: Ankara (1 daily, overnight; 9hr 10min).

Buses

Amasra to: Bartin (every 30min; 25min); Sinop (6 daily; 6hr); Zonguldak (3 daily; 1hr 45min).

Bartin to: Ankara (3 daily; 5hr 30min); Safranbolu (8 daily; 1hr 20min); Zonguldak (hourly; 1hr 20min).

Giresun to: Ordu (every 30min; 30min); Tirebolu (hourly; 45min); Trabzon (hourly; 2hr 15min).

Hopa to: Artvin (hourly dolmuşes; 1hr 30min); Rize (hourly dolmuşes; 1hr 40min).

İnebolu to: Kastamonu (4 daily; 1hr 30min).

Ordu to: Giresun (every 30min; 30min); Perşembe (every 30min; 20min); Samsun (hourly; 2hr 45min); Ünye (hourly; 1hr 30min).

Rize to: Afyon (1 daily; 20hr); Ankara (1 daily; 14hr); Ayder (1 daily; 2hr); Bursa (3 daily; 18hr); Erzurum via İspir (1–2 daily; 7hr); Hopa (hourly; 1hr 40min); İkizdere (hourly; 1hr); İsparta (1 daily; 18hr); İspir (5 dolmuşes daily; 4hr); İstanbul (3 daily; 18hr); Samsun (every 30min; 7hr); Trabzon (every 30min; 1hr 30 min); Urfa (1 daily; 20hr).

Samsun to: Afyon (2 daily; 10hr); Amasya (10 daily; 2hr 30min); Ankara (6 daily; 7hr); Balıkesir (1 daily; 14hr); Erzurum (2 daily; 10hr); İstanbul (4 daily; 11hr); Rize (every 30min; 7hr); Sinop (every 30min; 3hr); Sivas (3 daily; 6hr 30min); Trabzon (4 daily; 6hr); Van (1 daily; 23hr).

Sinop to: Amasra (2 daily; 6hr); Kastamonu (4 daily; 3hr); Samsun (every 30min; 3hr).

Trabzon to: Alanya (2 daily; 22hr); Ankara (6 daily; 12hr); Antalya (2 daily; 20hr); Artvin (2 direct daily; 5hr); Bayburt (5 daily; 5hr); Diyarbakır (1 daily; 20hr); Erzurum (3 daily; 6hr); Giresun (hourly; 2hr 15min); Hopa (hourly; 3hr); İstanbul (8 daily; 17hr); İzmir (4 daily; 22hr); Kars (2 direct daily; 12hr); Of (every 30min; 1hr); Rize (every 30min; 1hr 30min); Samsun (hourly; 6hr).

Zonguldak to: Ankara (hourly; 5hr 30min); İstanbul (6 daily; 6hr).

International buses

Rize to: Batumi, Georgia (1 daily; 4hr); Tbilisi, Georgia (1 daily; 10hr); Erivan, Armenia (2 daily; 10hr).

Samsun to: Tbilisi, Georgia (1 daily; 17hr).

Trabzon to: Batumi, Georgia (1 daily; 3hr 30min); Tbilisi, Georgia (1 daily; 9hr 30min).

Ferries

Turkish Maritime Lines run a cruise ship from İstanbul to Rize and back in a week, between mid-April and mid-September (total journey time from İstanbul to Rize 60hr). Prices vary considerably depending on the class of cabin or seat required, and the length of your journey, but to give some idea, a Pullman seat from İstanbul to Trabzon costs $27, while a luxury-class cabin goes for $65, and the cheapest cabin $37. Pullman seats on short hops, for example from Trabzon to Giresun, are under $10. The tariff to take a car from İstanbul to Trabzon is $48, from Trabzon to Samsun $28. Meals are served on the boat.

Giresun to: Samsun (weekly, Thurs; 8hr); Trabzon (weekly, Wed; 5hr).

İstanbul to: Sinop (weekly, Mon; 22hr).

Samsun to: Giresun (weekly, Tues; 5hr); Sinop (weekly, Thurs; 6hr 30min).

Sinop to: Samsun (weekly, Tues; 6hr); İstanbul (weekly, Thurs; 22hr).

Trabzon to: Giresun (weekly, Wed; 6hr); Rize (weekly, Wed; 2hr 30min).

Rize to: Trabzon (weekly,Wed; 2hr 30min).

International ferries

Samsun to: Novrosky, Russia (1 weekly, no foot passengers; 17hr); Odessa, Ukraine (2 weekly, no foot passengers; 32hr); Sochi, Russia (twice-weekly catamarans; 7hr).

Trabzon to: Gelencik (1 weekly; 16hr); Sochi (4 weekly ferries, 18hr; plus daily catamarans, 5hr).

Flights

Samsun to: Ankara (2 weekly; 1hr); İstanbul (1 daily; 1hr 30min).

Trabzon to: Ankara (2 daily on *THY*, 1hr 30min; 4 weekly on *İstanbul Hava Yolları*, 1hr); Antalya (2 weekly; 1hr 10min); Baku, Azerbaijan (2 weekly; 1hr); İstanbul (2–3 daily on *THY*, 1hr 50min; 1–2 daily on *İstanbul Hava Yolları*, 1hr 20min); İzmir (1 weekly on *THY*, 1hr; 1 weekly on *İstanbul Hava Yolları*, 1hr).

CHAPTER TEN

NORTHEASTERN ANATOLIA

Bleak, inhospitable and melancholy, **Northeastern Anatolia** is Turkey's Siberia, the Outback and the North Slope rolled into one. Much of it is high, windswept plateau segmented by ranks of eroded mountains that seem barely higher despite impressive altitudes on the map. Four great rivers – the Çoruh, Kura, Aras and Euphrates (Fırat in Turkish) – rise here, beginning courses which take them to disparate ends in the Black, Caspian and Persian seas. Their sources almost meet at the forbidding roof of the steppe near Erzurum, but as the rivers descend through warmer canyons and valleys at the edge of the uplands, oases and towns appear, lending much of the interest and attraction of the region.

A great deal of governmental attention, both military and civilian, has been lavished on the provinces of Kars, Artvin and Erzurum, which form the heart of the region. But despite ambitious development projects, most of the terrain will never be suited to anything except cultivating grain and sugar beets, or the grazing of livestock. Given the treeless landscape, the making and stacking of cow-dung patties for fuel becomes a conspicuous necessity for villagers unable to buy coal, the dung vying in height with the equally ubiquitous haystacks. The harsh, six-month winters dictate a troglodytic architecture of semi-subterranean burrow-houses – and a stoic, self-contained character to go with it. Only the relatively prosperous and forested valleys around Yusufeli and Artvin have a lighter atmosphere, as a tangible Caucasian influence begins to be felt.

As a traveller, you will probably have the place largely to yourself because tourism has collapsed in the wake of Kurdish troubles in the southeast. Yet although the region is hemmed in by trouble – the aftermath of a Georgian civil war to the north, an Azeri-Armenian war nearby in Nagorno-Karabakh, turbulent Iran to the east and Kurdish separatism to the south – it remains largely unaffected by all of the excitement going on around it. Whether you approach from central Anatolia, the extreme southeast of Turkey or the Black Sea, your first stop is likely to be **Erzurum**, long a goal of armies and merchants alike and the only real urban centre. Today it's the main jumping-off

---

DRIVING IN THE NORTHEAST

Road surfaces in the northeast are by far and away the worst in Turkey, and many of the tracks that lead off to smaller villages and churches are impassable after heavy rain. The roads around Kars and Ani are particularly horrible. Petrol stations, nearly always *Turk Ofisi*, are few and far between off the main roads, and many of the smaller stations regularly run out of petrol. Try not to let your tank fall below a quarter full. Check your spare tyre and tool kit, and try to take a list of garages specialising in your make. Car rental agencies exist in Erzurum and Trabzon, and you can often return a car to a different city than you rented from. Finally take a good map, ideally the *GeoCenter/RV Euro Atlas*.

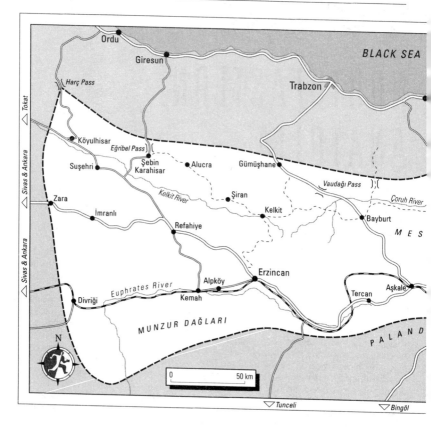

point to just about anywhere else in the region, with a clutch of post-Selçuk Turkish monuments to briefly distract you. To the northeast, **Kars**, the last major town before the Armenian frontier, is a dreary disappointment, but serves as the base for visits to the former Armenian capital of **Ani**, the single biggest tourist attraction in the region. North of Erzurum, the southernmost **valleys of early medieval Georgia**, now part of Turkey, hide nearly a dozen **churches** and almost as many **castles** – enchantingly set, little visited and arguably the most rewarding targets in the area. The provincial capital of **Artvin** and the pleasant town of **Yusufeli** are the logical overnight stops while in search of Georgian monuments, and Yusufeli also lies astride the most popular southern approach to the magnificent **Kaçkar Dağları**, a trekker's paradise that separates Northeast Anatolia from the Black Sea.

Some history

Perhaps because of the discouraging climate and meagre resources, this corner of the country was thinly settled until the second millennium BC. The Urartians had their northernmost city at today's **Altıntepe**, near Erzincan, between the ninth and sixth centuries, but the next real imperial power to make an appearance was the Roman Empire,

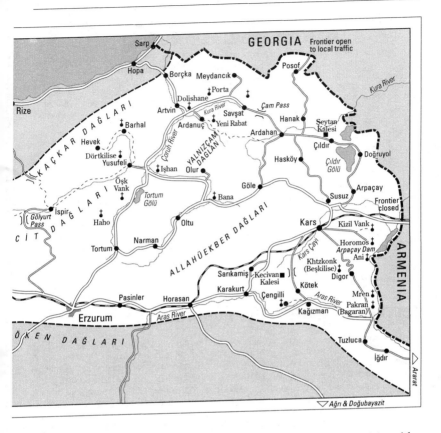

succeeded by the Byzantines and Armenians. The eleventh-century undermining of the Armenian state and the Byzantine defeat at Manzikert marked the start of a pattern of invasion and counterattack which was to continue until 1920. The Selçuks, their minor successor emirates and the newly ascendant Georgian kingdom jockeyed for position in the territory until swept aside by Mongol raids in the early thirteenth century, and Tamerlane's juggernaut in the next; the Ottomans finally reasserted some semblance of centralized control early in the sixteenth century.

Just as the northeast had been a remote frontier of the Byzantines, so it became the border of the new Anatolian empire, confronting an expansionist Tsarist Russia, which effectively ended what remained of Georgia's autonomy in 1783. As the Ottomans declined, Russia grew bolder, advancing out of Caucasian fortresses to lop off slices of the region on several occasions during the nineteenth century, though they got to keep their conquests only in 1829 and 1878. Until 1914 nearly half of the sites described in this chapter were under Russian rule, with additional conquests up to 1917 nullified by the Bolshevik Revolution and the collapse of the Caucasian front. Between 1915 and 1921 the area was the scene of almost uninterrupted warfare between White Russian, Armenian Dashnakist and Turkish Nationalist armies, and of massacres among the mixed civilian population which had historically been over a third Armenian and Georgian Christian.

By 1923 the northeast was all but prostrate, with ninety percent of its former population dead or dispersed. The present international boundaries between Turkey and Georgia or Armenia are the result of treaties between Atatürk and the Soviet Union in March and October 1921, and don't necessarily reflect historical divisions (indeed as late as 1945 Stalin was still demanding that Kars and Ardahan be returned to the Russian Motherland).

Towards Erzurum: the Euphrates valley route

Coming from the west, many travellers cover the lonely stretch of Highway 200/E88 between Sivas and Erzurum in one day – easily done and certainly recommended if you're in a hurry. With more time at your disposal, a leisurely approach via the valleys of the Euphrates River and its tributaries is preferable. Most of the countryside between Kangal and Kemah is all but trackless, the railway still the only dependable link to the rest of Turkey; during daylight hours a **train trip** through the spectacular, ruddy river gorges flecked with oases is certainly the most enjoyable and scenic introduction to northeastern Turkey. The river itself, green and opaque, is warm enough above the giant Keban Dam to support carp – an anomaly in a region famed for trout.

With more advance research and a taste for adventure, you can explore the river even more thoroughly by **kayak** or **raft**, albeit in the opposite direction. The favourite stretch, with highest water between May and July, is the two-day run between Erzincan and Kemah. Continuing further downstream is complicated by the difficulty of meeting a support vehicle on the largely roadless banks; the next place you could try might be Iliç, another two days' float beyond Kemah and accessible via a side road from Refahiye.

Divriği

Stuck in the middle of a mountainous nowhere between Sivas and Elâzığ, on a hill overlooking a tributary of the young Euphrates, **DİVRİĞİ** merits a visit for the sake of a single monument, the whimsical and unique **Ulu Cami** and its dependency, the **Darüşşifa** (sanitorium). These date from early in the thirteenth century, when the town was the seat of the tiny Mengüçeh emirate; the Mengüçehs were evicted by the Mongols in 1252, who demolished the castle here but left the religious foundations alone, and the place was not incorporated into the Ottoman Empire until 1516.

The main drawbacks to stopping in Divriği are the poor hotels and the limited number of options for moving on – transport schedules virtually dictate an overnight stay.

You'll probably arrive from either Sivas or Erzurum if dependent on public transport, most pleasantly by train; there are no links with Elâzaı.

The Town

Divriği is sleepy, dependent on the nearby iron and steel works, and has a ramshackle bazaar crisscrossed by cobbled lanes and grapevines. Architecturally the town sports distinctive wooden **minarets** and old houses with inverted-keyhole windows, neither of which are seen elsewhere in Anatolia. The conspicuous **Ulu Cami** and the **Darüşşifa** are joined in one complex at the top of a slope 250m east of town, commanding a fine view. The mosque, dedicated in 1228 by a certain Ahmet Zah, is noted for its outrageous external **portals**, most un-Islamic with their wealth of floral and faunal detail. Rather far-fetched comparisons have been made to Indian Mogul art but a simpler, more likely explanation is that Armenian or Selçuk craftsmen had a hand in the decoration. The north door, festooned with vegetal designs, is the most celebrated, although the northwestern one is more intricately worked – note the pair of double-headed eagles, not necessarily copied from the Byzantines since it's a very old Anatolian motif. Inside, sixteen columns and the ceiling they support are more suggestive of a Gothic cloister or a Byzantine cistern. There's rope-vaulting in one dome, while the northeastern one, at least until it's renovated, sports a peanut-brittle surface, in terms of both the relief work and variegated colouring; the central dome has been rather tastelessly restored. The *mihrab* is plain, flanked by an extravagant carved wooden *mimber*.

The adjoining **Darüşşifa** was also begun in 1228, by Adaletli Melike Turan Melek, Ahmet Şah's wife. Its **portal** is restrained in comparison to the mosque's, but still bears medallions lifted almost free from their background. The gate is usually locked, so you must find the caretaker to gain admission – easiest just after prayers next door. A $1 donation is requested after signing the guest register at the conclusion of the tour.

The caretaker proudly points out some of the more arcane features of the interior, which is asymmetrical in both ground plan and ornamentation, and even more eclectic than the mosque. Of four dissimilar columns surrounding a **fountain**, two are embossed; the eight-sided pool has a curlicue drain hole as well as two more conventional feeder spouts. Overhead, the dome has collapsed and been crudely replaced in the same manner as the mosque's, but four-pointed **groin vaulting** graces the entry hall, with even more elaborate ribbing over a raised platform in the *eyvan*, or domed side-chamber, at the rear of the nave. The fan-reliefs on the wall behind this once formed an elaborate **sundial**, catching rays through the second-floor window of the facade; it's claimed that the suspended carved cylinder in front of this opening once revolved, though it's unclear how this helped the sundial function – perhaps there was a prism mounted in it. Musicians may once have played on the raised platform to entertain the patients, whose rather poky bedrooms on both ground and upper storeys you're allowed to visit. One of the side rooms contains the **tombs** of Ahmet Şah and his father Süleyman Şah.

Practicalities

The **train station**, connected to Ankara and Erzurum, is down by the river, a twenty-minute walk from the bazaar; alternatively, taxis meet most arrivals, and don't cost more than a couple of dollars. The **otogar**, essentially a dirt car park with four or five daily departures to Sivas only, is 400m south of town on the road to Elâzığ; there's a **hamam** on the way there, which you may need to patronize if you spend the night here. The only two **hotels** stand across from each other on the main commercial street west of the inner bazaar: the depressingly basic *Ninni* (①) has passably clean rooms with a single hot shower on the first floor; its neighbour the *Diğer* (①) offers still less value for money. **Eating** is a little better, with a *kebap salonu* and an oven-food place near the hotels; the *Üçler Pide Salonu* in the bazaar; and the licensed *Belediye Restaurant* on the main square, below the Mengüçeh monuments.

The upper Euphrates valley

In addition to the long-distance expresses, a local "milk run" train sets out most days at 4.40am from Divriği to Erzincan and Erzurum. If you don't mind the risk of being stranded for half a day, you could alight at **KEMAH**, a historic town perched over a picturesque reach of river. There's a complex of **tombs** from different eras perched above the river, and a huge Byzantine-Selçuk **castle**, in better shape than Divriği's, with cellars to explore. The place is even smaller than Divriği, however, and can muster just a few tiny shops and one unmarked, rudimentary hotel. Except at weekends, **dolmuşes** along the paved 50km to Erzincan are fairly regular.

Kemah used to be a trailhead for treks across the **Munzur Dağları**, which tower snow-streaked above the Euphrates' south bank, but there have been sporadic Kurdish-related troubles since 1986, and if you inform the *jandarma* post of your intention to climb you may be prevented from doing so. **ALPKÖY**, twenty minutes further east along the tracks, is a better place to start – nobody will stop you here, and a giant canyon leading straight up to the heart of the mountains is very close to the station.

ERZİNCAN, once one of the most elegant cities in Turkey, with several Armenian monuments on the outskirts and dozens of mosques and *medrese*s in the town, was devastated by earthquakes in 1939 and again in 1983. There's therefore no reason to linger longer than the short time it takes to change buses or trains – connections on to Erzurum are frequent. Roughly halfway there, near the head of the Euphrates valley, you might – with your own transport – consider breaking the journey at **TERCAN**, graced by a **türbe**, **kervansaray** and **bridge** built by the Saltuk emirs of Erzurum at the beginning of the thirteenth century. The tomb in particular is bizarre, consisting of a lobed and cone-headed cylinder enclosed in a richly decorated circular boundary wall, a design found elsewhere only in Central Asian Turkestan.

Erzurum

Nearly two thousand metres up, its horizons defined by mountains a further thousand metres above, and rocked by frequent earthquakes, **ERZURUM** is Turkey's highest and most exposed city. Because of a strategic location astride the main trade routes to Persia, the Caucausus and western Anatolia, its sovereignty has always been contested, and today it's still a major garrison town of over a quarter of a million people. In this conservative backwater, far from the freedoms of Ankara, many women wear gunny-sack-like *çarşaf*s (full-length robes with hoods and veils) in the same dun colour as the surrounding steppe, and some even wear the black *chador*, a cultural import from nearby Iran; men often wear skullcaps, not just the ubiquitous Turkish bobble hat. All told, the combination of history, climate and earthquakes has resulted in a bleak, much-rebuilt place where sunlight seems wan even in midsummer, and where the landscaped, broad modern boulevards often end abruptly in quite literally the middle of nowhere.

After years as a transit stop for overlanders on the way to Iran, Afghanistan and India, mass tourism is still in its infancy in Erzurum. The city is increasingly used as a base and staging point for mountaineering and rafting expeditions bound for the Kaçkar Dağları and Ağrı Dağ, but it also deserves a full day in itself to see a compact group of very early Turkish monuments.

Some history

Although the site had been occupied for centuries before, a city only rose to prominence here towards the end of the fourth century AD, when the Byzantine emperor Theodosius fortified the place and renamed it **Theodosiopolis**. Over the next five hundred years the town changed hands frequently between Constantinople and assorted Arab dynasties, with a short period of Armenian rule.

After the decisive Battle of Manzikert in 1071, Erzurum – a corruption of Arz-er-Rum or "Domain of the Byzantines" in Arabic – fell into the hands of first the Selçuks and then the Saltuk clan of Turks. These were in turn displaced by the Alhanid Mongols during the fourteenth century, forerunners of Tamerlane himself, who used the city as a springboard for his brief blitzkrieg into western Anatolia.

Erzurum was incorporated into the Ottoman Empire by Selim I in 1515, where it remained securely until 1828, after which the Russians occupied it on three occasions. With the memory of the last Russian tenure (1916–17) still fresh in their minds, and the city held by renegade General Karabekir, supporters of the Nationalists convened a Congress here in July 1919, at which the present borders of the Turkish Republic were put forth as the minimum acceptable.

Arrival and information

Erzurum has two main bus terminals, the long-distance **otogar**, located almost 3km northwest of the city centre, and the **Gölbaşı Semt Garajı**, for Yusufeli and Artvin,

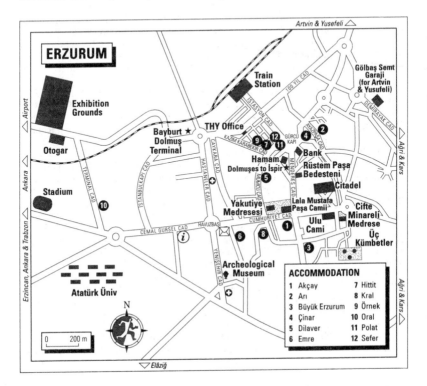

much more conveniently situated at just over 1km northeast of downtown. Many, though by no means all, long-distance buses stop at both of these stations – when it's time to move on from Erzurum, make sure you know exactly where your vehicle is starting from, easily enough checked when buying tickets at the terminals or at the numerous city-centre ticket offices scattered around town.

The **train station**, just over 1km directly north of the centre, is the most convenient of Erzurum's transport facilities, and also close to a major concentration of inexpensive accommodation; if you fly into the **airport**, 10km northeast of town at the end of the same road serving the *otogar*, try and catch the *THY* bus ($1.50) into town – a taxi will set you back $5.

From the main *otogar* a taxi fare to the centre won't exceed $2, and, aside from walking, **taxis** are really the way to get around Erzurum. There are municipal **buses** – particularly useful is the #2 which links the *otogar* with Cumhuriyet Caddesi, the main east–west thoroughfare – but it's tedious to hunt down ticket sales points, and taxi ranks are literally everywhere.

The **tourist information office** (June–Aug daily 8am–7pm; Sept–May Mon–Fri 8am–5pm; ☎0442/218 9127), rather inconveniently positioned on the south side of Cemal Gürsel Caddesi, 200m west of Havuzbaşı, is a helpful establishment where there's normally someone who speaks English. On winter weekends there is usually a caretaker on duty who can dish out basic city plans and glossy brochures.

Accommodation

The supply of **accommodation** in Erzurum usually exceeds demand, and you should have no trouble finding a decent room to suit any budget. Be aware however, that many hotels have a crazy pricing system, asking the same price for vastly different rooms, so it often pays to shop around and see a spread of rooms. If you're on a long haul overland, it's wise to break the journey here, since there's nowhere else as good to stay for hundreds of kilometres.

Several good choices lie **around Kâzım Karabekir Caddesi**, handy for the *THY* office and the train station, though all of them are plagued to a certain extent by traffic noise. Best bet is the *Örnek Otel* at no. 8 (☎0442/218 1203; ①), with clean doubles and excellent-value three-room corner suites, all with private bathrooms, though hot water can be temperamental on higher floors. The *Hittit Otel* at no. 26 (☎0442/218 1204; ②), a hangover from the days of the hippy trail to India, is about as rough and ready as you'd want, though passably clean and friendly, with en-suite bathrooms. A couple of blocks northeast, the basic *Otel Ar*s, Ayazpaşa Cad 22 (☎0442/218 3141; ①), and slightly better *Çınar Oteli*, Ayazpaza Cad 18 (☎0442/218 3580; ①), both with shared bath, are cheaper options, but you're really better off at the *Örnek*. Two slightly upmarket options nearby are the excellent *Hotel Sefer*, İstasyon Cad (☎0442/218 6714, fax 212 3775; ②), and the *Otel Polat*, Kâzım Karabekir Cad 4 (☎0442/218 1623, fax 234 4598; ②). Walk south along Mumcu Caddesi towards the Yakutiye Medresesi and you'll pass the *Hotel Dilaver* (☎0442/235 0068, fax 218 1148; ⑦), Erzurum's three-star finest.

The area immediately **south of Cumhuriyet Caddesi** is a good hunting ground for relatively quiet hotels. One block southeast of the PTT, the *Otel Emre* (☎0442/233 7725; ①) is a clean and bright budget option, which charges $1.50 extra for a shower down the hall. Closer to Erzurum's historic monuments are the quiet *Kral Otel*, Erzincankapı 18, near the southwest corner of the central park (☎0442/218 7783; ②), and the cheaper *Otel Akçay*, Kâmil Ağa Sok, off Cumhuriyet Cad (☎0442/235 2267; ①) – both are comfortable enough, with en-suite plumbing, and you can't get more central. Just down from the *Akçay,* on Ali Ravi Cad, is the overpriced *Büyük Erzurum Oteli* (☎0442/218 6528; ⑤), with nauseating lime-green and pale pink decor. Close to the **otogar** lies the *Otel Oral,* Terminal Cad 6 (☎0442/218 9740, fax 218 9749; ④), once Erzurum's top hotel and the traditional home of tour groups.

The City

All features of interest in Erzurum are along – or just off – Cumhuriyet Caddesi, and a leisurely tour shouldn't take more than half a day. Start at what is the de facto city park, a landscaped area with benches around the **Yakutiye Medresesi**. This was begun in 1310 by Hoca Yakut, a local governor of the Alhanid Mongols, and with its intricately worked portal, and truncated minaret featuring a knotted lattice of tilework, it's easily the most fanciful building in town. The minaret in particular seems displaced from somewhere in Central Asia or Persia – not such a far-fetched notion when you learn that the Alhanids had their seat in Tabriz. The beautiful interior of the *medrese* – note especially the stone stalactite carvings of the central dome – now holds an excellent **Museum of Islamic and Turkish Arts** (Tues–Fri 8.30am–noon & 1.30–5pm; $0.50), nicely arranged around *hujra* student cells. Exhibits include displays of local *oltu taşı* jewellery, various dervish accessories, *ehram* woven waistcoats and a selection of interesting old prints of Erzurum, among them a fine photograph taken from the roof of the old British consulate (Britain had a commercial agent in Erzurum as early as 1690).

A **türbe** at the east end of the *medrese* was intended for Yakut but never used. Just behind the tomb squats the uninspiring, mid-sixteenth-century **Lala Mustafa Paşa Camii**; it was supposedly designed by the famous architect Sinan but you'd never know it. The area around the mosque throngs with life during Friday *namaz.*

Continuing east about 300m along Cumhuriyet Caddesi, past an obscure *türbe* jostled by the surrounding shops, you pass the **Ulu Cami**, erected in 1179 by the third in the line of Saltuk emirs. Like most mosques of that age, it's a big square hall, with dozens of columns supporting bare vaults; the one note of fancy is the central skylight, led up to by a wedding cake of stalactite vaulting. At the *mihrab* the orderly rows of columns – seven aisles of six each – break up, yielding to an odd wooden dome built of overlapping timbers and pierced by two round windows.

Immediately adjacent stands the **Çifte Minareli Medrese**, the purported main tourist attraction in Erzurum but somewhat overrated. The name – meaning "double minareted" – derives from the most conspicuous feature of the seminary, two thirty-metre-high towers curiously devoid of a balcony for the muezzin to sound the call to prayer. There is some dispute about the structure's vintage, but the majority opinion holds that Hüdavênd Hatun, daughter of the Selçuk sultan Alâeddin Keykubad II, commissioned it in 1253, making it a contemporary of the similar Gök Medrese in Sivas. In conception the Çifte Minareli was the boldest and largest theological academy of its time, but was never finished. The stalactite portal, whose carved dragons and double-headed eagle designs hark somewhat sacrilegiously back to an earlier nomadic animism, gives onto a vast, bare courtyard, with stairways at the front corners leading to an upper storey of cells. At the rear looms an unusual cylindrical or *kümbet*-style tomb, thought to be that of the foundress; the sarcophagus, which may be empty, lies in a separate subterranean chamber below the dome.

A cluster of less enigmatic mausoleums, the **Üç Kümbetler**, graces another small park about 250m directly south. The oldest of the three tombs, and the most interesting, is probably that of the first Saltuk emir and dates from the early twelfth century, its octagonal base of alternating light and dark stone breached by half-oval windows demonstrating the mutual influence of Georgian, Armenian and early Turkish architecture. The other two *kümbet*s in the ensemble date from at least a century later and aren't nearly as compelling.

On the opposite side of Cumhuriyet Caddesi from the Çifte Minareli Medrese, a narrow lane leads past some of the oldest houses in town to the **citadel** (daily 8am–noon & 1.30–7pm; $0.75), whose vast rectangular bulk was originally laid out by Theodosius. The interior is bare except for a shoebox-like *mescit* or small mosque, capped by an afterthought of a dome, and a free-standing minaret, now a belltower. Stairs on the east side lead up to the ramparts, and while the citadel is no longer the highest point in town since Erzurum began to spread to its rim of hills, it still lends the best view over the city – and the great, intimidating vastness of the plateau beyond.

Just northwest of the castle, but easiest reached by retracing steps along Cumhuriyet Caddesi to Menderes Caddesi, is the **Rüstem Paşa Bedesteni**, the covered bazaar, endowed by Süleyman the Magnificent's mid-sixteenth-century grand vizier. Erzurum owed much of its wealth to transcontinental trade routes and even in the nineteenth century some 40,000 laden camels were passing through the city every year. Today trade is almost totally given over to **oltu taşı**, an obsidian-like material mined near Oltu, 150km northeast, and most frequently made into *tespih* (prayer beads) and *küpe* (earrings). Prices start at about $6 for a tiny, ten-centimetre *tespih*; silver clasps cost $2–3 extra. Earrings go for anywhere between $4 and $11, depending on the size and number of stones, but most importantly whether the setting is gold or silver.

Erzurum's remotest, least compelling sight is the **archeological museum** (daily except Mon 8am–noon & 1–5pm; $1), 400m south of Havuzbaşı. The ground floor has assorted Urartian and Caucasian pottery, plus some Roman and Hellenistic glassware and jewellery. There is also a rather unedifying "massacre room", containing items recently removed from two mass graves in the province – the property, it is claimed, of Turks slaughtered by Armenians between 1915 and 1918.

Eating and drinking

Restaurants in Erzurum tend to offer good value, with a concentration of sorts on or around Cumhuriyet Caddesi and the central park. Some of the fancier places like to style themselves as "salons" – for example the *Salon Çağın*, Cumhuriyet Cad 18, 100m west of the Yakutiye Medresesi, a dingily subterranean place with good food, *mantı* on Sunday and trout daily in summer; a big meal will set you back $6–7. The *Salon Asya*, nearby and still on Cumhuriyet Caddesi, has no fish, but the service is equally good and the decor a good deal cheerier. Neither is licensed; if you want **booze** with your food in this conservative town, you'll have to patronize the *Güzelyurt Restaurant*, directly across from the Yakutiye Medresesi on Cumhuriyet Caddesi. It looks expensive, but unless you intend to hit the wine and *rakı* it's difficult to spend more than $5–7. The *Park Pide Salonu*, immediately west of the *medrese* on the side street leading north from Cumhuriyet, is minuscule but does excellent, cheap *pide*s.

Listings

Airport bus Departs from in front of the *THY* office on 50 Yıl Cad 90min before each flight, with a stop at the *otogar* en route.

Car rental *Avis*, Terminal Cad 12/A (☎0442/218 8715, fax 233 2193); *Europcar*, Millet Bahçe Cad 2, Gez Mah (☎0442/234 6160).

Cirit This is a sort of cross between polo and warfare, with the players on horseback eliminating opponents from the field by thrusts of a blunted javelin. Ask at the tourist information office during spring and summer if a tournament is scheduled nearby.

CROSSING TO IRAN

International bus and train connections to the **Islamic Republic of Iran** have been suspended in recent years, but it's still perfectly possible to travel this most traditional of overland trails, and for the culturally sensitive traveller Iran can be one of the most friendly and rewarding places to travel in the Middle East.

Most travellers enter Iran on a week-long transit **visa** (routinely issued to travellers, with the exception of US citizens, from most Iranian consulates on proof of a Pakistani visa), which they then extend for up to a month, depending upon which town you choose to extend in (Tabriz is said to be a good choice, Tehran and Isfahan can be more problematic). It is generally better to get this visa in your home country as the Iranian consulates in Astanbul, Ankara and especially Erzurum have a reputation for being unhelpful.

To cross into Iran it's currently necessary to get yourself first to **Doğubeyazit**, in Turkey's troubled southeast – although surrounding areas are off-limits due to Kurdish-related security problems, the main road route to Doğubeyazit, from Erzurum via Horasan and Ağri, and, to a lesser degree, the back roads from Kars via Iqdar, are at the time of writing fairly safe and well travelled. Regular buses run from Ankara, Erzurum and Kars to Doğubeyazit, and if you get stuck, the town has a wide range of hotels and other facilities. From here take a dolmuş or taxi to the border post at Gürbulak, a taxi on to the Iranian town of Maku and then an onward Iranian bus to Tabriz. Other crossings east of Van are currently inadvisable.

Consulate *Iran*, Ali Ravi Cad (☎0442/218 3876); they don't issue visas at present but this may change in the future.

Exchange The only relatively efficient bank in town, prepared to accept both travellers' cheques and Eurocheques, is the main branch of the *Türk Ticaret Bankası*, situated near the Gürcü Kapı roundabout up at the top of İstasyon Cad. Avoid the truly hopeless banks up on Cumhuriyet Caddesi, and use *Erzurum Döviz*, next to the Toyota dealer, instead.

Hamam *Erzurum Hamamı*, at the Gürcü Kapı end of Astasyon Cad (daily 6am–10.30pm; $2; men only except by prior arrangement).

Hospitals One is north of Havuşbaşı on Hastaneler Cad, another south of Havuzbazı on Yenişehir Cad.

Newspapers English-language publications are sold only at *Kültürsarayı*, Cumhuriyet Cad 72, though the stock is limited to a few week-old *Time* magazines and *Turkish Daily News*.

Skiing A possible consolation for being stuck here in winter is the Palandöken ski resort, 6km away and said to be the best in the country. The single hotel, the *Palandöken Dedeman*, and chair lift operate between December and April.

THY office 50 Yıl Cad, SSK Rant Tesisleri no. 24 (☎0442/218 1904).

Northwest of Erzurum: Çoruh River citadels

As you head west (and then turning northwest) out of Erzurum on the way to the Black Sea, you'll follow either of the two roads away from the lorry route to Ankara. One follows the old Silk Route down to Trabzon via **Bayburt**; the other leads to Rize via **İspir**. After scaling the first range of peaks beyond Erzurum, both routes drop dizzyingly from 2300-metre passes to the **Çoruh River**, which flows through a deep trench that lies well below the level of the Anatolian plateau. This remote valley, reminiscent of deeper Central Asia or the American West, was the ancestral homeland of the Bagratid clan (see p.686), who went on to furnish early medieval Armenia and Georgia with so many of their rulers.

Bayburt

BAYBURT is dwarfed by the largest **fortress** in Turkey, its history virtually synonymous with the town. Thought to have been erected in the sixth century during Justinian's skirmishes with the Laz tribe from the Black Sea, it was later appropriated by the Bagratids, until being taken and renovated by the Saltuk Turks early in the thirteenth century. The citadel was a much-coveted prize in the Russo-Turkish wars of this century and the last, so it's something of a miracle that the perimeter walls are in such good condition – though this isn't true of the interior, where there's not much to see apart from the view.

Little else redeems Bayburt other than its position astride the young Çoruh River, best enjoyed at one of several riverside **restaurants** or **cafés** with wonderful views of the castle. There are **mosques** founded by Saltuk Turks and the İlhanid Mongol governor Yakut – he of the *medrese* in Erzurum – but these fall squarely in the category of time-filling exercises, and the main reason to pause here is to break a journey between Trabzon and Erzurum; otherwise content yourself with a glance at the fort while in transit.

Practicalities

Bayburt's small **otogar** is 500m south of the centre on the main highway, but buses to and from Erzurum often begin and end in the bazaar. If you need to **stay**, your best bets are two hotels on Cumhuriyet Caddesi, the main drag aiming right for the castle. The *Saracoğlu* at no. 13 (②) offers rooms with en-suite showers but toilets down the hall. The *Sevil* two doors down is much the same. A new top-range hotel is due to open soon.

For **eating out**, the enclosed *Yeni Zafer*, next to the central vehicle bridge over the Çoruh, is more appealing in winter, but the *Çoruh Lokantası* upstream, with riverbank seating, has the edge in the warm months. For summer dessert, good ice cream is dispensed on the quay between the two.

İspir

İSPİR once rivalled Bayburt in importance, but has precipitously declined. The setting, overlooking a bend of the Çoruh, with a monument-crowned acropolis, promises much but disappoints up close. There's not even a proper gate left to the Bagratid **castle**, which hardly rewards a climb through the town's shanties; inside there's a squat, little-used mosque from the Saltuk era, and a badly ruined Byzantine church. The town itself is shabby, the only foreigners passing through those on rafting trips on the Çoruh. The **hotels and restaurants** are among the worst in Turkey so it's a good idea to avoid getting stuck here; least loathsome of the three places to stay is the *Gürcüoğlu Hotel* (②) on the main street.

If you've arrived by **bus** from Rize on the way to Erzurum, or vice versa, you can get an onward bus the same day as long as you've made an early start. It's safest, though, to get a through service. If you deliberately alight here, much the most interesting thing to do if you're not waterborne is to cover the rough but scenic 75km of dirt road to Yusufeli (see p.690), sometimes by public transport (dolmuşes run almost half way, as far as Çamlıkaya) but more often than not by thumb.

Northeast of Erzurum towards Kars

Convoys of lorries clog the most heavily travelled route beyond Erzurum, bound for Iran and (in peaceful times) Georgia. **PASİNLER**, 40km along, is distinguished by the crumbled citadel of **Hasankale**, an originally Bagratid stronghold taken over by the Akkoyun Turcomans during the fifteenth century, and by its famous hot springs and mud baths. Twenty kilometres east at Köprüköy, the graceful **Çobandede bridge**, the finest medieval bridge in Turkey, attributed to Sinan, spans the Aras River near the beginning of its course, a particularly bewitching sight in soft early-morning light. The road, railway and river stick together until Horasan, where the highway to Iran – via Ağrı and Doğubeyazit – peels off to the southeast, and the train tracks meander north. It was around this region that the pivotal Battle of Manzikert took place in August 1071 between the Selçuks and Byzantines.

Soon the river forsakes the Kars trunk road too, and starts a sharp descent toward the Caspian Sea. The next place of any consequence, nestled off the main road among an unexpected forest of conifers, is **SARIKAMIŞ**, subject to the coldest climate in the country. The winter of 1914–15 proved lethal here for the Ottoman Third Army under the command of the megalomaniac Enver Paşa, when – in one of the worst Turkish defeats of World War I – 75,000 men froze to death or were killed attempting to halt a Tsarist force of roughly equal size; in the wake of the débâcle the Russians advanced to Erzurum and beyond. Today the thick seasonal snow supports a new and reportedly very good **ski resort**, and there are plans to develop the site further with a municipality hotel complex. Until then, your best bet is still the *Sançam Turistik Otel* on Halk Caddesi (☎474/0413 4176; ①), with its funky alpine-style lobby and spacious triple rooms for the price of a double.

Beyond Sarıkamış, the scenery becomes humdrum again as the mountains level out onto the high, grassy steppe which surrounds Kars. About 10km before Kars, 300m west of the road near the village of Kümbetla, you'll see the partly crumbled Armenian church of **Kümbet Kilise**, the first of various Armenian monuments in the province.

Kars

Hidden in a natural basin on the banks of the Kars Çayı, much reviled **KARS** is a dour and joyless town with only a few Russian Belle Epoque buildings to cheer it up. Although a couple of hundred metres lower than Erzurum, the climate is even more severe; the potholed streets never quite recover from the fierce winters; and when it rains, which it often does, the entire town becomes a treacherous swamp. The local economy is stagnant, hotels are substandard and overpriced. There are a few sites in town worth dallying for, but most visitors have made the long trek out here for the sole purpose of visiting the former Armenian capital of Ani.

Some history

Originally founded by the Armenians, Kars became the capital of their Bagratid dynasty early in the tenth century, when the citadel which still dominates the town was substantially improved. Later in that century the main seat of Armenian rule was transferred to nearby Ani, and Kars lost some of its importance. The Selçuks took it along with almost everything else in the area during the mid-eleventh century, but devastating Mongol raids made a mockery of any plans the new overlords had for Kars. In 1205 the Georgians, profiting from the wane of both Selçuk and Byzantine power in the area, seized the town and held it for three centuries until displaced by the Ottomans.

Kars defends the approaches to Erzurum just as the latter is the key to the rest of Anatolia; the Russians tried repeatedly during the nineteenth century to capture the place. Sieges in 1828 and 1855 were successful – the latter during the Crimean War, when a British and Turkish garrison was starved out of the citadel after five months – but on both occasions Kars reverted to Turkey by terms of peace treaties. Not so in 1878, when after a bloody eight-month war between the two powers, Kars was finally awarded to the Tsar. It remained in Russian hands until 1920, a period which bequeathed both the unusual grid layout of the city centre and the incongruous Belle

Epoque buildings found here. Today Kars is, not surprisingly, still a major forward military position, swarming with soldiers a long way from home.

Arrival and information

In the northeast of the town and within walking distance of most points of interest, the **old otogar**, on Küçük Kâzım Bey Caddesi, now houses dolmuşes to surrounding towns such as Yusufeli, Ardahan, Iğdır and Erzurum. *Servis* buses run from here to the new **long-distance otogar**, a few kilometres east of town. The **train station** is well to the southeast of the centre, off Cumhuriyet Caddesi on the way to the museum.

Staff at the **tourist information office** on the corner of Gazi Ahmed Muhtar and Faik Bey *caddesi*s (daily 8.30am–5.30pm; ☎0474/223 2300), worn down by the onerous task of vetting Ani-visit applications, are not terribly friendly and speak little English. They can however provide basic city plans and put you in contact with the local English-speaking "fixer" and self-proclaimed guide, Cecil Ersöloqlu, though he will probably find you first.

Accommodation

Accommodation in Kars is a dismal subject. Everything is expensive for what it is, and service often leaves much to be desired. The nominally budget hotels lining Faik Bey Caddesi are best left to the imagination, if the so-called "mid-range" establishments are anything to go by.

Three of the cheapest options are the dirty *Asya Otel*, Küçük Kâzım Bey Cad 50 (①), the labyrinthine *Hotel Kervansaray*, Faik Bey Cad 204 (①), whose drab rooms come equipped with a shower but no toilet, and the similarly depressing *Nursaray*, next door at no. 190. Establishments across the street slip into squalor with the *Hayut* and *Havut*. A much better budget choice is the clean and friendly *Hotel Yılmaz*, Küçük Kâzım Bey 24 (☎0474/223 1074; ①), across from the old *otogar*, for clean rooms with shower. A step up takes you to the *Hotel Temel*, just off Halit Paşa Cad (☎0474/223 1376; ②), with carpeted rooms and clean bathrooms. For the same price you can get a spacious room with shower at the faded *Güngören Otel*, just off Halit Paşa Cad at Millet Sok 4 (☎0474/212 0298; ②), where the gloomy lobby hides a decent grill restaurant. The only hotel in town to offer anything resembling semi-luxury is the new *Hotel Karabağ*, Faik Bey Cad 84 (☎0474/212 3480, fax 223 3089; ⑤), though even here the rooms are over-priced and nothing special. A couple of kilometres south of Kars in the middle of a muddy field, lies the surreal, pink *Arkar Anihan Motel* (☎0474/212 3517; ③), meant more for passing truck drivers and trysting couples than tourists.

The Town

The Russian grid plan makes central Kars easy to navigate: the most important east–west streets are Faik Bey Caddesi, essentially the continuation of the Erzurum–Armenia highway, and Halit Paşa Caddesi, home to many of Kars's restaurants. Lined with both humble and grandiose Russian structures, Atatürk Caddesi and the pedestrianized Kâzım Bey Caddesi lead approximately south–north to the river, on the far bank of which huddles the medieval settlement – now a shanty town.

Most items of interest cluster near this district, a few hundred metres north of the modern city centre. The obvious **Church of the Holy Apostles**, just the other side of the Kars Çayı on the way to the castle, was erected between 930 and 937 by the Armenian king Abbas I. Crude reliefs of the Twelve Apostles adorn the twelve arches of the dome, but otherwise it's a squat, functional bulk of dark basalt; the belfry and

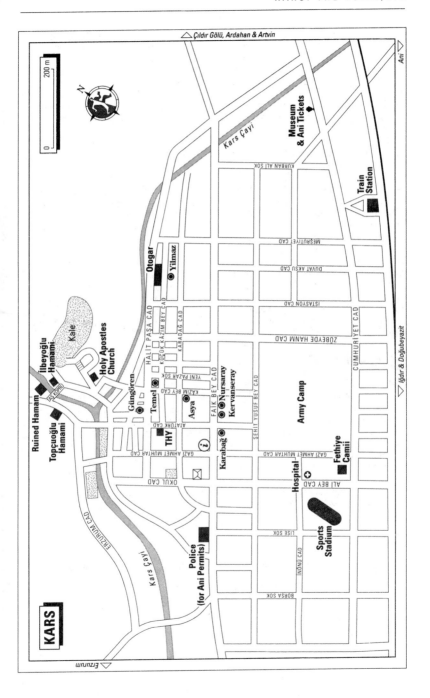

portico are relatively recent additions. A church when Christians held Kars, a mosque when Muslims ruled, and reconsecrated by the Russians, it briefly housed the town museum before becoming the locked warehouse of today.

Before climbing the short distance to the *kale* or castle, detour slightly up the tributary of the Kars Çayı to see the **Taş Köprü** or "Stone Bridge", made of the same volcanic rock as the nearby church and restored during the 1580s by order of Murat III. Several **hamams**, none dating from before the eighteenth century, huddle nearby: the still-functioning **İlbeyoğlu**, the **Mazlutağa** (in ruins) and the **Topçuoğlu** (still in use); see "Listings" below for details.

There has been a fortress of some kind on the hill overlooking the river confluence for well on two millennia. The Armeno-Byzantine structure was maintained by the Selçuks but levelled by the Mongols; the Ottomans rebuilt it as part of their late sixteenth-century urban overhaul, only to have the Russians blast it to bits, then put it back together again in the last century. After decades as an off-limits military reserve, **Kars Kalesi** as it's officially known (daily 9am–7pm), is now open as a park. Locals come to pay their respects at the tomb of Celal Baba, a holy man of the fourteenth century, and to enjoy the panorama over Kars, but there's little else to see other than the black-masoned military engineering.

The only other compelling attraction in Kars is the excellent **town museum** (daily 8.30am–5.30pm; $1.50), a fifteen-minute walk out to the east end of town, whose ethnographic section includes such curiosities as a *yayık* (butter churn) and a cradle, as well as jewellery, leatherwork and extensive exhibits on local carpets and kilims. Downstairs is given over to ancient pottery, and ecclesiastical artefacts of the departed Russians and Armenians, particularly a huge church bell and wooden doors which graced one of the cathedrals before 1920. On the way back pay a visit to the **Fethiye Camii**, housed in an old Russian church.

Eating and drinking

Fortunately the **restaurant** scene in Kars is a bit more varied than the hotel prospects. The *Cafe Kristal* on the corner of Halit Paşa and Atatürk *caddesi*s is recommended for its precooked *hazır yemek*, as is the *Bışım Lokanta* on Kâzim Bey Cad for its deep *pide*. The first-floor restaurant of the *Karabağ* is reasonably priced with the best selection of *meze*s and cleanest tablecloths in town. The *Konak* and the *Gemik* on Halit Paşa Caddesi are more modest but offer tasty fare. For **breakfast**, there are lots of places on Halit Paşa and Atatürk *caddesi*s near the *otogar*, featuring local *kaşar* cheese and the justifiably famous Kars honey, which you can stock up on at the *Seref Gida* honey shop on the corner of Kâzim Bey and Faik Bey. If you fancy a drink beware that a certain Russian-influenced, vodka-soaked desperation haunts many of the bars in Kars, including the *Efes Pub*, Halit Paşa Cad 113. However, the *Karybağ* has a pleasant ground-floor bar.

Listings

Exchange Try *not* to exchange money at the banks in Kars; in any case it's virtually impossible before 10.30am, when the day's rate is wired in from Ankara. *Vakif Bank* is probably your best bet, at Halit Paşa Cad 117. There are several efficient *döviz* on Kâzim Bey Cad.

Hamams Two of these, both near the Taş Köprü: the *Albeyoğlu* (men 8–10am & 6–11pm, women noon–6pm; $1.75); the *Topçuoğlu*, on the far side of the bridge, is for women only.

Hospital Near army camp on İnönü Cad.

PTT On Okul Cad; phone section open round-the-clock. There is also a useful *çarşi* branch on Kâzim Bey Cad.

THY Atatürk Cad 148 (☎0474/223 3839).

Ani and around

Once the capital of Bagratid Armenia, **ANİ** is today a melancholy, almost vacant triangular plateau, divided from Armenia by the Arpa Çayı (Ahuryan River) and very nearly separated from the rest of Turkey by two deep tributaries. It's mainly an expanse of rubble, but among this rise some of the finest examples of ecclesiastical and military architecture of its time. The Armenians were master stoneworkers, and the fortifications which defend the northern, exposed side of the plateau, and the handful of churches behind, are exquisite compositions in a blend of ruddy sandstone and darker volcanic rock. These, and the cliffs fringing the river, are the only vertical features here, dwarfed by an evocative but relentlessly horizontal landscape. Hillocks on the Armenian side and muddy Turkish pastures sprawl alike under a luminous sky chased by clouds. It is worth putting up with the deficiencies of Kars for a night or two to make the trip out, and inconceivable that you'd venture east of Erzurum or Artvin without fitting Ani into your plans.

Ani is 43km southeast of Kars, just beyond the village of **OCAKLI**. Without your own transport, you can take an early morning or mid-afternoon bus service between Kars and the ruins, but if you use the first service you'll be stuck at the site far longer than you'd like, and the later vehicle overnights in Ocaklı, leaving you stranded. The main alternative is a taxi tour, arranged either by yourself or the tourist office, for about $20 a vehicle. Solo travellers typically band together at the tourist information office; the taxis hold four people, and minibuses carrying up to nine passengers are also available. *Ani Tours* often run a dolmuş minibus or taxi from the new *otogar* to Ani for approximately $4 per person return; find them at the *otogar*.

Permits and admission

Because of its location in a restricted zone (see p.681), **Ani** (daily 8.30am–5pm; $2) would ordinarily be closed to visits, but in view of its artistic and historical interest both the Armenian and Turkish governments have made an exception. You'll still need a **permit**, routinely granted and requiring less than an hour to issue. Fill in a form at the Kars tourist information office, have this endorsed at the Security Police two blocks away, and proceed to the Kars museum to buy **tickets**. Tickets are usually *not* sold at the site, a measure designed to prevent people showing up unvetted.

The ruins are scattered, and many monuments are absorbing, so allow a good two hours at Ani, plus a similar period for going there and back – make sure your driver agrees to this. Prepare yourself also to be accosted, not always in a friendly manner, by hordes of village children and their elders hawking tepid Cokes, trinkets and fake (or sometimes real) antiquities. The ban on photography was lifted here in 1988, but mass tourism has yet to engulf Ani and you can often have the site to yourself. Mid-summer can be very hot, so you're advised to bring a hat, sun cream and water to tour the site, though the recent opening of the *Çunubirlik Tesisleri Restaurant* means that you can now at least get lunch at Ani.

Some history

There was a settlement here before Christian times, centred around the citadel near the southern tip of the upland; the name Ani is perhaps a corruption of "Anahit", a Persian water goddess who was one of the chief deities of the pagan Armenians. The city first came to prominence after the local instalment of the Armenian Gamsarkan clan during the fifth century. Situated astride a major east–west caravan route, Ani prospered, receiving fresh impetus when Ashot III, fifth in the line of the Bagratid kings of Armenia, transferred his capital here from Kars in 961. For three generations the kingdom and its capital, under the successive rule of Ashot, Smbat II and Gagik I, enjoyed

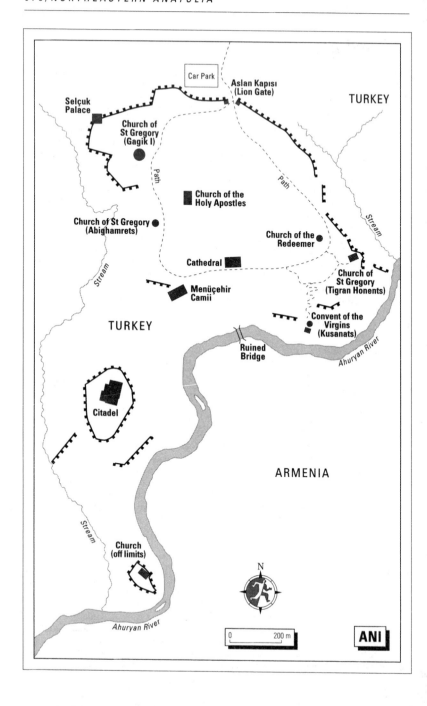

a golden age. Beautified and strengthened militarily, with a population exceeding 100,000, Ani rivalled Baghdad and Constantinople themselves.

By the middle of the eleventh century, however, wars of succession and the religiously motivated enmity of the Byzantines took their toll. The latter, having neutralized Bagratid power, annexed the city in 1045, but in the process they dissolved an effective bulwark against the approaching Selçuks, who took Ani with little resistance in 1064. After the collapse of the Selçuks, the Armenians returned in less than a century, this time with the assistance of the powerful Georgian kingdom. The Pahlavuni and Zakhariad clans ruled over a reduced but still semi-independent Armenia for two more centuries, continuing to endow Ani with churches and monasteries. The Mongol raids of the thirteenth century, a devasting earthquake in 1319 and realigned trade routes proved mortal blows to both Ani and its hinterland; thereafter the city was gradually abandoned, and forgotten until the last century.

The site

The vast **boundary walls** of Ani, dating from the late tenth century and studded with countless towers, are visible from several kilometres as you approach past villages teeming with sheep and buffalo. After handing over your ticket and permit, you enter via the **Aslan Kapısı**, so named because of a sculpted Selçuk lion on the wall just inside, and sole survivor of the four original gates.

Once inside you're confronted with the sight of the vast forlorn, weed-tufted plateau, dotted with only the sturdiest bits of masonry that have outlasted the ages. A system of **paths**, many of them remnants of the former main streets of Ani, lead to or past all of the principal remains. Bear slightly left and head first about 500m southeast to the **Church of the Redeemer**, built between 1034 and 1036. In 1957, half of the building was sheared away by lightning, so that the remainder, seen from the side, looks uncannily like a stage set, albeit one with the carved filigree crosses and Armenian inscriptions.

Church of Tigran Honents

Some 200m east, tucked down by a course of wall overlooking the Arpa Çayı, the charming **monastery church of St Gregory the Illuminator (Tigran Honents)** is the best preserved of Ani's monuments, and somewhat confusingly one of three dedicated to the saint who brought Christianity to Armenia at the start of the fourth century. The pious foundation of a merchant nobleman in 1215, it's unusually laid out in a rectangle divided width-wise into three (a colonnaded narthex has collapsed). The ground plan reflects the prominent Georgian influence in thirteenth-century Ani, and the fact that the Orthodox, not the Armenian Apostolic, rite was celebrated here. The church still sports delicate exterior relief work, including extensive animal designs and, on the south wall, a sundial, common in Armenian decoration.

But Tigran Honents is most rewarding for its **frescoes**, the only ones left at Ani, which cover most of the interior and spill out around the current entrance onto what was once the narthex wall, giving the church its Turkish name *Resimli Kilise* or "Painted Church". They are remarkable both for their high degree of realism and fluidity – especially compared to the static iconography of the neighbouring Byzantines – and for the subject matter, depicting episodes in early Armenian Christianity as well as the doings of ordinary people. As you enter the first of the three nave compartments, you'll see in the lower row of images on your right *The Trial of St Gregory by King Trdat III*, *The Martyrdom of Hrpsime* (an early female convert), and *The Torture of St Gregory*. All these events took place before Trdat's repentance and conversion, the earliest sovereign to do so; to the left are secular vignettes from the life of King Trdat. The transept is taken up by scenes from the life of Christ; on the south wall are *The Annunciation*,

The Nativity, The Entry into Jerusalem and *The Descent from the Cross*. To the north is *The Raising of Lazarus*, with *The Apostles* ringing the drum of the dome. All have had eyes and faces vandalized by pious muslims.

From Tigran Honents, a narrow trail leads past the Selçuk baths and skims the tops of the cliffs above the Arpa Çayı before finding a steep way down to the **Convent of the Virgins** (Kusanats), perched on a ledge even closer to the river. A minuscule, rocket-like rotunda church, contemporary with Tigran Honents, is flanked by a smaller chapel or baptistry, and the whole enclosed by a perimeter wall. Just upstream are the evocative stubs of the old **bridge** over the Arpa.

The cathedral and around

Rejoining the main plateau trail heading west from Tigran Honents, you reach the elegantly proportioned **cathedral**, completed between 989 and 1010. The architect, one Trdat Mendet, could present rather impressive credentials, having just previously completed restoration of the earthquake-damaged dome of Aya Sofya in Constantinople. However, this is a surprisingly plain, rectangular building, with just the generic blind arcades of Armenian churches and no external apse; the dome, once supported by four massive pillars, has long since vanished. The main entrance was – unusually – not to the west, opposite the apse, but on the side of the nave, through the south wall.

To the west, within sight of the cathedral, stands what's known as the **Menüçehir Camii**, billed as the earliest Selçuk mosque in Anatolia, though its lack of *mihrab*, its alternating red-and-black stonework, and its inlaid mosaic ceiling, invite suspicions of mixed antecedents. Certainly the view from the ornate gallery over the frontier river fits more with a role as a small palace. The truncated minaret was off-limits for a while after a tourist committed suicide by leaping off, but you can once again clamber up eroded steps for an unrivalled aerial view of the site.

At the southern tip of the triangular site lies the **citadel**, which was formerly in a forbidden zone but now appears to be fully accessible again. Little remains of the fortress, but the climb up is worth it for the haunting view of a fairytale monastery below, spectacularly sited above a sharp curve in the river gorge. The view back towards the main site gives an insight into the defence of the city, with steep gorges protecting the left and right and high walls linking the two sides. From the citadel head north again to visit the second **Church of St Gregory** (Abighamrets), begun in 1040 by the same individual responsible for the Church of the Redeemer. This rotunda is like no other at Ani – instead of blind arcades, the twelve-sided exterior is pierced by functional recessed vaults which alternate with the six rounded interior niches. The east side of the building is slowly but surely losing its dressed stone.

The nearby, so-called **Kervansaray** is really the eleventh-century Church of the Holy Apostles, today badly crumbled. The main circuit continues north to the sparse ruins of a third **Church of St Gregory** (Gagik I), begun in 998 by Trdat, architect of the cathedral. Intact it would have been one of the largest rotundas in medieval Armenia proper, but the design, based on the seventh-century rotunda at Zvartnots in Armenia, collapsed almost immediately, so that today only man-high outer walls and giant column stumps are left. Before completing your tour at the Aslan Kapısı, you might spare a glance for the facade of the **Selçuk Palace**, the only indisputably Islamic item at Ani, tucked into the northwest extremity of the ramparts – and, interestingly, the only structure to receive any degree of archeological investigation and maintenance.

Around Ani

A pair of churches are easily visited with your own transport on the way to or from Ani; you might even convince a minibus or taxi driver to detour to them. At Subatan, 25km from Kars, bear left 11km towards Başgedikler – about a kilometre before, turn left again for 2km to **OĞUZLU**, which shelters a half-fallen shrine of the tenth century. All told the picturesque village is probably of more interest than the church. Much more intact is the thirteenth-century church of **Kızıl Vank**, reached by driving through Başgedikler and proceeding 6km east to the hamlet of **BAIRAKDA**, where the track branches off left to the church, 2km away. This cruciform-plan building was restored in the last century and still retains its dome and facing stone. A family has set up house around the church, and you may need to engage their help to keep the overprotective dogs away.

Flanking Ani in the inner zone and currently off limits to tourists (see below) are the tenth-century fortress of **Magazbert**, about 5km southwest, and the monastic complex of **Horomos**, 6km northeast, about halfway to the dam over the Arpa Çaya. Founded in the tenth century, Horomos contains four later tombs of Armenian nobility, and two churches, in a walled enclosure at the brink of the Arpa Çaya. Two kilometres northeast stands **Daylar** (also in the inner zone), another church of the same vintage, near the modern village of the same name.

Other Armenian monuments around Kars

The present-day province of Kars formed an important part of the Bagratid kingdom between the sixth and the eleventh centuries, and of the Zakhariad clan's holdings during the thirteenth century, so it's not surprising that there are numerous Armenian churches and fortresses besides those around Ani. Visiting them is not necessarily straightforward, however; many are in bad condition, or are accessible only by atrocious roads or on foot, or else lie in military security zones – sometimes all three. You'll really need your own transport, enough Turkish to ask directions from villagers, and the *GeoCenter/RV* "Turkey East" map. As you may have gathered at Ani, the Armenians had a particular flair for poising their churches on sheer rock faces overlooking river canyons, and many of the remains detailed below adhere to this pattern; even in their ruinous state they are still among the most impressive sights in northeastern Turkey.

The only useful **public transport** in the area described here are buses from Kars to Iğdır and the hourly Kars–Digor minibuses. Hitching between the Tuzluca junction and Kağızman should not be a problem, but rides to Çengilli and Kecivan Kalesi are few and far between.

A word of warning

The border region abutting Armenia is subdivided into an **outer zone**, extending 5km into Turkey from the boundary – where photography, if not your very presence, will be strongly frowned on – and an **inner zone** consisting of the final 500m to the frontier, where it's claimed unauthorized entry might spark off an international incident. It's worth knowing that the entire region between the Digor–Tuzluca highway and the frontier is a no-go area after dark – even the villagers are not allowed to move about. You'll encounter plenty of *jandarma* road blocks on this road, but these are normally mere formalities for tourists.

If you want to tour any of the churches in the outer or inner zone (including Magazbert, Horomos and Daylar near Ani, described above, and Mren and Bagaran, described below, you'll need to contact the central military command in Ankara several weeks in advance, presenting yourself as a high-level university student of medieval art or architecture, with supporting documents; permission is more often denied than granted, and in practice most tourists simply don't have the time. A last-ditch option is to enquire at the local military headquarters just outside Kars – but don't hold your breath. Above all, don't just head off towards an inner-zone church hoping for the best: you'll certainly be detected by the military and turned back.

Neither should you appeal to the tourist information office or other civilian authorities in Kars. At the very least, you'll be fed disinformation or rather curtly discouraged, almost understandable when you consider that the past treatment of these churches is as sensitive a topic as the alleged mistreatment of the Armenians themselves in 1895 and 1915. Officially Armenians don't exist historically, and any archeological evidence of their past rule are non-monuments, either ignored or misattributed to Islamic builders. The continued presence of recognizable churches in this part of Turkey is a major embarrassment to the government, which sees them as the basis for potential Armenian territorial claims and demands for reparations.

Local authorities would rather that outsiders did not see the churches, and would probably be relieved if they disappeared altogether. It's claimed that army demolition units have helped the process along with dynamite or bulldozers in recent years, and while this is debatable, it's certainly true that nothing is being done to preserve these monuments. Such attitudes usually contrast sharply with those of the local villagers, who are often only too happy to show you the ruins they know of, have no ethnic axe to grind and are honoured that someone should bother to visit what for them is a barn – or a quarry for building stone. Incidentally, some degree of tourism is often enough to stop any ongoing vandalism, not so much in anticipation of the monetary benefit of increased tourist traffic, but because the village elders consider that they lose face if a "cultural" institution on their patch deteriorates.

Around Digor

There is fairly frequent public transport covering the 40km southeast of Kars to **DİGOR**, formerly Armenian Tekor, where the fifth-century church on a hill to the south is almost levelled. The dramatic setting of **BEŞKİLİSE** (Khtzkonk), a few kilometres upstream along the Digor Çayı gorge, is a far more rewarding destination. If you don't want to take a local guide along, have the bus set you down, or drive, 3.5km north of town, near the top of the pass, and turn onto a rough dirt track veering southwest from the asphalt, heading some 600m towards the gorge of the Digor Çayı. Walk behind the white pumice quarry and uphill for 200m and then turn left down a dried stream bed. The path follows the right-hand bank downhill and curves to the right to enter the gorge. Continue along the path, midway between the valley floor and cliff top above, for twenty minutes to reach **St Sergius**, an eleventh-century rotunda that is the sole survivor of the five churches (*beş kilise*) once perched at the edge of the narrow canyon here. The side walls are rent by fissures, but the dome is still intact and the west wall is covered in Armenian inscriptions.

A few kilometres south of Digor, near Doylalı, a track leads off west to the village of Kocaköy and the ruined church of **Nahçivan**. Another track leads southeast for 13km to Düzgeçit and 9km on to where the seventh-century cathedral of **MREN** – a restricted outer zone monument – overlooks the confluence of the Digor and Arpa streams. Once the focus of a town whose rubble litters the surrounding plateau, Mren exhibits marked Byzantine influence with its elongated cross-in-square ground plan and octagonal dome mounted on four pillars. Getting to the resricted site of **BAGARAN** (variously known as Bekren, Pakran or by the adjacent village name of Kilittaşı) involves retracing your route to the main road and then, 26km southeast of Digor, taking an unmarked seven-kilometre side road to Kilittaşı village. Final access to this ninth-century Bagratid capital is complicated by the terrain and its restricted status, but at least one early church is plainly visible on its pinnacle across the river.

Çengilli and Kecivan Kalesi

At the confluence of the Aras and Arpa rivers, right on the Armenian border, a junction leads south to Tuzluca and Iğdır (see below) or west to Kağızman. Just over the Kağızman bridge on the north bank of the Aras, a rough dirt track branches off west

---

THE ROUTE TO DOĞUBEYAZIT

Reasonably frequent long-distance buses from Kars to Doğubeyazit follow the Digor–Tuzluca–Iğdır route, with the Aras River for company much of the way; it's an area that is subject to current Kurdish-related troubles, but, at the time of writing at least, was incident-free. East of Tuzluca (named after some nearby rock-salt mines), the road skirts the Armenian frontier, with watchtowers plainly visible to the north, and drops sharply into a basin only 850m in elevation. The more temperate climate here permits the cultivation of rice, cotton, and grapes; the inhabitants are mostly Azeri Shiites, resettled here in the last century. Should you need to break the journey, **Iğdır** – a pleasant though unremarkable town at the southern corner of the valley – would be the place to do so: there are a handful of decent hotels, including the clean, mid-range *Azer* (③), with a decent restaurant attached. The Çilli Pass, about halfway between Iğdar and Doğubeyazit, is currently the best and safest place to get a clear (early morning) view of Mount Ararat (Aqra Daqa), though, as always, check the current local political situation before setting out.

---

and follows a tortuous route up into the mountains, through three timeless villages, to finally arrive at **ÇENGİLLİ**, home to an anomalous thirteenth-century **Georgian monastery**. Not only was the contemporary population of the area largely Armenian, but the architecture apes the tenth- and eleventh-century styles of Georgian specimens further north – specifically Tbeti (see p.698). The site can also be reached by a ninety-minute walk north from the twenty-first kilometre of the Kağızman–Karakurt highway – after heavy rain, this is probably the best way to reach the village as the Kağızman–Çengilli dirt track quickly disappears into a quagmire of mud.

Returning north towards Kars via Kötek, after about twenty kilometres a choice of side roads lead west towards **KECİVAN KALESİ** (Geçvan). Access is via Ortaköy, 3.5km off the asphalt, with a subsequent ninety-minute walk, or by a rough twelve-kilometre drive, the first 5km to Oluklu and then 7km southwest from there. The castle's western ramparts and gates are in fair condition, though little else remains of the third-century Armenian fortified town sacked by the Persians after a year's siege. Back on the main road, the route back to Kars crosses the Pasla Pass (2200m) and the ensuing plateau, before dropping back into the valley of the Kars Çayı.

North of Kars: around Çıldır Gölü

From Kars most travellers will want to move northwest towards Artvin without making the lengthy detour through Erzurum. There are basically three routes to consider: firstly via Çıldır Lake and Şeytan Kalesi to Ardahan and then Şavşat; secondly via Susuz to Ardahan and Şavşat; thirdly via Göle and Bana, taking you close to Yusufeli. The first, most northerly route is scenically superior but difficult without your own vehicle: bus services to Ardahan short-cut via the dull Susuz–Hasköy route, and the unpaved stretch between Ardahan and Şavşat isn't served by buses at all. Two dolmuşes a day run from Kars to Çıldır town, but only one morning minibus connects Çıldır to Ardahan, 30km further west. Note that the Turkish–Armenian border near Akyaka east of Kars remains closed at the time of writing, due to diplomatic wranglings and historical enmity between the two nations.

The slate-like expanse of **Çıldır Gölü**, nearly 2000m up, is the highest sizeable lake in Turkey, though only during the summer – when the hay and grain are growing along the shore – is there a hint of colour. The men on horseback, wielding their scythes and other farming implements, canter splendidly across the steppe against the backdrop of the Kasar Dağı, but their families have to live like moles, with the houses burrowed even deeper than the norm for this province. The shallow lake itself is frozen over for six months of the year, but there are plenty of birds during the warmer months, with handsome falcons and hawks swooping over your vehicle.

This region was an extension of medieval Georgia despite its proximity to Ani, and most of the local monuments are of relatively recent vintage. At **DOĞRUYOL**, the only substantial town on the lake's eastern shore, the thirteenth-century hilltop church of **Djala** masqueraded until recently as a mosque. A few kilometres further on, the islet of **Akçakale** (Argenkale) is crisscrossed by ruined walls and linked to the semifortified village opposite by a boulder causeway. There is also a badly ruined medieval chapel on the islet, but little else can be accurately dated. With its birds, fishing boats and changeable weather the lake here bears an uncanny resemblence to a Scottish highland loch. A modern hotel has just been built on the side of the islet (it wasn't yet open at time of writing, but it should be by now), and camping is allowed nearby; a small **restaurant**, next to the hotel, serves up fresh fish from the lake.

The town of **ÇILDIR** is an unprepossessing place north of the lake, out of sight of the water, but it does at least offer the basic *Otel Firhat* (②). It's also the jumping-off point for the **Şeytan Kalesi** (Satan's Castle), perched on a precipitous bend in the Bazköy Gorge, a thirty-minute walk downstream of Yıldırımtepe village, itself 2km west of Çıldır. A path winds into the gorge from just above the village and leads up to the brooding medieval keep and watchtower.

From Çıldır town you've a stretch of 47 fairly bleak kilometres west to **ARDA-HAN**, somehow reminiscent of Kars, with its Russian grid plan and turn-of-the-century architecture – and a pervasive military presence. There's nothing in particular to see except a fine old **bridge** over the Kura River, just opposite the massive **citadel**, originally Georgian but restored by Selim the Grim early in the sixteenth century. It's still an army camp, so no photography is allowed. There are a couple of basic hotels though the cheapest rooms are often booked up by Russian prostitutes who have crossed over from the Georgian border at nearby Posof (see p.647 for information about the border crossing). Best bet is the *Otel Sevimli*, Kocamustafa Cad (☎0478/211 3376; ①).

Ardahan sits in the midst of a vast plateau of hayfields, swaying even in summer to the winds gusting out of a livid sky. Geese waddle across the road, untamed horses gambol in the stubble, and others are lashed to wagons groaning with hay – all in all a more cheerful prospect than the norm for northeast Anatolia, as you begin the climb up to the **Çam Pass** (2840m), northeastern gateway to the Georgian valleys.

North from Erzurum: the southern Georgian valleys

Highway 950 heads north out of Erzurum across the steppe, aiming for an almost imperceptible gap, too trivial to call a pass, in the surrounding mountains. Almost without noticing it you're across the watershed, and as you begin a slow descent the landscape becomes more interesting, with the Tortum Çayı alongside and trees for the first time in a long while. Most buses bypass the nondescript town of Tortum, 54km from Erzurum; but 15km beyond here, you'll pass a pair of **castles** to left and right, crumbling away atop well-nigh inaccessible pinnacles, and announcing more effectively than any signpost that you've now reached the southern limits of medieval Georgia.

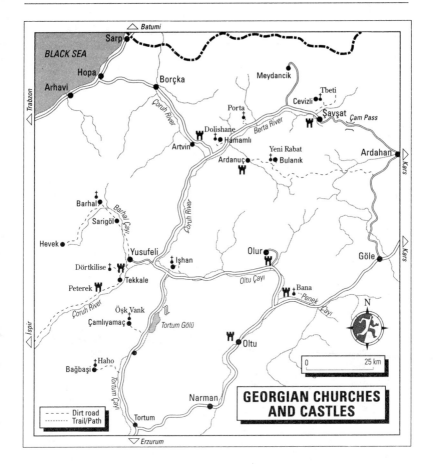

GEORGIAN CHURCHES AND CASTLES

---- Dirt road
.... Trail/Path

0   25 km

Haho

Twenty-six kilometres north of Tortum, turn off to the west at the Taş Köprü humpback bridge, take a left fork in the first large village you come to, then take a right a few minutes later by a new mosque; it's 7.5km in total from your first turn-off to the main square of Bağbaşi, a large community dispersed in a fertile valley. (There is supposedly a service of two buses a day covering the trip from the Gölbaşı Semt Garajı in Erzurum out to the village, but it's still a lot of to-ing and fro-ing just to see this one monument.) Beyond the *meydan* – really just a collection of teahouses loitering by a widening in the road – bear left, and after another 600m you will find, hidden behind some ablution toilets to the right, the dome of the late tenth-century church of **Haho** (Khakuli).

This is the first of several institutions that were constructed by David the Great, ruler of Tao between 961 and 1001. For once most of the monastery complex – the boundary wall, two satellite chapels, assorted galleries – is in good condition, the effect spoiled only by aluminium corrugated sheets on the roof, though the conical-topped dome is

---

THE GEORGIANS

Georgians have lived in the valleys of the Çoruh, Tortum, Kura and Berta rivers, now in Turkey, since the Bronze Age. Like the neighbouring Armenians, they were among the first Near Eastern nations to be evangelized, and were converted rapidly to Christianity by Saint Nino of Cappadocia in the mid-fourth century. Unlike the Armenians, they never broke with the Orthodox Patriarchate in Constantinople, and maintained good relations with Byzantium.

THE GEORGIAN KINGDOMS
An effective Georgian state only entered the local stage early in the ninth century, under the auspices of the **Bagratid** dynasty. This clan contributed rulers to both the Georgian and Armenian lines, and hence the medieval history of both kingdoms overlapped to some extent. They claimed direct descent from David and Bathsheba, which explains a preponderance of kings named David; a coat of arms laden with Old Testament symbols; and curiously Judaic Stars of David embossed on many of the churches they built.

Feudal Bagratid lords initially emerged in the nominally Byzantine-ruled districts of Tao (centred around today's Aspir, Yusufeli and Oltu) and Klarjeti (Ardanuç and Ardahan), from where **Ashot I Kuropalates** began the first stages of territorial aggrandizement at the expense of Byzantium and the Arab Caliphate – and the initial wave of church-building in the area, under the guidance of the monk **Gregory Khantzeli**. Ashot's descendants included **David the Great** of Oltu, a late tenth-century ruler responsible for several of the churches described below, and Bagrat III, who in 1008 succeeded in unifying the various Georgian principalities into one kingdom with a capital at Kutaisi.

A decade or so later the Byzantines compelled his successor Georgi I to evacuate Tao and Klarjeti, making it an easy matter for the Selçuks to step in during 1064. They ravaged Georgia and all of eastern Anatolia, but as soon as they turned to confront the Crusaders a Bagratid revival began. **David the Restorer** not only managed by 1125 to expel the Selçuks, but moved the Bagratid court to newly captured Tblisi, and reunited the various feuding principalities ruled by minor Bagratid warlords.

Under the rule of David's great-granddaughter **Tamara**, medieval Georgia acquired its greatest extent and prestige, controlling most of modern Georgia, Armenia and Azerbaijan from the Black Sea to the Caspian, as well as the ancestral Georgian valleys. The queen was not only a formidable military strategist and shrewd diplomat, but displayed a humanity and tolerance in her domestic administration unusual for the era. Many churches and monasteries were repaired or re-endowed by Tamara, and despite being a woman and a non-Muslim, her name still elicits respectful compliments and even a proprietary pride in the now-Turkish valleys of southern Georgia.

---

still covered in multicoloured tiles. Over the south transept windows, a vigilant stone eagle grasps a doe in his claws, before a fan of alternating light and dark masonry.

A narthex on the west side of the nave still exists, but the doors have been walled off; entry is now through a gallery on the south, a skilful addition of the thirteenth century that appears at first glance to be part of the original building. On either side of the old south entrance, now inside the **gallery**, there's a lion and a chimera in relief; on the right a whale that looks suspiciously like a dog devours Jonah, while below struts a cock (presumably the one of obstinate Pride, such as Jonah's). Inside, a small, well-executed swathe of frescoed angels and Apostles set on a blue background hovers over what was once the apse.

The excellent state of repair of Haho results mainly from its having been used as a mosque since the eighteenth century, so you may have to wait until prayer time for admission if you can't find the warden in the village; after your visit you'll sign the "guest register" and make a donation.

Following Tamara's death the Georgian kingdom began a slow but steady decline, precipitated by Mongol and Persian raids in the mid-thirteenth century but most of all by Tamerlane's apocalypse early in the next. Tamara's Georgia was effectively partitioned between the Ottoman and Persian empires, and although Bagratids continued to occupy thrones in Tblisi, they were essentially puppets. The rise of imperial Russia was a mixed blessing: while it prevented further Muslim encroachment, it signalled the end of any viable Georgian state, and the last semi-independent king effectively surrendered what was left of his autonomy to Catherine the Great in 1783.

GEORGIAN MONUMENTS

Tangible evidence of the Georgian heyday is still abundant in the northeastern parts of Turkey, not least in the common prefix "Ar-" (as in Ardahan, Artvin, Ardanuç etc), equivalent to "-ville" or to "-burg". The Bagratids were a prolific bunch, and they stuck **castles** on just about every height; generally a passing glance is what you'll have to be satisfied with, since access to many of these eyries has long been impossible. Most remarkable, however, are the early Bagratid monastic **churches**, all dating from before the move northeast to the Caucasus proper, and most sited amid oases at the heads of remote valleys. As a rule, the core conventions of Armenian religious architecture – domes supported on four freestanding columns, a cruciform, east-west ground plan with prominent transepts, blind exterior arcades and intricate relief work – were borrowed wholesale, and it takes a trained eye to distinguish the two styles. Georgian building has, however, been pinpointed as one of the major vehicles through which church architecture was transported to Russia.

You'll need your own wheels, or a lot of time for walking and hitching, to visit most of the churches. There's usually a small village nearby, or even surrounding the monument, but invariably bus services, where they exist, arrive in the afternoon and depart for the nearest town in the morning – exactly the opposite of tourist schedules. Many of the roads in are bad, but if you can assemble a group and find a taxi driver willing to risk his undercarriage, this can end up being far cheaper than renting a vehicle in Erzurum or Trabzon.

There's not nearly the degree of official stonewalling about Georgian Christians as there is concerning Armenians, and the churches have become semi-recognized as tourist attractions. We've only detailed the most intact examples; if you've a compulsive interest in the subject, there are numerous unsung others, slowly collapsing in isolated settings, that villagers will be happy to show you. Virtually every church has suffered some damage from dynamite- and pickaxe-wielding treasure-hunters: the locals have an unshakeable conviction that all of the Christians who left the area in 1923 or before, secreted precious items in or under their churches before departure in the mistaken belief that they'd eventually be able to return.

Önk Vank

Below the Haho turning, the Tortum valley widens appreciably, and the side road to the monastery church of **Öck Vank** (Oshkhi), just before Tortum lake, is prominently marked with the usual black-on-yellow archeologists' sign. It's an easy, well-graded 7km straight up to Çamlayamaç village, but the site, with houses built up to the very walls, is the least evocative of all in the area. Given the good road in, this is also the one church regularly mobbed by coach tours – there's even a teahouse and a shop, well used to foreigners, selling Pepsi to the right of the nave.

None of this should deter you, since Öck Vank is the most elaborate example of Georgian Gothic in these valleys. Another late tenth-century foundation of David the Great, it represents the culmination of Tao Georgian culture before the Bagratid dynasty's move northeast and the start of the Georgian "Golden Age" after 1125.

A protruding porch shelters the main entry through the **facade** of the south transept; blind arcades, topped by scallop-shell carving, flank it, with reliefs of the Archangels hovering high overhead. Alternatively you are able to enter from the southwest corner of the building, through a triple-arched **narthex** with an engaging zigzag roof; the interior colonnade exudes a European Gothic feel with its groin-vaulted ceiling and column capitals bearing sculpted angels. The roof over the nave, elongated to the west, has fallen in, leaving the dome stranded atop four essential pillars, two of which have their massive bases intricately worked in sinuous **geometric designs**. Halfway up the south transept wall, the vanished wooden floor of the mosque that once occupied the premises acted as protection for a stretch of **frescoes**, the best preserved in any of the Turkish Georgian churches, featuring half-a-dozen ethereal saints in hieratic poses.

Tortum Gölü and falls

A little way past the turn-off for Öşk Vank lies the inlet end of **Tortum Gölü**, a substantial body of water, roughly ten kilometres long by one wide, that forces the road up onto a hair-raising corniche bypass above the western shore. The water is by turns muddy green, milky beige or dull slate even on a bright day, so the idea of a swim doesn't necessarily appeal, though the locals try from the stone beach below the village of **BALIKLI**. The lake was formed by a landslide blocking the north end of the valley between two and three centuries ago. The famous *şelale* or **falls of Tortum** are today its natural outlet, accessible by a signposted dirt side road 12km north of the Öşk Vank turning. TEK, the Turkish Electric Foundation, has supplemented the natural dam with an artifical one and a turbine; you leave the asphalted highway where you see the power plant, and then proceed as indicated by a little red-and-white sign for just over a kilometre, until glimpsing a vast rock ledge with its 48-metre cascade on your left. You'll have to scramble down a path to the left to get a good look, and you won't see much except in spring, since the TEK diverts most available water for power generation later in the summer. Below the falls the valley narrows to an impressive canyon as the various arms of the Kara, Avsek and Dutlu ranges start to tighten their embrace.

Işhan

Seventeen kilometres below the falls there's an important intersection in the steadily descending highway. Continuing straight ahead will lead you to Yusufeli (see below); bearing right towards Olur, you reach, after approximately 5km, an archeological service sign pointing to **IŞHAN** (Ishkani), a bluff-top village 6km up a dirt road through the crumpled hills of a heavily eroded, lifeless moonscape. The gorgeous houses of this sleepy village and the dramatic views of the parched Oltu Valley in themselves make this one of the most attractive settlements in the region, well worth an exploratory stroll. Vehicles should be left near the central village fountain, with a final 300-metre walk down and left to the precincts of the sanctuary, where there's another fountain and nearby benches which are the perfect venue for a picnic.

The imposing **church**, originally dedicated to the Virgin, was constructed in stages between the seventh and eleventh centuries, ranking it among the oldest extant sacred Georgian architecture. The semicircular colonnade that lines the apse is the earliest surviving portion of the building, and was modelled consciously after the church at Bana (see below); great chunks of the roof are now missing, meaning that the 42-metre-high dome, built in a similar fashion to Öşk Vank's, rests in isolation on four columns. The acoustics however remain superb, as you can hear for yourself if you stand directly beneath the dome. There are some patches of fresco to be seen high up on the surviving walls, portraying portions of the Vision of Zaccharias, and in the cupola, there's an abstract cross. The external eleventh-century **relief work** is more interesting, though, particularly on the small baptistry with its bestiary and semicircular inscriptions, opposite a bricked-up southern portal where a lion and snake are locked in combat. Sadly, however, the church in general has been much mucked about with, particularly on the northwest corner – defaced with recent, ill-advised masonry – and in the nave, which is completely blocked by a modern wall.

Oltu and Bana

A detour via Narman and Oltu is time well spent, especially if you have your own vehicle. Invariably dismissed or underestimated, this alternative approach to Yusufeli compares well to similar landscapes in Afghanistan or the American Southwest. Stands of poplars and green fields are juxtaposed against a cobalt sky and reddish bluffs, often crowned with crumbling Georgian **castles**. Beyond Narman, the river rolls past **OLTU**, with the first of the citadels – well restored by the Ottomans and again in the 1970s – overhead (the castle remains locked but keys may be forthcoming from the local *Belediye*). A further 20km north brings you to an asphalt junction; continue left for 2km to the natural junction as the Penek River joins the Oltu on its dramatic journey to the Black Sea. Here on either side of the strategic Y-fork rise two castles – one backed into the cliff, the other freestanding and flanked by a small church. Continuing towards Işhan takes you past yet another redoubt, atop a rock spur by the road to Olur.

Bearing right instead leads towards Göle and Kars; 28km beyond Oltu (or 37km southwest of Göle) you'll see, just before the river valley narrows drastically, the seventh-century church of **Bana** on the north bank of the Penek (Irlağaç) Çayı. Perched on a knoll surveying water-meadows and dominated in turn by tawny crags, it's a commanding position. The Ottomans fortified Bana during the Crimean War, a century after it ceased to be used as a shrine. The Russians blasted the dome off during the 1877–78 war, and later carted off much of the masonry to build a turn-of-the-century church in Oltu.

What remains – the first floor of a vast rotunda half-submerged in its own ruins, with one talon of masonry protruding above – is still impressive, and in both architecture and setting seems a transition between Armenian shrines and the Georgian ones. The east apse houses a colonnade virtually identical to the later one at Işhan. To get to Bana, take the track that branches off left just before the gorge, where the main road crosses the river, and continue through the village of Penek, branching left after 3km to approach the church from the north.

Yusufeli and around

The area around the confluence of the Barhal and Çoruh rivers is scenically and climatically one of the most favoured corners of the northeast. During the balmy summers, every sort of fruit ripens, and you're treated to the incongruous spectacle of rice paddies by the Çoruh, within sight of parched cliffs overhead.

The rivers themselves are a magnet for visitors, making Yusufeli a popular base for **white-water rafters** finishing the challenging runs from İspir or Barhal upstream, or beginning the easier float down to Artvin. Highest water is from mid-June to mid-July, and the main outfitters for such trips are *Adrift* and *Sobek Expeditions* (see "Getting There" in *Basics*).

Tourism in general seems set to grow by leaps and bounds in the future, though so far the simplicity of local facilities has appealed mostly to the hardier breed of traveller. Even if you're not an outdoor sports enthusiast, you'll need a steady hand at the wheel

– or a strong stomach if you're a passenger – for the bumpy rides out to the local Georgian churches.

If you are unable to get a direct **bus** service to Yusufeli from Erzurum, ask to be set down at Su Kavuşumu junction, 9km below the town centre. The last Artvin–Yusufeli bus doesn't roll past the turn-off until about 4pm, but if you've missed it, or your heart is set on being in Barhal that evening (see below for onward schedules), don't panic and accept the offer of a **taxi** shuttle up to Yusufeli – they're pretty expensive at $6 per car and hitching can be rewarding. Heading in the other direction, the junction is also a good place to pick up transport east to Ardahan and Kars, and the aforementioned sights along the way.

Yusufeli

Straddling the Barhal Çayı just above its junction with the Çoruh, **YUSUFELİ** is an immediately likeable and friendly town with all essential services – including a **bank** and a **PTT**. It's a fairly conservative and devout anomaly in the secular, relatively progressive province of Artvin, a situation that can be partly explained by the fact that a high proportion of the inhabitants are descended from Bulgarian Muslim settlers of the turn of the century. Numerous travellers come to spend a night on their way to the Kaçkar mountains, but most end up staying two, making a day trip up one of the nearby river valleys.

Hotels in town are uniformly plain and dirt-cheap, though generally clean, and all are grouped within 100m of each other. When business is slack, it is often possible to get a three- or four-bed room for the same price as a single or double. One of the better choices is the *Barhal Hotel* (☎0466/811 3151; ①), next to the pedestrian suspension bridge, with clean, bright rooms with showers overlooking the foaming river. Above is the much more basic and even cheaper *Aydın* and opposite is the *Hotel Çoruh*, both worth avoiding. Another good choice is the clean *Otel Keleş*, on the main street, Halit Paşa Cad (☎0446/811 2305; ①). The nearby *Çiçek Palas Oteli* (☎0466/811 2393; ①) has cramped rooms but is bright, clean and friendly. Other less desirable options include the *Otel Ferah* (☎0446/811 2102; ①), *Hacioğlu Oteli* (☎0446/811 3566) and *Yeşil Kösk* (☎0446/811 2309; ①), which at least has a river view to compensate for dingy rooms. There are two **campsites**, the *Akın* and slightly better *Greenpeace Camping*, a couple of hundred metres upstream of the *Barhal*, on the far side of the river, but neither has any real facilities to boast of.

For something to eat head for the *Mavi Köşk*, a licensed full-menu **restaurant** next to the *Yeşil Kösk*, or try the *Mahzen Fıçı Bira* or the *Çınar Restorant*, whose balconies overhang either side of the river a hundred metres upstream – food is secondary to the drinking and spontaneous musical sessions here, though, and unless you arrive early they'll be packed out, often by tour groups. The *Lokanta Pide Salon* at the other end of town does excellent cheap *pide* and salad.

Yusufeli is also the start of **dolmuş routes** to various villages further upriver, including Barhal and Hevek. Service to these two high settlements is available daily all year, since both are inhabited in winter, but adheres to a somewhat informal schedule. The Barhal vehicle leaves Yusufeli between 3pm and 3.30pm, while there seem to be two Hevek departures, at around 2 and 5pm. In theory all are linked to the arrival of afternoon buses from Artvin. If you miss the Barhal service, you can often plead a seat on the Hevek dolmuş which has to pass through Barhal. All dolmuşes return to Yusufeli early in the morning.

Tekkale and Dörtkilise

TEKKALE lies 7km southwest of Yusufeli on the same bank of the Çoruh, connected by dolmuşes heading to either Kiliçkaya or Köprügören, 27km upriver and the last point served by public transport. The road to Tekkale passes two ruined chapels (one perched above the Çoruh in Yusufeli town, the second on the far side of the river a couple of kilometres upstream) and a vertiginous castle guarding the valley road, before curving the last 2km into the village. Next to the *Dörtkilise Resting Camp* (☎0466/811 2908; ①), you bear right and away from the Çoruh, and walk or drive the 6km further to **Dörtkilise** (Otkhta Eklesia). Despite the name – meaning "Four Churches" – only one still stands intact, but it's very fine and unlike most other Georgian places of worship. Domeless, with a steep gabled roof and relatively plain exterior, it's a twin of the church at nearby Barhal, though it was built several decades earlier; it was later renovated by David the Great. Since the closest *yayla* is about 2km away, Dörtkilise was never reconsecrated as a mosque, and is now home only to bats, swallows and occasionally livestock. Inside a double line of four columns supports the barrel ceiling hiding under the pitched roof; with a torch you can also pick out traces of fresco. The large half-ruined building to the northeast was the monastery refectory, joined to the main body of the church by an equally decrepit gallery which served as a narthex. Beyond Tekkale, the road from Yusufeli continues southwest past ancient Peterek castle, following the dramatic Çoruh valley for a further 60km to Aspir.

Barhal and Hevek

The most popular route out of Yusufeli follows the valley of the Barhal Çayı north through a landscape straight out of a Romantic engraving, complete with ruined Georgian castles on assorted crags – and an atrocious dirt track that hasn't changed much since the nineteenth century. After 18km, dolmuş drivers stop briefly at Sarıgöl to get the kinks out of their fingers and give their passengers a chance to eat (or just avoid being ill). Barhal, officially renamed **ALTIPARMAK** after the mountains behind, is reached 12km beyond, a two-hour drive in total from Yusufeli. With its scattered wooden buildings peeking out from lush pre-alpine vegetation at 1300m, Barhal conforms well to most people's notions of a mountain village. There are three **places to stay**: several treehouse-type chalets, with mattresses on the floor and a fridge full of cold beer, available by arrangement with the *Otel Karahan* in Artvin or direct with Mehmet Karahan (☎0446/826 2071; ①, including half-board), but often filled by trekking tours; the *Seher Köybaş Pansiyonu* (☎0446/826 2041; ①), a single room let out by a welcoming family; and the basic lodge (☎0466/826 2005; ①) run by Cemil Özyurt, above his combination **café-restaurant**, right by the dolmuş stop and the only place to eat out. Otherwise you can hunt for spots to **camp** on the banks of the trout-rich stream. The village facilities are completed by a bakery, well-stocked shop and well-attended teahouse.

The tenth-century **church of Barhal** (Parkhali), the final legacy of David the Great, is a ten-minute walk up the secondary track toward the Kaçkar mountains – not the main one headed toward Hevek – and then a muddy scramble up a lushly vegetated slope, starting opposite a single river-bank shed. It's virtually identical to Dörtkilise, except for being somewhat smaller – and in near-perfect condition owing to long use as the village mosque. As long as the church continued in this role it was difficult to gain admission, but a new mosque has been completed, and there is concern that the church, once abandoned, will be subject to the decay and vandalism that has beset the other Georgian monuments in Turkey. Optimistically, there also exists the possibility that the authorities might strip the church's interior whitewash to see what frescoes, if any, are hiding underneath. If the church is locked, enquire at the next-door school, but be prepared to be seconded into an impromptu English class.

HEVEK (Yaylalar) lies another two hours' drive along a steadily worsening, twenty-kilometre road. Well above tree-line at over 2000m, this substantial village is the highest trailhead for the Kaçkar, but its setting can't compare to Barhal's. So far the one **place to stay** is the *Altınay Pansiyon* (①), which is also probably the best place to track down food (there are plans to open another *pansiyon* nearby). Architecturally the village varies from new concrete to century-old houses, though the only specific sight is an Ottoman **bridge** just downstream. If you're determined to stay overnight here, it's prudent to consult Cemil Özyurt in Barhal, as he's originally from Hevek and may be able to arrange something with relatives.

The Kaçkar Dağları

A formidable barrier between the northeastern Anatolian plateau and the Black Sea, the **Kaçkar Dağları** are the high end of the Pontic coastal ranges – and Turkey's most rewarding and popular trekking area. Occupying a rough rectangle some 70km by 20km, the Kaçkars extend from the Rize–İspir road to the Hopa–Artvin highway, with the more abrupt southeast flank lapped by the Çoruh River, and the gentler northwest folds dropping more gradually to misty foothills. At 3972m, their summit ranks only third highest in Turkey after Ararat and Süphan Dağı, but in scenic and human interest they fully earn their aliases, "the Little Caucasus" and "the Pontic Alps".

"Kaçkar" is the Turkish spelling of *khatchkar*, sculpted Armenian votive crosses or gravestones once abundant in eastern Turkey – perhaps a reference to the complicated and tortured outline of the range, with multiple hanging valleys and secondary spurs. In addition to the principal summit area, several other major massifs are recognized: the Altıparmak and Marsis groups of about 3300m, at the north end of the Bulut ridge which links them with Point 3972; and the adjacent Tatos and Verçenik systems of about 3700m, at the extreme southwest of the chain. Oddly for Turkey, the Kaçkars are a young granite-diorite range instead of the usual karst, and were much transformed by the last Ice Age; there are still remnants of glaciers on the north slope of the highest peak, and literally hundreds of lakes spangle the alpine zone above 2600m.

Partly because of intensive human habitation, the Kaçkars support relatively few large mammals; bear and boar prefer the forested mid-altitude zones, while wolves and ibex are ruthlessly hunted in the treeless heights. Birds of prey and snow cocks are more easily seen and heard, while the summer months witness an explosion of wildflowers, butterflies – and vicious deer flies. Between May and September migration from the nearby lowlands to the *yayla*s, or summer pasture settlements, is the norm: the lower ones are occupied first, the higher ones once the snow recedes. Upper dwellings tend to be rudimentary, made mostly of stone, but the lower, sturdy chalets cluster in proper villages, some with jeep track access, others with power lines strung to them – an odd sight at 2100m.

Given the ethnic variety here, it's no surprise that local place names are similarly tangled – a discerning glance at the map will turn up plenty of Georgian and Armenian words, plus Turkified versions of same. Thus Pişkankara (the original form) has become Pişenkaya, "the cooking rock", while other more provocatively foreign ones like Sevcov Lake are camouflaged outright as Deniz Gölü. The recurring suffix "-evit" is an Armenian dialect particle meaning "yayla".

Practicalities

The four most popular **trailhead villages** are, on the Black Sea slopes, Çat and Ayder (see the *Black Sea Coast* chapter), and on the Çoruh side, Barhal and Hevek (see above). Approach from the Black Sea hills is gentler, with clearer trails, but the paths and villages can be crowded, and the almost daily mist rising up to 2800m is a problem. Hiking grades are tougher on the Çoruh flank, but the weather is more dependable. The best **season** is late June to September, with the mists less of a problem as autumn approaches. If you're hardy, it gets warm enough in midsummer for a quick swim in most of the lakes. Pure water, available everywhere from springs, is never scarce.

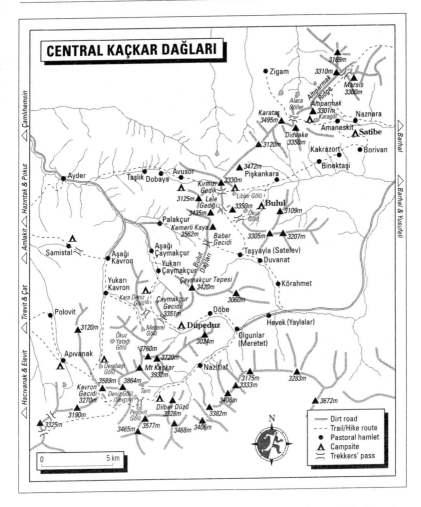

In terms of **itineraries**, the Kaçkar is infinitely versatile. If you're particularly manic, you can cross from Hevek to Ayder via certain passes in a single, gruelling day, but a more reasonable minimum time to switch sides of the mountains would be three or four days, and most people are happy to spend a week or ten days.

In any case you'll need a **full trekking kit**, including heavy-duty boots, tent, stove, all-weather clothing and food; hospitality may be offered in a *yayla*, but it cannot be counted on, as there's normally little extra to spare and they're only inhabited on a rota basis. Otherwise, there are few specific **dangers** or warnings, besides the absolute necessity of crossing all tricky passes early in the day before they're shrouded in mist. Territorial domestic bulls are also a nuisance, far more likely to charge a tent than any wild beast. It's useful to know that the ubiquitous Pontic azalea, from whose blossoms the notorious hallucinogenic *deli bal* is made (the "mad" honey that gave Xenophon's soldiers chronic diarrhoea), contains sufficient flammable resin to ignite even in damp conditions. The mountain people consider it a pest and uproot it with little compunction.

The Kaçkars seem to attract more and more crowds every season. There's no Nepal-style permit system yet, but such a situation is foreseeable; the lack of decent large-scale **maps** is another drawback. If this is all too daunting and you'd rather go with a **guide**, there are a couple of helpful individuals in Ayder (see p.657), as well as Bunyad Dinç in İstanbul (☎016/308 0568), who in 1990 led a dozen Dutch on the first complete traverse from İkizdere in the west to Barhal in the east. Özkan Şahin in Yusufeli may be able to help with route information and equipment hire; contact him via the *Çiçek Palas Oteli*. Otherwise virtually all of the adventure travel companies listed in *Basics* run some sort of Kaçkar group itinerary, though often through a local subcontractor.

Routes in the northern Kaçkar

Starting from **Barhal**, most trekkers head west to the top of the valley walled off by the Altıparmak chain, finishing a tough first day either near Karagöl or the nearby Satibe meadow. The following day usually involves a drop down to the Kışla valley just south, threading through the *yayla*s of Borivan, Binektaşı and Pişkankara before making camp higher up. If you choose to pitch tent at Libler Gölü, near the top of the main valley, the next day will see you over the tricky Kırmışı Gedik saddle for an easy descent to **Ayder**.

Alternatively you can bear south from Pişkankara up to a camp in the Bulul valley, at the head of which is the wonderful **Öküz Gölü** (Ox Lake) and an initially easy – but later steep – pass giving on to the **Körahmet valley**, still on the Çoruh side of the range. From an overnight next to Satelev *yayla*, you can choose between crossing the Bulut ridge via the Baber pass, dropping down to **Palakçur** just above Ayder; or rolling down-valley to **Hevek**, with the option of ending your hike or stocking up to continue into the central Kaçkar.

Routes in the central Kaçkar

Above Hevek, two more valleys lead up to the base of the highest Kaçkar peaks. At **Meretet**, the split occurs. Bearing right takes you to camping spots near spectacular wildflowers high up in the Düpedüz valley, just below the **Çaymakcur pass**, the easiest in the entire Kaçkar range. You should leave for the pass early the following day, when you'd camp at Kara Deniz Gölü beyond, with plenty of time for a day-hike to **Meterel Gölü** – and from a nearby overlook, your first, spectacular nose-to-nose view of Point 3972's north face. From Kara Deniz Gölü you can reach **Ayder** in another long walking day, via the upper and lower Çaymakcur *yayla*s.

The valley follows the Büyük Çay upstream to the apparent cul-de-sac of the **Dilber meadows**, a popular (and over-subscribed) camping venue at the formidable base of Point 3972 itself. Despite appearances there is a way up and out: first to the lake of **Sevcov** (Deniz Gölü), and then over the low crest just south to **Peşevit lake** with much better camping. But Sevcov is the veering-off point for the moderately difficult climb north to the **summit**, where the climbers' register is hidden underneath a rubble cairn.

From Peşevit lake it's a bit of a scramble due west until meeting a trail near the top of the Davali valley, aiming for the Kavron pass. Once back on the Black Sea side, you can choose between descending directly to Ayder through the *yayla*s of Apıvanak, Polovit, Amlakıt and Hazıntak, or slipping over the ridge west of Apıvanak to **Tirevit**, and the beginning of the western Kaçkar.

Routes in the western Kaçkar

Elevit *yayla* is roughly midway between Tirevit and **Çat**, and the starting point for the march up to **Yıldızlı Gölü** (Star Lake), just across the top of the valley from Hacıvanak *yayla*. The lake, named for the twinkles of light which appear on its surface early in the morning, offers good camping; the nearby, gentle Capug pass allows access to the headwaters of the Fırtına Çayı, though the onward route is briefly confused by the maze of bulldozer tracks around Başyayla and Kaleyayla. At the latter, bear south up toward campsites by a lake at the foot of Tatos peak; the following day you'd cross a saddle to another lake, Adalı, at the base of 3711-metre Verçenik.

From this point you'd either descend to Çat via Ortaköy and Varoş, using a morning bus if possible part of the way, or continue walking west for another day, past other lakes just below the ridge joining Verçenik to Germaniman peak. A final 3100-metre pass just north of Germaniman leads to the valley containing Saler and Başköy *yayla*s, linked by daily bus to **İkizdere**.

Artvin and beyond: the northern Georgian valleys

The northerly Georgian valleys form the heart of the **province of Artvin**, lying within a fifty-kilometre radius of the town of the same name. Nowhere else in Turkey, except for the Kaçkars, do you feel so close to the Caucasus; ornate wooden domestic and religious architecture, with green slopes or naked crags for a backdrop, clinch the impression of exoticism. Here, too, you may actually encounter native **Georgian speakers**, though they're mostly confined to the remote valleys centring on the towns of Camili, Meydancık and Posof, and the immediate surroundings of Şavşat. Whatever their antecedents, the people here are remarkable for their high literacy rate and left-of-centre polling practices – and their seasonal presence. Disgusted by the lack of local opportunities, many have emigrated internally to work ten months of the year at the factories around Bursa and İzmir, to the extent that there are now more *Artvinli*s out west than in the province itself.

The region, with its wet, alpine climate, has considerable potential as a winter sports playground, but for the moment most tourists come in summer to see the local **Georgian churches**. Individually these are not as impressive as their southern relatives, but their situations are almost always more picturesque. Visits should be uncomplicated if you follow the directions given; permits are only needed for access to points within 10km of the Georgian frontier – including, incidentally, all of the native-Georgian valleys listed above.

Artvin

As your vehicle winds up four kilometres' worth of zigzags from the Çoruh River, you begin to wonder just where **ARTVİN** is. Suddenly the town reveals itself, arrayed in sweeping tiers across a steep, east-facing slope, seeming much higher than its actual 550m of elevation. Unusually the obligatory ruined **castle** is down low by the river; the only other buildings with a patina of history are houses from the Russian era, tucked here and there on the hill above the centre. Certainly it has the least flat ground of any Turkish provincial capital, and – within the city limits at least – perhaps the fewest specific attractions. But Artvin is pleasant enough for a night or two, and becomes a destination in its own right every third week in June, when the **Kafkasör** festival takes place at a *yayla* above town. Highlight of this has traditionally been the pitting of bulls in rut against each other, but since the opening of the nearby frontier the event has taken on a genuinely international character, with revellers, vendors and performers from Georgia appearing among 75,000 locals. It's one of the last genuine folk fairs in the country, unlikely to be mucked about with by tourism officials, so be there if you can.

Practicalities

The **otogar** is way down by the castle, so the three main companies serving Artvin all run a *servis araba* or shuttle van up to town – don't get left behind, or end up paying over the odds for a taxi. Conversely, when it's time to leave, all the bus companies have ticket offices along İnönü **Caddesi**, the single high street running past the Hükümet Konağı (Government Hall) and **PTT**.

There's only one comfortable **hotel**, the *Karahan* at İnönü Cad 16 (☎0466/212 1800, fax 212 2420; ④), a bit overpriced, but all rooms have en-suite bath, the staff are willing and informative, and the attached restaurant is one of two places in town serving alcohol with meals. The *Otel Kaçkar* (☎0446/212 3397; ①), also on İnönü, has clean rooms with bathrooms (though the owner is threatening to move to İstanbul), and the *Hotel Güven*, Hamam Sok 9, down a side street running off İnönü (☎0446/212 1118; ①), is bright and modern, also with private bathrooms. The *Hotel Genya*, across from the *Karahan*, is noisy and run-down (①).

You may want to arrange beds at two basic **out-of-town establishments** while in Artvin. The *Otel Karahan* controls an inn for trekkers in Barhal (☎0466/212 2936; see p.691); they can also point you in the right direction for the municipal bungalows up at Kafkasör meadow.

Alternatives to the *Karahan* when **eating out** include the *Derya Restaurant*, up by the PTT, which has booze, grilled items and an atmosphere congenial enough for unescorted foreign women, or the cheerful *Kibar Pide Salonu*, up some stairs from the main drag. At the bottom end of İnönü, the *Efzar* is worth checking out for its views, while the *Hanedan* has the most refined ambience – though check the prices first; the *Merkez Lokantasi* is a dependable standby. The *Köşk Pastanesi*, up near the top of Anönü, has breakfast-time *börek* in addition to the usual range of sweeties.

Rounding off the list of amenities are a fairly useless **tourist information office** behind the *Otel Karahan* (everyone asks questions in the hotel instead) and a rather expensive **hamam** ($2.50 each), behind the PTT. Theoretically they shuffle clientele to accommodate either sex within the hour, but in practice this doesn't always happen.

Ardanuç and Yeni Rabat

The river valleys east of Artvin are no less spectacular than their counterparts around Yusufeli. The approach to **ARDANUÇ**, once the capital of Klarjeti Georgia, is through the spectacular, high-walled "Hell's Gorge". **Dolmuşes** from Artvin do the thirty-minute trip all morning, starting at 8am, with the last one back at 3pm. The dwindling old quarter of Ardanuç crouches at the foot of a giant wedding cake of crumbling orange rock, on top of which sits a giant Bagratid **castle**. With an early start to beat the heat, you can climb it, but to do that and see the church up the valley in one day you'll need your own transport – or be willing to overnight in the newer quarter. This, arranged around a delightful, plane-tree-studded green, can offer a single beer bar, some restaurants and a handful of very plain **hotels** worked by prostitutes.

Yeni Rabat

East of Ardanuç the paving ends, and the scenery gets ever more idyllic as the dirt road worsens. At a triple fork among the meadows and conifers 14km along, take the signed left option to **BULANIK** village and Yeni Rabat; most people come by car or walk, but considering the horrid surface there are a surprising number of Ardanuç-based dolmuşes lurching by, bound for Bulanık and Tosunlar, across the valley. You should be prepared for some serious detours as the fragile road has a tendency to disappear after bad weather.

From the middle of Bulanık, distinguished by fine vernacular log cabins, a recent bulldozer track leads east-northeast for most of the 45-minute walk to the tenth-century monastery church of **Yeni Rabat** (Shatberdi), nestled in the vegetable gardens of its four-house hamlet. The long-vanished monstery, founded a century earlier by Gregory Khantzeli, was renowned as a school for manuscript illuminators. The dome, nave and transept are still virtually intact, but the exterior has been stripped of most of its dressed stone, and the new track in – which will be extended west to replace the river bank route – has been routed dangerously close to the foundations.

The lower Berta valley: Dolishane and Porta

From the Ardanuç area, retrace your steps to the junction with Highway 965 linking Artvin and Şavşat, which parallels the Berta River (Imerhevi in Georgian). Exactly 300m upstream from the Ardanuç turning, a fine stone **bridge** leaps over the water, and directly opposite this a sign points up a dirt road to the village of **HAMAMLI**. In theory there's a dolmuş service, but it arrives in the afternoon and returns the next morning to Artvin, precisely the reverse of tourists' needs. After 6.5km all vehicles must park by the first house; it's two minutes more on foot to the tenth-century church of **Dolishane**, now the village mosque. The vegetable garden and house of the hospitable *imam* adjoin it, and he or his family will show you around. There are some faded frescoes in the "basement" created when wood planking split the building into top and bottom storeys; the whitewashed upper interior is of little interest. The exterior is more rewarding, the south dome window surrounded by such reliefs as the builder-king Smbat I (954–58) offering the church to Christ, a Star of David and an archangel.

Twelve kilometres above the turning for Ardanuç, an easily missed yellow metal sign – typical of those posted throughout the province by the energetic owners of the *Otel Karahan* – points to the start of the direct path up to **Porta**, modern name for the ninth-century monastery of Khantza, home to the architect-monk Gregory Khantzeli. It's an enjoyable but steep 35-minute climb up to the Bağlar district of Pırnallı village, though you'll need stout, treaded shoes, since the trail is very slippery; for the same reason reckon on the same amount of time down. The friendly hamlet, an oasis tucked into a side ravine of the main canyon running up to Pırnallı, is built higgledy-piggledy around and up against the dilapidated monuments.

The main tenth-century **church**, still impressive despite gaping holes in the dome and walls, was similar in plan to the one at Haho, with low-ceilinged aisles flanking the nave. To the west stands a separate, smaller sixteen-sided **cupola**, once part of either a belfry or a baptistry. Georgian inscriptions are chiselled across its two-toned masonry, which is in near-perfect condition. Of the monastery quarters themselves, orientated west-to-east, only the southeastern corner remains. Beside the path in, the eastern wall of an isolated chapel shelters an **ayazma** or sacred spring which supports the local orchards – a contrast to the endemic scrub oak (*pırnal*) which gives the main village its name.

The upper Berta valley: Tbeti and Şavşat

The last local Georgian church lies 10km off the Artvin–Şavşat road. Turn along the side road to Velaköy by the ruined castle, follow the Kalebonyu River for 6km and then bear right after the river bridge to get to the small hamlet of Ciritdüzü. Turn left here by a small shop, cross over a ridge into the Tbeti valley for 2.5km and then follow the Cevizli sign right for 750m. Park by the school, turn left and walk 200m more. There is a dolmuş service to and from nearby Şavşat, but it inconveniently arrives in the afternoon and goes back to town the next morning.

The remains of the tenth-century monastery church in **TBETİ**, peeking out of the trees at the head of a beautiful valley, are visible at a distance to the sharp-eyed, though up close the cloister – extensively damaged by local treasure-hunters a few decades ago – is heartbreaking. Tbeti was unique in its non-elongated cross-in-square ground plan, with only a church in far-off Çengilli approximating it. Now, only the south transept retains any relief work, with fine carved windows and cross details. According to tradition the great medieval Georgian poet, Shota Rustaveli, studied here for a time; he is said to have fallen hopelessly in love with Queen Tamara while serving as one of her ministers and, being summarily rejected, ended his days in a Jerusalem monastery. The finely carved wooden balconies and windows of the local houses, the lush saturated greens of the deep valleys and the humour of the local people all go towards making this area the most Georgian-feeling of Eastern Turkey.

A compact **castle**, just west of the town-limits sign, heralds your arrival in **ŞAVŞAT**, but there's little to stop for here other than the fine local **carpets** woven in a half-dozen villages of the district or, if you're desperate, a place to spend the night (try the *Hotel Sahara* in the centre of town). The road east from here through the forest to Ardahan, though nominally all-weather, deteriorates markedly as you approach the deserted wooden hamlets and extreme switchbacks that lead up to the high pass at the border between Artvin and Kars provinces.

travel details

Trains

Divriği to: Erzurum (daily at 4.40am; 8hr); Sivas (daily at 5am; 5hr).

Erzurum to: Ankara/İstanbul (daily at 12.40pm; 26/35hr); Kars (daily at 4.20am & 1pm; 5hr).

Kars to: Erzurum (daily at 7.10am & 2.40pm; 5–7hr).

Buses and dolmuşes

Artvin to: Ardahan, via Göle (2 daily; 5hr); Ardanuç (6 daily until 6pm; 30min); Erzurum (5 daily; 4hr); Hopa (hourly until 3pm; 3hr 15min); Kars (2 or 3 daily before noon; 7hr); Rize (hourly until 3pm; 3hr 15min); Şavşat (6 or 7 daily; 1hr 15min); Tblisi (Georgia) via Sarp (several weekly; 7hr); Trabzon (hourly until 3pm; 4hr 30min); Yusufeli (4 daily; 1hr).

Erzurum to: Ankara (hourly; 15hr); Artvin (5 daily; 4hr); Bayburt (hourly; 3hr); Doğubeyazit (4 daily; 4hr 30min); İspir (3 daily; 2hr 30min); Kars (hourly; 3hr 30min); Rize (1 or 2 direct daily; 7hr); Sivas (hourly; 8hr 30min); Trabzon (5 daily; 8hr); Van (3 or 4 daily; 7hr 30min); Yusufeli (3 direct daily; 3hr).

Kars to: Ardahan (hourly; 2hr); Artvin via Göle (1 daily at 7am; 7hr); Çıldır (2 daily; 1hr 30min); Digor (hourly; 45min); Doğubeyazit (6 daily until 2pm; 3hr 30min); Erzurum (10 daily; 3hr 30min); Iğdır (hourly; 2hr 45min); Trabzon (1 daily; 12hr).

Yusufeli to: Artvin (5 daily until 12.30pm; 2hr 30min); Erzurum (2 daily in the morning; 3hr).

Flights

Erzincan to: Ankara (3 weekly; 1hr 20min).

Erzurum to: Ankara (2 daily; 1hr 30min); İstanbul (2 daily; 4hr 30min).

Kars to: Ankara (daily; 1hr 50min).

International trains

Kars to: Ahuryan, just inside Armenia (summer Fri 10.45am, post train only, subject to state of relations between Turkey and Armenia).

CHAPTER ELEVEN

THE EUPHRATES AND TIGRIS BASIN

East of the Mediterranean coast, you leave touristic Turkey behind. The travelling is harder; there are no resorts, scarce travelling companions, and only a few items of conventional interest. Yet for many the **basin of the Euphrates and Tigris rivers**, a broad, fan-shaped floodplain ringed on three sides by the mountains containing their headwaters, is the most exotic part of Turkey, offering a handful of compelling ancient sites and some fascinating, isolated towns.

Historically this has always been a **border zone** where opposing empires and civilizations have met and often clashed. Settlements here formed an eastern outpost of the Roman Empire against the Parthians, and subsequently Byzantine local authority began to crumble during the seventh and eighth centuries under pressure from the Arabs to the south. Thereafter, almost everybody of any import in Middle Eastern affairs seems to have passed through at one time or another: Arabs, Crusaders, Selçuks, Mongols and finally the French, who invaded southeastern Turkey as part of a wider attempt by the victorious World War I Allies to break up the defeated Ottoman Empire.

Today a frontier atmosphere persists, and you'll notice that in many places ethnic Turks are in the minority. Close to the Syrian border **Arab influence** is strong, but moving further east or north, particularly into the remoter valleys of the Tigris and its tributaries, an ever-increasing proportion of the population is made up of **Kurds**. This sometimes volatile racial mix can be exacerbated by the fundamentalist or separatist sympathies of some of the population, not to mention the occasionally heavy-handed tactics of the Turkish authorities – all directly related to the chronic backwardness of the basin. Traditionally smallholding farmers and herdsmen have just barely scratched a living from the rocky and unrewarding land, although the government and locals

---

ACCOMMODATION PRICE CODES

In this guide, motels and nearly all hotels and *pansiyon*s have been categorized according to the price codes outlined below, which are based on US$ because of the high domestic Turkish inflation rate. These categories represent the minimum you can expect to pay for a **double room in high season**. Rates for hostels and for the most basic hotels and *pansiyon*s, where guests are charged **per person**, are given in US$, instead of being indicated by price code. For further information, including a rough outline of what you might expect in each category, see p.37.

① under $12	② $12–17	③ $18–25
④ $26–35	⑤ $36–45	⑥ $46–55
⑦ $56–75	⑧ over $75	

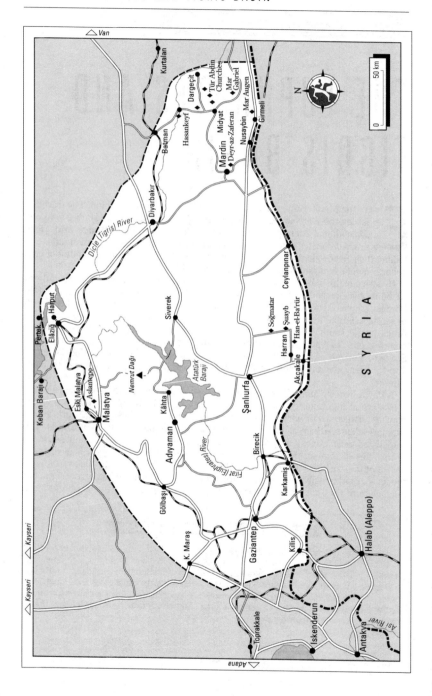

alike are optimistic that the recent completion of the massive Atatürk Dam project on the Euphrates, part of the Southeastern Anatolian Project (GAP), will raise the economy above subsistence levels and lessen discontent.

Travelling around is no problem in the western part of the region, with good bus links between all the major towns; but roads deteriorate dramatically east of Gaziantep province, and hotel facilities become correspondingly primitive. In summer the harsh terrain bakes in intense heat that will have you regretting your boldness in showing up; to enjoy the region at its best, visit during spring or autumn, when temperatures cool to more bearable levels. The main jumping-off point for **crossing to Syria** is not, in fact, in this region, but Antakya in the Hatay; for advice on this and other, less likely access points, see p.487.

Coming from the west on stretches of recently completed expressway, most visitors pass first through **Gaziantep**, an industrial centre and last outpost of Europeanized Turkey that has little to recommend it. From Gaziantep a much narrower road leads across the Euphrates to **Şanlıurfa**, an ancient city mentioned in the Bible as the birthplace of Abraham, and all told the region's most rewarding destination. Şanlıurfa also makes an ideal base for an excursion to **Harran** with its mud-brick beehive houses, and a convenient staging post for Nemrut-bound travellers.

In the mountains to the north of Gaziantep, the spectacular temple and tomb of **Nemrut Dağı** fully justifies a pilgrimage. The towns that surround the site, on the other hand, have little to offer: interesting only as possible bases for exploring Nemrut, **Adıyaman** and **Kâhta** are ugly modern developments, as is **Malatya** to the north, though the latter is more appealing and also offers the nearby attractions of **Eski Malatya** and **Aslantepe**.

From either Şanlıurfa or Malatya, it's a journey of half a day or less to **Diyarbakır**, a teeming, troubled city built on the banks of the River Tigris. South of Diyarbakır, the other major destination for travellers in the Tigris region is **Mardin**, with its atmospheric collection of beautiful vernacular houses set on a crag that overlooks the Syrian plain. To the east of Mardin, the isolated **Tür Abdin** plateau is home to most of the remaining Syrian Orthodox Christian population of Turkey and to a scattering of monasteries and churches. At its heart lies **Midyat**, a town of elegant mansions, once the equal of those in Mardin but now crumbling in seemingly irredeemable abandonment. Finally, taking a different route back to Diyarbakır, **Hasankeyf** is a good example of the numerous archeological sites scheduled to disappear under the GAP reservoirs.

THE EUPHRATES BASIN

As you approach from Adana, the **floodplain of the Euphrates** opens out to the east and northeast, reaching the southern fringes of the Anatolian plateau, from which the Euphrates river itself (*Fırat* in Turkish) winds its turbid way into Syria. The broad alluvial plain has been inhabited for several millennia and was once a lush, fertile region; indeed, remains of some of the world's oldest known human settlements have been discovered here. Unfortunately, centuries of continuous warfare, in particular the thirteenth-century Mongol destruction of the intricate irrigation canals which had existed since ancient times, aggravated by the depredations of nomadic herdsmen, have reduced much of the area to dusty steppeland.

Approaching from the west, the first major centre is **Gaziantep**, which, predominantly modern and industrial in character, has more in common with Mediterranean cities like Adana and Mersin than with the more traditional towns east of the Euphrates.

East of Gaziantep, the road shoots across the plain of the Euphrates, crossing the river at unremarkable Birecik before cutting through rocky uplands to the venerable town of **Şanlıurfa** (known locally as "Urfa"), worth a couple of days' sightseeing on its

THE SOUTHEASTERN ANATOLIAN PROJECT

The **GAP** or *Güneydoğu Anadolu Projesi* (Southeastern Anatolian Project) was begun in 1974 with the construction of the Keban Dam across the upper Euphrates near Elâzığ, and upon completion (originally scheduled for 1997, but unlikely to happen until well into next century) will total no less than 22 dams in the ring of foothills around the joint Euphrates–Tigris basin. A series of large-bore tunnels leading to spots as far-flung as Harran and Ceylanpınar near the Syrian border will irrigate 1.6 million hectares of what was previously wasteland. Moreover, seventeen of the dams will generate electric power, for a total hourly capacity of 26 billion kilowatts – a third of this from the massive Atatürk Dam, fourth largest in the world and weighing in at 80m high and 800m broad at the base, tapering gradually to 20m at the top. As evident from the mind-boggling numbers, it's an undertaking of pharaonic confidence and ambition, intended to be a panacea for most of the southeast's economic and social ills. GAP has even become something of a domestic tourist attraction: tours are advertised in the west of the country for Turks to go and see the gigantic (in many cases half-finished) engineering works.

Hydro-electrification is supposed to spur rapid **industrialization** of the basin, in conjunction with tax incentives offered by the government to companies who move some or all of their operations here. Proprietors of textile mills in western Turkey have even gone so far as to dismantle loss-making plants and machinery and ship them for re-assembly in the GAP area, where the cheap power and huge pool of inexpensive labour will allow them to run at a profit. However, in the wake of the increasing Kurdish troubles, such transfers and investment have nosedived. No matter, say the boosters – any excess power will be sent to western Turkey or even sold to Syria and Iraq.

At the moment, Turkey's two southern neighbours would far rather have water than power, and complain bitterly that their share of water from the Euphrates and Tigris has been halved since the completion of the Atatürk Dam. Diplomatic relations between Syria and Turkey have lately focused almost entirely on negotiations to raise the flow of water across the border towards the previous figure of 1000 cubic metres per second in return for an end to covert Syrian backing for insurgent Turkish Kurds.

During the late 1980s the late Turkish president Özal proposed two so-called **"Peace Pipelines"** to deliver surplus water to the thirsty Arab world: one through Syria and Jordan to the Saudi Arabian coast of the Red Sea, the other through Iraq to the Gulf Emirates. Both remain highly unlikely as the countries concerned are reluctant to make themselves even more dependent on the good will of Turkey.

As regards local benefits, only the **large landlords** will be able to qualify for credits for the fertilizer and machinery necessary to engage in the kind of large-scale agribusiness already typical of the irrigated areas around Adana. Many of the smaller farmers will be forced off the land, migrating to the cities to seek work in factories which will presumably have set up shop, contributing to the already serious **rural depopulation** in the area, as well as the creation of a permanent urban underclass of unskilled or semi-skilled labourers.

own; it also makes a good base for exploring local attractions like **Harran**, a village continuously inhabited for over 6000 years, and recommended despite swarming tour groups and suffocating summer heat.

But for many visitors the main attraction of the region is the Commagene mountain-top temple of **Nemrut Dağı**. Such is the appeal of the site that even highly unattractive nearby towns like **Adıyaman** and **Kâhta** have been able to cash in on the tourist boom, though in recent years visitor levels have dropped considerably in response to a perceived (rather than real) PKK threat, with many of the local hustlers packing up their bags and heading west. Many travellers are now approaching Nemrut Dağı from the north via **Malatya**, a blandly unobjectionable town in the middle of a bleak and empty territory dividing *İç* (Inner) from *Doğu Anadolu* (Eastern Anatolia). From Malatya it's also a fairly easy matter to make your way to **Elâzığ**, an ugly modern place interesting only for its archeological museum and the presence of the ruined city of **Harput** just outside town. North, and especially east, of Elâzığ you are heading into dangerous territory with the mountainous Kurdish centres around Tunceli and Bingöl and the heavily militarized road to Van.

Gaziantep

Approaching the Euphrates from the west, the main road passes through **GAZİANTEP**, a modern city with a population of well over half a million, the largest in the region but crowded, chaotic and busy with little of interest to offer. There is some fine Arab-style domestic architecture, but this is more easily seen in Şanlıurfa, Mardin or Midyat. Gaziantep can be used as a staging post on a journey to more compelling destinations to the north or further east, and rates an overnight stop at most, with perhaps a morning to shop for some of its crafts specialities.

The city is known to the locals and, more importantly for the traveller, to most bus companies as "Antep" (a corruption of the Arab *ayn teb* meaning "good spring"); indeed the "Gazi" prefix – meaning "warrior for Islam" – was only added in 1920, after Nationalist forces defending the city withstood a ten-month siege by the French, who had advanced up from their Syrian protectorate in an attempt to seize a portion of defeated Turkey. These days Gaziantep is probably best known for its incredible pistachio nuts – *şam fıstığı* – some of the best you'll taste anywhere in Turkey, though its booming growth as one of the main beneficiaries of GAP and of Turkish–Syrian trade will soon start to give the city a higher national profile.

The City

Gaziantep was first occupied during Hittite times and has since experienced the familiar round of occupations – Assyrian, Persian, Alexandrine, Roman, Selçuk, Crusader, Byzantine, Arab – shared by so many places in this part of Turkey. Industrialization based on textile mills has brought a degree of prosperity to the city, along with an influx of country people looking for a better standard of living. They tenant the vast *gecekondu* shanty towns, similar to those found in Ankara and İzmir, which spread up the surrounding hills.

The only interesting survivor from Gaziantep's past is the **kale** (castle), which dominates the town from the northeastern pair of hills – an artificial mound formed by layers of accumulated debris from thousands of years of human occupation. The castle dates back to late Roman times, but the present structure, with its 36 towers, owes more to the Selçuks. To reach it, take the road running up from İstasyon Caddesi, opposite the museum. If you bear right at the top you'll eventually come to a small mosque, opposite which a ramp leads up to the main doors. The surrounding **bazaar** quarter is of passing interest, and in some workshops you might find craftsmen manufacturing the local speciality: furniture inlaid with *sedef* (mother-of-pearl), although lately it's just as likely to be plastic. Other local souvenirs include copperware (samovars, *mangal*s or braziers, and *ibrik*s or ewers), *yemeni* (all-leather slippers) and *aba* – embroidered vests, usually adulterated these days with synthetic fibres. If you are serious about shopping, the tourist office (see below) keeps current lists of craftsmen and retail outlets.

Another worthwhile attraction just west of the castle hillock is the **Archeological Museum** on İstasyon Caddesi (Tues–Sun 8.30am–noon & 1–5pm; $1). This contains archeological and ethnological mementoes from Hittite through to late Ottoman times, including a number of draft Hittite reliefs from Yesenek, 100km west of Gaziantep, once one of the main open-air stone-carving centres of the entire Hittite empire.

By contrast the much-promoted **Hasan Süzer Ethnography Museum**, an old house in the town centre (daily 8am–noon and 1.30–5.30pm; $0.50), is missable if you've seen others in Turkey, owing to too many unlabelled dioramas with mannequins, though a small English brochure helps interpretation. Only the house itself is compelling, with its crypt-like basement, used for food stores and thirty degrees cooler than the surroundings. Finally, numerous candy-striped mosques such as the Alaybey and Eyüboğlu lend some atmosphere to the streets nearby, but none demands special attention.

Practicalities

Gaziantep's **otogar** lies almost 2km northwest of the centre, so you'll need to take a dolmuş or municipal bus from here into town. Get off near the junction of Suburcu and Hürriyet *caddesi*s, where you'll find most of the city's hotels and restaurants. The **train station**, logically enough, stands out at the north end of İstasyon Caddesi, a similar distance from downtown. *Havaş* buses ($1.50) will shuttle you in from Sazgın **airport** to the **THY terminal** at Atatürk Bul 30/B (☎0342/230 1565).

Gaziantep's **tourist information office**, 100 Yil Atatürk Kültür Park (☎0342/230 5969), lies hiding in waste ground 500m north and then west from the junction of Suburcu and Hürriyet *caddesi*s. They can provide basic sketch maps of the town and lists of accommodation but speak only basic English.

If you decide to stay, there are a score of **hotels**, with many top-of-the-range outfits, intended for the wealthier businessmen whom the GAP project hopes to attract, recently opened or under construction, but few good-value mid-range or budget options.

If you have well over $100 to blow, then try the remarkably luxurious *Hotel Tuğcan* at Atatürk Bul 34 (☎0342/220 4323; ⑨); a more sober-minded luxury choice would be the plush *Hotel Tilmen*, on the corner of İnönü and Hürriyet *caddesi*s (☎0342/220 2081, fax 220 2091; ⑥). The town's former top-end hotels have now slipped into the middle of the range; the *Hotel Kaleli* on Hürriyet Cad (☎0342/230 2655, fax 230 1597; ③) is reasonable enough, but a better choice for both rooms and location is the comfortable and quiet *Katan*, 100m from the archeological museum at İstasiyon Cad 58 (☎0342/230 6969, fax 220 8454; ④). It's a bit of a jump down in quality to the old-fashioned *Büyük Murat*, Suburcu Cad 16 (☎0342/231 8449, fax 342/231 1658; ②), the small but passable rooms of the next-door *Hotel Güllüoğlu*, Suburcu Cad 1/B (☎0342/232 4363, fax 220 8689; ②), or the bright, simple rooms of the *Hotel Velic*, Atatürk Bul 23 (☎0342/232 2341; ②). The rock-bottom options are a sorry bunch: choose from the basic *Seç*, Atatürk Bul (☎0342/231 5272; ①); the noisy and plain *Evin*, Kayacık Cad 11 (☎0342/231 3492; ①); or, cheaper still, the quiet and simple *Bulvar Palas*, İstasyon Cad 11 (☎0342/231 3238; ①), though at least the latter has some earthy character to commend it.

As with accommodation, so with **restaurants**: usually poor value, and located within sight of the Atatürk Bulvarı/Hürriyet Caddesi junction. The humble *Lezzet Lokantası*, just off Suburcu Caddesi near the *Büyük Murat Oteli*, is certainly preferable to the highly visible tourist trap *Keyvan Bey Restaurant*, whose only virtue seems to be provision of alcohol. Worth considering is the rooftop restaurant at the *Hotel Kaleli* which is not as expensive as you might imagine – you should be able to eat a two-course meal with a beer for about $7. Little else seems worth singling out in the centre, though you can have wonderful *dondurma* in premises directly opposite the State Hospital gate at the south end of Hürriyet Caddesi (it's the place that serves scoops in a bowl, and no *baklava*).

Finally, there are a number of **car rental** outfits in town – with either *Met-Kar*, Atatürk Bul 90/A (☎0342/232 0021), or *Al-Ser*, Gaşi Muhtar Paza Bul 19/B (☎0342/234 3084), likely to be cheaper than *Avis* at Ordu Cad 15/A (☎0342/336 1194) or *Hertz* at Ordu Cad 92/C (☎0342/336 7718).

East of Gaziantep: towards Şanlıurfa

East of Gaziantep most of the traffic seems to be oil tankers travelling nose to tail, to and from the oilfields around Batman and Siirt. If you're driving your own car, it's worth remembering that the drivers of these vehicles don't believe in switching their headlamps on until it gets *really* dark. To add to the excitement, road conditions deteriorate steadily the further east you go, and you'll notice a disturbing number of horrifically mangled vehicles in the fields by the roadside, contributing greatly to Turkey's rank as second-highest wreck-prone country worldwide. In summer, with temperatures edging into the mid-forties Centigrade, this route can be hellishly uncomfortable too; if you're travelling by bus, try and make sure you get a seat in the shade when buying your ticket.

About 50km from Gaziantep, amid a landscape of pistachio and olive groves stippled with hilltop villages, there's a turning south for **KARKAMIŞ**, the ancient Hittite city of Carchemish. A number of important reliefs were unearthed here by British archeologists (including T.E. Lawrence) during excavations financed by the British Museum between 1910 and 1915 and again in 1920, including scenes from the Assyrian epic of Gilgamesh.

These days, however, the site, which is just a few kilometres north of the border with Syria, is difficult to reach except on the one daily train from Gaziantep (leaves 7am, returns 2pm). You'll need authorization from the military authorities in Gaziantep if you want to visit – as the official tourist guide so shrewdly states "sweeping all the mines from this ancient city will make a big contribution to the tourism development . . . of the area". There's little to see anyway since reliefs were removed to the Museum of Anatolian Civilizations in Ankara. For more details enquire at the tourist office in Gaziantep.

The main road crosses the **Euphrates River** and the provincial border, deteriorating promptly at the shabby town of **BİRECİK** – of interest mainly to ornithologists as one of the few places in the world where you're likely to see a bald ibis (an ugly relative of the stork) nesting in the wild during the spring. Birecik's ruined **castle** was founded during the eleventh century as a frontier outpost for the Crusader-state of Edessa (see p.707), but isn't really worth going out of your way to inspect closely, though its entourage of old houses backed into the cliff face are appealing from a distance. Beyond Birecik, the orchards and villages which previously softened the landscape disappear completely, leaving a grim, featureless approach to Şanlıurfa.

Şanlıurfa

The name of **ŞANLIURFA** or "Glorious Urfa" (most of the locals just say Urfa) commemorates resistance to the French invasion and occupation of 1918–20. It's a place where you could easily spend a day or so taking in the local monuments, which include the reputed birthplace of the prophet Abraham and a poolside mosque complex of some beauty.

Just as compelling is Urfa's **Middle Eastern atmosphere**. For visitors coming from western Turkey, it's here that "the Orient" really seems to begin; at least half the town consists of *gecekondu* shanties, swathed in a pall of relentless dust which settles as mud during winter. A significant proportion of the population is Kurdish, and the few women on the streets are veiled and often tattooed with henna, while the men wear baggy trousers and Kurdish headdresses.

In Turkey this so-called "city of the prophets" has gained notoriety as a focus for Islamic fundamentalism – augmented during the late 1980s, when a mayor of Urfa was put on trial for allegedly undermining the secular nature of the Turkish state. Urfa is also notorious for the high incidence of gastric complaints among visitors during summer, when the intense heat turns every plate of food into a nursery for bacteria.

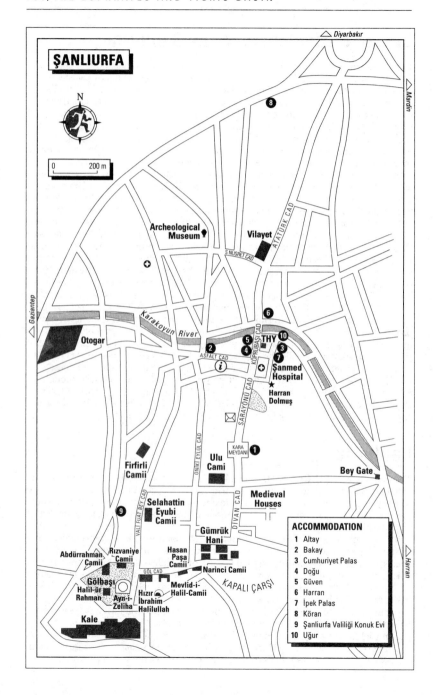

ŞANLIURFA

N

0   200 m

Diyarbakır

Mardin

Gaziantep

Archeological Museum

Vilayet

S NUSRET CAD

ATATÜRK CAD

Karakoyun River

Otogar

ASFALT CAD

KÖPRÜBAŞI CAD

THY

Şanmed Hospital

Harran Dolmuş

SARAYÖNÜ CAD

ONIKI EYLÜL CAD

KARA MEYDANI

Ulu Cami

Bey Gate

Fırfırlı Camii

Selahattin Eyubi Camii

Medieval Houses

DIVAN CAD

VALI FUAT BEY CAD

Gümrük Hani

Abdürrahman Camii

Rızvaniye Camii

Hasan Paşa Camii

GÖL CAD

Narinci Camii

KAPALI ÇARŞI

Gölbaşı

Halil-ür Rahman

Ayn-i-Zeliha

Hızır İbrahim Halilullah

Mevlid-i-Halil-Camii

Kale

Harran

ACCOMMODATION

1 Altay
2 Bakay
3 Cumhuriyet Palas
4 Doğu
5 Güven
6 Harran
7 İpek Palas
8 Köran
9 Şanliurfa Valiliği Konuk Evi
10 Uğur

Some history

Even by Turkish standards, Urfa is an old city. According to both Jewish and Muslim sources, Abraham received his summons from God to take himself and his family to Canaan while living in Urfa. Other stories record that the prophet Job was a resident for a while, though claims that the Garden of Eden was somewhere around here are probably based more on wishful thinking.

Whatever the factual basis of these legends, it's certain that people have been living on the site for thousands of years. The first settlers were the Hurri, members of one of Anatolia's earliest civilizations, who built a fortress on the site of the present citadel around 3500 BC and controlled much of the surrounding area. The Hurri, who probably named the place Orhoi – corrupted in modern times to Urfa – were followed by the Hittites and Assyrians, the latter remaining in control until Alexander the Great swept through after his victory at Issus; renamed Edessa after the Macedonian capital, the town was an important eastern outpost for the Romans against the Persians.

From the second century AD, Edessa was a thriving centre of Christianity, the Nestorian variant of it particularly taking root. Following the local collapse of Byzantine power the Arabs moved in, staying until the eleventh century, when, during the First Crusade, a French count, Baldwin of Boulogne, stopped off en route to Tripoli and the Holy Land to establish the county of Edessa, a short-lived Christian state. In 1144 the Arabs recaptured Edessa, giving the rulers of Europe a pretext to launch the Second Crusade, although the city was soon forgotten and never wrested back from the Arabs. In 1260 it was put to the sword by the Mongols and never really recovered, declining into obscurity before being absorbed (as Urfa) into the Ottoman Empire in 1637.

NESTORIAN CHRISTIANS

The history of the **Nestorian Church** parallels that of the Syrian Orthodox Church in many ways, although their respective theological positions are completely opposite. **Nestorius**, bishop of Constantinople from 428 to 431, formulated a doctrine which held Christ to be predominantly human in nature, and refused to recognize the divinity of the Virgin Mary. In 431, however, the Council of Ephesus declared his positions to be heretical. The works of Nestorius were burnt and he was deported to the Egyptian desert after suffering hideous tortures.

Despite his fate, Edessa (Şanlıurfa), Antioch (Antakya) and Nusaybin near Mardin became important Nestorian centres, though later the focus of the faith moved to Persia, where the Sassanid emperors officially encouraged it along with Zoroastrianism. After the Mongol attacks the Nestorians relocated again to the inaccessible Zagros mountains of western Iran, and the equally remote area around present-day Hakkâri in southeast Turkey.

During the latter half of the nineteenth century, however, the Kurds began to **massacre** the Nestorian men around Hakkâri and sell the women and children into slavery. Their fate was sealed in 1915 when the Nestorian patriarch came out in support of the World War I Allies. When the Russians withdrew from the region in 1918, the Nestorians deemed it wise not to linger as targets of reprisal, but more than half their number perished anyway in the attempted **flight** to Iran and Iraq. Today just a few tens of thousands survive in Iraq, Iran and Syria, with the patriarchate now in Chicago; in modern times adherents of this sect are confusingly referred to as Assyrians, because – like the Syrian Orthodox – most surviving believers speak Syriac.

Arrival and information

Şanlıurfa **otogar** is more than a kilometre west of the centre, so you should take a dolmuş into town (or a taxi if arriving late at night). Head for the *Hotel Harran* on Köprübaşı Caddesi, which makes a good orientation point as most of the hotels and other tourist facilities can found around here. The **airport** is about 6km south of town, on the road to Harran, with a *THY* bus to take you into the centre; the **THY office** is at Sarayönü Cad 74/A (☎0414/215 3344).

The **tourist information office** at Asfalt Cad 3/B (summer Mon–Fri 8am–noon & 1.30–5.30pm; winter Mon–Fri 8.30am–noon & 1–5pm; ☎0414/215 2467) has just one fluent English-speaking staff member; they hand out simple but adequate provincial and city maps, and may be able to help arrange group trips to Harran, Soğmatar (Sumatar) and Şuayb. There are a couple of convenient **dövüz** offices 100m south of the tourist office on Sarayönü Caddesi.

Accommodation

Many of Şanliurfa's older **hotels** have folded in the wake of plummeting tourist figures but there is still a decent choice in every price category. There are three **budget** hotels (all without private bathrooms) conveniently located behind the Şanmed Hospital (former Turban Urfa Hotel), on a street running parallel to Köprübaşı Caddesi. Best of the three is the friendly, clean and quiet *Otel Uğur*, Köprübaşı Cad 3 (☎0414/313 1340; ①), though the *Cumhuriyet Palas Oteli*, Köprübaşı Civarı 6 (☎0414/313 9797; ①), and the nearby and slightly more expensive *Hotel İpek Palas* (☎0414/215 1546; ①) are both satisfactory fallbacks. Worth the extra expense is the *Hotel Güven* on Köprübaşı Caddesi (☎0414/215 1700; ②), though you'll have to endure the alternately offhand and belligerent management to enjoy the power shower, fluffy towels and air conditioning of the obsessively clean rooms; ask to see a spread of rooms and don't be surprised if prices rise in the near future. The labyrinthine *Otel Doğu* next door is another budget option (①), as is the dingy *Hotel Altay* on Kara Meydanı (☎0414/215 1917; ①). The new *Bakay Hotel*, Asfalt Cad 24 (☎0414/15 2689; ③), due for opening at the time of writing, promises clean, modern rooms with bath.

Best of the **upper-range** hotels must be the *Şanliurfa Valiliği Konuk Evi* (☎0414/215 4678, fax 312 3368; ③), with just six traditional but comfortable rooms arranged around the *selâmlık* section of a restored nineteenth-century mansion; reservations are recommended. To find it follow the alley that leads off Vali Fuat Bey Caddesi just opposite the Selahattin Eyubi Camii. The traditional tour group hotel is the *Harran* on Atatürk Caddesi (☎0414/313 2860, fax 313 4918; ⑤), equipped with its own hamam and top-floor bar, and about to embark on renovation supposedly to upgrade it to five stars. If you have your own transport you may also want to consider the *Köran Hotel* (☎0414/313 1809, fax 312 1737; ④), on the main northern highway, for pleasant air-conditioned rooms with television and refrigerator.

Old Urfa

The extreme south end of Sarayönü Caddesi opens onto **Kara Meydan**, at the centre of which stands a venerable-looking nineteenth-century mosque. Beyond Kara Meydan, Sarayönü Caddesi turns into Divan Caddesi, to the southwest of which you'll notice the twelfth-century **Ulu Cami**, with a design based on that of the Grand Mosque in Halab (Halep, Aleppo) in Syria. You can take a look around the courtyard with its graves and octagonal minaret, originally the belfry of an earlier Byzantine church; inside the mosque is unexceptional.

East of Divan Caddesi lies an extensive warren of narrow streets lined with the best examples of Urfa's wonderful, stone-built **medieval houses**, whose distinctive features include lattice-windowed overhangs supported on ornate corbels. At the end of Divan Caddesi sprawls the **Gümrük Hanı**, a late sixteenth-century *kervansaray*, whose shady courtyard is taken up by the tables of tea houses and watch repairers. This is surrounded by the **Kapalı Çarşı** or covered bazaar, a maze-like commercial area spilling out into the narrow streets nearby. There are stalls and hole-in-the-wall shops selling everything imaginable, from spices to guns. Traders sell green Diyarbakır tobacco by the kilo out of plastic sacks, and domestic appliances are occasionally auctioned off the back of horse-drawn carts. The pungent stink of skins from freshly slaughtered sheep vies with the more pleasant odour of various powdered herbs. Turning right out of the Gümrük Hanı brings you to the *bedesten* next door, beyond which lies the Haci Kâmil Hanı and the coppersmith's bazaar. Further west lie the Sipahi and Hüseyniye bazaars, both left over from the time when camel caravans moved regularly between Urfa and Aleppo, Palmyra, Mari and Baghdad.

The Cave of Abraham

From the bazaar, make your way along Göl Caddesi, past the Narinci Camii and the Ottoman Hasan Paşa Camii, to the Mevlid-i Halil Camii, behind which is the entrance to **İbrahim Halilullah Dergâhı**, the Cave of Abraham (daily 8am–5.30pm; $0.50). According to local legend the prophet Abraham was born here, spending the first ten years of his life in hiding because a local Assyrian tyrant, Nemrut (Nimrod), had decreed that all new-born children be killed.

As Abraham is recognized as a prophet by Muslims, his birth-cave remains a place of worship, the majority of visitors being Muslim pilgrims from all over Turkey rather than tourists. Although there isn't actually much to see inside, the atmosphere is very reverential, with much praying in evidence; there are separate entrances for men and women, dress must be respectful and shoes removed. There are two other holy caves, one reputed to hold a hair plucked from Mohammed's head.

Northwest of the cave stands the **Hızır İbrahim Halilullah**, a colonnaded mosque and *medrese* complex named after the "Prophet Abraham and Friend of God", which has grown up to serve the large numbers of pilgrims – as have tables selling religious tracts. A huge new mosque is being constructed next door.

Gölbaşı and the Kale

It's a short walk from here to **Gölbaşı** – literally "at the lakeside" – where you'll find a shady park, a pair of mosques, and three pools filled with fat carp. According to a continuation of the local legend, Abraham, after he emerged from his cave, became an implacable opponent of King Nemrut and tried to smash the idols in the local temple. The tyrant was displeased, and had Abraham hurled from the citadel battlements into a fire below. Abraham was saved when, on a command from God, the flames turned into water and the firewood into carp. The smaller of the two pools at the foot of the citadel, the **Halil-ür Rahman**, adjacent to the larger **Ayn-i-Zeliha** pool (named after the daughter of Nimrod), is the one which saved Abraham from a fiery end.

There is a teahouse and restaurant (one of several in the area) beside the Ayn-i-Zeliha, where visitors like to sit in the shade after feeding the carp with special bait bought from poolside vendors. The carp have long been considered sacred, and it's said that anyone who eats them will go blind, a fate which supposedly befell a couple of soldiers in 1989 – according to another story the soldiers didn't lose their sight but were imprisoned. Another pool, the **Balıklı Göl**, just to the north, is the largest, most obvious and most popular carp pool, its banks swarming with bootblacks, bait-sellers and beggars. By a *şeyh*'s tomb on the south quay, there's even a stall selling Islamic reading matter.

The far western end of the Balıklı Göl is closed off by the seventeenth-century **Abdürrahman Camii**, which you are free to look around. The present mosque replaced an older twelfth-century building whose distinctive square minaret has survived. The entire north side of the pool is flanked by the **Rizvaniye Camii**, built by an Ottoman governor in 1716, with some intricately carved wooden doors giving onto its peaceful courtyard.

Above Gölbaşı is Urfa's **Kale** (unenclosed but $0.50 admission if guard present), a massive citadel whose construction is claimed by everybody who ever occupied the city. Much of what has survived probably dates from the time of the twelfth-century Frankish Crusader state. The fortifications are completely ruined now but it's worth climbing up there for the view of the mosques and pools down below. At the top are a couple of lone Corinthian columns, thought to be the remains of an early Christian chapel. They are referred to as the **Throne of Nemrut**, and local people will tell you that this is the spot from which Nemrut cast Abraham down into the flames.

North to the Archeological Museum

If you head north from Gölbaşı up Vali Fuat Bey Caddesi you'll come to the **Selahattin Eyubi Camii**, whose interior layout remains essentially unchanged from its previous incarnation as the Christian Church of St John. From here head north again for a glimpse of the former Armenian Church of the Twelve Apostles, now the neighbourhood **Firfirli Camii**. Echoes of former worship can be seen in the star and moon carvings on the old clocktower, which now serves as the mosque's minaret. Continue north to the Karakoyun River, the traditional northern boundary of the old town, and if you have time, check out the Byzantine aqueduct, built in 525 and now squeezed between two Ottoman bridges.

The city's excellent **Archeological Museum** (Tues–Sun 8.30am–noon & 1.30–5pm; $0.50) is just north of the town centre. To reach it follow Atatürk Caddesi as far as the *Vilayet* building and take a left turn onto S. Nusret Caddesi. You'll pass an ancient *kervansaray* on the right, still very much in use, and an old church to the left before reaching the museum garden, full of stone carvings and sarcophagi.

Inside, the various exhibits range from gold work to jewellery, mostly from funerary tumuli on the Euphrates floodplain, as well as from the sites of ancient Harran and Lidar. An ethnographic section devoted to more recent local lifestyles includes statuary from the province's vanished Christian communities, plus magnificent carved doors from demolished mansions. The outdoor collection of reliefs, with inscriptions ranging from Hittite to Armenian, is particularly fascinating, thanks to the sharpness and clarity of the carvings; look out also for numerous carved angels retrieved from caves all around Urfa.

Eating and drinking

Besides the *Harran* hotel, diners tend to eat at the *Sümer Lokantası*, on Köprübaşı Caddesi, or the *Kızılay Aile Lokantası*, in its own pleasant garden off the north end of Sarayönü Caddesi. The *Şanlıurfa Valiliği Konuk Evi* offers stylish romantic dinners (phone ahead to book) as well as afternoon coffee. There are numerous rather simpler eateries whose quality is pretty much the same, sometimes offering local specialities based on *bulgur* (cracked wheat), notably *çiğ köfte* or raw meatballs – eat at your own risk – and *dolmalı köfte* or stuffed meatballs, as well as *Urfa kebap* with skewered aubergine. The *Gulizar Doner Salonu* opposite the *Hotel Güven* is as good as any and has fine *iskender kebap*. Desserts such as *dondurma*, puddings and *baklava* can best be sampled in the congenial surroundings of *Bırlık Baklavarı*, in the Köprübaşı Çarşısı. Grab breakfast at the *Zahter Kahvaltı Salonu* near the *Hotel İpek Palas*.

Trips to Nemrut Dağı

A company called *Harran Dolmuş* (☎0414/215 1575), operating out of a small storefront near the *İpek Palas*, is currently the sole **tour operator** from Urfa to Nemrut Dağı. The chartered minibus goes for a flat rate of about $100, but the owner Özcan Aslan will run the tour for a minimum of three people at $20 each (including lunch and entrance fees) if you're prepared to pick up paying passengers en route. He will even stop for a look at the Atatürk Dam if you show willing. Tours usually depart in the morning and return at midnight; if you stay overnight on the mountain you'll have to figure in an extra sum for a motel or *pansiyon*.

Harran

Some 45km southeast of Urfa, the beehive-style houses in the village of **HARRAN** (also known as Altınbaşak) have become a major tourist attraction in recent years. It's the last surviving such community, the bleak plain around being dotted with the ruins of other mud-built villages in this Syrian-influenced style.

Harran has strong biblical links: in Genesis 11:31 and 12:4, the patriarch Abraham is described as having dwelt here for a while on his way from Ur to Canaan, and it's tempting to imagine the place hasn't changed much since – although visitors have in fact made big inroads over the last decade or so.

Harran is thought to have been continuously inhabited for at least 6000 years, which makes it one of the oldest settlements on earth. It first came to prominence under the Assyrians, who turned it into a prosperous trading centre, as well as a centre for the worship of Sin, god of the moon; there was a large temple here, later also used by the Sabian cult (see below), on the site now occupied by the ruins of a Crusader fortress. In 53 BC the Roman general Crassus's advance east was halted here, where he was defeated, crucified and had molten gold poured into his mouth by the Parthians. Despite this, the Romans were later able to convert Harran into an important centre of learning, a role it continued to play under the Byzantines and subsequently the Arabs, who founded a university in the town. The arrival of the Mongols during the thirteenth century meant devastation however, and was the end of Harran as a centre of anything other than archeological significance.

Arrival

The *Harran Dolmuş* company in Şanlıurfa runs four-hour **excursions** to Harran, departing late in the afternoon during summer to avoid the horrific heat, for $15 per car (maximum three people). Full-day tours are also offered at about $25 per car and include stops at the Han-el-Ba'rür *kervansaray*, 23km east of Harran, and the ruins of Şuayb and Soğmatar beyond (see "Around Harran" below). Tours will drop you off at the western end of the village by the *jandarma* post and a small café, adjacent to the ruined Urfa Gate and a small ticket booth whose occupant will charge you $1.50 admission if he's around. The villagers themselves use the single **dolmuş**, which leaves Urfa at around 4pm – implying staying overnight if you ride on it.

If you have your **own transport**, take the road south from Urfa towards Akçakale – signposted only as "*Havalimanı*" (Airport) – for 35km, following irrigation canals that bring water from the Atatürk Dam, until you reach a yellow-signposted turning; Harran is about 10km east of here.

The village and site

These days semi-nomadic Arabs and a few Kurds live amid the ruins of old Harran, surviving by farming and smuggling sheep (in exchange for instant coffee, Ceylon tea and other foreign luxury goods) across the Syrian border 10km to the south. It is they who have built – and to some extent still live in – the mud-brick beehive-shaped buildings which dot the area, the distinctive shape of which is owing to the fact that no wood is used as support. However, if you're expecting a homogenous community of gumdrop houses, you'll be disappointed, as they're interspersed with conventional cottages, and increasingly used for storage or animal – not human – habitation.

Most of the people here are fairly amiable, and amused by the fascination their way of life exerts on visitors. Many are likely to want to talk and show you around. If possible try to visit out of season, when the place is less likely to be crawling with tour groups and the heat won't be quite so intense. For soft drinks there are cafés to the east and west of the main site. It's possible to **stay** the night at *Harran House* (①), a purpose-built but traditional 18-domed compound up near the Ulu Cami; the interior is extremely basic but fun for one evening, catering principally to occasional overland truck-tour groups. If you wish, the management will cook supper – over the standard cow-pat fire in this treeless region – as there's no proper restaurant in Harran. The locals themselves pass the torrid summer nights outdoors, on peculiar raised platforms.

The site

The enigmatic ruins of old Harran have a kind of tragic grandeur, dwarfing the beehive dwellings, and it's not difficult to picture the town as it must have been before the arrival of the Mongols. The usual drop-off point is near an artificial tumulus thought to mark the site of the original settlement. Just north of here stands the most impressive of the ruins, the **Ulu Cami**, with its graceful square tower, built by an Arab caliph during the eighth century, and mistaken for a cathedral belfry by T.E. Lawrence when he passed through in 1909. Scattered around are broken pillars, a central water pool with carved seats, and remnants of the Arab university, which, judging from the surviving fragments, must have been an exceptionally beautiful complex.

By now you'll have certainly been approached by the village kids who'll beg for *para* (money) and *stilo* (pens). If you take pictures of the little girls in traditional costume they'll demand presents, and throw tantrums if you don't cough up. At this point a couple of them will probably attach themselves to you, offering to be your guides. Some of the older ones are gifted linguists with good twenty-word vocabularies in English, German and French; in addition, they all speak Arabic (their first language), Turkish (learned in school) and often Kurdish.

With your new entourage, make your way to the eleventh-century **Crusader fortress**, built on the site of the ancient moon temple at the eastern end of the village. Here there are plenty of ruins to scramble around, although much of the structure looks in a dangerous state of near-collapse. Watch out for the distinctive ten-sided tower, part of the ramparts which once ringed the city, sections of which are still visible to the south. Your young guides may also offer to show you the lion relief on the **Aslan Kapısı** (Lion Gate) at the northeast edge of the ancient town.

Around Harran

Northeast of Harran are the **Tek Tek Dağı**, a range of dusty hills dotted with ruins and remains, the most accessible and interesting of which can be reached on the *Harran Dolmuş* tours – or with your own vehicle, as the roads there are passable; be warned however that the dense network of trails makes navigation frustrating.

Twenty-five kilometres east of the uninspiring twelfth-century *kervansaray* of **Han-el-Ba'rür**, itself 23km from Harran, you'll reach **Şuayb**, an ancient, partially subterranean village founded in Roman times, and fully inhabited until the Mongol raids. Many of the caves and chambers are still occupied, and various lintels and archways remain above ground.

Soğmatar

From Şuayb, continue north 17km to the site of ancient **SOĞMATAR** (Sumatar on some maps), about 65km from Harran and Urfa. Soğmatar was the main centre of the

Sabians, inheritors and elaborators of the local moon-cult at Harran, who worshipped here from early Christian times onwards. Though nominally monotheistic, referring to the deity as Marilaha, the sect in fact was steeped in ancient Chaldean astrology, revering all the planetary bodies. By most accounts they were a pretty wild bunch, engaging in lurid orgies and performing ample human sacrifice in the course of their worship of the stars and planets. Even more amazing is the fact that they managed to elude Byzantine Christian censure well into the ninth and tenth centuries, at which time the Arabs – disgusted by their rites – gave them the choice of death or conversion to Islam.

Ringing the contemporary village are seven circular hilltop ruins believed to have formed the Sabians' principal observatory and temple complex, with some ancient Syriac inscriptions on the walls. There are also carved statues and lunar insignia in a cave near the centre of the village. Local boys are happy to show strangers around and this desperately poor Arab settlement will be grateful for any deserving tip.

Adıyaman, Kâhta and Nemrut Dağı

A day's journey northeast of Gaziantep, the mountain-top sanctuary at **Nemrut Dağı** is a giant tumulus flanked by massive, shattered statues of classical gods and the local king in whose name it was erected. It's an unforgettable place, remote and grandiose, drawing countless visitors who trek up the mountainside by minibus and car. Their enthusiasm is usually rewarded, but until the recent local troubles scared away most tourists, the sheer numbers of trippers processed up to the summit by local tour operators had begun to detract from the splendour of the site.

The towns of **Adıyaman** and **Kâhta** make the most obvious bases if you're spending a couple of days exploring this area. Of the two, Kâhta is the better bet – it's served by about three daily buses direct from Gaziantep, is only 75km from the summit and has slightly more character than Adıyaman, which is nothing but a low-rise concrete sprawl. Several hotels lie higher up on the flanks of the mountain, but they don't organize excursions and are really for those with their own transport. Other possible alternatives would be to visit Nemrut Dağı from Malatya, Şanlıurfa, or even Cappadocia.

Adıyaman

If you're *not* travelling to Nemrut Dağı, **ADIYAMAN** is worth missing altogether, a one-street concrete eyesore lined with broken garage forecourts and a few desultory hotels. Most of the town's **hotels** line the main street, nominally called Atatürk Bulvarı but in reality little more than a continuation of the main highway to Kâhta. The best is the comfortable but dull *Bozdoğan Hotel* at the western end of Atatürk Bulvarı (☎0416/216 3999; ⑤). To the east past the *otogar* lies the comfortable and quiet *Motel Beyaz Seray*, Atatürk Bul 136 (☎0416/216 4907; ①), probably the best budget choice with the unexpected luxury of a garden swimming pool. A further kilometre east lies the modern three-star *Hotel Antiochos*, Atatürk Bul 141 (☎0416/216 3377; ③), again with a nice swimming pool but marred by thumping music that may keep you awake if the highway traffic doesn't. Next door is the plain and overpriced *Arsemia Turistik Tesisleri*, Atatürk Bul 148 (☎0416/213 9895; ②). Back in the centre of town are a couple of fairly uninspiring options, the *Otel Yoluç*, Harıkçı Cad 26 (☎0416/213 5226; ②) and the *Unal Turistik Tesisleri*, Harıkçı Cad 14 (☎0416/ 216 1508; ①), which, though inconvenient for onward transport, have the advantage of being close to restaurants and shops. The town has a rather sleepy **tourist information office** next to the PTT at Atatürk Bul 41 (Mon–Fri 9am–noon & 1–5pm; ☎0416/216 1008).

EXCURSIONS TO NEMRUT DAĞI

It's possible to take organized **minibus trips** to Nemrut Dağı from Adıyaman, Kâhta, Malatya, Şanlıurfa, or even Cappadocia, and, given the distances involved, these are about the only way of getting there unless you have your own transport. Making the journey from Malatya or Şanlıurfa is relatively hassle-free but takes longer and always costs more because of extra petrol and the usual necessity of an overnight stop.

From Adıyaman and Kâhta

In Adıyaman, the local tourist information office occasionally charters minibuses to Nemrut, but most buses operate out of Kâhta, where business is in the hands of the hotels who provide excursions at an extra charge to guests.

The excursions most in demand are those timed to get you to Nemrut for sunset or sunrise; sunset trips leave at 1pm and return at 9pm, those for the sunrise leave at 3am, returning at 11am. Expect to pay about $45 per minibus (seating eight) for an excursion also taking in the **subsidiary sites** of the Karakuş tumulus, Cendere bridge and the ancient Commagene capital of Arsameia. If you're not particularly bothered about catching sunset or sunrise, it's also possible to tour the site during the day. Some tours miss out the subsidiary sites – try to make sure any trip you go on *does* include them as they're worth a visit. Some places also offer an overnight tour catching both sunset and sunrise for about $55 per bus.

From Malatya

Although visiting Nemrut from Malatya is a slightly more complicated and expensive process, it does cut out having to spend time in Adıyaman or Kâhta. Full details and bookings are best made the day before at the tourist information office in the town *Vilayet*. Departures are usually at about noon, but can be as late as four hours before dark, still reaching the summit in good time for sunset. You spend the night at *Güneş Hotel* on the northern side of Nemrut, though for hardier souls there's always the cheaper option of spending the night in the site café on the other side of the summit. The return trip starts at about 7am, allowing you time to first admire the sunrise, reaching Malatya about 11am. Assuming a fifteen-person minibus chartered from the tourist office, the cost per person will be about $30 for transport, lodging and two meals, but not inclusive of lunch or entrance fees. Transport alone costs $15 per person, with a minimum group size of three.

From Şanlıurfa

Visiting Nemrut from Şanlıurfa also has the advantage of cutting out Adıyaman and Kâhta and can include a trip to see the Atatürk Dam, but the 420-kilometre round trip is time-consuming. Just one company – *Harran Dolmuş* – currently offers very gruelling day trips (depart 9am, return at midnight) for about $20 per person depending on the number of participants (for further details, see p.710).

Kâhta

From Adıyaman regular dolmuşes make the hour-long journey to **KÂHTA**, a dusty town of low houses which looks like it's just heaved itself up out of the earth. Like Adıyaman its only attraction is as a base for Nemrut Dağı, and the recent troubles have decimated local enterprise, with many operators folding. The **tourist information office** is on the main drag (☎0416/725 5007), though a more useful source of information is the town *otogar* information office.

One of the least expensive **hotels** in Kâhta is the *Mezopotamya* (☎0416/725 5112; ①) at the west edge of town, with bathrooms down the hall; they also have a decent restaurant. Similar budget establishments include the *Hotel Kommagene* (☎0416/715 1092; ③), at the junction with the road up to Nemrut, which can offer rooms with toilet only and a congenial backpackers' atmosphere; and the *Anatolia Pension* (☎0416/715 1774; ③), a basic but relaxed family-run place set in an attractive courtyard a couple of blocks east of the *otogar*. The best hotel in Kâhta is the comfortable *Nemrut Tur* (☎0416/715 1967, fax 725 6881; ⑤), with its own restaurant. The *Kommagene* has rudimentary **camping facilities**, but if you've brought a tent you're probably best off at the *Zeus Camping* across the road. All establishments arrange **minibus trips** up to Nemrut, charging about $10 for the round trip, including stops at the minor sites.

There are a few cheap and basic **restaurants** on Kâhta's broad main street; the only one worth specifically recommending, for its leafy setting, is the *Yayla Çay Bahçesi ve İzgara*, south of and well below the main boulevard. There are some nice fish restaurants overlooking the Atatürk reservoir a couple of kilometres east of town, but you really need your own transport to reach them.

Finally, if you're driving yourself, a tip on **access to Kâhta**: the road east, shown on many maps as linking up with the main Urfa–Diyarbakır road, is now submerged under the Atatürk reservoir. However a single ferry crosses the lake every hour until dusk at a point near Köklüce (follow the road east from Narince) to link up with the road to Bucak and then the main Urfa–Diyarbakır road at Siverek, saving you a long detour west back to Adıyaman. A car costs $2.50; if you're in a hurry you can requisition the entire ferry for $8. Other ferries may soon operate from Akıncılar to Çaylarbaşı; ask locally for details.

The road to Nemrut Dağı

The 75-kilometre road up the mountain is generally fairly good, mostly paved but potholed and therefore slow-going. A new road financed by the oil companies now connects Karakuş to Narince but misses out many of the interesting subsidiary sights on the way. The trip is easily done in your own transport but make sure you fill up with fuel in Kâhta; only the last few kilometres pose any danger to your car's suspension.

Karakuş tumulus and Cendere bridge

The first attraction is about 9km north of Kâhta, where a huge mound suddenly rises up by the roadside, just past a small oil-drilling field. This is the **Karakuş tumulus**, said to be the funeral mound of Antiochus's wife. It's surrounded by pillars bearing animal motifs, the best of these an intact eagle which gives the site its name "black bird". From the top you can look out across a valley recently flooded by the waters trapped behind the Atatürk Dam and catch views of Nemrut Dağı to the northeast.

Another 9km along, the **Cendere bridge** is a Roman structure built between 193 and 211 AD during the reign of Emperor Septimius Severus, and still in use. It's a graceful, single-arched, humpbacked structure with tremendous views all around – especially up the Cendere canyon adjacent. Three of the original four columns at each end are still in place. Just beyond it are a couple of cafés and souvenir stands, where your custom will be solicited assiduously.

Eski Kâhta and Arsameia

After another 6km or so you come to the turning for **ESKI KÂHTA**, a traditional village layered onto the hills behind and dominated by the Mameluke **Yeni Kale**. The castle's fine keep and watchtower are ripe for exploration and give access to several hundred steps chiselled out of the sheer rock face which once led into the thundering gorge below. Just past the Eski Kâhta turning, an alternative road goes over a Selçuk bridge, from where you can get down into the scenic river canyon below for a dip.

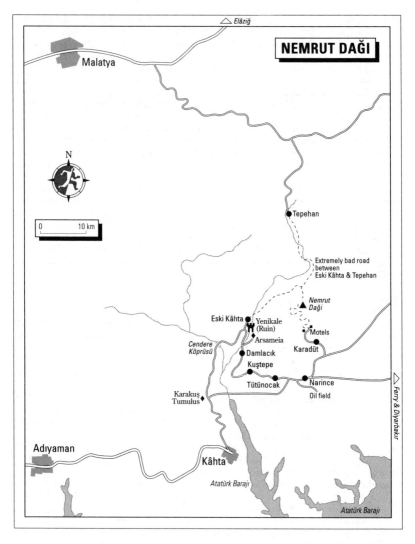

Signposts a kilometre or two beyond the bridge point the way to the ancient site of **ARSAMEIA** (unfenced; $1 when guard present), the capital of the ancient Commagene kingdom, nearly another 2km away at the end of an unsurfaced track. This was excavated by German archeologists during the 1950s, and is worth a quick detour for the chance to admire the mountainous local scenery as well as the site itself.

Members of a local family responsible for **the site** will collect admission and sell you soft drinks, postcards or souvenirs, as well as escorting you around. From a rudimentary parking space a path leads along the hillside, where steps detour to a truncated relief stele of the god Mithras, before the trail forks left past two fingers of rock (one inscribed) to a cave with a tunnel running to a cistern. Just below the cave is another damaged stele, this one showing Mithridates I Callinicus, the founder of the Commagene kingdom, and perhaps Apollo.

From here the trail proceeds up the hillside to the highlight of the site, a sizeable, perfectly preserved **relief** depicting Hercules and Callinicus shaking hands; next to it is another **tunnel** with steps leading down into the earth, emerging – according to some locals – either at the other side of the hill near the parking place, or somewhere in the valley below. In reality, as the Germans discovered after much painstaking digging, it currently terminates in a cave-in after about 150 metres. It's steep and roughly surfaced inside, and you'll need a lamp if you want to take more than a cursory look. Above the tunnel entrance a huge, 25-line inscription tells you that Mithridates I Callinicus, father of Antiochus, is buried in the vicinity, and that the site is consecrated to him.

Just above the relief depicting Hercules and Mithridates sprawls a kind of plateau with some sketchy foundations – so sketchy that it's difficult to determine what they once were. Also scattered around are bits of masonry and fragments of what must have been quite large statues – look out for a giant, sandal-clad foot hiding in the grass. The Germans uncovered a number of mosaics here, but these have all been removed to the Museum of Anatolian Civilizations in Ankara.

Damlacık, Narince and Karadüt

Beyond the Arsameia turn-off the road heads due south for such a distance that you begin to think you may have made a wrong turn. About 2km along, the village of **DAMLACIK** can offer a swimming pool and restaurant in the guise of the *Garden Camping*, but not much else.

After Damlacik the road veers east again, passing through a number of small villages (such as Kuştepe and Tütünocak) where the local kids seem to be unsure whether to wave or throw stones. The largest of these is **NARİNCE**, where if you ask directions you'll make the acquaintance of the local Kurds, many of whom profess to be loyally pro-government; if you announce your intention to travel further east into Diyarbakır and Mardin provinces, you may be discouraged from doing so and assured that "those Kurds" are *çok berbat* (really disgusting) – an aversion that probably predates the current troubles.

The settlements on Nemrut Dağı, however, are not noticeably better off than their neighbours', eking out a living from subsistence farming: tobacco and wheat on the high ground, cotton and rice in the river valleys, livestock on the hills. The Atatürk Dam has so far brought few tangible benefits to the area, and is unlikely to, given that Nemrut Dağı lies upstream, beyond the reach of irrigation schemes. The only remarkable effect has been the elimination of the most direct road link between Kâhta and Diyarbakır – a possibly deliberate ploy to make infiltration of the mountain by PKK operatives more difficult.

Nine kilometres out of Narince, just after the awful *Boğaziçi Camping ve Motel*, there's a properly signposted turning left for Nemrut Dağı. Three kilometres further on, **KARADÜT** is the last village served by local dolmuşes from Kâhta and the home of the *Karadüt Motel Pansiyon* (☎0416/737 2169; ①), the last budget accommodation before the summit and a good if spartan choice, with enjoyable walks to the nearby village to fill time before or after a summit visit.

A few kilometres further up you'll pass the *Hotel Euphrat* (☎0416/737 2175; ③), and the pleasant *Otel Kervansaray Nemrut* (☎0416/737 2190; ③), a better choice with good bathrooms and a shady pool. Further up you'll see the defunct *Zeus Motel* and a last-stop cafeteria, above which the road deteriorates noticeably, paved with basalt cobbles that guarantee a bone-shaking ride for the final 7km to the summit. Winter frosts have heaved up many of the blocks, whose sharp edges are capable of shredding a tyre, so drive with care.

Nemrut Dağı

The mighty stone heads of **Nemrut Dağı**, adorning the temple and tomb of king Antiochus, have become one of the best-known images of eastern Turkey. They are recycled endlessly on postcards and souvenirs, and if you find yourself anywhere within a couple of hundred kilometres of the place people will naturally assume that you're here to see them.

You'll be told that the best time to visit Nemrut is at dawn in order to watch the sun rise. This is debatable, and will probably involve setting out at 2am; upon arriving at the 2150-metre summit you will almost inevitably find that at least several dozen other people are there with the same idea. You might also find that it's quite cold, so come prepared; if you're visiting out of season check up on weather conditions before you leave. There's often snow on the ground from late October until May, and it's not unknown for the summit roads to be blocked even as late as April.

Some history

Nemrut Dağı is entirely the result of one man's delusions of grandeur, a great tomb and temple complex built by Antiochus I Epiphanes (64–38 BC), son of Mithridates I Callinicus, the founder of the Commagene kingdom. The Commagene dynasty was a breakaway from the Seleucid Empire, covering only a small territory from modern Adıyaman to Gaziantep, and it wouldn't rate much more than a passing mention in histories of the region were it not for the fact that Antiochus chose to build this temple as a colossal monument to himself. Despite having shown early promise as a statesman by concluding a non-aggression treaty with the Romans, Antiochus later decided he was divine in nature, or at the very least an equal of the gods, declaring: "I, the great King Antiochus have ordered the construction of these temples . . . on a foundation which will never be demolished . . . to prove my faith in the gods. At the conclusion of my life I will enter my eternal repose here, and my spirit will ascend to join that of Zeus in heaven."

Antiochus's vanity knew no bounds – he claimed descent from Darius the Great of Persia and Alexander the Great – but eventually he went too far, siding with the Parthians against Rome, and was deposed. This was effectively the end of the Commagene kingdom, which afterwards passed into Roman hands, leaving only Antiochus's massive funereal folly as a reminder of its brief existence.

Even this was forgotten by the outside world until the late nineteenth century, when Karl Puchstein, a German engineer, came across the site while making a survey in 1881. In 1883 he returned with Karl Humann (the man who removed the Pergamon altar to Berlin) to carry out a more thorough investigation, but it wasn't until 1953 that a comprehensive archeological survey of the site began, under the direction of an American team. Since then Nemrut Dağı, hitherto only reached after an arduous journey of several days, has been put back on the map.

The summit

You may well find yourself travelling the last few kilometres in a convoy of minibuses, and at first sight the summit of Nemrut Dağı seems basically a parking area full of milling crowds. Just adjacent are a small café and souvenir shop, and toilet facilities. The café provides tea, soft drinks and low-alcohol beer, and sometimes omelettes, though more often than not they only have dry biscuits, so it makes sense to bring your own food. They rent out dormitory beds here too (①), but you'd be well advised to bring your own sleeping bag.

The site

Behind the car park buildings is the entrance to the **site** ($2.50), beyond which is a fifty-metre-high tumulus of small rocks, thought to cover the tomb of Antiochus; signs tell you that it's forbidden to climb the mound. In any case you don't need to be at the very top to enjoy the awesome views for hundreds of kilometres around; Antiochus selected virtually the highest peak in his kingdom to give free rein to his megalomania.

A rocky path leads along the south side of the tumulus for ten to fifteen minutes to a terrace area, on which stands the **eastern temple** with six decapitated **seated statues**, each several metres in height. From left to right they represent: Apollo, Fortuna, Zeus, Antiochus and Hercules plus an unidentified figure. Scattered in front of these truncated figures are the much-photographed **detached heads** – just three in the case of the eastern terrace, and perhaps a little disappointing after all the hype, but remarkably intact bar the odd missing nose or two, each measuring a couple of metres in height.

They were meant to incorporate several similar deities drawn from different cultures, according to the principle of syncretism, which Alexander the Great had promoted to try and foster a sense of unity among the disparate peoples of his empire. On the date of Antiochus's birthday and the anniversary of his coronation, the Commagene people would file up to the mountain top to witness the dawn sacrifice and make offerings, carried out in strict accordance with the Greek inscriptions carved onto the back of the royal statues. The sacrificial altar still stands in front of the statues in a space now used as a helipad for VIP visitors.

The altar makes a good vantage point from which to admire the statues, and wonder at the immense effort that must have gone into the construction of this huge piece of self-aggrandizement. Scattered around about are fragments of a massive stone eagle and a lion, symbolic temple guardians that once stood like bookends at either end of the royal line-up.

A path leads around the northern base of the tumulus to the **western temple**, which has not been treated so benevolently by time. None of the statues are even partially intact, although the dispersed **heads** here are much less weathered than those on the other side of the tumulus, and there are more statues – a complete set of five, plus two eagle-heads to flank them – which argues in favour of a sunset visit. The line-up is the same, although it's harder to work out who's who. Look out for Fortuna, symbol of the Commagene kingdom, with a garland of leaves and vines in her hair, and Apollo, claimed by some to be a dead ringer for Elvis Presley.

A number of **reliefs** have, however, survived adjacent to the statuary debris – three depict Antiochus shaking hands with Apollo, Zeus and Hercules, while another shows a lion with the planets of Jupiter, Mars and Mercury and a moon representing the Commagene kingdom draped around his neck, thought to be an astrological chart possibly referring to an important date.

Malatya and around

North of Nemrut Dağı, and well served by public transport, **MALATYA** is a lively city with a surprisingly metropolitan atmosphere: smart shops lining tree-shaded boulevards, the easternmost examples of both in Turkey. There's little actually to see within the city limits, but it's a pleasant enough place for an overnight stop and makes a possible base for expeditions to Eski Malatya, Aslantepe and Nemrut Dağı.

Malatya is the centre of a fertile fruit-growing region particularly famed for apricot production, attested to by abundant supplies of dried, unpitted apricots for sale. Apart from that there's a university and a huge army base. It's a large place of nearly 300,000 people, but the centre is fairly compact, and though the **otogar** and **train station** (served by bus #11 from opposite the *Vilayet*) are 1km and 2km respectively from the centre in the west of town, most of the hotels and restaurants are within walking distance of each other.

Information and accommodation

There's a helpful **tourist information office** (Mon–Sat 8.30am–noon & 1–5pm; ☎0422/323 3025) in the *Vilayet* building behind the statue of Inönü, which exists mainly to sign you up for a trip to Nemrut Dağı (see box on p.714). Neither their hand-out sketch plan of the city, nor the street corner orientation placards, make it clear that the main boulevard is called İnönü Caddesi west of the *Vilayet* building, but Atatürk Caddesi east of it – and the whole referred to as İstasyon Caddesi by some sources.

Malatya's **hotels** tend either to be noisy, or unsavoury, or both – with a few exceptions. Most options are on the town's double-named main drag within 200m of the central square, with a grouping of budget hotels on or near PTT Caddesi, which branches diagonally off the high street between the *Yapı Kredi* and *İş* banks. Of these, the *Ozler* at PTT Cad 16 (①) and *Mercan Palas* next door at no. 14 (①) are marginally better than the *Tahran* at no. 20 (①) and the nearby *Merkez* (①), though all are very basic and lack en-suite bathroom facilities – choosing a room entails a tricky choice between bright and noisy rooms overlooking the street or quiet, dingy rooms in the bowels of the buildings. Also nearby is the plush *Yeni Kent Otel*, PTT Cad 33 (☎0422/321 1053, fax 324 9243; ④), which has double glazing and air conditioning to keep the outside world at bay, with nice extras such as refrigerator and bathtub to complete the cocoon like effect. Major credit cards are accepted, making this a tempting location for a minor splurge. There's a cluster of upper budget options on Atatürk Caddesi, of much the same dinginess as their cheaper rivals but equipped with en-suite showers. Of these the best choice is probably the noisy but clean *Otel Park*, Atatürk Cad 17 (☎0422/321 1691; ①).

Malatya has one or two good hotels higher up the price scale. Apart from the aforementioned *Yeni Kent*, there's the good-value *Kent Otel*, Atatürk Cad 131 (☎0422/321 2175; ②), and the two-star *Malatya Buyuk Hotel*, Yeni Cami Karşısı (☎0422/321 1400, fax 321 5367; ③), which has well-furnished rooms with fine views of Malatya's main mosque – though the 3.30am call to prayer is ear-splitting. Top of the range is the four-star *Hotel Altin Kayısı* (Golden Apricot), İstasyon Cad (☎0422/238 0533, fax 238 0083; ⑦), inconveniently located out of town near the train station, but equipped with a mouthwatering array of top-notch facilities.

The Town

The **Archeological Museum** (Tues–Sun 8am–5pm; $1), well signposted at the south end of Fuzuli Caddesi, is worth a visit, even though a confusing chronology can leave you leapfrogging the centuries like a gymnastic time traveller. Currently the best displays from Aslantepe include early Bronze Age bone idols, some of the earliest swords ever found and a Hittite stele of a winged supernatural being. There are also some amazingly intricate cuneiform seals that point to an early trade with Assyria and Mesopotamia, and some rare Commagene coins from the nearby kingdom based at Nemrut Dağı. Upstairs in the ethnological collection, the most engaging item is not even local but an imported Safavid bronze tray from medieval Persia.

A little way north of the centre, Malatya's **copper bazaar**, next to the main apricot bazaar, contains little that you'd specifically wish to buy, though it gives you an opportunity to watch the craftsmen hammering away, and tin-plating surfaces intended for use with food.

Eating, drinking and other practicalities

There are plenty of **places to eat** in town, but few are outstanding. Worth singling out is the simply named *Lokanta*, next to the *Tahran Otel*, unlicensed but offering both *sulu yemek* and grills. The *Kışla Restaurant*, Atatürk Cad 82, is a basic grill redeemed mostly by its nice *sütlaç*; the *Güngör*, at the intersection of Atatürk and PTT *caddesi*s, has more variety and stays open later. The *Beyaz Saray Lokantasi*, near the *Otel Park*, is also a good dependable choice. If you're craving **booze** with your meal, there are only two choices: the *Melita* near the *Otel Park*, an expensive clip-joint with an Arabian-Nights-type floor show for visiting businessmen, and the *Yeni Emniyet* behind the *Belediye* building, essentially a *meyhane* with old-fashioned decor. In terms of **light meals or snacks**, *Öz Malatya Mutfağı*, also called *Ayşe Abla'nin Yeri*, at the south end of Fuzuli Caddesi near the museum, serves home-style lunches (including *mantı*); and *Magdalena Burger*, at Şehit Hamit Fendoğlu Cad 35, is a pleasant café which stays open late – not much else does in Malatya, where food has vanished and the sidewalks roll up by 9.30pm.

Other facilities in Malatya include the **THY** terminal at Kanal Boyu Cad 10 (☎0422/321 1920); a women's **hamam** behind the *Yeni Emniyet* restaurant; and the **PTT** at the very start of İnönü Caddesi.

Eski Malatya

About 12km north of the modern city, **ESKİ MALATYA** or "Old Malatya", a ruined Roman-Byzantine town, is served by city buses heading for the village of Batalgazi from a stop on Sivas Caddesi, a few hundred metres east of the city centre. The old town walls are still visible, but much of the original settlement, which boasted 53 churches and a couple of dozen monasteries, has been built over by the inhabitants of the modern village. Buses arrive at the main square, from where it's a 200-metre walk southwest to a partially restored seventeenth-century *kervansaray*, and a further couple of hundred metres south to the Selçuk **Ulu Cami**, which has an elegant blue-tiled interior worth a quick look. Just south of the mosque is a ruined *medrese*, and 200m west lies the stranded Melik Sunullah minaret (1394) with traces of tilework still clinging to it.

Aslantepe

Currently the most actively excavated ancient site in central Anatolia, **ASLANTEPE** lies just over 4km from the northeastern edge of Malatya; city bus #36, labelled "Orduzu", passes within 800m of the site.

Like many similar settlements in Turkey, the mound here is mostly artificial, raised up a convenient distance from a river in the midst of what has always been an oasis; up top there's a view over well-watered apricot groves. The name – "Lion Hill" – derives from the stone lions found guarding the north gate of the Hittite city, now in Ankara's Anatolian Civilizations Museum. They, and many other Hittite treasures, were uncovered by French scholars in the 1930s using the now-discredited technique of deep, rapidly cut exploratory trenches. Since 1962 Aslantepe has been more meticulously uncovered by Italian archeologists, in residence each August to October – the best time for a visit (daily 8.30am–5pm), since many members of the team speak good English and will escort you around, making sense of a dig which is otherwise still very much of specialist interest and unprepared for the demands of tourism.

The most exciting discovery to date is a vast **palace complex**, the earliest known, built of mud bricks on a stone foundation, dating from the end of the fourth millennium BC. Also unusual are a pair of eerie **wall paintings** from approximately 3200 BC. The room with the painted wall is flanked by storehouses in which were found pots and clay seals for accounting and administration of foodstuff, since writing was as yet unknown.

Adjoining the palace to the west is a **temple** to an unknown deity, with concentric oval decorations stamped into its walls. On the northwest of the tumulus, some Neolithic remains predate the palace, while the northeast slope, now overgrown, was the location of the Hittite town and its spectacular finds. Beside the Hittite excavations, you can make out a bit of the Roman village; the Byzantines moved the population to Eski Malatya in the fifth century, ending more than 4000 years of habitation on this spot.

Northeast of Malatya: Elâzığ and around

One hundred kilometres northeast of Malatya, and easily accessible by dolmuş, **ELÂZIĞ** was founded in 1862 by Sultan Abdülaziz to house the overspill population from the old settlement of Harput (see below). It's an important grape-producing town, the centre of an area where *okuzgözü* (ox-eye) grapes, used to produce the red *Buzbağ* wine, are harvested. Elâzığ itself is predominantly modern and soulless, but it has a decent **Archeological Museum**, on the campus of the Euphrates University just outside town, displaying objects from various local ancient sites submerged by flooding after the completion of the Keban dam project to the north of Elâzığ in 1974. There's a remarkable collection of Urartian jewellery, as well as an ethnological section with some unexciting costumes and carpets.

Elâzığ's **tourist information office** is nominally found at İstasyon Caddesi 35 but has effectively shut down. **THY** can be found on Şehit İlhanlar Cad 26/D (☎0424/218 3730) for daily flights to Ankara. If you want to stay overnight, the cheapest palatable **hotel** in town is the *Erdem Hotel*, İstasyon Cad 19 (☎0424/218 2212; ②), though the two-star *Büyük Elâzığ Oteli*, located at Harput Cad 9 (☎0424/218 1484; ④), is much more pleasant.

Harput

The all-but-abandoned city of **HARPUT** lies a five-kilometre ride to the north of Elâzığ, on red city bus #19, at the end of a road lined by military installations guarding the Keban dam. It was a thriving commercial town of many thousands as recently as the end of the last century, since when a series of disastrous earthquakes has led to mass emigration to Elâzığ.

Today the sleepy hilltop village, as well as the valleys to the north, are studded with yellow signs pointing to numerous **mosques**, **hamams** and **tombs** of much-venerated saints, though none is especially distinguished and all told the detour up here is frankly a time-filler. Well marked at the northeast edge of town, the originally Byzantine **castle** is essentially a shell except for its fine restored gateway and a small church inside. Despite apparent impregnability on top of a rocky outcrop, it was captured by Tamerlane during the second Mongol wave and again by Sultan Selim I in 1515.

Back in the centre of Harput, the **Meydan Camii** and its attached hamam are the focus of what's still alive here. Nearby is the **Arap Baba Türbesi** housing the body of a local holy man; once in a while an attendant at this small mausoleum will raise the lid of the wooden coffin to reveal a startling mummified brown body. The oldest local survivor in town is the box-like twelfth-century **Ulu Cami**, with its brick minaret leaning at a crazy angle.

In the blissfully peaceful, leafy park adjoining the simple **Kurşunlu Cami**, you can get *ayran*, tea and simple snacks, perhaps even the eponymous *Harput köfte*, the extent of most people's knowledge of the town.

Eski Pertek

Heading northwest out of Elâzığ, you can follow what was once the main Erzurum-bound road – now unmarked – 25km north until it disappears into the Keban reservoir, where the fourteenth-century castle of **Eski Pertek** has been turned into a dramatic island fortress. The castle is in a good general condition but sadly is no longer easily reached; the only realistic way of getting there is to take the infrequent car ferry to Pertek on the other side of the lake and rent a boat, although this is by no means a simple operation.

THE TIGRIS VALLEY

From Malatya to the **valley of the River Tigris** (*Dicle* in Turkish), your approach is relatively appealing, threading through an Asiatic canyonscape with the scenic Hazar Gölü en route the only natural lake in a land of reservoirs. But the landscape eastwards from Urfa to Mardin and Diyarbakır is another story: grim and barren, and perhaps a more fitting introduction to the most underdeveloped corner of Turkey. By Turkish standards the region is unhealthy, too: cholera and malaria cases are still reported seasonally, and virtually every traveller succumbs to gastric distress at some point.

Most points of interest lie on the southwest bank of the Tigris, including **Diyarbakır**, a large, Kurd-populated city and the natural gateway to the region. However, another, heavily potholed road from Şanlıurfa does bypass Diyarbakır, heading due east to **Mardin**, a town separated from the rest of Turkey by distance and by a way of life apparently frozen in the past.

The Diyarbakır–Mardin road effectively marks the limit of the area affected by the Kurdish separatist unrest that has disrupted much of southeastern Turkey since the beginning of the 1980s. In recent years, there have been occasional isolated incidents east of this line in the area covered by this chapter, specifically in the semi-desert close to the Syrian border east of Nusaybin and in the mountains around Hasankeyf, but in general this region lacks the wild and remote terrain favoured by the PKK separatists further east and northeast. Nevertheless, it's worth checking out the political situation before setting off east of the Diyarbakır–Mardin road. Although it's highly unlikely that you'll experience trouble during daylight hours, you will notice heavy troop concentrations, armoured cars and tanks at strategic junctions, and a tangibly tense atmosphere in many provincial towns.

East of Mardin, **Midyat** and its hinterland is the traditional home of Turkey's Syrian Orthodox Christian community, who split with the rest of Christendom 1400 years ago. A steadily dwindling community of about 15,000 Christians live in the villages of the **Tür Abdin** plateau that extends to the east of Midyat, dotted with semi-ruined churches and monasteries, a few still functioning.

Independent travel in the region is still possible: daytime bus services continue to operate, and military checkpoints are rarely more than a formality, at worst an irritation. If anything, the state of the road surfaces is the most consistent threat to your health, especially that of your kidneys. However, depending on the timing and venue of the latest incident, any of the places covered in the balance of this chapter can turn quite nasty at short notice: you may be denied entry, stopped, or even briefly detained by the *jandarma*. As a foreigner you should be accorded every courtesy as long as you remain polite and there's no evidence that you've tried to establish contact with banned organizations.

Diyarbakır

Despite its superb position at the edge of the Tigris flood plain, **DİYARBAKIR** is essentially a sprawl of modern buildings hiding a few beautiful mosques, and enclosed by vast walls of black basalt. It's not particularly attractive but it does have a certain atmosphere, albeit of the kind that might start to wear on your nerves after more than a day or two – as will the intense summer heat.

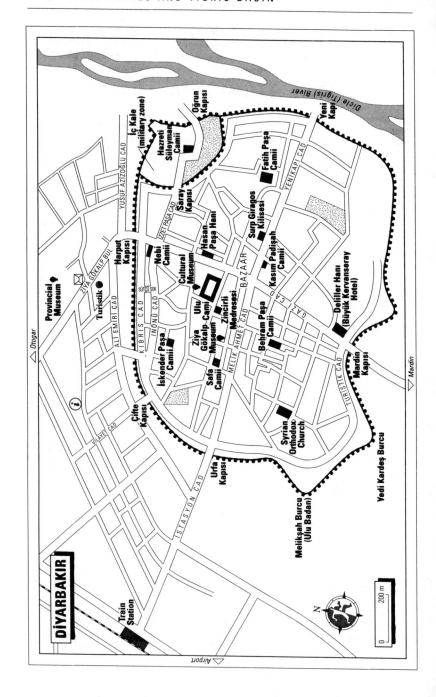

DİYARBAKIR

Train Station

Airport

Otogar

Provincial Museum

Turistik

ZIYA GÖKALP BUL

YUSUF AZIZOĞLU CAD

İç Kale (military zone)

Dicle (Tigris) River

Oğrun Kapısı

Hazreti Süleyman Camii

Yeni Kapısı

Fatih Paşa Camii

Saray Kapısı

İZET PAŞA CAD

Harput Kapısı

Nebi Camii

Cultural Museum

Hasan Paşa Hanı

Surp Giragos Kilisesi

YENIKAPI CAD

ALTMIRI CAD

KIBRIS CAD

İNÖNÜ CAD

SÜTCÜ SOK

Ulu Camii

Ziya Gökalp Müzesi

Zincirli Medresesi

BAZAAR

Kasım Padişah Camii

Deliller Hanı (Büyük Kervanseray Hotel)

İskender Paşa Camii

Safa Camii

Behram Paşa Camii

MELIK AHMET CAD

Mardin Kapısı

Çifte Kapısı

VILAYET CAD

Syrian Orthodox Church

TURISTIK CAD

Mardin

Urfa Kapısı

İSTASYON CAD

Melikşah Burcu (Ulu Badan)

Yedi Kardeş Burcu

N

200 m
0

Airport

A chaotic place with a population of almost half a million, Diyarbakır has something of a bad reputation in other parts of Turkey. Most of the alarming tales of terrorism can be dismissed, since police and soldiers are the intended targets of the violence; if you keep your wits about you, this is no more dangerous than any other large Turkish city. The biggest hazard you're likely to encounter are the carpet-shop **hustlers,** many of whom introduce themselves as "students" eager to give you a guided tour of the town and who won't take offence if you don't want to buy anything at the carpet shop which you'll visit – as if by chance – en route.

Talking to these young entrepreneurs is a good way to learn about Diyarbakır. It's a largely Kurdish town, and you may encounter overt displays of anti-Turkish feeling for the first time. Long a focus of tension, the place's reputation can probably be traced back to the anarchic days that preceded the 1980 military coup when the city was a hotbed of separatist activity.

Despite the fact that things are somewhat calmer now, the plight of the Kurds still makes its existence felt in Diyarbakır. The men and women you'll see in the streets dressed in distinctive headgear and costumes are some of the nearly half-million Kurds who have recently fled Iraq in two waves: first in 1988, when Saddam Hussein launched poison-gas attacks on Halabja and other towns, and the later – much greater – exodus following the end of the 1991 Gulf War. These **Iraqi Kurds** have been joined by Turkish Kurds fleeing the lack of opportunity and civil strife in the surrounding countryside.

This influx has done nothing to alleviate this grindingly poor city's already precarious **economic situation:** eight-to-ten-children families are the norm, many of the streets are frankly squalid and beggars are not an uncommon sight. Unemployment approaches forty percent, with no real industry to speak of; the only significant product is **watermelons,** grown on the banks of the Tigris with pigeon droppings as fertilizer. Fifty-kilo monsters are the result, but it's claimed that in the old days Diyarbakır melons weighed as much as 100kg and had to be transported by camel and cut using a sword.

Diyarbakır has long since burst out of its confining walls, and it's difficult to say which neighbourhoods are more unappealing: the tenements of the old town, or the soulless tower blocks of the new extension. Recently a significant proportion of the city's male population has sought solace in Islamic fundamentalism, possibly with semi-official encouragement since this diverts support from the PKK separatist movement.

Given the prevailing instability, and strategic location, it's not surprising that Diyarbakır is a big military outpost. Outside town is the headquarters of the Turkish Seventh Army, entrusted with the task of containing the PKK (see p.781 in *Contexts*), who keep them busy in the mountains. To the north sprawls a large NATO airbase, with the scream of jet engines and drumming of helicopter rotors a constant fact of life in the city.

Some history

Diyarbakır is not only the capital of the upper Tigris valley, but has some claim to being one of the oldest cities on earth, so not surprisingly it has a colourful and violent history. Certainly the city existed at the time of the Hurrian Empire, some 5000 years ago, and it subsequently saw successive periods of Urartian, Assyrian and Persian hegemony before falling to Alexander the Great and his successors, the Seleucids.

The Romans appeared on the scene in 115 AD, and over the next few centuries they and their successors, the Byzantines, struggled violently over the town with the Sassanid Persians. The Romans, who knew Diyarbakır as **Amida,** built the first substantial **walls** around the city in 297 – the ones you see today were erected in Byzantine times on top of the Roman originals. Their threatening, basalt bulwarks gave the place its popular ancient name, "Amid the Black". The modern name comes from the Arabs; in 638 the Bakr tribe of Arabs arrived and renamed the city Diyar Bakr or "Place of the Bakr". With the decline of Arab influence in the region Diyarbakır became a Selçuk, then a Turcoman and finally an Ottoman stronghold.

In 1925, after the new Republican government had dashed Kurdish hopes of autonomy, a rebellion erupted in the area around Diyarbakır. The city was besieged and Turkish troops were rushed in by train through French-occupied territory. The siege was soon lifted and hundreds of rebels were hanged on the spot, though the bloodshed didn't end here: over the next few years the lives of between 40,000 and quarter of a million Kurdish villagers are thought to have been taken in reprisals.

Arrival, orientation and information

Most of what you need in Diyarbakır is in the old city, within the great walls. The **train station** lies a kilometre west of town at the end of İstasyon Caddesi, the **otogar** 2km northwest at the top of Ziya Gökalp Bulvarı. Dolmuşes are on hand to ferry new arrivals into the centre from either terminal; don't believe any taxi drivers who tell you that there are no dolmuşes. You'll be dropped off near the Atatürk statue (under 24-hour armed guard, as the locals will gleefully tell you) in front of the Harput Kapısı, one of several gigantic city gateways. *Habur Tours* dolmuşes from Mardin arrive at the central crossroads where Gazi Caddesi and Melik Ahmet Caddesi intersect. Kaplaner **airport**, 3km southwest of town, is served by *THY* buses, which will drop you at their office at İnönü Cad 8 (☎0412/221 2314); alternatively, a taxi will set you back about $4.

The town itself is straightforward enough if you keep to the main roads; from Harput Kapısı, **Gazi Caddesi** running south to the Mardin Kapısı bisects the city from north to south, and **Melik Ahmet Caddesi**, later becoming **Yenikapı Caddesi**, does the same from west to east. The backstreets, however, are a narrow maze of sometimes filthy alleys, where it's easy to lose your bearings. The local **tourist office** is nominally at Lise Cad 24, but it seems to have gone into temporary hiding to protest at the lack of tourists.

Most banks line Gazi Caddesi, but – as ever in the east of Turkey – **money exchange** is a long, drawn-out rigamarole best avoided if possible. For Eurocheques in particular, *Emlak Bankası* charges a reasonable commission, while *Garanti Bankası* does not. You might have better luck at the main **PTT**, outside the Harput Kapısı on Gökalp Bulvarı, or at the fancier hotels. Most convenient, as ever, are the *döviz* offices, on Gazi Caddesi.

Accommodation

The most desirable accommodation in town lies within a short walk of the Harput Kapısı – the further away from it, the quieter it's likely to be, though nothing is quite as noisy as that found in Şanlıurfa or Gaziantep. Many of the bottom-end hotels are pretty grim, so you'd do best to avoid them if possible; we've only listed the most passable. Given the wide range of affordable mid-range choices, you really shouldn't need to patronize them, and unless another Gulf War has broken out, bed supply in Diyarbakır almost always exceeds demand.

Budget

All of the following are similarly basic but acceptable, offering rooms with and without showers.

Hotel Akdağ, İzzet Paşa Cad 23 (☎0412/221 3545). ①.

Hotel Kenan, İzzet Paşa Cad 20/B (☎0412/221 6614); with an attached hamam. ①.

Hotel Köprücü, İnönü Cad 1, Birinci Çıkmaz, an alley behind Nebi Camii (☎0412/221 2963). ①.

Hotel Malkoç, Sütçü Sok 6 (☎0412/221 2975). ①.

Otel Surkent, İzzet Paşa Cad 19 (☎0412/221 6616). ①.

Otel Van Palas, İnönü Cad 3, Çikmaz 3 (☎0412/221 1218). Squalid bathrooms but a very friendly atmosphere. ①.

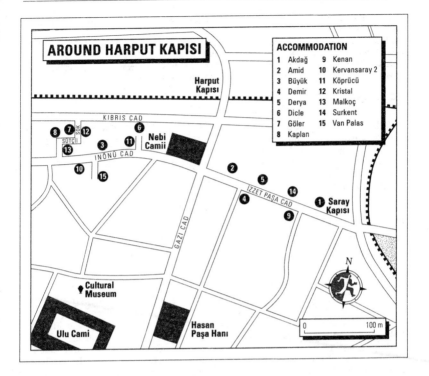

AROUND HARPUT KAPISI

ACCOMMODATION

1	Akdağ	9	Kenan
2	Amid	10	Kervansaray 2
3	Büyük	11	Köprücü
4	Demir	12	Kristal
5	Derya	13	Malkoç
6	Dicle	14	Surkent
7	Göler	15	Van Palas
8	Kaplan		

Mid-range

Most of the listings below will have proper bathrooms and fairly constant hot water, and be more used to Western tourists than the really inexpensive hotels.

Amid Otel, Suakar Sok 7, off Gazi Cad (☎0412/224 3331). Its eighth-floor bar sometimes features traditional Kurdish music. ②.

Hotel Derya, İnönü Cad 13 (☎0412/221 4966). A bit frayed at the edges, but a useful fall-back. ③.

Dicle Oteli, Kıbrıs Cad 3 (☎0412/223 5326). A large place, so tends to fill last, but starting to fall into a state of disrepair. ①.

Hotel Kaplan, Sütçü Sok 14, side street to the north of İnönü Cad (☎0412/221 3358). Friendly reception, with showers and TVs in the rooms, in a quiet location. ①.

Hotel Kristal, Sütçü Sok 10 (☎0412/224 1642). Best of the mid-range options. ③.

Expensive

In this category you should expect amenities such as mini-bars, air conditioning and even the occasional full-size bathtub. Prices include breakfast.

Büyük Otel, İnönü Cad 4 (☎0412/228 1295, fax 221 2444). Recently renovated and best value in this category. ③.

Büyük Kervansaray, Gazi Cad, Deliller Hanı (☎0412/228 9606, fax 223 7731). Characterful rooms in a converted *kervansaray* with a nice pool, where most of the West's press corps stayed during the Gulf War; still very popular, so reservations suggested. Singles are unusually good value, but avoid weekends when caterwauling chanteuse in courtyard defeats sleep. ⑤.

Demir Otel, İzzet Paşa Cad 8 (☎0412/221 2315, fax 222 4300). Refurbished in 1990 with all mod cons, but overpriced and lacking the *Büyük Kervansaray*'s charm. ⑦.

Hotel Güler, Yoğurtçu Sok 7, off Kıbrıs Cad (☎0412/224 0294, fax 224 0294). Well-appointed rooms, a good choice. ④.

Otel Kervansaray 2, İnönü Cad 13 (☎0412/221 4966, fax 223 5933). The *Büyük*'s overspill is charmless and inferior, though comfortable enough. ③.

Turistik Oteli, Ziya Gökalp Bul 7 (☎0412/224 7550, fax 224 4274). Grossly overpriced, but at least the rooms have bathtubs and the air conditioning actually works. ⑦.

The walls

Diyarbakır's six-kilometre-long **city wall**, breached by four huge main gateways plus several smaller ones, and dotted with 72 defensive towers, is the city's most famous attraction. Although the foundations are Roman and Byzantine, most of what can be seen today dates from the eleventh-century Selçuk kingdom of Melek Ahmet Şah – like the Great Wall of China, it is claimed that they are the only man-made structures on earth visible from space.

The best way to explore is on foot: near Mardin Kapısı you can ascend the ramparts, which should present no problems unless you suffer from extreme vertigo. From here onwards most sections are still intact, and in circling the city you'll only have to descend to ground level for a couple of short stretches. In hot weather be sure to take water and a head covering along – there are long intervals where you won't be able to descend for shade or refreshment.

Harput Kapısı and the İç Kale

The obvious place to start is at the **Harput Kapısı**, the best preserved of the city gates – an angular and unbreachable-looking black tower. You can't actually climb up onto the battlements at this point, however, so make your way down Gazi Caddesi and turn left onto İzzet Paşa Caddesi; this leads to **Saray Kapısı**, the entrance to the **İç Kale**, Diyarbakır's citadel and probably the oldest part of town. Beyond here the road dips before passing through the **Oğrun Kapısı** into a slum area overlooking the Tigris, outside the city walls. The view is undeniably impressive, with the broad, languid river further away than it looks, and spread below you the alluvial plain on which Diyarbakır's famous shit-nourished melons grow in special holes dug in the sandy river banks.

The citadel itself is a military zone, its walls patrolled by soldiers, a fact which restricts your wanderings somewhat. The only accessible building is the **Hazreti Süleyman Camii**, a black stone structure with a huge square minaret, built in 1160 by the Artukids, and looking these days rather like a grim Victorian workhouse. The cool spring that supplies the mosque's *şadırvan* is probably the city's original water source. In the domain of the army are a couple of churches: the **Church of St George** and the **Küçük Kilise**. Not much is known about either of these, and with the former purported to be in use as a prison it could be a while before our knowledge is extended.

Mardin Kapısı to Urfa Kapısı

The stretch of wall running between **Mardin Kapısı** and **Urfa Kapısı** is the best preserved and most impressive. Head down Gazi Caddesi until you reach the **Deliller Hanı**, now restored as the *Otel Büyük Kervansaray*. Nearby is the Mardin Kapısı, near to which you can ascend the wall – though if you don't feel up to the scramble it's slightly easier to go up at the Urfa Kapısı.

From Mardin Kapısı you can walk west along the battlements, which most of the way are wide enough for three people walking abreast – only in a couple of places do things get slightly hair-raising, requiring sturdy footwear. After about 400m you come to the **Yedi Kardeş Burcu** (Seven Brothers Tower), a huge circular bastion decorated with Selçuk lions and a double-headed eagle, from where there's a fantastic view out towards the Tigris. The view over the town is less inspiring, but enables you to appreciate the way it has developed over the centuries within the city walls. At this point they curve round to the northwest for 300m until you reach another tower, the **Melikşah Burcu** (also known as the Ulu Badan), which is again decorated with Selçuk motifs. From here a path, one of the few running parallel to the ramparts, also leads along them to the Urfa Kapısı.

At the **Urfa Kapısı** you'll have to descend to street level, but you can re-ascend a little further north. Continuing, the walls curve around to the northeast over the minor **Çifte Kapısı** (Double Gate). Grazing sheep aside, there isn't much to see for the remainder of the circuit to the Harput Kapısı.

The City

The Harput Kapısı also makes a good starting point for an exploration of the city proper. Immediately to the south of the gateway, at the intersection of Gazi Caddesi and İnönü Caddesi, stands the **Nebi Camii** or Mosque of the Prophet, a late fifteenth-century foundation of the Akkoyun Turcomans. The mosque's most distinctive feature is the alternating bands of black basalt and white sandstone used in its construction, and especially effective in the minaret; you'll come across this striped effect frequently in Diyarbakır, as both stones are quarried locally, and their combination is considerably less threatening than the unrelenting black of the walls.

Continuing down Gazi Caddesi will bring you to the **Hasan Paşa Hanı** on the left-hand (eastern) side of the street, and more bands of black and white stone. The *han* dates from the late sixteenth century and is still in commercial use, mainly for carpet and jewellery shops, while the city's main bazaar area occupies the small, twisting streets all around.

The Ulu Cami and around

Opposite the *han* stands the rather Victorian-looking gatehouse and funky teahouses of the **Ulu Cami**, Diyarbakır's most important mosque. The first of Anatolia's great Selçuk mosques, it was probably built in 1091 by Melik Şah, the Selçuk conqueror of the city. Legend claims that it was built on the site of, and with masonry from, the Byzantine church of Saint Thomas at the time of the Arab conquest in 639, giving rise to the assertion that this is the oldest mosque in Anatolia. It was gutted by fire in 1155 and extensively refurbished, but has been little altered since. In support of the later foundation date, many have noted that the Ulu Cami closely resembles the Umayyad mosque in Damascus.

On passing through the entrance portal decorated with bull and lion motifs, you find yourself in a large **courtyard**, perhaps the most impressive part of the building. Two *şadırvan*s occupy the centre of this courtyard, with its two-storeyed facades at the eastern and western ends. The north and west sides sport true arcades, constructed using pillars salvaged from earlier Roman and Byzantine buildings; on some of the columns and capitals are visible fragments of Greek inscription. The wing to the east and above the arch, with storks nesting on its roof, is actually a library, while at the northeast corner of the courtyard is the locked entrance to the **Mesudiye Medresesi**. Built in 1198 by the Artukids, this became the first university of Anatolia and is still in use as a Koran school.

The mosque itself is entered via a doorway on the southern side of the courtyard; a carved white *mimber* graces the cavernous interior. The minaret is tall and angular, like many such structures in Diyarbakır.

Leaving the Ulu Cami's tiny north gate and following Ziya Gökalp Sokak, you'll find the **Cultural Museum** ($0.50), occupying the former home of **Cahit Sıtkı Tarancı**, a prominent modern poet. There are exhibits about the man's life and work, as well as ethnographic memorabilia, but as so often in Turkey, the building itself matches or overshadows the displays.

If you leave the mosque courtyard via a door in the southwestern corner you enter a narrow alleyway. Turn left into the clothes bazaar and then right, and you will eventually come to the **Ziya Gökalp Museum**, former home of a turn-of-the-century Turkish nationalist, which again houses sections devoted to the man's life and work and an unexceptional ethnographic collection.

Diyarbakır's other mosques

Heading west from the the the Ziya Gökalp Museum brings you to the stunning fifteenth-century **Safa Camii**, a mosque of notably graceful design and construction. Its tall, round minaret, a departure from the city norm of stubby, square ones, still bears traces of blue tilework on its white, relief-worked surface. Archway masonry in the courtyard alternates between black and white in the local fashion, while the interior ceiling is accented by blue and green tilework.

Some way southeast across Melik Ahmet Caddesi stands the **Behram Paşa Camii**, Diyarbakır's largest mosque, built in 1572 by Behram Paşa, the governor of Diyarbakır, and also featuring the familiar black-and-white stonework. It is said that the mosque was constructed using a medieval form of pre-stressed concrete.

Also worth seeking out, east of Gazi Caddesi, is the early sixteenth-century **Kasım Padişah Camii** on Yenikapı Caddesi, in the Balıkcılarbaşı bazaar, virtually the last Akkoyun monument before the Ottomans took over. Its tall, square detached minaret, set on four two-metre basalt pillars, is known colloquially as the *Dört Ayaklı Minare* or "Four-Legged Minaret". According to legend if you walk around the minaret seven times and make a wish, it will be granted.

Other mosques, like the İskender Paşa Camii and the Fatih Paşa Camii, both dating from the fifteenth century, are only really worth tracking down if you're a real enthusiast.

Diyarbakır's churches

Near the Kasım Padişah Camii hides the **Surp Giragos Kilisesi**, an Armenian church, signposted as the "*Keldani Kilisesi*". It's a very simple barn-like place looked after by an ancient caretaker, a member of one of Diyarbakır's few surviving Armenian families. A priest comes by once every couple of weeks to conduct a service. The interior, though spartan, is a little garish in its details – icons in boxes with coloured lights are some of the more outré features.

There's also a Syrian Orthodox compound, the **Church of the Virgin Mary**, to the southwest of the Behram Paşa Camii – you'll probably have to ask someone directions to find it. A small door (keep knocking until someone answers) leads onto a paved courtyard surrounded by buildings which were once part of a seventh-century monastery.

Bear in mind when visiting these churches that Diyarbakır's Christian community keeps a fairly low profile in these times of Islamic and Kurdish resurgence, and that the people who show you around are putting themselves out especially for you. Most of the churches have collection boxes and the least you can do is make a small **contribution**.

The Provincial Museum

Diyarbakır's **Provincial Museum** (Tues–Sun 8.30am–noon & 1.30–5.30pm; $1) lies just outside the old city near the main PTT. To reach it head out along Ziya Gökalp Caddesi. You'll see a fairground on the northeastern (right) side of the road, and the typical black-on-yellow sign in the vicinity will lead you down a side street to the museum. It contains the usual archeological and ethnological titbits and also has a section devoted to the Akkoyun and Karakoyun Turcoman dynasties who ruled much of eastern Anatolia and western Persia in medieval times.

Eating and drinking

Finding a place to **eat** should be no problem in Diyarbakır, since there are kebab places on virtually every street corner near the Harput Kapısı. Modest places to try include the *Şanlı Urfa Kebap Evi* on İzzet Paşa Caddesi; or the *Hacı Baba Kebapçısı* and *Şehrin Kebapçısı*, both opposite the Nebi Camii on Gazi Caddesi. There are also a couple of good choices west of Harput Kapısı on Kıbrıs Caddesi: the *Neşem Yemek Salonu* and, a little further along at no. 17, the slightly more expensive *Büryan Salonu*. The cheapest licensed restaurant (and one of the best) is that attached to the *Dicle Oteli*, where tasty, largish portions are served in summer on a rooftop terrace. For something a bit special, try the lamb *kuburga* (ribs stuffed with rice), served at lunchtime at the *Selim Amca Sofra Salonu* on Ali Emiri Caddesi, a five-minute walk west of Harput Kapısı; reservations must be made a day in advance.

A particular Diyarbakır institution are the sidewalk liver-heart-and-offal **grill stalls** that set up shop on summer evenings along Gazi Caddesi; there are also a few such premises indoors, like *Manolya Ocakbaşı*. The meat bits are skewered and grilled as you watch, then served up hot and savoury with a raw vegetable garnish. Portions are generous and you can eat well for a couple of dollars, but don't go overboard the first time or you'll regret it the next day.

For **snacks and pastries** try the *Şeyhmus Pastanesi*, at the junction of İzzet Paşa Caddesi and Gazi Caddesi, or the smaller and cheaper *Sinem Pastanesi* on İzzet Paşa.

If you want to drink **alcohol** with or without food, you'll have to patronize the restaurants and bars attached to the hotels; the courtyard of the *Büyük Kervansaray* hosts the closest thing to a **nightclub** in the city centre. Diyarbakır's two main **cinemas**, the *Emek* and the better *Dılan*, on Izzet Paşa Caddesi and Ali Emiri Caddesi respectively, show fairly modern Western releases at rock-bottom prices; a ticket and a Coke will cost less than a dollar.

Mardin and around

Seen from the south at a distance, **MARDİN** can look almost spectacular, rising out of the flat surrounding landscape as a tiered cluster of buildings clinging to an eerie-looking rock. Closer up, it's a provincial centre of 60,000, more intriguing than beautiful with its mix of ugly concrete structures and fine old mansions, perched 1325m above sea level overlooking the Syrian plain. This position has always made it a strategic military outpost – the higher of the two castellated bluffs today sports golf-ball radar domes. The town also has a grandiose *medrese*, a couple of old mosques and a hotel or two which could serve as the base for excursions into the southeastern corner of the Tigris Basin.

Mardin's population is a mix of Kurds and Arabs, though in this part of Turkey it is probably more accurate to speak of Arabicized Kurds; thus the town has recently been a focus of tension, with strong separatist and Islamic undercurrents at work. There were riots here at the beginning of 1990, resulting in the drafting of several hundred extra police here from other parts of Turkey, recently replaced by more heavily armed gendarmes and army units.

The Town

Mardin's probable Roman origins are lost in the welter of war and conquest that forms this region's historical backdrop. The town's later history is tied up with the development of early Christianity; the first Christians to settle here were Syrian Orthodox who arrived during the fifth century AD, and today three churches hidden away in the backstreets still serve that dwindling community.

The Christians survived the period of Arab occupation from 640 to 1104, and were left largely unaffected by the arrival of the Selçuks and later the Turcomans. In 1394 the Mongols under Tamerlane captured the town, doling out death and misery in equal measures to Christian and Muslim alike, before handing Mardin over to the Karakoyun Turcoman tribe in 1408. The town fell to the Ottomans under Selim I in 1517 and an era of torpor began that was not significantly disrupted until the Kurdish rebellion of 1832, when a number of public buildings were blown up. There was a brief Egyptian occupation in 1839–40, after which the town sank back into somnolence until World War I.

From 1915 onwards Mardin's **Christian population** was drastically reduced by massacre and emigration, and today less than a thousand practising Christians remain. Immediately above the two car parks at Cumhuriyet Meydanı, the town's **cathedral** – largest of the trio of churches in town – is rarely used since there's no longer a resident priest. If you can gain admission to the badly damp-damaged but handsomely vaulted interior (donations invited), you'll be shown a kitsch crèche and an icon of the Virgin.

Although there's no shortage of featureless concrete, the architecture of Mardin's old **Arab-style houses** is stunning in places. Following Mardin's main street, **Birinci Caddesi**, east from **Cumhuriyet Meydanı** leads you to a famous example of Mardin's architecture – a beautiful stone facade with three arches, on the north side of the street. This is one of the finest private houses in town, and now serves as home to an extended family.

Several hundred metres beyond the house, the easterly of two sets of stone steps lead up to the **Sultan İsa Medresesi**, built in 1385, a striking, albeit crumbling, white structure with a magnificent Selçuk doorway, from which you can look out across the town towards Syria. If the caretaker is around it may be possible to take a look inside the eastern end of the building, which is still used as a Koran school. The *medrese* also houses the **Mardin Museum** (unreliable hours), home to a number of Christian carvings from Midyat and Hasankeyf. Another relief, housed in a chamber adjoining the museum's central courtyard, is unusual in that it features three figures carved out of a single block of stone, thought to represent Sumerian gods. The future of the museum, however, looks decidedly shaky and it may soon close down altogether.

Above the Sultan İsa Medresesi is the **kale**, originally built by the Romans and extended by the Byzantines. The Arabs and then the Selçuks occupied it for a while, and from the twelfth century through until the fourteenth century the citadel served the Artukid Turcoman tribe as a capital. From here they were able to beat off the Arabs and endure an eight-month siege during the first Mongol onslaught, falling only to the second Mongol wave in 1394. The Karakoyun Turcomans built the (now ruined) palace and mosque inside the walls; you may be able to enjoy the views from the terrace, but the castle interior and the golfball-crowned summit is a strictly off-limits military zone.

South of Cumhuriyet Meydanı stands Mardin's **Ulu Cami**, an eleventh-century Selçuk mosque with a fluted dome, blown up during the 1832 rebellion and much restored since. Nearby is the **Latifiye Camii**, dating from the fourteenth century. It has a carved Selçuk-style portal, and a courtyard with a shady garden – just the place to escape the blinding summer heat. At the western end of town, south of the main road (you'll have to ask directions), is the fifteenth-century **Kasım Paşa Medresesi**, similar in design to the Sultan İsa Medresesi.

Practicalities

Mardin can be confusing at first. One road bears north of the citadel bluff on its way to Midyat; another main road skirts the southern edge of the town before heading off to the southeast and the Syrian border. The town itself lies between this latter road and the citadel. Mardin's principal street, **Birinci Caddesi**, branches off from the main road at the western end of town and rejoins it at the eastern end. There's a small otogar on the main Syria-bound road at the eastern end of town, with frequent dolmuşes to Cumhuriyet Meydanı; there's another at the western end of Birinci Caddesi, with dolmuşes to Diyarbakır in particular, where you'll have a better selection of buses to other Turkish destinations.

Mardin's **tourist information office** on Birinci Caddesi, just west of Cumhuriyet Caddesi (☎0482/212 5845), is next to useless, and its hotels aren't much better – you may want to consider visiting the town as a day trip from Diyarbakır, though you'll probably need to stay here if you wish to visit the surrounding monasteries. Mardin's only budget hotel is the *Bayraktar* (☎0482/212 1338; ①), at the Cumhuriyet Meydanı end of Birinci Caddesi, whose plain but passable rooms with tepid-water bathrooms command fabulous views of the Syrian plain to the south. If you have your own transport, it's better to stay at the new and comfortable *Otel Bilen* (☎0482/212 5568, fax 212 2575; ④), 1500m out of town at its northwestern entrance; bargain them down.

There are a few of **places to eat** along Birinci Caddesi, of which the only vaguely upscale option is the restaurant attached to the *Hotel Bayraktar*, where you'll pay slightly over the odds for the privilege of being able to drink alcohol with your meal. The *Otel Bilen* also has a licensed restaurant, with overpriced, mediocre food. You really won't be much worse off at smaller places like the *Unsalyemek Salonu* on Birinci Caddesi or any other of the numerous kebab places in the town centre. At the eastern end of Mardin, oppostite the **PTT**, is a small and leafy terrace tea garden, where you can watch the sun set over Syria.

East of Mardin: Deyr-az-Zaferan (Deyrülzafran)

DEYR-AZ-ZAFERAN (also known as Deyrülzafran, or the "Saffron Monastery", so named for the yellowish rock from which it's built) lies 6km southeast of Mardin, the most accessible of the area's surviving Syrian Orthodox religious communities. Founded in 493 AD, it was, from 1160 until the 1920s, the seat of the Syrian Orthodox patriarch – though he has since relocated to Damascus. A surprisingly large rectangular building of three storeys, set on a low bluff overlooking an approach road, it wouldn't look out of place in southern Italy or Spain, and, judging the different styles of stonework, was built in stages, with frequent pauses for restoration. Now only two monks remain, running a school for about 25 orphans with the assistance of a few lay helpers.

Visiting is easy enough. You can walk to it in an hour and a half from Mardin, following the yellow signs leading southeast: first adopt the Nusaybin road, then turn off left following a little yellow sign, passing through the village of Eskikale. Eventually you'll come to another signposted turning leading you to the monastery. Failing that, pick up a taxi from Cumhuriyet Meydanı or the *otogar*, reckon on paying $5 (possibly more if business is booming) for a return trip with waiting time – though you'll have to bargain for this.

From the hills, ancient but still intact rock channels bring water to the Deyr-az-Zaferan monastery, whose entrance portal bears an inscription in Syriac. Some of the monks have a smattering of English, and after being greeted and perhaps offered a glass of tea, visitors are usually entrusted to one of the older orphans or visiting students and taken on a guided tour.

First stop is an **underground vault**, said to have been used as a temple by sun worshippers as long ago as 2000 BC. A now-blocked window at the eastern end enabled them to watch the sunrise, while a niche on the southern wall served as an altar (possibly sacrificial). The vault is enclosed by a ceiling of self-supporting stone built without the use of mortar. The room above, entered via huge 300-year-old walnut doors, is a **mausoleum**, whose walls contain the grave niches of seven Syrian Orthodox patriarchs and metropolitans (the equivalent of bishops).

Tours move on from here to the **chapel**, with fine relief-decorated arches and a carved stone altar (replacing a wooden one destroyed by fire fifty years ago), and the

THE SYRIAN ORTHODOX CHURCH

The area around Mardin has been a stronghold of the **Syrian Orthodox** or **Jacobite** church since 543 AD, when one Yakoub Al-Bardai (better known in the West as Jacobus Baradaeus), was appointed bishop of Edessa (Şanlıurfa). A native of Mesopotamia, Baradaeus was – like most of the Christians in the eastern and southern reaches of the Byzantine Empire – a **Monophysite**, subscribing to an anathemized doctrine locked in a century-old theological dispute with the patriarchate in Constantinople about the divine nature of Christ. According to the ecclesiastical Council of Chalcedon convened in 451 AD, Christ had both a human and a divine nature, but dissenting bishops throughout the Middle East held that Christ had only a divine nature – a creed known as Monophysitism, whose adherents risked condemnation as heretics and excommunication.

Present-day Syrian Orthodox Christians deny explicit Monophysitic leanings calling themselves "non-Chalcedonian Orthodox". In fact, the core and uniqueness of Syrian Orthodox observance, which has enabled the church to endure over time, is its liturgy in the **Syriac language**. Written from right to left in its own script, this had already evolved from ancient Aramaic – the purported mother tongue of Jesus – by the second century, when the first recognizable Syriac New Testament translations appeared. Between 541 and 578 AD, Baradaeus served as an energetic and peripatetic proselytizer throughout what is now the Hatay and Syria, helping to revive his church as it suffered determined attack by the agents of Constantinopolitan orthodoxy. From the advent of local Arab dominion in the seventh century, Syrian Orthodox Christians enjoyed considerable religious freedom, and by the time of the First Crusade at the end of the eleventh century the Tür Abdin in particular encompassed four bishoprics and eighty monasteries, the ruins of which are dotted across the plateau. Ironically, it was Christian Crusaders from Edessa and Antioch (Antakya) who unleashed the first wave of persecution against what they regarded as a heretical church, forcing abandonment of the traditional Syrian patriarchal seat in Antioch. They were followed by the Mongols whose motives had little to do with religion – they massacred and pillaged everybody regardless of race, colour and creed.

Under the Ottoman Empire order was restored, and the Christian community once again enjoyed a long period of tolerance and stability. Unfortunately, during World War I, they were tainted by association with Allied plans to dismember the Ottoman Empire and suffered widespread persecution and massacre, a fate they shared with the Anatolian Armenian and Greek minorities. Today the number of Syrian Christians worldwide totals nearly three million, though this figure may in fact include members of the breakaway **Syrian Catholic (Uniate) Church** which acknowledges the authority of the pope. The largest surviving national community is, perhaps surprisingly, in Kerala, India; in Turkey there remain just the bishoprics of Tür Abdin, Mardin (currently vacant), and İstanbul, where many thousands of beleaguered Tür Abdin residents have fled.

patriarch's or metropolitan's throne, on which are carved the names of all the patriarchs since 792 AD. Services in the chapel are held in Aramaic, and if you can manage to be here at around 6pm you may be able to attend one of them.

Beyond are a couple of rooms containing sedan chairs once used to transport the patriarchs; you'll also be shown a carved walnut altar, made without using nails, and an ancient mosaic said to come from the grotto of Sen Piyer in Antakya.

Upstairs, across the peaceful courtyard, you may also be shown the monastery's guest rooms (it is possible to stay overnight, but bear in mind that the quarters are intended for people visiting for religious reasons) and a more personalized suite intended for the use of the patriarch on his rare visits from Damascus. Lastly, you'll be taken out onto the roof terrace for fine views south into Syria, and the orphans will point out surrounding abandoned cave hermitages and two ruined monastic churches: Mar Yakoub and Miryam Anna. At the end of the tour you may want to make a donation or perhaps tip your guide, who may refuse your offer at first but will accept if you persist a little.

Southeast of Mardin: Nusaybin and Mar Augen

About 50km southeast of Mardin is **NUSAYBİN**, on the frontier with Syria, from where you can reach the abandoned monastery of Mar Augen. The last 33km of the journey runs parallel to the border, delineated by barbed wire and watchtowers. Nusaybin was the site of the Roman town of Nisibis but apart from a triumphal arch there's not much left to see. More interesting is a sporadically functioning Syrian Orthodox church, **Mar Yakoub**, and the town's ornate **railway station**, built by the Germans just before World War I and the last stop in Turkey on the Berlin–Baghdad railway; there are currently no international services, and just one slow local train daily at dawn to Gaziantep.

Unless you've got your own wheels, the monastery of **Mar Augen** is awkward to reach, and any trip will invariably involve a lot of messing around with taxis, dolmuşes and hitching. Just before the village of Girmeli (about 20km east of Nusaybin), the *Nezirhan* service station is an oasis-like motel and restaurant complex (④), living off the passing truck trade and overpriced for what it is. About a kilometre beyond, take the turning for Girmeli, cross the bridge just past the village and take the road on the extreme right at the triple junction, travelling towards the hills for about 3km. Eventually you'll have to abandon your transport and make your way up to the monastery on foot – a climb of about 45 minutes. During 1996 the local *jandarma* were not allowing visits to the monastery due to supposed PKK activity; check locally before leaving the main road.

Once home to a huge monastic community, Mar Augen is now the unlikely residence of a Muslim family who use the grounds as a farm. It's the most evocatively set and most poignant of all the abandoned monasteries in the area, though only the bare fifth-century monastery church is intact, with all traces of decoration long since erased.

The Tür Abdin plateau

Less than 100km east of Mardin spreads the undulating plateau of the **Tür Abdin**, a traditional homeland of the Syrian Orthodox Church – whose independence from the Greek Orthodox Church was formalized by theological disputes of the sixth century (see box opposite). Scattered across the area are numerous churches and monasteries; many of these are deserted but a few continue to function, reflecting the fact that the Tür Abdin is still home to some 3,000 Christians, who coexist uneasily with the local Kurds and account for most of Turkey's Christian minority outside of İstanbul. Aside from a traditional livelihood in grapevines, the rocky, parched plateau is a poor region, even by the standards of eastern Turkey, and in the towns and villages from Midyat eastwards you may well see obviously undernourished and unhealthy children. The government has set up aid programmes but local people claim that the authorities neglect them deliberately – and moreover do little to protect them from the attacks of their local enemies.

Midyat

From Mardin, **MİDYAT** is an uneventful journey of just under an hour. It's actually a double town: westerly, unremarkable, Kurd-inhabited Estel, and – 2km east, unsignposted – the originally Christian portion of half-abandoned medieval mansions. In theory, **old Midyat**, with its half-dozen churches and intricate architecture, should be a place people head for in droves; however, there are **no tourist facilities** other than a single, simple restaurant at the crossroads, all else having closed in response to the current troubles. Soldiers or **gendarmes** may ostentatiously patrol the streets during daylight hours, but the townspeople huddle indoors by night in a self-imposed curfew.

There is no *otogar*; dolmuşes stop at a junction at the foot of the **old town**, immediately east of which lies a small bazaar on level ground. Above this the residential quarter climbs up a slight hill, all cracked streets with open drains, and mysterious gateways opening onto the hidden courtyards of imposing mansions, inhabited by extended families of Kurds, Syrian Orthodox Christians, and a very few Armenians.

As recently as 1974 there were nearly 5000 Syrian Orthodox Christians in residence here, the men mostly engaged in gold- or silver-smithing, but this **population** has dwindled lately to about 300, in response to the PKK's extortion of money from the merchants and death threats by Muslim bigots, which have caused all but one of the town's priests to flee. The few remaining young people talk matter-of-factly of following their elders overseas to Canada, France or Germany, and it seems that unless conditions change the 2000-year history of Christianity here will end within another generation.

The town's **churches** are easily spotted by virtue of their graceful belfries and can all be reached on foot. Usually a member of a caretaking family living nearby will show you around if you hang about purposefully. The shrines aren't breathtaking, but strolling around their whitewashed interiors you can't help but marvel that they've survived intact, and many of the altars and shrines inside are touching in their simplicity. A few preserve illuminated Syriac missals, antiquarians' delights between 300 and 1000 years old, which you can ask to see.

Churches and monasteries around Midyat

Midyat is the western gateway to the **Tür Abdin** proper, which still has 32 villages wholly or partly inhabited by Syrian Orthodox Christians, plus 46 **monasteries and churches** in varying states of repair and use. To reach them you'll really need your own transport or a taxi, since walking or hitching cannot be recommended in current conditions. The positions of several are shown more or less correctly on the *GeoCenter/RV* map of eastern Turkey.

Mar Gabriel (Deyrulumur)

Southeast of Midyat, the monastery of **Mar Gabriel** is the geographical and spiritual centre of the plateau, and – if darkness is approaching – also the safest place of refuge in the area. To get there, leave Midyat on the half-paved, half-gravel Cizre-bound road; after 20km, just before an unmarked village, turn northeast onto a similarly unsignposted dirt driveway, which leads to the monastery gate in just over 2km.

Founded in 397 AD, Mar Gabriel is not only the oldest surviving Syrian Orthodox monastery, but the most vital in Turkey, with fourteen nuns and three monks occupying separate wings, as well as a fluctuating number of local lay workers, guests and students sent by Turkish emigrants to learn the Syriac language and retie hazy cultural connections. It is also the seat of the metropolitan bishop of Tür Abdin, who speaks good English, and with whom you may be granted an audience.

Compared with the showcase of Deyr-az-Zaferan, Mar Gabriel is a working community, set among gardens and orchards, and somewhat disfigured by a 1960s-vintage hostelry. The monastery's primary purpose is to keep Syrian Orthodox Christianity alive in the land of its birth by providing schooling, ordination of native-born monks, and – if necessary – physical protection to the faithful. You visit for the opportunity to gain some insight into the Church through a guided tour, and secondarily to stay the night, for which you need to ask permission. This will readily be granted late in the day, since the heavy steel gates of what in effect is a fortress are locked tightly at sunset, not opening until dawn except for life-or-death emergencies. The high walls of the compound have retained their medieval function as barriers to marauders, since the Syrian Orthodox communities of the Tür Abdin live in fear of attacks from both the PKK and Islamic fanatics; the bishop receives regular phone calls from villagers requesting guidance as to how to respond to the latest provocation.

On summer nights, accommodation may be a simple cot on the terrace roof, with an equally basic evening meal provided. At dawn, noon and dusk you are welcome to attend the liturgy conducted in the **subterranean church** underneath the belfry, a heady mix of Aramaic chants, swirling incense and Islamic-style prostration.

Village churches

In the opposite direction from Midyat – travelling north 4km towards Hasankeyf, then east along the secondary road to Dargeçit – lie the rest of the Tür Abdin's historic churches. Finest, though also remotest, is the monastic church of **Meryemanna** (El Hadra), about 24km away (17km along the road and then a further 7km south) in the village of Anıtlı (Hah). This fifth-century foundation sports a two-storey wedding-cake turret with blind arches atop a pyramidal roof; archways and lintels are also heavily ornamented.

Closer in, 10km along the Dargeçit road and then 3km north on a tertiary dirt track, the **Mar Yakoub** monastic church in Barıştepe (Salah) village is similarly ancient and impressive, with its barrel-vaulted nave and intricate relief work. Returning to the Dargeçit road, continuing east for 2km and then turning south for a further couple of kilometres, you reach the slightly later church of **Mar Kyriakos**, with its small courtyard, in the mixed Christian-Kurdish village of Bağlarbaşı (Arnas); its architect also built the **Mar Azazael** church on a knoll at the edge of Altıntaş (Keferzeh) village, about 7km east of Mar Kyriakos.

Hasankeyf

The journey north from Midyat to **HASANKEYF**, the spectacular site of a now-ruined city built by the Artukid Turcoman tribe on the banks of the Tigris, involves a gradual, scenic descent towards the river. With your own transport, it provides an excellent return route to Diyarbakır, without having to backtrack to Mardin, but check locally before setting out since not only is the area worryingly close to several known centres of PKK activity, but it is also subject to topographical changes as the full effects of the İlisu Dam project come into play. There are regular dolmuşes to Batman from Hasankeyf, via a gorge of the Tigris, but again get current information before venturing as far as Batman, a smelly oil town with only that improbable name to its credit.

The original settlement, founded by the Romans as an eastern bastion of Asia Minor, later became the Byzantine bishopric of Cephe. In 640 the conquering Arabs changed the town's name to Hisn Kayfa. During the twelfth century the Artukid Turcomans made it the capital of their realm, which it remained until the Mongols arrived in 1260. Hasankeyf then served as the stronghold of the Ayyubids, a clan of Kurdish chieftains supplanted by the Ottomans early in the fifteenth century.

Unfortunately the quality of the approach from any direction isn't matched by the modern town: it trails along for several hundred metres, overshadowed by the ruined Artukid city to the southwest, which covers two square kilometres on a clifftop above the right bank of the Tigris. The site is reached by turning west down a narrow paved street, later a dirt track, just before the modern Tigris bridge. After a kilometre look out for a ruined gateway halfway up the right side of the gorge, beyond which a stone pathway leads uphill to the twelfth-century **palace** of the Artukid kings, perched high above the Tigris. From here there is a fine view of the Tigris, a sheer drop of several hundred metres below, while behind you stretches the rest of the city. Although they look like standard-isssue ruins from the road, many of its skeletal houses contain intricate decorative features. Particularly impressive are the well-preserved **mosque**, and a couple of domed **tombs**.

To get a closer look at the Tigris, head back towards town and turn left by a gorgeous carved minaret to drop down to the river bank, where families come to paddle and wash their cars. Look out for the several hundred steps carved into the sheer cliff face, which give secret access to the Artukid palace above. Just downstream are the four pillars of an old **Artukid bridge** that in its day was apparently one of the finest in Anatolia.

But the best single bit of Hasankeyf, and unfortunately the one most threatened by the dam, is the fifteenth-century **Zeyn El-Abdin Türbesi**, a sizeable cylindrical building clad in glazed turquoise tiles and red brick, conspicuously isolated in a walled orchard on the north bank. This tomb, perhaps the most Timurid-influenced monument in Turkey, is easily reached on foot, via mud tracks starting opposite a filling station on the main road towards Batman.

travel details

Buses and dolmuşes

Adıyaman to: Adana (8 daily; 4hr); Kâhta (hourly; 1hr); Kayseri (4 daily; 7hr); Malatya (6 daily; 3hr); Şanlıurfa (4 daily; 2hr).

Diyarbakır to: Adana (4 daily; 10hr); Ankara (5 daily; 13hr); Bitlis (5 daily; 3hr 30min); Malatya (8 daily; 5hr); Mardin (6 daily; 1hr 45min); Şanlıurfa (6 daily; 3hr); Sivas (4 daily; 9hr); Tatvan (5 daily; 4hr); Van (4 daily; 7hr).

Gaziantep to: Adana via Mersin (10 daily; 3hr 30min); Adıyaman (3 daily; 4hr); Ankara (8 daily; 12hr); Antakya (8 daily; 4hr); Diyarbakır (4 daily; 5hr 30min); Mardin (5 daily; 6hr); Şanlıurfa (10 daily; 3hr).

Kâhta to: Adıyaman (hourly; 1hr).

Malatya to: Adana (5 daily; 8hr); Adıyaman (10 daily; 3hr); Ankara (8 daily; 12hr); Diyarbakır (3 daily; 4hr 30min); Elâzığ (8 daily; 1hr 40min); Erzurum (1 daily; 7hr).

Mardin to: Ankara (2 daily; 15hr); Diyarbakır (6 daily; 1hr 45min); Midyat (5 daily; 1hr 15min); Şanlıurfa (4 daily; 3hr).

Şanlıurfa to: Adana (3 daily; 6hr); Adıyaman (3 daily; 3hr); Ankara (3 daily; 16hr); Diyarbakır (3 daily; 3hr); Gaziantep (8 daily; 2hr); Malatya (3 daily; 6hr); Mardin (3 daily; 3hr).

Trains

Diyarbakır to: Ankara (4 weekly; 26hr 15min); Kayseri (4 weekly; 18hr); Sivas (4 weekly; 13hr).

Gaziantep to: İstanbul (3 weekly; 29hr); Konya (3 weekly; 16hr).

Malatya to: Adana (daily; 8hr 30min); Ankara (daily; 20hr); Diyarbakır (3 weekly; 6hr 30min); Tatvan (3 weekly; 10hr 30min).

Planes

Diyarbakır to: Ankara (2 daily; 1hr 30min); İstanbul (1 daily; 2hr).

Elâzığ to: Ankara (6 weekly; 2hr).

Gaziantep to: Ankara (daily; 1hr 20min); Baku (weekly; 2hr); Istanbul (daily; 2hr).

Malatya to: Ankara (daily; 1hr 15min).

Şanlıurfa to: Ankara (5 weekly; 2hr).

PART THREE

THE
CONTEXTS

THE
HISTORICAL
FRAMEWORK

So many cultures and states have held sway on the Anatolian peninsula that a thorough unravelling of its past would demand scholars of comparative religion, linguistics and archeology as well as historians. The present-day Turkish Republic is but the core remnant of a vast, late-medieval empire which extended at one point from the Indian Ocean to the Atlantic – and all of these realms contributed personalities and events. What follows is only the barest outline of a complex subject.

THE EARLIEST CULTURES

Discoveries in the heart of modern Turkey – the region known historically as Anatolia or Asia Minor – suggest that there has been settled habitation since the eighth millennium BC, among the oldest on earth. The **earliest finds**, including cave deposits in the region of Antalya, and surface finds from the Ankara and Hatay regions, prove that Anatolia was inhabited in the Paleolithic Age. More extensive discoveries from the **Neolithic** period include whole farming communities, of which the best known is **Çatal Höyük** near Konya (c.6500–5650 BC), demonstrating that early settlers lived in sizeable villages consisting of networks of houses crammed one against the other and surrounded by defensive outer walls. Their tools were made

from locally found obsidian and flint; pottery was beautifully burnished, and included stylized figures representing the mother goddess.

Oriental influence brought southeast Anatolia into the **Chalcolithic Age**. The interaction of cultures, which was probably of a commercial and technical nature, is particularly noticeable in pottery types and the use of metal tools; shared features are found through Upper Mesopotamia, northern Syria and into eastern Anatolia (especially the Lake Van region and Cilicia). Sites of this period were more like fortified towns, and frequent evidence of violent destruction suggests that they existed in a hostile environment, regularly at war with each other or with new arrivals. In central Anatolia and the west Anatolian lakeland there was less influence from the east; cultures that developed here are characterized by bright, burnished pottery and idols of local deities.

The third-millennium BC **Bronze Age** witnessed the rise of local dynasties, and the organization of land resources by communities inhabiting fortified settlements. The sophisticated metal equipment found in the royal cemetery of **Alaca Höyük** suggests metallurgy was one of the principal reasons for the economic rise of the early Anatolian kings. Religious art included standards crowned with highly stylized deer and bulls, and hoards of gold jewellery as well as musical instruments were prominent among the finds in the tombs. It is thought that the Alaca dynasty originated in northeast Anatolia, since their culture shows similarities to those in the Caucasian and Pontic border zones.

Meanwhile, on the south and west **coasts**, trade was becoming increasingly important, as were the piratic activities of local rulers, whose bases appear from their architecture to have had affinities with later Indo-European cultures. On the Aegean, **Troy** was in trading contact with the Aegean islands and mainland Greece, and with other Anatolian rulers in the southeast, around present-day Tarsus and Mersin. Anatolian metals, jewellery, weapons and tableware were exported in exchange for exotic goods such as lapis lazuli, rock crystal and ivory. The material advantages of a coastal situation, which provided naval contacts with the Aegean and the Orient (particularly Syrian trading ports), are obvious from the comparative wealth amassed by the rulers of cities like Troy, evidenced in finds such as the so-called "Treasure of Priam", a third-millennium hoard of jewellery and tableware discovered in the late nineteenth century.

The **Middle and Late Bronze Ages**, during the second millennium BC, began with a period of violent destruction and turbulence, out of which a race of people known as the **Hatti** emerged in central Anatolia. Their traditions and culture were later to be assimilated by the Hittites. This was an age of highly organized and regular commerce along fixed trading routes, and many Anatolian cities were annexed by colonies of Assyrian business agents. Their meticulous records have been discovered in many places, including the most famous of all these trade centres, Karum near Kaneş (modern Kültepe) in South Central Anatolia. Textiles and tin were the main imports, and the principal export was copper. The city itself was a fortified citadel with a number of large buildings surrounding open courtyards. Pottery was ornamental and showed a high degree of skill in its craftsmanship.

THE HITTITES

Perhaps the first really major civilization to emerge in Anatolia was the **Hittite** one. The Hittites seem to have first appeared, moving into Hatti territory, around 2000 BC, but their so-called "Old Kingdom" is reckoned to have been founded by King Labarnas around 1700–1600 BC. The capital at Hattuşaş was created by his son and successor, Hattusilis I, remaining a power to be reckoned with – though outlying territories in northern Syria and Babylonia were lost earlier – until 1200 BC.

Hattuşaş was a huge city for its time, surrounded by a six-kilometre-long fortified wall. The kings resided in a fortified citadel located on a rock overlooking a gorge to the north of the city; within were domestic quarters, administrative buildings, storage units and archives. The Hittites developed their artistic style from traditions of their Anatolian predecessors, and unlike their Syrian neighbours were never overwhelmed by Mesopotamian and Egyptian art. The principal examples are enormous rock-cut reliefs, including warrior gods and stylized sphinx-like beings, adapted from the Egyptian tradition to Hittite stylistic principles.

At **Yazılıkaya**, a temple site not far from the capital, processions of gods and goddesses –

one of whom is shown embracing a Hittite king, in an obvious expression of supposed kinship – are carved on the walls of an open chamber. While the warlike, imperialist nature of the Hittite rulers left an enduring impression on a previously non-aggressive Anatolia, the Hittites are also known for the humanity of their constitution and religion, and for a highly developed sense of ethics. Diplomacy was preferred to warfare, and often cemented by royal marriages. A queen ruled as an equal with her husband, and prisoners of war were not horribly tortured as they were elsewhere in the Middle East. Libraries, archives and bureaucracy all had their place in Hittite society, and rulers were not despotic but tied to a constitution like their subjects. The Old Kingdom dynasty lasted several generations before being riven, apparently by succession struggles: after a confused interlude, the state was re-established as the Hittite Empire by Tudhaliyas II, in about 1430 BC. By this time a rival power had arisen in Upper Mesopotamia. The Mitanni, ruled by an Indo-European dynasty, were basically East Anatolian Hurrians. They exerted an important cultural influence on the Hittite Empire before being defeated in battle by the Hittite ruler Suppiluliumas (1385–1345 BC).

Under Muwatallis the Hittites confirmed their military strength at the Battle of Kadesh (1290 BC), where they defeated the Egyptians under Ramses II. After the battle, friendship between the two dynasties was cemented by the division of Syria and by the marriage of Ramses II to a daughter of another Hittite ruler, Hattusilis III, in 1250 BC. The real threat to both, however, lay with the arrival of the **"Sea Peoples"**, early Iron Age merchants from the Greek archipelagos and mainland, which was to have widespread repercussions and eventually destroy the old order completely.

The land-bound Hittite Empire was surrounded by **smaller states**. The southern and western coasts were inhabited by tribes of Indo-European stock, with their own kings, languages and feuds, and a major interest in seaborne trade. In the southeast Mediterranean, the land originally known as Cilicia was taken from the Hittites by Hurrians, and referred to as Kizzuwadna. They remained closely related to the Hittites, however, with regular intermarriage between the respective ruling families.

On the west coast, a greater degree of independence on the part of local dynasties meant that their activities were not well documented in Hittite records, but excavations at the site of Troy show that, simultaneous with the apogee of Hittite power, Troy was being rebuilt by a new dynasty, and great supplies were amassed inside the large citadel. The second-millennium BC Trojans were serious rivals to the Greeks in the Aegean, and Troy was ultimately sacked by the Greeks around 1200 BC in the **Trojan War**, at about the same time as the Hittite Empire finally collapsed.

THE POST-HITTITE ERA

The same factors can ultimately account for the demise of both civilizations: migrations, invasions, and sudden increased pressures from all sides. New tribes, of Indo-European origin, poured into Anatolia from east and west. The Hittite capital and other centres of Hittite rule were attacked and burnt as Anatolia entered a long cultural Dark Age.

Small city-states were founded in the southeast by the surviving Hittites and their Anatolian allies, and these **neo-Hittite** centres, for instance at Malatya, Sakça Gözü and Karatepe, managed to salvage something of the old culture from the destruction of the empire. Cities were better fortified, with inner and outer defensive walls, but the traditional lions which stood guard at their gates were crudely carved in comparison with those which had performed the same task in the Old Hittite cities. The neo-Hittite culture was important as a bridge between the Bronze and Iron Ages, rescuing Hittite traditions and at the same time creating lively trading centres for the first Greek **Iron Age** merchants. Thus early Greek art was confronted by Hittite reliefs and statuary, and knowledge of oriental mythology and religion was also transmitted to Greece via the neo-Hittites. The neo-Hittite city-states were finally conquered and destroyed by the Arameans and the Assyrians in the eighth century BC.

To the east, in the region which was later to be known as Armenia, the kingdom of **Urartu** was founded by a people thought to be descendants of the native Anatolian Hurrian race. Their cities, including the capital at Tushpa near Lake Van, were well engineered, with walled citadels and elaborate tunnel systems for escape or survival under attack. The Urartians extended their power into central Anatolia and northern Syria before they were curbed, in the second half of the eighth century BC, by the Assyrians. The Urartians specialized in metalwork, and their bronzeware was traded as far away as Greece.

To the west, a new tribe of immigrants who attained some prominence in the eighth century BC, especially under their most famous king Midas, were the **Phrygians**. Their origins are unknown, but the historical connection between Greeks and Phrygians can perhaps be ascribed to a blood relationship between them. Their capital was at Gordion, on a strategic east–west trading route, by the River Sangarius (today the Sakarya). **King Midas**, according to Greek tradition, had a Greek wife and dedicated a throne at the sanctuary of Delphi. His kingdom reached its height during his rule, around 725 BC, but when Cimmerian horsemen came to loot and burn Gordion, he is said to have committed suicide in despair, and the Phrygian kingdom came to an abrupt end. The tumulus ascribed to King Midas bears witness to his power: nearly fifty metres high, it contained a profuse collection of artefacts, including textiles and richly carved furniture, from as far away as Urartu.

The southwest coast was inhabited during the Iron Age by the **Lycians**, probably the survivors of a nation of sailors and pirates referred to as the "Lukka" in Bronze Age records. Their language and culture had a local pedigree, suggesting that they were descendants of the native Anatolian Luvians, and their architecture, timber forms copied in stone, was strikingly unique. Greek influence on the Lycians is attested to in the Bronze Age by the legend of Bellerophon and the Chimera, and in the sixth century BC Lycia became gradually more imbued with Greek influence.

The country of the **Lydians** was an inland district of western Anatolia, its capital at Sardis in the Hermus valley. The Lydians survived the Bronze Age with a language of Anatolian derivation, emerging from the turmoil of the eighth century BC to dominate western Anatolia, including areas which had previously been Phrygian. Lydian ivories, textiles, perfumes and jewellery were exported to Greece and the East, and their refined and elegant art forms influenced those of Greek Ionia and even Persia.

THE PERSIANS AND ALEXANDER

Lydian power lasted until 546 BC, when their last king, **Croesus**, was defeated by the newly ascendant **Persian Empire** under **Cyrus**. Over the next half-century, the Persians subdued the Greek coastal trading colonies as well as the entire interior, ending the last vestiges of Anatolian self-rule. **Satraps** (compliant locally born puppets) were installed in various seats of power and obliged to pay tribute to the self-styled Great King of the Persians; even more rankling was the fact that Persian allies, such as the Phoenicians, were favoured at the expense of the Greek Anatolian cities in their role as commercial intermediaries with the west. In 499 BC, western Anatolia, under the leadership of Miletus, **revolted** against Persian rule, but in the absence of massive aid from mainland Greece, the rebellion was doomed to fail. Even so, it took the Persians under Darius I five years to suppress the insurrection, which culminated in the naval battle of Lade island, just off Miletus.

Enraged by even the token support of the Athenians for the rebels, **Darius** and his successor **Xerxes** crossed into Greece proper and were soundly defeated at the famous land battles of Marathon and Plataea, and the sea engagements of Salamis and Mycale, the latter in the straits between Samos and Anatolia. This blunting of Persian strength initially availed the cities of Asia Minor little, though as time went on they were able to exploit the growing rivalry between Athens and Sparta to negotiate a bit more autonomy. Indeed by the middle of the fourth century BC, some virtually independent dynasties had arisen in western Anatolia, the most notable being the **Hecatomnid** clan at Halicarnassus, whose more illustrious rulers included the Hellenizing **Mausolus** (377–353 BC) and his wife and successor **Artemisia II**.

In spring 334 BC, a new power swept out of Macedonia and across Asia Minor: **Alexander**, later the Great, possessed of little other than a guiding vision and some Corinthian volunteers to supplement his small Macedonian army. Having crossed the Dardanelles near present-day Çanakkale, he quickly defeated the Persians at nearby Granicus (today Biga), and proceeded down the west coast via all of the major cities, treating them with lenience or harshness depending on whether or not they rallied to his standard. Having wintered in Lycia, Alexander and his juggernaut rolled on across Pamphylia, inland to Gordion where he cut the eponymous knot with his sword, then crossed the Toros (Taurus) range into coastal Cilicia, intent on attacking the Persian heartland beyond Syria. **Darius III** awaited Alexander at **Issus** (modern Dörtyol), but was soundly defeated by the Macedonians despite outnumbering them two to one; this conquest of Anatolia in less than a year was indicative as much of rottenness at the core of Persian rule as it was of Alexander's military genius.

The prodigy swept on through Persia proper as far as the Indus valley, but died of a fever – or possibly poisoning – at Babylon on the return trip, in 323 BC. Following his death, Alexander's generals divided the vast Anatolian empire between them: **Lysimachus** took the west, while **Seleucus** – succeeded by **Antiochus** – received most of the southeast of the peninsula; much of the centre and north remained independent. Lysimachus' most important successor was **Philetarus**, who contrived to keep the treasure of Pergamon intact and made it the greatest Hellenistic city of Asia Minor. By the end of the second century BC, however, his heir **Attalus III** virtually invited the Romans into Anatolia by dying without issue, having willed the kingdom of Pergamon to them.

ROMAN RULE

Almost immediately Roman rule in Asia Minor was challenged by **Mithridates of Pontus** (ruled 110–63 BC), a brilliant, resourceful polymath and unscrupulous opponent. From 89 BC on, his rebellious campaigns kept an assortment of Roman generals occupied, most notably Sulla, Lucullus and Pompey. In 72 BC, at a low point in his fortunes, Mithridates sought refuge at the court of Tigranes the Great of **Armenia**, whose kingdom had enjoyed three decades of regional power and prosperity; this now came to an end as the Romans invaded Armenian territory in response to Tigranes' cooperation with Mithridates. It suited the Romans to maintain Armenia as a buffer principality between themselves and the **Parthians** on the east, successors to the Persian Empire; the accession of the first emperor Augustus marked the start of fairly durable peace in Anatolia proper, though the eastern frontier would always be problematic, with Romans and Parthians quarrelling ostensibly over who should designate the occupant of the Armenian throne, but in reality probing for a military opening.

In general, however, Anatolia prospered under Roman imperial rule, as witness the vast quantity of ruined cities dating from this period, especially those endowed during the reign of **Hadrian** (117–138 AD). Politically, however, it always remained a backwater, with only the ethnographic and geographic comments of such writers as Strabo and Pliny to flesh out life here – as well as the first-century AD biblical writings of **Saint Paul** during his various evangelical tours of Asia Minor.

In 284 AD, the emperor **Diocletian** attempted a solution to pressing imperial problems by dividing the empire into two administrative units, each ruled by an emperor (or *Augustus*) acting in concert with a designated successor (or *Caesar*), together comprising the so-called tetrarchy. Early in the fourth century, however, this system collapsed into civil war. The victor, **Constantine**, moved the headquarters of the eastern portion from Salonica to the minor, but strategically located, ancient Greek town of **Byzantium**, on the western shores of the Bosphorus straits linking the Black Sea and the Sea of Marmara. This new capital – "New Rome" – was enlarged and consciously rebuilt in imitation of the "old" Rome, and presently renamed **Constantinople** in the emperor's honour. Soon afterwards Constantine announced his espousal of Christianity, which by the end of the century became the state religion of an empire which had long persecuted Christians.

The unity of the empire, too unwieldy to be governed from a single centre, did not survive long beyond the forceful rule of Constantine. **Theodosius the Great**, during whose 379–395 reign paganism was officially proscribed, was the last sovereign of a united empire, which upon his death was formally **divided** into two realms: the western one Latin-speaking and Rome-based, the eastern part Greek-speaking and focused on Constantinople.

THE BYZANTINE EMPIRE

The western provinces had always been financially dependent on the east, and ineffective rule in the west meant that it could not easily survive the loss of this revenue – or the invasions of "barbarian" tribes from the north. The wealthier, more densely populated **Byzantine**

Empire – as the east came to be known – had abler rulers and, after a brief period of over-extension, more defensible frontiers. But internal **religious disputes** would contribute heavily to weakening the empire. Rule from Constantinople was resented in the southern and eastern border provinces of Egypt, Palestine, Syria and Armenia, not only because the indigenous cultures were so different from Classical Greece and Rome, but also because the churches in these areas embraced the **Monophysite doctrine**, which maintained that Christ had a single divine nature. Until the thirteenth century clerics in the capital would persecute the "heretics" on the periphery, at the same time resenting claims to papal supremacy in Rome and quarrelling over points of belief with the west. All this would ultimately culminate in the separation of the eastern **Orthodox** and western **Roman Catholic** churches in 1054.

Byzantium's response to the collapse of the west, brought on by the "barbarian" raids of the fifth and sixth centuries, was vehement and expansionist – or more accurately, nostalgic. The energetic emperor **Justinian** (527–565) and his empress Theodora, attempted to recapture the glory and territory of ancient Rome in a series of military campaigns throughout the Mediterranean basin. The imperial generals Narses and Belisarius reabsorbed Italy, North Africa and southern Spain into the empire, though the Byzantines were unable to stem the flow of Slavs into the Balkans, and were forced to adopt an uneasy truce with the Persian Empire after a long and inconclusive war.

After the quelling of the **Nika revolt** in 532, when Theodora saved her husband from deposition by the Hippodrome factions, Justinian was also able to carry out an ambitious **domestic agenda**. He inaugurated a widespread programme of construction and public works, particularly in Constantinople, which resulted in such masterpieces as the church of **Aya Sofya** (Haghia Sophia) in the capital and San Vitale in Ravenna. Justinian's streamlining and codification of the huge and often contradictory body of old Roman **law** was perhaps his most enduring achievement: the new code became the basis for the medieval legal systems of France, Germany and Italy. In his attempts to mediate between the Monophysites of the east and the papacy, however, the emperor was less successful – the extent of the "heresy" can be judged by the fact that Theodora herself is said to have been sympathetic to the Monophysites.

Justinian's reign marked the definitive emergence of a strictly Byzantine, as opposed to Roman, identity, with institutions that were to sustain the empire for the balance of its life. Having widened its boundaries to their maximum extent and established the theocratic nature of Byzantium, he can be reckoned one of the greatest of Byzantine emperors. In the long run, though, many of his achievements proved ephemeral, and so exhausted the empire's resources that it had difficulty withstanding subsequent outside attacks.

LATER BYZANTIUM . . . AND DECLINE

In the two centuries following Justinian's death the character of the empire changed radically. All of his peripheral conquests were lost: the western realms to the Lombards and Goths, the southeastern provinces in the seventh century to the Persians and Arab raiders. By 711, the Byzantine Empire consisted only of the Balkan coasts, parts of Italy, and **Anatolia**, which would henceforth be the most important part of the empire. Equally significant, the empire had acquired a strongly Greek character, both linguistically and philosophically, and Latin influence faded as relations with Rome worsened, particularly during the reign of Irene, whom the pope refused to recognize as empress.

It was only from 867 onward that the empire regained any of its old resilience. The so-called **Macedonian** dynasty, founded by **Basil I**, a former stable boy who rendered Justinian's law code into Greek, reversed Byzantium's fortunes. Under **Basil II** (976–1025), nicknamed "Bulgar-Slayer" for his ruthless campaigns against the Slavs, the empire again swelled its frontiers well into present-day eastern Turkey and up the Balkan peninsula, while Constantinople itself enjoyed unparalleled prosperity at the crossroads of the new Eurasian trade routes. Literature and the arts flourished, and missionaries converted many Balkan Slavs to the Orthodox Church.

After the reign of the second Basil, however, the empire began its **final decline**, slow but relentless over the course of four centuries. Although by the early eleventh century the empire seemed consolidated into a stable state

centred on most of the Balkans, the Aegean islands and Anatolia, the potential for both internal and external disruption was great. For the first six decades of the new millennium, Anatolia was in a state of virtual **civil war**, with the clique of civilian bureaucrats in Constantinople pitted against the caste of landed generals out in the countryside. Each promoted their own candidates for the throne, resulting in a succession of nonentities as emperors, amenable to manipulation by either faction, and utterly unequal to the external threats the empire would soon face. Simultaneously the Orthodox patriarchate renewed its vendetta against the **Monophysite Churches**, whose members were concentrated in the critical eastern borderlands. The warlords reduced the free peasantry to serfdom, eliminating the main source of revenue and military recruitment; the bureaucrats, usually in control at Constantinople, matched their own extravagance with stinginess toward the army – which increasingly came to be staffed by unreliable mercenaries.

The first major threats came from the west. The **Normans**, their greed excited by the reputation of Byzantine craftsmanship and splendour, invaded the Balkans late in the eleventh century, and were only repulsed with help from the **Venetians**, who in return demanded extensive trading concessions within the empire – as did the **Genoese**. Government tolls and taxes plummeted as imperial monopolies were broken by the new Latin maritime powers, and western covetousness – which would culminate in the sacking of Constantinople by the Fourth Crusade in 1204 – knew no bounds. Though able emperors did emerge from the twelfth-century **Comnenus** dynasty and the later **Paleologus** line, without consistent western aid the Byzantines were doomed to fight a long, rearguard action against enemies from the east and north. The imperial twilight was distinguished by a final flourishing of sacred art and architecture, as Anatolia and the Balkans – as if in defiance of the political facts – were adorned with numerous beautiful **churches** which were this period's main contribution to posterity.

THE ARRIVAL OF THE TURKS

Early in the eleventh century a new people had begun raiding Byzantine territory from the east. They had originally emerged in Mongolia during the seventh or eighth century, a shamanistic, nomadic bunch whom the Chinese called "Tu-kueh" or *Dürkö* – **Turks** to the West. Driven by drought and population pressure to seek new pastures, the Turkish tribes began migrating westward, encountering the Arabs by the ninth century. The latter, recognizing their martial virtues, recruited them as auxiliaries and began converting them to Islam, a process mostly completed by the tenth century.

One branch of the Turkish tribes, followers of the chieftain **Selçuk**, adopted a settled life and **Sunni** Islam, setting down roots in Baghdad. The majority, however, referred to by the convenient catch-all of "Turcoman", remained nomadic and heterodox in belief, drawing on the **Shi'ite and pagan** heritages, and rarely amenable to control by any state. The Selçuk rulers took advantage of their warrior zeal by diverting them from their own realms into those of the Byzantines.

The raiders penetrated as an advance guard deep into Byzantine Armenia, and it was as much to restrain them as to confront the Byzantines that the Selçuk ruler Alparslan marched north from Baghdad in **1071**. Meeting, almost accidentally, the motley, demoralized armies of Byzantine emperor Romanus IV Diogenes, he defeated them easily at **Manzikert** (Malazgirt). The Selçuks didn't follow up this victory, but it did leave the way open to redoubled rampages by the Turcomans across all of Anatolia. The Byzantines, alternately menaced and assisted by Latin Crusaders, managed to reoccupy the western third of Anatolia, plus the Black Sea and Mediterranean coasts, by the mid-twelfth century, by which time the Selçuks had established a state in the area devastated by the unruly Turcomans. This was the **Sultanate of Rum**, with its capital at Konya (Iconium). After winning the battle of **Myriokephalo**, nearby, in 1176, the new Selçuk state came to terms with the Byzantines.

After the occupation of Constantinople by the **Fourth Crusade** in 1204, the Selçuks continued their good relations with the provisional Byzantine Empire based at Nicaea; with peace assured, the Sultanate of Rum evolved into a highly cultured mini-empire at the heart of Anatolia, reaching its zenith in the first half of the thirteenth century. Their territories were endowed with a system of imposing *kervansarays*, *medreses*, bridges and other public monuments, with the encouragement of trade

being paramount. On a smaller scale, the Selçuks excelled in tile and relief work, and in the spiritual field the Sultanate, despite its Sunni orientation, provided a refuge for many heterodox religious figures, including Celâleddin Rumi, founder of the Mevlevi dervish order.

Before long, however, a new scourge appeared in the form of the **Mongols**; they crushed the Selçuk armies at the battle of **Köse Dağ** in 1243, and although the sultanate lingered on until the turn of the century, the Turcoman tribes, never fully pacified, took the opportunity to swarm over the lands of both the Selçuks and the Byzantines, who had virtually abandoned Asia Minor after returning to Constantinople in 1261. There was to be a two-century gap in which there was no single political authority on the Anatolian peninsula, but during which time the process of Turkification and Islamization, begun in 1071, continued gradually nonetheless.

THE RISE OF THE OTTOMANS

In the turmoil following the collapse of the Selçuk state, Anatolia fragmented into numerous petty, mostly Turcoman **emirates**: the Saltuks and Mongol İlhanids in the northeast, the Mengüçeh near Erzincan, the Aydınoğlu clan in the central Aegean, the Menteşe in the southwest Aegean, the Karamanids in the Toros mountains, the Artukids in the Euphrates basin, the Danişmendids, occupying a huge swathe from Malatya to Amasya, and the Hamidoğlu around the Pisidian lakes, are just a few of the short-lived principalities who left monuments scattered across modern Turkey.

The emirate centred around Söğüt, near Eskişehir, settled on lands granted to the chieftain Ertoğrul by Selçuk ruler Alâeddin, was not initially an important one. Ertoğrul was a typical *gazi*, a recent convert to Islam patrolling the frontier marches between Selçuk and Byzantine territory, carrying the faith ever westward in the face of infidel opposition. His son **Osman**, however, head of the clan from the 1290s onwards, was to give his name to a dynasty: *Osmanlı* in Turkish, "**Ottoman**" to the West. Spurred by proximity to Constantinople, the emirate began to expand under Osman's son **Orhan**, who took the important Byzantine centres of Bursa and İznik by the 1330s, and married into the Byzantine nobility, the first of several Ottoman princes who would have Greek Orthodox in-laws.

Anatolian culture had for some time been a hybrid one, with frequent intermarriage between Muslims and Christians, many descendants or converts bilingual in Greek and Turkish, and certain dervish orders – particularly the Bektaşi – effecting a synthesis between Islam and numerically declining Christianity. As Byzantine authority in a given area diminished, the assets and facilities of Christian monasteries were often appropriated by the **vakıfs** or Islamic pious foundations, which sponsored various public welfare projects; the demoralized Christian priesthood and population often converted to Islam simultaneously, though this was by no means mandatory or encouraged since under Islamic law this reduced tax revenue.

Complementing these processes was the **devşirme**, a custom that arose in the fourteenth century whereby a certain percentage of boys from conquered Christian districts were levied by the Ottomans to serve as an elite force, the **janissaries**. They became slaves of the sultan, were admitted to the more eclectic Bektaşi branch of Islam, and were given the best training available with an eye to their becoming not only warriors but Ottoman administrators. Free-born Muslims were expressly ineligible for elevation to the corps, and promotion was strictly on grounds of ability, so that (until abuses crept in) the Ottoman state, up to and including the office of grand vizier, was run by converts from Christianity. The only chance for advancement for those born Muslim was within the **ulema**, the body of Koranic sages who decreed on religious matters, or as a member of the **defterdar** or "accountant" class – a huge bureaucracy overseeing the empire's various sources of revenue.

Though the janissaries formed a powerful pretorian guard, they were supplemented by a standing army, whose members were paid indirectly by assignment of a **timar** or land grant. All conquered territory remained the property of the sultan, who dispensed such grants with the understanding that the man's "salary" was the proceeds of the estate – and that he remained liable for armed service whenever his ruler summoned him. Initially *timar*s reverted to the crown upon the holder's death, with his sons having to re-earn their portion by service. This system, based heavily on Byzantine practice, was not genuinely feudal, and resulted in a stability of rule that often prompted immigration of Christian peasantry from mis-administered neighbouring territory.

Despite religious tolerance shown to Christians of whatever rank, Ottoman society was **hierarchical**, with distinctions between Muslims and infidels – known as *raya*, or "cattle" – preserved in every particular from dress code to unequal status before the law. Christians – chiefly Armenians and Greeks – were not conscripted for campaigns, and hence could not qualify for land grants; instead they paid a tax in lieu of military service, and tended to congregate in towns and cities as tradesmen.

To continue the system of *timar*s, more land had to be made available for awarding, and the *gazi* mentality continued. By the mid-fourteenth century the Ottomans had crossed the Sea of Marmara to Thrace, and in 1362 **Sultan Murat I** took Edirne. Constantinople was virtually surrounded by Turkish territory, and indeed the almost-vanished Byzantine Empire existed on Ottoman sufferance, reduced to vassaldom and the necessity of calling on Turkish aid (and marrying its princesses to Ottoman chieftains) to fend off challenges from Catalans, Slavs and Hungarians. With the Latin and Orthodox Christians at each other's throats, Ottoman ascendancy was virtually assured, and Murat further isolated Constantinople with new acquisitions in the lower Balkans, routing a Serbian coalition at **Kosovo** in 1389. Murdered on the battlefield by a Serbian infiltrator, he was succeeded by his elder son **Beyazit I**, who established an unfortunate precedent by promptly strangling his brother Yakub to assure his own succession. Beyazit, nicknamed **Yıldırım** or "Lightning" for his swift deployments in battle, bested a huge Hungarian/Crusader army at Bulgarian Nicopolis in 1396, and the fall of Constantinople seemed imminent.

However, in expanding eastwards into Anatolia, Beyazit – more impulsive and less methodical than his father – had both overextended himself and antagonized the great Mongol warrior **Tamerlane**. Tamerlane routed Beyazit's armies at the **Battle of Ankara** in 1402, trundling the captive sultan about in a cage for a year before his demise, and proceeded to lay waste to much of Anatolia. Even though the Mongols soon vanished, the remnant of the Byzantine Empire was granted a fifty-year reprieve, and for a decade the fate of the Ottoman line hung in the balance as

Beyazit's four sons fought a civil war. The victor, Mehmet I, and his successor the mystically inclined Murat II, restored Ottoman fortunes, the latter deflecting one last half-hearted Latin Crusade in 1444.

But the greatest prize – **Constantinople** – still eluded the Ottomans. Both symbolically, as the seat of two prior empires, and practically – as a naval base controlling passage between the Black Sea and the Mediterranean – its capture was imperative. **Mehmet II**, who ascended the throne in 1451, immediately began preparations for the deed, studding the sea approaches to the now half-depopulated capital with fortresses, engaging ballistics and artillery experts from Europe with an eye to breaching the city walls, and for the first time outfitting a substantial Ottoman fleet. His Byzantine adversaries hastily concluded a union with the Catholic Church, expecting Latin aid to materialize forthwith, but only a trickle of Genoese and Venetian ships and men arrived. The final siege of Constantinople, in the spring of 1453, lasted seven weeks, ending on **29 May** when the sultan's armies finally succeeded in entering the city while the last Byzantine emperor died unnoticed in the melee.

Mehmet's epithet was henceforth *Fatih*, "the Conqueror", and there was no longer any room for doubt that the Ottoman Empire was the legitimate successor of the Roman and Byzantine ones. The imitation of Roman and Byzantine models in Ottoman imperial practice, begun in the preceeding century and a half, increased.

Mehmet immediately set about refurbishing the city, now renamed İstanbul, as a worthy capital of the empire, repopulating it with both Muslims and Christians from rural areas, establishing markets and public welfare institutions, and constructing a fine palace at Topkapı. The non-Muslim communities were organized into **millets** or "nations", headed by a patriarch or rabbi, answerable for his flock's good behaviour and under whom Greek or Slavic Orthodox, Armenian and Jew were governed by their own communal laws; this system, which tended to minimize sectarian disorder and guaranteed more freedom of worship than prevalent in contemporary Europe, persisted until 1926.

Overseas, Mehmet's mixed military record demonstrated that such a feat as the capture of Constantinople was not easily duplicated. Defeats along the Danube were followed by easier mop-up campaigns during 1458–60 in the Peloponnese and along the Black Sea, eliminating satellite Byzantine states and their Genoese cohorts. Persisting in the pre-conquest pattern of alternating European and Asian campaigns, Mehmet returned to the Balkans, adding Wallachia, most of present-day Greece, Bosnia-Herzegovina and part of Albania to his domains, while simultaneously building up his navy to better counter his main rivals, the Venetians. Back in Anatolia, the Conqueror annexed the Karamanid emirate and neutralized the forces of the Akkoyun Turcomans in eastern Anatolia.

Mehmet was succeeded in 1481 by his son **Beyazit II**, "the Pious", who despite a retiring disposition presided over the final relegation of Venice to secondary naval-power status – often by the enlistment of pirates into the Ottoman navy – and realized his father's ambition of revitalizing the core territory of the Byzantine Empire. The skills of Greek renegade statesmen and Italian mercenaries were supplemented in 1493 by the scientific knowledge of **Iberian Jews**, the ancestors of most contemporary Turkish Jewry, fetched by "mercy ships" sent by the sultan upon their expulsion from Spain and Portugal.

In 1512 Beyazit was forced to abdicate by his son **Selim I**, a vigorous personality in the mould of his grandfather, but with an added streak of wanton cruelty and bigotry, hence his epithet *Yavuz* ("the Fierce" – known as "the Grim" to the West). Both of Selim's predecessors had privately toyed with Sufic and heterodox Persian doctrines, but now religious orthodoxy was seen as vital within the Ottoman realm, since neighbour and rival Shah Ismail of Persia was starting to promote **Shi'ism** both within and without his frontiers. In an echo of the Catholic-Protestant bloodletting in Europe, Selim massacred 40,000 Shi'ites in Anatolia, and went on to defeat the Shah at east Anatolian **Çaldıran** in 1514. Rather than press on into Persia, however, Selim turned his armies south against the Mamluks, overrunning Mesopotamia, Syria and Egypt by 1516 and occupying at one fell swoop most of the **holy cities** of Islam. By capturing the caliph resident in Cairo and transporting him back to İstanbul, Selim essentially proved his claim to be the Defender of the (Sunni) Faith – and the **caliphate** effectively became identical with the Ottoman sultanate.

Though the empire would reach its greatest physical extent after his death, it was **Süleyman the Magnificent** who laid the foundations for this expansion during a 46-year reign which began in 1520. In his first few years on the throne, the strongholds of the Knights of Saint John at Rhodes and Bodrum – from where they controlled the sea lanes to Egypt – were taken, as was Belgrade, leaving the way further up the Danube valley unguarded. By 1526 Budapest, and most of Hungary, was in Ottoman hands, with the Habsburgs compelled to pay tribute for retaining a small portion. Campaigns in Persia and the Arabian peninsula were successful, but the first siege of Vienna in 1529 was not – and nor was an attempt to drive the Portuguese out of the Indian Ocean. The Ottomans were better able to control the Mediterranean, with such admirals as Greek-born Barbaros Hayrettin (**Barbarossa**) and his protégé Turgut Reis besting Venetian-Habsburg fleets. But in 1565 the siege of Malta, where the Knights of Saint John had retreated, failed, marking the end of the Mediterranean as an Ottoman lake. None the less the Ottoman Empire, however unwieldy, heterogenous and difficult to defend, was arguably the leading power of the sixteenth century.

It was, not surprisingly, regarded with a mixture of terror and fascination by the states of Europe; only the **French**, under Francis I, saw the possibility of alliance and manipulation, concluding a treaty with the Ottomans in **1536**. In addition to granting France trading advantages in the empire, the treaty's commercial clauses set forth various privileges for French nationals which came to be known as the **Capitulations**: exemption from most Ottoman taxes, and the right to be judged by their own consuls under foreign law. What began as an inducement to increased trade offered from a position of strength became, as time passed, a pernicious erosion of Turkish sovereignty, as many European nations and overseas companies secured such Capitulations for themselves, extending rights of immunity to local employees (usually Christian) provided with appropriate passports.

Domestically Süleyman distinguished himself as an administrator, legislator, builder and patron of the arts, and indeed in Turkey he is known as *Kanuni*, "the Lawgiver". In his personal life, however, his judgement was to have enduringly harmful consequences for the Ottoman state. He became so enamoured of his favourite concubine **Roxelana** that he broke with Ottoman precedent and actually married her. Scheming and ambitious, she used her influence over the sultan to turn him against his capable son and heir (by a previous liaison), **Mustafa**, inciting Süleyman to murder him and later her own son Beyazit – as well as his first grand vizier, İbrahim. Perhaps a bad conscience over these deeds heightened Süleyman's basic moroseness and introversion, and he died a lonely man on his last campaign on the Danube in 1566. With his two ablest sons gone, there were no obstacles to the succession of Roxelana's oldest son, the useless Selim.

THE CENTURIES OF DECLINE

While it's impossible to assign an exact date to the beginning of the Ottoman Empire's **decline**, the reign of the ineffectual **Selim II** (Selim the Sot to the west) is as good a start as any. He was followed by sixteen other, generally mediocre sultans, of whom only the bloodthirsty but resolute **Murat IV**, and the peace-loving aesthete **Ahmet II**, who instituted the cult of the tulip, did much to prevent the gradual deterioration. The decay of the empire was nevertheless almost imperceptibly gradual over a period of nearly three centuries, with spells of retrenchment and even territorial expansion.

It is far easier to catalogue the **causes** of the decline. From Roxelana's time onwards the **harem** was moved onto the grounds of the Topkapı palace itself, so that the intrigues of its tenants bore directly on day-to-day government. At the start of the seventeenth century the previous, grisly custom of fratricide upon the enthronement of a new sultan was abandoned in favour of the confinement of the other heirs-apparent; sequestered in the so-called **Kafes** or **Cage** for years (previously, heirs would serve an "apprenticeship" as a provincial governor), the next-in-line was not just inexperienced, but frequently emerged from captivity mentally and physically deranged. Few sultans campaigned overseas any longer, or presided personally over the *divan* (council of state), instead delegating most authority to their **grand viziers**.

When these viziers were able and honest, like those from the Albanian Köprülü clan of the seventeenth century, the downward slide of the empire was halted or reversed, but on the whole nepotism and **corruption** flourished in the decadent palace atmosphere. The early Ottoman principle of meritocracy was replaced by a **hereditary aristocracy**; the *devşirme* or levy of Christian boys was all but abandoned by the end of the seventeenth century, and the janissary corps was no longer celibate or religiously exclusive: sinecure passed from father to son, and the corps (with its payroll) expanded further as free Muslims rushed to enrol. Many – in direct contradiction of the institution's purpose – were artisans whose only martial act was to show up to collect pay, demands for more of which often prompted the inefficient, swollen corps to rebel, extorting money from hapless villagers and sultans alike, and on several occasions to depose and murder the latter. Similarly, land grants to the *sipahı* (cavalry) tended to become hereditary, and the holders evolved into a class of local warlord (the *derebeys* or "lords of the valley"). Both janissary and *sipahı* proved increasingly reluctant to fight the long wars now common, especially when booty or pay was not forthcoming. Revolts of these and other idle, underpaid troops devastated Anatolia, already wracked by population pressure and land shortage; thus began a steady rural depopulation which continues today.

Much of the impetus for decline came, however, from **outside** the empire. The influx into the Mediterranean of gold and silver from the Spanish conquests in the New World set off a spiral of inflation and debased coinage. The Age of Exploration saw new sea routes forged around Africa to the East Indies, reducing the importance of overland caravan routes through Ottoman territories. Most importantly, Europe underwent the **Renaissance** and **industrialization**, while the Ottomans remained stagnant under the influence of the conservative *ulema*. The Turks had become used to easily despatching the ragtag armies of assorted principalities during the fifteenth and sixteenth centuries, and failed to grasp the reasons for their frequent defeats thereafter. New, highly centralized nation-states in the West had established rigorously trained standing armies and navies, availing themselves of the benefits of new arma-

ments, ships and navigation, direct outgrowths of the Renaissance's spur to scientific enquiry. To these manifestations of European superiority the Ottomans – especially the janissary corps – generally reacted disdainfully, seeing no reason to learn from the infidels given the perfection of Islam.

External **evidence** of the rot took nearly a century to show: although the defeat of an Ottoman fleet at **Lepanto** (today Greek Nafpaktos) in 1571, by a combined Venetian, Spanish and papal armada, shattered the myth of Turkish invincibility, the victory was essentially neutralized by the capture of Cyprus from Venice the same year, and the reconquest of North Africa by 1578. The 1600s proceeded well, with the successful siege of Crete and seizure of parts of Poland, but already the Ottomans were compelled to draw up treaties with their adversaries as **equals** – a far cry from the days when victorious sultans condescended to suppliant Christian kings. Worse was to follow during the second half of the seventeenth century, when the most notorious of several defeats at the hands of the Austrians and allies was the bungled **second siege of Vienna** in 1683, where an entire Turkish army was decimated. Most of Hungary and other east European territory was lost as well before the **treaties of Carlowitz** (1699) and **Passarowitz** (1718) stabilized the Balkan frontier for nearly two centuries. In lieu of a formal Ottoman foreign service, necessary diplomatic initiatives were handled by the **Dragoman**, always a Christian with knowledge of the foreign languages which Muslim Ottomans lacked.

During the eighteenth century most of the territorial attrition at the Turks' expense was to be courtesy of the **Russian Empire**, newly consolidated under Peter the Great. Russo-Turkish enmity was to be a constant in Turkish history thereafter until the twentieth century. After a slow beginning, when French support had stiffened Ottoman resolve, Russia went on under Catherine the Great to thoroughly humiliate the Turks, presenting them with the **treaties of Küçük Kaynarca** (1774) and **Jassy** (1792), which ceded extensive territory to the Tsarina, gave Russia long-coveted access to the Black Sea and the straits guarding İstanbul – and the right to interfere, anywhere in the Ottoman Empire, to protect the interests of Orthodox Christian subjects.

THE START OF THE REFORM ERA

Selim III's accession to the throne in 1789 coincided with the advent of revolutionary regimes in France and the USA; thus the name of his proposed reforms, the **Nizam-i-Cedid** or "New Order", was a deliberate tip of the hat to them. Though the proliferation of the *derebeys* and their defiance of central authority was the most pressing domestic problem, Selim addressed military reorganization first. With the Napoleonic wars as a background and warning, he enlisted foreign experts to set up an army, trained, equipped and attired along Western lines. This aroused the hostility of the janissary corps and their allies among the *ulema*, and Selim was deposed, then murdered, in 1808, after he had dissolved his new army as a futile sop to the conservatives.

The new sultan, **Mahmut II**, was more tactful, moving gradually towards innovation. He managed to outlast both Russian and French designs on his realm only to be confronted by the major crisis of his reign: **full-scale rebellion in Greece**, which broke out in 1821. This proved impossible to crush, even after the Westernized army of **Mehmet Ali**, semi-autonomous ruler of Egypt, was despatched to the scene under the command of his son İbrahim. The destruction of an Ottoman fleet at Navarino by French, Russian and English ships in 1827, an overland attack by Russia on İstanbul in 1829, and a treaty in 1830 guaranteed the emergence of an **independent Greece** – the first substantial loss of Turkish territory in the south Balkans. The French simultaneously invaded Algeria, and Mehmet Ali chose this moment for an attack on Anatolia, which went unchecked until the Russians, this time as allies of Mahmut, landed on the Bosphorus. In consideration for services rendered they extracted the **Treaty of Hunkâr İskelesi** from the sultanate, which effectively gave the Tsar exclusive unimpeded access to the straits, reconfirmed the Russians' right to meddle in Ottoman internal affairs, and ensured that the British would try and act as a counter to all such intrigues.

Despite this disastrous record abroad, Mahmut II had notably more success **at home**. In 1826 the janissaries had mutinied once again, but the sultan, carefully baiting the trap, liquidated them with loyal forces – and a massive artillery bombardment – in what came to be known as the "**Auspicious Incident**". The Bektaşi sect, the "house religion" of the janissaries, was simultaneously suppressed, and a Western-style army created. During the 1830s Prussian and Austrian advisers came to train it, beginning a tradition of Teutonic involvement in Turkey's military which was to endure for nearly a century. A military academy and medical school were established, with French the language of instruction.

A formal **foreign service** and a **civil service** were also created, and the *ulema* was brought to heel by subordination to the secular bureaucracy. An approximation of Western dress for all except clerics became mandatory – including the replacement of the turban by the more "progressive" **fez**. Along with a notably less successful attempt to introduce a uniform law code and squelch corruption, the entire programme represented a quantum increase in **centralization** – and unintentionally a widening gap between the Ottoman masses and the new elite.

THE TANZIMAT AND THE YOUNG OTTOMANS

Mahmut's strenuous efforts bore more fruit posthumously when his son Sultan Abdülmecid and minister Mustafa Reşid proclaimed the **Tanzimat** or "Reorganization" in 1839, essentially an Ottoman Magna Carta which delegated some of the sultan's law-making authority to advisers, promised an end to taxation irregularities and stipulated equal treatment of Muslim and non-Muslim before the law. Although the climate engendered by such noble sentiments permitted the founding of newspapers and private, secular schools in the ensuing decades, the proposal of infidel equality deeply offended most of the population, who were not prepared to contemplate – for example – the enlistment of Christians in the armed forces (they were in fact restricted to the navy until the twentieth century).

Foreign economic penetration of the Ottoman Empire increased suddenly, with growing commercial activity in all coastal cities, and massive imports of European products; in the process the Greek, Armenian and foreign-Christian merchant class of the ports benefited in a disproportionate manner. Simultaneously inland centres and traditional bazaar crafts went into precipitous decline, unable to compete with the products of the industrial revolution. Along with the establishment of banks and a currency reform came **loans** from overseas to the Ottoman government – the first in the 1850s, then eight more until bankruptcy ensued in the worldwide depression of 1873–75.

By mid-century the empire had become thoroughly enmeshed in the **power struggles of Europe** – a far cry from the smug aloofness of 250 years before, and a consequence of the fact that England and France had determined that, for better or worse, the Ottomans must be propped up as a counter to Russian expansionism. Thus the empire found itself on the winning side of the 1853–56 **Crimean War**, which began as a dispute between Russia and France over the protection to be extended by each to respectively the Orthodox and Catholic churches in Ottoman Palestine. The war ended with little significant territorial adjustment, but did bring a twenty-year interval of peace for the Ottomans.

Abdülmecid had been a well-meaning but weak and extravagant ruler, and was succeeded in 1861 by his brother **Abdülaziz**, who combined all of his predecessor's defects with a despotic manner. There sprung up in reaction, from the ranks of the first graduates of the empire's secular schools, the **Society of Young Ottomans**, which strove for the evolution of a constitutional monarchy along British lines. Its most enduring figure was the poet and essayist **Namik Kemal**, and it made extensive use of the newly admitted media of the press, drama and literature to get its points across. Predictably the group aroused the ire of the sultan, who exiled the boldest; undeterred, the Young Ottomans overseas mounted a barrage of written material, much of it smuggled back into the empire to good effect.

Faced with Abdülaziz's flagrant financial irresponsibility in the period preceding the crash of 1873–75, and his growing mental instability, together with new Russian mischief in İstanbul and brutally suppressed revolts in the Balkans, the Young Ottomans among the bureaucratic elite – particularly **Mithat Paşa** – deposed him on **May 30, 1876**. The crown was passed to his promising nephew Murat, but he shortly suffered a nervous breakdown, aggravated by the suicide of his uncle in captivity, was declared unfit to rule and in turn placed in seclusion. The next heir apparent was his younger brother **Abdülhamid**, an unknown quantity, who was offered the throne on condition that he accept various Young Ottomans as advisers and rule under a constitution.

ABDÜLHAMID AND THE YOUNG TURK REVOLUTION

The new sultan did in fact promulgate the **constitution** drafted by the Young Ottomans, presided over the opening of the first Ottoman parliament and retained – for a time – his hapless brother's advisers, including Mithat. But Abdülhamid soon moved to forestall a government-by-ministers, exiling Mithat (and later having him murdered).

As so often in late Ottoman history, the implementation of liberal reforms was interpreted by the great powers as a sign of weakness. Accordingly Russia attacked on two fronts in **1877**, at the Caucasus and in the Balkans, with an explicitly pan-Slavic agenda. The war went badly for the Ottomans, with extensive territorial losses confirmed by the ruinous peace treaty of San Stefano (at the ceasefire line just a stone's throw from İstanbul), later modified, under British pressure, at the 1878 **Conference of Berlin**. The final settlement provided for the independence of Romania, Montenegro and Serbia; an autonomous if truncated Bulgaria; the cession of Thessaly to Greece, and Kars and Ardahan districts to Russia; and the occupation of Bosnia and Herzegovina by Austria. **Nationalism** had been unleashed – and rewarded – in the Balkans, and would be a theme for the next forty years, and indeed to this day. Britain, in compensation for fending off further Russian advances, was given the right to "administer" – and garrison – **Cyprus**.

Throughout all this the young **parliament** displayed altogether too much independence for the sultan's taste, criticizing war policy and summoning certain government ministers to answer for their conduct. In early 1878, between the San Stefano and Berlin negotiation sessions, Abdülhamid finally dropped all pretence of consultative government and dissolved the Chamber of Deputies; it was not to meet again for thirty years.

With any restraining influence safely out of the way, Abdülhamid chose to rule despotically and directly – for the balance of his reign ministers were ciphers who rarely stayed in office for even a year. Thanks both to the circumstances of his accession and his innate character, Abdülhamid developed a fear of sedition and conspiracy bordering on paranoia. A **police state** emerged, attended by huge numbers of spies and rigorous press censorship; the introduction of a **telegraph network** provided a tremendous boost to the surveillance system. The only clause of the constitution still honoured was the repeatedly invoked one that entitled the sultan to exile troublemakers.

After the disastrous wars marking the start of his reign, Abdülhamid's **foreign policy** was xenophobic and Asian-orientated, espousing Islam as a unifying force and, for the first time in centuries, emphasizing the sultan's second role as **caliph**. This ideology didn't, however, prevent the loss of Tunis and Egypt, and had as a corollary the steadily worsening treatment of the **Armenians** of eastern Anatolia, who began to show the same nationalist sentiments as the Christians of the Balkans. The abuses culminated in the organized pogroms of **1895–96**, in which nearly 150,000 Armenians died, provoking (albeit short-lived) outrage abroad. In 1897, war with Greece and a revolt on Crete coincided; even though the Prussian-trained army defeated the Greeks in the field, the Ottomans were forced to grant the island autonomy.

Despite his political obscurantism, Abdülhamid presided over widespread **technological Westernization**; carefully cultivated ties with Germany resulted in much-needed development projects – most famously the German-built **rail system** across Anatolia, aimed at (but never reaching) Baghdad. Important investment credits were also extended, and a **Public Debt Administration** was created, which gathered revenues of the various state monopolies to service the enormous debt run up earlier in the century. At the same time, secular schooling and technical training were encouraged, as long as they didn't directly challenge the sultan's rule – but the creation of an educated elite inevitably resulted in change.

In 1889 the Ottoman Society for Union and Progress – later the **Committee for Union and Progress** (CUP) – arose, mainly among army medical staff but also drawing on the talents of the huge European exile community. Soon it took strongest root in **Macedonia**, the worst-administered and most polyglot of the Ottoman provinces, and completely infiltrated the officer ranks of the Third Army at Salonica

(Thessaloniki), a city where the sultan's repression was less, and where Westernizing Jews and Masons were influential. Threats of further intervention by the great powers in Macedonia – where disorderly Greek, Bulgarian and other nationalist guerrilla bands were rampant – coincided with failure to pay the army, providing the spark for the revolt of the "**Young Turks**", as the CUP plotters were nicknamed. In July 1908, the Macedonian army units demanded by telegraph that Abdülhamid restore the 1876 constitution, or face unpleasant consequences. Abdülhamid's spies had either been oblivious to the threat, or he had chosen not to believe them, and on **July 24**, the sultan assented. There was widespread rejoicing on the streets of the major imperial cities, as mullahs fraternized with bishops, and Bulgarians walked arm in arm with Greeks. With the sultan's despotism over, surely the millennium was imminent.

AFTER THE REVOLUTION – THE BALKAN WARS

The euphoria prompted by the re-enactment of the 1876 constitution soon subsided as the **revolutionary government** fumbled for a coherent policy. The coup itself had had as immediate goals the curbing of Abdülhamid's powers and the physical preservation of the empire – but even these limited aims proved beyond it. By October 1908 Bulgaria had declared full independence, and Austria had formally annexed Bosnia and Herzegovina, occupied since 1878. **Elections** for the reconvened parliament were reasonably fair, and the "Young Turks", their CUP newly organized as a political party, gained a majority. Opposition to the Westernization and autocracy represented by the CUP simmered, however, and in spring 1909 a joint **revolt** of low-ranking soldiers, anti-CUP politicians and religious elements ousted the new government and took control of İstanbul. Abdülhamid, overestimating the rebels' strength, unwisely came out in their support. The CUP fought back from its base in Salonika, sending Third Army general Mahmut Şevket to crush the insurrection, and topped this off by **deposing the sultan**, banishing him to house arrest in Salonika. His younger brother ascended the throne as Mehmet V, promising to respect the "will of the nation".

The revolution had been saved, but there was still no agreement on a programme. Three main ideas vied for consideration. **Ottomanism**, essentially a recycled version of the Tanzimat reforms of the mid-nineteenth century, asserted that a Eurasian empire, federal in stucture, in which all ethnic and religious minorities had equal rights – and who in turn were loyal to the central government – was both viable and desirable. The adherents of **Pan-Islamism**, the pet creed of Abdülhamid, stressed the Islamic nature of the Ottoman Empire and the ties between Muslim Albanians, Caucasians, Kurds, Arabs and Turks. **Pan-Turanism** was more blatantly racial, dwelling on the affinities between all Turkic peoples between central Asia and the Balkans; as time went on it was modified to a more realistic **Turkism**, or the promotion of the interests of the Turkish-speaking Muslims of Anatolia, and it was in fact this notion which would eventually carry the day.

With the lifting of the Hamidian repression, discussion of these alternatives – and cultural life in general – flourished uninhibitedly for a while. Between 1908 and 1912 the CUP, beset by internal disputes, was by no means monolithic, and parliamentary opposition was not completely quelled until 1912.

The growing **authoritarianism** of CUP rule coincided with renewed **external threats** to the empire. Italy invaded Tripolitania (today's Libya) in 1911, and the next year took all of the Dodecanese islands. In late 1912, the Balkan states of Bulgaria, Serbia, Montenegro and Greece united for the first and last time in history, driving Turkey out of Europe in the **First Balkan War** and indeed approaching within a few miles of İstanbul by the beginning of 1913. Ottomanism as a doctrine was a dead letter, since the European minorities had opted for nationalism, leaving a far more homogeneous, truncated Asian empire. Enraged at attempts to limit the army's, and the CUP's, involvement in government, and the unfavourable terms of a pending peace treaty, key CUP officers staged a coup, murdering the Minister of War and continuing the war; when the new grand vizier Mahmut Şevket was assassinated in retaliation soon after, the CUP used it as an excuse to suppress all dissent and establish a **military junta**.

The unlikely Balkan alliance soon fell apart, with Bulgaria turning on Serbia and Greece in the **Second Balkan War**, and the Ottomans taking the opportunity to regain eastern Thrace

up to Edirne. This action made temporary heroes of the junta, which by now was in effect a triumvirate: **Enver Paşa**, an officer of humble origins, dashing, courageous, abstemious, as well as vain, ambitious and megalomaniac; **Talat Paşa**, a brutal Thracian civilian who would eventually be responsible for ordering the 1915 deportation of the Armenians; and **Cemal Paşa**, a ruthless but competent professional soldier from an old family.

WORLD WAR I

CUP ideology was now resolutely Turkish-nationalist, secular and technocratic, as well as anti-democratic – and increasingly pro-German. Public opinion, and the more level-headed CUP members, hoped that the Ottoman Empire would remain neutral in the obviously impending conflict, but Germanophile Enver had signed a secret agreement with the Kaiser on August 2, 1914. By coincidence Britain committed a major blunder the same day, impounding two half-built battleships which had already been paid for by public subscription in Turkey. The German government pulled off a major public relations coup by sailing two **replacement ships** through the Allied Mediterranean blockade to İstanbul in October, presenting them to the Turkish navy – whose German commander promptly forced Turkey's hand by sending them off to bombard Russian Black Sea ports. By November Turkey was officially **at war** with the Allies, though various CUP ministers resigned in protest. "This will be our ruin," said one prophetically, "even if we win."

Despite appearances, the CUP did not become puppets of the Germans, nor Turkey a complete satellite; though men and weaponry were diverted to the European eastern front and Anatolia used as a granary by the Central powers, the Capitulations were unilaterally abolished over German protests (they affected the French and English more anyway), and monetary policy was determined without outside interference for the first time in sixty years – as evidenced by the inflationary printing of paper notes. These measures counted on military successes to reinforce them, though, and the **Turkish war effort**, carried out on five fronts simultaneously, was an almost unmitigated disaster. Over the four-year duration, the empire lost all of its Middle Eastern domains, as the Arabs threw in their lot with the British on the promise of subsequent autonomy, thus proving pan-Islamism as dead as Ottomanism. Enver Paşa demonstrated his incompetence by losing an entire army on the Russian front during the winter of 1914–15; the subsequent Tsarist advance deep into Anatolia was only reversed after the Bolshevik revolution.

The single bright spot from the Turkish point of view was the successful defence of the **Gallipoli peninsula**, guarding the Dardanelles and thus the sea approaches to İstanbul. Allied armadas attempting to force the straits had been repelled in late 1914 and early 1915, after which it was decided to make an amphibious landing on the fortified promontory. This was launched on April 24, 1915, but foundered immediately, and the Allies finally withdrew just after New Year 1916. Credit for the successful Turkish resistance belonged largely to a hitherto unknown colonel named **Mustafa Kemal**, later Atatürk, ranking Turkish officer in the operations. Born in Salonica in 1881 of a lower middle-class family, and educated at Harbiye Military College in İstanbul, he had come of age in the midst of the pre-1908 Young Turk agitation, and like many other junior officers had been sent into internal exile for "disloyal" activities. Though an early member of the CUP, he had opposed its autocratic tendencies and entry into the war on Germany's side. The Turkish public craved a hero at this point, but upon Kemal's return to İstanbul the jealous Enver deprived them of this satisfaction, shuttling Kemal between various backwoods commands, until war's end saw him overseeing a strategic retreat to the hills on the Syrian border.

For the Ottoman Empire's **Armenians**, April 24, 1915 was also a fateful day, on which the CUP authorities ordered the disarming of all Armenians serving in the Turkish army, and the round-up of Armenian civilians from Anatolian cities, towns and villages; only those living in İstanbul and İzmir were exempted, for economic reasons. Over the next ten months of deportations, the men were usually shot immediately by gendarmes, Kurdish irregulars or bands of thugs recruited for the purpose, while women and children were forced to march, under conditions that guaranteed their abuse and death, hundreds of kilometres towards concentration camps in the Mesopotamian desert. The Armenians' homes and businesses were appropriated, often by CUP functionaries. Estimating

total casualties is difficult and controversial, but Ottoman and foreign censuses at the turn of the century showed nearly 1.5 million Armenians living in Anatolia. Allowing for the half-million refugees who managed to escape abroad by 1923, most of the one-million difference can be assumed to have perished, making it the first deliberate, large-scale genocide of this century.

The above scenario is hotly disputed by the current Turkish government, which denies that any officially sanctioned, systematic expulsion or killing took place, and admits at most 300,000 Armenian fatalities from unspecified causes – but implying that most of these were combatants in treasonous alliance with Russia or France. While it is true that many Armenians, particularly in Van, Kars and Adana provinces, sided with those two powers in the hopes of securing a post-war state for themselves, this happened *after* the deportation and massacre orders were issued, and could be construed as legitimate self-defence. In any event, the issue is still very much alive, with relatively clumsy Turkish propaganda recently developed to counter vigorous Armenian lobbying for international recognition of the tragedy.

On **October 30, 1918**, Turkish and British officers signed an armistice on the Greek island of Límnos. Two weeks later an Allied fleet sailed into İstanbul, and strategic points around the Sea of Marmara were occupied by the victors, though Turkish civil administration was allowed to continue on condition that no "disturbances" took place. In the interim the CUP triumvirate had fled on German ships, and all met violent deaths in the following years: Talat killed in revenge by an orphaned Armenian in Berlin; Cemal assassinated in Caucasian Georgia; and Enver – dying as flamboyantly as he had lived – as a self-styled emir fighting the Bolsheviks in central Asia.

THE STRUGGLE FOR INDEPENDENCE

The Allies were now in a position to carry out their long-deferred **designs on the Ottoman heartland**, based on various secret protocols of 1915–17. By early 1919 French troops were in occupation of parts of southeast Anatolia near the present Syrian and Iraqi frontiers, the Italians landed on the coast between Bodrum and Antalya, and the Greeks disembarked at

İzmir, where Greek civilians numbered a large part of the population. The British concentrated their strength in İstanbul and Thrace, and along with the other victors garrisoned in the capital effectively dictated policy to the defeated Ottoman regime. The new sultan **Mehmet VI** was by all accounts a collaborationist interested only in retaining his throne, and prepared to make any necessary territorial or administrative concessions to that end – including the dissolution of the last wartime parliament.

İstanbul, under de facto occupation, and with nationalist Turks forced into hiding, was a poor seedbed for a war of independence. In Thrace and Anatolia, however, various **Committees for the Defence of (Turkish) Rights** – patriotic Turkish guerrilla bands – had sprung up, and a substantial remnant of the Ottoman armies survived at Erzurum, under the control of **Kâzım Karabekir**. Together these would form the nucleus of the liberation forces. All that was lacking was visionary leadership, and further provocations from the Allies; neither were long in coming.

Mustafa Kemal, the hero of Gallipoli and the Syrian front, was the only undefeated Ottoman general at war's end; was not compromised by close association with the CUP leadership; and could hardly be accused of being pro-German. Popular and outspoken, he was considered too dangerous by the Allies to be kept idle in the capital. For his part, Kemal itched to cross over to Anatolia and begin organizing some sort of resistance to the pending imperialist schemes, but dared not do so without a suitable pretext. This was provided in the spring of 1919, when Kemal managed to wangle from the collaborationist war ministry a commission as a military inspector for all Anatolia, empowered to halt the activities of the various Committees for the Defence of Rights and seize their arms. His first stop was to be the Black Sea, where Turkish guerrillas had been fighting it out with Greeks bent on setting up a Pontic republic. On **May 19, 1919**, Mustafa Kemal landed at Samsun, four days after Greek operations began at İzmir – the last straw for many hitherto passive Turks. Contrary to his brief, Kemal promptly began organizing and strengthening the Turkish guerrillas. The puppet government in İstanbul, realizing too late what he was up to, attempted to recall him, then summarily relieved him of duties, and finally

ordered his arrest; he returned the compliment by resigning his commission. Kemal and Karabekir, along with **Rauf**, **Ali Fuad** and **Refet** – three high-ranking officers of old Ottoman families – drew up a provisional plan for resistance, with the strong support of the Anatolian religious authorities. Two **ideological congresses** were scheduled, with delegates often appearing after arduous journeys in disguise: one at Erzurum in July, and another in Sivas in September. Both gatherings elected Kemal as chairman, and both ratified the so-called **National Pact**, which demanded viable Turkish borders approximating those of today, an end to the Capitulations, and a guarantee of rights to all minorities. At the same time the pact reaffirmed its loyalty to the institution of the caliphate, if not the sultan himself, who was deemed a prisoner of the Allies. It was still far too early in the game to antagonize the religious elements, and indeed secularization was probably still a gleam in Kemal's eye.

Throughout these manoeuvres the Nationalists, as they came to be called, made good use of the **telegraph lines** installed by Abdülhamid, ensuring that telegraphists loyal to their cause manned the keys, and often conducting convoluted arguments with the İstanbul regime over the wires. By the autumn of 1919, they forced the resignation of the grand vizier and the announcement of elections for a new parliament. These, in early 1920, returned a large Nationalist majority, which openly proclaimed the National Pact – and created a climate where thefts from Allied arms depots, often with the connivance of the French and Italians who opposed Greek aims in Anatolia, became a routine occurrence. At the instigation of the outraged Ottoman court, the British placed İstanbul under formal military occupation on **March 16, 1920**, raiding parliament and bundling a few score deputies into exile on Malta. Luckier MPs escaped to Ankara, where Kemal and others had prudently remained, and on **April 23** opened the first **Grand National Assembly**, in direct defiance of the sundry Allied encroachments. Turkey's first Ankara-based parliament met in a Wild West atmosphere, lit by oil-lamps for several years, while its members tethered their horses to wooden railings out front.

The sultanate reacted vehemently to all this, securing a **fetva** (ruling) from the Islamic authorities sanctioning a holy war against the "rebels" and condemning the Nationalist leadership to death in absentia. Kemal and friends secured a counter-*fetva* from sympathetic religious figures in Ankara, and soon afterwards the head of the Bektaşi dervish order publicly commanded his followers to help the Nationalists.

Such moral support was vital to the beleaguered guerrillas, who were now fighting for their lives in a **multiple-front war**: against the French in the southeast, the Italians in the southwest, Armenians in the northeast, irregular bands supporting the sultan and – most dangerously – the Greeks in western Anatolia. The only consistent aid came from the newborn Soviet Union, which sent gold and weapons, and partitioned the short-lived Armenian republic between herself and Turkey, thus ending that theatre of war by late 1920.

The Allied governments, oblivious of the new reality on the ground in Turkey, attempted to legitimize their claims to Turkish territory by presenting the humiliating **Treaty of Sèvres** to the Ottoman government in May 1920. By its terms, partly motivated by the Wilsonian Fourteen Points, but more by unalloyed greed, an independent Armenia and an autonomous Kurdistan were created; the straits of the Sea of Marmara and İstanbul were placed under international control; Thrace, İzmir and its hinterland were given to Greece; France and Italy were assigned spheres of influence in those portions of Anatolia remaining to the Ottomans; and Turkish finances were placed under Allied supervision, with a revival of the Capitulations. By signing this document, the demoralized sultanate sacrificed its last shred of credibility, convinced any remaining waverers of the necessity of the Nationalist movement – and sparked a predictable Greek response.

The **Greek expeditionary armies**, acting with the authorization of British prime minister Lloyd George, not only pressed inland from İzmir but captured Edirne, İzmit and Bursa, seeking to revive notions of a Greater Greece straddling both shores of the Aegean. Only French and Italian objections caused them to halt just short of the strategic Afyon–Eskişehir railway. In early 1921 the Greeks were on the move again, but Nationalist general İsmet Paşa stopped them twice, in January and April, at the defile of **İnönü**, from which he would later take his sur-

name. Both sides had undergone subtle changes: since the fall of the republican Venizelos government in Greece, and the return of the Royalists, the Greek Anatolian armies had become progressively more corrupt, incompetently led and brutal, sustained for the time being by the momentum of superior numbers and weaponry. Kemal's forces, on the other hand, had become more cohesive and professional, with irregular bands either defeated or absorbed.

But when the Greeks advanced east once more in July 1921, they swiftly captured Afyon, Eskişehir and the vital railway that linked them; the Nationalists strategically retreated east of the Sakarya River, less than 100km from Ankara, to buy time and extend the enemy's supply lines. Panic and gloom reigned in Ankara, with calls for Kemal to be instated as commander-in-chief at the head of the defending army, to share its fate. This was done, and soon the Greeks went for the bait, sniffing an easy chance to finish off the Nationalists. But in the ferocious, three-week **Battle of the Sakarya** beginning on August 13, they failed to make further headway towards Ankara. Although most of the Greek army survived, anything less than its capture of the Nationalist headquarters was a decisive defeat. The jubilant Grand National Assembly conferred on Kemal the title *Gazi*, or "Warrior for the Faith".

The victory at Sakarya greatly enhanced the Nationalists' international position: both the **French and Italians** soon concluded peace treaties, withdrawing from southern Anatolia; and contributions from various Asian Muslim countries poured in to finance the "holy war". With remaining support for the Greek adventure evaporating, the British tried unsuccessfully to arrange an armistice between Greece and the Nationalists. Both camps dug in and waited until, on **August 26, 1922**, Kemal launched his final offensive at **Dumlupınar** near Afyon, designed to drive the Greeks out of Anatolia. Surprised by a dawn artillery barrage, the Greek lines crumbled, and those not taken prisoner or killed, fled down-valley in a disorderly rout towards waiting boats in İzmir, committing atrocities against the Turkish population, destroying the harvest, and abandoning Greek civilians to the inevitable Turkish reprisals. The latter included the **sacking and burning of İzmir** within four days of the triumphant entry of the Nationalists. Never again would Greece aspire to be a Mediterranean power, let alone a global one.

Despite this resounding triumph, the war was not yet over, and indeed the threat of a larger conflict loomed. A large Greek army remained intact in **Thrace**, determined to fight on, and British contingents guarding the strategically vital **Dardanelles** faced off against the Nationalist army sent north to cross the straits. Some of Kemal's associates even urged him to retake western Thrace and Greek Macedonia, a sure invitation to renewed world war. Cooler heads prevailed at the last minute, however, and at Mudanya on **October 11, 1922**, an armistice was signed, accepting accomplished facts and obliging the last Greek troops to depart from eastern Thrace. A week later British premier Lloyd George, his pro-Greek policy utterly discredited, was forced to **resign**.

There remained just one obstacle to full Nationalist control of Turkey: Sultan Mehmet VI still presided over a diminished realm, consisting of İstanbul alone. Few in Ankara had a good word to say about the man himself, but many expressed reluctance to abolish his office, favouring a constitutional monarchy with royalty exercising a stabilizing influence as in Britain. The Allies themselves helped decide the matter by extending a clumsy double invitation to a final peace conference at Lausanne – one addressed to the sultanate, the other to the Grand National Assembly. The outrage thus provoked in the latter quarters made it an easy matter for Kemal to persuade the deputies to **abolish the sultanate** on November 1, effective retroactively as from March 16, 1920, the date of British direct rule in İstanbul. Within two weeks Mehmet VI, last of the House of Osman, sneaked ignominiously out of the old imperial capital on a British warship, bound for exile in Italy; his cousin Abdülmecid was sworn in as caliph, but with no temporal powers whatsoever.

The **peace conference** at Lausanne was convened immediately, with İsmet Paşa as the sole Turkish representative. If the Allies were hoping to dictate terms as at Versailles and Sèvres, they were quickly disappointed; İsmet soon proved as dogged at the negotiating table as on the battlefield, reducing seasoned diplomats to despair by his repetitive insistence on the tenets of the Erzurum-Sivas National Pact.

The conference was suspended for two months in early 1923, the Allies doubtless hoping to wear İsmet down, but in the end it was they who gave in. The **Treaty of Lausanne**, signed on July 24, recognized the frontiers won in the recent war of independence; abolished the Capitulations; demilitarized the Dardanelles and the islands at its mouth; and postponed a decision on the status of the Mesopotamian district of Mosul.

More drastically, Greece and Turkey agreed to an **exchange of minority populations** to eliminate future outbreaks of communal conflict. Nearly half a million Muslims in Greece were sent to Turkey, and the remaining 1.3 million Greek Orthodox Christians in Turkey were despatched to Greece. The only exceptions were the Turkish minority in western Thrace, and Greeks with Ottoman citizenship resident in İstanbul and on Imvros and Tenedos islands at the mouth of the Dardanelles. The sole criterion was religious affiliation, and incalculable suffering was caused, especially among Turkish-speaking Christians and Greek-speaking Muslims who suddenly found themselves in a wholly alien environment.

The pact marked the true end of World War I, and saw Turkey, alone of the defeated nations, emerge in dignity, with defendable territory and modest demands made of her. Compared to the old empire, it was a compact state – 97 percent Anatolian and Muslim. Towards the end of the Lausanne conference, the first Grand National Assembly was dissolved, its work declared finished. A new political party, the **Republican People's Party** (RPP), incorporating the resources and personnel of the various Committees for the Defence of Rights, and the precepts of the National Pact, was formed, and a new parliament was swiftly created, its members drawn from the ranks of the new entity.

THE YOUNG REPUBLIC AND KEMAL ATATÜRK'S REFORMS

The Nationalists may have won the military battle for political sovereignty in Anatolia, but after ten years of constant warfare the country was physically devastated and economically a shambles. Export agriculture and urban commerce had largely been in the hands of the Greek and Armenian minorities, who had accounted for twenty percent of the pre-1914 population within the boundaries of the new state, and up to fifty percent in İzmir, İstanbul and along the Black Sea and Sea of Marmara. With their departure or demise, and that of the foreigners who had benefited from the Capitulations, the Turks were obliged to start from the ground up agriculturally and commercially, which they failed to do for many years.

Kemal had little patience for or understanding of intricate economics, and preferred to emphasize sweeping social change by fiat, skilfully delivered in the maximum increments tolerable at any given moment. In October 1923 the Grand National Assembly officially moved the capital to **Ankara** and proclaimed the **Republic**, to which there was little practical obstacle since the last sultan had absconded. Kemal was designated head of state – numerous abstentions were as much as his opponents dared – and İsmet İnönü was named prime minister. Though the sultan was gone, the caliph Abdülmecid was still around and very much a public personality – an intolerable situation for Kemal and the other Westernizers; since the war had been won they no longer felt the need for the legitimizing function of Islam. In March 1924 the caliphate was abolished and all members of the House of Osman exiled, the *medreses* and religious courts closed, and the assets of the *vakıfs* supervised by a new Ministry of Religious Affairs.

Even some of Kemal's long-time supporters were dismayed by his increasingly autocratic ways, and a few – including military men Ali Fuad, Rauf Orbay and Kâzım Karabekir – resigned from the RPP in October 1924 to form an opposition, the **Progressive Republican Party** (PRP). At first Kemal tolerated the new party as a means of blowing off steam, even replacing the unpopular İsmet as prime minister to placate them, but the RPP became alarmed when PRP speakers attracted large crowds and elements of the less supervised İstanbul press began siding with them.

Events soon provided Kemal with a basis for more action. In February 1925 the first of several **Kurdish revolts** this century erupted at Palu, near Elâzığ, under the leadership of a Naqshbandi dervish leader. The revolt was both fundamentalist Muslim and separatist-nationalist in ideology, and it took the central government two months to suppress it. (Diehards staged a comeback on Mount Ararat from 1926

to 1929, and there was a major flare-up in Tunceli between 1936 and 1938 – both in turn related to the current troubles.) Kemal, demanding unity in a time of crisis, secured the abolition of the PRP and established a series of sanguinary **Independence Tribunals** invested with summary powers; not only the leaders of the revolt but a few minor members of the PRP found themselves on the wrong end of a rope, and freedom of the press was quickly curtailed. By autumn 1925 all the **dervish orders** had been made illegal throughout Turkey (though they were never completely suppressed), and the veneration of saints at their tombs was forbidden. Simultaneously, Kemal embarked on a campaign against **traditional headgear**, in particular women's veils, the turban and the fez. Although the caliphate had been dissolved with hardly a murmur, the sartorial laws outlawing the turban and fez, and requiring the donning of the hated European hat, were met with stiff resistance; dress for the Ottomans had always served as a vital indicator of rank. Not a few offenders were hung from lampposts by the reactivated Independence Tribunals, but the secularists have never to this day succeeded in altogether eliminating the cloaking of women in the rural areas.

More drastic measures followed at a dizzying pace. By 1926, the **Gregorian calendar** had replaced the Muslim lunar one for official use, and the *şeriat* or Islamic **law code** was replaced by adaptations of the Western European versions. The same year, the Jewish, Armenian and Greek minorities relinquished the last vestiges of their communal laws; henceforth all citizens of the Republic were to be judged by a uniform legal system. Parallel with the introduction of a secular law code came the relative **emancipation of women**: marriage and divorce became civil rather than religious or customary, polygamy was abolished, and within four years women were given the vote.

Not surprisingly all this inflamed the existing opposition to Kemal, and in mid-1926 a **plot** to assassinate him while on a visit to İzmir was uncovered. Those involved were mostly disgruntled minor deputies and ex-CUP men, but Kemal took the opportunity to charge and try most of the former Progressive Republican Party's leadership, including war hero Karabekir. Many, including all the surviving CUP leadership, were hanged, and even those acquitted were effectively barred from public life in the future. This was the last mass purge, however, and soon after, the feared Independence Tribunals were disbanded, having served their purpose. There was to be no more public opposition to Kemal during his lifetime, except for a period in 1930 when a second short-lived opposition party was again judged to be a "premature experiment".

Kemal now felt secure enough to press on with his agenda, and chose as his next field **alphabet reform**. A special commission prepared a Roman script within six weeks in 1928, and by the end of the year its universal use was law, with the Gazi himself touring the country to give lessons in public parks. Reform was extended to the entire language over the next few years, with the founding of a language commission charged with the duty of purging Turkish of its Arabic and Persian accretions and reviving old Turkish words, coining new ones, or adopting French words to underline the break with the Islamic past. Nowadays most observers admit that the process was carried too far, with the language soon as top-heavy with borrowed Western words as it had been with Eastern ones, but together with the script change the measures resulted in a substantial increase in literacy and comprehension.

Less successful, and ultimately embarrassing, were programmes purporting to rewrite history, in which it was variously asserted that all other languages derived from Turkish; that the Turks were an Aryan race (and other racial nonsense uncomfortably close to Nazi theories), or that they were the descendants of the Hittites or Sumerians. After a few years these hypotheses, springing from a mix of inferiority feelings and a need for political legitimacy, were allowed to die quiet deaths. (A deliberate side effect of the language reform, for whose advocates 1919 was the Year One, was to isolate many Turks from their own history – unable to read Ottoman Turkish, they felt, and feel, estranged from their imperial past.) More constructive, in 1934, was full **suffrage for women** in national elections and the mandatory adoption of **surnames** by the entire population; previously this had been discretionary. Kemal chose for himself the unique **Atatürk**, "Father-Turk", dropping his first name Mustafa.

Belatedly Atatürk and his associates had turned their attention to the **economic** sphere, where Turkey's weaknesses had been accentuated by the Crash of 1929. Despite public discontent at deprivation and stagnation, Kemalism, as Kemal Atatürk's ideology was named, continued to stress industrial self-sufficiency through state investment in heavy industry with a goal of complete import substitution (except for factory equipment). Development banks had been set up in 1925, and subsequently the strategically important rail network was extended, and mining, steel, cement and paper works heavily subsidized on a pattern modelled on Italian Fascism. This paternalistic programme was, however, grossly inefficient, and proceeded at the expense of the agricultural sector, which remained in abject condition until the 1950s. The east of the country was effectively condemned to a subsistence existence – aggravating Kurdish feelings of punitive neglect – a situation unchanged until the massive, controversial irrigation and hydroelectric projects of the 1970s and 1980s.

Turkey's **foreign policy** during the post-independence years was rooted in non-interventionism and isolationism, though the country did join the League of Nations in 1934, and opposed appeasement of the Fascist regimes in Europe. Atatürk's slogan "Peace at home, peace in the world" may have had an unfortunate resemblance to Chamberlain's utterances after Munich, but in practice secured for Turkey years of calm which were badly needed. As much as the ruling party may have admired aspects of the European totalitarian systems then prevalent, it could see clearly that on the international stage Germany, Italy and the USSR were headed for cataclysm. Atatürk removed a remaining irritant to Anglo-Turkish relations by consenting to the cession of the Mosul region to Iraq, but began in 1936 an ultimately successful campaign to annexe the Hatay, part of the French protectorate of Syria with a large Turkish population. Alliances of the 1930s, with Greece, Yugoslavia and Romania to the west, and with Iraq, Iran and Afghanistan to the east, tended to be opportunistic and short-lived, nowhere near as durable as a Treaty of Friendship promulgated, partly for reasons of certain affinities between Bolshevism and Kemalism, with the Soviet Union.

Fortunately for Turkey Atatürk had accomplished the bulk of his intended life's work by **1938**, for his health, after a lifetime of heavy drinking, was steadily worsening. He died of cirrhosis of the liver in İstanbul's Dolmabahçe

Palace at 9.05am on November 10, 1938. Thousands of mourners bearing torches lined the route of his funeral cortege-train between İstanbul and Ankara.

Atatürk's legacy is a considerable one: unlike the totalitarian rulers of his day, he refrained from expansionist designs and racial/ethnic hatred, leaving behind a stable, defensible state and a guiding ideology, however uneven, expressly intended to outlive him. Personally he was a complex, even tragic figure: his charisma, energy and quick grasp of situations and people were unparalleled, but he had little inclination for methodical planning or systematic study. While respected, even revered, he was not loved by his associates or particularly loveable – despite his sponsorship of the advancement of women, he was himself a callous, compulsive womanizer, with one brief spell of unhappy marriage. In his fundamental loneliness, he nursed grudges and suspicions which often had deadly consequences for those who, as partners, might have been able to extricate Turkey from later awkward situations. By his stature and temperament Atatürk, like a giant tree that allows nothing to grow underneath, deprived Turkey, albeit inadvertently, of a succeeding generation of leadership. The cult of his personality, obvious from the silhouettes and signs on every hillside, is in some ways symptomatic of an inability to conceive of alternatives in ideology or heroes, though since 1983 reverence of the economic principles of Kemalism has fallen completely by the wayside.

WORLD WAR II AND THE RISE OF MULTI-PARTY POLITICS

Atatürk was succeeded as president by his long-time general and prime minister **İsmet İnönü**, and his policy concerning the **Hatay** was posthumously vindicated in 1939, when annexation of the nominally independent Hatay republic was ratified. France, eager for Turkish support in the impending war, acquiesced, and was apparently rewarded by the Turkish signing of a deliberately vaguely worded treaty of alliance with France and Britain in 1939.

In the event the treaty turned out to be a dead letter: France was swiftly defeated, and German propaganda convinced the Turkish government that Britain was probably doomed as well, and that the Axis would also dispatch Russia, the hereditary Turkish enemy. Accordingly a "Treaty of Friendship" was signed with Nazi Germany in 1941, guaranteeing at least Turkish non-belligerence. Entry into the war on either side had in fact been doubtful from the start, since Turkey's armed forces had become desperately antiquated, a match for neither German nor Allied weaponry. Memories of the Ottoman Empire's humiliation at the hands of the World War I Entente powers remained strong too. Turkey instead remained **neutral**, selling strategically vital chromium ore to both Germany and Britain. Despite this fence-sitting, the country was essentially on a war footing, with all able-bodied men mobilized, and the economy subject to the stresses of shortages, black markets, profiteering, and huge government budget deficits.

All these, and the partial infiltration of Nazi ideology, provoked the institution in 1942 of the so-called **Varlık Vergisi** or "Wealth Levy", a confiscatory tax applied in a discriminatory manner against businessmen of Armenian, Greek, Jewish and *Dönme* (nominal Muslims, ex-disciples of a false Jewish messiah) descent. It was in effect an attack by the Ankara-based nationalist bureaucrats against the remnants, in İzmir and İstanbul, of the Ottoman bourgeois merchant class: there was no appeal against assessments, and sums due had to be forwarded within absurdly short time limits. Defaulters had their property confiscated and/or were deported to labour camps in the interior, where many died. The measure, having in fact raised very little money, was rescinded in 1944, but not before urban commerce had been set back a decade, and the Republic's credibility with its non-Muslim minorities severely damaged.

Even after the collapse of the Italians, Turkey still declined to enter the war, despite assurances of Allied support. Turkey only declared war on Germany in early 1945 to qualify for membership of the UN, not soon enough to prevent the USSR from renewing demands for the return of the Kars and Ardahan districts, and joint control of the straits at each end of the Sea of Marmara. Though these were summarily rejected, Turkey badly needed a protective ally in the international arena, and found it in the **United States**. The arrival in İstanbul of the American warship USS *Missouri* in 1946 was greeted with such euphoria that the city fathers, in a famous instance of Turkish hospitality later worked into popular literature, ordered the local bordellos thrown open for free to the sailors.

The eventual results of the mutual wooing were, first, Turkey's participation in the Korean War, and soon after admission to **NATO** after an initial application had been rejected. This new pro-Western stance had several further consequences: the expulsion from Warsaw Pact Bulgaria into Turkey of vast numbers of ethnic Turks, a harbinger of an identical act four decades later; consistently bad relations with neighbouring Arab states, particularly after Turkey's recognition of Israel and the overthrow of the Iraqi monarchy by the Ba'ath Party; and a short-lived alliance with Greece and Yugoslavia, effectively dissolved by the first Cyprus crisis of the mid-1950s.

On the home front, discontent with one-party rule, secularization and the stiflingly centralized economy came to a head when four politicians – including Celâl Bayar and Adnan Menderes – having been expelled from the RPP, formed the **Democrat Party** in early 1946. Despite prematurely scheduled elections of that summer and widespread balloting irregularities, the new opposition managed to gain nearly fifteen percent of the parliamentary seats. The fact that this gain was not reversed by force was due as much to the climate of Turkish public opinion, demanding a change, as to any subtle pressure exerted by the Americans, whose **economic aid** was now pouring into the country.

A showdown could not be long postponed, however, and campaigning for the nationwide **elections of May 14, 1950** was strenuous and unimpeded. The Democrat Party's platform promised something to every disgruntled element in the electorate: an end to anti-business strictures for the embryonic middle class, freer religious observance for the devout, and attention to the badly neglected agricultural sector. Though it was a safe bet that the Democrats would win, the scale of their victory – 55 percent of the vote, and, by virtue of the winner-take-all, slate-of-candidates system, over 80 percent of parliamentary seats – caught everyone by surprise. Bayar replaced İnönü as president, and **Menderes** took office as prime minister.

"POPULIST GOVERNMENTS"

Virtually the first act of the new government was to permit, after a seventeen-year gap, the recitation of the call to prayer in Arabic – a decree neatly coinciding with the start of Ramadan. Simultaneously, rashes of fez- or turban-wearing, polygamy and use of the Arabic script were noted in the provinces. There followed far-reaching programmes of rural loans and public works, an end to various government monopolies and restrictions on investment by foreigners, and massive imports of luxury goods and farm machinery, based on the assumption that Turkey's allies would quietly subsidize all this. Many projects, including a Soviet-sponsored oil refinery on the Aegean, were controversial, though in retrospect Menderes can be credited with opening up a country where for three decades very little in the way of people, capital or goods had moved in or out. Despite lip service paid to private enterprise, however, much of this development was unplanned, uncoordinated investment in state enterprises, and most of it took the form of expensive rewards to supporters, a mere continuation of the old RPP system of patronage. Menderes himself, a largely self-taught farmer/lawyer, had his colossal vanity aggravated by the adulation of the peasants, who not only sacrificed livestock in his honour at his public appearances, but went so far as to name boy-children after him.

The honeymoon with the electorate continued through the first years of the 1950s, aided by bumper harvests, though by 1954 clouds loomed on the horizon: the **national debt** and trade deficit were enormous, and the black-market value of the Turkish lira was one-fourth the official exchange rate. But the increasingly sensitive Democrats would not tolerate even mutterings of criticism: in 1953 assets and institutions of the ousted RPP had been expropriated and abolished, and the small, right-wing/religious National Party, with its handful of seats in parliament, was proscribed. The first of a series of **repressive press laws** was passed in early 1954, further poisoning the atmosphere just before the May elections. These the Democrats won even more easily than four years previously, but instead of imbuing them with more confidence, they took the result as a mandate to clamp down harder on dissent and to run the country ever more shamelessly for the benefit of their clientele. The economy continued to worsen, with the first bouts of rampant **inflation** which was thereafter to be a constant feature of Turkish life. During 1955 the government, looking for a distraction from, and scapegoats for, domestic problems, found both in the form of the Cyprus issue and minorities – especially İstanbul Greeks. DP-orchestrated street demonstrations got out of hand, ending in destructive **riots** aimed at the wealthy and the foreigners in all three major cities.

In the wake of all this, support for the government tumbled, but probably not enough that it would have lost honestly contested elections in 1957. These, however, were heavily rigged, and the results – trimming the Democrats' strength to just over two-thirds of total – were never officially announced. Turkey thus approached the end of the decade in a parlous state, with a huge, dangerous gulf between the rural, largely pro-DP population and the intellectual/commercial elite in the towns – and, more dangerously, an alienated, antagonized military.

THE FIRST MILITARY INTERVENTION AND THE 1960S

Nowhere had dismay over the intentions and policies of the Democrat government been felt more keenly than in the military, who considered themselves the guardians of Atatürk's secular reforms (and indeed were enshrined as such in the military code of the Republic). The officer corps, debarred from voting and watching the value of their fixed salaries erode in the face of inflation, felt betrayed and neglected as the new middle class and Democrat apparatchiks surpassed them economically and socially. Cliques of officers had begun to formulate plans for action as far back as 1954, but it was not until May 27, 1960 that middle-ranking officers, enlisting a few commanders as figureheads, staged a **coup**. The month preceding the action was marked by student demonstrations in İstanbul and Ankara, which were fired on with some loss of life by elements of the army and police still loyal to Menderes.

The putsch was bloodless, swift and complete. Democrat Party MPs and ministers were jailed, and there was rejoicing on the streets of the larger cities. For the next sixteen months, a **National Unity Committee** (NUC) ruled the country, and oversaw the preparation of a new, extremely liberal constitution to supercede that of 1924. The ruling committee, however, was an uneasy marriage of convenience, incorporating as it did not only idealistic top brass hoping for a

speedy return to civilian rule, but junior officers who wished for an indefinite period of authoritarian military government, and who in fact embarked on disruptive purges of university faculties and the officer corps themselves. Committee chief and acting head of state **Cemal Gürsel** adroitly outflanked this element, exiling their representatives overseas to minor posts and lifting the ban on political activity early in 1961. The new constitution, which provided for a bicameral legislature, proportional representation in the lower house and a constitutional court, was submitted to public referendum in July, with elections scheduled for October.

The **referendum**, which was essentially a vote of confidence in the NUC, showed just 62 percent in favour of the new constitution. This was hardly gratifying to the junta, who panicked at the display of lingering support for the Democrat Party. Since the coup, several hundred leading DP members, including Menderes and Bayar, had been imprisoned and on trial at bleak Yassıada in the Sea of Marmara, on charges of undermining the 1924 constitution, corruption and complicity in the riots of 1955 – among others. Upon the return of guilty verdicts and fifteen death sentences, the NUC hastily ratified three of these – against Menderes, foreign minister Zorlu and finance minister Polatkan – while commuting the others, including that of Bayar, to life imprisonment. The three hangings, carried out a month before the elections, backfired badly, making Menderes a martyr and ensuring a long electoral life for the Justice Party, the new incarnation of the now-banned Democrat Party.

The inconclusive **parliamentary elections** proved a further disappointment to the NUC; neither the Justice Party nor a refurbished RPP gained a majority, with the balance of power held by splinter groups. Under threat of another coup, the two major parties were induced to enter into a coalition, with Cemal Gürsel as president and İnönü again prime minister for the first time since 1938. These compromises rankled certain disaffected junior officers who had hoped to be rid of the Democrats once and for all, and they resolved to clean up the "mess" with two subsequent coup attempts, one in February 1962 and another fourteen months later. The latter, involving the occupation of the state radio station by veterans of 27 May, was quelled and its leader executed. There would be no more putsches from below.

Civilian political life settled into a semblance of **normality**, with more unstable coalitions until 1965. In terms of standards of living, the promised economic reforms of the NUC had not borne fruit; the import substitution policies of the old RPP, whereby industrial self-sufficiency, however uneconomic, was subsidized, were quietly revived, while land reform and rural development was again deferred. The first wave of **emigration** to Germany and other Western European countries acted as a social safety valve, and the "guest workers" would return at holiday time with cars, consumer durables and – to a limited extent – European notions and wives. For the first time, independent labour unions began organizing and recruiting inside Turkey, with the right to strike finally confirmed in 1963. The growing urban proletariat found a political voice in the newly formed Turkish Workers Party, whose very existence nudged the RPP, now led by future prime minister **Bülent Ecevit**, leftward into a social-democratic mould. **Süleyman Demirel**, who was to emerge as one of the most enduring political figures over the next three decades, became leader in 1964 of the JP, which was obliged to come out strongly for free enterprise and foreign investment. In October 1965, Demirel's Justice Party gained a majority of votes in national elections, with the RPP and TWP together tallying less than a third.

But international events were to assume increasing importance in the Turkish domestic scene. Neighbouring **Cyprus** had gained independence in 1960 by terms of a treaty between the new Cypriot republic and the guarantors Britain, Greece and Turkey. Incorporated in the Treaty of Guarantee and the Cypriot constitution were extensive concessions to the Turkish Cypriot minority, who constituted roughly one-fifth of the island's population. By 1963 Cypriot president Makarios declared these clauses unworkable, and sought to limit the veto power of the Turkish community. Members of EOKA, the right-wing paramilitary force of the Greek population, took this as a cue to commence attacks on Turkish settlements, who replied in kind. Virtual civil war beset the island through much of 1964, with the ranks of both sides swelled by illegal, smuggled-in Greek and Turkish troops. A full-scale Greco-Turkish war was only narrowly avoided. The Turkish government had to confine its response to retaliations against the Greek population of their two Aegean islands and İstanbul, while communal violence recurred sporadically across Cyprus, despite the imposition of a UN-supervised truce, for the rest of the decade.

Turkey was also not immune from the spirit of May 1968, which here took the form of increased **anti-Americanism** and leftist sentiments, particularly on and around university campuses. At the height of the Vietnam War the US was easily labelled an imperialist power, a diagnosis confirmed by the deferred publication of a secret 1964 letter from President Johnson to İnönü, warning Turkey against military intervention on Cyprus. Many Turks felt betrayed by the US's lack of support on the Cyprus issue, having studiously followed the American lead on foreign policy issues since the end of World War II. Even the ruling establishment found the obviousness of American tutelage offensive to sentiments of national independence, and most of the half-dozen US military installations were quietly given over either to Turkish sovereign control or at worst that of NATO. At the same time, relations with the Soviet Union improved dramatically. Ironically perhaps, the most lasting American legacy to Turkey would be swarms of automobiles and 110-volt household appliances, provided as part of Marshall Plan assistance during the 1950s or sold off by departing diplomatic and military personnel throughout the 1960s.

Demirel was returned in **1969** for a second term as prime minister, but his majority and authority were soon eroded by the loss of a crucial budget vote and the defection of sixteen percent of the JP to legally reform the Democrat Party. More ominous was the upsurge in **political violence** on the streets and around the universities which was to be a pervasive feature of Turkish life until 1980. Extreme left-wing groups such as Dev Sol (Revolutionary Youth), who had emerged in response to the impotence and subsequent break-up of the TWP, fought it out with right-wing and/or Islamic activists such as the infamous Grey Wolves, who had set up paramilitary training camps as far back as 1966, under the tutelage of **Alpaslan Türkeş**, founder of the fascist Nationalist Action Party (NAP).

THE SECOND MILITARY INTERVENTION AND THE 1970S

Against this backdrop of domestic unrest, lingering corruption and continued non-productive parliamentary manoeuvres, the generals acted again. On March 12, 1971, they issued a proclamation forcing Demirel and his cabinet to resign in favour of an "above-party" government composed of reformist technocrats. This measure, often called the "**coup by memorandum**", allowed parliament to continue functioning, while stealing the wind from the sails of a considerable body of restive NCOs who had hoped for a full-scale military regime. Martial law was, however, imposed on the major cities and the ever-troublesome southeast, and thousands from the university community, the press and broadcasting were arrested and tried, mostly on charges of inciting violence or class conflict, in a wave of **repression** every bit as comprehensive as the more publicized one of 1980. In September amendments were promulgated to limit the freedoms granted by the 1961 constitution, but soon the "above-party" regime, effectively stymied by JP operatives in the Grand National Assembly, was forced to resign. Despite, or because of, the threat of another putsch, acting premier Nihat Erim managed to cobble together a merry-go-round of successively less radical and more acceptable cabinets, and preserved a semblance of civilian rule for two more years. The army, mindful of the hash which the colonels' junta had made of neighbouring Greece since 1967, decided to let the politicians take the blame for any adverse results in Turkey.

The surprise winners of the freely contested **elections in October 1973** were Bülent Ecevit and his RPP, though they were soon forced into uneasy alliance with Necmettin Erbakan's Islamic National Salvation Party (NSP), which gained control of several ministries. During Ecevit's short but momentous period of office, the economy was savaged by OPEC's oil price hike, which preceded the Turkish **military intervention in Cyprus**.

The military junta then ruling Greece had ousted President Makarios in July 1974 and replaced him with EOKA extremists supporting union with Greece. Ecevit's pro forma appeal to Britain to intervene in accordance with the Treaty of Guarantee went unheeded, so he gave the order for Turkish troops to invade the island on July 20. The EOKA regime fell three days later, after the Turks had secured a bridgehead around Kyrenia. A ceasefire was declared while furious negotiations between the Greek, Turkish and British foreign ministers continued over several weeks; on August 14, after the Greek Cypriots refused an ultimatum from Turkey, its army advanced further to occupy the northern third of the island.

Over two decades later the situation remains essentially unchanged, with a negotiated settlement as elusive as ever. The **ceasefire** (hostilities have not formally ended) is policed by a UN peace-keeping force sandwiched in a buffer zone called the "Green Line" between the Greek Cypriot-controlled south and the self-proclaimed Turkish Republic of Northern Cyprus. There has long been considerable unity of opinion in Turkey on the Cyprus issue, in that the status quo is seen as the only viable option, but lately Turkey has slowly begun withdrawing some troops from Cyprus and hinting to the intransigent and sometimes ungrateful Turkish Cypriot leadership that some accommodation with the South would end the international isolation of the North – and on this issue, of Turkey as well, in such international forums as the UN and the EC.

Back on the domestic front, Ecevit – riding a tide of popularity not unlike Mrs Thatcher's after the Falklands War – resigned in September to seek early elections and hopefully a workable parliamentary majority. This proved a major blunder, for opposition foot-dragging ensured that polling was delayed until April 1975, when Süleyman Demirel was able to assemble a coalition government along with the Islamic National Salvation Party and the fascist Nationalist Action Party, and hung on to power after inconclusive elections two years later.

All this served only to further polarize feelings in the country, which from 1976 onwards was beset by steadily increasing political **violence** by extremists at each end of the political spectrum. Death tolls escalated from 300 during 1976–77, to over 3000 during 1980, with the number of wounded and bomb explosions during this period well into five figures. While the perpetrators initially confined their activities to each other, a steady deterioration of parliamentary decorum and the politicization of trade unions and the civil service meant that incidents – and victims – were soon almost universal.

Ecevit regained power for about eighteen months beginning at the close of 1977, and attempted to address the **dire economic situation** which had been aggravated not only by the endemic disorder, but by successive governments' profligate public spending, trade deficits and other inflationary policies. International assistance was secured, but on condition that the budget was balanced, protectionism reduced and the lira devalued, and in the event the political resolve to apply such strict controls was lacking. In December 1978, street battles in the southern city of Maraş between right-wing, fundamentalist Sunni gunmen and left-wing Alevîs claimed more than a hundred lives within a week; the NAP were blamed by many for having orchestrated the clashes. Martial law was declared with some reluctance by Ecevit in many provinces, but this failed to prevent the establishment of an Alevî commune in the Black Sea town of Fatsa, where the army eventually sent in tanks against street barricades. Against such a background of events, Demirel regained power in October 1979, but he also failed to halt the slide into **civil and economic chaos**. Random, tit-for-tat murders in İstanbul reached twenty per day, with some neighbourhoods run by various factions – entry to these with the wrong newspaper in hand guaranteed a beating or worse.

THE 1980 COUP AND ITS AFTERMATH

The armed forces, initially reluctant to act because of the apparent ineffectiveness of the 1960 and 1971 interventions, soon decided that the Republic was facing its gravest crisis yet. A planning group for a military takeover apparently existed as early as 1978, but public rumblings first surfaced in the form of a warning letter to the two major political parties at New Year 1980. By this time **martial law** was in force in all of the major cities as well as the southeast, and an economist and engineer named **Turgut Özal** had been appointed head of the State Planning Organization, in which capacity he jettisoned the import-substitution policies prevalent since the founding of the Republic in favour of an **export-orientated economy**.

Now international events intervened. Turkey's strategic importance to the West had been emphasized by the Iranian revolution and Soviet invasion of Afghanistan, and the Americans in particular were anxious to secure a stable base in the Middle East. After five years of cool relations, prompted by an embargo of arms to Turkey in the wake of the Cyprus action, rapprochement feelers were put forth. By the time the Iran–Iraq war began in April 1980, these began to include signals of tacit approval for a coup. Some sources have also alleged that, given the existing martial law controls, the continued escalation of domestic violence was inconceivable without the military's toleration of it – even to the extent of using *agents provocateurs* to guarantee a solid pretext for a full-scale takeover.

This occurred bloodlessly on **September 12, 1980**, to the initial relief of a vast majority of the population. The frenzied killings ceased; Demirel and Ecevit, Erbakan and Türkeş were all detained; all political parties were disbanded shortly after; and all trade unions and associations were closed down. Turgut Özal was, however, left in charge of the economy, since his reforms were seen as both effective and essential to Western support.

It soon became apparent that this coup represented a drastic break from the pattern of the previous two. A junta of generals, not junior officers – the **National Security Council** – were firmly in control from the start, and return to civilian rule would be long delayed, and within a new framework. Meanwhile, bannings, indictments and purges punctuated the early 1980s, and while the radical right was by no means immune from prosecution, it became clear that the left would bear the brunt of the crackdown. Nationalist right-wing beliefs, if not explicitly violent or fascist, were compatible with the generals' agenda – as was an encouragement of mildly Islamic views on society as an antidote to secular Marxism, as long as the fundamentalists stayed out of the military itself.

The new rulers' principal **targets** which had been relatively untouched in previous putsches, were labour syndicates, internationalist or separatist groups and the left-leaning intelligentsia, previously influential in Turkish politics. DİSK, the far-left trade union confederation, had 1477 of its members put on trial after its dissolution; 264 were convicted, despite lack of evidence of advocacy of violence, though the proceedings dragged on for so long – until 1990, in fact – that many defendants qualified for immediate release on the basis of time served on remand. Even more controversial was the six-year court case against the Turkish Peace Association, with twelve defendants, including an ex-ambassador, sentenced. An example of the relatively lenient treatment of the Islamicists was the acquittal, on appeal, of fundamentalist National Salvation Party leader Necmettin Erbakan, on charges of attempting to create an Islamic state. The Nationalist Action Party was, however, decimated, with eight capital verdicts and dozens of longer prison terms for its members – though Türkeş himself was acquitted.

The military attacked the **universities** less directly, purging 1475 academic staff as of 1984 by outright dismissal, placement on non-renewed short-term contracts, or transfer to less desirable positions. All campuses were put under the control of a new body, the Higher Education Council (YÖK), subject to the direct authority of the acting head of state.

In a process somewhat like the drafting of the 1960 constitution, a 160-strong Consultative Committee of carefully vetted applicants was convened, which promulgated a new, highly **restrictive constitution** in 1982, expressly reversing most clauses of its predecessor. This was ratified by ninety percent of the electorate in a controversially coercive referendum which was also an election for the presidency. No campaigning against was allowed; the only candidate was **General Kenan Evren**, head of the National Security Council and coup leader, and it was presented as an all-or-nothing package.

RETURN TO CIVILIAN RULE AND THE RISE OF ANAP

Civilian authority was tentatively re-established in the **general elections of November 1983**, although severe controls were placed on parties and candidates. Pre-coup parties and their leaders remained excluded from politics until 1990, and only three of the fourteen newly formed parties were allowed to contest the elections, the rest being deemed successors of banned organizations. Nonetheless, the centrist slate backed by the generals came last, and Turgut Özal's centre-right Motherland Party (initials ANAP in Turkish) won just under half the votes and just over fifty percent of the parliamentary seats.

ANAP was a party of uneasy alliance, incorporating a wide range of opinion from economic liberals to Islamists. Özal, as party leader and prime minister, managed the almost impossible

task of balancing the opposing forces in the new party, by virtue of being both a technocrat with experience abroad, and a devout Muslim, ex-member of the NSP and adherent of the still-clandestine Naqshbandi dervish order. Simultaneously he set a scorching pace of **economic reform** during his first term, with exports reaching record levels and growth rates averaging more than six percent during the period 1983–88. Inflation, however, continued to soar, as public budgets were reflated to buy support, especially among the farmers and civil servants, and by 1986 foreign indebtedness and spiralling prices were again critical issues.

In retrospect, ANAP during its heyday – and by extension Özal – can be credited with sweeping economic and legal **reforms** bringing Turkey more into line with the international economy – and at the same time blamed for the **vulgarization** of public culture. Under ANAP, money and its ostentation assumed paramount importance, with the exact means of earning it secondary – creating an ethical climate conducive to sharp practice and the growing wave of public scandals (see below). A provincial elite, matching Özal's small-town, lower-middle-class background, came in on his coat-tails, earning an initial reputation of being able to "get things done", in contrast to the fumbling of the 1970s. Though trained abroad, they hadn't necessarily absorbed Western values, and when they had, their cue was taken from the US rather than the EC. **English** became the preferred language of this nouveau riche class, and of the best universities, which in the wake of the National Security Council's efforts during the early Eighties had become little more than apolitical polytechnics geared to cranking out technicians. Thatcher-Reaganism was the order of the day, unlike the noblesse oblige of the earlier RPP elite: large conglomerates and holding companies, numerous in Turkey, were expressly favoured, and many small businesses were forced to the wall. Larger units were seen as best suited for the pursuit of an **export-led economy** to replace the old import-substitution strategies. Along with the export earnings – and mass tourism should be included in this – came a flood of luxury goods that contrasted with the shortages of the 1970s: just about anything became available, for a price, flaunted avidly by the new consuming classes. This of course aggravated the ballooning trade deficit, since Turkish manufactured products – despite vast improvements since the 1970s – were (and are) still not competitive on most markets.

In local elections of 1984 and 1986, opposition parties gained some ground, particularly Erdal İnönü's Social Democrat Party (SHP in Turkish), and the True Path (DYP) and Democratic Left (DSP) parties, fronts respectively for the activities of still-proscribed Demirel and Ecevit. Another banned politician to return to the hustings was Necmettin Erbakan, whose old Islamist apparatus regrouped itself as the Welfare Party (*Refah Partisi* in Turkish). Popular pressure grew for a **lifting of the ban** on pre-coup politicians, which was narrowly approved in mid-1987. Parliamentary elections in November of that year showed just 36 percent support for ANAP but, because of the non-proportional-representation system put into effect especially for the occasion, they took nearly two-thirds of the seats in the Grand National Assembly. The SHP emerged as the main opposition, with nearly a quarter of the seats, though their performance was impeded somewhat by public perception of **Erdal İnönü**, a university professor turned politician, as a nice but ineffectual individual whom the unkind nicknamed "ET" after his tortoise-like resemblance to Spielberg's hero.

The DYP did badly; and Ecevit, his DSP party failing to poll the ten percent nationwide required for parliamentary representation, tearfully announced his retirement – temporarily as it turned out – from politics.

THE LATE 1980S: TRENDS AND PROBLEMS

Özal's two prime ministerial terms were marked, not surprisingly in view of his background, by a dramatic increase in **Islamic activity**. The Department of Religious Affairs received extra staffing and funding, and the mandatory teaching hours devoted to Muslim issues in schools saw a similar rise. Much of this can be attributed to a conscious effort to offset or channel the influence of Iranian-style fundamentalism, but there seems also to have been a deliberate policy of promoting moderate Islamic sentiment as a safeguard against resurgence of communist ideology. Outside of the government apparatus, the *vakıfs* or pious endowments also grew spectacularly, support-ed largely by donations from Saudi Arabia. Educational and welfare programmes run by the *vakıfs* offered, and continue to offer, some hope and relief to those trapped in the burgeoning *gecekondus* of the principal cities, where life is most precarious, but the assistance also encouraged fanatical and intolerant elements. On the other hand, the military periodically conducted purges of Islamicists who managed to infiltrate the ranks, in a continuation of their post-coup stance.

Kurdish separatism, an intermittent issue since the foundation of the Republic, resurfaced in a violent form in the southeastern provinces. The main group involved, the Marxist-Leninist Kurdish Workers' Party (PKK), was founded in 1978, and based partly overseas (though the French and German governments banned their activities in late 1993). Its guerrilla war of attrition against the Turkish government and its representatives since 1984 did not initially win it widespread support, but its position was undoubtedly strengthened by the frequent over-zealous actions and policies of the Turkish authorities. (For a complete discussion, see p.780).

Turkey's relations with most of her neighbours remained uneasy. **Ties with Greece** were strained not only by the Cyprus issue but by ongoing disputes over airspace, seabed exploitation rights and territorial waters in the Aegean, and by the Greek government's maltreatment of and denial of full civil rights to the Turkish minority in Greek Thrace. **Bulgarian–Turkish relations** made international headlines throughout the summer of 1989, as the Communist Bulgarian regime's policy of forced Slavification of the Bulgarian Turkish minority resulted in dozens of deaths and ultimately escalated into the largest European mass emigration since World War II. Between May and August, over 300,000 ethnic Turks fled Bulgaria for Turkey, which initially welcomed them (the government had in fact invited them as part of a war of words with Bulgaria) and attempted to some extent to capitalize politically on the exodus. The reality of the number of refugees to be settled soon hit home, however, the border was closed, and by 1990 the new government in Sofia had formally renounced the heavy-handed assimilationist campaign of their predecessors, while most of the new arrivals eventually decided to return to Bulgaria.

In direct contrast to the Turkish government's concern for the rights of Turkish minorities abroad, there was an ongoing pattern of **human rights violations** at home. This took the form principally of inhumane conditions in prisons but more importantly torture of suspects by law-enforcement agencies, and continual harassment of the press. At various times government spokesmen admitted that torture was practised during the 1980–83 period of military rule, when hundreds of thousands of individuals were taken into custody, but until recently declined to comment on, or denied, allegations of continuing incidents. In the late 1980s and early 1990s several cases of official torture during the subsequent period of civilian rule were admitted, and some prosecutions of those responsible conducted, but their numbers were token, with the guilty often quietly promoted out of harm's way rather than being jailed.

Abuses continued into the 1990s, particularly in police stations during the initial periods of detention, though the extent was difficult to establish, as was the issue of whether it was sanctioned at the highest levels. Amnesty International claimed that torture was still widespread and systematic; other monitoring organizations maintained that, while admittedly widespread, it was no longer officially condoned. However, only after the national elections of 1991 was their an official proclamation forbidding the maltreatment of non-political suspects prior to formal charging, the period for which was reduced from two weeks to 24 hours. Simultaneously, the Turkish Human Rights Foundation founded a chain of medical rehabilitation centres where victims of torture could apply for treatment.

If torture may eventually cease to be a feature of Turkish civic life, restrictions on the press show no signs of abating. The record number of prosecutions of journalists, editors and publishers between 1984 and 1996 may paradoxically have been a result of the media's growing boldness in testing the limits of censorship. An unsettling echo of the Menderes years was the increasing sensitivity of Turgut Özal to even the mildest criticism in print, with dozens of libel and slander suits filed by government prosecutors.

Meanwhile, in not entirely unrelated developments, Turkey's European-orientated **foreign policy** suffered various setbacks towards the end of the decade. Turkey had been an associate member of the EC since 1964, but her 1987 application for full membership was shelved indefinitely by the Community shortly after, ostensibly because of the need to concentrate on increased integration of the existing Twelve.

At the same time substantial public relations efforts were devoted to beating back repeated proposals in the United States Congress, sponsored by the international **Armenian lobby**, to designate April 24 as a day of "national remembrance" for the alleged genocide perpetrated against the Armenian community in 1915. This marked an increase in the sophistication of the more extreme Armenian advocates, who appeared to have mostly abandoned the policy of terrorist attacks on Turkish diplomats and installations which characterized the years 1973–82.

Finally, the dramatic changes in eastern Europe further marginalized the country, as Soviet influence in the region nearly vanished and doubts were cast on the future strategic importance of a post-Cold War NATO in general and Turkey in particular. In short, Turkish foreign policy was at sea by the late 1980s, deprived of a coherent position and often reduced to reacting to, rather than influencing, events.

THE PRESIDENCY AND DEATH OF ÖZAL

ANAP's influence was also already waning by early 1989, when municipal elections showed strong support for the opposition SHP and DYP at their expense. This was due to continuing high domestic inflation, the blatant nepotism benefiting Özal's cronies and large extended family – including his flamboyant, cigar-smoking, whisky-drinking wife Semra – and the inevitable corruption which attended this. Under the circumstances, most observers found Özal's self-nomination for the **presidency** – and election to it in November 1989 by a parliament half-empty owing to an opposition boycott – presumptuous in the extreme.

As prime minister, Özal had skilfully maintained a balance between the religious and secular wings of ANAP; now, as only the second civilian president in Turkish history, he strategically distanced himself from the nationalist/religious wing of the party in favour of the liberal one. Despite his official description as being "above-party", Özal was still widely perceived as the real leader of ANAP. He was instrumental in choosing the next prime minister, **Yıldırım Akbulut**, a lacklustre yes-man unable to command much respect either within the party or in the general population, where the repetition and even publishing of jokes at his expense became a favourite pastime. Akbulut's position was repeatedly undermined by Özal himself, who – in apparent contravention of the constitution – assumed many of the executive functions of the prime minister.

Özal's **interference** – including but not limited to highly quotable, foot-in-mouth utterances that were the despair of his cabinet ministers – prompted the resignations of several of them, including foreign minister Mesut Yılmaz in early 1990 (though he eventually replaced Akbulut as prime minister in July 1991), his successor Ali Bozer in October 1990 and army chief of staff Necip Torumtay – the latter originally appointed during 1987 in a manner expressly designed to snub the National Security Council and demonstrate Özal's independence from the military establishment.

Iraq's **invasion of Kuwait** in August 1990 reinforced Özal's position, and also reminded NATO and the US of Turkey's continuing strategic position. Özal – not Akbulut, Bozer or Torumtay – contacted other heads of state and was central in defining Turkey's stance as an enthusiastic adherent of the UN sanctions, perhaps in anticipation of tangible rewards from the West for such support. The Gulf crisis provided a needed, if temporary, boost to Özal's popularity, which had slumped following his election as head of state. He enthusiastically provided the US with landing facilities at İncirlik and Diyarbakır air bases, despite the risk of Iraqi attack, and incurred considerable financial loss by complying with UN sanctions, closing the pipeline which shipped Iraqi oil out through Turkish territory. Later in 1991 he permitted the stationing of coalition troops near the Kurdish "safe haven" across the Iraqi border as part of Operation Poised Hammer.

Özal perhaps entertained hopes that Turkey would be rewarded after the war by the return of the oil-rich province of Mosul. All he got tangibly for Turkey's cooperation was President Bush's undertaking that an independent Kurdistan would not be set up by dismembering Iraq. In the long term the Coalition treated Turkey shabbily, failing to compensate it adequately for its losses – or for their admittedly

reluctant hosting of hundreds of thousands of terrified Iraqi Kurdish refugees. Closer to home, participation in the anti-Iraq alliance sparked fundamentalist and leftist **attacks** on American and foreign property and personnel throughout early 1991, and sporadic street demonstrations against the war. A police crackdown on all this ensured a calm environment for President Bush's visit in July, the first of an American leader to Turkey in several decades and growing evidence of Turkey's importance for the US as a reliable regional ally.

Moreover, a nationwide **political vacuum** in terms of maturity and substance was growing both before and after the war. ANAP, beset by resignations, defections and factions, had lost its original energy and direction, but the opposition was not yet able to turn this to their advantage. The SHP, rent by an internal power struggle in which chairman İnönü ousted general secretary Deniz Baykal, accordingly slipped from its 1989 electoral standing, while Bülent Ecevit's DSP rebounded from a nadir in its fortunes by doing extremely well at the SHP's and DYP's expense in August 1990 municipal elections. İnönü renewed his oft-repeated call for a merger of the two left-of-centre parties but was rebuffed by Ecevit.

Overall the electorate was uninspired by the politics of personalities and almost complete lack of coherent party agendas or manifestos. The only consensus that in fact developed by the end of 1990 was the posthumous **rehabilitation of Menderes** and his cronies, an act of contrition that has taken the form of naming streets and public facilities after Menderes, and – on the thirtieth anniversary of the hangings of the three ministers – their solemn reburial in a special mausoleum.

By June 1991 Prime Minister Akbulut had been eased out of office, in tandem with Özal's increasing support for ANAP's liberal wing. The new premier and party leader **Mesut Yılmaz** decided to go to the polls considerably earlier than the November 1992 limit stipulated: with the economy worsening, he felt it better earlier than later, while some of Özal's post-war support might rub off on ANAP.

But the **October 1991 elections**, considered the fairest since 1980, produced a surprise result: the DYP was top finisher, with ANAP a strong second, and İnönü's SHP third. The biggest surprise, however, was the Welfare

Party's unprecedented seventeen percent of the vote. But since no party secured an absolute majority, a **coalition** was inevitable, and in the event was the one many had wished for throughout the 1970s: between DYP and SHP, forged after several weeks of negotiations. Demirel was designated prime minister, İnönü deputy prime minister, with the various lower ministries divided between their two parties.

The coalition began with considerable optimism and goodwill (or at least forbearance) on all sides, even from the excluded ANAP; both parties pledged to pull together in tackling the country's pressing economic problems. Rapid privatization of the state firms was envisioned, along with a better deal for labour, and tax reform to make the wealthy pay their fair share after the jamboree of the ANAP years. The unenviable task of tackling inflation was assigned to **Tansu Çiller**, state minister for economy and the sole woman cabinet member.

There were also promises to make Turkey a *konuşan* (talking) society, where opinions were freely aired without fear of retribution, in contrast to the intimidated silence of the past. This intention ran into an immediate snag, however, when some of the 22 parliamentary deputies of **HEP** (the Kurdish-dominated Popular Labour Party, accused of ties with the PKK) – legally compelled to run on the SHP ticket but winning a quarter of the party's seats – caused an uproar when they refused to recite the standard loyalty oath upon being sworn in. **Deniz Baykal** further destabilized the SHP by repeatedly challenging İnönü for its top post, branding him responsible for the declining party fortunes since 1989, with the latter maintaining his position mainly by predicting the demise of the coalition should Baykal replace him.

National legislation **un-banning pre-1980 parties** saw the Republican People's Party reopened, setting off a scramble as to who would assume its leadership: 1979 chief Ecevit, İnönü (envisioning its incorporation into the coalition) or his persistent adversary Deniz Baykal. Baykal won, and as defections to his standard from DSP and SHP mounted, coupled with resignations of HEP deputies from SHP, the coalition's governing majority dwindled to a slim three. Simultaneously ANAP again showed signs of disintegrating into its constituent factions, while the briefly reactivated Justice Party closed down at the request of its ex-chief Demirel.

Throughout 1992 **Özal** played an increasingly negative, spoiling role, much of it a function of the personal antipathy between him and Demirel, who openly sought a way to have him impeached. Özal also sparred with current ANAP leader Yılmaz for influence in a party which as president he constitutionally could no longer head, eventually attempting to unseat his old protégé. When this failed, he flip-flopped again and hinted he would resign the presidency to participate in a party dominated by defected ANAP conservatives. In his capacity as president, Özal delayed the signing of many bills, prompting serious discussion of having him removed from office, a drawn-out procedure requiring a two-thirds majority in parliament. In the event, this proved unnecessary; Özal **died suddenly** of a heart attack on April 17, 1993.

It was impossible for anyone to remain indifferent to Özal, despite his many faults the most eloquent and influential head of state since Atatürk, having opened up the country to the outside world even more than Menderes. Respected by many for his energy, courage and vision, despised by an equal number for his overbearing manner and shameless self-aggrandizing, he remains an ambiguous figure who sometimes did the right thing (for example his advocacy of concessions to the Kurds) for opportunistic reasons. His passing incontestably marked the end of an era, but the beginning of another where Turkey would have an increasingly high global profile.

AFTER ÖZAL

Demirel eventually emerged as president, while economic adviser **Tansu Çiller** – not Demirel's favoured candidate – became **prime minister** in June 1993. Like Özal and Demirel on the centre-right of Turkish politics, she was a US-educated academic-technocrat who had been brought into politics by Demirel in 1989 as part of an effort to modernize his party's image. With her assertive style and telegenic manner, she attracted considerable popular support, and her rise to power was initially viewed with optimism both within and without the DYP.

Such hopes, however, were soon dashed as the new prime minister proved herself woefully inadequate to the task at hand. Expectations of a fresh look at the **Kurdish problem** vanished as Çiller relegated all initiative to military hardliners, while she retreated into shrill, jingoistic rhetoric. Despite repeated assurances that the PKK was on the verge of defeat, the death toll in the undeclared civil war in east Anatolia continued to mount, exceeding a rate of 3000 per year. A controversial policy of expulsion of villagers from affected areas resulted in a tide of internal refugees, while efforts to bring about a political solution foundered when the pro-Kurdish Democracy Party (DEP) was proscribed and most of its MPs prosecuted (see p.782).

The government's **economic policy** was characterized by hasty improvisation. Inflation shot up from 66 percent in 1993 to a staggering 120 percent during 1994, hovering around 80 percent in subsequent years. During early 1994 the prime minister's persistent and confused meddling in monetary policy led to the Turkish lira losing nearly half its value within a month. April stabilization measures managed to contain the crisis at the cost of a year-long recession and a five-percent fall in national income. A boldly announced programme of privatizations and tax reform failed to materialize in practice, since given the complete lack of unemployment or early retirement benefits, or retraining schemes, such moves would have caused enormous social distress and threatened social stability. As it was, a spate of industrial disasters — particularly mine and factory explosions, with large loss of life — made headlines despite a commitment to a better social contract for labour, while massive strikes by public-sector workers in 1994 and 1995 won them only paltry wage increases. In late November 1994, a privatization bill was finally passed by the Turkish parliament, eleven years after being first discussed; so far the only tangible result has been the hiving off of the telecom division of the PTT in early 1996.

In the matter of **foreign affairs**, hesitation replaced Özal's active (if at times bumbling) intervention in Balkan, Central Asian and Middle Eastern affairs. Seven foreign ministers within thirty months prevented the emergence of a consistent policy direction. A much-heralded project to carry Azerbaijani petroleum to Mediterranean ports through a Turkish-built pipeline seemed, by early 1996, to have stalled in the face of Russian opposition; Moscow's displeasure also resulted in the toning down of noisy public support for the Chechen rebels. Equally vociferous Turkish sympathy for the Muslim cause in Bosnia failed to translate into a coherent policy initiative. Tensions with Greece flared periodically into crises which were aggravated by demagogic posturing by political leaders in both countries; in February 1996 the two countries nearly went to war over the sovereignty of the Kardak/Ímia archipelago, a pair of uninhabited rocky islets in the Aegean Sea.

The only significant – but still controversial – foreign policy success of the Çiller-led coalition was the conclusion in March 1995 of a **customs union** agreement with the EU. Overseas, there was considerable opposition in view of Turkey's poor human rights record (see below); within the country, opponents (including ANAP's Yılmaz and Refah's Necmettin Erbakan) pointed out that billions of dollars in annual import duties were being forfeited, while Turks would still not have freedom of movement to and within Europe. Though falling considerably short of the ideal of full EU membership for Turkey, the agreement, which took effect at the start of 1996, was still trumpeted as a triumph by the increasingly beleaguered government.

UNCIVIL LIBERTIES AND CORRUPTION

Turkey's dismal **human rights record** has been a perennial irritant in relations with the EU. Despite Demirel's 1991 election pledge that police stations would have "walls of glass", international human-rights monitoring organizations reported little substantive change in subsequent years, with torture and suspicious deaths in custody routine occurrences. Turkey is still a long way from being a *konuşan* society, given the nearly two thousand indictments returned yearly by State Security Tribunals against "seditious" publications. Despite parliamentary modification during 1995 of many objectionable clauses of the 1982 constitution, and of the notorious Article 8 of the 1991 anti-terrorism law, Turkish prisons still contain nearly 150 non-violent political prisoners. The civilian government abjectly and habitually defers to chiefs of the internal security forces which, together with elements of the State Security Tribunals, the police and the gendarmerie, form a virtual para-state, accountable to none.

Since 1990 a sharp rise in urban terrorism has occurred, with literally scores of **political assassinations** perpetrated by Islamic fundamentalists, far-leftists and possibly rogue civilian operatives of the Special Warfare Department, whose common feature has been the inability of police to identify or apprehend any suspects. Targets have included American personnel during and after the Gulf War; officers in the army and security forces; secularist professors, including the head of the national bar society; and (after a two-decade hiatus) members of Turkey's Jewish community. But it was the demise of **Uğur Mumcu** in an Ankara car bombing of January 1993 which caused the most widespread revulsion. His funeral, attended by hundreds of thousands (including the National Security Council), was the occasion for mass demonstrations of support for his ideals of secularism and pluralistic democracy. As ever, nobody significant has been apprehended in the case, with his relatives alleging a cover-up amidst wider murmurings of involvement by radical fundamentalists, in connivance with elements in the security forces. Meanwhile, police devoted most of their energies to crushing the Marxist terrorist group Dev Sol with a series of spectacular shoot-ups of alleged safehouses in İstanbul and elsewhere. Another feature of the Çiller era was the huge upsurge in the number of **"disappeared" persons** – usually left-wing or Kurdish activists who vanished after being detained by police or by unidentified civilians. In 1995, relatives of "disappeared" persons began to rally in İstanbul's Galatasaray Square each Saturday, defying police harassment and occasional mass arrests.

Perhaps the most important civic issue facing Çiller's government was its handling of the major **corruption scandals** which seemed to erupt almost every week. As in the broadly similar case of Italy, it's not so much more that there's more graft than in earlier times, but that the ethos of the Özal years encouraged a certain brazenness in its practice, which sorely tried public patience following lurid disclosures in the press. Again as in Italy, no party was immune from guilt, as all had governed in recent years. Most of the scandals concerned public firms and entities such as the PTT, the Health Ministry and the Social Security Administration, whose officials allegedly took kickbacks for the award of contracts to private companies. In the most spectacular case, Özal's widow and daughter were accused of contracting a mafia hit-team to shoot **Engin Civan**, chairman of a

state bank, who allegedly received a $5 million bribe to fix a credit deal but failed to deliver the goods. Civan eventually fled to the US after serving several months in jail; Mrs Özal deemed it prudent to make a long journey to the same country coincide with the court proceedings where she was named as a prime suspect; the daughter of the mafia boss who leaked the Özal connection to the press was murdered at a ski resort; and the hit-man who had attempted to shoot Mr Civan during a court hearing was himself gunned down at a popular İstanbul café, along with half a dozen innocent bystanders at adjacent tables. Another name which figured prominently in graft stories was that of the prime minister's husband, **Özer Çiller**, a businessman who apparently amassed $50 million worth of real estate (partly in the US) during his wife's term in office. A story circulated by Associated Press in September 1996 listed Tansu Çiller among the world's ten most corrupt politicians of the 1990s, so it was hardly surprising that she did little to combat this endemic feature of Turkish political culture.

THE COALITION DISSOLVES

Even before mid-1993, there had been widespread public disillusionment with the coalition, and the inadequacies of Çiller's leadership soon also fuelled discontent within the parties concerned. Old DYP bosses led the internal opposition to Çiller with the tacit backing of President Demirel, whose dislike of his former protégée became apparent soon after she had taken office. The anti-Çiller front found a ready ally in ANAP leader **Mesut Yılmaz**, whose opposition strategy seemed motivated principally by an intense personal hatred of "that woman".

The junior partner of the coalition fared no better. Shortly after Çiller's elevation, Erdal İnönü announced his **retirement** as leader of SHP. Former Ankara mayor Murat Karayalçın, who replaced him in September 1993, proved unable to defuse factional tensions in the party, nor to subordinate his personal rivalry with CHP leader Deniz Baykal in the interests of a long-awaited merger with the latter party. By late 1994, paralyzed by infighting, saddled with the dismal performance of SHP municipalities elected in 1989, and rent by increased radicalism within the traditionally centre-left Alevî community, the SHP had disintegrated into its constituent factions. In February 1995, the party formally dissolved itself to merge with the CHP, with a former foreign minister, **Hikmet Çetin**, designated as the most broadly acceptable leader of the unified party, and by extension Çiller's newest deputy prime minister. But in September 1995, Deniz Baykal returned as head of the neo-CHP, and having failed to reach agreement with Çiller on several crucial issues, announced the end of the coalition. Elections were set for December 24, with the tattered coalition presiding as a caretaker government in the interim.

THE 1995 ELECTIONS AND THE RISE OF REFAH

When they came around, the **elections** provided a rude shock for the established parties of both right and left. DYP did poorly with 19.2 percent of the vote, down eight points from its 1991 performance; the European Parliament's ratification of the customs union agreement just the week before had clearly furnished little benefit to Çiller's party. ANAP, which languished under the vacillating and unimaginative leadership of Mesut Yılmaz, tied for second place with an almost identical share of the votes, down five points from its showing four years earlier. The CHP, with 10.8 percent of the vote, came within a whisker of failing the statutory ten-percent nationwide minimum for parliamentary representation; the other centre-left party, Ecevit's DSP, performed only slightly better at 14 percent. HADEP, the latest incarnation of the HEP-DEP ethos, failed to gain seats with its 4.8 percent, though it scored a majority in several Kurdish-populated provinces; Turkeş's quasi-fascist MHP also missed the barrier at 8.7 percent. The only clear winner in the election was top-polling **Refah** with 21.3 percent of votes cast, taking 197 out of 550 seats in the recently enlarged parliament, despite assertions by Çiller that a Refah victory would mean a return to the Dark Ages.

The result was hardly surprising, as political Islam had been making impressive gains since the late 1980s, when Özal and the National Security Council had both given its milder expressions their blessing. Refah had established itself as the most active party in terms of grassroots organization; alone among political groups, it harnessed the energies of women (however conservatively attired) and employed door-to-door canvassing techniques, relying on campaign material that addressed — in however

lopsided a manner — social issues such as prostitution and income inequality, rather than stressing personalities and platitudes. In the burgeoning *gecekondus*, it alone seemed to represent the values and aspirations of the newly urbanized underclass, attracting it with populist rhetoric. To the lower-middle-class bazaar craftsman most at risk from the trappings of liberal capitalism, Refah promised protection in the form of a sharply renegotiated customs union. In the conservative east, its Islamic ecumenicism seemed to provide a reasonable alternative to many Kurds alienated by the more usual forms of Turkish nationalism. Last but not least, many voters threw in their lot with Refah simply in protest at the corruption and inertia of the discredited mainstream parties.

In the March 1994 **municipal elections**, Refah had carried a plurality of cities across the country, including both metropolitan İstanbul and Ankara (by contrast, it did poorly in rural areas and small towns). In İstanbul, initial fears of puritanism run amok — alcohol-free pubs, obligatory gender segregation on buses, *Swan Lake* in harem pants — were quickly dispelled as the administration of mayor **Tayyip Erdoğan** proved itself pragmatic, efficient and remarkably honest by Turkish standards. Pollution was substantively addressed, extra buses laid on, the rubbish collected regularly and facilities provided for the handicapped. Cynics said the rabbits would stop coming out of the Refah skullcap as soon as clandestine donations from the Saudis dried up; others, and by no means all of them Islamists, pointed out that Refah's success was earned both by their opponents' moral bankruptcy and by their own organizational skill. Relative Refah competence in Turkey's largest city had helped convert many voters in time for the national elections, and seemed to establish young Erdoğan as heir apparent to the party's septuagenarian leader Erbakan.

The **Islamic revivalism** which has gripped increasingly broader segments of Turkish society from the mid-1980s can just be seen as the latest in successive cycles of reaction against the Atatürkist secular republic. In Turkey, secularism has always been a matter of suppressing the public expression of Islam and keeping it out of politics, quite different from its Western manifestation as freedom of belief and equal treatment for all religions. The longstanding official ban on traditional Islamic dress meant in practice that many young people of conservative social background could never expect to enter a public career, or even be admitted to university. A December 1989 decree empowering individual universities to allow, at their discretion, attendance by women wearing headscarves was viewed alarmingly by secularists as the thin edge of a wedge of increased religiosity; by the mid-1990s, wearers of the scarf or the prophetic beard had grown from an initial radical fringe to include some of the brightest members of the academic community.

The prohibition of dervish orders had also begun to grate, as the various mystical brotherhoods emerged from underground and gained renewed popularity in the 1980s. For a majority of the population, Islam remained a much stronger cultural presence than the assertive Westernizing of the elites, and a more homespun expression of the national spirit than the quasi-colonial arrogance often associated with the Atatürkist establishment. On a wider level there was a general distrust of the West, regarded as the wellspring of Christian prejudice and capitalist exploitation, sworn enemy of the Muslim world, and betrayer of the Bosnians, Azeris and Palestinians. From this posture it was not too far a leap to overt anti-Semitism and hostility towards Israel; opposition to a series of military cooperation agreements signed between Turkey and Israel during the final months of the DYP–CHP coalition formed a key plank to Refah's campaign.

BETWEEN ALLAH AND THE IMF: REFAH TAKES POWER

The political establishment reacted to the December 1995 election results by hastily patching up a **DYP–ANAP coalition** of second-bests, expressly designed to keep Refah from assuming power. But even together they could only muster 267 seats out of the 276 needed for a parliamentary majority, and were forced to put out unsuccessful feelers to both of the left-of-centre parties in order to form a three-way, right–left coalition. In the event, Mesut Yılmaz presided over an unstable minority government, characterized by intensified mutual loathing between himself and Çiller, and constant sniping from Refah – which felt cheated of its electoral spoils – and from the rest of the opposition, which finally rang down the curtain in June 1996 with a motion of censure.

Virtually the only event inside Turkey during early 1996 to receive attention internationally, aside from the annual spring offensive against the PKK, was the conclusion of the year-long court proceedings against the internationally acclaimed novelist **Yaşar Kemal**. He had been charged with promulgating "separatist propaganda" and fomenting "hatred between races", as a result of his January 1995 article in *Der Spiegel* describing the Turkish state as a "system of unbearable repression and atrocity" and claiming that the Kurdish rebellion was a justifiable response to seventy years of official repression (a similar, English-language article appears in the special "File on Turkey" of *Index on Censorship*, Vol. 24 1/1995). With the eyes of the world on Turkey so soon after the customs union ratification, he was given a suspended twenty-month sentence in March, but not before 99 other prosecutions under Article 8 had been brought against artists and intellectuals who had rallied to his support.

All this indicated the pervasive, resurgent influence of the ex-security-service chiefs who had infiltrated Çiller's entourage at her express invitation, giving the DYP the nickname of the "Police Academy". But they would not be able to protect her against impending investigations into corruption, and in particular allegations that she'd helped herself to $6.5 million from the central bank to finance the recent elections. To save herself, in mid-July she negotiated a **DYP coalition with Refah**, something she'd sworn she would never do, with Erbakan as prime minister and herself as foreign minister; her price was the dropping of all proceedings against her, which Erbakan had encouraged. Secularist, professional women, who had believed her claim to be their last line of defence against the *hocas*, faxed their resentment in plenitude to DYP headquarters; feelings ran equally high in parliament, where punch-ups flared and handguns were drawn as the coalition was approved by a narrow vote of 278 to 265. Lurid headlines in the Turkish press predicted coup and disaster as Erbakan immediately embarked on a series of controversial trips to Iran and Libya, sent emissaries to Iraq and generally made friendly noises towards other notorious global pariahs.

Erbakan, however, proved nimbler than his detractors. While the secularists conjured up spectres of turbaned *kadi*s (Islamic judges) and obligatorily veiled women, Refah moved quickly to divest itself, in public at least, of its threatening image. Within weeks of taking office, after a discreet word in its ear from the military's US minders, the government meekly signed a new military treaty with Israel, making mockery of its campaign promise to tear up such documents. Authorization for the use by NATO aircraft of two airbases in the southeast as part of Operation Provide Comfort was quietly extended, despite prior characterization of NATO as a "formal occupation". An IMF negotiating team, in Ankara to sort through the morass of Turkish finances (its foreign debt ranks among the top ten worldwide), was pleasantly surprised to hear nothing further about either zero-interest banking or a proposed "Islamic currency". Non-veiled wives of Refah MPs began making the social rounds, and soon Erbakan himself was spotted committing the ultimate Islamist sacrilege: laying the customary wreath at Atatürk's tomb.

It's premature to pronounce on whether Refah is seeking to reinvent itself as a democratic party of the secular centre-right ground, previously occupied by Menderes' Democrat Party, Demirel's Justice Party and Özal's ANAP. A September party conference jettisoned much of the radical vocabulary which the Islamists had accumulated over 23 years in opposition, and Refah has trodden softly in the cities which it controls. However, the stability of its present configuration is debatable: Refah still includes a radical fringe proposing a return to the Islamic *sharia* law code, from which the party leadership has nominally dissociated itself, as well as technocrat refugees from ANAP, and numerous young graduates of the *imam hatip okulular* (religious schools) which burgeoned after 1980, fired as much by careerist as religious zeal. Radical application of the *sharia* along Afghan, Saudi or Sudani lines is not presently proposed, and the hardliners may leave the party, allowing it to evolve along more secular lines. On the other hand, critics allege that Refah is merely practicing **taqiya** – the concealment or temporary compromising of one's true aims in the interest of Islam – and that given a clear electoral majority, a radical fundamentalist programme would in fact be implemented.

In terms of day-to-day administration, the performance of the new government has thus far been disappointing. There have been no

imaginative policy initiatives against the spectres of hyperinflation and the mayhem in the east. And in November 1996, a fatal, high-speed car wreck outside Ankara seemed to prove long-muttered assertions of a link between right-wing-nationalist assasins, top police chiefs, the anti-PKK Kurdish drug mafia, and certain elements of the DYP. A representative member of each faction was found dead or dying in the wreckage, along with a fair quantity of weaponry, and the DYP Interior Minister, **Mehmet Ağar**, was compelled to resign when his close ties to the group were demonstrated.

IN AND AROUND TURKEY: TRENDS FOR THE 21ST CENTURY

It would be rash to predict a successful Iranian-style **Islamic revolution** in Turkey. The country's large Alevî minority – up to one in five inhabitants – could be counted on to oppose it, as would other powerful elements of Turkish society: big business, big media, academia, and much of the middle classes and the army. Although "Islamic" banks have already set up shop in Turkey, a complete ban on interest would throttle the vital inward flow of international credit and completely decouple Turkey from the European economy, which accounts for eighty percent of its trade. Strategic realities also make it unlikely that Turkey will leave NATO, however unappreciated it feels for doing the US's bidding in the region; Russia remains a dangerous, unknown quantity, and relations with Iran, Iraq and Syria always proceed on a rollercoaster basis, with Israel too remote, tiny and problematic to serve as a consistent ally.

By the same token, another **coup** appears almost as improbable in the immediate future, despite the long litany of destabilizing internal woes. A fresh military intervention would have neither public nor overseas support, since such action is demonstrably ineffective in the long term; the period since 1987 has witnessed the gradual yet total reversal of the 1980–83 regime's political agenda. Everything and everyone that the generals sought to eradicate is back – including DİSK, which has helped the workforce regain the (regularly exercised) right to strike. Cynics observe that the army does as it pleases anyway, having grown more sophisticated over the years in using civilian politicians as window-dressing for foreign consumption.

Yet the effects of ANAP's (and the old junta's) **economic policies** will not be so easily reversed: wide disparities in income are institutionalized now, the seventh largest such gap in the world, to the advantage of speculators and wheelerdealers, and the detriment of farmers, tradesmen and wage-earners. Whatever the fate of Refah, such iniquities – strongly correlated with a galloping rate of inflation that's fuelled by the world's largest arms-import programme – will continue to provide grist for demagogues taking advantage of social discontent.

Another military intervention or a full-scale fundamentalist revival would sink any chance of **admission to the EU**, which anyway seems an increasingly remote possibility. Already 16 million East Germans have jumped the queue, as have Austria, Finland, and Sweden, with Poland and the Czech Republic probably next up. Other formidable obstacles to full membership include Turkey's appalling human rights record, remaining unacceptable clauses of the 1982 constitution, the seemingly intractable under-development and strife in the east, plus the continued partition of Cyprus, but most of all attitudes in Europe which see Turkey as a Third World country inherently unsuitable for membership in a "white, Christian" club. Some Turkish intellectuals consider that full EU membership should be a reward for past services rendered to NATO, or imagine that Turkey will thus be passively insured against further rule by its military. European parliamentarians, however, periodically point out that three EU members – Spain, Portugal and Greece – with a recent history of authoritarian regimes had disposed of them and most of their legacy well in advance of joining, and that more active remedial measures on the part of Turkey are expected.

In the face of this rejection, there is no doubt that Turkey's slavish, century-long commitment to the West is now facing its most serious challenge since Atatürk's time. Disillusion with his restrictive ideology, if not the cult of his personality, is widespread, and the main question seems to be what the change in national direction will be, not whether there will be one. Since the precipitate collapse of the Soviet Union, and the realignment of the Balkans and Middle East in a fashion vastly to Turkey's advantage, even some moderate pundits pronounce themselves not too bothered about

Europe, with **regionalist options** coming to the fore as some familiar dynamics of Turkish history reassert themselves.

The recently independent republics of **Central Asia and the Caucausus** have been assiduously courted in mildly **pan-Turkic** terms. Such overtures, specifically elaborated to compete with those of fundamentalist Shia Iran, have met with the quiet approval of the US, which seeks a mildly Sunni counterbalance in the region – what *Le Monde* has called "Soft Islam". Ambassadorial links were almost immediately established, along with cultural outreaches (including special satellite-boosted TV broadcasts), and after a meagre start in the early Nineties, Turkish business investment in Kazakhstan, Uzbekistan, Turkmenistan and Kirghizia topped $6.5 billion as of 1995. Oil pipelines are frequently proposed from these regions, both to lessen dependence on Russian natural gas, and so that Turkey may act as a rent-collecting conduit for such petroleum products to the West.

Azerbaijan, the most closely linked to Turkey by language, history and (via Nakichevan) a common border, has seen the greatest direct political involvement by Turkey, if minimal industrial investment. Successive Turkish governments have had to buck a rising tide of public opinion calling for active official military assistance to the Azeris in their long-running struggle with the Armenians, mindful of the dire consequences of such an intervention since Cyprus – though "freelance" Turkish volunteers and weaponry have certainly found their way to the theatre of war. Of late there has been a slight thaw in Turkish relations with Armenia, pending a negotiated settlement of the Nagorno-Karabagh issue.

Hand in hand with pan-Turkism has come a hint of old-fashioned **Ottomanism**, as Turkey takes an increased interest in its former Balkan possessions, specifically those from which the forefathers of many contemporary Turks emigrated and which retain some Muslim population. This has caused grave consternation in Greece, which sees its influence waning in the region – and in Brussels, where Turkey is (rightly or otherwise) regarded as more reasonable and internationally cooperative than its Aegean neighbour. At Özal's urging, Turkey sent officers to retrain the army of predominantly Muslim **Albania**, as well as civilian economic aid and advisors. Relations – including joint military exercises – with **Bulgaria** are vastly improved since the ethnic-Turkish-dominated DPS party served as a partner in the ruling coalition there. Turkey was among the first countries to recognize the republic of **Macedonia** under that name, much to the outrage of Greece, and the very first to send an ambassador. A new Turkish-funded superhighway, expressly designed to compete with and bypass Greece's Via Egnatia project, was mooted to transit Bulgaria, Macedonia and Albania, ending on the Adriatic, but seems to have been suspended by Turkey's parlous financial state. Another personal pet of Özal's which may endure is the **Black Sea Economic Cooperation Zone**, inaugurated with great fanfare in June 1992 as a forum for tackling trade, environmental and ethnic difficulties.

Any or all of these venues and activities may help foster a constructive sense of identity – or at least relatively benign diversions – which could protect Turkey from unadulterated introversion or fundamentalism. Indeed the country seems poised to become a major regional power, a role not actively played since World War I. On the other hand, the past two centuries of Turkish history have exhibited a consistently destructive pattern of alternating trends of Islamism and forcible Westernization, increasingly in tandem with a virulently exclusive Turkish nationalism. If the country is to have a stable, responsible future, then some recognition of its multi-ethnic heritage and present makeup is imperative. At the time of writing, political leadership of the necessary stature and courage, with a coherently articulated programme, seems singularly lacking.

THE KURDISH QUESTION

The majority of people in the Tigris valley, the Lake Van region and in the mountains between Erzurum, Erzincan and Diyarbakır are Kurds, an originally nomadic people speaking an Indo-European language related to Farsi. They have been here for millennia, though their exact origins are obscure, and it seems most likely that they are the offspring of more than one ethnic group.

Some authorities consider them descended from, or identical to, the "Karduchi" who gave Xenophon's Ten Thousand so much trouble; others have described the nursery of the Kurds as either the Hakkâri mountains in present-day Turkey, or the Zagros range in western Iran. Their traditional **nomadic culture** focused on horse-breeding and pastoralism, practices which brought Kurds into perennial conflict with farmers and town-dwellers; today a far higher proportion have adopted a settled lifestyle.

The Kurds have never been united as a state, owing partly to their traditional organization in **clans** – not unlike Scottish Highland ones – further grouped into tribes headed by all-powerful hereditary *ağa*s or chieftains. There exist four mutually unintelligible **dialects** of the Kurdish tongue, two of them (Kurmanji and Zaza) spoken in Turkey. Kurds are further subdivided by **religious affiliation**, being both Sunni and Shiite Muslim – proportions varying by region – or members of two small heterodox sects, the Yezidis and the Ahl-i-Haqqi. In Turkey, Shiite (Alevî) Kurds are concentrated near Erzincan and Tunceli, while in the southeast the Naqshbandi and Qadiri dervish orders have historically claimed many Kurdish adherents.

The **number** of Kurds in Turkey is a contentious subject, but sober estimates reckon over 10 million out of a population of nearly 60 million, the largest Kurdish population in the Middle East. (Percentage-wise, Iraqi Kurds – so much in the news recently – constitute, at 23 percent, a much greater proportion of that country, but at only four million a much smaller absolute number.) Modern Turkish governments have always disputed Kurdish numbers and their geographic distribution, and indeed have usually denied that Kurds have a distinct ethnic and linguistic identity at all, describing them as "mountain Turks" who have forgotten their racial origins.

THE KURDS IN PRE-REPUBLICAN TURKEY

Under the Ottomans, the majority **Sunni Kurds** were regarded in the same way as other Muslim but non-Turkic subjects such as the Arabs or Circassians, enjoying no special *millet* (nation) status like the Christian and Jewish religious minorities. The sultans found their warlike qualities useful, using them often as a mobile, irregular raiding force on the frontiers with Russia and Persia. Under Sultan Abdülhamid, they were also allowed to terrorize both Alevî Kurds and the Armenians, their settled neighbours and hereditary enemies across much of eastern Anatolia.

After the Ottoman collapse in 1918, the victorious Allies, in response to pleas from certain Kurdish nationalists, briefly mooted the establishment of a Kurdish state straddling the current borders of Iraq, Turkey and Iran. Most Kurds, however, continued in their martial tradition, standing by the Kemalists in their struggle against the Armenians in the east and the Greeks in the west, the two greatest threats to a Muslim-dominated Anatolian state. But following the Turkish Nationalist victory in 1922, the Kurds found themselves poorly rewarded for their loyalty, as any special privileges for them were explicitly withdrawn.

THE FIRST MODERN REBELLIONS

At the same time as the abolition of the caliphate in 1924, all Kurdish-interest societies were banned. **Resistance** to these measures was not long in coming, though at first it was Islamic fundamentalist, rather than explicitly Kurdish nationalist, in character: in 1925, a Naqshbandi *şeyh* (dervish leader) north of Diyarbakır mounted a rebellion which took two months for the government to crush; at its conclusion all dervish orders were suppressed nationwide. Almost immediately another insurrection, this of a more overtly nationalist and secular character and supported by Iran, broke out near Mount Ararat. Only in 1929 was this completely quelled, when Iranian backing for the rebels was withdrawn. In 1936 yet another revolt, by the Alevî Kurds of

Dersim (thereafter renamed Tunceli), took the Turkish army two years to put down. To each of these rebellions the central Turkish goverment responded harshly with executions and deportations of villagers to the west, as well as suppression of any local Kurdish cultural manifestations. Most of the east was designated as a **military zone** – long before relations with the USSR had soured – in order to give the army a free hand against the Kurds.

Thereafter Kurds could participate in Turkish public life only insomuch as they **assimilated**. Kurdish concerns had to be addressed under the vaguer rubric of "development of the East", and – after 1960 – in conjunction with generalist left-wing parties where Kurds could have a voice. Before this Sunni Kurdish society had been essentially semi-feudal, subject to the *ağa*s who would deliver their charges' vote in return for minimal benefits from Ankara. Alevî Kurds in particular, however, have since the Sixties tended to espouse left-wing beliefs, making them the target of pogroms by Muslim fundamentalist and/or rightist activists, most notably in Kahraman Maraş in 1978. The military interventions of 1971 and 1980 were notably hard on leftist parties in general and anything specifically smacking of Kurdish sectarianism, providing fertile ground for the rise of the PKK (*Partia Karkaris Kurdistan*, the "Kurdistan Workers' Party"). This group therefore represents a continuation, albeit an ideologically extreme one, of Kurdish rejection of forced assimilation or marginalization.

THE PKK: BEGINNINGS

The **PKK** was founded in November 1978 by **Abdullah Öcalan**, a political science student in Ankara, with the express intent of establishing a Marxist, Kurdist-run state in southeastern Turkey. While other Kurdish-separatist manifestos of the 1970s may have been better articulated, the PKK (pronounced "Peh-Ka-Ka" in Turkey) was able to appeal to numerous poor and badly educated Kurdish youths, without realistic prospects in the underdeveloped southeast, with the possibility of direct guerrilla action.

After the 1980 military intervention, "**Apo**" – as Öcalan came to be known – fled to Syria and established training camps with the assistance of the Syrian government and the PLO; more camps were opened later in Lebanon's Bekaa

Valley. By summer 1984, the PKK felt strong enough to begin its **guerrilla campaign**, infiltrating southeastern Turkey and initially targeting isolated gendarmerie posts. The Turkish government responded by declaring **martial law** in the twelve affected provinces (later reduced to ten), sealing the border with Syria, and raiding PKK installations across the Syrian frontier.

The PKK quickly widened its attacks to include civilians it branded as accomplices of the Turkish state and representatives of the old "feudal" order, namely large landowners and conservative tribal chiefs. In 1986 the central government effectively augmented this class by creating the **village guards**, Kurds demonstrably loyal to the government who were provided with antiquated weapons. The better-armed PKK had no difficulty in dispatching them, often massacring their entire families in the process. **Schools**, seen by the PKK as centres for government indoctrination and Turkification, were also routinely destroyed, and teachers targeted, further aggravating the already high local illiteracy rate. Village life in much of the Tigris basin and Van region gradually became unbearable, with populations divided into pro- and anti-PKK factions – often merely covers for pursuing old feuds. Most of the rural population was threatened by each side with dire consequences for co-operating with the other, and both the government and the PKK used increasingly coercive techniques for recruiting young men.

By 1988, the regular **army** had replaced the gendarmerie in the suppression of the PKK, which in turn forged a provisional alliance with urban terrorist groups such as Dev Sol, allowing it to commit outrages in the larger western cities. Apo granted a few interviews to Turkish journalists, publication of which sparked court proceedings and a progressively more stringent **blackout** on media coverage of PKK statements.

THE PKK IN POLITICS . . . AND IN BATTLE

Between late 1989 and early 1991, the Kurdish question as a whole came increasingly to dominate Turkish public opinion, as well as perceptions of Turkey abroad. By its various actions the PKK succeeded indirectly in splitting both the ANAP government, and the DYP–SDP coalition which succeeded it in October 1991, between those favouring a more conciliatory approach to the Kurds and those advocating the continuation of the iron fist.

October 1989 marked the inauguration of a specifically Kurdish-based parliamentary **political party**, though of course under existing laws it could not and cannot be identified as such. Seven deputies from the opposition SHP (Social Democrat Party), who had attended an international conference on Kurdish affairs, were expelled upon return to Turkey for "weakening national feeling by appealing to narrow class or ethnic interests". They formed the **HEP** (the Popular Labour Party), which drew more defectors from the ranks of the SHP as time went on, especially after the autumn 1991 elections. In June 1993 the HEP was forcibly disbanded, only to quickly reform as the **DEP** (the Democracy Party), with essentially the same personnel and aims. DEP in turn was compulsorily shut down in June 1994, to be succeeded by the broadly similar **HADEP** (People's Democratic Party), which seems certain to share the fate of its predecessors. By year's end, ten former HEP deputies and six DEP MPs, stripped of parliamentary immunity, had been tried by State Security Courts and sentenced to terms of up to fifteen years for "separatist activities" (ie, clandestine PKK membership) – verdicts widely condemned by American and European parliamentarians. Once in jail, lower-ranking PKK activists or fellow-travellers can expect miserable treatment even by the appalling standards of Turkish prisons; mid-1996 saw hunger strikes by more than two hundred inmates in protest at prevailing conditions.

In the eastern hills, a **yearly pattern** had been established by 1990: the government would announce sweeping military measures to crush the rebels over the winter, when they were at their most vulnerable, with specially trained commando units wielding increasingly sophisticated hardware. (Purchase of such overseas technology, in defiance of human-rights-group-inspired embargos, has occasionally had international repercussions, as in the 1992 resignation of a German defence minister who had approved the surreptitious transfer of tanks to Turkey; the Turkish reaction has been to conclude arms deals with the less fastidious Russian Federation, and to start constructing its own aircraft.) The PKK in turn would usually

"celebrate" **Nawroz**, the Kurdish New Year, by some particularly bloody atrocity, inaugurating the summer season of incidents. As the decade wore on, the PKK grew bolder militarily, mounting attacks not just in the mountains but near, and within, sizeable towns. By 1995 the PKK could muster an estimated 15,000 guerrillas in the field, plus perhaps 75,000 "part-time" militants. Already by 1992 there had been mass resignations of village guards who no longer wished to risk their lives for an administration which did not protect them adequately. Subsequently there was a marked increase in the severity of the government's punitive responses; by the end of 1996 nearly 2000 villages in both the southeast and Tunceli had been either bombed or forcibly evacuated, and then burnt to the ground, on suspicion of cooperating with the PKK, or merely for not enrolling in the village-guard scheme.

The two main Iraqi Kurdish factions, hostile to the PKK for various reasons – among them its support for Saddam Hussein – have since 1991 been persuaded to cooperate in regular Turkish cross-border efforts to eradicate PKK bases in **Iraq**. These increased in frequency and magnitude as the US-proclaimed safe-haven zone effectively became a farce; the biggest incursion took place in late March 1995, when 35,000 Turkish troops plus supporting air cover and artillery crossed the frontier in a bid to definitively wipe out PKK training camps in the area. Four months, and numerous civilian casualties later, the last Turkish forces pulled out, with uncertain results, though judging from further, briefer raids in 1996 it would seem that Turkey has since created a permanent "zone of influence" inside the Iraqi frontier similar to the one deployed by the Israelis in Lebanon.

The PKK has become more sophisticated in its repertoire of **unarmed actions**, mobilizing large street demonstrations, staging ostentatious funerals of slain HEP, DEP or PKK personnel, and inspiring shopkeeper strikes in large southeastern towns. The government has played into its hands with a string of decrees muzzling press coverage of events and authorizing the deportations of troublemakers or the relocation of villagers from sensitive areas.

Those funerals were evidence of an ominous trend, parallel to a general one in Turkish society at large: the regular **assassination or "disappearance"** of non-violent activists and politicians (HEP/DEP/HADEP in these cases), by "unknown assailants", never apprehended or charged, but widely believed to be shadowy, organized groups of Hizbollah fundamentalists or far-right Turkish nationalists operating with the indulgence of the army and gendarmerie. Such killings continue unabated at the time of writing, averaging several individuals per month, with corpses often found mutilated by the roadside or buried in rubbish tips.

The PKK further **diversified tactics** between 1992 and 1996, with demonstrations and attacks on Turkish property and diplomatic missions **overseas**, as well as the abduction of numerous foreigners in the southeast. In early 1993 they offered a unilateral ceasefire, to include the traditional Nawroz offensive season. When that did not elicit a matching government response, the PKK announced the targeting of Turkey's **tourist industry**, one of the country's main foreign-exchange earners, with warnings that the battle would be carried to the resorts. Thus numerous bombings in İstanbul, Fethiye, Marmaris, Antalya and Kuşadası were carried out during 1993 and 1994, with 26 fatalities and many more wounded, accompanied by a brief dip in tourist numbers.

The PKK's **inner command circle** is by most accounts a very unpleasant bunch, steeped in Stalinist cant (and methodology) of the 1950s and 1960s, allegedly financing their operations by opium-smuggling in the Van area now that conventional Eastern Bloc support has dried up, and valuing the lives of their ever younger and more inexperienced recruits as little as those of their victims. Despite all this, **Europeans** have been apt to romanticize the PKK, thanks partly to its "public relations" efforts overseas. Of late, however, there has been a mixed but increasingly hostile reaction by various European governments to the PKK. While the Netherlands, to the considerable ire of Turkey, tolerated the convening of a self-styled "Kurdish Parliament in Exile" in April 1995, and the Greeks have provided consistent, surreptitious support for PKK activities, the German and French governments shut down PKK offices in their countries later that year, and the Belgians (presumably at Turkish instigation) in mid-1996 raided the Brussels-based satellite station **MED TV**, which had been broadcasting in the various Kurdish dialects.

PUBLIC OPINION AND REALISTIC PROSPECTS FOR A SOLUTION

The establishment of an **independent Kurdish state** is simply not on the cards, being viewed with extreme disfavour (to say the least) by all of the existing Middle Eastern governments concerned, as well as by major overseas powers. Turkey itself has invested far too much money and effort in its gargantuan **GAP project**, mostly on the territory of any proposed Kurdistan, not to mention the oil fields of Batman and Siirt, and would certainly prefer to completely depopulate and denude the area rather than surrender it. West Anatolian, urban Kurds – the legacy of previous population movements, voluntary or otherwise – would face a stark choice: retaining Turkish citizenship and lucrative employment in exchange for renouncing any Kurdish identity, or returning to a grindingly poor "homeland" and the dubious benefits of its nationality.

Though some parlour conversations in western Turkey ventilate opinions that the southeast is an unending, ungrateful hole for public money and that cutting it loose would be cutting Turkish losses in the long run, any Turkish civilian politician rash enough to make far-reaching **political or territorial concessions** to the Kurds would measure their remaining tenure in office – and perhaps their remaining life span – in days, if not hours. For the foreseeable future the Turkish army and air force trust in their ability to massively outgun the guerrillas, especially now that the PKK's main sponsor, Syria, no longer enjoys Soviet material and ideological backing.

In its present hard-line stance towards crushing the insurgency, the government retains considerable support among the western population, where majority opinion has hardened with the continuing loss of soldiers' lives; by late 1996, nearly 17,000 people had died on all sides since the start of the troubles, and funerals of soldiers were often pretexts for anti-Kurdish demonstrations or violence. Many Turks harbour a racial hatred towards Kurds, according them a low status on a par with gypsies, and seem prepared to endorse whatever means necessary to secure obedience – or at least docility – in Tunceli, the Tigris valley and Van hinterlands. But that will come at a price, not least the continual frustration of Turkey's attempts to improve its image overseas.

So far the only significant **conciliatory moves** on the government's part have been the easing, since 1991 and at the late President Özal's behest, of some bans on Kurdish cultural expression, such as public Kurdish musical performances and recordings, and (in theory but not in practice) Kurdish publications. Özal, himself half-Kurdish, was known to have favoured extending this policy to the electronic media, but died before anything substantive was done. A brief, but perhaps significant stir was created in August 1995 when **Tomris Özden**, widow of a gendarmerie officer killed near Mardin, made public statements repudiating a military solution to the Kurdish crisis, and publicly embraced the sister of a dead PKK activist at an İstanbul peace celebration. For these actions – and her allegedly unacceptably "Western" appearance and "schizophrenic" character – she was roundly attacked by her late husband's colleagues and by certain sectors of the press, and had to back down from proposed executive membership in the CHP party; however, the taboo on dissent from the socially acceptable line on the conflict had finally been broken.

For the indefinite future the Ankara elite seems to lack the political courage to accord the Kurdish language legitimate status (especially in primary education) and grant a degree of meaningful self-government to the ten southeastern provinces still under martial law, or at the very least find non-PKK Kurds to negotiate with. The result is a lengthy guerrilla war that neither side can decisively win.

TURKISH MUSIC

There's a tremendous variety of music in Turkey: arriving at your first Turkish cassette stall you'll be confronted by a vast choice, and probably won't have a clue where to start. The best advice is to keep your ears and eyes open as you travel.

Probably the first sort of music you'll hear will be either **arabesk** or **taverna**, which account for around eighty percent of the country's cassette sales. If you don't like them, don't despair – there's plenty of good music to be had, though, as everywhere, there is also a lot of dross. During your stay, you'll hear tapes on coaches, in teahouses and shops. Don't be afraid to ask someone what they are listening to – it's the best way to discover what you like. Tapes are cheap (around $3–6 at the current rate of exchange) and generally of adequate quality.

To see **live music** in cities, the likeliest spots are restaurants. Venues are listed in the weekly music paper **Müzik Magazin** under the section *Türkiye'deki Tüm Gazinolar*. The magazine also carries six charts, useful for reference purposes, under the following categories: **Türk müziği** (*sanat* or "art" music); **halk müziği** (folk music); **arabesk**; **taverna**; **özgün** (protest music); and **pop müziği** (Turkish and Western pop).

FOLK MUSIC

Folk music (*halk müziği*), which falls into three rough categories, Turkish rural, *ozan* and Kurdish, is still a living tradition in Turkey. There are signs of decline, caused partly by the broad-

casting and recording industries, but recently folklore groups have been founded in many areas, often with state assistance, to preserve the art. Such official intervention, however, has not always been so benign: immediately after the foundation of the Republic, "genuine" folk music and Western classical were decreed to be the oddly twinned musical destinies of the nation. Accordingly musicologists fanned out across Anatolia in the 1920s, charged with the responsibility of finding material that would flatter the racially based vanity of nationalist ideologues. Incalculable harm was done as melodies were standardized, lyrics were purged of "vulgarities" (ie non-Turkish words) and ensemble playing was mandated. Spontaneity and improvisation – central to the anti-authoritarian *ozan* tradition – was banished, as (briefly) was unsupervised folk on the radio.

TURKISH RURAL MUSIC

In general, the folk music styles of the western and central Turkish provinces are very similar; striking differences are found only around the eastern Black Sea, close to the Syrian border and in the predominantly Kurdish eastern region (see below).

In Turkish villages, music primarily accompanies **celebrations** such as weddings or annual festivals. Weddings can often last for three days, and from mid-morning to midnight, loud dance music of the *davul* and *zurna* or *klarnet* (see box for an introduction to these instruments) is audible some distance away. **Dances** are performed by segregated groups of men or women, who link hands and arms to form a long line – if you're watching you will invariably be asked to join in. Wedding music, together with dance tunes, children's songs and game songs, are all forms of *kırık hava* or "broken melody", and are characterized by incessant but very danceable rhythms. Many of these itinerant festival musicians are still gypsies, who specialize in the belly-dance tunes that originally emanated from the Thracian gypsy ghettos.

In the area around Trabzon and Rize on the Black Sea, the *kemençe* is the most popular instrument, used not only at weddings and other festivities, but also for personal enjoyment – you'll often see shopkeepers or barbers playing for themselves when there are no customers about. *Kemençe* music is played at an exceptionally fast tempo, marked out by drums

INSTRUMENTS

PERCUSSION

Bendir or *bendil* Frame drums of assorted sizes.

Davul or *ramzalla* A large double-sided drum. Each side is used with different-sized sticks to create a bass-and-snare-drum-like effect.

Deblek, dümbelek or *dar(a)buka* (*demblik* in Kurdish) A goblet-shaped drum made of pottery, wood or metal and played with the hands.

Def Kurdish bass drum.

Erbane Kurdish tambourine.

Kaşık A set of wooden or metal spoons, often brightly painted, that are manipulated like chopsticks by placing the handles of the spoons between the fingers.

Küdüm Small kettledrums usually played in pairs, with sticks.

Tef A frame drum with added snares or metal rings inside the frame.

Zil A pair of small cymbals.

WIND/REED INSTRUMENTS

Blur A Kurdish shepherd's flute made from a branch of either mulberry or walnut, with seven or nine finger-holes.

Çifte or *arghul* A double instrument sounding similar to the clarinet, with two mouthpieces and two sets of finger-holes on a pair of reed pipes. Often one set is used as a continuous drone. The *arghul* is found only in a small area near the Syrian border, and is related to the *arghoul* played in Egypt and Syria. The *çifte* is particular to the environs of Ereğli on the western Black Sea.

Kaval An end-blown flute made of wood, with seven finger-holes in the front and one thumb-hole at the back, and sometimes another at the side. A favourite instrument of Turkish shepherds.

Klarnet The Western clarinet.

Mey and *düdük* These are essentially the same, being called *mey* in western Turkey and *düdük* in eastern Turkey and in neighbouring Caucasian republics. Both are small and oboe-like instruments with a very large reed and a much sweeter tone than the *zurna*. Confusingly, *düdük* is also the name given to a simple duct flute which you see on sale at markets throughout the country.

Ney An end-blown flute requiring enormous skill to play, despite its simple design. It is made from calamus reed or hardwood, with six finger-holes in front and a thumb-hole at the back.

Tulum A bagpipe found in Rize and Artvin provinces, near the Georgian border. It generally has two pipes, each with five finger-holes, inserted into a goatskin bag which the player inflates before he begins. In Turkish Thrace, a nearly identical instrument is called a *gayda*.

Zurna (*zirne* in Kurdish) A very loud double-reed oboe-type instrument with seven finger-holes, made of wood with a conical body ending in a large bell.

STRING INSTRUMENTS

Cümbüş A fretless banjo-type lute which substitutes for the *ud* when playing with louder instruments. It has a large resonating metal bowl covered with skin or plastic.

Kanun A trapezoidal zither with between forty and a hundred strings, and a system of levers for tuning to different scales quickly.

Keman Originally a round-bodied version of the *kemençe*; now the name more commonly refers to a Western violin, often preferred for its tone.

Kemençe or *kemançe* A fiddle with three strings, originally used by the shepherds of the Black Sea coast. It has an oblong wooden body and a short neck. The *kemençe* is held vertically and played with a bow of horsehair or, more recently, nylon.

Rebab A pear-shaped relative of the *kemençe* used in classical and Mevlevi dervish music.

Saz A long-necked fretted lute, usually with seven strings (two pairs, and one set of three) played with a very thin plectrum. Variations include the *divan saz*, with eight strings; the *cura saz*, with six strings; and the *bağlama*, with seven strings on a shorter neck and a large bulbous body.

Saz tambur A smaller fretted version of the *cümbüş*.

Tanbur or *tambur* A very long-necked lute with three strings and a large, almost rectangular body, noted for its very deep tone.

Ud A fretless lute with eleven strings (five pairs and one single), and nearly identical to the oud found throughout the Arab world.

Yaylı tanbur Bowed version of the *tanbur*, its tone somewhere between a cello and double bass.

or stamping feet; at celebrations in the area between Rize and the Georgian border you may also hear the *tulum* (bagpipe).

OZAN

Ozan is the music of the folk-poets of Anatolia, who are usually referred to as *aşıks*, meaning "the ones in love". The *aşıks* have wandered the plains of Anatolia since around the tenth century, putting music to the words of legendary poets like Yunus Emre, Pir Sultan Abdal and Sefil Ali, as well as writing their own songs. *Aşıks* belong to the **Bektaşi/Alevî** faith, which stresses intersectarian tolerance, the teachings of its bards or troubadours, and equality between all men and women. Despite this, many *aşıks* have been the subject of mistrust and contempt from orthodox Sunni Muslims, often officially condoned. Most blatantly, a Sivas hotel hosting a leftist/Alevî conference was attacked on July 2, 1993 by a fundamentalist mob and set alight; 37 poets and *aşıks* died, and 128 accused of the incident were either released or given risibly light sentences at their 1994 trial.

Aşıks accompany themselves on the *saz*, a long-necked lute which has three sets of strings, representing the fundamental trinity of their faith: Allah, Mohammed and Ali. Today a large number of *aşıks* still make cassettes, and even more play in the villages and towns of central Anatolia. One of the greatest in recent years was **Aşık Veysel**, a blind minstrel who died in 1974. There are still several tapes of his available, and many of his songs, such as *Bülbül* (The Nightingale) and *Kara Toprak* (My Faithful, Beloved Black Earth), are sung by other *aşıks* and singers of *türkü* (see below). His best recordings are available on the French *Ocora* label, and are the only ones made in a village setting – those cut in the sterile environment of the Radio Ankara studios are like hearing a caged bird sing.

A group worth seeking out is **Muhabbet**, which combines the talents of some of the best *aşıks* in Turkey today. **Arif Sağ**, **Musa Eroğlu**, **Muhlis Akarsu** and **Yavuz Top** alternate between releasing solo cassettes and playing with Muhabbet. Together they have released numerous tapes and there are dozens more solo offerings. Of the many other *aşıks* with tapes available, **Ali Ekber Çiçek**, **Murat Çobanoğlu, Feyzullah Çınar** and **Mazlumi and Asım Mırık** all deserve a listen.

KURDISH MUSIC

Around ten million Kurds live within the political boundaries of Turkey, a fact not yet acknowledged by the central government, which obligatorily labelled their music and dance as "Turkish" during its 1920s musicological expeditions. Traditionally, Kurdish folklore and national identity have been preserved with the help of the *dengbey* (bard), the *stranbey* (popular singer) and the *cirokbey* (storyteller). A *dengbey* is a singer with an exceptional memory, effectively the guardian of the Kurdish national heritage, since he must know hundreds of songs for which there is no written notation. *Dengbeys* sing about the Kurdish myths and legends, the struggle for freedom and the successive rulers and occupiers of their land, as well as love songs and lighter entertainment. Sadly some of the best Kurdish *dengbeys*, like **Şivan Perwer** and **Temo**, now live in exile in Europe, though recently there has been a slight relaxation on the ban of public Kurdish musical events and cassette sales.

The main instruments used in Kurdish music are reed instruments such as the *blur* and the *düdük* – found in the mountainous regions where the echo from the hills is taken advantage of – and string instruments, such as the *tembur* and the *saz*, used in the towns of the plains.

URBAN MUSIC

Throughout Turkish history, urban music has generally meant the music of İstanbul or İzmir, with composers and performers from ethnic or religious minorities disproportionately represented. As such it was viewed with extreme suspicion by the Turkic ideologues of the young Republic. The teaching and dissemination of the *sanat*, *fasıl* and Ottoman classical styles, all deemed hopelessly tainted by undesirable cosmopolitan influences and associations, were officially prohibited in public, in favour of allegedly superior Western classical music.

Despite such strictures, these forms survived to a considerable degree, as witness recent, welcome reissues of recordings made between the 1920s and 1950s. Non-Muslim musicians, who continued to dominate urban music until mid-century, were feted by no less than Atatürk himself, and an Armenian *kanun* player, Artaki Candan-Terzian, was head of the *Sahibinin Sesi* (HMV-Turkey) recording studios from 1925 until 1948. Performers were often extremely versatile, so the stylistic distinctions made below and in the discography overleaf should not be viewed as rigid; *sanat* and *fasıl* practitioners overlapped considerably, and classical musicians would even perform *türkü* on demand, sometimes singing in Anatolian dialect.

The early 1990s saw a huge, if brief, local upsurge in interest in both contemporary and old **Greek music** among the urban intelligentsia, and a less dramatic but hopefully more durable appetite for quality urban music performed in bygone styles. The former was sparked by the local release in 1992 – after nearly a decade in the censors' limbo – of the Greek musical film *Rembetiko*. This can be seen as part of a larger reconciliation with the long-suppressed, multicultural Ottoman heritage of Anatolia.

SANAT

Sanat means "art", and until the 1960s the term accurately described the music, with its vocal forms *gazel* (improvisation), *şarkı* and *rubai* largely unchanged since the late eighteenth century. Times and tastes have changed, however, and the once-great **Bülent Ersoy** and **Emel Sayın** and their contemporaries are now just crooning their way to old age on autopilot. Indeed Ersoy is as notorious for being the most publicized of Turkey's transsexual entertainers as for any artistic merit; following the 1980 operation, she was forbidden from performing publicly on moral grounds. Yet her recordings still sold by the carload, and Ersöy successfully lobbied then-President Özal (a big fan) to lift the bar both to her stage appearances and to her (and other transsexuals') marrying.

The cassette-buying public, hungry for such sensational new sounds and personalities, have all but forgotten the golden era of top singers like **Münir Nurettin Selçuk**, **Müzeyyen Senar**, **Ağyazar Garabetyan Efendi**, the Jew **İsak el-Gazi**, and Atatürk's favourite, **Safiye Ayla**. Similarly abandoned are the rich textures of their orchestral backing; prominent instrumental soloists of prior decades include clarinetist **Şükrü Tunar**, Zeki Müren's first bandleader, violinists Macedonian **Kemani Haydar Taltlıyay** and Armenian **Kemani Nubar Çömlekçiyan**, as well as the great Armenian oudists **Udi Hrant Kenkuliyan** and **Marko Melkon Alemsherian**, plus the İstanbul Greek **Yorgo Bacanos**.

The more contemporary **Zeki Müren** was a gay tranvestite who topped the *sanat* chart consistently from the 1960s until the 1980s. Earlier in his career, his music was based on classical style with room for his voice to flourish; by the late 1980s he was definitely past his prime. He died dramatically onstage of heart failure in autumn 1996, while staging a comeback concert in İzmir.

TÜRKÜ

Türkü is folk-based popular music which has found a home in the cities; its roots largely protected it from the pressures exerted on other urban musical styles during the 1920s and 1930s. Melodies taken from the folk tradition are rendered on a mixture of folk, Western and Arabic instruments. The weekly *halk müziği* chart prominently features *türkü* music, and stars like **Belkis Akkale**, **Burhan Çaçan** and **Nuray Hafiftaş** constantly battle for top positions. Other artists worth hearing include **Beşir Kaya**, **İzzet Altımeşe** and the group **Yeni Türkü**.

ÖZGÜN

Özgün is the leftist urban protest music of Turkey, sounding quite sombre on first impression, but often very moving and sometimes danceable; like its Latin American equivalents, it first rose to prominence in the late 1960s. The lyrics are central to *özgün* music, so for non-Turkish-speakers most of the impact is lost; by political definition, its audience is even more limited within the country, where many consider the music's left-wing politics passé and its purveyors hypocritical. *Özgün* mixes elements of folk, *ozan*, *türkü* and Western music, with considerable variation between artists. **Ruhi Su** plays in a style and with instrumentation which have much in common with the music of the *aşık*s, whereas **Selda** shows more *türkü* influence. Stalwarts **Zülfü Livaneli**, who narrowly missed election as mayor of İstanbul in 1994, and **Fatih Kısparmak** are prone to lushly arranged orchestral backing, and collaborations with Greek artists like Maria Farandouri and Mikis Theodorakis.

ARABESK AND TAVERNA

Arabesk and *taverna* represent the eminently disposable side of urban popular music, full of catchy choruses that have you humming the tune in five minutes and forgetting it in ten. If you go to a tape shop (there are as yet relatively few CDs in these ephemeral genres), either *arabesk* or *taverna* will invariably be playing and, if you like it, the shopkeeper will show you hundreds of other new releases to tempt you.

Superficially, **arabesk** mixes the insipid side of Arab *chaabi* (pop music) with the gaudiness of Western showbiz; its instrumental heart consists of electrified strings (including a solo *bağlama*), keyboards and percussion. Long-established stars like **Coşkun Sabah**, **İbrahim Tatlıses** (a Kurdish ex-construction worker from Urfa) and **Orhan Gencebay**, plus up-and-coming stars like **Küçük Emrah**, sell tapes by the millions, and lead often lurid but comfortable soap-opera lives at odds with their lyrics' sentiments.

For such a dismissable style, the music has had a chequered history; its defenders have included the late President Özal, who used an *arabesk* song as the theme for his 1988 election campaign. From its first appearance in the early 1970s, as a deteriorated offshoot of *fasıl* and *sanat* but with the scales adapted to fit the intervals of Arab music (hence the name), it grew to take the country by storm from the mid-1980s. Also known as *minibüs müziği*, after its blaring from such vehicles taking workers into the cities from surrounding slums, it was (and is) as much a stance towards life – complete with windscreen ornaments, tacky postcards, day-glo coloured stickers, and associated Grade-B films – as a music. Establishment apparatchiks were properly horrified, as Atatürk would have been; the bathetically tragic lyrics were said to encourage the retrograde oriental vices of despair, fatalism and even suicide. Accordingly industrial-strength *arabesk* was banned from the airwaves in 1989, and the Minister of Culture attempted to promote a sanitized alternative, *acısız arabesk* (arabesk without sorrow); it flopped spectacularly, and the prohibition was soon rescinded.

Taverna is a more recent innovation, the bastard offspring of Greek taverna music and Turkish cabaret, drawing to a limited extent on *arabesk*. Even more disposable than the latter, *taverna* is the staple of tatty hotel clubs and *gazinos*, but could be used equally well as elevator or supermarket muzak. Its instrumentation, using the term loosely, consists primarily of Yamaha keyboards and drumming machines

(whose importers must be making a fortune). In recent years sales have been catching up with *arabesk*, and stars like **Cengiz Kurtoğlu**, **Metin Kaya** and **Karışık** are always topping the chart. Late in the 1980s, Karışık had eight cassettes in the top 25 simultaneously.

OTTOMAN CLASSICAL AND RELIGIOUS MUSIC

Turkish classical music, which includes the music of the Mevlevi dervish order, is the product of Ottoman urban civilization. It is based on modal systems or *makams*, an analogue to the Western scale system formulated over five centuries ago. The traditional classical repertoire in Turkey is today selected almost entirely from notated sources preserving the works of such composers as **Abdülkadir Meragi** (died 1435), **Prince Dimitri Cantemir** (seventeenth–eighteenth century), **Sultan Selim III** and **Tanburi Cemil Bey** (1873–1916).

The Mevlevi order of dervishes provided their own, related body of ritual music which contains many of the most highly regarded compositions from the sixteenth to the twentieth century. The best-known Mevlevi composers are **Köçek Derviş Mustafa Dede** (seventeenth century), **Dede Efendi** (eighteenth–nineteenth century), and **Rauf Yekta** (nineteenth–twentieth century).

Both sorts of music were attacked by Republican ideological purists with special zeal, even more than urban songs and Alevî ballads; Atatürk considered the Ottoman classical and devotional repertoire thoroughly decadent because of its reliance on Arabic, Byzantine and Persian forms, not to mention the importance of non-"Turkish" composers. The formal teaching and radio broadcasting of Turkish classical was forbidden between 1923 and 1976, with the dervish *tekkes* – which had served as informal conservatories for religious music – being similarly suppressed. Although the public ban on such music was relaxed at about the same time (not coincidentally) that *arabesk* made its first appearance, the damage had been done. Despite the existence of some superb archival tapes from the early 1960s, featuring such master practitioners as **Niyazi Sayın** and **Akagündüz Kutbay** on *ney*, **Necdet Yaşar** on *tanbur*, **İhsan Özgen** on *kemençe* and **Hurşit**

Üngay on *kudum*, they were essentially "private reserve" material, not intended for broadcast to the masses, and the lineal tradition of discipleship on which this type of music depends had been broken. Even after 1976, many of the best players chose to emigrate to France (the Ergüner clan, Talip Özkan), Germany and the US (Necdet Yaşar).

Today, public concerts of classical music are given in concert halls and in radio or television broadcasts, often with large ensembles of over thirty instrumentalists and singers. One of the most famous is the İstanbul Municipal Conservatory's **Klâsik İcra Heyeti**, which often gives concerts around İstanbul, and on Sunday mornings these and other such performances may be broadcast live on Radio İstanbul. The instruments normally used by classical ensembles include *tambur*, *ney*, *rebab* or *kemençe*, *keman*, *kanun*, *ud*, and *küdüm*.

The most famous Mevlevi musical event remains the annual **Mevlâna festival**, held in Konya during the week preceding December 17. Compositions for the ceremony are called *ayin*, and the musicians known collectively as the *mutrip*. The *mutrip* predominantly play the two traditional Mevlevi instruments, *ney* and *küdüm*, although *tambur*, *kanun* and *rebab* are sometimes used.

FASIL

The *fasıl*, or semi-classical, style can be described as an urban nightclub version of classical Turkish music, essentially a vocal suite interspersed with light orchestral ensemble pieces and solo *taksims* or improvisations. The music often has a distinctly gypsy flavour (not least because of the many gypsies who have excelled at particular instruments), and every short rest (*fasıl* means "interval") is filled with flourishes and improvisations from the stars of the orchestra, frowned upon in strictly classical circles. Like *sanat*, this style was also officially suppressed or at least discouraged, though privately enjoyed, by Atatürk and his retinue.

The main instruments used are *klarnet*, *keman*, *ud*, *cümbüş*, *kanun*, *darbuka* and *yaylı tambur*. Distinguished and versatile artists of this genre to look out for on commercially available recordings include the great gypsy clarinetist **Mustafa Kandırali**, the gypsy *kanun* player **Ahmet Yatman**, the oudist **Kardi Şençalar**, and vocalists **Perihan Altındağ,**

Mahmut Celalettin, Denizkışı Eftalya and **Kemal Gürses**.

SELECTED DISCOGRAPHY

Pressings from American or German labels such as Rounder or Music of the World can be obtained, often by special order, from major retail chains such as *Tower*, *HMV* or *Virgin*. Most *Crossroads* (US) and *MBI* (Greece) productions are released under licence by *Kalan* in İstanbul. If you have any trouble finding these discs overseas, contact *Traditional Crossroads Records*, PO Box 20320, Greeley Square Station, New York NY 10001-9992, USA, or *Music Box International*, Alímou 76, Aryiroúpoli 16452, Athens (☎01/9953 613). Turkish-label pressings are available only in Turkey, or overseas in speciality music shops catering to Turkish emigrant communities. In Britain, there's an excellent Turkish **record/cassette shop** with a good stock, ten-day special-order service and reasonable mark-up: *Melodi Müzik*, 121 Green Lanes, London N16 (☎0171/359 0038; ask for Salih, who speaks perfect English).

OZAN

Aşık Veysel: one disc of *Voyages d'Alain Gheerbrant en Anatolie* (Ocora 558634). The only recording of Veysel in a village setting. Wonderfully supported by his constant companion Küçük Veysel, who sings in imitating unison with the master. Produced in France and easily available.

Aşık Veysel *Dostlar Beni Hatırlasın* (Diskotür DTK 503, JEPA). The best of his Radio Ankara recordings; rather sterile sound but contains many of his most treasured songs.

Mazlumi ve Asım Mırık *Şölende Sohbet-2* (Şölen 013). Two relatively unknown *saz* players accompanied by the *mey*. An atmospheric and melodic collection of songs.

Muhabbet *Beş (5)* (Zirve 1008) & *Seksensekiz (88)* (Pınar 003). The combined talent of four of the greatest *saz* players. All have deep, resonating voices, which add soulful respite to the wash of fine *saz* interludes.

Arif Sağ *Halay* (Nora/ASM 001). Arif Sağ has for many years been one of Turkey's favourite singers, releasing dozens of records and tapes, both alone and with Muhabbet. This tape features complex rhythms, superb *saz* playing and solos from many Turkish folk instruments.

Yavuz Top *Değişler-1* (Sembol Plak 1048). A fast and vibrant tape from another member of Muhabbet. The flutes and *saz* play melodic interchanges over pulsating rhythms.

Özalarımızla Doksan Dakika (Harika 4052). A ninety-minute compilation of different *aşıks*, including Murat Çobanoğlu, Ali Ekber Çiçek, Feyzullah Çınar and Reyhani. A good introduction to *ozan* music.

Song Creators of Eastern Turkey (Smithsonian/Folkways, US). An anthology of contemporary *aşıks*, with good notes and lyric translations.

ÖZGÜN AND TURKU

Belkis Akkale *Türkü Türkü Türkiyem* (Sembol Plak 1011). Possibly the greatest living *türkü* singer at her best. Almost all of the traditional instruments of Turkey are in here somewhere.

Ruhi Su *Zeybekler* (IMECE 27). One of the greatest *özgün* singers with a collection of old west Anatolian ballads sung in Ruhi's forceful style.

Selda (Uzelli 1155). Selda is equally at home singing *türkü* or *özgün*. This collection features both and includes the wonderful *Dost Merhaba*.

Şivan Perwer vols 9 & 11 (Kurdistan Yekitiya Hunermenden 9 & 11, Germany). Arguably the finest Kurdish singer. Both collections contain Şivan's powerful voice and *saz* accompaniment, backed by *düdük* and *blur*, together with Western keyboards and classical Arabic instruments like *ud* and *kanun*.

Sümeyra *Kadınlarımızın Yüzleri* (Yeni Dünya). Female *özgün* singer with one of the most soulful voices in Turkey, accompanying herself on the *saz*.

Türküler Gecidi (Türküola 2265). A wonderful ninety-minute hit-parade from the world of *türkü*, featuring Belkis Akkale, Burhan Çaçan, Mahmut Tunçer and others.

Diyarbakırlı Beşir Kaya *Derman Kalmadı* (Özdemir 023). The sound of *düdük*, *saz* and *mey* blend beautifully with bass guitar, kit drums and Beşir's soaring voice. The modern sound of eastern Turkey and very danceable.

Folk Music of Turkey (Topic 12 TS 333). An excellent selection of many styles of Turkish folk music. Produced in Britain as part of a high-quality series covering Balkan and Middle Eastern music.

SANAT AND FASIL

Istanbul 1925 (Crossroads CD 4266). The best *sanat* played by Turkish, Armenian and Greek musicians in the city during the first years of the Republic, varied by the odd urban *türkü* song and *fasıl* instrumental. Highly recommended, with intelligent notes.

Masters of Turkish Music, Vol. 1 & Vol. 2 (Rounder CD 1051 & 1111, USA). These remasterings of early recordings make another excellent introduction to genuine *sanat*, and include plenty of *türküs* and classicized *taksims* as well. Vol. 1 is half *gazel* or *şarkı*, half instrumental solos, though liner notes are often missing; Vol. 2, starting off with Safiye Ayla's rendition of the famous İstanbul *türkü* "Kâtibim", is less rigidly divided and has more reliable notes, compiled by the University of Maryland's Center for Turkish Music, including translated lyrics.

Mustafa Kandırali *Turkey* (World Network, Germany). The archetypal "belly dance" clarinetist gives a wild performance with a small ensemble.

Udi Hrant Kenkuliyan (Crossroads 4265/Kalan 068). The great blind oudist sings on many of these wonderful tracks from a 1950s concert tour of the US. Look also for his *Early Recordings, Vol. 1* (Crossroads 4270) & *Vol 2* (Crossroads 4271), made in Turkey during the 1920s.

Marko Melkon (Crossroads 4281). Another Armenian oudist, a long-term resident in New York during the 1920s and 1930s, more forceful in style than Udi Hrant.

Fanari tis Anatolis/Anadolu Fener *Fanari tis Anatolis, Valkania Oneira, Last Boat from Halki* (MBI-Lyra, Athens/Kalan, Istanbul). Not strictly *sanat*, but a modern "crossover" effort in the best sense – an attempt to produce a genuinely Balkan/Anatolian style by drawing on the Greek folk and Turkish *ozan* tradition, overseen by Nikiforos Metaxas, coordinator of this successor group to Boğaziçi/Vosporos (see below). The first two discs feature alternating vocals by Vasiliki Papayeoryiou and Melda Kurt, backed by accomplished Turkish musicians; the last has Greek lyrics coupled to traditional İstanbul melodies.

Nesrin Sipahi *Love Songs of İstanbul* (CMP, Germany). *Şarkı* or love songs are a melancholy subdivision of *sanat*; many such compositions are three centuries old. Backing here provided by the Kudsi Ergüner Ensemble, based in Paris.

DEVOTIONAL CLASSICAL MUSIC

Abdi Coşkun & Fahreddin Çenli *Turquie: L'art du tambur Ottoman* (CVDE Gallo). Plucked and bowed technique on the *tambur*, one of the most soulful Asian instruments. Available only in French, Belgian or Swiss shops, or by faxing 41/24 33 17 18 in Geneva.

M. Sadreddin Özçimi *Ney Taksimleri* (Kalite Plak 022). Introspective solo *ney* improvisation from a contemporary master.

Mevlâna *Mistik Türk Müziği Şaheserleri serisi*, vols 1–6 (Kent). One of the best sets of Mevlevi music. Any of them will provide a good introduction to the beautiful and soothing music of the Mevlevi, though the earlier volumes may prove difficult to find.

Mevlâna Beyâti Ayini (Aras/Nora AR20). Considered the definitive version of the Mevlevi *sema* accompaniment; far better than the badly recorded schlock usually offloaded to hapless tourists in Konya.

Turquie: Musique Soufi (Ocora). Hypnotic, evocative incantations with *ney*, *bendir* and voice.

Talip Özkan *L'art du tanbûr* (Ocora C560042). Wonderfully meditative foray into classical *tanbur* by a practitioner better known for his *türkü*-style *saz* playing; thus the recording is varied by folk airs, and unexpectedly delicate singing. If you get hooked, seek out also his *L'art vivant de Talip Özkan* (Ocora C580047), various regional dances performed on *cura saz* and *tanbur*, or

Mysteries of Turkey (Music of the World CDT 115, Chapel Hill, North Carolina), more regional pieces performed on *saz*, with occasional vocal passages.

Boğaziçi *Türk Müziğinde Rum Bestekârlar* (Columbia TCP 2239, Turkey). A mixture of Greek and Turkish musicians playing music of the Byzantine, Ottoman and Mevlevi traditions. Beautiful, landmark recording of courtly classical and sacred music.

Vosporos *Zontani Ihografisi sto Irodheio* (MBI CD 10634, Athens). Vosporos is the Greek title and packaging of the identical group Boğaziçi, coordinated between 1987 and 1993 by Nikiforos Metaxas in İstanbul; this records a 1990 concert in Athens. Disc 1 features Greek composers of Ottoman music; Disc 2 (more interesting) has songs of the Alevî *aşık*s, with Kani Karaca, Melda Kurt and Sibel Sezal on vocals.

The Necdet Yaşar Ensemble (Music of the World CDT 128, Chapel Hill, North Carolina). Extracts from a 1989 concert of this master of the *tanbur*, a disciple of Tanburi Cemil Bey's son; imaginative instrumental suites, capped by a vocal medley.

Tanburi Cemil Bey (Crossroads 4264/Kalan 067). Pieces performed on various stringed instruments by one of the last great Ottoman composers, recorded between 1910 and 1914. *Tanburi Cemil Bey, Vol. 2 & 3* (double CD; Crossroads 4274) may also be of interest.

TURKISH CINEMA

The films of Yılmaz Güney aside, Turkish cinema is little known outside Turkey, a result perhaps of its historic preoccupations with what most foreign critics have perceived as strictly local issues such as rural to urban population drift and the dislocation of traditional lifestyles. Throughout the 1970s and 1980s, however, Turkish directors produced a number of powerful movies worthy of wider recognition. More recently, economic problems in the industry, and the country in general, have ravaged the film-making sector, just as Turkish art-house cinema was gaining a growing, if still small, number of followers.

Although cinema as an art form has only emerged in Turkey over the last couple of decades or so, the local film industry has been churning out low-budget melodrama for the better part of seventy years, and indeed continues to do so. All forms of film-making have been handicapped by a relative lack of finance and technical resources, and directors and writers wishing to address social or political issues have also had to contend with state censorship in varying degrees over the years, which has given rise to a tendency to portray everyday life lyrically or through allegory.

THE GROWTH OF THE INDUSTRY

The history of public cinema in Turkey began in 1897 when **Sigmund Weinberg**, a Romanian café owner in the Pera district of İstanbul,

staged the city's first film show. It was not until World War I, however, that the government, realizing the propaganda value of film, set up several **army film units**. These units put together a number of documentaries, although the first film ever produced under Turkish government auspices (recording the demolition of a Russian monument in İstanbul) was shot under the direction of an Austrian military crew. A Turkish projectionist, **Fuat Uzkınay**, took the largely symbolic role of holding the camera, under close Austrian supervision.

By the end of the world war, Turkish military film-makers had mastered their trade sufficiently to go on and make documentaries on the War of Independence. With the end of all hostilities a number of **production companies** were set up, including one owned jointly by Sigmund Weinberg and Fuat Uzkınay, and Turkey's feature film industry came into existence.

During the 1920s a trend for ham-fisted adaptations of works by seventeenth-century French playwrights like Molière was established, a field that was dominated by two companies, İpek Film and Kemal Film. The leading director of the period was **Muhsin Ertuğrul**, who made 29 films between 1922 and 1953. His CV includes a couple of features based on the independence war: *Ateş'ten Gömlek* (Shirt Of Fire; 1923) and *Bir Millet Uyaniyor* (The Awakening Of A Nation; 1932). These films did refer to actual events, but they never sought to challenge the official line of Kemalist Turkey, nor did they break any new ground artistically.

Any attempts to do either would probably have foundered against the government's rigorous **censorship** laws, codified in 1932. All films faced a three-tiered process; first, scripts were censored before filming began, then the police controlled sequences as they were shot, and finally government censors inspected the finished work, excising contentious material. Governmental stifling of creativity was exacerbated by chronic lack of cash and equipment, with the result that by World War II the staple fare of Turkish picture houses was Hollywood productions and risible B-movies churned out in Egypt by a Turkish producer, **V.O. Bengü**.

In quantitative terms the output of the Turkish film industry picked up significantly in the Fifties with the establishment of a genre of mass-entertainment **melodrama** which continues to this day, lapped up by rural and small-town audiences. These films had a very basic premise that was to prove successful time and time again: rural boy meets rural girl, the world tries to keep them apart (in more sophisticated variants, one is temporarily blind to the virtues of the other) but, ultimately, they triumph over tragedy and live happily ever after, having achieved fame and fortune along the way.

One positive effect of this increased cinematic activity was that it enabled a **new generation** of young film-makers to master the skills of cinematography, among them Yılmaz Güney and others who, in the Sixties and Seventies, would go on to develop a homegrown Turkish cinematic identity.

THE NEW WAVE – AND YILMAZ GÜNEY

It was during the Sixties that the first attempts were made to produce films that moved away from melodrama into the realm of social criticism. A leading director of the period was **Lüfti Ö. Akad** who, having cut his teeth on melodramas and a few derivative gangster pictures during the Forties and Fifties, went on to direct *Tanrı'nın Bağışı Orman* (The Forest, God's Gift) in 1964, a documentary study of the feudal hierarchy in Anatolia. In 1966 he made *Hudutların Kanunu* (The Law Of The Frontier), a dramatic treatment of similar issues, dealing with the stranglehold of wealthy landlords on the rural population in the southeast. He later directed *Kızılırmak-Karakoyun* (Red River, Black Sheep), based on a play by poet Nazim Hikmet. Between 1973 and 1975 Akad produced an important trilogy, exploring the drift of population from rural Anatolia to the cities, and the conflict between traditional lifestyles and modern, Westernized city life: *Gelin* (The Bride), *Düğün* (The Wedding) and *Diyet* (Retribution).

During the 1970s **Yılmaz Güney** took over as Turkey's leading serious director and became, in the process, the only Turkish director to gain real recognition outside his native land. After serving his apprenticeship on the melodramas of the Fifties, Güney had scripted *Hudutların Kanunu* for Akad and took the lead acting role in *Kızılırmak-Karakoyun*. The first major film he directed, in 1970, was *Umut* (Hope), the story of a cab-driver who loses his house and stakes his remaining money on a mad treasure-hunting venture. Though not an outstanding film, it is indicative of the thematic direction that Güney's

later films were to take, and certain scenes, notably the final one where the maddened hero circles a hole in the ground blindfolded, are echoed in later films.

Umut was followed in 1971 by *Ağıt* (Lament), in which a man is forced to resort to smuggling by economic circumstance, and *Acık* (Sorrow), a film about lost love and revenge. Güney was imprisoned after the 1971 coup, remaining in jail until 1974. Upon his release he made the film *Arkadaş* (The Friend), which, like the earlier *Umutsuzlar* (The Hopeless) and *Baba* (The Father), dealt with the lot of Turkey's urban poor, an area in which Güney was less confident as a director. In the same year Güney was imprisoned again, accused of murdering a judge. He began directing films from his cell, writing scripts and passing on instructions to fellow-directors; paradoxically, some of his finest work was produced in this period.

In 1979 *Sürü* (The Herd), written by Güney with **Zeki Ökten** directing, was released; like Güney's earlier films its theme is rural dislocation. Life among feuding nomadic families in the south is the starting point; with their traditional grazing lands threatened by development, a Kurdish family decide to take their sheep to the markets of Ankara. Visually the film is dominated by the road and rail journey of the shepherds and their flocks, and this is used to highlight the dichotomy between their lifestyle and city ways. The political turmoil that surrounds them, but which they are barely aware of, is suggested by characteristic Güney touches: almost impressionistic sequences of manacled prisoners and a youth being shot for distributing pamphlets.

Güney also worked on his most famous film, **Yol** (The Road), from the confines of his prison cell, with the outside directorial assistance of **Şerif Gören**. It's an extraordinary film, taking an allegorical look at the state of the nation by following the fortunes of five prisoners who have been allowed a week's parole. Even when temporarily released they are unable to make their own way through a society that seems unreal to them, and their behaviour is determined by social conditions over which they have no control. One prisoner, Ömer, returns to his Kurdish village and is faced with a choice between returning to prison or taking to the hills. He eventually opts for the latter but there is a strong sense that the decision is forced on him. The film focuses, though, on Seyit Ali, who returns to his village to find that his wife, who has become a prostitute, is being held by his brothers, who expect him to kill her. He refuses to do so outright by abandoning her in the snow – after a change of heart he returns to save her, only to find that she's dead. Güney, having escaped from jail, was able to edit this film in exile in France, and the final result, released in 1982, is permeated by a strong sense of longing for his homeland. *Yol* shared the Cannes Film Festival's Palme d'Or for that year with Costa-Gavras' *Missing*, greatly elevating Turkish cinema's international standing.

Güney's last film was **Duvar** (The Wall), made during his French exile and released in 1983. Unrelentingly brutal, it's a composite portrait of Turkish prison life, focusing on the experiences of a group of young detainees, little more than children. The prison of the film becomes a microcosm of Turkish society as seen through the eyes of its inmates. The prison hierarchy, with the director of prisons at the top, is shown as unmerciful and inflexible; complaints are responded to with violence and the prisoners have no chance of redress for the wrongs done to them. This is graphically demonstrated by the fate of Şabah, one of the young inmates; he is sexually assaulted byone of the guards and, encouraged by his fellow-inmates, decides to report the incident to the prison doctor. At the last moment his nerve fails him. His friends ostracize him, and in despair he attempts to escape, and is killed. Güney died of cancer, aged 46, the year after *Duvar's* release.

An important contemporary of Güney was **Ömer Kavur**, whose first film, *Emine*, was released in 1974. Set in a small provincial town at the turn of the century, the film looked at the role of women in traditional society. In 1979 Ömer directed *Yusuf İle Kenan* (Yusuf And Kenan), the story of two young boys forced to leave their village after their father is killed in a blood feud. An increasingly important element of modern Turkish life, the experience of the migrant worker, was explored in *Otobüs* (The Bus) by **Tunç Okan**. This 1977 film examines the dislocating effect of having to leave the homeland in search of work through the eyes of a group of Turks who, having come to Sweden in search of work, find themselves abandoned in Stockholm, ripped off by a fellow countryman.

THE EIGHTIES

Turkish film output actually peaked numerically in 1972 with 299 films, but as the decade progressed there was a steady decline amidst the political turmoil and violence preceding the 1980 coup. In that year, however, **Ali Özgentürk** released *Hazal*, a dramatic depiction of life in a spectacularly isolated, semi-feudal village, where a young woman attempts to escape from an arranged marriage to a ten-year-old boy in order to be with her lover, but finds swift, harsh retribution. In the wake of the 1980 coup, however, the work of many directors was banned, and the Turkish film industry was effectively driven into exile.

The early to mid-Eighties saw something of a revival. In 1982 Ali Özgentürk made *At* (The Horse), a co-production with West Germany which has been described as a harsher reworking of *The Bicycle Thief*. The film tells the story of a peasant and his son who arrive in İstanbul in search of a better life. The father hopes to be able to earn enough as a street trader to put his son through school, but is inevitably overwhelmed by life in the big city.

In 1983 *Hakkâri'de Bir Mevsim* (A Season In Hakkâri), directed by **Erdan Kıral** in another German-funded co-production, was released. Arguably the best Turkish film of the Eighties, and certainly the one which won most international acclaim, this visually stunning film examines the experiences of a young teacher sent to a distant Kurdish village to staff the local school. He is shocked by the poverty and isolated from the locals by vast linguistic and cultural gaps. Gradually, however, through his relationship with two local orphans, the girl Zazi and her brother Halit (a smuggler, also excluded from village life), he comes to identify with his surroundings, a process helped when the locals call on his aid during an epidemic. When he receives notice from the authorities that he can leave the village he is reluctant to go, having found a stability previously absent from his rootless existence.

Although many Turkish films of the decade were notably subdued, focusing on themes of individual struggle to skirt direct political comment, a few made after the middle of the decade addressed issues such as social hypocrisy, or the position of women in Turkish society. *Bir Yudum Sevgi* (A Sip Of Love), directed by **Atif Yılmaz** in 1984, looks at one woman's struggle to win her personal independence. Related themes emerge in *Asiye*, an unusual musical adapted from a stage play, lambasting the notion of the woman as male property through the tale of a peasant woman who becomes a prostitute and later brothel madam.

The director **Başar Sabuncu** chalked up a number of noteworthy films during the later 1980s. *Çıplak Vatandaş* (The Naked Citizen) is a fairly light-hearted 1986 satire, following the fortunes of a man who, while temporarily deranged by economic misfortune and confrontation with bureaucracy, runs almost naked through his home town, only to be subsequently exploited by an advertising firm who use him in a TV ad for bath salts. *Kupa Kızı* (Queen Of Hearts), released the following year, is an acidic reworking of *Belle de Jour*, telling of a woman who turns part-time prostitute and uses sex as a means of revenge. In *Asılacak Kadın* (A Woman To Be Hanged), a young woman becomes a judicial scapegoat for the murder of an old man who has sexually abused her. The film fell foul of the censors and its release resulted in the banning of the novel which inspired it, for "offending national morality". Sabuncu's next film, in 1988, was *Zengin Mutfağı* (Kitchen Of The Rich), an adaption of a stage play set among the servants in the kitchen of a wealthy family, intended as an allegory of the situation immediately before the 1971 military coup.

Other Eighties films worthy of mention include **Nesli Çölgecen**'s 1986 effort *Ağa* (The Landlord) and Ömer Kavur's 1986 return to the director's chair, *Anayurt Oteli* (The Motherland Hotel). The former examines the struggles of a wealthy landlord in the southeast, unable to come to terms with changes in rural life. Here a severe drought is substituted for the socio-economic forces that might have caused these changes had the film been made a decade earlier. Kavur's film is set in a small town near İzmir where an obsessive and lonely hotel owner's life falls apart when an attractive female guest breaks a promise to make a return visit. The film breaks new ground for Turkish cinema, exploring psychological and emotive issues with a previously unknown depth. Another important late Eighties film was *Kırk Metre Kare Almanya'da* (Forty Square Metres Of Germany),

directed by **Tevfik Başer** in 1987, looking at the experience of Turkish migrant workers through the eyes of a village woman brought to Hamburg and confined in a dismal flat while her husband goes off to work.

Films made towards the end of the decade indicated that Turkish directors once again felt secure enough to question openly the way their society functions, and to refer directly to political conditions within Turkey. **Tunç Başaran**'s *Uçurtmayı Vurmasınlar* (Don't Let Them Shoot The Kite; 1989), about the relationship that develops in jail between a sensitive inmate and the five-year-old son of a woman doing time for drug-dealing, touches on an area of Turkish life that, earlier in the decade, would have been out of bounds to film-makers. *Blackout Nights* (1990), by **Yusuf Kürçenli**, went even further. Based on an autobiographical novel by the poet Rifat Ilgaz, arrested as a suspected communist at the end of World War II, it questioned the need for censorship and attacked political oppression.

THE NINETIES

While the rest of the world was celebrating the hundredth anniversary of film in 1995, Turkey's industry remained in crisis. Multinational production companies dominated cinema screens so that independent Turkish operators, whose films were still plagued with technical difficulties, most noticeably their poor sound quality, found it hard to find outlets for their productions. A general lack of interest on the part of the Ministry of Culture, who withdrew funding for the subtitling of Turkish films to be shown abroad, compounded the problems.

Despite the difficulties there have been a few notable productions in an otherwise uneventful decade. In 1990, Ömer Kavur managed to release his acclaimed movie *Gizli Yüz* (The Secret Face), based on a story by writer Orhan Pamuk about a nightclub photographer and his pursuit of a beautiful woman who disappears with a watchmaker. In 1994, **Erden Kıral**'s *Mavi Sürgün* (The Blue Exile) gained worldwide attention and was nominated (unsuccessfully) for an Academy Award for Best Foreign Film. Beautifully photographed and acted, it tells of journalist Cevat Şakir's 1925 exile to Turkey's then-remote southwestern coast. By the end of his journey, he has come to terms with his past and started a new life based on self-understanding and his role in his adopted home.

One encouraging trend has been the emergence of **women directors**, most notably **Tomris Giritlioğlu**, whose films have received both national and international recognition. Her first, *Yaz Yağmuru* (A Passing Summer Rain), released in 1994, concerns a writer who is overwhelmed by images inspired by a young woman he sees in his garden one day; *80 Adim* (The Eightieth Step), winner of the best movie award at the İstanbul Film Festival in 1996, is about a committed left-wing political activist released from jail in 1980 as the country reels from the September 12 military coup, and deals with his personal conflicts in a changing society. Another female director, **Biket İlhan**, explores İstanbul's underworld in a thriller made in 1995, *Sokaktaki Adam* (The Man In The Street), about a ship's steward who becomes involved in smuggling and then falls for a famous prostitute.

One of the most highly acclaimed works of the decade has been *İstanbul Kanatlarımın Altında* (İstanbul Beneath My Wings), made in 1995 by **Mustafa Altıoklar**. Set in seventeenth-century İstanbul during the reign of tyrant Murat IV, four close friends are tussling with the theories of flight while Murat and his janissary guards rampage around the city closing down its more riotous drinking establishments by lynching everyone they discover on the premises. Murat eventually catches up with the four heroes, whose number includes the travel chronicler Evliya Çelebi, and is advised of their appropriate fate by reactionary forces in his divan council. The film, based on a true story, disguises its contemporary political overtones with tongue-in-cheek dialogue and farcical comedy, but its plea for enlightenment in the face of fundamentalist zeal is a timely message in modern Turkey.

After the success of *İstanbul Kanatlarımın Altında*, Turkey's filmgoers decided to give the domestic industry another chance in 1996. Financial constraints forced a group of the country's best-known directors to collaborate on two releases made up of five short made-for-TV films, *Aşık Üzerine Söylenmiş Her Şey* (Everything Untold About Love) and *Yerçekimli Aşıklar* (Loves With Gravity). These anthologies are snapshots of contemporary Turkish society, covering domestic themes with little overtly political content. More upfront, *Işıklar Sönmesin* (The Lights Must Not Go Out), directed by **Reis Çelik** in 1996, was the first action film to deal with the civil war in the southeast, and attracted large audiences across the country. The plot revolves around a captured PKK guerrilla and his captor, a gendarme captain. Wandering lost in a blizzard after their men have been killed, they justify themselves and attack the morality of one another's cause. Interestingly ambiguous, the film risks censorship, as the guerrilla is given a humanity and idealism hitherto unknown in Turkey's coverage of its "troubles".

TURKISH WRITERS

Turkish literature, like so much else about the country, is virtually unknown abroad except for the epic works of Yaşar Kemal. This is regrettable, because Turkish authors particularly excel in the genre of short stories and memoirs. On the whole, writing in the country is heavily biased towards accounts of city life, particularly İstanbul, a reflection perhaps of the cultural dominance of the city. The pieces below, however, show more of a cross-section of Turkish society.

İRFAN ORGA

İRFAN ORGA was born into a wealthy Ottoman family in old İstanbul in 1908. The lives of the family were irrevocably shattered by World War I and the Nationalist revolution. Brought up in extreme poverty after 1915, Orga was enrolled as a cadet in the Kuleli military academy, which was seen by his widowed mother as the only way of advancement. Later, as an officer of the air force, he arrived in wartime England in 1941 speaking no English, and soon began living with a married woman. Despite the unhappiness and dislocation this precipitated – court cases, trouble with the Home Office, the loss of his officer's commission, and eventually a permanent ban on return to Turkey – Orga quickly learned English and within eight years had penned the memoir excerpted below, currently in print and published by Eland Books. This was phenomenally well received, a success he was never to repeat despite producing numerous subsequent works on Turkish subjects. Orga died in 1970, survived by a son, and able to live in some semblance of comfort only in his later years.

PORTRAIT OF A TURKISH FAMILY

I had become very restless at home and was often insubordinate. My mother worried incessantly about my education, but all the schools were still disorganised and many teachers had never come back from the war. I used to haunt the streets, playing a corrupted version of football near the gardens of the Mosque, for I had nothing to keep my mind constantly occupied. My mother and I used to have fierce and bitter quarrels and, because I could not bear being confined to the house, I took to roaming farther and farther away from home. No doubt had I had a father to discipline me I should never have dared to do these things, but I would not listen to my mother or grandmother, flying into a passion if they attempted to interfere with me.

My mother was rebelling against life too – but for a different reason. Her rebellion was, unexpectedly enough, against wearing the veil, for she had noticed that none of the foreign women wore them and that even a few of the more daring Turkish women from good families had ceased the practice also. She used to complain about it to my grandmother, declaring she was sick and tired of keeping her face covered, and I would interrupt, with lordly ten-year oldness, saying I would not have her going about the streets with her face open. I would chastise her too for her many goings-out.

"You are never at home," I would declare and although usually I was told to mind my own affairs, one day I was very surprised when my grandmother actually agreed with me.

"It is quite true," she said heatedly. "You are always out these days. And it is not right for you to complain that you have to wear the veil. Why, many women are still behind the kafes and they never see the colour of the sky, excepting from behind their veils. But at least you cannot complain of that for you tore the kafes from here and it is a wonder to me that you were ever accepted in this street, for you behaved exactly like a fast woman looking for another husband or like a prostitute. Yes, you did!" she assured my mother's astonished face. "And now you talk of leaving aside your veil. Why, I lived for thirty years with my husband and I never went out without his permission and I had to keep my face covered all the time. If I went out in the carriage with Murat, immediately all the windows were closed and sometimes the blinds were drawn too. I say it is a scandal that women are today revealing their faces. God will punish them! Do not let me hear another word from you, my daughter, for surely the sky will open on you for such impiety."

Never had I heard my grandmother talk at such length or with such obvious passion. My mother replied:

"You are talking a great deal of old-fashioned nonsense, mother! My place is not in the home these days. If I were to sit at home all day, or you either for that matter, who would go to market for us? Do you expect me to stay here all day, reading the Koran and wearing my veil for fear the passers-by should see me from the street? I tell you again, from now on I shall go without my veil!"

And she angrily tore the pretty veil from her face and threw it petulantly on the floor.

My grandmother lifted her hands to heaven.

"I never thought I should live to see this day," she said.

"Times are changing," said my mother.

"They will say you are a prostitute!" wailed my grandmother, genuinely distressed, totally incapable of accepting such a fierce gesture as the "opening" of the face.

"If they do, it will not worry me," retorted my mother. "Their words will not bring bread to me. And from now on, you will throw aside your veil too, mother."

"Oh no, no, no!" said my grandmother in superstitious horror. "God forbid I should invite punishment upon me!"

But the next morning when my mother went into Beyoğlu, with a box of embroidered articles under her arm and her lovely face naked to the world, she was stoned by some children near Bayazit and received a nasty cut on the side of her head. After that she was cautious about going anywhere alone, but was adamant about not re-veiling herself; Mehmet or I would go with her to Beyoğlu, my grandmother steadfastly refusing to be seen with her. The reaction to her in the street was mixed. The older ones were stricken with horror, more especially since they had always recognised my mother as a good woman, and now their faith in her was sadly battered. She was still young and attractive – she was twenty-five – and despite the shadows that lingered now and then in her eyes, was so unusually beautiful that people could not help but stare at her, and certain sections of the street wondered if she were trying to catch a husband. They came in their droves, the old men as well, to remonstrate with my grandmother, urging her to put a stop to this terrible thing, and my grandmother, thoroughly enjoying herself, would groan to them that she had no authority left in this wayward family of

hers. But the younger women sided with my mother, and some of them even began to follow her example. Their fathers, however, in the absence of dead husbands, took a stick to them muttering piously that no woman in their family would so disgrace themselves. So they put on their veils again in a hurry.

Not a few wished to apply the chastening stick to my mother also. They gave my grandmother sympathy until she was sick of it and prophesied gloomily – but with a little bit of anticipatory relish too, I think – that my mother would come to a bad end.

And indeed she very nearly did!

For one day in Bayazit, when she was alone, an impressionable Frenchman attempted to flirt with her. She tried walking hurriedly on but this had no effect at all, or if anything a worse effect, for the gallant Frenchman became more than ever aware of the swing of her silk skirts and the little dark curls that twined so coquettishly at the nape of her neck. Naturally he followed her. And all the little boys of the district became aware, as is the way of all little boys, of the one-sided flirtation which was in progress. And naturally enough they followed the tall Frenchman, so there was that day in Bayazit the very, very unusual sight of a young Turkish woman, with open face, followed by a foreigner and an innumerable number of small, dirty-nosed boys. When my mother made the mistake of stopping, trying to explain in her totally inadequate French that the gentleman was making a great mistake, he took off his hat, bowed elegantly and declared with obvious feeling:

"Vous êtes ravissante!"

And all the small boys who could not understand a word of what he said, cheered or jeered, according to their several temperaments, and my mother – very properly – hurried on, blushing and breathless and perhaps wishing a little bit for the security of her veil.

So it was that when she came down our street, with her procession behind her, the neighbours were more than ever scandalised and ran into their houses to tell the ones inside. But when my mother called out to them in Turkish that she was being followed, and very much against her will, they set to with a vengeance and brought out sticks and brooms and shooed off the gallant representative of

Gallicism in no uncertain manner. Mehmet and I, who were watching the whole proceedings from the window, were bursting with laughter but my poor grandmother was quite ready to die with shame.

"Such a disgrace!" she kept saying. "We shall never be able to live in this street again."

But in this she was wrong for when the street had finally disposed of the amorous Frenchman, and a few old men had in fact chased him half-way to Bayazit with tin buckets in their hands, to break his head, the street settled down again to lethargy, exonerating my mother from all blame. All excepting the old women, that is.

Reprinted by permission of Eland Books.

SAİT FAİK

SAİT FAİK was born in 1906, the son of a wealthy Adapazarı businessman, but spent most of his later years at the family villa on Burgaz, one of the Princes' Islands. He was fortunate in being able to rely on a small inheritance, because he was intrinsically unsuited for conventional employment, never holding any job longer than a few weeks. Nor did he spend much time away from the İstanbul area, except for a brief period of study and travel in Switzerland and France, where he failed to complete university. Instead he spent most of his life strolling the quays and backstreets of his beloved city, cultivating friendships with all sorts of people, who were astonished to learn, after his death, of his profession and class, since he kept both a secret – along with his homosexuality. His stories, available in English in the collection A Dot on the Map, first published in 1983, are rarely strong on plot, often verging on the indulgent; but they have an unerring eye for characterization, dialogue and description. Faik died in 1954 of cirrhosis of the liver, doubtless prompted by long hours tippling with the fishermen, bootblacks and idlers of İstanbul's meyhanes and coffee houses.

THE SILK HANDKERCHIEF

The broad façade of the silk factory was bathed in moonlight. Several people hurried past the gate. As I was moving listlessly with steps that did not know where they were heading, the gatekeeper called after me, "Where are you going?"

"Just taking a stroll," I said.

"Aren't you going to the circus?"

When I didn't answer, he added, "Everyone is going. Nothing like this has ever come to Bursa before."

"I don't feel like going at all," I said.

He begged and begged, and persuaded me to guard the factory. I sat a little while, smoked a cigarette, sang a song. Then I became bored. "What should I do?" I wondered, got up, took the spiked stick from the gatekeeper's room, and started making the rounds of the factory.

As soon as I passed through the shop where the girls process the silk cocoons, I heard the sound of rapid footsteps. I turned on the flashlight I had been carrying in my pocket and scanned the place. In the bright beam of the flashlight there appeared two bare feet that were trying to run away. I hurried after them and caught the fugitive.

We entered the gatekeeper's room together, the thief and I. I turned on the yellow light. Oh, what a little thief this was! The hand that I squeezed to the verge of crushing was minute. His eyes were shining. After a while I let go of his hand because I had to laugh – to laugh my head off. At this point the tiny fellow rushed at me with a penknife. The rascal wounded my little finger. I firmly grasped the scamp and searched his pockets. I found a handful of illicit tobacco, some contraband cigarette paper, and a fairly clean handkerchief. I pressed some of the tobacco on my bleeding finger, tore the handkerchief, and made him bind my hand. With the remaining tobacco we rolled two thick cigarettes and had a friendly chat.

He was fifteen. Now this kind of thing was not his habit, but there you are, sin of youth. You understand, my friend, someone wanted a silk handkerchief from him, his sweetheart, his beloved, the girl next door. He of course didn't have the money to go and buy it at the market. He thought and thought and in the end hit upon this solution. I said, "All right, but the manufacturing plant is over there, what were you doing over here?" He laughed. How was he to know the location of the manufacturing plant?

Both of us smoked my cheap-brand cigarettes and became good friends. A genuine native of Bursa, born and bred there, he had never been to İstanbul, and just once to Mudanya in his long life – you should have seen his face as he said this.

At Emir Sultan, where we used to go sledding in the moonlight, I had other friends of this same type. I was sure that the skin of this one, just like theirs, turned dark in the pools of Gökdere, whose sound I could hear from afar. I know how they turn the same color as the skin of the fruits according to the season.

I looked and saw that he had a complexion as swarthy as a walnut whose green peel has fallen off. He also had white and brittle teeth like the white meat of a fresh walnut. I know that from the beginning of the summer until the walnut season only the hands of Bursa children smell like plums and peaches, and only the chests that appear through the holes left by the torn buttons of their striped shirts smell like hazelnut leaves.

At that point the gatekeeper's clock chimed midnight. The circus was going to be over any minute.

"I must be off," he said.

As I was thinking, troubled that I had sent him away without giving him a silk handkerchief, I was startled by a noise from outside. The gatekeeper was coming in grumbling. Behind him, the thief. . .

This time I pulled his ears and the gatekeeper gave him a searing whipping with a slender willow branch on the soles of his feet. Thank God the boss wasn't there. Otherwise he would surely have handed him over to the police with the words, "A child this young, and a thief! Sir, let him sit in jail and wise up!"

However much we tried to scare him he did not cry. His eyes took the expression of the eyes of children ready to cry, but not even the slightest tremor appeared on his lips, and his eyebrows remained just as firmly set; they were just a little dishevelled.

When he was let go, he shot out like a swallow that has been set free. Like a sharp wing that swipes at the moonlight and the corn field, he dashed off.

At that time I lived in the upper level of the manufacturing plant where the goods were stored. My room was really beautiful, especially pleasant on moonlit nights. There was a mulberry tree right in front of my window. Moonlight would slip through the foliage of the tree and pour in shafts over the room. Almost invariably, summer and winter, I left my window open. How cool and strange were the gusts that blew in! Because I had often worked on ships, I could tell

from their smell which were the southwest, the northeast, the northwest, and the west winds — I knew them all. What winds passed over my blankets, each like an erotic dream!

I was sleeping lightly as usual. Morning was approaching. I could hear a noise from outside. It was as if someone were on the mulberry tree. I must have been frightened, for I did not get up or shout. At this very moment a shadow appeared in the window.

It was the boy, quietly slipping through the window. As he passed by me, I shut my eyes. He rummaged in the closets, searching for quite a while through the stacked goods. I didn't make a sound. To tell the truth, faced with this daring, I wasn't going to utter a word even if he had taken all the goods. I knew that the next day the boss would say, "Idiot, were you a corpse in a grave? You bastard!" He would kick me in the rear and fire me. But I didn't make a peep.

The boy, however, slipped away through the window emptyhanded just as he had come, without a sound. At this moment I heard the cracking sound of a branch. He fell to the ground. As I came down, the gatekeeper and a few other people had gathered around him.

He was dying. The gatekeeper wrenched open his fist, which was tightly clenched. From inside its palm, a silk handkerchief spurted out like water.

Yes, genuine, pure silk handkerchiefs are all like that. No matter how much you squeeze and crease them inside your palm, once the fist has opened, they spurt out of your hand like water.

Translated by Svat Soucek; reprinted by permission of Indiana University Press.

EDOUARD RODITI

EDOUARD RODITI *was born of Turkish Sephardic Jewish parents, but left İstanbul relatively early in life. Though for many years dividing his time between Paris and California, he still retained an obvious affection for his roots; he died in Spain in 1992 in a motoring accident. Roditi was above all a versatile writer, having translated some of Yaşar Kemal's work into English and penned a history of Magellan's circumnavigation of the globe, in addition to being an important surrealist poet. The following piece, taken from a collection called* The Delights of Turkey, *first published in the 1970s, demonstrates that he was also an elegant prose stylist.*

THREE FAITHS, ONE GOD

In one of the boxes of secondhand books that the Latin Quarter dealers of Paris display on the parapets of the embankments of the Seine, I once picked up an old guidebook of Istanbul. It attracted my attention because it contained more explanatory text and fewer illustrations than those that are now published for hasty semiliterate and camera-clicking tourists who know things only by sight, and, no longer finding enough time for reading, generally remain a mine of misinformation about all that they have seen. To prepare myself for a more thorough exploration of the Byzantine and Ottoman monuments of the former Turkish capital, I therefore began to read this book a couple of months before I was actually able to leave Paris for Turkey. Somewhere among the learned author's very factual descriptions of Byzantine monuments and other Greek-Orthodox monuments, I found a story that fascinated me because it contrasted so oddly with the otherwise sober tone of his historical explanations.

In 1453, when the besieged Byzantine capital finally fell to the Turks, it had been resisting their attacks for so long that most of the surrounding territory was already living fairly peacefully behind the Turkish lines. Close to the besieged city, a Greek-Orthodox monastery thus went about its daily business without ever being disturbed by constant warfare which seemed to have become part of the natural order of things. Among its bearded and black-robed brethren, it harbored a particularly lazy, gluttonous, and ignorant monk who never displayed much interest in anything but the immediate satisfaction of his own gross appetite. Brother Dositheos, since we must give him a name, happened one day to be preparing to fry himself some fish in a pan when a breathless messenger reached the monastery, bringing news that the Imperial city had at long last fallen to the Turks.

"Impossible," Brother Dositheos replied, calmly continuing to season his fish, perhaps even sprinkling a pinch of oregano herbs in the pan while the rest of the monastery interrupted their occupations to listen in dismay to the messenger's account of bloodshed, plunder, and rape. "Impossible," Brother Dositheos repeated. "Haven't we all seen them displaying every day for weeks, on their rounds along the top of the city's battlements, all the miraculous ikons under whose protection the city has been placed by our saintly Patriarch Gennadios? Haven't we all heard that the Patriarch has revolted against the usurping authority of the new Roman Legate and proclaimed again the full independence of our Church? How can you believe that the Most Holy Virgin and all our Saints have deserted a city thus placed under their protection?"

The messenger and the other monks continued to argue with Brother Dositheos while he began to fry his fish as if nothing of any importance had happened. Finally, he rebuked them: "I'll believe you if the fish that I'm now frying come back to life in my pan."

Immediately, the three fish that he was frying jumped out of the pan, live and unharmed, and fell into the waters of a nearby pool that was fed by a natural spring. But all three fish bore, on one side, black marks where their skin had already been charred by the pan, whereas their other side remained silvery and unharmed. Ever since, there has always been, in the monastery's pool, which has thus become a *haghiasma* of waters that perform miraculous cures, the same number of fish that continue to display the same unique markings.

I decided to investigate this tale in Istanbul and, shortly after my arrival there, repeated it to a friend, a well-known Turkish historian. He too was fascinated by it, but admitted that he had never yet heard of the monastery and its miraculous pool. Inquiries made in various quarters then revealed that a few older people could remember having once heard the legend of the miraculous fish, but nobody that I knew had ever seen them or could tell me where the monastery and its pool might still be found.

In my wanderings in the more distant section of Old Istanbul where the last Byzantine Emperors had lived in the Vlachernae Palace, I asked again and again, in the following weeks, whether anyone there knew where I might find the *balikli kilisi*, the Church of the Fish. Many had heard of it and informed me that it was somewhere beyond the city's battlements, but nobody could tell me near which gate I might find it along the great fortified stretch that protected the city from land attacks all the way from the shores of the Golden Horn to those of the Sea of Marmara, where the city was then defended against attacks from the sea by the sinister Fortress of the Seven Towers.

Though I still failed to find the object of my search, the search itself proved fruitful, however, in that it now led me to discover a number of little-known mosques and Byzantine monuments which I might otherwise have neglected. I was thus encouraged to continue my explorations, especially as the spring weather was ideal for such long walks in little-frequented neighborhoods on the outskirts of Old İstanbul, where the fruit trees were blossoming in the many gardens scattered among almost rural slums and the ruins of abandoned monuments.

Among other monuments, I then discovered, close to the Fortress of the Seven Towers where I had just visited the dungeons and deciphered on their walls some of the messages left there by desperate prisoners, the ruins of what is now called Imrahor Djami, the Mosque of the Executioner. Situated among unidentifiable Byzantine ruins which an old Turkish woman with a passion for flowers, cats, and caged songbirds had transformed into a fantastic garden that she watered diligently with rain from a well-head that still communicated with vast underground Byzantine cisterns, this abandoned Byzantine church had once been rebuilt as a mosque by the pious executioner employed at the nearby fortress. It had previously been attached to the Monastery of Saint John of Studion, reputed in ecclesiastical history to have been the first Christian monastic community endowed with a rule, as opposed to earlier communities of hermits grouped together without having a common rule of life.

One day, close to one of the gates of the Old City, I then discovered another old mosque that was not listed in any of my guidebooks. It had been built to commemorate a holy man who, on the day that Baghdad had fallen to the armies of the Sultan, had stood there proclaiming the great news by the gate of the city, having been vouchsafed a vision of the fall of Baghdad, though the messengers sent to the Ottoman capital to bring the news of victory reached İstanbul only several weeks later, having come all the way from Baghdad by camel or on horseback.

In any other city, this little mosque might have attracted the tourist's attention. Though its proportions were modest, its architecture was in the same delicately classical style as the famous Baghdad Kiosk in the gardens of the Imperial Palace of Top Kapu. Its decoration was more simple, but in exquisite taste, and its *mihrab*, toward which the Faithful turn when they must face the east in prayer, was of finely carved marble and flanked with beautiful flowered panels of brightly colored İznik ceramic tiles. As I was quietly admiring all this, I was approached by the mosque's *Imam*, a surprisingly young Moslem ecclesiastic for these days of weakened faith when so few men of his generation choose a religious way of life. As he greeted me, he seemed to be proud to discover a foreigner visiting his otherwise deserted mosque. In broken Turkish, I told him that I found the *mihrab* truly beautiful, *chok güzel*. Seeing that I was bareheaded but wore an embroidered cap that I always carry in my pocket for such occasions, and that I had dutifully removed my shoes before entering the sacred precincts, he asked me if I was a Moslem. When I told him without further ado that I'm a Jew, an American poet, he remarked that we are all brothers if we still believe in one and the same God, especially in days when all too many men have lost their faith.

Suddenly, it occurred to me that he might know where I could find the *balikli kilisi*. To my inquiry, he replied that he knew it well. One of the Greek priests there was his friend. I would find the monastery only about half a mile from here, just beyond the nearest gate in the Old City's battlements. He then decided to lock the door of his mosque and accompany me to the gate, where he pointed out to me, in the suburban countryside beyond it, a few buildings that were almost concealed behind a slight tree-capped rising that was skirted by a rough road leading from the walled city's gate.

Together, we followed this road till we reached a group of monumental buildings that appeared to have been built in the early nineteenth century, in the Russian neo-Classical style of many Greek Orthodox monasteries that I had already visited on Mount Athos or elsewhere in Greece. Wealthy and pious Russians once devoted vast sums to the task of rebuilding such hallowed ecclesiastical monuments which, since the fall of Byzantium, had slowly been allowed to go to rack and ruin. But these particular buildings now seemed to have fallen on evil days again. At first, they appeared to be deserted, left almost in a state of ruin. Suddenly, a black-robed Greek ecclesiastic appeared in a doorway. Recognizing my guide, he greeted him cordially and volubly in fluent Turkish. I was then introduced to him somewhat abruptly as an American Jew, a poet who believed in God and who had come to visit the *haghiasma*.

The Greek priest led us through a paved yard where grass grew between the disjointed stone flags, to a huge church built in neo-Classical Russian imitation of a pillared Greek temple. Unlocking its main door, he revealed to me its once majestic and splendidly decorated aisles, which now offered every evidence of having but recently been wrecked by a mob of sacrilegious Vandals. From the vaulted ceilings, heavily wrought brass lamps had been torn and still lay scattered on the floor. The painted *iconostasis*, or icon screen, with its neo-Gothic woodwork and its saints depicted in the "Pre-Raphaelite" manner of Russian Romantic painters who studied in Rome instead of remaining faithful to traditional Byzantine styles, was sorely battered. Though much had already been hastily repaired, I could see that great effort and expense would still be necessary in order to restore all that had been so wantonly destroyed or damaged.

We stood there for a while, embarrassed by what we saw and by the Greek priest's silent sorrow as he contemplated the ruin of the splendid church of which he had once been so proud. Then he sighed, shrugged his shoulders and, through another door, led us into a small walled churchyard where all the marble tombs had been desecrated, disfigured, or overturned. From their Greek inscriptions, I was able to read the names of a couple of nineteenth-century Patriarchs of Constantinople as well as of several formerly aristocratic Phanariot families: Photiadis, Zarifi, Eliasco, Mavrogordato. In a corner of the yard, a pile of human bones had been gathered, after the Turkish mob had torn them from their sepulchers and scattered them to the winds during the anti-Greek riots which the Menderes government encouraged, a few years earlier, as an expression of protest against Greek oppression of the Turkish minority in Cyprus.

The Greek priest patted the young *Imam's* shoulder affectionately, then explained to me in Turkish: "When he heard that the mob was coming here, he came and fetched us and hid us all in his mosque. God will remember what he did for us on that dreadful day."

Returning to one of the other buildings of the almost deserted monastery, the Greek priest opened a small and nondescript door, then led us down some steps to a marble-lined and quite undamaged crypt that had escaped the attentions of the mob. In the marble basin of a fountain into which the waters of the natural spring now flowed, the three fish were swimming. They had black markings on one side, as if they had been burned, but their other side was immaculately silvery. The miraculous fish seemed to have lived over four hundred years, ever since the fall of Byzantium, and only recently to have escaped by another miracle the destructive frenzy of a rioting Turkish mob. I felt down my spine a shiver, like the devastating touch of the finger of God in a poem by Gerard Manley Hopkins. We stood there, all three, in silence, each one of us confirmed in his own different faith, but united in our common respect for all who try sincerely to be worthy of their faith.

Reprinted by permission of New Directions Publishing.

AYSEL ÖZAKIN

***AYSEL ÖZAKIN** was born in Urfa in 1942, and educated in Ankara, teaching French in İstanbul before beginning her career as a novelist and short-story writer. Shortly after the 1980 coup, Özakın moved to Germany where she has lived ever since. The following extract is from the novel she wrote shortly before leaving Turkey,* The Prizegiving *(published in the UK by The Women's Press) – in part an autobiographical work that was one of the first Turkish works of literature to question the institution of marriage.*

THE PRIZEGIVING

"Is this Polatlı?" asked the young girl sitting next to Nuray.

All the women in the compartment looked outside simultaneously, at the soldiers sitting in groups on the flat ground.

"Yes," said Nuray, "it's Polatlı."

The woman of thirty or thirty-five, with short, blonde hair, who was sitting on the other side of Nuray, next to the window, looked at the soldiers too, in an absent-minded way, and nodded her head. Of all the occupants of the compartment she was the one who had spoken least. She had either leant her head back and slept, or opened and read the notebook which she was holding on her knees. While she was reading she would hold the notebook upright, with the blue plastic cover facing towards Nuray, trying to hide what was written inside. Nuray respected this effort on her part, and refrained from looking into the notebook. Is it a diary? she wondered. Or the draft of a novel? For a moment Nuray looked at her pale face, turned towards the window. It seemed as if deep thoughts and anxieties lay hidden in that face. It looked tired but meaningful . . . From such observations Nuray began to imagine that she and the silent woman sitting next to her had qualities in common. From time to time the woman would raise her head from the notebook and scrutinize the other women in the compartment.

The women had acquired small pieces of information about one another. They had found out in which district of Ankara or İstanbul each lived. In the process, each of them had expressed her views on İstanbul or Ankara as a city. İstanbul was chaotic, dirty, out of control and so on . . . Ankara, for its part, had polluted air, but on the other hand was orderly and easy to live in . . . The conversation dragged on along these lines. The women were more or less equally divided into two camps: those who favoured İstanbul in spite of everything, and those who would not exchange Ankara for any other city. Eventually they tired of this discussion, and remained silent for a long while.

The train stopped at many stations along the way. Village women and men would get on to the train with their baskets, string bags and sacks and would open the doors of the compartments to ask if there were any seats free. The city-dwelling passengers sitting inside would say there were no seats free, even if there were. The villagers would either, with silent stubbornness, come in and sit down, or else travel quietly in the corridors, keeping themselves to themselves. They would get off at another intermediate station. A village girl, wearing a long, loose-fitting coat, *şalvar* (baggy trousers) of floral-printed cotton material and a traditional head-covering, had come in and perched herself beside Nuray. The man waiting outside, with the sun-tanned face, wearing a cloth cap and aged about thirty-five, was her

father. The girl was sixteen. She had bound her *yemeni* (headscarf) tightly round her brow. She had a tiny nose, and sparkling, black, childlike eyes. Her father had taken her to a *hoca*. They were on their way back. She pointed to her forehead and the back of her neck. Her head ached constantly. The *hoca* had written her an amulet. She put her henna-dyed, chapped hand down inside her clothing, brought out the amulet, and showed it to them. A small, triangular-shaped object, wrapped in a piece of flannel cloth, had been hung around her neck. One of the women, who was about Nuray's age, immediately reproached the girl.

"What good is a *hoca* going to do your headache? Tell your father to take you to a good doctor." Then, addressing herself to the other women in the compartment, she said, "What age are we living in? They still haven't managed to break away from these absurd things . . . "

The village girl, sitting with her back hunched, like an old woman, looked at her in bewilderment. After that, she did not speak at all until her father opened the door and said to her, "Come on, now." As she left she turned back towards them with a shy smile and said, "Have a good journey."

The train stopped for quite a long time at that station. Was there a mechanical fault, or did the crowd of people on the opposite platform mean another train was expected? Some cloth-capped, dark-skinned, poorly dressed men had gathered round a pillar and were talking idly, puffing at their cigarettes. Two women in black *feraces*, their heads covered in finely embroidered *yemenis*, carrying baskets in their hands and their children on their backs, walked quickly away on to the road behind the station, which led to a village. Three other women, dressed in *çarşafs*, and a man wearing a wide cloth cap and loose-fitting trousers, were squatting on the ground at the foot of the wall, eating food laid out on newspaper. There was a little girl standing waiting, her back leant against the station wall. Like the other women, she was fully covered. Only her small, red-cheeked face was exposed. She was about eleven or twelve. The people who were taking most interest in the train were some thin village youths in blue jeans. They were smoking and walking up and down in front of the windows. One of them was peering impatiently into the women's compartment where Nuray was sitting, as if he wanted to say something, or was waiting for something. He had a pale, spotty face and narrow shoulders. There was a shameless desire and a sad longing in his gaze. A very old man with a white beard, wearing şalvar and a green skull-cap, walked on bow legs away from the station, carrying a *heybe* (saddle-bag) on his back.

The young girl sitting on Nuray's right took out of her bag a hardback book with gold lettering on the cover and began to read it. Nuray had a daughter the same age as her; she gave the girl a motherly smile, and asked what she was reading. It was a novel. The title was *When You Choose Freedom*. Nuray looked at the cover of the book. She had never heard of the author before.

The girl was wearing tight-fitting jeans. Her fingernails were painted dark red, and she would frequently insert one of them into her mouth and nibble at it. After discovering the train had arrived at Polatlı, she put the book back in her bag and took out a black metal box, which she opened. There was a mirror in the lid, and the compartments inside contained blue, green, black and grey eyepencils, lipsticks of various shades, powder compacts, tweezers, toilet water and a hairbrush. She started to clean her dark-skinned face with a piece of cotton wool wetted with toilet water. She worked in a bank, and lived in the Ayrancı district of Ankara.

Nuray folded her arms and heaved a sigh. She thought about her daughter, who carried no make-up articles in her bag apart from a comb and a cheap mirror bought from a street stall, and who merely washed her face with soap every morning before going out with a large canvas bag full of books and papers hanging from her shoulder. Nuray felt the pain of her love for her daughter.

Translated by Celia Kerslake; reprinted by permission of The Women's Press.

CELALEDDİN RUMİ

CELALEDDİN RUMİ *(1207–1273) was a Sufi mystic who founded the Mevlevi Whirling Dervish order, and whose writings helped reshape Islamic thought. The Mathnawi, his master work, was composed from 1248 onwards, after the death of his spiritual companion Shams of Tabriz, and so strong is the presence and inspiration of Tabriz that Rumi's work is also often known as the Divan of Shams-i-Tabriz. Written in Persian, the Mathnawi is a sprawling, six-volume epic varying widely in tone, content and style, alternating between prose invocations of Allah, Sufi teaching parables, ecstatic love odes, practical advice for meditation, jokes and frankly raunchy sections. It is still one of the best-loved pieces of medieval Persian literature. The only complete English translation is the terribly dry one of Reynold Nicholson (8 vols, London: Luzac & Co, 1925–40), but in recent years, more lively and contemporary renderings of selected passages have appeared. The following are versions by Coleman Barks, who has produced nine small volumes in the past decade or so. For more on Rumi, see p.511.*

THE SEED MARKET
(Book IV, Stanzas 2611–2625)

Can you find another market like this?

Where,
for one seed
you get a whole wilderness?

For one weak breath,
the divine wind?

You've been fearful
of being absorbed in the ground,
or drawn up by the air.

Now, your waterbead lets go
and drops into the ocean,
where it came from.

It no longer has the form it had,
but it's still water.
The essence is the same.

This giving up is not a repenting.
It's a deep honoring of yourself.

When the ocean comes to you as a lover,
marry, at once, quickly,
for God's sake!

Don't postpone it!
Existence has no better gift.

No amount of searching
will find this.

A perfect falcon, for no reason,
has landed on your shoulder,
and become yours.

THE INDIAN PARROT

(Book I, Stanzas 1814–1833, 1845–1848)

There was a merchant setting out for India.

He asked each male and female servant
what they wanted to be brought as a gift.

Each told him a different exotic object:
A piece of silk, a brass figurine,
a pearl necklace.

Then he asked his beautiful caged parrot,
the one with such a lovely voice,
and she said,
"When you see the Indian parrots,
describe my cage. Say that I need guidance
here in my separation from them. Ask how
our friendship can continue with me so confined
and them flying about freely in the meadow
mist.

Tell them that I remember well our mornings
moving together from tree to tree.

Tell them to drink one cup of ecstatic wine
in honor of me here in the dregs of my life.

Tell them that the sound of their quarreling
high in the trees would be sweeter
to hear than any music."

This parrot is the spirit-bird in all of us,
that part that wants to return to freedom
and is the freedom. What she wants
from India is *herself!*

So this parrot gave her message to the merchant,
and when he reached India, he saw a field
full of parrots. He stopped
and called out what she had told him.

One of the nearest parrots shivered
and stiffened and fell down dead.

The merchant said, "This one is surely kin
to my parrot. I shouldn't have spoken."

He finished his trading and returned home
with the presents for his workers.

When he got to the parrot, she demanded her
gift.
"What happened when you told my story
to the Indian parrots?"
"I'm afraid to say."
"Master, you must!"
"When I spoke your complaint to the field
of chattering parrots, it broke
one of their hearts.

She must have been a close companion,
or a relative, for when she heard about you
she grew quiet and trembled, and died."

As the caged parrot heard this, she herself
quivered and sank to the cage floor.

This merchant was a good man.
He grieved deeply for his parrot, murmuring
distracted phrases, self-contradictory –
cold, then loving – clear, then
murky with symbolism.

A drowning man reaches for anything!
The Friend loves this flailing about
better than any lying still.

The One who lives inside existence
stays constantly in motion,
and whatever you do, that king
watches through the window.

When the merchant threw the "dead" parrot
out of the cage, it spread its wings
and glided to a nearby tree!

The merchant suddenly understood the mystery.
"Sweet singer, what was in the message
that taught you this trick?"

"She told me that it was the charm
of my voice that kept me caged.
Give it up, and be released!"

The parrot told the merchant one or two more
spiritual truths. Then a tender goodbye.

"God protect you", said the merchant.
"As you go on your new way.
I hope to follow you!"

THE MOUSE AND THE FROG
(Book VI, Stanzas 2632, 2665–69, 2681–84)

A mouse and a frog meet every morning
on the riverbank.
They sit in a nook of the ground and talk.

Each morning, the second they see each other,
they open easily, telling stories and dreams and
secrets,
empty of any fear or suspicious holding-back.
To watch and listen to these two
is to understand how, as it's written,
sometimes when two beings come together,
Christ becomes visible.

The mouse starts laughing out a story he hasn't
thought of
in five years, and the telling might take five
years!
There's no blocking the speechflow-river run-
ning-all-carrying momentum
that true intimacy is.

The God-Messenger, Khidr, touches a roasted
fish.
It leaps off the grill
back into the water.

Friend sits by Friend, and the tablets appear.
They read the mysteries
off each other's foreheads.
But one day the mouse complains, "There are
times
when I want *sohbet* (mystical communion), and
you're out in the water,
jumping around where you can't hear me.

We meet at this appointed time,
but the text says, *Lovers pray constantly.*

Once a day, once a week, five times an hour,
is not enough. Fish like we are
need the ocean around us!"

Do camel-bells say, *Let's meet back here
Thursday night?*
Ridiculous. They jingle
together continuously,
talking while the camel walks.

Do you pay regular visits to *yourself?*
Don't you argue rationally.

Let us die,
and dying, reply.

BOOKS

There are numerous books about every aspect of Turkey in English, many published or reissued in recent years. Two publishers specifically or partly dedicated to Turkology, and worth contacting for their latest offerings, are *I.B. Tauris*, 45 Bloomsbury Square, London WC1A 2HY (☎0171/916 1069), or c/o *St Martin's Press*, 257 Park Avenue South, 18th Floor, New York, NY 10010 (☎212/982 3900); and *The Eothen Press*, Huntingdon, Cambridgeshire, PE18 9BX (☎01480/466106). Books with Turkish publishers are rarely available outside Turkey.

One particularly reliable retail source for Turk-related literature in the UK, whether in person or by mail order, is *Daunt Books*, 83 Marylebone High St, London W1M 4DE (☎0171/224 2295, fax 224 6893), and 193 Haverstock Hill, London NW3 4QL (☎0171/794 4006, fax 431 2732). Publishers are detailed below, where applicable, in the form British/American, although not all titles have editions in both the UK and US; "o/p" means out of print.

ANCIENT AND MEDIEVAL HISTORY

Ekrem Akurgal *Ancient Civilisations and Ruins of Turkey* (Türk Tarih Kurum Basımevi). Excellent detailed survey of Anatolian sites from prehistoric times to the end of the Roman Empire. Includes site plans and interesting graphic reconstructions of monuments, as well as a few dated photos.

Anna Comnena *The Alexiad* (Penguin, UK/US). The daughter of Emperor Alexius Comnenus I, perhaps the first woman historian, wrote a history of the First Crusade from the Byzantine point of view. Accounts of military campaigns predominate, and it's all a bit dry, but holds its own historical interest.

O.R. Gurney *The Hittites* (Penguin, UK/US). Non-specialist's history of the first great Anatolian civilization.

Herodotus *The Histories* (Penguin, UK/US). The fifth-century BC native of what is now Bodrum, Herodotus is revered as the father of both systematic history and anthropology, providing descriptions of the Persian Wars and the assorted tribes and nations who inhabited Anatolia in his time.

Seton Lloyd *Ancient Turkey – A Traveller's History of Anatolia* (British Museum Publications/University of California Press). Written by a former head of the British Archeological Institute in Ankara, this is indispensable on the ancient civilizations. Without sacrificing detail and convincing research, it's written in an accessible, compelling style, avoiding the dull, encyclopedic approach of most writing on the subject.

J.G. MacQueen *The Hittites* (Thames and Hudson, UK only). Well-illustrated general history; more accessible than Gurney.

Cyril Mango *Byzantium: The Empire of the New Rome* (Weidenfeld & Nicolson/Scribner o/p). A single volume that makes a good, accessible introduction to Byzantium, taking in daily life, economic policy and taxation, scholarship and universities, cosmology and superstition, among other topics.

Otto F.A. Meinardus *St John of Patmos and the Seven Churches of the Apocalypse* (Lycabettus Press, Athens/Caratzas, New York). The Seven Churches were all in western Anatolia, and this volume, though mostly ecclesiastical history, is also a practical handbook to the sites.

John Julius Norwich *Byzantium: The Early Centuries*, *The Apogee* and *The Decline* (Penguin/Viking). An astonishingly detailed trilogy, well informed and above all the most readable account of a fascinating period of world history up to 1453.

Andrew Palmer *Monk and Mason on the Tigris Frontier: an Early History of the Tür Abdin* (Cambridge UP, UK/US). Origins of the Syrian Orthodox Church; expensive and fairly specialist.

Procopius *The Secret History* (Penguin Classics/University of Michigan). Extraordinarily raunchy account of the murkier side of the reigns of Justinian and his procuress empress, Theodora, from no less an authority than the emperor's official war historian. Bitterly dirt-digging; compulsive reading.

Michael Psellus *Fourteen Byzantine Rulers* (Penguin, UK/US). Covers the turbulent period between 976 and 1078, when the scholarly author was adviser to several of the emperors of whom he writes.

Jonathan Riley-Smith *What were the Crusades?* (Macmillan). A slim, readable discourse on the nature of the Crusades, including recently unearthed material throwing new light on the whole movement.

Steven Runciman *Byzantine Style and Civilisation* (Penguin, UK/US). Eleven centuries of Byzantine art in one small paperback, and still fascinating. Facts are presented in interesting contexts, theories are well argued. His *The Fall of Constantinople, 1453* (Canto/Cambridge UP) remains the classic study of the event, while his *The Great Church in Captivity* (Canto/Cambridge UP), a history of Orthodoxy under the Ottomans, continues the saga in a readable if partisan manner.

Strabo *Geography* (Harvard UP; 8 vols as a Loeb Library edition). A native of Pontus, Strabo travelled widely across the Mediterranean; our best document of Roman Anatolia.

David Trall *Schliemann of Troy: Treasure and Deceit* (John Murray). The man versus the myth of his self-publicity: not strictly ancient history, but if you're intending to visit the ruins of ancient Troy, this volume, portraying the crumbling edifice of Schliemann's reputation as an archeologist, will certainly help to bring the old walls to life.

Speros Vryonis, Jr *The Decline of Medieval Hellenism in Asia Minor and the Process of Islamization from the Eleventh through the Fifteenth Century* (University of California Press, UK/US; both o/p). Heavy, footnoted going, but the definitive study of how the Byzantine Empire culturally became the Ottoman Empire.

Xenophon *Anabasis (The March Up-Country)* (Penguin o/p/University of Michigan Press). The Athenian leader of the Ten Thousand, mercenaries for the Persian king Cyrus the Younger, led the long retreat from the Cunaxa battlefield in Mesopotamia to the Black Sea. A travel classic still mined for titbits of ethnology, archeology and geography.

OTTOMAN AND MODERN HISTORY

Feroz Ahmad *The Making of Modern Turkey* (Routledge, UK/US). Not the most orthodox of histories but lively, partisan and replete with wonderful anecdotes and quotes you'll find nowhere else.

Mehmet Ali Birand *Shirts of Steel: An Anatomy of the Turkish Armed Forces* (I.B. Tauris/St Martin's). Based on interviews by one of Turkey's top journalists, this gives a good idea of the officer corps' world view and their justifications for the numerous military interventions. Hardback only, so pricy.

Roderic Davison and C.H. Dodd *Turkey, a Short History* (Eothen Press, UK only). Non-chronological text which touches on everything, particularly good for late Ottoman and early Republican events.

F.W. Hasluck *Christianity and Islam under the Sultans* (2 vols; Oxford UP o/p/Octagon o/p). Invaluable if you can find it; ample material on the history of shrines and festivals, their veneration and attendance by different sects at the turn of the last century, plus Christian and pagan contributions to the dervish rites.

Michael Hickey *Gallipoli* (John Murray, UK only). Currently the best single-volume history of the campaign.

Halil İnalcık *The Ottoman Empire: The Classical Age, 1300–1600* (Weidenfeld & Nicolson, UK only). As the title says; the standard work, not superseded since its 1973 appearance.

Cağlar Keyder *State and Class in Turkey: A Study in Capitalist Development* (Verso, UK/US). Intertwined with the Marxist and academic rhetoric is a very useful economic history of the Republic.

Lord Kinross *The Ottoman Centuries* (Weidenfeld & Nicolson/Morrow o/p). Readable, balanced summary of Ottoman history from the fourteenth to the twentieth century; *Atatürk, the Rebirth of a Nation*, by the same author (Weidenfeld & Nicolson), is considered the definitive English biography – as opposed to hagiography – of the father of the Republic.

M. Fuad Köprülü *The Origins of the Ottoman Empire* (State University Press of New York). The recent translation, by Gary Leiser, of an early twentieth-century classic covers much the same ground as İnalcık's work.

Metin Kunt and Christine Woodhead *Suleyman the Magnificent and His Age* (Longman). Concise summary of the reign of the greatest Ottoman sultan, and of the cultural renaissance over which he presided.

Bernard Lewis *The Emergence of Modern Turkey* (Oxford UP, UK/US; both o/p). Analysis of the roots of the Republic in the reform movements of the late Ottoman Empire; as such strong on cultural history, weak on events.

Geoffrey L. Lewis *Turkey* (Ernest Benn/Praeger; both o/p). Hard to find, but a much more witty and readable choice than Davison and Dodd – a little uneven, though, and coverage ceases at 1974.

A.L. Macfie *Atatürk* (Longman). Concise overview for those daunted by the longer, if racier, Kinross study.

Philip Mansel *Constantinople: City of the World's Desire, 1453–1924* (John Murray, UK only). Readable, nostalgic, faintly anti-Republican popular history, focusing on the imperial capital and organized topically as well as chronologically. Obscure factoids and scandals are all here, to wit: Boğaziçi University began life as a hotbed of Bulgarian nationalism; Russian floozies have previously (1920–22) held Turkish men in thrall; coffee-consumption was periodically a capital crime until the eighteenth century.

Philip Mansel *Sultans in Splendour – the Last Years of the Ottoman World* (Andre Deutsch/Vendome; both o/p). The illustrations make this book: a collection of rare photos depicting unbelievable characters from the end of the Ottoman Empire. It's also well written, and contains much information not available in other sources.

Faik Okte *The Tragedy of the Turkish Capital Tax* (Croom Helm/Longwood; both o/p). Short, remorseful monograph on the discriminatory World War II tax, written by the İstanbul director of finance who was responsible for its implementation.

Yaşar Nuri Öztürk *The Eye of the Heart: An Introduction to Sufism and the Tariqats of Anatolia and the Balkans* (Redhouse Press,

İstanbul). A frustratingly brief description of the tenets of mystical Islam and the main dervish orders in Turkey; lavishly illustrated, easily available in the country.

Alan Palmer *The Decline and Fall of the Ottoman Empire* (John Murray, UK only). Particularly good for manoeuvres and machinations of the European powers versus Turkey in the mid-nineteenth century; spotty on the periods before and after.

Hugh Poulton *Top Hat, the Grey Wolves and the Crescent: Turkish Nationalism and the Turkish Republic* (C. Hurst, UK only). Expensive, but anything by Poulton is likely to be definitive for its chosen topic, if a bit gloomy.

Nigel Steel and Peter Hart *Defeat at Gallipoli* (Macmillan). Uses contemporary accounts to give a vivid impression of the siege.

Richard Stoneman *A Traveller's History of Turkey* (Windrush Press/Interlink Publishing Group, Northampton, MA). An easy-reading addition to an expanding series, and at less than 200 pages inevitably superficial, but it does touch on all salient points from Paleolithic times to 1992.

Richard Tapper, ed. *Islam in Modern Turkey: Religion, Politics and Literature in a Secular State* (I.B. Tauris/St Martin's). Short collection of essays by various specialists on the resurgence of religion in Turkish life. An affordable paperback.

Tezer Taşkıran *Women in Turkey* (Redhouse Press/IBD Ltd; both o/p). Pro-Republican, non-feminist review of the history of women in Turkish political and public life.

Pars Tuğlacı *The Ottoman Palace Women* (Cem Yayınevi, İstanbul). Bilingual (English and Turkish) account of life in the palace harem, with loads of bizarre illustrations.

Andrew Wheatcroft *The Ottomans* (Penguin, UK/US). Not an event-focused, chronological history but an analysis of trends in Ottoman life, and its stereotypical perceptions by the West – usefully demonstrated by period art, cartoons and photos.

Erik J. Zürcher *Turkey, A Modern History* (I.B. Tauris/St Martin's). If you have time for only one volume covering the post-1800 period, make it this one; it's well written and breathes some revisionist fresh air over sacred cows and received truths. Also with an opinionated, annotated bibliography.

MINORITIES IN THE OTTOMAN EMPIRE AND THE REPUBLIC

Alexandris *The Greek Minority of İstanbul and Greek Turkish Relations 1918–1974* (Centre for Asia Minor Studies, Athens, o/p). Effectively illustrates how the treatment of this community, whose rights were guaranteed by the Treaty of Lausanne, has functioned as a gauge of general relations between Greece and Turkey during the period in question.

Esther Benbassa and Aron Rodrigue *The Jews of the Balkans: The Judeo-Spanish Community, 15th to 20th Centuries* (Basil Blackwell, UK/US). Dense but brief overview of the Sephardic community in the European core of the Ottoman Empire, decimated this century by assorted nationalisms, the Nazis and emigration to Palestine. Pricy and of specialist interest, so wait for the paperback.

Sirarpie Der Nersessian *The Armenians* (Thames and Hudson o/p/Praeger). Less controversial than Walker (see below), focusing on the medieval period.

John Guest *Survival among the Kurds: A History of the Yezidis* (Kegan Paul Int/Routledge). An expensive hardback but the last word on this little-known heterodox sect scattered astride Turkey's eastern borders.

Sheri Laizer *Martyrs, Traitors and Patriots: Kurdistan after the Gulf War* (Zed Books, UK/US). Only two chapters specifically on Turkey, and these marred by factual errors and blatantly pro-PKK polemics, but relatively current (1996).

David McDowall *The Kurds: A Nation Denied* (Minority Rights Publications/Cultural Survival). About one-third of this more objective book is devoted to the Kurds of Turkey, though they are now distributed over the territory of several modern states – few of whose governments get high marks here for their treatment of Kurds, up to 1992. See also McDowall's more recent *A Modern History of the Kurds* (I.B. Tauris/St Martin's), out in paperback.

Jonathan Rugman and Roger Hutchings *Atatürk's Children: Turkey and the Kurds* (Cassell). Excellent, even-handed exploration of the topic by (in part) the *Guardian's* Turkey correspondent.

Stanford Shaw *The Jews of the Ottoman Empire and the Turkish Republic* (Macmillan, UK/US). The story of the one Turkish minority which has usually managed to stay on the good side of those in power; pricy in hardback, so best to wait for the paperback.

Christopher Walker *Armenia: The Survival of a Nation* (Routledge/St Martin's). A far-reaching if partisan history, with extended discussion on Armenian relations with the Turks – particularly the 1895–96 and 1915 massacres. His more recent *Visions of Ararat* (I.B. Tauris/St Martin's) is a collection of literary excerpts, mostly views of the Armenians by outsiders over the centuries.

TRAVEL AND GENERAL

Neal Ascherson *Black Sea* (Vintage/Hill & Wang). Subtitled "The Birthplace of Civilisation and Barbarism", this excellent historical, ethnological and ecological meditation explores these supposed antitheses around Turkey's northerly sea; only two chapters specifically on the Pontus and Bosphorus, but still highly recommended.

John Ash *A Byzantine Journey* (I.B. Tauris/Random House). Historically inclined reflections of a poet as he takes in all the major, and some of the minor, Byzantine sites in Anatolia; better than it sounds, and recommended.

Arın Bayraktaroğlu *Culture Shock: Turkey* (Kuperard). A useful volume, especially on a prolonged stay or business trip, which serves to make the Turks a little less inscrutable by explaining some of their more bizarre customs.

Frederick G. Burnaby *On Horseback through Asia Minor* (Oxford UP, UK/US). Victorian officer's thousand-mile ride through snowy northeast Anatolia to spy on the Russians in the run-up to the 1877 war. Prophetically observant (especially in light of the Chechen war) and gruesomely, if inadvertently humourous (sample conversational opener: "Are people ever impaled here?"). Anti-Armenian, condescendingly Turkophilic, plus Russophobic appendices.

Katherine Creon *London–İstanbul without even a Screwdriver* (Minerva Press). Musings of an intrepid traveller crossing Tito's Yugoslavia in an old banger thirty years ago and exploring İstanbul and western Turkey, in between tussles with Turkish bureaucracy.

John A. Cuddon *The Owl's Watch-song* (Century/Random o/p). Backstreet and *meyhane* İstanbul of the 1950s, on the eve of the first Cyprus crisis.

John Freely *Stamboul Sketches* (Redhouse Press, İstanbul, o/p). Lyrical rendering of the author's personal impressions of İstanbul, combined with fascinating historical detail. His most recent effort, *Istanbul: The Imperial City* (Viking), is worthy but comparatively dull.

Laurence Kelly, ed. *Istanbul: A Traveller's Companion* (Constable). Well-selected historical writing concerning various aspects of the city, and fascinating eye-witness accounts of historical events such as the Crusaders' sack of Constantinople.

Tim Kelsey *Dervish: The Invention of Modern Turkey* (Hamish Hamilton/Penguin). The troubled soul of the country, sought amongst minority communities, faith healers, the bulging prisons, the brothels, and the transsexual underground, plus the mystics of the title; bleak and pitiless dissection of Republican Turkish angst, with little optimism for Turkey's future.

Lord Kinross *Europa Minor* (John Murray/Morrow; both o/p). Good yarns interspersed with a comprehensive coastal ramble from the Hatay to İstanbul during the early 1950s; *Within the Taurus* (John Murray, o/p) is the companion volume covering the interior.

John and Kirsten Miller *Istanbul* (Chronicle). An attractively produced compendium of relatively modern views on the city, including the likes of Gore Vidal and Michael Palin.

Michael Pereira *East of Trebizond* (Geoffrey Bles, UK only, o/p). Travels between the Black Sea and northeast Anatolia during the late 1960s, interspersed with readable history of the area. Common in second-hand travel bookshops.

Jeremy Seal *A Fez of the Heart: Travels through Turkey in Search of a Hat* (Picador). Modern Turkey, ostensibly viewed through the vagaries of the fez. No claims to profundity or accuracy (eg, *antep* does not mean "pistachio"), at times downright sophomoric.

Freya Stark *Ionia – a Quest* (Century Hutchinson o/p/Transaction Pubs), *Alexander's Path* (Arrow/Overlook Press), *Lycian Shore* (John Murray o/p), and *Riding to the Tigris* (John Murray o/p). Some of the most evocative travel writing available on Turkey.

Mary Wortley Montagu *Letters* (Everyman/Oxford UP), and the newer *Turkish Embassy Letters* (Virago). Impressions of an eccentric but perceptive traveller, resident in İstanbul during 1716–18, whose disregard for convention and popular prejudice gave her the edge over contemporary historians.

ARCHITECTURE AND THE ARTS

Metin And *Turkish Miniature Painting – the Ottoman Period* (Dost Yayınları, İstanbul). Attractive, interesting account of the most important Ottoman art form. Loads of colour plates, mostly excellent production.

John Freely and Augusto Romano Burelli *Sinan: Architect of Süleyman the Magnificent and the Ottoman Golden Age* (Thames & Hudson, UK/US). Photos by Ara Güler complement this reverential catalogue of the great sixteenth-century genius's work; expensive coffee-table volume.

Godfrey Goodwin *A History of Ottoman Architecture* (Thames & Hudson, UK only). Definitive guide to Ottoman architecture, covering the whole of Turkey and providing a sound historical and ethno-geographical context for any Ottoman construction you care to name. Affordable paperback. Goodwin's *Sinan* (Saqi Books) provides fascinating insights into the architect, his life and influences, made eminently readable by the author's passion for his subject.

Chris Hellier and Francesco Venturi *Splendours of the Bosphorus: Houses and Palaces of İstanbul* (Tauris Parke/Abbeville Press). Not the usual coffee-table fare – inviting photographs of interiors you'd never otherwise see are supported by intelligent text that puts the shoreline *yalıs* and opulent palaces into their social and artistic context.

Jean Jenkins and Poul Rovsing Olsen *Music and Musical Instruments in the World of Islam* (Horniman Museum, UK only, o/p). Interesting introduction, not too technical but usefully illustrated with photos and line drawings.

Spiro Kostoff *Caves of God – Cappadocia and its Churches* (Oxford UP, UK/US; both o/p). Dry rendering of a fascinating subject, but there's no rival, and it is thorough.

Richard Krautheimer *Early Christian and Byzantine Architecture* (Penguin, UK/US). An excellent survey from the Pelican "History of Art" series.

Raymond Lifchez, ed. *The Dervish Lodge: Architecture, Art and Sufism in Ottoman Turkey*

(University of California Press, UK/US). Collection of relatively readable essays on various aspects of the *tekkes*, including liturgical music.

Cyril Mango *Byzantine Architecture* (Faber and Faber, UK/US). A complete survey of the most significant Byzantine structures, around a quarter of which fall within modern Turkey.

T.A. Sinclair *Eastern Turkey: An Archaeological and Architectural Survey* (4 vols; Pindar Press, UK only). The standard reference, covering just about every monument east of Cappadocia, but prohibitively priced. Try a specialist library.

Metin Sözen *The Evolution of Turkish Art and Architecture* (Haşet Kitabevi, İstanbul). Lavishly illustrated, erudite survey of major Turkish monuments by period, followed by detailed discussion of the fine arts.

David Talbot Rice et al. *The Church of Hagia Sophia in Trebizond* (Edinburgh University Press, UK only). The last word, from the team that restored the frescoes in this landmark church. Talbot Rice's *Islamic Art* (Thames & Hudson/Oxford UP) covers an enormous timescale and geographical area, giving useful perspectives on Ottoman and Selçuk art forms alongside those of Persia and Muslim Spain. Look also for his *Art of the Byzantine Era* (Thames & Hudson), in the same "World of Art" series.

Stephane Yerasimos, Ara Güler and Samih Rifat *Living in Turkey* (Thames and Hudson/Abbeville Press). Covers some of the same ground as Hellier and Venturi, but with less of a focus on nobility and more on the nouveau riche. Landscapes and interiors to drool over, in photos by Güler and Rifat; a bit prettified but still alluring as an ideal.

CARPETS

W Bruggeman and H. Böhmer *Rugs of the Peasants and Nomads of Anatolia* (K & A, Munich); **Cathryn M Cootner** *Anatolian Kilims: The Caroline and H McCoy Jones Collection and The Fine Arts Museum of San Francisco* (Hali Publications, UK only). Two focusing especially on Turkey.

Alastair Hull *Kilims: The Complete Guide* (Thames and Hudson/Chronicle Books). Comprehensive and thoroughly illustrated survey of Turkish *kilims*.

James Opie *Tribal Rugs* (Thames and Hudson, UK only). Contains examples of Turcoman and Kurdish rugs as part of a general Central Asian survey.

Orient Stars (E. Heinrich Kirchheim and Hali Publications, UK only). Despite the silly title, the ultimate rug book; 250 colour plates, with excellent representation of classical Turkish carpets.

Jon Thompson *Carpets from the Tents, Cottages and Workshops of Asia* (Lawrence King). A good general introduction.

Kurt Zipper and Claudia Fritzsche *The Carpets of Turkey* (Antique Collectors, UK/US). Volume 4 of the series entitled "Oriental Rugs". Extensive discussion of weaving techniques, symbols and rug categories, and the weavers themselves, along with a regional survey of distinctive patterns.

If you catch the rug bug, you might consider subscribing to Hali Magazine *(6 issues yearly, £62/$118), which publishes numerous articles on Turkish textiles and the latest in rug scholarship. Contact Hali Publications, Kingsgate House, Kingsgate Place, London NW6 4TA, UK (☎0171/328 9341). The same organization also publishes* İstanbul: The Hali Rug Guide, *a comprehensive handbook to carpet-shopping in the city.*

SPECIALIST GUIDES

Haldun Aydıngün *Aladağlar: An Introduction* (Redhouse Press, İstanbul). Details approaches and scrambling routes in this compact karst range near Niğde.

George E. Bean *Turkey's Southern Shore* (John Murray, UK/US), *Turkey Beyond the Maeander* (John Murray, UK/US), *Lycian Turkey* (John Murray, UK/US), *Aegean Turkey* (John Murray, UK/US, both o/p). A series of scholarly guides to the archeological sites of Turkey written from the original research of Professor Bean, much of which has never been superseded.

Everett Blake and Anna Edmonds *Biblical Sites in Turkey* (Redhouse Press, İstanbul). If it's mentioned in the Bible, it appears here too, with current description of sites; regularly updated.

Fatih Çimok *Cappadocia* (A Turizm Yayınları). Attractively illustrated coffee-table type format, more detailed and better researched than its competitors.

Marc Dubin and Enver Lucas *Trekking in Turkey* (Lonely Planet, UK/US; both o/p). Long and short treks – still navigable – in every Turkish mountain range, plus an obsolete section on the Turquoise Coast; worth trying to get a copy second-hand, as the maps are still the best available.

John Freely *Blue Guide to İstanbul* (A & C Black/Norton). Thorough but a bit pompous.

Karl Smith *The Mountains of Turkey* (Cicerone/Hunter). More up-to-date and more widely available than *Trekking in Turkey*, but the maps are poor.

Hilary Sumner-Boyd and John Freely *Strolling through İstanbul – A Guide to the City* (Kegan Paul Int/Routledge). Thorough, but covers much the same ground as the *Blue Guide*.

Sally Taylor *A Traveller's Guide to the Woody Plants of Turkey* (Redhouse Press, İstanbul). Coverage of all native trees and shrubs of Turkey, with keying sections and an especially useful glossary of Turkish species names.

FICTION AND POETRY

Hüseyin Avni Dede *Byzantine Coffin Nails* (Gümüş Basınevi, İstanbul). Translator Richard McKane calls Avni a "poet of the people", and his works are certainly accessible even to an audience who know nothing of the poverty-riven life of an İstanbul coin-seller.

Coleman Barks and John Moyne, trans. *Open Secret* (Threshold Books, US only). Translation of Rumi poetry.

Coleman Barks, trans. *Like This* (Maypop, US only) and *Now We are Three* (Maypop, US only). Two of several lively volumes of Rumi poetry. In the UK they can be ordered inexpensively through the London Sufi Centre at Beauchamp Lodge, 2 Warwick Crescent, London W2 6NE (☎0171/266 3099). Some selections are reproduced on pp.806–808.

Yunus Emre *The City of the Heart: Verses of Wisdom and Love* (Element Books, UK only). Along with Rumi, the most highly regarded Turkish medieval Sufi poet; translated by Süha Faiz.

Sait Faik *A Dot on the Map* (Indiana University Turkish Studies, US only). A large collection of short stories, translated by various scholars, from the acknowledged Turkish master of the genre; most are set in and around İstanbul and the Sea of Marmara during the early Republican years. One of these tales is reproduced on p.800.

Maureen Freely *The Life of the Party* (Penguin/Warner, both o/p). Salacious, desperate cavortings of a Bosphorus University faculty during the Sixties, including a thinly disguised amalgam of the author's father John Freely and others. An excellent read.

Talat S. Halman *Living Poets of Turkey* (Dost Yayınları, İstanbul). A wide selection of modern Turkish poetry, with an introduction giving the socio-political context. Halman also edited *Yunus Emre and his Mystical Poetry* (Indiana University Turkish Studies, o/p), the works of the medieval Islamic folk poet, with explanatory essays.

Kabir Edmund Helminski *Love is a Stranger* (Threshold Books, US only). Alternative translations of Rumi.

Nazim Hikmet *A Sad State of Freedom* (Greville Press Pamphlets, UK only). Gentle, moving poems – many of which were written in prison – from the internationally renowned Turkish poet who died in exile in 1963.

Yaşar Kemal The best-known Turkish novelist in the West, thanks to English translations by his wife Thilda of virtually every one of his titles. Except where noted, Harvill do the current editions in the UK, Pantheon in the US. Oldest are the epics, somewhat turgid and folksy, set in inner Anatolia: *Mehmed My Hawk*, its sequel *They Burn the Thistles* (o/p), and *The Lords of Akchasaz: Murder in Ironsmith's Market* (o/p). The trilogy *The Wind from the Plain, Iron Earth, Copper Sky* and *The Undying Grass* is strong in human observations and detail rather than plot. Better are some later novels, mostly set in and around İstanbul, including *The Sea-Crossed Fishermen* (Methuen, o/p), a psychological drama set against the background of an İstanbul sea-fishing village, and contrasting an old man's struggle to save the dolphins in the Sea of Marmara with the fortunes of a desperate hoodlum at bay in the city; and *The Birds have also Gone* (o/p), a symbolic, gentle story about bird-catchers near İstanbul.

Geoffrey L. Lewis, trans. *The Book of Dede Korkut* (Penguin, UK/US). The Turkish national epic, set in the age of the Oğuz Turks: by turns racy, formulaic, elegant and redundant.

Pierre Loti *Aziyade* (Kegan Paul Int/Routledge). For what's essentially romantic twaddle set in nineteenth-century Ottoman İstanbul, this is surprisingly racy, with good insights into Ottoman life and Western attitudes to the Orient.

Rose Macaulay *The Towers of Trebizond* (Flamingo/Carroll & Graf). Classic send-up of Low and High Church intrigue, British ethnocentricity and proselytizing naivety, with generous slices of Turkey in the 1950s.

Aziz Nesin *İstanbul Boy* (2 vols; University of Texas, US only). Set in the same era and milieu as Orga's work, and strong on local colour, but not such a good read.

İrfan Orga *Portrait of a Turkish Family* (Eland, UK only). Heartbreaking story following the Orga family from an idyllic existence in late Ottoman İstanbul through grim survival in the early Republican era; some of it is excerpted on p.798.

Aysel Özakın *The Prizegiving* (The Women's Press, UK only, o/p). Interesting insights into Turkish society, but lacks momentum as a novel, and it can be a bit predictable. The opening passage is given on p.804.

Orhan Pamuk *The White Castle* (Faber & Faber/Braziller). Excellent historical meditation in which a seventeenth-century Italian scholar is enslaved in the service of an Ottoman astronomer. His recent *The Black Book* (Faber &

Faber/Farrar Straus Giroux), set in modern İstanbul, is altogether more convoluted and surreal.

Edouard Roditi *The Delights of Turkey* (New Directions, US only, o/p). Twenty short stories, by turns touching or bawdy, set in rural Turkey and İstanbul, by a Sephardic Jew of Turkish descent long resident in Paris and America. One of the best is reproduced on p.801.

Daniel de Souza *Under a Crescent Moon* (Serpent's Tail, UK only). Turkish society seen from the bottom looking up: an excellent volume of prison vignettes by a jailed foreigner, and in its compassion the antithesis of *Midnight Express*. Compellingly written and spiced with interesting prejudices on the part of the writer.

Haldun Taner *Thickhead and Other Turkish Stories* (Forest Books/UNESCO). Mostly set in İstanbul from the 1950s to 1970s, translated by Geoffrey L. Lewis.

Latife Tekin *Berji Kristin: Tales from the Garbage Hills* (Marion Boyars, UK/US). The hard underbelly of Turkish life, in this surreal allegory set in a shanty town founded on an İstanbul rubbish dump (one of which exploded in 1993 from accumulated methane).

Barry Unsworth *The Rage of the Vulture* (Granada, UK/US). Set in the twilight years of the Ottoman Empire, with the paranoid sultan, Abdülhamid, centrestage.

LANGUAGE

It's worth learning as much Turkish as you can while you're out there; if you travel far from the tourist centres you may well need it, and Turks will always appreciate foreigners who show enough interest and courtesy to learn at least basic greetings. The main advantages of the language from the learner's point of view are that it's phonetically spelt, and grammatically regular. The disadvantages are that the vocabulary is unrelated to any language you're likely to have encountered, and the grammar, relying heavily on suffixes, gets more alien the further you delve into it. Concepts like vowel harmony, beyond the scope of this brief primer, further complicate matters. Trying to grasp at least the basics, though, is well worth the effort.

PRONUNCIATION

Pronunciation in Turkish is worth mastering, since once you've got it the phonetic spelling and regularity helps you progress fast. The following letters differ significantly from English pronunciation.

Aa short a similar to that in far.

Ââ softly aspirated a, can sound as if preceded by a faint y or h.

Ee as in bet.

Iı unstressed vowel similar to the a in probable.

İi as in pit.

Oo as in note.

Öö like ur in burn.

Uu as in blue.

Üü like ew in few.

Cc like j in jelly.

Çç like ch in chat.

Gg hard g as in get.

Ğğ generally silent, but lengthens the preceding vowel and between two vowels can be a y sound.

Hh as in hen, never silent.

Jj like the s in pleasure.

Ss as in six.

Şş like sh in shape.

Vv soft, somewhere between v and w.

PHRASEBOOKS AND DICTIONARIES

For a **phrasebook**, look no further than *Turkish: A Rough Guide Phrasebook* (Rough Guides), with useful two-way glossaries and a brief and simple grammar section. If you want to learn more, Geoffrey L. Lewis's *Teach Yourself Turkish* (Hodder) still probably has a slight edge over Yusuf Mardin's *Colloquial Turkish* (Routledge); or buy both, since they complement each other well. Alternatively, there's Geoffrey Lewis's *Turkish Grammar* (Oxford UP), a one-volume solution. If you're serious about learning Turkish when you get out there, the best series published in Turkey is a set of three textbooks and tapes, available in good bookshops in İstanbul and Ankara, *Türkçe Öğreniyoruz* (Engin Yayınevi).

Among widely available Turkish **dictionaries**, the best are probably the Langenscheidt/Lilliput miniature or coat-pocket sizes, or the *Concise Oxford Turkish Dictionary* (distributed in Turkey by ABC Kitabevi), a hardback suitable for serious students. In Turkey, locally produced Redhouse dictionaries are the best value: the affordable four-and-a-half-inch *Mini Sözlük* has the same number of entries as the seven-and-a-half-inch desk edition and is adequate for most demands; the definitive, two-tome version even gives Ottoman Turkish script and etymologies for each word, but it costs the earth and isn't exactly portable.

WORDS AND PHRASES

BASICS

Good morning	Günaydın	I live in . . .	. . .'de/da oturuyorum
Good afternoon	İyi Günler	Today	Bugün
Good evening	İyi Akşamlar	Tomorrow	Yarın
Good night	İyi Geceler	The day after tomorrow	Öbür gün/Ertesi gün
Hello	Merhaba	Yesterday	Dün
Goodbye	Allahaısmarladık	Now	Şimdi
Yes	Evet	Later	Sonra
No	Hayır	Wait a minute!	Bir dakika!
No (there isn't any)	Yok	In the morning	Sabahleyin
Please	Lütfen	In the afternoon	Öğleden sonra
Thank you	Teşekkürederim/	In the evening	Akşamleyin
	Mersi/Sağol	Here/there/over there	Burada/şurada/orada
You're welcome/that's	Bir şey değil	Good/bad	İyi/kötü
OK		Big/small	Büyük/küçük
How are you?	Nasılsınız? Nasılsın?	Cheap/expensive	Ucuz/pahalı
	Ne haber?	Early/late	Erken/geç
I'm fine (thank you)	(Sağol) İyiyim/İyilik	Hot/cold	Sıcak/soğuk
	sağlık	Near/far	Yakın/uzak
Do you speak English?	İngilizce biliyor-	Vacant/occupied	Boş/dolu
	musunuz?	Quickly/slowly	Hızlı/yavaş
I don't understand	Anlamadım/Anlamıyorum	With/without milk	Sutlu/sutsuz
I don't know	Bilmiyorum	With/without meat	Etli/etsiz
I beg your pardon/sorry	Affedersiniz	Enough	Yeter
Excuse me (in a crowd)	Pardon	Mr . . .	. . . Bey
I'm sightseeing	Geziyorum/Dolaşiyorum	Mrs . . .	. . . Hanım
I'm English/Scottish/	İngilizim/İskoçyalım/İrlan	Miss . . . (used with	Bayan . . .
Irish/Australian	dalıyım/Avustralyalım	forenames)	

DRIVING

Left	Sol	No entry	Araç giremez
Right	Sağ	No through road	Çıkmaz sokak
Straight ahead	Direk	Slow down	Yavaşla
Turn left/right	Sola dön/Sağa dön	Road closed	Yol kapalı
Parking	Park edilir	Crossroads	Dörtyol
No parking	Park edilmez	Pedestrian crossing	Yaya geçidi
One-way street	Tek yön		

SOME SIGNS

Entrance/exit	Giriş/çıkış	Beware	Dikkat
Free/paid entrance	Giriş ücretsiz/ücretli	First aid	İlk yardım
Gentlemen	Baylar	No smoking	Sigara ıçilmez
Ladies	Bayanlar	Don't tread on the grass	Çimenlere basmayınız
WC	Wc/tuvalet/umumî	Military area	Askeri bölge
Open/closed	Açık/kapalı	Stop/halt	Dur
Arrivals/departures	Varış/kalkış	Entry forbidden	Girmek yasaktır
Pull/push	Çekiniz/ıtiniz	No entry without a	Biletsiz/Damsız girilmez
Out of order	Arızalı	ticket/for women	
Drinking water	İçilebilir su	Please take off your	Lütfen ayakkabılarınızı
To let/for hire	Kiralık	shoes	çıkartınız
Foreign exchange	Kambiyo	No entry on foot	Yaya girimez
Ticket office	Gişe		

ACCOMMODATION

Hotel	*Hotel/otel*	For one/two weeks	*Bir/iki haftalık*
Pension, boarding house	*Pansiyon*	With an extra bed	*İlave yataklı*
Campsite	*Kamping*	With a double bed	*Fransiz yataklı*
Hostel	*Yurt*	With a shower	*Duşlu*
Tent	*Çadır*	Hot water	*Sicak su*
Is there a hotel nearby?	*Yakinda otel var mı?*	Cold water	*Soğuk su*
Do you have a room?	*Boş odanız var mı?*	Can I see it?	*Bakabilirmiyim?*
Single/double/triple	*Tek/çift/üç kişilik*	I have a booking	*Reservasyonım var*
Do you have a double room for one/two/ three nights?	*Bir/İki/Üç gecelik çift yataklı odanızvar mı?*	Can we camp here?	*Burda kamp edebilirmiyiz?*

QUESTIONS AND DIRECTIONS

Where is the . . . ?	*. . . nerede?*	How far is it to . . . ?	*. . .'a/e ne kadar uzakta?*
When?	*Ne zaman?*	Can you give me a lift to . . . ?	*Beni . . . 'a/e götüre- bilirmisiniz?*
What?/What is it?	*Ne?/Ne dir?*		
How much (does it cost)?	*Ne kadar?/Kaça?*	What time does it open?	*Kaçta açılıcak?*
How many?	*Kaç tane?*		
Why?	*Niye?*	What time does it close?	*Kaçta kapanacak?*
What time is it?	(polite) *Saatınız var mı?* (informal) *Saat kaç?*	What's it called in Turkish?	*Türkcesi ne dir?/Türkçe nasıl söylersiniz?*
How do I get to . . . ?	*. . .'a/e nasıl giderim?*		

TRAVELLING

Aeroplane	*Uçak*	What time does it leave?	*Kaçta kalkıyor?*
Bus	*Otobus*		
Train	*Tren*	When is the next bus/train/ferry?	*Bir sonraki otobus/tren /vapur kaçta kalkıyor?*
Car	*Araba*		
Taxi	*Taksi*	Do I have to change?	*Aktarma var mı?*
Bicycle	*Bisiklet*	Where does it leave from?	*Nereden kalkıyor?*
Ferry	*Vapur/feribot*		
Ship	*Gemi*	What platform does it leave from?	*Hangi perondan kalkıyor?*
Hitch-hiking	*Otostop*		
On foot	*Yaya*	How many kilometres is it?	*Kaç kilometredir?*
Bus station	*Otogar*		
Railway station	*Tren ıstasyonu*	How long does it take?	*Ne kadar sürerbilir?*
Ferry terminal/jetty	*İskele*	Which bus goes to . . . ?	*Hangi otobus . . . 'a gider?*
Port	*Liman*		
A ticket to . . .	*. . . 'a bir bilet*	Which road leads to . . . ?	*Hangi yol . . . 'a çıkar?*
Return	*Gidiş-dönüş*		
Can I book a seat?	*Reservasyon yapabilirmiyim?*	Can I get out at a convenient place?	*Müsait bir yerde inebilirmiyim?*

DAYS OF THE WEEK AND MONTHS

Sunday	*Pazar*	January	*Ocak*	August	*Agusto*
Monday	*Pazartesi*	February	*Subat*	September	*Eylül*
Tuesday	*Salı*	March	*Mart*	October	*Ekim*
Wednesday	*Çarşamba*	April	*Nisan*	November	*Kasim*
Thursday	*Perşembe*	May	*Mais*	December	*Aralık*
Friday	*Cuma*	June	*Haziran*		
Saturday	*Cumartesl*	July	*Temmuz*		

WORDS AND PHRASES (cont)

SEASONS

Spring *İlkbahar*	Summer *Yaz*	Autumn *Sonbahar*	Winter *Kış*

NUMBERS

1	*Bir*	8	*Sekiz*	30	*Otuz*	100	*Yüz*
2	*İki*	9	*Dokuz*	40	*Kırk*	140	*Yüz kırk*
3	*Üç*	10	*On*	50	*Elli*	200	*İki yüz*
4	*Dört*	11	*On bir*	60	*Altmış*	700	*Yedi yüz*
5	*Beş*	12	*On iki*	70	*Yetmiş*	1000	*Bin*
6	*Altı*	13	*On üç*	80	*Seksen*	9000	*Dokuz bin*
7	*Yedi*	20	*Yirmi*	90	*Doksan*	1,000,000	*Bir milyon*

Compounded numbers tend to be run together in spelling:
50,784 *Ellibinyediyüzseksendört*

The most important ordinals, as in class of train, restaurant, etc, are:
First *Birinci*   Second *İkinci*   Third *Üçüncü*

TIME CONVENTIONS

(At) 3 o'clock	*Saat üç(ta)*	It's 8.10	*Sekizi on geçiyor*
Two hours (duration)	*İki saat*	It's 10.45	*On bire çeyrek var*
Half-hour (duration)	*Yarım saat*	At 8.10	*Sekizi on geçe*
Five-thirty	*Beş büçük*	At 10.45	*On bire çeyrek kala*

GLOSSARY

Many of the Turkish terms below will change their form according to where they appear (eg *ada*, island, but *Eşek Adası*, Donkey Island); the genitive suffix is appended in brackets, or the form written separately when appropriate.

ACROPOLIS Ancient fortified hilltop.

ADA(SI) Island.

AGORA Marketplace and meeting area of an ancient Lycian, Greek or Roman city.

AĞA A minor rank of nobility in the Ottoman Empire, and still a term of respect applied to a local worthy; follows the name (eg Ismail Ağa).

AHİ Medieval Turkish apprentice craftsmen's guild, with religious overtones.

APSE Curved or polygonal recess at the altar end of a church.

ARABESK Popular, degenerated form of Turkish *sanat* or "art" music, which plagues travellers on long bus rides and at nightspots.

ARASTA Marketplace built into the foundations of a mosque, a portion of whose revenues goes to the upkeep of the latter.

AYAZMA Sacred spring.

BAHÇE(Sİ) Garden.

BEDESTEN Covered market hall, often lockable.

BEKÇİ Caretaker at an archeological site or monument.

BELEDIYE(Sİ) Municipality – both the corporation and the actual town hall, for a community of under 2000.

BEY Another minor Ottoman title like *ağa*, still in use; follows the first name.

BOULEUTERION Council hall of a Hellenistic or Roman city.

CAMEKÂN Changing rooms in a hamam.

CAMİ(İ) Mosque.

CAPITAL The top, often ornamented, of a column.

CAVEA The seating-curve of an ancient theatre.

ÇARŞAF A bedsheet, or the full-length, baggy dress-with-hood worn by religious Turkish women.

ÇARŞI(SI) Bazaar, market.

ÇAY(I) 1) Tea, the national drink; 2) a stream or torrent.

ÇEŞME(Sİ) Streetcorner fountain.

ÇIKMAZ(I) Dead-end alley.

DAĞ(I) Mount.

DAĞLAR(I) Mountains.

DEESIS or **DEISIS** Portrayal of Christ with the Virgin and John the Baptist.

DOLMUŞ Literally "filled" – the shared taxi system operating in larger Turkish towns; some confusing overlap with "minibus", since not all of the latter are dolmuşes, and vice versa.

ENTEL Short for *entelektüel* – the arty, trendy set which patronizes Western-style pubs and bars in the larger cities and resorts.

ESKİ Old (frequent modifier of place names).

EXEDRA Semicircular niche.

EYVAN Domed side-chamber of an Ottoman religious building; also applies to three-sided alcoves in secular mansions.

EZAN The Muslim call to prayer.

FERACE Similar to a *çarşaf*, but less all-enveloping.

GAZİ Warrior for the (Islamic) faith; also a common epithet of Atatürk.

GAZİNO Open-air nightclub, usually adorned with coloured lights and featuring live or taped *arabesk* or *taverna* music.

GECEKONDU Literally "founded-by-night" – a reference to the Ottoman law whereby houses begun in darkness which had acquired a roof and four walls by dawn were inviolable. The continuance of the tradition is responsible for the huge *gecekondu* shanty towns around all large Turkish cities.

GİŞE Ticket window or booth.

GÖBEK TAŞI Literally "navel stone" – the hot central platform of a hamam.

GÖL(Ü) Lake.

HACI Honorific of someone who has made the pilgrimage to Mecca; precedes the name.

HALVET Semi-private corner rooms in a hamam.

HAMAM(I) Turkish bath.

HAMSİ The Black Sea anchovy; by extension, nickname for any native of this area.

HAN(I) Traditionally a tradesmen's hall, or an urban inn; now can also mean an office block.

HANIM "Lady" – polite title from Ottoman times, and still in use; follows the first name.

HARABE Ruin; *harabeler* in the plural, abbreviated "Hb" on old maps.

HARARET The hottest room of a hamam.

HAREM The women's quarters in Ottoman residences.

HASTANE(Sİ) Hospital.

HITTITE First great civilization (*c.*1800–1200 BC) to emerge in Anatolia.

HİCRÎ The Muslim dating system, beginning with Mohammed's flight to Medina in 622 AD, and based on the thirteen-month lunar calendar; approximately six centuries behind the *Miladî* calendar. Abbreviated "H" on monuments and inscriptions.

HİSAR Same as *kale*.

HOCA Teacher in charge of religious instruction for children.

ILICA Hot spring.

IRMAK River, eg Yeşilırmak (Green River).

İL(İ) Province, the largest administrative division in Turkey, subdivided into *ilces* (counties).

İMAM Usually just the prayer leader at a mosque, though it can mean a more important spiritual authority.

İMARET(İ) Soup kitchen and hostel for dervishes and wayfarers, usually attached to a *medrese*.

İSKELE(Sİ) Jetty, dock.

KAABA Shrine at Mecca containing a sacred black stone.

KALE(Sİ) Castle, fort.

KAPI(SI) Gate, door.

KAPLICA Developed hot springs, spa.

KATHOLIKON Central shrine of a monastery.

KEMER Series of vaults, or an aqueduct.

KERVANSARAY(I) Strategically located "hotel", often Selçuk, for pack animals and men on Anatolian trade routes; some overlap with *han*.

KİLİM Flat-weave rug without a pile.

KİLİSE(Sİ) Church.

KONAK Large private residence, also the main government building of a province or city; genitive form *konağı*.

KONUT Same as *Tatil köyü* (see below).

KÖŞK(Ü) Kiosk, pavilion, gazebo, folly.

KUBBE Dome, cupola – as in *Kubbeli Kilise* (the Domed Church).

KULE(Sİ) Tower, turret.

KURNA Hewn stone basins of a hamam.

KÜLLIYE(Sİ) Building complex – term for a mosque and dependent buildings taken as a whole.

KÜMBET Vault, dome; by analogy the cylindrical "hatted" Selçuk tombs of central Anatolia.

LOKANTA Restaurant; rendition of Italian *locanda*.

MABET Temple, at archeological sites; genitive *mabedi*.

MAĞARA(SI) Cave.

MAHALLE(Sİ) District or neighbourhood of a larger municipality or postal area.

MEDRESE(Sİ) Islamic theological academy.

MESCIT Small mosque with no *mimber*; Islamic equivalent of a chapel; genitive *mescidi*.

MEYDAN(I) Public square or plaza.

MEYHANE Tavern where alcohol and food are both served.

MEZAR(I) Grave, tomb; thus *mezarlık*, cemetery.

MİHRAB Niche in a mosque indicating the direction of Mecca, and prayer.

MİLÂDÎ The Christian year-numbering system; abbreviated "M" on inscriptions and monuments.

MİMBER Pulpit in a mosque, from where the *imam* delivers homilies; often beautifully carved in wood or stone.

MİNARE(Sİ) Turkish for "minaret", the tower from which the call to prayer is delivered.

MUEZZIN Man who pronounces call to prayer from the minaret of a mosque; the call is often taped these days.

MUHTAR Village headman.

MUHTARLIK The office of the *muhtar*, both in the abstract and concrete sense; also designates the status of any community of under 2000.

NAMAZ The Muslim rite of prayer, performed five times daily.

NAOS The inner sanctum of an ancient temple.

NARTHEX Vestibule or entrance hall of a church; also *exonarthex*, the outer vestibule when there is more than one.

NAVE The principal lengthwise aisle of a church.

NECROPOLIS Place of burial in an ancient Greek or Roman city.

NEHİR (NEHRİ) River.

NYMPHAEUM Ornate, multistoreyed facade, often with statue niches, surrounding a public fountain in an ancient city.

OTOGAR Bus station.

OVA(SI) Plain, plateau.

ÖREN Alternative term for *harabe*, "ruin"; common village name.

PANSİYON Typical accommodation in Turkish resorts.

PENDENTIVE Curved, triangular surface, by means of which a dome can be supported over a square ground plan.

PIER A mass of supportive masonry.

PORPHYRY A hard red or purple rock containing mineral crystals.

RAMADAN The Muslim month of fasting and prayer; spelt *Ramazan* in Turkish.

REVETMENT Facing of stone, marble or tile on a wall.

SARAY(I) Palace.

SAZ Long-necked, fretted stringed instrument central to Turkish folk ballads and Alevî/Bektaşi devotional music.

SEBİL Public drinking fountain, either free-standing or built into the wall of an Ottoman structure.

SELÂMLİK Area where men receive guests in any sort of dwelling.

SELÇUK The first centralized, Turkish state based in Anatolia, lasting from the eleventh to the thirteenth centuries.

SEMA A dervish ceremony; thus *semahane*, a hall where such ceremonies are conducted.

SON CEMAAT YERİ Literally "Place of the last congregation" – a mosque porch where latecomers pray.

STOA Colonnaded walkway in ancient Greek marketplace.

SUFİ Dervish – more properly an adherent of one of the heterodox mystical branches of Islam. In Turkey the most important sects were (and to some extent still are) the Bektaşi, Mevlevi, Helveti, Naqshbandi and Kadiri orders.

SULTAN VALİDE The Sultan's mother.

SYNTHRONON Semicircular seating for clergy, usually in the apse of a Byzantine church.

ŞADIRVAN Ritual ablutions fountain of a mosque.

ŞEHZADE Prince, heir apparent.

ŞEREFE Balcony of a minaret.

ŞEYH Head of a Sufi order.

TABHANE Hospice for travelling dervishes or *ahis*, often housed in an *eyvan*.

TAPINAK Alternative term for "temple" at archeological sites; genitive *tapınağı*.

TATİL KÖYÜ or **SİTE(Sİ)** Holiday development, either for Turkish civil servants or a private co-operative – not geared for foreign tourists.

TEKEL The government monopoly, now no longer exclusive, on alcohol, cigarettes, matches etc.

TEKKE(Sİ) Gathering place of a Sufi order.

TERSANE(Sİ) Shipyard, dry-dock.

TRANSEPT The "wings" of a church, perpendicular to the nave.

TUFF Soft, carvable rock formed from volcanic ash.

TUĞRA Monogram or seal of a sultan.

TÜRBE(Sİ) Freestanding, usually domed, tomb.

TYMPANUM The surface, often adorned, enclosed by the top of an arch; found in churches or more ancient ruins.

ULEMA The corps of Islamic scholars and authorities in Ottoman times.

USTA An honorific term, often half-jokingly bestowed on any tradesman, meaning "master craftsman"; follows the first name.

VAKIF Islamic religious trust or foundation, responsible for social welfare and upkeep of religious buildings.

VERD ANTIQUE Type of green marble.

VEZIR Vizier, the principal Ottoman minister of state, responsible for the day-to-day running of the empire.

VİLÂYET(İ) Formal word for province; also a common term for the provincial headquarters building itself.

VOUSSOIR Stripes of wedge-shaped blocks at the edge of an arch.

YALI Ornate wooden residence along the Bosphorus.

YAYLA(Sİ) Pastoral mountain hamlet occupied only in summer.

YENİ New (common component of Turkish place names).

ZAVİYE Mosque built specifically as a hospice for dervishes, usually along a T-plan.

ACRONYMS AND ABBREVIATIONS

ANAP *Anavatan Partisi* or Motherland Party: the centre-right party founded by the late president Turgut Özal, now headed by Mesut Yılmaz.

AŞ Initials of *Anonim Şirket*, Turkish equivalent of "Ltd" or "Inc".

BUL Standard abbreviation for *bulvar(ı)* (boulevard).

CAD Standard abbreviation for *cadde(si)* (avenue).

CHP *Cumhuriyetçi Halk Partisi* or Republican People's Party (RPP) – founded by Atatürk, disbanded in 1980, revived in 1992.

DSP *Demokratik Sol Partisi* or Democratic Left Party: leftist party headed by Bülent Ecevit.

DYP *Doğru Yol Partisi* or True Path Party: centre-right party headed by Tansu Çiller, part of the current coalition government.

KDV Acronym of the Turkish VAT.

MHP *Milliyet Hareket Partisi* or National Action Party; quasi-fascist group headed by Alpaslan Türkeş.

PKK *Partia Karkaris Kurdistan* or Kurdish Workers' Party, actually an armed guerrilla movement, which was formed in 1978.

PTT *Post Telefon ve Telegraf*, the joint postal and phone service in Turkey, and by extension its offices.

RP *Refah Partisi* or Welfare Party; Islamic party headed by Necmettin Erbakan, part of the current coalition government.

SHP *Sosyal Demokratik Halkçı Partisi* or Social Democratic Party: centre-left party, absorbed into the CHP in 1994.

SOK Abbreviation for *sokak* (*sokağı*) or street.

THY *Türk Hava Yolları*, Turkish Airways.

TIR (pronounced "turr" locally) *Transport International Routière* – large, slow trucks.

TL Standard symbol for Turkish lira.

TML English acronym of *Turkish Maritime Lines; TDİ* in Turkish.

TRT Acronym of *Türk Radyo ve Televizyon*, the Turkish public broadcasting corporation.

TT *Türk Telekom* – body recently hived off the *PTT*, devoted exclusively to telecommunications services.

INDEX

		£	US$	CAN$
Amsterdam	1-85828-086-9	7.99	13.95	16.99
Andalucia	1-85828-094-X	8.99	14.95	18.99
Australia	1-85828-141-5	12.99	19.95	25.99
Bali	1-85828-134-2	8.99	14.95	19.99
Barcelona	1-85828-221-7	8.99	14.95	19.99
Berlin	1-85828-129-6	8.99	14.95	19.99
Brazil	1-85828-102-4	9.99	15.95	19.99
Britain	1-85828-208-X	12.99	19.95	25.99
Brittany & Normandy	1-85828-224-1	9.99	16.95	22.99
Bulgaria	1-85828-183-0	9.99	16.95	22.99
California	1-85828-181-4	10.99	16.95	22.99
Canada	1-85828-130-X	10.99	14.95	19.99
China	1-85828-225-X	15.99	24.95	32.95
Corsica	1-85828-089-3	8.99	14.95	18.99
Costa Rica	1-85828-136-9	9.99	15.95	21.99
Crete	1-85828-132-6	8.99	14.95	18.99
Cyprus	1-85828-182-2	9.99	16.95	22.99
Czech & Slovak Republics	1-85828-121-0	9.99	16.95	22.99
Egypt	1-85828-188-1	10.99	17.95	23.99
Europe	1-85828-159-8	14.99	19.95	25.99
England	1-85828-160-1	10.99	17.95	23.99
First Time Europe	1-85828-270-5	7.99	9.95	12.99
Florida	1-85828-184-4	10.99	16.95	22.99
France	1-85828-124-5	10.99	16.95	21.99
Germany	1-85828-128-8	11.99	17.95	23.99
Goa	1-85828-156-3	8.99	14.95	19.99
Greece	1-85828-131-8	9.99	16.95	20.99
Greek Islands	1-85828-163-6	8.99	14.95	19.99
Guatemala	1-85828-189-X	10.99	16.95	22.99
Hawaii: Big Island	1-85828-158-X	8.99	12.95	16.99
Hawaii	1-85828-206-3	10.99	16.95	22.99
Holland, Belgium & Luxembourg	1-85828-087-7	9.99	15.95	20.99
Hong Kong	1-85828-187-3	8.99	14.95	19.99
Hungary	1-85828-123-7	8.99	14.95	19.99
India	1-85828-200-4	14.99	23.95	31.99
Ireland	1-85828-179-2	10.99	17.95	23.99
Italy	1-85828-167-9	12.99	19.95	25.99
Kenya	1-85828-192-X	11.99	18.95	24.99
London	1-85828-231-4	9.99	15.95	21.99
Mallorca & Menorca	1-85828-165-2	8.99	14.95	19.99
Malaysia, Singapore & Brunei	1-85828-103-2	9.99	16.95	20.99
Mexico	1-85828-044-3	10.99	16.95	22.99
Morocco	1-85828-040-0	9.99	16.95	21.99
Moscow	1-85828-118-0	8.99	14.95	19.99
Nepal	1-85828-190-3	10.99	17.95	23.99
New York	1-85828-171-7	9.99	15.95	21.99
Pacific Northwest	1-85828-092-3	9.99	14.95	19.99

Paris	1-85828-235-7	8.99	14.95	19.99
Poland	1-85828-168-7	10.99	17.95	23.99
Portugal	1-85828-180-6	9.99	16.95	22.99
Prague	1-85828-122-9	8.99	14.95	19.99
Provence	1-85828-127-X	9.99	16.95	22.99
Pyrenees	1-85828-093-1	8.99	15.95	19.99
Rhodes & the Dodecanese	1-85828-120-2	8.99	14.95	19.99
Romania	1-85828-097-4	9.99	15.95	21.99
San Francisco	1-85828-185-7	8.99	14.95	19.99
Scandinavia	1-85828-039-7	10.99	16.99	21.99
Scotland	1-85828-166-0	9.99	16.95	22.99
Sicily	1-85828-178-4	9.99	16.95	22.99
Singapore	1-85828-135-0	8.99	14.95	19.99
Spain	1-85828-240-3	11.99	18.95	24.99
St Petersburg	1-85828-133-4	8.99	14.95	19.99
Thailand	1-85828-140-7	10.99	17.95	24.99
Tunisia	1-85828-139-3	10.99	17.95	24.99
Turkey	1-85828-242-X	12.99	19.95	25.99
Tuscany & Umbria	1-85828-243-8	10.99	17.95	23.99
USA	1-85828-161-X	14.99	19.95	25.99
Venice	1-85828-170-9	8.99	14.95	19.99
Vietnam	1-85828-191-1	9.99	15.95	21.99
Wales	1-85828-245-4	10.99	17.95	23.99
Washington DC	1-85828-246-2	8.99	14.95	19.99
West Africa	1-85828-101-6	15.99	24.95	34.99
More Women Travel	1-85828-098-2	9.99	14.95	19.99
Zimbabwe & Botswana	1-85828-186-5	11.99	18.95	24.99

Phrasebooks

Czech	1-85828-148-2	3.50	5.00	7.00
French	1-85828-144-X	3.50	5.00	7.00
German	1-85828-146-6	3.50	5.00	7.00
Greek	1-85828-145-8	3.50	5.00	7.00
Italian	1-85828-143-1	3.50	5.00	7.00
Mexican	1-85828-176-8	3.50	5.00	7.00
Portuguese	1-85828-175-X	3.50	5.00	7.00
Polish	1-85828-174-1	3.50	5.00	7.00
Spanish	1-85828-147-4	3.50	5.00	7.00
Thai	1-85828-177-6	3.50	5.00	7.00
Turkish	1-85828-173-3	3.50	5.00	7.00
Vietnamese	1-85828-172-5	3.50	5.00	7.00

Reference

Classical Music	1-85828-113-X	12.99	19.95	25.99
Internet	1-85828-198-9	5.00	8.00	10.00
Jazz	1-85828-137-7	16.99	24.95	34.99
Opera	1-85828-138-5	£16.99	24.95	34.99
Rock	1-85828-201-2	17.99	26.95	35.00
World Music	1-85828-017-6	16.99	22.95	29.99

In the USA, or for international orders, charge your order by Master Card or Visa (US$15.00 minimum order): call 1-800-253-6476; or send orders, with complete name, address and zip code, and list price, plus $2.00 shipping and handling per order to: Consumer Sales, Penguin USA, PO Box 999 – Dept #17109, Bergenfield, NJ 07621. No COD. Prepay foreign orders by international money order, a cheque drawn on a US bank, or US currency. No postage stamps are accepted. All orders are subject to stock availability at the time they are processed. Refunds will be made for books not available at that time. Please

Good Vibrations!

Rough Guides on the Web

Visit our websites www.roughguides.com and www.hotwired.com/rough for news about the latest books, online travel guides and updates, and the full text of our Rough Guide to Rock – all 1058 entries!

AT GOOD BOOKSHOPS • DISTRIBUTED BY PENGUIN

Stay in touch with us!

ROUGH*NEWS* is Rough Guides' free newsletter. In three issues a year we give you news, travel issues, music reviews, readers' letters and the latest dispatches from authors on the road.

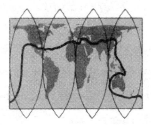

TAPESTRY
HOLIDAYS

Offering

The very best of

uncommercial

Turkey

0181-742 0055

PLEASE FEEL WELCOME TO CALL
FOR A BROCHURE OR A CHAT